# Paul Krugman • Robin Wells
# MACROECONOMICS
### THIRD EDITION

# Applications in Macroeconomics

Green type indicates global example

# MACROECONOMICS

## Third Edition

## Paul Krugman • Robin Wells
PRINCETON UNIVERSITY

WORTH PUBLISHERS

**Senior V.P., Editorial and Production:**
Catherine Woods

**Publisher:** Charles Linsmeier

**Executive Marketing Manager:** Scott Guile

**Marketing Assistant:** Julie Tompkins

**Executive Development Editor:** Sharon Balbos

**Development Editor:** Marilyn Freedman

**Senior Consultant:** Andreas Bentz

**Senior Media Editor:** Marie McHale

**Assistant Editor:** Mary Melis

**Director of Market Research and Development:**
Steven Rigolosi

**Director of Digital and Print Development:**
Tracey Kuehn

**Associate Managing Editor:** Lisa Kinne

**Project Editor:** Anthony Calcara

**Art Director:** Babs Reingold

**Cover Designers:** Lyndall Culbertson and Babs Reingold

**Interior Designer:** Charles Yuen

**Layout Designer and Illustrations:**
TSI Graphics and Lyndall Culbertson

**Photo Editor:** Cecilia Varas

**Photo Researcher:** Elyse Rieder

**Production Manager:** Barbara Anne Seixas

**Supplements Production Manager:** Stacey Alexander

**Supplements Project Editor:** Edgar Bonilla

**Composition:** TSI Graphics

**Printing and Binding:** RR Donnelley


ISBN-13: 978-1-4292-8343-4
ISBN-10: 1-4292-8343-2


Library of Congress Control Number: 2012930400

Printed in the United States of America


Second printing

Worth Publishers
41 Madison Avenue
New York, NY 10010
www.worthpublishers.com

**Cover Photos Credits**

Image of business people looking at screen: Hans Neleman/Getty Images; **First Row:** Bike rider: *Flat Earth Images;* Cornstalks: *Stockbyte;* Chevron workers: *Copyrights and trademarks held by Chevron on behalf of Chevron U.S.A. Inc. and used with permission.";* Logs on truck: *Photodisc;* Oil refinery: *Photodisc;* Machine worker: *Digitalvision.* **Second Row:** Collection of dyes: *Digital Vision/ Getty Images;* Zappos Kentucky warehouse: © 2010 Zappos.com, Inc.; Steam: *Photodisc;* Pineapples: *Photodisc;* Cows: *Stockbyte;* Couple buying car: *Photodisc.* **Third Row:** Woman smiling: *Photodisc;* Highways: *Fotosearch;* Powerlines: *Digitalvision;* Red Factory shot: *Digitalvision;* ING Sign: *Courtesy ING Group;* Flowers in a field: *Stockbyte.* **Fourth Row:** Cars in traffic: *PhotoDisc;* High-speed train: *Flat Earth Images;* Hong Kong intersection: *Photodisc;* Boy: *Photodisc;* Big truck: *Phil Whitehouse/Flickr;* Surgeon: *Stockbyte.* **Fifth Row:** GE Energy Smart® Soft White and Reveal® Hybrid Halogen CFL Bulbs: *Image courtesy of General Electric Company;* Flags: *Photodisc;* Steam: *PhotoDisc;* Tugboat: *Flat Earth Images;* Fisher: *Photodisc;* Boy with flowers: *Photodisc.* **Sixth Row:** Hybrid car: *istockphoto;* Wind turbines: *Beverett/Dreamstime.com;* Man with sign during Great Depression: *Archive Holdings Inc./Getty Images;* Wall Street sign: *Nikada/ iStockphoto;* Ship: *Photodisc;* Skyline: *Photodisc;* Sewage treatment plant: *Digital Vision.* **Seventh Row:** Tax form: *D. Hurst/Alamy;* Cisco headquarters: *Copyright Cisco Systems, Inc.;* Evening dining: *Photodisc;* Grocers: *Photodisc;* Woman with blue scarf: *Photodisc;* Wheat: *Stockbyte;* Oil refinery at night: *Digitalvision.* **Eighth Row:** NY Stock Exchange: *Image Source;* Chemical plant: *Brand X Pictures;* Gas prices: *Photodisc;* Wiretubes: *Digitalvision;* Currency: *Photodisc;* Golden Gate Bridge: *Photodisc;* Pipes in oil field: *Photodisc.* **Ninth Row:** Girl smiling: *Photodisc;* Can tops: *Brand X Pictures;* Tokyo Stock Exchange: *Media Bakery;* Smiling woman: *Photodisc;* Oil worker: *Corbis;* Trees: *Photodisc;* Double-decker bus: *Flat Earth Images.*

*To beginning students everywhere,*
*which we all were at one time.*

**Paul Krugman,** recipient of the 2008 Nobel Memorial Prize in Economic Sciences, is Professor of Economics at Princeton University, where he regularly teaches the principles course. He received his BA from Yale and his PhD from MIT. Prior to his current position, he taught at Yale, Stanford, and MIT. He also spent a year on the staff of the Council of Economic Advisers in 1982–1983. His research is mainly in the area of international trade, where he is one of the founders of the "new trade theory," which focuses on increasing returns and imperfect competition. He also works in international finance, with a concentration in currency crises. In 1991, Krugman received the American Economic Association's John Bates Clark medal. In addition to his teaching and academic research, Krugman writes extensively for nontechnical audiences. He is a regular op-ed columnist for the *New York Times*. His latest trade books, both best-sellers, include *The Return of Depression Economics and the Crisis of 2008,* a history of recent economic troubles and their implications for economic policy, and *The Conscience of a Liberal,* a study of the political economy of economic inequality and its relationship with political polarization from the Gilded Age to the present. His earlier books, *Peddling Prosperity* and *The Age of Diminished Expectations,* have become modern classics.

**Robin Wells** was a Lecturer and Researcher in Economics at Princeton University. She received her BA from the University of Chicago and her PhD from the University of California at Berkeley; she then did postdoctoral work at MIT. She has taught at the University of Michigan, the University of Southampton (United Kingdom), Stanford, and MIT. The subject of her teaching and research is the theory of organizations and incentives.

# BRIEF CONTENTS

# CONTENTS

## FROM PAUL AND ROBIN

More than a decade ago, when we began writing the first edition of this textbook, we had many small ideas: particular aspects of economics that we believed weren't covered the right way in existing textbooks. But we also had one big idea: the belief that an economics textbook could and should be built around narratives, that it should never lose sight of the fact that economics is, in the end, a set of stories about what people do.

Many of the stories economists tell take the form of models—for whatever else they are, economic models are stories about how the world works. But we believed that students' understanding of and appreciation for models would be greatly enhanced if they were presented, as much as possible, in the context of stories about the real world, stories that both illustrate economic concepts and touch on the concerns we all face as individuals living in a world shaped by economic forces.

Those stories have been integrated into every edition, including this one, which contains more stories than our earlier editions. Once again, you'll find them in the openers, in boxed features like Economics in Action, For Inquiring Minds, and Global Comparisons, but now in our new Business Cases as well.

As in the previous edition, we've made extensive changes and updates in coverage to reflect current events—events that have come thick and fast in a turbulent, troubled world economy, which is affecting the lives and prospects of students everywhere. Currency is very important to us.

We have also expanded our coverage of business issues, both because business experience is a key source of economic lessons and because most students will eventually find themselves working in the business world. We are especially pleased with how the new Business Cases have turned out and how they augment the overall number and richness of our stories.

And we've made a major effort to streamline and simplify in places where our zeal to get it right ran ahead of our commitment to keep it clear.

We remain extremely fortunate in our reviewers, who have put in an immense amount of work helping us to make this book even better. And we are also deeply thankful to all the users who have given us feedback, telling us what works and, even more important, what doesn't. (We also received useful comments from those who chose not to use our book and explained why!)

Many things have changed since the second edition of this book. As you'll see, there's a great deal of new material, and there are some significant changes (and, we hope, improvements) in pedagogy. But we've tried to keep the spirit the same. This is a book about economics as the study of what people do and how they interact, a study very much informed by real-world experience.

## The Third Edition: What's New

Although the second edition was a resounding success, further establishing *Macroeconomics* as one of the best-selling macroeconomics textbooks, we learn with each new edition that there is always room for improvement. So, for the third edition, we undertook a revision with three goals in mind:

1. To expand the book's appeal to business students
2. To be as current and cutting edge as possible in topics covered and examples included
3. To make the book more teachable and accessible

We hope that the following revisions lead to a more successful teaching experience for you.

### New Business Case Studies

Now, more than ever, students entering the business community need a strong understanding of economic principles and their applications to business decisions. To meet this demand, almost every chapter now concludes with a real-world Business Case, showing how the economic issues discussed in the chapter play out in the world of entrepreneurs and bottom lines.

The cases range from the 2009 bankruptcy of General Motors, once the symbol of American economic success, and its rebound in 2010, to a look at companies like Macroeconomic Advisers and the nonprofit Institute of Supply Management that forecast changes in GDP, to an examination of the productivity surge in retailing driven by improvements in global logistics at Walmart. They also place the individual consumer and firm in the macroeconomy with examples that illustrate the changing job market during a recession (Monster.com), the role of gift cards in secondary markets (PlasticJungle.com), and the value of "breakage" when individual consumers fail to pay down their gift cards completely.

Each case is followed by critical thinking questions that prompt students to apply the economics they learned in the chapter to real-life business situations (answers to these questions are found in the Instructor's Resource Manual). See a full list of the Business Cases on the inside front cover.

### An Emphasis on Currency

The third edition has been updated to remain the most current textbook on the market in its content, data and examples.

**New Chapter: "Crises and Consequences"** This new chapter provides an up-to-date look at the recent financial crisis and the aspects of the banking system that allowed it to take place. Starting with the story of the Lehman Brothers collapse, the chapter integrates coverage on the dangers of banking, the trade-off between liquidity and rate of return, the emergence of "shadow banks," and the early bank runs of the recession. Also covered: asset bubbles, financial contagion, financial panic, and a look at how the financial crisis of 2008 fits into a long history of economic crises. The chapter concludes with a discussion of why banking crises are so bad for so many, and the role the government and regulation play in crises.

**Economics in Action: A Richer Story to Be Told** Students and instructors alike have always championed *Macroeconomics* for its applications of economic principles, especially our Economics in Action feature. In the third edition, we have revised or replaced a significant number of Economics in Action applications in every chapter to ensure that the book remains fresh and cutting edge. We believe this provides the richness of content that drives student and instructor interest. All Economics in Action features are listed on the inside cover.

**Opening Stories** We have always taken great care to ensure that each chapter's opening story illustrates the key concepts of that chapter in a compelling and accessible way. And, as always, we update most of these in each edition and provide many completely new stories—nearly a third were replaced in an effort to bridge the gap between economic concepts and student interest in the world around them. New openers include the story of Facebook and the huge amounts of funding needed to obtain its large server farms; the story behind the American Recovery and Reinvestment Act and the two main reactions to the stimulus; the story of China's economic rise, surpassing Japan as the second largest economy, and the means economists use to measure such trends; and the story of Ben Bernanke, *Time* magazine's person of the year in 2009, and his high-profile role as Federal Reserve chairman in the wake of the financial crisis.

### A More Teachable and Accessible Presentation

**Streamlined Chapters** Because less is often more, we've streamlined the exposition in a number of places where our desire for thoroughness got a little ahead of our pedagogy. The chapters on fiscal policy and monetary policy, in particular, are a lot smoother in this edition.

**A New Location for Coverage of Present Value** To enhance teachability, coverage of present value has moved from elsewhere in the book to Chapter 10, "Savings, Investment Spending, and the Financial System"—where many instructors are likely to cover it. Basic coverage appears in the chapter and a more detailed look at present value follows in a new appendix to the chapter. This newly added content will give students a better understanding of how money appreciates over time and affects important investment decisions.

**A More Focused Treatment of the Keynesian Cross** The main coverage of the Keynesian Cross in the chapters on aggregate expenditure and *AD/AS* has been retained, but coverage of the integrated 45-degree diagrams in later chapters on fiscal policy and monetary policy has been cut back. This change was made in response to input from instructors who were vocal in their request for less integrated coverage of the Keynesian Cross to make our book more accessible to their students. Keynesian coverage remains as important as ever in these chapters. But the treatment is now more focused and, we hope, free of unnecessary complexity.

**A More Visual Exposition** The research tells us that students read more online, in shorter bursts, and respond better to visual representations of information than ever before. In the third edition, we've worked hard to present information in the format that best teaches students.

We've shortened our paragraphs for easier reading and included numbered and bulleted lists whenever content would allow. You will find helpful new summary tables in this edition. And, most helpful, are the visual displays in the book, including dynamic representations that turn paragraphs of text into a more accessible, and appealing, visual presentation.

## Advantages of This Book

Our basic approach to textbook writing remains unchanged:

- **Chapters build intuition through realistic examples.** In every chapter, we use real-world examples, stories, applications, and case studies to teach the core concepts and motivate student learning. The best way to introduce concepts and reinforce them is through real-world examples; students simply relate more easily to them.

- **Pedagogical features reinforce learning.** We've crafted a genuinely helpful set of features, our "tools for learning," that are presented in a visual walk-through format starting on the next page.

# CHAPTER 3

# Supply and Demand

## BLUE JEAN BLUES

How did flood-ravaged cotton crops in Pakistan lead to higher-priced blue jeans and more polyester in T-shirts?

Matt Nager Photography

IF YOU BOUGHT A PAIR OF BLUE jeans in 2011, you may have been shocked at the price. Or maybe not: fashions change, and maybe you thought you were paying the price for being fashionable. But you weren't—you were paying for cotton. Jeans are made of denim, which is a particular weave of cotton, and by late 2010, when jeans manufacturers were buying supplies for the coming year, cotton prices were more than triple their level just two years earlier. By December 2010, the price of a pound of cotton had hit a 140-year high, the highest cotton price since records began in 1870.

And why were cotton prices so high?

On one side, demand for clothing of all kinds was surging. In 2008–2009, as the world struggled with the effects of a financial crisis, nervous consumers cut back on clothing purchases. But by 20__ with the worst apparently over, b

production. Most notably, Pakistan, the world's fourth-largest cotton producer, was hit by devastating floods that put one-fifth of the country underwater and virtually destroyed its cotton crop.

Fearing that consumers had limited tolerance for large increases in the price of cotton clothing, apparel makers began scrambling to find ways to reduce costs without offending consumers' fashion sense. They adopted changes like smaller buttons, cheaper linings, and—yes—polyester, doubting that consumers would be willing to pay more for cotton goods. In fact, some experts on the cotton market warned that the sky-high prices of cotton in 2010–2011 might lead to a permanent shift in tastes, with consumers becoming more willing to wear synthetics even when cotton prices came down.

At the same time, it was not all bad news for everyone connected with the

weather and were relishing the higher prices. American farmers responded to sky-high cotton prices by sharply increasing the acreage devoted to the crop. None of this was enough, however, to produce immediate price relief.

Wait a minute: how, exactly, does flooding in Pakistan translate into higher jeans prices and more polyester in your T-shirts? It's a matter of supply and demand—but what does that mean? Many people use "supply and demand" as a sort of catchphrase to mean "the laws of the marketplace at work." To economists, however, the concept of supply and demand has a precise meaning: it is a *model of how a market behaves* that is extremely useful for understanding many—but not all—markets.

In this chapter, we lay out the pieces that make up the *supply and demand model*, put them together, and show how this model can be used to understand how many—but not all—markets behave. ■

**Economics in Action** cases conclude every major text section. This much-lauded feature lets students immediately apply concepts they've read about to real phenomena.

## ECONOMICS > *IN ACTION*

### BEATING THE TRAFFIC

All big cities have traffic problems, and many local authorities try to discourage driving in the crowded city center. If we think of an automobile to the city center as a good that people consume, we analyze anti-traffic policies.

One common strategy is to reduce the prices of substitutes. Many metropolitan hoping to lure commuters out of their cars. An alternative is to raise the price of complements: several major U.S. cities impose high taxes on commercial parking garages and impose short time limits on parking meters, both to raise revenue and to discourage people from driving into the city.

A few major cities—including Singapore, London, Oslo, Stockholm, and Milan—have been willing to adopt a direct and politically controversial approach: reducing congestion by raising the price of driving. Under "congestion pricing" (or "congestion charging" in the United Kingdom), a charge is imposed on cars entering the city center during business hours. Drivers buy passes, which are then debited electronically as they drive by monitoring stations. Compliance is monitored with automatic cameras that photograph license plates. Moscow is currently contemplating a congestion charge scheme to tackle the worst traffic jams of all major cities, with 40% of drivers reporting traffic jams exceeding three hours.

The current daily cost of driving in London ranges from £9 to £12 (about $13 to $19). And drivers who don't pay and are caught pay a fine of £120 (about $192) for each transgression.

Not surprisingly, studies have shown that after the implementation of congestion pricing, traffic does indeed decrease. In the 1990s, London had some of the worst traffic in Europe. The introduction of its congestion charge in 2003 immediately reduced traffic in the London city center by about 15%, with overall traffic falling by [...] increased use of substitutes, such as [...] ride-sharing.

In the United S[...] implemented pilot programs in [...] ansportation experts have even [...] g prices during peak commuti[...] ontroversial, it appears to be sl[...]

**Global Stamps** identify which boxes, cases, and applications are global in focus.

Cities can reduce traffic congestion by raising the price of driving.

### ▼ Quick Review

- The **supply and demand model** is a model of a **competitive market**—one in which there are many buyers and sellers of the same good or service.

- The **demand schedule** shows how the **quantity demanded** changes as the price changes. A **demand curve** illustrates this relationship.

- The **law of demand** asserts that a higher price reduces the quantity demanded and demand curves normally slope downward.

- An increase in demand corresponds to a rightward **shift of the demand curve:** the quantity demanded rises for any given price. A decrease in demand is a leftward shift: the quantity demanded falls for any given price. A change in price results in a change in the quantity demanded and a **movement along the demand curve.**

- The five main factors that can shift the demand curve are changes in (1) the price of a related good, such as a **substitute** or a **complement,** (2) income, (3) tastes, (4) expectations, and (5) the number of consumers.

- The market demand curve is the horizontal sum of the i[...]l demand

**Check Your Understanding** questions allow students to immediately test their understanding of a section. Solutions appear at the back of the book.

### CHECK YOUR UNDERSTANDING 3-1

1. Explain whether each of the following events represents (i) a *shift of* the demand curve or (ii) a *movement along* the demand curve.
   a. A store owner finds that customers are willing to pay more for umbrellas on rainy days.
   b. When XYZ Telecom, a long-distance telephone service provider, offered reduced rates on weekends, its volume of weekend calling increased sharply.
   c. People buy more long-stem roses the week of Valentine's Day, even though the prices are higher than at other times during the year.
   d. The sharp rise in the price of gasoline leads many commuters to join carpools in order to [...]e their gasoline purchases.

Solutions appear at back of book.

**Quick Reviews** offer students a short, bulleted summary of key concepts in the section to aid understanding.

## GLOBAL COMPARISON

### PAY MORE, PUMP LESS

For a real-world illustration of the law of demand, consider how gasoline consumption varies according to the prices consumers pay at the pump. Because of high taxes, gasoline and diesel fuel are more than twice as expensive in most European countries as in the United States. According to the law of demand, this should lead Europeans to buy less gasoline than Americans—and they do. As you can see from the figure, per person, Europeans consume less than half as much fuel as Americans, mainly because they drive smaller cars with better mileage.

Prices aren't the only factor affecting fuel consumption, but they're probably the main cause of the difference between European and American fuel consumption per person.

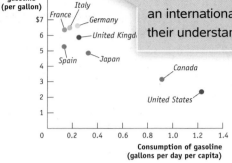

*Source:* U.S. Energy Information Administratio[n]

**Global Comparison** boxes use real data from several countries and colorful graphs to illustrate how and why countries reach different economic outcomes. The boxes give students an international perspective that will expand their understanding of economics.

## FOR INQUIRING MINDS

### TRIBULATIONS ON THE RUNWAY

You probably don't spend much time worrying about the trials and tribulations of [fash]ion models. Most of them don't lead [glam]orous lives; in fact, except for a lucky [few,] life as a fashion model today can be [frus]trating and not very lucrative. And it's [all b]ecause of supply and demand.

[C]onsider the case of Bianca Gomez, [a wi]llowy 18-year-old from Los Angeles, [with g]reen eyes, honey-colored hair, and [fair s]kin, whose experience was [told in a] *Wall Street Journal* article. [She] began modeling while still in high [scho]ol, earning about $30,000 in mod-[elin]g fees during her senior year. Having [attr]acted the interest of some top [desi]gners in New York, she moved there [afte]r graduation, hoping to land jobs [with l]eading fashion houses and photo-[sho]ots for leading fashion magazines. [B]ut once in New York, Bianca entered

Bianca Gomez on the runway before intense global competition got her thinking about switching careers.

by a rightward shift of the supply curve in the market for fashion models, which would by itself tend to lower the price paid to models. And that wasn't the only change in the market. Unfortunately for Bianca and others like her, the tastes of many of those who hire models have changed as well. Over the past few years, fashion magazines have come to prefer using celebrities such as Angelina Jolie on their pages rather than anonymous models, believing that their readers connect better with a familiar face. This amounts to a leftward shift of the demand curve for models—again reducing the equilibrium price paid to them.

This was borne out in Bianca's experiences. After paying her rent, her transportation, all her modeling expenses, and 20% of her earnings to her modeling agency (which markets

**For Inquiring Minds** boxes apply economic concepts to real-world events in unexpected and sometimes surprising ways, generating a sense of the power and breadth of economics. The feature furthers the book's goal of helping students build intuition with real-world examples.

## ⚠ PITFALLS

### DEMAND VERSUS QUANTITY DEMANDED

When economists say "an increase in demand," they mean a rightward shift of the demand curve, and when they say "a decrease in demand," they mean a leftward shift of the demand curve—that is, when they're being careful. In ordinary speech most people, including professional economists, use the word *demand* casually. For

example, an economist might say "the demand for air travel has doubled over the past 15 years, partly because of falling air-fares" w[hen the] *quantit[y . . .]*

It's [. . .] conver[. . .] nomic [. . .] distinct[. . .] deman[. . .]

**Pitfalls** boxes clarify concepts that are easily misunderstood by students new to economics.

**TABLE 3-1** Factors That Shift Demand

| When this happens . . . | . . . demand increases | But when this happens . . . | . . . demand decreases |
|---|---|---|---|
| When the price of a substitute rises . . . | . . . demand for the original good increases. | When the price of a substitute falls . . . | . . . demand for the original good decreases. |
| When the price of a complement falls . . . | . . . demand for the original good increases. | When the price of a substitute rises . . . | . . . demand for the original good decreases. |

**New! Summary Tables** serve as a helpful study aid for readers. Many incorporate visuals to help students grasp important economic concepts.

## BUSINESS CASE : The Chicago Board of Trade

Jim West/Photolibrary

To understand the concept of an equilibrium price, it's helpful to do what we did in the discussion of demand: imagine that buyers are wandering around comparing the prices offered by different sellers. Some markets really do work this way. But cotton, wheat, and many other commodities are traded on "exchanges" which make prices much more transparent and make the movement to equilibrium almost instantaneous.

Modern exchanges began with wheat trading at the Chicago Board of [Trade], founded in 1848. But in 1848, St. Louis, not Chicago, was the leading city of the American West, and it dominated the wheat trade. The wheat market in St. Louis was freewheeling and a lot like the story we told in the text. There [was] no marketplace; sellers set up in various warehouses, or even stacked sacks of wheat on the levee, and buyers wandered around looking for the best deal.

In Chicago, however, sellers had a better idea. The Chicago Board of Trade, an association of the city's leading grain dealers, created a system in which would-be traders gathered in one place—the "pit"—where they called out or accepted offers to buy or sell. The Board guaranteed that these contracts would be fulfilled. This system meant that buyers could very quickly find sellers and vice versa, lowering the costs of doing business. It also ensured that everyone could see the latest price, so the price rose and fell very rapidly to clear the market. For example, news of bad weather in a wheat-growing area hundreds of miles away would send the price in Chicago soaring in a matter of minutes.

The Chicago Board of Trade went on to become the world's most important trading center for wheat and many other agricultural commodities, a status it retains to this day. And the Board's rise helped the rise of Chicago, too. The city, as Carl Sandburg put it in his famous poem, became

Hog Butcher for the World,
Tool Maker, Stacker of Wheat,
Player with Railroads and the Nation's Freight Handler

By 1890, Chicago had more than a million people, second only to New York. Making a better market, it turned out, was very good business indeed.

### QUESTIONS FOR THOUGHT

1. In the text we mentioned how prices can vary in a tourist trap. Why was the wheat market in St. Louis a bit like a tourist trap, and why was Chicago different?

2. What was the advantage of having buyers and sellers gathered in one place?

---

**New!**
**Business Cases** close each chapter, applying key economic principles to real-life business situations in both American and international companies. Each case concludes with critical thinking questions.

---

### SUMMARY

1. The **supply and demand model** illustrates how a **competitive market**, one with many buyers and sellers, none of whom can influence the market price [takers].

2. The [demand] **schedule** shows the **quantity** [demanded] [repr]esented graphi[cally] [law] **of demand** says [that]; that is, a higher [price makes] people to demand a

ing supply, they mean **shifts of the supply curve**—a change in the quantity supplied at any given price. An increase in supply causes a rightward shift of the supply curve. A decrease in supply causes a leftward shift.

8. There are five main factors that shift the supply curve:
   • A change in **input** prices
   • A change in the prices of related goods and services
   • A change in technology
   • A change in expectations
   • A change in the number of producers

---

**End-of-Chapter Reviews** include a brief but complete summary of key concepts, a list of key terms, and a comprehensive, high-quality set of end-of-chapter Problems.

---

### PROBLEMS

1. A survey indicated that chocolate is Americans' favorite ice-cream flavor. For each of the following, indicate the possible effects on demand, supply, or both as well as equilibrium price and quantity of chocolate ice cream.

   **a.** A severe drought in the Midwest causes dairy farmers to reduce the number of milk-producing cattle in their herds by a third. These dairy farmers supply cream that is used to manufacture chocolate ice cream.

   **b.** A new report by the American Medical Association reveals that chocolate does, in fact, have significant [health benefits.]

   Case 2: There i[s a big news event in your town] which is repor[ted]

   **b.** The market fo[r]
   Case 1: The Ra[]
   Case 2: The pr[]

   **c.** The market fo[r]
   Case 1: People[]
   Case 2: People[]
   cooked breakf[ast]

   **d.** The market fo[r]

---

### KEY TERMS

# Organization of This Book: What's Core, What's Optional

We realize that some of our chapters will be considered optional. Below and on the facing page is a list of what we view as core chapters and those that could be considered optional. We've annotated the list of chapters to indicate what they cover should you wish to incorporate them.

| Core | Optional |
|---|---|
| | **Introduction: The Ordinary Business of Life** <br> Initiates students into the study of economics with basic terms and explains the difference between microeconomics and macroeconomics. |
| **1. First Principles** <br> Outlines 12 principles underlying the study of economics: principles of individual choice, interaction between individuals, and economy-wide interaction. | |
| **2. Economic Models: Trade-offs and Trade** <br> Employs two economic models—the production possibilities frontier and comparative advantage—as an introduction from gains from trade and international comparisons. | **Chapter 2 Appendix: Graphs in Economics** <br> Offers a comprehensive review of graphing and math skills for students who would find a refresher helpful to prepare them for better economic literacy. |
| **3. Supply and Demand** <br> Covers the essentials of supply, demand, market equilibrium, surplus, and shortage. | |
| **4. Price Controls and Quotas: Meddling with Markets** <br> Covers market interventions and their consequences: price and quantity controls, inefficiency, and deadweight loss. | |
| | **5. International Trade** <br> Here we trace the sources of comparative advantage, consider tariffs and quotas, and explore the politics of trade protection, including coverage on the controversy over imports from low-wage countries. |
| | **Chapter 5 Appendix: Consumer and Producer Surplus** <br> Introduces students to market efficiency, the ways markets fail, the roles of prices as signals, and property rights. |
| **6. Macroeconomics: The Big Picture** <br> Introduces the big ideas of macroeconomics with an overview of recessions and expansions, employment and unemployment, long-run growth, inflation versus deflation, and the open economy. | |
| **7. Tracking the Macroeconomy** <br> Explains how the numbers macroeconomists use are calculated and why, including the basics of national income accounting and price indexes. | |
| **8. Unemployment and Inflation** <br> Covers the measurement of unemployment, the reasons why positive employment exists even in booms, and the problems posed by inflation. | |
| **9. Long-Run Economic Growth** <br> Emphasizes an international perspective—economic growth is about the world as a whole—and explains why some countries have been more successful than others. | |
| **10. Savings, Investment Spending, and the Financial System** <br> Introduces students to financial markets and institutions, loanable funds and the determination of interest rates. Includes new coverage on present value in the chapter proper and in a new appendix. | **Chapter 10 Appendix: Toward a Fuller Understanding of Present Value** <br> Expands on the coverage of present value added to the chapter. |

| Core | Optional |
|---|---|
| **11. Income and Expenditure**<br>Addresses the determinants of consumer and investment spending, introduces the famous 45-degree diagram, and explains the logic of the multiplier. | **Chapter 11 Appendix: Deriving the Multiplier Algebraically**<br>A rigorous and mathematical approach to deriving the multiplier. |
| **12. Aggregate Demand and Aggregate Supply**<br>Provides the traditional focus on aggregate price level using the traditional approach to AD/AS. It also covers the ability of the economy to recover in the long run. | |
| **13. Fiscal Policy**<br>Provides an analysis of the role of discretionary fiscal policy, automatic stabilizers, and long-run issues of debt and solvency. | **Chapter 13 Appendix: Taxes and the Multiplier**<br>A rigorous derivation of the roles of taxes in reducing the size of the multiplier and acting as an automatic stabilizer. |
| **14. Money, Banking, and the Federal Reserve System**<br>Covers the roles of money, the ways in which banks create money, and the structure and the role of the Federal Reserve and other central banks. | |
| **15. Monetary Policy**<br>Covers the role of Federal Reserve policy in driving interest rates and aggregate demand. It includes a section bridging the short and long run by showing how interest rates set in the short run reflects the supply and demand of savings in the long run. | **Chapter 15 Appendix: Reconciling the Two Models of the Interest Rate**<br>This appendix explains why the loanable funds model (long-run discussions) and the liquidity preference approach (short-run discussions) are both valuable approaches. |
| **16. Inflation, Disinflation, and Deflation**<br>Covers the causes and consequences of inflation, the large cost deflation imposes on the economy, and the danger that disinflation leads the economy into a liquidity trap. | |
| | **17. Crises and Consequences**<br>Provides an up-to-date look at the recent financial crisis, starting with the Lehman Brothers collapse, integrating coverage about the dangers posed by banking, shadow banking, asset bubbles, and financial contagion. |
| | **18. Macroeconomics: Events and Ideas**<br>Provides a unique overview of the history of macroeconomic thought, set in the context of changing policy concerns, and the current state of macroeconomic debates. |
| | **19. Open-Economy Macroeconomics**<br>Analyzes special issues raised for macroeconomics in an open economy: a weak dollar, foreign accumulation of dollar reserves, and debates surrounding the euro. |

- **Chapters are accessible and entertaining.** We use a fluid and friendly writing style to make concepts accessible and, whenever possible, we use examples that are familiar to students.
- **Although easy to understand, the book also prepares students for further coursework.** There's no need to choose between two unappealing alternatives: a textbook that is "easy to teach" but leaves major gaps in students' understanding, or a textbook that is "hard to teach" but adequately prepares students for future coursework. We offer the best of both worlds.

# Supplements and Media

Worth Publishers is pleased to offer an enhanced and completely revised supplements and media package to accompany this textbook. The package has been crafted to help instructors teach their principles course and to give students the tools to develop their skills in economics.

## For Instructors

### Instructor's Resource Manual with Solutions Manual

The Instructor's Resource Manual, revised by Nora Underwood, University of Central Florida, is a resource meant to provide materials and tips to enhance the classroom experience. The Instructor's Resource Manual provides the following:

- Chapter-by-chapter learning objectives
- Chapter outlines
- Teaching tips and ideas that include:
  - Hints on how to create student interest
  - Tips on presenting the material in class
- Discussion of the examples used in the text, including points to emphasize with your students
- Activities that can be conducted in or out of the classroom
- Hints for dealing with common misunderstandings that are typical among students
- Web resources (includes tips for using EconPortal)
- Solutions manual with detailed solutions to all of the end-of-chapter Problems from the textbook

### Printed Test Bank

*Coordinator and Consultant:* Doris Bennett, Jacksonville State University. The Test Bank provides a wide range of questions appropriate for assessing your students' comprehension, interpretation, analysis, and synthesis skills. Totaling over 4,500 questions, the Test Bank offers multiple-choice, true/false, and short-answer questions designed for comprehensive coverage of the text concepts. Questions have been checked for continuity with the text content, overall usability, and accuracy.

*The Test Bank features include the following:*

- To aid instructors in building tests, each question has been categorized according to its general *degree of difficulty*. The three levels are: *easy, moderate,* and *difficult*.
  - *Easy* questions require students to recognize concepts and definitions. These are questions that can be answered by direct reference to the textbook.
  - *Moderate* questions require some analysis on the student's part.
  - *Difficult* questions usually require more detailed analysis by the student.
- Each question has also been categorized according to a *skill descriptor*. These include: *Fact-Based, Definitional, Concept-Based, Critical Thinking,* and *Analytical Thinking*.
  - *Fact-Based Questions* require students to identify facts presented in the text.
  - *Definitional Questions* require students to define an economic term or concept.
  - *Concept-Based Questions* require a straightforward knowledge of basic concepts.
  - *Critical Thinking Questions* require the student to apply a concept to a particular situation.
  - *Analytical Thinking Questions* require another level of analysis to answer the question. Students must be able to apply a concept and use this knowledge for further analysis of a situation or scenario.
- To further aid instructors in building tests, each question is conveniently cross-referenced to the appropriate topic heading in the textbook. Questions are presented in the order in which concepts are presented in the text.
- The Test Bank includes questions with tables that students must analyze to solve for numerical answers. It also contains questions based on the graphs that appear in the book. These questions ask students to use the graphical models developed in the textbook and to interpret the information presented in the graph. Selected questions are paired with scenarios to reinforce comprehension.
- Questions have been designed to correlate with the various questions in the text. *Study Guide Questions* are also available in each chapter. This is a unique set of 25–30 questions per chapter that are parallel to the *Chapter Review Questions* in the printed Study Guide. These questions focus on the key concepts from the text that students should grasp after reading the chapter. These questions reflect the types of questions that the students have likely already worked through in

homework assignments or in self-testing. These questions can also be used for testing or for brief in-class quizzes.

**Computerized Test Bank** The printed Test Bank is available in CD-ROM format for both Windows and Macintosh users. With this program, instructors can easily create and print tests and write and edit questions. Tests can be printed in a wide range of formats. The software's unique synthesis of flexible word-processing and database features creates a program that is extremely intuitive and capable.

**Lecture PowerPoint Presentation** Created by Can Erbil, Brandeis University, the enhanced PowerPoint presentation slides are designed to assist you with lecture preparation and presentations. The slides are organized by topic and contain graphs, data tables, and bulleted lists of key concepts suitable for lecture presentation. Key figures from the text are replicated and animated to demonstrate how they build. *Notes to the Instructor* are also included to provide added tips, class exercises, examples, and explanations to enhance classroom presentations. The slides have been designed to allow for easy editing of graphs and text. These slides can be customized to suit your individual needs by adding your own data, questions, and lecture notes. These files may be accessed on the instructor's side of the website or on the Instructor's Resource CD-ROM.

**Instructor's Resource CD-ROM** Using the Instructor's Resource CD-ROM, you can easily build classroom presentations or enhance your online courses. This CD-ROM contains all text figures (in JPEG and PPT formats), PowerPoint lecture slides, and detailed solutions to all end-of-chapter Problems. You can choose from the various resources, edit, and save for use in your classroom.

The Instructor's Resource CD-ROM includes:

- **Instructor's Resource Manual** (PDF): a resource containing chapter-by-chapter learning objectives, chapter outlines, teaching tips, examples used in the text, activities, hints for dealing with common student misunderstandings, and web resources.
- **Solutions Manual** (PDF): a manual including detailed solutions to all of the end-of-chapter Problems from the textbook.
- **Lecture PowerPoint Presentations** (PPT): PowerPoint slides including graphs, data tables, and bulleted lists of key concepts suitable for lecture presentation.
- **Images from the Textbook** (JPEG): a complete set of textbook images in high-res and low-res JPEG formats.
- **Illustration PowerPoint Slides** (PPT): a complete set of figures and tables from the textbook in PPT format.

## For Students

**Study Guide** Prepared by Elizabeth Sawyer-Kelly, University of Wisconsin–Madison, the Study Guide reinforces the topics and key concepts covered in the text. For each chapter, the Study Guide is organized as follows:

*Before You Read the Chapter*

- Summary: an opening paragraph that provides a brief overview of the chapter.
- Objectives: a numbered list outlining and describing the material that the student should have learned in the chapter. These objectives can be easily used as a study tool for students.
- Key Terms: a list of boldface key terms with their definitions—including room for note-taking.

*After You Read the Chapter*

- Tips: numbered list of learning tips with graphical analysis.
- Problems and Exercises: a set of 10–15 comprehensive problems.

*Before You Take the Test*

- Chapter Review Questions: a set of 30 multiple-choice questions that focus on the key concepts from the text students should grasp after reading the chapter. These questions are designed for student exam preparation. A parallel set of these questions is also available to instructors in the Test Bank.

*Answer Key*

- Answers to Problems and Exercises: detailed solutions to the Problems and Exercises in the Study Guide.
- Answers to Chapter Review Questions: solutions to the multiple-choice questions in the Study Guide— along with thorough explanations.

## Online Offerings

### Aplia

Worth/Aplia courses are all available with digital textbooks, interactive assignments, and detailed feedback. With Aplia, you retain complete control of and flexibility for your course. You choose the content you want students to cover, and you decide how to organize it. You decide whether online activities are practice (ungraded or graded). For a preview of Aplia materials and to learn more, visit http://www.aplia.com/worth.

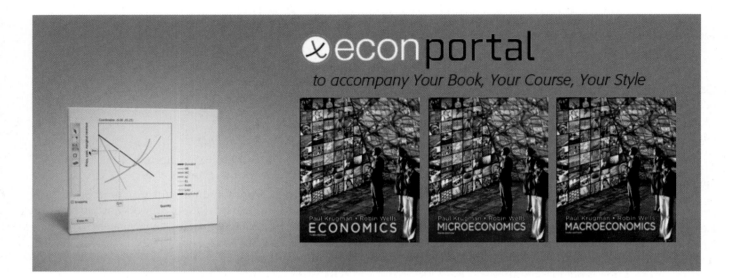

## ECONPORTAL

### Low Investment. High Return.

EconPortal provides a powerful, easy-to-use, completely customizeable teaching and learning management system designed for the principles course with resources created specifically for the Krugman/Wells textbooks. EconPortal marries an even richer variety of resources with a streamlined interface, proving that power and simplicity need not be mutually exclusive. Features include:

- **Clear, consistent interface.** The eBook, resources, and assessment tools are integrated into a single interface for students and instructors.

- **Everything is assignable.** All course materials are assignable and computer gradeable: eBook sections, videos, discussion forums, and RSS Feeds, as well as traditionally assignable items like quizzes.

- **Easy Course Management Integration.** EconPortal is simple to integrate with exisiting campus Learning Management Systems. Grades can be easily imported into campus learning management systems. Single sign-on and one-click grade importing is also available on many local campus management systems.

- **Tailored to Your Syllabus by People You Know.** We understand the opportunity costs involved in switching to a new homework service. That is why Worth Economics is committed to providing you with a single contact at Worth who will tailor your EconPortal course to reflect your syllabus and include the content and assessment elements most important to you. While our commitment to service may begin with your choice to use EconPortal, it does not diminish over time. At Worth, we understand the importance of our role in providing a homework service that is accurate, efficient, and effective.

Request a live demo of EconPortal, find ordering information, or receive trial access at
**www.youreconportal.com.**

### One Location. One Login.

EconPortal integrates the grading homework system, interactive eBook, student tutorials, *The Economist* RSS NewsFeed, course management, and the gradebook into one common interface. Features include:

- **Robust, interactive eBook.** The eBook enables a range of note-sharing options from instructor-to-student to student-to-student notes to actual discussions in the margins of the eBook page.

- **LAUNCH PAD – Pre-loaded assignments for easy startup.** Launch Pad units are pre-built assignments, vetted by practicing economists, that include pre-assembled quizzes (practice and graded), eBook sections, and LearningCurve activities pre-assembled for each chapter. Instructors simply choose which units to assign and customize them by adding or deleting content as they wish. Additional content available for Launch Pad units include *student tutorials, video activities, enhanced Economics in Action activities, and Check Your Understanding quizzes.*

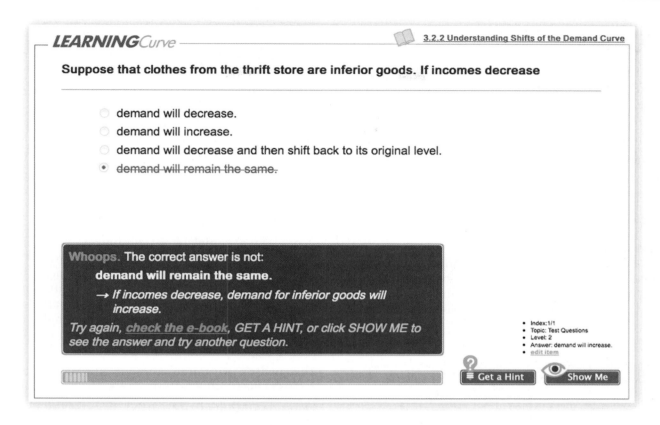

- **LearningCurve – Personalized, formative assessments.** LearningCurve is a smart quizzing program that incorporates adaptive question selection, personalized study plans, and state-of-the-art question analysis reports in a game-like environment that keeps students engaged with the material. Integrated eBook sections are one-click away and an innovative scoring system ensures that students who need more help with the material spend more time in the formative quizzing program than students who are already proficient.

- **Powerful online quizzing and homework.** In addition to the LaunchPad units, instructors can create their own assignments using their own questions or drawing on quiz items within EconPortal, including:

  - **The complete Test Bank** for the textbook for use in creating exams, quizzes, or homework problems. Instructors can use built-in filters and settings to ensure the right questions are chosen and displayed to their preferences.

  - An alternative bank of **Practice Quiz** questions for use in creating homework assignments.

  - The **End-of-Chapter Problem Sets** from the textbook which are carefully edited and available in a self-graded format – perfect for in-class quizzes and homework assignments.

  - **A Graphing Tool** that replicates the pencil and paper experience better than any product on the market by asking students to create curves, not simply shift them. There are an average of 20 graphing problems per chapter, ranging in difficulty, skill, and topic.

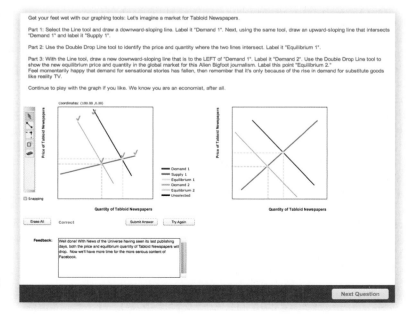

The integrated online version of the Aplia media and the Krugman/Wells text includes:

- Extra problem sets (derived from in-chapter questions in the book) suitable for homework and keyed to specific topics from each chapter
- Regularly updated news analyses
- Real-time online simulations of market interactions
- Interactive tutorials to assist with math and graphing
- Instant online reports that allow instructors to target student trouble areas more efficiently

## sapling learning
**www.saplinglearning.com**

Sapling Learning provides the most effective interactive homework and instruction that improves student-learning outcomes for the problem-solving disciplines.

Sapling Learning offers an enjoyable teaching and effective learning experience that is distinctive in three important ways:

- **Ease of Use:** Sapling Learning's easy-to-use interface keeps students engaged in problem-solving, not struggling with the software.
- **Targeted Instructional Content:** Sapling Learning increases student engagement and comprehension by delivering immediate feedback and targeted instructional content.
- **Unsurpassed Service and Support:** Sapling Learning makes teaching more enjoyable by providing a dedicated Masters- or PhD-level colleague to service instructors' unique needs throughout the course, including content customization.

**CoursePacks** Plug our content into your course management system. Whatever you teach, or whether you use Blackboard, WebCT, Desire2Learn, Angel, Sakai, or Moodle to manage your course, we have free content and support available. Registered instructors can download cartridges with no hassle, no strings attached. Content includes our most popular free resources and book-specific content. For more information, go to http://worthpublishers.com/catalog/Other/Coursepack.

### Companion Website for Students and Instructors
**www.worthpublishers.com/krugmanwells**

The companion website for the Krugman/Wells text offers valuable tools for both the instructor and students. For instructors, the site gives you the ability to track students' interaction with graded activities and gives you access to additional instructor resources.

*The following instructor resources are available:*

- **Quiz Gradebook:** The site gives you the ability to track students' work by accessing an online gradebook.
- **Lecture PowerPoint Presentations:** Instructors have access to helpful lecture material in PowerPoint format. These PowerPoint slides are designed to assist instructors with lecture preparation and presentation.
- **Illustration PowerPoint Slides:** A complete set of figures and tables from the textbook in PowerPoint format is available.
- **Images from the Textbook:** Instructors have access to a complete set of figures and tables from the textbook in high-res and low-res JPEG formats. The textbook art has been processed for "high-resolution" (150 dpi). These figures and photographs have been especially formatted for maximum readability in large lecture halls and follow standards that were set and tested in a real university auditorium.
- **Instructor's Resource Manual:** Instructors have access to the files for the Instructor's Resource Manual.
- **Solutions Manual:** Instructors have access to the files for the detailed solutions to the text's end-of-chapter Problems.

For students, the site offers many opportunities for self-testing and review.

*The following resources are available for students:*

- **Self-Test Quizzes:** This quizzing engine provides 20 multiple-choice question quizzes for every chapter. Immediate and appropriate feedback is provided to students along with topic references for further review.
- **Key Term Flashcards:** Students can test themselves on the key terms with these pop-up electronic flashcards.
- **Web Links:** These Web Links allow students to easily locate outside resources and readings that relate to topics covered in the textbook (or to articles by Paul Krugman). This allows students to effectively conduct research and explore related readings on specific topics.

## Further Resources Offered

### CourseSmart eBooks
**http://www.coursesmart.com/ourproducts**

CourseSmart eBooks offer the complete book in PDF format. Students can save money, up to 60% off the price of print textbooks. With the CourseSmart eBook, students have the ability to take notes, highlight, print pages, and more. A great alternative to renting print textbooks!

**Faculty Lounge** Faculty Lounge is an online community of economics instructors. At this unique forum, economics instructors can connect, interact, and collaborate with fellow teachers and economics researchers, sharing thoughts and teaching resources. Instructors can upload their own resources and search for peer-reviewed content to use in class. Faculty Lounge is a great place to connect with colleagues nationwide who face the same challenges in the classroom as you do. To learn more, ask your Worth representative or visit www.worthpublishers.com/facultylounge.

**Worth Noting** Worth Noting keeps you connected to your textbook authors in real time. Whether they were just on CNBC or published in the *New York Times*, this is the place to find out about it. Visit Worth Noting at http://blogs.worthpublishers.com/econblog/.

**i>clicker** Developed by a team of University of Illinois physicists, i>clicker is the most flexible and reliable classroom response system available. It is the only solution created *for* educators, *by* educators—with continuous product improvements made through direct classroom testing and faculty feedback. You'll love i>clicker, no matter your level of technical expertise, because the focus is on *your* teaching, *not the technology*. To learn more about packaging i>clicker with this textbook, please contact your local sales rep or visit www.iclicker.com.

**Dismal Scientist** A high-powered business database and analysis service comes to the classroom! Dismal Scientist offers real-time monitoring of the global economy, produced locally by economists and professionals at Economy.com's London, Sydney, and West Chester offices. Dismal Scientist is *free* when packaged with the Krugman/Wells textbook. Please contact your local sales rep for more information or go to www.dismal.com.

## Acknowledgments

We are indebted to the following reviewers, focus group participants, and other consultants for their suggestions and advice on the second edition.

Rebecca Achée Thornton, *University of Houston*
Carlos Aguilar, *El Paso Community College*
Terence Alexander, *Iowa State University*

Morris Altman, *University of Saskatchewan*
Farhad Ameen, *State University of New York, Westchester Community College*
Christopher P. Ball, *Quinnipiac University*
Sue Bartlett, *University of South Florida*
Scott Beaulier, *Mercer University*
David Bernotas, *University of Georgia*
Marc Bilodeau, *Indiana University and Purdue University, Indianapolis*
Kelly Blanchard, *Purdue University*
Anne Bresnock, *California State Polytechnic University*
Douglas M. Brown, *Georgetown University*
Joseph Calhoun, *Florida State University*
Douglas Campbell, *University of Memphis*
Kevin Carlson, *University of Massachusetts, Boston*
Andrew J. Cassey, *Washington State University*
Shirley Cassing, *University of Pittsburgh*
Sewin Chan, *New York University*
Mitchell M. Charkiewicz, *Central Connecticut State University*
Joni S. Charles, *Texas State University, San Marcos*
Adhip Chaudhuri, *Georgetown University*
Eric P. Chiang, *Florida Atlantic University*
Hayley H. Chouinard, *Washington State University*
Kenny Christianson, *Binghamton University*
Lisa Citron, *Cascadia Community College*
Steven L. Cobb, *University of North Texas*
Barbara Z. Connolly, *Westchester Community College*
Stephen Conroy, *University of San Diego*
Thomas E. Cooper, *Georgetown University*
Cesar Corredor, *Texas A&M University and University of Texas, Tyler*
Jim F. Couch, *University of Northern Alabama*
Daniel Daly, *Regis University*
H. Evren Damar, *Pacific Lutheran University*
Antony Davies, *Duquesne University*
Greg Delemeester, *Marietta College*
Patrick Dolenc, *Keene State College*
Christine Doyle-Burke, *Framingham State College*
Ding Du, *South Dakota State University*
Jerry Dunn, *Southwestern Oklahoma State University*
Robert R. Dunn, *Washington and Jefferson College*
Ann Eike, *University of Kentucky*
Tisha L. N. Emerson, *Baylor University*
Hadi Salehi Esfahani, *University of Illinois*
William Feipel, *Illinois Central College*
Rudy Fichtenbaum, *Wright State University*
David W. Findlay, *Colby College*
Mary Flannery, *University of California, Santa Cruz*
Robert Francis, *Shoreline Community College*
Shelby Frost, *Georgia State University*
Frank Gallant, *George Fox University*
Robert Gazzale, *Williams College*
Robert Godby, *University of Wyoming*
Michael Goode, *Central Piedmont Community College*
Douglas E. Goodman, *University of Puget Sound*
Marvin Gordon, *University of Illinois at Chicago*

Kathryn Graddy, *Brandeis University*

Alan Day Haight, *State University of New York, Cortland*

Mehdi Haririan, *Bloomsburg University*

Clyde A. Haulman, *College of William and Mary*

Richard R. Hawkins, *University of West Florida*

Mickey A. Hepner, *University of Central Oklahoma*

Michael Hilmer, *San Diego State University*

Tia Hilmer, *San Diego State University*

Jane Himarios, *University of Texas, Arlington*

Jim Holcomb, *University of Texas, El Paso*

Don Holley, *Boise State University*

Alexander Holmes, *University of Oklahoma*

Julie Holzner, *Los Angeles City College*

Robert N. Horn, *James Madison University*

Steven Husted, *University of Pittsburgh*

John O. Ifediora, *University of Wisconsin, Platteville*

Hiro Ito, *Portland State University*

Mike Javanmard, *RioHondo Community College*

Robert T. Jerome, *James Madison University*

Shirley Johnson-Lans, *Vassar College*

David Kalist, *Shippensburg University*

Lillian Kamal, *Northwestern University*

Roger T. Kaufman, *Smith College*

Herb Kessel, *St. Michael's College*

Rehim Kilic, *Georgia Institute of Technology*

Grace Kim, *University of Michigan, Dearborn*

Michael Kimmitt, *University of Hawaii, Manoa*

Robert Kling, *Colorado State University*

Sherrie Kossoudji, *University of Michigan*

Charles Kroncke, *College of Mount Saint Joseph*

Reuben Kyle, *Middle Tennessee State University (retired)*

Katherine Lande-Schmeiser, *University of Minnesota, Twin Cities*

David Lehr, *Longwood College*

Mary Jane Lenon, *Providence College*

Mary H. Lesser, *Iona College*

Solina Lindahl, *California Polytechnic Institute, San Luis Obispo*

Haiyong Liu, *East Carolina University*

Jane S. Lopus, *California State University, East Bay*

María José Luengo-Prado, *Northeastern University*

Rotua Lumbantobing, *North Carolina State University*

Ed Lyell, *Adams State College*

John Marangos, *Colorado State University*

Ralph D. May, *Southwestern Oklahoma State University*

Wayne McCaffery, *University of Wisconsin, Madison*

Larry McRae, *Appalachian State University*

Mary Ruth J. McRae, *Appalachian State University*

Ellen E. Meade, *American University*

Meghan Millea, *Mississippi State University*

Norman C. Miller, *Miami University (of Ohio)*

Khan A. Mohabbat, *Northern Illinois University*

Myra L. Moore, *University of Georgia*

Jay Morris, *Champlain College in Burlington*

Akira Motomura, *Stonehill College*

Kevin J. Murphy, *Oakland University*

Robert Murphy, *Boston College*

Ranganath Murthy, *Bucknell University*

Anthony Myatt, *University of New Brunswick, Canada*

Randy A. Nelson, *Colby College*

Charles Newton, *Houston Community College*

Daniel X. Nguyen, *Purdue University*

Dmitri Nizovtsev, *Washburn University*

Thomas A. Odegaard, *Baylor University*

Constantin Oglobin, *Georgia Southern University*

Charles C. Okeke, *College of Southern Nevada*

Una Okonkwo Osili, *Indiana University and Purdue University, Indianapolis*

Terry Olson, *Truman State University*

Maxwell Oteng, *University of California, Davis*

P. Marcelo Oviedo, *Iowa State University*

Jeff Owen, *Gustavus Adolphus College*

James Palmieri, *Simpson College*

Walter G. Park, *American University*

Elliott Parker, *University of Nevada, Reno*

Michael Perelman, *California State University, Chico*

Nathan Perry, *Utah State University*

Dean Peterson, *Seattle University*

Ken Peterson, *Furman University*

Paul Pieper, *University of Illinois at Chicago*

Dennis L. Placone, *Clemson University*

Michael Polcen, *Northern Virginia Community College*

Raymond A. Polchow, *Zane State College*

Linnea Polgreen, *University of Iowa*

Eileen Rabach, *Santa Monica College*

Matthew Rafferty, *Quinnipiac University*

Jaishankar Raman, *Valparaiso University*

Margaret Ray, *Mary Washington College*

Helen Roberts, *University of Illinois at Chicago*

Jeffrey Rubin, *Rutgers University, New Brunswick*

Rose M. Rubin, *University of Memphis*

Lynda Rush, *California State Polytechnic University, Pomona*

Michael Ryan, *Western Michigan University*

Sara Saderion, *Houston Community College*

Djavad Salehi-Isfahani, *Virginia Tech*

Elizabeth Sawyer Kelly, *University of Wisconsin, Madison*

Jesse A. Schwartz, *Kennesaw State University*

Chad Settle, *University of Tulsa*

Steve Shapiro, *University of North Florida*

Robert L. Shoffner III, *Central Piedmont Community College*

Joseph Sicilian, *University of Kansas*

Judy Smrha, *Baker University*

John Solow, *University of Iowa*

John Somers, *Portland Community College*

Stephen Stageberg, *University of Mary Washington*

Monty Stanford, *DeVry University*

Rebecca Stein, *University of Pennsylvania*

William K. Tabb, *Queens College, City University of New York (retired)*

Sarinda Taengnoi, *University of Wisconsin, Oshkosh*

Henry Terrell, *University of Maryland*

Michael Toma, *Armstrong Atlantic State University*

Brian Trinque, *University of Texas, Austin*

Boone A. Turchi, *University of North Carolina, Chapel Hill*

Nora Underwood, *University of Central Florida*
J. S. Uppal, *State University of New York, Albany*
John Vahaly, *University of Louisville*
Jose J. Vazquez-Cognet, *University of Illinois, Urbana–Champaign*
Daniel Vazzana, *Georgetown College*
Roger H. von Haefen, *North Carolina State University*
Andreas Waldkirch, *Colby College*
Christopher Waller, *University of Notre Dame*
Gregory Wassall, *Northeastern University*
Robert Whaples, *Wake Forest University*
Thomas White, *Assumption College*
Jennifer P. Wissink, *Cornell University*
Mark Witte, *Northwestern University*
Kristen M. Wolfe, *St. Johns River Community College*
Larry Wolfenbarger, *Macon State College*
Louise B. Wolitz, *University of Texas, Austin*
Gavin Wright, *Stanford University*
Bill Yang, *Georgia Southern University*
Jason Zimmerman, *South Dakota State University*

Our deep appreciation and heartfelt thanks to the following reviewers, class-testers, and contributors whose input helped us shape this third edition.

Carlos Aguilar, *El Paso Community College*
Seemi Ahmad, *Dutchess Community College*
Farhad Ameen, *Westchester Community College*
Dean Baim, *Pepperdine University*
David Barber, *Quinnipiac College*
Janis Barry-Figuero, *Fordham University at Lincoln Center*
Hamid Bastin, *Shippensburg University*
Michael Bonnal, *University of Tennessee, Chattanooga*
Milicia Bookman, *Saint Joseph's University*
Anne Bresnock, *California State Polytechnic University, Pomona*
Colleen Callahan, *American University*
Giuliana Campanelli Andreopoulos, *William Patterson University*
Charles Campbell, *Mississippi State University*
Randall Campbell, *Mississippi State University*
Joel Carton, *Florida International University*
Andrew Cassey, *Washington State University*
Sanjukta Chaudhuri, *University of Wisconsin, Eau Claire*
Eric Chiang, *Florida Atlantic University*
Abdur Chowdhury, *Marquette University*
Chad Cotti, *University of Wisconsin, Oshkosh*
Maria DaCosta, *University of Wisconsin, Eau Claire*
James P. D'Angelo, *University of Cincinnati*
Orgul Demet Ozturk, *University of South Carolina*
Harold Elder, *University of Alabama*
Rudy Fichenbaum, *Wright State University*
Sherman Folland, *Oakland University*
Amanda Freeman, *Kansas State University*
Shelby Frost, *Georgia State University*
Sarah Ghosh, *University of Scranton*
Satyajit Ghosh, *University of Scranton*
Fidel Gonzalez, *Sam Houston State University*

Michael G. Goode, *Central Piedmont Community College*
Alan Gummerson, *Florida International University*
Eran Guse, *West Virginia University*
Don Holley, *Boise State University*
Scott Houser, *Colorado School of Mines*
Russell A. Janis, *University of Massachusetts, Amherst*
Jonatan Jelen, *The City College of New York*
Miles Kimball, *University of Michigan*
Colin Knapp, *University of Florida*
Stephan Kroll, *Colorado State University*
Vicky Langston, *Columbus State University*
Richard B. Le, *Cosumnes River College*
Yu-Feng Lee, *New Mexico State University*
Mary Lesser, *Iona College*
Solina Lindahl, *California Polytechnic State University*
Volodymyr Lugovskyy, *Indiana University*
Mark E. McBride, *Miami University*
Michael Mogavero, *University of Notre Dame*
Gary Murphy, *Case Western Reserve University*
Anna Musatti, *Columbia University*
Christopher Mushrush, *Illinois State University*
ABM Nasir, *North Carolina Central University*
Gerardo Nebbia, *El Camino College*
Pattabiraman Neelakantan, *East Stroudsburg University*
Pamela Nickless, *University of North Carolina, Asheville*
Nick Noble, *Miami University (Ohio)*
Walter Park, *American University*
Brian Peterson, *Central College*
Michael Polcen, *Northern Virginia Community College*
Reza Ramazani, *Saint Michael's College*
Ryan Ratcliff, *University of San Diego*
Robert Rebelein, *Vassar College*
Ken Roberts, *Southwestern University*
Greg Rose, *Sacramento City College*
Jeff Rubin, *Rutgers University, New Brunswick*
Jason C. Rudbeck, *University of Georgia*
Michael Sattinger, *State University of New York, Albany*
Elizabeth Sawyer Kelly, *University of Wisconsin, Madison*
Arzu Sen, *West Virginia University*
Marcia Snyder, *College of Charleston*
Liliana V. Stern, *Auburn University*
Adam Stevenson, *University of Michigan*
Eric Stuen, *University of Idaho*
Christine Tarasevich, *Del Mar College*
Henry S. Terrell, *George Washington University*
Mickey Wu, *Coe College*

A special thanks to Michael Sattinger, State University of New York at Albany, for his thoughtful evaluation of chapters in the second edition and timely guidance on key changes in this third edition. Many thanks also to Kathryn Graddy, Brandeis University, for her invaluable contributions to this and previous revisions. Special thanks also to David Barber, who encouraged us to make this edition more visual so it could be more accessible to students. As in the first and second editions, we found ourselves trusting Andreas Bentz and his indefatigable eye for detail as we focused on the larger issues conveyed in this edition. We count ourselves extremely fortunate to have found Andreas. Andreas's efforts were also supported by accuracy checkers Myra Moore, University of Georgia; Nora Underwood, University of Central Florida; Martha Olney, University of California–Berkeley; James Watson, Salt Lake Community College; and Rod Hill, University of New Brunswick.

Thanks as well for the contributions of Jose J. Vasquez-Cognet, University of Illinois at Urbana–Champaign, and Solina Lindahl, California Polytechnic State University, each provided expert guidance on the media program associated with the textbook.

We must also thank the many people at Worth Publishers for their contributions. Elizabeth Widdicombe, president of Freeman and Worth, and Catherine Woods, senior vice president, played an important role in planning for this revision. We have Liz to thank for the idea that became the Business Case in each chapter. Charles Linsmeier, publisher, ably oversaw the revision and contributed throughout. A special thanks to Craig Bleyer, our original publisher at Worth and now national sales director, who put so much of his effort into making each edition a success. His keen instincts showed again in the revision plan for this edition.

Once again, we have had an incredible production and design team on this book, people whose hard work, creativity, dedication, and patience continue to amaze us. Once again, you have outdone yourselves. Thank you all: Tracey Kuehn, Lisa Kinne, and Anthony Calcara for producing this book; Babs Reingold and Lyndall Culbertson for their beautiful interior design and the spectacular cover; Karen Osborne for her thoughtful copyedit; Barbara Seixas, who worked her magic yet again despite the vagaries of the project schedule; Cecilia Varas and Elyse Rieder for photo research; Stacey Alexander and Edgar Bonilla for coordinating all the production of the supplemental materials; and Mary Melis, assistant editor, who wore many hats in this revision and each of them well.

Many thanks to Marie McHale for devising and coordinating the impressive collection of media and supplements that accompany our book. Thanks to the incredible team of supplements writers and coordinators who worked with Marie on the supplements and media package; we are forever grateful for your tireless efforts.

Thanks to Scott Guile, executive marketing manager, for his tireless advocacy of this book; to Steve Rigolosi and Kerri Russini for their contributions in market development; and to Tom Kling for his advocacy of this book with the sales department.

And most of all, special thanks to Sharon Balbos, executive development editor on each of our editions. Much of the success of this book is owed to Sharon's dedication and professionalism. As always, she kept her cool through rough spots. Sharon, we're not sure we deserved an editor as good as you, but we're sure that everyone involved as well as our adopters and their students have been made better off by your presence.

Paul Krugman                    Robin Wells

# Introduction: The Ordinary Business of Life

## ANY GIVEN SUNDAY

Robert Landau/Corbis

**Delivering the goods: the market economy in action.**

IT'S SUNDAY AFTERNOON IN THE spring of 2011, and Route 1 in central New Jersey is a busy place. Thousands of people crowd the shopping malls that line the road for 20 miles, all the way from Trenton to New Brunswick. Most of the shoppers are cheerful—and why not? The stores in those malls offer an extraordinary range of choice; you can buy everything from sophisticated electronic equipment to fashionable clothes to organic carrots. There are probably 100,000 distinct items available along that stretch of road. And most of these items are not luxury goods that only the rich can afford; they are products that millions of Americans can and do purchase every day.

The scene along Route 1 on this spring day is, of course, perfectly ordinary—very much like the scene along hundreds of other stretches of road, all across America, that same afternoon. And the discipline of economics is mainly concerned with ordinary things. As the great nineteenth-century economist Alfred Marshall put it, economics is "a study of mankind in the ordinary business of life."

What can economics say about this "ordinary business"? Quite a lot, it turns out. What we'll see in this book is that even familiar scenes of economic life pose some very important questions—questions that economics can help answer. Among these questions are:

- How does our economic system work? That is, how does it manage to deliver the goods?
- When and why does our economic system go astray, leading people into counterproductive behavior?
- Why are there ups and downs in the economy? That is, why does the economy sometimes have a "bad year"?
- Finally, why is the long run mainly a story of ups rather than downs? That is, why has America, along with other advanced nations, become so much richer over time?

Let's take a look at these questions and offer a brief preview of what you will learn in this book. ■

# The Invisible Hand

That ordinary scene in central New Jersey would not have looked at all ordinary to an American from colonial times—say, one of the patriots who helped George Washington win the Battle of Trenton in 1776. At the time, Trenton was a small village, and farms lined the route of Washington's epic night march from Trenton to Princeton—a march that took him right past the future site of the giant Quakerbridge shopping mall.

Imagine that you could transport an American from the colonial period forward in time to our own era. (Isn't that the plot of a movie? Several, actually.) What would this time-traveler find amazing?

Surely the most amazing thing would be the sheer prosperity of modern America—the range of goods and services that ordinary families can afford. Looking at all that wealth, our transplanted colonial would wonder, "How can I get some of that?" Or perhaps he would ask himself, "How can my society get some of that?"

The answer is that to get this kind of prosperity, you need a well-functioning system for coordinating productive activities—the activities that create the goods and services people want and get them to the people who want them. That kind of system is what we mean when we talk about the **economy.** And **economics** is the social science that studies the production, distribution, and consumption of goods and services.

An economy succeeds to the extent that it, literally, delivers the goods. A time-traveler from the eighteenth century—or even from 1950—would be amazed at how many goods and services the modern American economy delivers and at how many people can afford them. Compared with any past economy and with all but a few other countries today, America has an incredibly high standard of living.

So our economy must be doing something right, and the time-traveler might want to compliment the person in charge. But guess what? There isn't anyone in charge. The United States has a **market economy,** in which production and consumption are the result of decentralized decisions by many firms and individuals. There is no central authority telling people what to produce or where to ship it. Each individual producer makes what he or she thinks will be most profitable; each consumer buys what he or she chooses.

The alternative to a market economy is a *command economy,* in which there *is* a central authority making decisions about production and consumption. Command economies have been tried, most notably in the Soviet Union between 1917 and 1991. But they didn't work very well. Producers in the Soviet Union routinely found themselves unable to produce because they did not have crucial raw materials, or they succeeded in producing but then found that nobody wanted their products. Consumers were often unable to find necessary items—command economies are famous for long lines at shops.

Market economies, however, are able to coordinate even highly complex activities and to reliably provide consumers with the goods and services they want. Indeed, people quite casually trust their lives to the market system: residents of any major city would starve in days if the unplanned yet somehow orderly actions of thousands of businesses did not deliver a steady supply of food. Surprisingly, the unplanned "chaos" of a market economy turns out to be far more orderly than the "planning" of a command economy.

In 1776, in a famous passage in his book *The Wealth of Nations,* the pioneering Scottish economist Adam Smith wrote about how individuals, in pursuing their own interests, often end up serving the interests of society as a whole. Of a businessman whose pursuit of profit makes the nation wealthier, Smith wrote: "[H]e intends only his own gain, and he is in this, as in many other cases, led by an invisible hand to promote an end which was no part of his intention." Ever since, economists have used the term **invisible hand** to refer to the way a market

An **economy** is a system for coordinating society's productive activities.

**Economics** is the social science that studies the production, distribution, and consumption of goods and services.

A **market economy** is an economy in which decisions about production and consumption are made by individual producers and consumers.

The **invisible hand** refers to the way in which the individual pursuit of self-interest can lead to good results for society as a whole.

economy manages to harness the power of self-interest for the good of society.

The study of how individuals make decisions and how these decisions interact is called **microeconomics.** One of the key themes in microeconomics is the validity of Adam Smith's insight: individuals pursuing their own interests often do promote the interests of society as a whole.

So part of the answer to our time-traveler's question—"How can my society achieve the kind of prosperity you take for granted?"—is that his society should learn to appreciate the virtues of a market economy and the power of the invisible hand.

But the invisible hand isn't always our friend. It's also important to understand when and why the individual pursuit of self-interest can lead to counterproductive behavior.

## My Benefit, Your Cost

One thing that our time-traveler would not admire about modern Route 1 is the traffic. In fact, although most things have gotten better in America over time, traffic congestion has gotten a lot worse.

When traffic is congested, each driver is imposing a cost on all the other drivers on the road—he is literally getting in their way (and they are getting in his way). This cost can be substantial: in major metropolitan areas, each time someone drives to work, instead of taking public transportation or working at home, he can easily impose $15 or more in hidden costs on other drivers. Yet when deciding whether or not to drive, commuters have no incentive to take the costs they impose on others into account.

Traffic congestion is a familiar example of a much broader problem: sometimes the individual pursuit of one's own interest, instead of promoting the interests of society as a whole, can actually make society worse off. When this happens, it is known as **market failure.** Other important examples of market failure involve air and water pollution as well as the overexploitation of natural resources such as fish and forests.

The good news, as you will learn as you use this book to study microeconomics, is that economic analysis can be used to diagnose cases of market failure. And often, economic analysis can also be used to devise solutions for the problem.

## Good Times, Bad Times

Route 1 was bustling on that day in 2011. But if you'd visited the malls in 2008, the scene wouldn't have been quite as cheerful. That's because New Jersey's economy, along with that of the United States as a whole, was depressed in 2008: in early 2007, businesses began laying off workers in large numbers, and employment didn't start bouncing back until the summer of 2009.

Such troubled periods are a regular feature of modern economies. The fact is that the economy does not always run smoothly: it experiences fluctuations, a series of ups and downs. By middle age, a typical American will have experienced three or four downs, known as **recessions.** (The U.S. economy experienced serious recessions beginning in 1973, 1981, 1990, 2001, and 2007.) During a severe recession, millions of workers may be laid off.

**Microeconomics** is the branch of economics that studies how people make decisions and how these decisions interact.

When the individual pursuit of self-interest leads to bad results for society as a whole, there is **market failure.**

A **recession** is a downturn in the economy.

**Macroeconomics** is the branch of economics that is concerned with overall ups and downs in the economy.

**Economic growth** is the growing ability of the economy to produce goods and services.

Like market failure, recessions are a fact of life; but also like market failure, they are a problem for which economic analysis offers some solutions. Recessions are one of the main concerns of the branch of economics known as **macroeconomics,** which is concerned with the overall ups and downs of the economy. If you study macroeconomics, you will learn how economists explain recessions and how government policies can be used to minimize the damage from economic fluctuations.

Despite the occasional recession, however, over the long run the story of the U.S. economy contains many more ups than downs. And that long-run ascent is the subject of our final question.

## Onward and Upward

At the beginning of the twentieth century, most Americans lived under conditions that we would now think of as extreme poverty. Only 10% of homes had flush toilets, only 8% had central heating, only 2% had electricity, and almost nobody had a car, let alone a washing machine or air conditioning.

Such comparisons are a stark reminder of how much our lives have been changed by **economic growth,** the growing ability of the economy to produce goods and services. Why does the economy grow over time? And why does economic growth occur faster in some times and places than in others? These are key questions for economics because economic growth is a good thing, as those shoppers on Route 1 can attest, and most of us want more of it.

## An Engine for Discovery

We hope we have convinced you that the "ordinary business of life" is really quite extraordinary, if you stop to think about it, and that it can lead us to ask some very interesting and important questions.

In this book, we will describe the answers economists have given to these questions. But this book, like economics as a whole, isn't a list of answers: it's an introduction to a discipline, a way to address questions like those we have just asked. Or as Alfred Marshall, who described economics as a study of the "ordinary business of life," put it: "Economics . . . is not a body of concrete truth, but an engine for the discovery of concrete truth."

So let's turn the key and start the ignition.

### KEY TERMS

| | | |
|---|---|---|
| Economy, p. 2 | Invisible hand, p. 2 | Recession, p. 3 |
| Economics, p. 2 | Microeconomics, p. 3 | Macroeconomics, p. 4 |
| Market economy, p. 2 | Market failure, p. 3 | Economic growth, p. 4 |

# First Principles

## COMMON GROUND

❯ A set of principles for understanding the economics of how individuals make choices

❯ A set of principles for understanding how economies work through the interaction of individual choices

❯ A set of principles for understanding economy-wide interactions

Seongloon Cho//bloomsberg via Getty Images

**One must choose.**

THE ANNUAL MEETING OF THE American Economic Association draws thousands of economists, young and old, famous and obscure. There are booksellers, business meetings, and quite a few job interviews. But mainly the economists gather to talk and listen. During the busiest times, 60 or more presentations may be taking place simultaneously, on questions that range from financial market crises to who does the cooking in two-earner families.

What do these people have in common? An expert on financial markets probably knows very little about the economics of housework, and vice versa. Yet an economist who wanders into the wrong seminar and ends up listening to presentations on some unfamiliar topic is nonetheless likely to hear much that is familiar. The reason is that all economic analysis is based on a set of common principles that apply to many different issues.

Some of these principles involve *individual choice*—for economics is, first of all, about the choices that individuals make. Do you save your money and take the bus or do you buy a car? Do you keep your old smart-phone or upgrade to a new one? These decisions involve *making a choice* from among a limited number of alternatives—limited because no one can have everything that he or she wants. Every question in economics at its most basic level involves individuals making choices.

But to understand how an economy works, you need to understand more than how individuals make choices. None of us are Robinson Crusoe, alone on an island. We must make decisions in an environment that is shaped by the decisions of others. Indeed, in a modern economy even the simplest decisions you make—say, what to have for breakfast—are shaped by the decisions of thousands of other people, from the banana grower in Costa Rica who decided to grow the

fruit you eat to the farmer in Iowa who provided the corn in your cornflakes.

Because each of us in a market economy depends on so many others—and they, in turn, depend on us—our choices interact. So although all economics at a basic level is about individual choice, in order to understand how market economies behave we must also understand *economic interaction*—how my choices affect your choices, and vice versa.

Many important economic interactions can be understood by looking at the markets for individual goods, like the market for corn. But an economy as a whole has ups and downs, and we therefore need to understand economy-wide interactions as well as the more limited interactions that occur in individual markets.

In this chapter, we will look at twelve basic principles of economics—four principles involving individual choice, five involving the way individual choices interact, and three more involving economy-wide interactions. ■

# Principles That Underlie Individual Choice: The Core of Economics

Every economic issue involves, at its most basic level, **individual choice—** decisions by an individual about what to do and what not to do. In fact, you might say that it isn't economics if it isn't about choice.

Step into a big store like a Walmart or Target. There are thousands of different products available, and it is extremely unlikely that you—or anyone else—could afford to buy everything you might want to have. And anyway, there's only so much space in your dorm room or apartment. So will you buy another bookcase or a mini-refrigerator? Given limitations on your budget and your living space, you must choose which products to buy and which to leave on the shelf.

The fact that those products are on the shelf in the first place involves choice—the store manager chose to put them there, and the manufacturers of the products chose to produce them. All economic activities involve individual choice.

Four economic principles underlie the economics of individual choice, as shown in Table 1-1. We'll now examine each of these principles in more detail.

| TABLE 1-1   The Principles of Individual Choice |
|---|
| 1. People must make choices because resources are scarce. |
| 2. The opportunity cost of an item—what you must give up in order to get it—is its true cost. |
| 3. "How much" decisions require making trade-offs at the margin: comparing the costs and benefits of doing a little bit more of an activity versus doing a little bit less. |
| 4. People usually respond to incentives, exploiting opportunities to make themselves better off. |

## Principle #1: Choices Are Necessary Because Resources Are Scarce

You can't always get what you want. Everyone would like to have a beautiful house in a great location (and have help with the housecleaning), a new car or two, and a nice vacation in a fancy hotel. But even in a rich country like the United States, not many families can afford all that. So they must make choices—whether to go to Disney World this year or buy a better car, whether to make do with a small backyard or accept a longer commute in order to live where land is cheaper.

Limited income isn't the only thing that keeps people from having everything they want. Time is also in limited supply: there are only 24 hours in a day. And because the time we have is limited, choosing to spend time on one activity also means choosing not to spend time on a different activity—spending time studying for an exam means forgoing a night spent watching a movie. Indeed, many people are so limited by the number of hours in the day that they are willing to trade money for time. For example, convenience stores normally charge higher prices than a regular supermarket. But they fulfill a valuable role by catering to time-pressured customers who would rather pay more than travel farther to the supermarket.

This leads us to our first principle of individual choice:

*People must make choices because resources are scarce.*

A **resource** is anything that can be used to produce something else. Lists of the economy's resources usually begin with land, labor (the time of workers), capital (machinery, buildings, and other man-made productive assets), and human capital (the educational achievements and skills of workers). A resource is **scarce** when there's not enough of the resource available to satisfy all the ways a society wants to use it. There are many scarce resources. These include natural resources—resources that come from the physical environment, such as minerals, lumber, and petroleum. There is also a limited quantity of human resources—labor, skill, and intelligence. And in a growing world economy with a rapidly increasing human population, even clean air and water have become scarce resources.

**Individual choice** is the decision by an individual of what to do, which necessarily involves a decision of what not to do.

A **resource** is anything that can be used to produce something else.

Resources are **scarce**—not enough of the resources are available to satisfy all the various ways a society wants to use them.

Just as individuals must make choices, the scarcity of resources means that society as a whole must make choices. One way a society makes choices is by allowing them to emerge as the result of many individual choices, which is what usually happens in a market economy. For example, Americans as a group have only so many hours in a week: how many of those hours will they spend going to supermarkets to get lower prices, rather than saving time by shopping at convenience stores? The answer is the sum of individual decisions: each of the millions of individuals in the economy makes his or her own choice about where to shop, and the overall choice is simply the sum of those individual decisions.

But for various reasons, there are some decisions that a society decides are best not left to individual choice. For example, the authors live in an area that until recently was mainly farmland but is now being rapidly built up. Most local residents feel that the community would be a more pleasant place to live if some of the land was left undeveloped. But no individual has an incentive to keep his or her land as open space, rather than sell it to a developer. So a trend has emerged in many communities across the United States of local governments purchasing undeveloped land and preserving it as open space. We'll see in later chapters why decisions about how to use scarce resources are often best left to individuals but sometimes should be made at a higher, community-wide, level.

The real cost of an item is its **opportunity cost**: what you must give up in order to get it.

## Principle #2: The True Cost of Something Is Its Opportunity Cost

It is the last term before you graduate, and your class schedule allows you to take only one elective. There are two, however, that you would really like to take: Intro to Computer Graphics and History of Jazz.

Suppose you decide to take the History of Jazz course. What's the cost of that decision? It is the fact that you can't take the computer graphics class, your next best alternative choice. Economists call that kind of cost—what you must give up in order to get an item you want—the **opportunity cost** of that item. This leads us to our second principle of individual choice:

*The opportunity cost of an item—what you must give up in order to get it—is its true cost.*

So the opportunity cost of taking the History of Jazz class is the benefit you would have derived from the Intro to Computer Graphics class.

The concept of opportunity cost is crucial to understanding individual choice because, in the end, all costs are opportunity costs. That's because every choice you make means forgoing some other alternative. Sometimes critics claim that economists are concerned only with costs and benefits that can be measured in dollars and cents. But that is not true. Much economic analysis involves cases like our elective course example, where it costs no extra tuition to take one elective course—that is, there is no direct monetary cost. Nonetheless, the elective you choose has an opportunity cost—the other desirable elective course that you must forgo because your limited time permits taking only one. More specifically, the opportunity cost of a choice is what you forgo by not choosing your next best alternative.

You might think that opportunity cost is an add-on—that is, something *additional* to the monetary cost of an item. Suppose that an elective class costs additional tuition of $750; now there is a monetary cost to taking History of Jazz. Is the opportunity cost of taking that course something separate from that monetary cost?

Well, consider two cases. First, suppose that taking Intro to Computer Graphics also costs $750. In this case, you would have to spend that $750 no matter which class you take. So what you give up to take the History of Jazz class is still the computer graphics class, period—you would have to spend that $750

You make a **trade-off** when you compare the costs with the benefits of doing something.

AP Photo/Jeff Chiu

**Mark Zuckerberg understood the concept of opportunity cost.**

either way. But suppose there isn't any fee for the computer graphics class. In that case, what you give up to take the jazz class is the benefit from the computer graphics class *plus* the benefit you could have gained from spending the $750 on other things.

Either way, the real cost of taking your preferred class is what you must give up to get it. As you expand the set of decisions that underlie each choice—whether to take an elective or not, whether to finish this term or not, whether to drop out or not—you'll realize that all costs are ultimately opportunity costs.

Sometimes the money you have to pay for something is a good indication of its opportunity cost. But many times it is not. One very important example of how poorly monetary cost can indicate opportunity cost is the cost of attending college. Tuition and housing are major monetary expenses for most students; but even if these things were free, attending college would still be an expensive proposition because most college students, if they were not in college, would have a job. That is, by going to college, students *forgo* the income they could have earned if they had worked instead. This means that the opportunity cost of attending college is what you pay for tuition and housing plus the forgone income you would have earned in a job.

It's easy to see that the opportunity cost of going to college is especially high for people who could be earning a lot during what would otherwise have been their college years. That is why star athletes like LeBron James and entrepreneurs like Mark Zuckerberg, founder of Facebook, often skip or drop out of college.

## Principle #3: "How Much" Is a Decision at the Margin

Some important decisions involve an "either–or" choice—for example, you decide either to go to college or to begin working; you decide either to take economics or to take something else. But other important decisions involve "how much" choices—for example, if you are taking both economics and chemistry this semester, you must decide how much time to spend studying for each. When it comes to understanding "how much" decisions, economics has an important insight to offer: "how much" is a decision made at the margin.

Suppose you are taking both economics and chemistry. And suppose you are a pre-med student, so your grade in chemistry matters more to you than your grade in economics. Does that therefore imply that you should spend *all* your study time on chemistry and wing it on the economics exam? Probably not; even if you think your chemistry grade is more important, you should put some effort into studying economics.

Spending more time studying chemistry involves a benefit (a higher expected grade in that course) and a cost (you could have spent that time doing something else, such as studying to get a higher grade in economics). That is, your decision involves a **trade-off**—a comparison of costs and benefits.

How do you decide this kind of "how much" question? The typical answer is that you make the decision a bit at a time, by asking how you should spend the next hour. Say both exams are on the same day, and the night before you spend time reviewing your notes for both courses. At 6:00 P.M., you decide that it's a good idea to spend at least an hour on each course. At 8:00 P.M., you decide you'd better spend another hour on each course. At 10:00 P.M., you are getting tired and figure you have one more hour to study before bed—chemistry or economics? If you are pre-med, it's likely to be chemistry; if you are pre-MBA, it's likely to be economics.

Note how you've made the decision to allocate your time: at each point the question is whether or not to spend *one more hour* on either course. And in deciding whether to spend another hour studying for chemistry, you weigh the costs (an hour forgone of studying for economics or an hour forgone of sleeping) versus the benefits (a likely increase in your chemistry grade). As long as the benefit of studying chemistry for one more hour outweighs the cost, you should choose to study for that additional hour.

Decisions of this type—whether to do a bit more or a bit less of an activity, like what to do with your next hour, your next dollar, and so on—are **marginal decisions.** This brings us to our third principle of individual choice:

> *"How much" decisions require making trade-offs at the margin: comparing the costs and benefits of doing a little bit more of an activity versus doing a little bit less.*

The study of such decisions is known as **marginal analysis.** Many of the questions that we face in economics—as well as in real life—involve marginal analysis: How many workers should I hire in my shop? At what mileage should I change the oil in my car? What is an acceptable rate of negative side effects from a new medicine? Marginal analysis plays a central role in economics because it is the key to deciding "how much" of an activity to do.

## Principle #4: People Usually Respond to Incentives, Exploiting Opportunities to Make Themselves Better Off

One day, while listening to the morning financial news, the authors heard a great tip about how to park cheaply in Manhattan. Garages in the Wall Street area charge as much as $30 per day. But according to the newscaster, some people had found a better way: instead of parking in a garage, they had their oil changed at the Manhattan Jiffy Lube, where it costs $19.95 to change your oil—and they keep your car all day!

It's a great story, but unfortunately it turned out not to be true—in fact, there is no Jiffy Lube in Manhattan. But if there were, you can be sure there would be a lot of oil changes there. Why? Because when people are offered opportunities to make themselves better off, they normally take them—and if they could find a way to park their car all day for $19.95 rather than $30, they would.

In this example economists say that people are responding to an **incentive**—an opportunity to make themselves better off. We can now state our fourth principle of individual choice:

> *People usually respond to incentives, exploiting opportunities to make themselves better off.*

When you try to predict how individuals will behave in an economic situation, it is a very good bet that they will respond to incentives—that is, exploit opportunities to make themselves better off. Furthermore, individuals will *continue* to exploit these opportunities until they have been fully exhausted. If there really were a Manhattan Jiffy Lube and an oil change really were a cheap way to park your car, we can safely predict that before long the waiting list for oil changes would be weeks, if not months.

In fact, the principle that people will exploit opportunities to make themselves better off is the basis of *all* predictions by economists about individual behavior. If the earnings of those who get MBAs soar while the earnings of those who get law degrees decline, we can expect more students to go to business school and fewer to go to law school. If the price of gasoline rises and stays high for an extended period of time, we can expect people to buy smaller cars with higher gas mileage—making themselves better off in the presence of higher gas prices by driving more fuel-efficient cars.

One last point: economists tend to be skeptical of any attempt to change people's behavior that *doesn't* change their incentives. For example, a plan that calls on manufacturers to reduce pollution voluntarily probably won't be effective because it hasn't changed manufacturers' incentives. In contrast, a plan that gives them a financial reward to reduce pollution is a lot more likely to work because it has changed their incentives.

Decisions about whether to do a bit more or a bit less of an activity are **marginal decisions**. The study of such decisions is known as **marginal analysis**.

An **incentive** is anything that offers rewards to people who change their behavior.

## FOR INQUIRING MINDS

### CASHING IN AT SCHOOL

The true reward for learning is, of course, the learning itself. Many students, however, struggle with their motivation to study and work hard. Teachers and policy makers have been particularly challenged to help students from disadvantaged backgrounds, who often have poor school attendance, high dropout rates, and low standardized test scores. In a 2007–2008 study, Harvard economist Roland Fryer Jr. found that monetary incentives—cash rewards—could improve students' academic performance in schools in economically disadvantaged areas. How cash incentives work, however, is both surprising and predictable.

Fryer conducted his research in four different school districts, employing a different set of incentives and a different measure of performance in each. In New York, students were paid according to their scores on standardized tests; in Chicago, they were paid according to their grades; in Washington, D.C., they were paid according to attendance and good behavior as well as their grades; in Dallas, second-graders were paid each time they read a book. Fryer evaluated the results by comparing the performance of students who were in the program to other students in the same school who were not.

In New York, the program had no perceptible effect on test scores. In Chicago, students in the program got better grades and attended class more. In Washington, the program boosted the outcomes of the kids who are normally the hardest to reach, those with serious behavioral problems, raising their test scores by an amount equivalent to attending five extra months of school. The most dramatic results occurred in Dallas, where students significantly boosted their reading-comprehension test scores; results continued into the next year, after the cash rewards had ended.

So what explains the various results?

To motivate students with cash rewards, Fryer found that students had to believe that they could have a significant effect on the performance measure. So in Chicago, Washington, and Dallas—where students had a significant amount of control over outcomes such as grades, attendance, behavior, and the number of books read—the program produced significant results. But because New York students had little idea how to affect their score on a standardized test, the prospect of a reward had little influence on their behavior. Also, the timing of the reward matters: a $1

Cash incentives have been shown to improve student performance.

reward has more effect on behavior if performance is measured at shorter intervals and the reward is delivered soon after.

Fryer's experiment revealed some critical insights about how to motivate behavior with incentives. How incentives are designed is very important: the relationship between effort and outcome, as well as the speed of reward, matters a lot. Moreover, the design of incentives may depend quite a lot on the characteristics of the people you are trying to motivate: what motivates a student from an economically privileged background may not motivate a student from an economically disadvantaged one. Fryer's insights give teachers and policy makers an important new tool for helping disadvantaged students succeed in school.

So are we ready to do economics? Not yet—because most of the interesting things that happen in the economy are the result not merely of individual choices but of the way in which individual choices interact.

## ECONOMICS ▸ *IN ACTION*

### BOY OR GIRL? IT DEPENDS ON THE COST

One fact about China is indisputable: it's a big country with lots of people. As of 2009, the population of China was 1,331,460,000. That's right: over *one billion three hundred million.*

In 1978, the government of China introduced the "one-child policy" to address the economic and demographic challenges presented by China's large population. China was very, very poor in 1978, and its leaders worried that the country could not afford to adequately educate and care for its growing population. The average Chinese woman in the 1970s was giving birth to more than five children during her lifetime. So the government restricted most couples, particularly those in urban areas, to one child, imposing penalties on those who defied the mandate. As a result, by 2009 the average number of births for a woman in China was only 1.8.

But the one-child policy had an unfortunate unintended consequence. Because China is an overwhelmingly rural country and sons can perform the manual labor of farming, families had a strong preference for sons over daughters. In addition, tradition dictates that brides become part of their husbands' families and that sons take care of their elderly parents. As a result of the one-child policy, China soon had too many "unwanted girls." Some were given up for adoption abroad, but all too many simply "disappeared" during the first year of life, the victims of neglect and mistreatment.

India, another highly rural poor country with high demographic pressures, also has a significant problem with "disappearing girls." In 1990, Amartya Sen, an Indian-born British economist who would go on to win the Nobel Prize in 1998, estimated that there were up to 100 million "missing women" in Asia. (The exact figure is in dispute, but it is clear that Sen identified a real and pervasive problem.)

Demographers have recently noted a distinct turn of events in China, which is quickly urbanizing. In all but one of the provinces with urban centers, the gender imbalance between boys and girls peaked in 1995 and has steadily fallen toward the biologically natural ratio since then. Many believe that the source of the change is China's strong economic growth and increasing urbanization. As people move to cities to take advantage of job growth there, they don't need sons to work the fields. Moreover, land prices in Chinese cities are skyrocketing, making the custom of parents buying an apartment for a son before he can marry unaffordable for many. To be sure, sons are still preferred in the rural areas. But as a sure mark of how times have changed, Internet websites have recently popped up that advise couples on how to have a girl rather than a boy.

The cost of China's "one-child policy" was a generation of "disappeared" daughters—a phenomenon that has itself begun to disappear as economic conditions have changed.

▷●●

### CHECK YOUR UNDERSTANDING    1-1

1. Explain how each of the following situations illustrates one of the four principles of individual choice.
   a. You are on your third trip to a restaurant's all-you-can-eat dessert buffet and are feeling very full. Although it would cost you no additional money, you forgo a slice of coconut cream pie but have a slice of chocolate cake.
   b. Even if there were more resources in the world, there would still be scarcity.
   c. Different teaching assistants teach several Economics 101 tutorials. Those taught by the teaching assistants with the best reputations fill up quickly, with spaces left unfilled in the ones taught by assistants with poor reputations.
   d. To decide how many hours per week to exercise, you compare the health benefits of one more hour of exercise to the effect on your grades of one fewer hour spent studying.

2. You make $45,000 per year at your current job with Whiz Kids Consultants. You are considering a job offer from Brainiacs, Inc., that will pay you $50,000 per year. Which of the following are elements of the opportunity cost of accepting the new job at Brainiacs, Inc.?
   a. The increased time spent commuting to your new job
   b. The $45,000 salary from your old job
   c. The more spacious office at your new job

*Solutions appear at back of book.*

## Interaction: How Economies Work

As we learned in the Introduction, an economy is a system for coordinating the productive activities of many people. In a market economy like we live in, coordination takes place without any coordinator: each individual makes his or her own choices. Yet those choices are by no means independent of one another: each individual's opportunities, and hence choices, depend to a large extent on the choices made by other people. So to understand how a market economy behaves, we have to examine this **interaction** in which my choices affect your choices, and vice versa.

**Interaction** of choices—my choices affect your choices, and vice versa—is a feature of most economic situations. The results of this interaction are often quite different from what the individuals intend.

When studying economic interaction, we quickly learn that the end result of individual choices may be quite different from what any one individual intends. For example, over the past century farmers in the United States have eagerly adopted new farming techniques and crop strains that have reduced their costs and increased their yields. Clearly, it's in the interest of each farmer to keep up with the latest farming techniques.

But the end result of each farmer trying to increase his or her own income has actually been to drive many farmers out of business. Because American farmers have been so successful at producing larger yields, agricultural prices have steadily fallen. These falling prices have reduced the incomes of many farmers, and as a result fewer and fewer people find farming worth doing. That is, an individual farmer who plants a better variety of corn is better off; but when many farmers plant a better variety of corn, the result may be to make farmers as a group worse off.

A farmer who plants a new, more productive corn variety doesn't just grow more corn. Such a farmer also affects the market for corn through the increased yields attained, with consequences that will be felt by other farmers, consumers, and beyond.

Just as there are four economic principles that underlie individual choice, there are five principles that underlie the economics of interaction. These five principles are summarized in Table 1-2. We will now examine each of these principles more closely.

| TABLE **1-2** The Principles of the Interaction of Individual Choices |
|---|
| 5. There are gains from trade. |
| 6. Because people respond to incentives, markets move toward equilibrium. |
| 7. Resources should be used as efficiently as possible to achieve society's goals. |
| 8. Because people usually exploit gains from trade, markets usually lead to efficiency. |
| 9. When markets don't achieve efficiency, government intervention can improve society's welfare. |

## Principle #5: There Are Gains from Trade

Why do the choices I make interact with the choices you make? A family could try to take care of all its own needs—growing its own food, sewing its own clothing, providing itself with entertainment, writing its own economics textbooks. But trying to live that way would be very hard. The key to a much better standard of living for everyone is **trade,** in which people divide tasks among themselves and each person provides a good or service that other people want in return for different goods and services that he or she wants.

The reason we have an economy, not many self-sufficient individuals, is that there are **gains from trade:** by dividing tasks and trading, two people (or 6 billion people) can each get more of what they want than they could get by being self-sufficient. This leads us to our fifth principle:

> *There are gains from trade.*

Gains from trade arise from this division of tasks, which economists call **specialization**—a situation in which different people each engage in a different task, specializing in those tasks that they are good at performing. The advantages of specialization, and the resulting gains from trade, were the starting point for Adam Smith's 1776 book *The Wealth of Nations*, which many regard as the beginning of economics as a discipline. Smith's book begins with a description of an eighteenth-century pin factory where, rather than each of the 10 workers making a pin from start to finish, each worker specialized in one of the many steps in pin-making:

One man draws out the wire, another straights it, a third cuts it, a fourth points it, a fifth grinds it at the top for receiving the head; to make the head requires two or three distinct operations; to put it on, is a particular business, to whiten the pins is another; it is even a trade by itself to put them into the paper; and the important business of making a pin is, in this manner, divided into about eighteen distinct operations. . . . Those ten persons, therefore, could make among them upwards of forty-eight thousand pins in a day. But if they had all wrought separately and independently, and without any of them having been educated to this particular business, they certainly could not each of them have made twenty, perhaps not one pin a day. . . .

In a market economy, individuals engage in **trade**: they provide goods and services to others and receive goods and services in return.

There are **gains from trade**: people can get more of what they want through trade than they could if they tried to be self-sufficient. This increase in output is due to **specialization**: each person specializes in the task that he or she is good at performing.

The same principle applies when we look at how people divide tasks among themselves and trade in an economy. *The economy, as a whole, can produce more when each person specializes in a task and trades with others.*

The benefits of specialization are the reason a person typically chooses only one career. It takes many years of study and experience to become a doctor; it also takes many years of study and experience to become a commercial airline pilot. Many doctors might well have had the potential to become excellent pilots, and vice versa; but it is very unlikely that anyone who decided to pursue both careers would be as good a pilot or as good a doctor as someone who decided at the beginning to specialize in that field. So it is to everyone's advantage that individuals specialize in their career choices.

Markets are what allow a doctor and a pilot to specialize in their own fields. Because markets for commercial flights and for doctors' services exist, a doctor is assured that she can find a flight and a pilot is assured that he can find a doctor. As long as individuals know that they can find the goods and services they want in the market, they are willing to forgo self-sufficiency and to specialize. But what assures people that markets will deliver what they want? The answer to that question leads us to our second principle of how individual choices interact.

*"I hunt and she gathers—otherwise we couldn't make ends meet."*

## Principle #6: Markets Move Toward Equilibrium

It's a busy afternoon at the supermarket; there are long lines at the checkout counters. Then one of the previously closed cash registers opens. What happens? The first thing, of course, is a rush to that register. After a couple of minutes, however, things will have settled down; shoppers will have rearranged themselves so that the line at the newly opened register is about the same length as the lines at all the other registers.

How do we know that? We know from our fourth principle that people will exploit opportunities to make themselves better off. This means that people will rush to the newly opened register in order to save time standing in line. And things will settle down when shoppers can no longer improve their position by switching lines—that is, when the opportunities to make themselves better off have all been exploited.

A story about supermarket checkout lines may seem to have little to do with how individual choices interact, but in fact it illustrates an important principle. A situation in which individuals cannot make themselves better off by doing something different—the situation in which all the checkout lines are the same length—is what economists call an **equilibrium.** An economic situation is in equilibrium when no individual would be better off doing something different.

Recall the story about the mythical Jiffy Lube, where it was supposedly cheaper to leave your car for an oil change than to pay for parking. If the opportunity had really existed and people were still paying $30 to park in garages, the situation would *not* have been an equilibrium. And that should have been a giveaway that the story couldn't be true. In reality, people would have seized an opportunity to park cheaply, just as they seize opportunities to save time at the checkout line. And in so doing they would have eliminated the opportunity! Either it would have become very hard to get an appointment for an oil change or the price of a lube job would have increased to the point that it was no longer an attractive option (unless you really needed a lube job). This brings us to our sixth principle:

> ***Because people respond to incentives, markets move toward equilibrium.***

As we will see, markets usually reach equilibrium via changes in prices, which rise or fall until no opportunities for individuals to make themselves better off remain.

An economic situation is in **equilibrium** when no individual would be better off doing something different.

## FOR INQUIRING MINDS

### CHOOSING SIDES

Why do people in America drive on the right side of the road? Of course, it's the law. But long before it was the law, it was an equilibrium.

Before there were formal traffic laws, there were informal "rules of the road," practices that everyone expected everyone else to follow. These rules included an understanding that people would normally keep to one side of the road. In some places, such as England, the rule was to keep to the left; in others, such as France, it was to keep to the right.

Why would some places choose the right and others, the left? That's not completely clear, although it may have

depended on the dominant form of traffic. Men riding horses and carrying swords on their left hip preferred to ride on the left (think about getting on or off the horse, and you'll see why). On the other hand, right-handed people walking but leading horses apparently preferred to walk on the right.

In any case, once a rule of the road was established, there were strong incentives for each individual to stay on the "usual" side of the road: those who didn't would keep colliding with oncoming traffic. So once established, the rule of the road would be self-enforcing—that is, it would be an equilibrium. Nowadays,

of course, which side you drive on is determined by law; some countries have even changed sides (Sweden went from left to right in 1967).

But what about pedestrians? There are no laws—but there are informal rules. In the United States, urban pedestrians normally keep to the right. But if you should happen to visit a country where people drive on the left, watch out: people who drive on the left also typically walk on the left. So when in a foreign country, do as the locals do. You won't be arrested if you walk on the right, but you will be worse off than if you accept the equilibium and walk on the left.

The concept of equilibrium is extremely helpful in understanding economic interactions because it provides a way of cutting through the sometimes complex details of those interactions. To understand what happens when a new line is opened at a supermarket, you don't need to worry about exactly how shoppers rearrange themselves, who moves ahead of whom, which register just opened, and so on. What you need to know is that any time there is a change, the situation will move to an equilibrium.

The fact that markets move toward equilibrium is why we can depend on them to work in a predictable way. In fact, we can trust markets to supply us with the essentials of life. For example, people who live in big cities can be sure that the supermarket shelves will always be fully stocked. Why? Because if some merchants who distribute food *didn't* make deliveries, a big profit opportunity would be created for any merchant who did—and there would be a rush to supply food, just like the rush to a newly opened cash register. So the market ensures that food will always be available for city dwellers. And, returning to our fifth principle, this allows city dwellers to be city dwellers—to specialize in doing city jobs rather than living on farms and growing their own food.

A market economy, as we have seen, allows people to achieve gains from trade. But how do we know how well such an economy is doing? The next principle gives us a standard to use in evaluating an economy's performance.

## Principle #7: Resources Should Be Used Efficiently to Achieve Society's Goals

Suppose you are taking a course in which the classroom is too small for the number of students—many people are forced to stand or sit on the floor—despite the fact that large, empty classrooms are available nearby. You would say, correctly, that this is no way to run a college. Economists would call this an *inefficient* use of resources. But if an inefficient use of resources is undesirable, just what does it mean to use resources *efficiently*? You might imagine that the efficient use of resources has something to do with money, maybe that it is measured in dollars-and-cents terms. But in economics, as in life, money is only a means to other ends. The measure that economists really care about is not money but people's happiness or welfare. Economists say that *an economy's resources are used efficiently when they are used in a way that has fully exploited all opportunities to make every-*

*one better off.* To put it another way, an economy is **efficient** if it takes all opportunities to make some people better off without making other people worse off.

In our classroom example, there clearly was a way to make everyone better off—moving the class to a larger room would make people in the class better off without hurting anyone else in the college. Assigning the course to the smaller classroom was an inefficient use of the college's resources, whereas assigning the course to the larger classroom would have been an efficient use of the college's resources.

When an economy is efficient, it is producing the maximum gains from trade possible given the resources available. Why? Because there is no way to rearrange how resources are used in a way that can make everyone better off. When an economy is efficient, one person can be made better off by rearranging how resources are used *only* by making someone else worse off. In our classroom example, if all larger classrooms were already occupied, the college would have been run in an efficient way: your class could be made better off by moving to a larger classroom only by making people in the larger classroom worse off by making them move to a smaller classroom.

We can now state our seventh principle:

> *Resources should be used as efficiently as possible to achieve society's goals.*

Should economic policy makers always strive to achieve economic efficiency? Well, not quite, because efficiency is only a means to achieving society's goals. Sometimes efficiency may conflict with a goal that society has deemed worthwhile to achieve. For example, in most societies, people also care about issues of fairness, or **equity.** And there is typically a trade-off between equity and efficiency: policies that promote equity often come at a cost of decreased efficiency in the economy, and vice versa.

To see this, consider the case of disabled-designated parking spaces in public parking lots. Many people have difficulty walking due to age or disability, so it seems only fair to assign closer parking spaces specifically for their use. You may have noticed, however, that a certain amount of inefficiency is involved. To make sure that there is always a parking space available should a disabled person want one, there are typically more such spaces available than there are disabled people who want one. As a result, desirable parking spaces are unused. (And the temptation for nondisabled people to use them is so great that we must be dissuaded by fear of getting a ticket.) So, short of hiring parking valets to allocate spaces, there is a conflict between *equity*, making life "fairer" for disabled people, and *efficiency*, making sure that all opportunities to make people better off have been fully exploited by never letting close-in parking spaces go unused.

Exactly how far policy makers should go in promoting equity over efficiency is a difficult question that goes to the heart of the political process. As such, it is not a question that economists can answer. What is important for economists, however, is always to seek to use the economy's resources as efficiently as possible in the pursuit of society's goals, whatever those goals may be.

## Principle #8: Markets Usually Lead to Efficiency

No branch of the U.S. government is entrusted with ensuring the general economic efficiency of our market economy—we don't have agents who go around making sure that brain surgeons aren't plowing fields or that Minnesota farmers aren't trying to grow oranges. The government doesn't need to enforce the efficient use of resources, because in most cases the invisible hand does the job.

The incentives built into a market economy ensure that resources are usually put to good use and that opportunities to make people better off are not wasted. If a college were known for its habit of crowding students into small

An economy is **efficient** if it takes all opportunities to make some people better off without making other people worse off.

**Equity** means that everyone gets his or her fair share. Since people can disagree about what's "fair," equity isn't as well defined a concept as efficiency.

Sometimes equity trumps efficiency.

classrooms while large classrooms went unused, it would soon find its enrollment dropping, putting the jobs of its administrators at risk. The "market" for college students would respond in a way that induced administrators to run the college efficiently.

A detailed explanation of why markets are usually very good at making sure that resources are used well will have to wait until we have studied how markets actually work. But the most basic reason is that in a market economy, in which individuals are free to choose what to consume and what to produce, people normally take opportunities for mutual gain—that is, gains from trade. If there is a way in which some people can be made better off, people will usually be able to take advantage of that opportunity. And that is exactly what defines efficiency: all the opportunities to make some people better off without making other people worse off have been exploited. This gives rise to our eighth principle:

> *Because people usually exploit gains from trade, markets usually lead to efficiency.*

As we learned in the Introduction, however, there are exceptions to this principle that markets are generally efficient. In cases of *market failure*, the individual pursuit of self-interest found in markets makes society worse off—that is, the market outcome is inefficient. And, as we will see in examining the next principle, when markets fail, government intervention can help. But short of instances of market failure, the general rule is that markets are a remarkably good way of organizing an economy.

## Principle #9: When Markets Don't Achieve Efficiency, Government Intervention Can Improve Society's Welfare

Let's recall from the Introduction the nature of the market failure caused by traffic congestion—a commuter driving to work has no incentive to take into account the cost that his or her action inflicts on other drivers in the form of increased traffic congestion. There are several possible remedies to this situation; examples include charging road tolls, subsidizing the cost of public transportation, and taxing sales of gasoline to individual drivers. All these remedies work by changing the incentives of would-be drivers, motivating them to drive less and use alternative transportation. But they also share another feature: each relies on government intervention in the market. This brings us to our ninth principle:

> *When markets don't achieve efficiency, government intervention can improve society's welfare.*

That is, when markets go wrong, an appropriately designed government policy can sometimes move society closer to an efficient outcome by changing how society's resources are used.

A very important branch of economics is devoted to studying why markets fail and what policies should be adopted to improve social welfare. We will study these problems and their remedies in depth in later chapters, but, briefly, there are three principal ways in which they fail:

- Individual actions have side effects that are not properly taken into account by the market. An example is an action that causes pollution.
- One party prevents mutually beneficial trades from occurring in an attempt to capture a greater share of resources for itself. An example is a drug company that prices a drug higher than the cost of producing it, making it unaffordable for some people who would benefit from it.
- Some goods, by their very nature, are unsuited for efficient management by markets. An example of such a good is air traffic control.

An important part of your education in economics is learning to identify not just when markets work but also when they don't work, and to judge what government policies are appropriate in each situation.

## ECONOMICS ▶ IN ACTION

### RESTORING EQUILIBRIUM ON THE FREEWAYS

**B**ack in 1994 a powerful earthquake struck the Los Angeles area, causing several freeway bridges to collapse and thereby disrupting the normal commuting routes of hundreds of thousands of drivers. The events that followed offer a particularly clear example of interdependent decision making—in this case, the decisions of commuters about how to get to work.

In the immediate aftermath of the earthquake, there was great concern about the impact on traffic, since motorists would now have to crowd onto alternative routes or detour around the blockages by using city streets. Public officials and news programs warned commuters to expect massive delays and urged them to avoid unnecessary travel, reschedule their work to commute before or after the rush, or use mass transit. These warnings were unexpectedly effective. In fact, so many people heeded them that in the first few days following the quake, those who maintained their regular commuting routine actually found the drive to and from work faster than before.

Of course, this situation could not last. As word spread that traffic was relatively light, people abandoned their less convenient new commuting methods and reverted to

Witness equilibrium in action on a Los Angeles freeway.

their cars—and traffic got steadily worse. Within a few weeks after the quake, serious traffic jams had appeared. After a few more weeks, however, the situation stabilized: the reality of worse-than-usual congestion discouraged enough drivers to prevent the nightmare of citywide gridlock from materializing. Los Angeles traffic, in short, had settled into a new equilibrium, in which each commuter was making the best choice he or she could, given what everyone else was doing.

This was not, by the way, the end of the story: fears that the city would strangle on traffic led local authorities to repair the roads with record speed. Within only 18 months after the quake, all the freeways were back to normal, ready for the next one.

### CHECK YOUR UNDERSTANDING    1-2

1. Explain how each of the following situations illustrates one of the five principles of interaction.
   a. Using the college website, any student who wants to sell a used textbook for at least $30 is able to sell it to someone who is willing to pay $30.
   b. At a college tutoring co-op, students can arrange to provide tutoring in subjects they are good in (like economics) in return for receiving tutoring in subjects they are poor in (like philosophy).
   c. The local municipality imposes a law that requires bars and nightclubs near residential areas to keep their noise levels below a certain threshold.
   d. To provide better care for low-income patients, the local municipality has decided to close some underutilized neighborhood clinics and shift funds to the main hospital.
   e. On the college website, books of a given title with approximately the same level of wear and tear sell for about the same price.

### ▼ Quick Review

- Most economic situations involve the **interaction** of choices, sometimes with unintended results. In a market economy, interaction occurs via **trade** between individuals.

- Individuals trade because there are **gains from trade,** which arise from **specialization.** Markets usually move toward **equilibrium** because people exploit gains from trade.

- To achieve society's goals, the use of resources should be **efficient.** But **equity,** as well as efficiency, may be desirable in an economy. There is often a trade-off between equity and efficiency.

- Except for certain well-defined exceptions, markets are normally efficient. When markets fail to achieve efficiency, government intervention can improve society's welfare.

2. Which of the following describes an equilibrium situation? Which does not? Explain your answer.
   a. The restaurants across the street from the university dining hall serve better-tasting and cheaper meals than those served at the university dining hall. The vast majority of students continue to eat at the dining hall.
   b. You currently take the subway to work. Although taking the bus is cheaper, the ride takes longer. So you are willing to pay the higher subway fare in order to save time.

Solutions appear at back of book.

# Economy-Wide Interactions

**TABLE 1-3 The Principles of Economy-Wide Interactions**

| |
|---|
| 10. One person's spending is another person's income. |
| 11. Overall spending sometimes gets out of line with the economy's productive capacity. |
| 12. Government policies can change spending. |

As we mentioned in the Introduction, the economy as a whole has its ups and downs. For example, business in America's shopping malls was depressed in 2008, because the economy was in a recession. By 2011, the economy had somewhat recovered. To understand recessions and recoveries, we need to understand economy-wide interactions, and understanding the big picture of the economy requires understanding three more important economic principles. Those three economy-wide principles are summarized in Table 1-3.

## Principle #10: One Person's Spending Is Another Person's Income

In 2006, home construction in America began a rapid decline because builders found it increasingly hard to make sales. At first the damage was mainly limited to the construction industry. But over time the slump spread into just about every part of the economy, with consumer spending falling across the board.

But why should a fall in home construction mean empty stores in the shopping malls? After all, malls are places where families, not builders, do their shopping. The answer is that lower spending on construction led to lower incomes throughout the economy; people who had been employed either directly in construction, producing goods and services builders need (like wallboard), or in producing goods and services new homeowners need (like new furniture), either lost their jobs or were forced to take pay cuts. And as incomes fell, so did spending by consumers. This example illustrates our tenth principle:

*One person's spending is another person's income.*

In a market economy, people make a living selling things—including their labor—to other people. If some group in the economy decides, for whatever reason, to spend more, the income of other groups will rise. If some group decides to spend less, the income of other groups will fall.

Because one person's spending is another person's income, a chain reaction of changes in spending behavior tends to have repercussions that spread through the economy. For example, a cut in business investment spending, like the one that happened in 2008, leads to reduced family incomes; families respond by reducing consumer spending; this leads to another round of income cuts; and so on. These repercussions play an important role in our understanding of recessions and recoveries.

## Principle #11: Overall Spending Sometimes Gets Out of Line with the Economy's Productive Capacity

Macroeconomics emerged as a separate branch of economics in the 1930s, when a collapse of consumer and business spending, a crisis in the banking industry, and other factors led to a plunge in overall spending. This plunge in spending, in turn, led to a period of very high unemployment known as the Great Depression.

The lesson economists learned from the troubles of the 1930s is that overall spending—the amount of goods and services that consumers and businesses want to buy—sometimes doesn't match the amount of goods and services the economy is capable of producing. In the 1930s, spending fell far short of what was needed to keep American workers employed, and the result was a severe economic slump. In fact, shortfalls in spending are responsible for most, though not all, recessions.

It's also possible for overall spending to be too high. In that case, the economy experiences *inflation*, a rise in prices throughout the economy. This rise in prices occurs because when the amount that people want to buy outstrips the supply, producers can raise their prices and still find willing customers. Taking account of both shortfalls in spending and excesses in spending brings us to our eleventh principle:

*Overall spending sometimes gets out of line with the economy's productive capacity.*

## Principle #12: Government Policies Can Change Spending

Overall spending sometimes gets out of line with the economy's productive capacity. But can anything be done about that? Yes—which leads to our twelfth and last principle:

*Government policies can change spending.*

In fact, government policies can dramatically affect spending.

For one thing, the government itself does a lot of spending on everything from military equipment to education—and it can choose to do more or less. The government can also vary how much it collects from the public in taxes, which in turn affects how much income consumers and businesses have left to spend. And the government's control of the quantity of money in circulation, it turns out, gives it another powerful tool with which to affect total spending. Government spending, taxes, and control of money are the tools of *macroeconomic policy*.

Modern governments deploy these macroeconomic policy tools in an effort to manage overall spending in the economy, trying to steer it between the perils of recession and inflation. These efforts aren't always successful—recessions still happen, and so do periods of inflation. But it's widely believed that aggressive efforts to sustain spending in 2008 and 2009 helped prevent the financial crisis of 2008 from turning into a full-blown depression.

## ECONOMICS ▶ IN ACTION

### ADVENTURES IN BABYSITTING

The website, myarmyonesource.com, which offers advice to army families, suggests that parents join a babysitting cooperative—an arrangement that is common in many walks of life. In a babysitting cooperative, a number of parents exchange babysitting services rather than hire someone to babysit. But how do these organizations make sure that all members do their fair share of the work? As myarmyonesource.com explained, "Instead of money, most co-ops exchange tickets or points. When you need a sitter, you call a friend on the list, and you pay them with tickets. You earn tickets by babysitting other children within the co-op."

As participants in a babysitting co-op soon discovered, fewer nights out made everyone worse off.

In other words, a babysitting co-op is a miniature economy in which people buy and sell babysitting services. And it happens to be a type of economy that can have macroeconomic problems. A famous article titled "Monetary Theory and the Great Capitol Hill Babysitting Co-Op Crisis," published in 1977, described the troubles of a babysitting cooperative that issued too few tickets. Bear in mind that, on average, people in a babysitting co-op want to have a reserve of tickets stashed away in case they need to go out several times before they can replenish their stash by doing some more babysitting.

In this case, because there weren't that many tickets out there to begin with, most parents were anxious to add to their reserves by babysitting but reluctant to run them down by going out. But one parent's decision to go out was another's chance to babysit, so it became difficult to earn tickets. Knowing this, parents became even more reluctant to use their reserves except on special occasions.

In short, the co-op had fallen into a recession. Recessions in the larger, nonbabysitting economy are a bit more complicated than this, but the troubles of the Capitol Hill babysitting co-op demonstrate two of our three principles of economy-wide interactions. One person's spending is another person's income: opportunities to babysit arose only to the extent that other people went out. And an economy can suffer from too little spending: when not enough people were willing to go out, everyone was frustrated at the lack of babysitting opportunities.

And what about government policies to change spending? Actually, the Capitol Hill co-op did that, too. Eventually, it solved its problem by handing out more tickets, and with increased reserves, people were willing to go out more.

## ▼ Quick Review

- In a market economy, one person's spending is another person's income. As a result, changes in spending behavior have repercussions that spread through the economy.

- Overall spending sometimes gets out of line with the economy's capacity to produce goods and services. When spending is too low, the result is a recession. When spending is too high, it causes inflation.

- Modern governments use macroeconomic policy tools to affect the overall level of spending in an effort to steer the economy between recession and inflation.

### CHECK YOUR UNDERSTANDING    1-3

1. Explain how each of the following examples illustrates one of the three principles of economy-wide interactions.
   a. The White House urged Congress to pass a package of temporary spending increases and tax cuts in early 2009, a time when employment was plunging and unemployment soaring.
   b. Oil companies are investing heavily in projects that will extract oil from the "oil sands" of Canada. In Edmonton, Alberta, near the projects, restaurants and other consumer businesses are booming.
   c. In the mid-2000s, Spain, which was experiencing a big housing boom, also had the highest inflation rate in Europe.

Solutions appear at back of book.

# BUSINESS CASE • How Priceline.com Revolutionized the Travel Industry

Courtesy priceline.com

In 2001 and 2002, the travel industry was in deep trouble. After the terrorist attacks of September 11, 2001, many people simply stopped flying. As the economy went into a deep slump, airplanes sat empty on the tarmac and the airlines lost billions of dollars. When several major airlines spiraled toward bankruptcy and laid off 100,000 workers, Congress passed a $15 billion aid package that proved to be critical in stabilizing the airline industry.

This was also a particularly difficult time for Priceline.com, the online travel service. Just four years after its founding, Priceline.com was in danger of going under. The change in the company's fortunes had been dramatic. In 1999, one year after Priceline.com was formed, investors were so impressed by its potential for revolutionizing the travel industry that they valued the company at $9 billion dollars. But by 2002 investors had taken a decidedly dimmer view of the company, reducing its valuation by 95% to only $425 million.

To make matters worse, Priceline.com was losing several million dollars a year. Yet the company managed to survive; as of the time of writing in 2010, it was valued by investors at $8.8 billion. Not only has it survived, it has thrived.

So exactly how did Priceline.com bring such dramatic change to the travel industry? And what has allowed it to survive and prosper as a company in the face of dire economic conditions?

Priceline.com's success lies in its ability to spot exploitable opportunities for itself and its customers. The company understood that when a plane departs with empty seats or a hotel has empty beds, it bears a cost—the revenue that would have been earned if that seat or bed had been filled. And although some travelers like the security of booking their flights and hotels well in advance and are willing to pay for that, others are quite happy to wait until the last minute, risking not getting the flight or hotel they want but enjoying a lower price.

Customers specify the price they are willing to pay for a given trip or hotel location, and then Priceline.com presents them with a list of options from airlines or hotels that are willing to accept that price, with the price typically declining as the date of the trip nears. By bringing airlines and hotels with unsold capacity together with travelers who are willing to sacrifice some of their preferences for a lower price, Priceline.com made everyone better off—including itself, since it charged a small commission for each trade it facilitated.

Priceline.com was also quick on its feet when it saw its market challenged by newcomers Expedia and Orbitz. In response, it began aggressively moving more of its business toward hotel bookings and into Europe, where the online travel industry was still quite small. Its network was particularly valuable in the European hotel market, which is comprised of many more small hotels in comparison to the U.S. market, which is dominated by nationwide chains. The efforts paid off, and by 2003 Priceline.com had turned its first profit.

Priceline.com now operates within a network of more than 100,000 hotels in over 90 countries. As of 2010, its revenues had grown at least 24% over each of the previous three years, even growing 34% during the 2008 recession.

Clearly, the travel industry will never be the same again.

## QUESTION FOR THOUGHT

**1.** Explain how each of the twelve principles of economics is illustrated in this story.

## SUMMARY

1. All economic analysis is based on a set of basic principles that apply to three levels of economic activity. First, we study how individuals make choices; second, we study how these choices interact; and third, we study how the economy functions overall.

2. Everyone has to make choices about what to do and what *not* to do. **Individual choice** is the basis of economics—if it doesn't involve choice, it isn't economics.

3. The reason choices must be made is that **resources**—anything that can be used to produce something else—are **scarce.** Individuals are limited in their choices by money and time; economies are limited by their supplies of human and natural resources.

4. Because you must choose among limited alternatives, the true cost of anything is what you must give up to get it—all costs are **opportunity costs.**

5. Many economic decisions involve questions not of "whether" but of "how much"—how much to spend on some good, how much to produce, and so on. Such decisions must be made by performing a **trade-off** *at the margin*—by comparing the costs and benefits of doing a bit more or a bit less. Decisions of this type are called **marginal decisions,** and the study of them, **marginal analysis,** plays a central role in economics.

6. The study of how people *should* make decisions is also a good way to understand actual behavior. Individuals usually respond to **incentives**—exploiting opportunities to make themselves better off.

7. The next level of economic analysis is the study of **interaction**—how my choices depend on your choices, and vice versa. When individuals interact, the end result may be different from what anyone intends.

8. Individuals interact because there are **gains from trade:** by engaging in the **trade** of goods and services with one another, the members of an economy can all be made better off. **Specialization**—each person specializes in the task he or she is good at—is the source of gains from trade.

9. Because individuals usually respond to incentives, markets normally move toward **equilibrium**—a situation in which no individual can make himself or herself better off by taking a different action.

10. An economy is **efficient** if all opportunities to make some people better off without making other people worse off are taken. Resources should be used as efficiently as possible to achieve society's goals. But efficiency is not the sole way to evaluate an economy: **equity,** or fairness, is also desirable, and there is often a trade-off between equity and efficiency.

11. Markets usually lead to efficiency, with some well-defined exceptions.

12. When markets fail and do not achieve efficiency, government intervention can improve society's welfare.

13. Because people in a market economy earn income by selling things, including their own labor, one person's spending is another person's income. As a result, changes in spending behavior can spread throughout the economy.

14. Overall spending in the economy can get out of line with the economy's productive capacity. Spending below the economy's productive capacity leads to a recession; spending in excess of the economy's productive capacity leads to inflation.

15. Governments have the ability to strongly affect overall spending, an ability they use in an effort to steer the economy between recession and inflation.

## KEY TERMS

Individual choice, p. 6
Resource, p. 6
Scarce, p. 6
Opportunity cost, p. 7
Trade-off, p. 8
Marginal decisions, p. 9
Marginal analysis, p. 9
Incentive, p. 9
Interaction, p. 11
Trade, p. 12
Gains from trade, p. 12
Specialization, p. 12
Equilibrium, p. 13
Efficient, p. 15
Equity, p. 15

## PROBLEMS

1. In each of the following situations, identify which of the twelve principles is at work.

   a. You choose to shop at the local discount store rather than paying a higher price for the same merchandise at the local department store.

   b. On your spring break trip, your budget is limited to $35 a day.

   c. The student union provides a website on which departing students can sell items such as used books, appliances, and furniture rather than give them away to their roommates as they formerly did.

   d. After a hurricane did extensive damage to homes on the island of St. Crispin, homeowners wanted to purchase many more building materials and hire many more workers than were available on the island. As a result, prices for goods and services rose dramatically across the board.

   e. You buy a used textbook from your roommate. Your roommate uses the money to buy songs from iTunes.

   f. You decide how many cups of coffee to have when studying the night before an exam by considering how much more work you can do by having another cup versus how jittery it will make you feel.

   g. There is limited lab space available to do the project required in Chemistry 101. The lab supervisor assigns lab time to each student based on when that student is able to come.

   h. You realize that you can graduate a semester early by forgoing a semester of study abroad.

   i. At the student union, there is a bulletin board on which people advertise used items for sale, such as bicycles. Once you have adjusted for differences in quality, all the bikes sell for about the same price.

   j. You are better at performing lab experiments, and your lab partner is better at writing lab reports. So the two of you agree that you will do all the experiments and she will write up all the reports.

   k. State governments mandate that it is illegal to drive without passing a driving exam.

   l. Your parents' after-tax income has increased because of a tax cut passed by Congress. They therefore increase your allowance, which you spend on a spring break vacation.

2. Describe some of the opportunity costs when you decide to do the following.

   a. Attend college instead of taking a job

   b. Watch a movie instead of studying for an exam

   c. Ride the bus instead of driving your car

3. Liza needs to buy a textbook for the next economics class. The price at the college bookstore is $65. One online site offers it for $55 and another site, for $57. All prices include sales tax. The accompanying table indicates the typical shipping and handling charges for the textbook ordered online.

| Shipping method | Delivery time | Charge |
|---|---|---|
| Standard shipping | 3–7 days | $3.99 |
| Second-day air | 2 business days | 8.98 |
| Next-day air | 1 business day | 13.98 |

   a. What is the opportunity cost of buying online instead of at the bookstore? Note that if you buy the book online, you must wait to get it.

   b. Show the relevant choices for this student. What determines which of these options the student will choose?

4. Use the concept of opportunity cost to explain the following.

   a. More people choose to get graduate degrees when the job market is poor.

   b. More people choose to do their own home repairs when the economy is slow and hourly wages are down.

   c. There are more parks in suburban than in urban areas.

   d. Convenience stores, which have higher prices than supermarkets, cater to busy people.

   e. Fewer students enroll in classes that meet before 10:00 A.M.

5. In the following examples, state how you would use the principle of marginal analysis to make a decision.

   a. Deciding how many days to wait before doing your laundry

   b. Deciding how much library research to do before writing your term paper

   c. Deciding how many bags of chips to eat

   d. Deciding how many lectures of a class to skip

6. This morning you made the following individual choices: you bought a bagel and coffee at the local café, you drove to school in your car during rush hour, and you typed your roommate's term paper because you are a fast typist—in return for which she will do your laundry for a month. For each of these actions, describe how your individual choices interacted with the individual choices made by others. Were other people left better off or worse off by your choices in each case?

7. The Hatfield family lives on the east side of the Hatatoochie River, and the McCoy family lives on the west side. Each family's diet consists of fried chicken and corn-on-the-cob, and each is self-sufficient, raising their own chickens and growing their own corn.

Explain the conditions under which each of the following would be true.

a. The two families are made better off when the Hatfields specialize in raising chickens, the McCoys specialize in growing corn, and the two families trade.

b. The two families are made better off when the McCoys specialize in raising chickens, the Hatfields specialize in growing corn, and the two families trade.

8. Which of the following situations describes an equilibrium? Which does not? If the situation does not describe an equilibrium, what would an equilibrium look like?

a. Many people regularly commute from the suburbs to downtown Pleasantville. Due to traffic congestion, the trip takes 30 minutes when you travel by highway but only 15 minutes when you go by side streets.

b. At the intersection of Main and Broadway are two gas stations. One station charges $3.00 per gallon for regular gas and the other charges $2.85 per gallon. Customers can get service immediately at the first station but must wait in a long line at the second.

c. Every student enrolled in Economics 101 must also attend a weekly tutorial. This year there are two sections offered: section A and section B, which meet at the same time in adjoining classrooms and are taught by equally competent instructors. Section A is overcrowded, with people sitting on the floor and often unable to see the chalkboard. Section B has many empty seats.

9. In each of the following cases, explain whether you think the situation is efficient or not. If it is not efficient, why not? What actions would make the situation efficient?

a. Electricity is included in the rent at your dorm. Some residents in your dorm leave lights, computers, and appliances on when they are not in their rooms.

b. Although they cost the same amount to prepare, the cafeteria in your dorm consistently provides too many dishes that diners don't like, such as tofu casserole, and too few dishes that diners do like, such as roast turkey with dressing.

c. The enrollment for a particular course exceeds the spaces available. Some students who need to take this course to complete their major are unable to get a space even though others who are taking it as an elective do get a space.

10. Discuss the efficiency and equity implications of each of the following policies. How would you go about balancing the concerns of equity and efficiency in these areas?

a. The government pays the full tuition for every college student to study whatever subject he or she wishes.

b. When people lose their jobs, the government provides unemployment benefits until they find new ones.

11. Governments often adopt certain policies in order to promote desired behavior among their citizens. For each of the following policies, determine what the incentive is and what behavior the government wishes to promote. In each case, why do you think that the government might wish to change people's behavior, rather than allow their actions to be solely determined by individual choice?

a. A tax of $5 per pack is imposed on cigarettes.

b. The government pays parents $100 when their child is vaccinated for measles.

c. The government pays college students to tutor children from low-income families.

d. The government imposes a tax on the amount of air pollution that a company discharges.

12. In each of the following situations, explain how government intervention could improve society's welfare by changing people's incentives. In what sense is the market going wrong?

a. Pollution from auto emissions has reached unhealthy levels.

b. Everyone in Woodville would be better off if streetlights were installed in the town. But no individual resident is willing to pay for installation of a streetlight in front of his or her house because it is impossible to recoup the cost by charging other residents for the benefit they receive from it.

13. On August 2, 2010, Tim Geithner, the Treasury secretary, published an article defending the administration's policies. In it he said, "The recession that began in late 2007 was extraordinarily severe. But the actions we took at its height to stimulate the economy helped arrest the free fall, preventing an even deeper collapse and putting the economy on the road to recovery." Which two of the three principles of economy-wide interaction are at work in this statement?

14. In August 2007, a sharp downturn in the U.S. housing market reduced the income of many who worked in the home construction industry. A *Wall Street Journal* news article reported that Walmart's wire-transfer business was likely to suffer because many construction workers are Hispanics who regularly send part of their wages back to relatives in their home countries via Walmart. With this information, use one of the principles of economy-wide interaction to trace a chain of links that explains how reduced spending for U.S. home purchases is likely to affect the performance of the Mexican economy.

15. In 2005, Hurricane Katrina caused massive destruction to the U.S. Gulf Coast. Tens of thousands of people lost their homes and possessions. Even those who weren't directly affected by the destruction were hurt because businesses failed or contracted and jobs dried up. Using one of the principles of economy-wide interaction, explain how government intervention can help in this situation.

16. During the Great Depression, food was left to rot in the fields or fields that had once been actively cultivated were left fallow. Use one of the principles of economy-wide interaction to explain how this could have occurred.

# Economic Models: Trade-offs and Trade

## FROM KITTY HAWK TO DREAMLINER

Mark Ralston/AFP/Getty Images

The Wright Brothers' model made modern airplanes, including the Dreamliner, possible.

AP Photo

**WHAT YOU WILL LEARN IN THIS CHAPTER**

❭ Why **models**—simplified representations of reality—play a crucial role in economics

❭ Two simple but important models: the **production possibility frontier** and **comparative advantage**

❭ The **circular-flow diagram,** a schematic representation of the economy

❭ The difference between **positive economics,** which analyzes how the economy works, and **normative economics,** which prescribes economic policy

❭ When economists agree and why they sometimes disagree

O N DECEMBER 15, 2009, BOEING'S newest jet, the 787 Dreamliner, took its first three-hour test flight. It was a historic moment: the Dreamliner was the result of an aerodynamic revolution—a superefficient airplane designed to cut airline operating costs and the first to use superlight composite materials. To ensure that the Dreamliner was sufficiently lightweight and aerodynamic, it underwent over 15,000 hours of wind tunnel tests—tests that resulted in subtle design changes that improved its performance, making it 20% more fuel efficient and 20% less pollutant emitting than existing passenger jets.

The first flight of the Dreamliner was a spectacular advance from the 1903 maiden voyage of the Wright Flyer, the first successful powered airplane, in Kitty Hawk, North Carolina. Yet the Boeing engineers—and all aeronautic engineers—owe an enormous debt to the Wright Flyer's inventors, Wilbur and Orville Wright. What made the Wrights truly visionary was their invention of the wind tunnel, an apparatus that let them experiment with many different designs for wings and control surfaces. Doing experiments with a miniature airplane, inside a wind tunnel the size of a shipping crate, gave the Wright Brothers the knowledge that would make heavier-than-air flight possible.

Neither a miniature airplane inside a packing crate nor a miniature model of the Dreamliner inside Boeing's state-of-the-art Transonic Wind Tunnel is the same thing as an actual aircraft in flight. But it is a very useful *model* of a flying plane—a simplified representation of the real thing that can be used to answer crucial questions, such as how much lift a given wing shape will generate at a given airspeed.

Needless to say, testing an airplane design in a wind tunnel is cheaper and safer than building a full-scale version and hoping it will fly. More generally, models play a crucial role in almost all scientific research—economics very much included.

In fact, you could say that economic theory consists mainly of a collection of models, a series of simplified representations of economic reality that allow us to understand a variety of economic issues. In this chapter, we'll look at two economic models that are crucially important in their own right and also illustrate why such models are so useful. We'll conclude with a look at how economists actually use models in their work. ■

A **model** is a simplified representation of a real situation that is used to better understand real-life situations.

The **other things equal assumption** means that all other relevant factors remain unchanged.

# Models in Economics: Some Important Examples

A model is any simplified representation of reality that is used to better understand real-life situations. But how do we create a simplified representation of an economic situation?

One possibility—an economist's equivalent of a wind tunnel—is to find or create a real but simplified economy. For example, economists interested in the economic role of money have studied the system of exchange that developed in World War II prison camps, in which cigarettes became a universally accepted form of payment even among prisoners who didn't smoke.

Another possibility is to simulate the workings of the economy on a computer. For example, when changes in tax law are proposed, government officials use *tax models*—large mathematical computer programs—to assess how the proposed changes would affect different types of people.

Models are important because their simplicity allows economists to focus on the effects of only one change at a time. That is, they allow us to hold everything else constant and study how one change affects the overall economic outcome. So an important assumption when building economic models is the **other things equal assumption,** which means that all other relevant factors remain unchanged.

But you can't always find or create a small-scale version of the whole economy, and a computer program is only as good as the data it uses. (Programmers have a saying: "garbage in, garbage out.") For many purposes, the most effective form of economic modeling is the construction of "thought experiments": simplified, hypothetical versions of real-life situations.

In Chapter 1 we illustrated the concept of equilibrium with the example of how customers at a supermarket would rearrange themselves when a new cash register opens. Though we didn't say it, this was an example of a simple model—an imaginary supermarket, in which many details were ignored. (What were customers buying? Never mind.) This simple model can be used to answer a "what if" question: what if another cash register were opened?

As the cash register story showed, it is often possible to describe and analyze a useful economic model in plain English. However, because much of economics involves changes in quantities—in the price of a product, the number of units produced, or the number of workers employed in its production—economists often find that using some mathematics helps clarify an issue. In particular, a numerical example, a simple equation, or—especially—a graph can be key to understanding an economic concept.

Whatever form it takes, a good economic model can be a tremendous aid to understanding. The best way to grasp this point is to consider some simple but important economic models and what they tell us. First, we will look at the *production possibility frontier*, a model that helps economists think about the trade-offs every economy faces. Then we will turn to *comparative advantage*, a model that clarifies the principle of gains from trade—trade both between individuals and between countries. In addition, we'll examine the *circular-flow diagram*, a schematic representation that helps us understand how flows of money, goods, and services are channeled through the economy.

In discussing these models, we make considerable use of graphs to represent mathematical relationships. Graphs play an important role throughout this book. If you are already familiar with the use of graphs, you may feel free to skip the appendix to this chapter, which provides a brief introduction to the use of graphs in economics. If not, this would be a good time to turn to it.

## FOR INQUIRING MINDS

### THE MODEL THAT ATE THE ECONOMY

A model is just a model, right? So how much damage can it do? Economists probably would have answered that question quite differently before the financial meltdown of 2008–2009 than after it. The financial crisis continues to reverberate today—a testament to why economic models are so important. For an economic model—a *bad* economic model, it turned out—played a significant role in the origins of the crisis.

"The model that ate the economy" originated in finance theory, the branch of economics that seeks to understand what assets like stocks and bonds are worth. Financial theorists often get hired (at very high salaries, mind you) to devise complex mathematical models to help investment companies decide what assets to buy and sell and at what price.

Finance theory has become increasingly important as Wall Street (a district in New York City where nearly all major investment companies have their headquarters) has shifted from trading simple assets like stocks and bonds to more complex assets—notably, mortgage-backed securities (or MBS's for short). An MBS is an asset that entitles its owner to a stream of earnings based on the payments made by thousands of people on their home loans. Investors wanted to know how risky these complex assets were. That is, how likely was it that an investor would lose money on an MBS?

Although we won't go into the details, estimating the likelihood of losing money on an MBS is a complicated problem. It involves calculating the probability that a significant number of the thousands of homeowners backing your security will stop paying their mortgages. Until that probability could be calculated, investors didn't want to buy MBS's. In order to generate sales, Wall Street firms needed to provide potential MBS buyers with some estimate of their risk.

In 2000, a Wall Street financial theorist announced that he had solved the problem by employing a huge statistical abstraction—assuming that current homeowners were no more likely to stop paying their mortgages than in previous decades. With this assumption, he devised a simple model for estimating the risk of buying an MBS. Financial traders loved the model as it opened up a huge and extraordinarily profitable market for them. Using this simple model, Wall Street was able to create and sell billions of MBS's, generating billions in profits for itself.

Or investors *thought* they had calculated the risk of losing money on an MBS. Some financial experts—particularly Darrell Duffie, a Stanford University finance professor—warned from the sidelines that the estimates of risk calculated by this simple model were just plain wrong. He, and other critics, said that in the search for simplicity, the model seriously underestimated the likelihood that many homeowners would stop paying their mortgages at the same time, leaving MBS investors in danger of incurring huge losses.

The warnings fell on deaf ears—no doubt because Wall Street was making so much money. Billions of dollars worth of MBS's were sold to investors both in the United States and abroad. In 2008–2009, the problems critics warned about exploded in catastrophic fashion. Over the previous decade, American home prices had risen too high, and mortgages had been extended to many who were unable to pay. As home prices fell to earth, millions of homeowners didn't pay their mortgages. With losses mounting for MBS investors, it became all too clear that the model had indeed underestimated the risks. When investors and financial institutions around the world realized the extent of their losses, the worldwide economy ground to an abrupt halt. To this day, it has not fully recovered.

## Trade-offs: The Production Possibility Frontier

The first principle of economics we introduced in Chapter 1 was that resources are scarce and that, as a result, any economy—whether it's an isolated group of a few dozen hunter-gatherers or the 6 billion people making up the twenty-first-century global economy—faces trade-offs. No matter how lightweight the Boeing Dreamliner is, no matter how efficient Boeing's assembly line, producing Dreamliners means using resources that therefore can't be used to produce something else.

The **production possibility frontier** illustrates the trade-offs facing an economy that produces only two goods. It shows the maximum quantity of one good that can be produced for any given quantity produced of the other.

To think about the trade-offs that face any economy, economists often use the model known as the **production possibility frontier.** The idea behind this model is to improve our understanding of trade-offs by considering a simplified economy that produces only two goods. This simplification enables us to show the trade-off graphically.

Suppose, for a moment, that the United States was a one-company economy, with Boeing its sole employer and aircraft its only product. But there would still be a choice of what kinds of aircraft to produce—say, Dreamliners versus small commuter jets. Figure 2-1 shows a hypothetical production possibility frontier representing the trade-off this one-company economy would face. The frontier—the line in the diagram—shows the maximum quantity of small jets that Boeing can produce per year *given* the quantity of Dreamliners it produces per year, and vice versa. That is, it answers questions of the form, "What is the maximum quantity of small jets that Boeing can produce in a year if it also produces 9 (or 15, or 30) Dreamliners that year?"

There is a crucial distinction between points *inside* or *on* the production possibility frontier (the shaded area) and *outside* the frontier. If a production point lies inside or on the frontier—like point *C*, at which Boeing produces 20 small jets and 9 Dreamliners in a year—it is feasible. After all, the frontier tells us that if Boeing produces 20 small jets, it could also produce a maximum of 15 Dreamliners that year, so it could certainly make 9 Dreamliners. However, a production point that lies outside the frontier—such as the hypothetical production point *D*, where Boeing produces 40 small jets and 30 Dreamliners—isn't feasible. Boeing can produce 40 small jets and no Dreamliners, *or* it can produce 30 Dreamliners and no small jets, but it can't do both.

In Figure 2-1 the production possibility frontier intersects the horizontal axis at 40 small jets. This means that if Boeing dedicated all its production capacity to making small jets, it could produce 40 small jets per year but could produce no Dreamliners. The production possibility frontier intersects the vertical axis at 30 Dreamliners. This means that if Boeing dedicated all its production capacity to making Dreamliners, it could produce 30 Dreamliners per year but no small jets.

The figure also shows less extreme trade-offs. For example, if Boeing's managers decide to make 20 small jets this year, they can produce at most 15 Dreamliners; this production choice is illustrated by point *A*. And if Boeing's

**FIGURE   2-1   The Production Possibility Frontier**

The production possibility frontier illustrates the trade-offs Boeing faces in producing Dreamliners and small jets. It shows the maximum quantity of one good that can be produced given the quantity of the other good produced. Here, the maximum quantity of Dreamliners manufactured per year depends on the quantity of small jets manufactured that year, and vice versa. Boeing's feasible production is shown by the area *inside* or *on* the curve. Production at point *C* is feasible but not efficient. Points *A* and *B* are feasible and efficient in production, but point *D* is not feasible.

managers decide to produce 28 small jets, they can make at most 9 Dreamliners, as shown by point *B*.

Thinking in terms of a production possibility frontier simplifies the complexities of reality. The real-world U.S. economy produces millions of different goods. Even Boeing can produce more than two different types of planes. Yet it's important to realize that even in its simplicity, this stripped-down model gives us important insights about the real world.

By simplifying reality, the production possibility frontier helps us understand some aspects of the real economy better than we could without the model: efficiency, opportunity cost, and economic growth.

**Efficiency** First of all, the production possibility frontier is a good way to illustrate the general economic concept of *efficiency*. Recall from Chapter 1 that an economy is efficient if there are no missed opportunities—there is no way to make some people better off without making other people worse off.

One key element of efficiency is that there are no missed opportunities in production—there is no way to produce more of one good without producing less of other goods. As long as Boeing operates on its production possibility frontier, its production is efficient. At point *A*, 15 Dreamliners are the maximum quantity feasible given that Boeing has also committed to producing 20 small jets; at point *B*, 9 Dreamliners are the maximum number that can be made given the choice to produce 28 small jets; and so on. But suppose for some reason that Boeing was operating at point *C*, making 20 small jets and 9 Dreamliners. In this case, it would not be operating efficiently and would therefore be *inefficient:* it could be producing more of both planes.

Although we have used an example of the production choices of a one-firm, two-good economy to illustrate efficiency and inefficiency, these concepts also carry over to the real economy, which contains many firms and produces many goods. If the economy as a whole could not produce more of any one good without producing less of something else—that is, if it is on its production possibility frontier—then we say that the economy is *efficient in production*. If, however, the economy could produce more of some things without producing less of others—which typically means that it could produce more of everything—then it is inefficient in production. For example, an economy in which large numbers of workers are involuntarily unemployed is clearly inefficient in production. And that's a bad thing, because the economy could be producing more useful goods and services.

Although the production possibility frontier helps clarify what it means for an economy to be efficient in production, it's important to understand that efficiency in production is only *part* of what's required for the economy as a whole to be efficient. Efficiency also requires that the economy allocate its resources so that consumers are as well off as possible. If an economy does this, we say that it is *efficient in allocation*. To see why efficiency in allocation is as important as efficiency in production, notice that points *A* and *B* in Figure 2-1 both represent situations in which the economy is efficient in production, because in each case it can't produce more of one good without producing less of the other. But these two situations may not be equally desirable from society's point of view. Suppose that society prefers to have more small jets and fewer Dreamliners than at point *A*; say, it prefers to have 28 small jets and 9 Dreamliners, corresponding to point *B*. In this case, point *A* is inefficient in allocation from the point of view of the economy as a whole because it would rather have Boeing produce at point *B* rather than at point *A*.

This example shows that efficiency for the economy as a whole requires *both* efficiency in production and efficiency in allocation: to be efficient, an economy must produce as much of each good as it can given the production of other goods, and it must also produce the mix of goods that people want to consume. (And it must also deliver those goods to the right people: an economy that gives small jets to international airlines and Dreamliners to commuter airlines serving small rural airports is inefficient, too.)

In the real world, command economies, such as the former Soviet Union, are notorious for inefficiency in allocation. For example, it was common for consumers to find stores well stocked with items few people wanted but lacking such basics as soap and toilet paper.

**Opportunity Cost** The production possibility frontier is also useful as a reminder of the fundamental point that the true cost of any good isn't the money it costs to buy, but what must be given up in order to get that good—the *opportunity cost*. If, for example, Boeing decides to change its production from point *A* to point *B*, it will produce 8 more small jets but 6 fewer Dreamliners. So the opportunity cost of 8 small jets is 6 Dreamliners—the 6 Dreamliners that must be forgone in order to produce 8 more small jets. This means that each small jet has an opportunity cost of 6/8 = 3/4 of a Dreamliner.

Is the opportunity cost of an extra small jet in terms of Dreamliners always the same, no matter how many small jets and Dreamliners are currently produced? In the example illustrated by Figure 2-1, the answer is yes. If Boeing increases its production of small jets from 28 to 40, the number of Dreamliners it produces falls from 9 to zero. So Boeing's opportunity cost per additional small jet is 9/12 = 3/4 of a Dreamliner, the same as it was when Boeing went from 20 small jets produced to 28. However, the fact that in this example the opportunity cost of a small jet in terms of a Dreamliner is always the same is a result of an assumption we've made, an assumption that's reflected in how Figure 2-1 is drawn. Specifically, whenever we assume that the opportunity cost of an additional unit of a good doesn't change regardless of the output mix, the production possibility frontier is a straight line.

Moreover, as you might have already guessed, the slope of a straight-line production possibility frontier is equal to the opportunity cost—specifically, the opportunity cost for the good measured on the horizontal axis in terms of the good measured on the vertical axis. In Figure 2-1, the production possibility frontier has a *constant slope* of −3/4, implying that Boeing faces a *constant opportunity cost* for 1 small jet equal to 3/4 of a Dreamliner. (A review of how to calculate the slope of a straight line is found in this chapter's appendix.) This is the simplest case, but the production possibility frontier model can also be used to examine situations in which opportunity costs change as the mix of output changes.

Figure 2-2 illustrates a different assumption, a case in which Boeing faces *increasing opportunity cost*. Here, the more small jets it produces, the more costly it is to produce yet another small jet in terms of forgone production of a

FIGURE **2-2** Increasing Opportunity Cost

The bowed-out shape of the production possibility frontier reflects increasing opportunity cost. In this example, to produce the first 20 small jets, Boeing must forgo producing 5 Dreamliners. But to produce an additional 20 small jets, Boeing must forgo manufacturing 25 more Dreamliners.

Dreamliner. And the same holds true in reverse: the more Dreamliners Boeing produces, the more costly it is to produce yet another Dreamliner in terms of forgone production of small jets. For example, to go from producing zero small jets to producing 20, Boeing has to forgo producing 5 Dreamliners. That is, the opportunity cost of those 20 small jets is 5 Dreamliners. But to increase its production of small jets to 40—that is, to produce an additional 20 small jets—it must forgo producing 25 more Dreamliners, a much higher opportunity cost. As you can see in Figure 2-2, when opportunity costs are increasing rather than constant, the production possibility frontier is a bowed-out curve rather than a straight line.

Although it's often useful to work with the simple assumption that the production possibility frontier is a straight line, economists believe that in reality opportunity costs are typically increasing. When only a small amount of a good is produced, the opportunity cost of producing that good is relatively low because the economy needs to use only those resources that are especially well suited for its production. For example, if an economy grows only a small amount of corn, that corn can be grown in places where the soil and climate are perfect for corn-growing but less suitable for growing anything else, like wheat. So growing that corn involves giving up only a small amount of potential wheat output. Once the economy grows a lot of corn, however, land that is well suited for wheat but isn't so great for corn must be used to produce corn anyway. As a result, the additional corn production involves sacrificing considerably more wheat production. In other words, as more of a good is produced, its opportunity cost typically rises because well-suited inputs are used up and less adaptable inputs must be used instead.

**Economic Growth**    Finally, the production possibility frontier helps us understand what it means to talk about *economic growth*. We introduced the concept of economic growth in the Introduction, defining it as *the growing ability of the economy to produce goods and services*. As we saw, economic growth is one of the fundamental features of the real economy. But are we really justified in saying that the economy has grown over time? After all, although the U.S. economy produces more of many things than it did a century ago, it produces less of other things—for example, horse-drawn carriages. Production of many goods, in other words, is actually down. So how can we say for sure that the economy as a whole has grown?

The answer is illustrated in Figure 2-3, where we have drawn two hypothetical production possibility frontiers for the economy. In them we have assumed once

FIGURE **2-3**  Economic Growth

Economic growth results in an *outward shift* of the production possibility frontier because production possibilities are expanded. The economy can now produce more of everything. For example, if production is initially at point *A* (25 Dreamliners and 20 small jets), economic growth means that the economy could move to point *E* (30 Dreamliners and 25 small jets).

**Factors of production** are resources used to produce goods and services.

**Technology** is the technical means for producing goods and services.

again that everyone in the economy works for Boeing and, consequently, the economy produces only two goods, Dreamliners and small jets. Notice how the two curves are nested, with the one labeled "Original *PPF*" lying completely inside the one labeled "New *PPF*." Now we can see graphically what we mean by economic growth of the economy: economic growth means an *expansion of the economy's production possibilities;* that is, the economy *can* produce more of everything. For example, if the economy initially produces at point *A* (25 Dreamliners and 20 small jets), economic growth means that the economy could move to point *E* (30 Dreamliners and 25 small jets). *E* lies outside the original frontier; so in the production possibility frontier model, growth is shown as an outward shift of the frontier.

What can lead the production possibility frontier to shift outward? There are basically two sources of economic growth. One is an increase in the economy's **factors of production,** the resources used to produce goods and services. Economists usually use the term *factor of production* to refer to a resource that is not used up in production. For example, in traditional airplane manufacture workers used riveting machines to connect metal sheets when constructing a plane's fuselage; the workers and the riveters are factors of production, but the rivets and the sheet metal are not. Once a fuselage is made, a worker and riveter can be used to make another fuselage, but the sheet metal and rivets used to make one fuselage cannot be used to make another.

Broadly speaking, the main factors of production are the resources land, labor, physical capital, and human capital. Land is a resource supplied by nature; labor is the economy's pool of workers; physical capital refers to created resources such as machines and buildings; and human capital refers to the educational achievements and skills of the labor force, which enhance its productivity. Of course, each of these is really a category rather than a single factor: land in North Dakota is quite different from land in Florida.

To see how adding to an economy's factors of production leads to economic growth, suppose that Boeing builds another construction hangar that allows it to increase the number of planes—small jets or Dreamliners or both—it can produce in a year. The new construction hangar is a factor of production, a resource Boeing can use to increase its yearly output. We can't say how many more planes of each type Boeing will produce; that's a management decision that will depend on, among other things, customer demand. But we can say that Boeing's production possibility frontier has shifted outward because it can now produce more small jets without reducing the number of Dreamliners it makes, or it can make more Dreamliners without reducing the number of small jets produced.

The other source of economic growth is progress in **technology,** the technical means for the production of goods and services. Composite materials had been used in some parts of aircraft before the Boeing Dreamliner was developed. But Boeing engineers realized that there were large additional advantages to building a whole plane out of composites. The plane would be lighter, stronger, and have better aerodynamics than a plane built in the traditional way. It would therefore have longer range, be able to carry more people, and use less fuel, in addition to being able to maintain higher cabin pressure. So in a real sense Boeing's innovation—a whole plane built out of composites—was a way to do more with any given amount of resources, pushing out the production possibility frontier.

Because improved jet technology has pushed out the production possibility frontier, it has made it possible for the economy to produce more of everything, not just jets and air travel. Over the past 30 years, the biggest technological advances have taken place in information technology, not in construction or food services. Yet Americans have chosen to buy bigger houses and eat out more than they used to because the economy's growth has made it possible to do so.

The production possibility frontier is a very simplified model of an economy. Yet it teaches us important lessons about real-life economies. It gives us our first clear sense of what constitutes economic efficiency, it illustrates the concept of opportunity cost, and it makes clear what economic growth is all about.

## Comparative Advantage and Gains from Trade

Among the twelve principles of economics described in Chapter 1 was the principle of *gains from trade*—the mutual gains that individuals can achieve by specializing in doing different things and trading with one another. Our second illustration of an economic model is a particularly useful model of gains from trade—trade based on *comparative advantage*.

One of the most important insights in all of economics is that there are gains from trade—that it makes sense to produce the things you're especially good at producing and to buy from other people the things you aren't as good at producing. This would be true even if you could produce everything for yourself: even if a brilliant brain surgeon *could* repair her own dripping faucet, it's probably a better idea for her to call in a professional plumber.

How can we model the gains from trade? Let's stay with our aircraft example and once again imagine that the United States is a one-company economy where everyone works for Boeing, producing airplanes. Let's now assume, however, that the United States has the ability to trade with Brazil—another one-company economy where everyone works for the Brazilian aircraft company Embraer, which is, in the real world, a successful producer of small commuter jets. (If you fly from one major U.S. city to another, your plane is likely to be a Boeing, but if you fly into a small city, the odds are good that your plane will be an Embraer.)

In our example, the only two goods produced are large jets and small jets. Both countries could produce both kinds of jets. But as we'll see in a moment, they can gain by producing different things and trading with each other. For the purposes of this example, let's return to the simpler case of straight-line production possibility frontiers. America's production possibilities are represented by the production possibility frontier in panel (a) of Figure 2-4, which is similar to the production possibility frontier in Figure 2-1. According to this diagram, the United States can produce 40 small jets if it makes no large jets and can manufacture 30 large jets if it produces no small jets. Recall that this means that the slope of the U.S. production possibility frontier is $-\frac{3}{4}$: its opportunity cost of 1 small jet is $\frac{3}{4}$ of a large jet.

**FIGURE  2-4  Production Possibilities for Two Countries**

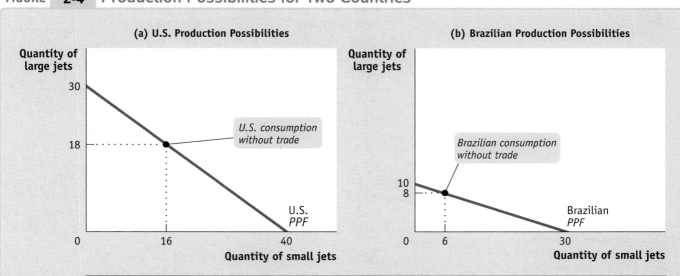

Here, both the United States and Brazil have a constant opportunity cost of small jets, illustrated by a straight-line production possibility frontier. For the United States, each small jet has an opportunity cost of ¾ of a large jet. Brazil has an opportunity cost of a small jet equal to ⅓ of a large jet.

Panel (b) of Figure 2-4 shows Brazil's production possibilities. Like the United States, Brazil's production possibility frontier is a straight line, implying a constant opportunity cost of a small jet in terms of large jets. Brazil's production possibility frontier has a constant slope of $-\frac{1}{3}$. Brazil can't produce as much of anything as the United States can: at most it can produce 30 small jets or 10 large jets. But it is relatively better at manufacturing small jets than the United States; whereas the United States sacrifices $\frac{3}{4}$ of a large jet per small jet produced, for Brazil the opportunity cost of a small jet is only $\frac{1}{3}$ of a large jet. Table 2-1 summarizes the two countries' opportunity costs of small jets and large jets.

Now, the United States and Brazil could each choose to make their own large and small jets, not trading any airplanes and consuming only what each produced within its own country. (A country "consumes" an airplane when it is owned by a domestic resident.) Let's suppose that the two countries start out this way and make the consumption choices shown in Figure 2-4: in the absence of trade, the United States produces and consumes 16 small jets and 18 large jets per year, while Brazil produces and consumes 6 small jets and 8 large jets per year.

But is this the best the two countries can do? No, it isn't. Given that the two producers—and therefore the two countries—have different opportunity costs, the United States and Brazil can strike a deal that makes both of them better off.

Table 2-2 shows how such a deal works: the United States specializes in the production of large jets, manufacturing 30 per year, and sells 10 to Brazil. Meanwhile, Brazil specializes in the production of small jets, producing 30 per year, and sells 20 to the United States. The result is shown in Figure 2-5. The United States now consumes more of both small jets and large jets than before: instead of 16 small jets and 18 large jets, it now consumes 20 small jets and 20 large jets. Brazil also consumes more, going from 6 small jets and 8 large jets to 10 small jets and 10 large jets. As Table 2-2 also shows, both the United States and Brazil reap gains from trade, consuming more of both types of plane than they would have without trade.

**TABLE 2-1** U.S. and Brazilian Opportunity Costs of Small Jets and Large Jets

|  | U.S. Opportunity Cost |  | Brazilian Opportunity Cost |
|---|---|---|---|
| One small jet | ¾ large jet | > | ⅓ large jet |
| One large jet | 4/3 small jets | < | 3 small jets |

**TABLE 2-2** How the United States and Brazil Gain from Trade

|  |  | Without Trade | | With Trade | | Gains from Trade |
|---|---|---|---|---|---|---|
|  |  | Production | Consumption | Production | Consumption | |
| United States | Large jets | 18 | 18 | 30 | 20 | +2 |
|  | Small jets | 16 | 16 | 0 | 20 | +4 |
| Brazil | Large jets | 8 | 8 | 0 | 10 | +2 |
|  | Small jets | 6 | 6 | 30 | 10 | +4 |

Both countries are better off when they each specialize in what they are good at and trade. It's a good idea for the United States to specialize in the production of large jets because its opportunity cost of a large jet is smaller than Brazil's: $\frac{4}{3} < 3$. Correspondingly, Brazil should specialize in the production of small jets because its opportunity cost of a small jet is smaller than the United States: $\frac{1}{3} < \frac{3}{4}$.

What we would say in this case is that the United States has a comparative advantage in the production of large jets and Brazil has a comparative advantage in the production of small jets. A country has a **comparative advantage** in producing something if the opportunity cost of that production is lower for that country than for other countries. The same concept applies to firms and people: a firm or an individual has a comparative advantage in producing something if its, his, or her opportunity cost of production is lower than for others.

A country has a **comparative advantage** in producing a good or service if its opportunity cost of producing the good or service is lower than other countries'. Likewise, an individual has a comparative advantage in producing a good or service if his or her opportunity cost of producing the good or service is lower than for other people.

**FIGURE** **2-5** **Comparative Advantage and Gains from Trade**

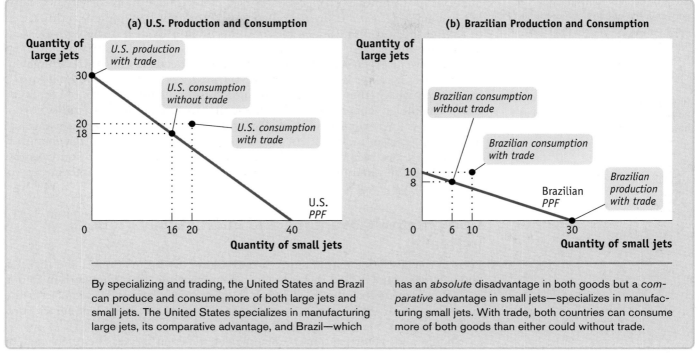

By specializing and trading, the United States and Brazil can produce and consume more of both large jets and small jets. The United States specializes in manufacturing large jets, its comparative advantage, and Brazil—which has an *absolute* disadvantage in both goods but a *comparative* advantage in small jets—specializes in manufacturing small jets. With trade, both countries can consume more of both goods than either could without trade.

One point of clarification before we proceed further. You may have wondered why the United States traded 10 large jets to Brazil in return for 20 small jets. Why not some other deal, like trading 10 large jets for 12 small jets? The answer to that question has two parts. First, there may indeed be other trades that the United States and Brazil might agree to. Second, there are some deals that we can safely rule out— one like 10 large jets for 10 small jets.

To understand why, reexamine Table 2-1 and consider the United States first. Without trading with Brazil, the U.S. opportunity cost of a small jet is ¾ of a large jet. So it's clear that the United States will not accept any trade that requires it to give up more than ¾ of a large jet for a small jet. Trading 10 jets in return for 12 small jets would require the United States to pay an opportunity cost of 10/12 = 5/6 of a large jet for a small jet. Because 5/6 > than ¾, this is a deal that the United States would reject. Similarly, Brazil won't accept a trade that gives it less than ⅓ of a large jet for a small jet.

The point to remember is that the United States and Brazil will be willing to trade only if the "price" of the good each country obtains in the trade is less than its own opportunity cost of producing the good domestically. Moreover, this is a general statement that is true whenever two parties—countries, firms, or individuals—trade voluntarily.

While our story clearly simplifies reality, it teaches us some very important lessons that apply to the real economy, too.

First, the model provides a clear illustration of the gains from trade: through specialization and trade, both countries produce more and consume more than if they were self-sufficient.

Second, the model demonstrates a very important point that is often overlooked in real-world arguments: each country has a comparative advantage in producing something. This applies to firms and people as well: *everyone has a comparative advantage in something, and everyone has a comparative disadvantage in something.*

Crucially, in our example it doesn't matter if, as is probably the case in real life, U.S. workers are just as good as or even better than Brazilian workers at producing small jets. Suppose that the United States is actually better than Brazil at all kinds of aircraft production. In that case, we would say that the

A country has an **absolute advantage** in producing a good or service if the country can produce more output per worker than other countries. Likewise, an individual has an absolute advantage in producing a good or service if he or she is better at producing it than other people. Having an absolute advantage is not the same thing as having a comparative advantage.

United States has an **absolute advantage** in both large-jet and small-jet production: in an hour, an American worker can produce more of either a large jet or a small jet than a Brazilian worker. You might be tempted to think that in that case the United States has nothing to gain from trading with the less productive Brazil.

But we've just seen that the United States can indeed benefit from trading with Brazil because *comparative, not absolute, advantage is the basis for mutual gain*. It doesn't matter whether it takes Brazil more resources than the United States to make a small jet; what matters for trade is that for Brazil the opportunity cost of a small jet is lower than the U.S. opportunity cost. So Brazil, despite its absolute disadvantage, even in small jets, has a comparative advantage in the manufacture of small jets. Meanwhile the United States, which can use its resources most productively by manufacturing large jets, has a comparative *dis*advantage in manufacturing small jets.

## Comparative Advantage and International Trade, in Reality

Look at the label on a manufactured good sold in the United States, and there's a good chance you will find that it was produced in some other country—in China, or Japan, or even in Canada, eh? On the other side, many U.S. industries sell a large fraction of their output overseas. (This is particularly true of agriculture, high technology, and entertainment.)

Should all this international exchange of goods and services be celebrated, or is it cause for concern? Politicians and the public often question the desirability of international trade, arguing that the nation should produce goods for itself rather than buying them from foreigners. Industries around the world demand protection from foreign competition: Japanese farmers want to keep out American rice, American steelworkers want to keep out European steel. And these demands are often supported by public opinion.

Economists, however, have a very positive view of international trade. Why? Because they view it in terms of comparative advantage. As we learned from our example of U.S. large jets and Brazilian small jets, international trade benefits both countries. Each country can consume more than if it didn't trade and remained self-sufficient. Moreover, these mutual gains don't depend on each country being better than other countries at producing one kind of good. Even if one country has, say, higher output per worker in both industries—that is, even if one country has an absolute advantage in both industries—there are still gains from trade. The upcoming Global Comparison, which explains the pattern of clothing production throughout the global economy, illustrates just this point.

---

## ⚠ PITFALLS

**MISUNDERSTANDING COMPARATIVE ADVANTAGE**

Students do it, pundits do it, and politicians do it all the time: they confuse *comparative* advantage with *absolute* advantage. For example, back in the 1980s, when the U.S. economy seemed to be lagging behind that of Japan, one often heard commentators warn that if we didn't improve our productivity, we would soon have no comparative advantage in anything.

What those commentators meant was that we would have no *absolute* advantage in anything—that there might come a time when the Japanese were better at everything than we were. (It didn't turn out that way, but that's another story.) And they had the idea that in that case we would no longer be able to benefit from trade with Japan.

But just as Brazil, in our example, was able to benefit from trade with the United States (and vice versa) despite the fact that the United States was better at manufacturing both large and small jets, in real life nations can still gain from trade even if they are less productive in all industries than the countries they trade with.

## PAJAMA REPUBLICS

Poor countries tend to have low productivity in clothing manufacture, but even lower productivity in other industries (see the upcoming Economics in Action), giving them a comparative advantage in clothing manufacture. As a result, the clothing industry tends to dominate their economies. An official from one such country once joked, "We are not a banana republic—we are a pajama republic."

The figure to the right plots per capita income (the total income of the country divided by the size of the population) against the share of manufacturing employment devoted to clothing production for several countries. The graph shows just how strongly negative the relationship is between a country's per capita income level and the size of its clothing industry: poor countries have relatively large clothing industries, while rich countries have relatively small ones.

According to the U.S. Department of Commerce, Bangladesh's clothing industry has "low productivity, largely low literacy levels, frequent labor unrest, and out- dated technology." Yet Bangladesh devotes most of its manufacturing workforce to clothing, the sector in which it nonetheless has a comparative advantage because its

productivity in non-clothing industries is even lower. In contrast, Costa Rica has "relatively high productivity" in clothing. Yet, a much smaller and declining fraction of Costa Rica's workforce is employed in clothing produc- tion. That's because productivity in non-clothing industries is somewhat higher in Costa Rica than in Bangladesh.

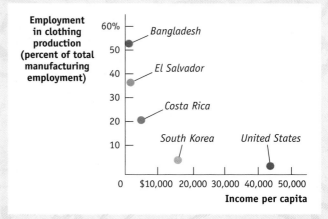

*Source:* World Bank, World Development Indicators; Nicita A. and M. Olarreaga, "Trade, Production and Protection 1976–2004," *World Bank Economic Review* 21, no. 1 (2007): 165–171.

## Transactions: The Circular-Flow Diagram

The model economies that we've studied so far—each containing only one firm—are a huge simplification. We've also greatly simplified trade between the United States and Brazil, assuming that they engage only in the simplest of economic transac- tions, **barter,** in which one party directly trades a good or service for another good or service without using money. In a modern economy, simple barter is rare: usually people trade goods or services for money—pieces of colored paper with no inherent value—and then trade those pieces of colored paper for the goods or services they want. That is, they sell goods or services and buy other goods or services.

And they both sell and buy a lot of different things. The U.S. economy is a vastly complex entity, with more than a hundred million workers employed by millions of companies, producing millions of different goods and services. Yet you can learn some very important things about the economy by considering the simple graphic shown in Figure 2-6 on the next page, the **circular-flow diagram.** This diagram rep- resents the transactions that take place in an economy by two kinds of flows around a circle: flows of physical things such as goods, services, labor, or raw materials in one direction, and flows of money that pay for these physical things in the opposite direc- tion. In this case the physical flows are shown in yellow, the money flows in green.

The simplest circular-flow diagram illustrates an economy that contains only two kinds of inhabitants: **households** and **firms.** A household consists of either an individual or a group of people (usually, but not necessarily, a family) that share their income. A firm is an organization that produces goods and services for sale—and that employs members of households.

As you can see in Figure 2-6, there are two kinds of markets in this simple economy. On one side (here the left side) there are **markets for goods and services** in which households buy the goods and services they want from firms.

Trade takes the form of **barter** when people directly exchange goods or services that they have for goods or services that they want.

The **circular-flow diagram** represents the transactions in an economy by flows around a circle.

A **household** is a person or a group of people that share their income.

A **firm** is an organization that produces goods and services for sale.

Firms sell goods and services that they produce to households in **markets for goods and services.**

FIGURE **2-6** The Circular-Flow Diagram

This diagram represents the flows of money and of goods and services in the economy. In the markets for goods and services, households purchase goods and services from firms, generating a flow of money to the firms and a flow of goods and services to the households. The money flows back to households as firms purchase factors of production from the households in factor markets.

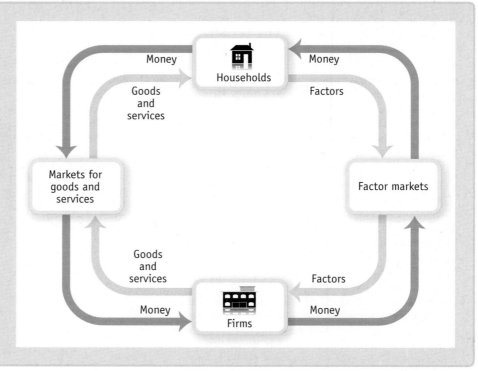

This produces a flow of goods and services to households and a return flow of money to firms.

On the other side, there are **factor markets** in which firms buy the resources they need to produce goods and services. Recall from earlier in the chapter that the main factors of production are land, labor, physical capital, and human capital.

The factor market most of us know best is the labor market, in which workers sell their services. In addition, we can think of households as owning and selling the other factors of production to firms. For example, when a firm buys physical capital in the form of machines, the payment ultimately goes to the households that own the machine-making firm. In this case, the transactions are occurring in the *capital market,* the market in which capital is bought and sold. As we'll examine in detail later, factor markets ultimately determine an economy's **income distribution,** how the total income created in an economy is allocated between less skilled workers, highly skilled workers, and the owners of capital and land.

The circular-flow diagram ignores a number of real-world complications in the interests of simplicity. A few examples:

- In the real world, the distinction between firms and households isn't always that clear-cut. Consider a small, family-run business—a farm, a shop, a small hotel. Is this a firm or a household? A more complete picture would include a separate box for family businesses.

- Many of the sales firms make are not to households but to other firms; for example, steel companies sell mainly to other companies such as auto manufacturers, not to households. A more complete picture would include these flows of goods, services, and money within the business sector.

- The figure doesn't show the government, which in the real world diverts quite a lot of money out of the circular flow in the form of taxes but also injects a lot of money back into the flow in the form of spending.

Firms buy the resources they need to produce goods and services in **factor markets.**

An economy's **income distribution** is the way in which total income is divided among the owners of the various factors of production.

Figure 2-6, in other words, is by no means a complete picture either of all the types of inhabitants of the real economy or of all the flows of money and physical items that take place among these inhabitants.

Despite its simplicity, the circular-flow diagram is a very useful aid to thinking about the economy.

## ECONOMICS ▶ IN ACTION

### RICH NATION, POOR NATION

Try taking off your clothes—at a suitable time and in a suitable place, of course—and taking a look at the labels inside that say where they were made. It's a very good bet that much, if not most, of your clothing was manufactured overseas, in a country that is much poorer than the United States—say, in El Salvador, Sri Lanka, or Bangladesh.

Why are these countries so much poorer than we are? The immediate reason is that their economies are much less *productive*—firms in these countries are just not able to produce as much from a given quantity of resources as comparable firms in the United States or other wealthy countries. Why countries differ so much in productivity is a deep question—indeed, one of the main questions that preoccupy economists. But in any case, the difference in productivity is a fact.

But if the economies of these countries are so much less productive than ours, how is it that they make so much of our clothing? Why don't we do it for ourselves?

The answer is "comparative advantage." Just about every industry in Bangladesh is much less productive than the corresponding industry in the United States. But the productivity difference between rich and poor countries varies across goods; it is very large in the production of sophisticated goods like aircraft but not that large in the production of simpler goods like clothing. So Bangladesh's position with regard to clothing production is like Embraer's position with respect to producing small jets: it's not as good at it as Boeing, but it's the thing Embraer does comparatively well.

Bangladesh, though it is at an absolute disadvantage compared with the United States in almost everything, has a comparative advantage in clothing production. This means that both the United States and Bangladesh are able to consume more because they specialize in producing different things, with Bangladesh supplying our clothing and the United States supplying Bangladesh with more sophisticated goods.

Although less productive than American workers, Bangladeshi workers have a comparative advantage in clothing production.

### CHECK YOUR UNDERSTANDING   2-1

1. True or false? Explain your answer.
   a. An increase in the amount of resources available to Boeing for use in producing Dreamliners and small jets does not change its production possibility frontier.
   b. A technological change that allows Boeing to build more small jets for any amount of Dreamliners built results in a change in its production possibility frontier.
   c. The production possibility frontier is useful because it illustrates how much of one good an economy must give up to get more of another good regardless of whether resources are being used efficiently.

2. In Italy, an automobile can be produced by 8 workers in one day and a washing machine by 3 workers in one day. In the United States, an automobile can be produced by 6 workers in one day and a washing machine by 2 workers in one day.
   a. Which country has an absolute advantage in the production of automobiles? In washing machines?

> ▼ **Quick Review**
>
> • Most economic **models** are "thought experiments" or simplified representations of reality that rely on the **other things equal assumption.**
>
> • The **production possibility frontier** model illustrates the concepts of efficiency, opportunity cost, and economic growth.
>
> • Every person and every country has a **comparative advantage** in something, giving rise to gains from trade. Comparative advantage is often confused with **absolute advantage.**
>
> • In the simplest economies people **barter** rather than transact with money. The **circular-flow diagram** illustrates transactions within the economy as flows of goods and services, **factors of production,** and money between **households** and **firms.** These transactions occur in **markets for goods and services** and **factor markets.** Ultimately, factor markets determine the economy's **income distribution.**

Robert Nickelsberg/Getty Images

**Positive economics** is the branch of economic analysis that describes the way the economy actually works.

**Normative economics** makes prescriptions about the way the economy should work.

A **forecast** is a simple prediction of the future.

    **b.** Which country has a comparative advantage in the production of washing machines? In automobiles?

    **c.** What pattern of specialization results in the greatest gains from trade between the two countries?

**3.** Using the numbers from Table 2-1, explain why the United States and Brazil are willing to engage in a trade of 10 large jets for 15 small jets.

**4.** Use the circular-flow diagram to explain how an increase in the amount of money spent by households results in an increase in the number of jobs in the economy. Describe in words what the circular-flow diagram predicts.

Solutions appear at back of book.

## Using Models

Economics, we have now learned, is mainly a matter of creating models that draw on a set of basic principles but add some more specific assumptions that allow the modeler to apply those principles to a particular situation. But what do economists actually *do* with their models?

### Positive versus Normative Economics

Imagine that you are an economic adviser to the governor of your state. What kinds of questions might the governor ask you to answer?

Well, here are three possible questions:

1. How much revenue will the tolls on the state turnpike yield next year?

2. How much would that revenue increase if the toll were raised from $1 to $1.50?

3. Should the toll be raised, bearing in mind that a toll increase will reduce traffic and air pollution near the road but will impose some financial hardship on frequent commuters?

There is a big difference between the first two questions and the third one. The first two are questions about facts. Your forecast of next year's toll collection will be proved right or wrong when the numbers actually come in. Your estimate of the impact of a change in the toll is a little harder to check—revenue depends on other factors besides the toll, and it may be hard to disentangle the causes of any change in revenue. Still, in principle there is only one right answer.

But the question of whether tolls should be raised may not have a "right" answer—two people who agree on the effects of a higher toll could still disagree about whether raising the toll is a good idea. For example, someone who lives near the turnpike but doesn't commute on it will care a lot about noise and air pollution but not so much about commuting costs. A regular commuter who doesn't live near the turnpike will have the opposite priorities.

This example highlights a key distinction between two roles of economic analysis. Analysis that tries to answer questions about the way the world works, which have definite right and wrong answers, is known as **positive economics.** In contrast, analysis that involves saying how the world *should* work is known as **normative economics.** To put it another way, positive economics is about description; normative economics is about prescription.

Positive economics occupies most of the time and effort of the economics profession. And models play a crucial role in almost all positive economics. As we mentioned earlier, the U.S. government uses a computer model to assess proposed changes in national tax policy, and many state governments have similar models to assess the effects of their own tax policy.

It's worth noting that there is a subtle but important difference between the first and second questions we imagined the governor asking. Question 1 asked for a simple prediction about next year's revenue—a **forecast.** Question 2 was a "what if" question, asking how revenue would change if the tax law were changed. Economists are often called upon to answer both types of questions, but models are especially useful for answering "what if" questions.

The answers to such questions often serve as a guide to policy, but they are still predictions, not prescriptions. That is, they tell you what will happen if a policy were changed; they don't tell you whether or not that result is good. Suppose your economic model tells you that the governor's proposed increase in highway tolls will raise property values in communities near the road but will hurt people who must use the turnpike to get to work. Does that make this proposed toll increase a good idea or a bad one? It depends on whom you ask. As we've just seen, someone who is very concerned with the communities near the road will support the increase, but someone who is very concerned with the welfare of drivers will feel differently. That's a value judgment—it's not a question of economic analysis.

Still, economists often do engage in normative economics and give policy advice. How can they do this when there may be no "right" answer?

One answer is that economists are also citizens, and we all have our opinions. But economic analysis can often be used to show that some policies are clearly better than others, regardless of anyone's opinions.

Suppose that policies A and B achieve the same goal, but policy A makes everyone better off than policy B—or at least makes some people better off without making other people worse off. Then A is clearly more efficient than B. That's not a value judgment: we're talking about how best to achieve a goal, not about the goal itself.

For example, two different policies have been used to help low-income families obtain housing: rent control, which limits the rents landlords are allowed to charge, and rent subsidies, which provide families with additional money to pay rent. Almost all economists agree that subsidies are the more efficient policy. And so the great majority of economists, whatever their personal politics, favor subsidies over rent control.

When policies can be clearly ranked in this way, then economists generally agree. But it is no secret that economists sometimes disagree.

## When and Why Economists Disagree

Economists have a reputation for arguing with each other. Where does this reputation come from, and is it justified?

One important answer is that media coverage tends to exaggerate the real differences in views among economists. If nearly all economists agree on an issue—for example, the proposition that rent controls lead to housing shortages—reporters and editors are likely to conclude that it's not a story worth covering, leaving the professional consensus tends to go unreported. But an issue on which prominent economists take opposing sides—for example, whether cutting taxes right now would help the economy—makes a news story worth reporting. So you hear much more about the areas of disagreement within economics than you do about the large areas of agreement.

It is also worth remembering that economics is, unavoidably, often tied up in politics. On a number of issues powerful interest groups know what opinions they want to hear; they therefore have an incentive to find and promote economists who profess those opinions, giving these economists a prominence and visibility out of proportion to their support among their colleagues.

While the appearance of disagreement among economists exceeds the reality, it remains true that economists often *do* disagree about important things. For example, some well respected economists argue vehemently that the U.S. government should replace the income tax with a *value-added tax* (a national sales tax, which is the main source of government revenue in many European countries). Other equally respected economists disagree. Why this difference of opinion?

## FOR INQUIRING MINDS

### WHEN ECONOMISTS AGREE

"If all the economists in the world were laid end to end, they still couldn't reach a conclusion." So goes one popular economist joke. But do economists really disagree that much?

Not according to a classic survey of members of the American Economic Association, reported in the May 1992 issue of the *American Economic Review*. The authors asked respondents to agree or disagree with a number of statements

about the economy; what they found was a high level of agreement among professional economists on many of the statements. At the top, with more than 90 percent of the economists agreeing, were "Tariffs and import quotas usually reduce general economic welfare" and "A ceiling on rents reduces the quantity and quality of housing available." What's striking about these two statements is that many noneconomists disagree:

tariffs and import quotas to keep out foreign-produced goods are favored by many voters, and proposals to do away with rent control in cities like New York and San Francisco have met fierce political opposition.

So is the stereotype of quarreling economists a myth? Not entirely: economists do disagree quite a lot on some issues, especially in macroeconomics. But there is a large area of common ground.

---

One important source of differences lies in values: as in any diverse group of individuals, reasonable people can differ. In comparison to an income tax, a value-added tax typically falls more heavily on people of modest means. So an economist who values a society with more social and income equality for its own sake will tend to oppose a value-added tax. An economist with different values will be less likely to oppose it.

A second important source of differences arises from economic modeling. Because economists base their conclusions on models, which are simplified representations of reality, two economists can legitimately disagree about which simplifications are appropriate—and therefore arrive at different conclusions.

Suppose that the U.S. government were considering introducing a value-added tax. Economist A may rely on a model that focuses on the administrative costs of tax systems—that is, the costs of monitoring, processing papers, collecting the tax, and so on. This economist might then point to the well-known high costs of administering a value-added tax and argue against the change. But economist B may think that the right way to approach the question is to ignore the administrative costs and focus on how the proposed law would change savings behavior. This economist might point to studies suggesting that value-added taxes promote higher consumer saving, a desirable result.

Because the economists have used different models—that is, made different simplifying assumptions—they arrive at different conclusions. And so the two economists may find themselves on different sides of the issue.

In most cases such disputes are eventually resolved by the accumulation of evidence showing which of the various models proposed by economists does a better job of fitting the facts. However, in economics, as in any science, it can take a long time before research settles important disputes—decades, in some cases. And since the economy is always changing, in ways that make old models invalid or raise new policy questions, there are always new issues on which economists disagree. The policy maker must then decide which economist to believe.

The important point is that economic analysis is a method, not a set of conclusions.

## ECONOMICS ▸ *IN ACTION*

### ECONOMISTS, BEYOND THE IVORY TOWER

**M**any economists are mainly engaged in teaching and research. But quite a few economists have a more direct hand in events.

As described earlier in this chapter (For Inquiring Minds, "The Model That Ate the Economy"), one specific branch of economics, finance theory, plays an important role on Wall Street—not always to good effect. But pricing assets is by no means the only useful function economists serve in the business world. Businesses need forecasts of the future demand for their products, predictions of future raw-material prices, assessments of their future financing needs, and more; for all of these purposes, economic analysis is essential.

Some of the economists employed in the business world work directly for the institutions that need their input. Top financial firms like Goldman Sachs and Morgan Stanley, in particular, maintain high-quality economics groups, which produce analyses of forces and events likely to affect financial markets. Other economists are employed by consulting firms like Macro Advisers, which sells analysis and advice to a wide range of other businesses.

While chair of the Council of Economic Advisers, Christine Romer provided critical input in the making and implementation of economic policy.

Last but not least, economists participate extensively in government. According to the Bureau of Labor Statistics, government agencies employ about half of the professional economists in the United States. This shouldn't be surprising: one of the most important functions of government is to make economic policy, and almost every government policy decision must take economic effects into consideration. So governments around the world employ economists in a variety of roles.

In the U.S. government, a key role is played by the Council of Economic Advisers, whose sole purpose is to advise the president on economic matters. Unlike most government employees, most economists at the Council aren't long-time civil servants; instead, they are mainly professors on leave for one or two years from their universities. Many of the nation's best-known economists have served at the Council of Economic Advisers at some point in their careers.

Economists also play an important role in many other parts of the government, from the Department of Commerce to the Labor Department. Economists dominate the staff of the Federal Reserve, a government agency that controls the economy's money supply as well as overseeing banks. And economists play an especially important role in two international organizations headquartered in Washington, D.C.: the International Monetary Fund, which provides advice and loans to countries experiencing economic difficulties, and the World Bank, which provides advice and loans to promote long-term economic development.

In the past, it wasn't that easy to track what all these economists working on practical affairs were up to. These days, however, there is a very lively online discussion of economic prospects and policy, on websites that range from the home page of the International Monetary Fund (www.imf.org), to business-oriented sites like economy.com, to the blogs of individual economists, like that of Mark Thoma (economistsview.typepad.com) or, yes, our own blog, which is among the Technorati top 100 blogs, at krugman.blogs.nytimes.com.

## CHECK YOUR UNDERSTANDING   2-2

1. Which of the following statements is a positive statement? Which is a normative statement?
   a. Society should take measures to prevent people from engaging in dangerous personal behavior.
   b. People who engage in dangerous personal behavior impose higher costs on society through higher medical costs.

2. True or false? Explain your answer.
   a. Policy choice A and policy choice B attempt to achieve the same social goal. Policy choice A, however, results in a much less efficient use of resources than policy choice B. Therefore, economists are more likely to agree on choosing policy choice B.
   b. When two economists disagree on the desirability of a policy, it's typically because one of them has made a mistake.
   c. Policy makers can always use economics to figure out which goals a society should try to achieve.

▼ **Quick Review**

- **Positive economics**—the focus of most economic research—is the analysis of the way the world works, in which there are definite right and wrong answers. If often involves making **forecasts.** But in **normative economics,** which makes prescriptions about how things ought to be, there are often no right answers and only value judgments.

- Economists do disagree—though not as much as legend has it—for two main reasons. One, they may disagree about which simplifications to make in a model. Two, economists may disagree—like everyone else—about values.

# Efficiency, Opportunity Cost, and the Logic of Lean Production at Boeing

Corbis/Photolibrary

In the summer and fall of 2010, workers were rearranging the furniture in Boeing's final assembly plant in Everett, Washington, in preparation for the production of the Boeing 767. It was a difficult and time-consuming process, however, because the items of "furniture"—Boeing's assembly equipment—weighed on the order of 200 tons each. It was a necessary part of setting up a production system based on "lean manufacturing," also called "just-in-time" production. Lean manufacturing, pioneered by Toyota Motors of Japan, is based on the practice of having parts arrive on the factory floor just as they are needed for production. This reduces the amount of parts Boeing holds in inventory as well as the amount of the factory floor needed for production—in this case, reducing the square footage required for manufacture of the 767 by 40%.

Boeing had adopted lean manufacturing in 1999 in the manufacture of the 737, the most popular commercial airplane. By 2005, after constant refinement, Boeing had achieved a 50% reduction in the time it takes to produce a plane and a nearly 60% reduction in parts inventory. An important feature is a continuously moving assembly line, moving products from one assembly team to the next at a steady pace and eliminating the need for workers to wander across the factory floor from task to task or in search of tools and parts.

Toyota's lean production techniques have been the most widely adopted of all manufacturing techniques and have revolutionized manufacturing worldwide. In simple terms, lean production is focused on organization and communication. Workers and parts are organized so as to ensure a smooth and consistent workflow that minimizes wasted effort and materials. Lean production is also designed to be highly responsive to changes in the desired mix of output—for example, quickly producing more sedans and fewer minivans according to changes in customers' demands.

Toyota's lean production methods were so successful that they transformed the global auto industry and severely threatened once-dominant American automakers. Until the 1980s, the "Big Three"—Chrysler, Ford, and General Motors—dominated the American auto industry, with virtually no foreign-made cars sold in the United States. In the 1980s, however, Toyotas became increasingly popular in the United States due to their high quality and relatively low price—so popular that the Big Three eventually prevailed upon the U.S. government to protect them by restricting the sale of Japanese autos in the U.S. Over time, Toyota responded by building assembly plants in the United States, bringing along its lean production techniques, which then spread throughout American manufacturing. Toyota's growth continued, and by 2008 it had eclipsed General Motors as the largest automaker in the world.

### QUESTIONS FOR THOUGHT

1. What is the opportunity cost associated with having a worker wander across the factory floor from task to task or in search of tools and parts?

2. Explain how lean manufacturing improves the economy's efficiency in allocation.

3. Before lean manufacturing innovations, Japan mostly sold consumer electronics to the United States. How did lean manufacturing innovations alter Japan's comparative advantage vis-à-vis the United States?

4. Predict how the shift in the location of Toyota's production from Japan to the United States is likely to alter the pattern of comparative advantage in automaking between the two countries.

1. Almost all economics is based on **models,** "thought experiments" or simplified versions of reality, many of which use mathematical tools such as graphs. An important assumption in economic models is the **other things equal assumption,** which allows analysis of the effect of a change in one factor by holding all other relevant factors unchanged.

2. One important economic model is the **production possibility frontier.** It illustrates *opportunity cost* (showing how much less of one good can be produced if more of the other good is produced); *efficiency* (an economy is efficient in production if it produces on the production possibility frontier and efficient in allocation if it produces the mix of goods and services that people want to consume); and *economic growth* (an outward shift of the production possibility frontier). There are two basic sources of growth: an increase in **factors of production**—resources such as land, labor, capital, and human capital, inputs that are not used up in production—and improved **technology.**

3. Another important model is **comparative advantage,** which explains the source of gains from trade between individuals and countries. Everyone has a comparative advantage in something—some good or service in which that person has a lower opportunity cost than everyone else. But it is often confused with **absolute advantage,** an ability to produce a particular good or service better than anyone else. This confusion leads some to erroneously conclude that there are no gains from trade between people or countries.

4. In the simplest economies people **barter**—trade goods and services for one another—rather than trade them for money, as in a modern economy. The **circular-flow diagram** represents transactions within the economy as flows of goods, services, and money between **households** and **firms.** These transactions occur in **markets for goods and services** and **factor markets,** markets for **factors of production**—land, labor, physical capital, and human capital. It is useful in understanding how spending, production, employment, income, and growth are related in the economy. Ultimately, factor markets determine the economy's **income distribution,** how an economy's total income is allocated to the owners of the factors of production.

5. Economists use economic models for both **positive economics,** which describes how the economy works, and for **normative economics,** which prescribes how the economy *should* work. Positive economics often involves making **forecasts.** Economists can determine correct answers for positive questions but typically not for normative questions, which involve value judgments. The exceptions are when policies designed to achieve a certain objective can be clearly ranked in terms of efficiency.

6. There are two main reasons economists disagree. One, they may disagree about which simplifications to make in a model. Two, economists may disagree—like everyone else—about values.

Model, p. 26
Other things equal assumption, p. 26
Production possibility frontier, p. 28
Factors of production, p. 32
Technology, p. 32
Comparative advantage, p. 34

Absolute advantage, p. 36
Barter, p. 37
Circular-flow diagram, p. 37
Household, p. 37
Firm, p. 37
Markets for goods and services, p. 37

Factor markets, p. 38
Income distribution, p. 38
Positive economics, p. 40
Normative economics, p. 40
Forecast, p. 40

1. Two important industries on the island of Bermuda are fishing and tourism. According to data from the Food and Agriculture Organization of the United Nations and the Bermuda Department of Statistics, in the year 2009 the 306 registered fishermen in Bermuda caught 387 metric tons of marine fish. And the 2,719 people employed by hotels produced 554,400 hotel stays (measured by the number of visitor arrivals). Suppose that this production point is efficient in production. Assume also that the opportunity cost of 1 additional metric ton of fish is 2,000 hotel stays and that this opportunity cost is constant (the opportunity cost does not change).

   a. If all 306 registered fishermen were to be employed by hotels (in addition to the 2,719 people already working in hotels), how many hotel stays could Bermuda produce?

   b. If all 2,719 hotel employees were to become fishermen (in addition to the 306 fishermen already working in the fishing industry), how many metric tons of fish could Bermuda produce?

**c.** Draw a production possibility frontier for Bermuda, with fish on the horizontal axis and hotel stays on the vertical axis, and label Bermuda's actual production point for the year 2009.

**2.** Atlantis is a small, isolated island in the South Atlantic. The inhabitants grow potatoes and catch fish. The accompanying table shows the maximum annual output combinations of potatoes and fish that can be produced. Obviously, given their limited resources and available technology, as they use more of their resources for potato production, there are fewer resources available for catching fish.

| Maximum annual output options | Quantity of potatoes (pounds) | Quantity of fish (pounds) |
|---|---|---|
| A | 1,000 | 0 |
| B | 800 | 300 |
| C | 600 | 500 |
| D | 400 | 600 |
| E | 200 | 650 |
| F | 0 | 675 |

**a.** Draw a production possibility frontier with potatoes on the horizontal axis and fish on the vertical axis illustrating these options, showing points *A–F*.

**b.** Can Atlantis produce 500 pounds of fish and 800 pounds of potatoes? Explain. Where would this point lie relative to the production possibility frontier?

**c.** What is the opportunity cost of increasing the annual output of potatoes from 600 to 800 pounds?

**d.** What is the opportunity cost of increasing the annual output of potatoes from 200 to 400 pounds?

**e.** Can you explain why the answers to parts c and d are not the same? What does this imply about the slope of the production possibility frontier?

**3.** According to data from the U.S. Department of Agriculture's National Agricultural Statistics Service, 124 million acres of land in the United States were used for wheat or corn farming in 2004. Of those 124 million acres, farmers used 50 million acres to grow 2.158 billion bushels of wheat and 74 million acres of land to grow 11.807 billion bushels of corn. Suppose that U.S. wheat and corn farming is efficient in production. At that production point, the opportunity cost of producing 1 additional bushel of wheat is 1.7 fewer bushels of corn. However, because farmers have increasing opportunity costs, additional bushels of wheat have an opportunity cost greater than 1.7 bushels of corn. For each of the following production points, decide whether that production point is (i) feasible and efficient in production, (ii) feasible but not efficient in production, (iii) not feasible, or (iv) unclear as to whether or not it is feasible.

**a.** Farmers use 40 million acres of land to produce 1.8 billion bushels of wheat, and they use 60 million acres of land to produce 9 billion bushels of corn. The remaining 24 million acres are left unused.

**b.** From their original production point, farmers transfer 40 million acres of land from corn to wheat production. They now produce 3.158 billion bushels of wheat and 10.107 bushels of corn.

**c.** Farmers reduce their production of wheat to 2 billion bushels and increase their production of corn to 12.044 billion bushels. Along the production possibility frontier, the opportunity cost of going from 11.807 billion bushels of corn to 12.044 billion bushels of corn is 0.666 bushel of wheat per bushel of corn.

**4.** In the ancient country of Roma, only two goods, spaghetti and meatballs, are produced. There are two tribes in Roma, the Tivoli and the Frivoli. By themselves, the Tivoli each month can produce either 30 pounds of spaghetti and no meatballs, or 50 pounds of meatballs and no spaghetti, or any combination in between. The Frivoli, by themselves, each month can produce 40 pounds of spaghetti and no meatballs, or 30 pounds of meatballs and no spaghetti, or any combination in between.

**a.** Assume that all production possibility frontiers are straight lines. Draw one diagram showing the monthly production possibility frontier for the Tivoli and another showing the monthly production possibility frontier for the Frivoli. Show how you calculated them.

**b.** Which tribe has the comparative advantage in spaghetti production? In meatball production?

In A.D. 100 the Frivoli discover a new technique for making meatballs that doubles the quantity of meatballs they can produce each month.

**c.** Draw the new monthly production possibility frontier for the Frivoli.

**d.** After the innovation, which tribe now has an absolute advantage in producing meatballs? In producing spaghetti? Which has the comparative advantage in meatball production? In spaghetti production?

**5.** According to the U.S. Census Bureau, in July 2006 the United States sold aircraft worth $1 billion to China and bought aircraft worth only $19,000 from China. During the same month, however, the United States bought $83 million worth of men's trousers, slacks, and jeans from China but sold only $8,000 worth of trousers, slacks, and jeans to China. Using what you have learned about how trade is determined by comparative advantage, answer the following questions.

**a.** Which country has the comparative advantage in aircraft production? In production of trousers, slacks, and jeans?

**b.** Can you determine which country has the absolute advantage in aircraft production? In production of trousers, slacks, and jeans?

**6.** Peter Pundit, an economics reporter, states that the European Union (EU) is increasing its productivity very rapidly in all industries. He claims that this productivity advance is so rapid that output from the EU in these industries will soon exceed that of the United States and, as a result, the United States will no longer benefit from trade with the EU.

**a.** Do you think Peter Pundit is correct or not? If not, what do you think is the source of his mistake?

**b.** If the EU and the United States continue to trade, what do you think will characterize the goods that the EU sells to the United States and the goods that the United States sells to the EU?

**7.** You are in charge of allocating residents to your dormitory's baseball and basketball teams. You are down to the last four people, two of whom must be allocated to baseball and two to basketball. The accompanying table gives each person's batting average and free-throw average.

| Name | Batting average | Free-throw average |
|------|-----------------|--------------------|
| Kelley | 70% | 60% |
| Jackie | 50% | 50% |
| Curt | 10% | 30% |
| Gerry | 80% | 70% |

**a.** Explain how you would use the concept of comparative advantage to allocate the players. Begin by establishing each player's opportunity cost of free throws in terms of batting average.

**b.** Why is it likely that the other basketball players will be unhappy about this arrangement but the other baseball players will be satisfied? Nonetheless, why would an economist say that this is an efficient way to allocate players for your dormitory's sports teams?

**8.** The inhabitants of the fictional economy of Atlantis use money in the form of cowry shells. Draw a circular-flow diagram showing households and firms. Firms produce potatoes and fish, and households buy potatoes and fish. Households also provide the land and labor to firms. Identify where in the flows of cowry shells or physical things (goods and services, or resources) each of the following impacts would occur. Describe how this impact spreads around the circle.

**a.** A devastating hurricane floods many of the potato fields.

**b.** A very productive fishing season yields a very large number of fish caught.

**c.** The inhabitants of Atlantis discover Shakira and spend several days a month at dancing festivals.

**9.** An economist might say that colleges and universities "produce" education, using faculty members and students as inputs. According to this line of reasoning, education is then "consumed" by households. Construct a circular-flow diagram to represent the sector of the economy devoted to college education: colleges and universities represent firms, and households both consume education and provide faculty and students to universities. What are the relevant markets in this diagram? What is being bought and sold in each direction?

What would happen in the diagram if the government decided to subsidize 50% of all college students' tuition?

**10.** Your dormitory roommate plays loud music most of the time; you, however, would prefer more peace and quiet. You suggest that she buy some earphones. She responds that although she would be happy to use earphones, she has many other things that she would prefer to spend her money on right now. You discuss this situation with a friend who is an economics major. The following exchange takes place:

*He: How much would it cost to buy earphones?*

*You: $15.*

*He: How much do you value having some peace and quiet for the rest of the semester?*

*You: $30.*

*He: It is efficient for you to buy the earphones and give them to your roommate. You gain more than you lose; the benefit exceeds the cost. You should do that.*

*You: It just isn't fair that I have to pay for the earphones when I'm not the one making the noise.*

**a.** Which parts of this conversation contain positive statements and which parts contain normative statements?

**b.** Construct an argument supporting your viewpoint that your roommate should be the one to change her behavior. Similarly, construct an argument from the viewpoint of your roommate that you should be the one to buy the earphones. If your dormitory has a policy that gives residents the unlimited right to play music, whose argument is likely to win? If your dormitory has a rule that a person must stop playing music whenever a roommate complains, whose argument is likely to win?

**11.** A representative of the American clothing industry recently made the following statement: "Workers in Asia often work in sweatshop conditions earning only pennies an hour. American workers are more productive and as a result earn higher wages. In order to preserve the dignity of the American workplace, the government should enact legislation banning imports of low-wage Asian clothing."

**a.** Which parts of this quote are positive statements? Which parts are normative statements?

**b.** Is the policy that is being advocated consistent with the preceding statements about the wages and productivities of American and Asian workers?

**c.** Would such a policy make some Americans better off without making any other Americans worse off? That is, would this policy be efficient from the viewpoint of all Americans?

**d.** Would low-wage Asian workers benefit from or be hurt by such a policy?

**12.** Are the following statements true or false? Explain your answers.

**a.** "When people must pay higher taxes on their wage earnings, it reduces their incentive to work" is a positive statement.

b. "We should lower taxes to encourage more work" is a positive statement.

c. Economics cannot always be used to completely decide what society ought to do.

d. "The system of public education in this country generates greater benefits to society than the cost of running the system" is a normative statement.

e. All disagreements among economists are generated by the media.

13. Evaluate the following statement: "It is easier to build an economic model that accurately reflects events that have already occurred than to build an economic model to forecast future events." Do you think this is true or not? Why? What does this imply about the difficulties of building good economic models?

14. Economists who work for the government are often called on to make policy recommendations. Why do you think it is important for the public to be able to differentiate normative statements from positive statements in these recommendations?

15. The mayor of Gotham City, worried about a potential epidemic of deadly influenza this winter, asks an economic adviser the following series of questions. Determine whether a question requires the economic adviser to make a positive assessment or a normative assessment.

a. How much vaccine will be in stock in the city by the end of November?

b. If we offer to pay 10% more per dose to the pharmaceutical companies providing the vaccines, will they provide additional doses?

c. If there is a shortage of vaccine in the city, whom should we vaccinate first—the elderly or the very young? (Assume that a person from one group has an equal likelihood of dying from influenza as a person from the other group.)

d. If the city charges $25 per shot, how many people will pay?

e. If the city charges $25 per shot, it will make a profit of $10 per shot, money that can go to pay for inoculating poor people. Should the city engage in such a scheme?

16. Assess the following statement: "If economists just had enough data, they could solve all policy questions in a way that maximizes the social good. There would be no need for divisive political debates, such as whether the government should provide free medical care for all."

# Graphs in Economics

A quantity that can take on more than one value is called a **variable**.

## Getting the Picture

Whether you're reading about economics in the *Wall Street Journal* or in your economics textbook, you will see many graphs. Visual images can make it much easier to understand verbal descriptions, numerical information, or ideas. In economics, graphs are the type of visual image used to facilitate understanding. To fully understand the ideas and information being discussed, you need to be familiar with how to interpret these visual aids. This appendix explains how graphs are constructed and interpreted and how they are used in economics.

## Graphs, Variables, and Economic Models

One reason to attend college is that a bachelor's degree provides access to higher-paying jobs. Additional degrees, such as MBAs or law degrees, increase earnings even more. If you were to read an article about the relationship between educational attainment and income, you would probably see a graph showing the income levels for workers with different amounts of education. And this graph would depict the idea that, in general, more education increases income. This graph, like most of those in economics, would depict the relationship between two economic variables. A **variable** is a quantity that can take on more than one value, such as the number of years of education a person has, the price of a can of soda, or a household's income.

As you learned in this chapter, economic analysis relies heavily on *models*, simplified descriptions of real situations. Most economic models describe the relationship between two variables, simplified by holding constant other variables that may affect the relationship. For example, an economic model might describe the relationship between the price of a can of soda and the number of cans of soda that consumers will buy, assuming that everything else that affects consumers' purchases of soda stays constant. This type of model can be described mathematically or verbally, but illustrating the relationship in a graph makes it easier to understand. Next we show how graphs that depict economic models are constructed and interpreted.

## How Graphs Work

Most graphs in economics are based on a grid built around two perpendicular lines that show the values of two variables, helping you visualize the relationship between them. So a first step in understanding the use of such graphs is to see how this system works.

### Two-Variable Graphs

Figure 2A-1 shows a typical two-variable graph. It illustrates the data in the accompanying table on outside temperature and the number of sodas a typical vendor can expect to sell at a baseball stadium during one game. The first column shows the values of outside temperature (the first variable) and the second column shows the values of the number of sodas sold (the second variable). Five combinations or pairs of the two variables are shown, each denoted by *A* through *E* in the third column.

Now let's turn to graphing the data in this table. In any two-variable graph, one variable is called the *x*-variable and the other is called the *y*-variable. Here

FIGURE **2A-1** Plotting Points on a Two-Variable Graph

| x-variable outside temperature | y-variable number of sodas sold | Point |
|---|---|---|
| 0°F | 10 | A |
| 10 | 0 | B |
| 40 | 30 | C |
| 60 | 50 | D |
| 80 | 70 | E |

The data from the table are plotted where outside temperature (the independent variable) is measured along the horizontal axis and number of sodas sold (the dependent variable) is measured along the vertical axis. Each of the five combinations of temperature and sodas sold is represented by a point: *A, B, C, D,* and *E.* Each point in the graph is identified by a pair of values. For example, point *C* corresponds to the pair (40, 30)—an outside temperature of 40°F (the value of the *x*-variable) and 30 sodas sold (the value of the *y*-variable).

The line along which values of the *x*-variable are measured is called the **horizontal axis** or *x*-axis. The line along which values of the *y*-variable are measured is called the **vertical axis** or *y*-axis. The point where the axes of a two-variable graph meet is the **origin.**

A **causal relationship** exists between two variables when the value taken by one variable directly influences or determines the value taken by the other variable. In a causal relationship, the determining variable is called the **independent variable;** the variable it determines is called the **dependent variable.**

we have made outside temperature the *x*-variable and number of sodas sold the *y*-variable. The solid horizontal line in the graph is called the **horizontal axis** or *x*-**axis,** and values of the *x*-variable—outside temperature—are measured along it. Similarly, the solid vertical line in the graph is called the **vertical axis** or *y*-**axis,** and values of the *y*-variable—number of sodas sold—are measured along it. At the **origin,** the point where the two axes meet, each variable is equal to zero. As you move rightward from the origin along the *x*-axis, values of the *x*-variable are positive and increasing. As you move up from the origin along the *y*-axis, values of the *y*-variable are positive and increasing.

You can plot each of the five points *A* through *E* on this graph by using a pair of numbers—the values that the *x*-variable and the *y*-variable take on for a given point. In Figure 2A-1, at point *C,* the *x*-variable takes on the value 40 and the *y*-variable takes on the value 30. You plot point *C* by drawing a line straight up from 40 on the *x*-axis and a horizontal line across from 30 on the *y*-axis. We write point *C* as (40, 30). We write the origin as (0, 0).

Looking at point *A* and point *B* in Figure 2A-1, you can see that when one of the variables for a point has a value of zero, it will lie on one of the axes. If the value of the *x*-variable is zero, the point will lie on the vertical axis, like point *A.* If the value of the *y*-variable is zero, the point will lie on the horizontal axis, like point *B.*

Most graphs that depict relationships between two economic variables represent a **causal relationship,** a relationship in which the value taken by one variable directly influences or determines the value taken by the other variable. In a causal relationship, the determining variable is called the **independent variable;** the variable it determines is called the **dependent variable.** In our example of soda sales, the outside temperature is the independent variable. It directly influences the number of sodas that are sold, the dependent variable in this case.

By convention, we put the independent variable on the horizontal axis and the dependent variable on the vertical axis. Figure 2A-1 is constructed consistent with this convention; the independent variable (outside temperature) is on the horizontal axis and the dependent variable (number of sodas sold) is on the vertical axis. An important exception to this convention is in graphs showing the economic relationship between the price of a product and quantity of the product: although price is generally the independent variable that determines quantity, it is always measured on the vertical axis.

> A **curve** is a line on a graph that depicts a relationship between two variables. It may be either a straight line or a curved line. If the curve is a straight line, the variables have a **linear relationship**. If the curve is not a straight line, the variables have a **nonlinear relationship.**

## Curves on a Graph

Panel (a) of Figure 2A-2 contains some of the same information as Figure 2A-1, with a line drawn through the points *B, C, D,* and *E.* Such a line on a graph is called a **curve,** regardless of whether it is a straight line or a curved line. If the curve that shows the relationship between two variables is a straight line, or linear, the variables have a **linear relationship.** When the curve is not a straight line, or nonlinear, the variables have a **nonlinear relationship.**

A point on a curve indicates the value of the *y*-variable for a specific value of the *x*-variable. For example, point *D* indicates that at a temperature of 60°F, a vendor can expect to sell 50 sodas. The shape and orientation of a curve reveal

**FIGURE   2A-2   Drawing Curves**

The curve in panel (a) illustrates the relationship between the two variables, outside temperature and number of sodas sold. The two variables have a positive linear relationship: positive because the curve has an upward tilt, and linear because it is a straight line. It implies that an increase in the *x*-variable (outside temperature) leads to an increase in the *y*-variable (number of sodas sold). The curve in panel (b) is also a straight line, but it tilts downward. The two variables

here, outside temperature and number of hot drinks sold, have a negative linear relationship: an increase in the *x*-variable (outside temperature) leads to a decrease in the *y*-variable (number of hot drinks sold). The curve in panel (a) has a horizontal intercept at point *B,* where it hits the horizontal axis. The curve in panel (b) has a vertical intercept at point *J,* where it hits the vertical axis, and a horizontal intercept at point *M,* where it hits the horizontal axis.

Two variables have a **positive relationship** when an increase in the value of one variable is associated with an increase in the value of the other variable. It is illustrated by a curve that slopes upward from left to right.

Two variables have a **negative relationship** when an increase in the value of one variable is associated with a decrease in the value of the other variable. It is illustrated by a curve that slopes downward from left to right.

The **horizontal intercept** of a curve is the point at which it hits the horizontal axis; it indicates the value of the *x*-variable when the value of the *y*-variable is zero.

The **vertical intercept** of a curve is the point at which it hits the vertical axis; it shows the value of the *y*-variable when the value of the *x*-variable is zero.

The **slope** of a line or curve is a measure of how steep it is. The slope of a line is measured by "rise over run"—the change in the *y*-variable between two points on the line divided by the change in the *x*-variable between those same two points.

the general nature of the relationship between the two variables. The upward tilt of the curve in panel (a) of Figure 2A-2 means that vendors can expect to sell more sodas at higher outside temperatures.

When variables are related this way—that is, when an increase in one variable is associated with an increase in the other variable—the variables are said to have a **positive relationship.** It is illustrated by a curve that slopes upward from left to right. Because this curve is also linear, the relationship between outside temperature and number of sodas sold illustrated by the curve in panel (a) of Figure 2A-2 is a positive linear relationship.

When an increase in one variable is associated with a decrease in the other variable, the two variables are said to have a **negative relationship.** It is illustrated by a curve that slopes downward from left to right, like the curve in panel (b) of Figure 2A-2. Because this curve is also linear, the relationship it depicts is a negative linear relationship. Two variables that might have such a relationship are the outside temperature and the number of hot drinks a vendor can expect to sell at a baseball stadium.

Return for a moment to the curve in panel (a) of Figure 2A-2 and you can see that it hits the horizontal axis at point *B*. This point, known as the **horizontal intercept,** shows the value of the *x*-variable when the value of the *y*-variable is zero. In panel (b) of Figure 2A-2, the curve hits the vertical axis at point *J*. This point, called the **vertical intercept,** indicates the value of the *y*-variable when the value of the *x*-variable is zero.

## A Key Concept: The Slope of a Curve

The **slope** of a curve is a measure of how steep it is and indicates how sensitive the *y*-variable is to a change in the *x*-variable. In our example of outside temperature and the number of cans of soda a vendor can expect to sell, the slope of the curve would indicate how many more cans of soda the vendor could expect to sell with each 1 degree increase in temperature. Interpreted this way, the slope gives meaningful information. Even without numbers for *x* and *y*, it is possible to arrive at important conclusions about the relationship between the two variables by examining the slope of a curve at various points.

### The Slope of a Linear Curve

Along a linear curve the slope, or steepness, is measured by dividing the "rise" between two points on the curve by the "run" between those same two points. The rise is the amount that *y* changes, and the run is the amount that *x* changes. Here is the formula:

$$\frac{\text{Change in } y}{\text{Change in } x} = \frac{\Delta y}{\Delta x} = \text{Slope}$$

In the formula, the symbol $\Delta$ (the Greek uppercase delta) stands for "change in." When a variable increases, the change in that variable is positive; when a variable decreases, the change in that variable is negative.

The slope of a curve is positive when the rise (the change in the *y*-variable) has the same sign as the run (the change in the *x*-variable). That's because when two numbers have the same sign, the ratio of those two numbers is positive. The curve in panel (a) of Figure 2A-2 has a positive slope: along the curve, both the *y*-variable and the *x*-variable increase. The slope of a curve is negative when the rise and the run have different signs. That's because when two numbers have different signs, the ratio of those two numbers is negative. The curve in panel (b) of Figure 2A-2 has a negative slope: along the curve, an increase in the *x*-variable is associated with a decrease in the *y*-variable.

Figure 2A-3 illustrates how to calculate the slope of a linear curve. Let's focus first on panel (a). From point *A* to point *B* the value of the *y*-variable changes from

FIGURE  **2A-3**  Calculating the Slope

Panels (a) and (b) show two linear curves. Between points $A$ and $B$ on the curve in panel (a), the change in $y$ (the rise) is −5 and the change in $x$ (the run) is 10. So the slope from $A$ to $B$ is $\frac{\Delta y}{\Delta x} = \frac{-5}{10} = -\frac{1}{2} = -0.5$, where the negative sign indicates that the curve is downward sloping. In panel (b), the curve has a slope from $A$ to $B$ of $\frac{\Delta y}{\Delta x} = \frac{10}{2} = 5$. The slope from $C$ to

$D$ is $\frac{\Delta y}{\Delta x} = \frac{20}{4} = 5$. The slope is positive, indicating that the curve is upward sloping. Furthermore, the slope between $A$ and $B$ is the same as the slope between $C$ and $D$, making this a linear curve. The slope of a linear curve is constant: it is the same regardless of where it is measured along the curve.

25 to 20 and the value of the $x$-variable changes from 10 to 20. So the slope of the line between these two points is:

$$\frac{\text{Change in } y}{\text{Change in } x} = \frac{\Delta y}{\Delta x} = \frac{-5}{10} = -\frac{1}{2} = -0.5$$

Because a straight line is equally steep at all points, the slope of a straight line is the same at all points. In other words, a straight line has a constant slope. You can check this by calculating the slope of the linear curve between points $A$ and $B$ and between points $C$ and $D$ in panel (b) of Figure 2A-3.

Between $A$ and $B$:  $\qquad\qquad \frac{\Delta y}{\Delta x} = \frac{10}{2} = 5$

Between $C$ and $D$:  $\qquad\qquad \frac{\Delta y}{\Delta x} = \frac{20}{4} = 5$

## Horizontal and Vertical Curves and Their Slopes

When a curve is horizontal, the value of the $y$-variable along that curve never changes—it is constant. Everywhere along the curve, the change in $y$ is zero. Now, zero divided by any number is zero. So, regardless of the value of the change in $x$, the slope of a horizontal curve is always zero.

If a curve is vertical, the value of the $x$-variable along the curve never changes— it is constant. Everywhere along the curve, the change in $x$ is zero. This means that the slope of a vertical curve is a ratio with zero in the denominator. A ratio with zero in the denominator is equal to infinity—that is, an infinitely large number. So the slope of a vertical curve is equal to infinity.

A **nonlinear curve** is one in which the slope is not the same between every pair of points.

The **absolute value** of a negative number is the value of the negative number without the minus sign.

A vertical or a horizontal curve has a special implication: it means that the *x*-variable and the *y*-variable are unrelated. Two variables are unrelated when a change in one variable (the independent variable) has no effect on the other variable (the dependent variable). Or to put it a slightly different way, two variables are unrelated when the dependent variable is constant regardless of the value of the independent variable. If, as is usual, the *y*-variable is the dependent variable, the curve is horizontal. If the dependent variable is the *x*-variable, the curve is vertical.

## The Slope of a Nonlinear Curve

A **nonlinear curve** is one in which the slope changes as you move along it. Panels (a), (b), (c), and (d) of Figure 2A-4 show various nonlinear curves. Panels (a) and (b) show nonlinear curves whose slopes change as you move along them, but the slopes always remain positive. Although both curves tilt upward, the curve in panel (a) gets steeper as you move from left to right in contrast to the curve in panel (b), which gets flatter. A curve that is upward sloping and gets steeper, as in panel (a), is said to have *positive increasing* slope. A curve that is upward sloping but gets flatter, as in panel (b), is said to have *positive decreasing* slope.

When we calculate the slope along these nonlinear curves, we obtain different values for the slope at different points. How the slope changes along the curve determines the curve's shape. For example, in panel (a) of Figure 2A-4, the slope of the curve is a positive number that steadily increases as you move from left to right, whereas in panel (b), the slope is a positive number that steadily decreases.

The slopes of the curves in panels (c) and (d) are negative numbers. Economists often prefer to express a negative number as its **absolute value,** which is the value of the negative number without the minus sign. In general, we denote the absolute value of a number by two parallel bars around the number; for example, the absolute value of −4 is written as |−4| = 4. In panel (c), the absolute value of the slope steadily increases as you move from left to right. The curve therefore has *negative increasing* slope. And in panel (d), the absolute value of the slope of the curve steadily decreases along the curve. This curve therefore has *negative decreasing* slope.

## Calculating the Slope Along a Nonlinear Curve

We've just seen that along a nonlinear curve, the value of the slope depends on where you are on that curve. So how do you calculate the slope of a nonlinear curve? We will focus on two methods: the *arc method* and the *point method*.

### The Arc Method of Calculating the Slope
An arc of a curve is some piece or segment of that curve. For example, panel (a) of Figure 2A-4 shows an arc consisting of the segment of the curve between points *A* and *B*. To calculate the slope along a nonlinear curve using the arc method, you draw a straight line between the two end-points of the arc. The slope of that straight line is a measure of the average slope of the curve between those two end-points. You can see from panel (a) of Figure 2A-4 that the straight line drawn between points *A* and *B* increases along the *x*-axis from 6 to 10 (so that $\Delta x = 4$) as it increases along the *y*-axis from 10 to 20 (so that $\Delta y = 10$). Therefore the slope of the straight line connecting points *A* and *B* is:

$$\frac{\Delta y}{\Delta x} = \frac{10}{4} = 2.5$$

This means that the average slope of the curve between points *A* and *B* is 2.5.

FIGURE  **2A-4**  Nonlinear Curves

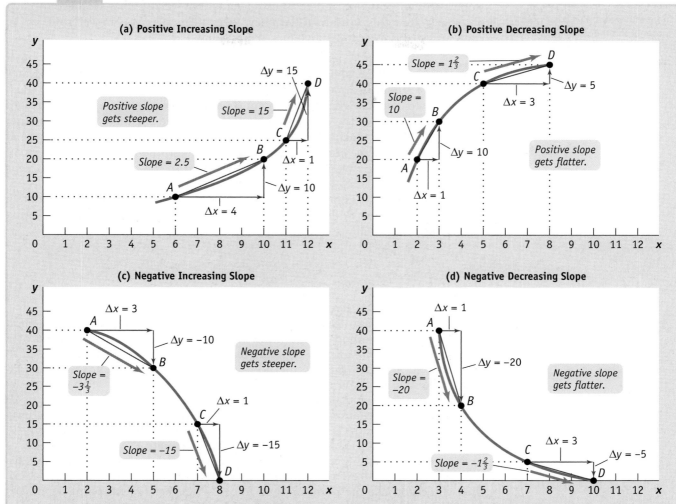

In panel (a) the slope of the curve from A to B is $\frac{\Delta y}{\Delta x} = \frac{10}{4} = 2.5$, and from C to D it is $\frac{\Delta y}{\Delta x} = \frac{15}{1} = 15$. The slope is positive and increasing; the curve gets steeper as you move to the right. In panel (b) the slope of the curve from A to B is $\frac{\Delta y}{\Delta x} = \frac{10}{1} = 10$, and from C to D it is $\frac{\Delta y}{\Delta x} = \frac{5}{3} = 1\frac{2}{3}$. The slope is positive and decreasing; the curve gets flatter as you move to the right. In panel (c) the slope from A to B is $\frac{\Delta y}{\Delta x} = \frac{-10}{3} = -3\frac{1}{3}$, and from C to D it is $\frac{\Delta y}{\Delta x} = \frac{-15}{1} = -15$. The slope is negative and increasing;

the curve gets steeper as you move to the right. And in panel (d) the slope from A to B is $\frac{\Delta y}{\Delta x} = \frac{-20}{1} = -20$, and from C to D it is $\frac{\Delta y}{\Delta x} = \frac{-5}{3} = -1\frac{2}{3}$. The slope is negative and decreasing; the curve gets flatter as you move to the right. The slope in each case has been calculated by using the arc method—that is, by drawing a straight line connecting two points along a curve. The average slope between those two points is equal to the slope of the straight line between those two points.

Now consider the arc on the same curve between points C and D. A straight line drawn through these two points increases along the x-axis from 11 to 12 ($\Delta x = 1$) as it increases along the y-axis from 25 to 40 ($\Delta y = 15$). So the average slope between points C and D is:

$$\frac{\Delta y}{\Delta x} = \frac{15}{1} = 15$$

A **tangent line** is a straight line that just touches, or is tangent to, a nonlinear curve at a particular point. The slope of the tangent line is equal to the slope of the nonlinear curve at that point.

Therefore the average slope between points *C* and *D* is larger than the average slope between points *A* and *B*. These calculations verify what we have already observed—that this upward-tilted curve gets steeper as you move from left to right and therefore has positive increasing slope.

**The Point Method of Calculating the Slope**  The point method calculates the slope of a nonlinear curve at a specific point on that curve. Figure 2A-5 illustrates how to calculate the slope at point *B* on the curve. First, we draw a straight line that just touches the curve at point *B*. Such a line is called a **tangent line:** the fact that it just touches the curve at point *B* and does not touch the curve at any other point on the curve means that the straight line is *tangent* to the curve at point *B*. The slope of this tangent line is equal to the slope of the nonlinear curve at point *B*.

You can see from Figure 2A-5 how the slope of the tangent line is calculated: from point *A* to point *C*, the change in *y* is 15 and the change in *x* is 5, generating a slope of:

$$\frac{\Delta y}{\Delta x} = \frac{15}{5} = 3$$

By the point method, the slope of the curve at point *B* is equal to 3.

A natural question to ask at this point is how to determine which method to use—the arc method or the point method—in calculating the slope of a nonlinear curve. The answer depends on the curve itself and the data used to construct it. You use the arc method when you don't have enough information to be able to draw a smooth curve. For example, suppose that in panel (a) of Figure 2A-4 you have only the data represented by points *A*, *C*, and *D* and don't have the data represented by point *B* or any of the rest of the curve. Clearly, then, you can't use the point method to calculate the slope at point *B*; you would have to use the arc method to approximate the slope of the curve in this area by drawing a straight line between points *A* and *C*. But if you have sufficient data to draw the smooth curve shown in panel (a) of Figure 2A-4, then you could use the point method to calculate the slope at point *B*—and at every other point along the curve as well.

FIGURE  **2A-5**  **Calculating the Slope Using the Point Method**

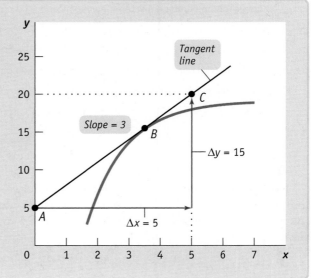

Here a tangent line has been drawn, a line that just touches the curve at point *B*. The slope of this line is equal to the slope of the curve at point *B*. The slope of the tangent line, measuring from *A* to *C*, is $\frac{\Delta y}{\Delta x} = \frac{15}{5} = 3$.

## Maximum and Minimum Points

The slope of a nonlinear curve can change from positive to negative or vice versa. When the slope of a curve changes from positive to negative, it creates what is called a *maximum* point of the curve. When the slope of a curve changes from negative to positive, it creates a *minimum* point.

Panel (a) of Figure 2A-6 illustrates a curve in which the slope changes from positive to negative as you move from left to right. When *x* is between 0 and 50, the slope of the curve is positive. At *x* equal to 50, the curve attains its highest point—the largest value of *y* along the curve. This point is called the **maximum** of the curve. When *x* exceeds 50, the slope becomes negative as the curve turns downward. Many important curves in economics, such as the curve that represents how the profit of a firm changes as it produces more output, are hill-shaped like this.

A nonlinear curve may have a **maximum** point, the highest point along the curve. At the maximum, the slope of the curve changes from positive to negative.

A nonlinear curve may have a **minimum** point, the lowest point along the curve. At the minimum, the slope of the curve changes from negative to positive.

**FIGURE    2A-6    Maximum and Minimum Points**

Panel (a) shows a curve with a maximum point, the point at which the slope changes from positive to negative.

Panel (b) shows a curve with a minimum point, the point at which the slope changes from negative to positive.

In contrast, the curve shown in panel (b) of Figure 2A-6 is U-shaped: it has a slope that changes from negative to positive. At *x* equal to 50, the curve reaches its lowest point—the smallest value of *y* along the curve. This point is called the **minimum** of the curve. Various important curves in economics, such as the curve that represents how per-unit the costs of some firms change as output increases, are U–shaped like this.

## Calculating the Area Below or Above a Curve

Sometimes it is useful to be able to measure the size of the area below or above a curve. We will encounter one such case in an upcoming chapter. To keep things simple, we'll only calculate the area below or above a linear curve.

How large is the shaded area below the linear curve in panel (a) of Figure 2A-7? First note that this area has the shape of a right triangle. A right triangle is a triangle that has two sides that make a right angle with each other. We will refer to one of these sides as the *height* of the triangle and the other side as the *base* of the triangle. For our purposes, it doesn't matter which of these two sides

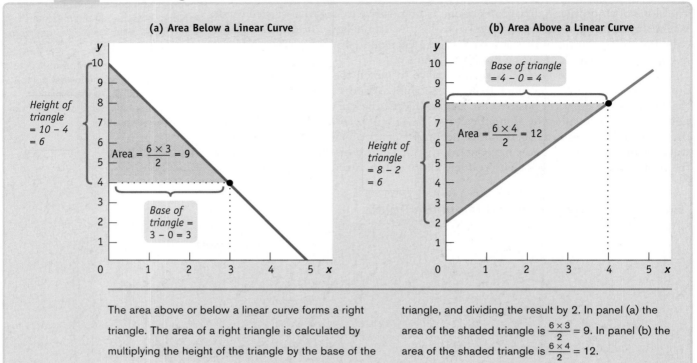

The area above or below a linear curve forms a right triangle. The area of a right triangle is calculated by multiplying the height of the triangle by the base of the triangle, and dividing the result by 2. In panel (a) the area of the shaded triangle is $\frac{6 \times 3}{2} = 9$. In panel (b) the area of the shaded triangle is $\frac{6 \times 4}{2} = 12$.

we refer to as the base and which as the height. Calculating the area of a right triangle is straightforward: multiply the height of the triangle by the base of the triangle, and divide the result by 2. The height of the triangle in panel (a) of Figure 2A-7 is $10 - 4 = 6$. And the base of the triangle is $3 - 0 = 3$. So the area of that triangle is

$$\frac{6 \times 3}{2} = 9$$

How about the shaded area above the linear curve in panel (b) of Figure 2A-7? We can use the same formula to calculate the area of this right triangle. The height of the triangle is $8 - 2 = 6$. And the base of the triangle is $4 - 0 = 4$. So the area of that triangle is

$$\frac{6 \times 4}{2} = 12$$

# Graphs That Depict Numerical Information

Graphs can also be used as a convenient way to summarize and display data without assuming some underlying causal relationship. Graphs that simply display numerical information are called *numerical graphs*. Here we will consider four types of numerical graphs: *time-series graphs*, *scatter diagrams*, *pie charts*, and *bar graphs*. These are widely used to display real, empirical data about different economic variables because they often help economists and policy makers identify patterns or trends in the economy. But as we will also see, you must be careful not to misinterpret or draw unwarranted conclusions from numerical graphs. That is, you must be aware of both the usefulness and the limitations of numerical graphs.

FIGURE **2A-8** Time-Series Graph

Time-series graphs show successive dates on the *x*-axis and values for a variable on the *y*-axis. This time-series graph shows real gross domestic product per capita, a measure of a country's standard of living, in the United States from 1947 to late 2010.
*Source:* Bureau of Economic Analysis.

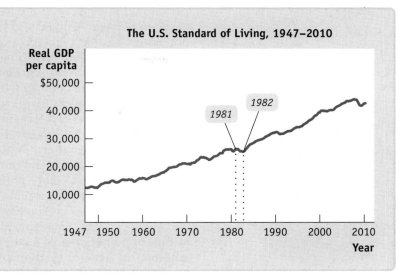

The U.S. Standard of Living, 1947–2010

## Types of Numerical Graphs

You have probably seen graphs in newspapers that show what has happened over time to economic variables such as the unemployment rate or stock prices. A **time-series graph** has successive dates on the horizontal axis and the values of a variable that occurred on those dates on the vertical axis. For example, Figure 2A-8 shows real gross domestic product (GDP) per capita—a rough measure of a country's standard of living—in the United States from 1947 to late 2010. A line connecting the points that correspond to real GDP per capita for each calendar quarter during those years gives a clear idea of the overall trend in the standard of living over these years.

Figure 2A-9 is an example of a different kind of numerical graph. It represents information from a sample of 184 countries on the standard of living,

A **time-series graph** has dates on the horizontal axis and values of a variable that occurred on those dates on the vertical axis.

FIGURE **2A-9** Scatter Diagram

In a scatter diagram, each point represents the corresponding values of the *x*- and *y*-variables for a given observation. Here, each point indicates the GDP per capita and the amount of carbon emissions per capita for a given country for a sample of 184 countries. The upward-sloping fitted line here is the best approximation of the general relationship between the two variables.
*Source:* World Bank.

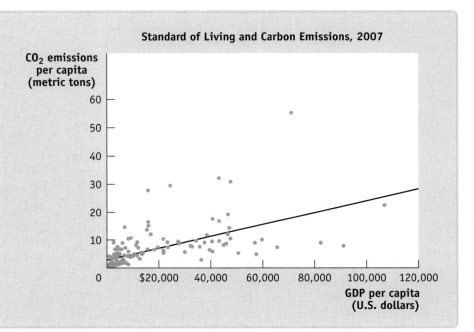

Standard of Living and Carbon Emissions, 2007

FIGURE **2A-10** Pie Chart

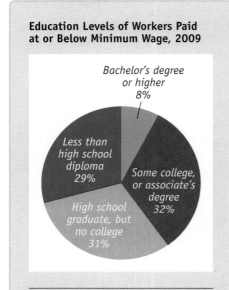

**Education Levels of Workers Paid at or Below Minimum Wage, 2009**

Bachelor's degree or higher 8%

Less than high school diploma 29%

Some college, or associate's degree 32%

High school graduate, but no college 31%

A pie chart shows the percentages of a total amount that can be attributed to various components. This pie chart shows the percentages of workers with given education levels who were paid at or below the federal minimum wage in 2009.

Source: Bureau of Labor Statistics.

again measured by GDP per capita, and the amount of carbon emissions per capita, a measure of environmental pollution. Each point here indicates an average resident's standard of living and his or her annual carbon emissions for a given country. The points lying in the upper right of the graph, which show combinations of a high standard of living and high carbon emissions, represent economically advanced countries such as the United States. (The country with the highest carbon emissions, at the top of the graph, is Qatar.) Points lying in the bottom left of the graph, which show combinations of a low standard of living and low carbon emissions, represent economically less advanced countries such as Afghanistan and Sierra Leone. The pattern of points indicates that there is a positive relationship between living standard and carbon emissions per capita: on the whole, people create more pollution in countries with a higher standard of living. This type of graph is called a **scatter diagram,** a diagram in which each point corresponds to an actual observation of the $x$-variable and the $y$-variable. In scatter diagrams, a curve is typically fitted to the scatter of points; that is, a curve is drawn that approximates as closely as possible the general relationship between the variables. As you can see, the fitted line in Figure 2A-9 is upward sloping, indicating the underlying positive relationship between the two variables. Scatter diagrams are often used to show how a general relationship can be inferred from a set of data.

A **pie chart** shows the share of a total amount that is accounted for by various components, usually expressed in percentages. For example, Figure 2A-10 is a pie chart that depicts the education levels of workers who in 2009 were paid the federal minimum wage or less. As you can see, the majority of workers paid at or below the minimum wage had no college degree. Only 8% of workers who were paid at or below the minimum wage had a bachelor's degree or higher.

**Bar graphs** use bars of various heights or lengths to indicate values of a variable. In the bar graph in Figure 2A-11, the bars show the percent change in the number of unemployed workers in the United States from 2009 to 2010, separately for White, Black or African-American, and Asian workers. Exact values of the variable that is being measured may be written at the end of the bar, as in this figure. For instance, the number of unemployed Black or African-American workers in the United States increased by 9.4% between 2009 and 2010. But even without the precise values, comparing the heights or lengths of the bars can give useful insight into the relative magnitudes of the different values of the variable.

## Problems in Interpreting Numerical Graphs

Although the beginning of this appendix emphasized that graphs are visual images that make ideas or information easier to understand, graphs can be constructed (intentionally or unintentionally) in ways that are misleading and can lead to inaccurate conclusions. This section raises some issues that you should be aware of when you interpret graphs.

FIGURE **2A-11** Bar Graph

**Changes in the Number of Unemployed by Race (2009–2010)**

| | Percent change in number of unemployed | Change in number of unemployed |
|---|---|---|
| White | 2.5% | 268,000 |
| Black or African-American | 9.4% | 246,000 |
| Asian | 4.0% | 21,000 |

A bar graph measures a variable by using bars of various heights or lengths. This bar graph shows the percent change in the number of unemployed workers between 2009 and 2010, separately for White, Black or African-American, and Asian workers.

Source: Bureau of Labor Statistics.

**Features of Construction** Before drawing any conclusions about what a numerical graph implies, you should pay attention to the scale, or size of increments, shown on the axes. Small increments tend to visually exaggerate changes in the variables, whereas large increments tend to visually diminish them. So the scale used in construction of a graph can influence your interpretation of the significance of the changes it illustrates—perhaps in an unwarranted way.

Take, for example, Figure 2A-12, which shows real GDP per capita in the United States from 1981 to 1982 using increments of $500. You can see that real GDP per capita fell from $26,208 to $25,189. A decrease, sure, but is it as enormous as the scale chosen for the vertical axis makes it seem? If you go back and reexamine Figure 2A-8, which shows real GDP per capita in the United States from 1947 to late 2010, you can see that this would be a misguided conclusion. Figure 2A-8 includes the same data shown in Figure 2A-12, but it is constructed with a scale having increments of $10,000 rather than $500. From it you can see that the fall in real GDP per capita from 1981 to 1982 was, in fact, relatively insignificant. In fact, the story of real GDP per capita—a measure of the standard of living—in the United States is mostly a story of ups, not downs. This comparison shows that if you are not careful to factor in the choice of scale in interpreting a graph, you can arrive at very different, and possibly misguided, conclusions.

Related to the choice of scale is the use of *truncation* in constructing a graph. An axis is **truncated** when part of the range is omitted. This is indicated by two slashes (//) in the axis near the origin. You can see that the vertical axis of Figure 2A-12 has been truncated—some of the range of values from 0 to $25,000 has been omitted and a // appears in the axis. Truncation saves space in the presentation of a graph and allows smaller increments to be used in constructing it. As a result, changes in the variable depicted on a graph that has been truncated appear larger compared to a graph that has not been truncated and that uses larger increments.

You must also pay close attention to exactly what a graph is illustrating. For example, in Figure 2A-11, you should recognize that what is being shown here are percentage changes in the number of unemployed, not numerical changes. The unemployment rate for Black or African-American workers increased by the highest percentage, 9.4% in this example. If you confused numerical changes with percentage changes, you would erroneously conclude that the greatest number of newly unemployed workers were Black or African-American. But, in fact, a correct interpretation of Figure 2A-11 shows that the greatest number of newly unemployed workers were White: the total number of unemployed White

A **scatter diagram** shows points that correspond to actual observations of the *x*- and *y*-variables. A curve is usually fitted to the scatter of points.

A **pie chart** shows how some total is divided among its components, usually expressed in percentages.

A **bar graph** uses bars of varying height or length to show the comparative sizes of different observations of a variable.

An axis is **truncated** when some of the values on the axis are omitted, usually to save space.

FIGURE **2A-12** Interpreting Graphs: The Effect of Scale

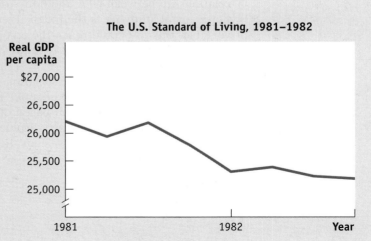

Some of the same data for the years 1981 and 1982 used in Figure 2A-8 are represented here, except that here they are shown using increments of $500 rather than increments of $10,000. As a result of this change in scale, changes in the standard of living look much larger in this figure compared to Figure 2A-8.
*Source:* Bureau of Labor Statistics.

An **omitted variable** is an unobserved variable that, through its influence on other variables, creates the erroneous appearance of a direct causal relationship among those variables.

The error of **reverse causality** is committed when the true direction of causality between two variables is reversed.

workers grew by 268,000 workers, which is greater than the increase in the number of unemployed Black or African-American workers, which is 246,000 in this example. Although there was a higher percentage increase in the number of unemployed Black or African-American workers, the number of unemployed Black or African-American workers in the United States in 2009 was smaller than the number of unemployed White workers, leading to a smaller number of newly unemployed Black or African-American workers than White workers.

**Omitted Variables** From a scatter diagram that shows two variables moving either positively or negatively in relation to each other, it is easy to conclude that there is a causal relationship. But relationships between two variables are not always due to direct cause and effect. Quite possibly an observed relationship between two variables is due to the *unobserved* effect of a third variable on each of the other two variables. An unobserved variable that, through its influence on other variables, creates the erroneous appearance of a direct causal relationship among those variables is called an **omitted variable.** For example, in New England, a greater amount of snowfall during a given week will typically cause people to buy more snow shovels. It will also cause people to buy more de-icer fluid. But if you omitted the influence of the snowfall and simply plotted the number of snow shovels sold versus the number of bottles of de-icer fluid sold, you would produce a scatter diagram that showed an upward tilt in the pattern of points, indicating a positive relationship between snow shovels sold and de-icer fluid sold. To attribute a causal relationship between these two variables, however, is misguided; more snow shovels sold do not cause more de-icer fluid to be sold, or vice versa. They move together because they are both influenced by a third, determining, variable—the weekly snowfall, which is the omitted variable in this case. So before assuming that a pattern in a scatter diagram implies a cause-and-effect relationship, it is important to consider whether the pattern is instead the result of an omitted variable. Or to put it succinctly: correlation is not causation.

**Reverse Causality** Even when you are confident that there is no omitted variable and that there is a causal relationship between two variables shown in a numerical graph, you must also be careful that you don't make the mistake of **reverse causality**—coming to an erroneous conclusion about which is the dependent and which is the independent variable by reversing the true direction of causality between the two variables. For example, imagine a scatter diagram that depicts the grade point averages (GPAs) of 20 of your classmates on one axis and the number of hours that each of them spends studying on the other. A line fitted between the points will probably have a positive slope, showing a positive relationship between GPA and hours of studying. We could reasonably infer that hours spent studying is the independent variable and that GPA is the dependent variable. But you could make the error of reverse causality: you could infer that a high GPA causes a student to study more, whereas a low GPA causes a student to study less.

The significance of understanding how graphs can mislead or be incorrectly interpreted is not purely academic. Policy decisions, business decisions, and political arguments are often based on interpretation of the types of numerical graphs that we've just discussed. Problems of misleading features of construction, omitted variables, and reverse causality can lead to very important and undesirable consequences.

## PROBLEMS

1. Study the four accompanying diagrams. Consider the following statements and indicate which diagram matches each statement. Which variable would appear on the horizontal and which on the vertical axis? In each of these statements, is the slope positive, negative, zero, or infinity?

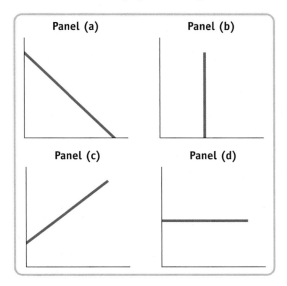

a. If the price of movies increases, fewer consumers go to see movies.

b. More experienced workers typically have higher incomes than less experienced workers.

c. Whatever the temperature outside, Americans consume the same number of hot dogs per day.

d. Consumers buy more frozen yogurt when the price of ice cream goes up.

e. Research finds no relationship between the number of diet books purchased and the number of pounds lost by the average dieter.

f. Regardless of its price, Americans buy the same quantity of salt.

2. During the Reagan administration, economist Arthur Laffer argued in favor of lowering income tax rates in order to increase tax revenues. Like most economists, he believed that at tax rates above a certain level, tax revenue would fall because high taxes would discourage some people from working and that people would refuse to work at all if they received no income after paying taxes. This relationship between tax rates and tax revenue is graphically summarized in what is widely known as the Laffer curve. Plot the Laffer curve relationship assuming that it has the shape of a nonlinear curve. The following questions will help you construct the graph.

a. Which is the independent variable? Which is the dependent variable? On which axis do you therefore measure the income tax rate? On which axis do you measure income tax revenue?

b. What would tax revenue be at a 0% income tax rate?

c. The maximum possible income tax rate is 100%. What would tax revenue be at a 100% income tax rate?

d. Estimates now show that the maximum point on the Laffer curve is (approximately) at a tax rate of 80%. For tax rates less than 80%, how would you describe the relationship between the tax rate and tax revenue, and how is this relationship reflected in the slope? For tax rates higher than 80%, how would you describe the relationship between the tax rate and tax revenue, and how is this relationship reflected in the slope?

3. In the accompanying figures, the numbers on the axes have been lost. All you know is that the units shown on the vertical axis are the same as the units on the horizontal axis.

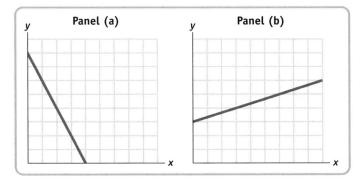

a. In panel (a), what is the slope of the line? Show that the slope is constant along the line.

b. In panel (b), what is the slope of the line? Show that the slope is constant along the line.

4. Answer each of the following questions by drawing a schematic diagram.

a. Taking measurements of the slope of a curve at three points farther and farther to the right along the horizontal axis, the slope of the curve changes from −0.3, to −0.8, to −2.5, measured by the point method. Draw a schematic diagram of this curve. How would you describe the relationship illustrated in your diagram?

b. Taking measurements of the slope of a curve at five points farther and farther to the right along the horizontal axis, the slope of the curve changes from 1.5, to 0.5, to 0, to −0.5, to −1.5, measured by the point method. Draw a schematic diagram of this curve. Does it have a maximum or a minimum?

5. For each of the accompanying diagrams, calculate the area of the shaded right triangle.

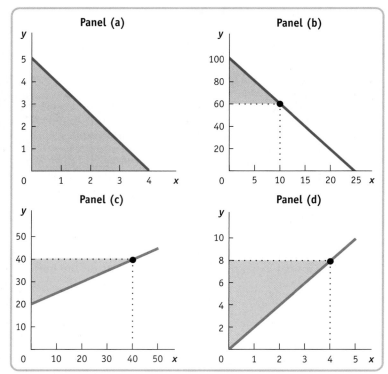

6. The base of a right triangle is 10, and its area is 20. What is the height of this right triangle?

7. The accompanying table shows the relationship between workers' hours of work per week and their hourly wage rate. Apart from the fact that they receive a different hourly wage rate and work different hours, these five workers are otherwise identical.

| Name | Quantity of labor (hours per week) | Wage rate (per hour) |
|---|---|---|
| Athena | 30 | $15 |
| Boris | 35 | 30 |
| Curt | 37 | 45 |
| Diego | 36 | 60 |
| Emily | 32 | 75 |

a. Which variable is the independent variable? Which is the dependent variable?

b. Draw a scatter diagram illustrating this relationship. Draw a (nonlinear) curve that connects the points. Put the hourly wage rate on the vertical axis.

c. As the wage rate increases from $15 to $30, how does the number of hours worked respond according to the relationship depicted here? What is the average slope of the curve between Athena's and Boris's data points using the arc method?

d. As the wage rate increases from $60 to $75, how does the number of hours worked respond according to the relationship depicted here? What is the average slope of the curve between Diego's and Emily's data points using the arc method?

8. Studies have found a relationship between a country's yearly rate of economic growth and the yearly rate of increase in airborne pollutants. It is believed that a higher rate of economic growth allows a country's residents to have more cars and travel more, thereby releasing more airborne pollutants.

a. Which variable is the independent variable? Which is the dependent variable?

b. Suppose that in the country of Sudland, when the yearly rate of economic growth fell from 3.0% to 1.5%, the yearly rate of increase in airborne pollutants fell from 6% to 5%. What is the average slope of a nonlinear curve between these points using the arc method?

c. Now suppose that when the yearly rate of economic growth rose from 3.5% to 4.5%, the yearly rate of increase in airborne pollutants rose from 5.5% to 7.5%. What is the average slope of a nonlinear curve between these two points using the arc method?

d. How would you describe the relationship between the two variables here?

9. An insurance company has found that the severity of property damage in a fire is positively related to the number of firefighters arriving at the scene.

a. Draw a diagram that depicts this finding with number of firefighters on the horizontal axis and amount of property damage on the vertical axis. What is the argument made by this diagram? Suppose you reverse what is measured on the two axes. What is the argument made then?

b. In order to reduce its payouts to policyholders, should the insurance company therefore ask the city to send fewer firefighters to any fire?

10. The accompanying table illustrates annual salaries and income tax owed by five individuals. Apart from the fact that they receive different salaries and owe different amounts of income tax, these five individuals are otherwise identical.

| Name | Annual salary | Annual income tax owed |
|---|---|---|
| Susan | $22,000 | $3,304 |
| Eduardo | 63,000 | 14,317 |
| John | 3,000 | 454 |
| Camila | 94,000 | 23,927 |
| Peter | 37,000 | 7,020 |

a. If you were to plot these points on a graph, what would be the average slope of the curve between the points for Eduardo's and Camila's salaries and taxes using the arc method? How would you interpret this value for slope?

b. What is the average slope of the curve between the points for John's and Susan's salaries and taxes using the arc method? How would you interpret that value for slope?

c. What happens to the slope as salary increases? What does this relationship imply about how the level of income taxes affects a person's incentive to earn a higher salary?

# CHAPTER 3

# Supply and Demand

## BLUE JEAN BLUES

How did flood-ravaged cotton crops in Pakistan lead to higher-priced blue jeans and more polyester in T-shirts?

Matt Nager Photography

**WHAT YOU WILL LEARN IN THIS CHAPTER**

❭ What a **competitive market** is and how it is described by the **supply and demand model**

❭ What the **demand curve** and the **supply curve** are

❭ The difference between **movements along a curve** and **shifts of a curve**

❭ How the supply and demand curves determine a market's **equilibrium price** and **equilibrium quantity**

❭ In the case of a **shortage** or **surplus,** how price moves the market back to equilibrium

**I**F YOU BOUGHT A PAIR OF BLUE jeans in 2011, you may have been shocked at the price. Or maybe not: fashions change, and maybe you thought you were paying the price for being fashionable. But you weren't—you were paying for cotton. Jeans are made of denim, which is a particular weave of cotton, and by late 2010, when jeans manufacturers were buying supplies for the coming year, cotton prices were more than triple their level just two years earlier. By December 2010, the price of a pound of cotton had hit a 140-year high, the highest cotton price since records began in 1870.

And why were cotton prices so high?

On one side, demand for clothing of all kinds was surging. In 2008–2009, as the world struggled with the effects of a financial crisis, nervous consumers cut back on clothing purchases. But by 2010, with the worst apparently over, buyers were back in force. On the supply side, severe weather events hit world cotton production. Most notably, Pakistan, the world's fourth-largest cotton producer, was hit by devastating floods that put one-fifth of the country underwater and virtually destroyed its cotton crop.

Fearing that consumers had limited tolerance for large increases in the price of cotton clothing, apparel makers began scrambling to find ways to reduce costs without offending consumers' fashion sense. They adopted changes like smaller buttons, cheaper linings, and—yes—polyester, doubting that consumers would be willing to pay more for cotton goods. In fact, some experts on the cotton market warned that the sky-high prices of cotton in 2010–2011 might lead to a permanent shift in tastes, with consumers becoming more willing to wear synthetics even when cotton prices came down.

At the same time, it was not all bad news for everyone connected with the cotton trade. In the United States, cotton producers had not been hit by bad weather and were relishing the higher prices. American farmers responded to sky-high cotton prices by sharply increasing the acreage devoted to the crop. None of this was enough, however, to produce immediate price relief.

Wait a minute: how, exactly, does flooding in Pakistan translate into higher jeans prices and more polyester in your T-shirts? It's a matter of supply and demand—but what does that mean? Many people use "supply and demand" as a sort of catchphrase to mean "the laws of the marketplace at work." To economists, however, the concept of supply and demand has a precise meaning: it is a *model of how a market behaves* that is extremely useful for understanding many—but not all—markets.

In this chapter, we lay out the pieces that make up the *supply and demand model*, put them together, and show how this model can be used to understand how many—but not all—markets behave. ■

A **competitive market** is a market in which there are many buyers and sellers of the same good or service, none of whom can influence the price at which the good or service is sold.

The **supply and demand model** is a model of how a competitive market behaves.

# Supply and Demand: A Model of a Competitive Market

Cotton sellers and cotton buyers constitute a market—a group of producers and consumers who exchange a good or service for payment. In this chapter, we'll focus on a particular type of market known as a *competitive market*. Roughly, a **competitive market** is a market in which there are many buyers and sellers of the same good or service. More precisely, the key feature of a competitive market is that no individual's actions have a noticeable effect on the price at which the good or service is sold. It's important to understand, however, that this is not an accurate description of every market.

For example, it's not an accurate description of the market for cola beverages. That's because in the market for cola beverages, Coca-Cola and Pepsi account for such a large proportion of total sales that they are able to influence the price at which cola beverages are bought and sold. But it is an accurate description of the market for cotton. The global marketplace for cotton is so huge that even a jeans maker as large as Levi Strauss & Co. accounts for only a tiny fraction of transactions, making it unable to influence the price at which cotton is bought and sold.

It's a little hard to explain why competitive markets are different from other markets until we've seen how a competitive market works. So let's take a rain check—we'll return to that issue at the end of this chapter. For now, let's just say that it's easier to model competitive markets than other markets. When taking an exam, it's always a good strategy to begin by answering the easier questions. In this book, we're going to do the same thing. So we will start with competitive markets.

When a market is competitive, its behavior is well described by the **supply and demand model.** Because many markets are competitive, the supply and demand model is a very useful one indeed.

There are five key elements in this model:

- The *demand curve*
- The *supply curve*
- The set of factors that cause the demand curve to shift and the set of factors that cause the supply curve to shift
- The *market equilibrium*, which includes the *equilibrium price* and *equilibrium quantity*
- The way the market equilibrium changes when the supply curve or demand curve shifts

To understand the supply and demand model, we will examine each of these elements.

# The Demand Curve

How many pounds of cotton, packaged in the form of blue jeans, do consumers around the world want to buy in a given year? You might at first think that we can answer this question by looking at the total number of pairs of blue jeans purchased around the world each day, multiply that number by the amount of cotton it takes to make a pair of jeans, and then multiply by 365. But that's not enough to answer the question, because how many pairs of jeans—in other words, how many pounds of cotton—consumers want to buy depends on the price of a pound of cotton.

When the price of cotton rises, as it did in 2010, some people will respond to the higher price of cotton clothing by buying fewer cotton garments or, perhaps, by switching completely to garments made from other materials, such as synthetics or linen. In general, the quantity of cotton clothing, or of any good or service that people want to buy, depends on the price. The higher the price, the less of the good or service people want to purchase; alternatively, the lower the price, the more they want to purchase.

So the answer to the question "How many pounds of cotton do consumers want to buy?" depends on the price of a pound of cotton. If you don't yet know what the price will be, you can start by making a table of how many pounds of cotton people would want to buy at a number of different prices. Such a table is known as a *demand schedule*. This, in turn, can be used to draw a *demand curve*, which is one of the key elements of the supply and demand model.

## The Demand Schedule and the Demand Curve

A **demand schedule** is a table showing how much of a good or service consumers will want to buy at different prices. At the right of Figure 3-1, we show a hypothetical demand schedule for cotton. It's hypothetical in that it doesn't use actual data on the world demand for cotton and it assumes that all cotton is of equal quality.

According to the table, if a pound of cotton costs $1, consumers around the world will want to purchase 10 billion pounds of cotton over the course of a year. If the price is $1.25 a pound, they will want to buy only 8.9 billion pounds; if the price is only $0.75 a pound, they will want to buy 11.5 billion pounds; and so on. The higher the price, the fewer pounds of cotton consumers will want to purchase. So, as the price rises, the **quantity demanded** of cotton—the actual amount consumers are willing to buy at some specific price—falls.

The graph in Figure 3-1 is a visual representation of the information in the table. (You might want to review the discussion of graphs in economics in the appendix to Chapter 2.) The vertical axis shows the price of a pound of cotton and the horizontal axis shows the quantity of cotton in pounds. Each point on the graph corresponds

A **demand schedule** shows how much of a good or service consumers will want to buy at different prices.

The **quantity demanded** is the actual amount of a good or service consumers are willing to buy at some specific price.

FIGURE **3-1**   The Demand Schedule and the Demand Curve

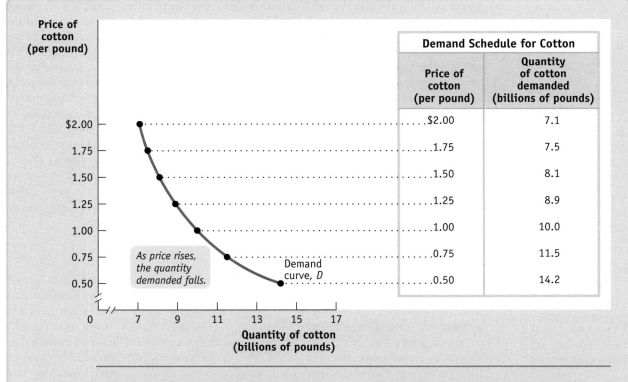

| Demand Schedule for Cotton | |
| --- | --- |
| Price of cotton (per pound) | Quantity of cotton demanded (billions of pounds) |
| $2.00 | 7.1 |
| 1.75 | 7.5 |
| 1.50 | 8.1 |
| 1.25 | 8.9 |
| 1.00 | 10.0 |
| 0.75 | 11.5 |
| 0.50 | 14.2 |

The demand schedule for cotton yields the corresponding demand curve, which shows how much of a good or service consumers want to buy at any given price. The demand curve and the demand schedule reflect the law of demand: As price rises, the quantity demanded falls. Similarly, a fall in price raises the quantity demanded. As a result, the demand curve is downward sloping.

## PAY MORE, PUMP LESS

For a real-world illustration of the law of demand, consider how gasoline consumption varies according to the prices consumers pay at the pump. Because of high taxes, gasoline and diesel fuel are more than twice as expensive in most European countries as in the United States. According to the law of demand, this should lead Europeans to buy less gasoline than Americans—and they do. As you can see from the figure, per person, Europeans consume less than half as much fuel as Americans, mainly because they drive smaller cars with better mileage.

Prices aren't the only factor affecting fuel consumption, but they're probably the main cause of the difference between European and American fuel consumption per person.

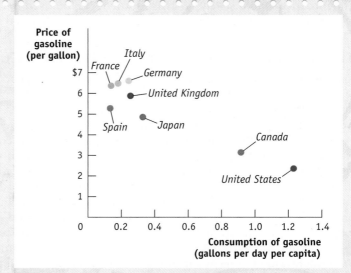

*Source:* U.S. Energy Information Administration, 2009.

to one of the entries in the table. The curve that connects these points is a **demand curve.** A demand curve is a graphical representation of the demand schedule, another way of showing the relationship between the quantity demanded and price.

Note that the demand curve shown in Figure 3-1 slopes downward. This reflects the general proposition that a higher price reduces the quantity demanded. For example, jeans-makers know that they will sell fewer pairs when the price of a pair of jeans is higher, reflecting a $2 price for a pound of cotton, compared to the number they will sell when the price of a pair is lower, reflecting a price of only $1 for a pound of cotton. Similarly, someone who buys a pair of cotton jeans when its price is relatively low will switch to synthetic or linen when the price of cotton jeans is relatively high. So in the real world, demand curves almost always *do* slope downward. (The exceptions are so rare that for practical purposes we can ignore them.) Generally, the proposition that a higher price for a good, *other things equal,* leads people to demand a smaller quantity of that good is so reliable that economists are willing to call it a "law"—the **law of demand.**

### Shifts of the Demand Curve

Although cotton prices in 2010 were higher than they had been in 2007, total world consumption of cotton was higher in 2010. How can we reconcile this fact with the law of demand, which says that a higher price reduces the quantity demanded, other things equal?

The answer lies in the crucial phrase *other things equal.* In this case, other things weren't equal: the world had changed between 2007 and 2010, in ways that increased the quantity of cotton demanded at any given price. For one thing, the world's population, and therefore the number of potential cotton clothing wearers, increased. In addition, the growing popularity of cotton clothing, as well as higher incomes in countries like China that allowed people to buy more clothing than before, led to an increase in the quantity of cotton demanded at any given price. Figure 3-2 illustrates this phenomenon using the

A **demand curve** is a graphical representation of the demand schedule. It shows the relationship between quantity demanded and price.

The **law of demand** says that a higher price for a good or service, other things equal, leads people to demand a smaller quantity of that good or service.

FIGURE  **3-2**  **An Increase in Demand**

| Demand Schedules for Cotton | | |
|---|---|---|
| Price of cotton (per pound) | Quantity of cotton demanded (billions of pounds) | |
| | in 2007 | in 2010 |
| $2.00 | 7.1 | 8.5 |
| 1.75 | 7.5 | 9.0 |
| 1.50 | 8.1 | 9.7 |
| 1.25 | 8.9 | 10.7 |
| 1.00 | 10.0 | 12.0 |
| 0.75 | 11.5 | 13.8 |
| 0.50 | 14.2 | 17.0 |

An increase in the population is one factor that generates an increase in demand—a rise in the quantity demanded at any given price. This is represented by the two demand schedules—one showing demand in 2007, before the rise in population, the other showing demand in 2010, after the rise in population—and their corresponding demand curves. The increase in demand shifts the demand curve to the right.

demand schedule and demand curve for cotton. (As before, the numbers in Figure 3-2 are hypothetical.)

The table in Figure 3-2 shows two demand schedules. The first is the demand schedule for 2007, the same as shown in Figure 3-1. The second is the demand schedule for 2010. It differs from the 2007 demand schedule due to factors such as a larger population and the increased popularity of cotton clothing, factors that led to an increase in the quantity of cotton demanded at any given price. So at each price the 2010 schedule shows a larger quantity demanded than the 2007 schedule. For example, the quantity of cotton consumers wanted to buy at a price of $1 per pound increased from 10 billion to 12 billion pounds per year, the quantity demanded at $1.25 per pound went from 8.9 billion to 10.7 billion, and so on.

What is clear from this example is that the changes that occurred between 2007 and 2010 generated a *new* demand schedule, one in which the quantity demanded was greater at any given price than in the original demand schedule. The two curves in Figure 3-2 show the same information graphically. As you can see, the demand schedule for 2010 corresponds to a new demand curve, $D_2$, that is to the right of the demand schedule for 2007, $D_1$. This **shift of the demand curve** shows the change in the quantity demanded at any given price, represented by the change in position of the original demand curve $D_1$ to its new location at $D_2$.

It's crucial to make the distinction between such shifts of the demand curve and **movements along the demand curve,** changes in the quantity demanded of a good arising from a change in that good's price. Figure 3-3 on the next page illustrates the difference.

The movement from point *A* to point *B* is a movement along the demand curve: the quantity demanded rises due to a fall in price as you move down $D_1$. Here, a fall in the price of cotton from $1.50 to $1 per pound generates a rise in the quantity demanded from 8.1 billion to 10 billion pounds per year. But the quantity demanded can also rise

A **shift of the demand curve** is a change in the quantity demanded at any given price, represented by the change of the original demand curve to a new position, denoted by a new demand curve.

A **movement along the demand curve** is a change in the quantity demanded of a good arising from a change in the good's price.

FIGURE **3-3**  Movement Along the Demand Curve versus Shift of the Demand Curve

The rise in quantity demanded when going from point *A* to point *B* reflects a movement along the demand curve: it is the result of a fall in the price of the good. The rise in quantity demanded when going from point *A* to point *C* reflects a shift of the demand curve: it is the result of a rise in the quantity demanded at any given price.

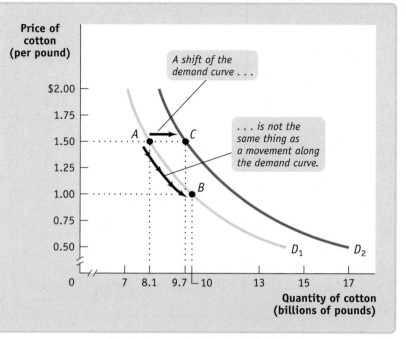

when the price is unchanged if there is an *increase in demand*—a rightward shift of the demand curve. This is illustrated in Figure 3-3 by the shift of the demand curve from $D_1$ to $D_2$. Holding the price constant at $1.50 a pound, the quantity demanded rises from 8.1 billion pounds at point *A* on $D_1$ to 9.7 billion pounds at point *C* on $D_2$.

When economists say "the demand for *X* increased" or "the demand for *Y* decreased," they mean that the demand curve for *X* or *Y* shifted—not that the quantity demanded rose or fell because of a change in the price.

 PITFALLS

**DEMAND VERSUS QUANTITY DEMANDED**

When economists say "an increase in demand," they mean a rightward shift of the demand curve, and when they say "a decrease in demand," they mean a leftward shift of the demand curve—that is, when they're being careful. In ordinary speech most people, including professional economists, use the word *demand* casually. For example, an economist might say "the

demand for air travel has doubled over the past 15 years, partly because of falling air-fares" when he or she really means that the *quantity demanded* has doubled.

It's OK to be a bit sloppy in ordinary conversation. But when you're doing economic analysis, it's important to make the distinction between changes in the quantity demanded, which involve movements along a demand curve, and shifts of the demand curve (See

Figure 3-3 for an illustration). Sometimes students end up writing something like this: "If demand increases, the price will go up, but that will lead to a fall in demand, which pushes the price down . . ." and then go around in circles. If you make a clear distinction between changes in *demand*, which mean shifts of the demand curve, and changes in *quantity demanded*, you can avoid a lot of confusion.

## Understanding Shifts of the Demand Curve

Figure 3-4 illustrates the two basic ways in which demand curves can shift. When economists talk about an "increase in demand," they mean a *rightward* shift of the demand curve: at any given price, consumers demand a larger quantity of the good or service than before. This is shown by the rightward shift of the original demand curve $D_1$ to $D_2$. And when economists talk about a "decrease in demand," they mean a *leftward* shift of the demand curve: at any given price, consumers demand a smaller quantity of the good or service than before. This is shown by the leftward shift of the original demand curve $D_1$ to $D_3$.

FIGURE   **3-4**   Shifts of the Demand Curve

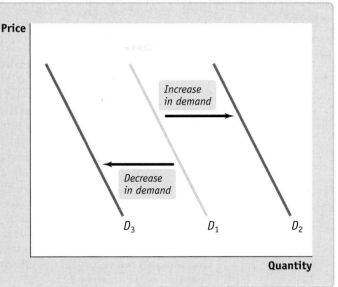

Any event that increases demand shifts the demand curve to the right, reflecting a rise in the quantity demanded at any given price. Any event that decreases demand shifts the demand curve to the left, reflecting a fall in the quantity demanded at any given price.

What caused the demand curve for cotton to shift? We have already mentioned two reasons: changes in population and a change in the popularity of cotton clothing. If you think about it, you can come up with other things that would be likely to shift the demand curve for cotton. For example, suppose that the price of polyester rises. This will induce some people who previously bought polyester clothing to buy cotton clothing instead, increasing the demand for cotton.

Economists believe that there are five principal factors that shift the demand curve for a good or service:

• Changes in the prices of related goods or services
• Changes in income
• Changes in tastes
• Changes in expectations
• Changes in the number of consumers

Although this is not an exhaustive list, it contains the five most important factors that can shift demand curves. So when we say that the quantity of a good or service demanded falls as its price rises, *other things equal*, we are in fact stating that the factors that shift demand are remaining unchanged. Let's now explore, in more detail, how those factors shift the demand curve.

**Changes in the Prices of Related Goods or Services** Although there's nothing quite like a comfortable pair of all-cotton blue jeans, for some purposes khakis—generally made from polyester blends—aren't a bad alternative. Khakis are what economists call a *substitute* for jeans. A pair of goods are **substitutes** if a rise in the price of one good (jeans) makes consumers more willing to buy the other good (khakis). Substitutes are usually goods that in some way serve a similar function: coffee and tea, muffins and doughnuts, train rides and air flights. A rise in the price of the alternative good induces some consumers to purchase the original good *instead* of it, shifting demand for the original good to the right.

But sometimes a rise in the price of one good makes consumers *less* willing to buy another good. Such pairs of goods are known as **complements.** Complements are usually goods that in some sense are consumed together: computers and software, cappuccinos and cookies, cars and gasoline. Because consumers like to consume a good and its complement together, a change in the price

Two goods are **substitutes** if a rise in the price of one of the goods leads to an increase in the demand for the other good.

Two goods are **complements** if a rise in the price of one good leads to a decrease in the demand for the other good.

When a rise in income increases the demand for a good—the normal case—it is a **normal good.**

When a rise in income decreases the demand for a good, it is an **inferior good.**

of one of the goods will affect the demand for its complement. In particular, when the price of one good rises, the demand for its complement decreases, shifting the demand curve for the complement to the left. So, for example, when the price of gasoline rose in 2007–2008, the demand for gas-guzzling cars fell.

**Changes in Income** When individuals have more income, they are normally more likely to purchase a good at any given price. For example, if a family's income rises, it is more likely to take that long-anticipated summer trip to Disney World—and therefore also more likely to buy plane tickets. So a rise in consumer incomes will cause the demand curves for most goods to shift to the right.

Why do we say "most goods," not "all goods"? Most goods are **normal goods**—the demand for them increases when consumer income rises. However, the demand for some products falls when income rises. Goods for which demand decreases when income rises are known as **inferior goods.** Usually an inferior good is one that is considered less desirable than more expensive alternatives—such as a bus ride versus a taxi ride. When they can afford to, people stop buying an inferior good and switch their consumption to the preferred, more expensive alternative. So when a good is inferior, a rise in income shifts the demand curve to the left. And, not surprisingly, a fall in income shifts the demand curve to the right.

One example of the distinction between normal and inferior goods that has drawn considerable attention in the business press is the difference between so-called casual-dining restaurants such as Applebee's or Olive Garden and fast-food chains such as McDonald's and KFC. When Americans' income rises, they tend to eat out more at casual-dining restaurants. However, some of this increased dining out comes at the expense of fast-food venues—to some extent, people visit McDonald's less once they can afford to move upscale. So casual dining is a normal good, whereas fast-food consumption appears to be an inferior good.

**Changes in Tastes** Why do people want what they want? Fortunately, we don't need to answer that question—we just need to acknowledge that people have certain preferences, or tastes, that determine what they choose to consume and that these tastes can change. Economists usually lump together changes in demand due to fads, beliefs, cultural shifts, and so on under the heading of changes in tastes or preferences.

For example, once upon a time men wore hats. Up until around World War II, a respectable man wasn't fully dressed unless he wore a dignified hat along with his suit. But the returning GIs adopted a more informal style, perhaps due to the rigors of the war. And President Eisenhower, who had been supreme commander of Allied Forces before becoming president, often went hatless. After World War II, it was clear that the demand curve for hats had shifted leftward, reflecting a decrease in the demand for hats.

Economists have relatively little to say about the forces that influence consumers' tastes. (Although marketers and advertisers have plenty to say about them!) However, a change in tastes has a predictable impact on demand. When tastes change in favor of a good, more people want to buy it at any given price, so the demand curve shifts to the right. When tastes change against a good, fewer people want to buy it at any given price, so the demand curve shifts to the left.

**Changes in Expectations** When consumers have some choice about when to make a purchase, current demand for a good is often affected by expectations about its future price. For example, savvy shoppers often wait for seasonal sales—say, buying next year's holiday gifts during the post-holiday markdowns. In this case, expectations of a future drop in price lead to a decrease in demand today. Alternatively, expectations of a future rise in price are likely to cause an increase in demand today. For example, as cotton prices began to rise in 2010, many textile mills began purchasing more cotton and stockpiling it in anticipation of further price increases.

Expected changes in future income can also lead to changes in demand: if you expect your income to rise in the future, you will typically borrow today and increase your demand for certain goods; if you expect your income to fall in the future, you are likely to save today and reduce your demand for some goods.

**Changes in the Number of Consumers** As we've already noted, one of the reasons for rising cotton demand between 2007 and 2010 was a growing world population. Because of population growth, overall demand for cotton would have risen even if the demand of each individual wearer of cotton clothing had remained unchanged.

Let's introduce a new concept: the **individual demand curve,** which shows the relationship between quantity demanded and price for an individual consumer. For example, suppose that Darla is a consumer of cotton blue jeans; also suppose that all pairs of jeans are the same, so they sell for the same price. Panel (a) of Figure 3-5 shows how many pairs of jeans she will buy per year at any given price. Then $D_{Darla}$ is Darla's individual demand curve.

The *market demand curve* shows how the combined quantity demanded by all consumers depends on the market price of that good. (Most of the time, when economists refer to the demand curve, they mean the market demand curve.) The market demand curve is the *horizontal sum* of the individual demand curves of all consumers in that market. To see what we mean by the term *horizontal sum*, assume for a moment that there are only two consumers of blue jeans, Darla and Dino. Dino's individual demand curve, $D_{Dino}$, is shown in panel (b). Panel (c) shows the market demand curve. At any given price, the quantity demanded by the market is the sum of the quantities demanded by Darla and Dino. For example, at a price of $30 per pair, Darla demands 3 pairs of jeans per year and Dino demands 2 pairs per year. So the quantity demanded by the market is 5 pairs per year.

Clearly, the quantity demanded by the market at any given price is larger with Dino present than it would be if Darla were the only consumer. The quantity demanded at

An **individual demand curve** illustrates the relationship between quantity demanded and price for an individual consumer.

---

**FIGURE** **3-5** **Individual Demand Curves and the Market Demand Curve**

Darla and Dino are the only two consumers of blue jeans in the market. Panel (a) shows Darla's individual demand curve: the number of pairs of blue jeans she will buy per year at any given price. Panel (b) shows Dino's individual demand curve. Given that Darla and Dino are the only two consumers, the *market demand curve*, which shows the quantity of blue jeans demanded by all consumers at any given price, is shown in panel (c). The market demand curve is the *horizontal sum* of the individual demand curves of all consumers. In this case, at any given price, the quantity demanded by the market is the sum of the quantities demanded by Darla and Dino.

any given price would be even larger if we added a third consumer, then a fourth, and so on. So an increase in the number of consumers leads to an increase in demand.

For a review of the factors that shift demand, see Table 3-1.

## ECONOMICS ➤ IN ACTION

### BEATING THE TRAFFIC

**A**ll big cities have traffic problems, and many local authorities try to discourage driving in the crowded city center. If we think of an auto trip to the city center as a good that people consume, we can use the economics of demand to analyze anti-traffic policies.

One common strategy is to reduce the demand for auto trips by lowering the prices of substitutes. Many metropolitan areas subsidize bus and rail service, hoping to lure commuters out of their cars. An alternative is to raise the price of complements: several major U.S. cities impose high taxes on commercial parking garages and impose short time limits on parking meters, both to raise revenue and to discourage people from driving into the city.

A few major cities—including Singapore, London, Oslo, Stockholm, and Milan—have been willing to adopt a direct and politically controversial approach: reducing congestion by raising the price of driving. Under "congestion pricing" (or "congestion charging" in the United Kingdom), a charge is imposed on cars entering the city center during business hours. Drivers buy passes, which are then debited electronically as they drive by monitoring stations. Compliance is monitored with automatic cameras that photograph license plates. Moscow is currently contemplating a congestion charge scheme to tackle the worst traffic jams of all major cities, with 40% of drivers reporting traffic jams exceeding three hours.

The current daily cost of driving in London ranges from £9 to £12 (about $13 to $19). And drivers who don't pay and are caught pay a fine of £120 (about $192) for each transgression.

Not surprisingly, studies have shown that after the implementation of congestion pricing, traffic does indeed decrease. In the 1990s, London had some of the worst traffic in Europe. The introduction of its congestion charge in 2003 immediately reduced traffic in the London city center by about 15%, with overall traffic falling by 21% between 2002 and 2006. And there was increased use of substitutes, such as public transportation, bicycles, motorbikes, and ride-sharing.

In the United States, the U.S. Department of Transportation has implemented pilot programs in five locations to study congestion pricing. Some transportation experts have even suggested using variable congestion prices, raising prices during peak commuting hours. So although congestion pricing may be controversial, it appears to be slowly gaining acceptance.

Global Warming Images/Alamy

Cities can reduce traffic congestion by raising the price of driving.

## CHECK YOUR UNDERSTANDING   3-1

1. Explain whether each of the following events represents (i) a *shift of* the demand curve or (ii) a *movement along* the demand curve.
   a. A store owner finds that customers are willing to pay more for umbrellas on rainy days.
   b. When XYZ Telecom, a long-distance telephone service provider, offered reduced rates on weekends, its volume of weekend calling increased sharply.
   c. People buy more long-stem roses the week of Valentine's Day, even though the prices are higher than at other times during the year.
   d. A sharp rise in the price of gasoline leads many commuters to join carpools in order to reduce their gasoline purchases.

**TABLE   3-1   Factors That Shift Demand**

| When this happens . . . | . . . demand increases | But when this happens . . . | . . . demand decreases |
|---|---|---|---|
| When the price of a substitute rises . . . | Price / $D_1$ $D_2$ / Quantity | When the price of a substitute falls . . . | Price / $D_2$ $D_1$ / Quantity |
| . . . demand for the original good increases. | | . . . demand for the original good decreases. | |
| When the price of a complement falls . . . | Price / $D_1$ $D_2$ / Quantity | When the price of a complement rises . . . | Price / $D_2$ $D_1$ / Quantity |
| . . . demand for the original good increases. | | . . . demand for the original good decreases. | |
| When income rises . . . | Price / $D_1$ $D_2$ / Quantity | When income falls . . . | Price / $D_2$ $D_1$ / Quantity |
| . . . demand for a normal good increases. | | . . . demand for a normal good decreases. | |
| When income falls . . . | Price / $D_1$ $D_2$ / Quantity | When income rises . . . | Price / $D_2$ $D_1$ / Quantity |
| . . . demand for an inferior good increases. | | . . . demand for an inferior good decreases. | |
| When tastes change in favor of a good . . . | Price / $D_1$ $D_2$ / Quantity | When tastes change against a good . . . | Price / $D_2$ $D_1$ / Quantity |
| . . . demand for the good increases. | | . . . demand for the good decreases. | |
| When the price is expected to rise in the future . . . | Price / $D_1$ $D_2$ / Quantity | When the price is expected to fall in the future . . . | Price / $D_2$ $D_1$ / Quantity |
| . . . demand for the good increases today. | | . . . demand for the good decreases today. | |
| When the number of consumers rises . . . | Price / $D_1$ $D_2$ / Quantity | When the number of consumers falls . . . | Price / $D_2$ $D_1$ / Quantity |
| . . . market demand for the good increases. | | . . . market demand for the good decreases. | |

The **quantity supplied** is the actual amount of a good or service people are willing to sell at some specific price.

A **supply schedule** shows how much of a good or service would be supplied at different prices.

# The Supply Curve

Some parts of the world are especially well suited to growing cotton, and the United States is one of those. But even in the United States, some land is better suited to growing cotton than other land. Whether American farmers restrict their cotton-growing to only the most ideal locations or expand it to less suitable land depends on the price they expect to get for their cotton. Moreover, there are many other areas in the world where cotton could be grown—such as Pakistan, Brazil, Turkey, and China. Whether farmers there actually grow cotton depends, again, on the price.

So just as the quantity of cotton that consumers want to buy depends on the price they have to pay, the quantity that producers are willing to produce and sell—the **quantity supplied**—depends on the price they are offered.

## The Supply Schedule and the Supply Curve

The table in Figure 3-6 shows how the quantity of cotton made available varies with the price—that is, it shows a hypothetical **supply schedule** for cotton.

A supply schedule works the same way as the demand schedule shown in Figure 3-1: in this case, the table shows the number of pounds of cotton farmers are willing to sell at different prices. At a price of $0.50 per pound, farmers are willing to sell only 8 billion pounds of cotton per year. At $0.75 per pound, they're willing to sell 9.1 billion pounds. At $1, they're willing to sell 10 billion pounds, and so on.

**FIGURE** **3-6** **The Supply Schedule and the Supply Curve**

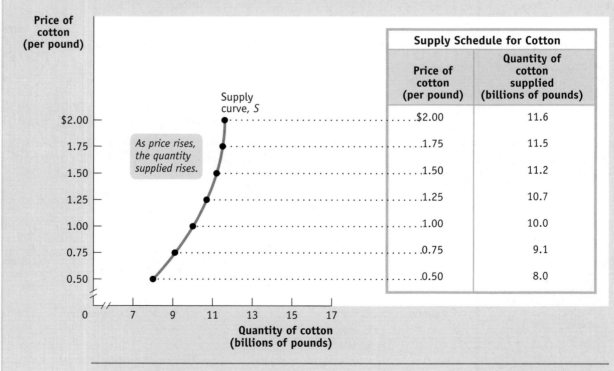

| Supply Schedule for Cotton | |
| --- | --- |
| Price of cotton (per pound) | Quantity of cotton supplied (billions of pounds) |
| $2.00 | 11.6 |
| 1.75 | 11.5 |
| 1.50 | 11.2 |
| 1.25 | 10.7 |
| 1.00 | 10.0 |
| 0.75 | 9.1 |
| 0.50 | 8.0 |

The supply schedule for cotton is plotted to yield the corresponding supply curve, which shows how much of a good producers are willing to sell at any given price. The supply curve and the sup-ply schedule reflect the fact that supply curves are usually upward sloping: the quantity supplied rises when the price rises.

In the same way that a demand schedule can be represented graphically by a demand curve, a supply schedule can be represented by a **supply curve,** as shown in Figure 3-6. Each point on the curve represents an entry from the table.

Suppose that the price of cotton rises from $1 to $1.25; we can see that the quantity of cotton farmers are willing to sell rises from 10 billion to 10.7 billion pounds. This is the normal situation for a supply curve, that a higher price leads to a higher quantity supplied. So just as demand curves normally slope downward, supply curves normally slope upward: the higher the price being offered, the more of any good or service producers will be willing to sell.

A **supply curve** shows the relationship between quantity supplied and price.

A **shift of the supply curve** is a change in the quantity supplied of a good or service at any given price. It is represented by the change of the original supply curve to a new position, denoted by a new supply curve.

## Shifts of the Supply Curve

Until recently, cotton remained relatively cheap over the past several decades. One reason is that the amount of land cultivated for cotton expanded over 35% from 1945 to 2007. However, the major factor accounting for cotton's relative cheapness was advances in the production technology, with output per acre more than quadrupling from 1945 to 2007. Figure 3-7 illustrates these events in terms of the supply schedule and the supply curve for cotton.

The table in Figure 3-7 shows two supply schedules. The schedule before improved cotton-growing technology was adopted is the same one as in Figure 3-6. The second schedule shows the supply of cotton *after* the improved technology was adopted. Just as a change in demand schedules leads to a shift of the demand curve, a change in supply schedules leads to a **shift of the supply curve**—a change in the quantity supplied at any given price. This is shown in Figure 3-7 by the shift of the supply curve before the adoption of new cotton-growing technology, $S_1$, to its new position after the adoption of new cotton-growing technology, $S_2$. Notice that $S_2$ lies to the right of $S_1$, a reflection of the fact that quantity supplied rises at any given price.

**FIGURE  3-7  An Increase in Supply**

| Supply Schedules for Cotton | | |
|---|---|---|
| Price of cotton (per pound) | Quantity of cotton supplied (billions of pounds) | |
| | Before new technology | After new technology |
| $2.00 | 11.6 | 13.9 |
| 1.75 | 11.5 | 13.8 |
| 1.50 | 11.2 | 13.4 |
| 1.25 | 10.7 | 12.8 |
| 1.00 | 10.0 | 12.0 |
| 0.75 | 9.1 | 10.9 |
| 0.50 | 8.0 | 9.6 |

The adoption of improved cotton-growing technology generated an increase in supply—a rise in the quantity supplied at any given price. This event is represented by the two supply schedules—one showing supply before the new technology was adopted, the other showing supply after the new technology was adopted—and their corresponding supply curves. The increase in supply shifts the supply curve to the right.

A **movement along the supply curve** is a change in the quantity supplied of a good arising from a change in the good's price.

As in the analysis of demand, it's crucial to draw a distinction between such shifts of the supply curve and **movements along the supply curve**—changes in the quantity supplied arising from a change in price. We can see this difference in Figure 3-8. The movement from point *A* to point *B* is a movement along the supply curve: the quantity supplied rises along $S_1$ due to a rise in price. Here, a rise in price from $1 to $1.50 leads to a rise in the quantity supplied from 10 billion to 11.2 billion pounds of cotton. But the quantity supplied can also rise when the price is unchanged if there is an increase in supply—a rightward shift of the supply curve. This is shown by the rightward shift of the supply curve from $S_1$ to $S_2$. Holding the price constant at $1, the quantity supplied rises from 10 billion pounds at point *A* on $S_1$ to 12 billion pounds at point *C* on $S_2$.

**FIGURE   3-8   Movement Along the Supply Curve versus Shift of the Supply Curve**

The increase in quantity supplied when going from point *A* to point *B* reflects a movement along the supply curve: it is the result of a rise in the price of the good. The increase in quantity supplied when going from point *A* to point *C* reflects a shift of the supply curve: it is the result of an increase in the quantity supplied at any given price.

## Understanding Shifts of the Supply Curve

Figure 3-9 illustrates the two basic ways in which supply curves can shift. When economists talk about an "increase in supply," they mean a *rightward* shift of the supply curve: at any given price, producers supply a larger quantity of the good than before. This is shown in Figure 3-9 by the rightward shift of the original supply curve $S_1$ to $S_2$. And when economists talk about a "decrease in supply," they mean a *leftward* shift of the supply curve: at any given price, producers supply a smaller quantity of the good than before. This is represented by the leftward shift of $S_1$ to $S_3$.

Economists believe that shifts of the supply curve for a good or service are mainly the result of five factors (though, as in the case of demand, there are other possible causes):

• Changes in input prices
• Changes in the prices of related goods or services
• Changes in technology
• Changes in expectations
• Changes in the number of producers

FIGURE    **3-9**    **Shifts of the Supply Curve**

Any event that increases supply shifts the supply curve to the right, reflecting a rise in the quantity supplied at any given price. Any event that decreases supply shifts the supply curve to the left, reflecting a fall in the quantity supplied at any given price.

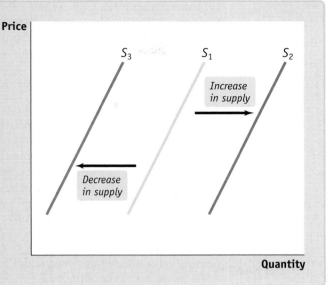

### Changes in Input Prices

To produce output, you need inputs. For example, to make vanilla ice cream, you need vanilla beans, cream, sugar, and so on. An **input** is any good or service that is used to produce another good or service. Inputs, like outputs, have prices. And an increase in the price of an input makes the production of the final good more costly for those who produce and sell it. So producers are less willing to supply the final good at any given price, and the supply curve shifts to the left. For example, fuel is a major cost for airlines. When oil prices surged in 2007–2008, airlines began cutting back on their flight schedules and some went out of business. Similarly, a fall in the price of an input makes the production of the final good less costly for sellers. They are more willing to supply the good at any given price, and the supply curve shifts to the right.

### Changes in the Prices of Related Goods or Services

A single producer often produces a mix of goods rather than a single product. For example, an oil refinery produces gasoline from crude oil, but it also produces heating oil and other products from the same raw material. When a producer sells several products, the quantity of any one good it is willing to supply at any given price depends on the prices of its other co-produced goods.

This effect can run in either direction. An oil refiner will supply less gasoline at any given price when the price of heating oil rises, shifting the supply curve for gasoline to the left. But it will supply more gasoline at any given price when the price of heating oil falls, shifting the supply curve for gasoline to the right. This means that gasoline and other co-produced oil products are *substitutes in production* for refiners.

In contrast, due to the nature of the production process, other goods can be *complements in production*. For example, producers of crude oil—oil-well drillers—often find that oil wells also produce natural gas as a by-product of oil extraction. The higher the price at which a driller can sell its natural gas, the more oil wells it will drill and the more oil it will supply at any given price for oil. As a result, natural gas is a complement in production for crude oil.

### Changes in Technology

When economists talk about "technology," they don't necessarily mean high technology—they mean all the methods people can use to turn inputs into useful goods and services. In that sense, the whole complex sequence of activities that turn cotton from Pakistan into the pair of jeans hanging in your closet is technology.

An **input** is a good or service that is used to produce another good or service.

An **individual supply curve** illustrates the relationship between quantity supplied and price for an individual producer.

Improvements in technology enable producers to spend less on inputs yet still produce the same output. When a better technology becomes available, reducing the cost of production, supply increases, and the supply curve shifts to the right. As we have already mentioned, improved technology enabled farmers to more than quadruple cotton output per acre planted over the past several decades. Improved technology is the main reason that, until recently, cotton remained relatively cheap even as worldwide demand grew.

**Changes in Expectations** Just as changes in expectations can shift the demand curve, they can also shift the supply curve. When suppliers have some choice about when they put their good up for sale, changes in the expected future price of the good can lead a supplier to supply less or more of the good today.

For example, consider the fact that gasoline and other oil products are often stored for significant periods of time at oil refineries before being sold to consumers. In fact, storage is normally part of producers' business strategy. Knowing that the demand for gasoline peaks in the summer, oil refiners normally store some of their gasoline produced during the spring for summer sale. Similarly, knowing that the demand for heating oil peaks in the winter, they normally store some of their heating oil produced during the fall for winter sale. In each case, there's a decision to be made between selling the product now versus storing it for later sale. Which choice a producer makes depends on a comparison of the current price versus the expected future price. This example illustrates how changes in expectations can alter supply: An increase in the anticipated future price of a good or service reduces supply today, a leftward shift of the supply curve. But a fall in the anticipated future price increases supply today, a rightward shift of the supply curve.

**Changes in the Number of Producers** Just as changes in the number of consumers affect the demand curve, changes in the number of producers affect the supply curve. Let's examine the **individual supply curve,** by looking at panel (a) in Figure 3-10. The individual supply curve shows

**FIGURE** **3-10** The Individual Supply Curve and the Market Supply Curve

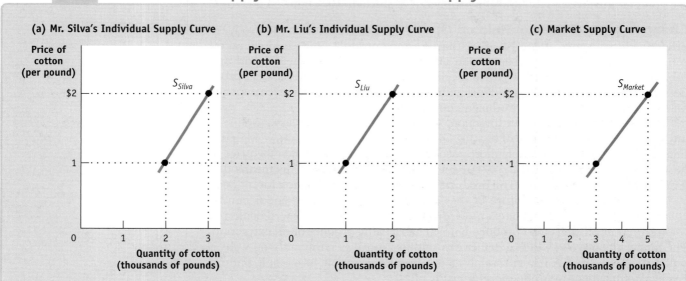

Panel (a) shows the individual supply curve for Mr. Silva, $S_{Silva}$, the quantity of cotton he will sell at any given price. Panel (b) shows the individual supply curve for Mr. Liu, $S_{Liu}$. The market supply curve, which shows the quantity of cotton supplied by all producers at any given price, is shown in panel (c). The market supply curve is the horizontal sum of the individual supply curves of all producers.

the relationship between quantity supplied and price for an individual producer. For example, suppose that Mr. Silva is a Brazilian cotton farmer and that panel (a) of Figure 3-10 shows how many pounds of cotton he will supply per year at any given price. Then $S_{Silva}$ is his individual supply curve.

The *market supply curve* shows how the combined total quantity supplied by all individual producers in the market depends on the market price of that good. Just as the market demand curve is the horizontal sum of the individual demand curves of all consumers, the market supply curve is the horizontal sum of the individual supply curves of all producers. Assume for a moment that there are only two producers of cotton, Mr. Silva and Mr. Liu, a Chinese cotton farmer. Mr. Liu's individual supply curve is shown in panel (b). Panel (c) shows the market supply curve. At any given price, the quantity supplied to the market is the sum of the quantities supplied by Mr. Silva and Mr. Liu. For example, at a price of $2 per pound, Mr. Silva supplies 3,000 pounds of cotton per year and Mr. Liu supplies 2,000 pounds per year, making the quantity supplied to the market 5,000 pounds.

Clearly, the quantity supplied to the market at any given price is larger with Mr. Liu present than it would be if Mr. Silva were the only supplier. The quantity supplied at a given price would be even larger if we added a third producer, then a fourth, and so on. So an increase in the number of producers leads to an increase in supply and a rightward shift of the supply curve.

For a review of the factors that shift supply, see Table 3-2.

## ECONOMICS ▸ *IN ACTION*

### ONLY CREATURES SMALL AND PAMPERED

During the 1970s, British television featured a popular show titled *All Creatures Great and Small*. It chronicled the real life of James Herriot, a country veterinarian who tended to cows, pigs, sheep, horses, and the occasional house pet, often under arduous conditions, in rural England during the 1930s. The show made it clear that in those days the local vet was a critical member of farming communities, saving valuable farm animals and helping farmers survive financially. And it was also clear that Mr. Herriot considered his life's work well spent.

But that was then and this is now. According to a recent article in the *New York Times*, the United States has experienced a severe decline in the number of farm veterinarians over the past two decades. The source of the problem is competition. As the number of household pets has increased and the incomes of pet owners have grown, the demand for pet veterinarians has increased sharply. As a result, vets are being drawn away from the business of caring for farm animals into the more lucrative business of caring for pets. As one vet stated, she began her career caring for farm animals but changed her mind after "doing a C-section on a cow and it's 50 bucks. Do a C-section on a Chihuahua and you get $300. It's the money. I hate to say that."

How can we translate this into supply and demand curves? Farm veterinary services and pet veterinary services are like gasoline and fuel oil: they're related goods that are substitutes in production. A veterinarian typically specializes in one type of practice or the other, and that decision often depends on the going price for the service. America's growing pet population, combined with the

Higher spending on pets means fewer veterinarians are available to tend to farm animals.

increased willingness of doting owners to spend on their companions' care, has driven up the price of pet veterinary services. As a result, fewer and fewer veterinarians have gone into farm animal practice. So the supply curve of farm veterinarians has shifted leftward—fewer farm veterinarians are offering their services at any given price.

**TABLE   3-2   Factors That Shift Supply**

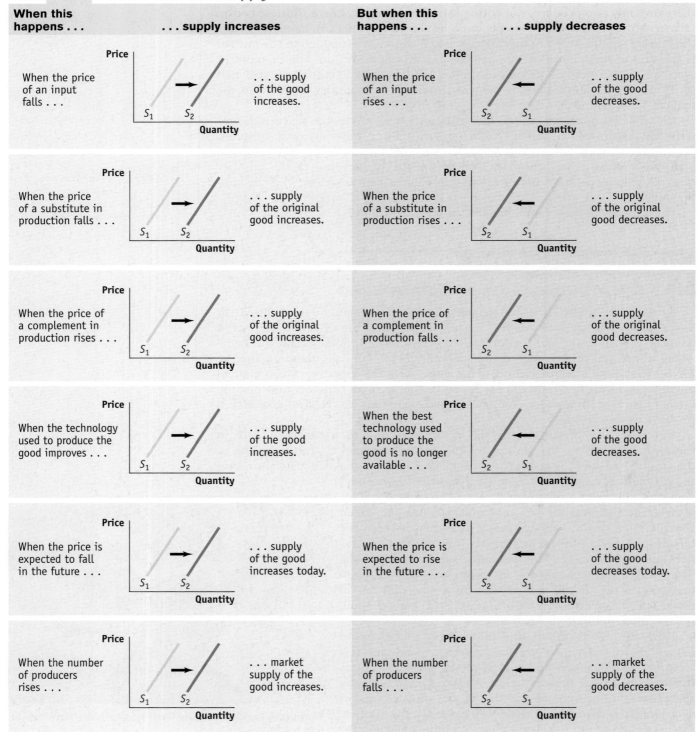

| When this happens . . . | . . . supply increases | But when this happens . . . | . . . supply decreases |
|---|---|---|---|
| When the price of an input falls . . . | . . . supply of the good increases. | When the price of an input rises . . . | . . . supply of the good decreases. |
| When the price of a substitute in production falls . . . | . . . supply of the original good increases. | When the price of a substitute in production rises . . . | . . . supply of the original good decreases. |
| When the price of a complement in production rises . . . | . . . supply of the original good increases. | When the price of a complement in production falls . . . | . . . supply of the original good decreases. |
| When the technology used to produce the good improves . . . | . . . supply of the good increases. | When the best technology used to produce the good is no longer available . . . | . . . supply of the good decreases. |
| When the price is expected to fall in the future . . . | . . . supply of the good increases today. | When the price is expected to rise in the future . . . | . . . supply of the good decreases today. |
| When the number of producers rises . . . | . . . market supply of the good increases. | When the number of producers falls . . . | . . . market supply of the good decreases. |

In the end, farmers understand that it is all a matter of dollars and cents; they get fewer veterinarians because they are unwilling to pay more. As one farmer, who had recently lost an expensive cow due to the unavailability of a veterinarian, stated, "The fact that there's nothing you can do, you accept it as a business expense now. You didn't used to. If you have livestock, sooner or later you're going to have deadstock." (Although we should note that this farmer could have chosen to pay more for a vet who would have then saved his cow.)

---

**CHECK YOUR UNDERSTANDING** 3-2

1. Explain whether each of the following events represents (i) a *shift of* the supply curve or (ii) a *movement along* the supply curve.
   a. More homeowners put their houses up for sale during a real estate boom that causes house prices to rise.
   b. Many strawberry farmers open temporary roadside stands during harvest season, even though prices are usually low at that time.
   c. Immediately after the school year begins, fast-food chains must raise wages, which represent the price of labor, to attract workers.
   d. Many construction workers temporarily move to areas that have suffered hurricane damage, lured by higher wages.
   e. Since new technologies have made it possible to build larger cruise ships (which are cheaper to run per passenger), Caribbean cruise lines offer more cabins, at lower prices, than before.

*Solutions appear at back of book.*

▼ **Quick Review**

- The **supply schedule** shows how the **quantity supplied** depends on the price. The **supply curve** illustrates this relationship.
- Supply curves are normally upward sloping: at a higher price, producers are willing to supply more of a good or service.
- A change in price results in a **movement along the supply curve** and a change in the quantity supplied.
- Increases or decreases in supply lead to **shifts of the supply curve.** An increase in supply is a rightward shift: the quantity supplied rises for any given price. A decrease in supply is a leftward shift: the quantity supplied falls for any given price.
- The five main factors that can shift the supply curve are changes in (1) **input** prices, (2) prices of related goods or services, (3) technology, (4) expectations, and (5) number of producers.
- The market supply curve is the horizontal sum of the **individual supply curves** of all producers in the market.

## Supply, Demand, and Equilibrium

We have now covered the first three key elements in the supply and demand model: the demand curve, the supply curve, and the set of factors that shift each curve. The next step is to put these elements together to show how they can be used to predict the actual price at which the good is bought and sold, as well as the actual quantity transacted.

What determines the price at which a good or service is bought and sold? What determines the quantity transacted of the good or service? In Chapter 1 we learned the general principle that *markets move toward equilibrium,* a situation in which no individual would be better off taking a different action. In the case of a competitive market, we can be more specific: a competitive market is in equilibrium when the price has moved to a level

---

⚠ **PITFALLS**

**BOUGHT AND SOLD?**
We have been talking about the price at which a good or service is bought *and* sold, as if the two were the same. But shouldn't we make a distinction between the price received by sellers and the price paid by buyers? In principle, yes; but it is helpful at this point to sacrifice a bit of realism in the interest of simplicity—by assuming away the difference between the prices received by sellers and those paid by buyers.

In reality, there is often a middleman—someone who brings buyers and sellers together. The middleman buys from suppliers, then sells to consumers at a markup—for example, cotton brokers who buy from cotton farmers and sell to textile mills—which turn the cotton into clothing for you and me. The farmers generally receive less than the mills, who eventually buy their bales of cotton, pay. No mystery there: that difference is how cotton brokers or any other middlemen make a living. In many markets, however, the difference between the buying and selling price is quite small. So it's not a bad approximation to think of the price paid by buyers as being the *same* as the price received by sellers. And that is what we assume in this chapter.

A competitive market is in equilibrium when price has moved to a level at which the quantity of a good or service demanded equals the quantity of that good or service supplied. The price at which this takes place is the **equilibrium price,** also referred to as the **market-clearing price.** The quantity of the good or service bought and sold at that price is the **equilibrium quantity.**

at which the quantity of a good demanded equals the quantity of that good supplied. At that price, no individual seller could make herself better off by offering to sell either more or less of the good and no individual buyer could make himself better off by offering to buy more or less of the good. In other words, at the market equilibrium, price has moved to a level that exactly matches the quantity demanded by consumers to the quantity supplied by sellers.

The price that matches the quantity supplied and the quantity demanded is the **equilibrium price;** the quantity bought and sold at that price is the **equilibrium quantity.** The equilibrium price is also known as the **market-clearing price:** it is the price that "clears the market" by ensuring that every buyer willing to pay that price finds a seller willing to sell at that price, and vice versa. So how do we find the equilibrium price and quantity?

## Finding the Equilibrium Price and Quantity

The easiest way to determine the equilibrium price and quantity in a market is by putting the supply curve and the demand curve on the same diagram. Since the supply curve shows the quantity supplied at any given price and the demand curve shows the quantity demanded at any given price, the price at which the two curves cross is the equilibrium price: the price at which quantity supplied equals quantity demanded.

Figure 3-11 combines the demand curve from Figure 3-1 and the supply curve from Figure 3-6. They *intersect* at point *E*, which is the equilibrium of this market; $1 is the equilibrium price and 10 billion pounds is the equilibrium quantity.

Let's confirm that point *E* fits our definition of equilibrium. At a price of $1 per pound, cotton farmers are willing to sell 10 billion pounds a year and cotton consumers want to buy 10 billion pounds a year. So at the price of $1

**FIGURE** **3-11** Market Equilibrium

Market equilibrium occurs at point *E*, where the supply curve and the demand curve intersect. In equilibrium, the quantity demanded is equal to the quantity supplied. In this market, the equilibrium price is $1 per pound and the equilibrium quantity is 10 billion pounds per year.

a pound, the quantity of cotton supplied equals the quantity demanded. Notice that at any other price the market would not clear: every willing buyer would not be able to find a willing seller, or vice versa. More specifically, if the price were more than $1, the quantity supplied would exceed the quantity demanded; if the price were less than $1, the quantity demanded would exceed the quantity supplied.

The model of supply and demand, then, predicts that given the demand and supply curves shown in Figure 3-11, 10 billion pounds of cotton would change hands at a price of $1 per pound. But how can we be sure that the market will arrive at the equilibrium price? We begin by answering three simple questions:

1. Why do all sales and purchases in a market take place at the same price?

2. Why does the market price fall if it is above the equilibrium price?

3. Why does the market price rise if it is below the equilibrium price?

YEAH, I KNOW IT'S PRICEY, BUT I ONLY GOTTA SELL *ONE* GLASS AND I'M SET FOR LIFE.

Lemonade $1,000,000 a glass

Dan Piraro, 1996 Dist. by Universal Press Syndicate

## Why Do All Sales and Purchases in a Market Take Place at the Same Price?

There are some markets where the same good can sell for many different prices, depending on who is selling or who is buying. For example, have you ever bought a souvenir in a "tourist trap" and then seen the same item on sale somewhere else (perhaps even in the shop next door) for a lower price? Because tourists don't know which shops offer the best deals and don't have time for comparison shopping, sellers in tourist areas can charge different prices for the same good.

But in any market where the buyers and sellers have both been around for some time, sales and purchases tend to converge at a generally uniform price, so we can safely talk about *the* market price. It's easy to see why. Suppose a seller offered a potential buyer a price noticeably above what the buyer knew other people to be paying. The buyer would clearly be better off shopping elsewhere—unless the seller were prepared to offer a better deal. Conversely, a seller would not be willing to sell for significantly less than the amount he knew most buyers were paying; he would be better off waiting to get a more reasonable customer. So in any well-established, ongoing market, all sellers receive and all buyers pay approximately the same price. This is what we call the *market price*.

## Why Does the Market Price Fall if It Is Above the Equilibrium Price?

Suppose the supply and demand curves are as shown in Figure 3-11 but the market price is above the equilibrium level of $1—say, $1.50. This situation is illustrated in Figure 3-12. Why can't the price stay there?

As the figure shows, at a price of $1.50 there would be more pounds of cotton available than consumers wanted to buy: 11.2 billion pounds versus 8.1 billion pounds. The difference of 3.1 billion pounds is the **surplus**—also known as the *excess supply*—of cotton at $1.50.

This surplus means that some cotton farmers are frustrated: at the current price, they cannot find consumers who want to buy their cotton. The surplus offers an incentive for those frustrated would-be sellers to offer a lower price in order to poach business from other producers and entice more consumers to buy. The result of this price cutting will be to push the prevailing price

There is a **surplus** of a good or service when the quantity supplied exceeds the quantity demanded. Surpluses occur when the price is above its equilibrium level.

FIGURE **3-12** Price Above Its Equilibrium Level Creates a Surplus

The market price of $1.50 is above the equilibrium price of $1. This creates a surplus: at a price of $1.50, producers would like to sell 11.2 billion pounds but consumers want to buy only 8.1 billion pounds, so there is a surplus of 3.1 billion pounds. This surplus will push the price down until it reaches the equilibrium price of $1.

down until it reaches the equilibrium price. So the price of a good will fall whenever there is a surplus—that is, whenever the market price is above its equilibrium level.

## Why Does the Market Price Rise if It Is Below the Equilibrium Price?

Now suppose the price is below its equilibrium level—say, at $0.75 per pound, as shown in Figure 3-13. In this case, the quantity demanded, 11.5 billion pounds, exceeds the quantity supplied, 9.1 billion pounds, implying that there are would-be buyers who cannot find cotton: there is a **shortage,** also known as an *excess demand,* of 2.4 billion pounds.

When there is a shortage, there are frustrated would-be buyers—people who want to purchase cotton but cannot find willing sellers at the current price. In this situation, either buyers will offer more than the prevailing price or sellers will realize that they can charge higher prices. Either way, the result is to drive up the prevailing price. This bidding up of prices happens whenever there are shortages—and there will be shortages whenever the price is below its equilibrium level. So the market price will always rise if it is below the equilibrium level.

## Using Equilibrium to Describe Markets

We have now seen that a market tends to have a single price, the equilibrium price. If the market price is above the equilibrium level, the ensuing surplus leads buyers and sellers to take actions that lower the price. And if the market price is below the equilibrium level, the ensuing shortage leads buyers and sellers to take actions that raise the price. So the market price always *moves toward* the equilibrium price, the price at which there is neither surplus nor shortage.

There is a **shortage** of a good or service when the quantity demanded exceeds the quantity supplied. Shortages occur when the price is below its equilibrium level.

FIGURE   **3-13**   **Price Below Its Equilibrium Level Creates a Shortage**

The market price of $0.75 is below the equilibrium price of $1. This creates a shortage: consumers want to buy 11.5 billion pounds, but only 9.1 billion pounds are for sale, so there is a shortage of 2.4 billion pounds. This shortage will push the price up until it reaches the equilibrium price of $1.

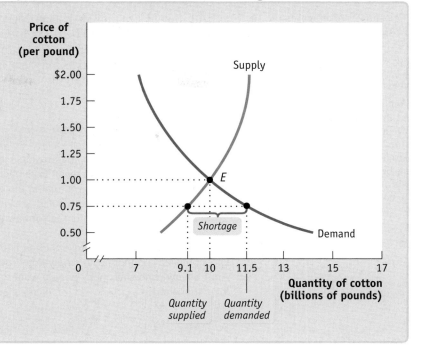

# ECONOMICS ➤ IN ACTION

## THE PRICE OF ADMISSION

The market equilibrium, so the theory goes, is pretty egalitarian because the equilibrium price applies to everyone. That is, all buyers pay the same price—the equilibrium price—and all sellers receive that same price. But is this realistic?

The market for concert tickets is an example that seems to contradict the theory—there's one price at the box office, and there's another price (typically much higher) for the same event on Internet sites where people who already have tickets resell them, such as StubHub.com or eBay. For example, compare the box office price for a recent Drake concert in Miami, Florida, to the StubHub.com price for seats in the same location: $88.50 versus $155.

Puzzling as this may seem, there is no contradiction once we take opportunity costs and tastes into account. For major events, buying tickets from the box office means waiting in very long lines. Ticket buyers who use Internet resellers have decided that the opportunity cost of their time is too high to spend waiting in line. And tickets for major events being sold at face value by online box offices often sell out within minutes. In this case, some people who want to go to the concert badly but have missed out on the opportunity to buy cheaper tickets from the online box office are willing to pay the higher Internet reseller price.

Not only that—perusing the StubHub.com website, you can see that markets really do move to equilibrium. You'll notice that the prices quoted by different sellers for seats close to one another are also very close: $184.99 versus $185 for seats on the main floor of the Drake concert. As the competitive market model predicts, units of the same good end up selling for the same price. And prices

The competitive market model determines the price you pay for concert tickets.

move in response to demand and supply. According to an article in the *New York Times,* tickets on StubHub.com can sell for less than the face value for events with little appeal, but prices can skyrocket for events that are in high demand. (The article quotes a price of $3,530 for a Madonna concert.) Even StubHub.com's chief executive says his site is "the embodiment of supply-and-demand economics."

So the theory of competitive markets isn't just speculation. If you want to experience it for yourself, try buying tickets to a concert.

### CHECK YOUR UNDERSTANDING 3-3

1. In the following three situations, the market is initially in equilibrium. Explain the changes in either supply or demand that result from each event. After each event described below, does a surplus or shortage exist at the original equilibrium price? What will happen to the equilibrium price as a result?
   a. 2009 was a very good year for California wine-grape growers, who produced a bumper crop.
   b. After a hurricane, Florida hoteliers often find that many people cancel their upcoming vacations, leaving them with empty hotel rooms.
   c. After a heavy snowfall, many people want to buy second-hand snowblowers at the local tool shop.

Solutions appear at back of book.

## Changes in Supply and Demand

The 2010 floods in Pakistan came as a surprise, but the subsequent increase in the price of cotton was no surprise at all. Suddenly there was a fall in supply: the quantity of cotton available at any given price fell. Predictably, a fall in supply raises the equilibrium price.

The flooding in Pakistan is an example of an event that shifted the supply curve for a good without having much effect on the demand curve. There are many such events. There are also events that shift the demand curve without shifting the supply curve. For example, a medical report that chocolate is good for you increases the demand for chocolate but does not affect the supply. Events often shift either the supply curve or the demand curve, but not both; it is therefore useful to ask what happens in each case.

We have seen that when a curve shifts, the equilibrium price and quantity change. We will now concentrate on exactly how the shift of a curve alters the equilibrium price and quantity.

### What Happens When the Demand Curve Shifts

Cotton and polyester are substitutes: if the price of polyester rises, the demand for cotton will increase, and if the price of polyester falls, the demand for cotton will decrease. But how does the price of polyester affect the *market equilibrium* for cotton?

Figure 3-14 shows the effect of a rise in the price of polyester on the market for cotton. The rise in the price of polyester increases the demand for cotton. Point $E_1$ shows the equilibrium corresponding to the original demand curve, with $P_1$ the equilibrium price and $Q_1$ the equilibrium quantity bought and sold.

An increase in demand is indicated by a *rightward* shift of the demand curve from $D_1$ to $D_2$. At the original market price $P_1$, this market is no longer in equilibrium: a shortage occurs because the quantity demanded exceeds the quantity supplied. So the price of cotton rises and generates an increase in the quantity supplied, an upward *movement along the supply curve.* A new

## FIGURE 3-14 Equilibrium and Shifts of the Demand Curve

The original equilibrium in the market for cotton is at $E_1$, at the intersection of the supply curve and the original demand curve, $D_1$. A rise in the price of polyester, a substitute, shifts the demand curve rightward to $D_2$. A shortage exists at the original price, $P_1$, causing both the price and quantity supplied to rise, a movement along the supply curve. A new equilibrium is reached at $E_2$, with a higher equilibrium price, $P_2$, and a higher equilibrium quantity, $Q_2$. When demand for a good or service increases, the equilibrium price and the equilibrium quantity of the good or service both rise.

equilibrium is established at point $E_2$, with a higher equilibrium price, $P_2$, and higher equilibrium quantity, $Q_2$. This sequence of events reflects a general principle: *When demand for a good or service increases, the equilibrium price and the equilibrium quantity of the good or service both rise.*

What would happen in the reverse case, a fall in the price of polyester? A fall in the price of polyester reduces the demand for cotton, shifting the demand curve to the *left*. At the original price, a surplus occurs as quantity supplied exceeds quantity demanded. The price falls and leads to a decrease in the quantity supplied, resulting in a lower equilibrium price and a lower equilibrium quantity. This illustrates another general principle: *When demand for a good or service decreases, the equilibrium price and the equilibrium quantity of the good or service both fall.*

To summarize how a market responds to a change in demand: *An increase in demand leads to a rise in both the equilibrium price and the equilibrium quantity. A decrease in demand leads to a fall in both the equilibrium price and the equilibrium quantity.*

## What Happens When the Supply Curve Shifts

In the real world, it is a bit easier to predict changes in supply than changes in demand. Physical factors that affect supply, like weather or the availability of inputs, are easier to get a handle on than the fickle tastes that affect demand. Still, with supply as with demand, what we can best predict are the *effects* of shifts of the supply curve.

As we mentioned in this chapter's opening story, devastating floods in Pakistan sharply reduced the supply of cotton in 2010. Figure 3-15 shows how this shift affected the market equilibrium. The original equilibrium is at $E_1$, the point of intersection of the original supply curve, $S_1$, and the demand curve, with an equilibrium price $P_1$ and equilibrium quantity $Q_1$. As a result of the bad weather, supply falls and $S_1$ shifts *leftward* to $S_2$. At the original price $P_1$, a shortage of cotton now exists and the market is no longer in equilibrium. The shortage causes a rise in price and a fall in quantity demanded, an upward movement along the demand curve. The new equilibrium is at $E_2$,

FIGURE **3-15** Equilibrium and Shifts of the Supply Curve

The original equilibrium in the market for cotton is at $E_1$. Bad weather in cotton-growing areas causes a fall in the supply of cotton and shifts the supply curve leftward from $S_1$ to $S_2$. A new equilibrium is established at $E_2$, with a higher equilibrium price, $P_2$, and a lower equilibrium quantity, $Q_2$.

## PITFALLS

**WHICH CURVE IS IT, ANYWAY?**
When the price of some good or service changes, in general, we can say that this reflects a change in either supply or demand. But it is easy to get confused about which one. A helpful clue is the direction of change in the quantity. If the quantity sold changes in the *same* direction as the price—for example, if both the price and the quantity rise—this suggests that the demand curve has shifted. If the price and the quantity move in *opposite* directions, the likely cause is a shift of the supply curve.

with an equilibrium price $P_2$ and an equilibrium quantity $Q_2$. In the new equilibrium, $E_2$, the price is higher and the equilibrium quantity lower than before. This can be stated as a general principle: *When supply of a good or service decreases, the equilibrium price of the good or service rises and the equilibrium quantity of the good or service falls.*

What happens to the market when supply increases? An increase in supply leads to a *rightward* shift of the supply curve. At the original price, a surplus now exists; as a result, the equilibrium price falls and the quantity demanded rises. This describes what happened to the market for cotton as new technology increased cotton yields. We can formulate a general principle: *When supply of a good or service increases, the equilibrium price of the good or service falls and the equilibrium quantity of the good or service rises.*

To summarize how a market responds to a change in supply: *An increase in supply leads to a fall in the equilibrium price and a rise in the equilibrium quantity. A decrease in supply leads to a rise in the equilibrium price and a fall in the equilibrium quantity.*

## Simultaneous Shifts of Supply and Demand Curves

Finally, it sometimes happens that events shift *both* the demand and supply curves at the same time. This is not unusual; in real life, supply curves and demand curves for many goods and services shift quite often because the economic environment continually changes. Figure 3-16 illustrates two examples of simultaneous shifts. In both panels there is an increase in demand—that is, a rightward shift of the demand curve, from $D_1$ to $D_2$—say, for example, representing an increase in the demand for cotton due to changing tastes. Notice that the rightward shift in panel (a) is larger than the one in panel (b): we can suppose that panel (a) represents a year in which many more people than usual choose to buy jeans and cotton T-shirts and panel (b) represents a normal year. Both panels also show a decrease in supply—that is, a leftward shift of the supply curve from

FIGURE   **3-16**   **Simultaneous Shifts of the Demand and Supply Curves**

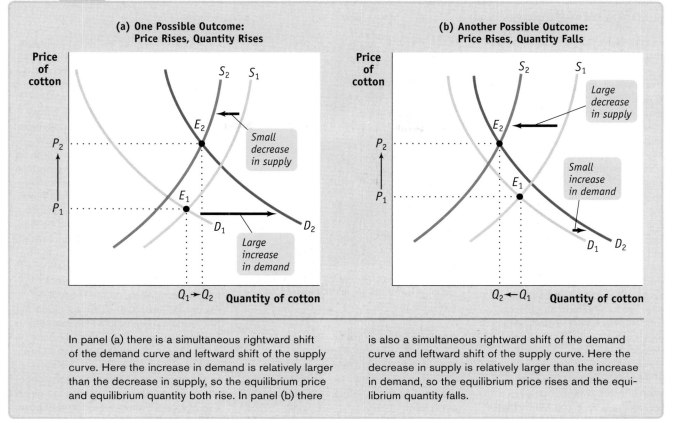

In panel (a) there is a simultaneous rightward shift of the demand curve and leftward shift of the supply curve. Here the increase in demand is relatively larger than the decrease in supply, so the equilibrium price and equilibrium quantity both rise. In panel (b) there is also a simultaneous rightward shift of the demand curve and leftward shift of the supply curve. Here the decrease in supply is relatively larger than the increase in demand, so the equilibrium price rises and the equilibrium quantity falls.

$S_1$ to $S_2$. Also notice that the leftward shift in panel (b) is relatively larger than the one in panel (a): we can suppose that panel (b) represents the effect of particularly bad weather in Pakistan and panel (a) represents the effect of a much less severe weather event.

In both cases, the equilibrium price rises from $P_1$ to $P_2$, as the equilibrium moves from $E_1$ to $E_2$. But what happens to the equilibrium quantity, the quantity of cotton bought and sold? In panel (a) the increase in demand is large relative to the decrease in supply, and the equilibrium quantity rises as a result. In panel (b), the decrease in supply is large relative to the increase in demand, and the equilibrium quantity falls as a result. That is, when demand increases and supply decreases, the actual quantity bought and sold can go either way, depending on *how much* the demand and supply curves have shifted.

In general, when supply and demand shift in opposite directions, we can't predict what the ultimate effect will be on the quantity bought and sold. What we can say is that a curve that shifts a disproportionately greater distance than the other curve will have a disproportionately greater effect on the quantity bought and sold. That said, we can make the following prediction about the outcome when the supply and demand curves shift in opposite directions:

• When demand increases and supply decreases, the equilibrium price rises but the change in the equilibrium quantity is ambiguous.

• When demand decreases and supply increases, the equilibrium price falls but the change in the equilibrium quantity is ambiguous.

But suppose that the demand and supply curves shift in the same direction. Before 2010, this was the case in the global market for cotton, where both supply

## FOR INQUIRING MINDS

### TRIBULATIONS ON THE RUNWAY

You probably don't spend much time worrying about the trials and tribulations of fashion models. Most of them don't lead glamorous lives; in fact, except for a lucky few, life as a fashion model today can be very trying and not very lucrative. And it's all because of supply and demand.

Consider the case of Bianca Gomez, a willowy 18-year-old from Los Angeles, with green eyes, honey-colored hair, and flawless skin, whose experience was detailed in a *Wall Street Journal* article. Bianca began modeling while still in high school, earning about $30,000 in modeling fees during her senior year. Having attracted the interest of some top designers in New York, she moved there after graduation, hoping to land jobs in leading fashion houses and photoshoots for leading fashion magazines.

But once in New York, Bianca entered the global market for fashion models. And it wasn't very pretty. Due to the ease of transmitting photos over the Internet and the relatively low cost of international travel, top fashion centers such as New York and Milan, Italy, are now deluged with beautiful young women from all over the world, eagerly trying to make it as models. Although Russians, other Eastern Europeans,

Bianca Gomez on the runway before intense global competition got her thinking about switching careers.

and Brazilians are particularly numerous, some hail from places such as Kazakhstan and Mozambique. As one designer said, "There are so many models now. . . . There are just thousands every year."

Returning to our (less glamorous) economic model of supply and demand, the influx of aspiring fashion models from around the world can be represented

by a rightward shift of the supply curve in the market for fashion models, which would by itself tend to lower the price paid to models. And that wasn't the only change in the market. Unfortunately for Bianca and others like her, the tastes of many of those who hire models have changed as well. Over the past few years, fashion magazines have come to prefer using celebrities such as Angelina Jolie on their pages rather than anonymous models, believing that their readers connect better with a familiar face. This amounts to a leftward shift of the demand curve for models—again reducing the equilibrium price paid to them.

This was borne out in Bianca's experiences. After paying her rent, her transportation, all her modeling expenses, and 20% of her earnings to her modeling agency (which markets her to prospective clients and books her jobs), Bianca found that she was barely breaking even. Sometimes she even had to dip into savings from her high school years. To save money, she ate macaroni and hot dogs; she traveled to auditions, often four or five in one day, by subway. As the *Wall Street Journal* reported, Bianca was seriously considering quitting modeling altogether.

and demand had increased over the past decade. Can we safely make any predictions about the changes in price and quantity? In this situation, the change in quantity bought and sold can be predicted, but the change in price is ambiguous. The two possible outcomes when the supply and demand curves shift in the same direction (which you should check for yourself) are as follows:

• When both demand and supply increase, the equilibrium quantity rises but the change in equilibrium price is ambiguous.

• When both demand and supply decrease, the equilibrium quantity falls but the change in equilibrium price is ambiguous.

## ECONOMICS › *IN ACTION*

### THE RICE RUN OF 2008

In April 2008, the price of rice exported from Thailand—a global benchmark for the price of rice traded in international markets—reached $950 per ton, up from $360 per ton at the beginning of 2008. Within hours, prices for rice at major rice-trading exchanges around the world were breaking record levels. The factors that lay behind the surge in rice prices were both demand-related and supply-related: growing incomes in China and India, traditionally large consumers of rice; drought in Australia; and pest infestation in Vietnam. But it was hoarding by farmers, panic buying by consumers, and an export ban by India, one of the largest exporters of rice, that explained the breathtaking speed of the rise in price.

In much of Asia, governments are major buyers of rice. They buy rice from their rice farmers, who are paid a government-set price, and then sell it to the poor at subsidized prices (prices lower than the market equilibrium price). In the past, the government-set price was better than anything farmers could get in the private market.

Now, even farmers in rural areas of Asia have access to the Internet and can see the price quotes on global rice exchanges. And as rice prices rose in response to changes in demand and supply, farmers grew dissatisfied with the government price and instead hoarded their rice in the belief that they would eventually get higher prices. This was a self-fulfilling belief, as the hoarding shifted the supply curve leftward and raised the price of rice even further.

At the same time, India, one of the largest growers of rice, banned Indian exports of rice in order to protect its domestic consumers, causing yet another leftward shift of the supply curve and pushing the price of rice even higher.

As shown in Figure 3-17, the effects even spilled over to the United States, which had not suffered any fall in its rice production. American rice consumers grew alarmed when large retailers limited some bulk rice purchases by consumers in response to the turmoil in the global rice market.

Fearful of paying even higher prices in the future, panic buying set in. As one woman who was in the process of buying 30 pounds of rice said, "We don't even eat that much rice. But I read about it in the newspaper and decided to buy some." In San Francisco, some Asian markets reported runs on rice. And, predictably, this led to even higher prices as panic buying shifted the demand curve rightward, further feeding the buying frenzy. As one market owner said, "People are afraid. We tell them, 'There's no shortage yet' but it was crazy in here."

**FIGURE  3-17**  **Rising Rice Prices in the United States, 2003–2011**

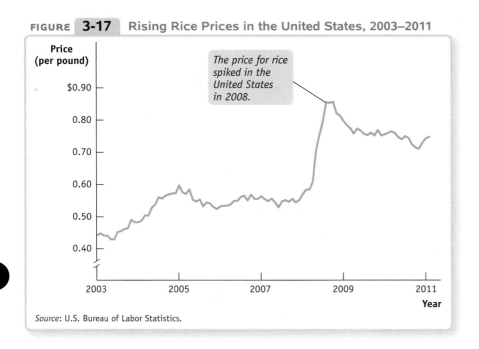

*Source*: U.S. Bureau of Labor Statistics.

**CHECK YOUR UNDERSTANDING** **3-4**

1. In each of the following examples, determine (i) the market in question; (ii) whether a shift in demand or supply occurred, the direction of the shift, and what induced the shift; and (iii) the effect of the shift on the equilibrium price and the equilibrium quantity.
   a. As the price of gasoline fell in the United States during the 1990s, more people bought large cars.
   b. As technological innovation has lowered the cost of recycling used paper, fresh paper made from recycled stock is used more frequently.
   c. When a local cable company offers cheaper on-demand films, local movie theaters have more unfilled seats.

2. When a new, faster computer chip is introduced, demand for computers using the older, slower chips decreases. Simultaneously, computer makers increase their production of computers containing the old chips in order to clear out their stocks of old chips.
   Draw two diagrams of the market for computers containing the old chips:
   a. one in which the equilibrium quantity falls in response to these events and
   b. one in which the equilibrium quantity rises. What happens to the equilibrium price in each diagram?

*Solutions appear at back of book.*

## Competitive Markets—And Others

Early in this chapter, we defined a competitive market and explained that the supply and demand framework is a model of competitive markets. But we took a rain check on the question of why it matters whether or not a market is competitive. Now that we've seen how the supply and demand model works, we can offer some explanation.

To understand why competitive markets are different from other markets, compare the problems facing two individuals: a wheat farmer who must decide whether to grow more wheat and the president of a giant aluminum company—say, Alcoa—who must decide whether to produce more aluminum.

For the wheat farmer, the question is simply whether the extra wheat can be sold at a price high enough to justify the extra production cost. The farmer need not worry about whether producing more wheat will affect the price of the wheat he or she was already planning to grow. That's because the wheat market is competitive. There are thousands of wheat farmers, and no one farmer's decision will have any impact on the market price.

For the Alcoa executive, things are not that simple because the aluminum market is *not* competitive. There are only a few big producers, including Alcoa, and each of them is well aware that its actions *do* have a noticeable impact on the market price. This adds a whole new level of complexity to the decisions producers have to make. Alcoa can't decide whether or not to produce more aluminum just by asking whether the additional product will sell for more than it costs to make. The company also has to ask whether producing more aluminum will drive down the market price and reduce its *profit*, its net gain from producing and selling its output.

When a market is competitive, individuals can base decisions on less complicated analyses than those used in a noncompetitive market. This in turn means that it's easier for economists to build a model of a competitive market than of a noncompetitive market.

Don't take this to mean that economic analysis has nothing to say about noncompetitive markets. On the contrary, economists can offer some very important insights into how other kinds of markets work. But those insights require other models, which we will learn about later in this text.

# The Chicago Board of Trade

Jim West/Photolibrary

Around the world, commodities are bought and sold on "exchanges," markets organized in a specific location, where buyers and sellers meet to trade. But it wasn't always like this.

The first modern commodity exchange was the Chicago Board of Trade, founded in 1848. At the time, the United States was already a major wheat producer. And St. Louis, not Chicago, was the leading city of the American West and the dominant location for wheat trading. But the St. Louis wheat market suffered from a major flaw: there was no central marketplace, no specific location where everyone met to buy and sell wheat. Instead, sellers would sell their grain from various warehouses or from stacked sacks of grain on the river levee. Buyers would wander around town, looking for the best price.

In Chicago, however, sellers had a better idea. The Chicago Board of Trade, an association of the city's leading grain dealers, created a much more efficient method for trading wheat. There, traders gathered in one place—the "pit"—where they called out offers to sell and accepted offers to buy. The Board guaranteed that these contracts would be fulfilled, removing the need for the wheat to be physically in place when a trade was agreed upon.

This system meant that buyers could very quickly find sellers and vice-versa, reducing the cost of doing business. It also ensured that everyone could see the latest price, leading the price to rise or fall quickly in response to market conditions. For example, news of bad weather in a wheat-growing area hundreds of miles away would send the price in the Chicago pit soaring in a matter of minutes.

The Chicago Board of Trade went on to become the world's most important trading center for wheat and many other agricultural commodities, a distinction it retains to this day. And the Board's rise helped the rise of Chicago, too. The city, as Carl Sandburg put it in his famous poem, "Chicago," became:

> **Hog Butcher for the World,**
> **Tool Maker, Stacker of Wheat,**
> **Player with Railroads and the Nation's Freight Handler;**
> **Stormy, husky, brawling,**
> **City of the Big Shoulders**

By 1890, Chicago had more than a million people, second only to New York and far out-pacing St. Louis. Making a better market, it turned out, was very good business indeed.

### QUESTIONS FOR THOUGHT

1. In the chapter we mention how prices can vary in a tourist trap. Which market, St. Louis or Chicago, was more likely to behave like a tourist trap? Explain.

2. What was the advantage to buyers from buying their wheat in the Chicago pit instead of in St. Louis? What was the advantage to sellers?

3. Based on what you have learned from this case, explain why eBay is like the Chicago pit. Why has it been so successful as a marketplace for second-hand items compared to a market composed of various flea markets and dealers?

1. The **supply and demand model** illustrates how a **competitive market,** one with many buyers and sellers, none of whom can influence the market price, works.

2. The **demand schedule** shows the **quantity demanded** at each price and is represented graphically by a **demand curve.** The **law of demand** says that demand curves slope downward; that is, a higher price for a good or service leads people to demand a smaller quantity, other things equal.

3. A **movement along the demand curve** occurs when a price change leads to a change in the quantity demanded. When economists talk of increasing or decreasing demand, they mean **shifts of the demand curve**—a change in the quantity demanded at any given price. An increase in demand causes a rightward shift of the demand curve. A decrease in demand causes a leftward shift.

4. There are five main factors that shift the demand curve:
   - A change in the prices of related goods or services, such as **substitutes** or **complements**
   - A change in income: when income rises, the demand for **normal goods** increases and the demand for **inferior goods** decreases.
   - A change in tastes
   - A change in expectations
   - A change in the number of consumers

5. The market demand curve for a good or service is the horizontal sum of the **individual demand curves** of all consumers in the market.

6. The **supply schedule** shows the **quantity supplied** at each price and is represented graphically by a **supply curve.** Supply curves usually slope upward.

7. A **movement along the supply curve** occurs when a price change leads to a change in the quantity supplied. When economists talk of increasing or decreas-ing supply, they mean **shifts of the supply curve**—a change in the quantity supplied at any given price. An increase in supply causes a rightward shift of the sup-ply curve. A decrease in supply causes a leftward shift.

8. There are five main factors that shift the supply curve:
   - A change in **input** prices
   - A change in the prices of related goods and services
   - A change in technology
   - A change in expectations
   - A change in the number of producers

9. The market supply curve for a good or service is the horizontal sum of the **individual supply curves** of all producers in the market.

10. The supply and demand model is based on the prin-ciple that the price in a market moves to its **equilib-rium price,** or **market-clearing price,** the price at which the quantity demanded is equal to the quantity supplied. This quantity is the **equilibrium quantity.** When the price is above its market-clearing level, there is a **surplus** that pushes the price down. When the price is below its market-clearing level, there is a **shortage** that pushes the price up.

11. An increase in demand increases both the equilib-rium price and the equilibrium quantity; a decrease in demand has the opposite effect. An increase in supply reduces the equilibrium price and increases the equilibrium quantity; a decrease in supply has the opposite effect.

12. Shifts of the demand curve and the supply curve can happen simultaneously. When they shift in opposite directions, the change in equilibrium price is predict-able but the change in equilibrium quantity is not. When they shift in the same direction, the change in equilibrium quantity is predictable but the change in equilibrium price is not. In general, the curve that shifts the greater distance has a greater effect on the changes in equilibrium price and quantity.

Competitive market, p. 66
Supply and demand model, p. 66
Demand schedule, p. 67
Quantity demanded, p. 67
Demand curve, p. 68
Law of demand, p. 68
Shift of the demand curve, p. 69
Movement along the demand curve, p. 69

Substitutes, p. 71
Complements, p. 71
Normal good, p. 72
Inferior good, p. 72
Individual demand curve, p. 73
Quantity supplied, p. 76
Supply schedule, p. 76
Supply curve, p. 77
Shift of the supply curve, p. 77

Movement along the supply curve, p. 78
Input, p. 79
Individual supply curve, p. 80
Equilibrium price, p. 84
Equilibrium quantity, p. 84
Market-clearing price, p. 84
Surplus, p. 85
Shortage, p. 86

## PROBLEMS

1. A survey indicated that chocolate is Americans' favorite ice-cream flavor. For each of the following, indicate the possible effects on demand, supply, or both as well as equilibrium price and quantity of chocolate ice cream.

   a. A severe drought in the Midwest causes dairy farmers to reduce the number of milk-producing cattle in their herds by a third. These dairy farmers supply cream that is used to manufacture chocolate ice cream.

   b. A new report by the American Medical Association reveals that chocolate does, in fact, have significant health benefits.

   c. The discovery of cheaper synthetic vanilla flavoring lowers the price of vanilla ice cream.

   d. New technology for mixing and freezing ice cream lowers manufacturers' costs of producing chocolate ice cream.

2. In a supply and demand diagram, draw the shift of the demand curve for hamburgers in your hometown due to the following events. In each case, show the effect on equilibrium price and quantity.

   a. The price of tacos increases.

   b. All hamburger sellers raise the price of their french fries.

   c. Income falls in town. Assume that hamburgers are a normal good for most people.

   d. Income falls in town. Assume that hamburgers are an inferior good for most people.

   e. Hot dog stands cut the price of hot dogs.

3. The market for many goods changes in predictable ways according to the time of year, in response to events such as holidays, vacation times, seasonal changes in production, and so on. Using supply and demand, explain the change in price in each of the following cases. Note that supply and demand may shift simultaneously.

   a. Lobster prices usually fall during the summer peak lobster harvest season, despite the fact that people like to eat lobster during the summer more than at any other time of year.

   b. The price of a Christmas tree is lower after Christmas than before but fewer trees are sold.

   c. The price of a round-trip ticket to Paris on Air France falls by more than $200 after the end of school vacation in September. This happens despite the fact that generally worsening weather increases the cost of operating flights to Paris, and Air France therefore reduces the number of flights to Paris at any given price.

4. Show in a diagram the effect on the demand curve, the supply curve, the equilibrium price, and the equilibrium quantity of each of the following events.

   a. The market for newspapers in your town
   Case 1: The salaries of journalists go up.

   Case 2: There is a big news event in your town, which is reported in the newspapers.

   b. The market for St. Louis Rams cotton T-shirts
   Case 1: The Rams win the Super Bowl.
   Case 2: The price of cotton increases.

   c. The market for bagels
   Case 1: People realize how fattening bagels are.
   Case 2: People have less time to make themselves a cooked breakfast.

   d. The market for the Krugman and Wells economics textbook
   Case 1: Your professor makes it required reading for all of his or her students.
   Case 2: Printing costs for textbooks are lowered by the use of synthetic paper.

5. The U.S. Department of Agriculture reported that in 2004 each person in the United States consumed an average of 37 gallons of soft drinks (nondiet) at an average price of $2 per gallon. Assume that, at a price of $1.50 per gallon, each individual consumer would demand 50 gallons of soft drinks. The U.S. population in 2004 was 294 million. From this information about the individual demand schedule, calculate the market demand schedule for soft drinks for the prices of $1.50 and $2 per gallon.

6. Suppose that the supply schedule of Maine lobsters is as follows:

| Price of lobster (per pound) | Quantity of lobster supplied (pounds) |
|---|---|
| $25 | 800 |
| 20 | 700 |
| 15 | 600 |
| 10 | 500 |
| 5 | 400 |

Suppose that Maine lobsters can be sold only in the United States. The U.S. demand schedule for Maine lobsters is as follows:

| Price of lobster (per pound) | Quantity of lobster demanded (pounds) |
|---|---|
| $25 | 200 |
| 20 | 400 |
| 15 | 600 |
| 10 | 800 |
| 5 | 1,000 |

   a. Draw the demand curve and the supply curve for Maine lobsters. What are the equilibrium price and quantity of lobsters?

Now suppose that Maine lobsters can be sold in France. The French demand schedule for Maine lobsters is as follows:

| Price of lobster (per pound) | Quantity of lobster supplied (pounds) |
| --- | --- |
| $25 | 100 |
| 20 | 300 |
| 15 | 500 |
| 10 | 700 |
| 5 | 900 |

**b.** What is the demand schedule for Maine lobsters now that French consumers can also buy them? Draw a supply and demand diagram that illustrates the new equilibrium price and quantity of lobsters. What will happen to the price at which fishermen can sell lobster? What will happen to the price paid by U.S. consumers? What will happen to the quantity consumed by U.S. consumers?

7. Find the flaws in reasoning in the following statements, paying particular attention to the distinction between shifts of and movements along the supply and demand curves. Draw a diagram to illustrate what actually happens in each situation.

   **a.** "A technological innovation that lowers the cost of producing a good might seem at first to result in a reduction in the price of the good to consumers. But a fall in price will increase demand for the good, and higher demand will send the price up again. It is not certain, therefore, that an innovation will really reduce price in the end."

   **b.** "A study shows that eating a clove of garlic a day can help prevent heart disease, causing many consumers to demand more garlic. This increase in demand results in a rise in the price of garlic. Consumers, seeing that the price of garlic has gone up, reduce their demand for garlic. This causes the demand for garlic to decrease and the price of garlic to fall. Therefore, the ultimate effect of the study on the price of garlic is uncertain."

8. The following table shows a demand schedule for a normal good.

| Price | Quantity demanded |
| --- | --- |
| $23 | 70 |
| 21 | 90 |
| 19 | 110 |
| 17 | 130 |

   **a.** Do you think that the increase in quantity demanded (say, from 90 to 110 in the table) when price decreases (from $21 to $19) is due to a rise in consumers' income? Explain clearly (and briefly) why or why not.

   **b.** Now suppose that the good is an inferior good. Would the demand schedule still be valid for an inferior good?

   **c.** Lastly, assume you do not know whether the good is normal or inferior. Devise an experiment that would allow you to determine which one it was. Explain.

9. According to the *New York Times* (November 18, 2006), the number of car producers in China is increasing rapidly. The newspaper reports that "China has more car brands now than the United States. . . . But while car sales have climbed 38 percent in the first three quarters of this year, automakers have increased their output even faster, causing fierce competition and a slow erosion in prices." At the same time, Chinese consumers' incomes have risen. Assume that cars are a normal good. Use a diagram of the supply and demand curves for cars in China to explain what has happened in the Chinese car market.

10. Aaron Hank is a star hitter for the Bay City baseball team. He is close to breaking the major league record for home runs hit during one season, and it is widely anticipated that in the next game he will break that record. As a result, tickets for the team's next game have been a hot commodity. But today it is announced that, due to a knee injury, he will not in fact play in the team's next game. Assume that season ticket-holders are able to resell their tickets if they wish. Use supply and demand diagrams to explain the following.

    **a.** Show the case in which this announcement results in a lower equilibrium price and a lower equilibrium quantity than before the announcement.

    **b.** Show the case in which this announcement results in a lower equilibrium price and a higher equilibrium quantity than before the announcement.

    **c.** What accounts for whether case a or case b occurs?

    **d.** Suppose that a scalper had secretly learned before the announcement that Aaron Hank would not play in the next game. What actions do you think he would take?

11. In *Rolling Stone* magazine, several fans and rock stars, including Pearl Jam, were bemoaning the high price of concert tickets. One superstar argued, "It just isn't worth $75 to see me play. No one should have to pay that much to go to a concert." Assume this star sold out arenas around the country at an average ticket price of $75.

    **a.** How would you evaluate the argument that ticket prices are too high?

    **b.** Suppose that due to this star's protests, ticket prices were lowered to $50. In what sense is this price too low? Draw a diagram using supply and demand curves to support your argument.

    **c.** Suppose Pearl Jam really wanted to bring down ticket prices. Since the band controls the supply of its services, what do you recommend they do? Explain using a supply and demand diagram.

    **d.** Suppose the band's next CD was a total dud. Do you think they would still have to worry about ticket prices being too high? Why or why not? Draw a supply and demand diagram to support your argument.

**e.** Suppose the group announced their next tour was going to be their last. What effect would this likely have on the demand for and price of tickets? Illustrate with a supply and demand diagram.

**12.** The accompanying table gives the annual U.S. demand and supply schedules for pickup trucks.

| Price of truck | Quantity of trucks demanded (millions) | Quantity of trucks supplied (millions) |
|---|---|---|
| $20,000 | 20 | 14 |
| 25,000 | 18 | 15 |
| 30,000 | 16 | 16 |
| 35,000 | 14 | 17 |
| 40,000 | 12 | 18 |

**a.** Plot the demand and supply curves using these schedules. Indicate the equilibrium price and quantity on your diagram.

**b.** Suppose the tires used on pickup trucks are found to be defective. What would you expect to happen in the market for pickup trucks? Show this on your diagram.

**c.** Suppose that the U.S. Department of Transportation imposes costly regulations on manufacturers that cause them to reduce supply by one-third at any given price. Calculate and plot the new supply schedule and indicate the new equilibrium price and quantity on your diagram.

**13.** After several years of decline, the market for handmade acoustic guitars is making a comeback. These guitars are usually made in small workshops employing relatively few highly skilled luthiers. Assess the impact on the equilibrium price and quantity of handmade acoustic guitars as a result of each of the following events. In your answers indicate which curve(s) shift(s) and in which direction.

**a.** Environmentalists succeed in having the use of Brazilian rosewood banned in the United States, forcing luthiers to seek out alternative, more costly woods.

**b.** A foreign producer reengineers the guitar-making process and floods the market with identical guitars.

**c.** Music featuring handmade acoustic guitars makes a comeback as audiences tire of heavy metal and alternative rock music.

**d.** The country goes into a deep recession and the income of the average American falls sharply.

**14.** *Demand twisters:* Sketch and explain the demand relationship in each of the following statements.

**a.** I would never buy a Britney Spears CD! You couldn't even give me one for nothing.

**b.** I generally buy a bit more coffee as the price falls. But once the price falls to $2 per pound, I'll buy out the entire stock of the supermarket.

**c.** I spend more on orange juice even as the price rises. (Does this mean that I must be violating the law of demand?)

**d.** Due to a tuition rise, most students at a college find themselves with less disposable income. Almost all of them eat more frequently at the school cafeteria and less often at restaurants, even though prices at the cafeteria have risen, too. (This one requires that you draw both the demand and the supply curves for school cafeteria meals.)

**15.** Will Shakespeare is a struggling playwright in sixteenth-century London. As the price he receives for writing a play increases, he is willing to write more plays. For the following situations, use a diagram to illustrate how each event affects the equilibrium price and quantity in the market for Shakespeare's plays.

**a.** The playwright Christopher Marlowe, Shakespeare's chief rival, is killed in a bar brawl.

**b.** The bubonic plague, a deadly infectious disease, breaks out in London.

**c.** To celebrate the defeat of the Spanish Armada, Queen Elizabeth declares several weeks of festivities, which involves commissioning new plays.

**16.** The small town of Middling experiences a sudden doubling of the birth rate. After three years, the birth rate returns to normal. Use a diagram to illustrate the effect of these events on the following.

**a.** The market for an hour of babysitting services in Middling today

**b.** The market for an hour of babysitting services 14 years into the future, after the birth rate has returned to normal, by which time children born today are old enough to work as babysitters

**c.** The market for an hour of babysitting services 30 years into the future, when children born today are likely to be having children of their own

**17.** Use a diagram to illustrate how each of the following events affects the equilibrium price and quantity of pizza.

**a.** The price of mozzarella cheese rises.

**b.** The health hazards of hamburgers are widely publicized.

**c.** The price of tomato sauce falls.

**d.** The incomes of consumers rise and pizza is an inferior good.

**e.** Consumers expect the price of pizza to fall next week.

**18.** Although he was a prolific artist, Pablo Picasso painted only 1,000 canvases during his "Blue Period." Picasso is now dead, and all of his Blue Period works are currently on display in museums and private galleries throughout Europe and the United States.

**a.** Draw a supply curve for Picasso Blue Period works. Why is this supply curve different from ones you have seen?

**b.** Given the supply curve from part a, the price of a Picasso Blue Period work will be entirely dependent on what factor(s)? Draw a diagram showing how the equilibrium price of such a work is determined.

**c.** Suppose rich art collectors decide that it is essential to acquire Picasso Blue Period art for their collec-

tions. Show the impact of this on the market for these paintings.

**19.** Draw the appropriate curve in each of the following cases. Is it like or unlike the curves you have seen so far? Explain.

**a.** The demand for cardiac bypass surgery, given that the government pays the full cost for any patient

**b.** The demand for elective cosmetic plastic surgery, given that the patient pays the full cost

**c.** The supply of reproductions of Rembrandt paintings

# CHAPTER 4

# Price Controls and Quotas: Meddling with Markets

## BIG CITY, NOT-SO-BRIGHT IDEAS

New York City: an empty taxi is hard to find.

> ❱ The meaning of **price controls** and **quantity controls,** two kinds of government intervention in markets

> ❱ How price and quantity controls create problems and can make a market inefficient

> ❱ Why the predictable side effects of intervention in markets often lead economists to be skeptical of its usefulness

> ❱ Who benefits and who loses from market interventions, and why they are used despite their well-known problems

NEW YORK CITY IS A PLACE WHERE you can find almost anything— that is, almost anything, except a taxicab when you need one or a decent apartment at a rent you can afford. You might think that New York's notorious shortages of cabs and apartments are the inevitable price of big-city living. However, they are largely the product of government policies—specifically, of government policies that have, one way or another, tried to prevail over the market forces of supply and demand.

In Chapter 3, we learned the principle that a market moves to equilibrium— that the market price rises or falls to the level at which the quantity of a good that people are willing to supply is equal to the quantity that other people demand.

But sometimes governments try to defy that principle. Whenever a government tries to dictate either a market price or a market quantity that's different from the equilibrium price or quantity, the market strikes back in predictable ways. Our ability to predict what will happen when governments try to defy supply and demand shows the power and usefulness of supply and demand analysis itself.

The shortages of apartments and taxicabs in New York are particular examples that illuminate what happens when the logic of the market is defied. New York's housing shortage is the result of *rent control,* a law that prevents landlords from raising rents except when specifically given permission. Rent control was introduced during World War II to protect the interests of tenants, and it still remains in force. Many other American cities have had rent control at one time or another, but with the notable exceptions of New York and San Francisco, these controls have largely been done away with. Similarly,

New York's limited supply of taxis is the result of a licensing system introduced in the 1930s. New York taxi licenses are known as "medallions," and only taxis with medallions are allowed to pick up passengers. Although this system was originally intended to protect the interests of both drivers and customers, it has generated a shortage of taxis in the city. The number of medallions remained fixed for nearly 60 years, with no significant increase until 2004.

In this chapter, we begin by examining what happens when governments try to control prices in a competitive market, keeping the price in a market either below its equilibrium level—a *price ceiling* such as rent control—or above it—a *price floor* such as the minimum wage paid to workers in many countries. We then turn to schemes such as taxi medallions that attempt to dictate the quantity of a good bought and sold. ■

**Price controls** are legal restrictions on how high or low a market price may go. They can take two forms: a **price ceiling,** a maximum price sellers are allowed to charge for a good or service, or a **price floor,** a minimum price buyers are required to pay for a good or service.

# Why Governments Control Prices

You learned in Chapter 3 that a market moves to equilibrium—that is, the market price moves to the level at which the quantity supplied equals the quantity demanded. But this equilibrium price does not necessarily please either buyers or sellers.

After all, buyers would always like to pay less if they could, and sometimes they can make a strong moral or political case that they should pay lower prices. For example, what if the equilibrium between supply and demand for apartments in a major city leads to rental rates that an average working person can't afford? In that case, a government might well be under pressure to impose limits on the rents landlords can charge.

Sellers, however, would always like to get more money for what they sell, and sometimes they can make a strong moral or political case that they should receive higher prices. For example, consider the labor market: the price for an hour of a worker's time is the wage rate. What if the equilibrium between supply and demand for less skilled workers leads to wage rates that yield an income below the poverty level? In that case, a government might well be pressured to require employers to pay a rate no lower than some specified minimum wage.

In other words, there is often a strong political demand for governments to intervene in markets. And powerful interests can make a compelling case that a market intervention favoring them is "fair." When a government intervenes to regulate prices, we say that it imposes **price controls.** These controls typically take the form either of an upper limit, a **price ceiling,** or a lower limit, a **price floor.**

Unfortunately, it's not that easy to tell a market what to do. As we will now see, when a government tries to legislate prices—whether it legislates them *down* by imposing a price ceiling or *up* by imposing a price floor—there are certain predictable and unpleasant side effects.

We make an important assumption in this chapter: the markets in question are efficient before price controls are imposed. But, markets can sometimes be inefficient—for example, a market dominated by a monopolist, a single seller that has the power to influence the market price. When markets are inefficient, price controls don't necessarily cause problems and can potentially move the market closer to efficiency. In practice, however, price controls are often imposed on efficient markets—like the New York apartment market. And so the analysis in this chapter applies to many important real-world situations.

# Price Ceilings

Aside from rent control, there are not many price ceilings in the United States today. But at times they have been widespread. Price ceilings are typically imposed during crises—wars, harvest failures, natural disasters—because these events often lead to sudden price increases that hurt many people but produce big gains for a lucky few. The U.S. government imposed ceilings on many prices during World War II: the war sharply increased demand for raw materials, such as aluminum and steel, and price controls prevented those with access to these raw materials from earning huge profits. Price controls on oil were imposed in 1973, when an embargo by Arab oil-exporting countries seemed likely to generate huge profits for U.S. oil companies. Price controls were imposed on California's wholesale electricity market in 2001, when a shortage created big profits for a few power-generating companies but led to higher electricity bills for consumers.

Rent control in New York is, believe it or not, a legacy of World War II: it was imposed because wartime production produced an economic boom, which increased demand for apartments at a time when the labor and raw materials that might have been used to build them were being used to win the war instead. Although most price controls were removed soon after the war ended, New York's rent limits were retained and gradually extended to buildings not previously covered, leading to some very strange situations.

You can rent a one-bedroom apartment in Manhattan on fairly short notice—if you are able and willing to pay several thousand dollars a month and live in a less-than-desirable area. Yet some people pay only a small fraction of this for comparable apartments, and others pay hardly more for bigger apartments in better locations.

Aside from producing great deals for some renters, however, what are the broader consequences of New York's rent-control system? To answer this question, we turn to the model we developed in Chapter 3: the supply and demand model.

## Modeling a Price Ceiling

To see what can go wrong when a government imposes a price ceiling on an efficient market, consider Figure 4-1, which shows a simplified model of the market for apartments in New York. For the sake of simplicity, we imagine that all apartments are exactly the same and so would rent for the same price in an unregulated market. The table in the figure shows the demand and supply schedules; the demand and supply curves are shown on the left. We show the quantity of apartments on the horizontal axis and the monthly rent per apartment on the vertical axis. You can see that in an unregulated market the equilibrium would be at point *E:* 2 million apartments would be rented for $1,000 each per month.

Now suppose that the government imposes a price ceiling, limiting rents to a price below the equilibrium price—say, no more than $800.

**FIGURE 4-1  The Market for Apartments in the Absence of Price Controls**

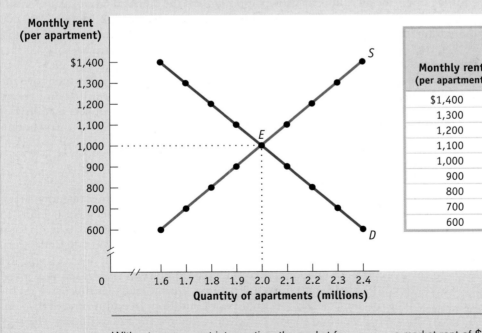

| Monthly rent (per apartment) | Quantity of apartments (millions) | |
| --- | --- | --- |
| | Quantity demanded | Quantity supplied |
| $1,400 | 1.6 | 2.4 |
| 1,300 | 1.7 | 2.3 |
| 1,200 | 1.8 | 2.2 |
| 1,100 | 1.9 | 2.1 |
| 1,000 | 2.0 | 2.0 |
| 900 | 2.1 | 1.9 |
| 800 | 2.2 | 1.8 |
| 700 | 2.3 | 1.7 |
| 600 | 2.4 | 1.6 |

Without government intervention, the market for apartments reaches equilibrium at point *E* with a market rent of $1,000 per month and 2 million apartments rented.

FIGURE **4-2** The Effects of a Price Ceiling

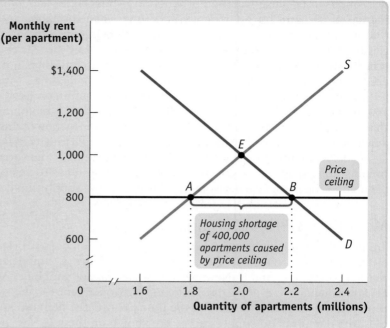

The black horizontal line represents the government-imposed price ceiling on rents of $800 per month. This price ceiling reduces the quantity of apartments supplied to 1.8 million, point *A*, and increases the quantity demanded to 2.2 million, point *B*. This creates a persistent shortage of 400,000 units: 400,000 people who want apartments at the legal rent of $800 but cannot get them.

Figure 4-2 shows the effect of the price ceiling, represented by the line at $800. At the enforced rental rate of $800, landlords have less incentive to offer apartments, so they won't be willing to supply as many as they would at the equilibrium rate of $1,000. They will choose point *A* on the supply curve, offering only 1.8 million apartments for rent, 200,000 fewer than in the unregulated market. At the same time, more people will want to rent apartments at a price of $800 than at the equilibrium price of $1,000; as shown at point *B* on the demand curve, at a monthly rent of $800 the quantity of apartments demanded rises to 2.2 million, 200,000 more than in the unregulated market and 400,000 more than are actually available at the price of $800. So there is now a persistent shortage of rental housing: at that price, 400,000 more people want to rent than are able to find apartments.

Do price ceilings always cause shortages? No. If a price ceiling is set above the equilibrium price, it won't have any effect. Suppose that the equilibrium rental rate on apartments is $1,000 per month and the city government sets a ceiling of $1,200. Who cares? In this case, the price ceiling won't be *binding*—it won't actually constrain market behavior—and it will have no effect.

## How a Price Ceiling Causes Inefficiency

The housing shortage shown in Figure 4-2 is not merely annoying: like any shortage induced by price controls, it can be seriously harmful because it leads to inefficiency. In other words, there are gains from trade that go unrealized. Rent control, like all price ceilings, creates inefficiency in at least four distinct ways. It reduces the quantity of apartments rented below the efficient level; it typically leads to misallocation of apartments among would-be renters; it leads to wasted time and effort as people search for apartments; and it leads landlords to maintain apartments in inefficiently low quality or condition. In addition to inefficiency, price ceilings give rise to illegal behavior as people try to circumvent them.

**Inefficiently Low Quantity** Because a price ceiling reduces the price of a good, it reduces the quantity that sellers are willing to supply. Buyers can't buy more units of a good than sellers are willing to sell; a price ceiling reduces the quantity of a good bought and sold below the market equilibrium quantity. Because rent control reduces the number of apartments supplied, it reduces the number of apartments rented, too. The low quantity sold is an inefficiency due to missed opportunities: price ceilings prevent mutually beneficial transactions from occurring, transactions that would benefit both buyers and sellers. Figure 4-3 shows the inefficiently low quantity of apartments supplied with rent control.

**Inefficient Allocation to Consumers** Rent control doesn't just lead to too few apartments being available. It can also lead to misallocation of the apartments that are available: people who badly need a place to live may not be able to find an apartment, but some apartments may be occupied by people with much less urgent needs.

In the case shown in Figure 4-2, 2.2 million people would like to rent an apartment at $800 per month, but only 1.8 million apartments are available. Of those 2.2 million who are seeking an apartment, some want an apartment badly and are willing to pay a high price to get one. Others have a less urgent need and are only willing to pay a low price, perhaps because they have alternative housing. An efficient allocation of apartments would reflect these differences: people who really want an apartment will get one and people who aren't all that anxious to find an apartment won't. In an inefficient distribution of apartments, the opposite will happen: some people who are not especially anxious to find an apartment will get one and others who are very anxious to find an apartment won't.

Because people usually get apartments through luck or personal connections under rent control, it generally results in an **inefficient allocation to consumers** of the few apartments available.

To see the inefficiency involved, consider the plight of the Lees, a family with young children who have no alternative housing and would be willing to pay up to $1,500 for an apartment—but are unable to find one. Also consider George, a retiree who lives most of the year in Florida but still has a lease on the New York apartment he moved into 40 years ago. George pays $800 per month for this

> Price ceilings often lead to inefficiency in the form of **inefficient allocation to consumers:** some people who want the good badly and are willing to pay a high price don't get it, and some who care relatively little about the good and are only willing to pay a low price do get it.

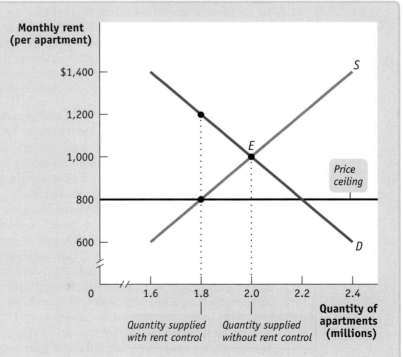

**FIGURE  4-3  A Price Ceiling Causes Inefficiently Low Quantity**

A price ceiling reduces the quantity supplied below the market equilibrium quantity. Because buyers can't buy more units of a good than sellers are willing to sell, a price ceiling reduces the quantity of a good bought and sold.

Quantity supplied with rent control

Quantity supplied without rent control

Price ceilings typically lead to inefficiency in the form of **wasted resources:** people expend money, effort, and time to cope with the shortages caused by the price ceiling.

Price ceilings often lead to inefficiency in that the goods being offered are of **inefficiently low quality:** sellers offer low-quality goods at a low price even though buyers would prefer a higher quality at a higher price.

apartment, but if the rent were even slightly more—say, $850—he would give it up and stay with his children when he is in New York.

This allocation of apartments—George has one and the Lees do not—is a missed opportunity: there is a way to make the Lees and George both better off at no additional cost. The Lees would be happy to pay George, say, $1,200 a month to sublease his apartment, which he would happily accept since the apartment is worth no more than $849 a month to him. George would prefer the money he gets from the Lees to keeping his apartment; the Lees would prefer to have the apartment rather than the money. So both would be made better off by this transaction—and nobody else would be made worse off.

Generally, if people who really want apartments could sublease them from people who are less eager to live there, both those who gain apartments and those who trade their occupancy for money would be better off. However, subletting is illegal under rent control because it would occur at prices above the price ceiling.

The fact that subletting is illegal doesn't mean it never happens. In fact, chasing down illegal subletting is a major business for New York private investigators. An article in the *New York Times* described how private investigators use hidden cameras and other tricks to prove that the legal tenants in rent-controlled apartments actually live in the suburbs, or even in other states, and have sublet their apartments at two or three times the controlled rent. This subletting is a kind of illegal activity, which we will discuss shortly. For now, just note that landlords and legal agencies actively discourage the practice of illegal subletting. As a result, the problem of inefficient allocation of apartments remains.

**Wasted Resources** Another reason a price ceiling causes inefficiency is that it leads to **wasted resources:** people expend money, effort, and time to cope with the shortages caused by the price ceiling. Back in 1979, U.S. price controls on gasoline led to shortages that forced millions of Americans to spend hours each week waiting in lines at gas stations. The opportunity cost of the time spent in gas lines—the wages not earned, the leisure time not enjoyed—constituted wasted resources from the point of view of consumers and of the economy as a whole.

Because of rent control, the Lees will spend all their spare time for several months searching for an apartment, time they would rather have spent working or in family activities. That is, there is an opportunity cost to the Lees' prolonged search for an apartment—the leisure or income they had to forgo. If the market for apartments worked freely, the Lees would quickly find an apartment at the equilibrium rent of $1,000, leaving them time to earn more or to enjoy themselves—an outcome that would make them better off without making anyone else worse off. Again, rent control creates missed opportunities.

**Inefficiently Low Quality** Yet another way a price ceiling creates inefficiency is by causing goods to be of inefficiently low quality. **Inefficiently low quality** means that sellers offer low-quality goods at a low price even though buyers would rather have higher quality and would be willing to pay a higher price for it.

Again, consider rent control. Landlords have no incentive to provide better conditions because they cannot raise rents to cover their repair costs but are able to find tenants easily. In many cases, tenants would be willing to pay much more for improved conditions than it would cost for the landlord to provide them—for example, the upgrade of an antiquated electrical system that cannot safely run air conditioners or computers. But any additional payment for such improvements would be legally considered a rent increase, which is prohibited. Indeed, rent-controlled apartments are notoriously badly maintained, rarely painted, subject to frequent electrical and plumbing problems, sometimes even hazardous to inhabit. As one former manager of Manhattan buildings described: "At unregulated apartments we'd do most things that the tenants requested. But on the rent-regulated units, we did absolutely only what the law required. . . . We had a perverse incentive to make those tenants unhappy."

## FOR INQUIRING MINDS

### RENT CONTROL, MUMBAI STYLE

How far would you go to keep a rent-controlled apartment? Some tenants in the city of Mumbai, India, went very far indeed. According to a *Wall Street Journal* article, three people were killed when four floors in a rent-controlled apartment building in Mumbai collapsed. Despite demands by the city government to vacate the deteriorated building, 58 other tenants refused to leave. They stayed put even after having their electricity and water shut off, being locked out of their apartments, and surviving a police raid. Tenants camped out on the building's veranda, vowing not to give up.

Not all of these tenants were desperately poor and lacking other options. One rent-controlled tenant, the owner of a thriving textile business, paid a total of $8.50 a month for a spacious two-bedroom apartment. (Luxury apartments in Mumbai can go for thousands of dollars a month.)

Although it's a world away, the dynamics of rent control in Mumbai are a lot like those in New York (although Mumbai has clearly had a much more extreme experience). Rent control began in Mumbai in 1947, to address a critical shortage of housing caused by a flood of refugees fleeing conflict between Hindus and

Muslims. Clearly intended to be a temporary measure, it was so popular politically that it has been extended 20 times and now applies to about 60% of the buildings in the city's center. Tenants pass apartments on to their heirs or sell the right to occupy to other tenants.

Despite the fact that home prices in Mumbai surged more than 60% between 2007 and 2010, landlords of rent-controlled buildings have suffered financially, with the result that across the city prime buildings have been abandoned to decay, even though half of the city's 12 million residents live in slums because of a lack of new housing.

---

This whole situation is a missed opportunity—some tenants would be happy to pay for better conditions, and landlords would be happy to provide them for payment. But such an exchange would occur only if the market were allowed to operate freely.

**Black Markets**  And that leads us to a last aspect of price ceilings: the incentive they provide for illegal activities, specifically the emergence of **black markets.** We have already described one kind of black market activity—illegal subletting by tenants. But it does not stop there. Clearly, there is a temptation for a landlord to say to a potential tenant, "Look, you can have the place if you slip me an extra few hundred in cash each month"—and for the tenant to agree if he or she is one of those people who would be willing to pay much more than the maximum legal rent.

What's wrong with black markets? In general, it's a bad thing if people break any law, because it encourages disrespect for the law in general. Worse yet, in this case illegal activity worsens the position of those who are honest. If the Lees are scrupulous about upholding the rent-control law but other people—who may need an apartment less than the Lees—are willing to bribe landlords, the Lees may never find an apartment.

## So Why Are There Price Ceilings?

We have seen three common results of price ceilings:

- A persistent shortage of the good
- Inefficiency arising from this persistent shortage in the form of inefficiently low quantity transacted, inefficient allocation of the good to consumers, resources wasted in searching for the good, and the inefficiently low quality of the good offered for sale
- The emergence of illegal, black market activity

Given these unpleasant consequences, why do governments still sometimes impose price ceilings? Why does rent control, in particular, persist in New York?

One answer is that although price ceilings may have adverse effects, they do benefit some people. In practice, New York's rent-control rules—which are more complex than our simple model—hurt most residents but give a small minority

A **black market** is a market in which goods or services are bought and sold illegally—either because it is illegal to sell them at all or because the prices charged are legally prohibited by a price ceiling.

of renters much cheaper housing than they would get in an unregulated market. And those who benefit from the controls are typically better organized and more vocal than those who are harmed by them.

Also, when price ceilings have been in effect for a long time, buyers may not have a realistic idea of what would happen without them. In our previous example, the rental rate in an unregulated market (Figure 4-1) would be only 25% higher than in the regulated market (Figure 4-2): $1,000 instead of $800. But how would renters know that? Indeed, they might have heard about black market transactions at much higher prices—the Lees or some other family paying George $1,200 or more—and would not realize that these black market prices are much higher than the price that would prevail in a fully unregulated market.

A last answer is that government officials often do not understand supply and demand analysis! It is a great mistake to suppose that economic policies in the real world are always sensible or well informed.

## ECONOMICS ▶ IN ACTION

### HUNGER AND PRICE CONTROLS IN VENEZUELA

Venezuela's food shortages offer a lesson in why price ceilings, however well intentioned, are usually never a good idea.

**S**omething was rotten in the state of Venezuela—specifically, 30,000 tons of decomposing food in Puerto Cabello in June 2010. The discovery was particularly embarrassing for President Hugo Chávez, who has governed Venezuela since 1998. He came to power on a platform denouncing the country's economic elite and promising policies favoring the poor and working classes. Among those policies were price controls on basic foodstuffs, which led to shortages that began in 2003 and had become severe by 2006.

Generous government policies led to higher spending by consumers and sharply rising prices for goods that weren't subject to price controls or which were bought on the black market. The result was a big increase in the demand for price-controlled goods. But a sharp decline in the value of Venezuela's currency led to a fall in imports of foreign food, and the result was empty shelves in the nation's food stores.

As the shortages persisted and inflation of food prices worsened (in the first five months of 2010, the prices of food and drink rose by 21%), Chávez declared "economic war" on the private sector, berating it for "hoarding and smuggling." The government expropriated farms, food manufacturers and grocery stores, creating in their place government-owned ones, which were corrupt and inefficient—it was the government-owned food-distribution company, PDVAL, that left tens of thousands of tons of food to rot in Venezuelan ports. Food production has also fallen, and Venezuela must now import 70% of its food.

Not surprisingly, the shelves have been far more bare in government-run grocery stores than in those still in private hands. The food shortages have been so severe that they have greatly diminished Chávez's popularity among working-class Venezuelans and halted his expropriation plans. As an old Venezuelan saying has it, "Love with hunger doesn't last."

### ▼ Quick Review

- **Price controls** take the form of either legal maximum prices—**price ceilings**—or legal minimum prices—**price floors.**

- A price ceiling below the equilibrium price benefits successful buyers but causes predictable adverse effects such as persistent shortages, which lead to four types of inefficiencies: inefficiently low quantity transacted, **inefficient allocation to consumers, wasted resources,** and **inefficiently low quality.**

- Price ceilings also lead to **black markets,** as buyers and sellers attempt to evade the price controls.

## CHECK YOUR UNDERSTANDING  4-1

1. On game days, homeowners near Middletown University's stadium used to rent parking spaces in their driveways to fans at a going rate of $11. A new town ordinance now sets a maximum parking fee of $7. Use the accompanying supply and demand diagram to explain how each of the following corresponds to a price-ceiling concept.

a. Some homeowners now think it's not worth the hassle to rent out spaces.

b. Some fans who used to carpool to the game now drive alone.

c. Some fans can't find parking and leave without seeing the game.

Explain how each of the following adverse effects arises from the price ceiling.

d. Some fans now arrive several hours early to find parking.

e. Friends of homeowners near the stadium regularly attend games, even if they aren't big fans. But some serious fans have given up because of the parking situation.

f. Some homeowners rent spaces for more than $7 but pretend that the buyers are nonpaying friends or family.

2. True or false? Explain your answer. A price ceiling below the equilibrium price of an otherwise efficient market does the following:

a. Increases quantity supplied

b. Makes some people who want to consume the good worse off

c. Makes all producers worse off

Solutions appear at back of book.

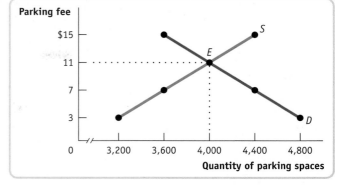

# Price Floors

Sometimes governments intervene to push market prices up instead of down. *Price floors* have been widely legislated for agricultural products, such as wheat and milk, as a way to support the incomes of farmers. Historically, there were also price floors on such services as trucking and air travel, although these were phased out by the U.S. government in the 1970s. If you have ever worked in a fast-food restaurant, you are likely to have encountered a price floor: governments in the United States and many other countries maintain a lower limit on the hourly wage rate of a worker's labor; that is, a floor on the price of labor—called the **minimum wage.**

Just like price ceilings, price floors are intended to help some people but generate predictable and undesirable side effects. Figure 4-4 shows hypothetical supply and demand curves for butter. Left to itself, the market would move to equilibrium at point *E*, with 10 million pounds of butter bought and sold at a price of $1 per pound.

Now suppose that the government, in order to help dairy farmers, imposes a price floor on butter of $1.20 per pound. Its effects are shown in Figure 4-5, where the line at $1.20 represents the price floor. At a price of $1.20 per pound, producers would want to supply 12 million pounds (point *B* on the supply curve) but consumers would want to buy only 9 million pounds (point *A* on the demand curve). So the price floor leads to a persistent surplus of 3 million pounds of butter.

Does a price floor always lead to an unwanted surplus? No. Just as in the case of a price ceiling, the floor may not be binding—that is, it may be irrelevant. If the equilibrium price of butter is $1 per pound but the floor is set at only $0.80, the floor has no effect.

But suppose that a price floor is binding: what happens to the unwanted surplus? The answer depends on government policy. In the case of agricultural price floors, governments buy up unwanted surplus. As a result, the U.S. government has at times found itself warehousing thousands of tons of butter, cheese, and other farm products. (The European Commission, which administers price floors for a number of European countries, once found itself the owner of a so-called butter mountain, equal in weight to the entire population of Austria.) The government then has to find a way to dispose of these unwanted goods.

Some countries pay exporters to sell products at a loss overseas; this is standard procedure for the European Union. The United States gives surplus food

The **minimum wage** is a legal floor on the wage rate, which is the market price of labor.

FIGURE **4-4** The Market for Butter in the Absence of Government Controls

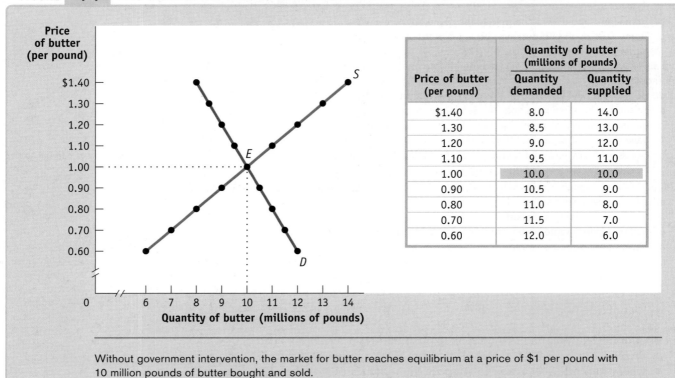

| Price of butter (per pound) | Quantity of butter (millions of pounds) | |
| --- | --- | --- |
| | Quantity demanded | Quantity supplied |
| $1.40 | 8.0 | 14.0 |
| 1.30 | 8.5 | 13.0 |
| 1.20 | 9.0 | 12.0 |
| 1.10 | 9.5 | 11.0 |
| 1.00 | 10.0 | 10.0 |
| 0.90 | 10.5 | 9.0 |
| 0.80 | 11.0 | 8.0 |
| 0.70 | 11.5 | 7.0 |
| 0.60 | 12.0 | 6.0 |

Without government intervention, the market for butter reaches equilibrium at a price of $1 per pound with 10 million pounds of butter bought and sold.

away to schools, which use the products in school lunches. In some cases, governments have actually destroyed the surplus production. To avoid the problem of dealing with the unwanted surplus, the U.S. government typically pays farmers not to produce the products at all.

FIGURE **4-5** The Effects of a Price Floor

The black horizontal line represents the government-imposed price floor of $1.20 per pound of butter. The quantity of butter demanded falls to 9 million pounds, and the quantity supplied rises to 12 million pounds, generating a persistent surplus of 3 million pounds of butter.

When the government is not prepared to purchase the unwanted surplus, a price floor means that would-be sellers cannot find buyers. This is what happens when there is a price floor on the wage rate paid for an hour of labor, the minimum wage: when the minimum wage is above the equilibrium wage rate, some people who are willing to work—that is, sell labor—cannot find buyers—that is, employers—willing to give them jobs.

## How a Price Floor Causes Inefficiency

The persistent surplus that results from a price floor creates missed opportunities—inefficiencies—that resemble those created by the shortage that results from a price ceiling. These include an inefficiently low quantity transacted, inefficient allocation of sales among sellers, wasted resources, inefficiently high quality, and the temptation to break the law by selling below the legal price.

**Inefficiently Low Quantity**  Because a price floor raises the price of a good to consumers, it reduces the quantity of that good demanded; because sellers can't sell more units of a good than buyers are willing to buy, a price floor reduces the quantity of a good bought and sold below the market equilibrium quantity. Notice that this is the *same* effect as a price ceiling. You might be tempted to think that a price floor and a price ceiling have opposite effects, but both have the effect of reducing the quantity of a good bought and sold (see Pitfalls at right).

As in the case of a price ceiling, the low quantity sold is an inefficiency due to missed opportunities: price floors prevent mutually beneficial transactions from occurring, transactions that would benefit both buyers and sellers. Figure 4-6 shows the inefficiently low quantity of butter sold with a price floor on the price of butter.

**PITFALLS**

**CEILINGS, FLOORS, AND QUANTITIES**
A price ceiling pushes the price of a good *down*. A price floor pushes the price of a good *up*. So it's easy to assume that the effects of a price floor are the opposite of the effects of a price ceiling. In particular, if a price ceiling reduces the quantity of a good bought and sold, doesn't a price floor increase the quantity?

No, it doesn't. In fact, both floors and ceilings reduce the quantity bought and sold. Why? When the quantity of a good supplied isn't equal to the quantity demanded, the actual quantity sold is determined by the "short side" of the market—whichever quantity is less. If sellers don't want to sell as much as buyers want to buy, it's the sellers who determine the actual quantity sold, because buyers can't force unwilling sellers to sell. If buyers don't want to buy as much as sellers want to sell, it's the buyers who determine the actual quantity sold, because sellers can't force unwilling buyers to buy.

**FIGURE** **4-6** A Price Floor Causes Inefficiently Low Quantity

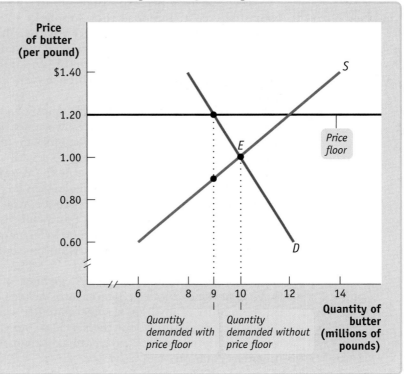

A price floor reduces the quantity demanded below the market equilibrium quantity. Because sellers can't sell more units of a good than buyers are willing to buy, a price floor reduces the quantity of a good bought and sold.

Price floors lead to **inefficient allocation of sales among sellers:** those who would be willing to sell the good at the lowest price are not always those who actually manage to sell it.

Price floors often lead to inefficiency in that goods of **inefficiently high quality** are offered: sellers offer high-quality goods at a high price, even though buyers would prefer a lower quality at a lower price.

**Inefficient Allocation of Sales Among Sellers** Like a price ceiling, a price floor can lead to *inefficient allocation*—but in this case **inefficient allocation of sales among sellers** rather than inefficient allocation to consumers.

An episode from the Belgian movie *Rosetta*, a realistic fictional story, illustrates the problem of inefficient allocation of selling opportunities quite well. Like many European countries, Belgium has a high minimum wage, and jobs for young people are scarce. At one point Rosetta, a young woman who is very anxious to work, loses her job at a fast-food stand because the owner of the stand replaces her with his son—a very reluctant worker. Rosetta would be willing to work for less money, and with the money he would save, the owner could give his son an allowance and let him do something else. But to hire Rosetta for less than the minimum wage would be illegal.

**Wasted Resources** Also like a price ceiling, a price floor generates inefficiency by *wasting resources*. The most graphic examples involve government purchases of the unwanted surpluses of agricultural products caused by price floors. The surplus production is sometimes destroyed, which is pure waste; in other cases the stored produce goes, as officials euphemistically put it, "out of condition" and must be thrown away.

Price floors also lead to wasted time and effort. Consider the minimum wage. Would-be workers who spend many hours searching for jobs, or waiting in line in the hope of getting jobs, play the same role in the case of price floors as hapless families searching for apartments in the case of price ceilings.

**Inefficiently High Quality** Again like price ceilings, price floors lead to inefficiency in the quality of goods produced.

We saw that when there is a price ceiling, suppliers produce products that are of inefficiently low quality: buyers prefer higher-quality products and are willing to pay for them, but sellers refuse to improve the quality of their products because the price ceiling prevents their being compensated for doing so. This same logic applies to price floors, but in reverse: suppliers offer goods of **inefficiently high quality.**

How can this be? Isn't high quality a good thing? Yes, but only if it is worth the cost. Suppose that suppliers spend a lot to make goods of very high quality but that this quality isn't worth much to consumers, who would rather receive the money spent on that quality in the form of a lower price. This represents a missed opportunity: suppliers and buyers could make a mutually beneficial deal in which buyers got goods of lower quality for a much lower price.

A good example of the inefficiency of excessive quality comes from the days when transatlantic airfares were set artificially high by international treaty. Forbidden to compete for customers by offering lower ticket prices, airlines instead offered expensive services, like lavish in-flight meals that went largely uneaten. At one point the regulators tried to restrict this practice by defining maximum service standards—for example, that snack service should consist of no more than a sandwich. One airline then introduced what it called a "Scandinavian Sandwich," a towering affair that forced the convening of another conference to define *sandwich*. All of this was wasteful, especially considering that what passengers really wanted was less food and lower airfares.

Since the deregulation of U.S. airlines in the 1970s, American passengers have experienced a large decrease in ticket prices accompanied by a decrease in the quality of in-flight service—smaller seats, lower-quality food, and so on. Everyone complains about the service—but thanks to lower fares, the number of people flying on U.S. carriers has grown several hundred percent since airline deregulation.

**Illegal Activity** Finally, like price ceilings, price floors provide incentives for illegal activity. For example, in countries where the minimum wage is far above the equilibrium wage rate, workers desperate for jobs sometimes agree to work off the books for employers who conceal their employment from the government—or bribe the government inspectors. This practice, known in Europe as "black labor," is especially common in Southern European countries such as Italy and Spain (see the upcoming Economics in Action).

## So Why Are There Price Floors?

To sum up, a price floor creates various negative side effects:

- A persistent surplus of the good
- Inefficiency arising from the persistent surplus in the form of inefficiently low quantity transacted, inefficient allocation of sales among sellers, wasted resources, and an inefficiently high level of quality offered by suppliers
- The temptation to engage in illegal activity, particularly bribery and corruption of government officials

So why do governments impose price floors when they have so many negative side effects? The reasons are similar to those for imposing price ceilings. Government officials often disregard warnings about the consequences of price floors either because they believe that the relevant market is poorly described by the supply and demand model or, more often, because they do not understand the model. Above all, just as price ceilings are often imposed because they benefit some influential buyers of a good, price floors are often imposed because they benefit some influential sellers.

## CHECK OUT OUR LOW, LOW WAGES!

The minimum wage rate in the United States, as you can see in this graph, is actually quite low compared with that in other rich countries. Since minimum wages are set in national currency—the British minimum wage is set in British pounds, the French minimum wage is set in euros, and so on—the comparison depends on the exchange rate on any given day. As of April 15, 2011, Australia had a minimum wage over twice as high as the U.S. rate, with France, Canada, and Ireland not far behind. You can see one effect of this difference in the supermarket checkout line. In the United States there is usually someone to bag your groceries—someone typically paid the minimum wage or at best slightly more. In Europe, where hiring a bagger is a lot more expensive, you're almost always expected to do the bagging yourself.

| | Minimum wage (per hour) |
|---|---|
| Australia | A$15.00 = US$15.84 |
| France | €8.86 = US$12.80 |
| Canada* | C$11.00* = US$11.44 |
| Ireland | €7.65 = US$11.05 |
| Britain | £5.93 = US$9.68 |
| United States | $7.25 |

*Source:* National Employment Rights Authority (Ireland); Ministère du Travail, de l'Emploi et de la Santé (France); Fair Work Australia (Australia); Department for Business, Innovation and Skills (Britain); Human Resources and Skills Development Canada (Canada); Department of Labor (U.S.); Federal Reserve Bank of St. Louis (exchange rates as of 04/15/2011).

*The Canadian minimum wage varies by province from C$8.00 to C$11.00.

## ECONOMICS > IN ACTION

### "BLACK LABOR" IN SOUTHERN EUROPE

The best-known example of a price floor is the minimum wage. Most economists believe, however, that the minimum wage has relatively little effect on the job market in the United States, mainly because the floor is set so low. In 1964 the U.S. minimum wage was 53% of the average wage of blue-collar production workers; by 2010, despite several recent increases, it had fallen to about 44%.

The generous minimum wage in many European countries has contributed to a high rate of unemployment and the flourishing of an illegal labor market.

The situation is different, however, in many European countries, where minimum wages have been set much higher than in the United States. This has happened despite the fact that workers in most European countries are somewhat less productive than their American counterparts, which means that the equilibrium wage in Europe—the wage that would clear the labor market—is probably lower in Europe than in the United States. Moreover, European countries often require employers to pay for health and retirement benefits, which are more extensive and so more costly than comparable American benefits. These mandated benefits make the actual cost of employing a European worker considerably more than the worker's paycheck.

The result is that in Europe the price floor on labor is definitely binding: the minimum wage is well above the wage rate that would make the quantity of labor supplied by workers equal to the quantity of labor demanded by employers.

The persistent surplus that results from this price floor appears in the form of high unemployment—millions of workers, especially young workers, seek jobs but cannot find them.

In countries where the enforcement of labor laws is lax, however, there is a second, entirely predictable result: widespread evasion of the law. In both Italy and Spain, officials believe there are hundreds of thousands, if not millions, of workers who are employed by companies that pay them less than the legal minimum, fail to provide the required health and retirement benefits, or both. In many cases the jobs are simply unreported: Spanish economists estimate that about a third of the country's reported unemployed are in the black labor market—working at unreported jobs. In fact, Spaniards waiting to collect checks from the unemployment office have been known to complain about the long lines that keep them from getting back to work!

Employers in these countries have also found legal ways to evade the wage floor. For example, Italy's labor regulations apply only to companies with 15 or more workers. This gives a big cost advantage to small Italian firms, many of which remain small in order to avoid paying higher wages and benefits. And sure enough, in some Italian industries there is an astonishing proliferation of tiny companies. For example, one of Italy's most successful industries is the manufacture of fine woolen cloth, centered in the Prato region. The average textile firm in that region employs only four workers!

### ▼ Quick Review

- The most familiar price floor is the **minimum wage.** Price floors are also commonly imposed on agricultural goods.

- A price floor above the equilibrium price benefits successful sellers but causes predictable adverse effects such as a persistent surplus, which leads to four kinds of inefficiencies: inefficiently low quantity transacted, **inefficient allocation of sales among sellers,** wasted resources, and **inefficiently high quality.**

- Price floors encourage illegal activity, such as workers who work off the books, often leading to official corruption.

### CHECK YOUR UNDERSTANDING   4-2

1. The state legislature mandates a price floor for gasoline of $P_F$ per gallon. Assess the following statements and illustrate your answer using the figure provided.

**a.** Proponents of the law claim it will increase the income of gas station owners. Opponents claim it will hurt gas station owners because they will lose customers.

**b.** Proponents claim consumers will be better off because gas stations will provide better service. Opponents claim consumers will be generally worse off because they prefer to buy gas at cheaper prices.

**c.** Proponents claim that they are helping gas station owners without hurting anyone else. Opponents claim that consumers are hurt and will end up doing things like buying gas in a nearby state or on the black market.

Solutions appear at back of book.

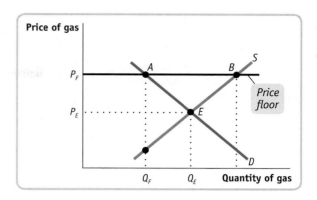

# Controlling Quantities

In the 1930s, New York City instituted a system of licensing for taxicabs: only taxis with a "medallion" were allowed to pick up passengers. Because this system was intended to assure quality, medallion owners were supposed to maintain certain standards, including safety and cleanliness. A total of 11,787 medallions were issued, with taxi owners paying $10 for each medallion.

In 1995, there were still only 11,787 licensed taxicabs in New York, even though the city had meanwhile become the financial capital of the world, a place where hundreds of thousands of people in a hurry tried to hail a cab every day. (An additional 400 medallions were issued in 1995, and after several rounds of sales of additional medallions, today there are 13,128 medallions.)

The result of this restriction on the number of taxis was that a New York City taxi medallion became very valuable: if you wanted to operate a taxi in New York, you had to lease a medallion from someone else or buy one for a going price of several hundred thousand dollars.

It turns out that this story is not unique; other cities introduced similar medallion systems in the 1930s and, like New York, have issued few new medallions since. In San Francisco and Boston, as in New York, taxi medallions trade for six-figure prices.

A taxi medallion system is a form of **quantity control,** or **quota,** by which the government regulates the quantity of a good that can be bought and sold rather than the price at which it is transacted. The total amount of the good that can be transacted under the quantity control is called the **quota limit.** Typically, the government limits quantity in a market by issuing **licenses;** only people with a license can legally supply the good.

A taxi medallion is just such a license. The government of New York City limits the number of taxi rides that can be sold by limiting the number of taxis to only those who hold medallions. There are many other cases of quantity controls, ranging from limits on how much foreign currency (for instance, British pounds or Mexican pesos) people are allowed to buy to the quantity of clams New Jersey fishing boats are allowed to catch. Notice, by the way, that although there are price controls on both sides of the equilibrium price—price ceilings and price floors—in the real world, quantity controls always set an upper, not a lower, limit on quantities. After all, nobody can be forced to buy or sell more than they want to!

Some attempts to control quantities are undertaken for good economic reasons, some for bad ones. In many cases, as we will see, quantity controls introduced to address a temporary problem become politically hard to remove later because the beneficiaries don't want them abolished, even after the original reason for their existence is long gone. But whatever the reasons for such controls, they have certain predictable—and usually undesirable—economic consequences.

A **quantity control,** or **quota,** is an upper limit on the quantity of some good that can be bought or sold. The total amount of the good that can be legally transacted is the **quota limit.**

A **license** gives its owner the right to supply a good.

The **demand price** of a given quantity is the price at which consumers will demand that quantity.

The **supply price** of a given quantity is the price at which producers will supply that quantity.

## The Anatomy of Quantity Controls

To understand why a New York taxi medallion is worth so much money, we consider a simplified version of the market for taxi rides, shown in Figure 4-7. Just as we assumed in the analysis of rent control that all apartments are the same, we now suppose that all taxi rides are the same—ignoring the real-world complication that some taxi rides are longer, and so more expensive, than others. The table in the figure shows supply and demand schedules. The equilibrium—indicated by point *E* in the figure and by the shaded entries in the table—is a fare of $5 per ride, with 10 million rides taken per year. (You'll see in a minute why we present the equilibrium this way.)

The New York medallion system limits the number of taxis, but each taxi driver can offer as many rides as he or she can manage. (Now you know why New York taxi drivers are so aggressive!) To simplify our analysis, however, we will assume that a medallion system limits the number of taxi rides that can legally be given to 8 million per year.

Until now, we have derived the demand curve by answering questions of the form: "How many taxi rides will passengers want to take if the price is $5 per ride?" But it is possible to reverse the question and ask instead: "At what price will consumers want to buy 10 million rides per year?" The price at which consumers want to buy a given quantity—in this case, 10 million rides at $5 per ride—is the **demand price** of that quantity. You can see from the demand schedule in Figure 4-7 that the demand price of 6 million rides is $7 per ride, the demand price of 7 million rides is $6.50 per ride, and so on.

Similarly, the supply curve represents the answer to questions of the form: "How many taxi rides would taxi drivers supply at a price of $5 each?" But we can also reverse this question to ask: "At what price will suppliers be willing to supply 10 million rides per year?" The price at which suppliers will supply a given quantity—in this case, 10 million rides at $5 per ride—is the **supply price** of that quantity. We can see from the supply schedule in Figure 4-7 that the supply

**FIGURE** **4-7** The Market for Taxi Rides in the Absence of Government Controls

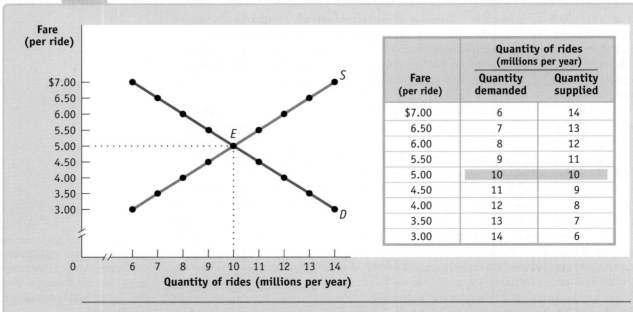

| Fare (per ride) | Quantity of rides (millions per year) | |
| --- | --- | --- |
| | Quantity demanded | Quantity supplied |
| $7.00 | 6 | 14 |
| 6.50 | 7 | 13 |
| 6.00 | 8 | 12 |
| 5.50 | 9 | 11 |
| 5.00 | 10 | 10 |
| 4.50 | 11 | 9 |
| 4.00 | 12 | 8 |
| 3.50 | 13 | 7 |
| 3.00 | 14 | 6 |

Without government intervention, the market reaches equilibrium with 10 million rides taken per year at a fare of $5 per ride.

price of 6 million rides is $3 per ride, the supply price of 7 million rides is $3.50 per ride, and so on.

Now we are ready to analyze a quota. We have assumed that the city government limits the quantity of taxi rides to 8 million per year. Medallions, each of which carries the right to provide a certain number of taxi rides per year, are made available to selected people in such a way that a total of 8 million rides will be provided. Medallion-holders may then either drive their own taxis or rent their medallions to others for a fee.

Figure 4-8 shows the resulting market for taxi rides, with the black vertical line at 8 million rides per year representing the quota limit. Because the quantity of rides is limited to 8 million, consumers must be at point A on the demand curve, corresponding to the shaded entry in the demand schedule: the demand price of 8 million rides is $6 per ride. Meanwhile, taxi drivers must be at point B on the supply curve, corresponding to the shaded entry in the supply schedule: the supply price of 8 million rides is $4 per ride.

But how can the price received by taxi drivers be $4 when the price paid by taxi riders is $6? The answer is that in addition to the market in taxi rides, there is also a market in medallions. Medallion-holders may not always want to drive their taxis: they may be ill or on vacation. Those who do not want to drive their own taxis will sell the right to use the medallion to someone else. So we need to consider two sets of transactions here, and so two prices: (1) the transactions in taxi rides and the price at which these will occur, and (2) the transactions in medallions and the price at which these will occur. It turns out that since we are looking at two markets, the $4 and $6 prices will both be right.

To see how this all works, consider two imaginary New York taxi drivers, Sunil and Harriet. Sunil has a medallion but can't use it because he's recovering from a

---

**FIGURE    4-8    Effect of a Quota on the Market for Taxi Rides**

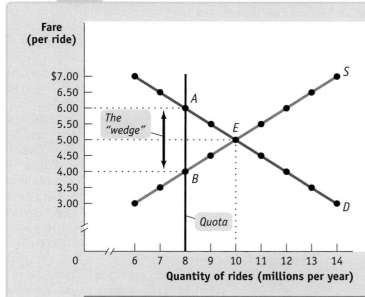

| Fare (per ride) | Quantity of rides (millions per year) | |
|---|---|---|
| | Quantity demanded | Quantity supplied |
| $7.00 | 6 | 14 |
| 6.50 | 7 | 13 |
| 6.00 | 8 | 12 |
| 5.50 | 9 | 11 |
| 5.00 | 10 | 10 |
| 4.50 | 11 | 9 |
| 4.00 | 12 | 8 |
| 3.50 | 13 | 7 |
| 3.00 | 14 | 6 |

The table shows the demand price and the supply price corresponding to each quantity: the price at which that quantity would be demanded and supplied, respectively. The city government imposes a quota of 8 million rides by selling licenses for only 8 million rides, represented by the black vertical line. The price paid by consumers rises to $6 per ride, the demand price of 8 million rides, shown by point A. The supply price of 8 million rides is only $4 per ride, shown by point B. The difference between these two prices is the quota rent per ride, the earnings that accrue to the owner of a license. The quota rent drives a wedge between the demand price and the supply price, and the quota discourages mutually beneficial transactions.

A quantity control, or quota, drives a **wedge** between the demand price and the supply price of a good; that is, the price paid by buyers ends up being higher than that received by sellers.

The difference between the demand and supply price at the quota limit is the **quota rent,** the earnings that accrue to the license-holder from ownership of the right to sell the good. It is equal to the market price of the license when the licenses are traded.

severely sprained wrist. So he's looking to rent his medallion out to someone else. Harriet doesn't have a medallion but would like to rent one. Furthermore, at any point in time there are many other people like Harriet who would like to rent a medallion. Suppose Sunil agrees to rent his medallion to Harriet. To make things simple, assume that any driver can give only one ride per day and that Sunil is renting his medallion to Harriet for one day. What rental price will they agree on?

To answer this question, we need to look at the transactions from the viewpoints of both drivers. Once she has the medallion, Harriet knows she can make $6 per day—the demand price of a ride under the quota. And she is willing to rent the medallion only if she makes at least $4 per day—the supply price of a ride under the quota. So Sunil cannot demand a rent of more than $2—the difference between $6 and $4. And if Harriet offered Sunil less than $2—say, $1.50—there would be other eager drivers willing to offer him more, up to $2. So, in order to get the medallion, Harriet must offer Sunil at least $2. Since the rent can be no more than $2 and no less than $2, it must be exactly $2.

It is no coincidence that $2 is exactly the difference between $6, the demand price of 8 million rides, and $4, the supply price of 8 million rides. In every case in which the supply of a good is legally restricted, there is a **wedge** between the demand price of the quantity transacted and the supply price of the quantity transacted. This wedge, illustrated by the double-headed arrow in Figure 4-8, has a special name: the **quota rent.** It is the earnings that accrue to the license-holder from ownership of a valuable commodity, the license. In the case of Sunil and Harriet, the quota rent of $2 goes to Sunil because he owns the license, and the remaining $4 from the total fare of $6 goes to Harriet.

So Figure 4-8 also illustrates the quota rent in the market for New York taxi rides. The quota limits the quantity of rides to 8 million per year, a quantity at which the demand price of $6 exceeds the supply price of $4. The wedge between these two prices, $2, is the quota rent that results from the restrictions placed on the quantity of taxi rides in this market.

But wait a second. What if Sunil doesn't rent out his medallion? What if he uses it himself? Doesn't this mean that he gets a price of $6? No, not really. Even if Sunil doesn't rent out his medallion, he could have rented it out, which means that the medallion has an *opportunity cost* of $2: if Sunil decides to use his own medallion and drive his own taxi rather than renting his medallion to Harriet, the $2 represents his opportunity cost of not renting out his medallion. That is, the $2 quota rent is now the rental income he forgoes by driving his own taxi.

In effect, Sunil is in two businesses—the taxi-driving business and the medallion-renting business. He makes $4 per ride from driving his taxi and $2 per ride from renting out his medallion. It doesn't make any difference that in this particular case he has rented his medallion to himself! So regardless of whether the medallion owner uses the medallion himself or herself, or rents it to others, it is a valuable asset. And this is represented in the going price for a New York City taxi medallion: in October 2011, it was $694,000. According to Simon Greenbaum, a broker of New York taxi medallions, an owner of a medallion who leases it to a driver can expect to earn about $2,500 per month, or a 3% return—an attractive rate of return compared to other investments.

Notice, by the way, that quotas—like price ceilings and price floors—don't always have a real effect. If the quota were set at 12 million rides—that is, above the equilibrium quantity in an unregulated market—it would have no effect because it would not be binding.

## The Costs of Quantity Controls

Like price controls, quantity controls can have some predictable and undesirable side effects. The first is the by-now-familiar problem of inefficiency due to missed opportunities: quantity controls prevent mutually beneficial transactions from occurring, transactions that would benefit both buyers and sellers. Looking back at Figure 4-8, you can see that starting at the quota limit of 8 million rides, New Yorkers would be willing to pay at least $5.50 per ride for an additional 1 million rides and that taxi drivers would be willing to provide those rides as long as they got at least $4.50 per ride. These are rides that would have taken place if there were no quota limit.

The same is true for the next 1 million rides: New Yorkers would be willing to pay at least $5 per ride when the quantity of rides is increased from 9 to 10 million, and taxi drivers would be willing to provide those rides as long as they got at least $5 per ride. Again, these rides would have occurred without the quota limit.

Only when the market has reached the unregulated market equilibrium quantity of 10 million rides are there no "missed-opportunity rides"—the quota limit of 8 million rides has caused 2 million "missed-opportunity rides."

Generally, *as long as the demand price of a given quantity exceeds the supply price, there is a missed opportunity.* A buyer would be willing to buy the good at a price that the seller would be willing to accept, but such a transaction does not occur because it is forbidden by the quota.

And because there are transactions that people would like to make but are not allowed to, quantity controls generate an incentive to evade them or even to break the law. New York's taxi industry again provides clear examples. Taxi regulation applies only to those drivers who are hailed by passengers on the street. A car service that makes prearranged pickups does not need a medallion. As a result, such hired cars provide much of the service that might otherwise be provided by taxis, as in other cities. In addition, there are substantial numbers of unlicensed cabs that simply defy the law by picking up passengers without a medallion. Because these cabs are illegal, their drivers are completely unregulated, and they generate a disproportionately large share of traffic accidents in New York City.

In fact, in 2004 the hardships caused by the limited number of New York taxis led city leaders to authorize an increase in the number of licensed taxis. In a series of sales, the city sold 900 new medallions, to bring the total number up to the current 13,128 medallions—a move that certainly cheered New York riders.

Dangerous, unlicensed cabs are one cost of quantity controls.

The Queens Ledger/Brooklyn Star Newspaper Group

But those who already owned medallions were less happy with the increase; they understood that the 900 new taxis would reduce or eliminate the shortage of taxis. As a result, taxi drivers anticipated a decline in their revenues because they would no longer always be assured of finding willing customers. And, in turn, the value of a medallion would fall. So to placate the medallion owners, city officials also raised taxi fares: by 25% in 2004, and again—by a smaller percentage—in 2006. Although taxis are now easier to find, a ride now costs more—and that price increase slightly diminished the newfound cheer of New York taxi riders.

In sum, quantity controls typically create the following undesirable side effects:

• Inefficiencies, or missed opportunities, in the form of mutually beneficial transactions that don't occur

• Incentives for illegal activities

## ECONOMICS ▶ IN ACTION

### THE CLAMS OF JERSEY SHORE

Forget the refineries along the Jersey Turnpike or reality TV shows; one industry that New Jersey *really* dominates is clam fishing. In 2009 the Garden State supplied 39% of the country's quahogs, which are used to make clam chowder, and 71% of the surf clams, whose tongues are used in fried-clam dinners.

Quotas helped to protect the clam beds of New Jersey but also transformed the clamming industry because boat owners found it more profitable to rent and sell licenses than to fish.

In the 1980s, however, excessive fishing threatened to wipe out New Jersey's clam beds. To save the resource, the U.S. government introduced a clam quota, which sets an overall limit on the number of bushels of clams that may be caught and allocates licenses to owners of fishing boats based on their historical catches.

Notice, by the way, that this is an example of a quota that is probably justified by broader economic and environmental considerations—unlike the New York taxicab quota, which has long since lost any economic rationale. Still, whatever its rationale, the New Jersey clam quota works the same way as any other quota.

Once the quota system was established, many boat owners stopped fishing for clams. They realized that rather than operate a boat part time, it was more profitable to sell or rent their licenses to someone else, who could then assemble enough licenses to operate a boat full time. Today, there are about 50 New Jersey boats fishing for clams; the license required to operate one is worth more than the boat itself.

### CHECK YOUR UNDERSTANDING 4-3

1. Suppose that the supply and demand for taxi rides is given by Figure 4-7 but the quota is set at 6 million rides instead of 8 million. Find the following and indicate them on Figure 4-7.
   **a.** The price of a ride
   **b.** The quota rent
   **c.** Suppose the quota limit on taxi rides is increased to 9 million. What happens to the quota rent?

2. Assume that the quota limit is 8 million rides. Suppose demand decreases due to a decline in tourism. What is the smallest parallel leftward shift in demand that would result in the quota no longer having an effect on the market? Illustrate your answer using Figure 4-7.

Solutions appear at back of book.

▼ **Quick Review**

● **Quantity controls,** or **quotas,** are government-imposed limits on how much of a good may be bought or sold. The quantity allowed for sale is the **quota limit.** The government then issues a **license**—the right to sell a given quantity of a good under the quota.

● When the quota limit is smaller than the equilibrium quantity in an unregulated market, the **demand price** is higher than the **supply price**—there is a **wedge** between them at the quota limit.

● This wedge is the **quota rent,** the earnings that accrue to the license-holder from ownership of the right to sell the good—whether by actually supplying the good or by renting the license to someone else. The market price of a license equals the quota rent.

● Like price controls, quantity controls create inefficiencies and encourage illegal activity.

# BUSINESS CASE : Medallion Financial: Cruising Right Along

Owaki/Kulla/Corbis

Back in 1937, before New York City froze its number of taxi medallions, Andrew Murstein's immigrant grandfather bought his first one for $10. Over time, the grandfather accumulated 500 medallions, which he rented to other drivers. Those 500 taxi medallions became the foundation for Medallion Financial: the company that would eventually pass to Andrew, its current president.

With a market value of over $200 million in late 2011, Medallion Financial has shifted its major line of business from renting out medallions to financing the purchase of new ones, lending money to those who want to buy a medallion but don't have the sizable amount of cash required to do so. Murstein believes that he is helping people who, like his Polish immigrant grandfather, want to buy a piece of the American dream.

Andrew Murstein carefully watches the value of a New York City taxi medallion: the more one costs, the more demand there is for loans from Medallion Financial, and the more interest the company makes on the loan. A loan from Medallion Financial is secured by the value of the medallion itself. If the borrower is unable to repay the loan, Medallion Financial takes possession of his or her medallion and resells it to offset the cost of the loan default. As of 2011, the value of a medallion has risen faster than stocks, oil, and gold. Over the past two decades, from 1990 through fall 2011, the value of a medallion rose 440% compared to only 255% for an index of stocks.

But medallion prices can fluctuate dramatically, threatening profits. During periods of a very strong economy, such as 1999 and 2001, the price of New York taxi medallions fell as drivers found jobs in other sectors. When the New York economy tanked in the aftermath of 9/11, the price of a medallion fell to $180,000, its lowest level in 12 years. In 2004, medallion owners were concerned about the impending sale by the New York City Taxi and Limousine Commission of an additional 900 medallions. As Peter Hernandez, a worried New York cabdriver who financed his medallion with a loan from Medallion Financial, said at the time: "If they pump new taxis into the industry, it devalues my medallion. It devalues my daily income, too."

Yet Murstein has always been optimistic that medallions would hold their value. He believed that a 25% fare increase would offset potential losses in their value caused by the sale of new medallions. In addition, more medallions would mean more loans for his company. As of 2011, Murstein's optimism had been justified. Because of the financial crisis of 2007–2009, many New York companies cut back the limousine services they ordinarily provided to their employees, forcing them to take taxis instead. As a result, the price of a medallion rose to an astonishing $694,000 in October 2011. And investors have noticed the value in Medallion Financial's line of business: from November 2010 to November 2011, shares of Medallion Financial have risen 44%.

## QUESTIONS FOR THOUGHT

1. How does Medallion Financial benefit from the restriction on the number of New York taxi medallions?

2. What will be the effect on Medallion Financial if New York companies resume widespread use of limousine services for their employees? What is the economic motivation that prompts companies to offer this perk to their employees? (Note that it is very difficult and expensive to own a personal car in New York City.)

3. Predict the effect on Medallion Financial's business if New York City eliminates restrictions on the number of taxis.

## SUMMARY

1. Even when a market is efficient, governments often intervene to pursue greater fairness or to please a powerful interest group. Interventions can take the form of **price controls** or quantity controls, both of which generate predictable and undesirable side effects consisting of various forms of inefficiency and illegal activity.

2. A **price ceiling,** a maximum market price below the equilibrium price, benefits successful buyers but creates persistent shortages. Because the price is maintained below the equilibrium price, the quantity demanded is increased and the quantity supplied is decreased compared to the equilibrium quantity. This leads to predictable problems: inefficiencies in the form of inefficiently low quantity transacted, **inefficient allocation to consumers, wasted resources,** and **inefficiently low quality.** It also encourages illegal activity as people turn to **black markets** to get the good. Because of these problems, price ceilings have generally lost favor as an economic policy tool. But some governments continue to impose them either because they don't understand the effects or because the price ceilings benefit some influential group.

3. A **price floor,** a minimum market price above the equilibrium price, benefits successful sellers but creates persistent surplus. Because the price is maintained above the equilibrium price, the quantity

demanded is decreased and the quantity supplied is increased compared to the equilibrium quantity. This leads to predictable problems: inefficiencies in the form of inefficiently low quantity transacted, **inefficient allocation of sales among sellers,** wasted resources, and **inefficiently high quality.** It also encourages illegal activity and black markets. The most well known kind of price floor is the **minimum wage,** but price floors are also commonly applied to agricultural products.

4. **Quantity controls,** or **quotas,** limit the quantity of a good that can be bought or sold. The quantity allowed for sale is the **quota limit.** The government issues **licenses** to individuals, the right to sell a given quantity of the good. The owner of a license earns a **quota rent,** earnings that accrue from ownership of the right to sell the good. It is equal to the difference between the **demand price** at the quota limit, what consumers are willing to pay for that quantity, and the **supply price** at the quota limit, what suppliers are willing to accept for that quantity. Economists say that a quota drives a **wedge** between the demand price and the supply price; this wedge is equal to the quota rent. Quantity controls lead to inefficiencies in the form of mutually beneficial transactions that do not occur in addition to encouraging illegal activity.

## KEY TERMS

Price controls, p. 102
Price ceiling, p. 102
Price floor, p. 102
Inefficient allocation to consumers, p. 105
Wasted resources, p. 106
Inefficiently low quality, p. 106

Black markets, p. 107
Minimum wage, p. 109
Inefficient allocation of sales among sellers, p. 112
Inefficiently high quality, p. 112
Quantity control, p. 115
Quota, p. 115

Quota limit, p. 115
License, p. 115
Demand price, p. 116
Supply price, p. 116
Wedge, p. 118
Quota rent, p. 118

## PROBLEMS

1. Suppose it is decided that rent control in New York City will be abolished and that market rents will now prevail. Assume that all rental units are identical and so are offered at the same rent. To address the plight of residents who may be unable to pay the market rent, an income supplement will be paid to all low-income households equal to the difference between the old controlled rent and the new market rent.

   a. Use a diagram to show the effect on the rental market of the elimination of rent control. What will happen to the quality and quantity of rental housing supplied?

   b. Use a second diagram to show the additional effect of the income-supplement policy on the market.

   What effect does it have on the market rent and quantity of rental housing supplied in comparison to your answers to part a?

   c. Are tenants better or worse off as a result of these policies? Are landlords better or worse off?

   d. From a political standpoint, why do you think cities have been more likely to resort to rent control rather than a policy of income supplements to help low-income people pay for housing?

2. In order to ingratiate himself with voters, the mayor of Gotham City decides to lower the price of taxi rides. Assume, for simplicity, that all taxi rides are the same

distance and therefore cost the same. The accompanying table shows the demand and supply schedules for taxi rides.

| | Quantity of rides (millions per year) | |
| --- | --- | --- |
| Fare (per ride) | Quantity demanded | Quantity supplied |
| $7.00 | 10 | 12 |
| 6.50 | 11 | 11 |
| 6.00 | 12 | 10 |
| 5.50 | 13 | 9 |
| 5.00 | 14 | 8 |
| 4.50 | 15 | 7 |

a. Assume that there are no restrictions on the number of taxi rides that can be supplied (there is no medallion system). Find the equilibrium price and quantity.

b. Suppose that the mayor sets a price ceiling at $5.50. How large is the shortage of rides? Illustrate with a diagram. Who loses and who benefits from this policy?

c. Suppose that the stock market crashes and, as a result, people in Gotham City are poorer. This reduces the quantity of taxi rides demanded by 6 million rides per year at any given price. What effect will the mayor's new policy have now? Illustrate with a diagram.

d. Suppose that the stock market rises and the demand for taxi rides returns to normal (that is, returns to the demand schedule given in the table). The mayor now decides to ingratiate himself with taxi drivers. He announces a policy in which operating licenses are given to existing taxi drivers; the number of licenses is restricted such that only 10 million rides per year can be given. Illustrate the effect of this policy on the market, and indicate the resulting price and quantity transacted. What is the quota rent per ride?

3. In the late eighteenth century, the price of bread in New York City was controlled, set at a predetermined price above the market price.

a. Draw a diagram showing the effect of the policy. Did the policy act as a price ceiling or a price floor?

b. What kinds of inefficiencies were likely to have arisen when the controlled price of bread was above the market price? Explain in detail.

One year during this period, a poor wheat harvest caused a leftward shift in the supply of bread and therefore an increase in its market price. New York bakers found that the controlled price of bread in New York was below the market price.

c. Draw a diagram showing the effect of the price control on the market for bread during this one-year period. Did the policy act as a price ceiling or a price floor?

d. What kinds of inefficiencies do you think occurred during this period? Explain in detail.

4. The U.S. Department of Agriculture (USDA) administers the price floor for butter, which the 2008 Farm Bill set at $1.05 per pound. At that price, according to data from the USDA, the quantity of butter supplied in 2010 was 1.7 billion pounds, and the quantity demanded was 1.6 billion

pounds. To support the price of butter at the price floor, the USDA therefore had to buy up 100 million pounds of butter. The accompanying diagram shows supply and demand curves illustrating the market for butter.

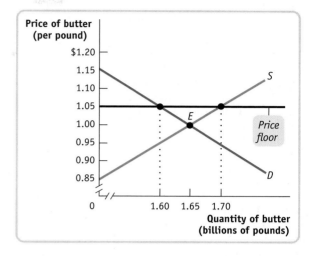

a. In the absence of a price floor, how much consumer surplus is created? How much producer surplus? What is the total surplus?

b. With the price floor at $1.05 per pound of butter, consumers buy 1.6 billion pounds of butter. How much consumer surplus is created now?

c. With the price floor at $1.05 per pound of butter, producers sell 1.7 billion pounds of butter (some to consumers and some to the USDA). How much producer surplus is created now?

d. How much money does the USDA spend on buying up surplus butter?

e. Taxes must be collected to pay for the purchases of surplus butter by the USDA. As a result, total surplus (producer plus consumer) is reduced by the amount the USDA spent on buying surplus butter. Using your answers for parts b–d, what is the total surplus when there is a price floor? How does this compare to the total surplus without a price floor from part a?

5. The accompanying table shows hypothetical demand and supply schedules for milk per year. The U.S. government decides that the incomes of dairy farmers should be maintained at a level that allows the traditional family dairy farm to survive. So it implements a price floor of $1 per pint by buying surplus milk until the market price is $1 per pint.

| | Quantity of milk (millions of pints per year) | |
| --- | --- | --- |
| Price of milk (per pint) | Quantity demanded | Quantity supplied |
| $1.20 | 550 | 850 |
| 1.10 | 600 | 800 |
| 1.00 | 650 | 750 |
| 0.90 | 700 | 700 |
| 0.80 | 750 | 650 |

**a.** How much surplus milk will be produced as a result of this policy?

**b.** What will be the cost to the government of this policy?

**c.** Since milk is an important source of protein and calcium, the government decides to provide the surplus milk it purchases to elementary schools at a price of only $0.60 per pint. Assume that schools will buy any amount of milk available at this low price. But parents now reduce their purchases of milk at any price by 50 million pints per year because they know their children are getting milk at school. How much will the dairy program now cost the government?

**d.** Explain how inefficiencies in the form of inefficient allocation to sellers and wasted resources arise from this policy.

**6.** European governments tend to make greater use of price controls than does the U.S. government. For example, the French government sets minimum starting yearly wages for new hires who have completed *le bac*, certification roughly equivalent to a high school diploma. The demand schedule for new hires with *le bac* and the supply schedule for similarly credentialed new job seekers are given in the accompanying table. The price here—given in euros, the currency used in France—is the same as the yearly wage.

| Wage (per year) | Quantity demanded (new job offers per year) | Quantity supplied (new job seekers per year) |
|---|---|---|
| €45,000 | 200,000 | 325,000 |
| 40,000 | 220,000 | 320,000 |
| 35,000 | 250,000 | 310,000 |
| 30,000 | 290,000 | 290,000 |
| 25,000 | 370,000 | 200,000 |

**a.** In the absence of government interference, what are the equilibrium wage and number of graduates hired per year? Illustrate with a diagram. Will there be anyone seeking a job at the equilibrium wage who is unable to find one—that is, will there be anyone who is involuntarily unemployed?

**b.** Suppose the French government sets a minimum yearly wage of €35,000. Is there any involuntary unemployment at this wage? If so, how much? Illustrate with a diagram. What if the minimum wage is set at €40,000? Also illustrate with a diagram.

**c.** Given your answer to part b and the information in the table, what do you think is the relationship between the level of involuntary unemployment and the level of the minimum wage? Who benefits from such a policy? Who loses? What is the missed opportunity here?

**7.** Until recently, the standard number of hours worked per week for a full-time job in France was 39 hours, just as in the United States. But in response to social unrest over high levels of involuntary unemployment, the French government instituted a 35-hour workweek—a worker could not work more than 35 hours per week even if both the worker and employer wanted it. The motivation behind this policy was that if current employees worked fewer hours, employers would be forced to hire more new workers. Assume that it is costly for employers to train new workers. French employers were greatly opposed to this policy and threatened to move their operations to neighboring countries that did not have such employment restrictions. Can you explain their attitude? Give an example of both an inefficiency and an illegal activity that are likely to arise from this policy.

**8.** For the last 70 years the U.S. government has used price supports to provide income assistance to American farmers. To implement these price supports, at times the government has used price floors, which it maintains by buying up the surplus farm products. At other times, it has used target prices, a policy by which the government gives the farmer an amount equal to the difference between the market price and the target price for each unit sold. Consider the market for corn depicted in the accompanying diagram.

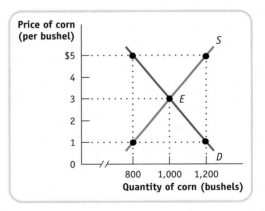

**a.** If the government sets a price floor of $5 per bushel, how many bushels of corn are produced? How many are purchased by consumers? By the government? How much does the program cost the government? How much revenue do corn farmers receive?

**b.** Suppose the government sets a target price of $5 per bushel for any quantity supplied up to 1,000 bushels. How many bushels of corn are purchased by consumers and at what price? By the government? How much does the program cost the government? How much revenue do corn farmers receive?

**c.** Which of these programs (in parts a and b) costs corn consumers more? Which program costs the government more? Explain.

**d.** Is one of these policies less inefficient than the other? Explain.

**9.** The waters off the North Atlantic coast were once teeming with fish. But because of overfishing by the commercial fishing industry, the stocks of fish became seriously depleted. In 1991, the National Marine Fishery Service of the U.S. government implemented a quota to allow fish stocks to recover. The quota limited the amount of swordfish caught per year by all U.S.-licensed fishing boats to 7 million pounds. As soon as the U.S. fishing fleet had met the quota limit, the swordfish catch was closed down for the rest of the year. The accompanying table gives the hypothetical demand and supply schedules for swordfish caught in the United States per year.

| Price of swordfish (per pound) | Quantity of swordfish (millions of pounds per year) | |
| --- | --- | --- |
| | Quantity demanded | Quantity supplied |
| $20 | 6 | 15 |
| 18 | 7 | 13 |
| 16 | 8 | 11 |
| 14 | 9 | 9 |
| 12 | 10 | 7 |

a. Use a diagram to show the effect of the quota on the market for swordfish in 1991.

b. How do you think fishermen will change how they fish in response to this policy?

10. In Maine, you must have a license to harvest lobster commercially; these licenses are issued yearly. The state of Maine is concerned about the dwindling supplies of lobsters found off its coast. The state fishery department has decided to place a yearly quota of 80,000 pounds of lobsters harvested in all Maine waters. It has also decided to give licenses this year only to those fishermen who had licenses last year. The accompanying diagram shows the demand and supply curves for Maine lobsters.

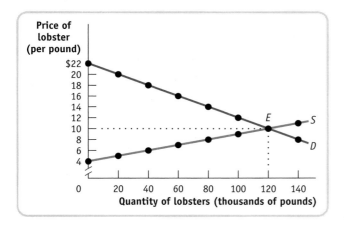

a. In the absence of government restrictions, what are the equilibrium price and quantity?

b. What is the *demand price* at which consumers wish to purchase 80,000 pounds of lobsters?

c. What is the *supply price* at which suppliers are willing to supply 80,000 pounds of lobsters?

d. What is the *quota rent* per pound of lobster when 80,000 pounds are sold?

e. Explain a transaction that benefits both buyer and seller but is prevented by the quota restriction.

11. The accompanying diagram shows data from the U.S. Bureau of Labor Statistics on the average price of an airline ticket in the United States from 1975 until 1985, adjusted to eliminate the effect of *inflation* (the general increase in the prices of all goods over time). In 1978, the United States Airline Deregulation Act removed the price floor on airline fares, and it also allowed the airlines greater flexibility to offer new routes.

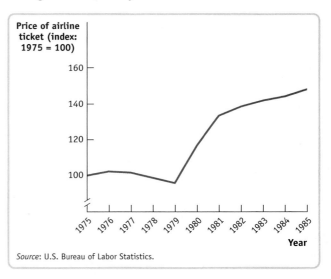

Source: U.S. Bureau of Labor Statistics.

a. Looking at the data on airline ticket prices in the diagram, do you think the price floor that existed before 1978 was binding or nonbinding? That is, do you think it was set above or below the equilibrium price? Draw a supply and demand diagram, showing where the price floor that existed before 1978 was in relation to the equilibrium price.

b. Most economists agree that the average airline ticket price per mile traveled actually *fell* as a result of the Airline Deregulation Act. How might you reconcile that view with what you see in the diagram?

# International Trade

## CAR PARTS AND SUCKING SOUNDS

**International trade improves the welfare of Mexican producers of auto parts as well as American car buyers and sellers.**

WHAT YOU WILL LEARN IN THIS CHAPTER

❯ How comparative advantage leads to mutually beneficial international trade

❯ The sources of international comparative advantage

❯ Who gains and who loses from international trade, and why the gains exceed the losses

❯ How **tariffs** and **import quotas** cause inefficiency and reduce total surplus

❯ Why governments often engage in **trade protection** and how **international trade agreements** counteract this

STOP IN AN AUTO SHOWROOM, and odds are that the majority of cars on display were produced in the United States. Even if they're Nissans, Hondas, or Volkswagens, most cars sold in this country were made here by the Big Three U.S. auto firms or by subsidiaries of foreign firms. The cars are assembled in "Auto Alley," a north–south corridor roughly defined as the space between Interstate 65, which runs from Chicago to Mobile, and Interstate 75, which runs from Detroit to western Florida.

Although that car you're looking at may have been made in America, a significant part of what's inside was probably made elsewhere, very likely in Mexico. Since the 1980s, U.S. auto production has increasingly relied on factories in Mexico to produce *labor-intensive* auto parts, such as seat parts—products that use a relatively high amount of labor in their production.

Changes in economic policy over the years have contributed greatly to the emergence of large-scale U.S. imports of auto parts from Mexico. Until the 1980s, Mexico had a system of *trade protection*—taxes and regulations limiting imports—that both kept out U.S. manufactured goods and encouraged Mexican industry to focus on selling to Mexican consumers rather than to

a wider market. In 1985, however, the Mexican government began dismantling much of its trade protection, boosting trade with the United States. A further boost came in 1993, when the United States, Mexico, and Canada signed the North American Free Trade Agreement (NAFTA), which eliminated most taxes on trade among the three nations and provided guarantees that business investments in Mexico would be protected from arbitrary changes in government policy.

NAFTA was deeply controversial when it went into effect: Mexican workers were paid only about 10% as much as their U.S. counterparts, and many expressed concern that U.S. jobs would be lost to low-wage competition. Most memorably, Ross Perot, a U.S. presidential candidate in 1992, warned that there would be a "giant sucking sound" as U.S. manufacturing moved south of the border. And although apocalyptic predictions about NAFTA's impact haven't come to pass, the agreement remains controversial even now.

Most economists disagreed with those who saw NAFTA as a threat to the U.S. economy. We saw in Chapter 2, how international trade can lead to mutual *gains from trade.* Economists, for the most part, believed that the same logic applied to NAFTA, that the treaty would make

both the United States and Mexico richer. But making a nation as a whole richer isn't the same thing as improving the welfare of everyone living in a country, and there were and are reasons to believe that NAFTA hurts some U.S. citizens.

Until now, we have analyzed the economy as if it were self-sufficient, as if the economy produces all the goods and services it consumes, and vice versa. This is, of course, true for the world economy as a whole. But it's not true for any individual country. Assuming self-sufficiency would have been far more accurate 50 years ago, when the United States exported only a small fraction of what it produced and imported only a small fraction of what it consumed.

Since then, however, both U.S. imports and exports have grown much faster than the U.S. economy as a whole. Moreover, compared to the United States, other countries engage in far more foreign trade relative to the size of their economies. To have a full picture of how national economies work, we must understand international trade.

This chapter examines the economics of international trade. We start from the model of comparative advantage, which, as we saw in Chapter 2, explains why there are gains from international trade. We will briefly recap that model here, and then extend our study to address deeper questions about international trade, such as why some individuals can be hurt by international trade while the country, as a whole, gains. At the conclusion of the chapter, we'll examine the effects of policies that countries use to limit imports or promote exports as well as how governments work together to overcome barriers to trade. ■

Goods and services purchased from other countries are **imports;** goods and services sold to other countries are **exports.**

**Globalization** is the phenomenon of growing economic linkages among countries.

# Comparative Advantage and International Trade

The United States buys auto parts—and many other goods and services—from other countries. At the same time, it sells many goods and services to other countries. Goods and services purchased from abroad are **imports;** goods and services sold abroad are **exports.**

As illustrated by the opening story, imports and exports have taken on an increasingly important role in the U.S. economy. Over the last 50 years, both imports into and exports from the United States have grown faster than the U.S. economy. Panel (a) of Figure 5-1 shows how the values of U.S. imports and exports have grown as a percentage of gross domestic product (GDP). Panel (b) shows imports and exports as a percentage of GDP for a number of countries. It shows that foreign trade is significantly more important for many other countries than it is for the United States. (Japan is the exception.)

Foreign trade isn't the only way countries interact economically. In the modern world, investors from one country often invest funds in another nation; many companies are multinational, with subsidiaries operating in several countries; and a growing number of individuals work in a country different from the one in which they were born. The growth of all these forms of economic linkages among countries is often called **globalization.**

**FIGURE   5-1   The Growing Importance of International Trade**

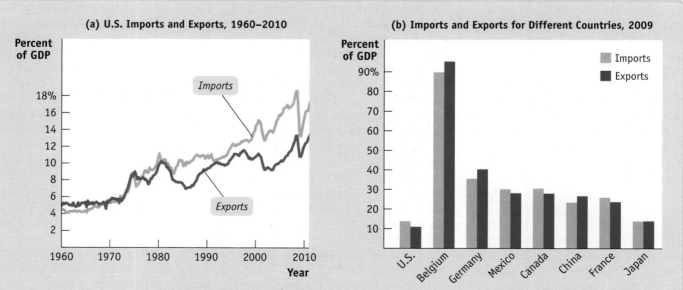

Panel (a) illustrates the fact that over the past 50 years, the United States has exported a steadily growing share of its GDP to other countries and imported a growing share of what it consumes. Panel (b) demonstrates that international trade is significantly more important to many other countries than it is to the United States, with the exception of Japan.

*Source:* Bureau of Economic Analysis [panel (a)] and World Trade Organization [panel (b)].

In this chapter, however, we'll focus mainly on international trade. To understand why international trade occurs and why economists believe it is beneficial to the economy, we will first review the concept of comparative advantage.

## Production Possibilities and Comparative Advantage, Revisited

To produce auto parts, any country must use resources—land, labor, capital, and so on—that could have been used to produce other things. The potential production of other goods a country must forgo to produce an auto part is the opportunity cost of that part.

In some cases, it's easy to see why the opportunity cost of producing a good is especially low in a given country. Consider, for example, shrimp—much of which now comes from seafood farms in Vietnam and Thailand. It's a lot easier to produce shrimp in Vietnam, where the climate is nearly ideal and there's plenty of coastal land suitable for shellfish farming, than it is in the United States. Conversely, other goods are not produced as easily in Vietnam as in the United States. For example, Vietnam doesn't have the base of skilled workers and technological know-how that makes the United States so good at producing high-technology goods. So the opportunity cost of a ton of shrimp, in terms of other goods such as aircraft, is much less in Vietnam than it is in the United States.

In other cases, matters are a bit less obvious. It's as easy to produce auto parts in the United States as it is in Mexico, and Mexican auto parts workers are, if anything, less efficient than their U.S. counterparts. But Mexican workers are a *lot* less productive than U.S. workers in other areas, such as aircraft and chemical production. This means that diverting a Mexican worker into auto parts production reduces output of other goods less than diverting a U.S. worker into auto parts production. That is, the opportunity cost of producing auto parts in Mexico is less than it is in the United States.

So we say that Mexico has a comparative advantage in producing auto parts. Let's repeat the definition of comparative advantage from Chapter 2: *A country has a comparative advantage in producing a good or service if the opportunity cost of producing the good or service is lower for that country than for other countries.*

Figure 5-2 provides a hypothetical numerical example of comparative advantage in international trade. We assume that only two goods are produced and consumed, auto parts and airplanes, and that there are only two countries in the world, the United States and Mexico. (In real life, auto parts aren't worth much without auto bodies to put them in, but let's set that issue aside). The figure shows hypothetical production possibility frontiers for the United States and Mexico.

As in Chapter 2, we simplify the model by assuming that the production possibility frontiers are straight lines, as shown in Figure 2-1, rather than the more realistic bowed-out shape shown in Figure 2-2. The straight-line shape implies that the opportunity cost of an auto part in terms of airplanes in each country is constant—it does not depend on how many units of each good the country produces. The analysis of international trade under the assumption that opportunity costs are constant, which makes production possibility frontiers straight lines, is known as the **Ricardian model of international trade,** named after the English economist David Ricardo, who introduced this analysis in the early nineteenth century.

In Figure 5-2 we have grouped auto parts into bundles of 10,000, so, for example, a country that produces 500 bundles of auto parts is producing 5 million individual auto parts. You can see in the figure that the United States can produce 2,000 airplanes if it produces no auto parts, or 1,000 bundles of auto

The **Ricardian model of international trade** analyzes international trade under the assumption that opportunity costs are constant.

FIGURE **5-2** Comparative Advantage and the Production Possibility Frontier

The U.S. opportunity cost of 1 bundle of auto parts in terms of airplanes is 2: for every additional bundle of auto parts, 2 airplanes must be forgone. The Mexican opportunity cost of 1 bundle of auto parts in terms of airplanes is ½: for every additional bundle of auto parts, only ½ of an airplane must be forgone. As a result, the

United States has a comparative advantage in airplane production, and Mexico has a comparative advantage in auto parts production. In autarky, each country is forced to consume only what it produces: 1,000 airplanes and 500 bundles of auto parts for the United States; 500 airplanes and 1,000 bundles of auto parts for Mexico.

**Autarky** is a situation in which a country does not trade with other countries.

parts if it produces no airplanes. Thus, the slope of the U.S. production possibility frontier, or PPF, is –2,000/1,000 = –2. That is, to produce an additional bundle of auto parts, the United States must forgo the production of 2 airplanes.

Similarly, Mexico can produce 1,000 airplanes if it produces no auto parts or 2,000 bundles of auto parts if it produces no airplanes. Thus, the slope of Mexico's PPF is –1,000/2,000 = –1/2. That is, to produce an additional bundle of auto parts, Mexico must forgo the production of 1/2 an airplane.

Economists use the term **autarky** to refer to a situation in which a country does not trade with other countries. We assume that in autarky the United States chooses to produce and consume 500 bundles of auto parts and 1,000 airplanes. We also assume that in autarky Mexico produces 1,000 bundles of auto parts and 500 airplanes.

The trade-offs facing the two countries when they don't trade are summarized in Table 5-1. As you can see, the United States has a comparative advantage in the production of airplanes because it has a lower opportunity cost in terms of auto parts than Mexico has: producing an airplane costs the United States only ½ a bundle of auto parts, while it costs Mexico 2 bundles of auto parts. Correspondingly, Mexico has a comparative advantage in auto parts production: 1 bundle costs it only ½ an airplane, while it costs the United States 2 airplanes.

TABLE **5-1** U.S. and Mexican Opportunity Costs of Auto Parts and Airplanes

| | **U.S. Opportunity Cost** | | **Mexican Opportunity Cost** |
|---|---|---|---|
| **1 bundle of auto parts** | 2 airplanes | > | 1/2 airplane |
| **1 airplane** | 1/2 bundle of auto parts | < | 2 bundles of auto parts |

As we learned in Chapter 2, each country can do better by engaging in trade than it could by not trading. A country can accomplish this by specializing in the production of the good in which it has a comparative advantage and exporting that good, while importing the good in which it has a comparative *dis*advantage. Let's see how this works.

FIGURE  **5-3**  The Gains from International Trade

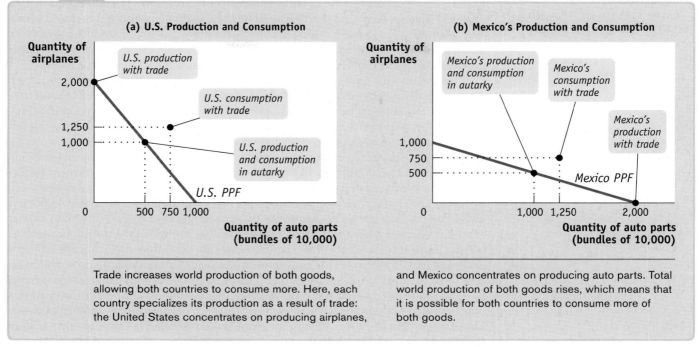

**Trade increases world production of both goods,** allowing both countries to consume more. Here, each country specializes its production as a result of trade: the United States concentrates on producing airplanes, **and Mexico concentrates on producing auto parts.** Total world production of both goods rises, which means that it is possible for both countries to consume more of both goods.

## The Gains from International Trade

Figure 5-3 illustrates how both countries can gain from specialization and trade, by showing a hypothetical rearrangement of production and consumption that allows *each* country to consume more of *both* goods. Again, panel (a) represents the United States and panel (b) represents Mexico. In each panel we indicate again the autarky production and consumption assumed in Figure 5-2. Once trade becomes possible, however, everything changes. With trade, each country can move to producing only the good in which it has a comparative advantage—airplanes for the United States and auto parts for Mexico. Because the world production of both goods is now higher than in autarky, trade makes it possible for each country to consume more of both goods.

Table 5-2 sums up the changes as a result of trade and shows why both countries can gain. The left part of the table shows the autarky situation, before trade, in which each country must produce the goods it consumes. The right part of the table shows what happens as a result of trade. After trade, the United States specializes in the production of airplanes, producing 2,000 airplanes and no auto parts; Mexico specializes in the production of auto parts, producing 2,000 bundles of auto parts and no airplanes.

TABLE  **5-2**  How the United States and Mexico Gain from Trade

|  |  | In Autarky | | With Trade | | |
|---|---|---|---|---|---|---|
|  |  | **Production** | **Consumption** | **Production** | **Consumption** | **Gains from trade** |
| **United States** | **Bundles of auto parts** | 500 | 500 | 0 | 750 | +250 |
|  | **Airplanes** | 1,000 | 1,000 | 2,000 | 1,250 | +250 |
| **Mexico** | **Bundles of auto parts** | 1,000 | 1,000 | 2,000 | 1,250 | +250 |
|  | **Airplanes** | 500 | 500 | 0 | 750 | +250 |

The result is a rise in total world production of both goods. As you can see in the Table 5-2 column at far right showing consumption with trade, the United States is able to consume both more airplanes and more auto parts than before, even though it no longer produces auto parts, because it can import parts from Mexico. Mexico can also consume more of both goods, even though it no longer produces airplanes, because it can import airplanes from the United States.

The key to this mutual gain is the fact that trade liberates both countries from self-sufficiency—from the need to produce the same mixes of goods they consume. Because each country can concentrate on producing the good in which it has a comparative advantage, total world production rises, making a higher standard of living possible in both nations.

Now, in this example we have simply assumed the post-trade consumption bundles of the two countries. In fact, the consumption choices of a country reflect both the preferences of its residents and the *relative prices*—the prices of one good in terms of another in international markets. Although we have not explicitly given the price of airplanes in terms of auto parts, that price is implicit in our example: Mexico sells the United States the 750 bundles of auto parts the U.S. consumes in return for the 750 airplanes Mexico consumes, so 1 bundle of parts is traded for 1 airplane. This tells us that the price of an airplane on world markets must be equal to the price of one bundle of 10,000 auto parts in our example.

One requirement that the relative price must satisfy is that no country pays a relative price greater than its opportunity cost of obtaining the good in autarky. That is, the United States won't pay more than 2 airplanes for each 1 bundle of 10,000 auto parts from Mexico, and Mexico won't pay more than 2 bundles of 10,000 auto parts for each 1 airplane from the United States. Once this requirement is satisfied, the actual relative price in international trade is determined by supply and demand—and we'll turn to supply and demand in international trade in the next section. However, first let's look more deeply into the nature of the gains from trade.

## Comparative Advantage versus Absolute Advantage

It's easy to accept the idea that Vietnam and Thailand have a comparative advantage in shrimp production: they have a tropical climate that's better suited to shrimp farming than that of the United States (even along the Gulf Coast), and they have a lot of usable coastal area. So the United States imports shrimp from Vietnam and Thailand. In other cases, however, it may be harder to understand why we import certain goods from abroad.

U.S. imports of auto parts from Mexico is a case in point. There's nothing about Mexico's climate or resources that makes it especially good at manufacturing auto parts. In fact, it almost surely takes *fewer* hours of labor to produce an auto seat or wiring harness in the United States than in Mexico.

Why, then, do we buy Mexican auto parts? Because the gains from trade depend on *comparative advantage*, not *absolute advantage*. Yes, it takes less labor to produce a wiring harness in the United States than in Mexico. That is, the productivity of Mexican auto parts workers is less than that of their U.S. counterparts. But what determines comparative advantage is not the amount of resources used to produce a good but the opportunity cost of that good—here, the quantity of other goods forgone in order to produce an auto seat. And the opportunity cost of auto parts is lower in Mexico than in the United States.

Here's how it works: Mexican workers have low productivity compared with U.S. workers in the auto parts industry. But Mexican workers have even lower productivity compared with U.S. workers in other

With their tropical climate, Vietnam and Thailand have a comparative advantage in shrimp production.

industries. Because Mexican labor productivity in industries other than auto parts is relatively very low, producing a wiring harness in Mexico, even though it takes a lot of labor, does not require forgoing the production of large quantities of other goods.

In the United States, the opposite is true: very high productivity in other industries (such as high-technology goods) means that producing an auto seat in the United States, even though it doesn't require much labor, requires sacrificing lots of other goods. So the opportunity cost of producing auto parts is less in Mexico than in the United States. Despite its lower labor productivity, Mexico has a comparative advantage in the production of many auto parts, although the United States has an absolute advantage.

Mexico's comparative advantage in auto parts is reflected in global markets by the wages Mexican workers are paid. That's because a country's wage rates, in general, reflect its labor productivity. In countries where labor is highly productive in many industries, employers are willing to pay high wages to attract workers, so competition among employers leads to an overall high wage rate. In countries where labor is less productive, competition for workers is less intense and wage rates are correspondingly lower.

As the accompanying Global Comparison shows, there is indeed a strong relationship between overall levels of productivity and wage rates around the world. Because Mexico has generally low productivity, it has a relatively low wage rate. Low wages, in turn, give Mexico a cost advantage in producing goods where its productivity is only moderately low, like auto parts. As a result, it's cheaper to produce these parts in Mexico than in the United States.

The kind of trade that takes place between low-wage, low-productivity economies like Mexico and high-wage, high-productivity economies like the United States gives rise to two common misperceptions. One, the *pauper labor fallacy*, is the belief that when a country with high wages imports goods produced by workers who are paid low wages, this must hurt the standard of living of workers in the importing country. The other, the *sweatshop labor fallacy*, is the belief that

## PRODUCTIVITY AND WAGES AROUND THE WORLD

Is it true that both the pauper labor argument and the sweatshop labor argument are fallacies? Yes, it is. The real explanation for low wages in poor countries is low overall productivity.

The graph shows estimates of labor productivity, measured by the value of output (GDP) per worker, and wages, measured by the monthly compensation of the average worker, for several countries in 2009. Both productivity and wages are expressed as percentages of U.S. productivity and wages; for example, productivity and wages in Japan were 79% and 91%, respectively, of their U.S. levels. You can see the strong positive relationship between productivity and wages. The relationship isn't perfect. For example, Germany has higher wages than its productivity might lead you to expect. But simple comparisons of wages give a misleading sense of labor costs in poor countries: their low-wage advantage is mostly offset by low productivity.

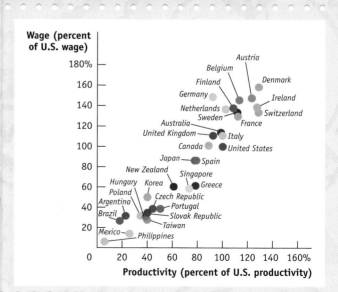

*Source:* Bureau of Labor Statistics; International Monetary Fund.

trade must be bad for workers in poor exporting countries because those workers are paid very low wages by our standards.

Both fallacies miss the nature of gains from trade: it's to the advantage of *both* countries if the poorer, lower-wage country exports goods in which it has a comparative advantage, even if its cost advantage in these goods depends on low wages. That is, both countries are able to achieve a higher standard of living through trade.

It's particularly important to understand that buying a good made by someone who is paid much lower wages than most U.S. workers doesn't necessarily imply that you're taking advantage of that person. It depends on the alternatives. Because workers in poor countries have low productivity across the board, they are offered low wages whether they produce goods exported to America or goods sold in local markets. A job that looks terrible by rich-country standards can be a step up for someone in a poor country.

International trade that depends on low-wage exports can nonetheless raise a country's standard of living. This is especially true of very-low-wage nations. For example, Bangladesh and similar countries would be much poorer than they are—their citizens might even be starving—if they weren't able to export goods such as clothing based on their low wage rates.

## Sources of Comparative Advantage

International trade is driven by comparative advantage, but where does comparative advantage come from? Economists who study international trade have found three main sources of comparative advantage: international differences in *climate*, international differences in *factor endowments*, and international differences in *technology*.

**Differences in Climate** One key reason the opportunity cost of producing shrimp in Vietnam and Thailand is less than in the United States is that shrimp need warm water—Vietnam has plenty of that, but America doesn't. In general, differences in climate play a significant role in international trade. Tropical countries export tropical products like coffee, sugar, bananas, and shrimp. Countries in the temperate zones export crops like wheat and corn. Some trade is even driven by the difference in seasons between the northern and southern hemispheres: winter deliveries of Chilean grapes and New Zealand apples have become commonplace in U.S. and European supermarkets.

**Differences in Factor Endowments** Canada is a major exporter of forest products—lumber and products derived from lumber, like pulp and paper—to the United States. These exports don't reflect the special skill of Canadian lumberjacks. Canada has a comparative advantage in forest products because its forested area is much greater compared to the size of its labor force than the ratio of forestland to the labor force in the United States.

Forestland, like labor and capital, is a *factor of production:* an input used to produce goods and services. (Recall from Chapter 2 that the factors of production are land, labor, capital, and human capital.) Due to history and geography, the mix of available factors of production differs among countries, providing an important source of comparative advantage. The relationship between comparative advantage and factor availability is found in an influential model of international trade, the *Heckscher–Ohlin model,* developed by two Swedish economists in the first half of the twentieth century.

Two key concepts in the model are *factor abundance* and *factor intensity.* Factor abundance refers to how large a country's supply of a factor is relative to its supply of other factors. Factor intensity refers to the fact that producers use different ratios of factors of production in the production of different goods. For example, oil refineries use much more capital per worker than clothing factories. Economists use the term **factor intensity** to describe this difference among goods: oil refining is capital-intensive, because it tends to use a high ratio of capital to labor, but auto seats production is labor-intensive, because it tends to use a high ratio of labor to capital.

According to the **Heckscher–Ohlin model,** *a country that has an abundant supply of a factor of production will have a comparative advantage in goods whose production is intensive in that factor.* So a country that has a relative abundance of capital will have a comparative advantage in capital-intensive industries such as oil refining, but a country that has a relative abundance of labor will have a comparative advantage in labor-intensive industries such as auto seats production.

The basic intuition behind this result is simple and based on opportunity cost. The opportunity cost of a given factor—the value that the factor would generate in alternative uses—is low for a country when it is relatively abundant in that factor. Relative to the United States, Mexico has an abundance of low-skilled labor. As a result, the opportunity cost of the production of low-skilled, labor-intensive goods is lower in Mexico than in the United States.

The most dramatic example of the validity of the Heckscher–Ohlin model is world trade in clothing. Clothing production is a labor-intensive activity: it doesn't take much physical capital, nor does it require a lot of human capital in the form of highly educated workers. So you would expect labor-abundant countries such as China and Bangladesh to have a comparative advantage in clothing production. And they do.

That much international trade is the result of differences in factor endowments helps explain another fact: international specialization of production is often *incomplete*. That is, a country often maintains some domestic production of a good that it imports. A good example of this is the United States and oil. Saudi Arabia exports oil to the United States because Saudi Arabia has an abundant supply of oil relative to its other factors of production; the United States exports medical devices to Saudi Arabia because it has an abundant supply of expertise in medical technology relative to its other factors of production. But the United States also produces some oil domestically because the size of its domestic oil reserves in Texas and Alaska makes it economical to do so.

In our supply and demand analysis in the next section, we'll consider incomplete specialization by a country to be the norm. We should emphasize, however, that the fact that countries often incompletely specialize does not in any way change the conclusion that there are gains from trade.

**Differences in Technology** In the 1970s and 1980s, Japan became by far the world's largest exporter of automobiles, selling large numbers to the United States and the rest of the world. Japan's comparative advantage in automobiles wasn't the result of climate. Nor can it easily be attributed to differences in factor endowments: aside from a scarcity of land, Japan's mix of available factors is quite similar to that in other advanced countries. Instead, as we discussed in the Chapter 2 Business Case on lean production at Toyota and Boeing, Japan's comparative advantage in automobiles was based on the superior production techniques developed by its manufacturers, which allowed them to produce more cars with a given amount of labor and capital than their American or European counterparts.

Japan's comparative advantage in automobiles was a case of comparative advantage caused by differences in technology—the techniques used in production.

The causes of differences in technology are somewhat mysterious. Sometimes they seem to be based on knowledge accumulated through experience—for

The **factor intensity** of production of a good is a measure of which factor is used in relatively greater quantities than other factors in production.

According to the **Heckscher–Ohlin model,** a country has a comparative advantage in a good whose production is intensive in the factors that are abundantly available in that country.

## FOR INQUIRING MINDS

### INCREASING RETURNS TO SCALE AND INTERNATIONAL TRADE

Most analysis of international trade focuses on how differences between countries—differences in climate, factor endowments, and technology—create national comparative advantage. However, economists have also pointed out another reason for international trade: the role of *increasing returns to scale.*

Production of a good is characterized by increasing returns to scale if the productivity of labor and other resources used in production rise with the quantity of output. For example, in an industry characterized by increasing returns to scale, increasing output by 10% might require only 8% more labor

and 9% more raw materials. Examples of industries with increasing returns to scale include auto manufacturing, oil refining, and the production of jumbo jets, all of which require large outlays of capital. Increasing returns to scale (sometimes also called economies of scale) can give rise to monopoly, a situation in which an industry is composed of only one producer, because it gives large firms a cost advantage over small ones.

But increasing returns to scale can also give rise to international trade. The logic runs as follows: If production of a good is characterized by increasing returns to scale, it makes sense to

concentrate production in only a few locations, so each location has a high level of output. But that also means production occurs in only a few countries that export the good to other countries. A commonly cited example is the North American auto industry: although both the United States and Canada produce automobiles and their components, each particular model or component tends to be produced in only one of the two countries and exported to the other.

Increasing returns to scale probably play a large role in the trade in manufactured goods between advanced countries, which is about 25% of the total value of world trade.

example, Switzerland's comparative advantage in watches reflects a long tradition of watchmaking. Sometimes they are the result of a set of innovations that for some reason occur in one country but not in others. Technological advantage, however, is often transitory. As we also discussed in the Chapter 2 Business Case, by adopting lean production, American auto manufacturers have now closed much of the gap in productivity with their Japanese competitors. In addition, Europe's aircraft industry has closed a similar gap with the U.S. aircraft industry. At any given point in time, however, differences in technology are a major source of comparative advantage.

## ECONOMICS ▸ *IN ACTION*

### SKILL AND COMPARATIVE ADVANTAGE

In 1953 U.S. workers were clearly better equipped with machinery than their counterparts in other countries. Most economists at the time thought that America's comparative advantage lay in capital-intensive goods. But Wassily Leontief made a surprising discovery: America's comparative advantage was in something other than capital-intensive goods. In fact, goods that the United States exported were slightly less capital-intensive than goods the country imported. This discovery came to be known as the Leontief paradox, and it led to a sustained effort to make sense of U.S. trade patterns.

The main resolution of this paradox, it turns out, depends on the definition of *capital.* U.S. exports aren't intensive in *physical* capital—machines and buildings. Instead, they are *skill-intensive*—that is, they are intensive in *human* capital. U.S. exporting industries use a substantially higher ratio of highly educated workers to other workers than is found in U.S. industries that compete against imports. For example, one of America's biggest export sectors is aircraft; the aircraft industry employs large numbers of engineers and other people with graduate degrees relative to the number of manual laborers. Conversely, we import a lot of clothing, which is often produced by workers with little formal education.

In general, countries with highly educated workforces tend to export skill-intensive goods, while countries with less educated workforces tend to export goods whose production requires little skilled labor. Figure 5-4 illustrates this point by comparing the goods the United States imports from Germany, a country with a highly educated labor force, with the goods the United States imports from Bangladesh, where about half of the adult population is still illiterate. In each country industries are ranked, first, according to how skill-intensive they are. Next, for each industry, we calculate its share of exports to the United States. This allows us to plot, for each country, various industries according to their skill intensity and their share of exports to the United States.

In Figure 5-4, the horizontal axis shows a measure of the skill intensity of different industries, and the vertical axes show the share of U.S. imports in each

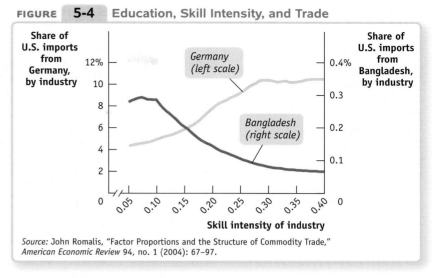

**FIGURE    5-4    Education, Skill Intensity, and Trade**

*Source:* John Romalis, "Factor Proportions and the Structure of Commodity Trade," *American Economic Review* 94, no. 1 (2004): 67–97.

industry coming from Germany (on the left) and Bangladesh (on the right). As you can see, each country's exports to the United States reflect its skill level. The curve representing Germany slopes upward: the more skill-intensive a German industry is, the higher its share of exports to the United States. In contrast, the curve representing Bangladesh slopes downward: the less skill-intensive a Bangladeshi industry is, the higher its share of exports to the United States.

## CHECK YOUR UNDERSTANDING  5-1

1. In the United States, the opportunity cost of 1 ton of corn is 50 bicycles. In China, the opportunity cost of 1 bicycle is 0.01 ton of corn.
   **a.** Determine the pattern of comparative advantage.
   **b.** In autarky, the United States can produce 200,000 bicycles if no corn is produced, and China can produce 3,000 tons of corn if no bicycles are produced. Draw each country's production possibility frontier assuming constant opportunity cost, with tons of corn on the vertical axis and bicycles on the horizontal axis.
   **c.** With trade, each country specializes its production. The United States consumes 1,000 tons of corn and 200,000 bicycles; China consumes 3,000 tons of corn and 100,000 bicycles. Indicate the production and consumption points on your diagrams, and use them to explain the gains from trade.

2. Explain the following patterns of trade using the Heckscher–Ohlin model.
   **a.** France exports wine to the United States, and the United States exports movies to France.
   **b.** Brazil exports shoes to the United States, and the United States exports shoe-making machinery to Brazil.

Solutions appear at back of book.

### ▼ Quick Review

● **Imports** and **exports** account for a growing share of the U.S. economy and the economies of many other countries.

● The growth of international trade and other international linkages is known as **globalization.**

● International trade is driven by comparative advantage. The **Ricardian model of international trade** shows that trade between two countries makes both countries better off than they would be in **autarky**—that is, there are gains from international trade.

● The main sources of comparative advantage are international differences in climate, factor endowments, and technology.

● The **Heckscher–Ohlin model** shows how comparative advantage can arise from differences in factor endowments: goods differ in their **factor intensity,** and countries tend to export goods that are intensive in the factors they have in abundance.

# Supply, Demand, and International Trade

Simple models of comparative advantage are helpful for understanding the fundamental causes of international trade. However, to analyze the effects of international trade at a more detailed level and to understand trade policy, it helps to return to the supply and demand model. We'll start by looking at the effects of imports on domestic producers and consumers, then turn to the effects of exports.

The **domestic demand curve** shows how the quantity of a good demanded by domestic consumers depends on the price of that good.

The **domestic supply curve** shows how the quantity of a good supplied by domestic producers depends on the price of that good.

The **world price** of a good is the price at which that good can be bought or sold abroad.

## The Effects of Imports

Figure 5-5 shows the U.S. market for auto seats, ignoring international trade for a moment. It introduces a few new concepts: the *domestic demand curve,* the *domestic supply curve,* and the domestic or autarky price.

The **domestic demand curve** shows how the quantity of a good demanded by residents of a country depends on the price of that good. Why "domestic"? Because people living in other countries may demand the good, too. Once we introduce international trade, we need to distinguish between purchases of a good by domestic consumers and purchases by foreign consumers. So the domestic demand curve reflects only the demand of residents of our own country. Similarly, the **domestic supply curve** shows how the quantity of a good supplied by producers inside our own country depends on the price of that good. Once we introduce international trade, we need to distinguish between the supply of domestic producers and foreign supply—supply brought in from abroad.

In autarky, with no international trade in auto seats, the equilibrium in this market would be determined by the intersection of the domestic demand and domestic supply curves, point *A.* The equilibrium price of auto seats would be $P_A$, and the equilibrium quantity of auto seats produced and consumed would be $Q_A$. As always, both consumers and producers gain from the existence of the domestic market. Economists refer to the net gain that buyers receive from the purchase of a good as *consumer surplus.* Likewise, *producer surplus* is the net gain to sellers from selling a good. *Total surplus* is the sum of consumer and producer surplus. We analyze these three concepts in detail in the appendix at the end of this chapter. In autarky, consumer surplus would be equal to the area of the blue-shaded triangle in Figure 5-5. Producer surplus would be equal to the area of the red-shaded triangle. And total surplus would be equal to the sum of these two shaded triangles.

Now let's imagine opening up this market to imports. To do this, we must make an assumption about the supply of imports. The simplest assumption, which we will adopt here, is that unlimited quantities of auto seats can be purchased from abroad at a fixed price, known as the **world price** of auto seats. Figure 5-6 shows a situation in which the world price of an auto seat, $P_W$, is lower than the price of an auto seat that would prevail in the domestic market in autarky, $P_A$.

**FIGURE** **5-5** **Consumer and Producer Surplus in Autarky**

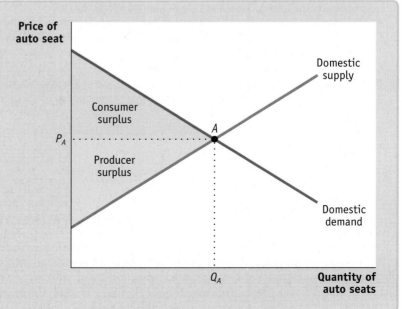

In the absence of trade, the domestic price is $P_A$, the autarky price at which the domestic supply curve and the domestic demand curve intersect. The quantity produced and consumed domestically is $Q_A$. Consumer surplus is represented by the blue-shaded area, and producer surplus is represented by the red-shaded area.

FIGURE   **5-6**   **The Domestic Market with Imports**

Here the world price of auto parts, $P_W$, is below the autarky price, $P_A$. When the economy is opened to international trade, imports enter the domestic market, and the domestic price falls from the autarky price, $P_A$, to the world price, $P_W$. As the price falls, the domestic quantity demanded rises from $Q_A$ to $Q_D$ and the domestic quantity supplied falls from $Q_A$ to $Q_S$. The difference between domestic quantity demanded and domestic quantity supplied at $P_W$, the quantity $Q_D - Q_S$, is filled by imports.

Given that the world price is below the domestic price of an auto seat, it is profitable for importers to buy auto seats abroad and resell them domestically. The imported auto seats increase the supply of auto seats in the domestic market, driving down the domestic market price. Auto seats will continue to be imported until the domestic price falls to a level equal to the world price.

The result is shown in Figure 5-6. Because of imports, the domestic price of an auto seat falls from $P_A$ to $P_W$. The quantity of auto seats demanded by domestic consumers rises from $Q_A$ to $Q_D$, and the quantity supplied by domestic producers falls from $Q_A$ to $Q_S$. The difference between the domestic quantity demanded and the domestic quantity supplied, $Q_D - Q_S$, is filled by imports.

Now let's turn to the effects of imports on consumer surplus and producer surplus. Because imports of auto seats lead to a fall in their domestic price, consumer surplus rises and producer surplus falls. Figure 5-7 shows how this works. We label four areas: $W$, $X$, $Y$, and $Z$. The autarky consumer surplus we identified in Figure 5-5 corresponds to $W$, and the autarky producer surplus corresponds to the sum of $X$ and $Y$. The fall in the domestic price to the world price leads to an increase in consumer surplus; it increases by $X$ and $Z$, so consumer surplus now equals the sum of $W$, $X$, and $Z$. At the same time, producers lose $X$ in surplus, so producer surplus now equals only $Y$.

The table in Figure 5-7 summarizes the changes in consumer and producer surplus when the auto seats market is opened to imports. Consumers gain surplus equal to the areas $X + Z$. Producers lose surplus equal to $X$. So the sum of producer and consumer surplus—the total surplus generated in the auto seats market—increases by $Z$. As a result of trade, consumers gain and producers lose, but the gain to consumers exceeds the loss to producers.

This is an important result. We have just shown that opening up a market to imports leads to a net gain in total surplus, which is what we should have

FIGURE **5-7** The Effects of Imports on Surplus

| | Changes in surplus | |
|---|---|---|
| | Gain | Loss |
| Consumer surplus | $X + Z$ | |
| Producer surplus | | $- X$ |
| **Change in total surplus** | **$+ Z$** | |

When the domestic price falls to $P_W$ as a result of international trade, consumers gain additional surplus (areas $X + Z$) and producers lose surplus (area $X$).

Because the gains to consumers outweigh the losses to producers, there is an increase in the total surplus in the economy as a whole (area $Z$).

expected given the proposition that there are gains from international trade. However, we have also learned that although the country as a whole gains, some groups—in this case, domestic producers of auto parts—lose as a result of international trade. As we'll see shortly, the fact that international trade typically creates losers as well as winners is crucial for understanding the politics of trade policy.

We turn next to the case in which a country exports a good.

## The Effects of Exports

Figure 5-8 shows the effects on a country when it exports a good, in this case airplanes. For this example, we assume that unlimited quantities of airplanes can be sold abroad at a given world price, $P_W$, which is higher than the price that would prevail in the domestic market in autarky, $P_A$.

The higher world price makes it profitable for exporters to buy airplanes domestically and sell them overseas. The purchases of domestic airplanes drive the domestic price up until it is equal to the world price. As a result, the quantity demanded by domestic consumers falls from $Q_A$ to $Q_D$ and the quantity supplied by domestic producers rises from $Q_A$ to $Q_S$. This difference between domestic production and domestic consumption, $Q_S - Q_D$, is exported.

Like imports, exports lead to an overall gain in total surplus for the exporting country but also create losers as well as winners. Figure 5-9 shows the effects of airplane exports on producer and consumer surplus. In the absence of trade, the price of each airplane would be $P_A$. Consumer surplus in the absence of trade is the sum of areas $W$ and $X$, and producer surplus is area $Y$. As a result of trade, price rises from $P_A$ to $P_W$, consumer surplus falls to $W$, and producer surplus rises to $Y + X + Z$. So producers gain $X + Z$, consumers lose $X$, and, as shown in the

FIGURE   **5-8**   The Domestic Market with Exports

Here the world price, $P_W$, is greater than the autarky price, $P_A$. When the economy is opened to international trade, some of the domestic supply is now exported. The domestic price rises from the autarky price, $P_A$, to the world price, $P_W$. As the price rises, the domestic quantity demanded falls from $Q_A$ to $Q_D$ and the domestic quantity supplied rises from $Q_A$ to $Q_S$. The portion of domestic production that is not consumed domestically, $Q_S - Q_D$, is exported.

table accompanying the figure, the economy as a whole gains total surplus in the amount of Z.

We have learned, then, that imports of a particular good hurt domestic producers of that good but help domestic consumers, whereas exports of a particular good hurt domestic consumers of that good but help domestic producers. In each case, the gains are larger than the losses.

**FIGURE** **5-9**   The Effects of Exports on Surplus

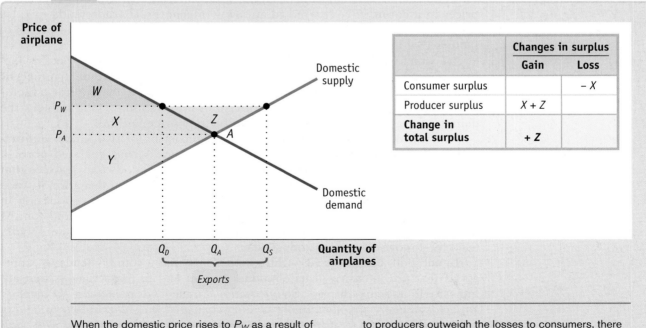

|  | Changes in surplus | |
|---|---|---|
|  | Gain | Loss |
| Consumer surplus |  | – X |
| Producer surplus | X + Z |  |
| **Change in total surplus** | **+ Z** |  |

When the domestic price rises to $P_W$ as a result of trade, producers gain additional surplus (areas X + Z) but consumers lose surplus (area X). Because the gains to producers outweigh the losses to consumers, there is an increase in the total surplus in the economy as a whole (area Z).

**Exporting industries** produce goods and services that are sold abroad.

**Import-competing industries** produce goods and services that are also imported.

## International Trade and Wages

So far we have focused on the effects of international trade on producers and consumers in a particular industry. For many purposes this is a very helpful approach. However, producers and consumers are not the only parts of society affected by trade—so are the owners of factors of production. In particular, the owners of labor, land, and capital employed in producing goods that are exported, or goods that compete with imported goods, can be deeply affected by trade.

Moreover, the effects of trade aren't limited to just those industries that export or compete with imports because *factors of production can often move between industries.* So now we turn our attention to the long-run effects of international trade on income distribution—how a country's total income is allocated among its various factors of production.

To begin our analysis, consider the position of Maria, an accountant at Midwest Auto Parts, Inc. If the economy is opened up to imports of auto parts from Mexico, the domestic auto parts industry will contract, and it will hire fewer accountants. But accounting is a profession with employment opportunities in many industries, and Maria might well find a better job in the aircraft industry, which expands as a result of international trade. So it may not be appropriate to think of her as a producer of auto parts who is hurt by competition from imported parts. Rather, we should think of her as an accountant who is affected by auto part imports only to the extent that these imports change the wages of accountants in the economy as a whole.

The wage rate of accountants is a *factor price*—the price employers have to pay for the services of a factor of production. One key question about international trade is how it affects factor prices—not just narrowly defined factors of production like accountants, but broadly defined factors such as capital, unskilled labor, and college-educated labor.

Earlier in this chapter we described the Heckscher–Ohlin model of trade, which states that comparative advantage is determined by a country's factor endowment. This model also suggests how international trade affects factor prices in a country: compared to autarky, international trade tends to raise the prices of factors that are abundantly available and reduce the prices of factors that are scarce.

We won't work this out in detail, but the idea is simple. The prices of factors of production, like the prices of goods and services, are determined by supply and demand. If international trade increases the demand for a factor of production, that factor's price will rise; if international trade reduces the demand for a factor of production, that factor's price will fall.

Now think of a country's industries as consisting of two kinds: **exporting industries,** which produce goods and services that are sold abroad, and **import-competing industries,** which produce goods and services that are also imported from abroad. Compared with autarky, international trade leads to higher production in exporting industries and lower production in import-competing industries. This indirectly increases the demand for the factors used by exporting industries and decreases the demand for factors used by import-competing industries.

In addition, the Heckscher–Ohlin model says that a country tends to export goods that are intensive in its abundant factors and to import goods that are intensive in its scarce factors. So *international trade tends to increase the demand for factors that are abundant in our country compared with other countries, and to decrease the demand for factors that are scarce in our country compared with other countries.* As a result, *the prices of abundant factors tend to rise, and the prices of scarce factors tend to fall as international trade grows.* In other words, international trade tends to redistribute income toward a country's abundant factors and away from its less abundant factors.

The Economics in Action at the end of the preceding section pointed out that U.S. exports tend to be human-capital-intensive and U.S. imports tend to be unskilled-labor-intensive. This suggests that the effect of international trade on U.S. factor markets is to raise the wage rate of highly educated American workers and reduce the wage rate of unskilled American workers.

This effect has been a source of much concern in recent years. Wage inequality—the gap between the wages of high-paid and low-paid workers—has increased substantially over the last 30 years. Some economists believe that growing international trade is an important factor in that trend. If international trade has the effects predicted by the Heckscher–Ohlin model, its growth raises the wages of highly educated American workers, who already have relatively high wages, and lowers the wages of less educated American workers, who already have relatively low wages. But keep in mind another phenomenon: trade reduces the income inequality *between* countries as poor countries improve their standard of living by exporting to rich countries.

How important are these effects? In some historical episodes, the impacts of international trade on factor prices have been very large. As we explain in the following Economics in Action, the opening of transatlantic trade in the late nineteenth century had a large negative impact on land rents in Europe, hurting landowners but helping workers and owners of capital.

The effects of trade on wages in the United States have generated considerable controversy in recent years. Most economists who have studied the issue agree that growing imports of labor-intensive products from newly industrializing economies, and the export of high-technology goods in return, have helped cause a widening wage gap between highly educated and less educated workers in this country. However, most economists believe that it is only one of several forces explaining the growth in American wage inequality.

## ECONOMICS ▸ IN ACTION

### TRADE, WAGES, AND LAND PRICES IN THE NINETEENTH CENTURY

**B**eginning around 1870, there was an explosive growth of world trade in agricultural products, based largely on the steam engine. Steam-powered ships could cross the ocean much more quickly and reliably than sailing ships. Until about 1860, steamships had higher costs than sailing ships, but after that costs dropped sharply. At the same time, steam-powered rail transport made it possible to bring grain and other bulk goods cheaply from the interior to ports. The result was that land-abundant countries—the United States, Canada, Argentina, and Australia—began shipping large quantities of agricultural goods to the densely populated, land-scarce countries of Europe.

This opening up of international trade led to higher prices of agricultural products, such as wheat, in exporting countries and a decline in their prices in importing countries. Notably,

International trade redistributes income toward a country's abundant factors and away from its less abundant factors.

## Quick Review

- The intersection of the **domestic demand curve** and the **domestic supply curve** determines the domestic price of a good. When a market is opened to international trade, the domestic price is driven to equal the **world price.**

- If the world price is lower than the autarky price, trade leads to imports and the domestic price falls to the world price. There are overall gains from international trade because the gain in consumer surplus exceeds the loss in producer surplus.

- If the world price is higher than the autarky price, trade leads to exports and the domestic price rises to the world price. There are overall gains from international trade because the gain in producer surplus exceeds the loss in consumer surplus.

- Trade leads to an expansion of **exporting industries,** which increases demand for a country's abundant factors, and a contraction of **import-competing industries,** which decreases demand for its scarce factors.

An economy has **free trade** when the government does not attempt either to reduce or to increase the levels of exports and imports that occur naturally as a result of supply and demand.

Policies that limit imports are known as **trade protection** or simply as **protection.**

A **tariff** is a tax levied on imports.

the difference between wheat prices in the midwestern United States and England plunged.

The change in agricultural prices created winners and losers on both sides of the Atlantic as factor prices adjusted. In England, land prices fell by half compared with average wages; landowners found their purchasing power sharply reduced, but workers benefited from cheaper food. In the United States, the reverse happened: land prices doubled compared with wages. Landowners did very well, but workers found the purchasing power of their wages dented by rising food prices.

### CHECK YOUR UNDERSTANDING 5-2

1. Due to a strike by truckers, trade in food between the United States and Mexico is halted. In autarky, the price of Mexican grapes is lower than that of U.S. grapes. Using a diagram of the U.S. domestic demand curve and the U.S. domestic supply curve for grapes, explain the effect of these events on the following.
   a. U.S. grape consumers' surplus
   b. U.S. grape producers' surplus
   c. U.S. total surplus
2. What effect do you think this event will have on Mexican grape producers? Mexican grape pickers? Mexican grape consumers? U.S. grape pickers?

Solutions appear at back of book.

# The Effects of Trade Protection

Ever since David Ricardo laid out the principle of comparative advantage in the early nineteenth century, most economists have advocated **free trade.** That is, they have argued that government policy should not attempt either to reduce or to increase the levels of exports and imports that occur naturally as a result of supply and demand. Despite the free-trade arguments of economists, however, many governments use taxes and other restrictions to limit imports. Less frequently, governments offer subsidies to encourage exports. Policies that limit imports, usually with the goal of protecting domestic producers in import-competing industries from foreign competition, are known as **trade protection** or simply as **protection.**

Let's look at the two most common protectionist policies, tariffs and import quotas, then turn to the reasons governments follow these policies.

## The Effects of a Tariff

A **tariff** is a form of excise tax, one that is levied only on sales of imported goods. For example, the U.S. government could declare that anyone bringing in auto seats must pay a tariff of $100 per unit. In the distant past, tariffs were an important source of government revenue because they were relatively easy to collect. But in the modern world, tariffs are usually intended to discourage imports and protect import-competing domestic producers rather than as a source of government revenue.

The tariff raises both the price received by domestic producers and the price paid by domestic consumers. Suppose, for example, that our country imports auto seats, and an auto seat costs $200 on the world market. As we saw earlier, under free trade the domestic price would also be $200. But if a tariff of $100 per

FIGURE   **5-10**   **The Effect of a Tariff**

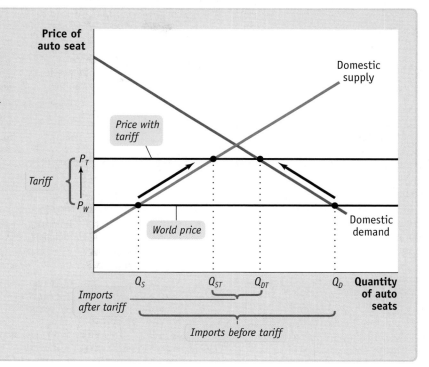

A tariff raises the domestic price of the good from $P_W$ to $P_T$. The domestic quantity demanded shrinks from $Q_D$ to $Q_{DT}$, and the domestic quantity supplied increases from $Q_S$ to $Q_{ST}$. As a result, imports—which had been $Q_D - Q_S$ before the tariff was imposed—shrink to $Q_{DT} - Q_{ST}$ after the tariff is imposed.

unit is imposed, the domestic price will rise to $300, because it won't be profitable to import auto seats unless the price in the domestic market is high enough to compensate importers for the cost of paying the tariff.

Figure 5-10 illustrates the effects of a tariff on imports of auto seats. As before, we assume that $P_W$ is the world price of an auto seat. Before the tariff is imposed, imports have driven the domestic price down to $P_W$, so that pre-tariff domestic production is $Q_S$, pre-tariff domestic consumption is $Q_D$, and pre-tariff imports are $Q_D - Q_S$.

Now suppose that the government imposes a tariff on each auto seat imported. As a consequence, it is no longer profitable to import auto seats unless the domestic price received by the importer is greater than or equal to the world price *plus* the tariff. So the domestic price rises to $P_T$, which is equal to the world price, $P_W$, plus the tariff. Domestic production rises to $Q_{ST}$, domestic consumption falls to $Q_{DT}$, and imports fall to $Q_{DT} - Q_{ST}$.

A tariff, then, raises domestic prices, leading to increased domestic production and reduced domestic consumption compared to the situation under free trade. Figure 5-11 shows the effects on surplus. There are three effects:

1. The higher domestic price increases producer surplus, a gain equal to area *A*.
2. The higher domestic price reduces consumer surplus, a reduction equal to the sum of areas *A*, *B*, *C*, and *D*.
3. The tariff yields revenue to the government. How much revenue? The government collects the tariff—which, remember, is equal to the difference between $P_T$ and $P_W$ on each of the $Q_{DT} - Q_{ST}$ units imported. So total revenue is $(P_T - P_W) \times (Q_{DT} - Q_{ST})$. This is equal to area *C*.

The welfare effects of a tariff are summarized in the table in Figure 5-11. Producers gain, consumers lose, and the government gains. But consumer losses are greater than the sum of producer and government gains, leading to a net reduction in total surplus equal to areas *B* + *D*.

FIGURE **5-11** A Tariff Reduces Total Surplus

When the domestic price rises as a result of a tariff, producers gain additional surplus (area *A*), the government gains revenue (area *C*), and consumers lose surplus (areas *A* + *B* + *C* + *D*). Because the losses to consumers outweigh the gains to producers and the government, the economy as a whole loses surplus (areas *B* + *D*).

An excise tax creates inefficiency, or deadweight loss, because it prevents mutually beneficial trades from occurring. The same is true of a tariff, where the deadweight loss imposed on society is equal to the loss in total surplus represented by areas $B + D$.

Tariffs generate deadweight losses because they create inefficiencies in two ways:

1. Some mutually beneficial trades go unexploited: some consumers who are willing to pay more than the world price, $P_W$, do not purchase the good, even though $P_W$ is the true cost of a unit of the good to the economy. The cost of this inefficiency is represented in Figure 5-11 by area *D*.

2. The economy's resources are wasted on inefficient production: some producers whose cost exceeds $P_W$ produce the good, even though an additional unit of the good can be purchased abroad for $P_W$. The cost of this inefficiency is represented in Figure 5-11 by area *B*.

## The Effects of an Import Quota

An **import quota,** another form of trade protection, is a legal limit on the quantity of a good that can be imported. For example, a U.S. import quota on Mexican auto seats might limit the quantity imported each year to 500,000 units. Import quotas are usually administered through licenses: a number of licenses are issued, each giving the license-holder the right to import a limited quantity of the good each year.

An **import quota** is a legal limit on the quantity of a good that can be imported.

A quota on sales has the same effect as an excise tax, with one difference: the money that would otherwise have accrued to the government as tax revenue under an excise tax becomes license-holders' revenue under a quota—also known as quota rents. ("Quota rent" was defined in Chapter 4.) Similarly, an import quota has the same effect as a tariff, with one difference: the money that would otherwise have been government revenue becomes quota rents to license-holders. Look again at Figure 5-11. An import quota that limits imports to $Q_{DT} - Q_{ST}$ will raise the domestic price of auto parts by the same amount as the tariff we considered previously. That is, it will raise the domestic price from $P_W$ to $P_T$. However, area $C$ will now represent quota rents rather than government revenue.

Who receives import licenses and so collects the quota rents? In the case of U.S. import protection, the answer may surprise you: the most important import licenses—mainly for clothing, to a lesser extent for sugar—are granted to foreign governments.

Because the quota rents for most U.S. import quotas go to foreigners, the cost to the nation of such quotas is larger than that of a comparable tariff (a tariff that leads to the same level of imports). In Figure 5-11 the net loss to the United States from such an import quota would be equal to areas $B + C + D$, the difference between consumer losses and producer gains.

## ECONOMICS ▸ *IN ACTION*

### TRADE PROTECTION IN THE UNITED STATES

The United States today generally follows a policy of free trade, both in comparison with other countries and in comparison with its own history. Most imports are subject to either no tariff or to a low tariff. So what are the major exceptions to this rule?

Most of the remaining protection involves agricultural products. Topping the list is ethanol, which in the United States is mainly produced from corn and used as an ingredient in motor fuel. Most imported ethanol is subject to a fairly high tariff, but some countries are allowed to sell a limited amount of ethanol in the United States, at high prices, without paying the tariff. Dairy products also receive substantial import protection, again through a combination of tariffs and quotas.

Until a few years ago, clothing and textiles were also strongly protected from import competition, thanks to an elaborate system of import quotas. However, this system was phased out in 2005 as part of a trade agreement reached a decade earlier. Some clothing imports are still subject to relatively high tariffs, but protection in the clothing industry is a shadow of what it used to be.

The most important thing to know about current U.S. trade protection is how limited it really is, and how little cost it imposes on the economy. Every two years the U.S. International Trade Commission, a government agency, produces estimates of the impact of "significant trade restrictions" on U.S. welfare. As Figure 5-12 shows, over the

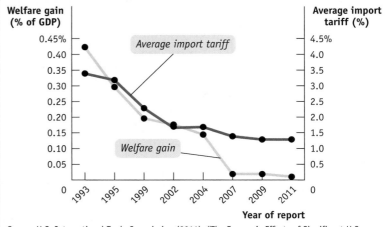

FIGURE **5-12** Tariff Rates and Estimated Welfare Gains, 1993–2011

*Source:* U.S. International Trade Commission (2011), "The Economic Effects of Significant U.S. Import Restraints."

past two decades both average tariff levels and the cost of trade restrictions as a share of national income, which weren't all that big to begin with, have fallen sharply.

### CHECK YOUR UNDERSTANDING 5-3

1. Suppose the world price of butter is $0.50 per pound and the domestic price in autarky is $1.00 per pound. Use a diagram similar to Figure 5-10 to show the following.
    a. If there is free trade, domestic butter producers want the government to impose a tariff of no less than $0.50 per pound.
    b. What happens if a tariff greater than $0.50 per pound is imposed?
2. Suppose the government imposes an import quota rather than a tariff on butter. What quota limit would generate the same quantity of imports as a tariff of $0.50 per pound?

Solutions appear at back of book.

# The Political Economy of Trade Protection

We have seen that international trade produces mutual benefits to the countries that engage in it. We have also seen that tariffs and import quotas, although they produce winners as well as losers, reduce total surplus. Yet many countries continue to impose tariffs and import quotas as well as to enact other protectionist measures.

To understand why trade protection takes place, we will first look at some common justifications for protection. Then we will look at the politics of trade protection. Finally, we will look at an important feature of trade protection in today's world: tariffs and import quotas are the subject of international negotiation and are policed by international organizations.

## Arguments for Trade Protection

Advocates for tariffs and import quotas offer a variety of arguments. Three common arguments are *national security, job creation,* and the *infant industry argument.*

The national security argument is based on the proposition that overseas sources of goods are vulnerable to disruption in times of international conflict; therefore, a country should protect domestic suppliers of crucial goods with the aim to be self-sufficient in those goods. In the 1960s, the United States—which had begun to import oil as domestic oil reserves ran low—had an import quota on oil, justified on national security grounds. Some people have argued that we should again have policies to discourage imports of oil, especially from the Middle East.

The job creation argument points to the additional jobs created in import-competing industries as a result of trade protection. Economists argue that these jobs are offset by the jobs lost elsewhere, such as industries that use imported inputs and now face higher input costs. But noneconomists don't always find this argument persuasive.

Finally, the infant industry argument, often raised in newly industrializing countries, holds that new industries require a temporary period of trade protection to get established. For example, in the 1950s many countries in Latin America imposed tariffs and import quotas on manufactured goods, in an effort to switch from their traditional role as exporters of raw materials to a new status as industrial countries.

In theory, the argument for infant industry protection can be compelling, particularly in high-tech industries that increase a country's overall skill level. Reality, however, is more complicated: it is most often industries that are politically influential that gain protection. In addition, governments tend to be poor predictors of the best emerging technologies. Finally, it is often very difficult to wean an industry from protection when it should be mature enough to stand on its own.

**International trade agreements** are treaties in which a country promises to engage in less trade protection against the exports of other countries in return for a promise by other countries to do the same for its own exports.

## The Politics of Trade Protection

In reality, much trade protection has little to do with the arguments just described. Instead, it reflects the political influence of import-competing producers.

We've seen that a tariff or import quota leads to gains for import-competing producers and losses for consumers. Producers, however, usually have much more influence over trade policy decisions. The producers who compete with imports of a particular good are usually a smaller, more cohesive group than the consumers of that good.

An example is trade protection for sugar: the United States has an import quota on sugar, which on average leads to a domestic price about twice the world price. This quota is difficult to rationalize in terms of any economic argument. However, consumers rarely complain about the quota because they are unaware that it exists: because no individual consumer buys large amounts of sugar, the cost of the quota is only a few dollars per family each year, not enough to attract notice. But there are only a few thousand sugar growers in the United States. They are very aware of the benefits they receive from the quota and make sure that their representatives in Congress are also aware of their interest in the matter.

Given these political realities, it may seem surprising that trade is as free as it is. For example, the United States has low tariffs, and its import quotas are mainly confined to clothing and a few agricultural products. It would be nice to say that the main reason trade protection is so limited is that economists have convinced governments of the virtues of free trade. A more important reason, however, is the role of *international trade agreements*.

## International Trade Agreements and the World Trade Organization

When a country engages in trade protection, it hurts two groups. We've already emphasized the adverse effect on domestic consumers, but protection also hurts foreign export industries. This means that countries care about one anothers' trade policies: the Canadian lumber industry, for example, has a strong interest in keeping U.S. tariffs on forest products low.

Because countries care about one anothers' trade policies, they enter into **international trade agreements:** treaties in which a country promises to engage in less trade protection against the exports of another country in return for a promise by the other country to do the same for its own exports. Most world trade is now governed by such agreements.

Some international trade agreements involve just two countries or a small group of countries. The United States, Canada, and Mexico are joined together

The **North American Free Trade Agreement,** or **NAFTA,** is a trade agreement between the United States, Canada, and Mexico.

The **European Union,** or **EU,** is a customs union among 27 European nations.

The **World Trade Organization,** or **WTO,** oversees international trade agreements and rules on disputes between countries over those agreements.

by the **North American Free Trade Agreement,** or **NAFTA.** This agreement, signed in 1993, will eventually remove all barriers to trade among the three nations. In Europe, 27 nations are part of an even more comprehensive agreement, the **European Union,** or **EU.** In NAFTA, the member countries set their own tariff rates against imports from other nonmember countries. The EU, however, is a *customs union:* tariffs are levied at the same rate on goods from outside the EU entering the union.

There are also global trade agreements covering most of the world. Such global agreements are overseen by the **World Trade Organization,** or **WTO,** an international organization composed of member countries, which plays two roles. First, it provides the framework for the massively complex negotiations involved in a major international trade agreement (the full text of the last major agreement, approved in 1994, was 24,000 pages long). Second, the WTO resolves disputes between its members. These disputes typically arise when one country claims that another country's policies violate its previous agreements. Currently, the WTO has 151 member countries, accounting for the bulk of world trade.

Here are two examples that illustrate the WTO's role. First, in 1999 the WTO ruled that the European Union's import restrictions on bananas, which discriminate in favor of banana producers in former European colonies and against Central American banana producers, are in violation of international trade rules. The United States took the side of the Central American countries, and the dispute threatened to become a major source of conflict between the European Union and the United States. Europe is currently in the process of revising its system. In 2009, the European Union agreed to reduce tariffs on Central American banana producers by 35% over seven years; in exchange, the United States and Central American countries dropped their case, ending the "banana wars."

A more recent example is the dispute between the United States and Brazil over American subsidies to its cotton farmers. These subsidies, in the amount of $3 billion to $4 billion a year, are illegal under WTO rules. Brazil argues that they artificially reduce the price of American cotton on world markets and hurt Brazilian cotton farmers. In 2005 the WTO ruled against the United States and in favor of Brazil, and the United States responded by cutting some export subsidies on cotton. However, in 2007 the WTO ruled that the United States had not done enough to fully comply, such as eliminating government loans to cotton farmers. After Brazil threatened, in turn, to impose import tariffs on U.S.-manufactured goods, in 2010 the two sides agreed to a framework for the solution to the cotton dispute.

By the way, Vietnam and Thailand are both members of the WTO. Yet the United States has, on and off, imposed tariffs on shrimp imports from these countries. The reason this is possible is that WTO rules do allow trade protection under certain circumstances. One circumstance is where the foreign competition is "unfair" under certain technical criteria. Trade protection is also allowed as a temporary measure when a sudden surge of imports threatens to disrupt a domestic industry. The response to Chinese tire exports, described in the accompanying For Inquiring Minds, is an important recent example.

The WTO is sometimes, with great exaggeration, described as a world government. In fact, it has no army, no police, and no direct enforcement power. The grain of truth in that description is that when a country joins the WTO, it agrees to accept the organization's judgments—and these judgments apply not only to tariffs and import quotas but also to domestic policies that the organization considers trade protection disguised under another name. So in joining the WTO a country does give up some of its sovereignty.

## FOR INQUIRING MINDS

### TIRES UNDER PRESSURE

In September 2009 the U.S. government imposed steep tariffs on imports of tires from China. The tariffs were imposed for three years: 35% in the first year, 30% in the second, and 25% in the third.

The tariffs were a response to union complaints about the effects of surging Chinese tire exports: between 2004 and 2008, U.S. imports of automobile tires from China had gone from 15 million to 46 million, and labor groups warned that this was costing American jobs. The unions wanted an import quota, but getting the tariff was still a political victory for organized labor.

But wasn't the tariff a violation of WTO rules? No, said the Obama administration. When China joined the WTO in 2001, it agreed to what is known, in trade policy jargon, as a "safeguard mechanism": importing countries were granted the right to impose temporary limits on Chinese exports in the event of an import surge. Despite this agreement, the government of China protested the U.S. action and appealed to the WTO to rule the tariff illegal. But in December 2010 the WTO came down on America's side, ruling

that the Obama administration had been within its rights.

You shouldn't be too cynical about this failure to achieve complete free trade in tires. World trade negotiations have always been based on the principle that half a loaf is better than none, that it's better to have an agreement that allows politically sensitive industries to retain some protection than to insist on free-trade purity. In spite of such actions as the tire tariff, world trade is, on the whole, remarkably free, and freer in many ways than it was just a few years ago.

## New Challenges to Globalization

The forward march of globalization over the past century is generally considered a major political and economic success. Economists and policy makers alike have viewed growing world trade, in particular, as a good thing. We would be remiss, however, if we failed to acknowledge that many people are having second thoughts about globalization. To a large extent, these second thoughts reflect two concerns shared by many economists: worries about the effects of globalization on inequality and worries that new developments, in particular the growth in *offshore outsourcing*, are increasing economic insecurity.

**Globalization and Inequality** We've already mentioned the implications of international trade for factor prices, such as wages: when wealthy countries like the United States export skill-intensive products like aircraft while importing labor-intensive products like clothing, they can expect to see the wage gap between more educated and less educated domestic workers widen. Thirty years ago, this wasn't a significant concern, because most of the goods wealthy countries imported from poorer countries were raw materials or goods where comparative advantage depended on climate. Today, however, many manufactured goods are imported from relatively poor countries, with a potentially much larger effect on the distribution of income.

Trade with China, in particular, raises concerns among labor groups trying to maintain wage levels in rich countries. Although China has experienced spectacular economic growth since the economic reforms that began in the late 1970s, it remains a poor, low-wage country: wages in Chinese manufacturing are estimated to be only about 4% of U.S. wages. Meanwhile, imports from China have soared. In 1983 less than 1% of U.S. imports came from China; by 2010, the figure was more than 19%. There's not much question that these surging imports from China put at least some downward pressure on the wages of less educated American workers.

**Outsourcing** Chinese exports to the United States overwhelmingly consist of labor-intensive manufactured goods. However, some U.S. workers have recently found themselves facing a new form of international competition. *Outsourcing,* in which a company hires another company to perform some

**Offshore outsourcing** takes place when businesses hire people in another country to perform various tasks.

task, such as running the corporate computer system, is a long-standing business practice. Until recently, however, outsourcing was normally done locally, with a company hiring another company in the same city or country.

Now, modern telecommunications increasingly makes it possible to engage in **offshore outsourcing,** in which businesses hire people in another country to perform various tasks. The classic example is call centers: the person answering the phone when you call a company's 1-800 help line may well be in India, which has taken the lead in attracting offshore outsourcing. Offshore outsourcing has also spread to fields such as software design and even health care: the radiologist examining your X-rays, like the person giving you computer help, may be on another continent.

Although offshore outsourcing has come as a shock to some U.S. workers, such as programmers whose jobs have been outsourced to India, it's still relatively small compared with more traditional trade. Some economists have warned, however, that millions or even tens of millions of workers who have never thought they could face foreign competition for their jobs may face unpleasant surprises in the not-too-distant future.

Concerns about income distribution and outsourcing, as we've said, are shared by many economists. There is also, however, widespread opposition to globalization in general, particularly among college students. In 1999, an attempt to start a major round of trade negotiations failed in part because the WTO meeting, in Seattle, was disrupted by antiglobalization demonstrators. However, the more important reason for its failure was disagreement among the countries represented. Another round of negotiations that began in 2001 in Doha, Qatar, and is therefore referred to as the "Doha development round," by 2008 had stalled, mainly because of disagreements over agricultural trade rules.

What motivates the antiglobalization movement? To some extent it's the sweatshop labor fallacy: it's easy to get outraged about the low wages paid to the person who made your shirt, and harder to appreciate how much worse off that person would be if denied the opportunity to sell goods in rich countries' markets. It's also true, however, that the movement represents a backlash against supporters of globalization who have oversold its benefits. Countries in Latin America, in particular, were promised that reducing their tariff rates would produce an economic takeoff; instead, they have experienced disappointing results. Some groups, such as poor farmers facing new competition from imported food, ended up worse off.

Do these new challenges to globalization undermine the argument that international trade is a good thing? The great majority of economists would argue that the gains from reducing trade protection still exceed the losses. However, it has become more important than before to make sure that the gains from international trade are widely spread. And the politics of international trade is becoming increasingly difficult as the extent of trade has grown.

To some extent, the antiglobalization movement is motivated by the sweatshop labor fallacy.

## ECONOMICS > IN ACTION

### BEEFING UP EXPORTS

In December 2010, negotiators from the United States and South Korea reached final agreement on a free-trade deal that would phase out many of the tariffs and other restrictions on trade between the two nations. The deal also involved changes in a variety of business regulations that were expected to make it easier for U.S. companies to operate in South Korea. This was, literally, a fairly big deal: South Korea's economy is comparable in size to Mexico's, so this was the most important free-trade agreement that the United States had been party to since NAFTA.

What made this deal possible? Estimates by the U.S. International Trade Commission found that the deal would raise average American incomes, although modestly: the commission put the gains at around one-tenth of one percent. Not bad when you consider the fact that South Korea, despite its relatively large economy, is still only America's seventh-most-important trading partner.

These overall gains played little role in the politics of the deal, however, which hinged on losses and gains for particular U.S. constituencies. Some opposition to the deal came from labor, especially from autoworkers, who feared that eliminating the 8% U.S. tariff on imports of Korean automobiles would lead to job losses. But there were also interest groups in America that badly wanted the deal, most notably the beef industry: Koreans are big beef-eaters, yet American access to that market was limited by a 38% Korean tariff.

And the Obama administration definitely wanted a deal, in part for reasons unrelated to economics: South Korea is an important U.S. ally, and military tensions with North Korea were ratcheting up even as the final negotiations were taking place. So a trade deal was viewed in part as a symbol of U.S.–South Korean cooperation. Even labor unions weren't as opposed as they might have been; the administration's imposition of tariffs on Chinese tires, just described in For Inquiring Minds, was seen as a demonstration that it was prepared to defend labor interests.

The 2010 trade agreement between South Korea and the United States was the most important free-trade deal since NAFTA and a boon for the U.S. beef industry.

It also helped that South Korea—unlike Mexico when NAFTA was signed—is both a fairly high-wage country and not right on the U.S. border, which meant less concern about massive shifts of manufacturing. In the end, the balance of interests was just favorable enough to make the deal politically possible. That said, at the time of writing, the U.S. Congress had yet to approve the deal.

## CHECK YOUR UNDERSTANDING 5-4

1. In 2002 the United States imposed tariffs on steel imports, which are an input in a large number and variety of U.S. industries. Explain why political lobbying to eliminate these tariffs is more likely to be effective than political lobbying to eliminate tariffs on consumer goods such as sugar or clothing.

2. Over the years, the WTO has increasingly found itself adjudicating trade disputes that involve not just tariffs or quota restrictions but also restrictions based on quality, health, and environmental considerations. Why do you think this has occurred? What method would you, as a WTO official, use to decide whether a quality, health, or environmental restriction is in violation of a free-trade agreement?

*Solutions appear at back of book.*

### ▼ Quick Review

● The three major justifications for trade protection are national security, job creation, and protection of infant industries.

● Despite the deadweight losses, import protections are often imposed because groups representing import-competing industries are more influential than groups of consumers.

● To further trade liberalization, countries engage in **international trade agreements.** Some agreements are among a small number of countries, such as the **North American Free Trade Agreement (NAFTA)** and the **European Union (EU).** The **World Trade Organization (WTO)** seeks to negotiate global trade agreements and referee trade disputes between members.

● Resistance to globalization has emerged in response to a surge in imports from relatively poor countries and the **offshore outsourcing** of many jobs that had been considered safe from foreign competition.

# Li & Fung: From Guangzhou to You

Daniel J. Groshong/Bloomberg via Getty Images

It's a very good bet that as you read this, you're wearing something manufactured in Asia. And if you are, it's also a good bet that the Hong Kong company Li & Fung was involved in getting your garment designed, produced, and shipped to your local store. From Levi's to The Limited to Walmart, Li & Fung is a critical conduit from factories around the world to the shopping mall nearest you.

The company was founded in 1906 in Guangzhou, China. According to Victor Fung, the company's chairman, his grandfather's "value added" was that he spoke English, allowing him to serve as an interpreter in business deals between Chinese and foreigners. When Mao's Communist Party seized control in mainland China, the company moved to Hong Kong. There, as Hong Kong's market economy took off during the 1960s and 1970s, Li & Fung grew as an export broker, bringing together Hong Kong manufacturers and foreign buyers.

The real transformation of the company came, however, as Asian economies grew and changed. Hong Kong's rapid growth led to rising wages, making Li & Fung increasingly uncompetitive in garments, its main business. So the company reinvented itself: rather than being a simple broker, it became a "supply chain manager." Not only would it allocate production of a good to a manufacturer, it would also break production down, allocate production of the inputs, and then allocate final assembly of the good among its 12,000+ suppliers around the globe. Sometimes production would be done in sophisticated economies like those of Hong Kong or even Japan, where wages are high but so is quality and productivity; sometimes it would be done in less advanced locations like mainland China or Thailand, where labor is less productive but cheaper.

For example, suppose you own a U.S. retail chain and want to sell garment-washed blue jeans. Rather than simply arrange for production of the jeans, Li & Fung will work with you on their design, providing you with the latest production and style information, like what materials and colors are hot. After the design has been finalized, Li & Fung will arrange for the creation of a prototype, find the most cost-effective way to manufacture it, and then place an order on your behalf. Through Li & Fung, the yarn might be made in Korea and dyed in Taiwan, and the jeans sewn in Thailand or mainland China. And because production is taking place in so many locations, Li & Fung provides transport logistics as well as quality control.

Li & Fung has been enormously successful. In 2010 the company had a market value of approximately $23.3 billion and business turnover of over $15 billion, with offices and distribution centers in more than 40 countries. Year after year, it has regularly doubled or tripled its profits.

## QUESTIONS FOR THOUGHT

1. Why do you think it was profitable for Li & Fung to go beyond brokering exports to becoming a supply chain manager, breaking down the production process and sourcing the inputs from various suppliers across many countries?

2. What principle do you think underlies Li & Fung's decisions on how to allocate production of a good's inputs and its final assembly among various countries?

3. Why do you think a retailer prefers to have Li & Fung arrange international production of its jeans rather than purchase them directly from a jeans manufacturer in mainland China?

4. What is the source of Li & Fung's success? Is it based on human capital, on ownership of a natural resource, or on ownership of capital?

## SUMMARY

1. International trade is of growing importance to the United States and of even greater importance to most other countries. International trade, like trade among individuals, arises from comparative advantage: the opportunity cost of producing an additional unit of a good is lower in some countries than in others. Goods and services purchased abroad are **imports;** those sold abroad are **exports.** Foreign trade, like other economic linkages between countries, has been growing rapidly, a phenomenon called **globalization.**

2. The **Ricardian model of international trade** assumes that opportunity costs are constant. It shows that there are gains from trade: two countries are better off with trade than in **autarky.**

3. In practice, comparative advantage reflects differences between countries in climate, factor endowments, and technology. The **Heckscher–Ohlin** model shows how differences in factor endowments determine comparative advantage: goods differ in **factor intensity,** and countries tend to export goods that are intensive in the factors they have in abundance.

4. The **domestic demand curve** and the **domestic supply curve** determine the price of a good in autarky. When international trade occurs, the domestic price is driven to equality with the **world price,** the price at which the good is bought and sold abroad.

5. If the world price is below the autarky price, a good is imported. This leads to an increase in consumer surplus, a fall in producer surplus, and a gain in total surplus. If the world price is above the autarky price, a good is exported. This leads to an increase in producer surplus, a fall in consumer surplus, and a gain in total surplus.

6. International trade leads to expansion in **exporting industries** and contraction in **import-competing industries.** This raises the domestic demand for abundant factors of production, reduces the demand for scarce factors, and so affects factor prices, such as wages.

7. Most economists advocate **free trade,** but in practice many governments engage in **trade protection.** The two most common forms of **protection** are tariffs and quotas. In rare occasions, export industries are subsidized.

8. A **tariff** is a tax levied on imports. It raises the domestic price above the world price, hurting consumers, benefiting domestic producers, and generating government revenue. As a result, total surplus falls. An **import quota** is a legal limit on the quantity of a good that can be imported. It has the same effects as a tariff, except that the revenue goes not to the government but to those who receive import licenses.

9. Although several popular arguments have been made in favor of trade protection, in practice the main reason for protection is probably political: import-competing industries are well organized and well informed about how they gain from trade protection, while consumers are unaware of the costs they pay. Still, U.S. trade is fairly free, mainly because of the role of **international trade agreements,** in which countries agree to reduce trade protection against one anothers' exports. The **North American Free Trade Agreement (NAFTA)** and the **European Union (EU)** cover a small number of countries. In contrast, the **World Trade Organization (WTO)** covers a much larger number of countries, accounting for the bulk of world trade. It oversees trade negotiations and adjudicates disputes among its members.

10. In the past few years, many concerns have been raised about the effects of globalization. One issue is the increase in income inequality due to the surge in imports from relatively poor countries over the past 20 years. Another concern is the increase in **offshore outsourcing,** as many jobs that were once considered safe from foreign competition have been moved abroad.

## KEY TERMS

Imports, p. 128
Exports, p. 128
Globalization, p. 128
Ricardian model of international trade, p. 129
Autarky, p. 130
Factor intensity, p. 135
Heckscher–Ohlin model, p. 135
Domestic demand curve, p. 138

Domestic supply curve, p. 138
World price, p. 138
Exporting industries, p. 142
Import-competing industries, p. 142
Free trade, p. 144
Trade protection, p. 144
Protection, p. 144
Tariff, p. 144
Import quota, p. 146

International trade agreements, p. 149
North American Free Trade Agreement (NAFTA), p. 150
European Union (EU), p. 150
World Trade Organization (WTO), p. 150
Offshore outsourcing, p. 152

## PROBLEMS

1. Assume Saudi Arabia and the United States face the production possibilities for oil and cars shown in the accompanying table.

| Saudi Arabia | | United States | |
|---|---|---|---|
| Quantity of oil (millions of barrels) | Quantity of cars (millions) | Quantity of oil (millions of barrels) | Quantity of cars (millions) |
| 0 | 4 | 0 | 10.0 |
| 200 | 3 | 100 | 7.5 |
| 400 | 2 | 200 | 5.0 |
| 600 | 1 | 300 | 2.5 |
| 800 | 0 | 400 | 0 |

**a.** What is the opportunity cost of producing a car in Saudi Arabia? In the United States? What is the opportunity cost of producing a barrel of oil in Saudi Arabia? In the United States?

**b.** Which country has the comparative advantage in producing oil? In producing cars?

**c.** Suppose that in autarky, Saudi Arabia produces 200 million barrels of oil and 3 million cars; similarly, that the United States produces 300 million barrels of oil and 2.5 million cars. Without trade, can Saudi Arabia produce more oil *and* more cars? Without trade, can the United States produce more oil *and* more cars?

2. The production possibilities for the United States and Saudi Arabia are given in Problem 1. Suppose now that each country specializes in the good in which it has the comparative advantage, and the two countries trade. Also assume that for each country the value of imports must equal the value of exports.

**a.** What is the total quantity of oil produced? What is the total quantity of cars produced?

**b.** Is it possible for Saudi Arabia to consume 400 million barrels of oil and 5 million cars and for the United States to consume 400 million barrels of oil and 5 million cars?

**c.** Suppose that, in fact, Saudi Arabia consumes 300 million barrels of oil and 4 million cars and the United States consumes 500 million barrels of oil and 6 million cars. How many barrels of oil does the United States import? How many cars does the United States export? Suppose a car costs $10,000 on the world market. How much, then, does a barrel of oil cost on the world market?

3. Both Canada and the United States produce lumber and music CDs with constant opportunity costs. The United States can produce either 10 tons of lumber and no CDs, or 1,000 CDs and no lumber, or any combination in between. Canada can produce either 8 tons of lumber and no CDs, or 400 CDs and no lumber, or any combination in between.

**a.** Draw the U.S. and Canadian production possibility frontiers in two separate diagrams, with CDs on the horizontal axis and lumber on the vertical axis.

**b.** In autarky, if the United States wants to consume 500 CDs, how much lumber can it consume at most? Label this point *A* in your diagram. Similarly, if Canada wants to consume 1 ton of lumber, how many CDs can it consume in autarky? Label this point *C* in your diagram.

**c.** Which country has the absolute advantage in lumber production?

**d.** Which country has the comparative advantage in lumber production?

Suppose each country specializes in the good in which it has the comparative advantage, and there is trade.

**e.** How many CDs does the United States produce? How much lumber does Canada produce?

**f.** Is it possible for the United States to consume 500 CDs and 7 tons of lumber? Label this point *B* in your diagram. Is it possible for Canada at the same time to consume 500 CDs and 1 ton of lumber? Label this point *D* in your diagram.

4. For each of the following trade relationships, explain the likely source of the comparative advantage of each of the exporting countries.

**a.** The United States exports software to Venezuela, and Venezuela exports oil to the United States.

**b.** The United States exports airplanes to China, and China exports clothing to the United States.

**c.** The United States exports wheat to Colombia, and Colombia exports coffee to the United States.

5. The U.S. Census Bureau keeps statistics on U.S. imports and exports on its website. The following steps will take you to the foreign trade statistics. Use them to answer the questions below.

**i.** Go to the U.S. Census Bureau's website at www.census.gov

**ii.** Under the heading "Business & Industry," select "Foreign Trade"

**iii.** At the top of the page, select "Data"

**iv.** Then select "Country/Product Trade"

**v.** Under the heading "North American Industry Classification System (NAICS)-Based," select "NAICS web application"

**vi.** In the drop-down menu "3-digit and 6-digit NAICS by country," select the product category you are interested in, and hit "Go"

**vii.** In the drop-down menu "Select 6-digit NAICS," select the good or service you are interested in, and hit "Go"

**viii.** In the drop-down menus that allow you to select a month and year, select "December" and "2010," and hit "Go"

**ix.** The right side of the table now shows the import and export statistics for the entire year 2010. For the questions below on U.S. imports, use the column for "Consumption Imports, Customs Value Basis."

a. Look up data for U.S. imports of hats and caps: in step (vi), select "(315) Apparel & Accessories" and in step (vii), select "(315991) Hats and Caps." From which country do we import the most hats and caps? Which of the three sources of comparative advantage (climate, factor endowments, and technology) accounts for that country's comparative advantage in hat and cap production?

b. Look up data for U.S. imports of grapes: in step (vi), select "(111) Agricultural Products" and in step (vii), select "(111332) Grapes." From which country do we import the most grapes? Which of the three sources of comparative advantage (climate, factor endowments, and technology) accounts for that country's comparative advantage in grape production?

c. Look up data for U.S. imports of food product machinery: in step (vi), select "(333) Machinery, Except Electrical" and in step (vii), select "(333294) Food Product Machinery." From which country do we import the most food product machinery? Which of the three sources of comparative advantage (climate, factor endowments, and technology) accounts for that country's comparative advantage in food product machinery?

6. Compare the data for U.S. imports of hats and caps from China in 2010 that you found in Problem 5 with the same data for the year 2000. Repeat the steps outlined in Problem 5, but in step (viii) select "December" and "2000."

a. What happened to the value of U.S. imports of hats and caps from China between 2000 and 2010?

b. What prediction does the Heckscher–Ohlin model make about the wages received by labor in China?

7. Shoes are labor-intensive and satellites are capital-intensive to produce. The United States has abundant capital. China has abundant labor. According to the Heckscher–Ohlin model, which good will China export? Which good will the United States export? In the United States, what will happen to the price of labor (the wage) and to the price of capital?

8. Before the North American Free Trade Agreement (NAFTA) gradually eliminated import tariffs on goods, the autarky price of tomatoes in Mexico was below the world price and in the United States was above the world price. Similarly, the autarky price of poultry in Mexico was above the world price and in the United States was below the world price. Draw diagrams with domestic supply and demand curves for each country and each of the two goods. As a result of NAFTA, the United States now imports tomatoes from Mexico and the United States now exports poultry to Mexico. How would you expect the following groups to be affected?

a. Mexican and U.S. consumers of tomatoes. Illustrate the effect on consumer surplus in your diagram.

b. Mexican and U.S. producers of tomatoes. Illustrate the effect on producer surplus in your diagram.

c. Mexican and U.S. tomato workers.

d. Mexican and U.S. consumers of poultry. Illustrate the effect on consumer surplus in your diagram.

e. Mexican and U.S. producers of poultry. Illustrate the effect on producer surplus in your diagram.

f. Mexican and U.S. poultry workers.

9. The accompanying table indicates the U.S. domestic demand schedule and domestic supply schedule for commercial jet airplanes. Suppose that the world price of a commercial jet airplane is $100 million.

| Price of jet (millions) | Quantity of jets demanded | Quantity of jets supplied |
|---|---|---|
| $120 | 100 | 1,000 |
| 110 | 150 | 900 |
| 100 | 200 | 800 |
| 90 | 250 | 700 |
| 80 | 300 | 600 |
| 70 | 350 | 500 |
| 60 | 400 | 400 |
| 50 | 450 | 300 |
| 40 | 500 | 200 |

a. In autarky, how many commercial jet airplanes does the United States produce, and at what price are they bought and sold?

b. With trade, what will the price for commercial jet airplanes be? Will the United States import or export airplanes? How many?

10. The accompanying table shows the U.S. domestic demand schedule and domestic supply schedule for oranges. Suppose that the world price of oranges is $0.30 per orange.

| Price of orange | Quantity of oranges demanded (thousands) | Quantity of oranges supplied (thousands) |
|---|---|---|
| $1.00 | 2 | 11 |
| 0.90 | 4 | 10 |
| 0.80 | 6 | 9 |
| 0.70 | 8 | 8 |
| 0.60 | 10 | 7 |
| 0.50 | 12 | 6 |
| 0.40 | 14 | 5 |
| 0.30 | 16 | 4 |
| 0.20 | 18 | 3 |

a. Draw the U.S. domestic supply curve and domestic demand curve.

b. With free trade, how many oranges will the United States import or export?

Suppose that the U.S. government imposes a tariff on oranges of $0.20 per orange.

**c.** How many oranges will the United States import or export after introduction of the tariff?

**d.** In your diagram, shade the gain or loss to the economy as a whole from the introduction of this tariff.

**11.** The U.S. domestic demand schedule and domestic supply schedule for oranges was given in Problem 10. Suppose that the world price of oranges is $0.30. The United States introduces an import quota of 3,000 oranges and assigns the quota rents to foreign orange exporters.

**a.** Draw the domestic demand and supply curves.

**b.** What will the domestic price of oranges be after introduction of the quota?

**c.** What is the value of the quota rents that foreign exporters of oranges receive?

**12.** The accompanying diagram illustrates the U.S. domestic demand curve and domestic supply curve for beef.

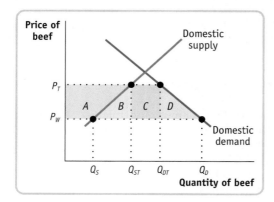

The world price of beef is $P_W$. The United States currently imposes an import tariff on beef, so the price of beef is $P_T$. Congress decides to eliminate the tariff. In terms of the areas marked in the diagram, answer the following questions.

**a.** What is the gain/loss in consumer surplus?

**b.** What is the gain/loss in producer surplus?

**c.** What is the gain/loss to the government?

**d.** What is the gain/loss to the economy as a whole?

**13.** As the United States has opened up to trade, it has lost many of its low-skill manufacturing jobs, but it has gained jobs in high-skill industries, such as the software industry. Explain whether the United States as a whole has been made better off by trade.

**14.** The United States is highly protective of its agricultural industry, imposing import tariffs, and sometimes quotas, on imports of agricultural goods. This chapter presented three arguments for trade protection. For each argument, discuss whether it is a valid justification for trade protection of U.S. agricultural products.

**15.** In World Trade Organization (WTO) negotiations, if a country agrees to reduce trade barriers (tariffs or quotas), it usually refers to this as a *concession* to other countries. Do you think that this terminology is appropriate?

**16.** Producers in import-competing industries often make the following argument: "Other countries have an advantage in production of certain goods purely because workers abroad are paid lower wages. In fact, American workers are much more productive than foreign workers. So import-competing industries need to be protected." Is this a valid argument? Explain your answer.

# CHAPTER 5

# Consumer and Producer Surplus

In the body of this chapter, we used the concepts of consumer and producer surplus to analyze how the welfare of consumers and producers is affected by trade and tariffs. The concepts of consumer surplus and producer surplus are extremely useful for analyzing a wide variety of economic issues. They let us calculate how much benefit producers and consumers receive from the existence of a market. They also allow us to calculate how the welfare of consumers and producers is affected by changes in market prices. Such calculations play a crucial role in evaluating many economic policies, and they are especially useful in understanding the effects of trade.

All we need in order to calculate consumer surplus are the demand and supply curves for a good. That is, the supply and demand model isn't just a model of how a competitive market works—it's also a model of how much consumers and producers gain from participating in that market. Our starting point is the market in used textbooks, a big business in terms of dollars and cents, approximately $3 billion in 2009. More importantly for us, it is useful for developing the concepts of consumer and producer surplus.

## Consumer Surplus and the Demand Curve

Let's look at the market for used textbooks, starting with the buyers. The key point, as we'll see in a minute, is that the demand curve is derived from their tastes or preferences—and that those same preferences also determine how much they gain from the opportunity to buy used books.

### Willingness to Pay and the Demand Curve

A used book is not as good as a new book—it will be battered and coffee-stained, may include someone else's highlighting, and may not be completely up to date. How much this bothers you depends on your preferences. Some potential buyers would prefer to buy the used book even if it is only slightly cheaper than a new one; others would buy the used book only if it is considerably cheaper. Let's define a potential buyer's **willingness to pay** as the maximum price at which he or she would buy a good, in this case a used textbook. An individual won't buy the book if it costs more than this amount but is eager to do so if it costs less. If the price is just equal to an individual's willingness to pay, he or she is indifferent between buying and not buying.

A consumer's **willingness to pay** for a good is the maximum price at which he or she would buy that good.

Table 5A-1 shows five potential buyers of a used book that costs $100 new, listed in order of their willingness to pay. At one extreme is Aleisha, who will buy a second-hand book even if the price is as high as $59. Brad is less willing to have a used book and will buy one only if the price is $45 or less. Claudia is willing to pay only $35; Darren, only $25. And Edwina, who really doesn't like the idea of a used book, will buy one only if it costs no more than $10.

How many of these five students will actually buy a used book? It depends on the

**TABLE 5A-1** Consumer Surplus If Price of a Used Textbook = $30

| Potential buyer | Willingness to pay | Price paid | Individual consumer surplus = Willingness to pay − Price paid |
|---|---|---|---|
| Aleisha | $59 | $30 | $29 |
| Brad | 45 | 30 | 15 |
| Claudia | 35 | 30 | 5 |
| Darren | 25 | — | — |
| Edwina | 10 | — | — |
| **All buyers** | | | **Total consumer surplus = $49** |

**Individual consumer surplus** is the net gain to an individual buyer from the purchase of a good. It is equal to the difference between the buyer's willingness to pay and the price paid.

**Total consumer surplus** is the sum of the individual consumer surpluses of all the buyers of a good in a market.

The term **consumer surplus** is often used to refer to both individual and total consumer surplus.

price. If the price of a used book is $55, only Aleisha buys one; if the price is $40, Aleisha and Brad both buy used books, and so on. So the information in the table on willingness to pay also defines the *demand schedule* for used textbooks.

## Willingness to Pay and Consumer Surplus

Suppose that the campus bookstore makes used textbooks available at a price of $30. In that case Aleisha, Brad, and Claudia will buy books. Do they gain from their purchases, and if so, how much?

The answer, also shown in Table 5A-1, is that each student who purchases a book does achieve a net gain but that the amount of the gain differs among students.

Aleisha would have been willing to pay $59, so her net gain is $59 – $30 = $29. Brad would have been willing to pay $45, so his net gain is $45 – $30 = $15. Claudia would have been willing to pay $35, so her net gain is $35 – $30 = $5. Darren and Edwina, however, won't be willing to buy a used book at a price of $30, so they neither gain nor lose.

The net gain that a buyer achieves from the purchase of a good is called that buyer's **individual consumer surplus.** What we learn from this example is that whenever a buyer pays a price less than his or her willingness to pay, the buyer achieves some individual consumer surplus.

The sum of the individual consumer surpluses achieved by all the buyers of a good is known as the **total consumer surplus** achieved in the market. In Table 5A-1, the total consumer surplus is the sum of the individual consumer surpluses achieved by Aleisha, Brad, and Claudia: $29 + $15 + $5 = $49.

Economists often use the term **consumer surplus** to refer to both individual and total consumer surplus. We will follow this practice; it will always be clear in context whether we are referring to the consumer surplus achieved by an individual or by all buyers.

Total consumer surplus can be represented graphically. As we saw in Chapter 3, we can use the demand schedule to derive the market demand curve shown in Figure 5A-1. Because we are considering only a small number of consumers, this curve doesn't look like the smooth demand curves of Chapter 3, where markets contained hundreds or thousands of consumers. Instead, this demand curve is stepped, with alternating horizontal and vertical segments. Each horizontal segment—each step—corresponds to one potential buyer's willingness to pay. Each step in that demand curve is one book wide and represents one consumer. For example, the height of Aleisha's step is $59, her willingness to pay. This step forms the top of a rectangle, with $30—the price she actually pays for a book—forming the bottom. The area of Aleisha's rectangle, ($59 – $30) × 1 = $29, is her consumer surplus from purchasing

**FIGURE 5A-1 Consumer Surplus in the Used-Textbook Market**

At a price of $30, Aleisha, Brad, and Claudia each buy a book but Darren and Edwina do not. Aleisha, Brad, and Claudia get individual consumer surpluses equal to the difference between their willingness to pay and the price, illustrated by the areas of the shaded rectangles. Both Darren and Edwina have a willingness to pay less than $30, so they are unwilling to buy a book in this market; they receive zero consumer surplus. The total consumer surplus is given by the entire shaded area—the sum of the individual consumer surpluses of Aleisha, Brad, and Claudia—equal to $29 + $15 + $5 = $49.

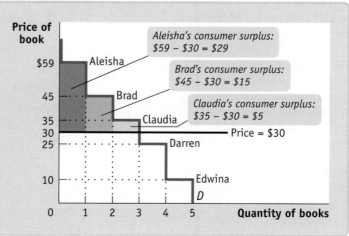

one book at $30. So the individual consumer surplus Aleisha gains is the *area of the dark blue rectangle* shown in Figure 5A-1.

In addition to Aleisha, Brad and Claudia will also each buy a book when the price is $30. Like Aleisha, they benefit from their purchases, though not as much, because they each have a lower willingness to pay. Figure 5A-1 also shows the consumer surplus gained by Brad and Claudia; again, this can be measured by the areas of the appropriate rectangles. Darren and Edwina, because they do not buy books at a price of $30, receive no consumer surplus.

The total consumer surplus achieved in this market is just the sum of the individual consumer surpluses received by Aleisha, Brad, and Claudia. So total consumer surplus is equal to the combined area of the three rectangles—the entire shaded area in Figure 5A-1. Another way to say this is that total consumer surplus is equal to the area below the demand curve but above the price.

This illustrates the following general principle: *the total consumer surplus generated by purchases of a good at a given price is equal to the area below the demand curve but above that price.* The same principle applies regardless of the number of consumers.

For large markets, such as the market for auto parts that was used in the chapter, this graphical representation of consumer surplus becomes extremely helpful. Consider, for example, the sales of iPads to millions of potential buyers. Each potential buyer has a maximum price that he or she is willing to pay. With so many potential buyers, the demand curve will be smooth, like the one shown in Figure 5A-2.

Suppose that at a price of $500, a total of 1 million iPads are purchased. How much do consumers gain from being able to buy those 1 million iPads? We could answer that question by calculating the consumer surplus of each individual buyer and then adding these numbers up to arrive at a total. But it is much easier just to look at Figure 5A-2 and use the fact that the total consumer surplus is equal to the shaded area. As in our original example, consumer surplus is equal to the area below the demand curve but above the price. (You can refresh your memory on how to calculate the area of a right triangle by reviewing the appendix to Chapter 2.)

**FIGURE 5A-2 Consumer Surplus**

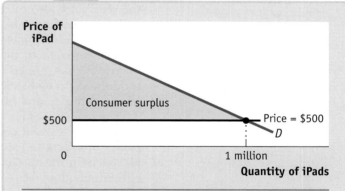

The demand curve for iPads is smooth because there are many potential buyers. At a price of $500, 1 million iPads are demanded. The consumer surplus at this price is equal to the shaded area: the area below the demand curve but above the price. This is the total net gain to consumers generated from buying and consuming iPads when the price is $500.

# Producer Surplus and the Supply Curve

Just as some buyers of a good would have been willing to pay more for their purchase than the price they actually pay, some sellers of a good would have been willing to sell it for less than the price they actually receive. So just as there are consumers who receive consumer surplus from buying in a market, there are producers who receive producer surplus from selling in a market.

## Cost and Producer Surplus

Consider a group of students who are potential sellers of used textbooks. Because they have different preferences, the various potential sellers differ in the price at which they are willing to sell their books. Table 5A-2 shows the prices at which several different students would be willing to sell. Andrew is willing to sell the book as long as he can get at least $5; Betty won't sell unless she can get at least $15; Carlos, unless he can get $25; Donna, unless she can get $35; Engelbert, unless he can get $45.

**TABLE 5A-2 Producer Surplus If Price of a Used Textbook = $30**

| Potential seller | Cost | Price received | Individual producer surplus = Price received − Cost |
|---|---|---|---|
| Andrew | $5 | $30 | $25 |
| Betty | 15 | 30 | 15 |
| Carlos | 25 | 30 | 5 |
| Donna | 35 | — | — |
| Engelbert | 45 | — | — |
| **All sellers** | | | **Total producer surplus = $45** |

A seller's **cost** is the lowest price at which he or she is willing to sell a good.

**Individual producer surplus** is the net gain to an individual seller from selling a good. It is equal to the difference between the price received and the seller's cost.

**Total producer surplus** in a market is the sum of the individual producer surpluses of all the sellers of a good in a market.

Economists use the term **producer surplus** to refer to either total or individual producer surplus.

The lowest price at which a potential seller is willing to sell has a special name in economics: it is called the seller's **cost.** So Andrew's cost is $5, Betty's is $15, and so on.

Using the term *cost*, which people normally associate with the monetary cost of producing a good, may sound a little strange when applied to sellers of used textbooks. The students don't have to manufacture the books, so it doesn't cost the student who sells a used textbook anything to make that book available for sale, does it?

Yes, it does. A student who sells a book won't have it later, as part of his or her personal collection. So there is an *opportunity cost* to selling a textbook, even if the owner has completed the course for which it was required. And remember that one of the basic principles of economics is that the true measure of the cost of doing something is always its opportunity cost. That is, the real cost of something is what you must give up to get it.

So it is good economics to talk of the minimum price at which someone will sell a good as the "cost" of selling that good, even if he or she doesn't spend any money to make the good available for sale. Of course, in most real-world markets the sellers are also those who produce the good and therefore *do* spend money to make the good available for sale. In this case the cost of making the good available for sale *includes* monetary costs, but it may also include other opportunity costs.

Getting back to the example, suppose that Andrew sells his book for $30. Clearly he has gained from the transaction: he would have been willing to sell for only $5, so he has gained $25. This net gain, the difference between the price he actually gets and his cost—the minimum price at which he would have been willing to sell—is known as his **individual producer surplus.**

As in the case of consumer surplus, we can add the individual producer surpluses of sellers to calculate the **total producer surplus,** the total net gain to all sellers in the market. Economists use the term **producer surplus** to refer to either individual or total producer surplus. Table 5A-2 shows the net gain to each of the students who would sell a used book at a price of $30: $25 for Andrew, $15 for Betty, and $5 for Carlos. The total producer surplus is $25 + $15 + $5 = $45.

As with consumer surplus, the producer surplus gained by those who sell books can be represented graphically. Just as we derived the demand curve from the willingness to pay of different consumers, we derive the supply curve from the cost of different producers. The step-shaped curve in Figure 5A-3 shows the supply curve implied by the cost shown in Table 5A-2. Each step in the supply curve is one book wide and represents one seller. The height of Andrew's step is $5, his cost. This forms the bottom of a rectangle, with $30, the price he actually receives for his book, forming the top. The area of this rectangle, ($30 − $5) × 1 = $25, is his

**FIGURE  5A-3**  Producer Surplus in the Used-Textbook Market

At a price of $30, Andrew, Betty, and Carlos each sell a book but Donna and Engelbert do not. Andrew, Betty, and Carlos get individual producer surpluses equal to the difference between the price and their cost, illustrated here by the shaded rectangles. Donna and Engelbert each have a cost that is greater than the price of $30, so they are unwilling to sell a book and so receive zero producer surplus. The total producer surplus is given by the entire shaded area, the sum of the individual producer surpluses of Andrew, Betty, and Carlos, equal to $25 + $15 + $5 = $45.

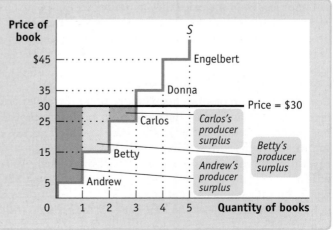

producer surplus. So the producer surplus Andrew gains from selling his book is the *area of the dark red rectangle* shown in the figure.

Let's assume that the campus bookstore is willing to buy all the used copies of this book that students are willing to sell at a price of $30. Then, in addition to Andrew, Betty and Carlos will also sell their books. They will also benefit from their sales, though not as much as Andrew, because they have higher costs. Andrew, as we have seen, gains $25. Betty gains a smaller amount: since her cost is $15, she gains only $15. Carlos gains even less, only $5.

Again, as with consumer surplus, we have a general rule for determining the total producer surplus from sales of a good: *The total producer surplus from sales of a good at a given price is the area above the supply curve but below that price.*

This rule applies both to examples like the one shown in Figure 5A-3, where there are a small number of producers and a step-shaped supply curve, and to more realistic examples, where there are many producers and the supply curve is smooth.

Consider, for example, the supply of wheat. Figure 5A-4 shows how producer surplus depends on the price per bushel. Suppose that, as shown in the figure, the price is $5 per bushel and farmers supply 1 million bushels. What is the benefit to the farmers from selling their wheat at a price of $5? Their producer surplus is equal to the shaded area in the figure—the area above the supply curve but below the price of $5 per bushel.

**FIGURE  5A-4  Producer Surplus**

Here is the supply curve for wheat. At a price of $5 per bushel, farmers supply 1 million bushels. The producer surplus at this price is equal to the shaded area: the area above the supply curve but below the price. This is the total gain to producers—farmers in this case—from supplying their product when the price is $5.

# The Gains from Trade

Let's return to the market for used textbooks, but now consider a much bigger market—say, one at a large state university. There are many potential buyers and sellers, so the market is competitive. Let's line up incoming students who are potential buyers of a book in order of their willingness to pay, so that the entering student with the highest willingness to pay is potential buyer number 1, the student with the next highest willingness to pay is number 2, and so on. Then we can use their willingness to pay to derive a demand curve like the one in Figure 5A-5. Similarly, we can line up outgoing students, who are potential sellers of the book, in order of their cost, starting

**FIGURE  5A-5  Total Surplus**

In the market for used textbooks, the equilibrium price is $30 and the equilibrium quantity is 1,000 books. Consumer surplus is given by the blue area, the area below the demand curve but above the price. Producer surplus is given by the red area, the area above the supply curve but below the price. The sum of the blue and the red areas is total surplus, the total benefit to society from the production and consumption of the good.

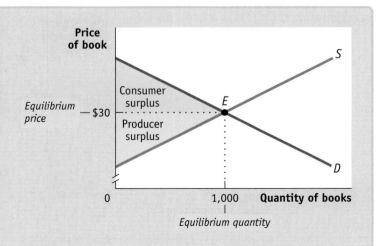

The **total surplus** generated in a market is the total net gain to consumers and producers from trading in the market. It is the sum of the consumer and the producer surplus.

with the student with the lowest cost, then the student with the next lowest cost, and so on, to derive a supply curve like the one shown in the same figure.

As we have drawn the curves, the market reaches equilibrium at a price of $30 per book, and 1,000 books are bought and sold at that price. The two shaded triangles show the consumer surplus (blue) and the producer surplus (red) generated by this market. The sum of consumer and producer surplus is known as the **total surplus** generated in a market.

The striking thing about this picture is that both consumers and producers gain—that is, both consumers and producers are better off because there is a market in this good. But this should come as no surprise—it illustrates another core principle of economics: *There are gains from trade*. These gains from trade are the reason everyone is better off participating in a market economy than they would be if each individual tried to be self-sufficient.

## PROBLEMS

1. Determine the amount of consumer surplus generated in each of the following situations.
   a. Leon goes to the clothing store to buy a new T-shirt, for which he is willing to pay up to $10. He picks out one he likes with a price tag of exactly $10. When he is paying for it, he learns that the T-shirt has been discounted by 50%.
   b. Alberto goes to the CD store hoping to find a used copy of *Nirvana's Greatest Hits* for up to $10. The store has one copy selling for $10, which he purchases.
   c. After soccer practice, Stacey is willing to pay $2 for a bottle of mineral water. The 7-Eleven sells mineral water for $2.25 per bottle, so she declines to purchase it.

2. Determine the amount of producer surplus generated in each of the following situations.
   a. Gordon lists his old Lionel electric trains on eBay. He sets a minimum acceptable price, known as his *reserve price*, of $75. After five days of bidding, the final high bid is exactly $75. He accepts the bid.
   b. So-Hee advertises her car for sale in the used-car section of the student newspaper for $2,000, but she is willing to sell the car for any price higher than $1,500. The best offer she gets is $1,200, which she declines.
   c. Sanjay likes his job so much that he would be willing to do it for free. However, his annual salary is $80,000.

3. You are the manager of Fun World, a small amusement park. The accompanying diagram shows the demand curve of a typical customer at Fun World.

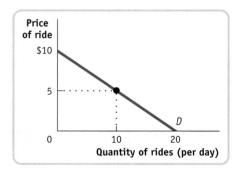

a. Suppose that the price of each ride is $5. At that price, how much consumer surplus does an individual consumer get? (Recall that the area of a right triangle is ½ × the height of the triangle × the base of the triangle.)
b. Suppose that Fun World considers charging an admission fee, even though it maintains the price of each ride at $5. What is the maximum admission fee it could charge? (Assume that all potential customers have enough money to pay the fee.)
c. Suppose that Fun World lowered the price of each ride to zero. How much consumer surplus does an individual consumer get? What is the maximum admission fee Fun World could charge?

4. The accompanying diagram illustrates a taxi driver's individual supply curve (assume that each taxi ride is the same distance).

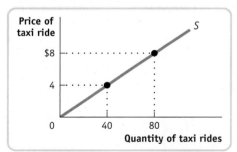

a. Suppose the city sets the price of taxi rides at $4 per ride, and at $4 the taxi driver is able to sell as many taxi rides as he desires. What is this taxi driver's producer surplus? (Recall that the area of a right triangle is ½ × the height of the triangle × the base of the triangle.)
b. Suppose that the city keeps the price of a taxi ride set at $4, but it decides to charge taxi drivers a "licensing fee." What is the maximum licensing fee the city could extract from this taxi driver?
c. Suppose that the city allowed the price of taxi rides to increase to $8 per ride. Again assume that, at this price, the taxi driver sells as many rides as he is willing to offer. How much producer surplus does an individual taxi driver now get? What is the maximum licensing fee the city could charge this taxi driver?

# Macroeconomics: The Big Picture

## HOOVERVILLES

During the Great Depression, Hoovervilles sprang up across America, named after the economically clueless President Herbert Hoover.

> **What makes macroeconomics different from microeconomics**
>
> **What a business cycle is and why policy makers seek to diminish the severity of business cycles**
>
> **How long-run economic growth determines a country's standard of living**
>
> **The meaning of inflation and deflation and why price stability is preferred**
>
> **The importance of open-economy macroeconomics and how economies interact through trade deficits and trade surpluses**

TODAY MANY PEOPLE ENJOY walking, biking, and horseback riding in New York's Central Park. But in 1932 there were also many people living there: Central Park contained one of the "Hoovervilles"—shantytowns—that had sprung up all across America as a result of a catastrophic economic slump that started in 1929, leaving millions of workers out of work, reduced to standing in breadlines or selling apples on street corners. The U.S. economy would stage a partial recovery beginning in 1933, but joblessness stayed high throughout the 1930s. The whole period would come to be known as the Great Depression.

Why Hoovervilles? The shantytowns got their derisive name from Herbert Hoover, who had been elected president in 1928—and who lost his bid for reelection because many Americans blamed him for the Depression. Hoover began his career as an engineer, and until he became president he had a reputation as a can-do, highly competent manager. But when the Depression struck, neither he nor his economic advisers had any idea what to do.

Hoover's cluelessness was no accident. At the time of the Great Depression, *microeconomics,* which is concerned with the consumption and production decisions of individual consumers and producers and with the allocation of scarce resources among industries, was already a well-developed branch of economics. But *macroeconomics,* which focuses on the behavior of the economy as a whole, was still in its infancy.

What happened between 1929 and 1933, and on a smaller scale on many other occasions (most recently between 2007 and 2009), was a blow to the economy as a whole. At any given moment there are always some industries laying off workers. For example, the number of independent record stores in America fell almost 30% between 2003 and 2007, as consumers turned to online purchases. But workers who lost their jobs at record stores had a good chance of finding new jobs elsewhere, because other industries were expanding even as record stores shut their doors. In the early 1930s, however, there were no expanding industries: everything was headed downward.

Macroeconomics came into its own as a branch of economics during the Great Depression. Economists realized that they needed to understand the nature of the catastrophe that had overtaken the United States and much of the rest of the world in order to extricate themselves as well as to learn how to avoid such catastrophes in the future. To this day, the effort to understand economic slumps and find ways to prevent them is at the core of macroeconomics. Over time, however, macroeconomics has broadened its reach to encompass a number of other subjects, such as *long-run economic growth, inflation,* and *open-economy macroeconomics.*

This chapter offers an overview of macroeconomics. We start with a general description of the difference between macroeconomics and microeconomics, then briefly describe some of the field's major concerns. ■

# The Nature of Macroeconomics

What makes macroeconomics different from microeconomics? The distinguishing feature of macroeconomics is that it focuses on the behavior of the economy as a whole.

## Macroeconomic Questions

Table 6-1 lists some typical questions that involve economics. A microeconomic version of the question appears on the left paired with a similar macroeconomic question on the right. By comparing the questions, you can begin to get a sense of the difference between microeconomics and macroeconomics.

As these questions illustrate, microeconomics focuses on how decisions are made by individuals and firms and the consequences of those decisions. For example, we use microeconomics to determine how much it would cost a university or college to offer a new course, which includes the instructor's salary, the cost of class materials, and so on. The school can then decide whether or not to offer the course by weighing the costs and benefits.

**TABLE 6-1** Microeconomic versus Macroeconomic Questions

| Microeconomic Questions | Macroeconomic Questions |
| --- | --- |
| Should I go to business school or take a job right now? | How many people are employed in the economy as a whole this year? |
| What determines the salary offered by Citibank to Cherie Camajo, a new MBA? | What determines the overall salary levels paid to workers in a given year? |
| What determines the cost to a university or college of offering a new course? | What determines the overall level of prices in the economy as a whole? |
| What government policies should be adopted to make it easier for low-income students to attend college? | What government policies should be adopted to promote employment and growth in the economy as a whole? |
| What determines whether Citibank opens a new office in Shanghai? | What determines the overall trade in goods, services, and financial assets between the United States and the rest of the world? |

Macroeconomics, in contrast, examines the *overall* behavior of the economy—how the actions of all the individuals and firms in the economy interact to produce a particular economy-wide level of economic performance. For example, macroeconomics is concerned with the general level of prices in the economy and how high or how low it is relative to prices last year, rather than with the price of one particular good or service.

You might imagine that macroeconomic questions can be answered simply by adding up microeconomic answers. For example, the model of supply and demand we introduced in Chapter 3 tells us how the equilibrium price of an individual good or service is determined in a competitive market. So you might think that applying supply and demand analysis to every good and service in the economy, then summing the results, is the way to understand the overall level of prices in the economy as a whole.

But that turns out not to be right: although basic concepts such as supply and demand are as essential to macroeconomics as they are to microeconomics, answering macroeconomic questions requires an additional set of tools and an expanded frame of reference.

## Macroeconomics: The Whole Is Greater Than the Sum of Its Parts

If you occasionally drive on a highway, you probably know what a rubber-necking traffic jam is and why it is so annoying. Someone pulls over to the side of the road for something minor, such as changing a flat tire, and, pretty soon, a long traffic jam occurs as drivers slow down to take a look. What makes it so annoying is that the length of the traffic jam is greatly out of proportion to the minor event that precipitated it. Because some drivers hit their brakes in order to rubber-neck, the drivers behind them must also hit their brakes, those behind them must do the same, and so on. The accumulation of all the individual hitting of brakes eventually leads to a long, wasteful traffic jam as each driver slows down a little bit more than the driver in front of him or her. In other words, each person's response leads to an amplified response by the next person.

Understanding a rubber-necking traffic jam gives us some insight into one very important way in which macroeconomics is different from microeconomics: many thousands or millions of individual actions compound upon one another to produce an outcome that isn't simply the sum of those individual actions.

Consider, for example, what macroeconomists call the *paradox of thrift:* when families and businesses are worried about the possibility of economic hard times, they prepare by cutting their spending. This reduction in spending depresses the economy as consumers spend less and businesses react by laying off workers. As a result, families and businesses may end up worse off than if they hadn't tried to act responsibly by cutting their spending. This is a paradox because seemingly virtuous behavior—preparing for hard times by saving more—ends up harming everyone. And there is a flip-side to this story: when families and businesses are feeling optimistic about the future, they spend more today. This stimulates the economy, leading businesses to hire more workers, which further expands the economy. Seemingly profligate behavior leads to good times for all.

Or consider what happens when something causes the quantity of cash circulating through the economy to rise. An individual with more cash on hand is richer. But if everyone has more cash, the long-run effect is simply to push the overall level of prices higher, taking the purchasing power of the total amount of cash in circulation right back to where it was before.

A key insight of macroeconomics, then, is that the combined effect of individual decisions can have results that are very different from what any one individual intended, results that are sometimes perverse. The behavior of the macroeconomy is, indeed, greater than the sum of individual actions and market outcomes.

In a **self-regulating economy,** problems such as unemployment are resolved without government intervention, through the working of the invisible hand.

According to **Keynesian economics,** economic slumps are caused by inadequate spending, and they can be mitigated by government intervention.

The behavior of the macroeconomy is greater than the sum of individual actions and market outcomes.

## Macroeconomics: Theory and Policy

To a much greater extent than microeconomists, macroeconomists are concerned with questions about *policy,* about what the government can do to make macroeconomic performance better. This policy focus was strongly shaped by history, in particular by the Great Depression of the 1930s.

Before the 1930s, economists tended to regard the economy as **self-regulating:** they believed that problems such as unemployment would be corrected through the working of the invisible hand and that government attempts to improve the economy's performance would be ineffective at best—and would probably make things worse.

The Great Depression changed all that. The sheer scale of the catastrophe, which left a quarter of the U.S. workforce without jobs and threatened the political stability of many countries—the Depression is widely believed to have been a major factor in the Nazi takeover of Germany—created a demand for action. It also led to a major effort on the part of economists to understand economic slumps and find ways to prevent them.

In 1936 the British economist John Maynard Keynes (pronounced "canes") published *The General Theory of Employment, Interest, and Money,* a book that transformed macroeconomics. According to **Keynesian economics,** a depressed economy is the result of inadequate spending. In addition, Keynes

**Monetary policy** uses changes in the quantity of money to alter interest rates and affect overall spending.

**Fiscal policy** uses changes in government spending and taxes to affect overall spending.

argued that government intervention can help a depressed economy through *monetary policy* and *fiscal policy*. **Monetary policy** uses changes in the quantity of money to alter interest rates, which in turn affect the level of overall spending. **Fiscal policy** uses changes in taxes and government spending to affect overall spending.

In general, Keynes established the idea that managing the economy is a government responsibility. Keynesian ideas continue to have a strong influence on both economic theory and public policy: in 2008 and 2009, Congress, the White House, and the Federal Reserve (a quasi-governmental agency that manages U.S. monetary policy) took steps to fend off an economic slump that were clearly Keynesian in spirit, as described in the following Economics in Action.

## ECONOMICS ▶ IN ACTION

### FENDING OFF DEPRESSION

I n 2008 the world economy experienced a severe financial crisis that was all too reminiscent of the early days of the Great Depression. Major banks teetered on the edge of collapse; world trade slumped. In the spring of 2009, the economic historians Barry Eichengreen and Kevin O'Rourke, reviewing the available data, pointed out that "globally we are tracking or even doing worse than the Great Depression."

But the worst did not, in the end, come to pass. Figure 6-1 shows one of Eichengreen and O'Rourke's measures of economic activity, world industrial production, during the Great Depression and during "the Great Recession," the now widely used term for the slump that followed the 2008 financial crisis. During the first year the two crises were indeed comparable. But this time, fortunately, world production leveled off and turned around. Why?

At least part of the answer is that policy makers responded very differently. During the Great Depression, it was widely argued that the slump should simply be allowed to run its course. Any attempt to mitigate the ongoing catastrophe, declared Joseph Schumpeter—the Austrian-born Harvard economist now famed for his work on innovation— would "leave the work of depression undone." In the early 1930s, some countries' monetary authorities actually raised interest rates in the face of the slump, while governments cut spending and raised taxes—actions that, as we'll see in later chapters, deepened the recession.

In the aftermath of the 2008 crisis, by contrast, interest rates were slashed, and a number of countries, the United States included, used temporary increases in spending and reductions in taxes in an attempt to sustain spending. Governments also moved to shore up their banks with loans, aid, and guarantees.

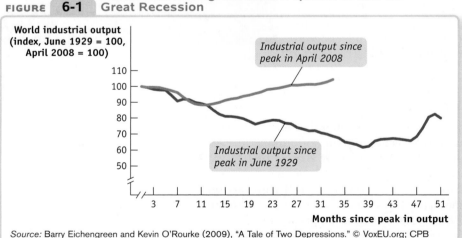

**FIGURE 6-1** Measures of Economic Activity and World Industrial Production During the Great Depression and the Great Recession

*Source:* Barry Eichengreen and Kevin O'Rourke (2009), "A Tale of Two Depressions." © VoxEU.org; CPB Netherlands Bureau for Economic Policy Analysis World Trade Monitor.

Many of these measures were controversial, to say the least. But most economists believe that by responding actively to the Great Recession—and doing so using the knowledge gained from the study of macroeconomics—governments helped avoid a global economic catastrophe.

▶●●

## CHECK YOUR UNDERSTANDING    6-1

1. Which of the following questions involve microeconomics, and which involve macroeconomics? In each case, explain your answer.
   a. Why did consumers switch to smaller cars in 2008?
   b. Why did overall consumer spending slow down in 2008?
   c. Why did the standard of living rise more rapidly in the first generation after World War II than in the second?
   d. Why have starting salaries for students with geology degrees risen sharply of late?
   e. What determines the choice between rail and road transportation?
   f. Why has salmon gotten cheaper over the past 20 years?
   g. Why did inflation fall in the 1990s?

2. In 2008, problems in the financial sector led to a drying up of credit around the country: home-buyers were unable to get mortgages, students were unable to get student loans, car buyers were unable to get car loans, and so on.
   a. Explain how the drying up of credit can lead to compounding effects throughout the economy and result in an economic slump.
   b. If you believe the economy is self-regulating, what would you advocate that policy makers do?
   c. If you believe in Keynesian economics, what would you advocate that policy makers do?

*Solutions appear at back of book.*

▼ **Quick Review**

● Microeconomics focuses on decision making by individuals and firms and the consequences of the decisions made. Macroeconomics focuses on the overall behavior of the economy.

● The combined effect of individual actions can have unintended consequences and lead to worse or better macroeconomic outcomes for everyone.

● Before the 1930s, economists tended to regard the economy as **self-regulating.** After the Great Depression, **Keynesian economics** provided the rationale for government intervention through **monetary policy** and **fiscal policy** to help a depressed economy.

# The Business Cycle

The Great Depression was by far the worst economic crisis in U.S. history. But although the economy managed to avoid catastrophe for the rest of the twentieth century, it has experienced many ups and downs.

It's true that the ups have consistently been bigger than the downs: a chart of any of the major numbers used to track the U.S. economy shows a strong upward trend over time. For example, panel (a) of Figure 6-2 shows total U.S. private-sector employment (the total number of jobs offered by private businesses) measured along the left vertical axis, with the data from 1988 to 2011 given by the purple line. The graph also shows the index of industrial production (a measure of the total output of U.S. factories) measured along the right vertical axis, with the data from 1988 to 2011 given by the red line. Both private-sector employment and industrial production were much higher at the end of this period than at the beginning, and in most years both measures rose.

But they didn't rise steadily. As you can see from the figure, there were three periods—in the early 1990s, in the early 2000s, and again beginning in late 2007—when both employment and industrial output stumbled. Panel (b) emphasizes these stumbles by showing the *rate of change* of employment and industrial production over the previous year. For example, the percent change in employment for December 2007 was 0.7, because employment in December 2007 was 0.7% higher than it had been in December 2006. The three big downturns stand out clearly. What's more, a detailed look at the data makes it clear that in each period the stumble wasn't confined to only a few industries: in each downturn, just about every sector of the U.S. economy cut back on production and on the number of people employed.

FIGURE **6-2** Growth, Interrupted, 1988–2011

**(a) Private–Sector Employment and Industrial Production Index**

**(b) Percent Change from Year Earlier**

Panel (a) shows two important economic numbers, the industrial production index and total private-sector employment. Both numbers grew substantially from 1988 to 2011, but they didn't grow steadily. Instead, both suffered from three downturns associated with *recessions*, which are indicated by the shaded areas in the figure. Panel (b) emphasizes those downturns by showing the annual rate of change of industrial production and employment, that is, the percentage increase over the past year. The simultaneous downturns in both numbers during the three recessions are clear.

*Source:* Federal Reserve Bank of St. Louis.

The economy's forward march, in other words, isn't smooth. And the uneven pace of the economy's progress, its ups and downs, is one of the main preoccupations of macroeconomics.

## Charting the Business Cycle

Figure 6-3 shows a stylized representation of the way the economy evolves over time. The vertical axis shows either employment or an indicator of how much the economy is producing, such as industrial production or *real gross domestic product (real GDP)*, a measure of the economy's overall output that we'll learn about in the next chapter. As the data in Figure 6-2 suggest, these two measures tend to move together. Their common movement is the starting point for a major theme of macroeconomics: the economy's alternation between short-run downturns and upturns.

A broad-based downturn, in which output and employment fall in

**Recessions,** or contractions, are periods of economic downturn when output and employment are falling.

**Expansions,** or recoveries, are periods of economic upturn when output and employment are rising.

The **business cycle** is the short-run alternation between recessions and expansions.

The point at which the economy turns from expansion to recession is a **business-cycle peak.**

The point at which the economy turns from recession to expansion is a **business-cycle trough.**

*"Please stand by for a series of tones. The first indicates the official end of the recession, the second indicates prosperity, and the third the return of the recession."*

FIGURE  **6-3**  The Business Cycle

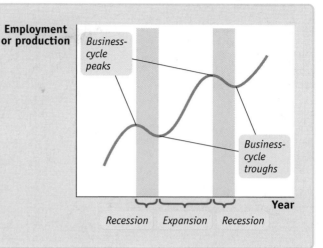

This is a stylized picture of the business cycle. The vertical axis measures either employment or total output in the economy. Periods when these two variables turn down are *recessions*; periods when they turn up are *expansions*. The point at which the economy turns down is a *business-cycle peak*; the point at which it turns up again is a *business-cycle trough*.

many industries, is called a **recession** (sometimes referred to as a *contraction*). Recessions, as officially declared by the National Bureau of Economic Research, or NBER (see the upcoming For Inquiring Minds), are indicated by the shaded areas in Figure 6-2. When the economy isn't in a recession, when most economic numbers are following their normal upward trend, the economy is said to be in an **expansion** (sometimes referred to as a *recovery*). The alternation between recessions and expansions is known as the **business cycle.** The point in time at which the economy shifts from expansion to recession is known as a **business-cycle peak;** the point at which the economy shifts from recession to expansion is known as a **business-cycle trough.**

The business cycle is an enduring feature of the economy. Table 6-2 shows the official list of business-cycle peaks and troughs. As you can see, there have been recessions and expansions for at least the past 155 years. Whenever there is a prolonged expansion, as there was in the 1960s and again in the 1990s, books and articles come out proclaiming the end of the business cycle. Such proclamations have always proved wrong: The cycle always comes back. But why does it matter?

## The Pain of Recession

Not many people complain about the business cycle when the economy is expanding. Recessions, however, create a great deal of pain.

The most important effect of a recession is its effect on the ability of workers to find and hold jobs. The most widely used indicator of conditions in the labor market is the *unemployment rate.* We'll explain how that rate is calculated in Chapter 7, but for now it's enough to say that a high unemployment rate tells us that jobs are scarce and a low unemployment rate tells us that jobs are easy to find.

TABLE  **6-2**  The History of the Business Cycle

| Business-Cycle Peak | Business-Cycle Trough |
|---|---|
| *no prior data available* | December 1854 |
| June 1857 | December 1858 |
| October 1860 | June 1861 |
| April 1865 | December 1867 |
| June 1869 | December 1870 |
| October 1873 | March 1879 |
| March 1882 | May 1885 |
| March 1887 | April 1888 |
| July 1890 | May 1891 |
| January 1893 | June 1894 |
| December 1895 | June 1897 |
| June 1899 | December 1900 |
| September 1902 | August 1904 |
| May 1907 | June 1908 |
| January 1910 | January 1912 |
| January 1913 | December 1914 |
| August 1918 | March 1919 |
| January 1920 | July 1921 |
| May 1923 | July 1924 |
| October 1926 | November 1927 |
| August 1929 | March 1933 |
| May 1937 | June 1938 |
| February 1945 | October 1945 |
| November 1948 | October 1949 |
| July 1953 | May 1954 |
| August 1957 | April 1958 |
| April 1960 | February 1961 |
| December 1969 | November 1970 |
| November 1973 | March 1975 |
| January 1980 | July 1980 |
| July 1981 | November 1982 |
| July 1990 | March 1991 |
| March 2001 | November 2001 |
| December 2007 | June 2009 |

*Source:* National Bureau of Economic Research.

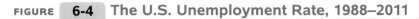

FIGURE **6-4** The U.S. Unemployment Rate, 1988–2011

The unemployment rate, a measure of joblessness, rises sharply during recessions and usually falls during expansions.

*Source:* Bureau of Labor Statistics.

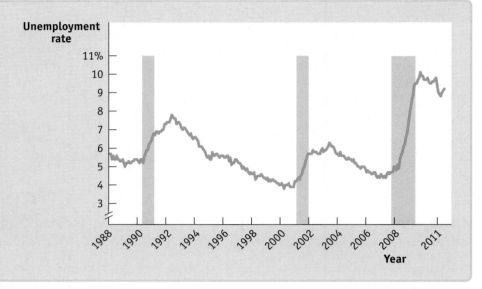

Figure 6-4 shows the unemployment rate from 1988 to 2011. As you can see, the U.S. unemployment rate surged during and after each recession but eventually fell during periods of expansion. The rising unemployment rate in 2008 was a sign that a new recession might be under way, which was later confirmed by the NBER to have begun in December 2007.

Because recessions cause many people to lose their jobs and also make it hard to find new ones, recessions hurt the standard of living of many families. Recessions are usually associated with a rise in the number of people living below the poverty line, an increase in the number of people who lose their houses because they can't afford the mortgage payments, and a fall in the percentage of Americans with health insurance coverage.

## FOR INQUIRING MINDS

### DEFINING RECESSIONS AND EXPANSIONS

Some readers may be wondering exactly how recessions and expansions are defined. The answer is that there is no exact definition!

In many countries, economists adopt the rule that a recession is a period of at least two consecutive quarters (a quarter is three months) during which the total output of the economy shrinks. The two-consecutive-quarters requirement is designed to avoid classifying brief hiccups in the economy's performance, with no lasting significance, as recessions.

Sometimes, however, this definition seems too strict. For example,

an economy that has three months of sharply declining output, then three months of slightly positive growth, then another three months of rapid decline, should surely be considered to have endured a nine-month recession.

In the United States, we try to avoid such misclassifications by assigning the task of determining when a recession begins and ends to an independent panel of experts at the National Bureau of Economic Research (NBER). This panel looks at a variety of economic indicators, with the main focus on employment and produc-

tion. But, ultimately, the panel makes a judgment call.

Sometimes this judgment is controversial. In fact, there is lingering controversy over the 2001 recession. According to the NBER, that recession began in March 2001 and ended in November 2001 when output began rising. Some critics argue, however, that the recession really began several months earlier, when industrial production began falling. Other critics argue that the recession didn't really end in 2001 because employment continued to fall and the job market remained weak for another year and a half.

You should not think, however, that workers are the only group that suffers during a recession. Recessions are also bad for firms: like employment and wages, profits suffer during recessions, with many small businesses failing, and do well during expansions.

All in all, then, recessions are bad for almost everyone. Can anything be done to reduce their frequency and severity?

## Taming the Business Cycle

Modern macroeconomics largely came into being as a response to the worst recession in history—the 43-month downturn that began in 1929 and continued into 1933, ushering in the Great Depression. The havoc wreaked by the 1929–1933 recession spurred economists to search both for understanding and for solutions: they wanted to know how such things could happen and how to prevent them.

As we explained earlier in this chapter, the work of John Maynard Keynes, published during the Great Depression, suggested that monetary and fiscal policies could be used to mitigate the effects of recessions, and to this day governments turn to Keynesian policies when recession strikes. Later work, notably that of another great macroeconomist, Milton Friedman, led to a consensus that it's important to rein in booms as well as to fight slumps. So modern policy makers try to "smooth out" the business cycle. They haven't been completely successful, as a look at Figure 6-2 makes clear. It's widely believed, however, that policy guided by macroeconomic analysis has helped make the economy more stable.

Although the business cycle is one of the main concerns of macroeconomics and historically played a crucial role in fostering the development of the field, macroeconomists are also concerned with other issues. We turn next to the question of long-run growth.

## GLOBAL COMPARISON | INTERNATIONAL BUSINESS CYCLES

This figure shows the annual rate of growth in industrial production—the percent change since the same month the previous year—for three economies from 1991 to 2011: the United States, Japan, and the euro area, the group of European countries that have adopted the euro as their common currency. Do other economies have business cycles similar to those in the United States?

The answer, which is clear from the figure, is yes. Furthermore, business cycles in different economies are often, although not always, synchronized. The U.S. recession of 2001 was paralleled by recessions in both the euro area and Japan; the Great Recession of 2007–2009 was a severe slump around the world, not just in America. But not all business cycles are international phenomena. Japan suffered a fairly severe recession in 1998, even as the United States and European economies continued to expand.

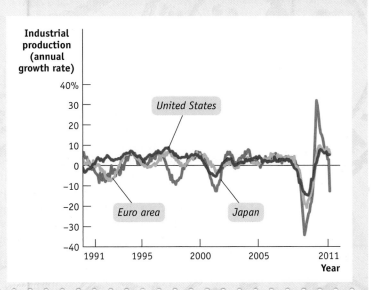

*Sources:* OECD; Eurostat.

## ECONOMICS ▸ IN ACTION

### COMPARING RECESSIONS

The alternation of recessions and expansions seems to be an enduring feature of economic life. However, not all business cycles are created equal. In particular, some recessions have been much worse than others.

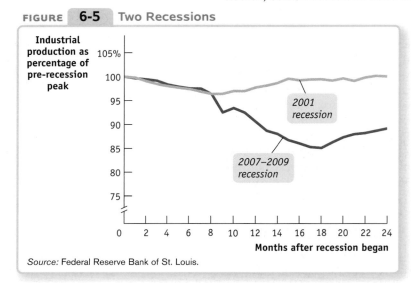

FIGURE **6-5**   Two Recessions

Industrial production as percentage of pre-recession peak

*Source:* Federal Reserve Bank of St. Louis.

Let's compare the two most recent recessions: the 2001 recession and the Great Recession of 2007–2009. These recessions differed in duration: the first lasted only eight months, the second more than twice as long. Even more important, however, they differed greatly in depth.

In Figure 6-5 we compare the depth of the recessions by looking at what happened to industrial production over the months after the recession began. In each case, production is measured as a percentage of its level at the recession's start. Thus the line for the 2007–2009 recession shows that industrial production eventually fell to about 85% of its initial level.

Clearly, the 2007–2009 recession hit the economy vastly harder than the 2001 recession. Indeed, by comparison to many recessions, the 2001 slump was very mild.

Of course, this was no consolation to the millions of American workers who lost their jobs, even in that mild recession.

### ▾ Quick Review

- The **business cycle,** the short-run alternation between **recessions** and **expansions,** is a major concern of modern macroeconomics.

- The point at which expansion shifts to recession is a **business-cycle peak.** The point at which recession shifts to expansion is a **business-cycle trough.**

### CHECK YOUR UNDERSTANDING   6-2

1. Why do we talk about business cycles for the economy as a whole, rather than just talking about the ups and downs of particular industries?

2. Describe who gets hurt in a recession, and how.

Solutions appear at back of book.

## Long-Run Economic Growth

In 1955, Americans were delighted with the nation's prosperity. The economy was expanding, consumer goods that had been rationed during World War II were available for everyone to buy, and most Americans believed, rightly, that they were better off than the citizens of any other nation, past or present. Yet by today's standards, Americans were quite poor in 1955. Figure 6-6 shows the percentage of American homes equipped with a variety of appliances in 1905, 1955, and 2005: in 1955 only 37% of American homes contained washing machines and hardly anyone had air conditioning. And if we turn the clock back another half-century, to 1905, we find that life for many Americans was startlingly primitive by today's standards.

Why are the vast majority of Americans today able to afford conveniences that many Americans lacked in 1955? The answer is **long-run economic growth,** the sustained rise in the quantity of goods and services the economy produces. Figure 6-7 shows the growth since 1900 in real GDP per capita, a measure of total output per person in the economy. The severe recession of 1929–1933 stands out, but business cycles between World War II and 2007 are almost invisible, dwarfed by the strong upward

**Long-run economic growth** is the sustained upward trend in the economy's output over time.

FIGURE **6-6**   The Fruits of Long-Run Growth in America

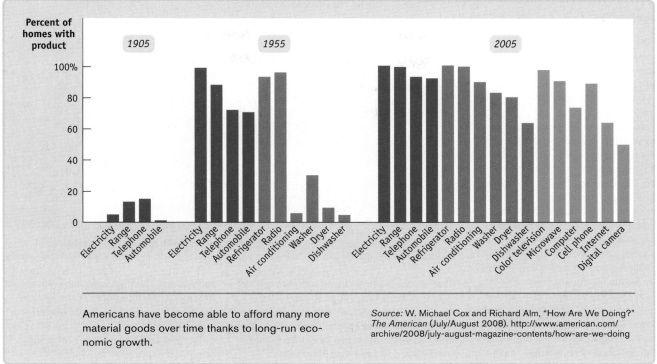

Americans have become able to afford many more material goods over time thanks to long-run economic growth.

*Source:* W. Michael Cox and Richard Alm, "How Are We Doing?" *The American* (July/August 2008). http://www.american.com/archive/2008/july-august-magazine-contents/how-are-we-doing

trend. Part of the long-run increase in output is accounted for by the fact that we have a growing population and workforce. But the economy's overall production has increased by much more than the population. On average, in 2010 the U.S. economy produced about $42,000 worth of goods and services per person, about twice as much as in 1971, about three times as much as in 1951, and almost eight times as much as in 1900.

Long-run economic growth is fundamental to many of the most pressing economic questions today. Responses to key policy questions, like the country's ability to bear the future costs of government programs such as Social Security and Medicare,

FIGURE   **6-7**   Growth, the Long View

Over the long run, growth in real GDP per capita has dwarfed the ups and downs of the business cycle. Except for the recession that began the Great Depression, recessions are almost invisible until 2007.

*Sources:* Angus Maddison, *Statistics on World Population, GDP, and Per Capita GDP, 1–2008AD,* http://www.ggdc.net/MADDISON/oriindex.htm; Bureau of Economic Analysis.

## FOR INQUIRING MINDS

### WHEN DID LONG-RUN GROWTH START?

Today, the United States is much richer than it was in 1955; in 1955 it was much richer than it had been in 1905. But how did 1855 compare with 1805? Or 1755? How far back does long-run economic growth go?

The answer is that long-run growth is a relatively modern phenomenon. The U.S. economy was already growing steadily by the mid-nineteenth century—think railroads. But if you go back to the period before 1800, you find a world economy that grew extremely slowly by today's standards. Furthermore, the population grew almost as fast as the economy, so there was very little increase in output per person. According to the economic historian Angus Maddison, from 1000 to 1800, real aggregate output around the world grew less than 0.2% per year, with population rising at about the same rate.

Economic stagnation meant unchanging living standards. For example, infor-

Economic stagnation and unchanging living standards prevailed for centuries until the Industrial Revolution in the mid-1800s ushered in a new era of wealth and sustained increases in living standards.

mation on prices and wages from sources such as monastery records shows that workers in England weren't significantly better off in the early eighteenth century than they had been five centuries earlier. And it's a good bet that they weren't

much better off than Egyptian peasants in the age of the pharaohs. However, long-run economic growth has increased significantly since 1800. In the last 50 years or so, real GDP per capita has grown about 3.5% per year.

depend in part on how fast the U.S. economy grows over the next few decades. More broadly, the public's sense that the country is making progress depends crucially on success in achieving long-run growth. When growth slows, as it did in the 1970s, it can help feed a national mood of pessimism. In particular, *long-run growth per capita*—a sustained upward trend in output per person—is the key to higher wages and a rising standard of living. A major concern of macroeconomics—and the theme of Chapter 9—is trying to understand the forces behind long-run growth.

Long-run growth is an even more urgent concern in poorer, less developed countries. In these countries, which would like to achieve a higher standard of living, the question of how to accelerate long-run growth is the central concern of economic policy.

As we'll see, macroeconomists don't use the same models to think about long-run growth that they use to think about the business cycle. It's always important to keep both sets of models in mind, because what is good in the long run can be bad in the short run, and vice versa. For example, we've already mentioned the paradox of thrift: an attempt by households to increase their savings can cause a recession. But a higher level of savings, as we'll see in Chapter 10, plays a crucial role in encouraging long-run economic growth.

## ECONOMICS ► *IN ACTION*

### A TALE OF TWO COUNTRIES

**M**any countries have experienced long-run growth, but not all have done equally well. One of the most informative contrasts is between Canada and Argentina, two countries that, at the beginning of the twentieth century, seemed to be in a good economic position.

From today's vantage point, it's surprising to realize that Canada and Argentina looked rather similar before World War I. Both were major exporters of agricultural products; both attracted large numbers of European immigrants; both also attracted large amounts of European investment, especially in the railroads that opened up their agricultural hinterlands. Economic historians believe that the average level of per capita income was about the same in the two countries as late as the 1930s.

After World War II, however, Argentina's economy performed poorly, largely due to political instability and bad macroeconomic policies. (Argentina experienced several periods of extremely high inflation, during which the cost of living soared.) Meanwhile, Canada made steady progress. Thanks to the fact that Canada has achieved sustained long-run growth since 1930, but Argentina has not, Canada today has almost as high a standard of living as the United States—and is about three times as high as Argentina's.

## CHECK YOUR UNDERSTANDING  6-3

1. Many poor countries have high rates of population growth. What does this imply about the long-run growth rates of overall output that they must achieve in order to generate a higher standard of living per person?

2. Argentina used to be as rich as Canada; now it's much poorer. Does this mean that Argentina is poorer than it was in the past? Explain.

Solutions appear at back of book.

# Inflation and Deflation

In January 1980 the average production worker in the United States was paid $6.57 an hour. By June 2011, the average hourly earnings for such a worker had risen to $19.41 an hour. Three cheers for economic progress!

But wait. American workers were paid much more in 2011, but they also faced a much higher cost of living. In early 1980, a dozen eggs cost only about $0.88; by June 2011, that was up to $1.68. The price of a loaf of white bread went from about $0.50 to $1.49. And the price of a gallon of gasoline rose from just $1.11 to $3.75. Figure 6-8 compares the percentage increase in hourly earnings between 1980 and 2011 with the increases in the prices of some standard items: the average worker's paycheck went further in terms

## FIGURE  6-8  Rising Prices

Between 1980 and 2011, American workers' hourly earnings rose by 195%. But the prices of just about all the goods bought by workers also rose, some by more, some by less. Overall, the rising cost of living offset most of the rise in the average U.S. worker's wage.
*Source:* Bureau of Labor Statistics.

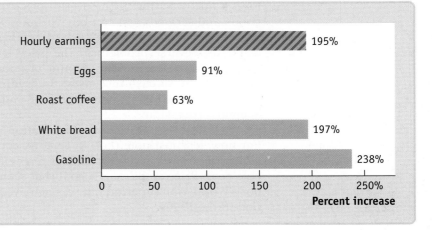

A rising overall level of prices is **inflation**.

A falling overall level of prices is **deflation**.

The economy has **price stability** when the overall level of prices changes slowly or not at all.

of some goods, but less far in terms of others. Overall, the rise in the cost of living wiped out many, if not all, of the wage gains of the typical worker from 1980 to 2011. In other words, once inflation is taken into account, the living standard of the typical U.S. worker has stagnated from 1980 to the present.

The point is that between 1980 and 2011 the economy experienced substantial **inflation:** a rise in the overall level of prices. Understanding the causes of inflation and its opposite, **deflation**—a fall in the overall level of prices—is another main concern of macroeconomics.

## The Causes of Inflation and Deflation

You might think that changes in the overall level of prices are just a matter of supply and demand. For example, higher gasoline prices reflect the higher price of crude oil, and higher crude oil prices reflect such factors as the exhaustion of major oil fields, growing demand from China and other emerging economies as more people grow rich enough to buy cars, and so on. Can't we just add up what happens in each of these markets to find out what happens to the overall level of prices?

The answer is no, we can't. Supply and demand can only explain why a particular good or service becomes more expensive *relative to other goods and services*. It can't explain why, for example, the price of chicken has risen over time in spite of the facts that chicken production has become more efficient (you don't want to know) and that chicken has become substantially cheaper compared to other goods.

What causes the overall level of prices to rise or fall? As we'll learn in Chapter 8, in the short run, movements in inflation are closely related to the business cycle. When the economy is depressed and jobs are hard to find, inflation tends to fall; when the economy is booming, inflation tends to rise. For example, prices of most goods and services fell sharply during the terrible recession of 1929–1933.

In the long run, by contrast, the overall level of prices is mainly determined by changes in the *money supply*, the total quantity of assets that can be readily used to make purchases. As we'll see in Chapter 16, *hyperinflation*, in which prices rise by thousands or hundreds of thousands of percent, invariably occurs when governments print money to pay a large part of their bills.

## The Pain of Inflation and Deflation

Both inflation and deflation can pose problems for the economy. Here are two examples: inflation discourages people from holding onto cash, because cash loses value over time if the overall price level is rising. That is, the amount of goods and services you can buy with a given amount of cash falls. In extreme cases, people stop holding cash altogether and turn to barter. Deflation can cause the reverse problem. If the price level is falling, cash gains value over time. In other words, the amount of goods and sevices you can buy with a given amount of cash increases. So holding on to it can become more attractive than investing in new factories and other productive assets. This can deepen a recession.

We'll describe other costs of inflation and deflation in Chapters 8 and 16. For now, let's just note that, in general, economists regard **price stability**—in which the overall level of prices is changing, if at all, only slowly—as a desirable goal. Price stability is a goal that seemed far out of reach for much of the post–World War II period but was achieved to most macroeconomists' satisfaction in the 1990s.

## ECONOMICS ▶ *IN ACTION*

### A FAST (FOOD) MEASURE OF INFLATION

The original McDonald's opened in 1954. It offered fast service—it was, indeed, the original fast-food restaurant. And it was also very inexpensive: hamburgers cost $0.15, $0.25 with fries. By 2010, a hamburger at a typical McDonald's cost 6 times as much, about $0.90. Has McDonald's lost touch with its fast-food roots? Have burgers become luxury cuisine?

No—in fact, compared with other consumer goods, a burger is a better bargain today than it was in 1954. Burger prices were about 6 times as high in 2010 as they were in 1954. But the consumer price index, the most widely used measure of the cost of living, was 8.2 times as high in 2010 as it was in 1954.

Even though a burger costs 6 times more than it did in 1954 when McDonald's first opened, it's still a good bargain compared to other consumer goods.

### CHECK YOUR UNDERSTANDING    6-4

1. Which of these sound like inflation, which sound like deflation, and which are ambiguous?
   a. Gasoline prices are up 10%, food prices are down 20%, and the prices of most services are up 1–2%.
   b. Gas prices have doubled, food prices are up 50%, and most services seem to be up 5% or 10%.
   c. Gas prices haven't changed, food prices are way down, and services have gotten cheaper, too.

*Solutions appear at back of book.*

▼ **Quick Review**

● A dollar today doesn't buy what it did in 1971, because the prices of most goods have risen. This rise in the overall price level has wiped out most if not all of the wage increases received by the typical American worker over the past 30 years.

● One area of macroeconomic study is in the overall level of prices. Because either **inflation** or **deflation** can cause problems for the economy, economists typically advocate maintaining **price stability.**

## International Imbalances

The United States is an **open economy:** an economy that trades goods and services with other countries. There have been times when that trade was more or less balanced—when the United States sold about as much to the rest of the world as it bought. But this isn't one of those times.

In 2010, the United States ran a big **trade deficit**—that is, the value of the goods and services U.S. residents bought from the rest of the world was a lot larger than the value of the goods and services American producers sold to customers abroad. Meanwhile, some other countries were in the opposite position, selling much more to foreigners than they bought. Figure 6-9 shows the exports and imports of goods for several important economies in 2010. As you can see, the United States imported much more than it exported, but Germany, China, and Saudi Arabia did the reverse: they each ran a **trade surplus.** A country runs a trade surplus when the value of the goods and services it buys from the rest of the world is smaller than the value of the goods and services it sells abroad. Was America's trade deficit a sign that something was wrong with our economy—that we weren't able to make things that people in other countries wanted to buy?

No, not really. Trade deficits and their opposite, trade surpluses, are macroeconomic phenomena. They're the result of situations in which the whole is very different from the sum of its parts. You might think that countries

An **open economy** is an economy that trades goods and services with other countries.

A country runs a **trade deficit** when the value of goods and services bought from foreigners is more than the value of goods and services it sells to them. It runs a **trade surplus** when the value of goods and services bought from foreigners is less than the value of the goods and services it sells to them.

FIGURE **6-9** Unbalanced Trade

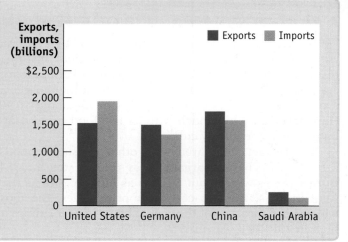

In 2010, the goods and services the United States bought from other countries were worth considerably more than the goods and services we sold abroad. Germany, China, and Saudi Arabia were in the reverse position. Trade deficits and trade surpluses reflect macroeconomic forces, especially differences in savings and investment spending.

*Source:* World Trade Organization.

with highly productive workers or widely desired products and services to sell run trade surpluses but countries with unproductive workers or poor-quality products and services run deficits. But the reality is that there's no simple relationship between the success of an economy and whether it runs trade surpluses or deficits.

Microeconomic analysis tells us why countries trade but not why they run trade surpluses or deficits. In Chapter 2 we learned that international trade is the result of comparative advantage: countries export goods they're relatively good at producing and import goods they're not as good at producing. That's why the United States exports wheat and imports coffee. One important thing the concept of comparative advantage doesn't explain, however, is why the value of a country's imports is sometimes much larger than the value of its exports, or vice versa.

So what does determine whether a country runs a trade surplus or a trade deficit? In Chapter 19 we'll learn the surprising answer: the determinants of the overall balance between exports and imports lie in decisions about savings and investment spending—spending on goods like machinery and factories that are in turn used to produce goods and services for consumers. Countries with high investment spending relative to savings run trade deficits; countries with low investment spending relative to savings run trade surpluses.

## ECONOMICS > IN ACTION

### BALTIC BALANCING ACT

The Soviet Union, once second only to the United States as a world power, broke up into 15 independent countries in 1991. Many of these countries have had a hard time finding a new place in the world, both politically and economically. However, the three small nations of Estonia, Latvia, and Lithuania—often referred to as the "Baltics" because they all have coastlines on the Baltic Sea—were quick both to establish democratic institutions and to move to market economies, building strong ties to the democratic market economies of Western Europe.

What has this meant for their international trade? Figure 6-10 shows the current account balances of the three countries—a broad definition of their trade balances—from 2000 to 2010. As you can see, in the middle years of that decade all three countries began running sizable deficits (amounting in each case to more than 10% of the total value of goods and services they produced.) Then, after 2008, all three suddenly moved into surplus.

Does this mean that these economies were doing badly around 2005 or 2006 and that they rapidly improved late in the decade? Actually, it was the opposite. During the period from 2000 to 2007, financial markets were extremely optimistic about the economic prospects of the Baltic nations and poured money into the countries, allowing them to engage in high rates of investment spending and, correspondingly, to run large trade deficits. When the world plunged into financial crisis, this inflow of funds dried up, forcing the Baltics to move into trade surplus. The adjustment was hard on the three countries, all of which saw unemployment rates rise to Depression-era levels.

FIGURE **6-10** Baltic Current Account Balances, 2000–2010

Source: International Monetary Fund.

### CHECK YOUR UNDERSTANDING 6-5

1. Which of the following reflect comparative advantage, and which reflect macroeconomic forces?
   a. Thanks to the development of huge oil sands in the province of Alberta, Canada has become an exporter of oil and an importer of manufactured goods.
   b. Like many consumer goods, the Apple iPod is assembled in China, although many of the components are made in other countries.
   c. Since 2002, Germany has been running huge trade surpluses, exporting much more than it imports.
   d. The United States, which had roughly balanced trade in the early 1990s, began running large trade deficits later in the decade, as the technology boom took off.

Solutions appear at back of book.

### ▼ Quick Review

- Comparative advantage can explain why an **open economy** exports some goods and services and imports others, but it can't explain why a country imports more than it exports, or vice versa.

- **Trade deficits** and **trade surpluses** are macroeonomic phenomena, determined by decisions about investment spending and savings.

# What's Good for America Is Good for General Motors

AP Photo/Paul Sancya, file

On June 1, 2009, General Motors filed for bankruptcy. It was a sad comedown for a company that had once been the very symbol of American economic success—so much so that in 1953 the company's CEO declared that the company's interests and those of the nation were identical: "For years I thought that what was good for the country was good for General Motors, and vice versa."

The 2009 bankruptcy didn't mean that GM shut down; the company was able to continue operating thanks to almost $50 billion in federal aid. In return for that aid, the government received stock in the restructured company. The government's intention was to sell off that stock later, once the company was profitable again.

But why did government officials believe that GM had a reasonable prospect of returning to profitability? Their case was based on an observation and a prediction.

The observation was that GM's troubles weren't unique. To be sure, the company had been badly run and needed both to make better cars and to reduce its costs. But all U.S. automakers were in trouble: overall car sales had slumped and, beyond that, overall manufacturing production had slumped. The association of weak auto sales with a general manufacturing slump fit the historical pattern. Figure 6-11 shows U.S. auto sales and total U.S. manufacturing production as a percentage of capacity; the two series have often, although not always, moved together.

The prediction was that both manufacturing production and auto sales would soon rebound, improving GM's bottom line. And this indeed proved to be the case: as the economy bounced back, so did General Motors, which returned to profitability in 2010. By late 2010, the government was able to start selling off its stock, and expectations were that taxpayers would eventually get most of their money back.

In this case, at least, the old line still applied: what was good for America was indeed good for General Motors, and vice versa.

**FIGURE 6-11** U.S. Auto Sales and Total Manufacturing Production, 1976–2011

Vehicle sales (millions)

Light weight vehicle sales: autos and light trucks

Manufacturing production (percentage of total capacity)

Capacity utilization: manufacturing

| Year | 1976 | 1980 | 1985 | 1990 | 1995 | 2000 | 2005 | 2011 |

*Source:* Federal Reserve Bank of St. Louis.

## QUESTIONS FOR THOUGHT

1. Why do overall manufacturing production and auto sales tend to move together?

2. Why was it reasonable in June 2009 to predict that auto sales would improve in the near future?

3. Why was the Obama administration especially lucky that it stepped in to rescue GM in June 2009 rather than, say, six months earlier?

## SUMMARY

1. Macroeconomics is the study of the behavior of the economy as a whole, which can be different from the sum of its parts. Macroeconomics differs from microeconomics in the type of questions it tries to answer. Macroeconomics also has a strong policy focus: **Keynesian economics,** which emerged during the Great Depression, advocates the use of **monetary policy** and **fiscal policy** to fight economic slumps. Prior to the Great Depression, the economy was thought to be **self-regulating.**

2. One key concern of macroeconomics is the **business cycle,** the short-run alternation between **recessions,** periods of falling employment and output, and **expansions,** periods of rising employment and output. The point at which expansion turns to recession is a **business-cycle peak.** The point at which recession turns to expansion is a **business-cycle trough.**

3. Another key area of macroeconomic study is **long-run economic growth,** the sustained upward trend in the economy's output over time. Long-run economic

growth is the force behind long-term increases in living standards and is important for financing some economic programs. It is especially important for poorer countries.

4. When the prices of most goods and services are rising, so that the overall level of prices is going up, the economy experiences **inflation.** When the overall level of prices is going down, the economy is experiencing **deflation.** In the short run, inflation and deflation are closely related to the business cycle. In the long run, prices tend to reflect changes in the overall quantity of money. Because both inflation and deflation can cause problems, economists and policy makers generally aim for **price stability.**

5. Although comparative advantage explains why **open economies** export some things and import others, macroeconomic analysis is needed to explain why countries run **trade surpluses** or **trade deficits.** The determinants of the overall balance between exports and imports lie in decisions about savings and investment spending.

## KEY TERMS

Self-regulating economy, p. 167
Keynesian economics, p. 167
Monetary policy, p. 168
Fiscal policy, p. 168
Recession, p. 170
Expansion, p. 170

Business cycle, p. 17
Business-cycle peak, p. 170
Business-cycle trough, p. 170
Long-run economic growth, p. 174
Inflation, p. 178
Deflation, p. 178

Price stability, p. 178
Open economy, p. 179
Trade deficit, p. 179
Trade surplus, p. 179

## PROBLEMS

1. Which of the following questions are relevant for the study of macroeconomics and which for microeconomics?

   a. How will Ms. Martin's tips change when a large manufacturing plant near the restaurant where she works closes?

   b. What will happen to spending by consumers when the economy enters a downturn?

   c. How will the price of oranges change when a late frost damages Florida's orange groves?

   d. How will wages at a manufacturing plant change when its workforce is unionized?

   e. What will happen to U.S. exports as the dollar becomes less expensive in terms of other currencies?

   f. What is the relationship between a nation's unemployment rate and its inflation rate?

2. When one person saves more, that person's wealth is increased, meaning that he or she can consume more

in the future. But when everyone saves more, everyone's income falls, meaning that everyone must consume less today. Explain this seeming contradiction.

3. Before the Great Depression, the conventional wisdom among economists and policy makers was that the economy is largely self-regulating.

   a. Is this view consistent or inconsistent with Keynesian economics? Explain.

   b. What effect did the Great Depression have on conventional wisdom?

   c. Contrast the response of policy makers during the 2007–2009 recession to the actions of policy makers during the Great Depression. What would have been the likely outcome of the 2007–2009 recession if policy makers had responded in the same fashion as policy makers during the Great Depression?

4. How do economists in the United States determine when a recession begins and when it ends? How do

other countries determine whether or not a recession is occurring?

5. The U.S. Department of Labor reports statistics on employment and earnings that are used as key indicators by many economists to gauge the health of the economy. Figure 6-4 in the text plots historical data on the unemployment rate each month. Noticeably, the numbers were high during the recessions in the early 1990s, in 2001, and in 2007–2009.

   a. Locate the latest data on the national unemployment rate. (*Hint:* Go to the website of the Bureau of Labor Statistics, www.bls.gov, and locate the latest release of the Employment Situation.)

   b. Compare the current numbers with the recessions in the early 1990s, in 2001, and in 2007–2009 as well as with the periods of relatively high economic growth just before the recessions. Are the current numbers indicative of a recessionary trend?

6. The accompanying figure shows the annual rate of growth in employment for the United Kingdom and Japan from 1991 to 2010. (The annual growth rate is the percent change in each year's employment over the previous year.)

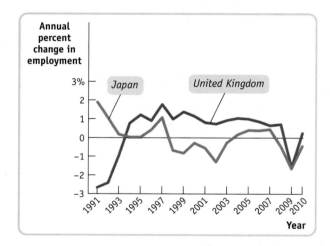

   a. Comment on the business cycles of these two economies. Are their business cycles similar or dissimilar?

   b. Use the accompanying figure and the figure in the Global Comparison on international business cycles in the chapter to compare the business cycles of each of these two economies with those of the United States and the euro area.

7. a. What three measures of the economy tend to move together during the business cycle? Which way do they move during an upturn? During a downturn?

   b. Who in the economy is hurt during a recession? How?

   c. How did Milton Friedman alter the consensus that had developed in the aftermath of the Great Depression on how the economy should be managed? What is the current goal of policy makers in managing the economy?

8. Why do we consider a business-cycle expansion different from long-run economic growth? Why do we care about the size of the long-run growth rate of real GDP versus the size of the growth rate of the population?

9. In 1798, Thomas Malthus's *Essay on the Principle of Population* was published. In it, he wrote: "Population, when unchecked, increases in a geometrical ratio. Subsistence increases only in an arithmetical ratio. . . . This implies a strong and constantly operating check on population from the difficulty of subsistence." Malthus was saying that the growth of the population is limited by the amount of food available to eat; people will live at the subsistence level forever. Why didn't Malthus's description apply to the world after 1800?

10. College tuition has risen significantly in the last few decades. From the 1979–1980 academic year to the 2009–2010 academic year, total tuition, room, and board paid by full-time undergraduate students went from $2,327 to $15,041 at public institutions and from $5,013 to $35,061 at private institutions. This is an average annual tuition increase of 6.4% at public institutions and 6.7% at private institutions. Over the same time, average personal income after taxes rose from $7,956 to $35,088 per year, which is an average annual rate of growth of personal income of 5.0%. Have these tuition increases made it more difficult for the average student to afford college tuition?

11. Each year, *The Economist* publishes data on the price of the Big Mac in different countries and exchange rates. The accompanying table shows some data used for the index from 2007 and 2011. Use this information to answer the following questions.

| | 2007 | | 2011 | |
| | Price of Big Mac (in local currrency) | Price of Big Mac (in U.S. dollars) | Price of Big Mac (in local currency) | Price of Big Mac (in U.S. dollars) |
| Country | | | | |
|---|---|---|---|---|
| Argentina | peso8.25 | $2.65 | peso20.0 | $4.84 |
| Canada | C$3.63 | $3.08 | C$4.73 | $5.00 |
| Euro area | €2.94 | $3.82 | €3.44 | $4.93 |
| Japan | ¥280 | $2.31 | ¥320 | $4.08 |
| United States | $3.22 | $3.22 | $4.07 | $4.07 |

   a. Where was it cheapest to buy a Big Mac in U.S. dollars in 2007?

   b. Where was it cheapest to buy a Big Mac in U.S. dollars in 2011?

   c. Using the increase in the local currency price of the Big Mac in each country to measure the percent change in the overall price level from 2007 to 2011, which nation experienced the most inflation? Did any of the nations experience deflation?

12. The accompanying figure illustrates the trade deficit of the United States since 1987. The United States has been

consistently and, on the whole, increasingly importing more goods than it has been exporting. One of the countries it runs a trade deficit with is China. Which of the following statements are valid possible explanations of this fact? Explain.

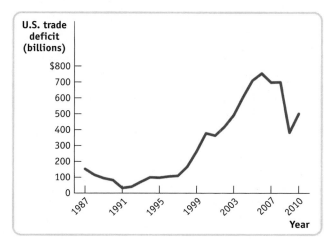

**U.S. trade deficit (billions)**

a. Many products, such as televisions, that were formerly manufactured in the United States are now manufactured in China.

b. The wages of the average Chinese worker are far lower than the wages of the average American worker.

c. Investment spending in the United States is high relative to its level of savings.

# CHAPTER 7

# GDP and the CPI:
# Tracking the Macroeconomy

## THE NEW #2

The 2010 economic data showed that China had become an economic superpower, surpassing Japan.

REUTERS/Aly Song

❱ How economists use aggregate measures to track the performance of the economy

❱ What **gross domestic product,** or **GDP,** is and the three ways of calculating it

❱ The difference between **real GDP** and **nominal GDP** and why real GDP is the appropriate measure of real economic activity

❱ What a **price index** is and how it is used to calculate the **inflation rate**

"CHINA PASSES JAPAN AS Second-Largest Economy." That was the headline in the *New York Times* on August 15, 2010. Citing economic data suggesting that Japan's economy was weakening while China's was roaring ahead, the article predicted—correctly, as it turned out—that 2010 would mark the first year in which the surging Chinese economy finally overtook Japan's, taking second place to the United States on the world economic stage. "The milestone," wrote the *Times,* "though anticipated for some time, is the most striking evidence yet that China's ascendance is for real and that the rest of the world will have to reckon with a new economic superpower."

But wait a minute—what does it mean to say that China's economy is larger than Japan's? The two economies are, after all, producing very different mixes of goods. Despite its rapid advance, China is still a fairly poor country whose greatest strength is in relatively low-tech production. Japan, by contrast, is very much a high-tech nation, and it dominates world output of some sophisticated goods, like electronic sensors for automobiles. That's why the 2011 earthquake in northeastern Japan, which put many factories out of action, temporarily caused major production disruptions for auto factories around the world.

How can you compare the sizes of two economies when they aren't producing the same things?

The answer is that comparisons of national economies are based on the *value* of their production. When news reports declared that China's economy had overtaken Japan's, they meant that China's *gross domestic product,* or *GDP*—a measure of the overall value of goods and services produced—had surpassed Japan's GDP.

GDP is one of the most important measures used to track the macroeconomy—that is, to quantify movements in the overall level of output and prices. Measures like GDP and *prices indexes* play an important role in formulating economic policy, since policy makers need to know what's going on, and anecdotes are no substitute for hard data. They're also important for business decisions—to such an extent that, as the business case at the end of the chapter illustrates, corporations and other players are willing to pay for early reads on what official economic measurements are likely to find.

In this chapter, we explain how macroeconomists measure key aspects of the economy. We first explore ways to measure the economy's total output and total income. We then turn to the problem of how to measure the level of prices and the change in prices in the economy. ◾

The **national income and product accounts,** or **national accounts,** keep track of the flows of money between different sectors of the economy.

**Consumer spending** is household spending on goods and services.

A **stock** is a share in the ownership of a company held by a shareholder.

A **bond** is borrowing in the form of an IOU that pays interest.

**Government transfers** are payments by the government to individuals for which no good or service is provided in return.

**Disposable income,** equal to income plus government transfers minus taxes, is the total amount of household income available to spend on consumption and to save.

# The National Accounts

Almost all countries calculate a set of numbers known as the *national income and product accounts*. In fact, the accuracy of a country's accounts is a remarkably reliable indicator of its state of economic development—in general, the more reliable the accounts, the more economically advanced the country. When international economic agencies seek to help a less developed country, typically the first order of business is to send a team of experts to audit and improve the country's accounts.

In the United States, these numbers are calculated by the Bureau of Economic Analysis, a division of the U.S. government's Department of Commerce. The **national income and product accounts,** often referred to simply as the **national accounts,** keep track of the spending of consumers, sales of producers, business investment spending, government purchases, and a variety of other flows of money between different sectors of the economy. Let's see how they work.

## The Circular-Flow Diagram, Revisited and Expanded

To understand the principles behind the national accounts, it helps to look at Figure 7-1, a revised and expanded *circular-flow diagram* similar to the one we introduced in Chapter 2. Recall that in Figure 2-7 we showed the flows of money, goods and services, and factors of production through the economy. Here we restrict ourselves to flows of money but add extra elements that allow us to show the key concepts behind the national accounts. As in our original version of the circular-flow diagram, the underlying principle is that the inflow of money into each market or sector is equal to the outflow of money coming from that market or sector.

Figure 2-7 showed a simplified world containing only two kinds of "inhabitants," households and firms. And it illustrated the circular flow of money between households and firms, which remains visible in Figure 7-1. In the markets for goods and services, households engage in **consumer spending,** buying goods and services from domestic firms and from firms in the rest of the world. Households also own factors of production—labor, land, physical capital, human capital, and financial capital. They sell the use of these factors of production to firms, receiving wages, profit, interest payments, and rent in return. Firms buy and pay households for the use of those factors of production in the factor markets. Most households derive the bulk of their income from wages earned by selling labor and human capital. But households derive additional income from their indirect ownership of the physical capital used by firms, mainly in the form of **stocks,** shares in the ownership of a company, and from **bonds,** by borrowing in the form of an IOU that pays interest. So the income households receive from the factor markets includes profits distributed to shareholders known as *dividends,* and the interest payments on bonds held by bondholders. Finally, households receive rent in return for allowing firms to use land or structures that they own. So households receive income in the form of wages, profit, interest payments, and rent via factor markets.

In our original, simplified circular-flow diagram, households spent all the income they received via factor markets on goods and services. Figure 7-1, however, illustrates a more complicated but more realistic diagram. There we see two reasons why goods and services don't in fact absorb all of households' income. First, households don't get to keep all the income they receive via the factor markets. They must pay part of their income to the government in the form of taxes, such as income taxes and sales taxes. In addition, some households receive **government transfers**—payments by the government to individuals for which no good or service is provided in return, such as Social Security benefits and unemployment insurance payments. The total income households have left after paying taxes and receiving government transfers is **disposable income.**

### FIGURE 7-1   An Expanded Circular-Flow Diagram: The Flows of Money Through the Economy

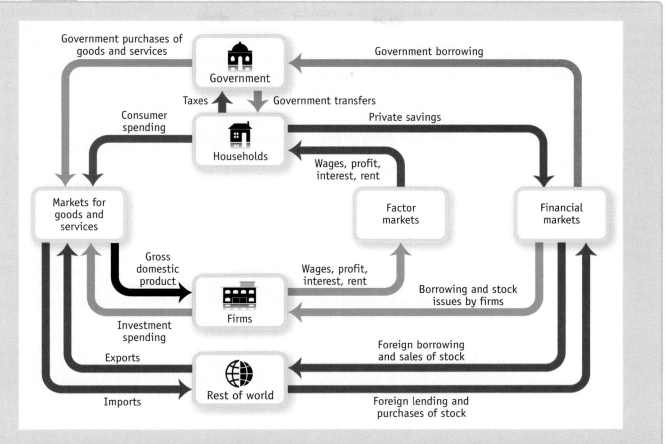

A circular flow of funds connects the four sectors of the economy—households, firms, government, and the rest of the world—via three types of markets: the factor markets, the markets for goods and services, and the *financial markets.* Funds flow from firms to households in the form of wages, profit, interest, and rent through the factor markets. After paying taxes to the government and receiving *government transfers,* households allocate the remaining income—*disposable income*—to private savings and consumer spending. Via the financial markets, *private savings* and funds from the rest of the world are channeled into investment spending by firms, government borrowing, foreign borrowing and lending, and foreign

transactions of stocks. In turn, funds flow from the government and households to firms to pay for purchases of goods and services. Finally, exports to the rest of the world generate a flow of funds into the economy and imports lead to a flow of funds out of the economy. If we add up consumer spending on goods and services, investment spending by firms, government purchases of goods and services, and exports, then subtract the value of imports, the total flow of funds represented by this calculation is total spending on final goods and services produced in the United States. Equivalently, it's the value of all the final goods and services produced in the United States—that is, the *gross domestic product* of the economy.

Second, households normally don't spend all their disposable income on goods and services. Instead, a portion of their income is typically set aside as **private savings,** which goes into **financial markets** where individuals, banks, and other institutions buy and sell stocks and bonds as well as make loans. As Figure 7-1 shows, the financial markets also receive funds from the rest of the world and provide funds to the government, to firms, and to the rest of the world.

Before going further, we can use the box representing households to illustrate an important general feature of the circular-flow diagram: the total sum of flows of money out of a given box is equal to the total sum of flows of money into that box. It's simply a matter of accounting: what goes in must come out. So, for example, the

**Private savings,** equal to disposable income minus consumer spending, is disposable income that is not spent on consumption.

The banking, stock, and bond markets, which channel private savings and foreign lending into investment spending, government borrowing, and foreign borrowing, are known as the **financial markets.**

**Government borrowing** is the total amount of funds borrowed by federal, state, and local governments in the financial markets.

**Government purchases of goods and services** are total expenditures on goods and services by federal, state, and local governments.

Goods and services sold to other countries are **exports.** Goods and services purchased from other countries are **imports.**

**Inventories** are stocks of goods and raw materials held to facilitate business operations.

**Investment spending** is spending on productive physical capital—such as machinery and construction of buildings, and on changes to inventories.

total flow of money out of households—the sum of taxes paid, consumer spending, and private savings—must equal the total flow of money into households—the sum of wages, profits, interest payments, rent, and government transfers.

Now let's look at the other types of inhabitants we've added to the circular-flow diagram, including the government—all federal, state, and local governments—and the rest of the world. The government returns a portion of the money it collects from taxes to households in the form of government transfers. However, it uses much of its tax revenue, plus additional funds borrowed in the financial markets through **government borrowing,** to buy goods and services. **Government purchases of goods and services,** the total purchases by federal, state, and local governments, include everything from military spending on ammunition to your local public school's spending on chalk, erasers, and teacher salaries.

The rest of the world participates in the U.S. economy in three ways.

1. Some of the goods and services produced in the United States are sold to residents of other countries. For example, more than half of America's annual wheat and cotton crops are sold abroad. Goods and services sold to other countries are known as **exports.** Export sales lead to a flow of funds from the rest of the world into the United States to pay for them.

2. Some of the goods and services purchased by residents of the United States are produced abroad. For example, many consumer goods are now made in China. Goods and services purchased from residents of other countries are known as **imports.** Import purchases lead to a flow of funds out of the United States to pay for them.

3. Foreigners can participate in U.S. financial markets by making transactions. Foreign lending—lending by foreigners to borrowers in the United States, and purchases by foreigners of shares of stock in American companies—generates a flow of funds into the United States from the rest of the world. Conversely, foreign borrowing—borrowing by foreigners from U.S. lenders and purchases by Americans of stock in foreign companies—leads to a flow of funds out of the United States to the rest of the world.

Finally, let's go back to the markets for goods and services. In Chapter 2 we focused only on purchases of goods and services by households. We now see that there are other types of spending on goods and services, including government purchases, *investment spending* by firms, imports, and exports.

Notice that firms also buy goods and services in our expanded economy. For example, an automobile company that is building a new factory will buy investment goods—machinery like stamping presses and welding robots that are used to produce goods and services for consumers—from companies that manufacture these items. It will also accumulate an inventory of finished cars in preparation for shipment to dealers. **Inventories,** then, are stocks of goods and raw materials that firms hold to facilitate their operations. The national accounts count this **investment spending**—spending on productive physical capital, such as machinery and construction of buildings, and on changes to inventories—as part of total spending on goods and services.

You might ask why *changes* to inventories are included in investment spending—finished cars aren't, after all, used to produce more cars. Changes to inventories of finished goods are counted as investment spending because, like machinery, they change the ability of a firm to make future sales. So spending on additions to inventories is a form of investment spending by a firm. Conversely, a drawing-down of inventories is counted as a fall in investment spending because it leads to lower future sales. It's also important to understand that investment spending includes spending on construction of any structure, regardless of whether it is an assembly plant or a new house. Why include construction of homes? Because, like a plant, a new house produces a future stream of output—housing services for its occupants.

Suppose we add up consumer spending on goods and services, investment spending, government purchases of goods and services, and the value of exports, then subtract the value of imports. This gives us a measure of the overall market value of the goods and services the economy produces. That measure has a name: it's a country's *gross domestic product.* But before we can formally define gross domestic product, or GDP, we have to examine an important distinction between classes of goods and services: the difference between *final goods and services* versus *intermediate goods and services.*

## Gross Domestic Product

A consumer's purchase of a new car from a dealer is one example of a sale of **final goods and services:** goods and services sold to the final, or end, user. But an automobile manufacturer's purchase of steel from a steel foundry or glass from a glassmaker is an example of purchasing **intermediate goods and services:** goods and services that are inputs for production of final goods and services. In the case of intermediate goods and services, the purchaser—another firm—is *not* the final user.

**Gross domestic product,** or **GDP,** is the total value of all *final goods and services* produced in an economy during a given period, usually a year. In 2010 the GDP of the United States was $14,527 billion, or about $46,844 per person. If you are an economist trying to construct a country's national accounts, *one way to calculate GDP is to calculate it directly: survey firms and add up the total value of their production of final goods and services.* We'll explain in detail in the next section why intermediate goods, and some other types of goods as well, are not included in the calculation of GDP.

But adding up the total value of final goods and services produced isn't the only way of calculating GDP. There is another way, based on total spending on final goods and services. Since GDP is equal to the total value of final goods and services produced in the economy, it must also equal the flow of funds received by firms from sales in the goods and services market.

If you look again at the circular-flow diagram in Figure 7-1, you will see that the arrow going from markets for goods and services to firms is indeed labeled "Gross domestic product." According to our basic rule of accounting, flows out of any box are equal to flows into the box; so the flow of funds out of the markets for goods and services to firms is equal to the total flow of funds into the markets for goods and services from other sectors. And as you can see from Figure 7-1, the total flow of funds into the markets for goods and services is total or **aggregate spending** on domestically produced final goods and services—the sum of consumer spending, investment spending, government purchases of goods and services, and exports minus imports. *So a second way of calculating GDP is to add up aggregate spending on domestically produced final goods and services in the economy.*

And there is yet a third way of calculating GDP, based on total income earned in the economy. Firms, and the factors of production that they employ, are owned by households. So firms must ultimately pay out what they earn to households. The flow from firms to the factor markets is the factor income paid out by firms to households in the form of wages, profit, interest, and rent. Again, by accounting rules, the value of the flow of factor income from firms to households must be equal to the flow of money into firms from the markets for goods and services. And this last value, we know, is the total value of production in the economy—GDP. Why is GDP equal to the total value of factor income paid by firms in the economy to households? Because each sale in the economy must accrue to someone as income— either as wages, profit, interest, or rent. *So a third way of calculating GDP is to sum the total factor income earned by households from firms in the economy.*

**Final goods and services** are goods and services sold to the final, or end, user.

**Intermediate goods and services** are goods and services—bought from one firm by another firm—that are inputs for production of final goods and services.

**Gross domestic product,** or **GDP,** is the total value of all final goods and services produced in the economy during a given year.

**Aggregate spending,** the sum of consumer spending, investment spending, government purchases of goods and services, and exports minus imports, is the total spending on domestically produced final goods and services in the economy.

*"You wouldn't think there'd be much money in potatoes, chickens, and woodchopping, but it all adds up."*

## Calculating GDP

We've just explained that there are in fact three methods for calculating GDP:

1. adding up total value of all final goods and services produced
2. adding up spending on all domestically produced goods and services
3. adding to total factor income earned by households from firms in the economy

Government statisticians use all three methods. To illustrate how these three methods work, we will consider a hypothetical economy, shown in Figure 7-2. This economy consists of three firms—American Motors, Inc., which produces one car per year; American Steel, Inc., which produces the steel that goes into the car; and American Ore, Inc., which mines the iron ore that goes into the steel. So GDP is $21,500, the value of the one car per year the economy produces. Let's look at how the three different methods of calculating GDP yield the same result.

**Measuring GDP as the Value of Production of Final Goods and Services** The first method for calculating GDP is to add up the value of all the final goods and services produced in the economy—a calculation that excludes the value of intermediate goods and services. Why are intermediate goods and services excluded? After all, don't they represent a very large and valuable portion of the economy?

To understand why only final goods and services are included in GDP, look at the simplified economy described in Figure 7-2. Should we measure the GDP of this economy by adding up the total sales of the iron ore producer, the steel producer, and the auto producer? If we did, we would in effect be counting the value of the steel twice—once when it is sold by the steel plant to the auto plant, and again when the steel auto body is sold to a consumer as a finished car. And we would be counting the value of the iron ore *three* times—once when it is mined and sold to the steel company, a second time when it is made into steel and sold to the auto producer, and a third time when the steel is made into a car and sold to the consumer.

**FIGURE 7-2 Calculating GDP**

In this hypothetical economy consisting of three firms, GDP can be calculated in three different ways: 1) measuring GDP as the value of production of final goods and services, by summing each firm's value added; 2) measuring GDP as aggregate spending on domestically produced final goods and services; and 3) measuring GDP as factor income earned by households from firms in the economy.

*2. Aggregate spending on domestically produced final goods and services = $21,500*

| | American Ore, Inc. | American Steel, Inc. | American Motors, Inc. | Total factor income | |
|---|---|---|---|---|---|
| **Value of sales** | $4,200 (ore) | $9,000 (steel) | $21,500 (car) | | |
| **Intermediate goods** | 0 | 4,200 (iron ore) | 9,000 (steel) | | |
| **Wages** | 2,000 | 3,700 | 10,000 | $15,700 | *3. Total payments to factors = $21,500* |
| **Interest payments** | 1,000 | 600 | 1,000 | 2,600 | |
| **Rent** | 200 | 300 | 500 | 1,000 | |
| **Profit** | 1,000 | 200 | 1,000 | 2,200 | |
| **Total expenditure by firm** | 4,200 | 9,000 | 21,500 | | |
| **Value added per firm** = **Value of sales − Cost of intermediate goods** | 4,200 | 4,800 | 12,500 | | |

*1. Value of production of final goods and services, sum of value added = $21,500*

So counting the full value of each producer's sales would cause us to count the same items several times and artificially inflate the calculation of GDP. For example, in Figure 7-2, the total value of all sales, intermediate and final, is $34,700: $21,500 from the sale of the car, plus $9,000 from the sale of the steel, plus $4,200 from the sale of the iron ore. Yet we know that GDP is only $21,500. The way we avoid double-counting is to count only each producer's **value added** in the calculation of GDP: the difference between the value of its sales and the value of the intermediate goods and services it purchases from other businesses.

That is, at each stage of the production process we subtract the cost of inputs—the intermediate goods—at that stage. In this case, the value added of the auto producer is the dollar value of the cars it manufactures *minus* the cost of the steel it buys, or $12,500. The value added of the steel producer is the dollar value of the steel it produces *minus* the cost of the ore it buys, or $4,800. Only the ore producer, which we have assumed doesn't buy any inputs, has value added equal to its total sales, $4,200. The sum of the three producers' value added is $21,500, equal to GDP.

The **value added** of a producer is the value of its sales minus the value of its purchases of intermediate goods and services.

**Measuring GDP as Spending on Domestically Produced Final Goods and Services** Another way to calculate GDP is by adding up aggregate spending on domestically produced final goods and services. That is, GDP can be measured by the flow of funds into firms. Like the method that estimates GDP as the value of domestic production of final goods and services, this measurement must be carried out in a way that avoids double-counting. In terms of our steel and auto example, we don't want to count both consumer spending on a car (represented in Figure 7-2 by $12,500, the sales price of the car) and the auto producer's spending on steel (represented in Figure 7-2 by $9,000, the price of a car's worth of steel). If we counted both, we would be counting the steel embodied in the car twice. We solve this problem by counting only the value of sales to *final buyers*, such as consumers, firms that purchase investment goods, the government, or foreign buyers. In other words, in order to avoid double-counting of spending, we omit sales of inputs from one business to another when estimating GDP using spending data. You can see from Figure 7-2 that aggregate spending on final goods and services—the finished car—is $21,500.

## FOR INQUIRING MINDS

### OUR IMPUTED LIVES

An old line says that when a person marries the household cook, GDP falls. And it's true: when someone provides services for pay, those services are counted as a part of GDP. But the services family members provide to each other are not. Some economists have produced alternative measures that try to "impute" the value of household work—that is, assign an estimate of what the market value of that work would have been if it had been paid for. But the standard measure of GDP doesn't contain that imputation.

GDP estimates do, however, include an imputation for the value of "owner-occupied housing." That is, if you buy the home you were formerly renting, GDP does not go down. It's true that because

you no longer pay rent to your landlord, the landlord no longer sells a service to you—namely, use of the house or apartment. But the statisticians make an estimate of what you would have paid if you rented whatever you live in, whether it's an apartment or a house. For the purposes of the statistics, it's as if you were renting your dwelling from yourself.

If you think about it, this makes a lot of sense. In a home-owning country like the United States, the pleasure we derive from our houses is an important part of the standard of living. So to be accurate, esti-

The value of the services that family members provide to each other is not counted as part of GDP.

mates of GDP must take into account the value of housing that is occupied by owners as well as the value of rental housing.

As we've already pointed out, the national accounts *do* include investment spending by firms as a part of final spending. That is, an auto company's purchase of steel to make a car isn't considered a part of final spending, but the company's purchase of new machinery for its factory *is* considered a part of final spending. What's the difference? Steel is an input that is used up in production; machinery will last for a number of years. Since purchases of capital goods that will last for a considerable time aren't closely tied to current production, the national accounts consider such purchases a form of final sales.

In later chapters, we will make use of the proposition that GDP is equal to aggregate spending on domestically produced goods and services by final buyers. We will also develop models of how final buyers decide how much to spend. With that in mind, we'll now examine the types of spending that make up GDP.

Look again at the markets for goods and services in Figure 7-1, and you will see that one component of sales by firms is consumer spending. Let's denote consumer spending with the symbol *C*. Figure 7-1 also shows three other components of sales: sales of investment goods to other businesses, or investment spending, which we will denote by *I*; government purchases of goods and services, which we will denote by *G*; and sales to foreigners—that is, exports—which we will denote by *X*.

In reality, not all of this final spending goes toward domestically produced goods and services. We must take account of spending on imports, which we will denote by *IM*. Income spent on imports is income not spent on domestic goods and services—it is income that has "leaked" across national borders. So to accurately value domestic production using spending data, we must subtract out spending on imports to arrive at spending on domestically produced goods and services. Putting this all together gives us the following equation that breaks GDP down by the four sources of aggregate spending:

**(7-1)** $GDP = C + I + G + X - IM$

We'll be seeing a lot of Equation 7-1 in later chapters.

---

## ⚠ PITFALLS

**GDP: WHAT'S IN AND WHAT'S OUT**
It's easy to confuse what is included and what is excluded from GDP. So let's stop here for a moment and make sure the distinction is clear. The most likely source of confusion is the difference between investment spending and spending on intermediate goods and services. Investment spending—spending on productive physical capital (including construction of residential and commercial structures), and changes to inventories—is included in GDP. But spending on intermediate goods and services is not.

Why the difference? Recall from Chapter 2 that we made a distinction between resources that are *used up* and those that are *not used up* in production. An input, like steel, is used up in production. An investment good, like a metal-stamping machine, is not. It will last for many years and will be used repeatedly

to make many cars. Since spending on productive physical capital—investment goods—and construction of structures is not directly tied to current output, economists consider such spending to be spending on final goods.

Spending on changes to inventories is considered a part of investment spending, so it is also included in GDP. Why? Because, like a machine, additional inventory is an investment in future sales. And when a good is released for sale from inventories, its value is subtracted from the value of inventories and so from GDP.

Used goods are not included in GDP because, as with inputs, to include them would be to double-count: counting them once when sold as new and again when sold as used.

Also, financial assets such as stocks and bonds are not included in GDP because they don't represent either the

production or the sale of final goods and services. Rather, a bond represents a promise to repay with interest, and a stock represents a proof of ownership. And for obvious reasons, foreign-produced goods and services are not included in calculations of GDP.

Here is a summary of what's included and not included in GDP:

*Included*

- Domestically produced final goods and services, including capital goods, new construction of structures, and changes to inventories

*Not Included*

- Intermediate goods and services
- Inputs
- Used goods
- Financial assets like stocks and bonds
- Foreign-produced goods and services

## Measuring GDP as Factor Income Earned from Firms in the Economy

A final way to calculate GDP is to add up all the income earned by factors of production from firms in the economy—the wages earned by labor; the interest paid to those who lend their savings to firms and the government; the rent earned by those who lease their land or structures to firms; and dividends, the profits paid to the shareholders, the owners of the firms' physical capital. This is a valid measure because the money firms earn by selling goods and services must go somewhere; whatever isn't paid as wages, interest, or rent is profit. Ultimately, profits are paid out to shareholders as dividends.

Figure 7-2 shows how this calculation works for our simplified economy. The shaded column at the far right shows the total wages, interest, and rent paid by all these firms as well as their total profit. Summing up all of these yields total factor income of $21,500—again, equal to GDP.

We won't emphasize factor income as much as the other two methods of calculating GDP. It's important to keep in mind, however, that all the money spent on domestically produced goods and services generates factor income to households—that is, there really is a circular flow.

**The Components of GDP** Now that we know how GDP is calculated in principle, let's see what it looks like in practice.

Figure 7-3 shows the first two methods of calculating GDP side by side. The height of each bar above the horizontal axis represents the GDP of the U.S. economy in 2010: $14,527 billion. Each bar is divided to show the breakdown of that total in terms of where the value was added and how the money was spent.

In the left bar in Figure 7-3, we see the breakdown of GDP by value added according to sector, the first method of calculating GDP. Of the $14,527 billion, $10,879 billion consisted of value added by businesses. Another $1,809 billion consisted of

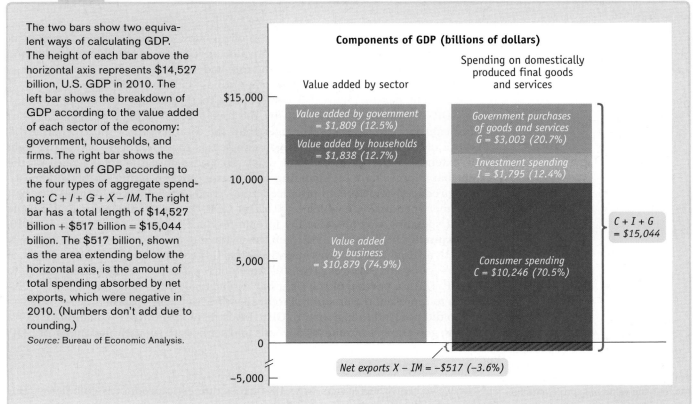

**FIGURE  7-3  U.S. GDP in 2010: Two Methods of Calculating GDP**

The two bars show two equivalent ways of calculating GDP. The height of each bar above the horizontal axis represents $14,527 billion, U.S. GDP in 2010. The left bar shows the breakdown of GDP according to the value added of each sector of the economy: government, households, and firms. The right bar shows the breakdown of GDP according to the four types of aggregate spending: $C + I + G + X - IM$. The right bar has a total length of $14,527 billion + $517 billion = $15,044 billion. The $517 billion, shown as the area extending below the horizontal axis, is the amount of total spending absorbed by net exports, which were negative in 2010. (Numbers don't add due to rounding.)

*Source:* Bureau of Economic Analysis.

**Components of GDP (billions of dollars)**

Value added by sector

Spending on domestically produced final goods and services

Value added by government = $1,809 (12.5%)

Value added by households = $1,838 (12.7%)

Government purchases of goods and services $G = $3,003 (20.7%)$

Investment spending $I = $1,795 (12.4%)$

Value added by business = $10,879 (74.9%)

Consumer spending $C = $10,246 (70.5%)$

$C + I + G = $15,044$

Net exports $X - IM = -$517 (-3.6%)$

## FOR INQUIRING MINDS

### GROSS WHAT?

Occasionally you may see references not to gross domestic product but to gross *national* product, or GNP. Is this just another name for the same thing? Not quite.

If you look at Figure 7-1 carefully, you may realize that there's a possibility that is missing from the figure. According to the figure, all factor income goes to domestic households. But what happens when profits are paid to foreigners who own stock in General Motors or Microsoft? And where do the profits earned by American companies operating overseas fit in?

To answer these questions, an alternative measure, GNP, was devised. GNP is defined as the total factor income earned by residents of a country. It *excludes* factor income earned by foreigners, like profits paid to foreign investors who own American stocks and payments to foreigners who work temporarily in the United States. And it *includes* factor income earned abroad by Americans, like the profits of IBM's European operations that accrue to IBM's American shareholders and the wages of Americans who work abroad temporarily.

In the early days of national income accounting, economists usually used GNP rather than GDP as a measure of the economy's size—although the measures were generally very close to each other. They switched to GDP mainly because it's considered a better indicator of short-run movements in production and because data on international flows of factor income are considered somewhat unreliable.

In practice, it doesn't make much difference which measure is used for large economies like that of the United States, where the flows of net factor income to other countries are relatively small. In 2010, America's GNP was about 1.3% larger than its GDP, mainly because of the overseas profit of U.S. companies. However, for smaller countries, which are likely to be hosts to a number of foreign companies,

GNP, the value of output produced within a country's borders, is typically smaller than GDP, the value of output produced worldwide that is owned by a country's citizens and firms.

GDP and GNP can diverge significantly. For example, much of Ireland's industry is owned by American corporations, whose profit must be deducted from Ireland's GNP. In addition, Ireland has become a host to many temporary workers from poorer regions of Europe, whose wages must also be deducted from Ireland's GNP. As a result, in 2010 Ireland's GNP was only 82% of its GDP.

---

value added by government, in the form of military, education, and other government services. Finally, $1,838 billion of value added was added by households and institutions; a large part of that was the imputed services of owner-occupied housing, described in the earlier For Inquiring Minds "Our Imputed Lives."

The right bar in Figure 7-3 corresponds to the second method of calculating GDP, showing the breakdown by the four types of aggregate spending. The total length of the right bar is longer than the total length of the left bar, a difference of $517 billion (which, as you can see, is the amount by which the right bar extends below the horizontal axis). That's because the total length of the right bar represents total spending in the economy, spending on both domestically produced and foreign-produced final goods and services. Within the bar, consumer spending ($C$), which is 70.5% of GDP, dominates the picture. But some of that spending was absorbed by foreign-produced goods and services. In 2010, **net exports,** the difference between the value of exports and the value of imports ($X - IM$ in Equation 7-1) was negative—the United States was a net importer of foreign goods and services. The 2010 value of $X - IM$ was –$517 billion, or –3.6% of GDP. Thus, a portion of the right bar extends below the horizontal axis by $517 billion to represent the amount of total spending that was absorbed by net imports and so did not lead to higher U.S. GDP. Investment spending ($I$) constituted 12.4% of GDP; government purchases of goods and services ($G$) constituted 20.7% of GDP.

### What GDP Tells Us

**Net exports** are the difference between the value of exports and the value of imports.

Now we've seen the various ways that gross domestic product is calculated. But what does the measurement of GDP tell us?

The most important use of GDP is as a measure of the size of the economy, providing us a scale against which to measure the economic performance of other years or to compare the economic performance of other countries. For example, suppose you want to compare the economies of different nations. A natural approach is to compare their GDPs. In 2010, as we've seen, U.S. GDP was $14,527 billion, Japan's GDP was $5,459 billion, and the combined GDP of the 27 countries that make up the European Union was $16,263 billion. This comparison tells us that Japan, although it has the world's second-largest national economy, carries considerably less economic weight than does the United States. When taken in aggregate, Europe is America's equal or superior.

Still, one must be careful when using GDP numbers, especially when making comparisons over time. That's because part of the increase in the value of GDP over time represents increases in the *prices* of goods and services rather than an increase in output. For example, U.S. GDP was $7,415 billion in 1995 and had approximately doubled to $14,527 billion by 2010. But the U.S. economy didn't actually double in size over that period. To measure actual changes in aggregate output, we need a modified version of GDP that is adjusted for price changes, known as *real GDP*. We'll see next how real GDP is calculated.

## ECONOMICS ➤ IN ACTION

## CREATING THE NATIONAL ACCOUNTS

The national accounts, like modern macroeconomics, owe their creation to the Great Depression. As the economy plunged into depression, government officials found their ability to respond crippled not only by the lack of adequate economic theories but also by the lack of adequate information. All they had were scattered statistics: railroad freight car loadings, stock prices, and incomplete indexes of industrial production. They could only guess at what was happening to the economy as a whole.

In response to this perceived lack of information, the Department of Commerce commissioned Simon Kuznets, a young Russian-born economist, to develop a set of national income accounts. (Kuznets later won the Nobel Prize in economics for his work.) The first version of these accounts was presented to Congress in 1937 and in a research report titled *National Income, 1929–35*.

Kuznets's initial estimates fell short of the full modern set of accounts because they focused on income, not production. The push to complete the national accounts came during World War II, when policy makers were in even more need of comprehensive measures of the economy's performance. The federal government began issuing estimates of gross domestic product and gross national product in 1942.

In January 2000, in its publication *Survey of Current Business*, the Department of Commerce ran an article titled "GDP: One of the Great Inventions of the 20th Century." This may seem a bit over the top, but national income accounting, invented in the United States, has since become a tool of economic analysis and policy making around the world.

## CHECK YOUR UNDERSTANDING  7-1

1. Explain why the three methods of calculating GDP produce the same estimate of GDP.

2. What are the various sectors to which firms make sales? What are the various ways in which households are linked with other sectors of the economy?

3. Consider Figure 7-2 and suppose you mistakenly believed that total value added was $30,500, the sum of the sales price of a car and a car's worth of steel. What items would you be counting twice?

Solutions appear at back of book.

### ▼ Quick Review

- A country's **national income and product accounts,** or **national accounts,** track flows of money among economic sectors.

- Households receive factor income in the form of wages, profit from ownership of **stocks,** interest paid on **bonds,** and rent. They also receive **government transfers.**

- Households allocate **disposable income** between **consumer spending** and **private savings**—funds that flow into the **financial markets,** financing **investment spending** and any **government borrowing.**

- **Government purchases of goods and services** are total expenditures by federal, state, and local governments on goods and services.

- **Exports** lead to a flow of funds into the country. **Imports** lead to a flow of funds out of the country.

- **Gross domestic product,** or **GDP,** can be calculated in three different ways: add up the **value added** by all firms; add up all spending on domestically produced **final goods and services,** an amount equal to **aggregate spending;** or add up all factor income paid by firms. **Intermediate goods and services** are not included in the calculation of GDP, while changes in **inventories** and **net exports** are.

**Aggregate output** is the economy's total quantity of output of final goods and services.

# Real GDP: A Measure of Aggregate Output

In this chapter's opening story, we described how China passed Japan as the world's second-largest economy in 2010. At the time, Japan's economy was weakening: during the second quarter of 2010, output declined by an annual rate of 6.3%. Oddly, however, GDP was up. In fact, Japan's GDP measured in yen, its national currency, rose by an annual rate of 4.8% during the quarter. How was that possible? The answer is that Japan was experiencing inflation at the time. As a result, the yen value of Japan's GDP rose although output actually fell.

The moral of this story is that the commonly cited GDP number is an interesting and useful statistic, one that provides a good way to compare the size of different economies, but it's not a good measure of the economy's growth over time. GDP can grow because the economy grows, but it can also grow simply because of inflation. Even if an economy's output doesn't change, GDP will go up if the prices of the goods and services the economy produces have increased. Likewise, GDP can fall either because the economy is producing less or because prices have fallen.

In order to accurately measure the economy's growth, we need a measure of **aggregate output:** the total quantity of final goods and services the economy produces. The measure that is used for this purpose is known as *real GDP*. By tracking real GDP over time, we avoid the problem of changes in prices distorting the value of changes in production of goods and services over time. Let's look first at how real GDP is calculated, then at what it means.

## Calculating Real GDP

To understand how real GDP is calculated, imagine an economy in which only two goods, apples and oranges, are produced and in which both goods are sold only to final consumers. The outputs and prices of the two fruits for two consecutive years are shown in Table 7-1.

The first thing we can say about these data is that the value of sales increased from year 1 to year 2. In the first year, the total value of sales was (2,000 billion × $0.25) + (1,000 billion × $0.50) = $1,000 billion; in the second it was (2,200 billion × $0.30) + (1,200 billion × $0.70) = $1,500 billion, which is 50% larger. But it is also clear from the table that this increase in the dollar value of GDP overstates the real growth in the economy. Although the quantities of both apples and oranges increased, the prices of both apples and oranges also rose. So part of the 50% increase in the dollar value of GDP from year 1 to year 2 simply reflects higher prices, not higher production of output.

To estimate the true increase in aggregate output produced, we have to ask the following question: how much would GDP have gone up if prices had *not*

**TABLE 7-1** Calculating GDP and Real GDP in a Simple Economy

|  | Year 1 | Year 2 |
|---|---|---|
| Quantity of apples (billions) | 2,000 | 2,200 |
| Price of apple | $0.25 | $0.30 |
| Quantity of oranges (billions) | 1,000 | 1,200 |
| Price of orange | $0.50 | $0.70 |
| GDP (billions of dollars) | $1,000 | $1,500 |
| Real GDP (billions of year 1 dollars) | $1,000 | $1,150 |

changed? To answer this question, we need to find the value of output in year 2 expressed in year 1 prices. In year 1 the price of apples was $0.25 each and the price of oranges $0.50 each. So year 2 output *at year 1 prices* is (2,200 billion × $0.25) + (1,200 billion × $0.50) = $1,150 billion. And output in year 1 at year 1 prices was $1,000 billion. So in this example GDP measured in year 1 prices rose 15%—from $1,000 billion to $1,150 billion.

Now we can define **real GDP:** it is the total value of final goods and services produced in the economy during a year, calculated as if prices had stayed constant at the level of some given base year. A real GDP number always comes with information about what the base year is.

A GDP number that has not been adjusted for changes in prices is calculated using the prices in the year in which the output is produced. Economists call this measure **nominal GDP,** GDP at current prices. If we had used nominal GDP to measure the true change in output from year 1 to year 2 in our apples and oranges example, we would have overstated the true growth in output: we would have claimed it to be 50%, when in fact it was only 15%. By comparing output in the two years using a common set of prices—the year 1 prices in this example—we are able to focus solely on changes in the quantity of output by eliminating the influence of changes in prices.

Table 7-2 shows a real-life version of our apples and oranges example. The second column shows nominal GDP in 1995, 2005, and 2010. The third column shows real GDP for each year in 2005 dollars. For 2005 the two numbers are the same. But real GDP in 1995 expressed in 2005 dollars was higher than nominal GDP in 1995, reflecting the fact that prices were in general higher in 2005 than in 1995. Real GDP in 2010 expressed in 2005 dollars, however, was less than nominal GDP in 2010 because prices in 2005 were lower than in 2010.

| TABLE **7-2** | Nominal versus Real GDP in 1995, 2005, and 2010 | |
| --- | --- | --- |
| | Nominal GDP (billions of current dollars) | Real GDP (billions of 2005 dollars) |
| 1995 | $7,415 | $9,086 |
| 2005 | 12,623 | 12,623 |
| 2010 | 14,527 | 13,088 |

You might have noticed that there is an alternative way to calculate real GDP using the data in Table 7-1. Why not measure it using the prices of year 2 rather than year 1 as the base-year prices? This procedure seems equally valid. According to that calculation, real GDP in year 1 at year 2 prices is (2,000 billion × $0.30) + (1,000 billion × $0.70) = $1,300 billion; real GDP in year 2 at year 2 prices is $1,500 billion, the same as nominal GDP in year 2. So using year 2 prices as the base year, the growth rate of real GDP is equal to ($1,500 billion – $1,300 billion)/$1,300 billion = 0.154, or 15.4%. This is slightly higher than the figure we got from the previous calculation, in which year 1 prices were the base-year prices. In that calculation, we found that real GDP increased by 15%. Neither answer, 15.4% versus 15%, is more "correct" than the other.

In reality, the government economists who put together the U.S. national accounts have adopted a method to measure the change in real GDP known as chain-linking, which uses the average between the GDP growth rate calculated using an early base year and the GDP growth rate calculated using a late base year. As a result, U.S. statistics on real GDP are always expressed in **chained dollars.**

## What Real GDP Doesn't Measure

GDP, nominal or real, is a measure of a country's aggregate output. Other things equal, a country with a larger population will have higher GDP simply because there are more people working. So if we want to compare GDP across countries but want to eliminate the effect of differences in population size, we use the measure **GDP per capita**—GDP divided by the size of the population, equivalent to the average GDP per person.

**Real GDP** is the total value of all final goods and services produced in the economy during a given year, calculated using the prices of a selected base year.

**Nominal GDP** is the value of all final goods and services produced in the economy during a given year, calculated using the prices current in the year in which the output is produced.

**Chained dollars** is the method of calculating changes in real GDP using the average between the growth rate calculated using an early base year and the growth rate calculated using a late base year.

**GDP per capita** is GDP divided by the size of the population; it is equivalent to the average GDP per person.

Real GDP per capita can be a useful measure in some circumstances, such as in a comparison of labor productivity between countries. However, despite the fact that it is a rough measure of the average real output per person, real GDP per capita has well-known limitations as a measure of a country's living standards. Every once in a while economists are accused of believing that growth in real GDP per capita is the only thing that matters—that is, thinking that increasing real GDP per capita is a goal in itself. In fact, economists rarely make that mistake; the idea that economists care only about real GDP per capita is a sort of urban legend. Let's take a moment to be clear about why a country's real GDP per capita is not a sufficient measure of human welfare in that country and why growth in real GDP per capita is not an appropriate policy goal in itself.

One way to think about this issue is to say that an increase in real GDP means an expansion in the economy's production possibility frontier. Because the economy has increased its productive capacity, there are more things that society can achieve. But whether society actually makes good use of that increased potential to improve living standards is another matter. To put it in a slightly different way,

## GDP AND THE MEANING OF LIFE

"I've been rich and I've been poor," the actress Mae West famously declared. "Believe me, rich is better." But is the same true for countries?

This figure shows two pieces of information for a number of countries: how rich they are, as measured by GDP per capita, and how people assess their well-being. Well-being was measured by a Gallup world survey that asked people to rate their lives at the current time and their expectations for the next five years. The graph shows the percentage of people who rated their well-being as "thriving." The figure seems to tell us three things:

1. *Rich is better.* Richer countries on average have higher well-being than poor countries.

2. *Money matters less as you grow richer.* The gain in life satisfaction as you go from GDP per capita of $5,000 to $20,000 is greater than the gain as you go from $20,000 to $35,000.

3. *Money isn't everything.* Israelis, though rich by world standards, are poorer than Americans—but they seem more satisfied with their lives. Japan is richer than most other nations, but by and large, quite miserable.

These results are consistent with the observation that high GDP per capita makes it easier to achieve a good life but that countries aren't equally successful in taking advantage of that possibility.

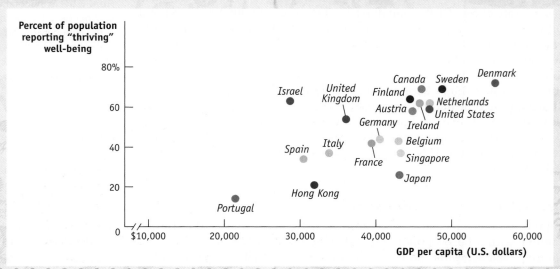

*Source:* Gallup; World Bank.

your income may be higher this year than last year, but whether you use that higher income to actually improve your quality of life is your choice.

So let's say it again: real GDP per capita is a measure of an economy's average aggregate output per person—and so of what it *can* do. It is not a sufficient goal in itself because it doesn't address how a country uses that output to affect living standards. A country with a high GDP can afford to be healthy, to be well educated, and in general to have a good quality of life. But there is not a one-to-one match between GDP and the quality of life.

## ECONOMICS ►*IN ACTION*

### MIRACLE IN VENEZUELA?

The South American nation of Venezuela has a distinction that may surprise you: in recent years, it has had one of the world's fastest-growing nominal GDPs. Between 2000 and 2010, Venezuelan nominal GDP grew by an average of 29% each year—much faster than nominal GDP in the United States or even in booming economies like China.

So is Venezuela experiencing an economic miracle? No, it's just suffering from unusually high inflation. Figure 7-4 shows Venezuela's nominal and real GDP from 2000 to 2010, with real GDP measured in 1997 prices. Real GDP did grow over the period, but at an annual rate of only 3%. That's about twice the U.S. growth rate over the same period, but it is far short of China's 10% growth.

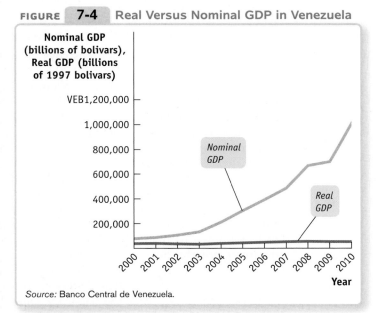

FIGURE **7-4**   Real Versus Nominal GDP in Venezuela

Source: Banco Central de Venezuela.

Solutions appear at back of book.

### CHECK YOUR UNDERSTANDING   7-2

1. Assume there are only two goods in the economy, french fries and onion rings. In 2011, 1,000,000 servings of french fries were sold at $0.40 each and 800,000 servings of onion rings at $0.60 each. From 2011 to 2012, the price of french fries rose by 25% and the servings sold fell by 10%; the price of onion rings fell by 15% and the servings sold rose by 5%.
   **a.** Calculate nominal GDP in 2011 and 2012. Calculate real GDP in 2012 using 2011 prices.
   **b.** Why would an assessment of growth using nominal GDP be misguided?

2. From 2005 to 2010, the price of electronic equipment fell dramatically and the price of housing rose dramatically. What are the implications of this in deciding whether to use 2005 or 2010 as the base year in calculating 2012 real GDP?

### ▼ Quick Review

● To determine the actual growth in **aggregate output,** we calculate **real GDP** using prices from some given base year. In contrast, **nominal GDP** is the value of aggregate output calculated with current prices. U.S. statistics on real GDP are always expressed in **chained dollars.**

● Real **GDP per capita** is a measure of the average aggregate output per person. But it is not a sufficient measure of human welfare, nor is it an appropriate goal in itself, because it does not reflect important aspects of living standards within an economy.

The **aggregate price level** is a measure of the overall level of prices in the economy.

A **market basket** is a hypothetical set of consumer purchases of goods and services.

# Price Indexes and the Aggregate Price Level

In the spring and summer of 2011, Americans were facing sticker shock at the gas pump: the price of a gallon of regular gasoline had risen from an average of $1.61 at the end of December 2008 to close to $4. Many other prices were also up. Some prices, though, were heading down: some foods, like eggs, were coming down from a run-up from late 2010, and virtually anything involving electronics was getting cheaper as well. Yet practically everyone felt that the overall cost of living was rising. But how fast?

Clearly, there was a need for a single number summarizing what was happening to consumer prices. Just as macroeconomists find it useful to have a single number representing the overall level of output, they also find it useful to have a single number representing the overall level of prices: the **aggregate price level.** Yet a huge variety of goods and services are produced and consumed in the economy. How can we summarize the prices of all these goods and services with a single number? The answer lies in the concept of a *price index*—a concept best introduced with an example.

## Market Baskets and Price Indexes

Suppose that a frost in Florida destroys most of the citrus harvest. As a result, the price of an orange rises from $0.20 each to $0.40, the price of grapefruit rises from $0.60 to $1.00, and the price of a lemon rises from $0.25 to $0.45. How much has the price of citrus fruit increased?

One way to answer that question is to state three numbers—the changes in prices for oranges, grapefruit, and lemons. But this is a very cumbersome method. Rather than having to recite three numbers in an effort to track changes in the prices of citrus fruit, we would prefer to have some kind of overall measure of the *average* price change.

To measure average price changes for consumer goods and services, economists track changes in the cost of a typical consumer's *consumption bundle*— the typical basket of goods and services purchased before the price changes. A hypothetical consumption bundle, used to measure changes in the overall price level, is known as a **market basket.** Suppose that before the frost a typical consumer bought 200 oranges, 50 grapefruit, and 100 lemons over the course of a year, our market basket for this example.

Table 7-3 shows the pre-frost and post-frost cost of this market basket. Before the frost, it cost $95; after the frost, the same bundle of goods cost $175. Since $175/$95 = 1.842, the post-frost basket costs 1.842 times the cost of the pre-frost basket, a cost increase of 84.2%. In this example, the average price of citrus fruit has increased 84.2% since the base year as a result of the frost, where the base year is the initial year used in the measurement of the price change.

**TABLE 7-3** Calculating the Cost of a Market Basket

| | Pre-frost | Post-frost |
|---|---|---|
| Price of orange | $0.20 | $0.40 |
| Price of grapefruit | 0.60 | 1.00 |
| Price of lemon | 0.25 | 0.45 |
| Cost of market basket (200 oranges, 50 grapefruit, 100 lemons) | (200 × $0.20) + (50 × $0.60) + (100 × $0.25) = $95.00 | (200 × $0.40) + (50 × $1.00) + (100 × $0.45) = $175.00 |

Economists use the same method to measure changes in the overall price level: they track changes in the cost of buying a given market basket. In addition, they perform another simplification in order to avoid having to keep track of the information that the market basket cost, for example, $95 in such-and-such a year. They *normalize* the measure of the aggregate price level, which means that they set the cost of the market basket equal to 100 in the chosen base year. Working with a market basket and a base year, and after performing normalization, we obtain what is known as a **price index,** a normalized measure of the overall price level. It is always cited along with the year for which the aggregate price level is being measured and the base year. A price index can be calculated using the following formula:

**(7-2)** Price index in a given year = $\dfrac{\text{Cost of market basket in a given year}}{\text{Cost of market basket in base year}} \times 100$

In our example, the citrus fruit market basket cost $95 in the base year, the year before the frost. So by Equation 7-2 we define the price index for citrus fruit as (cost of market basket in current year/$95) × 100, yielding an index of 100 for the period before the frost and 184.2 after the frost. You should note that the price index for the base year always results in a price index equal to 100. This is because the price index in the base year is equal to: (cost of market basket in base year/cost of market basket in base year) × 100 = 100.

Thus, the price index makes it clear that the average price of citrus has risen 84.2% as a consequence of the frost. Because of its simplicity and intuitive appeal, the method we've just described is used to calculate a variety of price indexes to track average price changes among a variety of different groups of goods and services. For example, the *consumer price index*, which we'll discuss shortly, is the most widely used measure of the aggregate price level, the overall price level of final consumer goods and services across the economy.

Price indexes are also the basis for measuring inflation. The **inflation rate** is the annual percent change in an official price index. The inflation rate from year 1 to year 2 is calculated using the following formula, where we assume that year 1 and year 2 are consecutive years.

**(7-3)** Inflation rate = $\dfrac{\text{Price index in year 2} - \text{Price index in year 1}}{\text{Price index in year 1}} \times 100$

Typically, a news report that cites "the inflation rate" is referring to the annual percent change in the consumer price index.

## The Consumer Price Index

The most widely used measure of prices in the United States is the **consumer price index** (often referred to simply as the **CPI**), which is intended to show how the cost of all purchases by a typical urban family has changed over time. It is calculated by surveying market prices for a market basket that is constructed to represent the consumption of a typical family of four living in a typical American city. The base period for the index is currently 1982–1984; that is, the index is calculated so that the average of consumer prices in 1982–1984 is 100.

The market basket used to calculate the CPI is far more complex than the three-fruit market basket we described above. In fact, to calculate the CPI, the Bureau of Labor Statistics sends its employees out to survey supermarkets, gas stations, hardware stores, and so on—some 23,000 retail outlets in 87 cities. Every month it tabulates about 80,000 prices, on everything from romaine lettuce to a medical check-up. Figure 7-5 shows the weight of major categories in the consumer price index as of December 2010. For example, motor fuel, mainly gasoline,

A **price index** measures the cost of purchasing a given market basket in a given year, where that cost is normalized so that it is equal to 100 in the selected base year.

The **inflation rate** is the percent change per year in a price index—typically the consumer price index.

The **consumer price index,** or **CPI,** measures the cost of the market basket of a typical urban American family.

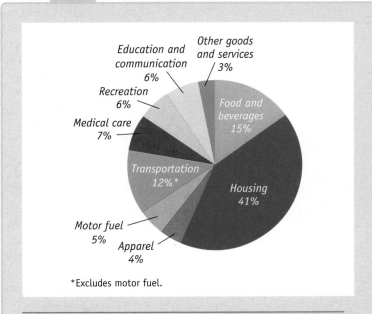

**The Makeup of the Consumer**

FIGURE **7-5**  **Price Index in 2010**

*Other goods and services*
*3%*

*Education and communication*
*6%*

*Recreation*
*6%*

*Medical care*
*7%*

*Food and beverages*
*15%*

*Transportation*
*12%\**

*Housing*
*41%*

*Motor fuel*
*5%*

*Apparel*
*4%*

\*Excludes motor fuel.

This chart shows the percentage shares of major types of spending in the CPI as of December 2010. Housing, food, transportation, and motor fuel made up about 73% of the CPI market basket. (Numbers don't add to 100% due to rounding.)

*Source:* Bureau of Labor Statistics.

FIGURE   **7-6**   **The CPI, 1913–2007**

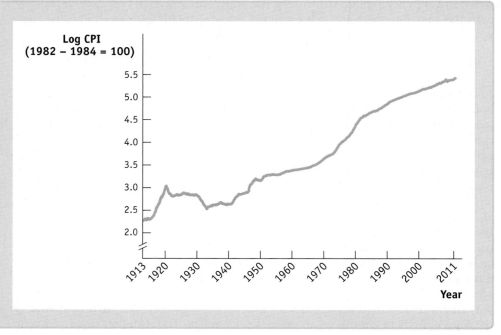

Since 1940, the CPI has risen steadily. But the annual percentage increases in recent years have been much smaller than those of the 1970s and early 1980s. (The vertical axis is measured on a logarithmic scale so that equal percent changes in the CPI have the same slope.)

*Source:* Bureau of Labor Statistics.

accounted for 5% of the CPI in December 2010. So when gas prices rose 150%, from about $1.61 a gallon in late 2008 to $3.96 a gallon in May 2011, the effect was to increase the CPI by about 1.5 times 5%—that is, around 7.5%.

Figure 7-6 shows how the CPI has changed since measurement began in 1913. Since 1940, the CPI has risen steadily, although its annual percent increases in recent years have been much smaller than those of the 1970s and early 1980s. A logarithmic scale is used so that equal percent changes in the CPI have the same slope.

The United States is not the only country that calculates a consumer price index. In fact, nearly every country has one. As you might expect, the market baskets that make up these indexes differ quite a lot from country to country. In poor countries, where people must spend a high proportion of their income just to feed themselves, food makes up a large share of the price index. Among high-income countries, differences in consumption patterns lead to differences in the price indexes: the Japanese price index puts a larger weight on raw fish and a smaller weight on beef than ours does, and the French price index puts a larger weight on wine.

## Other Price Measures

There are two other price measures that are also widely used to track economy-wide price changes. One is the **producer price index** (or **PPI,** which used to be known as the *wholesale price index*). As its name suggests, the producer price index measures the cost of a typical basket of goods and services—containing raw commodities such as steel, electricity, coal, and so on—purchased by producers. Because commodity producers are relatively quick to raise prices when they perceive a change in overall demand for their goods, the PPI often responds to inflationary or deflationary pressures more quickly than the CPI. As a result, the PPI is often regarded as an "early warning signal" of changes in the inflation rate.

The **producer price index,** or **PPI,** measures changes in the prices of goods purchased by producers.

The **GDP deflator** for a given year is 100 times the ratio of nominal GDP to real GDP in that year.

The other widely used price measure is the *GDP deflator;* it isn't exactly a price index, although it serves the same purpose. Recall how we distinguished between nominal GDP (GDP in current prices) and real GDP (GDP calculated using the prices of a base year). The **GDP deflator** for a given year is equal to 100 times the ratio of nominal GDP for that year to real GDP for that year. Since real GDP

FIGURE    **7-7**    The CPI, the PPI, and the GDP Deflator

As the figure shows, the three different measures of inflation, the PPI (orange), the CPI (green), and the GDP deflator (purple), usually move closely together. Each reveals a drastic acceleration of inflation during the 1970s and a return to relative price stability in the 1990s.

*Sources:* Bureau of Labor Statistics; Bureau of Economic Analysis.

is currently expressed in 2005 dollars, the GDP deflator for 2005 is equal to 100. If nominal GDP doubles but real GDP does not change, the GDP deflator indicates that the aggregate price level doubled.

Perhaps the most important point about the different inflation rates generated by these three measures of prices is that they usually move closely together (although the producer price index tends to fluctuate more than either of the other two measures). Figure 7-7 shows the annual percent changes in the three indexes since 1930. By all three measures, the U.S. economy experienced deflation during the early years of the Great Depression, inflation during World War II, accelerating inflation during the 1970s, and a return to relative price stability in the 1990s. Notice, by the way, the dramatic ups and downs in producer prices from 2000 to 2010 on the graph; this reflects large swings in energy and food prices, which play a much bigger role in the PPI than they do in either the CPI or the GDP deflator.

## ECONOMICS > IN ACTION

### INDEXING TO THE CPI

**A**lthough GDP is a very important number for shaping economic policy, official statistics on GDP don't have a direct effect on people's lives. The CPI, by contrast, has a direct and immediate impact on millions of Americans. The reason is that many payments are tied, or "indexed," to the CPI—the amount paid rises or falls when the CPI rises or falls.

The practice of indexing payments to consumer prices goes back to the dawn of the United States as a nation. In 1780 the Massachusetts State Legislature recognized that the pay of its soldiers fighting the British needed to be increased because of inflation that occurred during the Revolutionary War. The legislature adopted a formula that made a soldier's pay proportional to the cost of a market basket, consisting of 5 bushels of corn, 68⁴⁄₇ pounds of beef, 10 pounds of sheep's wool, and 16 pounds of sole leather.

Today, 54 million people, most of them old or disabled, receive payments from Social Security, a national retirement program that

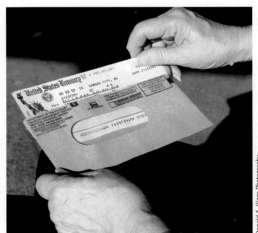

A small change in the CPI has large consequences for those dependent on Social Security payments.

accounts for almost a quarter of current total federal spending—more than the defense budget. The amount of an individual's Social Security payment is determined by a formula that reflects his or her previous payments into the system as well as other factors. In addition, all Social Security payments are adjusted each year to offset any increase in consumer prices over the previous year. The CPI is used to calculate the official estimate of the inflation rate used to adjust these payments yearly. So every percentage point added to the official estimate of the rate of inflation adds 1% to the checks received by tens of millions of individuals.

Other government payments are also indexed to the CPI. In addition, income tax brackets, the bands of income levels that determine a taxpayer's income tax rate, are also indexed to the CPI. (An individual in a higher income bracket pays a higher income tax rate in a progressive tax system like ours.) Indexing also extends to the private sector, where many private contracts, including some wage settlements, contain cost-of-living allowances (called COLAs) that adjust payments in proportion to changes in the CPI.

Because the CPI plays such an important and direct role in people's lives, it's a politically sensitive number. The Bureau of Labor Statistics, which calculates the CPI, takes great care in collecting and interpreting price and consumption data. It uses a complex method in which households are surveyed to determine what they buy and where they shop, and a carefully selected sample of stores are surveyed to get representative prices.

## ▼ Quick Review

- Changes in the **aggregate price level** are measured by the cost of buying a particular **market basket** during different years. A **price index** for a given year is the cost of the market basket in that year normalized so that the price index equals 100 in a selected base year.

- The **inflation rate** is calculated as the percent change in a price index. The most commonly used price index is the **consumer price index,** or **CPI,** which tracks the cost of a basket of consumer goods and services. The **producer price index,** or **PPI,** does the same for goods and services used as inputs by firms. The **GDP deflator** measures the aggregate price level as the ratio of nominal to real GDP times 100. These three measures normally behave quite similarly.

## CHECK YOUR UNDERSTANDING   7-3

1. Consider Table 7-3 but suppose that the market basket is composed of 100 oranges, 50 grapefruit, and 200 lemons. How does this change the pre-frost and post-frost price indexes? Explain. Generalize your explanation to how the construction of the market basket affects the price index.

2. For each of the following events, how would an economist using a 10-year-old market basket create a bias in measuring the change in the cost of living today?
   a. A typical family owns more cars than it would have a decade ago. Over that time, the average price of a car has increased more than the average prices of other goods.
   b. Virtually no households had broadband Internet access a decade ago. Now many households have it, and the price has regularly fallen each year.

3. The consumer price index in the United States (base period 1982–1984) was 214.537 in 2009 and 218.056 in 2010. Calculate the inflation rate from 2009 to 2010.

*Solutions appear at back of book.*

# BUSINESS CASE : Getting a Jump on GDP

REUTERS/Lucas Jackson

GDP matters. Investors and business leaders are always anxious to get the latest numbers. When the Bureau of Economic Analysis releases its first estimate of each quarter's GDP, normally on the 27th or 28th day of the month after the quarter ends, it's invariably a big news story.

In fact, many companies and other players in the economy are so eager to know what's happening to GDP that they don't want to wait for the official estimate. So a number of organizations produce numbers that can be used to predict what the official GDP number will say. Let's talk about two of those organizations, the economic consulting firm Macroeconomic Advisers and the nonprofit Institute of Supply Management.

Macroeconomic Advisers takes a direct approach: it produces its own estimates of GDP based on raw data from the U.S. government. But whereas the Bureau of Economic Analysis estimates GDP only on a quarterly basis, Macroeconomic Advisers produces monthly estimates. This means that clients can, for example, look at the estimates for January and February and make a pretty good guess at what first-quarter GDP, which also includes March, will turn out to be. The monthly estimates are derived by looking at a number of monthly measures that track purchases, such as car and truck sales, new housing construction, and exports.

The Institute for Supply Management (ISM) takes a very different approach. It relies on monthly surveys of purchasing managers—that is, executives in charge of buying supplies—who are basically asked whether their companies are increasing or reducing production. (We say "basically" because the ISM asks a longer list of questions.) Responses to the surveys are released in the form of indexes showing the percentage of companies that are expanding. Obviously, these indexes don't directly tell you what is happening to GDP. But historically, the ISM indexes have been strongly correlated with the rate of growth of GDP, and this historical relationship can be used to translate ISM data into "early warning" GDP estimates.

So if you just can't wait for those quarterly GDP numbers, you're not alone. The private sector has responded to demand, and you can get your data fix every month.

## QUESTIONS FOR THOUGHT

1. Why do businesses care about GDP to such an extent that they want early estimates?

2. How do the methods of Macroeconomic Advisers and the Institute of Supply Management fit into the three different ways to calculate GDP?

3. If private firms are producing GDP estimates, why do we need the Bureau of Economic Analysis?

1. Economists keep track of the flows of money between sectors with the **national income and product accounts,** or **national accounts.** Households earn income via the factor markets from wages, interest on **bonds,** profit accruing to owners of **stocks,** and rent on land. In addition, they receive **government transfers** from the government. **Disposable income,** total household income minus taxes plus government transfers, is allocated to **consumer spending** (C) and **private savings.** Via the **financial markets,** private savings and foreign lending are channeled to **investment spending** (I), government borrowing, and foreign borrowing. **Government purchases of goods and services** (G) are paid for by tax revenues and any **government borrowing. Exports** (X) generate an inflow of funds into the country from the rest of the world, but **imports** (IM) lead to an outflow of funds to the rest of the world. Foreigners can also buy stocks and bonds in the U.S. financial markets.

2. **Gross domestic product,** or **GDP,** measures the value of all **final goods and services** produced in the economy. It does not include the value of **intermediate goods and services,** but it does include **inventories** and **net exports** (X – IM). It can be calculated in three ways: add up the **value added** by all producers; add up all spending on domestically produced final goods and services, leading to the equation $GDP = C + I + G + X - IM$, also known as **aggregate spending;** or add up all the income paid by domestic firms to factors of production. These three methods are equivalent because in the economy as a whole, total income paid by domestic firms to factors of production must equal total spending on domestically produced final goods and services.

3. **Real GDP** is the value of the final goods and services produced calculated using the prices of a selected base year. Except in the base year, real GDP is not the same as **nominal GDP,** the value of **aggregate output** calculated using current prices. Analysis of the growth rate of aggregate output must use real GDP because doing so eliminates any change in the value of aggregate output due solely to price changes. Real **GDP per capita** is a measure of average aggregate output per person but is not in itself an appropriate policy goal. U.S. statistics on real GDP are always expressed in **chained dollars.**

4. To measure the **aggregate price level,** economists calculate the cost of purchasing a **market basket.** A **price index** is the ratio of the current cost of that market basket to the cost in a selected base year, multiplied by 100.

5. The **inflation rate** is the yearly percent change in a price index, typically based on the **consumer price index,** or **CPI,** the most common measure of the aggregate price level. A similar index for goods and services purchased by firms is the **producer price index,** or **PPI.** Finally, economists also use the **GDP deflator,** which measures the price level by calculating the ratio of nominal to real GDP times 100.

National income and product accounts (national accounts), p. 188
Consumer spending, p. 188
Stock, p. 188
Bond, p. 188
Government transfers, p. 188
Disposable income, p. 188
Private savings, p. 189
Financial markets, p. 189
Government borrowing, p. 190
Government purchases of goods and services, p. 190

Exports, p. 190
Imports, p. 190
Inventories, p. 190
Investment spending, p. 190
Final goods and services, p. 191
Intermediate goods and services, p. 191
Gross domestic product (GDP), p. 191
Aggregate spending, p. 191
Value added, p. 193
Net exports, p. 196
Aggregate output, p. 198
Real GDP, p. 199

Nominal GDP, p. 199
Chained dollars, p. 199
GDP per capita, p. 199
Aggregate price level, p. 202
Market basket, p. 202
Price index, p. 203
Inflation rate, p. 203
Consumer price index (CPI), p. 203
Producer price index (PPI), p. 204
GDP deflator, p. 204

## PROBLEMS

1. At right is a simplified circular-flow diagram for the economy of Micronia. (Note that there is no investment in Micronia.)

   a. What is the value of GDP in Micronia?

   b. What is the value of net exports?

   c. What is the value of disposable income?

   d. Does the total flow of money out of house-holds—the sum of taxes paid and consumer spending—equal the total flow of money into households?

   e. How does the government of Micronia finance its purchases of goods and services?

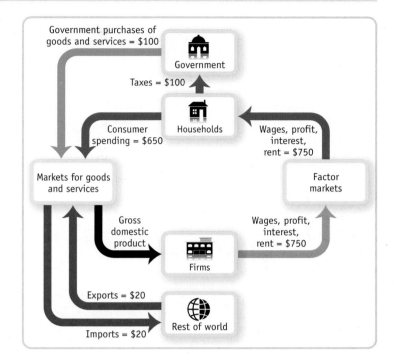

2. A more complex circular-flow diagram for the econo-my of Macronia is shown at right. (Note that Macronia has investment and financial markets.)

   a. What is the value of GDP in Macronia?

   b. What is the value of net exports?

   c. What is the value of dis-posable income?

   d. Does the total flow of money out of house-holds—the sum of taxes paid, consumer spending, and private savings—equal the total flow of money into households?

   e. How does the government finance its spending?

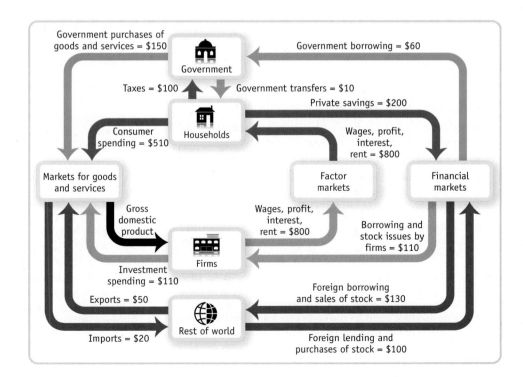

**3.** The components of GDP in the accompanying table were produced by the Bureau of Economic Analysis.

| Category | Components of GDP in 2010 (billions of dollars) |
|---|---|
| **Consumer spending** | |
| Durable goods | $1,085.5 |
| Nondurable goods | 2,301.5 |
| Services | 6,858.5 |
| **Private investment spending** | |
| Fixed investment spending | 1,728.2 |
| Nonresidential | 1,390.1 |
| Structures | 374.4 |
| Equipment and software | 1,015.7 |
| Residential | 338.1 |
| Change in private inventories | 66.9 |
| **Net exports** | |
| Exports | 1,839.8 |
| Imports | 2,356.7 |
| **Government purchases of goods and services and investment spending** | |
| Federal | 1,222.8 |
| National defense | 819.2 |
| Nondefense | 403.6 |
| State and local | 1,780.0 |

  **a.** Calculate 2010 consumer spending.

  **b.** Calculate 2010 private investment spending.

  **c.** Calculate 2010 net exports.

  **d.** Calculate 2010 government purchases of goods and services and investment spending.

  **e.** Calculate 2010 gross domestic product.

  **f.** Calculate consumer spending on services as a percentage of total consumer spending.

  **g.** Calculate 2010 exports as a percentage of imports.

  **h.** Calculate 2010 government purchases on national defense as a percentage of federal government purchases of goods and services.

**4.** The small economy of Pizzania produces three goods (bread, cheese, and pizza), each produced by a separate company. The bread and cheese companies produce all the inputs they need to make bread and cheese, respectively. The pizza company uses the bread and cheese from the other companies to make its pizzas. All three companies employ labor to help produce their goods, and the difference between the value of goods sold and the sum of labor and input costs is the firm's profit. The accompanying table summarizes the activities of the three companies when all the bread and cheese produced are sold to the pizza company as inputs in the production of pizzas.

| | Bread company | Cheese company | Pizza company |
|---|---|---|---|
| Cost of inputs | $0 | $0 | $50 (bread) |
| | | | 35 (cheese) |
| Wages | 15 | 20 | 75 |
| Value of output | 50 | 35 | 200 |

  **a.** Calculate GDP as the value added in production.

  **b.** Calculate GDP as spending on final goods and services.

  **c.** Calculate GDP as factor income.

**5.** In the economy of Pizzania (from Problem 4), bread and cheese produced are sold both to the pizza company for inputs in the production of pizzas and to consumers as final goods. The accompanying table summarizes the activities of the three companies.

| | Bread company | Cheese company | Pizza company |
|---|---|---|---|
| Cost of inputs | $0 | $0 | $50 (bread) |
| | | | 35 (cheese) |
| Wages | 25 | 30 | 75 |
| Value of output | 100 | 60 | 200 |

  **a.** Calculate GDP as the value added in production.

  **b.** Calculate GDP as spending on final goods and services.

  **c.** Calculate GDP as factor income.

**6.** Which of the following transactions will be included in GDP for the United States?

  **a.** Coca-Cola builds a new bottling plant in the United States.

  **b.** Delta sells one of its existing airplanes to Korean Air.

  **c.** Ms. Moneybags buys an existing share of Disney stock.

  **d.** A California winery produces a bottle of Chardonnay and sells it to a customer in Montreal, Canada.

  **e.** An American buys a bottle of French perfume in Paris.

  **f.** A book publisher produces too many copies of a new book; the books don't sell this year, so the publisher adds the surplus books to inventories.

**7.** The economy of Britannica produces three goods: computers, DVDs, and pizza. The accompanying table shows the prices and output of the three goods for the years 2010, 2011, and 2012.

| Year | Computers Price | Computers Quantity | DVDs Price | DVDs Quantity | Pizzas Price | Pizzas Quantity |
|---|---|---|---|---|---|---|
| 2010 | $900 | 10 | $10 | 100 | $15 | 2 |
| 2011 | 1,000 | 10.5 | 12 | 105 | 16 | 2 |
| 2012 | 1,050 | 12 | 14 | 110 | 17 | 3 |

**a.** What is the percent change in production of each of the goods from 2010 to 2011 and from 2011 to 2012?

**b.** What is the percent change in prices of each of the goods from 2010 to 2011 and from 2011 to 2012?

**c.** Calculate nominal GDP in Britannica for each of the three years. What is the percent change in nominal GDP from 2010 to 2011 and from 2011 to 2012?

**d.** Calculate real GDP in Britannica using 2010 prices for each of the three years. What is the percent change in real GDP from 2010 to 2011 and from 2011 to 2012?

**8.** The accompanying table shows data on nominal GDP (in billions of dollars), real GDP (in billions of 2005 dollars), and population (in thousands) of the United States in 1960, 1970, 1980, 1990, 2000, and 2010. The U.S. price level rose consistently over the period 1960–2010.

| Year | Nominal GDP (billions of dollars) | Real GDP (billions of 2005 dollars) | Population (thousands) |
|---|---|---|---|
| 1960 | $526.4 | $2,828.5 | 180,760 |
| 1970 | 1,038.5 | 4,266.3 | 205,089 |
| 1980 | 2,788.1 | 5,834.0 | 227,726 |
| 1990 | 5,800.5 | 8,027.1 | 250,181 |
| 2000 | 9,951.5 | 11,216.4 | 282,418 |
| 2010 | 14,526.5 | 13,088.0 | 310,106 |

**a.** Why is real GDP greater than nominal GDP for all years until 2000 and lower for 2010?

**b.** Calculate the percent change in real GDP from 1960 to 1970, 1970 to 1980, 1980 to 1990, 1990 to 2000, and 2000 to 2010. Which period had the highest growth rate?

**c.** Calculate real GDP per capita for each of the years in the table.

**d.** Calculate the percent change in real GDP per capita from 1960 to 1970, 1970 to 1980, 1980 to 1990, 1990 to 2000, and 2000 to 2010. Which period had the highest growth rate?

**e.** How do the percent change in real GDP and the percent change in real GDP per capita compare? Which is larger? Do we expect them to have this relationship?

**9.** Eastland College is concerned about the rising price of textbooks that students must purchase. To better identify the increase in the price of textbooks, the dean asks you, the Economics Department's star student, to create an index of textbook prices. The average student purchases three English, two math, and four economics textbooks per year. The prices of these books are given in the accompanying table.

|  | 2010 | 2011 | 2012 |
|---|---|---|---|
| English textbook | $50 | $55 | $57 |
| Math textbook | 70 | 72 | 74 |
| Economics textbook | 80 | 90 | 100 |

**a.** What is the percent change in the price of an English textbook from 2010 to 2012?

**b.** What is the percent change in the price of a math textbook from 2010 to 2012?

**c.** What is the percent change in the price of an economics textbook from 2010 to 2012?

**d.** Using 2010 as a base year, create a price index for these books for all years.

**e.** What is the percent change in the price index from 2010 to 2012?

**10.** The consumer price index, or CPI, measures the cost of living for a typical urban household by multiplying the price for each category of expenditure (housing, food, and so on) times a measure of the importance of that expenditure in the average consumer's market basket and summing over all categories. However, using data from the consumer price index, we can see that changes in the cost of living for different types of consumers can vary a great deal. Let's compare the cost of living for a hypothetical retired person and a hypothetical college student. Let's assume that the market basket of a retired person is allocated in the following way: 10% on housing, 15% on food, 5% on transportation, 60% on medical care, 0% on education, and 10% on recreation. The college student's market basket is allocated as follows: 5% on housing, 15% on food, 20% on transportation, 0% on medical care, 40% on education, and 20% on recreation. The accompanying table shows the July 2011 CPI for each of the relevant categories.

|  | CPI July 2011 |
|---|---|
| Housing | 220.2 |
| Food | 228.3 |
| Transportation | 216.2 |
| Medical care | 400.3 |
| Education | 206.2 |
| Recreation | 113.5 |

Calculate the overall CPI for the retired person and for the college student by multiplying the CPI for each of the categories by the relative importance of that category to the individual and then summing each of the categories. The CPI for all items in July 2011 was 225.9. How do your calculations for a CPI for the retired person and the college student compare to the overall CPI?

**11.** Each month the Bureau of Labor Statistics releases the Consumer Price Index Summary for the previous month. Go to the Bureau of Labor Statistics home page at www.bls.gov. Place the cursor over the "Economic Releases" tab and then click on "Major Economic Indicators" in the drop-down menu that appears. Once on the "Major Economic Indicators" page, click on "Consumer Price Index." Use the "not seasonally adjusted" figures. On that page, under "Table of Contents," click on "Consumer Price Index Summary." What was the CPI for the previous month? How did it change from the previous month? How does the CPI compare to the same month one year ago?

12. The accompanying table provides the annual real GDP (in billions of 2005 dollars) and nominal GDP (in billions of dollars) for the United States.

| | 2006 | 2007 | 2008 | 2009 | 2010 |
|---|---|---|---|---|---|
| Real GDP (billions of 2005 dollars) | 12,958.5 | 13,206.4 | 13,161.9 | 12,703.1 | 13,088.0 |
| Nominal GDP (billions of dollars) | 13,377.2 | 14,028.7 | 14,291.5 | 13,939.0 | 14,526.5 |

a. Calculate the GDP deflator for each year.

b. Use the GDP deflator to calculate the inflation rate for all years except 2006.

13. The accompanying table contains two price indexes for the years 2008, 2009, and 2010: the GDP deflator and the CPI. For each price index, calculate the inflation rate from 2008 to 2009 and from 2009 to 2010.

| Year | GDP deflator | CPI |
|---|---|---|
| 2008 | 108.582 | 215.303 |
| 2009 | 109.729 | 214.537 |
| 2010 | 110.992 | 218.056 |

14. The cost of a college education in the United States is rising at a rate faster than inflation. The table below shows the average cost of a college education in the United States during the academic year that began in 2009 and the academic year that began in 2010 for public and private colleges. Assume the costs listed in the table are the only costs experienced by the various college students in a single year.

a. Calculate the cost of living for an average college student in each category for 2009 and 2010.

b. Calculate an inflation rate for each type of college student between 2009 and 2010.

| | Cost of college education during academic year beginning 2009 (averages in 2009 dollars) | | | | |
|---|---|---|---|---|---|
| | Tuition and fees | Room and board | Books and supplies | Transportation | Other expenses |
| Two-year public college: commuter | $2,544 | $7,202 | $1,098 | $1,445 | $1,996 |
| Four-year public college: in-state, on-campus | 7,020 | 8,193 | 1,122 | 1,079 | 1,974 |
| Four-year public college: out-of-state, on-campus | 18,548 | 8,193 | 1,122 | 1,079 | 1,974 |
| Four-year private college: on-campus | 26,273 | 9,363 | 1,116 | 849 | 1,427 |
| | Cost of college education during academic year beginning 2010 (averages in 2010 dollars) | | | | |
| | Tuition and fees | Room and board | Books and supplies | Transportation | Other expenses |
| Two-year public college: commuter | $2,713 | $7,259 | $1,133 | $1,491 | $2,041 |
| Four-year public college: in-state, on-campus | 7,605 | 8,535 | 1,137 | 1,073 | 1,989 |
| Four-year public college: out-of-state, on-campus | 19,595 | 8,535 | 1,137 | 1,073 | 1,989 |
| Four-year private college: on-campus | 27,293 | 9,700 | 1,181 | 862 | 1,440 |

# Unemployment and Inflation

## A VERY BRITISH DILEMMA

❯ How **unemployment** is measured and how the **unemployment rate** is calculated

❯ The significance of the unemployment rate for the economy

❯ The relationship between the unemployment rate and economic growth

❯ The factors that determine the **natural rate of unemployment**

❯ The economic costs of inflation

❯ How inflation and deflation create winners and losers

❯ Why policy makers try to maintain a stable rate of inflation

Through good times and bad, the Old Lady of Threadneedle Street has been managing Great Britain's money supply for over 300 years.

Alex Segre/Alamy

David Levenson/Alamy

THE BANK OF ENGLAND IS A venerable institution—so venerable that it makes the Federal Reserve, its American counterpart, look like a youthful upstart. The Old Lady of Threadneedle Street, as the Bank is sometimes known, has been managing Great Britain's money supply for three centuries—pumping up the money supply when the economy needs a boost, putting on the brakes when inflation looms.

But in early 2011, it wasn't at all clear what the Bank should do. British inflation was rising: in February 2011 consumer prices were 4.4 percent higher than they had been a year earlier, a rate of increase far above the Bank's comfort level. At the same time, the British economy was still suffering the aftereffects of a severe recession, and unemployment,

especially among young people, was disturbingly high. So should the Bank have focused on fighting inflation, or should it have kept trying to bring down unemployment?

Opinion was sharply divided. The Bank faced "a genuine problem of credibility," declared Patrick Minford, a professor at Cardiff University, who urged the Bank to fight inflation by raising interest rates. The rise in inflation reflected temporary factors and would soon reverse course, countered Adam Posen, a member of the Bank's Policy Committee, who argued that any tightening would risk putting Britain into a prolonged slump.

Whoever was right, the dispute highlighted the key concerns of macroeconomic policy. Unemployment and inflation are the two great evils of

macroeconomics. So the two principal goals of macroeconomic policy are low unemployment and price stability, usually defined as a low but positive rate of inflation. Unfortunately, those goals sometimes appear to be in conflict with each other: economists often warn that policies intended to fight unemployment run the risk of increasing inflation; conversely, policies intended to bring down inflation can raise unemployment.

The nature of the trade-off between low unemployment and low inflation, along with the policy dilemma it creates, is a topic reserved for later chapters. This chapter provides an overview of the basic facts about unemployment and inflation: how they're measured, how they affect consumers and firms, and how they change over time. ∎

**Employment** is the number of people currently employed in the economy, either full time or part time.

**Unemployment** is the number of people who are actively looking for work but aren't currently employed.

# The Unemployment Rate

Britain had an unemployment rate of 7.7 percent in early 2011, up from just 5.7 percent in 2008. That was bad. But the U.S. unemployment rate was even worse. Figure 8-1 shows the U.S. unemployment rate from 1948 to mid-2011; as you can see, unemployment soared during the 2007–2009 recession and had fallen only modestly by 2011. What did the rise in the unemployment rate mean, and why was it such a big factor in people's lives? To understand why policy makers pay so much attention to employment and unemployment, we need to understand how they are both defined and measured.

FIGURE **8-1**  The U.S. Unemployment Rate, 1948–2011

The unemployment rate has fluctuated widely over time. It always rises during recessions, which are shown by the shaded bars. It usually, but not always, falls during periods of economic expansion.

*Sources:* Bureau of Labor Statistics; National Bureau of Economic Research.

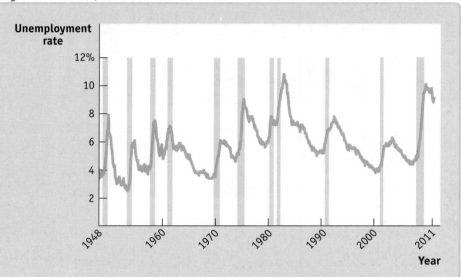

## Defining and Measuring Unemployment

It's easy to define employment: you're employed if and only if you have a job. **Employment** is the total number of people currently employed, either full time or part time.

Unemployment, however, is a more subtle concept. Just because a person isn't working doesn't mean that we consider that person unemployed. For example, as of January 2012, there were 35.8 million retired workers in the United States receiving Social Security checks. Most of them were probably happy that they were no longer working, so we wouldn't consider someone who has settled into a comfortable, well-earned retirement to be unemployed. There were also 8.6 million disabled U.S. workers receiving benefits because they were unable to work. Again, although they weren't working, we wouldn't normally consider them to be unemployed.

The U.S. Census Bureau, the federal agency tasked with collecting data on unemployment, considers the unemployed to be those who are "jobless, looking for jobs, and available for work." Retired people don't count because they aren't looking for jobs; the disabled don't count because they aren't available for work. More specifically, an individual is considered unemployed if he or she doesn't currently have a job and has been actively seeking a job during the past four weeks. So **unemployment** is defined as the total number of people who are actively looking for work but aren't currently employed.

A country's **labor force** is the sum of employment and unemployment—that is, of people who are currently working and people who are currently looking for work, respectively. The **labor force participation rate,** defined as the share of the working-age population that is in the labor force, is calculated as follows:

**(8-1)** Labor force participation rate $= \dfrac{\text{Labor force}}{\text{Population age 16 and older}} \times 100$

The **unemployment rate,** defined as the percentage of the total number of people in the labor force who are unemployed, is calculated as follows:

**(8-2)** Unemployment rate $= \dfrac{\text{Number of unemployed workers}}{\text{Labor force}} \times 100$

To estimate the numbers that go into calculating the unemployment rate, the U.S. Census Bureau carries out a monthly survey called the Current Population Survey, which involves interviewing a random sample of 60,000 American families. People are asked whether they are currently employed. If they are not employed, they are asked whether they have been looking for a job during the past four weeks. The results are then scaled up, using estimates of the total population, to estimate the total number of employed and unemployed Americans.

## The Significance of the Unemployment Rate

In general, the unemployment rate is a good indicator of how easy or difficult it is to find a job given the current state of the economy. When the unemployment rate is low, nearly everyone who wants a job can find one. In 2000, when the unemployment rate averaged 4%, jobs were so abundant that employers spoke of a "mirror test" for getting a job: if you were breathing (therefore your breath would fog a mirror), you could find work. By contrast, in 2010, with the unemployment rate above 9% all year, it was very hard to find work. In fact, there were almost five times as many Americans seeking work as there were job openings.

Although the unemployment rate is a good indicator of current labor market conditions, it's not a literal measure of the percentage of people who want a job but can't find one. That's because in some ways the unemployment rate exaggerates the difficulty people have in finding jobs. But in other ways, the opposite is true—a low unemployment rate can conceal deep frustration over the lack of job opportunities.

**How the Unemployment Rate Can Overstate the True Level of Unemployment** If you are searching for work, it's normal to take at least a few weeks to find a suitable job. Yet a worker who is quite confident of finding a job, but has not yet accepted a position, is counted as unemployed. As a consequence, the unemployment rate never falls to zero, even in boom times when jobs are plentiful. Even in the buoyant labor market of 2000, when it was easy to find work, the unemployment rate was still 4%. Later in this chapter, we'll discuss in greater depth the reasons that measured unemployment persists even when jobs are abundant.

**How the Unemployment Rate Can Understate the True Level of Unemployment** Frequently, people who would like to work but aren't working still don't get counted as unemployed. In particular, an individual who has given up looking for a job for the time being because there are no jobs available—say, a laid-off steelworker in a deeply depressed steel town—isn't counted as unemployed because he or she has not been searching for a job during the previous four weeks. Individuals who want to work but have told government researchers that they aren't currently searching because they see little prospect of finding a job given the state of the job market are called

The **labor force** is equal to the sum of employment and unemployment.

The **labor force participation rate** is the percentage of the population aged 16 or older that is in the labor force.

The **unemployment rate** is the percentage of the total number of people in the labor force who are unemployed.

**Discouraged workers** are nonworking people who are capable of working but have given up looking for a job given the state of the job market.

**Marginally attached workers** would like to be employed and have looked for a job in the recent past but are not currently looking for work.

**Underemployment** is the number of people who work part time because they cannot find full-time jobs.

**discouraged workers.** Because it does not count discouraged workers, the measured unemployment rate may understate the percentage of people who want to work but are unable to find jobs.

Discouraged workers are part of a larger group—**marginally attached workers.** These are people who say they would like to have a job and have looked for work in the recent past but are not currently looking for work. They, too, are not included when calculating the unemployment rate.

Finally, another category of workers who are frustrated in their ability to find work but aren't counted as unemployed are the **underemployed:** workers who would like to find full-time jobs but are currently working part time "for economic reasons"—that is, they can't find a full-time job. Again, they aren't counted in the unemployment rate.

The Bureau of Labor Statistics is the federal agency that calculates the official unemployment rate. It also calculates broader "measures of labor underutilization" that include the three categories of frustrated workers. Figure 8-2 shows what happens to the measured unemployment rate once discouraged workers, other marginally attached workers, and the underemployed are counted. The broadest measure of unemployment and underemployment, known as U-6, is the sum of these three measures plus the unemployed. It is substantially higher than the rate usually quoted by the news media. But U-6 and the unemployment rate move very much in parallel, so changes in the unemployment rate remain a good guide to what's happening in the overall labor market, including frustrated workers.

Finally, it's important to realize that the unemployment rate varies greatly among demographic groups. Other things equal, jobs are generally easier to find for more experienced workers and for workers during their "prime" working years, from ages 25 to 54. For younger workers, as well as workers nearing retirement age, jobs are typically harder to find, other things equal.

Figure 8-3 shows unemployment rates for different groups in December 2007, when the overall unemployment rate of 5.0% was low by historical standards. As you can see, at this time the unemployment rate for African-American workers was much higher than the national average; the unemployment rate for White teenagers (ages 16–19) was almost three times the national average; and the unemployment rate for African-American teenagers, at 33.1%, was over six times the national average. (Bear in mind that a teenager isn't considered unemployed,

FIGURE **8-2** **Alternative Measures of Unemployment, 1994–2011**

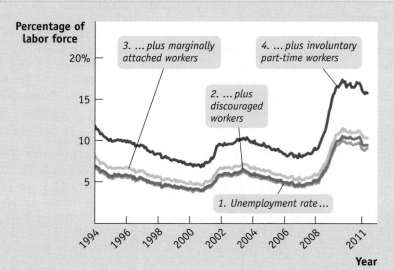

The unemployment number usually quoted in the news media counts someone as unemployed only if he or she has been looking for work during the past four weeks. Broader measures also count discouraged workers, marginally attached workers, and the underemployed. These broader measures show a higher unemployment rate, but they move closely in parallel with the standard rate.

*Source:* Bureau of Labor Statistics.

FIGURE  **8-3**  Unemployment Rates of Different Groups, 2007

FIGURE  **8-3**  Unemployment Rates of Different Groups, 2007

Unemployment rates vary greatly among different demographic groups. For example, although the overall unemployment rate in December 2007 was 5.0%, the unemployment rate among African-American teenagers was 33.1%. As a result, even during periods of low overall unemployment, unemployment remains a serious problem for some groups.

*Source:* Bureau of Labor Statistics.

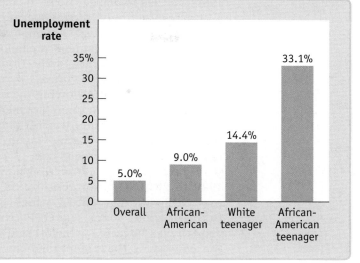

even if he or she isn't working, unless that teenager is looking for work but can't find it.) So even at a time when the overall unemployment rate was relatively low, jobs were hard to find for some groups.

So you should interpret the unemployment rate as an indicator of overall labor market conditions, not as an exact, literal measure of the percentage of people unable to find jobs. The unemployment rate is, however, a very good indicator: its ups and downs closely reflect economic changes that have a significant impact on people's lives. Let's turn now to the causes of these fluctuations.

## Growth and Unemployment

Compared to Figure 8-1, Figure 8-4 shows the U.S. unemployment rate over a somewhat shorter period, the 33 years from 1978 to 2011. The shaded bars represent periods of recession. As you can see, during every recession, without exception, the

FIGURE  **8-4**  Unemployment and Recessions, 1978–2011

This figure shows a close-up of the unemployment rate for the past three decades, with the shaded bars indicating recessions. It's clear that unemployment always rises during recessions and *usually* falls during expansions. But in both the early 1990s and the early 2000s, unemployment continued to rise for some time after the recession was officially declared over.

*Sources:* Bureau of Labor Statistics; National Bureau of Economic Research.

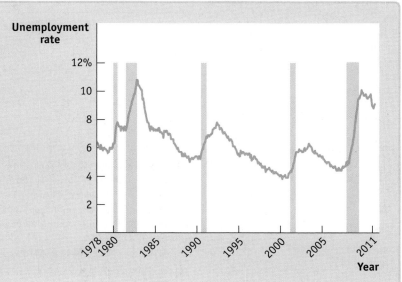

unemployment rate rose. The severe recession of 2007–2009, like the earlier one of 1981–1982, led to a huge rise in unemployment.

Correspondingly, during periods of economic expansion the unemployment rate usually falls. The long economic expansion of the 1990s eventually brought the unemployment rate below 4%, and the expansion of the mid-2000s brought the rate down to 4.7%. However, it's important to recognize that *economic expansions aren't always periods of falling unemployment.* Look at the periods immediately following the recessions of 1990–1991 and 2001 in Figure 8-4. In each case the unemployment rate continued to rise for more than a year after the recession was officially over. The explanation in both cases is that although the economy was growing, it was not growing fast enough to reduce the unemployment rate.

Figure 8-5 is a scatter diagram showing U.S. data for the period from 1949 to 2010. The horizontal axis measures the annual rate of growth in real GDP—the percent by which each year's real GDP changed compared to the previous year's real GDP. (Notice that there were nine years in which growth was negative—that is, real GDP shrank.) The vertical axis measures the *change* in the unemployment rate over the previous year in percentage points. Each dot represents the observed growth rate of real GDP and change in the unemployment rate for a given year. For example, in 2000 the average unemployment rate fell to 4.0% from 4.2% in 1999; this is shown as a value of –0.2 along the vertical axis for the year 2000. Over the same period, real GDP grew by 3.7%; this is the value shown along the horizontal axis for the year 2000.

**FIGURE 8-5** Growth and Changes in Unemployment, 1949–2010

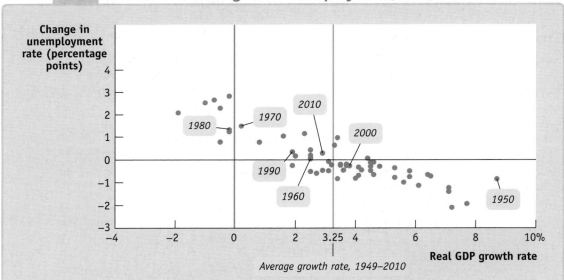

Each dot shows the growth rate of the economy and the change in the unemployment rate for a specific year between 1949 and 2010. For example, in 2000 the economy grew 3.7% and the unemployment rate fell 0.2 percentage point, from 4.2% to 4.0%. In general, the unemployment rate fell when growth was above its average rate of 3.25% a year and rose when growth was below average. Unemployment always rose when real GDP fell.

*Sources:* Bureau of Labor Statistics; Bureau of Economic Analysis.

The downward trend of the scatter diagram in Figure 8-5 shows that there is a generally strong negative relationship between growth in the economy and the rate of unemployment. Years of high growth in real GDP were also years in which the unemployment rate fell, and years of low or negative growth in real GDP were years in which the unemployment rate rose.

The green vertical line in Figure 8-5 at the value of 3.25% indicates the average growth rate of real GDP over the period from 1949 to 2010. Points lying to the right of the vertical line are years of above-average growth. In these years, the value on the vertical axis is usually negative, meaning that the unemployment rate fell. That is, years of above-average growth were usually years in which the unemployment rate was falling. Conversely, points lying to the left of the green vertical line were years of below-average growth. In these years, the value on the vertical axis is usually positive, meaning that the unemployment rate rose. That is, years of below-average growth were usually years in which the unemployment rate was rising.

A period in which real GDP is growing at a below-average rate and unemployment is rising is called a **jobless recovery** or a "growth recession." Since 1990, there have been three recessions, all of which have been followed by jobless recoveries. But true recessions, periods when real GDP falls, are especially painful for workers. As illustrated by the points to the left of the purple vertical line in Figure 8-5 (representing years in which the real GDP growth rate is negative), falling real GDP is always associated with a rising rate of unemployment, causing a great deal of hardship to families.

> A **jobless recovery** is a period in which the real GDP growth rate is positive but the unemployment rate is still rising.

## ECONOMICS ▶ IN ACTION

### FAILURE TO LAUNCH

In March 2010, when the U.S. job situation was near its worst, the *Harvard Law Record* published a brief note titled "Unemployed law student will work for $160K plus benefits." In a self-mocking tone, the author admitted to having graduated from Harvard Law School the previous year but not landing a job offer. "What mark on our résumé is so bad that it outweighs the crimson H?" the note asked.

The answer, of course, is that it wasn't about the résumé—it was about the economy. Times of high unemployment are especially hard on new graduates, who often find it hard to get any kind of full-time job.

How bad was it in March 2010, around the time that note was written? Researchers at the San Francisco Fed analyzed the employment experience of college graduates, ages 21–23, and their findings are in Figure 8-6.

Although the overall unemployment rate for college graduates 25 and older, even at its peak, was only about 5 percent, unemployment among recent graduates aged 21–23 peaked in 2010 at 10.7 percent. And many of those who *were* employed had been able to get only part-time jobs. In December 2007, at the beginning of the 2007–2009 recession, 83 percent of college graduates under the age of 24 who weren't still in school were employed full time. By December 2009, that number was down to just 72 percent. Quite simply, many college graduates were having a hard time getting their working lives started.

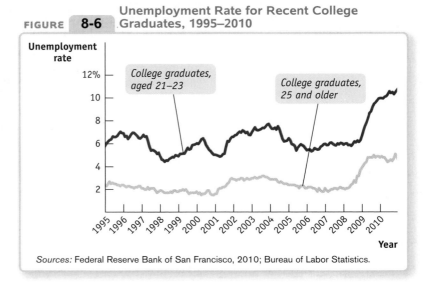

**FIGURE 8-6**  Unemployment Rate for Recent College Graduates, 1995–2010

*Sources:* Federal Reserve Bank of San Francisco, 2010; Bureau of Labor Statistics.

A year later, the situation was starting to improve, but slowly: in December 2010, 74 percent of recent graduates had full-time jobs. The U.S. labor market had a long way to go before being able to offer college graduates—and young people in general—the kinds of opportunities they deserved.

### CHECK YOUR UNDERSTANDING 8-1

1. Suppose that the advent of employment websites enables job-seekers to find suitable jobs more quickly. What effect will this have on the unemployment rate over time? Also suppose that these websites encourage job-seekers who had given up their searches to begin looking again. What effect will this have on the unemployment rate?

2. In which of the following cases is a worker counted as unemployed? Explain.
   a. Rosa, an older worker who has been laid off and who gave up looking for work months ago
   b. Anthony, a schoolteacher who is not working during his three-month summer break
   c. Grace, an investment banker who has been laid off and is currently searching for another position
   d. Sergio, a classically trained musician who can only find work playing for local parties
   e. Natasha, a graduate student who went back to school because jobs were scarce

3. Which of the following are consistent with the observed relationship between growth in real GDP and changes in the unemployment rate? Which are not?
   a. A rise in the unemployment rate accompanies a fall in real GDP.
   b. An exceptionally strong business recovery is associated with a greater percentage of the labor force being employed.
   c. Negative real GDP growth is associated with a fall in the unemployment rate.

Solutions appear at back of book.

# The Natural Rate of Unemployment

Fast economic growth tends to reduce the unemployment rate. So how low can the unemployment rate go? You might be tempted to say zero, but that isn't feasible. Over the past half-century, the national unemployment rate has never dropped below 2.9%.

How can there be so much unemployment even when many businesses are having a hard time finding workers? To answer this question, we need to examine the nature of labor markets and why they normally lead to substantial measured unemployment even when jobs are plentiful. Our starting point is the observation that even in the best of times, jobs are constantly being created and destroyed.

## Job Creation and Job Destruction

Even during good times, most Americans know someone who has lost his or her job. In July 2007, the U.S. unemployment rate was only 4.7%, relatively low by historical standards. Yet in that month there were 4.5 million "job separations"—terminations of employment that occur because a worker is either fired or quits voluntarily.

There are many reasons for such job loss. One is structural change in the economy: industries rise and fall as new technologies emerge and consumers' tastes change. For example, employment in high-tech industries such as telecommunications surged in the late 1990s but slumped severely after 2000. However, structural change also brings the creation of new jobs: after 2000, the number of jobs in the American healthcare sector surged as new medical technologies and the aging of the population increased the demand for medical care. Poor management performance or bad luck at individual companies also leads to job loss for their employees. For example, in 2005 General Motors announced plans to eliminate 30,000 jobs after several years of lagging sales, even as Japanese companies such as Toyota announced plans to open new plants in North America to meet growing demand for their cars.

Continual job creation and destruction are a feature of modern economies, making a naturally occurring amount of unemployment inevitable. Within this naturally occurring amount, there are two types of unemployment—*frictional* and *structural*.

*"At this point, I'm just happy to still have a job"*

## Frictional Unemployment

When a worker loses a job involuntarily due to job destruction, he or she often doesn't take the first new job offered. For example, suppose a skilled programmer, laid off because her software company's product line was unsuccessful, sees a help-wanted ad for clerical work online. She might respond to the ad and get the job—but that would be foolish. Instead, she should take the time to look for a job that takes advantage of her skills and pays accordingly. In addition, individual workers are constantly leaving jobs voluntarily, typically for personal reasons—family moves, dissatisfaction, and better job prospects elsewhere.

Economists say that workers who spend time looking for employment are engaged in **job search.** If all workers and all jobs were alike, job search wouldn't be necessary; if information about jobs and workers was perfect, job search would be very quick. In practice, however, it's normal for a worker who loses a job, or a young worker seeking a first job, to spend at least a few weeks searching.

**Frictional unemployment** is unemployment due to the time workers spend in job search. A certain amount of frictional unemployment is inevitable due to the constant process of economic change. Thus even in 2007, a year of low unemployment, there were 62 million "job separations," in which workers left or lost their jobs. Total employment grew because these separations were more than offset by more than 63 million hires. Inevitably, some of the workers who left or lost their jobs spent at least some time unemployed, as did some of the workers newly entering the labor force.

Figure 8-7 shows the 2007 average monthly flows of workers among three states: employed, unemployed, and not in the labor force. What the figure suggests

Workers who spend time looking for employment are engaged in **job search.**

**Frictional unemployment** is unemployment due to the time workers spend in job search.

---

**FIGURE** **8-7** Labor Market Flows in an Average Month in 2007

Even in 2007, a low-unemployment year, large numbers of workers moved into and out of both employment and unemployment each month. On average, each month in 2007, 1.781 million unemployed became employed, and 1.929 million employed became unemployed.
*Source:* Bureau of Labor Statistics.

Employed

1.781 million
1.929 million

4.118 million
3.920 million

Unemployed

1.601 million
1.798 million

Not in labor force

In **structural unemployment,** more people are seeking jobs in a particular labor market than there are jobs available at the current wage rate, even when the economy is at the peak of the business cycle.

is how much churning is constantly taking place in the labor market. An inevitable consequence of that churning is a significant number of workers who haven't yet found their next job—that is, frictional unemployment.

A limited amount of frictional unemployment is relatively harmless and may even be a good thing. The economy is more productive if workers take the time to find jobs that are well matched to their skills and workers who are unemployed for a brief period while searching for the right job don't experience great hardship. In fact, when there is a low unemployment rate, periods of unemployment tend to be quite short, suggesting that much of the unemployment is frictional.

Figure 8-8 shows the composition of unemployment for all of 2007, when the unemployment rate was only 4.6%. Thirty-six percent of the unemployed had been unemployed for less than 5 weeks, and only 33% had been unemployed for 15 or more weeks. Only about one in six unemployed workers were considered to be "long-term unemployed"—unemployed for 27 or more weeks.

In periods of higher unemployment, however, workers tend to be jobless for longer periods of time, suggesting that a smaller share of unemployment is frictional. By 2010, the fraction of unemployed workers considered "long-term unemployed" had jumped to 43%.

**FIGURE 8-8** Distribution of the Unemployed by Duration of Unemployment, 2007

In years when the unemployment rate is low, most unemployed workers are unemployed for only a short period. In 2007, a year of low unemployment, 36% of the unemployed had been unemployed for less than 5 weeks and 67% for less than 15 weeks. The short duration of unemployment for most workers suggests that most unemployment in 2007 was frictional.
*Source:* Bureau of Labor Statistics.

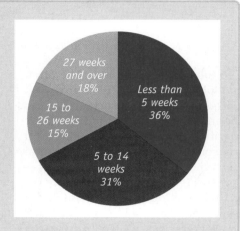

## Structural Unemployment

Frictional unemployment exists even when the number of people seeking jobs is equal to the number of jobs being offered—that is, the existence of frictional unemployment doesn't mean that there is a surplus of labor. Sometimes, however, there is a *persistent surplus* of job-seekers in a particular labor market, even when the economy is at the peak of the business cycle. There may be more workers with a particular skill than there are jobs available using that skill, or there may be more workers in a particular geographic region than there are jobs available in that region. **Structural unemployment** is unemployment that results when there are more people seeking jobs in a particular labor market than there are jobs available at the current wage rate.

The supply and demand model tells us that the price of a good, service, or factor of production tends to move toward an equilibrium level that matches the quantity supplied with the quantity demanded. This is equally true, in general, of labor markets.

Figure 8-9 shows a typical market for labor. The labor demand curve indicates that when the price of labor—the wage rate—increases, employers demand less labor. The labor supply curve indicates that when the price of labor increases, more workers are willing to supply labor at the prevailing wage rate. These two forces coincide to lead to an equilibrium wage rate for any given type of labor in a particular location. That equilibrium wage rate is shown as $W_E$.

Even at the equilibrium wage rate $W_E$, there will still be some frictional unemployment. That's because there will always be some workers engaged in job search even when the number of jobs available is equal to the number of workers seeking jobs. But there wouldn't be any structural unemployment in this labor market. *Structural unemployment occurs when the wage rate is, for some reason, persistently above $W_E$.* Several factors can lead to a wage rate in excess of $W_E$, the most important being minimum wages, labor unions, *efficiency wages,* the side effects of government policies, and mismatches between employees and employers.

FIGURE   **8-9**   The Effect of a Minimum Wage on a Labor Market

When the government sets a minimum wage, $W_F$, that exceeds the market equilibrium wage rate in that market, $W_E$, the number of workers, $Q_S$, who would like to work at that minimum wage is greater than the number of workers, $Q_D$, demanded at that wage rate. This surplus of labor is structural unemployment.

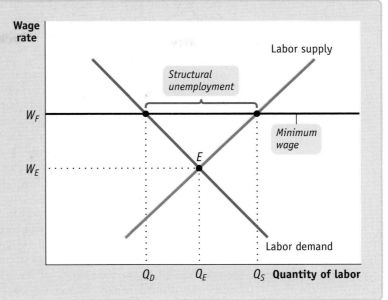

## Minimum Wages

A minimum wage is a government-mandated floor on the price of labor. In the United States, the national minimum wage in early 2012 was $7.25 an hour. For many American workers, the minimum wage is irrelevant; the market equilibrium wage for these workers is well above this price floor. But for less skilled workers, the minimum wage may be binding—it affects the wages that people are actually paid and can lead to structural unemployment in particular markets for labor. Other wealthy countries have higher minimum wages; for example, in 2012 the French minimum wage was 9.22 euros an hour, or around $11.90. In these countries, the range of workers for whom the minimum wage is binding is larger.

Figure 8-9 shows the effect of a binding minimum wage. In this market, there is a legal floor on wages, $W_F$, which is above the equilibrium wage rate, $W_E$. This leads to a persistent surplus in the labor market: the quantity of labor supplied, $Q_S$, is larger than the quantity demanded, $Q_D$. In other words, more people want to work than can find jobs at the minimum wage, leading to structural unemployment.

Given that minimum wages—that is, binding minimum wages—generally lead to structural unemployment, you might wonder why governments impose them. The rationale is to help ensure that people who work can earn enough income to afford at least a minimally comfortable lifestyle. However, this may come at a cost, because it may eliminate the opportunity to work for some workers who would have willingly worked for lower wages. As illustrated in Figure 8-9, not only are there more sellers of labor than there are buyers, but there are also fewer people working at a minimum wage ($Q_D$) than there would have been with no minimum wage at all ($Q_E$).

Although economists broadly agree that a high minimum wage has the employment-reducing effects shown in Figure 8-9, there is some question about whether this is a good description of how the U.S. minimum wage actually works. The minimum wage in the United States is quite low compared with that in other wealthy countries. For three decades, from the 1970s to the mid-2000s, the American minimum wage was so low that it was not binding for the vast majority of workers.

In addition, some researchers have produced evidence that increases in the minimum wage actually lead to higher employment when, as was the case in the United States at one time, the minimum wage is low compared to average wages.

**Efficiency wages** are wages that employers set above the equilibrium wage rate as an incentive for better employee performance.

They argue that firms that employ low-skilled workers sometimes restrict their hiring in order to keep wages low and that, as a result, the minimum wage can sometimes be increased without any loss of jobs. Most economists, however, agree that a sufficiently high minimum wage *does* lead to structural unemployment.

**Labor Unions** The actions of *labor unions* can have effects similar to those of minimum wages, leading to structural unemployment. By bargaining collectively for all of a firm's workers, unions can often win higher wages from employers than workers would have obtained by bargaining individually. This process, known as *collective bargaining,* is intended to tip the scales of bargaining power more toward workers and away from employers. Labor unions exercise bargaining power by threatening firms with a *labor strike,* a collective refusal to work. The threat of a strike can have serious consequences for firms. In such cases, workers acting collectively can exercise more power than they could if acting individually.

Employers have acted to counter the bargaining power of unions by threatening and enforcing lockouts—periods in which union workers are locked out and rendered unemployed—while hiring replacement workers.

When workers have increased bargaining power, they tend to demand and receive higher wages. Unions also bargain over benefits, such as health care and pensions, which we can think of as additional wages. Indeed, economists who study the effects of unions on wages find that unionized workers earn higher wages and more generous benefits than non-union workers with similar skills. The result of these increased wages can be the same as the result of a minimum wage: labor unions push the wage that workers receive above the equilibrium wage. Consequently, there are more people willing to work at the wage being paid than there are jobs available. Like a binding minimum wage, this leads to structural unemployment. In the United States, however, due to a low level of unionization, the amount of unemployment generated by union demands is likely to be very small.

**Efficiency Wages** Actions by firms can contribute to structural unemployment. Firms may choose to pay **efficiency wages**—wages that employers set above the equilibrium wage rate as an incentive for their workers to perform better.

Employers may feel the need for such incentives for several reasons. For example, employers often have difficulty observing directly how hard an employee works. They can, however, elicit more work effort by paying above-market wages: employees receiving these higher wages are more likely to work harder to ensure that they aren't fired, which would cause them to lose their higher wages.

When many firms pay efficiency wages, the result is a pool of workers who want jobs but can't find them. So the use of efficiency wages by firms leads to structural unemployment.

**Side Effects of Government Policies** In addition, government policies designed to help workers who lose their jobs can lead to structural unemployment as an unintended side effect. Most economically advanced countries provide benefits to laid-off workers as a way to tide them over until they find a new job. In the United States, these benefits typically replace only a small fraction of a worker's income and expire after 26 weeks. (This was extended in some cases to 99 weeks during the period of high unemployment in 2009–2011). In other countries, particularly in Europe, benefits are more generous and last longer. The drawback to this generosity is that it reduces a worker's incentive to quickly find a new job. Generous unemployment benefits in some European countries are often argued to be one of the causes of "Eurosclerosis," the persistent high unemployment that afflicts a number of European economies.

**Mismatches between Employees and Employers** It takes time for workers and firms to adjust to shifts in the economy. The result can be a mismatch between what employees have to offer and what employers are looking for. A skills mismatch is one form; for example, in the aftermath of the housing bust of 2009, there were more construction workers looking for jobs than were available. Another form is geographic as in Michigan, which has had a long-standing surplus of workers after its auto industry declined. Until the mismatch is resolved through a big enough fall in wages of the surplus workers that induces re-training or relocation, there will be structural unemployment.

## The Natural Rate of Unemployment

Because some frictional unemployment is inevitable and because many economies also suffer from structural unemployment, a certain amount of unemployment is normal, or "natural." Actual unemployment fluctuates around this normal level. The **natural rate of unemployment** is the normal unemployment rate around which the actual unemployment rate fluctuates. It is the rate of unemployment that arises from the effects of frictional plus structural unemployment. **Cyclical unemployment** is the deviation of the actual rate of unemployment from the natural rate; that is, it is the difference between the actual and natural rates of unemployment. As the name suggests, cyclical unemployment is the share of unemployment that arises from the downturns of the business cycle.

We'll see in Chapter 16 that an economy's natural rate of unemployment is a critical policy variable because government cannot keep the unemployment rate persistently below the natural rate without leading to accelerating inflation.

We can summarize the relationships between the various types of unemployment as follows:

> The **natural rate of unemployment** is the unemployment rate that arises from the effects of frictional plus structural unemployment.
>
> **Cyclical unemployment** is the deviation of the actual rate of unemployment from the natural rate due to downturns in the business cycle.

## NATURAL UNEMPLOYMENT AROUND THE OECD

The Organization for Economic Cooperation and Development (OECD) is an association of relatively wealthy countries, in Europe and North America but also including Japan, Korea, New Zealand, and Australia. Among other activities, the OECD collects data on unemployment rates for member nations. The figure shows average unemployment, which is a rough estimate of the natural rate of unemployment, for select OECD members, from 2000–2010. The purple bar in the middle shows the average across all the OECD countries.

The U.S. natural rate of unemployment appears to be somewhat below average; those of many European countries (including the major economies of Germany, Italy, and France) are above average. Many economists think that persistently high European unemployment rates are the result of government policies, such as high minimum wages and generous unemployment benefits, which discourage employers from offering jobs and discourage workers from accepting jobs, leading to high rates of structural unemployment.

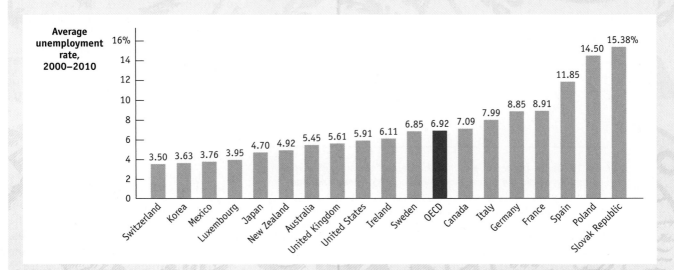

Average unemployment rate, 2000–2010

| Country | Rate |
|---|---|
| Switzerland | 3.50 |
| Korea | 3.63 |
| Mexico | 3.76 |
| Luxembourg | 3.95 |
| Japan | 4.70 |
| New Zealand | 4.92 |
| Australia | 5.45 |
| United Kingdom | 5.61 |
| United States | 5.91 |
| Ireland | 6.11 |
| Sweden | 6.85 |
| OECD | 6.92 |
| Canada | 7.09 |
| Italy | 7.99 |
| Germany | 8.85 |
| France | 8.91 |
| Spain | 11.85 |
| Poland | 14.50 |
| Slovak Republic | 15.38% |

*Source:* OECD.

**(8-3)** Natural unemployment =
Frictional unemployment + Structural unemployment

**(8-4)** Actual unemployment =
Natural unemployment + Cyclical unemployment

Perhaps because of its name, people often imagine that the natural rate of unemployment is a constant that doesn't change over time and can't be affected by government policy. Neither proposition is true. Let's take a moment to stress two facts: the natural rate of unemployment changes over time, and it can be affected by government policies.

## Changes in the Natural Rate of Unemployment

Private-sector economists and government agencies need estimates of the natural rate of unemployment both to make forecasts and to conduct policy analyses. Almost all these estimates show that the U.S. natural rate rises and falls over time. For example, the Congressional Budget Office, the independent agency that conducts budget and economic analyses for Congress, believes that the U.S. natural rate of unemployment was 5.3% in 1950, rose to 6.3% by the end of the 1970s, but has fallen to 5.2% today. European countries have experienced even larger swings in their natural rates of unemployment.

What causes the natural rate of unemployment to change? The most important factors are changes in labor force characteristics, changes in labor market institutions, and changes in government policies. Let's look briefly at each factor.

**Changes in Labor Force Characteristics**  In 2007 the overall rate of unemployment in the United States was 4.6%. Young workers, however, had much higher unemployment rates: 15.7% for teenagers and 8.2% for workers aged 20 to 24. Workers aged 25 to 54 had an unemployment rate of only 3.7%.

In general, unemployment rates tend to be lower for experienced than for inexperienced workers. Because experienced workers tend to stay in a given job longer than do inexperienced ones, they have lower frictional unemployment. Also, because older workers are more likely than young workers to be family breadwinners, they have a stronger incentive to find and keep jobs.

One reason the natural rate of unemployment rose during the 1970s was a large rise in the number of new workers—children of the post–World War II baby boom entered the labor force, as did a rising percentage of married women. As Figure 8-10 shows, both the percentage of the labor force less than 25 years old and the percentage of women in the labor force grew rapidly in the 1970s. By the end of the 1990s, however, the share of women in the labor force had leveled off and the percentage of workers under 25 had fallen sharply.

**FIGURE  8-10**

### The Changing Makeup of the U.S. Labor Force, 1948–2011

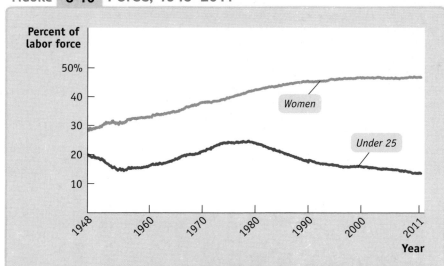

In the 1970s the percentage of the labor force consisting of women rose rapidly, as did the percentage under age 25. These changes reflected the entry of large numbers of women into the paid labor force for the first time and the fact that baby boomers were reaching working age. The natural rate of unemployment may have risen because many of these workers were relatively inexperienced. Today, the labor force is much more experienced, which is one possible reason the natural rate has fallen since the 1970s.

*Source:* Bureau of Labor Statistics.

As a result, the labor force as a whole is more experienced today than it was in the 1970s, one likely reason that the natural rate of unemployment is lower today than in the 1970s.

**Changes in Labor Market Institutions**  As we pointed out earlier, unions that negotiate wages above the equilibrium level can be a source of structural unemployment. Some economists believe that strong labor unions are one reason for the high natural rate of unemployment in Europe, discussed in the Global Comparison. In the United States, a sharp fall in union membership after 1980 may have been one reason the natural rate of unemployment fell between the 1970s and the 1990s.

Other institutional changes may also be at work. For example, some labor economists believe that temporary employment agencies, which have proliferated in recent years, have reduced frictional unemployment by helping match workers to jobs. Furthermore, as discussed in the Business Case at the end of the chapter, Internet websites such as Monster.com may have reduced frictional unemployment.

Technological change, coupled with labor market institutions, can also affect the natural rate of unemployment. Technological change tends to increase the demand for skilled workers who are familiar with the relevant technology and a reduction in the demand for unskilled workers. Economic theory predicts that wages should increase for skilled workers and decrease for unskilled workers. But if wages for unskilled workers cannot go down—say, due to a binding minimum wage—increased structural unemployment, and therefore a higher natural rate of unemployment, will result.

**Changes in Government Policies**  A high minimum wage can cause structural unemployment. Generous unemployment benefits can increase both structural and frictional unemployment. So government policies intended to help workers can have the undesirable side effect of raising the natural rate of unemployment.

Some government policies, however, may reduce the natural rate. Two examples are job training and employment subsidies. Job-training programs are supposed to provide unemployed workers with skills that widen the range of jobs they can perform. Employment subsidies are payments either to workers or to employers that provide a financial incentive to accept or offer jobs.

## ECONOMICS ▶ IN ACTION

### STRUCTURAL UNEMPLOYMENT IN EAST GERMANY

In one of the most dramatic events in world history, a spontaneous popular uprising in 1989 overthrew the communist dictatorship in East Germany. Citizens quickly tore down the wall that had divided Berlin, and in short order East and West Germany united into one democratic nation.

Then the trouble started.

After reunification, employment in East Germany plunged and the unemployment rate soared. This high unemployment rate has persisted: despite receiving massive aid from the federal German government, the economy of the former East Germany has remained persistently depressed, with an unemployment rate of more than 16% in 2008. Other parts of formerly communist Eastern Europe have done much better. For example, the Czech Republic, which was often cited along with East Germany as a relatively successful communist economy, had an unemployment rate of only 5.5% in July 2007. What went wrong in East Germany?

The answer is that, through nobody's fault, East Germany found itself suffering from severe structural unemployment. When Germany was reunified, it

After reunification in 1989, East Germany found itself suffering from severe structural unemployment that continues to this day.

Robert Wallis/Corbis

became clear that workers in East Germany were much less productive than their cousins in the west. Yet unions initially demanded and received wage rates equal to those in West Germany. These wage rates have been slow to come down because East German workers objected to being treated as inferior to their West German counterparts. Meanwhile, productivity in the former East Germany has remained well below West German levels, in part because of decades of misguided investment under the former dictatorship. The result has been a persistently large mismatch between the number of workers demanded and the number of those seeking jobs, and persistently high structural unemployment in the former East Germany.

### CHECK YOUR UNDERSTANDING  8-2

1. Explain the following.
   a. Frictional unemployment is higher when the pace of technological advance quickens.
   b. Structural unemployment is higher when the pace of technological advance quickens.
   c. Frictional unemployment accounts for a larger share of total unemployment when the unemployment rate is low.

2. Why does collective bargaining have the same general effect on unemployment as a minimum wage? Illustrate your answer with a diagram.

3. Suppose that at the peak of the business cycle the United States dramatically increases benefits for unemployed workers. Explain what will happen to the natural rate of unemployment.

*Solutions appear at back of book.*

## Inflation and Deflation

As we mentioned in the opening story, in early 2011 British officials were worried about two things: the unemployment rate was high and so was inflation. And there was a fierce debate about which concern should take priority.

Why is inflation something to worry about? Why do policy makers even now get anxious when they see the inflation rate moving upward? The answer is that inflation can impose costs on the economy—but not in the way most people think.

### The Level of Prices Doesn't Matter . . .

The most common complaint about inflation, an increase in the price level, is that it makes everyone poorer—after all, a given amount of money buys less. But inflation does not make everyone poorer. To see why, it's helpful to imagine what would happen if the United States did something other countries have done from time to time—replacing the dollar with a new currency.

An example of this kind of currency conversion happened in 2002, when France, like a number of other European countries, replaced its national currency, the franc, with the new pan-European currency, the euro. People turned in their franc coins and notes, and received euro coins and notes in exchange, at a rate of precisely 6.55957 francs per euro. At the same time, all contracts were restated in euros at the same rate of exchange. For example, if a French citizen had a home mortgage debt of 500,000 francs, this became a debt of 500,000/6.55957 = 76,224.51 euros. If a worker's contract specified that he or she should be paid 100 francs per hour, it became a contract specifying a wage of 100/6.55957 = 5.2449 euros per hour, and so on.

You could imagine doing the same thing here, replacing the dollar with a "new dollar" at a rate of exchange of, say, 7 to 1. If you owed $140,000 on your home, that would become a debt of 20,000 new dollars. If you had a wage rate of $14 an hour, it would become 2 new dollars an hour, and so on. This would bring the overall U.S. price level back to about what it was in 1962, when John F. Kennedy was president.

So would everyone be richer as a result because prices would be only one-seventh as high? Of course not. Prices would be lower, but so would wages and incomes in general. If you cut a worker's wage to one-seventh of its previous value, but also cut all prices to one-seventh of their previous level, the worker's **real wage**—the wage rate divided by the price level—hasn't changed. In fact, bringing the overall price level back to what it was during the Kennedy administration would have no effect on overall purchasing power because doing so would reduce income exactly as much as it reduced prices.

Conversely, the rise in prices that has actually taken place since the early 1960s hasn't made America poorer because it has also raised incomes by the same amount: **real incomes**—incomes divided by the price level—haven't been affected by the rise in overall prices.

The moral of this story is that the *level* of prices doesn't matter: the United States would be no richer than it is now if the overall level of prices was still as low as it was in 1961; conversely, the rise in prices over the past 50 years hasn't made us poorer.

> The **real wage** is the wage rate divided by the price level.
>
> **Real income** is income divided by the price level.

## . . . But the Rate of Change of Prices Does

The conclusion that the level of prices doesn't matter might seem to imply that the inflation rate doesn't matter either. But that's not true.

To see why, it's crucial to distinguish between the *level of prices* and the *inflation rate:* the percent increase in the overall level of prices per year. Recall from Chapter 7 that the inflation rate is defined as follows:

$$\text{Inflation rate} = \frac{\text{Price index in year 2} - \text{Price index in year 1}}{\text{Price index in year 1}} \times 100$$

Figure 8-11 highlights the difference between the price level and the inflation rate in the United States over the last half-century, with the price level measured along the left vertical axis and the inflation rate measured along

---

**FIGURE  8-11**  **The Price Level versus the Inflation Rate, 1960–2011**

With the exception of 2009, over the past half-century the consumer price index has continuously increased. But the *inflation rate*—the rate at which consumer prices are rising—has had both ups and downs. And in 2009, the inflation rate briefly turned negative, a phenomenon called *deflation.*

*Source:* Bureau of Labor Statistics.

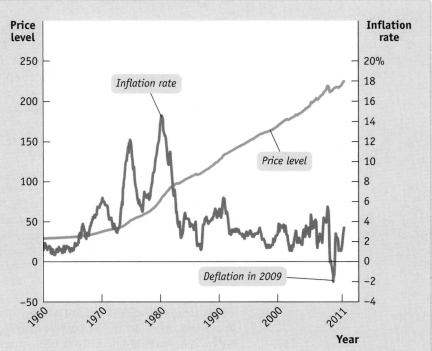

**Shoe-leather costs** are the increased costs of transactions caused by inflation.

The **menu cost** is the real cost of changing a listed price.

the right vertical axis. In the 2000s, the overall level of prices in America was much higher than it had been in 1960—but that, as we've learned, didn't matter. The inflation rate in the 2000s, however, was much lower than in the 1970s—and that almost certainly made the economy richer than it would have been if high inflation had continued.

Economists believe that high rates of inflation impose significant economic costs. The most important of these costs are *shoe-leather costs, menu costs,* and *unit-of-account costs.* We'll discuss each in turn.

**Shoe-Leather Costs** People hold money—cash in their wallets and bank deposits on which they can write checks—for convenience in making transactions. A high inflation rate, however, discourages people from holding money because the purchasing power of the cash in your wallet and the funds in your bank account steadily erodes as the overall level of prices rises. This leads people to search for ways to reduce the amount of money they hold, often at considerable economic cost.

The Economics in Action at the end of this section describes how Israelis spent a lot of time at the bank during the periods of high inflation rates that afflicted Israel in 1984–1985. During the most famous of all inflations, the German *hyperinflation* of 1921–1923, merchants employed runners to take their cash to the bank many times a day to convert it into something that would hold its value, such as a stable foreign currency. In each case, in an effort to avoid having the purchasing power of their money eroded, people used up valuable resources, such as time for Israeli citizens and the labor of those German runners that could have been used productively elsewhere. During the German hyperinflation, so many banking transactions were taking place that the number of employees at German banks nearly quadrupled—from around 100,000 in 1913 to 375,000 in 1923.

More recently, Brazil experienced hyperinflation during the early 1990s; during that episode, the Brazilian banking sector grew so large that it accounted for 15% of GDP, more than twice the size of the financial sector in the United States measured as a share of GDP. The large increase in the Brazilian banking sector needed to cope with the consequences of inflation represented a loss of real resources to its society.

Increased costs of transactions caused by inflation are known as **shoe-leather costs,** an allusion to the wear and tear caused by the extra running around that takes place when people are trying to avoid holding money. Shoe-leather costs are substantial in economies with very high inflation, as anyone who has lived in such an economy—say, one suffering inflation of 100% or more per year—can attest. Most estimates suggest, however, that the shoe-leather costs of inflation at the rates seen in the United States—which in peacetime has never had inflation above 15%—are quite small.

**Menu Costs** In a modern economy, most of the things we buy have a listed price. There's a price listed under each item on a supermarket shelf, a price printed on the back of a book, a price listed for each dish on a restaurant's menu. Changing a listed price has a real cost, called a **menu cost.** For example, to change prices in a supermarket requires sending clerks through the store to change the listed price under each item. In the face of inflation, of course, firms are forced to change prices more often than they would if the aggregate price level was more or less stable. This means higher costs for the economy as a whole.

In times of very high inflation, menu costs can be substantial. During the Brazilian inflation of the early 1990s, for instance, supermarket workers reportedly spent half of their time replacing old price stickers with new ones. When inflation is high, merchants may decide to stop listing prices in terms of the local currency and use either an artificial unit—in effect, measuring prices relative to one another—or a more stable currency, such as the U.S. dollar. This is exactly what the Israeli real estate market began doing in the mid-1980s: prices were quoted in U.S. dollars, even though payment was made in Israeli shekels. And this is also what happened in Zimbabwe when, in May 2008, official estimates of the inflation rate reached 1,694,000%. By 2009, the government had suspended the Zimbabwean dollar, allowing Zimbabweans to buy and sell goods using foreign currencies.

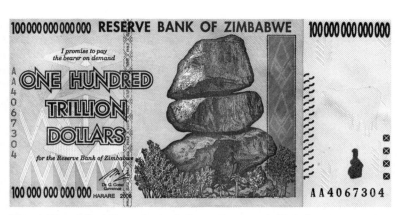

When trillion-dollar bills are in circulation as they were in Zimbabwe, menu costs are substantial.

Menu costs are also present in low-inflation economies, but they are not severe. In low-inflation economies, businesses might update their prices only sporadically—not daily or even more frequently, as is the case in high-inflation or hyperinflation economies. Also, with technological advances, menu costs are becoming less and less important, since prices can be changed electronically and fewer merchants attach price stickers to merchandise.

**Unit-of-Account Costs**  In the Middle Ages, contracts were often specified "in kind": a tenant might, for example, be obliged to provide his landlord with a certain number of cattle each year (the phrase *in kind* actually comes from an ancient word for *cattle)*. This may have made sense at the time, but it would be an awkward way to conduct modern business. Instead, we state contracts in monetary terms: a renter owes a certain number of dollars per month, a company that issues a bond promises to pay the bondholder the dollar value of the bond when it comes due, and so on. We also tend to make our economic calculations in dollars: a family planning its budget, or a small business owner trying to figure out how well the business is doing, makes estimates of the amount of money coming in and going out.

This role of the dollar as a basis for contracts and calculation is called the *unit-of-account* role of money. It's an important aspect of the modern economy. Yet it's a role that can be degraded by inflation, which causes the purchasing power of a dollar to change over time—a dollar next year is worth less than a dollar this year. The effect, many economists argue, is to reduce the quality of economic decisions: the economy as a whole makes less efficient use of its resources because of the uncertainty caused by changes in the unit of account, the dollar. The **unit-of-account costs** of inflation are the costs arising from the way inflation makes money a less reliable unit of measurement.

Unit-of-account costs may be particularly important in the tax system because inflation can distort the measures of income on which taxes are collected. Here's an example: Assume that the inflation rate is 10%, so the overall level of prices rises 10% each year. Suppose that a business buys an asset, such as a piece of land, for $100,000, then resells it a year later for $110,000. In a fundamental sense, the business didn't make a profit on the deal: in real terms, it got no more for the land than it paid for it. But U.S. tax law would say that the business made a capital gain of $10,000, and it would have to pay taxes on that phantom gain.

During the 1970s, when the United States had relatively high inflation, the distorting effects of inflation on the tax system were a serious problem. Some businesses were discouraged from productive investment spending because they

**Unit-of-account costs** arise from the way inflation makes money a less reliable unit of measurement.

The **interest rate** on a loan is the price, calculated as a percentage of the amount borrowed, that a lender charges a borrower for the use of their savings for one year.

The **nominal interest rate** is the interest rate expressed in dollar terms.

The **real interest rate** is the nominal interest rate minus the rate of inflation.

found themselves paying taxes on phantom gains. Meanwhile, some unproductive investments became attractive because they led to phantom losses that reduced tax bills. When inflation fell in the 1980s—and tax rates were reduced—these problems became much less important.

## Winners and Losers from Inflation

As we've just learned, a high inflation rate imposes overall costs on the economy. In addition, inflation can produce winners and losers within the economy. The main reason inflation sometimes helps some people while hurting others is that economic transactions often involve contracts that extend over a period of time, such as loans, and these contracts are normally specified in nominal—that is, in dollar—terms.

In the case of a loan, the borrower receives a certain amount of funds at the beginning, and the loan contract specifies the *interest rate* on the loan and when it must be paid off. The **interest rate** is the return a lender receives for allowing borrowers the use of their savings for one year, calculated as a percentage of the amount borrowed.

But what that dollar is worth in real terms—that is, in terms of purchasing power—depends greatly on the rate of inflation over the intervening years of the loan. Economists summarize the effect of inflation on borrowers and lenders by distinguishing between the *nominal* interest rate and the *real* interest rate. The **nominal interest rate** is the interest rate in dollar terms—for example, the interest rate on a student loan. The **real interest rate** is the nominal interest rate minus the rate of inflation. For example, if a loan carries an interest rate of 8%, but there is 5% inflation, the real interest rate is 8% – 5% = 3%.

When a borrower and a lender enter into a loan contract, the contract is normally written in dollar terms—that is, the interest rate it specifies is a nominal interest rate. (And in later chapters, when we say the interest rate we will mean the nominal interest rate unless noted otherwise.) But each party to a loan contract has an expectation about the future rate of inflation and therefore an expectation about the real interest rate on the loan. If the actual inflation rate is *higher* than expected, borrowers gain at the expense of lenders: borrowers will repay their loans with funds that have a lower real value than had been expected. Conversely, if the inflation rate is *lower* than expected, lenders will gain at the expense of borrowers: borrowers must repay their loans with funds that have a higher real value than had been expected.

Historically, the fact that inflation creates winners and losers has sometimes been a major source of political controversy. In 1896 William Jennings Bryan electrified the Democratic presidential convention with a speech in which he declared, "You shall not crucify mankind on a cross of gold." What he was actually demanding was an inflationary policy. At the time, the U.S. dollar had a fixed value in terms of gold. Bryan wanted to abandon that gold standard and have the U.S. government print more money, which would have raised the level of prices. The reason he wanted inflation was to help farmers, many of whom were deeply in debt.

In modern America, home mortgages are the most important source of gains and losses from inflation. Americans who took out mortgages in the early 1970s quickly found their real payments reduced by higher-than-expected inflation: by 1983, the purchasing power of a dollar was only 45% of what it had been in 1973. Those who took out mortgages in the early 1990s were not so lucky, because the inflation rate fell to lower-than-expected levels in the following years: in 2003 the purchasing power of a dollar was 78% of what it had been in 1993.

Because gains for some and losses for others result from inflation that is either higher or lower than expected, yet another problem arises: uncertainty about the future inflation rate discourages people from entering into any form of long-term contract. This is an additional cost of high inflation, because high rates of inflation are usually unpredictable. In countries with high and uncertain inflation, long-term loans are rare, which makes it difficult in many cases to make long-term investments.

One last point: unexpected *deflation*—a surprise fall in the price level—creates winners and losers, too. Between 1929 and 1933, as the U.S. economy plunged into the Great Depression, the consumer price index fell by 35%. This meant that debtors, including many farmers and homeowners, saw a sharp rise in the real value of their debts, which led to widespread bankruptcy and helped create a banking crisis, as lenders found their customers unable to pay back their loans. And as you can see in Figure 8-11, deflation occurred again in 2009, when the inflation rate fell to –2% at the trough of a deep recession. Like the Great Depression (but to a much lesser extent), the unexpected deflation of 2009 imposed heavy costs on debtors. We will discuss the effects of deflation in more detail in Chapter 16.

> **Disinflation** is the process of bringing the inflation rate down.

## Inflation Is Easy; Disinflation Is Hard

There is not much evidence that a rise in the inflation rate from, say, 2% to 5% would do a great deal of harm to the economy. Still, policy makers generally move forcefully to bring inflation back down when it creeps above 2% or 3%. Why? Because experience shows that bringing the inflation rate down—a process called **disinflation**—is very difficult and costly once a higher rate of inflation has become well established in the economy.

Figure 8-12 shows what happened during two major episodes of disinflation in the United States, in the mid-1970s and in the early 1980s. The horizontal axis shows the unemployment rate. The vertical axis shows "core" inflation over the previous year, a measure that excludes volatile food and energy prices and is widely considered a better measure of underlying inflation than overall consumer prices. Each marker represents the inflation rate and the unemployment rate for one month. In each episode, unemployment and inflation followed a sort of clockwise spiral, with high inflation gradually falling in the face of an extended period of very high unemployment.

According to many economists, these periods of high unemployment that temporarily depressed the economy were necessary to reduce inflation that had become deeply embedded in the economy. The best way to avoid having to put the economy through a wringer to reduce inflation, however, is to avoid having a serious inflation problem in the first place. So policy makers respond forcefully to signs that inflation may be accelerating as a form of preventive medicine for the economy.

**FIGURE   8-12**   The Cost of Disinflation

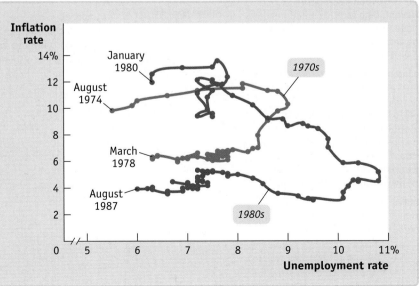

There were two major periods of disinflation in modern U.S. history, in the mid-1970s and the early 1980s. This figure shows the track of the unemployment rate and the "core" inflation rate, which excludes food and energy, during these two episodes. In each case bringing inflation down required a temporary but very large increase in the unemployment rate, demonstrating the high cost of disinflation.

*Source:* Bureau of Labor Statistics.

## ECONOMICS ▷ *IN ACTION*

### ISRAEL'S EXPERIENCE WITH INFLATION

It's often hard to see the costs of inflation clearly because serious inflation problems are often associated with other problems that disrupt economic life, notably war or political instability (or both). In the mid-1980s, however, Israel experienced a "clean" inflation: there was no war, the government was stable, and there was order in the streets. Yet a series of policy errors led to very high inflation, with prices often rising more than 10% a month.

As it happens, one of the authors spent a month visiting at Tel Aviv University at the height of the inflation, so we can give a first-hand account of the effects.

First, the shoe-leather costs of inflation were substantial. At the time, Israelis spent a lot of time in lines at the bank, moving money in and out of accounts that provided high enough interest rates to offset inflation. People walked around with very little cash in their wallets; they had to go to the bank whenever they needed to make even a moderately large cash payment. Banks responded by opening a lot of branches, a costly business expense.

Second, although menu costs weren't that visible to a visitor, what you could see were the efforts businesses made to minimize them. For example, restaurant menus often didn't list prices. Instead, they listed numbers that you had to multiply by another number, written on a chalkboard and changed every day, to figure out the price of a dish.

Finally, it was hard to make decisions because prices changed so much and so often. It was a common experience to walk out of a store because prices were 25% higher than at one's usual shopping destination, only to discover that prices had just been increased 25% there, too.

The shoe-leather costs of inflation in Israel: when the inflation rate hit 500% in 1985, people spent a lot of time in line at banks.

### ▼ Quick Review

- The **real wage** and **real income** are unaffected by the level of prices.

- Inflation, like unemployment, is a major concern of policy makers—so much so that in the past they have accepted high unemployment as the price of reducing inflation.

- While the overall level of prices is irrelevant, high rates of inflation impose real costs on the economy: **shoe-leather costs, menu costs,** and **unit-of-account costs.**

- The **interest rate** is the return a lender receives for use of his or her funds for a year. The **real interest rate** is equal to the **nominal interest rate** minus the inflation rate. As a result, unexpectedly high inflation helps borrowers and hurts lenders. With high and uncertain inflation, people will often avoid long-term investments.

- **Disinflation** is very costly, so policy makers try to avoid getting into situations of high inflation in the first place.

### CHECK YOUR UNDERSTANDING   8-3

1. The widespread use of technology has revolutionized the banking industry, making it much easier for customers to access and manage their assets. Does this mean that the shoe-leather costs of inflation are higher or lower than they used to be?

2. Most people in the United States have grown accustomed to a modest inflation rate of around 2% to 3%. Who would gain and who would lose if inflation unexpectedly came to a complete stop over the next 15 or 20 years?

Solutions appear at back of book.

# BUSINESS CASE : A Monster Slump

Courtesy of Monster Worldwide, Inc.

The 1990s were famously an era of business hype, a decade when numerous Internet-based companies were created, then sold their stock at incredibly high prices, and, in the end, went bust. Some of the dot-coms, however, turned out to have workable business models and have endured. Among them is Monster.com, a job-search company that, along with its competitors, has helped replace traditional help-wanted ads in newspapers with online listings.

Monster Worldwide (the company's current name) and its competitors sell services to both employers seeking workers and workers seeking jobs. The employers place job listings, to which workers can respond; in addition to responding to these listings, job-seekers can pay for premium services such as résumé-writing and priority listing of their résumés.

The growing importance of online job listings was brought home in 2007 when The Conference Board, a business group that has long tracked the economy by producing an index of help-wanted ads, added an index of online help-wanted ads. As Figure 8-13 shows, a plunge in online help-wanted ads heralded the surge in unemployment in 2008–2009; when online ads began to recover, unemployment stabilized and began a slow decline.

In the late 1990s, when the U.S. economy was experiencing unusually low unemployment, some economists suggested that Monster Worldwide and other Internet job services might be partly responsible, by making it easier for workers to get new jobs without a prolonged intervening period of unemployment. The evidence for this effect is, however, inconclusive.

You might have thought that the 2007–2009 recession, in which many laid-off workers were desperately seeking new jobs, would have been good for Monster. And the company did, in fact, receive a lot more business from workers wanting to post their résumés. But the company makes much more money from employer job listings, and these were sharply lower during the slump, hurting Monster's bottom line.

By late 2010, the economy seemed to be on the road to recovery, and so was Monster, with one caveat: by 2010, online job listings, which were cutting-edge a decade earlier, were losing ground to Twitter and social networks.

**FIGURE 8-13** A Plunge in Online Help-Wanted Ads Heralds a Surge in Unemployment, 2008–2009

Number of unemployed (millions) / Number of online ads (millions)

Unemployed

Online ads

2007  2008  2009  2010  2011
**Year**

*Sources:* The Conference Board; Bureau of Labor Statistics.

## QUESTIONS FOR THOUGHT

1. Use the flows shown in Figure 8-7 to explain the potential role of online job listings in the economy.

2. In light of our discussion of the determinants of the unemployment rate, how could improved matching of job-seekers and employers through online job listings help?

3. What does the fact that Monster did badly during the 2008–2009 surge in unemployment suggest about the nature of that surge?

1. Inflation and unemployment are the twin evils of macroeconomics and the main concerns of macroeconomic policy.

2. **Employment** is the number of people employed; **unemployment** is the number of people unemployed and actively looking for work. Their sum is equal to the **labor force,** and the **labor force participation rate** is the percentage of the population age 16 or older that is in the labor force.

3. The **unemployment rate,** the percentage of the labor force that is unemployed and actively looking for work, can both overstate and understate the true level of unemployment. It can overstate because it counts as unemployed those who are continuing to search for a job despite having been offered one. It can understate because it ignores frustrated workers, such as **discouraged workers, marginally attached workers,** and the **underemployed.** In addition, the unemployment rate varies greatly among different groups in the population; it is typically higher for younger workers and for workers near retirement age than for workers in their prime working years.

4. The unemployment rate is affected by the business cycle. The unemployment rate generally falls when the growth rate of real GDP is above average and generally increases when the growth rate of real GDP is below average. A **jobless recovery,** a period in which real GDP is growing but unemployment rises, often follows recessions.

5. Job creation and destruction, as well as voluntary job separations, lead to **job search** and **frictional unemployment.** In addition, a variety of factors such as minimum wages, unions, **efficiency wages,** government policies designed to help laid-off workers, and mismatch between employees and employers result in a situation in which there is a surplus of labor at the market wage rate, creating **structural unemployment.** As a result, the **natural rate of unemployment,** the sum of frictional and structural employment, is well above zero, even when jobs are plentiful.

6. The actual unemployment rate is equal to the natural rate of unemployment, the share of unemployment that is independent of the business cycle, plus **cyclical unemployment,** the share of unemployment that depends on fluctuations in the business cycle.

7. The natural rate of unemployment changes over time, largely in response to changes in labor force characteristics, labor market institutions, and government policies.

8. Inflation does not, as many assume, make everyone poorer by raising the level of prices. That's because wages and incomes are adjusted to take into account a rising price level, leaving **real wages** and **real income** unaffected. However, a high inflation rate imposes overall costs on the economy: **shoe-leather costs, menu costs,** and **unit-of-account costs.**

9. Inflation can produce winners and losers within the economy, because long-term contracts are generally written in dollar terms. The **interest rate** specified in a loan is typically a **nominal interest rate,** which differs from the **real interest rate** due to inflation. A higher-than-expected inflation rate is good for borrowers and bad for lenders. A lower-than-expected inflation rate is good for lenders and bad for borrowers.

10. Many believe policies that depress the economy and produce high unemployment are necessary to reduce embedded inflation. Because **disinflation** is very costly, policy makers try to prevent inflation from becoming excessive in the first place.

Employment, p. 214
Unemployment, p. 214
Labor force, p. 215
Labor force participation rate, p. 215
Unemployment rate, p. 215
Discouraged workers, p. 216
Marginally attached workers, p. 216
Underemployment, p. 216

Jobless recovery, p. 219
Job search, p. 221
Frictional unemployment, p. 221
Structural unemployment, p. 222
Efficiency wages, p. 224
Natural rate of unemployment, p. 225
Cyclical unemployment, p. 225
Real wage, p. 229

Real income, p. 229
Shoe-leather costs, p. 230
Menu costs, p. 230
Unit-of-account costs, p. 231
Interest rate, p. 232
Nominal interest rate, p. 232
Real interest rate, p. 232
Disinflation, p. 233

## PROBLEMS

1. Each month, usually on the first Friday of the month, the Bureau of Labor Statistics releases the Employment Situation Summary for the previous month. Go to www.bls.gov and find the latest report. (On the Bureau of Labor Statistics home page, at the top of the page, select the "Subject Areas" tab, find "Unemployment," and select "National Unemployment Rate." You will find the Employment Situation Summary under "News Releases" on the left side of the page.) How does the unemployment rate compare to the rate one month earlier? How does the unemployment rate compare to the rate one year earlier?

2. In general, how do changes in the unemployment rate vary with changes in real GDP? After several quarters of a severe recession, explain why we might observe a decrease in the official unemployment rate. Explain why we could see an increase in the official unemployment rate after several quarters of a strong expansion.

3. In each of the following situations, what type of unemployment is Melanie facing?

   a. After completing a complex programming project, Melanie is laid off. Her prospects for a new job requiring similar skills are good, and she has signed up with a programmer placement service. She has passed up offers for low-paying jobs.

   b. When Melanie and her co-workers refused to accept pay cuts, her employer outsourced their programming tasks to workers in another country. This phenomenon is occurring throughout the programming industry.

   c. Due to the current slump, Melanie has been laid off from her programming job. Her employer promises to rehire her when business picks up.

4. Part of the information released in the Employment Situation Summary concerns how long individuals have been unemployed. Go to www.bls.gov to find the latest report. Use the same technique as in Problem 1 to find the Employment Situation Summary. Near the end of the Employment Situation, click on Table A-12, titled "Unemployed persons by duration of unemployment." Use the seasonally adjusted numbers to answer the following questions.

   a. How many workers were unemployed less than 5 weeks? What percentage of all unemployed workers do these workers represent? How do these numbers compare to the previous month's data?

   b. How many workers were unemployed for 27 or more weeks? What percentage of all unemployed workers do these workers represent? How do these numbers compare to the previous month's data?

   c. How long has the average worker been unemployed (average duration, in weeks)? How does this compare to the average for the previous month's data?

   d. Comparing the latest month for which there are data with the previous month, has the problem of long-term unemployment improved or deteriorated?

5. There is only one labor market in Profunctia. All workers have the same skills, and all firms hire workers with these skills. Use the accompanying diagram, which shows the supply of and demand for labor, to answer the following questions. Illustrate each answer with a diagram.

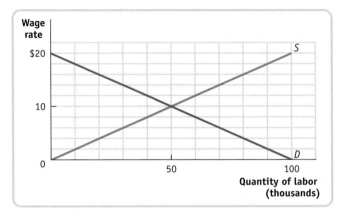

   a. What is the equilibrium wage rate in Profunctia? At this wage rate, what are the level of employment, the size of the labor force, and the unemployment rate?

   b. If the government of Profunctia sets a minimum wage equal to $12, what will be the level of employment, the size of the labor force, and the unemployment rate?

   c. If unions bargain with the firms in Profunctia and set a wage rate equal to $14, what will be the level of employment, the size of the labor force, and the unemployment rate?

   d. If the concern for retaining workers and encouraging high-quality work leads firms to set a wage rate equal to $16, what will be the level of employment, the size of the labor force, and the unemployment rate?

6. A country's labor force is the sum of the number of employed and unemployed workers. The accompanying table provides data on the size of the labor force and the number of unemployed workers for different regions of the United States.

| Region | Labor force (thousands) | | Unemployed (thousands) | |
|---|---|---|---|---|
| | May 2010 | May 2011 | May 2010 | May 2011 |
| Northeast | 28,303.7 | 28,201.9 | 2,482.7 | 2,254.1 |
| South | 55,223.5 | 55,544.1 | 5,126.3 | 4,896.6 |
| Midwest | 34,520.2 | 34,430.0 | 3,305.7 | 2,803.7 |
| West | 35,827.2 | 35,613.0 | 3,954.0 | 3,664.4 |

*Source:* Bureau of Labor Statistics.

**a.** Calculate the number of workers employed in each of the regions in May 2010 and May 2011. Use your answers to calculate the change in the total number of workers employed between May 2010 and May 2011.

**b.** For each region, calculate the growth in the labor force from May 2010 to May 2011.

**c.** Compute unemployment rates in the different regions of the country in May 2010 and May 2011.

**d.** What can you infer about the fall in unemployment rates over this period? Was it caused by a net gain in the number of jobs or by a large fall in the number of people seeking jobs?

7. In which of the following cases is it more likely for efficiency wages to exist? Why?

**a.** Jane and her boss work as a team selling ice cream.

**b.** Jane sells ice cream without any direct supervision by her boss.

**c.** Jane speaks Korean and sells ice cream in a neighborhood in which Korean is the primary language. It is difficult to find another worker who speaks Korean.

8. How will the following changes affect the natural rate of unemployment?

**a.** The government reduces the time during which an unemployed worker can receive unemployment benefits.

**b.** More teenagers focus on their studies and do not look for jobs until after college.

**c.** Greater access to the Internet leads both potential employers and potential employees to use the Internet to list and find jobs.

**d.** Union membership declines.

9. With its tradition of a job for life for most citizens, Japan once had a much lower unemployment rate than that of the United States; from 1960 to 1995, the unemployment rate in Japan exceeded 3% only once. However, since the crash of its stock market in 1989 and slow economic growth in the 1990s, the job-for-life system has broken down and unemployment rose to more than 5% in 2003.

**a.** Explain the likely effect of the breakdown of the job-for-life system in Japan on the Japanese natural rate of unemployment.

**b.** As the accompanying diagram shows, the rate of growth of real GDP picked up in Japan after 2001 and before the global economic crisis of 2007–2009. Explain the likely effect of this increase in real GDP growth on the unemployment rate. Was the likely cause of the change in the unemployment rate during this period a change in the natural rate of unemployment or a change in the cyclical unemployment rate?

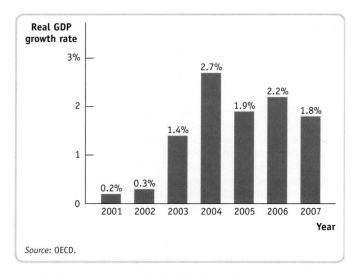

Source: OECD.

10. In the following examples, is inflation creating winners and losers at no net cost to the economy or is inflation imposing a net cost on the economy? If a net cost is being imposed, which type of cost is involved?

**a.** When inflation is expected to be high, workers get paid more frequently and make more trips to the bank.

**b.** Lanwei is reimbursed by her company for her work-related travel expenses. Sometimes, however, the company takes a long time to reimburse her. So when inflation is high, she is less willing to travel for her job.

**c.** Hector Homeowner has a mortgage with a fixed nominal 6% interest rate that he took out five years ago. Over the years, the inflation rate has crept up unexpectedly to its present level of 7%.

**d.** In response to unexpectedly high inflation, the manager of Cozy Cottages of Cape Cod must reprint and resend expensive color brochures correcting the price of rentals this season.

11. The accompanying diagram shows the interest rate on one-year loans and inflation during 1995–2010 in the economy of Albernia. When would one-year loans have been especially attractive and why?

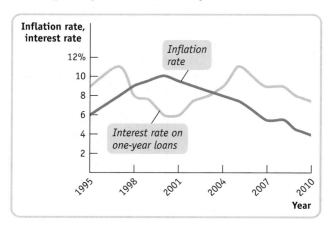

**12.** The accompanying table provides the inflation rate in the year 2000 and the average inflation rate over the period 2001–2010 for seven different countries.

| Country | Inflation rate in 2000 | Average inflation rate in 2001–2010 |
|---|---|---|
| Brazil | 7.06 | 6.70 |
| China | 0.4 | 2.16 |
| France | 1.83 | 1.86 |
| Indonesia | 3.77 | 8.55 |
| Japan | –0.78 | –0.25 |
| Turkey | 55.03 | 18.51 |
| United States | 3.37 | 2.40 |

*Source:* IMF.

**a.** Given the expected relationship between average inflation and menu costs, rank the countries in descending order of menu costs using average inflation over the period 2001–2010.

**b.** Rank the countries in order of inflation rates that most favored borrowers with ten-year loans that were taken out in 2000. Assume that the loans were agreed upon with the expectation that the inflation rate for 2001 to 2010 would be the same as the inflation rate in 2000.

**c.** Did borrowers who took out ten-year loans in Japan gain or lose overall versus lenders? Explain.

**13.** The accompanying diagram shows the inflation rate in the United Kingdom from 1980 to 2010.

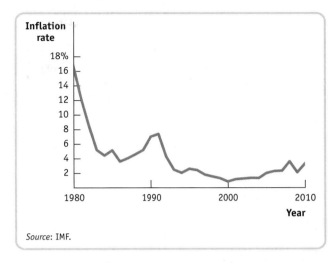

*Source:* IMF.

**a.** Between 1980 and 1985, policy makers in the United Kingdom worked to lower the inflation rate. What would you predict happened to unemployment between 1980 and 1985?

**b.** Policy makers in the United Kingdom react forcefully when the inflation rate rises above a target rate of 2%. Why would it be harmful if inflation rose from 3.4% (the level in 2010) to, say, a level of 5%?

# CHAPTER 9

# Long-Run Economic Growth

## TALL TALES

Yann Layma/Getty Images

As China illustrates, there is a positive relationship between a country's rate of long-run economic growth and its average population height.

> ❱ Why long-run economic growth is measured as the increase in real GDP per capita, how real GDP per capita has changed over time, and how it varies across countries

> ❱ Why **productivity** is the key to long-run economic growth and how productivity is driven by **physical capital, human capital,** and technological progress

> ❱ The factors that explain why long-run growth rates differ so much among countries

> ❱ How growth has varied among several important regions of the world and why the **convergence hypothesis** applies to economically advanced countries

> ❱ The question of **sustainability** and the challenges to growth posed by scarcity of natural resources and environmental degradation

**C**HINA IS GROWING—AND SO are the Chinese. According to official statistics, children in China are almost 2½ inches taller now than they were 30 years ago. The average Chinese citizen is still a lot shorter than the average American, but at the current rate of growth the difference may be largely gone in a couple of generations.

If that does happen, China will be following in Japan's footsteps. Older Americans tend to think of the Japanese as short, but today young Japanese men are more than 5 inches taller on average than they were in 1900, which makes them almost as tall as their American counterparts (and taller, on average, than either author of this book).

There's no mystery about why the Japanese grew taller—it's because they

grew richer. In the early twentieth century, Japan was a relatively poor country in which many families couldn't afford to give their children adequate nutrition. As a result, their children grew up to be short adults. However, since World War II, Japan has become an economic powerhouse in which food is ample and young adults are much taller than before.

The same phenomenon is now happening in China. Although it is still a relatively poor country, China has made great economic strides over the past 30 years. Its recent history is probably the world's most dramatic example of long-run economic growth—a sustained increase in output per capita. Yet despite its impressive performance, China is currently playing catch-up with economically advanced countries like

the United States and Japan. It's still a relatively poor country because these other nations began their own processes of long-run economic growth many decades ago—and in the case of the United States and European countries, more than a century ago.

Many economists have argued that long-run economic growth—why it happens and how to achieve it—is the single most important issue in macroeconomics. In this chapter, we present some facts about long-run growth, look at the factors that economists believe determine the pace at which long-run growth takes place, examine how government policies can help or hinder growth, and address questions about the environmental sustainability of long-run growth. ■

# Comparing Economies Across Time and Space

Before we analyze the sources of long-run economic growth, it's useful to have a sense of just how much the U.S. economy has grown over time and how large the gaps are between wealthy countries like the United States and countries that have yet to achieve comparable growth. So let's take a look at the numbers.

## Real GDP per Capita

The key statistic used to track economic growth is *real GDP per capita*—real GDP divided by the population size. We focus on GDP because, as we learned in Chapter 7, GDP measures the total value of an economy's production of final goods and services as well as the income earned in that economy in a given year. We use *real* GDP because we want to separate changes in the quantity of goods and services from the effects of a rising price level. We focus on real GDP *per capita* because we want to isolate the effect of changes in the population. For example, other things equal, an increase in the population lowers the standard of living for the average person—there are now more people to share a given amount of real GDP. An increase in real GDP that only matches an increase in population leaves the average standard of living unchanged.

Although we also learned in Chapter 7 that growth in real GDP per capita should not be a policy goal in and of itself, it does serve as a very useful summary measure of a country's economic progress over time. Figure 9-1 shows real GDP per capita for the United States, India, and China, measured in 1990 dollars, from 1900 to 2010. (We'll talk about India and China in a moment.) The vertical axis is drawn on a logarithmic scale so that equal percent changes in real GDP per capita across countries are the same size in the graph.

To give a sense of how much the U.S. economy grew during the last century, Table 9-1 shows real GDP per capita at selected years, expressed two ways: as a percentage of the 1900 level and as a percentage of the 2010 level. In 1920, the U.S.

**FIGURE** **9-1** **Economic Growth in the United States, India, and China over the Past Century**

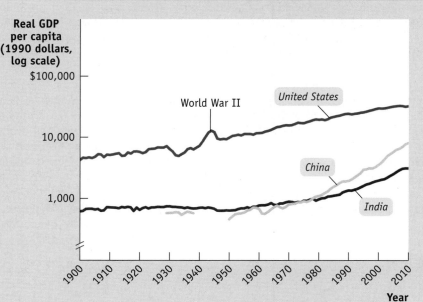

Real GDP per capita from 1900 to 2010, measured in 1990 dollars, is shown for the United States, India, and China. Equal percent changes in real GDP per capita are drawn the same size. As the steeper slopes of the lines representing China and India show, since 1980 India and China had a much higher growth rate than the United States. In 2000, China attained the standard of living achieved in the United States in 1900. In 2010, India was still poorer than the United States was in 1900. (Break in China data from 1940 to 1950 is due to war.)

*Sources:* Angus Maddison, *Statistics on World Population, GDP, and Per Capita GDP, 1–2008AD,* http://www.ggdc.net/maddison; International Monetary Fund.

economy already produced 136% as much per person as it did in 1900. In 2010, it produced 758% as much per person as it did in 1900, a more than sevenfold increase. Alternatively, in 1900 the U.S. economy produced only 13% as much per person as it did in 2010.

The income of the typical family normally grows more or less in proportion to per capita income. For example, a 1% increase in real GDP per capita corresponds, roughly, to a 1% increase in the income of the median or typical family—a family at the center of the income distribution. In 2010, the median American household had an income of about $50,000. Since Table 9-1 tells us that real GDP per capita in 1900 was only 13% of its 2010 level, a typical family in 1900 probably had a purchasing power only 13% as large as the purchasing power of a typical family in 2010. That's around $6,100 in today's dollars, representing a standard of living that we would now consider severe poverty. Today's typical American family, if transported back to the United States of 1900, would feel quite a lot of deprivation.

Yet many people in the world have a standard of living equal to or lower than that of the United States at the beginning of the last century. That's the message about China and India in Figure 9-1: despite dramatic economic growth in China over the last three decades and the less dramatic acceleration of economic growth in India, China has only recently exceeded the standard of living that the United States enjoyed in the early twentieth century, while India is still poorer than the United States was at that time. And much of the world today is poorer than China or India.

You can get a sense of how poor much of the world remains by looking at Figure 9-2, a map of the world in which countries are classified according to their 2010 levels of GDP per capita, in U.S. dollars. As you can see, large parts of the world have very low incomes. Generally speaking, the countries of Europe and North America, as well as a few in the Pacific, have high incomes. The rest of the world, containing most of its population, is dominated by countries with GDP

**TABLE 9-1 U.S. Real GDP per Capita**

| Year | Percentage of 1900 real GDP per capita | Percentage of 2010 real GDP per capita |
|------|------|------|
| 1900 | 100% | 13% |
| 1920 | 136 | 18 |
| 1940 | 171 | 23 |
| 1980 | 454 | 60 |
| 2000 | 696 | 92 |
| 2010 | 758 | 100 |

*Sources:* Angus Maddison, *Statistics on World Population, GDP, and Per Capita GDP, 1–2008AD,* http://www.ggdc.net/maddison; Bureau of Economic Analysis.

**FIGURE 9-2 Incomes Around the World, 2010**

Although the countries of Europe and North America—along with a few in the Pacific—have high incomes, much of the world is still very poor. Today, about 50% of the world's population lives in countries with a lower standard of living than the United States had a century ago.

*Source:* International Monetary Fund.

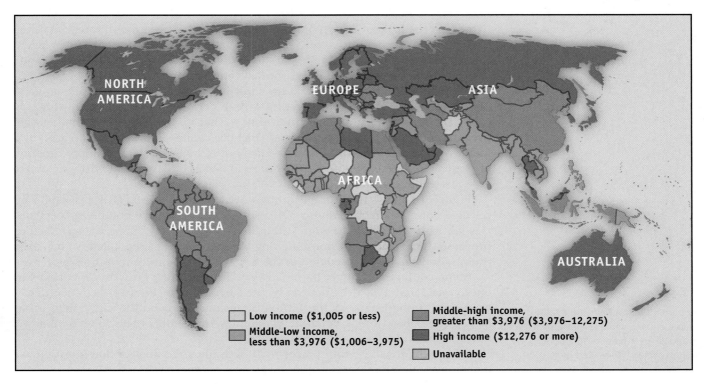

Low income ($1,005 or less)

Middle-low income, less than $3,976 ($1,006–3,975)

Middle-high income, greater than $3,976 ($3,976–12,275)

High income ($12,276 or more)

Unavailable

**PITFALLS**

**CHANGE IN LEVELS VERSUS RATE OF CHANGE**
When studying economic growth, it's vitally important to understand the difference between a change in level and a rate of change. When we say that real GDP "grew," we mean that the level of real GDP increased. For example, we might say that U.S. real GDP grew during 2010 by $385 billion.

If we knew the level of U.S. real GDP in 2009, we could also represent the amount of 2010 growth in terms of a rate of change. For example, if U.S. real GDP in 2009 was $12,703 billion, then U.S. real GDP in 2010 was $12,703 billion + $385 billion = $13,088 billion. We could calculate the rate of change, or the growth rate, of U.S. real GDP during 2010 as: (($13,088 billion − $12,703 billion)/$12,703 billion) × 100 = ($385 billion/$12,703 billion) × 100 = 3.03%. Statements about economic growth over a period of years almost always refer to changes in the growth rate.

When talking about growth or growth rates, economists often use phrases that appear to mix the two concepts and so can be confusing. For example, when we say that "U.S. growth fell during the 1970s," we are really saying that the U.S. growth rate of real GDP was lower in the 1970s in comparison to the 1960s. When we say that "growth accelerated during the early 1990s," we are saying that the growth rate increased year after year in the early 1990s—for example, going from 3% to 3.5% to 4%.

less than $3,976 per capita—and often much less. In fact, today about 50% of the world's people live in countries with a lower standard of living than the United States had a century ago.

## Growth Rates

How did the United States manage to produce over seven times as much per person in 2010 than in 1900? A little bit at a time. Long-run economic growth is normally a gradual process in which real GDP per capita grows at most a few percent per year. From 1900 to 2010, real GDP per capita in the United States increased an average of 1.9% each year.

To have a sense of the relationship between the annual growth rate of real GDP per capita and the long-run change in real GDP per capita, it's helpful to keep in mind the **Rule of 70,** a mathematical formula that tells us how long it takes real GDP per capita, or any other variable that grows gradually over time, to double. The approximate answer is:

**(9-1)** Number of years for variable to double = $\dfrac{70}{\text{Annual growth rate of variable}}$

(Note that the Rule of 70 can only be applied to a positive growth rate.) So if real GDP per capita grows at 1% per year, it will take 70 years to double. If it grows at 2% per year, it will take only 35 years to double. In fact, U.S. real GDP per capita rose on average 1.9% per year over the last century. Applying the Rule of 70 to this information implies that it should have taken 37 years for real GDP per capita to double; it would have taken 111 years—three periods of 37 years each—for U.S. real GDP per capita to double three times. That is, the Rule of 70 implies that over the course of 111 years, U.S. real GDP per capita should have increased by a factor of 2 × 2 × 2 = 8. And this does turn out to be a pretty good approximation of reality. Between 1899 and 2010—a period of 111 years—real GDP per capita rose just about eightfold.

Figure 9-3 shows the average annual rate of growth of real GDP per capita for selected countries from 1980 to 2010. Some countries were notable success stories: for example, China, though still quite a poor country, has made spectacular progress. India, although not matching China's performance, has also achieved impressive growth, as discussed in the following Economics in Action.

Some countries, though, have had very disappointing growth. Argentina was once considered a wealthy nation. In the early years of the twentieth century, it was in the same league as the United States and Canada. But since then it has lagged far behind more dynamic economies. And still others, like Zimbabwe, have slid backward.

What explains these differences in growth rates? To answer that question, we need to examine the sources of long-run economic growth.

According to the **Rule of 70,** the time it takes a variable that grows gradually over time to double is approximately 70 divided by that variable's annual growth rate.

FIGURE   **9-3**   Comparing Recent Growth Rates

The average annual rate of growth of real GDP per capita from 1980 to 2010 is shown here for selected countries. China and, to a lesser extent, India and Ireland achieved impressive growth. The United States and France had moderate growth. Once considered an economically advanced country, Argentina had more sluggish growth. Still others, such as Zimbabwe, slid backward.

*Source:* International Monetary Fund.

*Data for Zimbabwe is average annual growth rate 2000–2010 due to data limitations.

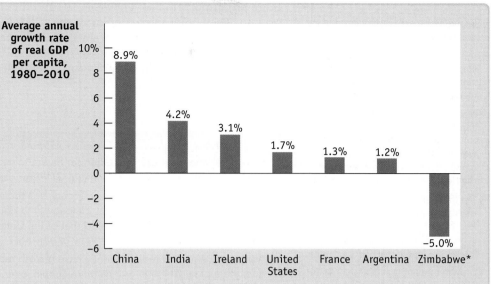

Average annual growth rate of real GDP per capita, 1980–2010

| | |
|---|---|
| China | 8.9% |
| India | 4.2% |
| Ireland | 3.1% |
| United States | 1.7% |
| France | 1.3% |
| Argentina | 1.2% |
| Zimbabwe* | –5.0% |

## ECONOMICS ▸ *IN ACTION*

### INDIA TAKES OFF

India achieved independence from Great Britain in 1947, becoming the world's most populous democracy—a status it has maintained to this day. For more than three decades after independence, however, this happy political story was partly overshadowed by economic disappointment. Despite ambitious economic development plans, India's performance was consistently sluggish. In 1980, India's real GDP per capita was only about 50% higher than it had been in 1947; the gap between Indian living standards and those in wealthy countries like the United States had been growing rather than shrinking.

Since then, however, India has done much better. As Figure 9-3 shows, real GDP per capita has grown at an average rate of 4.2% a year, more than tripling between 1980 and 2010. India now has a large and rapidly growing middle class. And yes, the well-fed children of that middle class are much taller than their parents.

What went right in India after 1980? Many economists point to policy reforms. For decades after independence, India had a tightly controlled, highly regulated economy. Today, things are very different: a series of reforms opened the economy to international trade and freed up domestic competition. Some economists, however, argue that this can't be the main story because the big policy reforms weren't adopted until 1991, yet growth accelerated around 1980.

Regardless of the explanation, India's economic rise has transformed it into a major new economic power—and allowed hundreds of millions of people to have a much better life, better than their grandparents could have dreamed.

Martin Harvey/Getty Images

India's high rate of economic growth since 1980 has raised living standards and led to the emergence of a rapidly growing middle class.

The big question now is whether this growth can continue. Skeptics argue that there are important bottlenecks in the Indian economy that may constrain future growth. They point in particular to the still low education level of much of India's population and inadequate infrastructure—that is, the poor quality and limited capacity of the country's roads, railroads, power supplies, and so on. But India's economy has defied the skeptics for several decades and the hope is that it can continue doing so.

### CHECK YOUR UNDERSTANDING 9-1

1. Why do economists use real GDP per capita to measure economic progress rather than some other measure, such as nominal GDP per capita or real GDP?

2. Apply the Rule of 70 to the data in Figure 9-3 to determine how long it will take each of the countries listed there (except Zimbabwe) to double its real GDP per capita. Would India's real GDP per capita exceed that of the United States in the future if growth rates remain as shown in Figure 9-3? Why or why not?

3. Although China and India currently have growth rates much higher than the U.S. growth rate, the typical Chinese or Indian household is far poorer than the typical American household. Explain why.

Solutions appear at back of book.

## The Sources of Long-Run Growth

Long-run economic growth depends almost entirely on one ingredient: rising *productivity*. However, a number of factors affect the growth of productivity. Let's look first at why productivity is the key ingredient and then examine what affects it.

### The Crucial Importance of Productivity

*Sustained economic growth occurs only when the amount of output produced by the average worker increases steadily.* The term **labor productivity,** or **productivity** for short, is used to refer either to output per worker or, in some cases, to output per hour. (The number of hours worked by an average worker differs to some extent across countries, although this isn't an important factor in the difference between living standards in, say, India and the United States.) In this book we'll focus on output per worker. For the economy as a whole, productivity—output per worker—is simply real GDP divided by the number of people working.

You might wonder why we say that higher productivity is the only source of long-run growth. Can't an economy also increase its real GDP per capita by putting more of the population to work? The answer is, yes, but . . . . For short periods of time, an economy can experience a burst of growth in output per capita by putting a higher percentage of the population to work. That happened in the United States during World War II, when millions of women who previously worked only in the home entered the paid workforce. The percentage of adult civilians employed outside the home rose from 50% in 1941 to 58% in 1944, and you can see the resulting bump in real GDP per capita during those years in Figure 9-1.

Over the longer run, however, the rate of employment growth is never very different from the rate of population growth. Over the course of the twentieth century, for example, the population of the United States rose at an average rate of 1.3% per year and employment rose 1.5% per year. Real GDP per capita rose 1.9% per year; of that, 1.7%—that is, almost 90% of the total—was the result of rising

**Labor productivity,** often referred to simply as **productivity,** is output per worker.

productivity. In general, overall real GDP can grow because of population growth, but any large increase in real GDP *per capita* must be the result of increased output *per worker.* That is, it must be due to higher productivity.

So increased productivity is the key to long-run economic growth. But what leads to higher productivity?

## Explaining Growth in Productivity

There are three main reasons why the average U.S. worker today produces far more than his or her counterpart a century ago. First, the modern worker has far more *physical capital,* such as machinery and office space, to work with. Second, the modern worker is much better educated and so possesses much more *human capital.* Finally, modern firms have the advantage of a century's accumulation of technical advancements reflecting a great deal of *technological progress.*

Let's look at each of these factors in turn.

**Increase in Physical Capital**   Economists define **physical capital** as manufactured resources such as buildings and machines. Physical capital makes workers more productive. For example, a worker operating a backhoe can dig a lot more feet of trench per day than one equipped only with a shovel.

The average U.S. private-sector worker today is backed up by more than $150,000 worth of physical capital—far more than a U.S. worker had 100 years ago and far more than the average worker in most other countries has today.

**Increase in Human Capital**   It's not enough for a worker to have good equipment—he or she must also know what to do with it. **Human capital** refers to the improvement in labor created by the education and knowledge embodied in the workforce.

The human capital of the United States has increased dramatically over the past century. A century ago, although most Americans were able to read and write, very few had an extensive education. In 1910, only 13.5% of Americans over 25 had graduated from high school and only 3% had four-year college degrees. By 2010, the percentages were 87% and 30%, respectively. It would be impossible to run today's economy with a population as poorly educated as that of a century ago.

Analyses based on *growth accounting,* described later in this chapter, suggest that education—and its effect on productivity—is an even more important determinant of growth than increases in physical capital.

**Technological Progress**   Probably the most important driver of productivity growth is **technological progress,** which is broadly defined as an advance in the technical means of the production of goods and services. We'll see shortly how economists measure the impact of technology on growth.

Workers today are able to produce more than those in the past, even with the same amount of physical and human capital, because technology has advanced over time. It's important to realize that economically important technological progress need not be flashy or rely on cutting-edge science. Historians have noted that past economic growth has been driven not only by major inventions, such as the railroad or the semiconductor chip, but also by thousands of modest innovations, such as the flat-bottomed paper bag, patented in 1870, which made packing groceries and many other goods much easier, and the Post-it® note, introduced in 1981, which has had surprisingly large benefits for office productivity. Experts attribute much of the productivity

**Physical capital** consists of human-made resources such as buildings and machines.

**Human capital** is the improvement in labor created by the education and knowledge embodied in the workforce.

**Technological progress** is an advance in the technical means of the production of goods and services.

I SHALL BE SO GLAD WHEN THEY INVENT THE INTERNET AND THIS STUFF CAN GO STRAIGHT ON TO OUR WEBSITE

ROGER BEALE

Roger Beale

The **aggregate production function** is a hypothetical function that shows how productivity (real GDP per worker) depends on the quantities of physical capital per worker and human capital per worker as well as the state of technology.

An aggregate production function exhibits **diminishing returns to physical capital** when, holding the amount of human capital per worker and the state of technology fixed, each successive increase in the amount of physical capital per worker leads to a smaller increase in productivity.

surge that took place in the United States late in the twentieth century to new technology adopted by retail companies like Walmart rather than to high-technology companies.

## Accounting for Growth: The Aggregate Production Function

Productivity is higher, other things equal, when workers are equipped with more physical capital, more human capital, better technology, or any combination of the three. But can we put numbers to these effects? To do this, economists make use of estimates of the **aggregate production function,** which shows how productivity depends on the quantities of physical capital per worker and human capital per worker as well as the state of technology. In general, all three factors tend to rise over time, as workers are equipped with more machinery, receive more education, and benefit from technological advances. What the aggregate production function does is allow economists to disentangle the effects of these three factors on overall productivity.

An example of an aggregate production function applied to real data comes from a comparative study of Chinese and Indian economic growth by the economists Barry Bosworth and Susan Collins of the Brookings Institution. They used the following aggregate production function:

$$\text{GDP per worker} = T \times (\text{Physical capital per worker})^{0.4} \times (\text{Human capital per worker})^{0.6}$$

where $T$ represented an estimate of the level of technology and they assumed that each year of education raises workers' human capital by 7%. Using this function, they tried to explain why China grew faster than India between 1978 and 2004. About half the difference, they found, was due to China's higher levels of investment spending, which raised its level of physical capital per worker faster than India's. The other half was due to faster Chinese technological progress.

In analyzing historical economic growth, economists have discovered a crucial fact about the estimated aggregate production function: it exhibits **diminishing returns to physical capital.** That is, when the amount of human capital per worker and the state of technology are held fixed, each successive increase in the amount of physical capital per worker leads to a smaller increase in productivity. Figure 9-4 and the table to its right give a hypothetical example of how the level of physical capital per worker might affect the level of real GDP per worker, holding human capital per worker and the state of technology fixed. In this example, we measure the quantity of physical capital in dollars.

To see why the relationship between physical capital per worker and productivity exhibits diminishing returns, think about how having farm equipment affects the productivity of farmworkers. A little bit of equipment makes a big difference: a worker equipped with a tractor can do much more than a worker without one. And a worker using more expensive equipment will, other things equal, be more productive: a worker with a $40,000 tractor will normally be able to cultivate more farmland in a given amount of time than a worker with a $20,000 tractor because the more expensive machine will be more powerful, perform more tasks, or both.

But will a worker with a $40,000 tractor, holding human capital and technology constant, be twice as productive as a worker with a $20,000 tractor? Probably not: there's a huge difference between not having a tractor at all and having even an inexpensive tractor; there's much less difference between having an inexpensive tractor and having a better tractor. And we can be sure that a worker with a $200,000 tractor won't be 10 times as productive: a tractor can be improved only so much. Because the same is true of other kinds of equipment, the aggregate production function shows diminishing returns to physical capital.

Diminishing returns to physical capital imply a relationship between physical capital per worker and output per worker like the one shown in Figure 9-4. As the

FIGURE    **9-4**    Physical Capital and Productivity

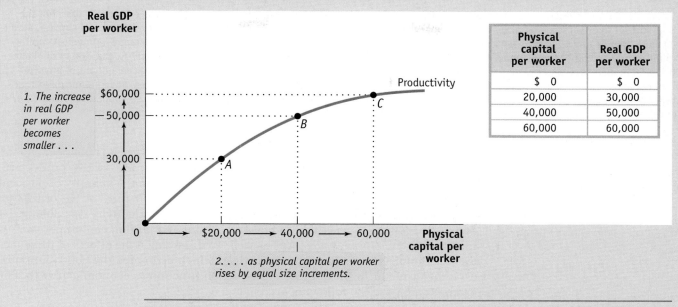

| Physical capital per worker | Real GDP per worker |
|---|---|
| $  0 | $  0 |
| 20,000 | 30,000 |
| 40,000 | 50,000 |
| 60,000 | 60,000 |

1. The increase in real GDP per worker becomes smaller . . .

2. . . . as physical capital per worker rises by equal size increments.

The aggregate production function shows how, in this case holding human capital per worker and technology fixed, productivity increases as physical capital per worker rises. Other things equal, a greater quantity of physical capital per worker leads to higher real GDP per worker but is subject to diminishing returns: each successive addition to physical capital per worker produces a smaller increase in productivity. Starting at the origin, 0, a $20,000 increase in physical capital per worker leads to an increase in real GDP per worker of $30,000, indicated by point A. Starting from point A, another $20,000 increase in physical capital per worker leads to an increase in real GDP per worker but only of $20,000, indicated by point B. Finally, a third $20,000 increase in physical capital per worker leads to only a $10,000 increase in real GDP per worker, indicated by point C.

productivity curve for physical capital and the accompanying table illustrate, more physical capital per worker leads to more output per worker. But each $20,000 increment in physical capital per worker adds less to productivity. As you can see from the table, there is a big payoff for the first $20,000 of physical capital: real GDP per worker rises by $30,000. The second $20,000 of physical capital also raises productivity, but not by as much: real GDP per worker goes up by only $20,000. The third $20,000 of physical capital raises real GDP per worker by only $10,000. By comparing points along the curve you can also see that as physical capital per worker rises, output per worker also rises—but at a diminishing rate. Going from the origin at 0 to point A, a $20,000 increase in physical capital per worker, leads to an increase of $30,000 in real GDP per worker. Going from point A to point B, a second $20,000 increase in physical capital per worker, leads to an increase of only $20,000 in real GDP per worker. And from point B to point C, a $20,000 increase in physical capital per worker increased real GDP per worker by only $10,000.

It's important to realize that diminishing returns to physical capital is an "other things equal" phenomenon: additional amounts of physical capital are less productive *when the amount of human capital per worker and the technology are held fixed*. Diminishing returns may disappear if we increase the amount of human capital per worker, or improve the technology, or both at the same time the amount of physical capital per worker is increased.

For example, a worker with a $40,000 tractor who has also been trained in the most advanced cultivation techniques may in fact be more than twice as productive as a worker with only a $20,000 tractor and no additional human capital. But

## ⚠ PITFALLS

**IT MAY BE DIMINISHED . . . BUT IT'S STILL POSITIVE**
It's important to understand what diminishing returns to physi-cal capital means and what it doesn't mean. As we've already explained, it's an "other things equal" statement: holding the amount of human capital per worker and the technology fixed, each successive increase in the amount of physical capital per worker results in a smaller increase in real GDP per worker. But this doesn't mean that real GDP per worker eventually falls

as more and more physical capital is added. It's just that the *increase* in real GDP per worker gets smaller and smaller, albeit remaining at or above zero. So an increase in physical capital per worker will never reduce productivity. But due to diminish-ing returns, at some point increasing the amount of physical capital per worker no longer produces an economic payoff: at some point the increase in output is so small that it is not worth the cost of the additional physical capital.

diminishing returns to any one input—regardless of whether it is physical capital, human capital, or number of workers—is a pervasive characteristic of production. Typical estimates suggest that in practice a 1% increase in the quantity of physical capital per worker increases output per worker by only one-third of 1%, or 0.33%.

In practice, all the factors contributing to higher productivity rise during the course of economic growth: both physical capital and human capital per worker increase, and technology advances as well. To disentangle the effects of these fac-tors, economists use **growth accounting,** which estimates the contribution of each major factor in the aggregate production function to economic growth. For example, suppose the following are true:

- The amount of physical capital per worker grows 3% a year.
- According to estimates of the aggregate production function, each 1% rise in physical capital per worker, holding human capital and technology constant, raises output per worker by one-third of 1%, or 0.33%.

In that case, we would estimate that growing physical capital per worker is responsible for 3% × 0.33 = 1 percentage point of productivity growth per year. A similar but more complex procedure is used to estimate the effects of growing human capital. The procedure is more complex because there aren't simple dollar measures of the quantity of human capital.

Growth accounting allows us to calculate the effects of greater physical and human capital on economic growth. But how can we estimate the effects of technological progress? We do so by estimating what is left over after the effects of physical and human capital have been taken into account. For example, let's imagine that there was no increase in human capital per worker so that we can focus on changes in physical capital and in technology.

In Figure 9-5, the lower curve shows the same hypothetical relationship between physical capital per worker and output per worker shown in Figure 9-4. Let's assume that this was the relationship given the technology available in 1940. The upper curve also shows a relationship between physical capital per worker and productivity, but this time given the technology available in 2010. (We've cho-sen a 70-year stretch to allow us to use the Rule of 70.) The 2010 curve is shifted up compared to the 1940 curve because technologies developed over the previous 70 years make it possible to produce more output for a given amount of physical capital per worker than was possible with the technology available in 1940. (Note that the two curves are measured in constant dollars.)

Let's assume that between 1940 and 2010 the amount of physical capital per worker rose from $20,000 to $60,000. If this increase in physical capital per work-er had taken place without any technological progress, the economy would have moved from A to C: output per worker would have risen, but only from $30,000 to $60,000, or 1% per year (using the Rule of 70 tells us that a 1% growth rate over 70 years doubles output). In fact, however, the economy moved from A to D: output rose from $30,000 to $120,000, or 2% per year. There was an increase in both physical capital per worker and technological progress, which shifted the aggregate production function.

**Growth accounting** estimates the contribution of each major factor in the aggregate production function to economic growth.

FIGURE    **9-5**    Technological Progress and Productivity Growth

Technological progress raises productivity at any given level of physical capital per worker, and therefore shifts the aggregate production function upward. Here we hold human capital per worker fixed. We assume that the lower curve (the same curve as in Figure 9-4) reflects technology in 1940 and the upper curve reflects technology in 2010. Holding technology and human capital fixed, tripling physical capital per worker from $20,000 to $60,000 leads to a doubling of real GDP per worker, from $30,000 to $60,000. This is shown by the movement from point A to point C, reflecting an approximately 1% per year rise in real GDP per worker. In reality, technological progress raised productivity at any given level of physical capital—shown here by the upward shift of the curve—and the actual rise in real GDP per worker is shown by the movement from point A to point D. Real GDP per worker grew 2% per year, leading to a quadrupling during the period. The extra 1% in growth of real GDP per worker is due to higher total factor productivity.

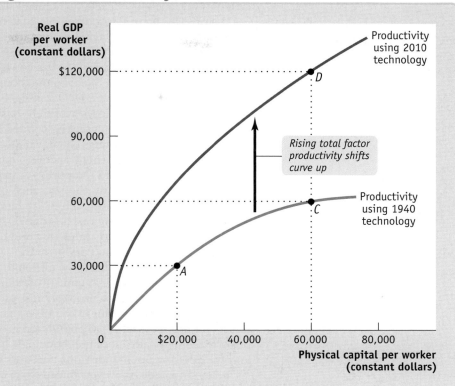

In this case, 50% of the annual 2% increase in productivity—that is, 1% in annual productivity growth—is due to higher **total factor productivity,** the amount of output that can be produced with a given amount of factor inputs. So when total factor productivity increases, the economy can produce more output with the same quantity of physical capital, human capital, and labor.

Most estimates find that increases in total factor productivity are central to a country's economic growth. We believe that observed increases in total factor productivity in fact measure the economic effects of technological progress. All of this implies that technological change is crucial to economic growth. The Bureau of Labor Statistics estimates the growth rate of both labor productivity and total factor productivity for nonfarm business in the United States. According to the Bureau's estimates, over the period from 1948 to 2010 American labor productivity rose 2.3% per year. Only 49% of that rise is explained by increases in physical and human capital per worker; the rest is explained by rising total factor productivity—that is, by technological progress.

## What About Natural Resources?

In our discussion so far, we haven't mentioned natural resources, which certainly have an effect on productivity. Other things equal, countries that are abundant in valuable natural resources, such as highly fertile land or rich mineral deposits, have higher real GDP per capita than less fortunate countries. The most obvious modern example is the Middle East, where enormous oil deposits have made a few sparsely populated countries very rich. For example, Kuwait has about the same level of real GDP per capita as Germany, but Kuwait's wealth is based on oil, not manufacturing, the source of Germany's high output per worker.

But other things are often not equal. In the modern world, natural resources are a much less important determinant of productivity than human or physical capital for the great majority of countries. For example, some nations with very high real

**Total factor productivity** is the amount of output that can be achieved with a given amount of factor inputs.

GDP per capita, such as Japan, have very few natural resources. Some resource-rich nations, such as Nigeria (which has sizable oil deposits), are very poor.

Historically, natural resources played a much more prominent role in determining productivity. In the nineteenth century, the countries with the highest real GDP per capita were those abundant in rich farmland and mineral deposits: the United States, Canada, Argentina, and Australia. As a consequence, natural resources figured prominently in the development of economic thought. In a famous book published in 1798, *An Essay on the Principle of Population,* the English economist Thomas Malthus made the fixed quantity of land in the world the basis of a pessimistic prediction about future productivity. As population grew, he pointed out, the amount of land per worker would decline. And this, other things equal, would cause productivity to fall.

His view, in fact, was that improvements in technology or increases in physical capital would lead only to temporary improvements in productivity because they would always be offset by the pressure of rising population and more workers on the supply of land. In the long run, he concluded, the great majority of people were condemned to living on the edge of starvation. Only then would death rates be high enough and birth rates low enough to prevent rapid population growth from outstripping productivity growth.

It hasn't turned out that way, although many historians believe that Malthus's prediction of falling or stagnant productivity was valid for much of human history. Population pressure probably did prevent large productivity increases until the eighteenth century. But in the time since Malthus wrote his book, any negative effects on productivity from population growth have been far outweighed by other, positive factors—advances in technology, increases in human and physical capital, and the opening up of enormous amounts of cultivable land in the New World.

It remains true, however, that we live on a finite planet, with limited supplies of resources such as oil and limited ability to absorb environmental damage. We address the concerns these limitations pose for economic growth in the final section of this chapter.

## ECONOMICS ▸ *IN ACTION*

### THE INFORMATION TECHNOLOGY PARADOX

From the early 1970s through the mid-1990s, the United States went through a slump in total factor productivity growth. Figure 9-6 shows Bureau of Labor Statistics estimates of annual total factor productivity growth, averaged for each 10-year period from 1948 to 2010. As you can see, there was a large fall in the total factor productivity growth rate beginning in the early 1970s. Because higher total factor productivity plays such a key role in long-run growth, the economy's overall growth was also disappointing, leading to a widespread sense that economic progress had ground to a halt.

Many economists were puzzled by the slowdown in total factor productivity growth after 1973, since in other ways the era seemed to be one of rapid technological progress. Modern information technology really began with the development of the first microprocessor—a computer on a chip—in 1971. In the 25 years that followed, a series of inventions that seemed revolutionary became standard equipment in the business world: fax machines, desktop computers, cell phones, and e-mail. Yet the rate of growth of total factor productivity remained stagnant. In a famous remark, MIT economics professor and Nobel laureate Robert Solow, a pioneer in the analysis of economic

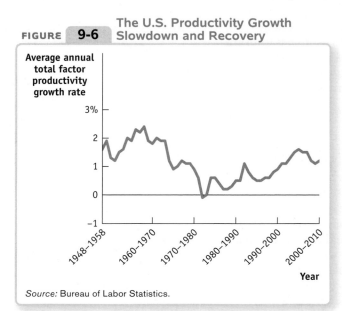

**FIGURE  9-6  The U.S. Productivity Growth Slowdown and Recovery**

Average annual total factor productivity growth rate

*Source:* Bureau of Labor Statistics.

growth, declared that the information technology revolution could be seen everywhere except in the economic statistics.

Why didn't information technology show large rewards? Paul David, a Stanford University economic historian, offered a theory and a prediction. He pointed out that 100 years earlier another miracle technology—electric power—had spread through the economy, again with surprisingly little impact on productivity growth at first. The reason, he suggested, was that a new technology doesn't yield its full potential if you use it in old ways.

For example, a traditional factory around 1900 was a multistory building, with the machinery tightly crowded together and designed to be powered by a steam engine in the basement. This design had problems: it was very difficult to move people and materials around. Yet owners who electrified their factories initially maintained the multistory, tightly packed layout. Only with the switch to spread-out, one-story factories that took advantage of the flexibility of electric power—most famously Henry Ford's auto assembly line—did productivity take off.

David suggested that the same phenomenon was happening with information technology. Productivity, he predicted, would take off when people really changed their way of doing business to take advantage of the new technology—such as replacing letters and phone calls with e-mail. Sure enough, productivity growth accelerated dramatically in the second half of the 1990s as companies like Walmart discovered how to effectively use information technology.

---

### CHECK YOUR UNDERSTANDING 9-2

1. Predict the effect of each of the following events on the growth rate of productivity.
   a. The amounts of physical and human capital per worker are unchanged, but there is significant technological progress.
   b. The amount of physical capital per worker grows at a steady pace, but the level of human capital per worker and technology are unchanged.

2. Output in the economy of Erewhon has grown 3% per year over the past 30 years. The labor force has grown at 1% per year, and the quantity of physical capital has grown at 4% per year. The average education level hasn't changed. Estimates by economists say that each 1% increase in physical capital per worker, other things equal, raises productivity by 0.3%. (*Hint:* % change in (X/Y) = % change in X – % change in Y.)
   a. How fast has productivity in Erewhon grown?
   b. How fast has physical capital per worker grown?
   c. How much has growing physical capital per worker contributed to productivity growth? What percentage of productivity growth is that?
   d. How much has technological progress contributed to productivity growth? What percentage of productivity growth is that?

3. Multinomics, Inc., is a large company with many offices around the country. It has just adopted a new computer system that will affect virtually every function performed within the company. Why might a period of time pass before employees' productivity is improved by the new computer system? Why might there be a temporary decrease in employees' productivity?

Solutions appear at back of book.

### ▼ Quick Review

● Long-run increases in living standards arise almost entirely from growing **labor productivity**, often simply referred to as **productivity.**

● An increase in **physical capital** is one source of higher productivity, but it is subject to **diminishing returns to physical capital.**

● **Human capital** and technological progress are also sources of increases in productivity.

● The **aggregate production function** is used to estimate the sources of increases in productivity. **Growth accounting** has shown that rising **total factor productivity,** interpreted as the effect of technological progress, is central to long-run economic growth.

● Natural resources are less important today than physical and human capital as sources of productivity growth in most economies.

---

# Why Growth Rates Differ

In 1820, according to estimates by the economic historian Angus Maddison, Mexico had somewhat higher real GDP per capita than Japan. Today, Japan has higher real GDP per capita than most European nations and Mexico is a poor country, though by no means among the poorest. The difference? Over the long run—since 1820—real GDP per capita grew at 1.9% per year in Japan but at only 1.3% per year in Mexico.

As this example illustrates, even small differences in growth rates have large consequences over the long run. So why do growth rates differ across countries and across periods of time?

## Explaining Differences in Growth Rates

As one might expect, economies with rapid growth tend to be economies that add physical capital, increase their human capital, or experience rapid technological progress. Striking economic success stories, like Japan in the 1950s and 1960s or China today, tend to be countries that do all three: that rapidly add to their physical capital through high savings and investment spending, upgrade their educational level, and make fast technological progress. Evidence also points to the importance of government policies, property rights, political stability, and good governance in fostering the sources of growth.

**Savings and Investment Spending** One reason for differences in growth rates between countries is that some countries are increasing their stock of physical capital much more rapidly than others, through high rates of investment spending. In the 1960s, Japan was the fastest-growing major economy; it also spent a much higher share of its GDP on investment goods than did other major economies. Today, China is the fastest-growing major economy, and it similarly spends a very large share of its GDP on investment goods. In 2010, investment spending was 38% of China's GDP, compared with only 16% in the United States.

Where does the money for high investment spending come from? From savings. In the next chapter, we'll analyze how financial markets channel savings into investment spending. For now, however, the key point is that investment spending must be paid for either out of savings from domestic households or by savings from foreign households—that is, an inflow of foreign capital.

Foreign capital has played an important role in the long-run economic growth of some countries, including the United States, which relied heavily on foreign funds during its early industrialization. For the most part, however, countries that invest a large share of their GDP are able to do so because they have high domestic savings. In fact, China in 2010 saved an even higher percentage of its GDP than it invested at home. The extra savings were invested abroad, largely in the United States.

One reason for differences in growth rates, then, is that countries add different amounts to their stocks of physical capital because they have different rates of savings and investment spending.

**Education** Just as countries differ substantially in the rate at which they add to their physical capital, there have been large differences in the rate at which countries add to their human capital through education.

A case in point is the comparison between Argentina and China. In both countries the average educational level has risen steadily over time, but it has risen much faster in China. Figure 9-7 shows the average years of education of adults in China, which we have highlighted as a spectacular example of long-run growth, and in Argentina, a country whose growth has been disappointing. Compared to China, sixty years ago, Argentina had a much more educated population, while many Chinese were still illiterate. Today, the average educational level in China is still slightly below that in Argentina—but that's mainly because there are still many elderly adults who never received basic education. In terms of secondary and tertiary education, China has outstripped once-rich Argentina.

**Research and Development** The advance of technology is a key force behind economic growth. What drives technological progress?

Scientific advances make new technologies possible. To take the most spectacular example in today's world, the semiconductor chip—which is the basis for all modern information technology—could not have been developed without the theory of quantum mechanics in physics.

FIGURE   **9-7**   China's Students Are Catching Up

In both China and Argentina, the average educational level—measured by the number of years the average adult aged 25 or older has spent in school—has risen over time. Although China is still lagging behind Argentina, it is catching up—and China's success at adding human capital is one key to its spectacular long-run growth.

*Source:* Robert Barro and Jong-Wha Lee, "A New Data Set of Educational Attainment in the World, 1950–2010," NBER Working Paper No. 15902 (April 2010).

But science alone is not enough: scientific knowledge must be translated into useful products and processes. And that often requires devoting a lot of resources to **research and development,** or **R&D,** spending to create new technologies and apply them to practical use.

Although some research and development is conducted by governments, much R&D is paid for by the private sector, as discussed below. The United States became the world's leading economy in large part because American businesses were among the first to make systematic research and development a part of their operations. The upcoming For Inquiring Minds describes how Thomas Edison created the first modern industrial research laboratory.

**Research and development,** or **R&D,** is spending to create and implement new technologies.

## FOR INQUIRING MINDS

### INVENTING R&D

Thomas Edison is best known as the inventor of the lightbulb and the phonograph. But his biggest invention may surprise you: he invented research and development.

Before Edison's time, there had, of course, been many inventors. Some of them worked in teams. But in 1875 Edison created something new: his Menlo Park, New Jersey, laboratory. It employed 25 men full time to generate new products and processes for business. In other words, he did not set out to pursue a particular idea and then cash in. He created an organization whose purpose was to create new ideas year after year.

Edison's Menlo Park lab is now a museum. "To name a few of the prod-

ucts that were developed in Menlo Park," says the museum's website, "we can list the following: the carbon button mouthpiece for the telephone, the phonograph, the incandescent light bulb and the electrical distribution system, the electric train, ore separation, the Edison effect bulb, early experiments in wireless, the grasshopper telegraph, and improvements in telegraphic transmission."

You could say that before Edison's lab, technology just sort of happened: people came up with ideas, but businesses didn't plan to make continuous technological progress. Now R&D operations, often much bigger

than Edison's original team, are standard practice throughout the business world.

Roads, power lines, ports, information networks, and other underpinnings for economic activity are known as **infrastructure.**

Developing new technology is one thing; applying it is another. There have often been notable differences in the pace at which different countries take advantage of new technologies. As this chapter's Global Comparison shows, America's surge in productivity growth after 1995, as firms learned to make use of information technology, was at least initially not matched in Europe.

## The Role of Government in Promoting Economic Growth

Governments can play an important role in promoting—or blocking—all three sources of long-term economic growth: physical capital, human capital, and technological progress. They can either affect growth directly through subsidies to factors that enhance growth, or by creating an environment that either fosters or hinders growth.

**Government Policies** Government policies can increase the economy's growth rate through four main channels.

**1. GOVERNMENT SUBSIDIES TO INFRASTRUCTURE** Governments play an important direct role in building **infrastructure:** roads, power lines, ports, information networks, and other large-scale physical capital projects that provide a foundation for economic activity. Although some infrastructure is provided by private companies, much of it is either provided by the government or requires a great deal of government regulation and support. Ireland is often cited as an example of the importance of government-provided infrastructure. After the government invested in an excellent telecommunications infrastructure in the 1980s, Ireland became a favored location for high-technology companies from abroad and its economy took off in the 1990s.

Poor infrastructure, such as a power grid that frequently fails and cuts off electricity, is a major obstacle to economic growth in many countries. To provide

### GLOBAL COMPARISON OLD EUROPE AND NEW TECHNOLOGY

The United States experienced a burst of productivity growth after 1995, probably because businesses finally figured out how to use modern information technology effectively. As we'll see in the Business Case at the end of this chapter, the acceleration of technological progress was especially dramatic in distribution—that is, in the business of getting goods to consumers. But did the rest of the world experience a similar takeoff?

The answer is, not everywhere. This figure shows 5-year average rates of growth in labor productivity in the United States and in the four big economies of Western Europe—France, Germany, Italy, and the United Kingdom—from 1970 to 2009. Up until the mid-1990s, Europe consistently achieved higher productivity growth than did the United States. But in the years that followed, European growth declined as U.S. growth surged for a decade. By the mid 2000s, the U.S. productivity growth rate had reverted to the pre-information technology boom levels.

There is great dispute both about why much of Europe didn't share in the productivity takeoff and about whether it will soon catch up to the United States. Some economists argue that high levels of government regulation made it hard for European businesses to reorganize themselves to take advantage of new technology. What is clear is that for at least a decade Europe lagged behind.

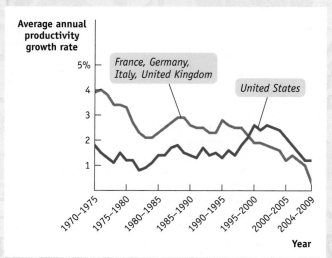

*Source:* Bureau of Labor Statistics.

good infrastructure, an economy must not only be able to afford it, but it must also have the political discipline to maintain it.

Perhaps the most crucial infrastructure is something we, in an advanced country, rarely think about: basic public health measures in the form of a clean water supply and disease control. As we'll see in the next section, poor health infrastructure is a major obstacle to economic growth in poor countries, especially those in Africa.

**2. GOVERNMENT SUBSIDIES TO EDUCATION** In contrast to physical capital, which is mainly created by private investment spending, much of an economy's human capital is the result of government spending on education. Government pays for the great bulk of primary and secondary education. And it pays for a significant share of higher education: 75% of students attend public colleges and universities, and government significantly subsidizes research performed at private colleges and universities. As a result, differences in the rate at which countries add to their human capital largely reflect government policy. As we saw in Figure 9-7, educational levels in China are increasing much more rapidly than in Argentina. This isn't because China is richer than Argentina; until recently, China was, on average, poorer than Argentina. Instead, it reflects the fact that the Chinese government has made education of the population a high priority.

**3. GOVERNMENT SUBSIDIES TO R&D** Technological progress is largely the result of private initiative. But in the more advanced countries, important R&D is done by government agencies as well. In the upcoming Economics in Action, we describe Brazil's agricultural boom, which was made possible by government researchers who made discoveries that expanded the amount of arable land in Brazil, as well as developing new varieties of crops that flourish in Brazil's climate.

**4. MAINTAINING A WELL-FUNCTIONING FINANCIAL SYSTEM** Governments play an important indirect role in making high rates of private investment spending possible. Both the amount of savings and the ability of an economy to direct savings into productive investment spending depend on the economy's institutions, especially its financial system. In particular, a well-regulated and well-functioning financial system is very important for economic growth because in most countries it is the principal way in which savings are channeled into investment spending.

If a country's citizens trust their banks, they will place their savings in bank deposits, which the banks will then lend to their business customers. But if people don't trust their banks, they will hoard gold or foreign currency, keeping their savings in safe deposit boxes or under the mattress, where it cannot be turned into productive investment spending. As we'll discuss later, a well-functioning financial system requires appropriate government regulation to assure depositors that their funds are protected from loss.

**Protection of Property Rights** *Property rights* are the rights of owners of valuable items to dispose of those items as they choose. A subset, *intellectual property rights*, are the rights of an innovator to accrue the rewards of her innovation. The state of property rights generally, and intellectual property rights in particular, are important factors in explaining differences in growth rates across economies. Why? Because no one would bother to spend the effort and resources required to innovate if someone else could appropriate that innovation and capture the rewards. So, for innovation to flourish, intellectual property rights must receive protection.

Sometimes this is accomplished by the nature of the innovation: it may be too difficult or expensive to copy. But, generally, the government has to protect intellectual property rights. A *patent* is a government-created temporary monopoly given to an innovator for the use or sale of his or her innovation. It's a temporary rather than permanent monopoly because while it's in society's interests to give an innovator an incentive to invent, it's also in society's interests to eventually encourage competition.

**Political Stability and Good Governance** There's not much point in investing in a business if rioting mobs are likely to destroy it, or saving your money if someone with political connections can steal it. Political stability and good governance

## FOR INQUIRING MINDS

### THE NEW GROWTH THEORY

Until the 1990s, economic models of technological progress assumed that what drove innovation was a mystery—unknown and unpredictable. In the words of economists, the sources of technological progress were *exogenous*—they were outside the models of economics and assumed to "just happen." Then, in a series of influential papers written in the 1980s and 1990s, Paul Romer founded what we now call "the New Growth Theory." In Romer's model, technological progress was explainable because it was in fact *endogenous*—the outcome of economic variables and incentives. And because technological progress was endogenous, policies could be adopted to foster its growth.

At any point in time, an economy has a stock of knowledge capital—the accumulated knowledge generated by past investments in research and development, education, and skill enhancement, as well as knowledge acquired from other economies. And that stock of knowledge capital is spread throughout the economy, so all firms benefit from it. According to the New Growth Theory, a rising stock of knowledge capital creates the foundation for further technological progress as innovation, shared by firms throughout the economy, makes further innovation possible. For example, touch-screen technology—developed in the 1970s and 1980s—became the basis for later developments such as smartphones and tablet computers.

Yet, as Romer pointed out, there is a severe wrinkle in this story: because knowledge is shared throughout the economy, it may be very difficult for an innovator to capture the rewards of his or her innovation as others exploit the innovation for their own interests. So in the New Growth Theory, government protection of intellectual property rights is critical to furthering technological progress. In addition, governments, institutions, and firms can enhance technological progress by subsidizing investments in education and research and development, which, in turn, can increase the stock of knowledge capital.

By giving us a better model of where technological progress comes from, the New Growth Theory makes clear how important the policies of government, institutions, and firms are in fostering it.

---

(including the protection of property rights) are essential ingredients in fostering economic growth in the long run.

Long-run economic growth in successful economies, like that of the United States, has been possible because there are good laws, institutions that enforce those laws, and a stable political system that maintains those institutions. The law must say that your property is really yours so that someone else can't take it away. The courts and the police must be honest so that they can't be bribed to ignore the law. And the political system must be stable so that laws don't change capriciously.

Americans take these preconditions for granted, but they are by no means guaranteed. Aside from the disruption caused by war or revolution, many countries find that their economic growth suffers due to corruption among the government officials who should be enforcing the law. For example, until 1991 the Indian government imposed many bureaucratic restrictions on businesses, which often had to bribe government officials to get approval for even routine activities—a tax on business, in effect. Economists have argued that a reduction in this burden of corruption is one reason Indian growth has been much faster in recent years.

Even when the government isn't corrupt, excessive government intervention can be a brake on economic growth. If large parts of the economy are supported by government subsidies, protected from imports, subject to unnecessary monopolization, or otherwise insulated from competition, productivity tends to suffer because of a lack of incentives. As we'll see in the next section, excessive government intervention is one often-cited explanation for slow growth in Latin America.

## ECONOMICS ▸ IN ACTION

### THE BRAZILIAN BREADBASKET

A wry Brazilian joke says that "Brazil is the country of the future—and always will be." The world's fifth most populous country has often been considered as a possible major economic power yet has never fulfilled that promise.

In recent years, however, Brazil's economy has made a better showing, especially in agriculture. This success depends on exploiting a natural resource, the tropical savanna land known as the *cerrado*. Until a quarter-century ago, the land was considered unsuitable for farming. A combination of three factors changed that: technological progress due to research and development, improved economic policies, and greater physical capital.

The Brazilian Enterprise for Agricultural and Livestock Research, a government-run agency, developed the crucial technologies. It showed that adding lime and phosphorus made *cerrado* land productive, and it developed breeds of cattle and varieties of soybeans suited for the climate. (Now they're working on wheat.) Also, until the 1980s, Brazilian international trade policies discouraged exports, as did an overvalued exchange rate that made the country's goods more expensive to foreigners. After economic reform, investing in Brazilian agriculture became much more profitable and companies began putting in place the farm machinery, buildings, and other forms of physical capital needed to exploit the land.

In Brazil, government-funded R&D has resulted in crucial agricultural technologies and economic reforms that turn unusable land into profitable farmland.

What still limits Brazil's growth? Infrastructure. According to a report in the *New York Times,* Brazilian farmers are "concerned about the lack of reliable highways, railways and barge routes, which adds to the cost of doing business." Recognizing this, the Brazilian government is investing in infrastructure, and Brazilian agriculture is continuing to expand. The country has already overtaken the United States as the world's largest beef exporter and may not be far behind in soybeans.

**CHECK YOUR UNDERSTANDING** 9-3

**1.** Explain the link between a country's growth rate, its investment spending as a percent of GDP, and its domestic savings.

**2.** U.S. centers of academic biotechnology research have closer connections with private biotechnology companies than do their European counterparts. What effect might this have on the pace of creation and development of new drugs in the United States versus Europe?

**3.** During the 1990s in the former U.S.S.R., a lot of property was seized and controlled by those in power. How might this have affected the country's growth rate at that time? Explain.

*Solutions appear at back of book.*

## ▼ Quick Review

- Countries differ greatly in their growth rates of real GDP per capita due to differences in the rates at which they accumulate physical capital and human capital as well as differences in technological progress. A prime cause of differences in growth rates is differences in rates of domestic savings and investment spending as well as differences in education levels, and **research and development,** or **R&D,** levels. R&D largely drives technological progress.

- Government actions can promote or hinder the sources of long-term growth.

- Government policies that directly promote growth are subsidies to **infrastructure,** particularly public health infrastructure, subsidies to education, subsidies to R&D, and the maintenance of a well-functioning financial system.

- Governments improve the environment for growth by protecting property rights (particularly intellectual property rights through patents), by providing political stability, and through good governance. Poor governance includes corruption and excessive government intervention.

# Success, Disappointment, and Failure

As we've seen, rates of long-run economic growth differ quite a lot around the world. Now let's look at three regions of the world that have had quite different experiences with economic growth over the last few decades.

Figure 9-8 shows trends since 1960 in real GDP per capita in 2000 dollars for three countries: Argentina, Nigeria, and South Korea. (As in Figure 9-1, the vertical axis is drawn in logarithmic scale.) We have chosen these countries because each is a particularly striking example of what has happened in its region. South Korea's amazing rise is part of a broad "economic miracle"

**FIGURE**  **9-8**  **Success and Disappointment**

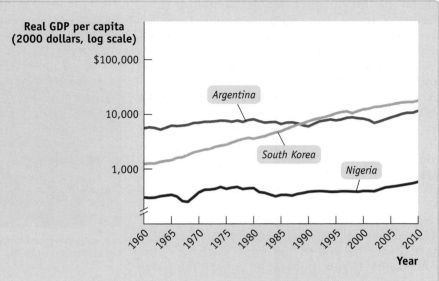

Real GDP per capita from 1960 to 2010, measured in 2000 dollars, is shown for Argentina, South Korea, and Nigeria, using a logarithmic scale. South Korea and some other East Asian countries have been highly successful at achieving economic growth. Argentina, like much of Latin America, has had several setbacks, slowing its growth. Nigeria's standard of living in 2010 was only barely higher than it had been in 1960, an experience shared by many African countries. Neither Argentina nor Nigeria exhibited much growth over the 50-year period, although both have had significantly higher growth in recent years.
*Source:* World Bank.

in East Asia. Argentina's slow progress, interrupted by repeated setbacks, is more or less typical of the disappointing growth that has characterized Latin America. And Nigeria's unhappy story until very recently—with little growth in real GDP until after 2000 —was, unfortunately, an experience shared by many African countries.

## East Asia's Miracle

In 1960 South Korea was a very poor country. In fact, in 1960 its real GDP per capita was lower than that of India today. But, as you can see from Figure 9-8, beginning in the early 1960s South Korea began an extremely rapid economic ascent: real GDP per capita grew about 7% per year for more than 30 years. Today South Korea, though still somewhat poorer than Europe or the United States, looks very much like an economically advanced country.

South Korea's economic growth is unprecedented in history: it took the country only 35 years to achieve growth that required centuries elsewhere. Yet South Korea is only part of a broader phenomenon, often referred to as the East Asian economic miracle. High growth rates first appeared in South Korea, Taiwan, Hong Kong, and Singapore but then spread across the region, most notably to China. Since 1975, the whole region has increased real GDP per capita by 6% per year, more than three times America's historical rate of growth.

How have the Asian countries achieved such high growth rates? The answer is that all of the sources of productivity growth have been firing on all cylinders. Very high savings rates, the percentage of GDP that is saved nationally in any given year, have allowed the countries to significantly increase the amount of physical capital per worker. Very good basic education has permitted a rapid improvement in human capital. And these countries have experienced substantial technological progress.

Why didn't any economy achieve this kind of growth in the past? Most economic analysts think that East Asia's growth spurt was possible because of its *relative* backwardness. That is, by the time that East Asian economies began to move into the modern world, they could benefit from adopting the technological advances that had been generated in technologically advanced countries such as the United States.

In 1900, the United States could not have moved quickly to a modern level of productivity because much of the technology that powers the modern economy, from jet planes to computers, hadn't been invented yet. In 1970, South Korea probably still had lower labor productivity than the United States had in 1900, but it could rapidly upgrade its productivity by adopting technology that had been developed in the United States, Europe, and Japan over the previous century. This was aided by a huge investment in human capital through widespread schooling.

The East Asian experience demonstrates that economic growth can be especially fast in countries that are playing catch-up to other countries with higher GDP per capita. On this basis, many economists have suggested a general principle known as the **convergence hypothesis.** It says that differences in real GDP per capita among countries tend to narrow over time because countries that start with lower real GDP per capita tend to have higher growth rates. We'll look at the evidence on the convergence hypothesis in the Economics in Action at the end of this section.

Even before we get to that evidence, however, we can say right away that starting with a relatively low level of real GDP per capita is no guarantee of rapid growth, as the examples of Latin America and Africa both demonstrate.

According to the **convergence hypothesis**, international differences in real GDP per capita tend to narrow over time.

## Latin America's Disappointment

In 1900, Latin America was not considered an economically backward region. Natural resources, including both minerals and cultivable land, were abundant. Some countries, notably Argentina, attracted millions of immigrants from Europe in search of a better life. Measures of real GDP per capita in Argentina, Uruguay, and southern Brazil were comparable to those in economically advanced countries.

Since about 1920, however, growth in Latin America has been disappointing. As Figure 9-8 shows in the case of Argentina, growth has been disappointing for many decades, until 2000 when it finally began to increase. The fact that South Korea is now much richer than Argentina would have seemed inconceivable a few generations ago.

Why did Latin America stagnate? Comparisons with East Asian success stories suggest several factors. The rates of savings and investment spending in Latin America have been much lower than in East Asia, partly as a result of irresponsible government policy that has eroded savings through high inflation, bank failures, and other disruptions. Education—especially broad basic education—has been underemphasized: even Latin American nations rich in natural resources often failed to channel that wealth into their educational systems. And political instability, leading to irresponsible economic policies, has taken a toll.

In the 1980s, many economists came to believe that Latin America was suffering from excessive government intervention in markets. They recommended opening the economies to imports, selling off government-owned companies, and, in general, freeing up individual initiative. The hope was that this would produce an East Asian–type economic surge. So far, however, only one Latin American nation, Chile, has achieved sustained rapid growth. It now seems that pulling off an economic miracle is harder than it looks. Although, in recent years Brazil and Argentina have seen their growth rates increase significantly as they exported large amounts of commodities to the advanced countries and rapidly developing China.

## Africa's Troubles and Promise

Africa south of the Sahara is home to about 780 million people, more than 2½ times the population of the United States. On average, they are very poor, nowhere close to U.S. living standards 100 or even 200 years ago. And economic progress has been both slow and uneven, as the example of Nigeria, the most populous nation in the region, suggests. In fact, real GDP per capita in sub-Saharan Africa actually fell 13 percent from 1980 to 1994, although it has recovered since then. The consequence of this poor growth performance has been intense and continuing poverty.

This is a very disheartening story. What explains it?

Several factors are probably crucial. Perhaps first and foremost is the problem of political instability. In the years since 1975, large parts of Africa have experienced savage civil wars (often with outside powers backing rival sides) that have killed millions of people and made productive investment spending impossible. The threat of war and general anarchy has also inhibited other important preconditions for growth, such as education and provision of necessary infrastructure.

Property rights are also a major problem. The lack of legal safeguards means that property owners are often subject to extortion because of government corruption, making them averse to owning property or improving it. This is especially damaging in a country that is very poor.

While many economists see political instability and government corruption as the leading causes of underdevelopment in Africa, some—most notably Jeffrey Sachs of Columbia University and the United Nations—believe the opposite. They argue that Africa is politically unstable because Africa is poor. And Africa's poverty, they go on to claim, stems from its extremely unfavorable geographic conditions—much of the continent is landlocked, hot, infested with tropical diseases, and cursed with poor soil.

Sachs, along with economists from the World Health Organization, has highlighted the importance of health problems in Africa. In poor countries, worker productivity is often severely hampered by malnutrition and disease. In particular, tropical diseases such as malaria can only be controlled with an effective public health infrastructure, something that is lacking in much of Africa. At the time of writing, economists are studying certain regions of Africa to determine whether modest amounts of aid given directly to residents for the purposes of increasing crop yields, reducing malaria, and increasing school attendance can produce self-sustaining gains in living standards.

Although the example of African countries represents a warning that long-run economic growth cannot be taken for granted, there are some signs of hope. As we noted in Figure 9-8, Nigeria's per capita GDP, after decades of stagnation, turned upward after 2000, achieving a 5.5% real GDP per capita growth rate in 2010. The same is true for sub-Saharan African economies as a whole. In 2011, real GDP per capita growth rates averaged around 5.5% across sub-Saharan African countries and are projected to be nearly 6% in 2012. Rising prices for their exports are part of the reason for recent success, but there is growing optimism among development experts that a period of relative peace and better government is ushering in a new era for Africa's economies.

## ECONOMICS > IN ACTION

### ARE ECONOMIES CONVERGING?

In the 1950s, much of Europe seemed quaint and backward to American visitors, and Japan seemed very poor. Today, a visitor to Paris or Tokyo sees a city that looks about as rich as New York. Although real GDP per capita is still somewhat higher in the United States, the differences in the standards of living among the United States, Europe, and Japan are relatively small.

Many economists have argued that this convergence in living standards is normal; the convergence hypothesis says that relatively poor countries should have higher rates of growth of real GDP per capita than relatively rich countries. And if we look at today's relatively well-off countries, the convergence hypothesis seems to be true. Panel (a) of Figure 9-9 shows data for a number of today's wealthy economies measured in 1990 dollars. On the horizontal axis is real GDP per capita in 1955; on the vertical axis is the average annual growth rate of real GDP per capita from 1955 to 2008. There is a clear negative relationship as can be seen from the line fitted through the points. The United States was the richest country in this group in 1955 and had the slowest rate of growth. Japan and Spain were the poorest countries in 1955 and had the fastest rates of growth. These data suggest that the convergence hypothesis is true.

But economists who looked at similar data realized that these results depend on the countries selected. If you look at successful economies that have a high standard of living today, you find that real GDP per capita has converged. But

FIGURE  **9-9**   Do Economies Converge?

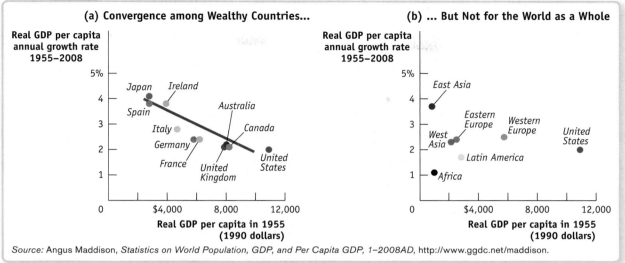

Source: Angus Maddison, *Statistics on World Population, GDP, and Per Capita GDP, 1–2008AD,* http://www.ggdc.net/maddison.

looking across the world as a whole, including countries that remain poor, there is little evidence of convergence. Panel (b) of Figure 9-9 illustrates this point using data for regions rather than individual countries (other than the United States). In 1955, East Asia and Africa were both very poor regions. Over the next 53 years, the East Asian regional economy grew quickly, as the convergence hypothesis would have predicted, but the African regional economy grew very slowly. In 1955, Western Europe had substantially higher real GDP per capita than Latin America. But, contrary to the convergence hypothesis, the Western European regional economy grew more quickly over the next 53 years, widening the gap between the regions.

So is the convergence hypothesis all wrong? No: economists still believe that countries with relatively low real GDP per capita tend to have higher rates of growth than countries with relatively high real GDP per capita, *other things equal.* But other things—education, infrastructure, rule of law, and so on—are often not equal. Statistical studies find that when you adjust for differences in these other factors, poorer countries do tend to have higher growth rates. This result is known as *conditional convergence.*

Because other factors differ, however, there is no clear tendency toward convergence in the world economy as a whole. Western Europe, North America, and parts of Asia are becoming more similar in real GDP per capita, but the gap between these regions and the rest of the world is growing.

## CHECK YOUR UNDERSTANDING  9-4

1. Some economists think the high rates of growth of productivity achieved by many Asian economies cannot be sustained. Why might they be right? What would have to happen for them to be wrong?

2. Consider Figure 9-9, panel (b). Based on the data there, which regions support the convergence hypothesis? Which do not? Explain.

3. Some economists think the best way to help African countries is for wealthier countries to provide more funds for basic infrastructure. Others think this policy will have no long-run effect unless African countries have the financial and political means to maintain this infrastructure. What policies would you suggest?

Solutions appear at back of book.

### ▼ Quick Review

● East Asia's spectacular growth was generated by high savings and investment spending rates, emphasis on education, and adoption of technological advances from other countries.

● Poor education, political instability, and irresponsible government policies are major factors in the slow growth of Latin America.

● In sub-Saharan Africa, severe instability, war, and poor infrastructure—particularly affecting public health—resulted in a catastrophic failure of growth. But economic performance in recent years has been much better than in preceding years.

● The **convergence hypothesis** seems to hold only when other things that affect economic growth—such as education, infrastructure, property rights, and so on—are held equal.

**Sustainable long-run economic growth** is long-run growth that can continue in the face of the limited supply of natural resources and the impact of growth on the environment.

# Is World Growth Sustainable?

E arlier in this chapter we described the views of Thomas Malthus, the early-nineteenth-century economist who warned that the pressure of population growth would tend to limit the standard of living. Malthus was right about the past: for around 58 centuries, from the origins of civilization until his own time, limited land supplies effectively prevented any large rise in real incomes per capita. Since then, however, technological progress and rapid accumulation of physical and human capital have allowed the world to defy Malthusian pessimism.

But will this always be the case? Some skeptics have expressed doubt about whether **sustainable long-run economic growth** is possible—whether it can continue in the face of the limited supply of natural resources and the impact of growth on the environment.

## Natural Resources and Growth, Revisited

In 1972 a group of scientists called The Club of Rome made a big splash with a book titled *The Limits to Growth,* which argued that long-run economic growth wasn't sustainable due to limited supplies of nonrenewable resources such as oil and natural gas. These "neo-Malthusian" concerns at first seemed to be validated by a sharp rise in resource prices in the 1970s, then came to seem foolish when resource prices fell sharply in the 1980s. After 2005, however, resource prices rose sharply again, leading to renewed concern about resource limitations to growth. Figure 9-10 shows the real price of oil—the price of oil adjusted for inflation in the rest of the economy. The rise, fall, and rise of concern about resource-based limits to growth have more or less followed the rise, fall, and rise of oil prices shown in the figure.

Differing views about the impact of limited natural resources on long-run economic growth turn on the answers to three questions:

- How large are the supplies of key natural resources?
- How effective will technology be at finding alternatives to natural resources?
- Can long-run economic growth continue in the face of resource scarcity?

FIGURE  **9-10**  The Real Price of Oil, 1949–2010

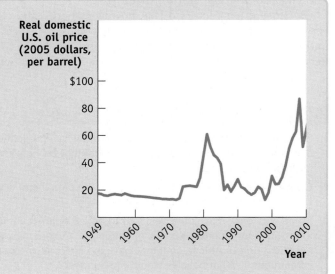

The real price of natural resources, like oil, rose dramatically in the 1970s and then fell just as dramatically in the 1980s. Since 2005, however, the real prices of natural resources have soared.
*Source:* Energy Information Administration.

It's mainly up to geologists to answer the first question. Unfortunately, there's wide disagreement among the experts, especially about the prospects for future oil production. Some analysts believe that there is enough untapped oil in the ground that world oil production can continue to rise for several decades. Others, including a number of oil company executives, believe that the growing difficulty of finding new oil fields will cause oil production to plateau—that is, stop growing and eventually begin a gradual decline—in the fairly near future. Some analysts believe that we have already reached that plateau.

The answer to the second question, whether there are alternatives to natural resources, has to come from engineers. There's no question that there are many alternatives to the natural resources currently being depleted, some of which are already being exploited. For example, "unconventional" oil extracted from Canadian tar sands is already making a significant contribution to world oil supplies, and electricity generated by wind turbines is rapidly becoming big business.

The third question, whether economies can continue to grow in the face of resource scarcity, is mainly a question for economists. And most, though not all, economists are optimistic: they believe that modern economies can find ways to work around limits on the supply of natural resources. One reason for this optimism is the fact that resource scarcity leads to high resource prices. These high prices in turn provide strong incentives to conserve the scarce resource and to find alternatives.

For example, after the sharp oil price increases of the 1970s, American consumers turned to smaller, more fuel-efficient cars, and U.S. industry also greatly intensified its efforts to reduce energy bills. The result is shown in Figure 9-11, which compares U.S. real GDP per capita and oil consumption before and after the 1970s energy crisis. In the United States before 1973, there seemed to be a more or less one-to-one relationship between economic growth and oil consumption. But after 1973 the U.S. economy continued to deliver growth in real GDP per capita even as it substantially reduced the use of oil. This move toward conservation paused after 1990, as low real oil prices encouraged consumers to shift back to gas-greedy larger cars and SUVs. But a sharp rise in oil prices

**FIGURE 9-11** U.S. Oil Consumption and Growth over Time

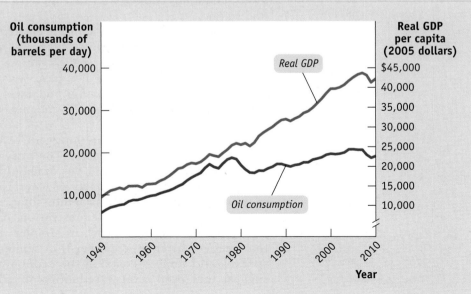

Until 1973, the real price of oil was relatively cheap and there was a more or less one-to-one relationship between economic growth and oil consumption. Conservation efforts increased sharply after the spike in the real price of oil in the mid-1970s. Yet the U.S. economy was still able to deliver growth despite cutting back on oil consumption.

*Sources:* Energy Information Administration; Bureau of Economic Analysis.

from 2005 to 2008, and again in 2010, encouraged renewed shifts toward oil conservation.

Given such responses to prices, economists generally tend to see resource scarcity as a problem that modern economies handle fairly well, and so not a fundamental limit to long-run economic growth. Environmental issues, however, pose a more difficult problem because dealing with them requires effective political action.

## Economic Growth and the Environment

Economic growth, other things equal, tends to increase the human impact on the environment. For example, China's spectacular economic growth has also brought a spectacular increase in air pollution in that nation's cities.

It's important to realize, however, that other things aren't necessarily equal: countries can and do take action to protect their environments. In fact, air and water quality in today's advanced countries is generally much better than it was a few decades ago. London's famous "fog"—actually a form of air pollution, which killed 4,000 people during a two-week episode in 1952—is gone, thanks to regulations that virtually eliminated the use of coal heat. The equally famous smog of Los Angeles, although not extinguished, is far less severe than it was in the 1960s and early 1970s, again thanks to pollution regulations.

Despite these past environmental success stories, there is widespread concern today about the environmental impacts of continuing economic growth, reflecting a change in the scale of the problem. Environmental success stories have mainly involved dealing with *local* impacts of economic growth, such as the effect of widespread car ownership on air quality in the Los Angeles basin. Today, however, we are faced with *global* environmental issues—the adverse impacts on the environment of the Earth as a whole by worldwide economic growth. The biggest of these issues involves the impact of fossil-fuel consumption on the world's climate.

Burning coal and oil releases carbon dioxide into the atmosphere. There is broad scientific consensus that rising levels of carbon dioxide and other gases are causing a greenhouse effect on the Earth, trapping more of the sun's energy and raising the planet's overall temperature. And rising temperatures may impose high human and economic costs: rising sea levels may flood coastal areas; changing climate may disrupt agriculture, especially in poor countries; and so on.

The problem of climate change is clearly linked to economic growth. Figure 9-12 shows carbon dioxide emissions from the United States, Europe, and China since 1980. Historically, the wealthy nations have been responsible for the bulk of these emissions because they have consumed far more energy per person than poorer countries. As China and other emerging economies have grown, however, they have begun to consume much more energy and emit much more carbon dioxide.

Is it possible to continue long-run economic growth while curbing the emissions of greenhouse gases? The answer, according to most economists who have studied the issue, is yes. It should be possible to reduce greenhouse gas emissions in a wide variety of ways, ranging from the use of non-fossil-fuel energy sources such as wind, solar, and nuclear power; to preventive measures such as carbon sequestration (capturing the carbon dioxide from power plants and storing it); to simpler things like designing buildings so that they're easier to keep warm in winter and cool in summer. Such measures would impose costs on the economy, but the best available estimates suggest that even a large reduction in greenhouse gas emissions over the

FIGURE   **9-12**   **Climate Change and Growth**

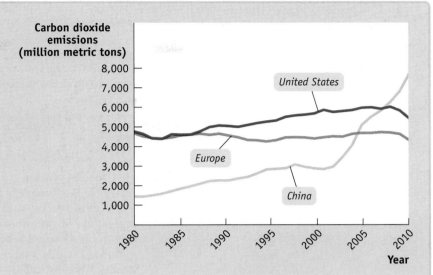

Greenhouse gas emissions are positively related to growth. As shown here by the United States and Europe, wealthy countries have historically been responsible for the great bulk of greenhouse gas emissions because of their richer and faster-growing economies. As China and other emerging economies have grown, they have begun to emit much more carbon dioxide.

*Source:* Energy Information Administration.

next few decades would only modestly dent the long-term rise in real GDP per capita.

The problem is how to make all of this happen. Unlike resource scarcity, environmental problems don't automatically provide incentives for changed behavior. Pollution is an example of a *negative externality*, a cost that individuals or firms impose on others without having to offer compensation. In the absence of government intervention, individuals and firms have no incentive to reduce negative externalities, which is why it took regulation to reduce air pollution in America's cities. And as Nicholas Stern, the author of an influential report on climate change, put it, greenhouse gas emissions are "the mother of all externalities."

So there is a broad consensus among economists—although there are some dissenters—that government action is needed to deal with climate change. There is also broad consensus that this action should take the form of market-based incentives, either in the form of a carbon tax—a tax per unit of carbon emitted—or a cap and trade system in which the total amount of emissions is capped, and producers must buy licenses to emit greenhouse gases. There is, however, considerable dispute about how much action is appropriate, reflecting both uncertainty about the costs and benefits and scientific uncertainty about the pace and extent of climate change.

There are also several aspects of the climate change problem that make it much more difficult to deal with than, say, smog in Los Angeles. One is the problem of taking the long view. The impact of greenhouse gas emissions on the climate is very gradual: carbon dioxide put into the atmosphere today won't have its full effect on the climate for several generations. As a result, there is the political problem of persuading voters to accept pain today in return for gains that will benefit their children, grandchildren, or even great-grandchildren.

There is also a difficult problem of international burden sharing. As Figure 9-12 shows, today's rich economies have historically been responsible for most greenhouse gas emissions, but newly emerging economies like China are responsible for most of the recent growth. Inevitably, rich countries are reluctant to pay the price of reducing emissions only to have their efforts frustrated by rapidly growing emissions from new players. On the other hand, countries like China, which are still relatively poor, consider it unfair that they should be expected to bear the burden of protecting an environment threatened by the past actions of rich nations.

The general moral of this story is that it is possible to reconcile long-run economic growth with environmental protection. The main question is one of getting political consensus around the necessary policies.

## ECONOMICS > IN ACTION

### THE COST OF CLIMATE PROTECTION

Reducing U.S. emissions of greenhouse gases over the long run would have few economic costs and many health benefits.

In recent years a number of bills have been introduced before the U.S. Congress, some of them with bipartisan sponsorship, calling for ambitious, long-term efforts to reduce U.S. emissions of greenhouse gases. For example, a bill sponsored by Senators Joseph Lieberman and John McCain would have used a cap and trade system to gradually reduce emissions over time, eventually—by 2050—reducing them to 60% below their 1990 level. Another bill, sponsored by Senators Barbara Boxer and Bernie Sanders, called for an 80% reduction by 2050.

Would implementing these bills, or others like them, put a stop to long-run economic growth? Not according to a comprehensive study by a team at MIT, which found that reducing emissions would impose significant but not overwhelming costs. Using an elaborate model of the interaction between environmental policy and the economy, the MIT group estimated that the Lieberman–McCain proposal would reduce real GDP per capita in 2050 by 1.11% and the more stringent Sanders–Boxer proposal would reduce real GDP per capita by 1.79%.

These may sound like big numbers—they would amount to between $200 billion and $250 billion today—but they would hardly make a dent in the economy's long-run growth rate. Remember that over the long run the U.S. economy has on average seen real GDP per capita rise by almost 2% a year. If the MIT group's estimates are correct, even a strong policy to avert climate change would, in effect, require that we give up less than one year's growth over the next four decades.

### ▼ Quick Review

- There's wide disagreement about whether it is possible to have **sustainable long-run economic growth.** However, economists generally believe that modern economies can find ways to alleviate limits to growth from natural resource scarcity through the price response that promotes conservation and the creation of alternatives.

- Overcoming the limits to growth arising from environmental degradation is more difficult because it requires effective government intervention. Limiting the emission of greenhouse gases would require only a modest reduction in the growth rate.

- There is broad consensus that government action to address climate change and greenhouse gases should be in the form of market-based incentives, like a carbon tax or a cap and trade system. It will also require rich and poor countries to come to some agreement on how the cost of emissions reductions will be shared.

### CHECK YOUR UNDERSTANDING 9-5

1. Are economists typically more concerned about the limits to growth imposed by environmental degradation or those imposed by resource scarcity? Explain, noting the role of negative externalities in your answer.

2. What is the link between greenhouse gas emissions and growth? What is the expected effect on growth from emissions reduction? Why is international burden sharing of greenhouse gas emissions reduction a contentious problem?

Solutions appear at back of book.

# BUSINESS CASE : Big Box Boom

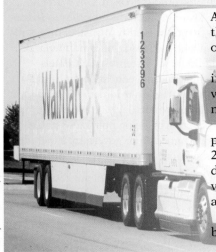

Courtesy Wal-Mart Stores, Inc.

After 20 years of being sluggish, U.S. productivity growth accelerated sharply in the late 1990s; that is, productivity began to grow at a much faster rate than previously. What caused that acceleration? Was it the rise of the Internet?

Not according to analysts at McKinsey and Co., the famous business consulting firm. They found that a major source of productivity improvement after 1995 was a surge in output per worker in retailing—stores were selling much more merchandise per worker.

Other analysts agree. Figure 9-13 shows the result of an analysis of total factor productivity growth in France, Germany, and the United States between 1995 and 2004, the decade of the U.S. productivity surge. As you can see, the United States did considerably better than either European nation. The key to the surge was very fast growth in the productivity of the distribution sector, that is, in wholesale and retail trade.

Why did productivity surge in retailing in the United States? "The reason can be explained in just two syllables: Walmart," wrote McKinsey.

Walmart is famed in the business world for its successful focus on the unglamorous but crucial area of *logistics*: getting stuff where it was needed, when it was needed. For example, it was one of the first companies to use computers to track inventory, to use bar-code scanners, to establish direct electronic links with suppliers, and so on. These practices gave it a huge advantage over competitors, leading to high profits and rapid expansion. Other firms, observing Walmart's success, have emulated its business practices, spreading productivity gains through the economy as a whole.

There are two lessons from the "Walmart effect," as McKinsey calls it. One is that how you apply a technology makes all the difference: everyone in the retail business knew about computers, but Walmart figured out what to do with them. The other is that a lot of economic growth comes from everyday improvements rather than flashy new technologies.

**FIGURE 9-13** U.S. and European Productivity Growth, 1995–2004

Annual average growth rate of total factor productivity

- Overall economy
- Distribution sector

France: 0.8%, 0.4%
Germany: 0.4%, 1.5%
United States: 1.4%, 3.2%

*Source*: Bart Van Ark, "Productivity, Sources of Growth and Potential Output in the Euro Area and the United States," *Intereconomics* 45, no. 1 (2010). Brussels: Center for European Policy Studies.

## QUESTIONS FOR THOUGHT

1. In the chapter we described several sources of productivity growth. Which of these sources corresponds to the "Walmart effect"?

2. How does our description of Walmart's role tie in with the New Growth Theory?

3. How does the Walmart story relate to the "information technology paradox"?

1. Growth is measured as changes in real GDP per capita in order to eliminate the effects of changes in the price level and changes in population size. Levels of real GDP per capita vary greatly around the world: more than half of the world's population lives in countries that are still poorer than the United States was in 1900. Over the course of the twentieth century, real GDP per capita in the United States increased more than fivefold.

2. Growth rates of real GDP per capita also vary widely. According to the **Rule of 70,** the number of years it takes for real GDP per capita to double is equal to 70 divided by the annual growth rate of real GDP per capita.

3. The key to long-run economic growth is rising **labor productivity,** or just **productivity,** which is output per worker. Increases in productivity arise from increases in **physical capital** per worker and **human capital** per worker as well as **technological progress.** The **aggregate production function** shows how real GDP per worker depends on these three factors. Other things equal, there are **diminishing returns to physical capital:** holding human capital per worker and technology fixed, each successive addition to physical capital per worker yields a smaller increase in productivity than the one before. Equivalently, more physical capital per worker results in a lower, but still positive, increase in productivity. **Growth accounting,** which estimates the contribution of each factor to a country's economic growth, has shown that rising **total factor productivity,** the amount of output produced from a given amount of factor inputs, is key to long-run growth. It is usually interpreted as the effect of technological progress. In contrast to earlier times, natural resources are a less significant source of productivity growth in most countries today.

4. The large differences in countries' growth rates are largely due to differences in their rates of accumulation of physical and human capital as well as differences in technological progress. Although inflows of foreign savings from abroad help, a prime factor is differences in domestic savings and investment spending rates, since most countries that have high investment spending in physical capital finance it by high domestic savings. Technological progress is largely a result of **research and development,** or **R&D.**

5. Governments can help or hinder growth. Government policies that directly foster growth are subsidies to **infrastructure,** particularly public health infrastructure, subsidies to education, subsidies to R&D, and maintenance of a well-functioning financial system that channels savings into investment spending, education, and R&D. Governments can enhance the environment for growth by protecting property rights (particularly intellectual property rights through patents), by being politically stable, and by providing good governance. Poor governance includes corruption and excessive government intervention.

6. The world economy contains examples of success and failure in the effort to achieve long-run economic growth. East Asian economies have done many things right and achieved very high growth rates. The low growth rates of Latin American and African economies over many years led economists to believe that the **convergence hypothesis,** the claim that differences in real GDP per capita across countries narrow over time, fits the data only when factors that affect growth, such as education, infrastructure, and favorable government policies and institutions, are held equal across countries. In recent years, there has been an uptick in growth among some Latin American and sub-Saharan African countries, largely due to a boom in commodity exports.

7. Economists generally believe that environmental degradation poses a greater challenge to **sustainable long-run economic growth** than does natural resource scarcity. Addressing environmental degradation requires effective governmental intervention, but the problem of natural resource scarcity is often well handled by the market price response.

8. The emission of greenhouse gases is clearly linked to growth, and limiting them will require some reduction in growth. However, the best available estimates suggest that a large reduction in emissions would require only a modest reduction in the growth rate.

9. There is broad consensus that government action to address climate change and greenhouse gases should be in the form of market-based incentives, like a carbon tax or a cap and trade system. It will also require rich and poor countries to come to some agreement on how the cost of emissions reductions will be shared.

Rule of 70, p. 244
Labor productivity, p. 246
Productivity, p. 246
Physical capital, p. 247
Human capital, p. 247
Technological progress, p. 247

Aggregate production function, p. 248
Diminishing returns to physical capital, p. 248
Growth accounting, p. 250
Total factor productivity, p. 251

Research and development (R&D), p. 255
Infrastructure, p. 256
Convergence hypothesis, p. 261
Sustainable long-run economic growth, p. 264

## PROBLEMS

1. The accompanying table shows data from the Penn World Table, Version 7.0, for real GDP per capita in 2005 U.S. dollars for Argentina, Ghana, South Korea, and the United States for 1960, 1970, 1980, 1990, 2000, and 2009.

   a. Complete the table by expressing each year's real GDP per capita as a percentage of its 1960 and 2009 levels.

   b. How does the growth in living standards from 1960 to 2009 compare across these four nations? What might account for these differences?

| | Argentina | | | Ghana | | | South Korea | | | United States | | |
|---|---|---|---|---|---|---|---|---|---|---|---|---|
| Year | Real GDP per capita (2005 dollars) | Percentage of 1960 real GDP per capita | Percentage of 2009 real GDP per capita | Real GDP per capita (2005 dollars) | Percentage of 1960 real GDP per capita | Percentage of 2009 real GDP per capita | Real GDP per capita (2005 dollars) | Percentage of 1960 real GDP per capita | Percentage of 2009 real GDP per capita | Real GDP per capita (2005 dollars) | Percentage of 1960 real GDP per capita | Percentage of 2009 real GDP per capita |
| 1960 | $6,243 | ? | ? | $603 | ? | ? | $1,782 | ? | ? | $15,438 | ? | ? |
| 1970 | $7,810 | ? | ? | $939 | ? | ? | $3,018 | ? | ? | $20,480 | ? | ? |
| 1980 | $8,638 | ? | ? | $807 | ? | ? | $5,339 | ? | ? | $25,090 | ? | ? |
| 1990 | $6,823 | ? | ? | $844 | ? | ? | $11,437 | ? | ? | $31,637 | ? | ? |
| 2000 | $9,172 | ? | ? | $887 | ? | ? | $18,926 | ? | ? | $39,175 | ? | ? |
| 2009 | $11,961 | ? | ? | $1,239 | ? | ? | $25,029 | ? | ? | $41,102 | ? | ? |

2. The accompanying table shows the average annual growth rate in real GDP per capita for Argentina, Ghana, and South Korea using data from the Penn World Table, Version 6.2, for the past few decades.

| | Average annual growth rate of real GDP per capita | | |
|---|---|---|---|
| Years | Argentina | Ghana | South Korea |
| 1960–1970 | 2.53% | 15.54% | 7.50% |
| 1970–1980 | 1.12 | 0.85 | 7.62 |
| 1980–1990 | −2.50 | 0.10 | 11.33 |
| 1990–2000 | 3.83 | 2.08 | 6.37 |

   a. For each decade and for each country, use the Rule of 70 where possible to calculate how long it would take for that country's real GDP per capita to double.

   b. Suppose that the average annual growth rate that each country achieved over the period 1990–2000 continues indefinitely into the future. Starting from 2000, use the Rule of 70 to calculate, where possible, the year in which a country will have doubled its real GDP per capita.

3. The accompanying table provides approximate statistics on per capita income levels and growth rates for regions defined by income levels. According to the Rule of 70, starting in 2010 the high-income countries are projected to double their per capita GDP in approximately 78 years, in 2088. Throughout this question, assume constant growth rates for each of the regions that are equal to their average value between 2000 and 2010.

| Region | GDP per capita (2010) | Average annual growth rate of real GDP per capita (2000–2010) |
|---|---|---|
| High-income countries | $38,293 | 0.9% |
| Middle-income countries | 3,980 | 4.8 |
| Low-income countries | 507 | 3.0 |

*Source:* World Bank.

   a. Calculate the ratio of per capita GDP in 2010 of the following:

   i. Middle-income to high-income countries

   ii. Low-income to high-income countries

   iii. Low-income to middle-income countries

   b. Calculate the number of years it will take the low-income and middle-income countries to double their per capita GDP.

   c. Calculate the per capita GDP of each of the regions in 2088. (*Hint:* How many times does their per capita GDP double in 78 years, the number of years from 2010 to 2088?)

   d. Repeat part a with the projected per capita GDP in 2088.

   e. Compare your answers to parts a and d. Comment on the change in economic inequality between the regions.

4. You are hired as an economic consultant to the countries of Albernia and Brittania. Each country's

current relationship between physical capital per worker and output per worker is given by the curve labeled "Productivity$_1$" in the accompanying diagram. Albernia is at point $A$ and Brittania is at point $B$.

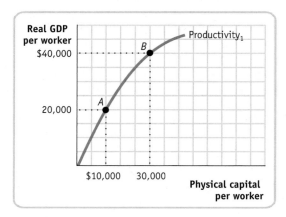

**a.** In the relationship depicted by the curve Productivity$_1$, what factors are held fixed? Do these countries experience diminishing returns to physical capital per worker?

**b.** Assuming that the amount of human capital per worker and the technology are held fixed in each country, can you recommend a policy to generate a doubling of real GDP per capita in Albernia?

**c.** How would your policy recommendation change if the amount of human capital per worker could be changed? Assume that an increase in human capital doubles the output per worker when physical capital per worker equals $10,000. Draw a curve on the diagram that represents this policy for Albernia.

**5.** The country of Androde is currently using Method 1 for its production function. By chance, scientists stumble onto a technological breakthrough that will enhance Androde's productivity. This technological breakthrough is reflected in another production function, Method 2. The accompanying table shows combinations of physical capital per worker and output per worker for both methods, assuming that human capital per worker is fixed.

| Method 1 | | Method 2 | |
|---|---|---|---|
| Physical capital per worker | Real GDP per worker | Physical capital per worker | Real GDP per worker |
| 0 | 0.00 | 0 | 0.00 |
| 50 | 35.36 | 50 | 70.71 |
| 100 | 50.00 | 100 | 100.00 |
| 150 | 61.24 | 150 | 122.47 |
| 200 | 70.71 | 200 | 141.42 |
| 250 | 79.06 | 250 | 158.11 |
| 300 | 86.60 | 300 | 173.21 |
| 350 | 93.54 | 350 | 187.08 |
| 400 | 100.00 | 400 | 200.00 |
| 450 | 106.07 | 450 | 212.13 |
| 500 | 111.80 | 500 | 223.61 |

**a.** Using the data in the accompanying table, draw the two production functions in one diagram. Androde's current amount of physical capital per worker is 100. In your figure, label that point $A$.

**b.** Starting from point $A$, over a period of 70 years, the amount of physical capital per worker in Androde rises to 400. Assuming Androde still uses Method 1, in your diagram, label the resulting point of production $B$. Using the Rule of 70, calculate by how many percent per year output per worker has grown.

**c.** Now assume that, starting from point $A$, over the same period of 70 years, the amount of physical capital per worker in Androde rises to 400, but that during that time period, Androde switches to Method 2. In your diagram, label the resulting point of production $C$. Using the Rule of 70, calculate by how many percent per year output per worker has grown now.

**d.** As the economy of Androde moves from point $A$ to point $C$, what share of the annual productivity growth is due to higher total factor productivity?

**6.** The Bureau of Labor Statistics regularly releases the "Productivity and Costs" report for the previous month. Go to www.bls.gov and find the latest report. (On the Bureau of Labor Statistics home page, from the tab "Subject Areas," select the link to "Labor Productivity & Costs"; then, from the heading "LPC News Releases," find the most recent "Productivity and Costs" report.) What were the percent changes in business and nonfarm business productivity for the previous quarter? How does the percent change in that quarter's productivity compare to data from the previous quarter?

**7.** What roles do physical capital, human capital, technology, and natural resources play in influencing long-run economic growth of aggregate output per capita?

**8.** How have U.S. policies and institutions influenced the country's long-run economic growth?

**9.** Over the next 100 years, real GDP per capita in Groland is expected to grow at an average annual rate of 2.0%. In Sloland, however, growth is expected to be somewhat slower, at an average annual growth rate of 1.5%. If both countries have a real GDP per capita today of $20,000, how will their real GDP per capita differ in 100 years? [*Hint:* A country that has a real GDP today of $x and grows at $y$% per year will achieve a real GDP of $x \times (1 + (y/100))^z$ in $z$ years. We assume that $0 \le y < 10$.]

**10.** The accompanying table shows data from the Penn World Table, Version 7.0, for real GDP per capita (2005 U.S. dollars) in France, Japan, the United Kingdom, and the United States in 1950 and 2009. Complete the table. Have these countries converged economically?

| | 1950 | | 2009 | |
|---|---|---|---|---|
| | Real GDP per capita (2005 dollars) | Percentage of U.S. real GDP per capita | Real GDP per capita (2005 dollars) | Percentage of U.S. real GDP per capita |
| France | $7,112 | ? | $30,821 | ? |
| Japan | 3,118 | ? | 31,958 | ? |
| United Kingdom | 10,401 | ? | 33,386 | ? |
| United States | 13,183 | ? | 41,102 | ? |

**11.** The accompanying table shows data from the Penn World Table, Version 7.0, for real GDP per capita (2005 U.S. dollars) for Argentina, Ghana, South Korea, and the United States in 1960 and 2009. Complete the table. Have these countries converged economically?

| | 1960 | | 2009 | |
|---|---|---|---|---|
| | Real GDP per capita (2005 dollars) | Percentage of U.S. real GDP per capita | Real GDP per capita (2005 dollars) | Percentage of U.S. real GDP per capita |
| Argentina | $6,243 | ? | $11,961 | ? |
| Ghana | 603 | ? | 1,239 | ? |
| South Korea | 1,782 | ? | 25,029 | ? |
| United States | 15,438 | ? | 41,102 | ? |

**12.** Why would you expect real GDP per capita in California and Pennsylvania to exhibit convergence but not in California and Baja California, a state of Mexico that borders the United States? What changes would allow California and Baja California to converge?

**13.** According to the *Oil & Gas Journal,* the proven oil reserves existing in the world in 2009 consisted of 1,342 billion barrels. In that year, the U.S. Energy Information Administration reported that the world daily oil production was 72.26 million barrels a day.

  **a.** At this rate, for how many years will the proven oil reserves last? Discuss the Malthusian view in the context of the number you just calculated.

  **b.** In order to do the calculations in part a, what did you assume about the total quantity of oil reserves

over time? About oil prices over time? Are these assumptions consistent with the Malthusian view on resource limits?

  **c.** Discuss how market forces may affect the amount of time the proven oil reserves will last, assuming that no new oil reserves are discovered and that the demand curve for oil remains unchanged.

**14.** The accompanying table shows the annual growth rate for the years 2000–2009 in per capita emissions of carbon dioxide ($CO_2$) and the annual growth rate in real GDP per capita for selected countries.

| | 2000–2009 average annual growth rate of: | |
|---|---|---|
| Country | Real GDP per capita | $CO_2$ emissions per capita |
| Argentina | 2.81% | 1.01% |
| Bangladesh | 4.17 | 5.47 |
| Canada | 0.68 | −1.46 |
| China | 9.85 | 11.11 |
| Germany | 0.59 | −1.23 |
| Ireland | 1.05 | −2.10 |
| Japan | 0.29 | −1.03 |
| South Korea | 3.48 | 1.68 |
| Mexico | 0.18 | 0.44 |
| Nigeria | 6.07 | −2.46 |
| Russia | 5.22 | 0.52 |
| South Africa | 2.39 | 0.80 |
| United Kingdom | 0.88 | −1.35 |
| United States | 0.58 | −1.78 |

*Sources:* Energy Information Administration; International Monetary Fund.

  **a.** Rank the countries in terms of their growth in $CO_2$ emissions, from highest to lowest. What five countries have the highest growth rate in emissions? What five countries have the lowest growth rate in emissions?

  **b.** Now rank the countries in terms of their growth in real GDP per capita, from highest to lowest. What five countries have the highest growth rate? What five countries have the lowest growth rate?

  **c.** Would you infer from your results that $CO_2$ emissions are linked to growth in output per capita?

  **d.** Do high growth rates necessarily lead to high $CO_2$ emissions?

 **www.worthpublishers.com/krugmanwells**

# CHAPTER 10

# Savings, Investment Spending, and the Financial System

## FUNDS FOR FACEBOOK

Facebook obtained millions of dollars in financing to pay for physical capital like the server farms it needed to expand.

Rainer Raffalski

> WHAT YOU WILL LEARN IN THIS CHAPTER

> ❯ The relationship between savings and investment spending

> ❯ Aspects of the **loanable funds market,** which show how savers are matched with borrowers

> ❯ The purpose of the five principal types of **financial assets:** stocks, bonds, **loans,** real estate, and **bank deposits**

> ❯ How **financial intermediaries** help investors achieve **diversification**

> ❯ Some competing views of what determines asset prices and why asset market fluctuations can be a source of macroeconomic instability

"**F**ACEBOOK IS HUNTING FOR More Money"—so read a 2009 headline in *Business Week,* which reported that the social networking site was seeking to borrow a $100 million credit line. Why would a wildly successful business like Facebook need to borrow money?

Everyone knows Facebook. Founded in 2004, it has gone on to become arguably the biggest business success story of the twenty-first century—so far. Currently, about 40% of Americans are reported to have Facebook pages. How did Facebook grow so big, so fast?

In large part, of course, the answer is that the company had a good idea. Personalized web pages providing information to friends turned out to be something many people really wanted. Equally important, since advertisers wanted access to the readers of those pages, Facebook could make a lot of money selling advertising space.

But having a good idea isn't enough to build a business. Entrepreneurs need funds: you have to spend money to make money. Although businesses like Facebook seem to exist solely in the virtual world of cyberspace, free of the worldly burdens of brick-and-mortar establishments, the

truth is that running such businesses requires a lot of very real and expensive hardware. Like Google, Yahoo!, and other Internet giants, Facebook maintains huge "server farms," arrays of linked computers that track and process all the information needed to provide the user experience.

So where did Facebook get the money to equip these server farms? Some of it came from investors who acquired shares in the business, but much of it was borrowed. As Facebook grew bigger, so did the amount it borrowed.

The ability of Facebook to raise large sums of money to finance its growth is, in its own way, as remarkable as the company's product. In effect, some young guy with a bright idea is able to lay his hands on hundreds of millions of dollars to build his business. It's an amazing story.

Yet this sort of thing is common in modern economies. The long-run growth we analyzed in the previous chapter depends crucially on a set of markets and institutions, collectively known as the *financial system,* that channels the funds of savers into productive investment spending. Without this system, businesses like Facebook would not be able

to purchase much of the physical capital that is an important source of productivity growth. And savers would be forced to accept a lower return on their funds. Historically, financial systems channeled funds into investment spending projects such as railroads and factories. Today, financial systems channel funds into new sources of growth such as green technology, social media, and investments in human capital. Without a well-functioning financial system, a country will suffer stunted economic growth.

In this chapter, we begin by focusing on the economy as a whole. We will examine the relationship between savings and investment spending. Next, we go behind this relationship and analyze the financial system, the means by which savings is transformed into investment spending. We'll see how the financial system works by creating assets, markets, and institutions that increase the welfare of both savers (those with funds to invest) and borrowers (those with investment spending projects to finance). Finally, we examine the behavior of financial markets and why they often resist economists' attempts at explanation. ∎

According to the **savings–investment spending identity,** savings and investment spending are always equal for the economy as a whole.

# Matching Up Savings and Investment Spending

We learned in the previous chapter that two of the essential ingredients in economic growth are increases in the economy's levels of *human capital* and *physical capital*. Human capital is largely provided by governments through public education. (In countries with a large private education sector, like the United States, private post-secondary education is also an important source of human capital.) But physical capital, with the exception of infrastructure, is mainly created through private investment spending—that is, spending by firms rather than by the government.

Who pays for private investment spending? In some cases it's the people or corporations that actually do the spending—for example, a family that owns a business might use its own savings to buy new equipment or a new building, or a corporation might reinvest some of its own profits to build a new factory. In the modern economy, however, individuals and firms that create physical capital often do it with other people's money—money that they borrow or raise by selling stock.

To understand how investment spending is financed, we need to look first at how savings and investment spending are related for the economy as a whole. Then we will examine how savings are allocated among investment spending projects.

## The Savings–Investment Spending Identity

The most basic point to understand about savings and investment spending is that they are always equal. This is not a theory; it's a fact of accounting called the **savings–investment spending identity.**

To see why the savings-investment spending identity must be true, let's look again at the national income accounting that we learned in Chapter 7. Recall that GDP is equal to total spending on domestically produced final goods and services, and that we can write the following equation (which is the same as Equation 7-1):

**(10-1)** $GDP = C + I + G + X - IM$

where $C$ is spending by consumers, $I$ is investment spending, $G$ is government purchases of goods and services, $X$ is the value of exports to other countries, and $IM$ is spending on imports from other countries.

### The Savings-Investment Spending Identity in a Closed Economy
In a closed economy, there are no exports or imports. So $X = 0$ and $IM = 0$, which makes Equation 10-1 simpler. As we learned in Chapter 7, the overall income of this simplified economy would, by definition, equal total spending. Why? Recall one of the basic principles of economics from Chapter 1, that one person's spending is another person's income: the only way people can earn income is by selling something to someone else, and every dollar spent in the economy creates income for somebody. This is represented by Equation 10-2: on the left, GDP represents total income earned in the economy, and on the right, $C + I + G$ represents total spending in the economy:

**(10-2)** $$GDP = C + I + G$$
Total income = Total spending

Now, what can be done with income? It can either be spent on consumption—consumer spending ($C$) plus government purchases of goods and service ($G$)—or saved ($S$). So it must be true that:

**PITFALLS**

**INVESTMENT VERSUS INVESTMENT SPENDING**

When macroeconomists use the term *investment spending*, they almost always mean "spending on new physical capital." This can be confusing, because in ordinary life we often say that someone who buys stocks or purchases an existing building is "investing." The important point to keep in mind is that only spending that adds to the economy's stock of physical capital is "investment spending." In contrast, the act of purchasing an asset such as a share of stock, a bond, or existing real estate is "making an investment."

**(10-3)** $$GDP = C + G + S$$
Total income = Consumption spending + Savings

where $S$ is savings. Meanwhile, as Equation 10-2 tells us, total spending consists of either consumption spending ($C + G$) or investment spending ($I$):

**(10-4)** $$GDP = C + G + I$$
Total income = Consumption spending + Investment spending

Putting Equations 10-3 and 10-4 together, we get:

**(10-5)** $$C + G + S = C + G + I$$
Consumption spending = Consumption Spending + Savings + Investment spending

Subtract consumption spending ($C + G$) from both sides, and we get:

**(10-6)** $$S = I$$
Savings = Investment spending

As we said, then, it's a basic accounting fact that savings equals investment spending for the economy as a whole.

Now, let's take a closer look at savings. Households are not the only parties that can save in an economy. In any given year, the government can save, too, if it collects more tax revenue than it spends. When this occurs, the difference is called a **budget surplus** and is equivalent to savings by government. If, alternatively, government spending exceeds tax revenue, there is a **budget deficit**—a negative budget surplus. In this case, we often say that the government is "dis-saving": by spending more than its tax revenues, the government is engaged in the opposite of savings. We'll define the term **budget balance** to refer to both cases, with the understanding that the budget balance can be positive (a budget surplus) or negative (a budget deficit). The budget balance is defined as:

**(10-7)** $S_{Government} = T - G - TR$

Where $T$ is the value of tax revenues and $TR$ is the value of government transfers. The budget balance is equivalent to savings by government—if it's positive, the government is saving; if it's negative, the government is dis-saving. **National savings,** which we just called savings, for short, is equal to the sum of the budget balance and private savings, where private savings is disposable income (income after taxes) minus consumption. It is given by:

**(10-8)** $S_{National} = S_{Government} + S_{Private}$

So Equations 10-6 and 10-8 tell us that, in a closed economy, the savings-investment spending identity has the following form:

**(10-9)** $S_{National} = I$
National savings = Investment

### The Savings-Investment Spending Identity in an Open Economy An

open economy is an economy in which goods and money can flow into and out of the country. This changes the savings-investment spending identity because savings need not be spent on investment spending projects in the same country in which the savings are generated. That's because the savings of people who live in any one country can be used to finance investment spending that takes place in other countries. So any given country can receive *inflows* of funds—foreign

The **budget surplus** is the difference between tax revenue and government spending when tax revenue exceeds government spending.

The **budget deficit** is the difference between tax revenue and government spending when government spending exceeds tax revenue.

The **budget balance** is the difference between tax revenue and government spending.

**National savings,** the sum of private savings and the budget balance, is the total amount of savings generated within the economy.

**Net capital inflow** is the total inflow of funds into a country minus the total outflow of funds out of a country.

savings that finance investment spending in that country. Any given country can also generate *outflows* of funds—domestic savings that finance investment spending in another country.

The net effect of international inflows and outflows of funds on the total savings available for investment spending in any given country is known as the **net capital inflow** into that country, equal to the total inflow of foreign funds minus the total outflow of domestic funds to other countries. Like the budget balance, a net capital inflow can be negative—that is, more capital can flow out of a country than flows into it. In recent years, the United States has experienced a consistent positive net capital inflow from foreigners, who view our economy as an attractive place to put their savings. In 2010, for example, net capital inflows into the United States were $471 billion.

It's important to note that, from a national perspective, a dollar generated by national savings and a dollar generated by capital inflow are not equivalent. Yes, they can both finance the same dollar's worth of investment spending. But any dollar borrowed from a saver must eventually be repaid with interest. A dollar that comes from national savings is repaid with interest to someone domestically—either a private party or the government. But a dollar that comes as capital inflow must be repaid with interest to a foreigner. So a dollar of investment spending financed by a capital inflow comes at a higher *national* cost—the interest that must eventually be paid to a foreigner—than a dollar of investment spending financed by national savings.

The fact that a net capital inflow represents funds borrowed from foreigners is an important aspect of the savings-investment spending identity in an open economy. Consider an individual who spends more than his or her income; that person must borrow the difference from others. Similarly, a country that spends more on imports than it earns from exports must borrow the difference from foreigners. And that difference, the amount of funds borrowed from foreigners, is the country's net capital inflow. As we will explain at greater length in Chapter 19, this means that the net capital inflow into a country is equal to the difference between imports and exports:

**(10-10)**   $NCI = IM - X$
Net capital inflow = Imports – Exports

Re-arranging Equation 10-1 we get:

**(10-11)** $I = (GDP - C - G) + (IM - X)$

Using Equation 10-3 and 10-9 we know that GDP – C – G is equal to National savings, so that:

**(10-12)** $I = S_{National} + (IM - X) = S_{National} + NCI$
Investment spending = National savings + Net capital inflow

So the application of the savings–investment spending identity to an economy that is open to inflows or outflows of capital means that investment spending is equal to savings, where savings is equal to national savings *plus* net capital inflow. That is, in an economy with a positive net capital inflow, some investment spending is funded by the savings of foreigners. And in an economy with a negative net capital inflow (that is, more capital is flowing out than flowing in), some portion of national savings is funding investment spending in other countries. In the United States in 2010, investment spending totaled $2,300 billion. Private savings totaled $3,119 billion, offset by a government budget deficit of $1,299 billion and supplemented by a net capital inflow of $471 billion. Notice that these numbers

## ⚠ PITFALLS

### THE DIFFERENT KINDS OF CAPITAL
It's important to understand clearly the three different kinds of capital: physical capital, human capital, and financial capital (as explained in the previous chapter):

1. Physical capital consists of manufactured resources such as buildings and machines.
2. Human capital is the improvement in the labor force generated by education and knowledge.
3. Financial capital is funds from savings that are available for investment spending. A country that has a positive net capital inflow is experiencing a flow of funds into the country from abroad that can be used for investment spending.

don't quite add up; because data collection isn't perfect, there is a "statistical discrepancy" of $9 billion. But we know that this is an error in the data, not in the theory, because the savings–investment spending identity must hold in reality.

It's also worth noting that 2010 was not a normal year. As we have pointed out in previous chapters, in 2008 the U.S. economy (along with the economies of many other nations) was struck by a severe financial crisis. This crisis led both to a plunge in investment spending and to large government budget deficits, effects that have continued up until the time of writing. In much of the rest of this chapter we'll focus on data from 2007, the last year before the crisis, because it gives a much better picture of what savings and investment look like in normal times.

Figure 10-1 shows what the savings–investment spending identity looked like in 2007 for two of the world's largest economies, those of the United States and Japan. To make the two economies easier to compare, we've measured savings and investment spending as percentages of GDP. In each panel the orange bars on the left show total investment spending and the multi-colored bars on the right show the components of savings. U.S. investment spending was 18.8% of GDP, financed by a combination of private savings (15.7% of GDP) and positive net capital inflow or capital inflow (5.2% of GDP) and partly offset by a government budget deficit (–1.6% of GDP). (These numbers sum to more than 18.8% due to statistical discrepancy.) Japanese investment spending was higher as a percentage of GDP, at 23.8%. It was financed by a higher level of private savings as a percentage of GDP (32.1%) and was offset by both a negative net capital inflow or capital outflow (–4.9% of GDP) and a budget deficit (–3.4% of GDP).

The economy's savings finance its investment spending. But how are these funds that are available for investment spending allocated among various projects? That is, what determines which projects get financed (such as Facebook's

**The Savings–Investment Spending Identity in Open Economies:**

FIGURE **10-1** The United States and Japan, 2007

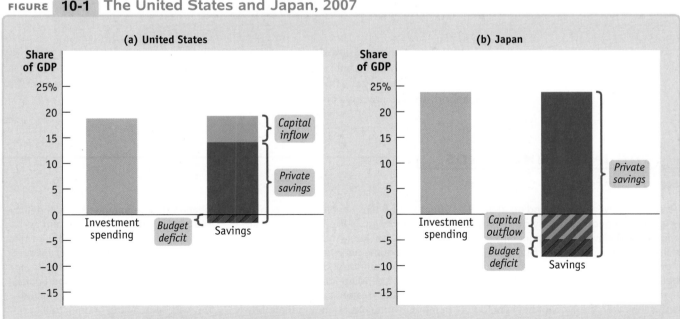

U.S. investment spending in 2007 (equal to 18.8% of GDP) was financed by a combination of private savings (15.7% of GDP) and a capital inflow (5.2% of GDP), which was partially offset by a government budget deficit (–1.6% of GDP). Japanese investment spending in 2007 was higher as a percentage of GDP (23.8%). It was financed by a higher level of private savings as a percentage of GDP (32.1%), which was offset by both a capital outflow (–4.9% of GDP) and a relatively high government budget deficit (–3.4% of GDP). *Source:* Bureau of Economic Analysis; OECD.

## GLOBAL COMPARISON

# AMERICA'S LOW SAVINGS

This figure shows national savings as a percentage of GDP for seven wealthy economies in 2007. (Again, we focus on 2007 as the last pre-crisis year). The United States had the lowest savings rate, although Britain's savings were only slightly higher.

In this respect, 2007 wasn't unusual. The United States has had consistently low national savings compared with other wealthy countries since the 1980s. The main source of these international differences in national savings lies in low U.S. private savings rather than in large U.S. government budget deficits.

Why do Americans save so little? The short answer is that economists aren't sure, although there are a number of theories. One is that consumers have easier access to credit in the United States than elsewhere. For example, Japanese lenders have traditionally demanded large down payments from home-buyers; but, until the recent housing bust, it

was possible for Americans to buy homes with little or no money down.

It's also argued that the U.S. Social Security system, by providing guaranteed income in retirement, may reduce the incentive for private saving. In any case, the United States has been able to maintain high levels of investment spending in spite of its low savings rate because it receives large positive net capital inflows.

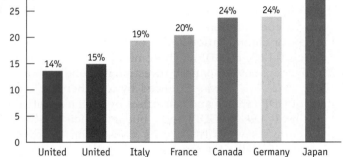

2007 savings rates (percent of GDP)

United States 14% | United Kingdom 15% | Italy 19% | France 20% | Canada 24% | Germany 24% | Japan 29%

*Source:* International Monetary Fund.
*Note:* IMF data differ slightly from other data sources.

server farms) and which don't (such as Microsoft's Courier tablet computer, an innovative concept that the software giant decided not to pursue)? We'll see shortly that funds get allocated to investment spending projects using a familiar method: by the market, via supply and demand.

## FOR INQUIRING MINDS

### WHO ENFORCES THE ACCOUNTING?

The savings–investment spending identity is a fact of accounting. By definition, savings equals investment spending for the economy as a whole. But who enforces the arithmetic? For example, what happens if the amount that businesses want to invest in capital equipment is less than the amount households want to save?

The short answer is that actual and *desired* investment spending aren't always equal. Suppose that households suddenly decide to save more by spending less—say, by putting off the purchase of new cars. The immediate

effect will be that unsold goods pile up—in this case, in the form of cars sitting in dealers' lots. And this increase in inventory counts as investment spending, albeit unintended. So the savings–investment spending identity still holds, because auto dealers end up engaging in more investment spending than they intended to. Similarly, if households suddenly decide to save less and spend more, inventories will drop—and this will be counted as *negative* investment spending.

A real-world example occurred in 2001. Savings and investment spending,

measured at an annual rate, both fell by $126 billion between the second and the fourth quarters of 2001. But on the investment spending side, $71 billion of that fall took the form of negative inventory investment spending. In particular, car dealers sold many of the vehicles that had been sitting on their lots.

Of course, businesses respond to changes in their inventories by changing their production. The inventory reduction in late 2001 prepared the ground for a spurt in output in early 2002. We'll examine the special role of inventories in economic fluctuations in Chapter 11.

# The Market for Loanable Funds

For the economy as a whole, savings always equals investment spending. In a closed economy, savings is equal to national savings. In an open economy, savings is equal to national savings plus capital inflow. At any given time, however, savers, the people with funds to lend, are usually not the same as borrowers, the people who want to borrow to finance their investment spending. How are savers and borrowers brought together?

Savers and borrowers are matched up with one another in much the same way producers and consumers are matched up: through markets governed by supply and demand. In Figure 7-1, the expanded circular-flow diagram, we noted that the *financial markets* channel the savings of households to businesses that want to borrow in order to purchase capital equipment. It's now time to take a look at how those financial markets work.

To do this, it helps to consider a somewhat simplified version of reality. As we noted in Chapter 7, there are a large number of different financial markets in the financial system, such as the bond market and the stock market. However, economists often work with a simplified model in which they assume that there is just one market that brings together those who want to lend money (savers) and those who want to borrow (firms with investment spending projects). This hypothetical market is known as the **loanable funds market.** The price that is determined in the loanable funds market is the interest rate, denoted by *r*. As we noted in Chapter 8, loans typically specify a nominal interest rate. So although we call *r* "the interest rate," it is with the understanding that *r* is a nominal interest rate—an interest rate that is unadjusted for inflation.

We're not quite done simplifying things. There are, in reality, many different kinds of interest rates, because there are many different kinds of loans— short-term loans, long-term loans, loans made to corporate borrowers, loans made to governments, and so on. In the interest of simplicity, we'll ignore those differences and assume that there is only one type of loan.

OK, now we're ready to analyze how savings and investment get matched up.

**The Demand for Loanable Funds** Figure 10-2 illustrates a hypothetical demand curve for loanable funds, *D*, which slopes downward. On the horizontal axis we show the quantity of loanable funds demanded. On the vertical axis

The **loanable funds market** is a hypothetical market that illustrates the market outcome of the demand for funds generated by borrowers and the supply of funds provided by lenders.

**FIGURE 10-2 The Demand for Loanable Funds**

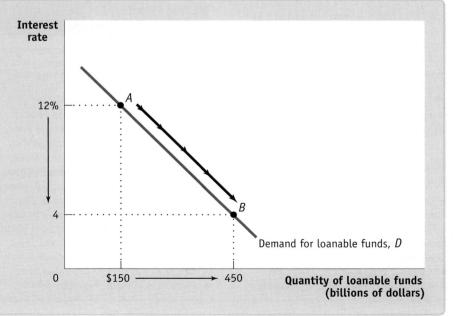

The demand curve for loanable funds slopes downward: the lower the interest rate, the greater the quantity of loanable funds demanded. Here, reducing the interest rate from 12% to 4% increases the quantity of loanable funds demanded from $150 billion to $450 billion.

The **present value** of X is the amount of money needed today in order to receive X at a future date given the interest rate.

we show the interest rate, which is the "price" of borrowing. But why does the demand curve for loanable funds slope downward?

To answer this question, consider what a firm is doing when it engages in investment spending—say, by buying new equipment. Investment spending means laying out money right now, expecting that this outlay will lead to higher profits at some point in the future. In fact, however, the promise of a dollar five or ten years from now is worth less than an actual dollar right now. So an investment is worth making only if it generates a future return that is *greater* than the monetary cost of making the investment today. How much greater? To answer that, we need to take into account the *present value* of the future return the firm expects to get. We examine the concept of present value in the accompanying For Inquiring Minds. Then, in the chapter's appendix, we show how the concept of present value can be applied to dollars earned multiple years in the future.

In present value calculations, we use the interest rate to determine how the value of a dollar in the future compares to the value of a dollar today. But the fact is that future dollars are worth less than a dollar today, and they are

## FOR INQUIRING MINDS

### USING PRESENT VALUE

An understanding of the concept of present value shows why the demand curve for loanable funds slopes downward. A simple way to grasp the essence of present value is to consider an example that illustrates the difference in value between having a sum of money today and having the same sum of money a year from now.

Suppose that exactly one year from today you will graduate, and you want to reward yourself by taking a trip that will cost $1,000. In order to have $1,000 a year from now, how much do you need today? It's not $1,000, and the reason why has to do with the interest rate. Let's call the amount you need today $X$. We'll use $r$ to represent the interest rate you receive on funds deposited in the bank. If you put $X$ into the bank today and earn interest rate $r$ on it, then after one year, the bank will pay you $X \times (1 + r)$. If what the bank will pay you a year from now is equal to $1,000, then the amount you need today is

$$X \times (1 + r) = \$1,000$$

You can apply some basic algebra to find that

$$X = \$1,000/(1 + r)$$

Notice that the value of $X$ depends on the interest rate $r$, which is always greater than 0. This fact implies that $X$ *is always less than* $1,000. For example, if $r$ = 5% (that is, $r$ = 0.05), then $X$ = $952.38. In other words, having

When making financial decisions, individuals and firms must always keep in mind that having $1,000 today is worth more than having $1,000 a year from now.

$952.38 today is equivalent to having $1,000 a year from now when the interest rate is 5%. That is, $952.38 is the value of $1,000 today given an interest rate of 5%. Now we can define the **present value** of $X$: it is the amount of money needed today in order to receive $X$ in the future given the interest rate. In this numerical example, $952.38 is the present value of $1,000 received one year from now given an interest rate of 5%.

The concept of present value also applies to decisions made by firms.

Think about a firm that has two potential investment projects in mind, each of which will yield $1,000 a year from now. However, each project has different initial costs—say, one requires that the firm borrow $900 right now and the other requires that the firm borrow $950. Which, if any, of these projects is worth borrowing money to finance and undertake?

The answer depends on the interest rate, which determines the present value of $1,000 a year from now. If the interest rate is 10%, the present value of $1,000 delivered a year from now is $909. So only the first project, which has an initial cost of less than $909, is profitable. With an interest rate of 10%, the return on any project costing more than $909 is less than the amount the firm had to repay on its loan and is therefore unprofitable. If the interest rate is only 5%, however, the present value of $1,000 rises to $952. At this interest rate, both projects are profitable because $952 exceeds both projects' initial cost. So a firm will borrow more and engage in more investment spending when the interest rate is lower.

Meanwhile, similar calculations will be taking place at other firms. So a lower interest rate will lead to higher investment spending in the economy as a whole: the demand curve for loanable funds slopes downward.

worth even less when the interest rate is higher. The intuition behind present value calculations is simple. The interest rate measures the opportunity cost of investment spending that results in a future return: instead of spending money on an investment spending project, a company could simply put the money into the bank and earn interest on it. And the higher the interest rate, the more attractive it is to simply put money into the bank instead of investing it in an investment spending project. In other words, the higher the interest rate, the higher the opportunity cost of investment spending. And, the higher the opportunity cost of investment spending, the lower the number of investment spending projects firms want to carry out, and therefore the lower the quantity of loanable funds demanded. It is this insight (discussed in the accompanying For Inquiring Minds) that explains why the demand curve for loanable funds is downward sloping.

When businesses engage in investment spending, they spend money right now in return for an expected payoff in the future. So, to evaluate whether a particular investment spending project is worth undertaking, a business must compare the present value of the future payoff with the current cost of that project. If the present value of the future payoff is greater than the current cost, a project is profitable and worth investing in. If the interest rate falls, then the present value of any given project rises, so more projects pass that test. If the interest rate rises, then the present value of any given project falls, then fewer projects pass that test. So total investment spending, and hence the demand for loanable funds to finance that spending, is negatively related to the interest rate. Thus, the demand curve for loanable funds slopes downward. You can see this in Figure 10-2. When the interest rate falls from 12% to 4%, the quantity of loanable funds demanded rises from $150 billion (point A) to $450 billion (point B).

**The Supply of Loanable Funds** Figure 10-3 shows a hypothetical supply curve for loanable funds, S. Again, the interest rate plays the same role that the price plays in ordinary supply and demand analysis. But why is this curve upward sloping?

FIGURE **10-3** The Supply of Loanable Funds

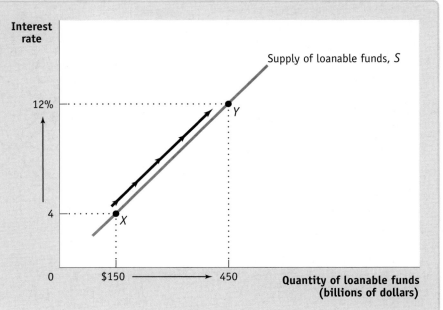

The supply curve for loanable funds slopes upward: the higher the interest rate, the greater the quantity of loanable funds supplied. Here, increasing the interest rate from 4% to 12% increases the quantity of loanable funds supplied from $150 billion to $450 billion.

The answer is that loanable funds are supplied by savers, and savers incur an opportunity cost when they lend to a business: the funds could instead be spent on consumption—say, a nice vacation. Whether a given saver becomes a lender by making funds available to borrowers depends on the interest rate received in return. By saving your money today and earning interest on it, you are rewarded with higher consumption in the future when the loan you made is repaid with interest. So it is a good assumption that more people are willing to forgo current consumption and make a loan to a borrower when the interest rate is higher. As a result, our hypothetical supply curve of loanable funds slopes upward. In Figure 10-3, lenders will supply $150 billion to the loanable funds market at an interest rate of 4% (point *X*); if the interest rate rises to 12%, the quantity of loanable funds supplied will rise to $450 billion (point *Y*).

**The Equilibrium Interest Rate** The equilibrium interest rate is the interest rate at which the quantity of loanable funds supplied equals the quantity of loanable funds demanded. As you can see in Figure 10-4, the equilibrium interest rate, *r**, and the total quantity of lending, *Q**, are determined by the intersection of the supply and demand curves, at point *E*. Here, the equilibrium interest rate is 8%, at which $300 billion is lent and borrowed. In this equilibrium, only investment spending projects that are profitable if the interest rate is 8% or higher are funded. Projects that would not be undertaken unless they are profitable only when the interest rate falls below 8% are not funded. Correspondingly, only lenders who are willing to accept an interest rate of 8% or less will have their offers to lend funds accepted; lenders who demand an interest rate higher than 8% do not have their offers to lend accepted.

Figure 10-4 shows how the market for loanable funds matches up desired savings with desired investment spending: in equilibrium, the quantity of funds that savers want to lend is equal to the quantity of funds that firms want to borrow. The figure also shows that this match-up is efficient, in two senses.

**FIGURE** **10-4** **Equilibrium in the Loanable Funds Market**

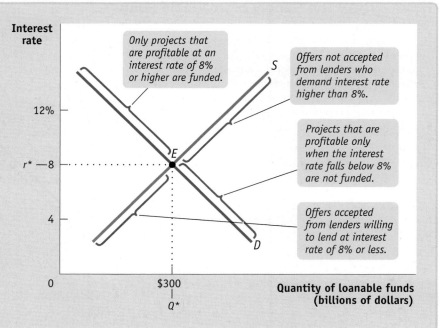

At the equilibrium interest rate, the quantity of loanable funds supplied equals the quantity of loanable funds demanded. Here, the equilibrium interest rate is 8%, with $300 billion of funds lent and borrowed. Lenders who demand an interest rate of 8% or lower have their offers of loans accepted; those who demand a higher interest rate do not. Projects that are profitable at an interest rate of 8% or higher are funded; those that are profitable only when the interest rate falls below 8% are not.

First, the right investments get made: the investment spending projects that are actually financed have higher payoffs (in terms of present value) than those that do not get financed. Second, the right people do the saving and lending: the savers who actually lend funds are willing to lend for lower interest rates than those who do not.

The insight that the loanable funds market leads to an efficient use of savings, although drawn from a highly simplified model, has important implications for real life. As we'll see shortly, it is the reason that a well-functioning financial system increases an economy's long-run economic growth rate.

Before we get to that, let's look at how the market for loanable funds responds to shifts of demand and supply. As in the standard model of supply and demand, where the equilibrium price changes in response to shifts of the demand or supply curves, here, the equilibrium interest rate changes when there are shifts of the demand curve for loanable funds, the supply curve for loanable funds, or both.

**Shifts of the Demand for Loanable Funds** Let's start by looking at the causes and effects of changes in demand.

The factors that can cause the demand curve for loanable funds to shift include the following:

1. *Changes in perceived business opportunities.* A change in beliefs about the payoff of investment spending can increase or reduce the amount of desired spending at any given interest rate. For example, during the 1990s there was great excitement over the business possibilities created by the Internet, which had just begun to be widely used. As a result, businesses rushed to buy computer equipment, put fiber-optic cables in the ground, and so on. This shifted the demand for loanable funds to the right. By 2001, the failure of many dot-com businesses had led to disillusionment with technology-related investment; this shifted the demand for loanable funds back to the left.

2. *Changes in government borrowing.* A government runs a budget deficit when, in a given year, it spends more than it receives. A government that runs budget deficits can be a major source of demand for loanable funds. As a result, changes in the government budget deficit can shift the demand curve for loanable funds. For example, between 2000 and 2003, as the U.S. federal government went from a budget surplus to a budget deficit, the government went from being a net saver that provided loanable funds to the market to being a net borrower, borrowing funds from the market. In 2000, net federal borrowing was *minus* $189 billion, as the federal government was paying off some of its pre-existing debt. But by 2003, net federal borrowing was *plus* $416 billion because the government had to borrow large sums to pay its bills. This change in the federal budget position had the effect, other things equal, of shifting the demand curve for loanable funds to the right.

Figure 10-5 shows the effects of an increase in the demand for loanable funds. $S$ is the supply of loanable funds, and $D_1$ is the initial demand curve. The initial equilibrium interest rate is $r_1$. An increase in the demand for loanable funds means that the quantity of funds demanded rises at any given interest rate, so the demand curve shifts rightward to $D_2$. As a result, the equilibrium interest rate rises to $r_2$.

The fact that an increase in the demand for loanable funds leads, other things equal, to a rise in the interest rate has one especially important implication: it tells us that increasing or persistent government budget deficits

FIGURE **10-5** An Increase in the Demand for Loanable Funds

If the quantity of funds demanded by borrowers rises at any given interest rate, the demand for loanable funds shifts rightward from $D_1$ to $D_2$. As a result, the equilibrium interest rate rises from $r_1$ to $r_2$.

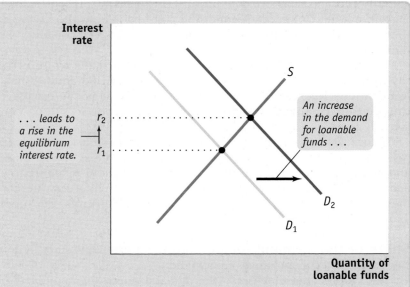

are cause for concern because an increase in the government's deficit shifts the demand curve for loanable funds to the right, which leads to a higher interest rate. If the interest rate rises, businesses will cut back on their investment spending. So, other things equal, a rise in the government budget deficit tends to reduce overall investment spending. Economists call the negative effect of government budget deficits on investment spending **crowding out.** Concerns about crowding out are one key reason to worry about increasing or persistent budget deficits.

However, it's important to add a qualification here: crowding out may not occur if the economy is depressed. When the economy is operating far below full employment, government spending can lead to higher incomes; and these higher incomes lead to increased savings at any given interest rate. Higher savings allows the government to borrow without raising interest rates. Many economists believe, for example, that the large budget deficits that the U.S. government ran from 2008 to 2012 (the time of writing), in the face of a depressed economy, caused little if any crowding out.

**Shifts of the Supply of Loanable Funds** Like the demand for loanable funds, the supply of loanable funds can shift. Among the factors that can cause the supply of loanable funds to shift are the following:

1. *Changes in private savings behavior.* A number of factors can cause the level of private savings to change at any given interest rate. For example, between 2000 and 2006 rising home prices in the United States made many homeowners feel richer, making them willing to spend more and save less. This had the effect of shifting the supply curve of loanable funds to the left.

2. *Changes in net capital inflows.* Capital flows into and out of a country can change as investors' perceptions of that country change. For example, Greece experienced large net capital inflows after the creation of the euro, Europe's common currency, in 1999, because investors believed that Greece's adoption of the euro as its currency had made it a safe place to put their funds. By 2009, however, worries about the Greek government's solvency (and the

**Crowding out** occurs when a government budget deficit drives up the interest rate and leads to reduced investment spending.

discovery that it had been understating its debt) led to a collapse in investor confidence, and the net inflow of funds dried up. The effect of shrinking capital inflows was to shift the supply curve in the Greek loanable funds market to the left.

As we've already seen, the United States has received large net capital inflows in recent years, with much of the money coming from China and the Middle East. Those inflows helped fuel a big increase in residential investment spending—newly constructed homes—from 2003 to 2006. As a result of the bursting of the U.S. housing bubble in 2008 and the subsequent deep recession, those inflows began to trail off in 2008.

Figure 10-6 shows the effects of an increase in the supply of loanable funds. $D$ is the demand for loanable funds, and $S_1$ is the initial supply curve. The initial equilibrium interest rate is $r_1$. An increase in the supply of loanable funds means that the quantity of funds supplied rises at any given interest rate, so the supply curve shifts rightward to $S_2$. As a result, the equilibrium interest rate falls to $r_2$.

**FIGURE  10-6  An Increase in the Supply of Loanable Funds**

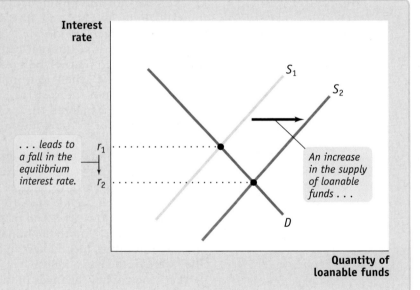

If the quantity of funds supplied by lenders rises at any given interest rate, the supply of loanable funds shifts rightward from $S_1$ to $S_2$. As a result, the equilibrium interest rate falls from $r_1$ to $r_2$.

. . . leads to a fall in the equilibrium interest rate.

An increase in the supply of loanable funds . . .

**Inflation and Interest Rates** Anything that shifts either the supply of loanable funds curve or the demand for loanable funds curve changes the interest rate. Historically, major changes in interest rates have been driven by many factors, including changes in government policy and technological innovations that created new investment opportunities. However, arguably the most important factor affecting interest rates over time—the reason, for example, that interest rates today are much lower than they were in the late 1970s and early 1980s—is changing expectations about future inflation, which shift both the supply and the demand for loanable funds.

To understand the effect of expected future inflation on interest rates, recall our discussion in Chapter 8 of the way inflation creates winners and losers—for example, the way that higher than expected U.S. inflation in the 1970s and 1980s reduced the real value of homeowners' mortgages, which was good for the homeowners but bad for the banks. In Chapter 8 we learned that economists summarize the effect of inflation on borrowers and lenders by distinguishing between the *nominal interest rate* and the *real interest rate,* where the difference is:

Real interest rate = Nominal interest rate – Inflation rate

The true cost of borrowing is the real interest rate, not the nominal interest rate. To see why, suppose a firm borrows $10,000 for one year at a 10% nominal interest rate. At the end of the year, it must repay $11,000—the amount borrowed plus the interest. But suppose that over the course of the year the average level of prices increases by 10%, so that the real interest rate is zero. Then the $11,000 repayment has the same purchasing power as the original $10,000 loan. In real terms, the borrower has received a zero-interest loan.

Similarly, the true payoff to lending is the real interest rate, not the nominal rate. Suppose that a bank makes a $10,000 loan for one year at a 10% nominal interest rate. At the end of the year, the bank receives an $11,000 repayment. But if the average level of prices rises by 10% per year, the purchasing power of the money the bank gets back is no more than that of the money it lent out. In real terms, the bank has made a zero-interest loan.

Now we can add an important detail to our analysis of the loanable funds market. Figures 10-5 and 10-6 are drawn with the vertical axis measuring the *nominal interest rate for a given expected future inflation rate.* Why do we use the nominal interest rate rather than the real interest rate? Because in the real world neither borrowers nor lenders know what the future inflation rate will be when they make a deal. Actual loan contracts therefore specify a nominal interest rate rather than a real interest rate. Because we are holding the expected future inflation rate fixed in Figures 10-5 and 10-6, however, changes in the nominal interest rate also lead to changes in the real interest rate.

The expectations of borrowers and lenders about future inflation rates are normally based on recent experience. In the late 1970s, after a decade of high inflation, borrowers and lenders expected future inflation to be high. By the late 1990s, after a decade of fairly low inflation, borrowers and lenders expected future inflation to be low. And these changing expectations about future inflation had a strong effect on the nominal interest rate, largely explaining why nominal interest rates were much lower in the early years of the twenty-first century than they were in the early 1980s.

Let's look at how changes in the expected future rate of inflation are reflected in the loanable funds model.

In Figure 10-7, the curves $S_0$ and $D_0$ show the supply and demand for loanable funds given that the expected future rate of inflation is 0%. In that case, equilibrium is at $E_0$ and the equilibrium nominal interest rate is 4%. Because expected future inflation is 0%, the equilibrium expected real interest rate over the life of the loan is also 4%.

Now suppose that the expected future inflation rate rises to 10%. The demand curve for loanable funds shifts upward to $D_{10}$: borrowers are now willing to borrow as much at a nominal interest rate of 14% as they were previously willing to borrow at 4%. That's because with a 10% inflation rate, a 14% nominal interest rate corresponds to a 4% real interest rate. Similarly, the supply curve of loanable funds shifts upward to $S_{10}$: lenders require a nominal interest rate of 14% to persuade them to lend as much as they would previously have lent at 4%. The new equilibrium is at $E_{10}$: the result of an expected future inflation rate of 10% is that the equilibrium nominal interest rate rises from 4% to 14%.

FIGURE **10-7** The Fisher Effect

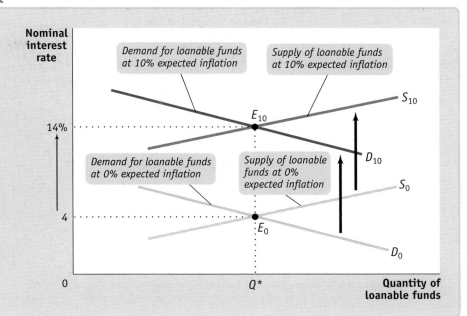

$D_0$ and $S_0$ are the demand and supply curves for loanable funds when the expected future inflation rate is 0%. At an expected inflation rate of 0%, the equilibrium nominal interest rate is 4%. An increase in expected future inflation pushes both the demand and supply curves upward by 1 percentage point for every percentage point increase in expected future inflation. $D_{10}$ and $S_{10}$ are the demand and supply curves for loanable funds when the expected future inflation rate is 10%. The 10 percentage point increase in expected future inflation raises the equilibrium nominal interest rate to 14%. The expected real interest rate remains at 4%, and the equilibrium quantity of loanable funds also remains unchanged.

This situation can be summarized as a general principle, known as the **Fisher effect** (after the American economist Irving Fisher, who proposed it in 1930): *The expected real interest rate is unaffected by changes in expected future inflation.* According to the Fisher effect, an increase in expected future inflation drives up the nominal interest rate, where each additional percentage point of expected future inflation drives up the nominal interest rate by 1 percentage point. The central point is that both lenders and borrowers base their decisions on the expected real interest rate. As a result, a change in the expected rate of inflation does not affect the equilibrium quantity of loanable funds or the expected real interest rate; all it affects is the equilibrium nominal interest rate.

## ECONOMICS ▸ *IN ACTION*

### FIFTY YEARS OF U.S. INTEREST RATES

There have been some large movements in U.S. interest rates over the past half-century. These movements clearly show how both changes in expected future inflation and changes in the expected return on investment spending move interest rates.

Panel (a) of Figure 10-8 illustrates the first effect. It shows the average interest rate on bonds issued by the U.S. government—specifically, bonds for which the government promises to repay the full amount after 10 years—from 1960 to mid-2011, along with the rate of consumer price inflation over the same period. As you can see, the big story about interest rates is the way they soared in the 1970s, before coming back down in the 1980s. It's not hard to see why that happened: inflation shot up during the 1970s, leading to widespread expectations that high inflation would continue. And as we've seen, expected inflation raises the equilibrium interest rate. As inflation came down in the 1980s, so did expectations of future inflation, and this brought interest rates down as well.

According to the **Fisher effect,** an increase in expected future inflation drives up the nominal interest rate, leaving the expected real interest rate unchanged.

FIGURE **10-8** Changes in U.S. Interest Rates Over Time

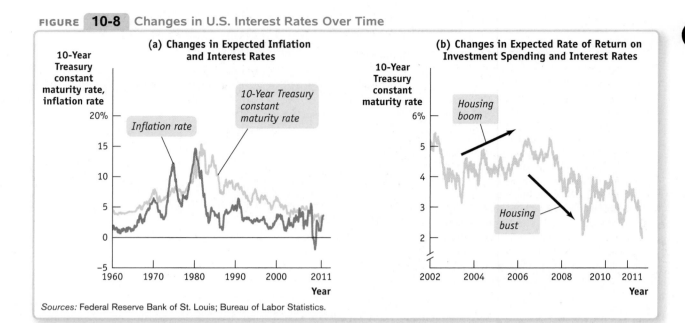

*Sources:* Federal Reserve Bank of St. Louis; Bureau of Labor Statistics.

## ▼ Quick Review

- The **savings–investment spending identity** is an accounting fact: savings is equal to investment spending for the economy as a whole.

- The government is a source of savings when it runs a positive **budget balance,** a **budget surplus.** It is a source of dis-savings when it runs a negative budget balance, a **budget deficit.**

- Savings is equal to **national savings** plus **net capital inflow,** which may be either positive or negative.

- When costs or benefits arrive at different times, you must take the complication created by time into account. This is done by transforming any dollars realized in the future into their **present value.**

- The **loanable funds market** matches savers to borrowers. In equilibrium, only investment spending projects with an expected return greater than or equal to the equilibrium interest rate are funded.

- Because the government competes with private borrowers in the loanable funds market, a government deficit can cause **crowding out.** However, crowding out is unlikely when the economy is in a slump.

- Higher expected future inflation raises the nominal interest rate through the **Fisher effect,** leaving the real interest rate unchanged.

Panel (b) illustrates the second effect: changes in the expected return on investment spending and interest rates, with a "close-up" of interest rates from 2002 to 2011. Notice the rise in interest rates during the middle years of the last decade, followed by a sharp drop. We know from other evidence (such as surveys of investor opinion) that expected inflation didn't change much over those years. What happened, instead, was the boom and bust in housing: interest rates rose as demand for housing soared, pushing the demand curve for loanable funds to the right, then fell as the housing boom collapsed, shifting the demand curve for loanable funds back to the left.

Throughout this whole process, total savings was equal to total investment spending, and the rise and fall of the interest rate played a key role in matching lenders with borrowers.

## CHECK YOUR UNDERSTANDING 10-1

1. Use a diagram of the loanable funds market to illustrate the effect of the following events on the equilibrium interest rate and investment spending.

   **a.** An economy is opened to international movements of capital, and a net capital inflow occurs.

   **b.** Retired people generally save less than working people at any interest rate. The proportion of retired people in the population goes up.

2. Explain what is wrong with the following statement: "Savings and investment spending may not be equal in the economy as a whole because when the interest rate rises, households will want to save more money than businesses will want to invest."

3. Suppose that expected inflation rises from 3% to 6%.

   **a.** How will the real interest rate be affected by this change?

   **b.** How will the nominal interest rate be affected by this change?

   **c.** What will happen to the equilibrium quantity of loanable funds?

Solutions appear at back of book.

# The Financial System

A well-functioning financial system that brought together the funds of investors and the ideas of brilliant nerds made the rise of Facebook possible. But to think that this is an exclusively modern phenomenon would be misguided. Financial markets raised the funds that were used to develop colonial markets in India, to build canals across Europe, and to finance the Napoleonic wars in the eighteenth and early nineteenth centuries. Capital inflows financed the early economic development of the United States, funding investment spending in mining, railroads, and canals. In fact, many of the principal features of financial markets and assets have been well understood in Europe and the United States since the eighteenth century. These features are no less relevant today. So let's begin by understanding exactly what is traded in financial markets.

Financial markets are where households invest their current savings and their accumulated savings, or **wealth,** by purchasing *financial assets.* A **financial asset** is a paper claim that entitles the buyer to future income from the seller. For example, when a saver lends funds to a company, the loan is a financial asset sold by the company that entitles the lender (the buyer of the financial asset) to future income from the company. A household can also invest its current savings or wealth by purchasing a **physical asset,** a tangible object that can be used to generate future income such as a preexisting house or preexisting piece of equipment. It gives the owner the right to dispose of the object as he or she wishes (for example, rent it or sell it).

Recall that the purchase of a financial or physical asset is typically called investing. So if you purchase a preexisting piece of equipment—say, a used airliner—you are investing in a physical asset. In contrast, if you spend funds that *add* to the stock of physical capital in the economy—say, purchasing a newly manufactured airplane—you are engaging in investment spending. (See the Pitfalls on investment versus investment spending that appears earlier in the chapter.)

If you get a loan from your local bank—say, to buy a new car—you and the bank are creating a financial asset: your loan. A *loan* is one important kind of financial asset in the real world, one that is owned by the lender—in this case, your local bank. In creating that loan, you and the bank are also creating a **liability,** a requirement to pay income in the future. So although your loan is a financial asset from the bank's point of view, it is a liability from your point of view: a requirement that you repay the loan, including any interest. In addition to loans, there are three other important kinds of financial assets: stocks, bonds, and *bank deposits.* Because a financial asset is a claim to future income that someone has to pay, it is also someone else's liability. We'll explain in detail shortly who bears the liability for each type of financial asset.

These four types of financial assets—loans, stocks, bonds, and bank deposits—exist because the economy has developed a set of specialized markets, like the stock market and the bond market, and specialized institutions, like banks, that facilitate the flow of funds from lenders to borrowers. In Chapter 7, in the context of the circular-flow diagram, we defined the financial markets and institutions that make up the financial system. A well-functioning financial system is a critical ingredient in achieving long-run growth because it encourages greater savings and investment spending. It also ensures that savings and investment spending are undertaken efficiently. To understand how this occurs, we first need to know what tasks the financial system needs to accomplish. Then we can see how the job gets done.

## Three Tasks of a Financial System

Our earlier analysis of the loanable funds market ignored three important problems facing borrowers and lenders: *transaction costs, risk,* and the desire for *liquidity.* The three tasks of a financial system are to reduce these problems in a cost-effective way. Doing so enhances the efficiency of financial markets: it

A household's **wealth** is the value of its accumulated savings.

A **financial asset** is a paper claim that entitles the buyer to future income from the seller.

A **physical asset** is a tangible object that can be used to generate future income.

A **liability** is a requirement to pay income in the future.

**Transaction costs** are the expenses of negotiating and executing a deal.

**Financial risk** is uncertainty about future outcomes that involve financial losses or gains.

makes it more likely that lenders and borrowers will make mutually beneficial trades—trades that make society as a whole richer. We'll turn now to examining how financial assets are designed and how institutions are developed to cope with these problems.

### Task 1: Reducing Transaction Costs
**Transaction costs** are the expenses of actually putting together and executing a deal. For example, arranging a loan requires spending time and money negotiating the terms of the deal, verifying the borrower's ability to pay, drawing up and executing legal documents, and so on. Suppose a large business decided that it wanted to raise $1 billion for investment spending. No individual would be willing to lend that much. And negotiating individual loans from thousands of different people, each willing to lend a modest amount, would impose very large total costs because each individual transaction would incur a cost. Total costs would be so large that the entire deal would probably be unprofitable for the business.

Fortunately, that's not necessary: when large businesses want to borrow money, they either go to a bank or sell bonds in the bond market. Obtaining a loan from a bank avoids large transaction costs because it involves only a single borrower and a single lender. We'll explain more about how bonds work in the next section. For now, it is enough to know that the principal reason there is a bond market is that it allows companies to borrow large sums of money without incurring large transaction costs.

### Task 2: Reducing Risk
A second problem that real-world borrowers and lenders face is **financial risk,** uncertainty about future outcomes that involve financial losses or gains. Financial risk, or simply risk, is a problem because the future is uncertain, containing the potential for losses as well as gains. For example, owning and driving a car entails the financial risk of a costly accident. Most people view potential losses and gains in an *asymmetrical* way: most people experience the loss in welfare from losing a given amount of money more intensely than they experience the increase in welfare from gaining the same amount of money. A person who is more sensitive to a loss than to a gain of an equal dollar amount is called *risk-averse*. Most people are risk-averse, although to differing degrees. For example, people who are wealthy are typically less risk-averse than those who are not so well-off.

A well-functioning financial system helps people reduce their exposure to risk, which risk-averse people would like to do. Suppose the owner of a business expects to make a greater profit if she buys additional capital equipment, but she isn't completely sure that this will indeed happen. She could pay for the equipment by using her savings or selling her house. But if the profit is significantly less than expected, she will have lost her savings, or her house, or both. That is, she would be exposing herself to a lot of risk due to uncertainty about how well or poorly the business performs. (This is why business owners, who typically have a significant portion of their own personal wealth tied up in their businesses, are usually people who are more tolerant of risk than the average person.)

So, being risk-averse, this business owner wants to share the risk of purchasing new capital equipment with someone, even if that requires sharing some of the profit if all goes well. How can she do this? By selling shares of her company to other people and using the money she receives from selling shares, rather than money from the sale of her other assets, to finance the equipment purchase. By selling shares in her company, she reduces her personal losses if the profit is less than expected: she won't have lost her other assets. But if things go well, the shareholders earn a share of the profit as a return on their investment.

By selling a share of her business, the owner has achieved *diversification:* she has been able to invest in several things in a way that lowers her total risk. She has maintained her investment in her bank account, a financial asset; in ownership of her house, a physical asset; and in ownership of the unsold portion of her business, a financial asset. These investments are likely to carry some risk of their own; for example, her bank may fail or her house may burn down (though in the modern United States it is likely that she is partly protected against these risks by insurance).

But even in the absence of insurance, she is better off having maintained investments in these different assets because their different risks are *unrelated,* or *independent, events.* This means, for example, that her house is no more likely to burn down if her business does poorly and that her bank is no more likely to fail if her house burns down. To put it another way, if one asset performs poorly, it is very likely that her other assets will be unaffected and, as a result, her total risk of loss has been reduced. But if she had invested all her wealth in her business, she would have faced the prospect of losing everything if the business had performed poorly. By engaging in **diversification**—investing in several assets with unrelated, or independent, risks—our business owner has lowered her total risk of loss.

The desire of individuals to reduce their total risk by engaging in diversification is why we have stocks and a stock market. In the next section on types of financial assets, we'll explain in more detail how certain features of the stock market increase the ability of individuals to manage and reduce risk.

**Task 3: Providing Liquidity**  The third and final task of the financial system is to provide investors with *liquidity,* a concern that—like risk—arises because the future is uncertain. Suppose that, having made a loan, a lender suddenly finds himself in need of cash—say, to meet a medical emergency. Unfortunately, if that loan was made to a business that used it to buy new equipment, the business cannot repay the loan on short notice to satisfy the lender's need to recover his money. Knowing in advance that there is a danger of needing to get his money back before the term of the loan is up, our lender might be reluctant to lock up his money by lending it to a business.

An asset is **liquid** if it can be quickly converted into cash with relatively little loss of value, **illiquid** if it cannot. As we'll see, stocks and bonds are a partial answer to the problem of liquidity. Banks provide an additional way for individuals to hold liquid assets and still finance illiquid investment spending projects.

To help lenders and borrowers make mutually beneficial deals, then, the economy needs ways to reduce transaction costs, to reduce and manage risk through diversification, and to provide liquidity. How does it achieve these tasks?

## Types of Financial Assets

In the modern economy there are four main types of financial assets: *loans,* bonds, stocks, and *bank deposits.* In addition, financial innovation has allowed the creation of a wide range of *loan-backed securities.* Each serves a somewhat different purpose. We'll examine loans, bonds, stocks, and loan-backed securities now, reserving our discussion of bank deposits until the following section.

**Loans**  A **loan** is a lending agreement between an individual lender and an individual borrower. Most people encounter loans in the form of a student loan or a bank loan to finance the purchase of a car or a house. And small businesses usually use bank loans to buy new equipment.

The good aspect of loans is that a given loan is usually tailored to the needs of the borrower. Before a small business can get a loan, it usually has to discuss its business plans, its profits, and so on with the lender. This results in a loan that meets the borrower's needs and ability to pay.

The bad aspect of loans is that making a loan to an individual person or a business typically involves a lot of transaction costs, such as the cost of negotiating the terms of the loan, investigating the borrower's credit history and ability to repay, and so on. To minimize these costs, large borrowers such as major corporations and governments often take a more streamlined approach: they sell (or issue) bonds.

An individual can engage in **diversification** by investing in several different things so that the possible losses are independent events.

An asset is **liquid** if it can be quickly converted into cash with relatively little loss of value.

An asset is **illiquid** if it cannot be quickly converted into cash with relatively little loss of value.

A **loan** is a lending agreement between an individual lender and an individual borrower.

A **default** occurs when a borrower fails to make payments as specified by the loan or bond contract.

A **loan-backed security** is an asset created by pooling individual loans and selling shares in that pool.

**Bonds** As we learned in Chapter 7, a bond is an IOU issued by the borrower. Normally, the seller of the bond promises to pay a fixed sum of interest each year and to repay the principal—the value stated on the face of the bond—to the owner of the bond on a particular date. So a bond is a financial asset from its owner's point of view and a liability from its issuer's point of view. A bond issuer sells a number of bonds with a given interest rate and maturity date to whoever is willing to buy them, a process that avoids costly negotiation of the terms of a loan with many individual lenders.

Bond purchasers can acquire information free of charge on the quality of the bond issuer, such as the bond issuer's credit history, from bond-rating agencies rather than having to incur the expense of investigating it themselves. A particular concern for investors is the possibility of **default,** the risk that the bond issuer will fail to make payments as specified by the bond contract. Once a bond's risk of default has been rated, it can be sold on the bond market as a more or less standardized product—a product with clearly defined terms and quality. In general, bonds with a higher default risk must pay a higher interest rate to attract investors.

Another important advantage of bonds is that they are easy to resell. This provides liquidity to bond purchasers. Indeed, a bond will often pass through many hands before it finally comes due. Loans, in contrast, are much more difficult to resell because, unlike bonds, they are not standardized: they differ in size, quality, terms, and so on. This makes them a lot less liquid than bonds.

**Loan-Backed Securities** **Loan-backed securities,** assets created by pooling individual loans and selling shares in that pool (a process called *securitization*), have become extremely popular over the past two decades. While mortgage-backed securities, in which thousands of individual home mortgages are pooled and shares sold to investors, are the best-known example, securitization has also been widely applied to student loans, credit card loans, and auto loans. These loan-backed securities are traded on financial markets like bonds; they are preferred by investors because they provide more diversification and liquidity than individual loans. However, with so many loans packaged together, it can be difficult to assess the true quality of the asset. That difficulty came to haunt investors during the financial crisis of 2008, when the bursting of the housing bubble led to widespread defaults on mortgages and large losses for holders of "supposedly safe" mortgage-backed securities, pain that spread throughout the entire financial system.

**Stocks** As we learned in Chapter 7, a stock is a share in the ownership of a company. A share of stock is a financial asset from its owner's point of view and a liability from the company's point of view. Not all companies sell shares of their stock; "privately held" companies are owned by an individual or a few partners, who get to keep all of the company's profit. Most large companies, however, do sell stock. For example, Microsoft has nearly 11 billion shares outstanding; if you buy one of those shares, you are entitled to one-eleven billionth of the company's profit, as well as 1 of 11 billion votes on company decisions.

Why does Microsoft, historically a very profitable company, allow you to buy a share in its ownership? Why don't Bill Gates and Paul Allen, the two founders of Microsoft, keep complete ownership for themselves and just sell bonds for their investment spending needs? The reason, as we have just learned, is risk: few individuals are risk-tolerant enough to face the risk involved in being the sole owner of a large company.

Reducing the risk that business owners face, however, is not the only way in which the existence of stocks improves society's welfare: it also improves the welfare of investors who buy stocks. Shareowners are able to enjoy the higher returns over time that stocks generally offer in comparison to bonds. Over the past century, stocks have typically yielded about 7% after adjusting for inflation; bonds have yielded only about 2%. But as investment companies warn you, "past performance is no guarantee of future performance." And there is a downside: owning the stock of a given company is riskier than owning a bond issued by the same company. Why? Loosely speaking, a bond is a promise while a stock is a hope: by law, a company must pay what it owes its lenders before it distributes any profit to its shareholders. And if the company should fail (that is, be unable to pay its interest obligations and declare bankruptcy), its physical and financial assets go to its bondholders—its lenders—while its shareholders generally receive nothing. So although a stock generally provides a higher return to an investor than a bond, it also carries higher risk.

But the financial system has devised ways to help investors as well as business owners simultaneously manage risk and enjoy somewhat higher returns. It does that through the services of institutions known as *financial intermediaries.*

## Financial Intermediaries

A **financial intermediary** is an institution that transforms funds gathered from many individuals into financial assets. The most important types of financial intermediaries are *mutual funds, pension funds, life insurance companies*, and *banks.* About three-quarters of the financial assets Americans own are held through these intermediaries rather than directly.

**Mutual Funds** As we've explained, owning shares of a company entails accepting risk in return for a higher potential reward. But it should come as no surprise that stock investors can lower their total risk by engaging in diversification. By owning a *diversified portfolio* of stocks—a group of stocks in which risks are unrelated to, or offset, one another—rather than concentrating investment in the shares of a single company or a group of related companies, investors can reduce their risk. In addition, financial advisers, aware that most people are risk-averse, almost always advise their clients to diversify not only their stock portfolio but also their entire wealth by holding other assets in addition to stock—assets such as bonds, real estate, and cash. (And, for good measure, to have plenty of insurance in case of accidental losses!)

However, for individuals who don't have a large amount of money to invest—say $1 million or more—building a diversified stock portfolio can incur high transaction costs (particularly fees paid to stockbrokers) because they are buying a few shares of a lot of companies. Fortunately for such investors, mutual funds help solve the problem of achieving diversification without high transaction costs. A **mutual fund** is a financial intermediary that creates a stock portfolio by buying and holding shares in companies and then selling shares of the stock portfolio to individual investors. By buying these shares, investors with a relatively small amount of money to invest can indirectly hold a diversified portfolio, achieving a better return for any given level of risk than they could otherwise achieve. Table 10-1 shows an example of a diversified mutual fund, the Vanguard 500 Index Fund. It shows the percentage of investors' money invested in the stocks of the largest companies in the mutual fund's portfolio.

Many mutual funds also perform market research on the companies they invest in. This is important because there are thousands of stock-issuing U.S. companies (not to mention foreign companies), each differing in terms of its likely profitability, dividend payments, and so on. It would be extremely time-consuming and costly for an individual investor to do adequate research on even a small number of companies. Mutual funds save transaction costs by doing this research for their customers.

The mutual fund industry represents a huge portion of the modern U.S. economy, not just of the U.S. financial system. In total, U.S. mutual

A **financial intermediary** is an institution that transforms the funds it gathers from many individuals into financial assets.

A **mutual fund** is a financial intermediary that creates a stock portfolio and then resells shares of this portfolio to individual investors.

TABLE **10-1** Vanguard 500 Index Fund Investor Shares, Top Holdings (as of June 2011)

| Company | Percent of mutual fund assets invested in a company |
|---|---|
| Exxon Mobil Corp. | 3.3% |
| Apple Inc. | 2.6 |
| International Business Machines Corp. | 1.7 |
| Chevron Corp. | 1.7 |
| General Electric Co. | 1.7 |
| Microsoft Corp. | 1.6 |
| AT&T Inc. | 1.5 |
| Johnson & Johnson | 1.5 |
| Procter & Gamble Co. | 1.5 |
| Pfizer Inc. | 1.4 |

*Source:* The Vanguard Group.

A **pension fund** is a type of mutual fund that holds assets in order to provide retirement income to its members.

A **life insurance company** sells policies that guarantee a payment to a policyholder's beneficiaries when the policyholder dies.

A **bank deposit** is a claim on a bank that obliges the bank to give the depositor his or her cash when demanded.

A **bank** is a financial intermediary that provides liquid assets in the form of bank deposits to lenders and uses those funds to finance the illiquid investment spending needs of borrowers.

funds had assets of $10.1 trillion in late 2011. In December 2011, the largest mutual fund company was The Vanguard Group, which managed $1.7 trillion in funds.

We should mention, by the way, that mutual funds charge fees for their services. These fees are quite small for mutual funds that simply hold a diversified portfolio of stocks, without trying to pick winners. But the fees charged by mutual funds that claim to have special expertise in investing your money can be quite high.

**Pension Funds and Life Insurance Companies** In addition to mutual funds, many Americans have holdings in **pension funds,** nonprofit institutions that collect the savings of their members and invest those funds in a wide variety of assets, providing their members with income when they retire. Although pension funds are subject to some special rules and receive special treatment for tax purposes, they function much like mutual funds. They invest in a diverse array of financial assets, allowing their members to achieve more cost-effective diversification and market research than they would be able to achieve individually. In late 2011, pension funds in the United States held almost $10 trillion in assets.

Americans also have substantial holdings in the policies of **life insurance companies,** which guarantee a payment to the policyholder's beneficiaries (typically, the family) when the policyholder dies. By enabling policyholders to cushion their beneficiaries from financial hardship arising from their death, life insurance companies also improve welfare by reducing risk.

**Banks** Recall the problem of liquidity: other things equal, people want assets that can be readily converted into cash. Bonds and stocks are much more liquid than physical assets or loans, yet the transaction cost of selling bonds or stocks to meet a sudden expense can be large. Furthermore, for many small and moderate-size companies, the cost of issuing bonds and stocks is too large given the modest amount of money they seek to raise. A *bank* is an institution that helps resolve the conflict between lenders' needs for liquidity and the financing needs of borrowers who don't want to use the stock or bond markets.

A bank works by first accepting funds from *depositors:* when you put your money in a bank, you are essentially becoming a lender by lending the bank your money. In return, you receive credit for a **bank deposit**—a claim on the bank, which is obliged to give you your cash if and when you demand it. So a bank deposit is a financial asset owned by the depositor and a liability of the bank that holds it.

A bank, however, keeps only a fraction of its customers' deposits in the form of ready cash. Most of its deposits are lent out to businesses, buyers of new homes, and other borrowers. These loans come with a long-term commitment by the bank to the borrower: as long as the borrower makes his or her payments on time, the loan cannot be recalled by the bank and converted into cash. So a bank enables those who wish to borrow for long lengths of time to use the funds of those who wish to lend but simultaneously want to maintain the ability to get their cash back on demand. More formally, a **bank** is a financial intermediary that provides liquid financial assets in the form of deposits to lenders and uses their funds to finance the illiquid investment spending needs of borrowers.

In essence, a bank is engaging in a kind of mismatch: lending for long periods of time while subject to the condition that its depositors could demand their funds back at any time. How can it manage that?

The bank counts on the fact that, on average, only a small fraction of its depositors will want their cash at the same time. On any given day, some people will make withdrawals and others will make new deposits; these will roughly cancel each other out. So the bank needs to keep only a limited amount of cash on hand to satisfy its depositors. In addition, if a bank becomes financially incapable of paying its depositors, individual bank deposits are guaranteed to depositors up to $250,000 by the Federal Deposit Insurance Corporation, or FDIC, a federal agency. This reduces the risk to a depositor of holding a bank deposit, in turn reducing the incentive to withdraw funds if concerns about the financial state of the bank should arise. So, under normal conditions, banks need hold only a fraction of their depositors' cash.

By reconciling the needs of savers for liquid assets with the needs of borrowers for long-term financing, banks play a key economic role. As the following Economics in Action explains, the creation of a well-functioning banking system was a key turning point in South Korea's economic success.

## ECONOMICS ➤ *IN ACTION*

### BANKS AND THE SOUTH KOREAN MIRACLE

South Korea is one of the great success stories of economic growth. In the early 1960s, it was a very poor nation. Then it experienced spectacularly high rates of economic growth. South Korean banks had a lot to do with it.

In the early 1960s, South Korea's banking system was a mess. Interest rates on deposits were very low by government regulation at a time when the country was experiencing high inflation. So savers didn't want to save by putting money in a bank, fearing that much of their purchasing power would be eroded by rising prices. Instead, they engaged in current consumption by spending their money on goods and services or used their wealth to buy physical assets such as real estate and gold. Because savers refused to make bank deposits, businesses found it very hard to borrow money to finance investment spending.

South Korea's experience with banks shows how important a good financial system is to economic growth.

In 1965 the South Korean government reformed the country's banks and increased interest rates to a level that was attractive to savers. Over the next five years the value of bank deposits increased seven-fold, and the national savings rate—the percentage of GDP going into national savings—more than doubled. The rejuvenated banking system made it possible for South Korean businesses to launch a great investment spending boom, a key element in the country's growth surge.

Many other factors besides banking were involved in South Korea's success, but the country's experience does show how important a good financial system is to economic growth.

### CHECK YOUR UNDERSTANDING   10-2

1. Rank the following assets in terms of (i) level of transaction costs, (ii) level of risk, (iii) level of liquidity.
   a. A bank deposit with a guaranteed interest rate
   b. A share of a highly diversified mutual fund, which can be quickly sold
   c. A share of the family business, which can be sold only if you find a buyer and all other family members agree to the sale

2. What relationship would you expect to find between the level of development of a country's financial system and its level of economic development? Explain in terms of the country's level of savings and level of investment spending.

*Solutions appear at back of book.*

### ▼ Quick Review

- Households can invest their current savings or their **wealth** by purchasing either **financial assets** or **physical assets.** A financial asset is a seller's **liability.**

- A well-functioning financial system reduces **transaction costs,** reduces **financial risk** by enabling **diversification,** and provides **liquid** assets, which investors prefer to **illiquid** assets.

- The four main types of financial assets are **loans,** bonds, stocks, and **bank deposits.** A recent innovation is **loan-backed securities,** which are more liquid and more diversified than individual loans. Bonds with a higher **default** risk typically must pay a higher interest rate.

- The most important types of **financial intermediaries** are **mutual funds, pension funds, life insurance companies,** and **banks.**

- A bank accepts bank deposits, which obliges it to return depositors' cash on demand, and lends those funds to borrowers for long lengths of time.

*Seokyong Lee/Bloomberg via Getty Images*

# Financial Fluctuations

We've learned that the financial system is an essential part of the economy; without stock markets, bond markets, and banks, long-run economic growth would be hard to achieve. Yet the news isn't entirely good: the financial system sometimes doesn't function well and instead is a source of instability in the short run. In fact, the financial consequences of a sharp fall in housing prices became a major problem for economic policy makers starting in the summer of 2007. By the fall of 2008, it was clear that the U.S. economy was facing a severe slump as it adjusted to the consequences of greatly reduced home values. And in 2012, the time of writing, the economy was only slowly recovering from a severe recession.

We could easily write a whole book on asset market fluctuations. In fact, many people have. Here, we briefly discuss the causes of asset price fluctuations.

## The Demand for Stocks

Once a company issues shares of stock to investors, those shares can then be resold to other investors in the stock market. And these days, thanks to cable TV and the Internet, you can easily spend all day watching stock market fluctuations—the movement up and down of the prices of individual stocks as well as summary measures of stock prices like the Dow Jones Industrial Average. These fluctuations reflect changes in supply and demand by investors. But what causes the supply and demand for stocks to shift?

Remember that stocks are financial assets: they are shares in the ownership of a company. Unlike a good or service, whose value to its owner comes from

---

### 🗨 FOR INQUIRING MINDS

#### HOW NOW, DOW JONES?

Financial news reports often lead with the day's stock market action, as measured by changes in the Dow Jones Industrial Average, the S&P 500, and the NASDAQ. What are these numbers, and what do they tell us?

All three are stock market indices. Like the consumer price index, they are numbers constructed as a summary of average prices—in this case, prices of stocks. The Dow, created by the financial analysis company Dow Jones, is an index of the prices of stock in 30 leading companies, such as Microsoft, Walmart, and General Electric. The S&P 500 is an index of 500 companies, created by Standard and Poor's, another financial company. The NASDAQ is compiled by the National Association of Securities Dealers, which trades the stocks of smaller new companies, like the satellite radio company Sirius XM Radio or the computer manufacturer Dell.

Because these indices contain different groups of stocks, they track somewhat different things. The Dow, because it con-

tains only 30 of the largest companies, tends to reflect the "old economy," traditional business powerhouses like Exxon Mobil. The NASDAQ is heavily influenced by technology stocks. The S&P 500, a broad measure, is in between.

Why are these indices important? Because the movement in an index gives investors a quick, snapshot view of how stocks from certain sectors of the economy are doing. As we'll explain shortly, the price of a stock at a given point in time embodies investors' expectations about the future prospects of the underlying company. By implication, an index composed of stocks drawn from companies in a particular sector embodies investors' expectations of the future prospects of that sector of the economy. So a day on which the NASDAQ moves up but

Dramatic fluctuations of the Dow, NASDAQ, S&P 500, and stock market indices early in 2011 suggested that the world might be facing another major economic crisis. The expressions on the faces of these stockbrokers were another indicator.

the Dow moves down implies that, on that day, prospects appear brighter for the high-tech sector than for the old-economy sector. The movement in the indices reflects the fact that investors are acting on their beliefs by selling stocks in the Dow and buying stocks in the NASDAQ.

its consumption, the value of an asset comes from its ability to generate higher future consumption of goods or services. A financial asset allows higher future consumption in two ways. First, many financial assets provide regular income to their owners in the form of interest payments or dividends. But many companies don't pay dividends; instead, they retain their earnings to finance future investment spending. Investors purchase non-dividend-paying stocks in the belief that they will earn income from selling the stock in the future at a profit, the second way of generating higher future income. Even in the cases of a bond or a dividend-paying stock, investors will not want to purchase an asset that they believe will sell for less in the future than today because such an asset will reduce their wealth when they sell it.

So the value of a financial asset today depends on investors' beliefs about the future value or price of the asset. If investors believe that it will be worth more in the future, they will demand more of the asset today at any given price; consequently, today's equilibrium price of the asset will rise. Conversely, if investors believe the asset will be worth less in the future, they will demand less today at any given price; consequently, today's equilibrium price of the asset will fall. Today's stock prices will change according to changes in investors' expectations about future stock prices.

Suppose an event occurs that leads to a rise in the expected future price of a company's shares—say, for example, Apple announces that it forecasts higher than expected profitability due to torrential sales of the latest version of the iPad. Demand for Apple shares will increase. At the same time, existing shareholders will be less willing to supply their shares to the market at any given price, leading to a decrease in the supply of Apple shares. And as we know, an increase in demand or a decrease in supply (or both) leads to a rise in price. Alternatively, suppose that an event occurs that leads to a fall in the expected future price of a company's shares—say, Home Depot announces that it expects lower profitability because the slump in home sales has depressed the demand for home improvements. Demand for Home Depot shares will decrease. At the same time, supply will increase because existing shareholders will be more willing to supply their Home Depot shares to the market. Both changes lead to a fall in the stock price.

So stock prices are determined by the supply and demand for shares—which, in turn, depend on investors' expectations about the future stock price.

Stock prices are also affected by changes in the attractiveness of substitute assets, like bonds. As we learned early on, the demand for a particular good decreases when purchasing a substitute good becomes more attractive—say, due to a fall in its price. The same lesson holds true for stocks: when purchasing bonds becomes more attractive due to a rise in interest rates, stock prices will fall. And when purchasing bonds becomes less attractive due to a fall in interest rates, stock prices will rise.

## The Demand for Other Assets

Everything we've just said about stocks applies to other assets as well, including physical assets. Consider the demand for commercial real estate—office buildings, shopping malls, and other structures that provide space for business activities. An investor who buys an office building does so for two reasons. First, because space in the building can be rented out, the owner of the building receives income in the form of rents. Second, the investor may expect the building to rise in value, meaning that it can be sold at a higher price at some future date. As in the case of stocks, the demand for commercial real estate also depends on the attractiveness of substitute assets, especially bonds. When interest rates rise, the demand for commercial real estate decreases; when interest rates fall, the demand for commercial real estate increases.

According to the **efficient markets hypothesis,** asset prices embody all publicly available information.

Most Americans don't own commercial real estate. Only half of the population owns any stock, even indirectly through mutual funds, and for most of those people stock ownership is well under $50,000. However, at the end of 2011 about 66% of American households owned another kind of asset: their own homes. What determines housing prices?

You might wonder whether home prices can be analyzed the same way we analyze stock prices or the price of commercial real estate. After all, stocks pay dividends, commercial real estate yields rents, but when a family lives in its own home, no money changes hands.

In economic terms, however, that doesn't matter very much. To a large extent, the benefit of owning your own home is the fact that you don't have to pay rent to someone else—or, to put it differently, it's as if you were paying rent to yourself. In fact, the U.S. government includes "implicit rent"—an estimate of the amount that homeowners, in effect, pay to themselves—in its estimates of GDP.

The amount people are willing to pay for a house depends in part on the implicit rent they expect to receive from that house. The demand for housing, like the demand for other assets, also depends on what people expect to happen to future prices: they're willing to pay more for a house if they believe they can sell it at a higher price sometime in the future. Last but not least, the demand for houses depends on interest rates: a rise in the interest rate increases the cost of a mortgage and leads to a decrease in housing demand; a fall in the interest rate reduces the cost of a mortgage and causes an increase in housing demand.

All asset prices, then, are determined by a similar set of factors. But we haven't yet fully answered the question of what determines asset prices because we haven't explained what determines investors' *expectations* about future asset prices.

## Asset Price Expectations

There are two principal competing views about how asset price expectations are determined. One view, which comes from traditional economic analysis, emphasizes the rational reasons why expectations *should* change. The other, widely held by market participants and also supported by some economists, emphasizes the irrationality of market participants.

**The Efficient Markets Hypothesis** Suppose you were trying to assess what Home Depot's stock is really worth. To do this, you would look at the *fundamentals,* the underlying determinants of the company's future profits. These would include factors like the changing shopping habits of the American public and the prospects for home remodeling. You would also want to compare the earnings you could expect to receive from Home Depot with the likely returns on other financial assets, such as bonds.

According to one view of asset prices, the value you would come up with after a careful study of this kind would, in fact, turn out to be the price at which Home Depot stock is already selling in the market. Why? Because all publicly available information about Home Depot's fundamentals is already embodied in its stock price. Any difference between the market price and the value suggested by a careful analysis of the underlying fundamentals indicates a profit opportunity to smart investors, who then sell Home Depot stock if it looks overpriced and buy it if it looks underpriced. The **efficient markets hypothesis** is the general form of this view; it means that asset prices always embody all publicly available information. An implication of the efficient markets hypothesis is that at any point in time stock prices are fairly valued: they reflect all currently available information about fundamentals. So they are neither overpriced nor underpriced.

One implication of the efficient markets hypothesis is that the prices of stocks and other assets should change only in response to new information about the underlying fundamentals. Since new information is by definition unpredictable— if it were predictable, it wouldn't be new information—movements in asset prices

## FOR INQUIRING MINDS

### BEHAVIORAL FINANCE

Individuals often make irrational—sometimes predictably irrational—choices that leave them worse off economically than would other, feasible alternatives. People also have a habit of repeating the same decision-making mistakes. This kind of behavior is the subject of *behavioral economics,* which includes the rapidly growing subfield of *behavioral finance,* the study of how investors in financial markets often make predictably irrational choices.

Like most people, investors depart from rationality in systematic ways. In particular, they are prone to *overconfidence,* as in having a misguided faith that they are able to spot a winning stock; to *loss aversion,* being unwilling to sell an unprofitable asset and accept the loss; and to a *herd mentality,* buying an asset when its price has already been driven high and selling it when its price has already been driven low.

This irrational behavior raises an important question: can investors who *are* rational make a lot of money at the expense of those investors who aren't—for example, by buying a company's stock if irrational fears make it cheap?

The answer to this question is sometimes yes and sometimes no. Some professional investors have made huge profits by betting against irrational moves in the market (buying when there is irrational selling and selling when there is irrational buying). For example, the billionaire hedge fund manager John Paulson made

$4 billion by betting against subprime mortgages during the U.S. housing bubble of 2007–2008 because he understood that financial asets containing subprime mortgages were being sold at inflated prices.

But sometimes even a rational investor cannot profit from market irrationality. For example, a money manager has to obey customers' orders to buy or sell even when those actions are irrational. Likewise, it can be much safer for professional money managers to follow the herd: If they do that and their investments go badly, they have the career-saving excuse that no one foresaw a problem. But if they've gone against the herd and their investments go south, they are likely to be fired for making poor choices. So rational investors can even exacerbate the irrational moves in financial markets.

Some observers of historical trends hypothesize that financial markets alter-

© Kal, CartoonArts International, Inc.

nate between periods of complacency and forgetfulness, which breed bubbles as investors irrationally believe that prices can only go up, followed by a crash, which in turn leads investors to avoid financial markets altogether and renders asset prices irrationally cheap. Clearly, the events of the past decade, with its huge housing bubble followed by extreme turmoil in financial markets, have given researchers in the area of behavioral finance a lot of material to work with.

---

are also unpredictable. As a result, the movement of, say, stock prices will follow a **random walk**—the general term for the movement over time of an unpredictable variable.

The efficient markets hypothesis plays an important role in understanding how financial markets work. Most investment professionals and many economists, however, regard it as an oversimplification. Investors, they claim, aren't that rational.

**Irrational Markets?** Many people who actually trade in the markets, such as individual investors and professional money managers, are skeptical of the efficient markets hypothesis. They believe that markets often behave irrationally and that a smart investor can engage in successful "market timing"—buying stocks when they are underpriced and selling them when they are overpriced.

Although economists are generally skeptical about claims that there are sure-fire ways to outsmart the market, many have also challenged the efficient markets hypothesis. It's important to understand, however, that finding particular examples where the market got it wrong does not disprove the efficient markets hypothesis. If the price of Home Depot stock plunges from $40 to $10 because of a sudden change in buying patterns, this doesn't mean that the market was inefficient in originally

A **random walk** is the movement over time of an unpredictable variable.

*Mike Smith King Features Syndicate*

*"…well, good for Barbie."*

pricing the stock at $40. The fact that buying patterns were about to change wasn't publicly available information, so it wasn't embodied in the earlier stock price.

Serious challenges to the efficient markets hypothesis focus instead either on evidence of systematic misbehavior of market prices or on evidence that individual investors don't behave in the way the theory suggests. For example, some economists believe they have found strong evidence that stock prices fluctuate more than can be explained by news about fundamentals. Others believe they have strong evidence that individual investors behave in systematically irrational ways. For example, people seem to expect that a stock that has risen in the past will keep on rising, even though the efficient markets hypothesis tells us there is no reason to expect this. The same appears to be true of other assets, especially housing: the great housing bubble, described in the Economics in Action that follows this section, arose in large part because home-buyers assumed that home prices would continue rising in the future.

## Asset Prices and Macroeconomics

How should macroeconomists and policy makers deal with the fact that asset prices fluctuate a lot and that these fluctuations can have important economic effects? This question has become one of the major problems facing macroeconomic policy. On one side, policy makers are reluctant to assume that the market is wrong—that asset prices are either too high or too low. In part, this reflects the efficient markets hypothesis, which says that any information that is publicly available is already accounted for in asset prices. More generally, it's hard to make the general case that government officials are better judges of appropriate prices than private investors who are putting their own money on the line.

On the other side, the past 15 years were marked by not one but two huge asset bubbles, each of which created major macroeconomic problems when it burst. In the late 1990s the prices of technology stocks, including but not limited to dot-com Internet firms, soared to hard-to-justify heights. When the bubble burst, these stocks lost, on average, two-thirds of their value in a short time, helping to cause the 2001 recession and a period of high unemployment. A few years later there was a major bubble in housing prices. The collapse of this bubble in 2008 triggered a severe financial crisis followed by a deep recession that was still ongoing as this book went to press.

These events have led to a fierce debate among economists over whether policy makers should try to pop asset bubbles before they get too big. We'll describe that debate in Chapter 17.

## ECONOMICS > IN ACTION

### THE GREAT AMERICAN HOUSING BUBBLE

**B**etween 2000 and 2006, there was a huge increase in the price of houses in America. By the summer of 2006, home prices were well over twice as high as they had been in January 2000 in a number of major U.S. metropolitan areas, including Los Angeles, San Diego, San Francisco, Washington, Miami, Las Vegas, and New York. By 2004, as the increase in home prices accelerated, a number of economists (including the authors of this textbook) argued that this price increase was excessive—that it was a bubble, a rise in asset prices driven by unrealistic expectations about future prices.

It was certainly true that home prices rose much more than the cost of renting a comparable place to live. Panel (a) of Figure 10-9 compares a widely used index

FIGURE **10-9** The Great American Housing Bubble

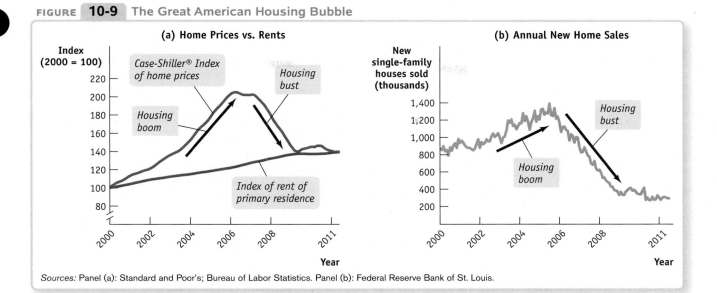

Sources: Panel (a): Standard and Poor's; Bureau of Labor Statistics. Panel (b): Federal Reserve Bank of St. Louis.

of U.S. housing prices with the U.S. government's index of the cost of renting, both shown as index numbers with January 2000 = 100. Home prices shot up, even though rental rates grew only gradually.

Yet there were also a number of economists who argued that the rise in housing prices was completely justified. They pointed, in particular, to the fact that interest rates were unusually low in the years of rapid price increases, and they argued that low interest rates combined with other factors, such as growing population, explained the surge in prices. Alan Greenspan, then chairman of the Federal Reserve, conceded in 2005 that there might be some "froth" in the markets but denied that there was any national bubble.

Unfortunately, it turned out that the skeptics were right. Greenspan himself would later concede that there had, in fact, been a huge national bubble. In 2006, as home prices began to level off, it became apparent that many buyers had held unrealistic expectations about future prices. As home prices began to fall, expectations of future increases in home prices were revised downward, precipitating a sudden and dramatic collapse in prices. And with home prices falling, the demand for housing fell drastically, as illustrated by panel (b) of Figure 10-9.

The implosion in housing, in turn, created numerous economic difficulties, including severe stress on the banking system, which we will examine in Chapter 14.

## CHECK YOUR UNDERSTANDING   10-3

1. What is the likely effect of each of the following events on the stock price of a company? Explain your answers.
   a. The company announces that although profits are low this year, it has discovered a new line of business that will generate high profits next year.
   b. The company announces that although it had high profits this year, those profits will be less than had been previously announced.
   c. Other companies in the same industry announce that sales are unexpectedly slow this year.
   d. The company announces that it is on track to meet its previously forecast profit target.

2. Assess the following statement: "Although many investors may be irrational, it is unlikely that over time they will behave irrationally in exactly the same way—such as always buying stocks the day after the Dow has risen by 1%."

Solutions appear at back of book.

### ▼ Quick Review

- Financial market fluctuations can be a source of short-run macroeconomic instability.

- Asset prices are driven by supply and demand as well as by the desirability of competing assets like bonds. Supply and demand also reflect expectations about future asset prices. One view of expectations is the **efficient markets hypothesis,** which leads to the view that stock prices follow a **random walk.**

- Market participants and some economists question the efficient markets hypothesis. In practice, policy makers don't assume that they can outsmart the market, but they also don't assume that markets will always behave rationally.

## SUMMARY

1. Investment in physical capital is necessary for long-run economic growth. So in order for an economy to grow, it must channel savings into investment spending.

2. According to the **savings–investment spending identity,** savings and investment spending are always equal for the economy as a whole. The government is a source of savings when it runs a positive **budget balance,** also known as a **budget surplus;** it is a source of dissavings when it runs a negative budget balance, also known as a **budget deficit.** In a closed economy, savings is equal to **national savings,** the sum of private savings plus the budget balance. In an open economy, savings is equal to national savings plus **net capital inflow** of foreign savings. When a negative net capital inflow occurs, some portion of national savings is funding investment spending in other countries.

3. The hypothetical **loanable funds market** shows how loans from savers are allocated among borrowers with investment spending projects. By showing how gains from trade between lenders and borrowers are maximized, the loanable funds market shows why a well-functioning financial system leads to greater long-run economic growth. Increasing or persistent government budget deficits can lead to **crowding out:** higher interest rates and reduced investment spending. Changes in perceived business opportunities and in government borrowing shift the demand curve for loanable funds; changes in private savings and capital inflows shift the supply curve.

4. In order to evaluate a project in which the return, $X$, is realized in the future, you must transform $X$ into its **present value** using the interest rate, $r$. The present value of \$1 received one year from now is \$1 / (1 + r), the amount of money you must lend out today to have \$1 one year from now. The present value of a given project rises as the interest rate falls and falls as the interest rate rises. This tells us that the demand curve for loanable funds is downward-sloping.

5. Because neither borrowers nor lenders can know the future inflation rate, loans specify a nominal interest rate rather than a real interest rate. For a given expected future inflation rate, shifts of the demand and supply curves of loanable funds result in changes in the underlying real interest rate, leading to changes in the nominal interest rate. According to the **Fisher effect,** an increase in expected future inflation raises the nominal interest rate one-to-one so that the expected real interest rate remains unchanged.

6. Households invest their current savings or **wealth**—their accumulated savings—by purchasing assets. Assets come in the form of either a **financial asset,** a paper claim that entitles the buyer to future income from the seller, or a **physical asset,** a tangible object that can generate future income. A financial asset is also a **liability** from the point of view of its seller. There are four main types of financial assets: **loans,** bonds, stocks, and **bank deposits.** Each of them serves a different purpose in addressing the three fundamental tasks of a financial system: reducing **transaction costs**—the cost of making a deal; reducing **financial risk**—uncertainty about future outcomes that involves financial gains and losses; and providing **liquid** assets—assets that can be quickly converted into cash without much loss of value (in contrast to **illiquid** assets, which are not easily converted).

7. Although many small and moderate-size borrowers use bank loans to fund investment spending, larger companies typically issue bonds. Bonds with a higher risk of **default** must typically pay a higher interest rate. Business owners reduce their risk by selling stock. Although stocks usually generate a higher return than bonds, investors typically wish to reduce their risk by engaging in **diversification,** owning a wide range of assets whose returns are based on unrelated, or independent, events. Most people are risk-averse, more sensitive to a loss than to an equal-sized gain. **Loan-backed securities,** a recent innovation, are assets created by pooling individual loans and selling shares of that pool to investors. Because they are more diversified and more liquid than individual loans, bonds are preferred by investors. It can be difficult, however, to assess a bond's quality.

8. **Financial intermediaries**—institutions such as **mutual funds, pension funds, life insurance companies,** and **banks**—are critical components of the financial system. Mutual funds and pension funds allow small investors to diversify, and life insurance companies reduce risk.

9. A bank allows individuals to hold liquid bank deposits that are then used to finance illiquid loans. Banks can perform this mismatch because on average only a small fraction of depositors withdraw their funds at any one time. A well-functioning banking sector is a key ingredient of long-run economic growth.

10. Asset market fluctuations can be a source of short-run macroeconomic instability. Asset prices are determined by supply and demand as well as by the desirability of competing assets, like bonds: when the interest rate rises, prices of stocks and physical assets such as real estate generally fall, and vice versa. Expectations drive the supply of and demand

for assets: expectations of higher future prices push today's asset prices higher, and expectations of lower future prices drive them lower. One view of how expectations are formed is the **efficient markets hypothesis,** which holds that the prices of assets embody all publicly available information. It implies that fluctuations are inherently unpredictable—they follow a **random walk.**

11. Many market participants and economists believe that, based on actual evidence, financial markets are not as rational as the efficient markets hypothesis claims. Such evidence includes the fact that stock price fluctuations are too great to be driven by fundamentals alone. Policy makers assume neither that markets always behave rationally nor that they can outsmart them.

## KEY TERMS

Savings–investment spending identity, p. 276
Budget surplus, p. 277
Budget deficit, p. 277
Budget balance, p. 277
National savings, p. 277
Net capital inflow, p. 278
Loanable funds market, p. 281
Present value, p. 282
Crowding out, p. 286
Fisher effect, p. 289

Wealth, p. 291
Financial asset, p. 291
Physical asset, p. 291
Liability, p. 291
Transaction costs, p. 292
Financial risk, p. 292
Diversification, p. 293
Liquid, p. 293
Illiquid, p. 293
Loan, p. 293
Default, p. 294

Loan-backed securities, p. 294
Financial intermediary, p. 295
Mutual fund, p. 295
Pension fund, p. 296
Life insurance company, p. 296
Bank deposit, p. 296
Bank, p. 296
Efficient markets hypothesis, p. 300
Random walk, p. 301

## PROBLEMS

1. Given the following information about the closed economy of Brittania, what is the level of investment spending and private savings, and what is the budget balance? What is the relationship among the three? Is national savings equal to investment spending? There are no government transfers.

   GDP = $1,000 million        $T$ = $50 million
   $C$ = $850 million          $G$ = $100 million

2. Given the following information about the open economy of Regalia, what is the level of investment spending and private savings, and what are the budget balance and net capital inflow? What is the relationship among the four? There are no government transfers. (*Hint:* net capital inflow equals the value of imports *(IM)* minus the value of exports *(X)*.)

   GDP = $1,000 million        $G$ = $100 million
   $C$ = $850 million          $X$ = $100 million
   $T$ = $50 million           $IM$ = $125 million

3. The accompanying table shows the percentage of GDP accounted for by private savings, investment spending, and net capital inflow in the economies of Capsland and Marsalia. Capsland is currently experiencing a positive net capital inflow and Marsalia, a negative net capital outflow. What is the budget balance (as a percentage of GDP) in both countries? Are Capsland and Marsalia running a budget deficit or surplus?

|  | Capsland | Marsalia |
|---|---|---|
| Investment spending as a percentage of GDP | 20% | 20% |
| Private savings as a percentage of GDP | 10 | 25 |
| Net capital inflow as a percentage of GDP | 5 | –2 |

4. Assume the economy is open to capital inflows and outflows and therefore net capital inflow equals imports *(IM)* minus exports *(X)*. Answer each of the following questions.

   **a.** $X$ = $125 million
   $IM$ = $80 million
   Budget balance = –$200 million
   $I$ = $350 million
   Calculate private savings.

   **b.** $X$ = $85 million
   $IM$ = $135 million
   Budget balance = $100 million
   Private savings = $250 million
   Calculate *I*.

   **c.** $X$ = $60 million
   $IM$ = $95 million
   Private savings = $325 million
   $I$ = $300 million
   Calculate the budget balance

   **d.** Private savings = $325 million
   $I$ = $400 million
   Budget balance = $10 million
   Calculate $IM - X$.

**5.** The accompanying table, taken from the National Income and Product Accounts Tables, shows the various components of U.S. GDP in 2009 and 2010 in billions of dollars.

| Year | Gross domestic product | Private consumption | Gross domestic investment | Government purchases of goods and services | Government savings (budget balance) | Net government taxes after transfers |
|---|---|---|---|---|---|---|
| | | | (billions of dollars) | | | |
| 2009 | $13,939.0 | $9,866.1 | $2,052.2 | $2,412.2 | –$1,296.0 | ? |
| 2010 | 14,526.5 | 10,245.5 | 2,300.4 | 2,497.5 | ? | 1,198.5 |

**a.** Complete the table by filling in the missing figures.

**b.** For each year, calculate taxes (after transfers) as a percentage of GDP.

**c.** For each year, calculate national savings and private savings.

**6.** Use the market for loanable funds shown in the accompanying diagram to explain what happens to private savings, private investment spending, and the interest rate if each of the following events occur. Assume that there are no capital inflows or outflows.

**a.** The government reduces the size of its deficit to zero.

**b.** At any given interest rate, consumers decide to save more. Assume the budget balance is zero.

**c.** At any given interest rate, businesses become very optimistic about the future profitability of investment spending. Assume the budget balance is zero.

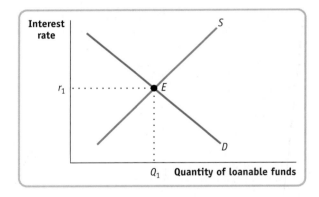

**7.** The government is running a budget balance of zero when it decides to increase education spending by $200 billion and finance the spending by selling bonds. The accompanying diagram shows the market for loanable funds before the government sells the bonds. Assume that there are no capital inflows or outflows. How will the equilibrium interest rate and the equilibrium quantity of loanable funds change? Is there any crowding out in the market?

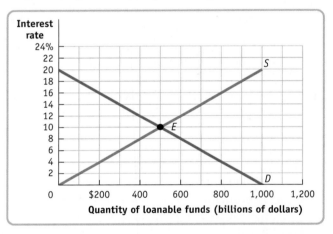

**8.** In 2010, Congress estimated that the cost of increasing the U.S. presence in Afghanistan by 30,000 troops was approximately $36 billion. Since the U.S. government was running a budget deficit at the time, assume that the surge in troop levels was financed by government borrowing, which increases the demand for loanable funds without affecting supply. This question considers the likely effect of this government expenditure on the interest rate.

**a.** Draw typical demand ($D_1$) and supply ($S_1$) curves for loanable funds without the cost of the surge in troop levels accounted for. Label the vertical axis "Interest rate" and the horizontal axis "Quantity of loanable funds." Label the equilibrium point ($E_1$) and the equilibrium interest rate ($r_1$).

**b.** Now draw a new diagram with the cost of the surge in troop levels included in the analysis. Shift the demand curve in the appropriate direction. Label the new equilibrium point ($E_2$) and the new equilibrium interest rate ($r_2$).

**c.** How does the equilibrium interest rate change in response to government expenditure on the troop surge? Explain.

9. Explain why equilibrium in the loanable funds market maximizes efficiency.

10. How would you respond to a friend who claims that the government should eliminate all purchases that are financed by borrowing because such borrowing crowds out private investment spending?

11. Boris Borrower and Lynn Lender agree that Lynn will lend Boris $10,000 and that Boris will repay the $10,000 with interest in one year. They agree to a nominal interest rate of 8%, reflecting a real interest rate of 3% on the loan and a commonly shared expected inflation rate of 5% over the next year.

    a. If the inflation rate is actually 4% over the next year, how does that lower-than-expected inflation rate affect Boris and Lynn? Who is better off?

    b. If the actual inflation rate is 7% over the next year, how does that affect Boris and Lynn? Who is better off?

12. Using the accompanying diagram, explain what will happen to the market for loanable funds when there is a fall of 2 percentage points in the expected future inflation rate. How will the change in the expected future inflation rate affect the equilibrium quantity of loanable funds?

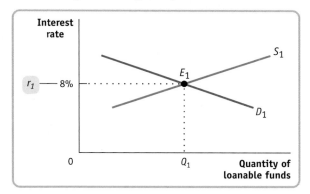

13. The accompanying diagram shows data for the interest rate on 10-year euro area government bonds and inflation rate for the euro area for 1991 through mid-2011, as reported by the European Central Bank. How would you describe the relationship between the two? How does the pattern compare to that of the United States in Figure 10-8?

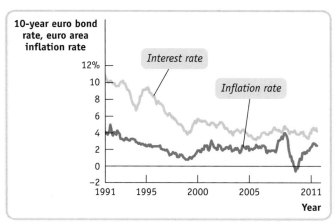

14. For each of the following, is it an example of investment spending, investing in financial assets, or investing in physical assets?

    a. Rupert Moneybucks buys 100 shares of existing Coca-Cola stock.

    b. Rhonda Moviestar spends $10 million to buy a mansion built in the 1970s.

    c. Ronald Basketballstar spends $10 million to build a new mansion with a view of the Pacific Ocean.

    d. Rawlings builds a new plant to make catcher's mitts.

    e. Russia buys $100 million in U.S. government bonds.

15. Explain how a well-functioning financial system increases savings and investment spending, holding the budget balance and any capital flows fixed.

16. What are the important types of financial intermediaries in the U.S. economy? What are the primary assets of these intermediaries, and how do they facilitate investment spending and saving?

17. Explain the effect on a company's stock price today of each of the following events, other things held constant.

    a. The interest rate on bonds falls.

    b. Several companies in the same sector announce surprisingly higher sales.

    c. A change in the tax law passed last year reduces this year's profit.

    d. The company unexpectedly announces that due to an accounting error, it must amend last year's accounting statement and reduce last year's reported profit by $5 million. It also announces that this change has no implications for future profits.

18. Sallie Mae is a quasi-governmental agency that packages individual student loans into pools of loans and sells shares of these pools to investors as Sallie Mae bonds.

    a. What is this process called? What effect will it have on investors compared to situations in which they could only buy and sell individual student loans?

    b. What effect do you think Sallie Mae's actions will have on the ability of students to get loans?

    c. Suppose that a very severe recession hits and, as a consequence, many graduating students cannot get jobs and default on their student loans. What effect will this have on Sallie Mae bonds? Why is it likely that investors now believe Sallie Mae bonds to be riskier than expected? What will be the effect on the availability of student loans?

# Toward a Fuller Understanding of Present Value

In the chapter, we showed that receiving $1,000 a year from now is worth less than $1,000 received today by calculating the present value of $1,000 received one year from now given an interest rate of 5%. You can apply the concept of present value more generally to calculate the value today of costs as well as benefits that arrive in the future.

The key point to keep in mind is that when businesses engage in investment spending, they are undertaking projects that involve a cost now in return for benefits in the future. The lower the interest rate, the more projects will be worth doing, and therefore the more businesses will spend on investment.

## How to Calculate the Present Value of One-Year Projects

Recall that the symbol $r$ represents the interest rate, either as a percentage or decimal (that is, $r = 5\% = 0.05$). Rather than work with units of $1,000, we will calculate present value for the simplest case, units of $1.

If you lend $X$, at the end of one year you will receive:

**(10A-1)** $X \times (1 + r) =$ Amount received at end of year in return for lending $X$

From Equation 10A-1, we can calculate how much you would have to lend today in order to receive $1 a year from now. To do that we set Equation 10A-1 equal to $1 and solve for $X$:

**(10A-2)** $X \times (1 + r) = \$1$

Solving for $X$ by dividing both sides of Equation 10A-2 by $(1 + r)$ gives:

**(10A-3)** $X = \$1/(1 + r)$

As we explained in the chapter, $X$ is the present value of $1 given an interest rate of $r$: it is the amount of money you would need today in order to generate a given amount of money one year from now given the interest rate $r$. Because $r$ is greater than zero, $X$ is less than $1; $1 to be delivered in the future is worth less than $1 delivered today.

Also recall from the chapter that as the interest rate goes up, the present value of a dollar delivered in the future falls. For example, the present value of $1 when $r = 0.10$ is $\$1/(1 + 0.10) = \$1/1.10 = \$0.91$, and the present value of $1 when $r = 0.02$ is $\$1/(1 + 0.02) = \$1/1.02 = \$0.98$.

## How to Calculate the Present Value of Multiyear Projects

Let's represent the value of $1 to be received two years from now as $X_{2\text{yrs}}$. If you lend out $X_{2\text{yrs}}$ today for two years, you will receive:

**(10A-4)** $X_{2\text{yrs}} \times (1 + r)$ at the end of one year

which you then reinvest to receive:

**(10A-5)** $X_{2\text{yrs}} \times (1 + r) \times (1 + r) = X_{2\text{yrs}} \times (1 + r)^2$ at the end of two years

From Equation 10A-5 we can calculate how much you would have to lend today in order to receive $1 two years from now:

**(10A-6)** $X_{2\text{yrs}} (1 + r)^2 = \$1$

To solve for $X_{2\text{yrs}}$, divide both sides of Equation 10A-5 by $(1 + r)^2$ to arrive at:

**(10A-7)** $X_{2\text{yrs}} = \$1/(1 + r)^2$

For example, if $r = 0.10$, then $X_{2\text{yrs}} = \$1/(1.10)^2 = \$1/1.21 = \$0.83$.

Equation 10A-7 points the way toward the general expression for present value, where $1 is paid after $N$ years. It is

**(10A-8)** $X_{\text{Nyrs}} = \$1/(1 + r)^N$

In other words, the present value of $1 to be received $N$ years from now is equal to $\$1/(1 + r)^N$.

## How to Calculate the Present Value of Projects with Revenues and Costs

Suppose you have to choose one of three projects to undertake. Project A gives you an immediate payoff of $100. Project B costs you $10 now and pays $115 a year from now. Project C gives you an immediate payoff of $119 but requires you to pay $20 a year from now. We will assume that $r = 0.10$.

In order to compare these three projects, you must evaluate costs and revenues that are expended or realized at different times. It is here, of course, that the concept of present value is extremely handy: by using present value to convert any dollars realized in the future into today's value, you can factor out differences in time. Once differences in time are factored out, you can compare the three projects by calculating each one's *net present value*, the present value of current and future revenues minus the present value of current and future costs. The best project to undertake is the one with the highest net present value.

Table 10A-1 shows how to calculate the net present value of each of the three projects. The second and third columns show how many dollars are realized and when they are realized; costs are indicated by a minus sign. The fourth column shows the equations used to convert the flows of dollars into their present value, and the fifth column shows the actual amounts of the total net present value for each of the three projects.

For instance, to calculate the net present value of project B, you need to calculate the present value of $115 received one year from now. The

TABLE **10A-1**  The Net Present Value of Three Hypothetical Projects

| Project | Dollars realized today | Dollars realized one year from today | Present value formula | Net present value given $r = 0.10$ |
|---------|-----------------------|--------------------------------------|----------------------|------------------------------------|
| A | $100 | — | $100 | $100.00 |
| B | –$10 | $115 | –$10 + $115/(1 + r) | $94.55 |
| C | $119 | –$20 | $119 – $20/(1 + r) | $100.82 |

present value of $1 received one year from now is $\$1/(1 + r)$. So the present value of $115 received one year from now is $115 \times \$1/(1 + r) = \$115/(1 + r)$. The net present value of project B is the present value of current and future revenues minus the present value of current and future costs: $-\$10 + \$115/(1 + r)$.

From the fifth column, we can immediately see that, at an interest rate of 10%, project C is the best project. It has the highest net present value, $100.82, which is higher than the net present value of project A ($100) and much higher than the net present value of project B ($94.55).

This example shows how important the concept of present value is. If we had failed to use the present value calculations and had instead simply added up the revenues and costs, we would have been misled into believing that project B was the best project and C was the worst one.

## PROBLEMS

1. Suppose that a major city's main thoroughfare, which is also an interstate highway, will be completely closed to traffic for two years, from January 2012 to December 2013, for reconstruction at a cost of $535 million. If the construction company were to keep the highway open for traffic during construction, the highway reconstruction project would take much longer and be more expensive. Suppose that construction would take four years if the highway were kept open, at a total cost of $800 million. The state department of transportation had to make its decision in 2011, one year before the start of construction (so that the first payment was one year away). So the department of transportation had the following choices:

   (i) Close the highway during construction, at an annual cost of $267.5 million per year for two years.

   (ii) Keep the highway open during construction, at an annual cost of $200 million per year for four years.

   a. Suppose the interest rate is 10%. Calculate the present value of the costs incurred under each plan. Which reconstruction plan is less expensive?

   b. Now suppose the interest rate is 80%. Calculate the present value of the costs incurred under each plan. Which reconstruction plan is now less expensive?

2. You have won the state lottery. There are two ways in which you can receive your prize. You can either have $1 million in cash now, or you can have $1.2 million that is paid out as follows: $300,000 now, $300,000 in one year's time, $300,000 in two years' time, and $300,000 in three years' time. The interest rate is 20%. How would you prefer to receive your prize?

3. The drug company Pfizer is considering whether to invest in the development of a new cancer drug. Development will require an initial investment of $10 million now; beginning one year from now, the drug will generate annual profits of $4 million for three years.

   a. If the interest rate is 12%, should Pfizer invest in the development of the new drug? Why or why not?

   b. If the interest rate is 8%, should Pfizer invest in the development of the new drug? Why or why not?

# CHAPTER 11

# Income and Expenditure

## FROM BOOM TO BUST

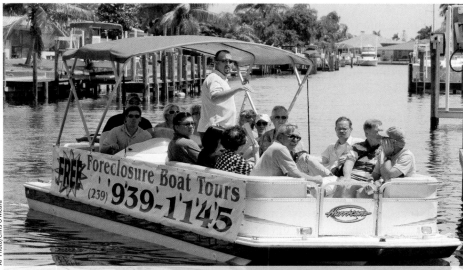

AP Photo/Chris O'Meara

The foreclosure-tour business flourished in Ft. Myers after its housing market went from boom to bust.

❭ The nature of the **multiplier,** which shows how initial changes in spending lead to further changes

❭ The meaning of the **aggregate consumption function,** which shows how current disposable income affects consumer spending

❭ How expected future income and aggregate wealth affect consumer spending

❭ The determinants of investment spending and the distinction between **planned investment spending** and **unplanned inventory investment**

❭ How the inventory adjustment process moves the economy to a new equilibrium after a change in demand

❭ Why investment spending is considered a leading indicator of the future state of the economy

FT. MYERS, FLORIDA, WAS A BOOM town from 2003 to 2005. Jobs were plentiful: the unemployment rate in the Ft. Myers–Cape Coral metropolitan area was less than 3%. Shopping malls were humming, and new stores were opening everywhere.

But then the boom went bust. Jobs became scarce, and by the middle of 2010, the unemployment rate was above 13%. Stores had few customers, and many were closing. One new business was flourishing, however. As the local economy plunged, real estate agents began offering "foreclosure tours": visits to homes that had been seized by banks after the owners were unable to make mortgage payments—and were available at bargain prices.

What happened? Ft. Myers boomed from 2003 to 2005 because of a surge in home construction, fueled in part by speculators who bought houses not to live in, but to resell at much higher prices. Home construction gave jobs to construction workers, electricians, roofers, real estate agents, and others. These

workers, in turn, spent money locally, creating jobs for waiters, gardeners, pool cleaners, sales people, and more. These workers, in turn, also spent money locally, creating further expansion, and so on.

The boom turned into a bust when home construction suddenly came to a virtual halt. It turned out that speculation had been feeding on itself: people were buying houses as investments, then selling them to others who were also buying houses as investments, and prices had risen to levels far beyond what people who actually wanted to live in houses were willing to pay. Eventually there was a "Wile E. Coyote moment"—named after the cartoon character who has a habit of running off the edge of cliffs but doesn't fall until he looks down and realizes that nothing is supporting him. In 2005 people looked down—and suddenly realized that home prices had lost touch with reality. And when they did, the housing market collapsed.

The local economy then collapsed, as the process that had created the earlier boom operated in reverse. The jobs cre-

ated by home construction went away, leading to a fall in local spending, leading to a loss of other local jobs, leading to further declines in spending, and so on.

The boom and bust in Ft. Myers illustrates, on a small scale, the way booms and busts happen for the economy as a whole. The business cycle is often driven by ups or downs in investment spending—either residential investment spending (that is, home construction) or nonresidential investment spending (such as the construction of office buildings, factories, and shopping malls). Changes in investment spending, in turn, indirectly lead to changes in consumer spending, which magnify—or, as economists usually say, *multiply*—the effect of the investment spending changes on the economy as a whole.

In this chapter we'll study how this process works, showing how *multiplier* analysis helps us understand the business cycle. As a first step, we introduce the concept of the multiplier informally. ■

The **marginal propensity to consume,** or **MPC,** is the increase in consumer spending when disposable income rises by $1.

The **marginal propensity to save,** or **MPS,** is the increase in household savings when disposable income rises by $1.

# The Multiplier: An Informal Introduction

The story of the boom and bust in Ft. Myers involves a sort of chain reaction in which an initial rise or fall in aggregate spending leads to changes in income, which lead to further changes in aggregate spending, and so on. Let's examine that chain reaction more closely, this time thinking through the effects of changes in aggregate spending in the economy as a whole.

For the sake of this analysis, we'll make four simplifying assumptions that will have to be reconsidered in later chapters.

1. We assume that *producers are willing to supply additional output at a fixed price*. That is, if consumers or businesses buying investment goods decide to spend an additional $1 billion, that will translate into the production of $1 billion worth of additional goods and services without driving up the overall level of prices. As a result, *changes in aggregate spending translate into changes in aggregate output*, as measured by real GDP. As we'll learn in the next chapter, this assumption isn't too unrealistic in the short run, but it needs to be changed when we think about the long-run effects of changes in demand.

2. We take the interest rate as given.

3. We assume that there is no government spending and no taxes.

4. We assume that exports and imports are zero.

Given these simplifying assumptions, consider what happens if there is a change in investment spending. Specifically, imagine that for some reason home builders decide to spend an extra $100 billion on home construction over the next year.

The direct effect of this increase in investment spending will be to increase income and the value of aggregate output by the same amount. That's because each dollar spent on home construction translates into a dollar's worth of income for construction workers, suppliers of building materials, electricians, and so on. If the process stopped there, the increase in housing investment spending would raise overall income by exactly $100 billion.

But the process doesn't stop there. The increase in aggregate output leads to an increase in disposable income that flows to households in the form of profits and wages. The increase in households' disposable income leads to a rise in consumer spending, which, in turn, induces firms to increase output yet again. This generates another rise in disposable income, which leads to another round of consumer spending increases, and so on. So there are multiple rounds of increases in aggregate output.

How large is the total effect on aggregate output if we sum the effect from all these rounds of spending increases? To answer this question, we need to introduce the concept of the **marginal propensity to consume,** or **MPC:** the increase in consumer spending when disposable income rises by $1. When consumer spending changes because of a rise or fall in disposable income, MPC is the change in consumer spending divided by the change in disposable income:

$$\textbf{(11-1)} \quad MPC = \frac{\Delta \text{ Consumer spending}}{\Delta \text{ Disposable income}}$$

where the symbol Δ (delta) means "change in." For example, if consumer spending goes up by $6 billion when disposable income goes up by $10 billion, MPC is $6 billion/$10 billion = 0.6.

Because consumers normally spend part but not all of an additional dollar of disposable income, MPC is a number between 0 and 1. The additional disposable income that consumers don't spend is saved; the **marginal propensity to save,** or **MPS,** is the fraction of an additional dollar of disposable income that is saved. MPS is equal to 1 − MPC.

Because we assumed that there are no taxes and no international trade, each $1 increase in aggregate spending raises both real GDP and disposable income by $1. So the $100 billion increase in investment spending initially raises real GDP by $100 billion. This leads to a second-round increase in consumer spending, which raises real GDP by a further $MPC \times$ $100 billion. It is followed by a third-round increase in consumer spending of $MPC \times MPC$ $\times$ $100 billion, and so on. After an infinite number of rounds, the total effect on real GDP is:

| | | |
|---|---|---|
| Increase in investment spending | = | $100 billion |
| + Second-round increase in consumer spending | = $MPC$ | $\times$ $100 billion |
| + Third-round increase in consumer spending | = $MPC^2$ | $\times$ $100 billion |
| + Fourth-round increase in consumer spending | = $MPC^3$ | $\times$ $100 billion |

$$\text{Total increase in real GDP} = (1 + MPC + MPC^2 + MPC^3 + \ldots) \times \$100 \text{ billion}$$

So the $100 billion increase in investment spending sets off a chain reaction in the economy. The net result of this chain reaction is that a $100 billion increase in investment spending leads to a change in real GDP that is a *multiple* of the size of that initial change in spending.

How large is this multiple? It's a mathematical fact that an infinite series of the form $1 + x + x^2 + x^3 + \ldots$, where $x$ is between 0 and 1, is equal to $1/(1 - x)$. So the total effect of a $100 billion increase in investment spending, $I$, taking into account all the subsequent increases in consumer spending (and assuming no taxes and no international trade), is given by:

**(11-2)** Total increase in real GDP from a $100 billion rise in $I$

$$= \frac{1}{1 - MPC} \times \$100 \text{ billion}$$

Let's consider a numerical example in which $MPC = 0.6$: each $1 in additional disposable income causes a $0.60 rise in consumer spending. In that case, a $100 billion increase in investment spending raises real GDP by $100 billion in the first round. The second-round increase in consumer spending raises real GDP by another 0.6 × $100 billion, or $60 billion. The third-round increase in consumer spending raises real GDP by another 0.6 × $60 billion, or $36 billion. Table 11-1 shows the successive stages of increases, where "..." means the process goes on an infinite number of times. In the end, real GDP rises by $250 billion as a consequence of the initial $100 billion rise in investment spending:

$$\frac{1}{1 - 0.6} \times \$100 \text{ billion} = 2.5 \times \$100 \text{ billion} = \$250 \text{ billion}$$

**TABLE 11-1  Rounds of Increases of Real GDP When $MPC = 0.6$**

| | Increase in real GDP (billions) | Total increase in real GDP (billions) |
|---|---|---|
| First round | $100 | $100 |
| Second round | 60 | 160 |
| Third round | 36 | 196 |
| Fourth round | 21.6 | 217.6 |
| ... | ... | ... |
| Final round | 0 | 250 |

Notice that even though there are an infinite number of rounds of expansion of real GDP, the total rise in real GDP is limited to $250 billion. The reason is that at each stage some of the rise in disposable income "leaks out" because it is saved. How much of an additional dollar of disposable income is saved depends on $MPS$, the marginal propensity to save.

We've described the effects of a change in investment spending, but the same analysis can be applied to any other change in aggregate spending. The important thing is to distinguish between the initial change in aggregate spending, before real GDP rises, and the additional change in aggregate spending caused by the change in real GDP as the chain reaction unfolds. For

An **autonomous change in aggregate spending** is an initial change in the desired level of spending by firms, households, or government at a given level of real GDP.

The **multiplier** is the ratio of the total change in real GDP caused by an autonomous change in aggregate spending to the size of that autonomous change.

example, suppose that a boom in housing prices makes consumers feel richer and that, as a result, they become willing to spend more at any given level of disposable income. This will lead to an initial rise in consumer spending, before real GDP rises. But it will also lead to second and later rounds of higher consumer spending as real GDP rises.

An initial rise or fall in aggregate spending at a given level of real GDP is called an **autonomous change in aggregate spending.** It's autonomous—which means "self-governing"—because it's the cause, not the result, of the chain reaction we've just described. Formally, the **multiplier** is the ratio of the total change in real GDP caused by an autonomous change in aggregate spending to the size of that autonomous change. If we let $\Delta AAS$ stand for autonomous change in aggregate spending and $\Delta Y$ stand for the change in real GDP, then the multiplier is equal to $\Delta Y/\Delta AAS$. And we've already seen how to find the value of the multiplier. Assuming no taxes and no trade, the change in real GDP caused by an autonomous change in spending is:

$$\textbf{(11-3)} \ \Delta Y = \frac{1}{1 - MPC} \times \Delta AAS$$

So the multiplier is:

$$\textbf{(11-4)} \ \text{Multiplier} = \frac{\Delta Y}{\Delta AAS} = \frac{1}{1 - MPC}$$

Notice that the size of the multiplier depends on *MPC*. If the marginal propensity to consume is high, so is the multiplier. This is true because the size of *MPC* determines how large each round of expansion is compared with the previous round. To put it another way, the higher *MPC* is, the less disposable income "leaks out" into savings at each round of expansion.

In later chapters we'll use the concept of the multiplier to analyze the effects of fiscal and monetary policies. We'll also see that the formula for the multiplier changes when we introduce various complications, including taxes and foreign trade. First, however, we need to look more deeply at what determines consumer spending.

## ECONOMICS > IN ACTION

### THE MULTIPLIER AND THE GREAT DEPRESSION

The concept of the multiplier was originally devised by economists trying to understand the greatest economic disaster in history, the collapse of output and employment from 1929 to 1933, which began the Great Depression. Most economists believe that the slump from 1929 to 1933 was driven by a collapse in investment spending. But as the economy shrank, consumer spending also fell sharply, multiplying the effect on real GDP.

Table 11-2 shows what happened to investment spending, consumer spending, and GDP during those four terrible years. All data are in 2005 dollars. What we see is that investment spending imploded, falling by more than 80%. But consumer spending also fell drastically and actually accounted for more of the fall in real GDP. (The total fall in real

**TABLE 11-2** Investment Spending, Consumer Spending, and Real GDP in the Great Depression (billions of 2005 dollars)

|                     | 1929    | 1933    | Change    |
|---------------------|---------|---------|-----------|
| Investment spending | $101.4  | $18.9   | –$82.5    |
| Consumer spending   | 736.3   | 600.8   | –135.5    |
| Real GDP            | 976.1   | 715.8   | –260.3    |

*Source:* Bureau of Economic Analysis.

GDP was larger than the combined fall in consumer and investment spending, mainly because of technical accounting issues.)

The numbers in Table 11-2 suggest that at the time of the Great Depression, the multiplier was around 3. Most current estimates put the size of the multiplier considerably lower—but there's a reason for that change. In 1929, government in the United States was very small by modern standards: taxes were low and major government programs like Social Security and Medicare had not yet come into being. In the modern U.S. economy, taxes are much higher, and so is government spending. Why does this matter? Because taxes and some government programs act as *automatic stabilizers,* reducing the size of the multiplier. The appendix to Chapter 13 explains how taxes change the multiplier.

### CHECK YOUR UNDERSTANDING    11-1

1. Explain why a decline in investment spending caused by a change in business expectations leads to a fall in consumer spending.

2. What is the multiplier if the marginal propensity to consume is 0.5? What is it if *MPC* is 0.8?

3. As a percentage of GDP, savings accounts for a larger share of the economy in the country of Scania compared to the country of Amerigo. Which country is likely to have the larger multiplier? Explain.

Solutions appear at back of book.

# Consumer Spending

Should you splurge on a restaurant meal or save money by eating at home? Should you buy a new car and, if so, how expensive a model? Should you redo that bathroom or live with it for another year? In the real world, households are constantly confronted with such choices—not just about the consumption mix but also about how much to spend in total. These choices, in turn, have a powerful effect on the economy: consumer spending normally accounts for two-thirds of total spending on final goods and services. In particular, as we've just seen, the decision about how much of an additional dollar in income to spend—the marginal propensity to consume—determines the size of the multiplier, which determines the ultimate effect on the economy of autonomous changes in spending.

But what determines how much consumers spend?

## Current Disposable Income and Consumer Spending

The most important factor affecting a family's consumer spending is its current disposable income—income after taxes are paid and government transfers are received. It's obvious from daily life that people with high disposable incomes on average drive more expensive cars, live in more expensive houses, and spend more on meals and clothing than people with lower disposable incomes. And the relationship between current disposable income and spending is clear in the data.

The Bureau of Labor Statistics (BLS) collects annual data on family income and spending. Families are grouped by levels of before-tax income, and after-tax income for each group is also reported. Since the income figures include transfers from the government, what the BLS calls a household's after-tax income is equivalent to its current disposable income.

Figure 11-1 is a scatter diagram illustrating the relationship between household current disposable income and household consumer spending for American households by income group in 2009. For example, point *A* shows that in 2009 the middle fifth of the population had an average current disposable income of

During recessions, consumers tend to avoid higher-priced brand-name goods in favor of generics that cost less.

## FIGURE 11-1 Current Disposable Income and Consumer Spending for American Households in 2009

For each income group of households, average current disposable income in 2009 is plotted versus average consumer spending in 2009. For example, the middle income group, with an annual income of $35,598 to $57,294, is represented by point *A*, indicating a household average current disposable income of $45,199 and average household consumer spending of $41,150. The data clearly show a positive relationship between current disposable income and consumer spending: families with higher current disposable income have higher consumer spending.

*Source:* Bureau of Labor Statistics.

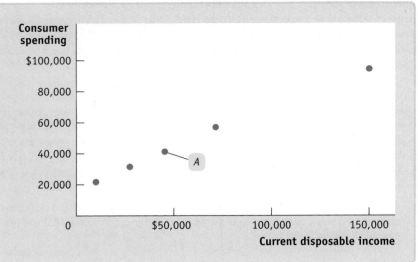

$45,199 and average spending of $41,150. The pattern of the dots slopes upward from left to right, making it clear that households with higher current disposable income had higher consumer spending.

It's very useful to represent the relationship between an individual household's current disposable income and its consumer spending with an equation. The **consumption function** is an equation showing how an individual household's consumer spending varies with the household's current disposable income. The simplest version of a consumption function is a linear equation:

**(11-5)** $c = a + MPC \times yd$

where lowercase letters indicate variables measured for an individual household.

In this equation, $c$ is individual household consumer spending and $yd$ is individual household current disposable income. Recall that *MPC*, the marginal propensity to consume, is the amount by which consumer spending rises if current disposable income rises by $1. Finally, $a$ is a constant term—individual household *autonomous consumer spending*, the amount of spending a household would do if it had zero disposable income. We assume that $a$ is greater than zero because a household with zero disposable income is able to fund some consumption by borrowing or using its savings. Notice, by the way, that we're using $y$ for income. That's standard practice in macroeconomics, even though *income* isn't actually spelled "yncome." The reason is that $I$ is reserved for investment spending.

Recall that we expressed *MPC* as the ratio of a change in consumer spending to the change in current disposable income. We've rewritten it for an individual household as Equation 11-6:

**(11-6)** $MPC = \Delta c / \Delta yd$

Multiplying both sides of Equation 11-6 by $\Delta yd$, we get:

**(11-7)** $MPC \times \Delta yd = \Delta c$

The **consumption function** is an equation showing how an individual household's consumer spending varies with the household's current disposable income.

Equation 11-7 tells us that when $yd$ goes up by $1, $c$ goes up by $MPC \times$ $1.

Figure 11-2 shows what Equation 11-5 looks like graphically, plotting $yd$ on the horizontal axis and $c$ on the vertical axis. Individual household autonomous

FIGURE **11-2**  The Consumption Function

The consumption function relates a household's current disposable income to its consumer spending. The vertical intercept, *a*, is individual household autonomous consumer spending: the amount of a household's consumer spending if its current disposable income is zero. The slope of the consumption function line, *cf*, is the marginal propensity to consume, or *MPC*: of every additional $1 of current disposable income, *MPC* × $1 is spent.

consumer spending, *a*, is the value of *c* when *yd* is zero—it is the vertical *intercept* of the consumption function, *cf*. *MPC* is the *slope* of the line, measured by rise over run. If current disposable income rises by $\Delta yd$, household consumer spending, *c*, rises by $\Delta c$. Since *MPC* is defined as $\Delta c/\Delta yd$, the slope of the consumption function is:

**(11-8)** Slope of consumption function
= Rise over run
= $\Delta c/\Delta yd$
= *MPC*

In reality, actual data never fit Equation 11-5 perfectly, but the fit can be pretty good. Figure 11-3 shows the data from Figure 11-1 again, together with a line drawn to fit the data as closely as possible. According to the data on households' consumer spending and current disposable income, the best estimate of *a* is $17,594 and of *MPC* is 0.518. So the consumption function fitted to the data is:

$$c = \$17,594 + 0.518 \times yd$$

That is, the data suggest a marginal propensity to consume of approximately 0.52. This implies that the marginal propensity to save (*MPS*)—the amount of an additional $1 of disposable income that is saved—is approximately 0.48, and the multiplier is approximately 1/0.48 = 2.08.

It's important to realize that Figure 11-3 shows a *microeconomic* relationship between the current disposable income of individual households and their spending on goods and services. However, macro-

FIGURE **11-3**  A Consumption Function Fitted to Data

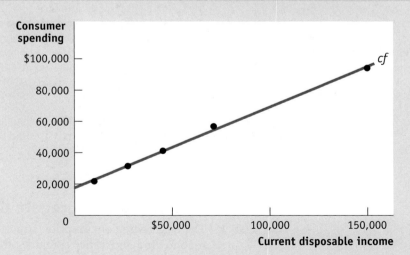

The data from Figure 11-1 are reproduced here, along with a line drawn to fit the data as closely as possible. For American households in 2009, the best estimate of the average household's autonomous consumer spending, *a*, is $17,594 and the best estimate of *MPC* is 0.518, or approximately 0.52.
*Source:* Bureau of Labor Statistics.

The **aggregate consumption function** is the relationship for the economy as a whole between aggregate current disposable income and aggregate consumer spending.

economists assume that a similar relationship holds *for the economy as a whole:* that there is a relationship, called the **aggregate consumption function,** between aggregate current disposable income and aggregate consumer spending. We'll assume that it has the same form as the household-level consumption function:

**(11-9)** $C = A + MPC \times YD$

Here, $C$ is aggregate consumer spending (called just "consumer spending"); $YD$ is aggregate current disposable income (called, for simplicity, just "disposable income"); and $A$ is aggregate autonomous consumer spending, the amount of consumer spending when $YD$ equals zero. This is the relationship represented in Figure 11-4 by $CF$, analogous to $cf$ in Figure 11-3.

**FIGURE 11-4** Shifts of the Aggregate Consumption Function

Panel (a) illustrates the effect of an increase in expected aggregate future disposable income. Consumers will spend more at every given level of aggregate current disposable income, $YD$. As a result, the initial aggregate consumption function $CF_1$, with aggregate autonomous consumer spending $A_1$, shifts up to a new position at $CF_2$ and aggregate autonomous consumer spending $A_2$. An increase in aggregate wealth will also shift the aggregate consumption function up. Panel (b), in

contrast, illustrates the effect of a reduction in expected aggregate future disposable income. Consumers will spend less at every given level of aggregate current disposable income, $YD$. Consequently, the initial aggregate consumption function $CF_1$, with aggregate autonomous consumer spending $A_1$, shifts down to a new position at $CF_2$ and aggregate autonomous consumer spending $A_2$. A reduction in aggregate wealth will have the same effect.

## Shifts of the Aggregate Consumption Function

The aggregate consumption function shows the relationship between disposable income and consumer spending for the economy as a whole, other things equal. When things other than disposable income change, the aggregate consumption function shifts. There are two principal causes of shifts of the aggregate consumption function: changes in expected future disposable income and changes in aggregate wealth.

**Changes in Expected Future Disposable Income** Suppose you land a really good, well-paying job on graduating from college in May—but the job, and the paychecks, won't start until September. So your disposable income hasn't risen yet. Even so, it's likely that you will start spending more on final goods and services right away—maybe buying nicer work clothes than you originally planned—because you know that higher income is coming.

Conversely, suppose you have a good job but learn that the company is planning to downsize your division, raising the possibility that you may lose your job and have to take a lower-paying one somewhere else. Even though your disposable income hasn't gone down yet, you might well cut back on spending even while still employed, to save for a rainy day.

Both of these examples show how expectations about future disposable income can affect consumer spending. The two panels of Figure 11-4, which plot disposable income against consumer spending, show how changes in expected future disposable income affect the aggregate consumption function. In both panels, $CF_1$ is the initial aggregate consumption function. Panel (a) shows the effect of good news: information that leads consumers to expect higher disposable income in the future than they did before. Consumers will now spend more at any given level of current disposable income, $YD$, corresponding to an increase in $A$, aggregate autonomous consumer spending, from $A_1$ to $A_2$. The effect is to shift the aggregate consumption function up, from $CF_1$ to $CF_2$. Panel (b) shows the effect of bad news: information that leads consumers to expect lower disposable income in the future than they did before. Consumers will now spend less at any given level of current disposable income, $YD$, corresponding to a fall in $A$ from $A_1$ to $A_2$. The effect is to shift the aggregate consumption function down, from $CF_1$ to $CF_2$.

In a famous 1956 book, *A Theory of the Consumption Function*, Milton Friedman showed that taking the effects of expected future income into account explains an otherwise puzzling fact about consumer behavior. If we look at consumer spending during any given year, we find that people with high current income save a larger fraction of their income than those with low current income. (This is obvious from the data in Figure 11-3: people in the highest income group spend considerably less than their income; those in the lowest income group spend more than their income.) You might think this implies that the overall savings rate will rise as the economy grows and average current incomes rise; in fact, however, this hasn't happened.

Friedman pointed out that when we look at individual incomes in a given year, there are systematic differences between current and expected future income that create a positive relationship between current income and the savings rate. On one side, people with low current incomes are often having an unusually bad year. For example, they may be workers who have been laid off but will probably find new jobs eventually. They are people whose expected future income is higher than their current income, so it makes sense for them to have low or even negative savings. On the other side, people with high current incomes in a given year are often having an unusually good year. For example, they may have investments that happened to do extremely well. They are people whose expected future income is lower than their current income, so it makes sense for them to save most of their windfall.

When the economy grows, by contrast, current and expected future incomes rise together. Higher current income tends to lead to higher savings today, but higher expected future income tends to lead to less savings today. As a result, there's a weaker relationship between current income and the savings rate.

Friedman argued that consumer spending ultimately depends mainly on the income people expect to have over the long term rather than on their current income. This argument is known as the *permanent income hypothesis*.

### Changes in Aggregate Wealth
Imagine two individuals, Maria and Mark, both of whom expect to earn $30,000 this year. Suppose, however, that they have different histories. Maria has been working steadily for the past 10 years, owns

her own home, and has $200,000 in the bank. Mark is the same age as Maria, but he has been in and out of work, hasn't managed to buy a house, and has very little in savings. In this case, Maria has something that Mark doesn't have: wealth. Even though they have the same disposable income, other things equal, you'd expect Maria to spend more on consumption than Mark. That is, *wealth* has an effect on consumer spending.

The effect of wealth on spending is emphasized by an influential economic model of how consumers make choices about spending versus saving called the *life-cycle hypothesis*. According to this hypothesis, consumers plan their spending over a lifetime, not just in response to their current disposable income. As a result, people try to smooth their consumption over their lifetimes—they save some of their current disposable income during their years of peak earnings (typically occurring during a worker's 40s and 50s) and during their retirement live off the wealth they accumulated while working. We won't go into the details of this hypothesis but will simply point out that it implies an important role for wealth in determining consumer spending. For example, a middle-aged couple who have accumulated a lot of wealth—who have paid off the mortgage on their house and already own plenty of stocks and bonds—will, other things equal, spend more on goods and services than a couple who have the same current disposable income but still need to save for their retirement.

Because wealth affects household consumer spending, changes in wealth across the economy can shift the aggregate consumption function. A rise in aggregate wealth—say, because of a booming stock market—increases the vertical intercept $A$, aggregate autonomous consumer spending. This, in turn, shifts the aggregate consumption function up in the same way as does an expected increase in future disposable income. A decline in aggregate wealth—say, because of a fall in housing prices as occurred in 2008—reduces $A$ and shifts the aggregate consumption function down.

## ECONOMICS > *IN ACTION*

### FAMOUS FIRST FORECASTING FAILURES

The Great Depression created modern macroeconomics. It also gave birth to the modern field of econometrics—the use of statistical techniques to fit economic models to empirical data. The aggregate consumption function was one of the first things econometricians studied. And, sure enough, they quickly experienced one of the first major failures of economic forecasting: consumer spending after World War II was much higher than estimates of the aggregate consumption function based on prewar data would have predicted.

Figure 11-5 tells the story. Panel (a) shows aggregate data on disposable income and consumer spending from 1929 to 1941, measured in billions of 2005 dollars. A simple linear consumption function, $CF_1$, seems to fit the data very well. And many economists thought this relationship would continue to hold in the future. But panel (b) shows what actually happened in later years. The points in the circle at the left are the data from the Great Depression shown in panel (a). The points in the circle at the right are data from 1946 to 1960. (Data from 1942 to 1945 aren't included because rationing during World War II prevented consumers from spending normally.) The solid line in the figure, $CF_1$, is the consumption function fitted to 1929–1941 data. As you can see, post–World War II consumer spending was much higher than the relationship from the Depression years would have predicted. For example, in 1960 consumer spending was 13.5% higher than the level predicted by $CF_1$.

Why was extrapolating from the earlier relationship so misleading? The answer is that from 1946 onward, both expected future disposable income and aggregate wealth were steadily rising. Consumers grew increasingly confident that the Great Depression wouldn't reemerge and that the post–World War II

FIGURE   **11-5**   Changes in the Aggregate Consumption Function Over Time

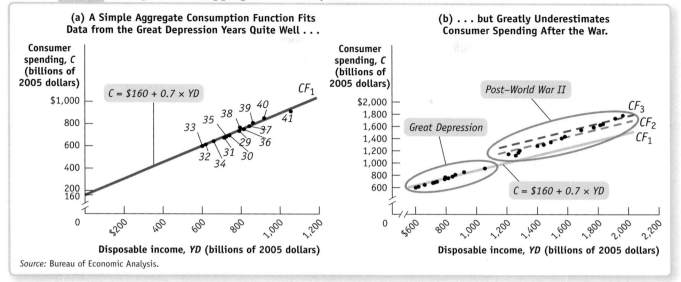

Source: Bureau of Economic Analysis.

economic boom would continue. At the same time, wealth was steadily increasing. As indicated by the dashed lines in panel (b), $CF_2$ and $CF_3$, the increases in expected future disposable income and in aggregate wealth shifted the aggregate consumption function up a number of times.

In macroeconomics, failure—whether of economic policy or of economic prediction—often leads to intellectual progress. The embarrassing failure of early estimates of the aggregate consumption function to predict post–World War II consumer spending led to important progress in our understanding of consumer behavior.

**CHECK YOUR UNDERSTANDING**   **11-2**

1. Suppose the economy consists of three people: Angelina, Felicia, and Marina. The table shows how their consumer spending varies as their current disposable income rises by $10,000.

   a. Derive each individual's consumption function, where *MPC* is calculated for a $10,000 change in current disposable income.

   b. Derive the aggregate consumption function.

| Current disposable income | Consumer spending | | |
|---|---|---|---|
| | Angelina | Felicia | Marina |
| $0 | $8,000 | $6,500 | $7,250 |
| 10,000 | 12,000 | 14,500 | 14,250 |

2. Suppose that problems in the capital markets make consumers unable either to borrow or to put money aside for future use. What implication does this have for the effects of expected future disposable income on consumer spending?

Solutions appear at back of book.

# Investment Spending

Although consumer spending is much larger than investment spending, booms and busts in investment spending tend to drive the business cycle. In fact, most recessions originate as a fall in investment spending. Figure 11-6 illustrates this point; it shows the annual percent change of investment spending and consumer spending in the United States, measured in real terms,

FIGURE    **11-6**    Fluctuations in Investment Spending and Consumer Spending

The bars illustrate the annual percent change in investment spending and consumer spending during six recent recessions. As the lengths of the bars show, swings in investment spending were much larger in percentage terms than those in consumer spending. This pattern has led economists to believe that recessions typically originate as a slump in investment spending.

*Source:* Bureau of Economic Analysis.

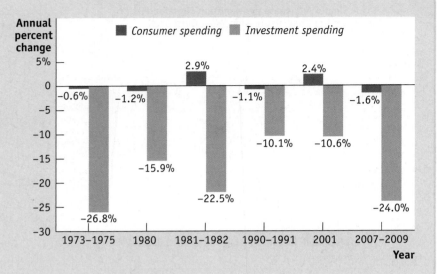

during six recessions from 1973 to 2009. As you can see, swings in investment spending are much more dramatic than those in consumer spending. In addition, due to the multiplier process, economists believe that declines in consumer spending are usually the result of a process that begins with a slump in investment spending. Soon we'll examine in more detail how a slump in investment spending generates a fall in consumer spending through the multiplier process.

Before we do that, however, let's analyze the factors that determine investment spending, which are somewhat different from those that determine consumer spending. The most important ones are the interest rate and expected future real GDP. We'll also revisit a fact that we noted in For Inquiring Minds in Chapter 10: the level of investment spending businesses *actually* carry out is sometimes not the same level as **planned investment spending,** the investment spending that firms *intend* to undertake during a given period. Planned investment spending depends on three principal factors: the interest rate, the expected future level of real GDP, and the current level of production capacity. First, we'll analyze the effect of the interest rate.

## The Interest Rate and Investment Spending

Interest rates have their clearest effect on one particular form of investment spending: spending on residential construction—that is, on the construction of homes. The reason is straightforward: home builders only build houses they think they can sell, and houses are more affordable—and so more likely to sell—when the interest rate is low. Consider a potential home-buying family that needs to borrow $150,000 to buy a house. At an interest rate of 7.5%, a 30-year home mortgage will mean payments of $1,048 per month. At an interest rate of 5.5%, those payments would be only $851 per month, making houses significantly more affordable. As described in the upcoming Economics in Action, interest rates actually did drop from roughly 7.5% to 5.5% between the late 1990s and 2003, helping set off the great housing boom described in this chapter's opening story.

Interest rates also affect other forms of investment spending. Firms with investment spending projects will only go ahead with a project if they expect a rate of return higher than the cost of the funds they would have to borrow to

**Planned investment spending** is the investment spending that businesses intend to undertake during a given period.

finance that project. As we saw in Chapter 10 the interest rate rises, fewer projects will pass that test, and as a result investment spending will be lower.

You might think that the trade-off a firm faces is different if it can fund its investment project with its past profits rather than through borrowing. Past profits used to finance investment spending are called *retained earnings*. But even if a firm pays for investment spending out of retained earnings, the trade-off it must make in deciding whether or not to fund a project remains the same because it must take into account the opportunity cost of its funds. For example, instead of purchasing new equipment, the firm could lend out the funds and earn interest. The forgone interest earned is the opportunity cost of using retained earnings to fund an investment project. So the trade-off the firm faces when comparing a project's rate of return to the market interest rate has not changed when it uses retained earnings rather than borrowed funds, which means that regardless of whether a firm funds investment spending through borrowing or retained earnings, a rise in the market interest rate makes any given investment project less profitable. Conversely, a fall in the interest rate makes some investment projects that were unprofitable before profitable at the now lower interest rate. So some projects that had been unfunded before will be funded now.

So planned investment spending—spending on investment projects that firms voluntarily decide whether or not to undertake—is negatively related to the interest rate. Other things equal, a higher interest rate leads to a lower level of planned investment spending.

## Expected Future Real GDP, Production Capacity, and Investment Spending

Suppose a firm has enough capacity to continue to produce the amount it is currently selling but doesn't expect its sales to grow in the future. Then it will engage in investment spending only to replace existing equipment and structures that wear out or are rendered obsolete by new technologies. But if, instead, the firm expects its sales to grow rapidly in the future, it will find its existing production capacity insufficient for its future production needs. So the firm will undertake investment spending to meet those needs. This implies that, other things equal, firms will undertake more investment spending when they expect their sales to grow.

Now suppose that the firm currently has considerably more capacity than necessary to meet current production needs. Even if it expects sales to grow, it won't have to undertake investment spending for a while—not until the growth in sales catches up with its excess capacity. This illustrates the fact that, other things equal, the current level of productive capacity has a negative effect on investment spending: other things equal, the higher the current capacity, the lower is investment spending.

If we put together the effects on investment spending of growth in expected future sales and the size of current production capacity, we can see one situation in which we can be reasonably sure that firms will undertake high levels of investment spending: when they expect sales to grow rapidly. In that case, even excess production capacity will soon be used up, leading firms to resume investment spending.

What is an indicator of high expected growth of future sales? It's a high expected future growth rate of real GDP. A higher expected future growth rate of real GDP results in a higher level of planned investment spending, but a lower expected future growth rate of real GDP leads to lower planned investment spending. This relationship is summarized in a proposition known as the **accelerator principle.** As we explain in the upcoming Economics in Action, in 2006, when expectations of future real GDP growth turned negative, planned investment spending—and, in particular, residential investment spending—plunged, accelerating the economy's slide into recession. Generally, the effects of the accelerator principle play an important role in *investment spending slumps*, periods of low investment spending.

According to the **accelerator principle,** a higher growth rate of real GDP leads to higher planned investment spending, but a lower growth rate of real GDP leads to lower planned investment spending.

**Inventories** are stocks of goods held to satisfy future sales.

**Inventory investment** is the value of the change in total inventories held in the economy during a given period.

**Unplanned inventory investment** occurs when actual sales are more or less than businesses expected, leading to unplanned changes in inventories.

**Actual investment spending** is the sum of planned investment spending and unplanned inventory investment.

## Inventories and Unplanned Investment Spending

Most firms maintain **inventories,** stocks of goods held to satisfy future sales. Firms hold inventories so they can quickly satisfy buyers—a consumer can purchase an item off the shelf rather than waiting for it to be manufactured. In addition, businesses often hold inventories of their inputs to be sure they have a steady supply of necessary materials and spare parts. At the end of the second quarter of 2011, the overall value of inventories in the U.S. economy was estimated at $2.3 trillion, just over 15% of GDP.

As we explained in Chapter 7, a firm that increases its inventories is engaging in a form of investment spending. Suppose, for example, that the U.S. auto industry produces 800,000 cars per month but sells only 700,000. The remaining 100,000 cars are added to the inventory at auto company warehouses or car dealerships, ready to be sold in the future. **Inventory investment** is the value of the change in total inventories held in the economy during a given period. Unlike other forms of investment spending, inventory investment can actually be negative. If, for example, the auto industry reduces its inventory over the course of a month, we say that it has engaged in negative inventory investment.

To understand inventory investment, think about a manager stocking the canned goods section of a supermarket. The manager tries to keep the store fully stocked so that shoppers can almost always find what they're looking for. But the manager does not want the shelves too heavily stocked because shelf space is limited and products can spoil. Similar considerations apply to many firms and typically lead them to manage their inventories carefully. However, sales fluctuate. And because firms cannot always accurately predict sales, they often find themselves holding more or less inventories than they had intended. These unintended swings in inventories due to unforeseen changes in sales are called **unplanned inventory investment.** They represent investment spending, positive or negative, that occurred but was unplanned.

So in any given period, **actual investment spending** is equal to planned investment spending plus unplanned inventory investment. If we let $I_{Unplanned}$ represent unplanned inventory investment, $I_{Planned}$ represent planned investment spending, and $I$ represent actual investment spending, then the relationship among all three can be represented as:

**(11-10)** $I = I_{Unplanned} + I_{Planned}$

To see how unplanned inventory investment can occur, let's continue to focus on the auto industry and make the following assumptions. First, let's assume that the industry must determine each month's production volume in advance, before it knows the volume of actual sales. Second, let's assume that it anticipates selling 800,000 cars next month and that it plans neither to add to nor subtract from existing inventories. In that case, it will produce 800,000 cars to match anticipated sales.

Now imagine that next month's actual sales are less than expected, only 700,000 cars. As a result, the value of 100,000 cars will be added to investment spending as unplanned inventory investment.

The auto industry will, of course, eventually adjust to this slowdown in sales and the resulting unplanned inventory investment. It is likely that it will cut next month's production volume in order to reduce inventories. In fact, economists who study macroeconomic variables in an attempt to determine the future path of the economy pay

In 2009, vehicles sat unsold on car dealership lots when the economy slumped and consumer spending plunged.

Fabrizio Costantini/The New York Times/Redux

careful attention to changes in inventory levels. Rising inventories typically indicate positive unplanned inventory investment and a slowing economy, as sales are less than had been forecast. Falling inventories typically indicate negative unplanned inventory investment and a growing economy, as sales are greater than forecast. In the next section, we will see how production adjustments in response to fluctuations in sales and inventories ensure that the value of final goods and services actually produced is equal to desired purchases of those final goods and services.

## ECONOMICS ➤ IN ACTION

### INTEREST RATES AND THE U.S. HOUSING BOOM

The housing boom in the Ft. Myers metropolitan area, described at the beginning of this chapter, was part of a broader housing boom in the country as a whole. There is little question that this housing boom was caused, in the first instance, by low interest rates.

Figure 11-7 shows the interest rate on 30-year home mortgages—the traditional way to borrow money for a home purchase—and the number of housing starts, the number of homes for which construction is started per month, from 1995 to the middle of 2011, in the United States. Panel (a), which shows the mortgage rate, gives you an idea of how much interest rates fell. In the second half of the 1990s, mortgage rates generally fluctuated between 7% and 8%; by 2003, they were down to between 5% and 6%. These lower rates were largely the result of Federal Reserve policy: the Fed cut rates in response to the 2001 recession and continued cutting them into 2003 out of concern that the economy's recovery was too weak to generate sustained job growth.

**FIGURE   11-7   Interest Rates and the U.S. Housing Boom**

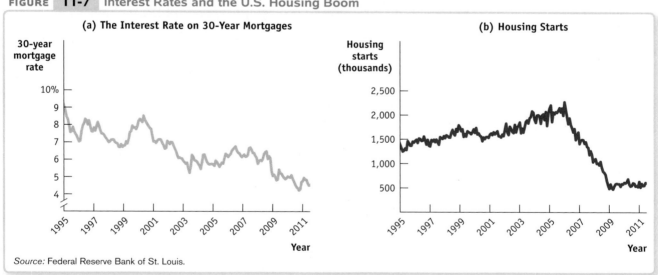

Source: Federal Reserve Bank of St. Louis.

The low interest rates led to a large increase in residential investment spending, reflected in a surge of housing starts, shown in panel (b). This rise in investment spending drove an overall economic expansion, both through its direct effects and through the multiplier process.

Unfortunately, the housing boom eventually turned into too much of a good thing. By 2006, it was clear that the U.S. housing market was experiencing a bubble: people were buying housing based on unrealistic expectations about future price increases. When the bubble burst, housing—and the U.S. economy—took a fall. The fall was so severe that even when the Fed cut rates to near zero, and mortgage rates consequently dropped to below 5% beginning in 2009, housing starts merely stabilized. By 2011, housing starts had not yet recovered.

## CHECK YOUR UNDERSTANDING 11-3

1. For each event, explain whether planned investment spending or unplanned inventory investment will change and in what direction.
   a. An unexpected increase in consumer spending
   b. A sharp rise in the cost of business borrowing
   c. A sharp increase in the economy's growth rate of real GDP
   d. An unanticipated fall in sales

2. Historically, investment spending has experienced more extreme upward and downward swings than consumer spending. Why do you think this is so? (*Hint:* Consider the marginal propensity to consume and the accelerator principle.)

3. Consumer spending was sluggish in late 2007, and economists worried that an *inventory overhang*—a high level of unplanned inventory investment throughout the economy—would make it difficult for the economy to recover anytime soon. Explain why an inventory overhang might, like the existence of too much production capacity, depress current economic activity.

*Solutions appear at back of book.*

# The Income–Expenditure Model

Earlier in this chapter, we described how autonomous changes in spending—such as a fall in investment spending when a housing bubble bursts—lead to a multistage process through the actions of the multiplier that magnifies the effect of these changes on real GDP. In this section, we will examine this multistage process more closely. We'll see that the multiple rounds of changes in real GDP are accomplished through changes in the amount of output produced by firms—changes that they make in response to changes in their inventories. We'll come to understand why inventories play a central role in macroeconomic models of the economy in the short run as well as why economists pay particular attention to the behavior of firms' inventories when trying to understand the likely future state of the economy.

Before we begin, let's quickly recap the assumptions underlying the multiplier process.

1. *Changes in overall spending lead to changes in aggregate output.* We assume that producers are willing to supply additional output at a fixed price level. As a result, changes in spending translate into changes in output rather than moves of the overall price level up or down. A fixed aggregate price level also implies that there is no difference between nominal GDP and real GDP. So we can use the two terms interchangeably in this chapter.

2. *The interest rate is fixed.* We'll take the interest rate as predetermined and unaffected by the factors we analyze in the model. As in the case of the aggregate price level, what we're really doing here is leaving the determinants of the interest rate outside the model. As we'll see, the model can still be used to study the effects of a change in the interest rate.

3. *Taxes, government transfers, and government purchases are all zero.*

4. *Exports and imports are both zero.*

In all subsequent chapters, we will drop the assumption that the aggregate price level is fixed. The Chapter 13 appendix addresses how taxes affect the multiplier process. We'll explain how the interest rate is determined in Chapter 15 and bring foreign trade back into the picture in Chapter 19.

**Planned aggregate spending** is the total amount of planned spending in the economy.

## Planned Aggregate Spending and Real GDP

In an economy with no government and no foreign trade, there are only two sources of aggregate spending: consumer spending, $C$, and investment spending, $I$. And since we assume that there are no taxes or transfers, aggregate disposable income is equal to GDP (which, since the aggregate price level is fixed, is the same as real GDP): the total value of final sales of goods and services ultimately accrues to households as income. So in this highly simplified economy, there are two basic equations of national income accounting:

**(11-11)** $GDP = C + I$

**(11-12)** $YD = GDP$

As we learned earlier in this chapter, the aggregate consumption function shows the relationship between disposable income and consumer spending. Let's continue to assume that the aggregate consumption function is of the same form as in Equation 11-9:

**(11-13)** $C = A + MPC \times YD$

In our simplified model, we will also assume planned investment spending, $I_{Planned}$, is fixed.

We need one more concept before putting the model together: **planned aggregate spending,** the total amount of planned spending in the economy. Unlike firms, households don't take unintended actions like unplanned inventory investment. So planned aggregate spending is equal to the sum of consumer spending and planned investment spending. We denote planned aggregate spending by $AE_{Planned}$, so:

**(11-14)** $AE_{Planned} = C + I_{Planned}$

The level of planned aggregate spending in a given year depends on the level of real GDP in that year. To see why, let's look at a specific example, shown in Table 11-3. We assume that the aggregate consumption function is:

**(11-15)** $C = 300 + 0.6 \times YD$

Real GDP, $YD$, $C$, $I_{Planned}$, and $AE_{Planned}$ are all measured in billions of dollars, and we assume that the level of planned investment, $I_{Planned}$, is fixed at $500 billion per year. The first column shows possible levels of real GDP. The second column shows disposable income, $YD$, which in our simplified model is equal to real GDP. The third column shows consumer spending, $C$, equal to $300 billion plus 0.6 times disposable income, $YD$. The fourth column shows planned investment spending, $I_{Planned}$, which we have assumed is $500 billion regardless of the level of real GDP. Finally, the last column shows planned aggregate spending, $AE_{Planned}$, the sum of aggregate consumer spending, $C$, and planned investment spending, $I_{Planned}$. (To economize on notation, we'll assume that it is understood from now on that all the variables in Table 11-3 are measured in billions of dollars per year.) As you can see, a higher level of real GDP leads to a higher

TABLE **11-3**

| Real GDP | YD | C | $I_{Planned}$ | $AE_{Planned}$ |
|---|---|---|---|---|
| (billions of dollars) | | | | |
| $0 | $0 | $300 | $500 | $800 |
| 500 | 500 | 600 | 500 | 1,100 |
| 1,000 | 1,000 | 900 | 500 | 1,400 |
| 1,500 | 1,500 | 1,200 | 500 | 1,700 |
| 2,000 | 2,000 | 1,500 | 500 | 2,000 |
| 2,500 | 2,500 | 1,800 | 500 | 2,300 |
| 3,000 | 3,000 | 2,100 | 500 | 2,600 |
| 3,500 | 3,500 | 2,400 | 500 | 2,900 |

**FIGURE 11-8** The Aggregate Consumption Function and Planned Aggregate Spending

The lower line, *CF*, is the aggregate consumption function constructed from the data in Table 11-3. The upper line, *AE*$_{Planned}$, is the planned aggregate spending line, also constructed from the data in Table 11-3. It is equivalent to the aggregate consumption function shifted up by $500 billion, the amount of planned investment spending, *I*$_{Planned}$.

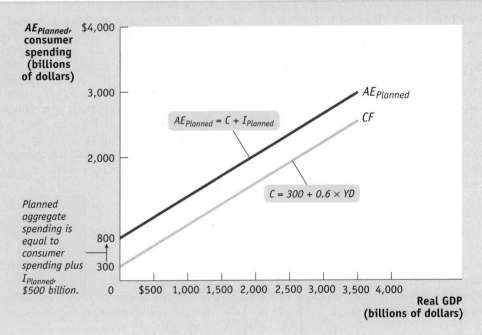

Planned aggregate spending is equal to consumer spending plus *I*$_{Planned}$, $500 billion.

level of disposable income: every 500 increase in real GDP raises *YD* by 500, which in turn raises *C* by 500 × 0.6 = 300 and *AE*$_{Planned}$ by 300.

Figure 11-8 illustrates the information in Table 11-3 graphically. Real GDP is measured on the horizontal axis. *CF* is the aggregate consumption function; it shows how consumer spending depends on real GDP. *AE*$_{Planned}$, the planned aggregate spending line, corresponds to the aggregate consumption function shifted up by 500 (the amount of *I*$_{Planned}$). It shows how planned aggregate spending depends on real GDP. Both lines have a slope of 0.6, equal to *MPC*, the marginal propensity to consume.

But this isn't the end of the story. Table 11-3 reveals that real GDP equals planned aggregate spending, *AE*$_{Planned}$, only when the level of real GDP is at 2,000. Real GDP does not equal *AE*$_{Planned}$ at any other level. Is that possible? Didn't we learn in Chapter 7, with the circular-flow diagram, that total spending on final goods and services in the economy is equal to the total value of output of final goods and services? The answer is that for *brief* periods of time, planned aggregate spending can differ from real GDP because of the role of *unplanned* aggregate spending—*I*$_{Unplanned}$, unplanned inventory investment. But as we'll see in the next section, the economy moves over time to a situation in which there is no unplanned inventory investment, a situation called *income–expenditure equilibrium*. And when the economy is in income–expenditure equilibrium, planned aggregate spending on final goods and services equals aggregate output.

## Income–Expenditure Equilibrium

For all but one value of real GDP shown in Table 11-3, real GDP is either more or less than *AE*$_{Planned}$, the sum of consumer spending and *planned* investment spending. For example, when real GDP is 1,000, consumer spending, *C*, is 900 and planned investment spending is 500, making planned aggregate spending 1,400. This is 400 *more* than the corresponding level of real GDP. Now consider what happens when real GDP is 2,500; consumer spending, *C*, is 1,800 and planned investment spending is 500, making planned aggregate spending only 2,300, 200 *less* than real GDP.

As we've just explained, planned aggregate spending can be different from real GDP only if there is unplanned inventory investment, $I_{Unplanned}$, in the economy. Let's examine Table 11-4, which includes the numbers for real GDP and for planned aggregate spending from Table 11-3. It also includes the levels of unplanned inventory investment, $I_{Unplanned}$, that each combination of real GDP and planned aggregate spending implies. For example, if real GDP is 2,500, planned aggregate spending is only 2,300. This 200 excess of real GDP over $AE_{Planned}$ must consist of positive unplanned inventory investment. This can happen only if firms have overestimated sales and produced too much, leading to unintended additions to inventories. More generally, any level of real GDP in excess of 2,000 corresponds to a situation in which firms are producing more than consumers and other firms want to purchase, creating an unintended increase in inventories.

Conversely, a level of real GDP below 2,000 implies that planned aggregate spending is *greater* than real GDP. For example, when real GDP is 1,000, planned aggregate spending is much larger, at 1,400. The 400 excess of $AE_{Planned}$ over real GDP corresponds to negative unplanned inventory investment equal to –400. More generally, any level of real GDP below 2,000 implies that firms have underestimated sales, leading to a negative level of unplanned inventory investment in the economy.

By putting together Equations 11-10, 11-11, and 11-14, we can summarize the general relationships among real GDP, planned aggregate spending, and unplanned inventory investment as follows:

**(11-16)** $GDP = C + I$
$= C + I_{Planned} + I_{Unplanned}$
$= AE_{Planned} + I_{Unplanned}$

So whenever real GDP exceeds $AE_{Planned}$, $I_{Unplanned}$ is positive; whenever real GDP is less than $AE_{Planned}$, $I_{Unplanned}$ is negative.

But firms will act to correct their mistakes. We've assumed that they don't change their prices, but they *can* adjust their output. Specifically, they will reduce production if they have experienced an unintended rise in inventories or increase production if they have experienced an unintended fall in inventories. And these responses will eventually eliminate the unanticipated changes in inventories and move the economy to a point at which real GDP is equal to planned aggregate spending. Staying with our example, if real GDP is 1,000, negative unplanned inventory investment will lead firms to increase production, leading to a rise in real GDP. In fact, this will happen whenever real GDP is less than 2,000—that is, whenever real GDP is less than planned aggregate spending. Conversely, if real GDP is 2,500, positive unplanned inventory investment will lead firms to reduce production, leading to a fall in real GDP. This will happen whenever real GDP is greater than planned aggregate spending.

The only situation in which firms won't have an incentive to change output in the next period is when aggregate output, measured by real GDP, is equal to planned aggregate spending in the current period, an outcome known as **income–expenditure equilibrium.** In Table 11-4, income–expenditure equilibrium is achieved when real GDP is 2,000, the only level of real GDP at which unplanned inventory investment is zero. From now on, we'll denote the real GDP level at which income–expenditure equilibrium occurs as *Y\** and call it the **income–expenditure equilibrium GDP.**

TABLE **11-4**

| Real GDP | $AE_{Planned}$ | $I_{Unplanned}$ |
|---|---|---|
| (billions of dollars) | | |
| $0 | $800 | –$800 |
| 500 | 1,100 | –600 |
| 1,000 | 1,400 | –400 |
| 1,500 | 1,700 | –200 |
| 2,000 | 2,000 | 0 |
| 2,500 | 2,300 | 200 |
| 3,000 | 2,600 | 400 |
| 3,500 | 2,900 | 600 |

The economy is in **income–expenditure equilibrium** when aggregate output, measured by real GDP, is equal to planned aggregate spending.

**Income–expenditure equilibrium GDP** is the level of real GDP at which real GDP equals planned aggregate spending.

FIGURE    **11-9**    Income–Expenditure Equilibrium

Income–expenditure equilibrium occurs at $E$, the point where the planned aggregate spending line, $AE_{Planned}$, crosses the 45-degree line. At $E$, the economy produces real GDP of $2,000 billion per year, the only point at which real GDP equals planned aggregate spending, $AE_{Planned}$, and unplanned inventory investment, $I_{Unplanned}$, is zero. This is the level of income–expenditure equilibrium GDP, $Y^*$. At any level of real GDP less than $Y^*$, $AE_{Planned}$ exceeds real GDP. As a result, unplanned inventory investment, $I_{Unplanned}$, is negative and firms respond by increasing production. At any level of real GDP greater than $Y^*$, real GDP exceeds $AE_{Planned}$. Unplanned inventory investment, $I_{Unplanned}$, is positive and firms respond by reducing production.

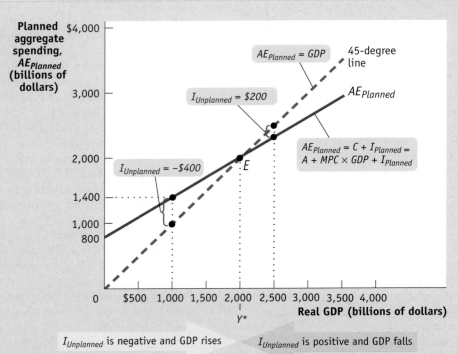

Figure 11-9 illustrates the concept of income–expenditure equilibrium graphically. Real GDP is on the horizontal axis and planned aggregate spending, $AE_{Planned}$, is on the vertical axis. There are two lines in the figure. The solid line is the planned aggregate spending line. It shows how $AE_{Planned}$, equal to $C + I_{Planned}$, depends on real GDP; it has a slope of 0.6, equal to the marginal propensity to consume, $MPC$, and a vertical intercept equal to $A + I_{Planned}$ (300 + 500 = 800). The dashed line, which goes through the origin with a slope of 1 (often called a 45-degree line), shows all the possible points at which planned aggregate spending is equal to real GDP. This line allows us to easily spot the point of income–expenditure equilibrium, which must lie on both the 45-degree line and the planned aggregate spending line. So the point of income–expenditure equilibrium is at $E$, where the two lines cross. And the income–expenditure equilibrium GDP, $Y^*$, is 2,000—the same outcome we derived in Table 11-4.

Now consider what happens if the economy isn't in income–expenditure equilibrium. We can see from Figure 11-9 that whenever real GDP is less than $Y^*$, the planned aggregate spending line lies above the 45-degree line and $AE_{Planned}$ exceeds real GDP. In this situation, $I_{Unplanned}$ is negative: as shown in the figure, at a real GDP of 1,000, $I_{Unplanned}$ is –400. As a consequence, real GDP will rise. In contrast, whenever real GDP is greater than $Y^*$, the planned aggregate expenditure line lies below the 45-degree line. Here, $I_{Unplanned}$ is positive: as shown, at a real GDP of 2,500, $I_{Unplanned}$ is 200. The unanticipated accumulation of inventory leads to a fall in real GDP.

The **Keynesian cross** diagram identifies income–expenditure equilibrium as the point where the planned aggregate spending line crosses the 45-degree line.

The type of diagram shown in Figure 11-9, which identifies income–expenditure equilibrium as the point at which the planned aggregate spending line crosses the 45-degree line, has a special place in the history of economic thought. Known as the **Keynesian cross,** it was developed by Paul Samuelson, one of the greatest economists of the twentieth century (as well as a Nobel Prize winner), to explain the ideas of John Maynard Keynes, the founder of macroeconomics as we know it.

## The Multiplier Process and Inventory Adjustment

We've just learned about a very important feature of the macroeconomy: when planned spending by households and firms does not equal the current aggregate output by firms, this difference shows up in changes in inventories. The response of firms to those inventory changes moves real GDP over time to the point at which real GDP and planned aggregate spending are equal. That's why, as we mentioned earlier, changes in inventories are considered a leading indicator of future economic activity.

Now that we understand how real GDP moves to achieve income–expenditure equilibrium for a given level of planned aggregate spending, let's turn to understanding what happens when there is *a shift of the planned aggregate spending line.* How does the economy move from the initial point of income–expenditure equilibrium to a new point of income–expenditure equilibrium? And what are the possible sources of changes in planned aggregate spending?

In our simple model there are only two possible sources of a shift of the planned aggregate spending line: a change in planned investment spending, $I_{Planned}$, or a shift of the aggregate consumption function, $CF$. For example, a change in $I_{Planned}$ can occur because of a change in the interest rate. (Remember, we're assuming that the interest rate is fixed by factors that are outside the model. But we can still ask what happens when the interest rate changes.) A shift of the aggregate consumption function (that is, a change in its vertical intercept, $A$) can occur because of a change in aggregate wealth— say, due to a rise in house prices. When the planned aggregate spending line shifts—when there is a change in the level of planned aggregate spending at any given level of real GDP—there is an autonomous change in planned aggregate spending. Recall from earlier in this chapter that an autonomous change in planned aggregate spending is a change in the desired level of spending by firms, households, and government at any given level of real GDP (although we've assumed away the government for the time being). How does an autonomous change in planned aggregate spending affect real GDP in income–expenditure equilibrium?

Table 11-5 and Figure 11-10 start from the same numerical example we used in Table 11-4 and Figure 11-9. They also show the effect of an autonomous increase in planned aggregate spending of 400—what happens when planned aggregate spending is 400 higher at each level of real GDP. Look first at Table 11-5. Before the autonomous increase in planned aggregate spending, the level of real GDP at which planned aggregate spending is equal to real GDP, $Y^*$, is 2,000. After the autonomous change, $Y^*$ has risen to 3,000. The same result is visible in Figure 11-10. The initial income–expenditure equilibrium is at $E_1$, where $Y_1^*$ is 2,000. The autonomous rise in planned aggregate spending shifts the planned aggregate spending line up, leading to a new income–expenditure equilibrium at $E_2$, where $Y_2^*$ is 3,000.

The fact that the rise in income–expenditure equilibrium GDP, from 2,000 to 3,000, is much larger than the autonomous increase in aggregate spending, which is only 400, has a familiar explanation: the multiplier process. In the specific example we have just described, an autonomous increase in planned aggregate spending of 400 leads to an increase in $Y^*$ from 2,000 to 3,000, a rise of 1,000. So the multiplier in this example is $1,000/400 = 2.5$.

We can examine in detail what underlies the multistage multiplier process by looking more closely at Figure 11-10. First, starting from $E_1$, the autonomous

**TABLE** **11-5**

| Real GDP | $AE_{Planned}$ before autonomous change | $AE_{Planned}$ after autonomous change |
|---|---|---|
| | (billions of dollars) | |
| $0 | $800 | $1,200 |
| 500 | 1,100 | 1,500 |
| 1,000 | 1,400 | 1,800 |
| 1,500 | 1,700 | 2,100 |
| 2,000 | 2,000 | 2,400 |
| 2,500 | 2,300 | 2,700 |
| 3,000 | 2,600 | 3,000 |
| 3,500 | 2,900 | 3,300 |
| 4,000 | 3,200 | 3,600 |

FIGURE **11-10** The Multiplier

This figure illustrates the change in $Y^*$ caused by an autonomous increase in planned aggregate spending. The economy is initially at equilibrium point $E_1$ with an income–expenditure equilibrium GDP, $Y_1^*$, equal to 2,000. An autonomous increase in $AE_{Planned}$ of 400 shifts the planned aggregate spending line upward by 400. The economy is no longer in income–expenditure equilibrium: real GDP is equal to 2,000 but $AE_{Planned}$ is now 2,400, represented by point $X$. The vertical distance between the two planned aggregate spending lines, equal to 400, represents $I_{Unplanned} = -400$—the negative inventory investment that the economy now experiences. Firms respond by increasing production, and the economy eventually reaches a new income–expenditure equilibrium at $E_2$ with a higher level of income–expenditure equilibrium GDP, $Y_2^*$, equal to 3,000.

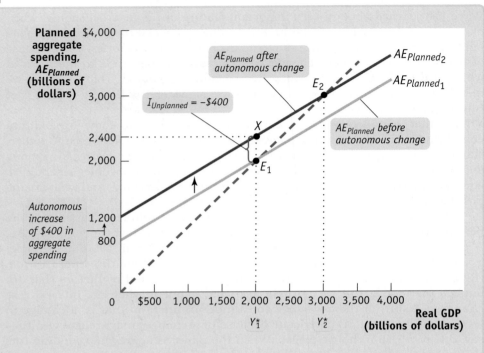

increase in planned aggregate spending leads to a gap between planned aggregate spending and real GDP. This is represented by the vertical distance between $X$, at 2,400, and $E_1$, at 2,000. This gap illustrates an unplanned fall in inventory investment: $I_{Unplanned} = -400$. Firms respond by increasing production, leading to a rise in real GDP from $Y_1^*$. The rise in real GDP translates into an increase in disposable income, $YD$. That's the first stage in the chain reaction. But it doesn't stop there—the increase in $YD$ leads to a rise in consumer spending, $C$, which sets off a second-round rise in real GDP. This in turn leads to a further rise in disposable income and consumer spending, and so on. And we could play this process in reverse: an autonomous fall in aggregate spending will lead to a chain reaction of reductions in real GDP and consumer spending.

We can summarize these results in an equation, where $\Delta AAE_{Planned}$ represents the autonomous change in $AE_{Planned}$, and $\Delta Y^* = Y_2^* - Y_1^*$, the subsequent change in income–expenditure equilibrium GDP:

$$(11\text{-}17) \quad \Delta Y^* = \text{Multiplier} \times \Delta AAE_{Planned} = \frac{1}{1 - MPC} \times \Delta AAE_{Planned}$$

Recalling that the multiplier, $1/(1 - MPC)$, is greater than 1, Equation 11-17 tells us that the change in income–expenditure equilibrium GDP, $\Delta Y^*$, is several times as large as the autonomous change in planned aggregate spending, $\Delta AAE_{Planned}$. It also helps us recall an important point: because the marginal propensity to consume is less than 1, each increase in disposable income and each corresponding increase in consumer spending is smaller than in the previous round. That's because at each round some of the increase in disposable income leaks out into savings. As a result, although real GDP grows at each round, the increase in real GDP diminishes from each round to the next. At some point the increase in real GDP is negligible, and the economy converges to a new income–expenditure equilibrium GDP at $Y_2^*$.

**The Paradox of Thrift** You may recall that in Chapter 6 we mentioned the paradox of thrift to illustrate the fact that in macroeconomics the outcome of many individual actions can generate a result that is different from and worse than the simple sum of those individual actions. In the paradox of thrift, households and firms cut their spending in anticipation of future tough economic times. These actions depress the economy, leaving households and firms worse off than if they hadn't acted virtuously to prepare for tough times. It is called a paradox because what's usually "good" (saving to provide for your family in hard times) is "bad" (because it can make everyone worse off).

Using the multiplier, we can now see exactly how this scenario unfolds. Suppose that there is a slump in consumer spending or investment spending, or both, just like the slump in residential construction investment spending leading up to the 2007–2009 recession. This causes a fall in income–expenditure equilibrium GDP that is several times larger than the original fall in spending. The fall in real GDP leaves consumers and producers worse off than they would have been if they hadn't cut their spending. Conversely, prodigal behavior is rewarded: if consumers or producers increase their spending, the resulting multiplier process makes the increase in income–expenditure equilibrium GDP several times larger than the original increase in spending. So prodigal spending makes consumers and producers better off than if they had been cautious spenders.

It's important to realize that our result that the multiplier is equal to $1/(1 - MPC)$ depends on the simplifying assumption that there are no taxes or transfers, so that disposable income is equal to real GDP. In the appendix to Chapter 28, we'll bring taxes into the picture, which makes the expression for the multiplier more complicated and the multiplier itself smaller. But the general principle we have just learned—an autonomous change in planned aggregate spending leads to a change in income–expenditure equilibrium GDP, both directly and through an induced change in consumer spending—remains valid.

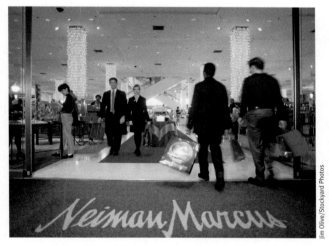

Extravagant spending on the part of producers and consumers makes everyone better off thanks to the multiplier process.

As we noted earlier in this chapter, declines in planned investment spending are usually the major factor causing recessions, because historically they have been the most common source of autonomous reductions in aggregate spending. The tendency of the consumption function to shift upward over time, which we pointed out earlier in Economics in Action, "Famous First Forecasting Failures," means that autonomous changes in both planned investment spending and consumer spending play important roles in expansions. But regardless of the source, there are multiplier effects in the economy that magnify the size of the initial change in aggregate spending.

## ECONOMICS > IN ACTION

### INVENTORIES AND THE END OF A RECESSION

A very clear example of the role of inventories in the multiplier process took place in late 2001, as that year's recession came to an end. The driving force behind the recession was a slump in business investment spending. It took several years before investment spending bounced back in the form of a housing boom. Still, the economy did start to recover in late 2001, largely because of an increase in consumer spending—especially on durable goods such as automobiles.

**FIGURE 11-11** Inventories and the End of a Recession

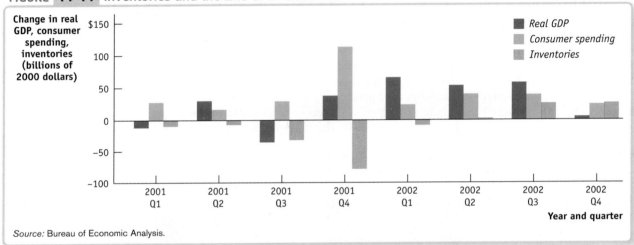

*Source:* Bureau of Economic Analysis.

Initially, this increase in consumer spending caught manufacturers by surprise. Figure 11-11 shows changes in real GDP, real consumer spending, and real inventories in each quarter of 2001 and 2002. Notice the surge in consumer spending in the fourth quarter of 2001. It didn't lead to a lot of GDP growth because it was offset by a plunge in inventories. But in the first quarter of 2002 producers greatly increased their production, leading to a jump in real GDP.

### CHECK YOUR UNDERSTANDING 11-4

1. Although economists believe that recessions typically begin as slumps in investment spending, they also believe that consumer spending eventually slumps during a recession. Explain why.

2. **a.** Use a diagram like Figure 11-10 to show what happens when there is an autonomous fall in planned aggregate spending. Describe how the economy adjusts to a new income–expenditure equilibrium.

   **b.** Suppose $Y^*$ is originally $500 billion, the autonomous reduction in planned aggregate spending is $300 million ($0.3 billion), and $MPC = 0.5$. Calculate $Y^*$ after such a change.

*Solutions appear at back of book.*

# BUSINESS CASE : Making It Through in Muskegon

Muskegon, Michigan, is no Ft. Myers. Unlike the Florida city whose boom and bust we described in this chapter's opening story, Muskegon didn't have a housing boom in the mid-2000s. And it didn't have that much of a housing bust, either. Since real estate wasn't a big part of the local economy, the housing bubble burst at the end of 2007 couldn't do much to drag that economy down. So you might think that Muskegon-area businesses were somewhat insulated from the resulting national downturn.

In fact, however, Muskegon businesses were hit hard by the recession. For example, Eagle Alloy—a manufacturing company that sells its products to a wide variety of industries, but not especially to the housing or construction sectors— saw its sales drop by 50% during the worst of the 2007–2009 recession. And it wasn't only manufacturers selling to a national market that were hit. As factories in the Muskegon–Norton Shores metropolitan area laid off workers, and the local unemployment rate increased from around 6% in 2001 to over 15% during 2010, local businesses that depended on these workers' paychecks were hurt as well; employment in retail businesses fell about 8% over the course of the recession.

This story does, however, have a somewhat happy ending. As the U.S. economy as a whole began to recover, so did Eagle Alloy and other Muskegon-area manufacturing companies. During the recession, Eagle had cut its workforce from 430 to 200, but by May 2011, the workforce was back to 400 and the company was planning to hire another 150 workers. At the end of 2011, Eagle Alloy's president Mark Fazakerley was predicting a 25% increase in sales, and he declared, "It's going to be a good year for manufacturing." In the broader Muskegon–Norton Shores metropolitan area, by the end of 2011, the local unemployment rate had fallen back down to 9%. And as manufacturing for the national market revived, businesses with local sales also bounced back; the redevelopment of Muskegon's downtown, which stalled during the recession, had resumed by 2011.

## QUESTIONS FOR THOUGHT

1. Why did a national slump that began with housing affect companies like Eagle Alloy that didn't sell much to the construction industry?

2. Why did the troubles of Muskegon manufacturers spread to other industries, like retailing?

3. How does this story about Muskegon help explain how a slump in housing—a relatively small part of the U.S. economy—could produce such a deep national recession?

## SUMMARY

1. An **autonomous change in aggregate spending** leads to a chain reaction in which the total change in real GDP is equal to the **multiplier** times the initial change in aggregate spending. The size of the multiplier, $1/(1 - MPC)$, depends on the **marginal propensity to consume, MPC,** the fraction of an additional dollar of disposable income spent on consumption. The larger the $MPC$, the larger the multiplier and the larger the change in real GDP for any given autonomous change in aggregate spending. The **marginal propensity to save, MPS,** is equal to $1 - MPC$.

2. The **consumption function** shows how an individual household's consumer spending is determined by its current disposable income. The **aggregate consumption function** shows the relationship for the entire economy. According to the life-cycle hypothesis, households try to smooth their consumption over their lifetimes. As a result, the aggregate consumption function shifts in response to changes in expected future disposable income and changes in aggregate wealth.

3. **Planned investment spending** depends negatively on the interest rate and on existing production capacity; it depends positively on expected future real GDP. The **accelerator principle** says that investment spending is greatly influenced by the expected growth rate of real GDP.

4. Firms hold **inventories** of goods so that they can satisfy consumer demand quickly. **Inventory investment** is positive when firms add to their inventories, negative when

they reduce them. Often, however, changes in inventories are not a deliberate decision but the result of mistakes in forecasts about sales. The result is **unplanned inventory investment,** which can be either positive or negative. **Actual investment spending** is the sum of planned investment spending and unplanned inventory investment.

5. In **income–expenditure equilibrium, planned aggregate spending,** which in a simplified model with no government and no trade is the sum of consumer spending and planned investment spending, is equal to real GDP. At the **income–expenditure equilibrium GDP,** or $Y^*$, unplanned inventory investment is zero. When planned aggregate spending is larger than $Y^*$, unplanned inventory investment is negative; there is an unanticipated reduction in inventories and firms increase production. When planned aggregate spending is less than $Y^*$, unplanned inventory investment is positive; there is an unanticipated increase in inventories and firms reduce production. The **Keynesian cross** shows how the economy self-adjusts to income–expenditure equilibrium through inventory adjustments.

6. After an autonomous change in planned aggregate spending, the inventory adjustment process moves the economy to a new income–expenditure equilibrium. The change in income–expenditure equilibrium GDP arising from an autonomous change in spending is equal to $(1/(1 - MPC)) \times \Delta AAE_{Planned}$.

## KEY TERMS

Marginal propensity to consume (*MPC*), p. 312
Marginal propensity to save (*MPS*), p. 312
Autonomous change in aggregate spending, p. 314
Multiplier, p. 314
Consumption function, p. 316

Aggregate consumption function, p. 318
Planned investment spending, p. 322
Accelerator principle, p. 323
Inventories, p. 324
Inventory investment, p. 324
Unplanned inventory investment, p. 324

Actual investment spending, p. 324
Planned aggregate spending, p. 327
Income–expenditure equilibrium, p. 329
Income–expenditure equilibrium GDP, p. 329
Keynesian cross, p. 330

## PROBLEMS

1. Due to an increase in consumer wealth, there is a $40 billion autonomous increase in consumer spending in the economies of Westlandia and Eastlandia. Assuming that the aggregate price level is constant, the interest rate is fixed in both countries, and there are no taxes and no foreign trade, complete the accompanying tables to show the various rounds of increased spending that will occur in both economies if the marginal propensity to consume is 0.5 in Westlandia and 0.75 in Eastlandia. What do your results indicate about the relationship between the size of the marginal propensity to consume and the multiplier?

| Rounds | Westlandia | | Total change in GDP |
|---|---|:---:|:---:|
| | Incremental change in GDP | | |
| 1 | $\Delta C = \$40$ billion | ? | ? |
| 2 | $MPC \times \Delta C =$ | ? | ? |
| 3 | $MPC \times MPC \times \Delta C =$ | ? | ? |
| 4 | $MPC \times MPC \times MPC \times \Delta C =$ | ? | ? |
| . . . | | . . . | . . . |
| Total change in GDP | $(1/(1 - MPC)) \times \Delta C =$ | | ? |

| Rounds | Eastlandia Incremental change in GDP | | Total change in GDP |
|---|---|---|---|
| 1 | | $\Delta C$ = $40 billion | ? |
| 2 | $MPC \times \Delta C$ = | ? | ? |
| 3 | $MPC \times MPC \times \Delta C$ = | ? | ? |
| 4 | $MPC \times MPC \times MPC \times \Delta C$ = | ? | ? |
| . . . | | . . . | . . . |
| **Total change in GDP** | $(1/(1 - MPC)) \times \Delta C$ = | | ? |

2. Assuming that the aggregate price level is constant, the interest rate is fixed, and there are no taxes and no foreign trade, what will be the change in GDP if the following events occur?

   a. There is an autonomous increase in consumer spending of $25 billion; the marginal propensity to consume is 2/3.

   b. Firms reduce investment spending by $40 billion; the marginal propensity to consume is 0.8.

   c. The government increases its purchases of military equipment by $60 billion; the marginal propensity to consume is 0.6.

3. Economists observed the only five residents of a very small economy and estimated each one's consumer spending at various levels of current disposable income. The accompanying table shows each resident's consumer spending at three income levels.

| Individual consumer spending by | Individual current disposable income | | |
|---|---|---|---|
| | **$0** | **$20,000** | **$40,000** |
| Andre | 1,000 | $15,000 | 29,000 |
| Barbara | 2,500 | 12,500 | 22,500 |
| Casey | 2,000 | 20,000 | 38,000 |
| Declan | 5,000 | 17,000 | 29,000 |
| Elena | 4,000 | 19,000 | 34,000 |

   a. What is each resident's consumption function? What is the marginal propensity to consume for each resident?

   b. What is the economy's aggregate consumption function? What is the marginal propensity to consume for the economy?

4. From 2003 to 2008, Eastlandia experienced large fluctuations in both aggregate consumer spending and disposable income, but wealth, the interest rate, and expected future disposable income did not change. The accompanying table shows the level of aggregate consumer spending and disposable income in millions of dollars for each of these years. Use this information to answer the following questions.

| Year | Disposable income (millions of dollars) | Consumer spending (millions of dollars) |
|---|---|---|
| 2003 | $100 | $180 |
| 2004 | 350 | 380 |
| 2005 | 300 | 340 |
| 2006 | 400 | 420 |
| 2007 | 375 | 400 |
| 2008 | 500 | 500 |

   a. Plot the aggregate consumption function for Eastlandia.

   b. What is the marginal propensity to consume? What is the marginal propensity to save?

   c. What is the aggregate consumption function?

5. The Bureau of Economic Analysis reported that, in real terms, overall consumer spending increased by $35.4 billion during October 2010.

   a. If the marginal propensity to consume is 0.52, by how much will real GDP change in response?

   b. If there are no other changes to autonomous spending other than the increase in consumer spending in part a, and unplanned inventory investment, $I_{Unplanned}$, decreased by $50 billion, what is the change in real GDP?

   c. GDP at the end of September 2010 was $13,139.5 billion. If GDP were to increase by the amount calculated in part b, what would be the percent increase in GDP?

6. During the early 2000s, the Case–Shiller U.S. Home Price Index, a measure of average home prices, rose continuously until it peaked in March 2006. From March 2006 to May 2009, the index lost 32% of its value. Meanwhile, the stock market experienced similar ups and downs. From March 2003 to October 2007, the Standard and Poor's 500 (S&P 500) stock index, a broad measure of stock market prices, almost doubled, from 800.73 to a high of 1,565.15. From that time until March 2009, the index fell by almost 60%, to a low of 676.53. How do you think the movements in home prices both influenced the growth in real GDP during the first half of the decade and added to the concern about maintaining consumer spending after the collapse in the housing market that began in 2006? To what extent did the movements in the stock market hurt or help consumer spending?

7. How will planned investment spending change as the following events occur?

   a. The interest rate falls as a result of Federal Reserve policy.

   b. The U.S. Environmental Protection Agency decrees that corporations must upgrade or replace their machinery in order to reduce their emissions of sulfur dioxide.

   c. Baby boomers begin to retire in large numbers and reduce their savings, resulting in higher interest rates.

8. Explain how each of the following actions will affect the level of planned investment spending and unplanned inventory investment. Assume the economy is initially in income–expenditure equilibrium.

   a. The Federal Reserve raises the interest rate.

b. There is a rise in the expected growth rate of real GDP.

c. A sizable inflow of foreign funds into the country lowers the interest rate.

9. a. The accompanying table shows gross domestic product (GDP), disposable income (YD), consumer spending (C), and planned investment spending ($I_{Planned}$) in an economy. Assume there is no government or foreign sector in this economy. Complete the table by calculating planned aggregate spending ($AE_{Planned}$) and unplanned inventory investment ($I_{Unplanned}$).

| GDP | YD | C | $I_{Planned}$ | $AE_{Planned}$ | $I_{Unplanned}$ |
|---|---|---|---|---|---|
| | | | (billions of dollars) | | |
| $0 | $0 | $100 | $300 | ? | ? |
| 400 | 400 | 400 | 300 | ? | ? |
| 800 | 800 | 700 | 300 | ? | ? |
| 1,200 | 1,200 | 1,000 | 300 | ? | ? |
| 1,600 | 1,600 | 1,300 | 300 | ? | ? |
| 2,000 | 2,000 | 1,600 | 300 | ? | ? |
| 2,400 | 2,400 | 1,900 | 300 | ? | ? |
| 2,800 | 2,800 | 2,200 | 300 | ? | ? |
| 3,200 | 3,200 | 2,500 | 300 | ? | ? |

b. What is the aggregate consumption function?

c. What is Y*, income–expenditure equilibrium GDP?

d. What is the value of the multiplier?

e. If planned investment spending falls to $200 billion, what will be the new Y*?

f. If autonomous consumer spending rises to $200 billion, what will be the new Y*?

10. In an economy with no government and no foreign sectors, autonomous consumer spending is $250 billion, planned investment spending is $350 billion, and the marginal propensity to consume is 2/3.

a. Plot the aggregate consumption function and planned aggregate spending.

b. What is unplanned inventory investment when real GDP equals $600 billion?

c. What is Y*, income–expenditure equilibrium GDP?

d. What is the value of the multiplier?

e. If planned investment spending rises to $450 billion, what will be the new Y*?

11. An economy has a marginal propensity to consume of 0.5, and Y*, income–expenditure equilibrium GDP, equals $500 billion. Given an autonomous increase in planned investment of $10 billion, show the rounds of increased spending that take place by completing the accompanying table. The first and second rows are filled in for you. In the first row, the increase of planned investment spending of $10 billion raises real GDP and YD by $10 billion, leading to an increase in consumer spending of $5 billion (MPC × change in disposable income) in row 2, raising real GDP and YD by a further $5 billion.

| | Change in $I_{Planned}$ or C | Change in real GDP | Change in YD |
|---|---|---|---|
| Rounds | | (billions of dollars) | |
| 1 | $\Delta I_{Planned}$ = $10.00 | $10.00 | $10.00 |
| 2 | $\Delta C$ = $5.00 | $5.00 | $5.00 |
| 3 | $\Delta C$ = ? | ? | ? |
| 4 | $\Delta C$ = ? | ? | ? |
| 5 | $\Delta C$ = ? | ? | ? |
| 6 | $\Delta C$ = ? | ? | ? |
| 7 | $\Delta C$ = ? | ? | ? |
| 8 | $\Delta C$ = ? | ? | ? |
| 9 | $\Delta C$ = ? | ? | ? |
| 10 | $\Delta C$ = ? | ? | ? |

a. What is the total change in real GDP after the 10 rounds? What is the value of the multiplier? What would you expect the total change in Y* to be based on the multiplier formula? How do your answers to the first and third questions compare?

b. Redo the table starting from round 2, assuming the marginal propensity to consume is 0.75. What is the total change in real GDP after 10 rounds? What is the value of the multiplier? As the marginal propensity to consume increases, what happens to the value of the multiplier?

12. Although the United States is one of the richest nations in the world, it is also the world's largest debtor nation. We often hear that the problem is the nation's low savings rate. Suppose policy makers attempt to rectify this by encouraging greater savings in the economy. What effect will their successful attempts have on real GDP?

13. The U.S. economy slowed significantly in early 2008, and policy makers were extremely concerned about growth. To boost the economy, Congress passed several relief packages (the Economic Stimulus Act of 2008 and the American Recovery and Reinvestment Act of 2009) that combined would deliver about $700 billion in government spending. Assume, for the sake of argument, that this spending was in the form of payments made directly to consumers. The objective was to boost the economy by increasing the disposable income of American consumers.

a. Calculate the initial change in aggregate consumer spending as a consequence of this policy measure if the marginal propensity to consume (MPC) in the United States is 0.5. Then calculate the resulting change in real GDP arising from the $700 billion in payments.

b. Illustrate the effect on real GDP with the use of a graph depicting the income–expenditure equilibrium. Label the vertical axis "Planned aggregate spending, $AE_{Planned}$" and the horizontal axis "Real GDP." Draw two planned aggregate expenditure curves ($AE_{Planned1}$ and $AE_{Planned2}$) and a 45-degree line to show the effect of the autonomous policy change on the equilibrium.

# Deriving the Multiplier Algebraically

This appendix shows how to derive the multiplier algebraically. First, recall that in this chapter planned aggregate spending, $AE_{Planned}$, is the sum of consumer spending, $C$, which is determined by the consumption function, and planned investment spending, $I_{Planned}$. That is, $AE_{Planned} = C + I_{Planned}$. Rewriting this equation to express all its terms fully, we have:

**(11A-1)** $AE_{Planned} = A + MPC \times YD + I_{Planned}$

Because there are no taxes or government transfers in this model, disposable income is equal to GDP, so Equation 11A-1 becomes:

**(11A-2)** $AE_{Planned} = A + MPC \times GDP + I_{Planned}$

The income–expenditure equilibrium GDP, $Y^*$, is equal to planned aggregate spending:

**(11A-3)** $Y^* = AE_{Planned}$
$\qquad = A + MPC \times Y^* + I_{Planned}$
$\qquad$ in income–expenditure equilibrium

Just two more steps. Subtract $MPC \times Y^*$ from both sides of Equation 11A-3:

**(11A-4)** $Y^* - MPC \times Y^* = Y^* \times (1 - MPC) = A + I_{Planned}$

Finally, divide both sides by $(1 - MPC)$:

**(11A-5)** $Y^* = \dfrac{A + I_{Planned}}{1 - MPC}$

Equation 11A-5 tells us that a \$1 autonomous change in planned aggregate spending—a change in either $A$ or $I_{Planned}$—causes a \$1/(1 - MPC)$ change in income–expenditure equilibrium GDP, $Y^*$. The multiplier in our simple model is therefore:

**(11A-6)** Multiplier $= 1/(1 - MPC)$

## PROBLEMS

**1.** In an economy without government purchases, transfers, or taxes, and without imports or exports, aggregate autonomous consumer spending is \$500 billion, planned investment spending is \$250 billion, and the marginal propensity to consume is 0.5.

  **a.** Write the expression for planned aggregate spending as in Equation 11A-1.

  **b.** Solve for $Y^*$ algebraically.

  **c.** What is the value of the multiplier?

  **d.** How will $Y^*$ change if autonomous consumer spending falls to \$450 billion?

**2.** Complete the following table by calculating the value of the multiplier and identifying the change in $Y^*$ due to the change in autonomous spending. How does the value of the multiplier change with the marginal propensity to consume?

| MPC | Value of multiplier | Change in spending | Change in $Y^*$ |
|---|---|---|---|
| 0.5 | ? | $\Delta C = + \$50$ million | ? |
| 0.6 | ? | $\Delta I = - \$10$ million | ? |
| 0.75 | ? | $\Delta C = - \$25$ million | ? |
| 0.8 | ? | $\Delta I = + \$20$ million | ? |
| 0.9 | ? | $\Delta C = - \$2.5$ million | ? |

# CHAPTER 12

# Aggregate Demand and Aggregate Supply

## SHOCKS TO THE SYSTEM

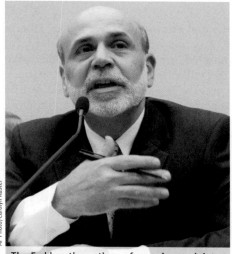

AP Photo/Carolyn Kaster

The Fed has the options of pumping cash into the economy to fight unemployment or pulling cash out of the economy to fight inflation.

❱ How the **aggregate demand curve** illustrates the relationship between the aggregate price level and the quantity of aggregate output demanded in the economy

❱ How the **aggregate supply curve** illustrates the relationship between the aggregate price level and the quantity of aggregate output supplied in the economy

❱ Why the aggregate supply curve is different in the short run compared to the long run

❱ How the *AD–AS* **model** is used to analyze economic fluctuations

❱ How monetary policy and fiscal policy can stabilize the economy

**S**OMETIMES IT'S NOT EASY BEING BEN.

In 2008 Ben Bernanke, a distinguished former Princeton economics professor, was chairman of the Federal Reserve—the institution that sets U.S. *monetary policy,* along with regulating the financial sector. The Federal Reserve's job is to help the economy avoid the twin evils of high inflation and high unemployment. It does this, loosely speaking, either by pumping cash into the economy to fight unemployment or by pulling cash out of the economy to fight inflation.

When the U.S. economy went into a recession in 2001, the Fed rushed cash into the system. It was an easy choice: unemployment was rising, and inflation was low and falling. In fact, for much of 2002 the Fed was actually worried about the possibility of *deflation.*

For much of 2008, however, Bernanke faced a much more difficult problem. In fact, he faced the problem people in his position dread most: a combination of unacceptably high inflation and rising unemployment, often referred to as *stagflation.* Stagflation was the scourge of the 1970s: the two deep recessions of 1973–1975 and 1979–1982 were both accompanied by soaring inflation. And in the first half of 2008, the threat of stagflation seemed to be back.

Why did the economic difficulties of early 2008 look so different from those of 2001? Because they had a different cause. The lesson of stagflation in the 1970s was that recessions can have different causes and that the appropriate policy response depends on the cause. Many recessions, from the great slump of 1929–1933 to the much milder recession of 2001, have been caused by a fall in investment and consumer spending. In these recessions high inflation isn't a threat. In fact, the 1929–1933 slump was accompanied by a sharp fall in the aggregate price level. And because inflation isn't a problem in such recessions, policy makers know what they must do: pump cash in, to fight rising unemployment.

The recessions of the 1970s, however, were largely caused by events in the Middle East that led to sharp cuts in world oil production and soaring prices for oil and other fuels. Not coincidentally, soaring oil prices also contributed to the economic difficulties of early 2008. In both periods, high energy prices led to a combination of unemployment and high inflation. They also created a dilemma: should the Fed fight the slump by pumping cash *into* the economy, or should it fight inflation by pulling cash *out* of the economy?

It's worth noting, by the way, that in 2011 the Fed faced some of the same problems it faced in 2008, as rising oil and food prices led to rising inflation despite high unemployment. In 2011, however, the Fed was fairly sure that demand was the main problem.

In the previous chapter we developed the *income–expenditure model,* which focuses on the determinants of aggregate spending. This model is extremely useful for understanding events like the recession of 2001 and the recovery that followed. However, the income–expenditure model takes the price level as given, and therefore it's much less helpful for understanding the problems policy makers faced in 2008.

In this chapter, we'll develop a model that goes beyond the income–expenditure model and shows us how to distinguish between different types of short-run economic fluctuations—*demand shocks,* like those of the Great Depression and the 2001 recession, and *supply shocks,* like those of the 1970s and 2008.

To develop this model, we'll proceed in three steps. First, we'll develop the concept of *aggregate demand.* Then we'll turn to the parallel concept of *aggregate supply.* Finally, we'll put them together in the *AD–AS model.* ■

The **aggregate demand curve** shows the relationship between the aggregate price level and the quantity of aggregate output demanded by households, businesses, the government, and the rest of the world.

# Aggregate Demand

The Great Depression, the great majority of economists agree, was the result of a massive negative demand shock. What does that mean? In Chapter 3 we explained that when economists talk about a fall in the demand for a particular good or service, they're referring to a leftward shift of the demand curve. Similarly, when economists talk about a negative demand shock to the economy as a whole, they're referring to a leftward shift of the **aggregate demand curve,** a curve that shows the relationship between the aggregate price level and the quantity of aggregate output demanded by households, firms, the government, and the rest of the world.

Figure 12-1 shows what the aggregate demand curve may have looked like in 1933, at the end of the 1929–1933 recession. The horizontal axis shows the total quantity of domestic goods and services demanded, measured in 2005 dollars. We use real GDP to measure aggregate output and will often use the two terms interchangeably. The vertical axis shows the aggregate price level, measured by the GDP deflator. With these variables on the axes, we can draw a curve, *AD*, showing how much aggregate output would have been demanded at any given aggregate price level. Since *AD* is meant to illustrate aggregate demand in 1933, one point on the curve corresponds to actual data for 1933, when the aggregate price level was 7.9 and the total quantity of domestic final goods and services purchased was $716 billion in 2005 dollars.

As drawn in Figure 12-1, the aggregate demand curve is downward sloping, indicating a negative relationship between the aggregate price level and the quantity of aggregate output demanded. A higher aggregate price level, other things equal, reduces the quantity of aggregate output demanded; a lower aggregate price level, other things equal, increases the quantity of aggregate output demanded. According to Figure 12-1, if the price level in 1933 had been 4.2 instead of 7.9, the total quantity of domestic final goods and services demanded would have been $1,000 billion in 2005 dollars instead of $716 billion.

The first key question about the aggregate demand curve is: why should the curve be downward sloping?

**FIGURE 12-1 The Aggregate Demand Curve**

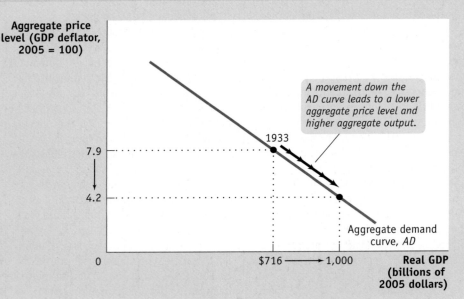

The aggregate demand curve shows the relationship between the aggregate price level and the quantity of aggregate output demanded. The curve is downward sloping due to the wealth effect of a change in the aggregate price level and the interest rate effect of a change in the aggregate price level. Corresponding to the actual 1933 data, here the total quantity of goods and services demanded at an aggregate price level of 7.9 is $716 billion in 2005 dollars. According to our hypothetical curve, however, if the aggregate price level had been only 4.2, the quantity of aggregate output demanded would have risen to $1,000 billion.

# Why Is the Aggregate Demand Curve Downward Sloping?

In Figure 12-1, the curve *AD* is downward sloping. Why? Recall the basic equation of national income accounting:

**(12-1)** GDP = *C* + *I* + *G* + *X* − *IM*

where *C* is consumer spending, *I* is investment spending, *G* is government purchases of goods and services, *X* is exports to other countries, and *IM* is imports. If we measure these variables in constant dollars—that is, in prices of a base year—then *C* + *I* + *G* + *X* − *IM* is the quantity of domestically produced final goods and services demanded during a given period. *G* is decided by the government, but the other variables are private-sector decisions. To understand why the aggregate demand curve slopes downward, we need to understand why a rise in the aggregate price level reduces *C*, *I*, and *X* − *IM*.

You might think that the downward slope of the aggregate demand curve is a natural consequence of the *law of demand* we defined back in Chapter 3. That is, since the demand curve for any one good is downward sloping, isn't it natural that the demand curve for aggregate output is also downward sloping? This turns out, however, to be a misleading parallel. The demand curve for any individual good shows how the quantity demanded depends on the price of that good, *holding the prices of other goods and services constant*. The main reason the quantity of a good demanded falls when the price of that good rises—that is, the quantity of a good demanded falls as we move up the demand curve—is that people switch their consumption to other goods and services.

But when we consider movements up or down the aggregate demand curve, we're considering *a simultaneous change in the prices of all final goods and services*. Furthermore, changes in the composition of goods and services in consumer spending aren't relevant to the aggregate demand curve: if consumers decide to buy fewer clothes but more cars, this doesn't necessarily change the total quantity of final goods and services they demand.

Why, then, does a rise in the aggregate price level lead to a fall in the quantity of all domestically produced final goods and services demanded? There are two main reasons: the *wealth effect* and the *interest rate effect* of a change in the aggregate price level.

**The Wealth Effect** An increase in the aggregate price level, other things equal, reduces the purchasing power of many assets. Consider, for example, someone who has $5,000 in a bank account. If the aggregate price level were to rise by 25%, what used to cost $5,000 would now cost $6,250, and would no longer be affordable. And what used to cost $4,000 would now cost $5,000, so that the $5,000 in the bank account would now buy only as much as $4,000 would have bought previously. With the loss in purchasing power, the owner of that bank account would probably scale back his or her consumption plans. Millions of other people would respond the same way, leading to a fall in spending on final goods and services, because a rise in the aggregate price level reduces the purchasing power of everyone's bank account. Correspondingly, a fall in the aggregate price level increases the purchasing power of consumers' assets and leads to more consumer demand. The **wealth effect of a change in the aggregate price level** is the effect on consumer spending caused by the effect of a change in the aggregate price level on the purchasing power of consumers' assets. Because of the wealth effect, consumer spending, *C*, falls when the aggregate price level rises, leading to a downward-sloping aggregate demand curve.

**The Interest Rate Effect** Economists use the term *money* in its narrowest sense to refer to cash and bank deposits on which people can write checks. People and firms hold money because it reduces the cost and inconvenience of making transactions. An increase in the aggregate price level, other things equal, reduces the purchasing power of a given amount of money holdings. To purchase the same basket of goods and services as before, people and firms now need to hold more money. So, in response to an increase in the aggregate price level, the public tries to increase its money holdings,

The **wealth effect of a change in the aggregate price level** is the effect on consumer spending caused by the effect of a change in the aggregate price level on the purchasing power of consumers' assets.

The **interest rate effect of a change in the aggregate price level** is the effect on consumer spending and investment spending caused by the effect of a change in the aggregate price level on the purchasing power of consumers' and firms' money holdings.

either by borrowing more or by selling assets such as bonds. This reduces the funds available for lending to other borrowers and drives interest rates up.

In Chapter 10 we learned that a rise in the interest rate reduces investment spending because it makes the cost of borrowing higher. It also reduces consumer spending because households save more of their disposable income. So a rise in the aggregate price level depresses investment spending, $I$, and consumer spending, $C$, through its effect on the purchasing power of money holdings, an effect known as the **interest rate effect of a change in the aggregate price level.** This also leads to a downward-sloping aggregate demand curve.

We'll have a lot more to say about money and interest rates in Chapter 15 on monetary policy. We'll also see, in Chapter 19, which covers open-economy macroeconomics, that a higher interest rate indirectly tends to reduce exports ($X$) and increase imports ($IM$). For now, the important point is that the aggregate demand curve is downward sloping due to both the wealth effect and the interest rate effect of a change in the aggregate price level.

## The Aggregate Demand Curve and the Income–Expenditure Model

In the preceding chapter we introduced the *income–expenditure model*, which shows how the economy arrives at *income–expenditure equilibrium*. Now we've introduced the aggregate demand curve, which relates the overall demand for goods and services to the overall price level. How do these concepts fit together?

Recall that one of the assumptions of the income–expenditure model is that the aggregate price level is fixed. We now drop that assumption. We can still use the income–expenditure model, however, to ask what aggregate spending would be *at any given aggregate price level*, which is precisely what the aggregate demand curve shows. So the $AD$ curve is actually derived from the income–expenditure model. Economists sometimes say that the income–expenditure model is "embedded" in the $AD$–$AS$ model.

Figure 12-2 shows, once again, how income–expenditure equilibrium is determined. Real GDP is on the horizontal axis; real planned aggregate spending

**FIGURE 12-2** How Changes in the Aggregate Price Level Affect Income–Expenditure Equilibrium

Income–expenditure equilibrium occurs at the point where the curve $AE_{Planned}$, which shows real aggregate planned spending, crosses the 45-degree line. A fall in the aggregate price level causes the $AE_{Planned}$ curve to shift from $AE_{Planned_1}$ to $AE_{Planned_2}$, leading to a rise in income-expenditure equilibrium GDP from $Y_1$ to $Y_2$.

is on the vertical axis. Other things equal, planned aggregate spending, equal to consumer spending plus planned investment spending, rises with real GDP. This is illustrated by the upward-sloping lines $AE_{Planned_1}$ and $AE_{Planned_2}$. Income–expenditure equilibrium, as we learned in Chapter 11, is at the point where the line representing planned aggregate spending crosses the 45-degree line. For example, if $AE_{Planned_1}$ is the relationship between real GDP and planned aggregate spending, then income–expenditure equilibrium is at point $E_1$, corresponding to a level of real GDP equal to $Y_1$.

We've just seen, however, that changes in the aggregate price level change the level of planned aggregate spending *at any given level of real GDP*. This means that when the aggregate price level changes, the $AE_{Planned}$ curve shifts. For example, suppose that the aggregate price level falls. As a result of both the wealth effect and the interest rate effect, the fall in the aggregate price level will lead to higher planned aggregate spending at any given level of real GDP. So the $AE_{Planned}$ curve will shift up, as illustrated in Figure 12-2 by the shift from $AE_{Planned_1}$ to $AE_{Planned_2}$. The increase in planned aggregate spending leads to a multiplier process that moves the income–expenditure equilibrium from point $E_1$ to point $E_2$, raising real GDP from $Y_1$ to $Y_2$.

Figure 12-3 shows how this result can be used to derive the aggregate demand curve. In Figure 12-3, we show a fall in the aggregate price level from $P_1$ to $P_2$. We saw in Figure 12-2 that a fall in the aggregate price level would lead to an upward shift of the $AE_{Planned}$ curve and hence a rise in real GDP. You can see this same result in Figure 12-3 as a movement along the $AD$ curve: as the aggregate price level falls, real GDP rises from $Y_1$ to $Y_2$.

So the aggregate demand curve doesn't replace the income–expenditure model. Instead, it's a way to summarize what the income–expenditure model says about the effects of changes in the aggregate price level.

In practice, economists often use the income–expenditure model to analyze short-run economic fluctuations, even though strictly speaking it should be seen as a component of a more complete model. In the short run, in particular, this is usually a reasonable shortcut.

**FIGURE   12-3   The Income–Expenditure Model and the Aggregate Demand Curve**

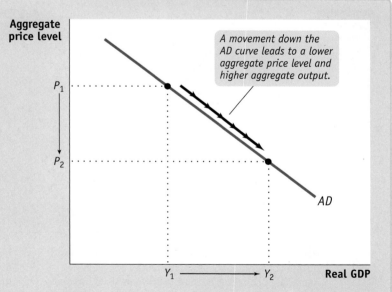

In Figure 12-2 we saw how a fall in the aggregate price level shifts the planned aggregate spending curve up, leading to a rise in real GDP. Here we show that same result as a movement along the aggregate demand curve. If the aggregate price level falls from $P_1$ to $P_2$, real GDP rises from $Y_1$ to $Y_2$. The $AD$ curve is therefore downward sloping.

A movement down the AD curve leads to a lower aggregate price level and higher aggregate output.

## Shifts of the Aggregate Demand Curve

In Chapter 3, where we introduced the analysis of supply and demand in the market for an individual good, we stressed the importance of the distinction between *movements along* the demand curve and *shifts of* the demand curve. The same distinction applies to the aggregate demand curve. Figure 12-1 shows a *movement along* the aggregate demand curve, a change in the aggregate quantity of goods and services demanded as the aggregate price level changes.

But there can also be *shifts of* the aggregate demand curve, changes in the quantity of goods and services demanded at any given price level, as shown in Figure 12-4. When we talk about an increase in aggregate demand, we mean a shift of the aggregate demand curve to the right, as shown in panel (a) by the shift from $AD_1$ to $AD_2$. A rightward shift occurs when the quantity of aggregate output demanded increases at any given aggregate price level. A decrease in aggregate demand means that the $AD$ curve shifts to the left, as in panel (b). A leftward shift implies that the quantity of aggregate output demanded falls at any given aggregate price level.

A number of factors can shift the aggregate demand curve. Among the most important factors are changes in expectations, changes in wealth, and the size of the existing stock of physical capital. In addition, both fiscal and monetary policy can shift the aggregate demand curve. All five factors set the multiplier process in motion. By causing an initial rise or fall in real GDP, they change disposable income, which leads to additional changes in aggregate spending, which lead to further changes in real GDP, and so on. For an overview of factors that shift the aggregate demand curve, see Table 12-1.

**Changes in Expectations**  As explained in Chapter 11, both consumer spending and planned investment spending depend in part on people's expectations about the future. Consumers base their spending not only on the income they have now but also on the income they expect to have in the future. Firms base

**FIGURE  12-4  Shifts of the Aggregate Demand Curve**

Panel (a) shows the effect of events that increase the quantity of aggregate output demanded at any given aggregate price level, such as improvements in business and consumer expectations or increased government spending. Such changes shift the aggregate demand curve to the right, from $AD_1$ to $AD_2$. Panel (b) shows the effect of events that decrease the quantity of aggregate output demanded at any given aggregate price level, such as a fall in wealth caused by a stock market decline. This shifts the aggregate demand curve leftward from $AD_1$ to $AD_2$.

**TABLE** **12-1**   Factors That Shift Aggregate Demand

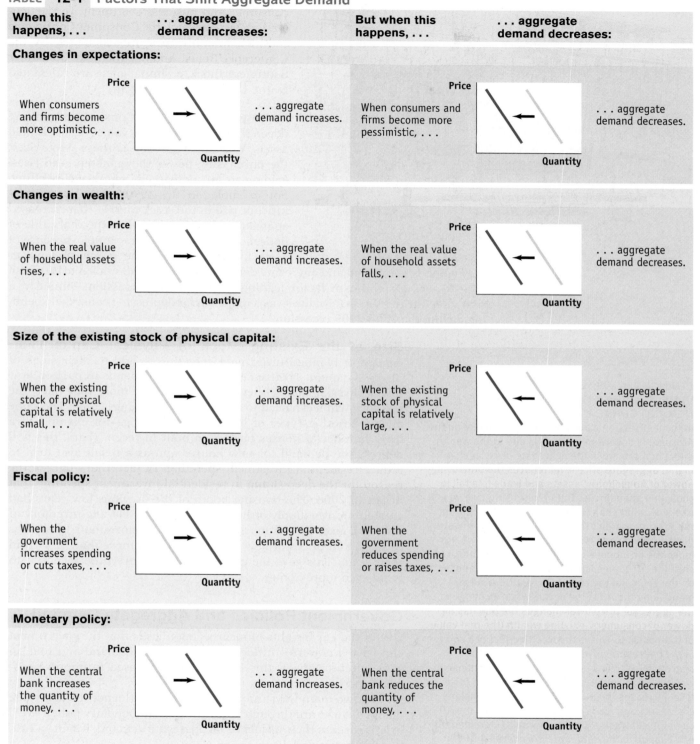

| When this happens, . . . | . . . aggregate demand increases: | | But when this happens, . . . | . . . aggregate demand decreases: | |
|---|---|---|---|---|---|
| **Changes in expectations:** | | | | | |
| When consumers and firms become more optimistic, . . . | | . . . aggregate demand increases. | When consumers and firms become more pessimistic, . . . | | . . . aggregate demand decreases. |
| **Changes in wealth:** | | | | | |
| When the real value of household assets rises, . . . | | . . . aggregate demand increases. | When the real value of household assets falls, . . . | | . . . aggregate demand decreases. |
| **Size of the existing stock of physical capital:** | | | | | |
| When the existing stock of physical capital is relatively small, . . . | | . . . aggregate demand increases. | When the existing stock of physical capital is relatively large, . . . | | . . . aggregate demand decreases. |
| **Fiscal policy:** | | | | | |
| When the government increases spending or cuts taxes, . . . | | . . . aggregate demand increases. | When the government reduces spending or raises taxes, . . . | | . . . aggregate demand decreases. |
| **Monetary policy:** | | | | | |
| When the central bank increases the quantity of money, . . . | | . . . aggregate demand increases. | When the central bank reduces the quantity of money, . . . | | . . . aggregate demand decreases. |

their planned investment spending not only on current conditions but also on the sales they expect to make in the future. As a result, changes in expectations can push consumer spending and planned investment spending up or down. If consumers and firms become more optimistic, aggregate spending rises; if they become more pessimistic, aggregate spending falls. In fact, short-run economic

*"CONSUMER CONFIDENCE CRISIS IN AISLE 3!"*

forecasters pay careful attention to surveys of consumer and business sentiment. In particular, forecasters watch the Consumer Confidence Index, a monthly measure calculated by the Conference Board, and the Michigan Consumer Sentiment Index, a similar measure calculated by the University of Michigan.

**Changes in Wealth** Consumer spending depends in part on the value of household assets. When the real value of these assets rises, the purchasing power they embody also rises, leading to an increase in aggregate spending. For example, in the 1990s there was a significant rise in the stock market that increased aggregate demand. And when the real value of household assets falls—for example, because of a stock market crash—the purchasing power they embody is reduced and aggregate demand also falls. The stock market crash of 1929 was a significant factor leading to the Great Depression. Similarly, a sharp decline in real estate values was a major factor depressing consumer spending during the 2007–2009 recession.

## ⚠ PITFALLS

### CHANGES IN WEALTH: A MOVEMENT ALONG VERSUS A SHIFT OF THE AGGREGATE DEMAND CURVE

In the last section we explained that one reason the *AD* curve is downward sloping is due to the wealth effect of a change in the aggregate price level: a higher aggregate price level reduces the purchasing power of households' assets and leads to a fall in consumer spending, *C*. But in this section we've just explained that changes in wealth lead to a shift of the *AD* curve. Aren't those two explanations contradictory? Which one is it—does a change in wealth move the economy along the *AD* curve or does it shift the *AD* curve? The answer is both: it depends on the *source* of the change in wealth. A movement along the *AD* curve occurs when a change in the aggregate price level changes the purchasing power of consumers' existing wealth (the real value of their assets). This is the *wealth effect of a change in the aggregate price level*—a change in the aggregate price level is the source of the change in wealth. For example, a fall in the aggregate price level increases the purchasing power of consumers' assets and leads to a movement down the *AD* curve. In contrast, a change in wealth *independent of a change in the aggregate price level* shifts the *AD* curve. For example, a rise in the stock market or a rise in real estate values leads to an increase in the real value of consumers' assets at any given aggregate price level. In this case, the source of the change in wealth is a change in the values of assets without any change in the aggregate price level— that is, a change in asset values holding the prices of all final goods and services constant.

**Size of the Existing Stock of Physical Capital** Firms engage in planned investment spending to add to their stock of physical capital. Their incentive to spend depends in part on how much physical capital they already have: the more they have, the less they will feel a need to add more, other things equal. The same applies to other types of investment spending—for example, if a large number of houses have been built in recent years, this will depress the demand for new houses and as a result also tend to reduce residential investment spending. In fact, that's part of the reason for the deep slump in residential investment spending that began in 2006. The housing boom of the previous few years had created an oversupply of houses: by spring 2009, the inventory of unsold houses on the market was equal to more than 14 months of sales, and prices of new homes had fallen more than 25% from their peak. This gave the construction industry little incentive to build even more homes.

## Government Policies and Aggregate Demand

One of the key insights of macroeconomics is that the government can have a powerful influence on aggregate demand and that, in some circumstances, this influence can be used to improve economic performance.

The two main ways the government can influence the aggregate demand curve are through fiscal policy and monetary policy. We'll briefly discuss their influence on aggregate demand, leaving a full-length discussion for upcoming chapters.

**Fiscal Policy** As we learned in Chapter 6, fiscal policy is the use of either government spending—government purchases of final goods and services and government transfers—or tax policy to stabilize the economy. In practice, governments often respond to recessions by increasing spending, cutting taxes, or both. They often respond to inflation by reducing spending or increasing taxes.

The effect of government purchases of final goods and services, *G*, on the aggregate demand curve is *direct* because government purchases are themselves a component of aggregate demand. So an increase in government purchases shifts the aggregate demand curve to the right and a decrease shifts it to the left. History's most dramatic example of how increased government purchases affect aggregate demand was the effect of wartime government spending during World War II. Because of the war, U.S. federal purchases surged 400%. This increase in purchases is usually credited with ending the Great Depression. In the 1990s Japan used large public works projects—such as government-financed construction of roads, bridges, and dams—in an effort to increase aggregate demand in the face of a slumping economy. Similarly, in 2009, the United States began spending more than $100 billion on infrastructure projects such as improving highways, bridges, public transportation, and more, to stimulate overall spending.

In contrast, changes in either tax rates or government transfers influence the economy *indirectly* through their effect on disposable income. A lower tax rate means that consumers get to keep more of what they earn, increasing their disposable income. An increase in government transfers also increases consumers' disposable income. In either case, this increases consumer spending and shifts the aggregate demand curve to the right. A higher tax rate or a reduction in transfers reduces the amount of disposable income received by consumers. This reduces consumer spending and shifts the aggregate demand curve to the left.

**Monetary Policy**  We opened this chapter by talking about the problems faced by the Federal Reserve, which controls monetary policy—the use of changes in the quantity of money or the interest rate to stabilize the economy. We've just discussed how a rise in the aggregate price level, by reducing the purchasing power of money holdings, causes a rise in the interest rate. That, in turn, reduces both investment spending and consumer spending.

But what happens if the quantity of money in the hands of households and firms changes? In modern economies, the quantity of money in circulation is largely determined by the decisions of a *central bank* created by the government. As we'll learn in Chapter 14, the Federal Reserve, the U.S. central bank, is a special institution that is neither exactly part of the government nor exactly a private institution. When the central bank increases the quantity of money in circulation, households and firms have more money, which they are willing to lend out. The effect is to drive the interest rate down at any given aggregate price level, leading to higher investment spending and higher consumer spending. That is, increasing the quantity of money shifts the aggregate demand curve to the right. Reducing the quantity of money has the opposite effect: households and firms have less money holdings than before, leading them to borrow more and lend less. This raises the interest rate, reduces investment spending and consumer spending, and shifts the aggregate demand curve to the left.

## ECONOMICS › IN ACTION

### MOVING ALONG THE AGGREGATE DEMAND CURVE, 1979–1980

When looking at data, it's often hard to distinguish between changes in spending that represent *movements along* the aggregate demand curve and *shifts of* the aggregate demand curve. One telling exception, however, is what happened right after the oil crisis of 1979, which we mentioned in this chapter's opening story. Faced with a sharp increase in the aggregate price level—the rate of consumer price inflation reached 14.8% in March of 1980—the Federal Reserve stuck to a policy of increasing

The interest rate effect of a rise in the aggregate price level lead to a drop in consumer and investment spending.

the quantity of money slowly. The aggregate price level was rising steeply, but the quantity of money circulating in the economy was growing slowly. The net result was that the purchasing power of the quantity of money in circulation fell.

This led to an increase in the demand for borrowing and a surge in interest rates. The *prime rate*, which is the interest rate banks charge their best customers, climbed above 20%. High interest rates, in turn, caused both consumer spending and investment spending to fall: in 1980 purchases of durable consumer goods like cars fell by 5.3% and real investment spending fell by 8.9%.

In other words, in 1979–1980 the economy responded just as we'd expect if it were moving upward along the aggregate demand curve from right to left: due to the wealth effect and the interest rate effect of a change in the aggregate price level, the quantity of aggregate output demanded fell as the aggregate price level rose. This does not explain, of course, why the aggregate price level rose. But as we'll see in the section "The *AD–AS* Model," the answer to that question lies in the behavior of the *short-run aggregate supply curve.*

**CHECK YOUR UNDERSTANDING** **12-1**

1. Determine the effect on aggregate demand of each of the following events. Explain whether it represents a movement along the aggregate demand curve (up or down) or a shift of the curve (leftward or rightward).
   a. A rise in the interest rate caused by a change in monetary policy
   b. A fall in the real value of money in the economy due to a higher aggregate price level
   c. News of a worse-than-expected job market next year
   d. A fall in tax rates
   e. A rise in the real value of assets in the economy due to a lower aggregate price level
   f. A rise in the real value of assets in the economy due to a surge in real estate values

   *Solutions appear at back of book.*

# Aggregate Supply

Between 1929 and 1933, there was a sharp fall in aggregate demand—a reduction in the quantity of goods and services demanded at any given price level. One consequence of the economy-wide decline in demand was a fall in the prices of most goods and services. By 1933, the GDP deflator (one of the price indexes we defined in Chapter 7) was 26% below its 1929 level, and other indexes were down by similar amounts. A second consequence was a decline in the output of most goods and services: by 1933, real GDP was 27% below its 1929 level. A third consequence, closely tied to the fall in real GDP, was a surge in the unemployment rate from 3% to 25%.

The association between the plunge in real GDP and the plunge in prices wasn't an accident. Between 1929 and 1933, the U.S. economy was moving down its **aggregate supply curve,** which shows the relationship between the economy's aggregate price level (the overall price level of final goods and services in the economy) and the total quantity of final goods and services, or aggregate output, producers are willing to supply. (As you will recall, we use real GDP to measure aggregate output. So we'll often use the two terms interchangeably.) More specifically, between 1929 and 1933 the U.S. economy moved down its *short-run aggregate supply curve.*

## The Short-Run Aggregate Supply Curve

The **aggregate supply curve** shows the relationship between the aggregate price level and the quantity of aggregate output supplied in the economy.

The period from 1929 to 1933 demonstrated that there is a positive relationship in the short run between the aggregate price level and the quantity of aggregate output supplied. That is, a rise in the aggregate price level is associated with a rise in the quantity of aggregate output supplied, other things equal; a fall in the aggregate price level is associated with a fall in the quantity of aggregate output supplied, other things equal. To understand why this positive relationship exists, consider the most basic question facing a producer: is producing a unit of output profitable or not? Let's define profit per unit:

**(12-2)** Profit per unit of output =
    Price per unit of output – Production cost per unit of output

Thus, the answer to the question depends on whether the price the producer receives for a unit of output is greater or less than the cost of producing that unit of output. At any given point in time, many of the costs producers face are fixed per unit of output and can't be changed for an extended period of time. Typically, the largest source of inflexible production cost is the wages paid to workers. *Wages* here refers to all forms of worker compensation, such as employer-paid health care and retirement benefits in addition to earnings.

Wages are typically an inflexible production cost because the dollar amount of any given wage paid, called the **nominal wage,** is often determined by contracts that were signed some time ago. And even when there are no formal contracts, there are often informal agreements between management and workers, making companies reluctant to change wages in response to economic conditions. For example, companies usually will not reduce wages during poor economic times—unless the downturn has been particularly long and severe—for fear of generating worker resentment. Correspondingly, they typically won't raise wages during better economic times—until they are at risk of losing workers to competitors—because they don't want to encourage workers to routinely demand higher wages.

As a result of both formal and informal agreements, then, the economy is characterized by **sticky wages:** nominal wages that are slow to fall even in the face of high unemployment and slow to rise even in the face of labor shortages. It's important to note, however, that nominal wages cannot be sticky forever: ultimately, formal contracts and informal agreements will be renegotiated to take into account changed economic circumstances. As the Pitfalls at the end of this section explains, how long it takes for nominal wages to become flexible is an integral component of what distinguishes the short run from the long run.

To understand how the fact that many costs are fixed in nominal terms gives rise to an upward-sloping short-run aggregate supply curve, it's helpful to know that prices are set somewhat differently in different kinds of markets. In *perfectly competitive markets,* producers take prices as given; in *imperfectly competitive markets,* producers have some ability to choose the prices they charge. In both kinds of markets, there is a short-run positive relationship between prices and output, but for slightly different reasons.

Let's start with the behavior of producers in perfectly competitive markets; remember, they take the price as given. Imagine that, for some reason, the aggregate price level falls, which means that the price received by the typical producer of a final good or service falls. Because many production costs are fixed in the short run, production cost per unit of output doesn't fall by the same proportion as the fall in the price of output. So the profit per unit of output declines, leading perfectly competitive producers to reduce the quantity supplied in the short run.

On the other hand, suppose that for some reason the aggregate price level rises. As a result, the typical producer receives a higher price for its final good or service. Again, many production costs are fixed in the short run, so production cost per unit of output doesn't rise by the same proportion as the rise in the price

The **nominal wage** is the dollar amount of the wage paid.

**Sticky wages** are nominal wages that are slow to fall even in the face of high unemployment and slow to rise even in the face of labor shortages.

The **short-run aggregate supply curve** shows the relationship between the aggregate price level and the quantity of aggregate output supplied that exists in the short run, the time period when many production costs can be taken as fixed.

of a unit. And since the typical perfectly competitive producer takes the price as given, profit per unit of output rises and output increases.

Now consider an imperfectly competitive producer that is able to set its own price. If there is a rise in the demand for this producer's product, it will be able to sell more at any given price. Given stronger demand for its products, it will probably choose to increase its prices as well as its output, as a way of increasing profit per unit of output. In fact, industry analysts often talk about variations in an industry's "pricing power": when demand is strong, firms with pricing power are able to raise prices—and they do.

Conversely, if there is a fall in demand, firms will normally try to limit the fall in their sales by cutting prices.

Both the responses of firms in perfectly competitive industries and those of firms in imperfectly competitive industries lead to an upward-sloping relationship between aggregate output and the aggregate price level. The positive relationship between the aggregate price level and the quantity of aggregate output producers are willing to supply during the time period when many production costs, particularly nominal wages, can be taken as fixed is illustrated by the **short-run aggregate supply curve.** The positive relationship between the aggregate price level and aggregate output in the short run gives the short-run aggregate supply curve its upward slope.

Figure 12-5 shows a hypothetical short-run aggregate supply curve, *SRAS*, which matches actual U.S. data for 1929 and 1933. On the horizontal axis is aggregate output (or, equivalently, real GDP)—the total quantity of final goods and services supplied in the economy—measured in 2005 dollars. On the vertical axis is the aggregate price level as measured by the GDP deflator, with the value for the year 2005 equal to 100. In 1929, the aggregate price level was 10.6 and real GDP was $976 billion. In 1933, the aggregate price level was 7.9 and real GDP was only $716 billion. The movement down the *SRAS* curve corresponds to the deflation and fall in aggregate output experienced over those years.

**FIGURE  12-5  The Short-Run Aggregate Supply Curve**

The short-run aggregate supply curve shows the relationship between the aggregate price level and the quantity of aggregate output supplied in the short run, the period in which many production costs such as nominal wages are fixed. It is upward sloping because a higher aggregate price level leads to higher profit per unit of output and higher aggregate output given fixed nominal wages. Here we show numbers corresponding to the Great Depression, from 1929 to 1933: when deflation occurred and the aggregate price level fell from 10.6 (in 1929) to 7.9 (in 1933), firms responded by reducing the quantity of aggregate output supplied from $976 billion to $716 billion measured in 2005 dollars.

**WHAT'S TRULY FLEXIBLE, WHAT'S TRULY STICKY**

Most macroeconomists agree that the basic picture shown in Figure 12-5 is correct: there is, other things equal, a positive short-run relationship between the aggregate price level and aggregate output. But many would argue that the details are a bit more complicated.

So far we've stressed a difference in the behavior of the aggregate price level and the behavior of nominal wages. That is, we've said that the aggregate price level is flexible but nominal wages are sticky in the short run. Although this assumption is a good way to explain why the short-run aggregate supply curve is upward sloping, empirical data on wages and prices don't wholly support a sharp distinction

between flexible prices of final goods and services and sticky nominal wages.

On one side, some nominal wages are in fact flexible even in the short run because some workers are not covered by a contract or informal agreement with their employers. Since some nominal wages are sticky but others are flexible, we observe that the *average nominal wage*—the nominal wage averaged over all workers in the economy—falls when there is a steep rise in unemployment. For example, nominal wages fell substantially in the early years of the Great Depression.

On the other side, some prices of final goods and services are sticky rather than flexible. For example, some

firms, particularly the makers of luxury or name-brand goods, are reluctant to cut prices even when demand falls. Instead they prefer to cut output even if their profit per unit hasn't declined.

These complications, as we've said, don't change the basic picture. When the aggregate price level falls, some producers cut output because the nominal wages they pay are sticky. And some producers don't cut their prices in the face of a falling aggregate price level, preferring instead to reduce their output. In both cases, the positive relationship between the aggregate price level and aggregate output is maintained. So, in the end, the short-run aggregate supply curve is still upward sloping.

## Shifts of the Short-Run Aggregate Supply Curve

Figure 12-5 shows a *movement along* the short-run aggregate supply curve, as the aggregate price level and aggregate output fell from 1929 to 1933. But there can also be *shifts of* the short-run aggregate supply curve, as shown in Figure 12-6. Panel (a) shows a *decrease in short-run aggregate supply*—a leftward shift of the short-run aggregate supply curve. Aggregate supply decreases when producers reduce the quantity of aggregate output they are willing to supply at any given aggregate price level. Panel (b)

**FIGURE 12-6 Shifts of the Short-Run Aggregate Supply Curve**

Panel (a) shows a decrease in short-run aggregate supply: the short-run aggregate supply curve shifts leftward from SRAS₁ to SRAS₂, and the quantity of aggregate output supplied at any given aggregate price level falls.

Panel (b) shows an increase in short-run aggregate supply: the short-run aggregate supply curve shifts rightward from SRAS₁ to SRAS₂, and the quantity of aggregate output supplied at any given aggregate price level rises.

shows an *increase in short-run aggregate supply*—a rightward shift of the short-run aggregate supply curve. Aggregate supply increases when producers increase the quantity of aggregate output they are willing to supply at any given aggregate price level.

To understand why the short-run aggregate supply curve can shift, it's important to recall that producers make output decisions based on their profit per unit of output. The short-run aggregate supply curve illustrates the relationship between the aggregate price level and aggregate output: because some production costs are fixed in the short run, a change in the aggregate price level leads to a change in producers' profit per unit of output and, in turn, leads to a change in aggregate output. But other factors besides the aggregate price level can affect profit per unit and, in turn, aggregate output. It is changes in these other factors that will shift the short-run aggregate supply curve.

To develop some intuition, suppose that something happens that raises production costs—say, an increase in the price of oil. At any given price of output, a producer now earns a smaller profit per unit of output. As a result, producers reduce the quantity supplied at any given aggregate price level, and the short-run aggregate supply curve shifts to the left. If, in contrast, something happens that lowers production costs—say, a fall in the nominal wage—a producer now earns a higher profit per unit of output at any given price of output. This leads producers to increase the quantity of aggregate output supplied at any given aggregate price level, and the short-run aggregate supply curve shifts to the right.

Now we'll discuss some of the important factors that affect producers' profit per unit and so can lead to shifts of the short-run aggregate supply curve.

### Changes in Commodity Prices

In this chapter's opening story, we described how a surge in the price of oil caused problems for the U.S. economy in the 1970s, early in 2008, and again in 2011. Oil is a commodity, a standardized input bought and sold in bulk quantities. An increase in the price of a commodity—oil—raised production costs across the economy and reduced the quantity of aggregate output supplied at any given aggregate price level, shifting the short-run aggregate supply curve to the left. Conversely, a decline in commodity prices reduces production costs, leading to an increase in the quantity supplied at any given aggregate price level and a rightward shift of the short-run aggregate supply curve.

Why isn't the influence of commodity prices already captured by the short-run aggregate supply curve? Because commodities—unlike, say, soft drinks—are not a final good, their prices are not included in the calculation of the aggregate price level. Further, commodities represent a significant cost of production to most suppliers, just like nominal wages do. So changes in commodity prices have large impacts on production costs. And in contrast to noncommodities, the prices of commodities can sometimes change drastically due to industry-specific shocks to supply—such as wars in the Middle East or rising Chinese demand that leaves less oil for the United States.

### Changes in Nominal Wages

At any given point in time, the dollar wages of many workers are fixed because they are set by contracts or informal agreements made in the past. Nominal wages can change, however, once enough time has passed for contracts and informal agreements to be renegotiated. Suppose, for example, that there is an economy-wide rise in the cost of health care insurance premiums paid by employers as part of employees' wages. From the employers' perspective, this is equivalent to a rise in nominal wages because it is an increase in employer-paid compensation. So this rise in nominal wages increases production costs and shifts the short-run aggregate supply curve to the left. Conversely, suppose there is an economy-wide fall in the cost of such premiums. This is equivalent to a fall in nominal wages from the point of view of employers; it reduces production costs and shifts the short-run aggregate supply curve to the right.

An important historical fact is that during the 1970s the surge in the price of oil had the indirect effect of also raising nominal wages. This "knock-on" effect occurred because many wage contracts included *cost-of-living allowances* that automatically raised the nominal wage when consumer prices increased. Through this channel, the surge in the price of oil—which led to an increase in overall consumer prices—ultimately caused a rise in nominal wages. So the economy, in the end, experienced two leftward shifts of the aggregate supply curve: the first generated by the initial surge in the price of oil, the second generated by the induced increase in nominal wages. The negative effect on the economy of rising oil prices was greatly magnified through the cost-of-living allowances in wage contracts. Today, cost-of-living allowances in wage contracts are rare.

**Changes in Productivity** An increase in productivity means that a worker can produce more units of output with the same quantity of inputs. For example, the introduction of bar-code scanners in retail stores greatly increased the ability of a single worker to stock, inventory, and resupply store shelves. As a result, the cost to a store of "producing" a dollar of sales fell and profit rose. And, correspondingly, the quantity supplied increased. (Think of Walmart and the increase in the number of its stores as an increase in aggregate supply.) So a rise in productivity, whatever the source, increases producers' profits and shifts the short-run aggregate supply curve to the right. Conversely, a fall in productivity—say, due to new regulations that require workers to spend more time filling out forms—reduces the number of units of output a worker can produce with the same quantity of inputs. Consequently, the cost per unit of output rises, profit falls, and quantity supplied falls. This shifts the short-run aggregate supply curve to the left.

For a summary of the factors that shift the short-run aggregate supply curve, see Table 12-2.

**TABLE 12-2 Factors That Shift Aggregate Supply**

| When this happens, . . . | . . . aggregate supply increases: | | But when this happens, . . . | . . . aggregate supply decreases: | |
| --- | --- | --- | --- | --- | --- |
| **Changes in commodity prices:** | | | | | |
| When commodity prices fall, . . . | | . . . aggregate supply increases. | When commodity prices rise, . . . | | . . . aggregate supply decreases. |
| **Changes in nominal wages:** | | | | | |
| When nominal wages fall, . . . | | . . . aggregate supply increases. | When nominal wages rise, . . . | | . . . aggregate supply decreases. |
| **Changes in productivity:** | | | | | |
| When workers become more productive, . . . | | . . . aggregate supply increases. | When workers become less productive, . . . | | . . . aggregate supply decreases. |

The **long-run aggregate supply curve** shows the relationship between the aggregate price level and the quantity of aggregate output supplied that would exist if all prices, including nominal wages, were fully flexible.

## The Long-Run Aggregate Supply Curve

We've just seen that in the short run a fall in the aggregate price level leads to a decline in the quantity of aggregate output supplied because nominal wages are sticky in the short run. But, as we mentioned earlier, contracts and informal agreements are renegotiated in the long run. So in the long run, nominal wages—like the aggregate price level—are flexible, not sticky. This fact greatly alters the long-run relationship between the aggregate price level and aggregate supply. In fact, in the long run the aggregate price level has *no* effect on the quantity of aggregate output supplied.

To see why, let's conduct a thought experiment. Imagine that you could wave a magic wand—or maybe a magic bar-code scanner—and cut *all prices* in the economy in half at the same time. By "all prices" we mean the prices of all inputs, including nominal wages, as well as the prices of final goods and services. What would happen to aggregate output, given that the aggregate price level has been halved and all input prices, including nominal wages, have been halved?

The answer is: nothing. Consider Equation 12-2 again: each producer would receive a lower price for its product, but costs would fall by the same proportion. As a result, every unit of output profitable to produce before the change in prices would still be profitable to produce after the change in prices. So a halving of *all* prices in the economy has no effect on the economy's aggregate output. In other words, changes in the aggregate price level now have no effect on the quantity of aggregate output supplied.

In reality, of course, no one can change all prices by the same proportion at the same time. But now, we'll consider the *long run, the period of time over which all prices are fully flexible.* In the long run, inflation or deflation has the same effect as someone changing all prices by the same proportion. *As a result, changes in the aggregate price level do not change the quantity of aggregate output supplied in the long run.* That's because changes in the aggregate price level will, in the long run, be accompanied by equal proportional changes in *all* input prices, including nominal wages.

The **long-run aggregate supply curve,** illustrated in Figure 12-7 by the curve *LRAS*, shows the relationship between the aggregate price level and the quantity of aggregate output supplied that would exist if all prices, including

**FIGURE 12-7 The Long-Run Aggregate Supply Curve**

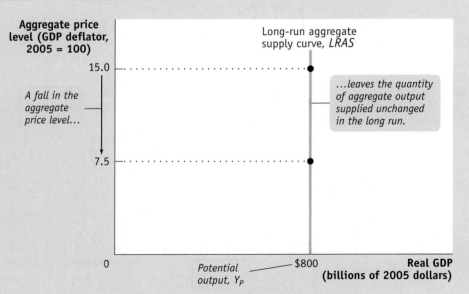

The long-run aggregate supply curve shows the quantity of aggregate output supplied when all prices, including nominal wages, are flexible. It is vertical at potential output, $Y_P$, because in the long run a change in the aggregate price level has no effect on the quantity of aggregate output supplied.

nominal wages, were fully flexible. The long-run aggregate supply curve is vertical because changes in the aggregate price level have *no* effect on aggregate output in the long run. At an aggregate price level of 15.0, the quantity of aggregate output supplied is $800 billion in 2005 dollars. If the aggregate price level falls by 50% to 7.5, the quantity of aggregate output supplied is unchanged in the long run at $800 billion in 2005 dollars.

It's important to understand not only that the *LRAS* curve is vertical but also that its position along the horizontal axis represents a significant measure. The horizontal intercept in Figure 12-7, where *LRAS* touches the horizontal axis ($800 billion in 2005 dollars), is the economy's **potential output,** $Y_P$: the level of real GDP the economy would produce if all prices, including nominal wages, were fully flexible.

In reality, the actual level of real GDP is almost always either above or below potential output. We'll see why later in this chapter, when we discuss the *AD–AS* model. Still, an economy's potential output is an important number because it defines the trend around which actual aggregate output fluctuates from year to year.

In the United States, the Congressional Budget Office, or CBO, estimates annual potential output for the purpose of federal budget analysis. In Figure 12-8, the CBO's estimates of U.S. potential output from 1990 to 2011 are represented by the orange line and the actual values of U.S. real GDP over the same period are represented by the blue line. Years shaded purple on the horizontal axis correspond to periods in which actual aggregate output fell short of potential output, years shaded green to periods in which actual aggregate output exceeded potential output.

> **Potential output** is the level of real GDP the economy would produce if all prices, including nominal wages, were fully flexible.

**FIGURE   12-8   Actual and Potential Output from 1990 to 2011**

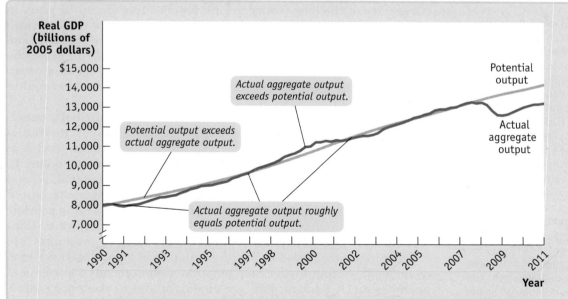

This figure shows the performance of actual and potential output in the United States from 1990 to 2011. The orange line shows estimates of U.S. potential output, produced by the Congressional Budget Office, and the blue line shows actual aggregate output. The purple-shaded years are periods in which actual aggregate output fell below potential output, and the green-shaded years are periods in which actual aggregate output exceeded potential output. As shown, significant shortfalls occurred in the recessions of the early 1990s and after 2000. Actual aggregate output was significantly above potential output in the boom of the late 1990s, and a huge shortfall occurred after the recession of 2007–2009.

*Sources:* Congressional Budget Office; Bureau of Economic Analysis.

As you can see, U.S. potential output has risen steadily over time—implying a series of rightward shifts of the *LRAS* curve. What has caused these rightward shifts? The answer lies in the factors related to long-run growth that we discussed in Chapter 9, such as increases in physical capital and human capital as well as technological progress. Over the long run, as the size of the labor force and the productivity of labor both rise, the level of real GDP that the economy is capable of producing also rises. Indeed, one way to think about long-run economic growth is that it is the growth in the economy's potential output. We generally think of the long-run aggregate supply curve as shifting to the right over time as an economy experiences long-run growth.

## From the Short Run to the Long Run

As you can see in Figure 12-8, the economy normally produces more or less than potential output: actual aggregate output was below potential output in the early 1990s, above potential output in the late 1990s, below potential output for most of the 2000s, and significantly below potential output after the recession of 2007–2009. So the economy is normally on its short-run aggregate supply curve—but not on its long-run aggregate supply curve. So why is the long-run curve relevant? Does the economy ever move from the short run to the long run? And if so, how?

The first step to answering these questions is to understand that the economy is always in one of only two states with respect to the short-run and long-run aggregate supply curves. It can be on both curves simultaneously by being at a point where the curves cross (as in the few years in Figure 12-8 in which actual aggregate output and potential output roughly coincided). Or it can be on the short-run aggregate supply curve but not the long-run aggregate supply curve (as in the years in which actual aggregate output and potential output *did not* coincide). But that is not the end of the story. If the economy is on the short-run but not the long-run aggregate supply curve, the short-run aggregate supply curve will shift over time until the economy is at a point where both curves cross—a point where actual aggregate output is equal to potential output.

Figure 12-9 illustrates how this process works. In both panels *LRAS* is the long-run aggregate supply curve, $SRAS_1$ is the initial short-run aggregate supply curve, and the aggregate price level is at $P_1$. In panel (a) the economy starts at the initial production point, $A_1$, which corresponds to a quantity of aggregate output supplied, $Y_1$, that is higher than potential output, $Y_P$. Producing an aggregate output level (such as $Y_1$) that is higher than potential output ($Y_P$) is possible only because nominal wages haven't yet fully adjusted upward. Until this upward adjustment in nominal wages occurs, producers are earning high profits and producing a high level of output. But a level of aggregate output higher than potential output means a low level of unemployment. Because jobs are abundant and workers are scarce, nominal wages will rise over time, gradually shifting the short-run aggregate supply curve leftward. Eventually it will be in a new position, such as $SRAS_2$. (Later in this chapter, we'll show where the short-run aggregate supply curve ends up. As we'll see, that depends on the aggregate demand curve as well.)

In panel (b), the initial production point, $A_1$, corresponds to an aggregate output level, $Y_1$, that is lower than potential output, $Y_P$. Producing an aggregate output level (such as $Y_1$) that is lower than potential output ($Y_P$) is possible only because nominal wages haven't yet fully adjusted downward. Until this downward adjustment occurs, producers are earning low (or negative) profits and producing a low level of output. An aggregate output level lower than potential output means high unemployment. Because workers are abundant and jobs

**PITFALLS**

**ARE WE THERE YET? WHAT THE LONG RUN REALLY MEANS**
We've used the term *long run* in two different contexts. In an earlier chapter we focused on *long-run economic growth*: growth that takes place over decades. In this chapter we introduced the *long-run aggregate supply curve*, which depicts the economy's potential output: the level of aggregate output that the economy would produce if all prices, including nominal wages, were fully flexible. It might seem that we're using the same term, *long run*, for two different concepts. But we aren't: these two concepts are really the same thing.

Because the economy always tends to return to potential output in the long run, actual aggregate output *fluctuates around* potential output, rarely getting too far from it. As a result, the economy's rate of growth over long periods of time—say, decades—is very close to the rate of growth of potential output. And potential output growth is determined by the factors we analyzed in the chapter on long-run economic growth. So that means that the "long run" of long-run growth and the "long run" of the long-run aggregate supply curve coincide.

FIGURE **12-9** From the Short Run to the Long Run

**(a) Leftward Shift of the Short-Run Aggregate Supply Curve**

**(b) Rightward Shift of the Short-Run Aggregate Supply Curve**

In panel (a), the initial short-run aggregate supply curve is $SRAS_1$. At the aggregate price level, $P_1$, the quantity of aggregate output supplied, $Y_1$, exceeds potential output, $Y_P$. Eventually, low unemployment will cause nominal wages to rise, leading to a leftward shift of the short-run aggregate supply curve from $SRAS_1$ to $SRAS_2$. In panel (b), the reverse happens: at the aggregate price level, $P_1$, the quantity of aggregate output supplied is less than potential output. High unemployment eventually leads to a fall in nominal wages over time and a rightward shift of the short-run aggregate supply curve.

are scarce, nominal wages will fall over time, shifting the short-run aggregate supply curve gradually to the right. Eventually it will be in a new position, such as $SRAS_2$.

We'll see shortly that these shifts of the short-run aggregate supply curve will return the economy to potential output in the long run.

## ECONOMICS ➤ IN ACTION

### PRICES AND OUTPUT DURING THE GREAT DEPRESSION

Figure 12-10 shows the actual track of the aggregate price level, as measured by the GDP deflator, and real GDP, from 1929 to 1942. As you can see, aggregate output and the aggregate price level fell together from 1929 to 1933 and rose together from 1933 to 1937. This is what we'd expect to see if the economy was moving down the short-run aggregate supply curve from 1929 to 1933 and moving up it (with a brief reversal in 1937–1938) thereafter.

But even in 1942 the aggregate price level was still lower than it was in 1929; yet real GDP was much higher. What happened?

The answer is that the short-run aggregate supply curve shifted to the right over time. This shift partly reflected rising productivity—a rightward shift of the underlying long-run aggregate supply curve.

FIGURE **12-10** Prices and Output During the Great Depression

---

**▼ Quick Review**

- The **aggregate supply curve** illustrates the relationship between the aggregate price level and the quantity of aggregate output supplied.

- The **short-run aggregate supply curve** is upward sloping: a higher aggregate price level leads to higher aggregate output given that **nominal wages** are **sticky**.

- Changes in commodity prices, nominal wages, and productivity shift the short-run aggregate supply curve.

- In the long run, all prices are flexible, and changes in the aggregate price level have no effect on aggregate output. The **long-run aggregate supply curve** is vertical at **potential output.**

- If actual aggregate output exceeds potential output, nominal wages eventually rise and the short-run aggregate supply curve shifts leftward. If potential output exceeds actual aggregate output, nominal wages eventually fall and the short-run aggregate supply curve shifts rightward.

---

But since the U.S. economy was producing below potential output and had high unemployment during this period, the rightward shift of the short-run aggregate supply curve also reflected the adjustment process shown in panel (b) of Figure 12-9. So the movement of aggregate output from 1929 to 1942 reflected both movements along and shifts of the short-run aggregate supply curve.

**CHECK YOUR UNDERSTANDING** 12-2

1. Determine the effect on short-run aggregate supply of each of the following events. Explain whether it represents a movement along the *SRAS* curve or a shift of the *SRAS* curve.

   **a.** A rise in the consumer price index (CPI) leads producers to increase output.

   **b.** A fall in the price of oil leads producers to increase output.

   **c.** A rise in legally mandated retirement benefits paid to workers leads producers to reduce output.

2. Suppose the economy is initially at potential output and the quantity of aggregate output supplied increases. What information would you need to determine whether this was due to a movement along the *SRAS* curve or a shift of the *LRAS* curve?

Solutions appear at back of book.

## The *AD–AS* Model

From 1929 to 1933, the U.S. economy moved down the short-run aggregate supply curve as the aggregate price level fell. In contrast, from 1979 to 1980 the U.S. economy moved up the aggregate demand curve as the aggregate price level rose. In each case, the cause of the movement along the curve was a shift of the other curve. In 1929–1933, it was a leftward shift of the aggregate demand curve—a major fall in consumer spending. In 1979–1980, it was a leftward shift of the short-run aggregate supply curve—a dramatic fall in short-run aggregate supply caused by the oil price shock.

So to understand the behavior of the economy, we must put the aggregate supply curve and the aggregate demand curve together. The result is the **AD–AS model,** the basic model we use to understand economic fluctuations.

### Short-Run Macroeconomic Equilibrium

We'll begin our analysis by focusing on the short run. Figure 12-11 shows the aggregate demand curve and the short-run aggregate supply curve on the same diagram. The point at which the *AD* and *SRAS* curves intersect, $E_{SR}$, is the **short-run macroeconomic equilibrium:** the point at which the quantity of aggregate output supplied is equal to the quantity demanded by domestic households, businesses, the government, and the rest of the world. The aggregate price level at $E_{SR}$, $P_E$, is the **short-run equilibrium aggregate price level.** The level of aggregate output at $E_{SR}$, $Y_E$, is the **short-run equilibrium aggregate output.**

In the supply and demand model of Chapter 3 we saw that a shortage of any individual good causes its market price to rise but a surplus of the good causes its market price to fall. These forces ensure that the market reaches equilibrium. The same logic applies to short-run macroeconomic equilibrium. If the aggregate price level is above its equilibrium level, the quantity of aggregate output supplied exceeds the quantity of aggregate output demanded. This leads to a fall in the aggregate price level and pushes it toward its equilibrium level. If

In the *AD–AS* **model,** the aggregate supply curve and the aggregate demand curve are used together to analyze economic fluctuations.

The economy is in **short-run macroeconomic equilibrium** when the quantity of aggregate output supplied is equal to the quantity demanded.

The **short-run equilibrium aggregate price level** is the aggregate price level in the short-run macroeconomic equilibrium.

**Short-run equilibrium aggregate output** is the quantity of aggregate output produced in the short-run macroeconomic equilibrium.

### FIGURE 12-11 The *AD–AS* Model

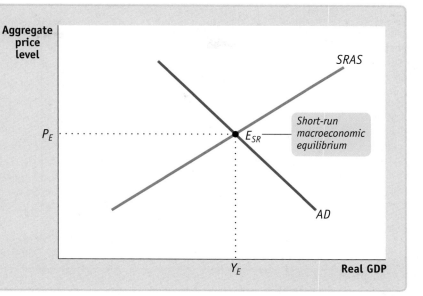

The *AD–AS* model combines the aggregate demand curve and the short-run aggregate supply curve. Their point of intersection, $E_{SR}$, is the point of short-run macroeconomic equilibrium where the quantity of aggregate output demanded is equal to the quantity of aggregate output supplied. $P_E$ is the short-run equilibrium aggregate price level, and $Y_E$ is the short-run equilibrium level of aggregate output.

the aggregate price level is below its equilibrium level, the quantity of aggregate output supplied is less than the quantity of aggregate output demanded. This leads to a rise in the aggregate price level, again pushing it toward its equilibrium level. In the discussion that follows, we'll assume that the economy is always in short-run macroeconomic equilibrium.

We'll also make another important simplification based on the observation that in reality there is a long-term upward trend in both aggregate output and the aggregate price level. We'll assume that a fall in either variable really means a fall compared to the long-run trend. For example, if the aggregate price level normally rises 4% per year, a year in which the aggregate price level rises only 3% would count, for our purposes, as a 1% decline. In fact, since the Great Depression there have been very few years in which the aggregate price level of any major nation actually declined—Japan's period of deflation since 1995 is one of the few exceptions. We'll explain why in Chapter 16. There have, however, been many cases in which the aggregate price level fell relative to the long-run trend.

Short-run equilibrium aggregate output and the short-run equilibrium aggregate price level can change either because of shifts of the *AD* curve or because of shifts of the *SRAS* curve. Let's look at each case in turn.

## Shifts of Aggregate Demand: Short-Run Effects

An event that shifts the aggregate demand curve, such as a change in expectations or wealth, the effect of the size of the existing stock of physical capital, or the use of fiscal or monetary policy, is known as a **demand shock.** The Great Depression was caused by a negative demand shock, the collapse of wealth and of business and consumer confidence that followed the stock market crash of 1929 and the banking crisis of 1930–1931. The Depression was ended by a positive demand shock—the huge increase in government purchases during World War II. In 2008 the U.S. economy experienced another significant negative demand shock as the housing market turned from boom to bust, leading consumers and firms to scale back their spending.

Figure 12-12 shows the short-run effects of negative and positive demand shocks. A negative demand shock shifts the aggregate demand curve, *AD*, to the

An event that shifts the aggregate demand curve is a **demand shock.**

FIGURE 12-12 Demand Shocks

A demand shock shifts the aggregate demand curve, moving the aggregate price level and aggregate output in the same direction. In panel (a), a negative demand shock shifts the aggregate demand curve leftward from $AD_1$ to $AD_2$, reducing the aggregate price level from $P_1$ to $P_2$ and aggregate output from $Y_1$ to $Y_2$. In panel (b), a positive demand shock shifts the aggregate demand curve rightward, increasing the aggregate price level from $P_1$ to $P_2$ and aggregate output from $Y_1$ to $Y_2$.

left, from $AD_1$ to $AD_2$, as shown in panel (a). The economy moves down along the $SRAS$ curve from $E_1$ to $E_2$, leading to lower short-run equilibrium aggregate output and a lower short-run equilibrium aggregate price level. A positive demand shock shifts the aggregate demand curve, $AD$, to the right, as shown in panel (b). Here, the economy moves up along the $SRAS$ curve, from $E_1$ to $E_2$. This leads to higher short-run equilibrium aggregate output and a higher short-run equilibrium aggregate price level. Demand shocks cause aggregate output and the aggregate price level to move in the same direction.

## Shifts of the *SRAS* Curve

An event that shifts the short-run aggregate supply curve, such as a change in commodity prices, nominal wages, or productivity, is known as a **supply shock.** A *negative* supply shock raises production costs and reduces the quantity producers are willing to supply at any given aggregate price level, leading to a leftward shift of the short-run aggregate supply curve. The U.S. economy experienced severe negative supply shocks following disruptions to world oil supplies in 1973 and 1979. In contrast, a *positive* supply shock reduces production costs and increases the quantity supplied at any given aggregate price level, leading to a rightward shift of the short-run aggregate supply curve. The United States experienced a positive supply shock between 1995 and 2000, when the increasing use of the Internet and other information technologies caused productivity growth to surge.

The effects of a negative supply shock are shown in panel (a) of Figure 12-13. The initial equilibrium is at $E_1$, with aggregate price level $P_1$ and aggregate output $Y_1$. The disruption in the oil supply causes the short-run aggregate supply curve to shift to the left, from $SRAS_1$ to $SRAS_2$. As a consequence, aggregate output falls and the aggregate price level rises, an upward movement along the $AD$ curve. At the new equilibrium, $E_2$, the short-run equilibrium aggregate price

An event that shifts the short-run aggregate supply curve is a **supply shock.**

FIGURE **12-13** Supply Shocks

**(a) A Negative Supply Shock**

A negative supply shock...

$SRAS_2$   $SRAS_1$

$E_2$

$P_2$
↑
$P_1$

...leads to lower aggregate output and a higher aggregate price level.

$E_1$

$AD$

$Y_2$←$Y_1$          **Real GDP**

Aggregate price level

**(b) A Positive Supply Shock**

A positive supply shock...

$SRAS_1$
$SRAS_2$

$E_1$

$P_1$
↓
$P_2$

...leads to higher aggregate output and a lower aggregate price level.

$E_2$

$AD$

$Y_1$→$Y_2$          **Real GDP**

Aggregate price level

A supply shock shifts the short-run aggregate supply curve, moving the aggregate price level and aggregate output in opposite directions. Panel (a) shows a negative supply shock, which shifts the short-run aggregate supply curve leftward and causes stagflation—lower aggregate output and a higher aggregate price level. Here the short-run aggregate supply curve shifts from $SRAS_1$ to $SRAS_2$, and the economy moves from $E_1$ to $E_2$. The aggregate price level rises from $P_1$ to $P_2$, and aggregate output falls from $Y_1$ to $Y_2$. Panel (b) shows a positive supply shock, which shifts the short-run aggregate supply curve rightward, generating higher aggregate output and a lower aggregate price level. The short-run aggregate supply curve shifts from $SRAS_1$ to $SRAS_2$, and the economy moves from $E_1$ to $E_2$. The aggregate price level falls from $P_1$ to $P_2$, and aggregate output rises from $Y_1$ to $Y_2$.

level, $P_2$, is higher, and the short-run equilibrium aggregate output level, $Y_2$, is lower than before.

The combination of inflation and falling aggregate output shown in panel (a) has a special name: **stagflation,** for "stagnation plus inflation." When an economy experiences stagflation, it's very unpleasant: falling aggregate output leads to rising unemployment, and people feel that their purchasing power is squeezed by rising prices. Stagflation in the 1970s led to a mood of national pessimism. It also, as we'll see shortly, poses a dilemma for policy makers.

A positive supply shock, shown in panel (b), has exactly the opposite effects. A rightward shift of the $SRAS$ curve from $SRAS_1$ to $SRAS_2$ results in a rise in aggregate output and a fall in the aggregate price level, a downward movement along the $AD$ curve. The favorable supply shocks of the late 1990s led to a combination of full employment and declining inflation. That is, the aggregate price level fell compared with the long-run trend. This combination produced, for a time, a great wave of national optimism.

The distinctive feature of supply shocks, both negative and positive, is that, unlike demand shocks, they cause the aggregate price level and aggregate output to move in *opposite* directions.

There's another important contrast between supply shocks and demand shocks. As we've seen, monetary policy and fiscal policy enable the government to shift the $AD$ curve, meaning that governments

**Stagflation** is the combination of inflation and falling aggregate output.

As you can see from the faces of these job seekers, pessimism prevails during stagflation as unemployment and prices rise.

## GLOBAL COMPARISON

## SUPPLY SHOCKS OF THE TWENTY-FIRST CENTURY

The price of oil and other raw materials has been highly unstable in recent years, with surging prices in 2007–2008, plunging prices in 2008–2009, and another surge starting in the second half of 2010. The reasons for these wild swings are somewhat controversial, but their macroeconomic implications are clear: much of the world has been subjected to a series of supply shocks. There was a negative shock in 2007–2008, a positive shock in 2008–2009, and another negative shock in 2010–2011.

You can see the effect of these shocks in the accompanying figure, which shows the rate of inflation, as measured by the percentage change in consumer prices over the previous year, in three large economies. Economic policies have been quite different in the United States, Germany (which shares a currency with many other European countries), and China. Yet in all three inflation rose sharply in 2007–2008, fell dramatically thereafter, and rose sharply again in 2011.

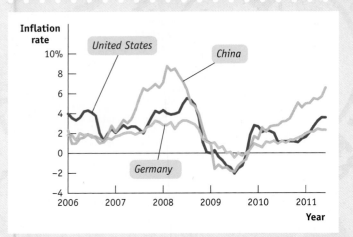

*Source:* Federal Reserve Bank of St. Louis.

are in a position to create the kinds of shocks shown in Figure 12-12. It's much harder for governments to shift the *AS* curve. Are there good policy reasons to shift the *AD* curve? We'll turn to that question soon. First, however, let's look at the difference between short-run macroeconomic equilibrium and long-run macroeconomic equilibrium.

## Long-Run Macroeconomic Equilibrium

Figure 12-14 combines the aggregate demand curve with both the short-run and long-run aggregate supply curves. The aggregate demand curve, *AD*, crosses the short-run aggregate supply curve, *SRAS*, at $E_{LR}$. Here we assume that enough time has elapsed that the economy is also on the long-run aggregate supply curve, *LRAS*. As a result, $E_{LR}$ is at the intersection of all three curves—*SRAS*, *LRAS*, and *AD*. So short-run equilibrium aggregate output is equal to potential output, $Y_P$. Such a situation, in which the point of short-run macroeconomic equilibrium is on the long-run aggregate supply curve, is known as **long-run macroeconomic equilibrium.**

To see the significance of long-run macroeconomic equilibrium, let's consider what happens if a demand shock moves the economy away from long-run macroeconomic equilibrium. In Figure 12-15, we assume that the initial aggregate demand curve is $AD_1$ and the initial short-run aggregate supply curve is $SRAS_1$. So the initial macroeconomic equilibrium is at $E_1$, which lies on the long-run aggregate supply curve, *LRAS*. The economy, then, starts from a point of short-run and long-run macroeconomic equilibrium, and short-run equilibrium aggregate output equals potential output at $Y_1$.

Now suppose that for some reason—such as a sudden worsening of business and consumer expectations—aggregate demand falls and the aggregate demand curve shifts leftward to $AD_2$. This results in a lower equilibrium aggregate price level at $P_2$ and a lower equilibrium aggregate output level at $Y_2$ as the economy settles in the short run at $E_2$. The short-run effect of such a fall in aggregate

The economy is in **long-run macroeconomic equilibrium** when the point of short-run macroeconomic equilibrium is on the long-run aggregate supply curve.

There is a **recessionary gap** when aggregate output is below potential output.

FIGURE **12-14** Long-Run Macroeconomic Equilibrium

Here the point of short-run macro-economic equilibrium also lies on the long-run aggregate supply curve, *LRAS*. As a result, short-run equilibrium aggregate output is equal to potential output, $Y_P$. The economy is in long-run macroeconomic equilibrium at $E_{LR}$.

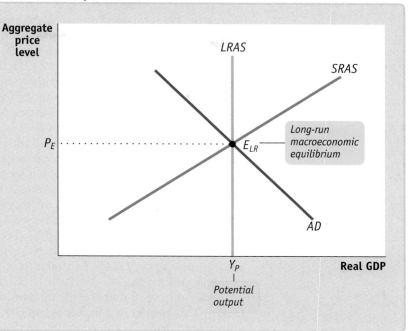

demand is what the U.S. economy experienced in 1929–1933: a falling aggregate price level and falling aggregate output.

Aggregate output in this new short-run equilibrium, $E_2$, is below potential output. When this happens, the economy faces a **recessionary gap.** A

FIGURE **12-15** Short-Run versus Long-Run Effects of a Negative Demand Shock

In the long run the economy is self-correcting: demand shocks have only a short-run effect on aggregate output. Starting at $E_1$, a negative demand shock shifts $AD_1$ leftward to $AD_2$. In the short run the economy moves to $E_2$ and a recessionary gap arises: the aggregate price level declines from $P_1$ to $P_2$, aggregate output declines from $Y_1$ to $Y_2$, and unemployment rises. But in the long run nominal wages fall in response to high unemployment at $Y_2$, and $SRAS_1$ shifts rightward to $SRAS_2$. Aggregate output rises from $Y_2$ to $Y_1$, and the aggregate price level declines again, from $P_2$ to $P_3$. Long-run macroeconomic equilibrium is eventually restored at $E_3$.

There is an **inflationary gap** when aggregate output is above potential output.

The **output gap** is the percentage difference between actual aggregate output and potential output.

recessionary gap inflicts a great deal of pain because it corresponds to high unemployment. The large recessionary gap that had opened up in the United States by 1933 caused intense social and political turmoil. And the devastating recessionary gap that opened up in Germany at the same time played an important role in Hitler's rise to power.

But this isn't the end of the story. In the face of high unemployment, nominal wages eventually fall, as do any other sticky prices, ultimately leading producers to increase output. As a result, a recessionary gap causes the short-run aggregate supply curve to gradually shift to the right over time. This process continues until $SRAS_1$ reaches its new position at $SRAS_2$, bringing the economy to equilibrium at $E_3$, where $AD_2$, $SRAS_2$, and $LRAS$ all intersect. At $E_3$, the economy is back in long-run macroeconomic equilibrium; it is back at potential output $Y_1$ but at a lower aggregate price level, $P_3$, reflecting a long-run fall in the aggregate price level. In the end, the economy is *self-correcting* in the long run.

What if, instead, there was an increase in aggregate demand? The results are shown in Figure 12-16, where we again assume that the initial aggregate demand curve is $AD_1$ and the initial short-run aggregate supply curve is $SRAS_1$, so that the initial macroeconomic equilibrium, at $E_1$, lies on the long-run aggregate supply curve, $LRAS$. Initially, then, the economy is in long-run macroeconomic equilibrium.

Now suppose that aggregate demand rises, and the $AD$ curve shifts rightward to $AD_2$. This results in a higher aggregate price level, at $P_2$, and a higher aggregate output level, at $Y_2$, as the economy settles in the short run at $E_2$. Aggregate output in this new short-run equilibrium is above potential output, and unemployment is low in order to produce this higher level of aggregate output. When this happens, the economy experiences an **inflationary gap.**

As in the case of a recessionary gap, this isn't the end of the story. In the face of low unemployment, nominal wages will rise, as will other sticky prices. An inflationary gap causes the short-run aggregate supply curve to shift gradually to the left as producers reduce output in the face of rising nominal wages. This process continues until $SRAS_1$ reaches its new position at $SRAS_2$, bringing the economy to equilibrium at $E_3$, where $AD_2$, $SRAS_2$, and $LRAS$ all intersect. At $E_3$, the economy is back in long-run macroeconomic equilibrium. It is back at potential output, but at a higher price level, $P_3$, reflecting a long-run rise in the aggregate price level. Again, the economy is self-correcting in the long run.

To summarize the analysis of how the economy responds to recessionary and inflationary gaps, we can focus on the **output gap,** the percentage difference

---

### FOR INQUIRING MINDS

#### WHERE'S THE DEFLATION?

The *AD–AS* model says that either a negative demand shock or a positive supply shock should lead to a fall in the aggregate price level—that is, deflation. However, since 1949, an actual fall in the aggregate price level has been a rare occurrence in the United States. Similarly, most other countries have had little or no experience with deflation. Japan, which experienced sustained mild deflation in the late 1990s and the early part of the next decade, is the big (and

much discussed) exception. What happened to deflation?

The basic answer is that since World War II economic fluctuations have largely taken place around a long-run inflationary trend. Before the war, it was common for prices to fall during recessions, but since then negative demand shocks have largely been reflected in a *decline in the rate of inflation* rather than an actual fall in prices. For example, the rate of consumer price inflation fell from

more than 3% at the beginning of the 2001 recession to 1.1% a year later, but it never went below zero.

All of this changed during the recession of 2007–2009. The negative demand shock that followed the 2008 financial crisis was so severe that, for most of 2009, consumer prices in the United States indeed fell. But the deflationary period didn't last long: Beginning in 2010, prices again rose, at a rate of between 1% and 4% per year.

FIGURE **12-16** Short-Run versus Long-Run Effects of a Positive Demand Shock

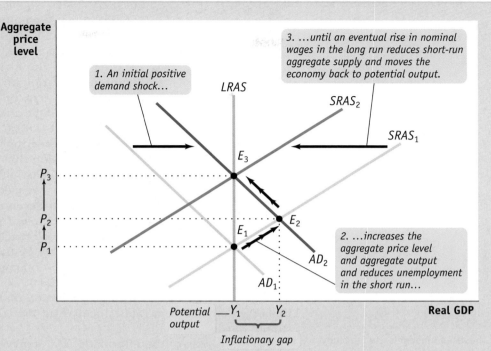

Starting at $E_1$, a positive demand shock shifts $AD_1$ rightward to $AD_2$, and the economy moves to $E_2$ in the short run. This results in an inflationary gap as aggregate output rises from $Y_1$ to $Y_2$, the aggregate price level rises from $P_1$ to $P_2$, and unemployment falls to a low level. In the long run, $SRAS_1$ shifts leftward to $SRAS_2$ as nominal wages rise in response to low unemployment at $Y_2$. Aggregate output falls back to $Y_1$, the aggregate price level rises again to $P_3$, and the economy self-corrects as it returns to long-run macroeconomic equilibrium at $E_3$.

1. An initial positive demand shock...

3. ...until an eventual rise in nominal wages in the long run reduces short-run aggregate supply and moves the economy back to potential output.

2. ...increases the aggregate price level and aggregate output and reduces unemployment in the short run...

between actual aggregate output and potential output. The output gap is calculated as follows:

**(12-3)** Output gap = $\dfrac{\text{Actual aggregate output} - \text{Potential output}}{\text{Potential output}} \times 100$

Our analysis says that the output gap always tends toward zero.

If there is a recessionary gap, so that the output gap is negative, nominal wages eventually fall, moving the economy back to potential output and bringing the output gap back to zero. If there is an inflationary gap, so that the output gap is positive, nominal wages eventually rise, also moving the economy back to potential output and again bringing the output gap back to zero. So in the long run the economy is **self-correcting:** shocks to aggregate demand affect aggregate output in the short run but not in the long run.

## ECONOMICS > IN ACTION

### SUPPLY SHOCKS VERSUS DEMAND SHOCKS IN PRACTICE

How often do supply shocks and demand shocks, respectively, cause recessions? The verdict of most, though not all, macroeconomists is that recessions are mainly caused by demand shocks. But when a negative supply shock does happen, the resulting recession tends to be particularly severe.

Let's get specific. Officially there have been twelve recessions in the United States since World War II. However, two of these, in 1979–1980 and 1981–1982, are often treated as a single "double-dip" recession, bringing the total number down to eleven. Of these eleven recessions, only two—the

The economy is **self-correcting** when shocks to aggregate demand affect aggregate output in the short run, but not in the long run.

**FIGURE 12-17** Negative Supply Shocks Are Relatively Rare but Nasty

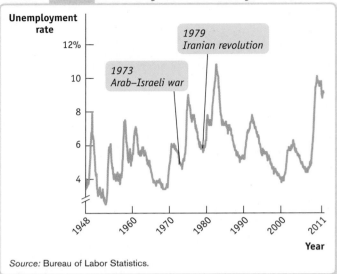

*Source:* Bureau of Labor Statistics.

recession of 1973–1975 and the double-dip recession of 1979–1982—showed the distinctive combination of falling aggregate output and a surge in the price level that we call stagflation. In each case, the cause of the supply shock was political turmoil in the Middle East—the Arab–Israeli war of 1973 and the Iranian revolution of 1979—that disrupted world oil supplies and sent oil prices skyrocketing. In fact, economists sometimes refer to the two slumps as "OPEC I" and "OPEC II," after the Organization of Petroleum Exporting Countries, the world oil cartel. A third recession that began in 2007 and lasted until 2009 was at least partially exacerbated, if not at least partially caused, by a spike in oil prices.

So eight of eleven postwar recessions were purely the result of demand shocks, not supply shocks. The few supply-shock recessions, however, were the worst as measured by the unemployment rate. Figure 12-17 shows the U.S. unemployment rate since 1948, with the dates of the 1973 Arab–Israeli war and the 1979 Iranian revolution marked on the graph. Some of the highest unemployment rates since World War II came after these big negative supply shocks.

There's a reason the aftermath of a supply shock tends to be particularly severe for the economy: macroeconomic policy has a much harder time dealing with supply shocks than with demand shocks. Indeed, the reason the Federal Reserve was having a hard time in 2008, as described in the opening story, was the fact that in early 2008 the U.S. economy was in a recession partially caused by a supply shock (although it was also facing a demand shock). We'll see in a moment why supply shocks present such a problem.

**CHECK YOUR UNDERSTANDING** **12-3**

1. Describe the short-run effects of each of the following shocks on the aggregate price level and on aggregate output.
   a. The government sharply increases the minimum wage, raising the wages of many workers.
   b. Solar energy firms launch a major program of investment spending.
   c. Congress raises taxes and cuts spending.
   d. Severe weather destroys crops around the world.

2. A rise in productivity increases potential output, but some worry that demand for the additional output will be insufficient even in the long run. How would you respond?

*Solutions appear at back of book.*

## Macroeconomic Policy

We've just seen that the economy is self-correcting in the long run: it will eventually trend back to potential output. Most macroeconomists believe, however, that the process of self-correction typically takes a decade or more. In particular, if aggregate output is below potential output, the economy can suffer an extended period of depressed aggregate output and high unemployment before it returns to normal.

This belief is the background to one of the most famous quotations in economics: John Maynard Keynes's declaration, "In the long run we are all dead." We explain the context in which he made this remark in the accompanying For Inquiring Minds.

Economists usually interpret Keynes as having recommended that governments not wait for the economy to correct itself. Instead, it is argued by many economists, but not all, that the government should use monetary and fiscal policy to get the economy back to potential output in the aftermath of a shift of the aggregate demand curve. This is the rationale for an active **stabilization policy,** which is the use of government policy to reduce the severity of recessions and rein in excessively strong expansions.

**Stabilization policy** is the use of government policy to reduce the severity of recessions and rein in excessively strong expansions.

**FOR INQUIRING MINDS**

**KEYNES AND THE LONG RUN**

The British economist Sir John Maynard Keynes (1883–1946), probably more than any other single economist, created the modern field of macroeconomics. We'll look at his role, and the controversies that still swirl around some aspects of his thought, in a later chapter on macroeconomic events and ideas. But for now let's just look at his most famous quote.

In 1923 Keynes published *A Tract on Monetary Reform*, a small book on the economic problems of Europe after World War I. In it he decried the tendency of many of his colleagues to focus on how things work out in the long run—as in the long-run macroeconomic equilibrium we have just analyzed—while ignoring the often very painful and possibly disastrous things that can happen along the way. Here's a fuller version of the quote:

> This *long run* is a misleading guide to current affairs. *In the long run* we are all dead. Economists set themselves too easy, too useless a task if in tempestuous seasons they can only tell us that when the storm is long past the sea is flat again.

Keynes focused the attention of economists of his day on the short run.

Can stabilization policy improve the economy's performance? If we reexamine Figure 12-8, the answer certainly appears to be yes. Under active stabilization policy, the U.S. economy returned to potential output in 1996 after an approximately five-year recessionary gap. Likewise, in 2001 it also returned to potential output after an approximately four-year inflationary gap. These periods are much shorter than the decade or more that economists believe it would take for the economy to self-correct in the absence of active stabilization policy. However, as we'll see shortly, the ability to improve the economy's performance is not always guaranteed. It depends on the kinds of shocks the economy faces.

## Policy in the Face of Demand Shocks

Imagine that the economy experiences a negative demand shock, like the one shown in Figure 12-15. As we've discussed in this chapter, monetary and fiscal policy shift the aggregate demand curve. If policy makers react quickly to the fall in aggregate demand, they can use monetary or fiscal policy to shift the aggregate demand curve back to the right. And if policy were able to perfectly anticipate shifts of the aggregate demand curve, it could short-circuit the whole process shown in Figure 12-15. Instead of going through a period of low aggregate output and falling prices, the government could manage the economy so that it would stay at $E_1$.

Why might a policy that short-circuits the adjustment shown in Figure 12-15 and maintains the economy at its original equilibrium be desirable? For two reasons. First, the temporary fall in aggregate output that would happen without policy intervention is a bad thing, particularly because such a decline is associated with high unemployment. Second, as we explained in Chapter 8, *price stability* is generally regarded as a desirable goal. So preventing deflation—a fall in the aggregate price level—is a good thing.

Does this mean that policy makers should always act to offset declines in aggregate demand? Not necessarily. As we'll see in later chapters, some policy measures to increase aggregate demand, especially those that increase budget deficits, may have long-term costs in terms of lower long-run growth. Furthermore, in the real world policy makers aren't perfectly informed, and the effects of their policies aren't perfectly predictable. This creates the danger that stabilization policy will do more harm than good; that is, attempts to stabilize the economy may end up creating more instability. We'll describe the long-running debate over macroeconomic policy in Chapter 18. Despite these qualifications, most economists believe that a good case can be made for using macroeconomic policy to offset major negative shocks to the *AD* curve.

Should policy makers also try to offset positive shocks to aggregate demand? It may not seem obvious that they should. After all, even though inflation may be a bad thing, isn't more output and lower unemployment a good thing? Not necessarily. Most economists now believe that any short-run gains from an inflationary gap must be paid back later. So policy makers today usually try to offset positive as well as negative demand shocks. For reasons we'll explain in Chapter 15, attempts to eliminate recessionary gaps and inflationary gaps usually rely on monetary rather than fiscal policy. In 2007 and 2008 the Federal Reserve sharply cut interest rates in an attempt to head off a rising recessionary gap; earlier in the decade, when the U.S. economy seemed headed for an inflationary gap, it raised interest rates to generate the opposite effect.

But how should macroeconomic policy respond to supply shocks?

## Responding to Supply Shocks

We've now come full circle to the story that began this chapter. We can now explain why people in Ben Bernanke's position dread stagflation.

Back in panel (a) of Figure 12-13 we showed the effects of a negative supply shock: in the short run such a shock leads to lower aggregate output but a higher aggregate price level. As we've noted, policy makers can respond to a negative *demand* shock by using monetary and fiscal policy to return aggregate demand to its original level. But what can or should they do about a negative *supply* shock?

In contrast to the aggregate demand curve, there are no easy policies that shift the short-run aggregate supply curve. That is, there is no government policy that can easily affect producers' profitability and so compensate for shifts of the short-run aggregate supply curve. So the policy response to a negative supply shock cannot aim to simply push the curve that shifted back to its original position.

And if you consider using monetary or fiscal policy to shift the aggregate demand curve in response to a supply shock, the right response isn't obvious. Two bad things are happening simultaneously: a fall in aggregate output, leading to a rise in unemployment, *and* a rise in the aggregate price level. Any policy that shifts the aggregate demand curve helps one problem only by making the other worse. If the government acts to increase aggregate demand and limit the rise in unemployment, it reduces the decline in output but causes even more inflation. If it acts to reduce aggregate demand, it curbs inflation but causes a further rise in unemployment.

It's a trade-off with no good answer. In the end, the United States and other economically advanced nations suffering from the supply shocks of the 1970s eventually chose to stabilize prices even at the cost of higher unemployment. But being an economic policy maker in the 1970s, or in early 2008, meant facing even harder choices than usual.

## ECONOMICS ➤ IN ACTION

### IS STABILIZATION POLICY STABILIZING?

We've described the theoretical rationale for stabilization policy as a way of responding to demand shocks. But does stabilization policy actually stabilize the economy? One way we might try to answer this question is to look at the long-term historical record. Before World War II, the U.S. government didn't really have a stabilization policy, largely because macroeconomics as we know it didn't exist, and there was no consensus about what to do. Since World War II, and especially since 1960, active stabilization policy has become standard practice.

So here's the question: has the economy actually become more stable since the government began trying to stabilize it? The answer is a qualified yes. It's qualified for two reasons. One is that data from the pre–World War II era are less reliable than more modern data. The other is that the severe and protracted slump that began in 2007 has shaken confidence in the effectiveness of government policy. Still, there seems to have been a reduction in the size of fluctuations.

Figure 12-18 shows the number of unemployed as a percentage of the nonfarm labor force since 1890. (We focus on nonfarm workers because farmers, though they often suffer economic hardship, are rarely reported as unemployed.) Even ignoring the huge spike in unemployment during the Great Depression, unemployment seems to have varied a lot more before World War II than after. It's also worth noticing that the peaks in postwar unemployment, in 1975, 1982, and, as we described earlier, to some extent in 2010, corresponded to major supply shocks—the kind of shock for which stabilization policy has no good answer.

It's possible that the greater stability of the economy reflects good luck rather than policy. But on the face of it, the evidence suggests that stabilization policy is indeed stabilizing.

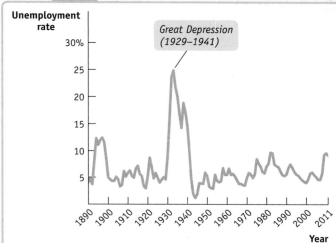

**FIGURE 12-18** Has Stabilization Policy Been Stabilizing?

*Sources:* Christina Romer, "Spurious Volatility in Historical Unemployment Data." *Journal of Political Economy* 94, no. 1 (1986): 1–37 (years 1890–1928); Bureau of Labor Statistics (years 1929–2011).

### CHECK YOUR UNDERSTANDING 12-4

1. Suppose someone says, "Using monetary or fiscal policy to pump up the economy is counterproductive—you get a brief high, but then you have the pain of inflation."
   a. Explain what this means in terms of the *AD–AS* model.
   b. Is this a valid argument against stabilization policy? Why or why not?

2. In 2008, in the aftermath of the collapse of the housing bubble and a sharp rise in the price of commodities, particularly oil, there was much internal disagreement within the Fed about how to respond, with some advocating lowering interest rates and others contending that this would set off a rise in inflation. Explain the reasoning behind each one of these views in terms of the *AD–AS* model.

Solutions appear at back of book.

▼ **Quick Review**

- **Stabilization policy** is the use of fiscal or monetary policy to offset demand shocks. There can be drawbacks, however. Such policies may lead to a long-term rise in the budget deficit and lower long-run growth because of crowding out. And, due to incorrect predictions, a misguided policy can increase economic instability.

- Negative supply shocks pose a policy dilemma because fighting the slump in aggregate output worsens inflation and fighting inflation worsens the slump.

## BUSINESS CASE : United In Pain

Bayne Stanley/Alamy

The airline industry is notoriously "cyclical." That is, instead of making profits all through the business cycle, it tends to plunge into losses during recessions, only regaining profitability sometime after recovery begins. Mainly this is because airlines have large fixed costs that remain high even if ticket sales slump. The cost of operating a flight from one city to another is pretty much the same whether the flight is fully booked or two-thirds empty, so when business slumps for whatever reason, even highly profitable routes quickly become money-losers. It's true that airlines can to some extent adapt to a decline in business by switching to smaller planes, consolidating flights, and so on, but this process takes time and still tends to leave costs per passenger higher than before.

But some recessions are worse for airlines than for other businesses, because operating costs rise even as demand falls. This was very much the case in early 2008. In the spring of that year, the so-called Great Recession of 2007–2009 was still in its early stages, with unemployment just starting to rise. Yet airlines were already, as an article in the *Los Angeles Times* put it, in a "sea of red ink." The article highlighted the case of United Airlines, which had suddenly plunged into large losses and was planning large layoffs.

Why was United in so much trouble? Business travel had started to slacken, but at that point leisure travel, such as flights to Disney World, was still holding up. What was hurting United and its sister airlines was the cost of fuel, which soared in late 2007 and early 2008.

Fuel prices fell back down in late 2008. But by that time United was suffering from a sharp drop in ticket sales. The airline finally returned to profitability in 2010, which was also the year it agreed to merge with Continental. But in early 2011 fuel prices rose again, putting airlines once more in a difficult position.

### QUESTIONS FOR THOUGHT

1. How did United's problems in early 2008 relate to our analysis of the causes of recessions?

2. Ben Bernanke had to make a choice between fighting two evils in early 2008. How would that choice affect United compared with, say, a company producing a service without expensive raw-material inputs, like health care?

3. In early 2008, business travel was beginning to slacken, but leisure travel was still holding up. Given the situation the overall economy was in, what would you expect to happen to leisure travel as the economy moved further into recession?

## SUMMARY

1. The **aggregate demand curve** shows the relationship between the aggregate price level and the quantity of aggregate output demanded.

2. The aggregate demand curve is downward sloping for two reasons. The first is the **wealth effect of a change in the aggregate price level**—a higher aggregate price level reduces the purchasing power of households' wealth and reduces consumer spending. The second is the **interest rate effect of a change in the aggregate price level**—a higher aggregate price level reduces the purchasing power of households' and firms' money holdings, leading to a rise in interest rates and a fall in investment spending and consumer spending.

3. The aggregate demand curve shifts because of changes in expectations, changes in wealth not due to changes in the aggregate price level, and the effect of the size of the existing stock of physical capital. Policy makers can use fiscal policy and monetary policy to shift the aggregate demand curve.

4. The **aggregate supply curve** shows the relationship between the aggregate price level and the quantity of aggregate output supplied.

5. The **short-run aggregate supply curve** is upward sloping because **nominal wages** are **sticky** in the short run: a higher aggregate price level leads to higher profit per unit of output and increased aggregate output in the short run.

6. Changes in commodity prices, nominal wages, and productivity lead to changes in producers' profits and shift the short-run aggregate supply curve.

7. In the long run, all prices, including nominal wages, are flexible and the economy produces at its **potential output.** If actual aggregate output exceeds potential output, nominal wages will eventually rise in response to low unemployment and aggregate output will fall. If potential output exceeds actual aggregate output, nominal wages will eventually fall in response to high unemployment and aggregate output will rise. So the **long-run aggregate supply curve** is vertical at potential output.

8. In the *AD–AS* **model,** the intersection of the short-run aggregate supply curve and the aggregate demand curve is the point of **short-run macroeconomic equilibrium.** It determines the **short-run equilibrium aggregate price level** and the level of **short-run equilibrium aggregate output.**

9. Economic fluctuations occur because of a shift of the aggregate demand curve (a *demand shock*) or the short-run aggregate supply curve (a *supply shock*). A **demand shock** causes the aggregate price level and aggregate output to move in the same direction as the economy moves along the short-run aggregate supply curve. A **supply shock** causes them to move in opposite directions as the economy moves along the aggregate demand curve. A particularly nasty occurrence is **stagflation**—inflation and falling aggregate output—which is caused by a negative supply shock.

10. Demand shocks have only short-run effects on aggregate output because the economy is **self-correcting** in the long run. In a **recessionary gap,** an eventual fall in nominal wages moves the economy to **long-run macroeconomic equilibrium,** where aggregate output is equal to potential output. In an **inflationary gap,** an eventual rise in nominal wages moves the economy to long-run macroeconomic equilibrium. We can use the **output gap,** the percentage difference between actual aggregate output and potential output, to summarize how the economy responds to recessionary and inflationary gaps. Because the economy tends to be self-correcting in the long run, the output gap always tends toward zero.

11. The high cost—in terms of unemployment—of a recessionary gap and the future adverse consequences of an inflationary gap lead many economists to advocate active **stabilization policy:** using fiscal or monetary policy to offset demand shocks. There can be drawbacks, however, because such policies may contribute to a long-term rise in the budget deficit and crowding out of private investment, leading to lower long-run growth. Also, poorly timed policies can increase economic instability.

12. Negative supply shocks pose a policy dilemma: a policy that counteracts the fall in aggregate output by increasing aggregate demand will lead to higher inflation, but a policy that counteracts inflation by reducing aggregate demand will deepen the output slump.

## KEY TERMS

Aggregate demand curve, p. 342
Wealth effect of a change in the aggregate price level, p. 343
Interest rate effect of a change in the aggregate price level, p. 344
Aggregate supply curve, p. 350
Nominal wage, p. 351
Sticky wages, p. 351
Short-run aggregate supply curve, p. 352
Long-run aggregate supply curve, p. 356
Potential output, p. 357
*AD–AS* model, p. 360
Short-run macroeconomic equilibrium, p. 360

## PROBLEMS

1. A fall in the value of the dollar against other currencies makes U.S. final goods and services cheaper to foreigners even though the U.S. aggregate price level stays the same. As a result, foreigners demand more American aggregate output. Your study partner says that this represents a movement down the aggregate demand curve because foreigners are demanding more in response to a lower price. You, however, insist that this represents a rightward shift of the aggregate demand curve. Who is right? Explain.

2. Your study partner is confused by the upward-sloping short-run aggregate supply curve and the vertical long-run aggregate supply curve. How would you explain this?

3. Suppose that in Wageland all workers sign annual wage contracts each year on January 1. No matter what happens to prices of final goods and services during the year, all workers earn the wage specified in their annual contract. This year, prices of final goods and services fall unexpectedly after the contracts are signed. Answer the following questions using a diagram and assume that the economy starts at potential output.

   a. In the short run, how will the quantity of aggregate output supplied respond to the fall in prices?

   b. What will happen when firms and workers renegotiate their wages?

4. In each of the following cases, in the short run, determine whether the events cause a shift of a curve or a movement along a curve. Determine which curve is involved and the direction of the change.

   a. As a result of an increase in the value of the dollar in relation to other currencies, American producers now pay less in dollar terms for foreign steel, a major commodity used in production.

   b. An increase in the quantity of money by the Federal Reserve increases the quantity of money that people wish to lend, lowering interest rates.

   c. Greater union activity leads to higher nominal wages.

   d. A fall in the aggregate price level increases the purchasing power of households' and firms' money holdings. As a result, they borrow less and lend more.

5. The economy is at point A in the accompanying diagram. Suppose that the aggregate price level rises from $P_1$ to $P_2$. How will aggregate supply adjust in the short run and in the long run to the increase in the aggregate price level? Illustrate with a diagram.

6. Suppose that all households hold all their wealth in assets that automatically rise in value when the aggregate price level rises (an example of this is what is called an "inflation-indexed bond"—a bond whose interest rate, among other things, changes one-for-one with the inflation rate). What happens to the wealth effect of a change in the aggregate price level as a result of this allocation of assets? What happens to the slope of the aggregate demand curve? Will it still slope downward? Explain.

7. Suppose that the economy is currently at potential output. Also suppose that you are an economic policy maker and that a college economics student asks you to rank, if possible, your most preferred to least preferred type of shock: positive demand shock, negative demand shock, positive supply shock, negative supply shock. How would you rank them and why?

8. Explain whether the following government policies affect the aggregate demand curve or the short-run aggregate supply curve and how.

   a. The government reduces the minimum nominal wage.

   b. The government increases Temporary Assistance to Needy Families (TANF) payments, government transfers to families with dependent children.

   c. To reduce the budget deficit, the government announces that households will pay much higher taxes beginning next year.

   d. The government reduces military spending.

9. In Wageland, all workers sign an annual wage contract each year on January 1. In late January, a new computer operating system is introduced that increases labor

productivity dramatically. Explain how Wageland will move from one short-run macroeconomic equilibrium to another. Illustrate with a diagram.

10. The Conference Board publishes the Consumer Confidence Index (CCI) every month based on a survey of 5,000 representative U.S. households. It is used by many economists to track the state of the economy. A press release by the Board on June 28, 2011 stated: "The Conference Board Consumer Confidence Index, which had declined in May, decreased again in June. The Index now stands at 58.5 (1985 = 100), down from 61.7 in May."

   **a.** As an economist, is this news encouraging for economic growth?

   **b.** Explain your answer to part a with the help of the *AD–AS* model. Draw a typical diagram showing two equilibrium points ($E_1$) and ($E_2$). Label the vertical axis "Aggregate price level" and the horizontal axis "Real GDP." Assume that all other major macroeconomic factors remain unchanged.

   **c.** How should the government respond to this news? What are some policy measures that could be used to help neutralize the effect of falling consumer confidence?

11. There were two major shocks to the U.S. economy in 2007, leading to the severe recession of 2007–2009. One shock was related to oil prices; the other was the slump in the housing market. This question analyzes the effect of these two shocks on GDP using the *AD–AS* framework.

   **a.** Draw typical aggregate demand and short-run aggregate supply curves. Label the horizontal axis "Real GDP" and the vertical axis "Aggregate price level." Label the equilibrium point $E_1$, the equilibrium quantity $Y_1$, and equilibrium price $P_1$.

   **b.** Data taken from the Department of Energy indicate that the average price of crude oil in the world increased from $54.63 per barrel on January 5, 2007, to $92.93 on December 28, 2007. Would an increase in oil prices cause a demand shock or a supply shock? Redraw the diagram from part a to illustrate the effect of this shock by shifting the appropriate curve.

   **c.** The Housing Price Index, published by the Office of Federal Housing Enterprise Oversight, calculates that U.S. home prices fell by an average of 3.0% in the 12 months between January 2007 and January 2008. Would the fall in home prices cause a supply shock or demand shock? Redraw the diagram from part b to illustrate the effect of this shock by shifting the appropriate curve. Label the new equilibrium point $E_3$, the equilibrium quantity $Y_3$, and equilibrium price $P_3$.

   **d.** Compare the equilibrium points $E_1$ and $E_3$ in your diagram for part c. What was the effect of the two shocks on real GDP and the aggregate price level (increase, decrease, or indeterminate)?

12. Using aggregate demand, short-run aggregate supply, and long-run aggregate supply curves, explain the process by which each of the following economic events will move the economy from one long-run macroeconomic equilibrium to another. Illustrate with diagrams. In each case, what are the short-run and long-run effects on the aggregate price level and aggregate output?

   **a.** There is a decrease in households' wealth due to a decline in the stock market.

   **b.** The government lowers taxes, leaving households with more disposable income, with no corresponding reduction in government purchases.

13. Using aggregate demand, short-run aggregate supply, and long-run aggregate supply curves, explain the process by which each of the following government policies will move the economy from one long-run macroeconomic equilibrium to another. Illustrate with diagrams. In each case, what are the short-run and long-run effects on the aggregate price level and aggregate output?

   **a.** There is an increase in taxes on households.

   **b.** There is an increase in the quantity of money.

   **c.** There is an increase in government spending.

14. The economy is in short-run macroeconomic equilibrium at point $E_1$ in the accompanying diagram. Based on the diagram, answer the following questions.

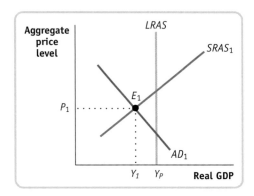

   **a.** Is the economy facing an inflationary or a recessionary gap?

   **b.** What policies can the government implement that might bring the economy back to long-run macroeconomic equilibrium? Illustrate with a diagram.

   **c.** If the government did not intervene to close this gap, would the economy return to long-run macroeconomic equilibrium? Explain and illustrate with a diagram.

   **d.** What are the advantages and disadvantages of the government implementing policies to close the gap?

**15.** In the accompanying diagram, the economy is in long-run macroeconomic equilibrium at point $E_1$ when an oil shock shifts the short-run aggregate supply curve to $SRAS_2$. Based on the diagram, answer the following questions.

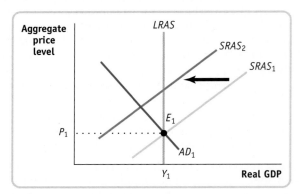

**a.** How do the aggregate price level and aggregate output change in the short run as a result of the oil shock? What is this phenomenon known as?

**b.** What fiscal or monetary policies can the government use to address the effects of the supply shock? Use a diagram that shows the effect of policies chosen to address the change in real GDP. Use another diagram to show the effect of policies chosen to address the change in the aggregate price level.

**c.** Why do supply shocks present a dilemma for government policy makers?

**16.** The late 1990s in the United States was characterized by substantial economic growth with low inflation; that is, real GDP increased with little, if any, increase in the aggregate price level. Explain this experience using aggregate demand and aggregate supply curves. Illustrate with a diagram.

# Fiscal Policy

## TO STIMULATE OR NOT TO STIMULATE?

"WE'RE GONNA NEED A BIGGER BOAT."

©2009 Karl Wimer

Denver Business Journal
cartoonistgroup.com

**WHAT YOU WILL LEARN IN THIS CHAPTER**

❯ **What fiscal policy is** and why it is an important tool in managing economic fluctuations

❯ Which policies constitute an **expansionary fiscal policy** and which constitute a **contractionary fiscal policy**

❯ Why fiscal policy has a multiplier effect and how this effect is influenced by **automatic stabilizers**

❯ Why governments calculate the **cyclically-adjusted budget balance**

❯ Why a large **public debt** may be a cause for concern

❯ Why **implicit liabilities** of the government are also a cause for concern

ON FEBRUARY 17, 2009, PRESIDENT Obama signed the American Recovery and Reinvestment Act, a $787 billion package of spending, aid, and tax cuts intended to help the struggling U.S. economy reverse a severe recession that began in December 2007. A week earlier, as the bill neared final passage in Congress, Obama hailed the measure: "It is the right size; it is the right scope. Broadly speaking it has the right priorities to create jobs that will jumpstart our economy and transform it for the twenty-first century."

Others weren't so sure. Some argued that the government should be cutting spending, not increasing it, at a time when American families were suffering. "It's time for government to tighten their belts and show the American people that we 'get' it," said John Boehner, the leader of Republicans in the House of Representatives. Some economic analysts warned that the stimulus bill, as the Recovery Act was commonly called, would drive up interest rates and increase the burden of national debt.

Others had the opposite complaint— that the stimulus was too small given the economy's troubles. For example, Joseph Stiglitz, the 2001 recipient of the Nobel Prize in economics, stated about the stimulus, "First of all that it was not enough should be pretty apparent from what I just said: It is trying to offset the deficiency in aggregate demand and it is just too small."

Nor did the passage of time resolve these disputes. True, some predictions were proved false. On one side, Obama's hope that the bill would "jumpstart" the economy fell short: although the recession officially ended in June 2009, unemployment remained high through 2011 and into 2012, by which time the stimulus had largely run its course. On the other side, the soaring interest rates predicted by stimulus opponents failed to materialize, as U.S. borrowing costs remained low by historical standards. But the net effect of the stimulus remained controversial, with opponents arguing that it had failed to help the economy and defenders arguing that things would have been much worse without the bill.

Whatever the verdict—and this is one of those issues that economists and historians will probably be arguing about for decades to come—the Recovery Act of 2009 was a classic example of *fiscal policy*, the use of government spending and taxes to manage aggregate demand. In this chapter we'll see how fiscal policy fits into the models of economic fluctuations we studied in Chapters 11 and 12. We'll also see why budget deficits and government debt can be a problem and how short-run and long-run concerns can pull fiscal policy in different directions. ■

**Social insurance** programs are government programs intended to protect families against economic hardship.

# Fiscal Policy: The Basics

Let's begin with the obvious: modern governments in economically advanced countries spend a great deal of money and collect a lot in taxes. Figure 13-1 shows government spending and tax revenue as percentages of GDP for a selection of high-income countries in 2007. (We focus on 2007, rather than a more recent year, because it was a largely "normal" year. The numbers for later years were very much affected by the financial crisis of 2008 and its aftermath.) As you can see, the Swedish government sector is relatively large, accounting for more than half of the Swedish economy. The government of the United States plays a smaller role in the economy than those of Canada or most European countries. But that role is still sizable, with the government playing a major role in the U.S. economy. As a result, changes in the federal budget—changes in government spending or in taxation—can have large effects on the American economy.

**FIGURE 13-1 Government Spending and Tax Revenue for Some High-Income Countries in 2007**

We focus on 2007 because it was a "normal" year, not a year of deep economic slump. Government spending and tax revenue are represented as a percentage of GDP. Sweden has a particularly large government sector, representing more than half of its GDP. The U.S. government sector, although sizable, is smaller than those of Canada and most European countries.
*Source:* OECD.

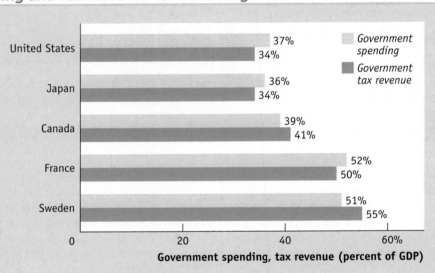

To analyze these effects, we begin by showing how taxes and government spending affect the economy's flow of income. Then we can see how changes in spending and tax policy affect aggregate demand.

## Taxes, Purchases of Goods and Services, Government Transfers, and Borrowing

In Figure 7-1 we showed the circular flow of income and spending in the economy as a whole. One of the sectors represented in that figure was the government. Funds flow *into* the government in the form of taxes and government borrowing; funds flow *out* in the form of government purchases of goods and services and government transfers to households.

What kinds of taxes do Americans pay, and where does the money go? Figure 13-2 shows the composition of U.S. tax revenue in 2007. Taxes, of course, are required payments to the government. In the United States, taxes are collected at the national level by the federal government; at the state level by each state government; and at local levels by counties, cities, and towns. At the federal level, the taxes that generate the greatest revenue are income taxes on both personal income and corporate profits as well as *social insurance* taxes, which we'll explain shortly. At the state and local levels, the picture is more complex: these governments rely on a mix of sales taxes, property taxes, income taxes, and fees of various kinds. Overall, taxes on personal income and corporate profits accounted for 48% of total government revenue in 2007; social insurance taxes accounted for 25%; and a variety of other taxes, collected mainly at the state and local levels, accounted for the rest.

Figure 13-3 shows the composition of total U.S. government spending in 2007, which takes two broad forms. One form is purchases of goods and services. This includes everything from ammunition for the military to the salaries of public school teachers (who are treated in the national accounts as providers of a service—education). The big items here are national defense and education. The large category labeled "Other goods and services" consists mainly of state and local spending on a variety of services, from police and firefighters to highway construction and maintenance.

The other form of government spending is government transfers, which are payments by the government to households for which no good or service is provided in return. In the modern United States, as well as in Canada and Europe, government transfers represent a very large proportion of the budget. Most U.S. government spending on transfer payments is accounted for by three big programs:

- Social Security, which provides guaranteed income to older Americans, disabled Americans, and the surviving spouses and dependent children of deceased or retired beneficiaries

- Medicare, which covers much of the cost of health care for Americans over age 65

- Medicaid, which covers much of the cost of health care for Americans with low incomes

The term **social insurance** is used to describe government programs that are intended to protect families against economic hardship. These include Social Security, Medicare, and Medicaid, as well as smaller programs such as unemployment insurance and food stamps. In the United States, social insurance programs are largely paid for with special, dedicated taxes on wages—the social insurance taxes we mentioned earlier.

But how do tax policy and government spending affect the economy? The answer is that taxation and government spending have a strong effect on total aggregate spending in the economy.

FIGURE **13-2**   Sources of Tax Revenue in the United States, 2007

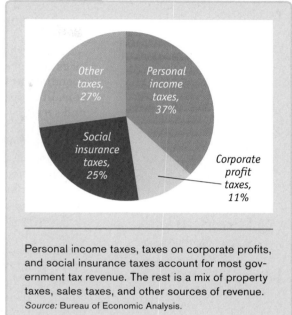

Personal income taxes, taxes on corporate profits, and social insurance taxes account for most government tax revenue. The rest is a mix of property taxes, sales taxes, and other sources of revenue.

*Source:* Bureau of Economic Analysis.

FIGURE **13-3**   Government Spending in the United States, 2007

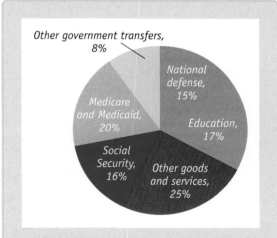

The two types of government spending are purchases of goods and services and government transfers. The big items in government purchases are national defense and education. The big items in government transfers are Social Security and the Medicare and Medicaid health care programs. (Numbers do not add to 100% due to rounding.)

*Source:* Bureau of Economic Analysis.

**Expansionary fiscal policy** is fiscal policy that increases aggregate demand.

## The Government Budget and Total Spending

Let's recall the basic equation of national income accounting:

**(13-1)** $GDP = C + I + G + X - IM$

The left-hand side of this equation is GDP, the value of all final goods and services produced in the economy. The right-hand side is aggregate spending, total spending on final goods and services produced in the economy. It is the sum of consumer spending ($C$), investment spending ($I$), government purchases of goods and services ($G$), and the value of exports ($X$) minus the value of imports ($IM$). It includes all the sources of aggregate demand.

The government directly controls one of the variables on the right-hand side of Equation 13-1: government purchases of goods and services ($G$). But that's not the only effect fiscal policy has on aggregate spending in the economy. Through changes in taxes and transfers, it also influences consumer spending ($C$) and, in some cases, investment spending ($I$).

To see why the budget affects consumer spending, recall that *disposable income,* the total income households have available to spend, is equal to the total income they receive from wages, dividends, interest, and rent, *minus* taxes, *plus* government transfers. So either an increase in taxes or a reduction in government transfers *reduces* disposable income. And a fall in disposable income, other things equal, leads to a fall in consumer spending. Conversely, either a decrease in taxes or an increase in government transfers *increases* disposable income. And a rise in disposable income, other things equal, leads to a rise in consumer spending.

The government's ability to affect investment spending is a more complex story, which we won't discuss in detail. The important point is that the government taxes profits, and changes in the rules that determine how much a business owes can increase or reduce the incentive to spend on investment goods.

Because the government itself is one source of spending in the economy, and because taxes and transfers can affect spending by consumers and firms, the government can use changes in taxes or government spending to *shift the aggregate demand curve.* And as we saw in Chapter 12, there are sometimes good reasons to shift the aggregate demand curve. In early 2009, as this chapter's opening story explained, the Obama administration believed it was crucial that the U.S. government act to increase aggregate demand—that is, to move the aggregate demand curve to the right of where it would otherwise be. The 2009 stimulus package was a classic example of *fiscal policy:* the use of taxes, government transfers, or government purchases of goods and services to stabilize the economy by shifting the aggregate demand curve.

## Expansionary and Contractionary Fiscal Policy

Why would the government want to shift the aggregate demand curve? Because it wants to close either a recessionary gap, created when aggregate output falls below potential output, or an inflationary gap, created when aggregate output exceeds potential output.

Figure 13-4 shows the case of an economy facing a recessionary gap. *SRAS* is the short-run aggregate supply curve, *LRAS* is the long-run aggregate supply curve, and $AD_1$ is the initial aggregate demand curve. At the initial short-run macroeconomic equilibrium, $E_1$, aggregate output is $Y_1$, below potential output, $Y_P$. What the government would like to do is increase aggregate demand, shifting the aggregate demand curve rightward to $AD_2$. This would increase aggregate output, making it equal to potential output. Fiscal policy that increases aggregate demand, called **expansionary fiscal policy,** normally takes one of three forms:

- An increase in government purchases of goods and services
- A cut in taxes
- An increase in government transfers

FIGURE  **13-4**  **Expansionary Fiscal Policy Can Close a Recessionary Gap**

The economy is in short-run macroeconomic equilibrium at $E_1$, where the aggregate demand curve,
$AD_1$, intersects the $SRAS$ curve. However, it is not
in long-run macroeconomic equilibrium. At $E_1$, there is
a recessionary gap of $Y_P - Y_1$. An expansionary
fiscal policy—an increase in government purchases
of goods and services, a reduction in taxes, or an
increase in government transfers—shifts the aggregate demand curve rightward. It can close the recessionary gap by shifting $AD_1$ to $AD_2$, moving the
economy to a new short-run macroeconomic equilibrium, $E_2$, which is also a long-run macroeconomic
equilibrium.

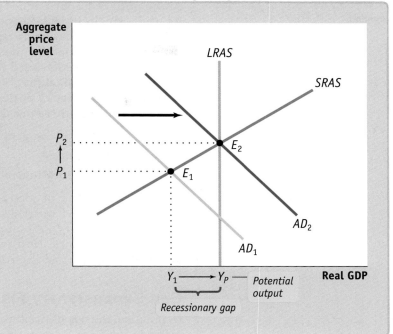

The 2009 American Recovery and Reinvestment Act or simply, the Recovery
Act, was a combination of all three: a direct increase in federal spending and aid
to state governments to help them maintain spending, tax cuts for most families,
and increased aid to the unemployed.

Figure 13-5 shows the opposite case—an economy facing an inflationary gap. Again, $SRAS$ is the short-run aggregate supply curve, $LRAS$ is the

FIGURE  **13-5**  **Contractionary Fiscal Policy Can Close an Inflationary Gap**

The economy is in short-run macroeconomic equilibrium at $E_1$, where the aggregate demand curve,
$AD_1$, intersects the $SRAS$ curve. But it is not in
long-run macroeconomic equilibrium. At $E_1$, there is
an inflationary gap of $Y_1 - Y_P$. A contractionary fiscal
policy—such as reduced government purchases of
goods and services, an increase in taxes, or a reduction in government transfers—shifts the aggregate
demand curve leftward. It closes the inflationary gap
by shifting $AD_1$ to $AD_2$, moving the economy to a new
short-run macroeconomic equilibrium, $E_2$, which is
also a long-run macroeconomic equilibrium.

**Contractionary fiscal policy** is fiscal policy that reduces aggregate demand.

long-run aggregate supply curve, and $AD_1$ is the initial aggregate demand curve. At the initial equilibrium, $E_1$, aggregate output is $Y_1$, above potential output, $Y_P$. As we'll explain in later chapters, policy makers often try to head off inflation by eliminating inflationary gaps. To eliminate the inflationary gap shown in Figure 13-5, fiscal policy must reduce aggregate demand and shift the aggregate demand curve leftward to $AD_2$. This reduces aggregate output and makes it equal to potential output. Fiscal policy that reduces aggregate demand, called **contractionary fiscal policy,** is the opposite of expansionary fiscal policy. It is implemented in three possible ways:

1. A reduction in government purchases of goods and services

2. An increase in taxes

3. A reduction in government transfers

A classic example of contractionary fiscal policy occurred in 1968, when U.S. policy makers grew worried about rising inflation. President Lyndon Johnson imposed a temporary 10% surcharge on taxable income—everyone's income taxes were increased by 10%. He also tried to scale back government purchases of goods and services, which had risen dramatically because of the cost of the Vietnam War.

## Can Expansionary Fiscal Policy Actually Work?

In practice, the use of fiscal policy—in particular, the use of expansionary fiscal policy in the face of a recessionary gap—is often controversial. We'll examine the origins of these controversies in detail in Chapter 17. But for now, let's quickly summarize the major points of the debate over expansionary fiscal policy, so we can understand when the critiques are justified and when they are not.

Broadly speaking, there are three arguments against the use of expansionary fiscal policy.

- Government spending always crowds out private spending
- Government borrowing always crowds out private investment spending
- Government budget deficits lead to reduced private spending

The first of these claims is wrong in principle, but it has nonetheless played a prominent role in public debates. The second is valid under some, but not all, circumstances. The third argument, although it raises some important issues, isn't a good reason to believe that expansionary fiscal policy doesn't work.

### Claim 1: "Government Spending Always Crowds Out Private Spending" Some claim that expansionary fiscal policy can never raise aggregate spending and therefore can never raise aggregate income, with reasons that go something like this: "Every dollar that the government spends is a dollar taken away from the private sector. So any rise in government spending must be offset by an equal fall in private spending." In other words, every dollar spent by the government *crowds out*, or displaces, a dollar of private spending. So what's wrong with this view? The answer is that the statement is wrong because it assumes that resources in the economy are always fully employed and, as a result, the aggregate income earned in the economy is always a fixed sum—which isn't true. In particular, when the economy is suffering from a recessionary gap, there are unemployed resources in the economy and output, and therefore income, is below its potential level. Expansionary fiscal policy during these periods puts unemployed resources to work and generates higher spending and higher income. So the argument that expansionary fiscal policy always crowds out private spending is wrong in principle.

### Claim 2: "Government Borrowing Always Crowds Out Private Investment Spending" In Chapter 10, we discussed the possibility that government borrowing uses funds that would have otherwise been used for private

investment spending—that is, it crowds out private investment spending. How valid is that argument?

The answer is "it depends." Specifically, it depends upon whether the economy is depressed or not. If the economy is not depressed, then increased government borrowing, by increasing the demand for loanable funds, can raise interest rates and crowd out private investment spending. However, what if the economy is depressed? In that case, crowding out is much less likely. When the economy is at far less than full employment, a fiscal expansion will lead to higher incomes, which in turn leads to increased savings at any given interest rate. This larger pool of savings allows the government to borrow without driving up interest rates. The Recovery Act of 2009 was a case in point: despite high levels of government borrowing, U.S. interest rates stayed near historic lows.

**Claim 3: "Government Budget Deficits Lead to Reduced Private Spending"** Other things equal, expansionary fiscal policy leads to a larger budget deficit and greater government debt. And higher debt will eventually require the government to raise taxes to pay it off. So, according to the third argument against expansionary fiscal policy, consumers, anticipating that they must pay higher taxes in the future to pay off today's government debt, will cut their spending today in order to save money. This argument, first made by the nineteenth-century economist David Ricardo, is known as *Ricardian equivalence*. It is an argument often taken to imply that expansionary fiscal policy will have no effect on the economy because far-sighted consumers will undo any attempts at expansion by the government. (And will also undo any contractionary fiscal policy, for that matter.)

In reality, however, it's doubtful that consumers behave with such foresight and budgeting discipline. Most people, when provided with extra cash (generated by the fiscal expansion), will spend at least some of it. So even fiscal policy that takes the form of temporary tax cuts or transfers of cash to consumers probably does have an expansionary effect.

Moreover, it's possible to show that even with Ricardian equivalence, a temporary rise in government spending that involves direct purchases of goods and services— such as a program of road construction—would still lead to a boost in total spending in the near term. That's because even if consumers cut back their current spending in anticipation of higher future taxes, their reduced spending will take place over an extended period as consumers save over time to pay the future tax bill. Meanwhile, the additional government spending will be concentrated in the near future, when the economy needs it. So although the effects emphasized by Ricardian equivalence may reduce the impact of fiscal expansion, the claim that it makes fiscal expansion completely ineffective is neither consistent with how consumers actually behave nor a reason to believe that increases in government spending have no effect. So, in the end, it's not a valid argument against expansionary fiscal policy.

In sum, then, the extent to which we should expect expansionary fiscal policy to work depends upon the circumstances. When the economy has a recessionary gap—as it did when the 2009 Recovery Act was passed—economics tells us that this is just the kind of situation in which expansionary fiscal policy helps the economy. However, when the economy is already at full employment, expansionary fiscal policy is the wrong policy and will lead to crowding out, an overheated economy, and higher inflation.

## A Cautionary Note: Lags in Fiscal Policy

Looking back at Figures 13-4 and 13-5, it may seem obvious that the government should actively use fiscal policy—always adopting an expansionary fiscal policy when the economy faces a recessionary gap and always adopting a contractionary fiscal policy when the economy faces an inflationary gap. But many economists caution against an extremely active stabilization policy, arguing that a government that tries too hard to stabilize the economy—through either fiscal policy or monetary policy—can end up making the economy less stable.

We'll leave discussion of the warnings associated with monetary policy to Chapter 19. In the case of fiscal policy, one key reason for caution is that there are important *time lags* between when the policy is decided upon and when it is implemented. To understand the nature of these lags, think about what has to happen before the government increases spending to fight a recessionary gap. First, the government has to realize that the recessionary gap exists: economic data take time to collect and analyze, and recessions are often recognized only months after they have begun. Second, the government has to develop a spending plan, which can itself take months, particularly if politicians take time debating how the money should be spent and passing legislation. Finally, it takes time to spend money. For example, a road construction project begins with activities such as surveying that don't involve spending large sums. It may be quite some time before the big spending begins.

Because of these lags, an attempt to increase spending to fight a recessionary gap may take so long to get going that the economy has already recovered on its own. In fact, the recessionary gap may have turned into an inflationary gap by the time the fiscal policy takes effect. In that case, the fiscal policy will make things worse instead of better.

This doesn't mean that fiscal policy should never be actively used. In early 2009 there was good reason to believe that the slump facing the U.S. economy would be both deep and long and that a fiscal stimulus designed to arrive over the next year or two would almost surely push aggregate demand in the right direction. In fact, as we'll see later in this chapter, the 2009 stimulus arguably faded out too soon, leaving the economy still deeply depressed. But the problem of lags makes the actual use of both fiscal and monetary policy harder than you might think from a simple analysis like the one we have just given.

## ECONOMICS ➤ *IN ACTION*

### WHAT WAS IN THE RECOVERY ACT?

As we've just learned, fiscal stimulus can take three forms: increased government purchases of goods and services, increased transfer payments, and tax cuts. So what form did the Recovery Act take? The answer is that it's a bit complicated.

Figure 13-6 shows the composition of the budget impact of the Recovery Act, a measure that adds up the dollar value of tax cuts, transfer payments, and government spending. Here, the numbers are broken down into *four* categories, not three. "Infrastructure and other spending" means spending on roads, bridges, and schools as well as "nontraditional" infrastructure like research and development, all of which fall under government purchases of goods and services. "Tax cuts" are self-explanatory. "Transfer payments to persons" mostly took the form of expanded benefits for the unemployed. But a fourth category, "transfers to state and local governments," accounted for roughly a third of the funds. Why this fourth category?

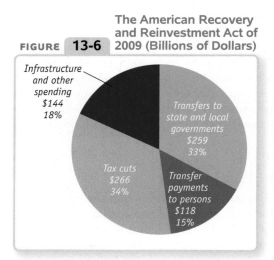

**FIGURE 13-6** The American Recovery and Reinvestment Act of 2009 (Billions of Dollars)

Infrastructure and other spending $144 18%

Transfers to state and local governments $259 33%

Tax cuts $266 34%

Transfer payments to persons $118 15%

Because America has multiple levels of government. The authors live in Princeton Township, which has its own budget, which is part of Mercer County, which has its own budget, which is part of the state of New Jersey, which has its own budget, which is part of the United States. One effect of the recession was a sharp drop in revenues at the state and local levels, which in turn forced these lower levels of government to cut spending. Federal aid—those transfers to state and local governments—was intended to mitigate these spending cuts.

Perhaps the most surprising aspect of the Recovery Act was how little direct federal spending on goods and services was involved. The great bulk of the program involved giving money to other people, one way or another, in the hope that they would spend it.

### CHECK YOUR UNDERSTANDING  13-1

1. In each of the following cases, determine whether the policy is an expansionary or contractionary fiscal policy.
   a. Several military bases around the country, which together employ tens of thousands of people, are closed.
   b. The number of weeks an unemployed person is eligible for unemployment benefits is increased.
   c. The federal tax on gasoline is increased.

2. Explain why federal disaster relief, which quickly disburses funds to victims of natural disasters such as hurricanes, floods, and large-scale crop failures, will stabilize the economy more effectively after a disaster than relief that must be legislated.

3. Is the following statement true or false? Explain. "When the government expands, the private sector shrinks; when the government shrinks, the private sector expands."

Solutions appear at back of book.

## Fiscal Policy and the Multiplier

An expansionary fiscal policy, like the 2009 U.S. stimulus, pushes the aggregate demand curve to the right. A contractionary fiscal policy, like Lyndon Johnson's tax surcharge, pushes the aggregate demand curve to the left. For policy makers, however, knowing the direction of the shift isn't enough: they need estimates of *how much* a given policy will shift the aggregate demand curve. To get these estimates, they use the concept of the multiplier, which we learned about in Chapter 11.

### Multiplier Effects of an Increase in Government Purchases of Goods and Services

Suppose that a government decides to spend $50 billion building bridges and roads. The government's purchases of goods and services will directly increase total spending on final goods and services by $50 billion. But as we learned in Chapter 11, there will also be an indirect effect: the government's purchases will start a chain reaction throughout the economy. The firms that produce the goods and services purchased by the government earn revenues that flow to households in the form of wages, profits, interest, and rent. This increase in disposable income leads to a rise in consumer spending. The rise in consumer spending, in turn, induces firms to increase output, leading to a further rise in disposable income, which leads to another round of consumer spending increases, and so on.

As we know, the *multiplier* is the ratio of the change in real GDP caused by an autonomous change in aggregate spending to the size of that autonomous change.

### ▼ Quick Review

- The main channels of fiscal policy are taxes and government spending. Government spending takes the form of purchases of goods and services as well as transfers.

- In the United States, most government transfers are accounted for by **social insurance** programs designed to alleviate economic hardship—principally Social Security, Medicare, and Medicaid.

- The government controls *G* directly and influences *C* and *I* through taxes and transfers.

- **Expansionary fiscal policy** is implemented by an increase in government spending, a cut in taxes, or an increase in government transfers. **Contractionary fiscal policy** is implemented by a reduction in government spending, an increase in taxes, or a reduction in government transfers.

- Arguments against the effectiveness of expansionary fiscal policy based upon crowding out are valid only when the economy is at full employment. The argument that expansionary fiscal policy won't work because of Ricardian equivalence—that consumers will cut back spending today to offset expected future tax increases—appears to be untrue in practice. What is clearly true is that time lags can reduce the effectiveness of fiscal policy, and potentially render it counterproductive.

An increase in government purchases of goods and services is a prime example of such an autonomous increase in aggregate spending.

In Chapter 11 we considered a simple case in which there are no taxes or international trade, so that any change in GDP accrues entirely to households. We also assumed that the aggregate price level is fixed, so that any increase in nominal GDP is also a rise in real GDP, and that the interest rate is fixed. In that case the multiplier is $1/(1 - MPC)$. Recall that *MPC* is the *marginal propensity to consume*, the fraction of an additional dollar in disposable income that is spent. For example, if the marginal propensity to consume is 0.5, the multiplier is $1/(1 - 0.5) = 1/0.5 = 2$. Given a multiplier of 2, a $50 billion increase in government purchases of goods and services would increase real GDP by $100 billion. Of that $100 billion, $50 billion is the initial effect from the increase in *G*, and the remaining $50 billion is the subsequent effect arising from the increase in consumer spending.

What happens if government purchases of goods and services are instead reduced? The math is exactly the same, except that there's a minus sign in front: if government purchases of goods and services fall by $50 billion and the marginal propensity to consume is 0.5, real GDP falls by $100 billion.

## Multiplier Effects of Changes in Government Transfers and Taxes

Expansionary or contractionary fiscal policy need not take the form of changes in government purchases of goods and services. Governments can also change transfer payments or taxes. In general, however, a change in government transfers or taxes shifts the aggregate demand curve by *less* than an equal-sized change in government purchases, resulting in a smaller effect on real GDP.

To see why, imagine that instead of spending $50 billion on building bridges, the government simply hands out $50 billion in the form of government transfers. In this case, there is no direct effect on aggregate demand, as there was with government purchases of goods and services. Real GDP goes up only because households spend some of that $50 billion—and they probably won't spend it all.

Table 13-1 shows a hypothetical comparison of two expansionary fiscal policies assuming an *MPC* equal to 0.5 and a multiplier equal to 2: one in which the government directly purchases $50 billion in goods and services and one in which the government makes transfer payments instead, sending out $50 billion in checks to consumers. In each case there is a first-round effect on real GDP, either from purchases by the government or from purchases by the consumers who received the checks, followed by a series of additional rounds as rising real GDP raises disposable income.

| TABLE **13-1** Hypothetical Effects of a Fiscal Policy with Multiplier of 2 | | |
| --- | --- | --- |
| Effect on real GDP | $50 billion rise in government purchases of goods and services | $50 billion rise in government transfer payments |
| First round | $50 billion | $25 billion |
| Second round | $25 billion | $12.5 billion |
| Third round | $12.5 billion | $6.25 billion |
| ⋮ | ⋮ | ⋮ |
| Eventual effect | $100 billion | $50 billion |

However, the first-round effect of the transfer program is smaller; because we have assumed that the *MPC* is 0.5, only $25 billion of the $50 billion is spent, with the other $25 billion saved. And as a result, all the further rounds are smaller, too. In the end, the transfer payment increases real GDP by only $50 billion. In comparison, a $50 billion increase in government purchases produces a $100 billion increase in real GDP.

Overall, when expansionary fiscal policy takes the form of a rise in transfer payments, real GDP may rise by either more or less than the initial government outlay—that is, the multiplier may be either more or less than 1 depending upon the size of the *MPC*. In Table 13-1, with an *MPC* equal to 0.5, the multiplier is exactly 1: a $50 billion rise in transfer payments increases real GDP by $50 billion. If the *MPC* is less than 0.5, so that a smaller share of the initial transfer is spent, the multiplier on that transfer is *less* than 1. If a larger share of the initial transfer is spent, the multiplier is *more* than 1.

A tax cut has an effect similar to the effect of a transfer. It increases disposable income, leading to a series of increases in consumer spending. But the overall effect is smaller than that of an equal-sized increase in government purchases of goods and services: the autonomous increase in aggregate spending is smaller because households save part of the amount of the tax cut.

We should also note that taxes introduce a further complication—they typically change the size of the multiplier. That's because in the real world governments rarely impose **lump-sum taxes,** in which the amount of tax a household owes is independent of its income. With lump-sum taxes there is no change in the multiplier. Instead, the great majority of tax revenue is raised via taxes that are not lump-sum, and so tax revenue depends upon the level of real GDP. As we'll discuss shortly, and analyze in detail in the appendix to this chapter, non-lump-sum taxes reduce the size of the multiplier.

In practice, economists often argue that the size of the multiplier determines *who* among the population should get tax cuts or increases in government transfers. For example, compare the effects of an increase in unemployment benefits with a cut in taxes on profits distributed to shareholders as dividends. Consumer surveys suggest that the average unemployed worker will spend a higher share of any increase in his or her disposable income than would the average recipient of dividend income. That is, people who are unemployed tend to have a higher *MPC* than people who own a lot of stocks because the latter tend to be wealthier and tend to save more of any increase in disposable income. If that's true, a dollar spent on unemployment benefits increases aggregate demand more than a dollar's worth of dividend tax cuts.

> **Lump-sum taxes** are taxes that don't depend on the taxpayer's income.

## How Taxes Affect the Multiplier

When we introduced the analysis of the multiplier in Chapter 11, we simplified matters by assuming that a $1 increase in real GDP raises disposable income by $1. In fact, however, government taxes capture some part of the increase in real GDP that occurs in each round of the multiplier process, since most government taxes depend positively on real GDP. As a result, disposable income increases by considerably less than $1 once we include taxes in the model.

The increase in government tax revenue when real GDP rises isn't the result of a deliberate decision or action by the government. It's a consequence of the way the tax laws are written, which causes most sources of government revenue to increase *automatically* when real GDP goes up. For example, income tax receipts increase when real GDP rises because the amount each individual owes in taxes depends positively on his or her income, and households' taxable income rises when real GDP rises. Sales tax receipts increase when real GDP rises because people with more income spend more on goods and services. And corporate profit tax receipts increase when real GDP rises because profits increase when the economy expands.

The effect of these automatic increases in tax revenue is to reduce the size of the multiplier. Remember, the multiplier is the result of a chain reaction in which higher real GDP leads to higher disposable income, which leads to higher consumer spending, which leads to further increases in real GDP. The fact that the government siphons off some of any increase in real GDP means that at each stage of this process, the increase in consumer spending is smaller than it would be if taxes weren't part of the picture. The result is to reduce the multiplier. The appendix to this chapter shows how to derive the multiplier when taxes that depend positively on real GDP are taken into account.

**Automatic stabilizers** are government spending and taxation rules that cause fiscal policy to be automatically expansionary when the economy contracts and automatically contractionary when the economy expands.

**Discretionary fiscal policy** is fiscal policy that is the result of deliberate actions by policy makers rather than rules.

Many macroeconomists believe it's a good thing that in real life taxes reduce the multiplier. In Chapter 12 we argued that most, though not all, recessions are the result of negative demand shocks. The same mechanism that causes tax revenue to increase when the economy expands causes it to decrease when the economy contracts. Since tax receipts decrease when real GDP falls, the effects of these negative demand shocks are smaller than they would be if there were no taxes. The decrease in tax revenue reduces the adverse effect of the initial fall in aggregate demand.

The automatic decrease in government tax revenue generated by a fall in real GDP—caused by a decrease in the amount of taxes households pay—acts like an automatic expansionary fiscal policy implemented in the face of a recession. Similarly, when the economy expands, the government finds itself automatically pursuing a contractionary fiscal policy—a tax increase. Government spending and taxation rules that cause fiscal policy to be automatically expansionary when the economy contracts and automatically contractionary when the economy expands, without requiring any deliberate action by policy makers, are called **automatic stabilizers.**

The rules that govern tax collection aren't the only automatic stabilizers, although they are the most important ones. Some types of government transfers also play a stabilizing role. For example, more people receive unemployment insurance when the economy is depressed than when it is booming. The same is true of Medicaid and food stamps. So transfer payments tend to rise when the economy is contracting and fall when the economy is expanding. Like changes in tax revenue, these automatic changes in transfers tend to reduce the size of the multiplier because the total change in disposable income that results from a given rise or fall in real GDP is smaller.

A historical example of discretionary fiscal policy was the Works Progress Administration (WPA), a relief measure established during the Great Depression that put millions of unemployed Americans to work building bridges, roads, buildings, and parks.

As in the case of government tax revenue, many macroeconomists believe that it's a good thing that government transfers reduce the multiplier. Expansionary and contractionary fiscal policies that are the result of automatic stabilizers are widely considered helpful to macroeconomic stabilization because they blunt the extremes of the business cycle.

But what about fiscal policy that *isn't* the result of automatic stabilizers? **Discretionary fiscal policy** is fiscal policy that is the direct result of deliberate actions by policy makers rather than automatic adjustment. For example, during a recession, the government may pass legislation that cuts taxes and increases government spending in order to stimulate the economy. In general, economists tend to support the use of discretionary fiscal policy only in special circumstances, such as an especially severe recession. We'll explain why, and describe the debates among macroeconomists on the appropriate role of fiscal policy, in Chapter 18.

## ECONOMICS ▸ *IN ACTION*

### MULTIPLIERS AND THE OBAMA STIMULUS

The American Recovery and Reinvestment Act, also known as the Obama stimulus, was the largest example of discretionary fiscal expansion in U.S. history. The total stimulus was $787 billion, although not all of that was spent at once: only about half, or roughly $400 billion, of the stimulus arrived in 2010, the year of peak impact. Still, even that was a lot—roughly 2.7% of GDP. But was that enough? From the beginning, there were doubts.

The first description of the planned stimulus and its expected effects came in early January 2009, from two of the incoming administration's top economists—Christina Romer, who would head the Council of Economic Advisers, and Jared Bernstein, who would serve as the vice president's chief economist. Romer and Bernstein were explicit about the assumed multipliers: based on models developed at the Federal Reserve and elsewhere, they assumed that government spending would have a multiplier of 1.57 and that tax cuts would have a multiplier of 0.99.

These assumptions yielded an overall multiplier for the stimulus of almost 1.4, implying that the stimulus would, at its peak in 2010, add about 3.7% to real GDP. It would also, they estimated, reduce unemployment by about 1.8 percentage points relative to what it would otherwise have been.

But here's the problem: the slump the Obama stimulus was intended to fight was brought on by a major financial crisis—and such crises tend to produce very deep, prolonged slumps. Shortly before Romer and Bernstein released their analysis, another team of economists—Carmen Reinhart of the University of Maryland and Kenneth Rogoff of Harvard—circulated a paper titled "The Aftermath of Financial Crises," based on historical episodes. Reinhart and Rogoff found that major crises are followed, on average, by a 7-percentage-point rise in the unemployment rate and that it takes years before unemployment falls to anything like normal levels.

Compared with the economy's problems, then, the Obama stimulus was actually small: it cut only 1.8 points off the unemployment rate in 2010 and faded out rapidly thereafter. And given its small size relative to the problem, the failure of the stimulus to avert persistently high unemployment should not have come as a surprise.

The Obama stimulus, although too small to significantly lower unemployment, did create jobs and added about 3.7% to real GDP.

---

**CHECK YOUR UNDERSTANDING    13-2**

1.  Explain why a $500 million increase in government purchases of goods and services will generate a larger rise in real GDP than a $500 million increase in government transfers.

2.  Explain why a $500 million reduction in government purchases of goods and services will generate a larger fall in real GDP than a $500 million reduction in government transfers.

3.  The country of Boldovia has no unemployment insurance benefits and a tax system using only lump-sum taxes. The neighboring country of Moldovia has generous unemployment benefits and a tax system in which residents must pay a percentage of their income. Which country will experience greater variation in real GDP in response to demand shocks, positive and negative? Explain.

*Solutions appear at back of book.*

> **▼ Quick Review**
>
> - The amount by which changes in government purchases raise real GDP is determined by the multiplier.
>
> - Changes in taxes and government transfers also move real GDP, but by less than equal-sized changes in government purchases.
>
> - Taxes reduce the size of the multiplier unless they are **lump-sum taxes**.
>
> - Taxes and some government transfers act as **automatic stabilizers** as tax revenue responds positively to changes in real GDP and some government transfers respond negatively to changes in real GDP. Many economists believe that it is a good thing that they reduce the size of the multiplier. In contrast, the use of **discretionary fiscal policy** is more controversial.

# The Budget Balance

Headlines about the government's budget tend to focus on just one point: whether the government is running a surplus or a deficit and, in either case, how big. People usually think of surpluses as good: when the federal government ran a record surplus in 2000, many people regarded it as a cause for celebration. Conversely, people usually think of deficits as bad: when the U.S. federal government ran record deficits in 2009 and 2010, many people regarded it as a cause for concern.

How do surpluses and deficits fit into the analysis of fiscal policy? Are deficits ever a good thing and surpluses a bad thing? To answer those questions, let's look at the causes and consequences of surpluses and deficits.

## The Budget Balance as a Measure of Fiscal Policy

What do we mean by surpluses and deficits? The budget balance, which we defined in Chapter 10, is the difference between the government's revenue, in the form of tax revenue, and its spending, both on goods and services and on government transfers, in a given year. That is, the budget balance—savings by government—is defined by Equation 13-2 (which is the same as Equation 10-1):

**(13-2)** $S_{Government} = T - G - TR$

where $T$ is the value of tax revenues, $G$ is government purchases of goods and services, and $TR$ is the value of government transfers. As we learned in Chapter 10, a budget surplus is a positive budget balance and a budget deficit is a negative budget balance.

Other things equal, expansionary fiscal policies—increased government purchases of goods and services, higher government transfers, or lower taxes—reduce the budget balance for that year. That is, expansionary fiscal policies make a budget surplus smaller or a budget deficit bigger. Conversely, contractionary fiscal policies—reduced government purchases of goods and services, lower government transfers, or higher taxes—increase the budget balance for that year, making a budget surplus bigger or a budget deficit smaller.

You might think this means that changes in the budget balance can be used to measure fiscal policy. In fact, economists often do just that: they use changes in the budget balance as a "quick-and-dirty" way to assess whether current fiscal policy is expansionary or contractionary. But they always keep in mind two reasons this quick-and-dirty approach is sometimes misleading:

1. Two different changes in fiscal policy that have equal-sized effects on the budget balance may have quite unequal effects on the economy. As we have already seen, changes in government purchases of goods and services have a larger effect on real GDP than equal-sized changes in taxes and government transfers.

2. Often, changes in the budget balance are themselves the result, not the cause, of fluctuations in the economy.

To understand the second point, we need to examine the effects of the business cycle on the budget.

## The Business Cycle and the Cyclically Adjusted Budget Balance

Historically there has been a strong relationship between the federal government's budget balance and the business cycle. The budget tends to move into deficit when the economy experiences a recession, but deficits tend to get smaller or even turn into surpluses when the economy is expanding. Figure 13-7 shows the federal budget deficit as a percentage of GDP from 1970 to 2011. Shaded areas indicate recessions; unshaded areas indicate expansions. As you can see, the federal budget deficit increased around the time of each recession and usually declined during expansions. In fact, in the late stages of the long expansion from 1991 to 2000, the deficit actually became negative—the budget deficit became a budget surplus.

The relationship between the business cycle and the budget balance is even clearer if we compare the budget deficit as a percentage of GDP with the

FIGURE **13-7** The U.S. Federal Budget Deficit and the Business Cycle, 1970–2011

The budget deficit as a percentage of GDP tends to rise during recessions (indicated by shaded areas) and fall during expansions.

*Sources:* Bureau of Economic Analysis; National Bureau of Economic Research.

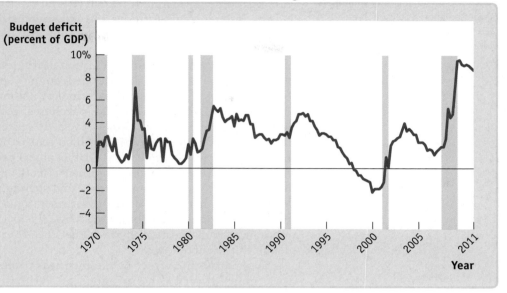

unemployment rate, as we do in Figure 13-8. The budget deficit almost always rises when the unemployment rate rises and falls when the unemployment rate falls.

Is this relationship between the business cycle and the budget balance evidence that policy makers engage in discretionary fiscal policy, using expansionary fiscal policy during recessions and contractionary fiscal policy during expansions? Not necessarily. To a large extent the relationship in Figure 13-8 reflects automatic stabilizers at work. As we learned in the discussion of automatic stabilizers, government tax revenue tends to rise and some government transfers, like unemployment benefit payments, tend to

FIGURE **13-8** The U.S. Federal Budget Deficit and the Unemployment Rate

There is a close relationship between the budget balance and the business cycle: a recession moves the budget balance toward deficit, but an expansion moves it toward surplus. Here, the unemployment rate serves as an indicator of the business cycle, and we should expect to see a higher unemployment rate associated with a higher budget deficit. This is confirmed by the figure: the budget deficit as a percentage of GDP moves closely in tandem with the unemployment rate.

*Sources:* Bureau of Economic Analysis; Bureau of Labor Statistics.

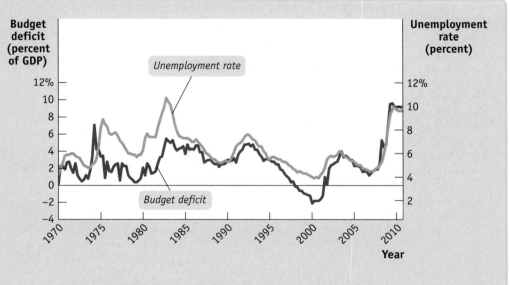

The **cyclically adjusted budget balance** is an estimate of what the budget balance would be if real GDP were exactly equal to potential output.

fall when the economy expands. Conversely, government tax revenue tends to fall and some government transfers tend to rise when the economy contracts. So the budget tends to move toward surplus during expansions and toward deficit during recessions even without any deliberate action on the part of policy makers.

In assessing budget policy, it's often useful to separate movements in the budget balance due to the business cycle from movements due to discretionary fiscal policy changes. The former are affected by automatic stabilizers and the latter by deliberate changes in government purchases, government transfers, or taxes. It's important to realize that business-cycle effects on the budget balance are temporary: both recessionary gaps (in which real GDP is below potential output) and inflationary gaps (in which real GDP is above potential output) tend to be eliminated in the long run. Removing their effects on the budget balance sheds light on whether the government's taxing and spending policies are sustainable in the long run. In other words, do the government's tax policies yield enough revenue to fund its spending in the long run? As we'll learn shortly, this is a fundamentally more important question than whether the government runs a budget surplus or deficit in the current year.

To separate the effect of the business cycle from the effects of other factors, many governments produce an estimate of what the budget balance would be if there were neither a recessionary nor an inflationary gap. The **cyclically adjusted budget balance** is an estimate of what the budget balance would be if real GDP were exactly equal to potential output. It takes into account the extra tax revenue the government would collect and the transfers it would save if a recessionary gap were eliminated—or the revenue the government would lose and the extra transfers it would make if an inflationary gap were eliminated.

Figure 13-9 shows the actual budget deficit and the Congressional Budget Office estimate of the cyclically adjusted budget deficit, both as a percentage of GDP, from 1970 to 2010. As you can see, the cyclically adjusted budget deficit doesn't fluctuate as much as the actual budget deficit. In particular, large actual deficits, such as those of 1975, 1983, and 2009 are usually caused in part by a depressed economy.

**FIGURE** **13-9** The Actual Budget Deficit versus the Cyclically Adjusted Budget Deficit

The cyclically adjusted budget deficit is an estimate of what the budget deficit would be if the economy was at potential output. It fluctuates less than the actual budget deficit because years of large budget deficits also tend to be years when the economy has a large recessionary gap.

*Sources:* Congressional Budget Office; Bureau of Economic Analysis.

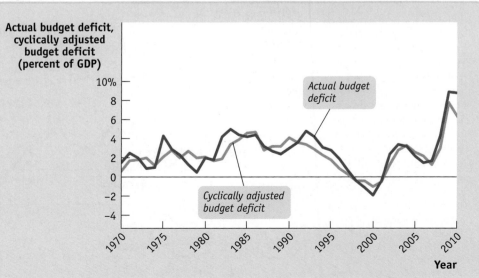

## Should the Budget Be Balanced?

As we'll see in the next section, persistent budget deficits can cause problems for both the government and the economy. Yet politicians are always tempted to run deficits because this allows them to cater to voters by cutting taxes without cutting spending or by increasing spending without increasing taxes. As a result, there are occasional attempts by policy makers to force fiscal discipline by introducing legislation—even a constitutional amendment— forbidding the government from running budget deficits. This is usually stated as a requirement that the budget be "balanced"—that revenues at least equal spending each fiscal year. Would it be a good idea to require a balanced budget annually?

Most economists don't think so. They believe that the government should only balance its budget on average—that it should be allowed to run deficits in bad years, offset by surpluses in good years. They don't believe the government should be forced to run a balanced budget *every year* because this would undermine the role of taxes and transfers as automatic stabilizers. As we learned earlier in this chapter, the tendency of tax revenue to fall and transfers to rise when the economy contracts helps to limit the size of recessions. But falling tax revenue and rising transfer payments generated by a downturn in the economy push the budget toward deficit. If constrained by a balanced-budget rule, the government would have to respond to this deficit with contractionary fiscal policies that would tend to deepen a recession.

Yet policy makers concerned about excessive deficits sometimes feel that rigid rules prohibiting—or at least setting an upper limit on—deficits are necessary. As the following Economics in Action explains, Europe has had a lot of trouble reconciling rules to enforce fiscal responsibility with the challenges of short-run fiscal policy.

## ECONOMICS > IN ACTION

### EUROPE'S SEARCH FOR A FISCAL RULE

In 1999 a group of European nations took a momentous step when they adopted a common currency, the euro, to replace their various national currencies, such as the French franc, the German mark, and the Italian lira. Along with the introduction of the euro came the creation of the European Central Bank, which sets monetary policy for the whole region.

As part of the agreement creating the new currency, governments of member countries signed on to the European "stability pact." This agreement required each government to keep its budget deficit—its actual deficit, not a cyclically adjusted number—below 3% of the country's GDP or face fines. The pact was intended to prevent irresponsible deficit spending arising from political pressure that might eventually undermine the new currency. The stability pact, however, had a serious downside: in principle, it would force countries to slash spending and/or raise taxes whenever an economic downturn pushed their deficits above the critical level. This would turn fiscal policy into a force that worsens recessions instead of fighting them.

Nonetheless, the stability pact proved impossible to enforce: European nations, including France and even Germany, with its reputation for fiscal probity, simply ignored the rule during the 2001 recession and its aftermath.

In 2011 the Europeans tried again, this time against the background of a severe debt crisis. In the wake of the 2008 financial

Nicolas Sarkozy of France and Angela Merkel of Germany discuss the new EU economic plan.

REUTERS/Philippe Wojazer

crisis, Greece, Ireland, Portugal, Spain, and Italy all lost the confidence of investors, who were worried about their ability and/or willingness to repay all their debt—and the efforts of these nations to reduce their deficits seemed likely to push Europe back into recession. Yet a return to the old stability pact didn't seem to make sense. Among other things, it was clear that the stability pact's rule on the size of budget deficits would not have done much to prevent the crisis—in 2007 all of the problem debtors except Greece were running deficits under 3% of GDP, with Ireland and Spain actually running surpluses.

So the agreement reached in December 2011 was framed in terms of the "structural" budget balance, more or less corresponding to the cyclically adjusted budget balance as defined in the text. According to the new rule, the structural budget balance of each country should be very nearly zero, with deficits not to exceed 0.5% of GDP. This seemed like a much better rule than the old stability pact.

Yet big problems remained. One was the question of how reliable were the estimates of the structural budget balances. Also, the new rule seemed to ban any use of discretionary fiscal policy, under any circumstances. Was this wise?

Before patting themselves on the back over the superiority of their own fiscal rules, Americans should note that the United States has its own version of the original, flawed European stability pact. The federal government's budget acts as an automatic stabilizer, but 49 of the 50 states are required by their state constitutions to balance their budgets every year. When recession struck in 2008, most states were forced to—guess what?—slash spending and raise taxes in the face of a recession, exactly the wrong thing from a macroeconomic point of view.

### CHECK YOUR UNDERSTANDING  13-3

1. Why is the cyclically adjusted budget balance a better measure of whether government policies are sustainable in the long run than the actual budget balance?

2. Explain why states required by their constitutions to balance their budgets are likely to experience more severe economic fluctuations than states not held to that requirement.

*Solutions appear at back of book.*

# Long-Run Implications of Fiscal Policy

In 2009 the government of Greece ran into a financial wall. Like most other governments in Europe (and the U.S. government, too), the Greek government was running a large budget deficit, which meant that it needed to keep borrowing more funds, both to cover its expenses and to pay off existing loans as they came due. But governments, like companies or individuals, can only borrow if lenders believe there's a good chance they are willing or able to repay their debts. By 2009 most investors, having lost confidence in Greece's financial future, were no longer willing to lend to the Greek government. Those few who were willing to lend demanded very high interest rates to compensate them for the risk of loss.

Figure 13-10 compares interest rates on 10-year bonds issued by the governments of Greece and Germany. At the beginning of 2007, Greece could borrow at almost the same rate as Germany, widely considered a very safe borrower. By the end of 2011, however, Greece was having to pay an interest rate around 10 times the rate Germany paid.

Why was Greece having these problems? Largely because investors had become deeply worried about the level of its debt (in part because it became

FIGURE  **13-10**  Greek and German Long-Term Interest Rates

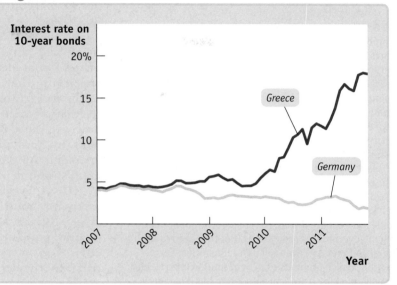

As late as 2008, the government of Greece could borrow at interest rates only slightly higher than those facing Germany, widely considered a very safe borrower. But in early 2009, as it became clear that both Greek debt and Greek deficits were larger than previously reported, investors lost confidence, sending Greek borrowing costs sky-high.

*Source:* European Central Bank.

Interest rate on 10-year bonds

clear that the Greek government had been using creative accounting to hide just how much debt it had already taken on). Government debt is, after all, a promise to make future payments to lenders. By 2009 it seemed likely that the Greek government had already promised more than it could possibly deliver.

The result was that Greece found itself unable to borrow more from private lenders; it received emergency loans from other European nations and the International Monetary Fund, but these loans came with the requirement that the Greek government make severe spending cuts, which wreaked havoc with its economy, imposed severe economic hardship on Greeks, and led to massive social unrest.

No discussion of fiscal policy is complete if it doesn't take into account the long-run implications of government budget surpluses and deficits, especially the implications for government debt. We now turn to those long-run implications.

Greeks angered by their government's harsh austerity measures took to the streets in protest.

## Deficits, Surpluses, and Debt

When a family spends more than it earns over the course of a year, it has to raise the extra funds either by selling assets or by borrowing. And if a family borrows year after year, it will eventually end up with a lot of debt.

The same is true for governments. With a few exceptions, governments don't raise large sums by selling assets such as national parkland. Instead, when a government spends more than the tax revenue it receives—when it runs a budget deficit—it almost always borrows the extra funds. And governments that run persistent budget deficits end up with substantial debts.

To interpret the numbers that follow, you need to know a slightly peculiar feature of federal government accounting. For historical reasons, the U.S. government does not keep books by calendar years. Instead, budget totals are kept by **fiscal years,** which run from October 1 to September 30 and are labeled

A **fiscal year** runs from October 1 to September 30 and is labeled according to the calendar year in which it ends.

## ⚠ PITFALLS

### DEFICITS VERSUS DEBT

One common mistake—it happens all the time in newspaper reports—is to confuse *deficits* with *debt*. Let's review the difference.

A *deficit* is the difference between the amount of money a government spends and the amount it receives in taxes over a given period—usually, though not always, a year. Deficit numbers always come with a statement about the time period to which they apply, as in "the U.S. budget deficit *in fiscal 2011* was $1.3 trillion."

A *debt* is the sum of money a government owes at a particular point in time. Debt numbers usually come with a specific date, as in "U.S. public debt *at the end of fiscal 2011* was $10.1 trillion."

Deficits and debt are linked, because government debt grows when governments run deficits. But they aren't the same thing, and they can even tell different stories. For example, Italy, which found itself in debt trouble in 2011, had a fairly small deficit by historical standards, but it had very high debt, a legacy of past policies.

by the calendar year in which they end. For example, fiscal 2010 began on October 1, 2009, and ended on September 30, 2010.

At the end of fiscal 2011, the U.S. federal government had total debt equal to $14.8 trillion. However, part of that debt represented special accounting rules specifying that the federal government as a whole owes funds to certain government programs, especially Social Security. We'll explain those rules shortly. For now, however, let's focus on **public debt:** government debt held by individuals and institutions outside the government. At the end of fiscal 2011, the federal government's public debt was "only" $10.1 trillion, or 68% of GDP. If we include the debts of state and local governments, total public debt at the end of fiscal 2011 was larger than it was at the end of fiscal 2010 because the federal government ran a budget deficit during fiscal 2011. A government that runs persistent budget deficits will experience a rising level of public debt. Why is this a problem?

## GLOBAL COMPARISON   THE AMERICAN WAY OF DEBT

How does the public debt of the United States stack up internationally? In dollar terms, we're number one—but this isn't very informative, since the U.S. economy and so the government's tax base are much larger than those of any other nation. A more informative comparison is the ratio of public debt to GDP.

The figure shows the *net public debt* of a number of rich countries as a percentage of GDP at the end of 2011. Net public debt is government debt minus any assets governments may have—an adjustment that can make a big difference. What you see here is that the United States is more or less in the middle of the pack.

It may not surprise you that Greece heads the list, and most of the other high net debt countries are European nations that have been making headlines for their debt problems. Interestingly, however, Japan is also high on the list because it used massive public spending to prop up its economy in the 1990s. Investors, however, still consider Japan a reliable government, so its borrowing costs remain low despite high net debt.

In contrast to the other countries, Norway has a large *negative*

net public debt. What's going on in Norway? In a word, oil. Norway is the world's third-largest oil exporter, thanks to large offshore deposits in the North Sea. Instead of spending its oil revenues immediately, the government of Norway has used them to build up an investment fund for future needs following the lead of traditional oil producers like Saudi Arabia. As a result, Norway has huge stock of government assets rather than a large government debt.

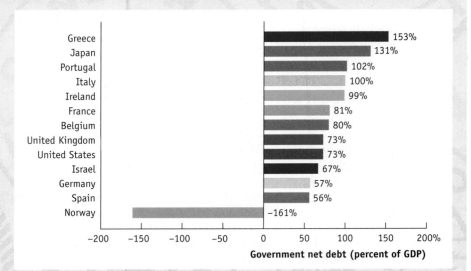

*Source:* International Monetary Fund.

## Problems Posed by Rising Government Debt

There are two reasons to be concerned when a government runs persistent budget deficits. We described one reason in Chapter 10: when the economy is at full employment and the government borrows funds in the financial markets, it is competing with firms that plan to borrow funds for investment spending. As a result, the government's borrowing may crowd out private investment spending, increasing interest rates and reducing the economy's long-run rate of growth.

But there's a second reason: today's deficits, by increasing the government's debt, place financial pressure on future budgets. The impact of current deficits on future budgets is straightforward. Like individuals, governments must pay their bills, including interest payments on their accumulated debt. When a government is deeply in debt, those interest payments can be substantial. In fiscal 2011, the U.S. federal government paid 1.8% of GDP—$266 billion—in interest on its debt. The more heavily indebted government of Italy paid interest of 4.7% of its GDP in 2011.

Other things equal, a government paying large sums in interest must raise more revenue from taxes or spend less than it would otherwise be able to afford—or it must borrow even more to cover the gap. And a government that borrows to pay interest on its outstanding debt pushes itself even deeper into debt. This process can eventually push a government to the point where lenders question its ability to repay. Like a consumer who has maxed out his or her credit cards, it will find that lenders are unwilling to lend any more funds. The result can be that the government defaults on its debt—it stops paying what it owes. Default is often followed by deep financial and economic turmoil.

Americans aren't used to the idea of government default, but such things do happen. In the 1990s Argentina, a relatively high-income developing country, was widely praised for its economic policies—and it was able to borrow large sums from foreign lenders. By 2001, however, Argentina's interest payments were spiraling out of control, and the country stopped paying the sums that were due. In the end, it reached a settlement with most of its lenders under which it paid less than a third of the amount originally due. By late 2011 investors were placing a fairly high probability on Argentine-type default by several European countries—namely, Greece, Ireland, and Portugal—and were seriously worried about Italy and Spain. Each one was forced to pay high interest rates on its debt by nervous lenders, exacerbating the risk of default.

Default creates havoc in a country's financial markets and badly shakes public confidence in both the government and the economy. Argentina's debt default was accompanied by a crisis in the country's banking system and a very severe recession. And even if a highly indebted government avoids default, a heavy debt burden typically forces it to slash spending or raise taxes, politically unpopular measures that can also damage the economy. In some cases, "austerity" measures intended to reassure lenders that the government can indeed pay end up depressing the economy so much that lender confidence continues to fall—a process we'll look at more closely in the Economics in Action that follows this section.

Some may ask why can't a government that has trouble borrowing just print money to pay its bills? Yes, it can if it has its own currency (which the troubled European nations don't). But printing money to pay the government's bills can lead to another problem: inflation. In fact, budget problems are the main cause of very severe inflation, as we'll see in Chapter 16. The point for now is that governments do not want to find themselves in a position where the choice is between defaulting on their debts and inflating those debts away by printing money.

Concerns about the long-run effects of deficits need not rule out the use of expansionary fiscal policy to stimulate the economy when it is depressed.

**Public debt** is government debt held by individuals and institutions outside the government.

The **debt–GDP ratio** is the government's debt as a percentage of GDP.

However, these concerns do mean that governments should try to offset budget deficits in bad years with budget surpluses in good years. In other words, governments should run a budget that is approximately balanced over time. Have they actually done so?

## Deficits and Debt in Practice

Figure 13-11 shows how the U.S. federal government's budget deficit and its debt evolved from 1940 to 2011. Panel (a) shows the federal deficit as a percentage of GDP. As you can see, the federal government ran huge deficits during World War II. It briefly ran surpluses after the war, but it has normally run deficits ever since, especially after 1980. This seems inconsistent with the advice that governments should offset deficits in bad times with surpluses in good times.

However, panel (b) of Figure 13-11 shows that for most of the period these persistent deficits didn't lead to runaway debt. To assess the ability of governments to pay their debt, we use the **debt–GDP ratio,** the government's debt as a percentage of GDP. We use this measure, rather than simply looking at the size of the debt, because GDP, which measures the size of the economy as a whole, is a good indicator of the potential taxes the government can collect. If the government's debt grows more slowly than GDP, the burden of paying that debt is actually falling compared with the government's potential tax revenue.

What we see from panel (b) is that although the federal debt grew in almost every year, the debt–GDP ratio fell for 30 years after the end of World War II. This shows that the debt–GDP ratio can fall, even when debt is rising, as long as GDP grows faster than debt. For Inquiring Minds, which focuses on the large debt the U.S. government ran up during World War II, explains how growth and inflation

**FIGURE 13-11** U.S. Federal Deficits and Debt

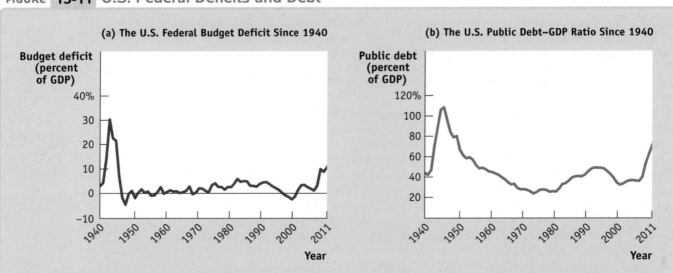

Panel (a) shows the U.S. federal budget deficit as a percentage of GDP from 1940 to 2011. The U.S. government ran huge deficits during World War II and has run smaller deficits ever since. Panel (b) shows the U.S. debt–GDP ratio. Comparing panels (a) and (b), you can see that in many years the debt–GDP ratio has declined in spite of government deficits. This seeming paradox reflects the fact that the debt–GDP ratio can fall, even when debt is rising, as long as GDP grows faster than debt.

*Source:* Office of Management and Budget.

## FOR INQUIRING MINDS

### WHAT HAPPENED TO THE DEBT FROM WORLD WAR II?

As you can see from Figure 13-11, the U.S. government paid for World War II by borrowing on a huge scale. By the war's end, the public debt was more than 100% of GDP, and many people worried about how it could ever be paid off.

The truth is that it never was paid off. In 1946 public debt was $242 bil-lion; that number dipped slightly in the next few years, as the United States ran postwar budget surpluses, but the government budget went back into deficit in 1950 with the start of the Korean War. By 1962 the public debt was back up to $248 billion.

But by that time nobody was worried about the fiscal health of the U.S.

government because the debt–GDP ratio had fallen by more than half. The reason? Vigorous economic growth, plus mild inflation, had led to a rapid rise in GDP. The experience was a clear lesson in the peculiar fact that modern governments can run deficits forever, as long as they aren't too large.

---

sometimes allow a government that runs persistent budget deficits to nevertheless have a declining debt–GDP ratio.

Still, a government that runs persistent *large* deficits will have a rising debt–GDP ratio when debt grows faster than GDP. In the aftermath of the financial crisis of 2008, the U.S. government began running deficits much larger than anything seen since World War II, and the debt–GDP ratio began rising sharply. Similar surges in the debt–GDP ratio could be seen in a number of other countries in 2008. Economists and policy makers agreed that this was not a sustainable trend, that governments would need to get their spending and revenues back in line. But *when* to bring spending in line with revenue was a source of great disagreement. Some argued for fiscal tightening right away; others argued that this tightening should be postponed until the major economies had recovered from their slump.

## Implicit Liabilities

Looking at Figure 13-11, you might be tempted to conclude that until the 2008 crisis struck, the U.S. federal budget was in fairly decent shape: the return to budget deficits after 2001 caused the debt–GDP ratio to rise a bit, but that ratio was still low compared with both historical experience and some other wealthy countries. In fact, however, experts on long-run budget issues view the situation of the United States (and other countries such as Japan and Italy) with alarm. The reason is the problem of *implicit liabilities*. **Implicit liabilities** are spending promises made by governments that are effectively a debt despite the fact that they are not included in the usual debt statistics.

The largest implicit liabilities of the U.S. government arise from two transfer programs that principally benefit older Americans: Social Security and Medicare. The third-largest implicit liability, Medicaid, benefits low-income families. In each of these cases, the government has promised to provide transfer payments to future as well as current beneficiaries. So these programs represent a future debt that must be honored, even though the debt does not currently show up in the usual statistics. Together, these three programs currently account for almost 40% of federal spending.

The implicit liabilities created by these transfer programs worry fiscal experts. Figure 13-12 shows why. It shows actual spending on Social Security and on Medicare, Medicaid, and CHIP (a program that provides health care coverage to uninsured children) as percentages of GDP from 2000 to 2010, together with Congressional Budget Office projections of spending through 2085. According to these projections, spending on Social Security will rise substantially over the next few decades and spending on the three health care programs will soar. Why?

**Implicit liabilities** are spending promises made by governments that are effectively a debt despite the fact that they are not included in the usual debt statistics.

FIGURE **13-12** Future Demands on the Federal Budget

This figure shows Congressional Budget Office projections of spending on social insurance programs as a share of GDP. Partly as a result of an aging population, but mainly because of rising health care costs, these programs are expected to become much more expensive over time, posing problems for the federal budget.

*Source:* Congressional Budget Office.

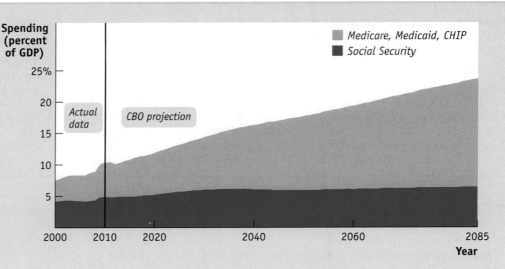

In the case of Social Security, the answer is demography. Social Security is a "pay-as-you-go" system: current workers pay payroll taxes that fund the benefits of current retirees. So the ratio of the number of retirees drawing benefits to the number of workers paying into Social Security has a major impact on the system's finances. There was a huge surge in the U.S. birth rate between 1946 and 1964, the years of what is commonly called the "baby boom." Most baby boomers are currently of working age—which means they are paying taxes, not collecting benefits. But some are starting to retire, and as more and more of them do so, they will stop earning taxable income and start collecting benefits. As a result, the ratio of retirees receiving benefits to workers paying into the Social Security system will rise. In 2010 there were 34 retirees receiving benefits for every 100 workers paying into the system. By 2030, according to the Social Security Administration, that number will rise to 46; by 2050, it will rise to 48; and by 2080, that number will be 51. So as baby boomers move into retirement, benefit payments will continue to rise relative to the size of the economy.

The aging of the baby boomers, by itself, poses only a moderately sized long-run fiscal problem. The projected rise in Medicare and Medicaid spending is a much more serious concern. The main story behind projections of higher Medicare and Medicaid spending is the long-run tendency of health care spending to rise faster than overall spending, both for government-funded and for privately funded health care.

To some extent, the implicit liabilities of the U.S. government are already reflected in debt statistics. We mentioned earlier that the government had a total debt of $14.8 trillion at the end of fiscal 2011 but that only $10.1 trillion of that total was owed to the public. The main explanation for that discrepancy is that both Social Security and part of Medicare (the hospital insurance program) are supported by *dedicated taxes:* their expenses are paid out of special taxes on wages. At times, these dedicated taxes yield more revenue than is needed to pay current benefits. In particular, since the mid-1980s the Social Security system has been taking in more revenue than it currently needs in order to prepare for the retirement of the baby boomers. This surplus in the Social Security system has been used to accumulate a *Social Security trust fund,* which was $2.9 trillion at the end of fiscal 2011.

The money in the trust fund is held in the form of U.S. government bonds, which are included in the $14.8 trillion in total debt. You could say that there's something funny about counting bonds in the Social Security trust fund as part of government debt. After all, these bonds are owed by one part of the government (the government outside the Social Security system) to another part of the government (the Social Security system itself). But the debt corresponds to a real, if implicit, liability: promises by the government to pay future retirement benefits. So many economists argue that the gross debt of $14.8 trillion, the sum of public debt and government debt held by Social Security and other trust funds, is a more accurate indication of the government's fiscal health than the smaller amount owed to the public alone.

## ECONOMICS > IN ACTION

### AUSTERITY DILEMMAS

Suppose that a country's economy hits a rough patch and lenders worry if the government, already deeply indebted, will be able to repay its loans. As a result, lenders cut off further lending. What's a government to do?

The usual prescription has been fiscal austerity: cut government spending and raise taxes, to both reduce the need to borrow more funds and to demonstrate to lenders the ability and determination to do what's necessary to honor its debts. But besides being painful and politically unpopular, does fiscal austerity really work to extricate a country from a crisis of lender confidence? Both economics and history indicate that the likely answer is no.

Fiscal austerity means contractionary fiscal policy. And we know from our earlier analysis that if an economy is already depressed, contractionary fiscal policy will depress it further. Moreover, the experiences of Argentina and Ireland show that the worsened state of an economy arising from austerity can further undermine the lender confidence that it was supposed to support.

Argentina presents a clear picture of the dynamic. Starting in the 1990s, Argentina was a favorite of foreign lenders and borrowed freely from abroad. But its debts accumulated, and by the late 2000s when the economy hit a downturn, lenders began to get worried. From 1997 to 2001, Argentina tried to reassure lenders that it was credit-worthy by repeatedly raising taxes and cutting government spending. But each round of austerity so weakened the economy that the government was unable to balance its budget. Finally, facing massive popular protests, the government collapsed and defaulted on its debts.

Since 2009, Ireland has gone through a similar experience, although the origins of its troubles were different. Until 2008, Ireland's government ran a more or less balanced budget. But during the 2000s, the Irish economy had a massive real estate bubble, fueled by excessive bank lending to real estate developers. When the bubble burst, Irish banks were left with massive losses. In order to prop them up, the Irish government guaranteed the banks' losses, making Irish taxpayers responsible for paying off the banks' debts. But, as it turns out, these debts were so large that the government's own solvency came into question, and the interest rate at which it had to borrow rose abruptly. This result can be seen in Figure 13-13, which shows how the interest rate spread between Irish government bonds and German government bonds (which are considered very safe) jumped in late 2008 and early 2009.

In an attempt to regain lender confidence, Ireland imposed severe austerity, even though the economy had already fallen into recession. For example, the government adopted a policy of reducing its workforce by 25,000; calculated

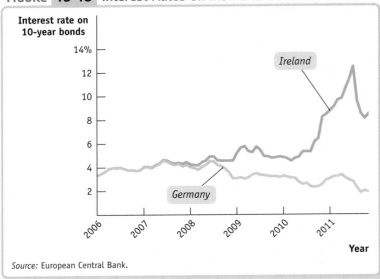

FIGURE **13-13** Interest Rates on Irish and German Bonds

Interest rate on
10-year bonds

*Source:* European Central Bank.

as a percentage of the population, this was equivalent to a loss of 2.5 million jobs in the United States.

By mid-2010, the Irish austerity policy appeared to be working, as rates on Irish bonds stabilized and even fell a bit from 2009 to 2010. But by 2011, it all fell apart as the size of the banks' losses continued to mushroom and it became clear that the austerity policies were pushing the economy deeper into a recession. By late 2010, Irish GDP was 12% lower than it had been at the end of 2007. The weaknesses of the Irish economy were depressing tax revenues, undoing much of the direct effect of austerity. Simultaneously, the decline in GDP had contributed to a surge in the debt-GDP ratio. At the time of writing, Irish officials were still hoping to regain lender confidence through even harsher austerity measures, although prospects did not look encouraging.

So why do lenders advocate, and indebted countries adopt, such self-defeating austerity measures? Because they make the mistake of thinking that an economy is like a household: if the family would just cut back on their spending, so the thinking goes, then they could pay their credit card bills. But as we know, an economy is not like a family; instead, one person's spending is another person's income. So austerity measures that reduce spending end up reducing income and making it even less likely that a country can repay its debts.

## ▼ Quick Review

- Persistent budget deficits lead to increases in **public debt.**

- Rising public debt can lead to government default. In less extreme cases, it can crowd out investment spending, reducing long-run growth. This suggests that budget deficits in bad **fiscal years** should be offset with budget surpluses in good fiscal years.

- A widely used indicator of fiscal health is the **debt–GDP ratio.** A country with rising GDP can have a stable or falling debt–GDP ratio even if it runs budget deficits if GDP is growing faster than the debt.

- In addition to their official public debt, modern governments have implicit liabilities. The U.S. government has large **implicit liabilities** in the form of Social Security, Medicare, and Medicaid.

## CHECK YOUR UNDERSTANDING  13-4

1. Explain how each of the following events would affect the public debt or implicit liabilities of the U.S. government, other things equal. Would the public debt or implicit liabilities be greater or smaller?
   a. A higher growth rate of real GDP
   b. Retirees live longer
   c. A decrease in tax revenue
   d. Government borrowing to pay interest on its current public debt

2. Suppose the economy is in a slump and the current public debt is quite large. Explain the trade-off of short-run versus long-run objectives that policy makers face when deciding whether or not to engage in deficit spending.

3. Explain how a policy of fiscal austerity can make it more likely that a government is unable to pay its debts.

Solutions appear at back of book.

# Priming the Pumps

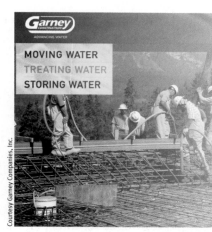

MOVING WATER
TREATING WATER
STORING WATER

Courtesy Garney Companies, Inc.

In the old days, when fewer Americans had cars but many more people lived in rural areas and drew their water from wells, advocates of fiscal expansion used different metaphors. Instead of talking, as President Obama did, about giving the economy a "jumpstart," they'd talk about "priming the pump." You see, it was often necessary to add water to old-fashioned hand pumps before they would work; similarly, people would argue, you need to add funds to the economy before it will get back to producing jobs and income.

In the case of the Obama stimulus, priming the pump was more than a metaphor: some of the most obvious beneficiaries were companies that made . . . pumps. The Recovery Act allocated $7 billion for drinking-water and wastewater projects, creating a number of new opportunities for companies in the business of moving water around.

A case in point was Garney Construction, a Kansas-City based company specializing in water and sewage projects whose slogan is "Advancing Water." By the summer of 2009, Garney had won contracts to work on nine water- and sewer-related projects that were being financed in whole or in part by the Recovery Act.

None of these infrastructure projects were dreamed up as ways to spend more money; they were all things that state or local governments had been planning to do eventually. "I think most of these projects were sitting on a shelf, waiting for funding," Garney's president told a local business journal.

Although the stimulus was good for Garney, it was not exactly a financial gusher. In 2007, the United States spent about $100 billion on water-supply and wastewater infrastructure; the extra $7 billion coming from the stimulus, not all of it coming in one year, was basically a, well, drop in the bucket by comparison. Indeed, Garney said that only about 10% of its business was coming from stimulus money. And despite the stimulus, the company had less business than it had two years earlier.

Still, Garney and other companies in the water-infrastructure business were clearly getting some benefit from the Recovery Act.

## QUESTIONS FOR THOUGHT

1. Some opponents of fiscal expansion have accused it of consisting of make-work projects of little social value. What does the Garney story say about this view?

2. Based on this case, would you say that government spending was competing with the private sector for scarce resources?

3. If a water or sewer project is something we want to do eventually, is the depth of a recession a good or a bad time to undertake that project? Why?

## SUMMARY

1. The government plays a large role in the economy, collecting a large share of GDP in taxes and spending a large share both to purchase goods and services and to make transfer payments, largely for **social insurance.** *Fiscal policy* is the use of taxes, government transfers, or government purchases of goods and services to shift the aggregate demand curve.

2. Government purchases of goods and services directly affect aggregate demand, and changes in taxes and government transfers affect aggregate demand indirectly by changing households' disposable income. **Expansionary fiscal policy** shifts the aggregate demand curve rightward; **contractionary fiscal policy** shifts the aggregate demand curve leftward.

3. Only when the economy is at full employment is there potential for crowding out of private spending and private investment spending by expansionary fiscal policy. The argument that expansionary fiscal policy won't work because of Ricardian equivalence—that consumers will cut back spending today to offset expected future tax increases—appears to be untrue in practice. What is clearly true is that very active fiscal policy may make the economy less stable due to time lags in policy formulation and implementation.

4. Fiscal policy has a multiplier effect on the economy, the size of which depends on the fiscal policy. Except in the case of lump-sum taxes, taxes reduce the size of the multiplier. Expansionary fiscal policy leads to an increase in real GDP, and contractionary fiscal policy leads to a reduction in real GDP. Because part of any change in taxes or transfers is absorbed by savings in the first round of spending, changes in government purchases of goods and services have a more powerful effect on the economy than equal-sized changes in taxes or transfers.

5. Rules governing taxes—with the exception of **lump-sum taxes**—and some transfers act as **automatic stabilizers,** reducing the size of the multiplier and automatically reducing the size of fluctuations in the business cycle. In contrast, **discretionary fiscal policy** arises from deliberate actions by policy makers rather than from the business cycle.

6. Some of the fluctuations in the budget balance are due to the effects of the business cycle. In order to separate the effects of the business cycle from the effects of discretionary fiscal policy, governments estimate the **cyclically adjusted budget balance,** an estimate of the budget balance if the economy were at potential output.

7. U.S. government budget accounting is calculated on the basis of **fiscal years.** Persistent budget deficits have long-run consequences because they lead to an increase in **public debt.** This can be a problem for two reasons. Public debt may crowd out investment spending, which reduces long-run economic growth. And in extreme cases, rising debt may lead to government default, resulting in economic and financial turmoil.

8. A widely used measure of fiscal health is the **debt–GDP ratio.** This number can remain stable or fall even in the face of moderate budget deficits if GDP rises over time. However, a stable debt–GDP ratio may give a misleading impression that all is well because modern governments often have large **implicit liabilities.** The largest implicit liabilities of the U.S. government come from Social Security, Medicare, and Medicaid, the costs of which are increasing due to the aging of the population and rising medical costs.

## KEY TERMS

Social insurance, p. 379
Expansionary fiscal policy, p. 380
Contractionary fiscal policy, p. 382
Lump-sum taxes, p. 387
Automatic stabilizers, p. 388
Discretionary fiscal policy, p. 388
Cyclically adjusted budget balance, p. 392
Fiscal year, p. 395
Public debt, p. 396
Debt–GDP ratio, p. 398
Implicit liabilities, p. 399

## PROBLEMS

1. The accompanying diagram shows the current macroeconomic situation for the economy of Albernia. You have been hired as an economic consultant to help the economy move to potential output, $Y_P$.

   a. Is Albernia facing a recessionary or inflationary gap?

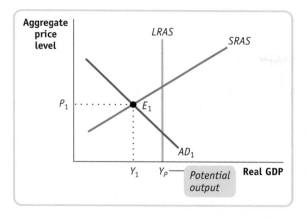

**b.** Which type of fiscal policy—expansionary or contractionary—would move the economy of Albernia to potential output, $Y_P$? What are some examples of such policies?

**c.** Illustrate the macroeconomic situation in Albernia with a diagram after the successful fiscal policy has been implemented.

**2.** The accompanying diagram shows the current macroeconomic situation for the economy of Brittania; real GDP is $Y_1$, and the aggregate price level is $P_1$. You have been hired as an economic consultant to help the economy move to potential output, $Y_P$.

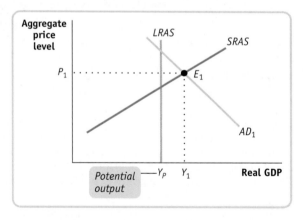

**a.** Is Brittania facing a recessionary or inflationary gap?

**b.** Which type of fiscal policy—expansionary or contractionary—would move the economy of Brittania to potential output, $Y_P$? What are some examples of such policies?

**c.** Illustrate the macroeconomic situation in Brittania with a diagram after the successful fiscal policy has been implemented.

**3.** An economy is in long-run macroeconomic equilibrium when each of the following aggregate demand shocks occurs. What kind of gap—inflationary or recessionary—will the economy face after the shock, and what type of fiscal policies would help move the economy back to potential output? How would your recommended fiscal policy shift the aggregate demand curve?

**a.** A stock market boom increases the value of stocks held by households.

**b.** Firms come to believe that a recession in the near future is likely.

**c.** Anticipating the possibility of war, the government increases its purchases of military equipment.

**d.** The quantity of money in the economy declines and interest rates increase.

**4.** During an interview in 2008, the German Finance Minister Peer Steinbrueck said, "We have to watch out that in Europe and beyond, nothing like a combination of downward economic [growth] and high inflation rates emerges—something that experts call stagflation." Such a situation can be depicted by the movement of the short-run aggregate supply curve from its original position, $SRAS_1$, to its new position, $SRAS_2$, with the new equilibrium point $E_2$ in the accompanying figure. In this question, we try to understand why stagflation is particularly hard to fix using fiscal policy.

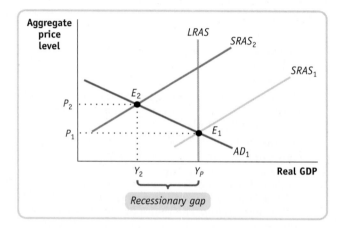

**a.** What would be the appropriate fiscal policy response to this situation if the primary concern of the government was to maintain economic growth? Illustrate the effect of the policy on the equilibrium point and the aggregate price level using the diagram.

**b.** What would be the appropriate fiscal policy response to this situation if the primary concern of the government was to maintain price stability? Illustrate the effect of the policy on the equilibrium point and the aggregate price level using the diagram.

**c.** Discuss the effectiveness of the policies in parts a and b in fighting stagflation.

**5.** Show why a $10 billion reduction in government purchases of goods and services will have a larger effect on real GDP than a $10 billion reduction in government transfers by completing the accompanying table for an economy with a marginal propensity to consume (*MPC*) of 0.6. The first and second rows of the table are filled in for you: on the left side of the table, in the first row, the $10 billion reduction in government purchases decreases real GDP and disposable income, *YD*, by $10 billion, leading to a reduction in consumer spending of $6 billion (*MPC* × change in disposable income) in row 2. However, on the right side of the table, the $10 billion reduction in transfers has no effect on real GDP in round 1 but does lower *YD* by $10 billion, resulting in a decrease in consumer spending of $6 billion in round 2.

| | Decrease in *G* = −$10 billion | | | Decrease in *TR* = −$10 billion | | |
|---|---|---|---|---|---|---|
| | Billions of dollars | | | Billions of dollars | | |
| Rounds | Change in *G* or *C* | Change in real GDP | Change in *YD* | Change in *TR* or *C* | Change in real GDP | Change in *YD* |
| 1 | Δ*G* = −$10.00 | −$10.00 | −$10.00 | Δ*TR* = −$10.00 | $0.00 | −$10.00 |
| 2 | Δ*C* = −6.00 | −6.00 | −6.00 | Δ*C* = −6.00 | −6.00 | −6.00 |
| 3 | Δ*C* = ? | ? | ? | Δ*C* = ? | ? | ? |
| 4 | Δ*C* = ? | ? | ? | Δ*C* = ? | ? | ? |
| 5 | Δ*C* = ? | ? | ? | Δ*C* = ? | ? | ? |
| 6 | Δ*C* = ? | ? | ? | Δ*C* = ? | ? | ? |
| 7 | Δ*C* = ? | ? | ? | Δ*C* = ? | ? | ? |
| 8 | Δ*C* = ? | ? | ? | Δ*C* = ? | ? | ? |
| 9 | Δ*C* = ? | ? | ? | Δ*C* = ? | ? | ? |
| 10 | Δ*C* = ? | ? | ? | Δ*C* = ? | ? | ? |

**a.** When government purchases decrease by $10 billion, what is the sum of the changes in real GDP after the 10 rounds?

**b.** When the government reduces transfers by $10 billion, what is the sum of the changes in real GDP after the 10 rounds?

**c.** Using the formula for the multiplier for changes in government purchases and for changes in transfers, calculate the total change in real GDP due to the $10 billion decrease in government purchases and the $10 billion reduction in transfers. What explains the difference? (*Hint:* The multiplier for government purchases of goods and services is $1/(1 - MPC)$. But since each $1 change in government transfers only leads to an initial change in real GDP of $MPC \times \$1$, the multiplier for government transfers is $MPC/(1 - MPC)$.)

**6.** In each of the following cases, either a recessionary or inflationary gap exists. Assume that the aggregate supply curve is horizontal, so that the change in real GDP arising from a shift of the aggregate demand curve equals the size of the shift of the curve. Calculate both the change in government purchases of goods and services and the change in government transfers necessary to close the gap.

**a.** Real GDP equals $100 billion, potential output equals $160 billion, and the marginal propensity to consume is 0.75.

**b.** Real GDP equals $250 billion, potential output equals $200 billion, and the marginal propensity to consume is 0.5.

**c.** Real GDP equals $180 billion, potential output equals $100 billion, and the marginal propensity to consume is 0.8.

**7.** Most macroeconomists believe it is a good thing that taxes act as automatic stabilizers and lower the size of the multiplier. However, a smaller multiplier means that the change in government purchases of goods and services, government transfers, or taxes needed to close

an inflationary or recessionary gap is larger. How can you explain this apparent inconsistency?

**8.** The accompanying table shows how consumers' marginal propensities to consume in a particular economy are related to their level of income.

| Income range | Marginal propensity to consume |
|---|---|
| $0–$20,000 | 0.9 |
| $20,001–$40,000 | 0.8 |
| $40,001–$60,000 | 0.7 |
| $60,001–$80,000 | 0.6 |
| Above $80,000 | 0.5 |

**a.** Suppose the government engages in increased purchases of goods and services. For each of the income groups in the table, what is the value of the multiplier—that is, what is the "bang for the buck" from each dollar the government spends on government purchases of goods and services in each income group?

**b.** If the government needed to close a recessionary or inflationary gap, at which group should it primarily aim its fiscal policy of changes in government purchases of goods and services?

**9.** The government's budget surplus in Macroland has risen consistently over the past five years. Two government policy makers disagree as to why this has happened. One argues that a rising budget surplus indicates a growing economy; the other argues that it shows that the government is using contractionary fiscal policy. Can you determine which policy maker is correct? If not, why not?

**10.** Figure 13-9 shows the actual budget deficit and the cyclically adjusted budget deficit as a percentage of GDP in the United States from 1970 to 2010. Assuming that potential output was unchanged, use this figure to determine which of the years from 1990 to 2009 the government used expansionary fiscal policy and in which years it used contractionary fiscal policy.

**11.** You are an economic adviser to a candidate for national office. She asks you for a summary of the economic consequences of a balanced-budget rule for the federal government and for your recommendation on whether she should support such a rule. How do you respond?

**12.** In 2012, the policy makers of the economy of Eastlandia projected the debt–GDP ratio and the ratio of the budget deficit to GDP for the economy for the next 10 years under different scenarios for growth in the government's deficit. Real GDP is currently $1,000 billion per year and is expected to grow by 3% per year, the public debt is $300 billion at the beginning of the year, and the deficit is $30 billion in 2012.

| Year | Real GDP (billions of dollars) | Debt (billions of dollars) | Budget deficit (billions of dollars) | Debt (percent of real GDP) | Budget deficit (percent of real GDP) |
|------|------|------|------|------|------|
| 2012 | $1,000 | $300 | $30 | ? | ? |
| 2013 | 1,030 | ? | ? | ? | ? |
| 2014 | 1,061 | ? | ? | ? | ? |
| 2015 | 1,093 | ? | ? | ? | ? |
| 2016 | 1,126 | ? | ? | ? | ? |
| 2017 | 1,159 | ? | ? | ? | ? |
| 2018 | 1,194 | ? | ? | ? | ? |
| 2019 | 1,230 | ? | ? | ? | ? |
| 2020 | 1,267 | ? | ? | ? | ? |
| 2021 | 1,305 | ? | ? | ? | ? |
| 2022 | 1,344 | ? | ? | ? | ? |

**a.** Complete the accompanying table to show the debt–GDP ratio and the ratio of the budget deficit to GDP for the economy if the government's budget deficit remains constant at $30 billion over the next 10 years. (Remember that the government's debt will grow by the previous year's deficit.)

**b.** Redo the table to show the debt–GDP ratio and the ratio of the budget deficit to GDP for the economy if the government's budget deficit grows by 3% per year over the next 10 years.

**c.** Redo the table again to show the debt–GDP ratio and the ratio of the budget deficit to GDP for the economy if the government's budget deficit grows by 20% per year over the next 10 years.

**d.** What happens to the debt–GDP ratio and the ratio of the budget deficit to GDP for the economy over time under the three different scenarios?

**13.** Your study partner argues that the distinction between the government's budget deficit and debt is similar to the distinction between consumer savings and wealth. He also argues that if you have large budget deficits,

you must have a large debt. In what ways is your study partner correct and in what ways is he incorrect?

**14.** In which of the following cases does the size of the government's debt and the size of the budget deficit indicate potential problems for the economy?

**a.** The government's debt is relatively low, but the government is running a large budget deficit as it builds a high-speed rail system to connect the major cities of the nation.

**b.** The government's debt is relatively high due to a recently ended deficit-financed war, but the government is now running only a small budget deficit.

**c.** The government's debt is relatively low, but the government is running a budget deficit to finance the interest payments on the debt.

**15.** How did or would the following affect the current public debt and implicit liabilities of the U.S. government?

**a.** In 2003, Congress passed and President Bush signed the Medicare Modernization Act, which provides seniors and individuals with disabilities with a prescription drug benefit. Some of the benefits under this law took effect immediately, but others will not begin until sometime in the future.

**b.** The age at which retired persons can receive full Social Security benefits is raised to age 70 for future retirees.

**c.** Social Security benefits for future retirees are limited to those with low incomes.

**d.** Because the cost of health care is increasing faster than the overall inflation rate, annual increases in Social Security benefits are increased by the annual increase in health care costs rather than the overall inflation rate.

**16.** Unlike households, governments are often able to sustain large debts. For example, in 2011, the U.S. government's total debt reached $14.8 trillion, approximately equal to 102.7% of GDP. At the time, according to the U.S. Treasury, the average interest rate paid by the government on its debt was 2.2%. However, running budget deficits becomes hard when very large debts are outstanding.

**a.** Calculate the dollar cost of the annual interest on the government's total debt assuming the interest rate and debt figures cited above.

**b.** If the government operates on a balanced budget before interest payments are taken into account, at what rate must GDP grow in order for the debt–GDP ratio to remain unchanged?

**c.** Calculate the total increase in national debt if the government incurs a deficit of $600 billion in 2012.

**d.** At what rate would GDP have to grow in order for the debt–GDP ratio to remain unchanged when the deficit in 2012 is $600 billion?

**e.** Why is the debt–GDP ratio the preferred measure of a country's debt rather than the dollar value of the debt? Why is it important for a government to keep this number under control?

# Taxes and the Multiplier

In the chapter, we described how taxes that depend positively on real GDP reduce the size of the multiplier and act as an automatic stabilizer for the economy. Let's look a little more closely at the mathematics of how this works.

Specifically, let's assume that the government "captures" a fraction $t$ of any increase in real GDP in the form of taxes, where $t$, the tax rate, is a fraction between 0 and 1. And let's repeat the exercise we carried out in Chapter 11, where we consider the effects of a $100 billion increase in investment spending. The same analysis holds for *any* autonomous increase in aggregate spending—in particular, it is also true for increases in government purchases of goods and services.

The $100 billion increase in investment spending initially raises real GDP by $100 billion (the first round). In the absence of taxes, disposable income would rise by $100 billion. But because part of the rise in real GDP is collected in the form of taxes, disposable income only rises by $(1 - t) \times$ $100 billion. The second-round increase in consumer spending, which is equal to the marginal propensity to consume *(MPC)* multiplied by the rise in disposable income, is $(MPC \times (1 - t)) \times$ $100 billion. This leads to a third-round increase in consumer spending of $(MPC \times (1 - t)) \times (MPC \times (1 - t)) \times$ $100 billion, and so on. So the total effect on real GDP is

| | | |
|---|---|---|
| Increase in investment spending | = | $100 billion |
| + Second-round increase in consumer spending | = $(MPC \times (1 - t))$ | × $100 billion |
| + Third-round increase in consumer spending | = $(MPC \times (1 - t))^2$ | × $100 billion |
| + Fourth-round increase in consumer spending | = $(MPC \times (1 - t))^3$ | × $100 billion |

•
•
•

Total increase in real GDP = $[1 + (MPC \times (1 - t)) + (MPC \times (1 - t))^2 + (MPC \times (1 - t))^3 + \ldots ] \times$ $100 billion

As we pointed out in Chapter 11, an infinite series of the form $1 + x + x^2 + \ldots$, with $0 < x < 1$, is equal to $1/(1 - x)$. In this example, $x = (MPC \times (1 - t))$. So the total effect of a $100 billion increase in investment spending, taking into account all the subsequent increases in consumer spending, is to raise real GDP by:

$$\frac{1}{1 - (MPC \times (1 - t))} \times \text{\$100 billion}$$

When we calculated the multiplier assuming away the effect of taxes, we found that it was $1/(1 - MPC)$. But when we assume that a fraction $t$ of any change in real GDP is collected in the form of taxes, the multiplier is:

$$\text{Multiplier} = \frac{1}{1 - (MPC \times (1 - t))}$$

This is always a smaller number than $1/(1 - MPC)$, and its size diminishes as $t$ grows. Suppose, for example, that $MPC = 0.6$. In the absence of taxes, this implies a multiplier of $1/(1 - 0.6) = 1/0.4 = 2.5$. But now let's assume that $t = 1/3$, that is, that 1/3 of any increase in real GDP is collected by the government. Then the multiplier is:

$$\frac{1}{1 - (0.6 \times (1 - 1/3))} = \frac{1}{1 - (0.6 \times 2/3)} = \frac{1}{1 - 0.4} = \frac{1}{0.6} = 1.667$$

## PROBLEMS

1. An economy has a marginal propensity to consume of 0.6, real GDP equals $500 billion, and the government collects 20% of GDP in taxes. If government purchases increase by $10 billion, show the rounds of increased spending that take place by completing the accompanying table. The first and second rows are filled in for you. In the first row, the increase in government purchases of $10 billion raises real GDP by $10 billion, taxes increase by $2 billion, and *YD* increases by $8 billion; in the second row, the increase in *YD* of $8 billion increases consumer spending by $4.80 billion (*MPC* × change in disposable income).

| Rounds | Change in G or C | Change in real GDP | Change in taxes | Change in *YD* |
|---|---|---|---|---|
| | | (billions of dollars) | | |
| 1 | Δ*G* = $10.00 | $10.00 | $2.00 | $8.00 |
| 2 | Δ*C* = 4.80 | 4.80 | 0.96 | 3.84 |
| 3 | Δ*C* = ? | ? | ? | ? |
| 4 | Δ*C* = ? | ? | ? | ? |
| 5 | Δ*C* = ? | ? | ? | ? |
| 6 | Δ*C* = ? | ? | ? | ? |
| 7 | Δ*C* = ? | ? | ? | ? |
| 8 | Δ*C* = ? | ? | ? | ? |
| 9 | Δ*C* = ? | ? | ? | ? |
| 10 | Δ*C* = ? | ? | ? | ? |

 a. What is the total change in real GDP after the 10 rounds? What is the value of the multiplier? What would you expect the total change in real GDP to be, based on the multiplier formula? How do your two answers compare?

 b. Redo the accompanying table, assuming the marginal propensity to consume is 0.75 and the government collects 10% of the rise in real GDP in taxes. What is the total change in real GDP after 10 rounds? What is the value of the multiplier? How do your two answers compare?

2. Calculate the change in government purchases of goods and services necessary to close the recessionary or inflationary gaps in the following cases. Assume that the short-run aggregate supply curve is horizontal, so that the change in real GDP arising from a shift of the aggregate demand curve equals the size of the shift of the curve.

 a. Real GDP equals $100 billion, potential output equals $160 billion, the government collects 20% of any change in real GDP in the form of taxes, and the marginal propensity to consume is 0.75.

 b. Real GDP equals $250 billion, potential output equals $200 billion, the government collects 10% of any change in real GDP in the form of taxes, and the marginal propensity to consume is 0.5.

 c. Real GDP equals $180 billion, potential output equals $100 billion, the government collects 25% of any change in real GDP in the form of taxes, and the marginal propensity to consume is 0.8.

# CHAPTER 14

# Money, Banking, and the Federal Reserve System

## FUNNY MONEY

"The A-train Is On the Banks," by James Flora, 1996, © Jim Flora Art LLC; Courtesy Irwin Chusid and Barbara Economon. www.JimFlora.

**Money is the essential channel that links the various parts of the modern economy.**

WHAT YOU WILL LEARN IN THIS CHAPTER

❯ The various roles **money** plays and the many forms it takes in the economy

❯ How the actions of private banks and the Federal Reserve determine the **money supply**

❯ How the Federal Reserve uses **open-market operations** to change the **monetary base**

ON OCTOBER 2, 2004, FBI AND Secret Service agents seized a shipping container that had just arrived in Newark, New Jersey, on a ship from China. Inside the container, under cardboard boxes containing plastic toys, they found what they were looking for: more than $300,000 in counterfeit $100 bills. Two months later, another shipment with $3 million in counterfeit bills was intercepted. Government and law enforcement officials began alleging publicly that these bills—high-quality fakes that were very hard to tell from the real thing—were being produced by the government of North Korea.

The funny thing is that elaborately decorated pieces of paper have little or no intrinsic value. Indeed, a $100 bill printed with blue or orange ink literally wouldn't be worth the paper it was printed on. But if the ink on that decorated piece of paper is just the right shade of green, people will think that it's money and will accept it as payment for very real goods and services. Why? Because they believe, correctly, that they can do the same thing: exchange that piece of green paper for real goods and services.

In fact, here's a riddle: if a fake $100 bill from North Korea enters the United States, and nobody ever realizes it's

fake, who gets hurt? Accepting a fake $100 bill isn't like buying a car that turns out to be a lemon or a meal that turns out to be inedible; as long as the bill's counterfeit nature remains undiscovered, it will pass from hand to hand just like a real $100 bill. The answer to the riddle, as we'll learn later in this chapter, is that the real victims of North Korean counterfeiting are U.S. taxpayers, because counterfeit dollars reduce the revenues available to pay for the operations of the U.S. government. Accordingly, the Secret Service diligently monitors the integrity of U.S. currency, promptly investigating any reports of counterfeit dollars.

The efforts of the Secret Service attest to the fact that money isn't like ordinary goods and services. It plays a unique role in the economy as the essential channel that links the various parts of the modern economy. In this chapter, we'll look at the role money plays, then look at how a modern monetary system works and at the institutions that sustain and regulate it. This topic is important in itself, and it's also essential background for the understanding of monetary policy, which we will examine in the next chapter. ◼

**Money** is any asset that can easily be used to purchase goods and services.

**Currency in circulation** is cash held by the public.

**Checkable bank deposits** are bank accounts on which people can write checks.

The **money supply** is the total value of financial assets in the economy that are considered money.

# The Meaning of Money

In everyday conversation, people often use the word *money* to mean "wealth." If you ask, "How much money does Bill Gates have?" the answer will be something like, "Oh, $50 billion or so, but who's counting?" That is, the number will include the value of the stocks, bonds, real estate, and other assets he owns.

But the economist's definition of money doesn't include all forms of wealth. The dollar bills in your wallet are money; other forms of wealth—such as cars, houses, and stock certificates—aren't money. What, according to economists, distinguishes money from other forms of wealth?

## What Is Money?

Money is defined in terms of what it does: **money** is any asset that can easily be used to purchase goods and services. In Chapter 10 we defined an asset as *liquid* if it can easily be converted into cash. Money consists of cash itself, which is liquid by definition, as well as other assets that are highly liquid.

You can see the distinction between money and other assets by asking yourself how you pay for groceries. The person at the cash register will accept dollar bills in return for milk and frozen pizza—but he or she won't accept stock certificates or a collection of vintage baseball cards. If you want to convert stock certificates or vintage baseball cards into groceries, you have to sell them—trade them for money—and then use the money to buy groceries.

Of course, many stores allow you to write a check on your bank account in payment for goods (or to pay with a debit card that is linked to your bank account). Does that make your bank account money, even if you haven't converted it into cash? Yes. **Currency in circulation**—actual cash in the hands of the public—is considered money. So are **checkable bank deposits**—bank accounts on which people can write checks.

Are currency and checkable bank deposits the only assets that are considered money? It depends. As we'll see later, there are two widely used definitions of the **money supply,** the total value of financial assets in the economy that are considered money. The narrower definition considers only the most liquid assets to be money: currency in circulation, traveler's checks, and checkable bank deposits. The broader definition includes these three categories plus other assets that are "almost" checkable, such as savings account deposits that can be transferred into a checking account with a phone call or a mouse click. Both definitions of the money supply, however, make a distinction between those assets that can easily be used to purchase goods and services and those that can't.

Money plays a crucial role in generating *gains from trade* because it makes indirect exchange possible. Think of what happens when a cardiac surgeon buys a new refrigerator. The surgeon has valuable services to offer—namely, heart operations. The owner of the store has valuable goods to offer—refrigerators and other appliances. It would be extremely difficult for both parties if, instead of using money, they had to directly barter the goods and services they sell. In a barter system, a cardiac surgeon and an appliance store owner could trade only if the store owner happened to want a heart operation and the surgeon happened to want a new refrigerator.

This is known as the problem of finding a "double coincidence of wants": in a barter system, two parties can trade only when each wants what the other has to offer. Money solves this problem: individuals can trade what they have to offer for money and trade money for what they want.

Because the ability to make transactions with money rather than relying on bartering makes it easier to achieve gains from trade, the existence of money increases welfare, even though money does not directly produce anything. As

Adam Smith put it, money "may very properly be compared to a highway, which, while it circulates and carries to market all the grass and corn of the country, produces itself not a single pile of either."

Let's take a closer look at the roles money plays in the economy.

## Roles of Money

Money plays three main roles in any modern economy: it is a *medium of exchange*, a *store of value*, and a *unit of account*.

**1. Medium of Exchange**  Our cardiac surgeon/refrigerator example illustrates the role of money as a **medium of exchange**—an asset that individuals use to trade for goods and services rather than for consumption. People can't eat dollar bills; rather, they use dollar bills to trade for edible goods and their accompanying services.

In normal times, the official money of a given country—the dollar in the United States, the peso in Mexico, and so on—is also the medium of exchange in virtually all transactions in that country. During troubled economic times, however, other goods or assets often play that role instead. For example, during economic turmoil people often turn to other countries' moneys as the medium of exchange: U.S. dollars have played this role in troubled Latin American countries, as have euros in troubled Eastern European countries. In a famous example, cigarettes functioned as the medium of exchange in World War II prisoner-of-war camps: even nonsmokers traded goods and services for cigarettes because the cigarettes could in turn be easily traded for other items. During the extreme German inflation of 1923, goods such as eggs and lumps of coal became, briefly, mediums of exchange.

**2. Store of Value**  In order to act as a medium of exchange, money must also be a **store of value**—a means of holding purchasing power over time. To see why this is necessary, imagine trying to operate an economy in which ice-cream cones were the medium of exchange. Such an economy would quickly

> A **medium of exchange** is an asset that individuals acquire for the purpose of trading goods and services rather than for their own consumption.
>
> A **store of value** is a means of holding purchasing power over time.

## GLOBAL COMPARISON  THE BIG MONEYS

Americans tend to think of the dollar as the world's leading currency—and it does remain the currency most likely to be accepted in payment around the globe. But there are other important currencies, too. One simple measure of a currency's importance is the value of the quantity of that currency in circulation. This figure shows the value, in billions of dollars, of the quantity of four major currencies in circulation at the end of 2010. The dollar, it turns out, is only number 2, behind the euro. The euro's prominence isn't that surprising, since the combined economies of the countries using the euro, the eurozone, are about as big as the U.S. economy. And despite the fact that its economy is much smaller, Japan is closely behind the United States, largely because the Japanese make much more use of cash, as opposed to checks

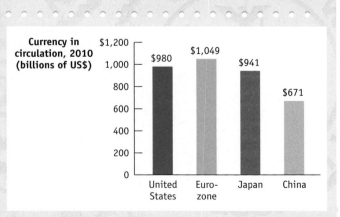

and credit cards, than either Europeans or Americans. And China, with its rapidly growing economy, is moving up the charts.

*Sources:* Federal Reserve Bank of St. Louis; European Central Bank; Bank of Japan; The People's Bank of China.

A **unit of account** is a measure used to set prices and make economic calculations.

**Commodity money** is a good used as a medium of exchange that has intrinsic value in other uses.

**Commodity-backed money** is a medium of exchange with no intrinsic value whose ultimate value is guaranteed by a promise that it can be converted into valuable goods.

suffer from, well, monetary meltdown: your medium of exchange would often turn into a sticky puddle before you could use it to buy something else. (As we'll see in Chapter 16, one of the problems caused by high inflation is that, in effect, it causes the value of money to "melt.") Of course, money is by no means the only store of value. Any asset that holds its purchasing power over time is a store of value. So the store-of-value role is a necessary but not distinctive feature of money.

**3. Unit of Account** Finally, money normally serves as the **unit of account**— the commonly accepted measure individuals use to set prices and make economic calculations. To understand the importance of this role, consider a historical fact: During the Middle Ages, peasants typically were required to provide land-owners with goods and labor rather than money. A peasant might, for example, be required to work on the lord's land one day a week and hand over one-fifth of his harvest.

Today, rents, like other prices, are almost always specified in money terms. That makes things much clearer: imagine how hard it would be to decide which apartment to rent if modern landlords followed medieval practice. Suppose, for example, that Mr. Smith says he'll let you have a place if you clean his house twice a week and bring him a pound of steak every day, whereas Ms. Jones wants you to clean her house just once a week but wants four pounds of chicken every day. Who's offering the better deal? It's hard to say. If, instead, Smith wants $600 a month and Jones wants $700, the comparison is easy. In other words, without a commonly accepted measure, the terms of a transaction are harder to determine, making it more difficult to make transactions and achieve gains from trade.

## Types of Money

In some form or another, money has been in use for thousands of years. For most of that period, people used **commodity money:** the medium of exchange was a good, normally gold or silver, that had intrinsic value in other uses. These alter-native uses gave commodity money value independent of its role as a medium of exchange. For example, cigarettes, which served as money in World War II pris-oner of war camps, were also valuable because many prisoners smoked. Gold was valuable because it was used for jewelry and ornamentation, aside from the fact that it was minted into coins.

By 1776, the year in which the United States declared independence and Adam Smith published *The Wealth of Nations*, there was widespread use of paper money in addition to gold or silver coins. Unlike modern dollar bills, how-ever, this paper money consisted of notes issued by private banks, which prom-ised to exchange their notes for gold or silver coins on demand. So the paper currency that initially replaced commodity money was **commodity-backed money,** a medium of exchange with no intrinsic value whose ultimate value was guaranteed by a promise that it could always be converted into valuable goods on demand.

The big advantage of commodity-backed money over simple commodity money, like gold and silver coins, was that it tied up fewer valuable resources. Although a note-issuing bank still had to keep some gold and silver on hand, it had to keep only enough to satisfy demands for redemption of its notes. And it could rely on the fact that on a normal day only a fraction of its paper notes would be redeemed. So the bank needed to keep only a portion of the total value of its notes in circulation in the form of gold and silver in its vaults. It could lend out the remaining gold and silver to those who wished to use it. This allowed society to use the remaining gold and silver for other purposes, all with no loss in the ability to achieve gains from trade.

In a famous passage in *The Wealth of Nations,* Adam Smith described paper money as a "waggon-way through the air." Smith was making an analogy between money and an imaginary highway that did not absorb valuable land beneath it. An actual highway provides a useful service but at a cost: land that could be used to grow crops is instead paved over. If the highway could be built through the air, it wouldn't destroy useful land. As Smith understood, when banks replaced gold and silver money with paper notes, they accomplished a similar feat: they reduced the amount of real resources used by society to provide the functions of money.

At this point you may ask: why make any use at all of gold and silver in the monetary system, even to back paper money? In fact, today's monetary system goes even further than the system Smith admired, having eliminated any role for gold and silver. A U.S. dollar bill isn't commodity money, and it isn't even commodity-backed. Rather, its value arises entirely from the fact that it is generally accepted as a means of payment, a role that is ultimately decreed by the U.S. government. Money whose value derives entirely from its official status as a means of exchange is known as **fiat money** because it exists by government fiat, a historical term for a policy declared by a ruler.

Fiat money has two major advantages over commodity-backed money. First, it is even more of a "waggon-way through the air"—creating it doesn't use up any real resources beyond the paper it's printed on. Second, the supply of money can be adjusted based on the needs of the economy, instead of being determined by the amount of gold and silver prospectors happen to discover.

Fiat money, though, poses some risks. In this chapter's opening story, we described one such risk—counterfeiting. Counterfeiters usurp a privilege of the U.S. government, which has the sole legal right to print dollar bills. And the benefit that counterfeiters get by exchanging fake bills for real goods and services comes at the expense of the U.S. federal government, which covers a small but nontrivial part of its own expenses by issuing new currency to meet a growing demand for money.

The larger risk is that governments that can create money whenever they feel like it will be tempted to abuse the privilege. In Chapter 16 we'll learn how governments sometimes rely too heavily on printing money to pay their bills, leading to high inflation. In this chapter, however, we'll stay focused on the question of what money is and how it is managed.

## Measuring the Money Supply

The Federal Reserve (an institution we'll talk about shortly) calculates the size of two **monetary aggregates,** overall measures of the money supply, which differ in how strictly money is defined. The two aggregates are known, rather cryptically, as M1 and M2. (There used to be a third aggregate named—you guessed it—M3, but in 2006 the Federal Reserve concluded that measuring it was no longer useful.)

M1, the narrowest definition, contains only currency in circulation (also known as cash), traveler's checks, and checkable bank deposits. M2 adds several other kinds of assets, often referred to as **near-moneys**—financial assets that aren't directly usable as a medium of exchange but can be readily converted into cash or checkable bank deposits, such as savings accounts. Examples are time deposits such

**Fiat money** is a medium of exchange whose value derives entirely from its official status as a means of payment.

A **monetary aggregate** is an overall measure of the money supply.

**Near-moneys** are financial assets that can't be directly used as a medium of exchange but can be readily converted into cash or checkable bank deposits.

⚠ **PITFALLS**

### WHAT'S NOT IN THE MONEY SUPPLY

Are financial assets like stocks and bonds part of the money supply? No, not under any definition, because they're not liquid enough.

M1 consists, roughly speaking, of assets you can use to buy groceries: currency, traveler's checks, and checkable deposits (which work as long as your grocery store accepts either checks or debit cards). M2 is broader, because it includes things like savings accounts that can easily and quickly be converted into M1. Normally, for example, you can switch funds between your savings and checking accounts with a click of a mouse or a call to an automated phone service.

By contrast, converting a stock or a bond into cash requires selling the stock or bond—something that usually takes some time and also involves paying a broker's fee. That makes these assets much less liquid than bank deposits. So stocks and bonds, unlike bank deposits, aren't considered money.

**FIGURE** **14-1** Monetary Aggregates, September 2011

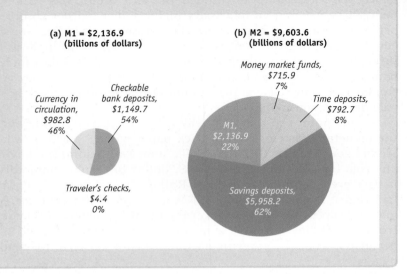

The Federal Reserve uses two definitions of the money supply, M1 and M2. As panel (a) shows, more than half of M1 consists of checkable bank deposits with currency in circulation making up virtually all of the rest. M2, as panel (b) shows, has a much broader definition: it includes M1 plus a range of other deposits and deposit-like assets, making it almost five times as large.

*Source:* Federal Reserve Bank of St. Louis.

as small-denomination CDs, which aren't checkable but can be withdrawn at any time before their maturity date by paying a penalty. Because currency and checkable deposits are directly usable as a medium of exchange, M1 is the most liquid measure of money.

Figure 14-1 shows the actual composition of M1 and M2 in September 2011, in billions of dollars. M1 was valued at $2,136.9 billion, with just under half accounted for by currency in circulation, almost all the rest accounted for by checkable bank deposits, and a tiny slice accounted for by traveler's checks. In turn, M1 made up 22% of M2, valued at $9,603.6 billion. M2 consists of M1 plus other types of assets: two types of bank deposits, known as savings deposits and time deposits, both of which are considered non-checkable, plus money market funds, which are mutual funds that invest only in liquid assets and bear a close resemblance to bank deposits. These near-moneys pay interest although cash (currency in circulation) does not, and they typically pay higher interest rates than any offered on checkable bank deposits.

## FOR INQUIRING MINDS

### WHAT'S WITH ALL THE CURRENCY?

Alert readers may be a bit startled at one of the numbers in the money supply: almost $1,000 billion of currency in circulation. That's just over $3,000 in cash for every man, woman, and child in the United States. How many people do you know who carry $3,000 in their wallets? Not many. So where is all that cash?

Part of the answer is that it isn't in individuals' wallets—it's in cash registers. Businesses as well as individuals need to hold cash.

Economists believe that cash also plays an important role in transactions that people want to keep hidden. Small businesses and the self-employed sometimes prefer to be paid in cash so they can avoid paying taxes by hiding income from the Internal Revenue Service. Also, drug dealers and other criminals obviously don't want bank records of their dealings. In fact, some analysts have tried to infer the amount of illegal activity in the economy from

the total amount of cash holdings held by the public.

The most important reason for those huge currency holdings, however, is foreign use of dollars. The Federal Reserve estimates that 60% of U.S. currency is actually held outside the United States—largely in countries in which residents are so distrustful of their national currencies that the U.S. dollar has become a widely accepted medium of exchange.

## ECONOMICS ▸ IN ACTION

### THE HISTORY OF THE DOLLAR

**U.S.** dollar bills are pure fiat money: they have no intrinsic value, and they are not backed by anything that does. But American money wasn't always like that. In the early days of European settlement, the colonies that would become the United States used commodity money, partly consisting of gold and silver coins minted in Europe. But such coins were scarce on this side of the Atlantic, so the colonists relied on a variety of other forms of commodity money. For example, settlers in Virginia used tobacco as money and settlers in the Northeast used "wampum," a type of clamshell.

Later in American history, commodity-backed paper money came into widespread use. But this wasn't paper money as we now know it, issued by the U.S. government and bearing the signature of the Secretary of the Treasury. Before the Civil War, the U.S. government didn't issue any paper money. Instead, dollar bills were issued by private banks, which promised that their bills could be redeemed for silver coins on demand. These promises weren't always credible because banks sometimes failed, leaving holders of their bills with worthless pieces of paper. Understandably, people were reluctant to accept currency from any bank rumored to be in financial trouble. In this private money system, some dollars were less valuable than others.

A curious legacy of that time was notes issued by the Citizens' Bank of Louisiana, based in New Orleans, that became among the most widely used bank notes in the southern states. These notes were printed in English on one side and French on the other. (At the time, many people in New Orleans, originally a colony of France, spoke French.) Thus, the $10 bill read *Ten* on one side and *Dix*, the French word for "ten," on the other. These $10 bills became known as "dixies," probably the source of the nickname of the U.S. South.

The U.S. government began issuing official paper money, called "greenbacks," during the Civil War, as a way to help pay for the war. At first greenbacks had no fixed value in terms of commodities. After 1873, the U.S. government guaranteed the value of a dollar in terms of gold, effectively turning dollars into commodity-backed money.

Not until the Civil War did the U.S. government issue official paper money.

In 1933, when President Franklin D. Roosevelt broke the link between dollars and gold, his own federal budget director—who feared that the public would lose confidence in the dollar if it wasn't ultimately backed by gold—declared ominously, "This will be the end of Western civilization." It wasn't. The link between the dollar and gold was restored a few years later, then dropped again—seemingly for good—in August 1971. Despite the warnings of doom, the U.S. dollar went on to become the world's most widely used currency. (Now it is the second-most widely used, after the euro.)

▶●●

### CHECK YOUR UNDERSTANDING    14-1

1. Suppose you hold a gift certificate, good for certain products at participating stores. Is this gift certificate money? Why or why not?

2. Although most bank accounts pay some interest, depositors can get a higher interest rate by buying a certificate of deposit, or CD. The difference between a CD and a checking account is that the depositor pays a penalty for withdrawing the money before the CD comes due—a period of months or even years. Small CDs are counted in M2 but not in M1. Explain why they are not part of M1.

3. Explain why a system of commodity-backed money uses resources more efficiently than a system of commodity money.

Solutions appear at back of book.

---

▼ **Quick Review**

- **Money** is any asset that can easily be used to purchase goods and services. **Currency in circulation** and **checkable bank deposits** are both part of the **money supply.**

- Money plays three roles: a **medium of exchange,** a **store of value,** and a **unit of account.**

- Historically, money took the form first of **commodity money,** then of **commodity-backed money.** Today the dollar is pure **fiat money.**

- The money supply is measured by two **monetary aggregates:** M1 and M2. M1 consists of currency in circulation, checkable bank deposits, and traveler's checks. M2 consists of M1 plus various kinds of **near-moneys.**

**Bank reserves** are the currency banks hold in their vaults plus their deposits at the Federal Reserve.

A **T-account** is a tool for analyzing a business's financial position by showing, in a single table, the business's assets (on the left) and liabilities (on the right).

# The Monetary Role of Banks

Roughly half of M1, the narrowest definition of the money supply, consists of currency in circulation—$1 bills, $5 bills, and so on. It's obvious where currency comes from: it's printed by the U.S. Treasury. But the rest of M1 consists of bank deposits, and deposits account for the great bulk of M2, the broader definition of the money supply. By either measure, then, bank deposits are a major component of the money supply. And this fact brings us to our next topic: the monetary role of banks.

## What Banks Do

As we learned in Chapter 10, a bank is a *financial intermediary* that uses liquid assets in the form of bank deposits to finance the illiquid investments of borrowers. Banks can create liquidity because it isn't necessary for a bank to keep all of the funds deposited with it in the form of highly liquid assets. Except in the case of a *bank run*—which we'll get to shortly—all of a bank's depositors won't want to withdraw their funds at the same time. So a bank can provide its depositors with liquid assets yet still invest much of the depositors' funds in illiquid assets, such as mortgages and business loans.

Banks can't, however, lend out all the funds placed in their hands by depositors because they have to satisfy any depositor who wants to withdraw his or her funds. In order to meet these demands, a bank must keep substantial quantities of liquid assets on hand. In the modern U.S. banking system, these assets take the form either of currency in the bank's vault or deposits held in the bank's own account at the Federal Reserve. As we'll see shortly, the latter can be converted into currency more or less instantly. Currency in bank vaults and bank deposits held at the Federal Reserve are called **bank reserves.** Because bank reserves are in bank vaults and at the Federal Reserve, not held by the public, they are not part of currency in circulation.

To understand the role of banks in determining the money supply, we start by introducing a simple tool for analyzing a bank's financial position: a **T-account.** A business's T-account summarizes its financial position by showing, in a single table, the business's assets and liabilities, with assets on the left and liabilities on the right.

Figure 14-2 shows the T-account for a hypothetical business that *isn't* a bank— Samantha's Smoothies. According to Figure 14-2, Samantha's Smoothies owns a building worth $30,000 and has $15,000 worth of smoothie-making equipment. These are assets, so they're on the left side of the table. To finance its opening, the business borrowed $20,000 from a local bank. That's a liability, so the loan is on the right side of the table. By looking at the T-account, you can immediately see what Samantha's Smoothies owns and what it owes. Oh, and it's called a T-account because the lines in the table make a T-shape.

Samantha's Smoothies is an ordinary, nonbank business. Now let's look at the T-account for a hypothetical bank, First Street Bank, which is the repository of $1 million in bank deposits.

**FIGURE** **14-2** A T-Account for Samantha's Smoothies

A T-account summarizes a business's financial position. Its assets, in this case consisting of a building and some smoothie-making machinery, are on the left side. Its liabilities, consisting of the money it owes to a local bank, are on the right side.

| Assets | | Liabilities | |
|---|---|---|---|
| Building | $30,000 | Loan from bank | $20,000 |
| Smoothie-making machines | $15,000 | | |

**14-3** Assets and Liabilities of First Street Bank

First Street Bank's assets consist of $1,200,000 in loans and $100,000 in reserves. Its liabilities consist of $1,000,000 in deposits—money owed to people who have placed funds in First Street's hands.

| Assets | | Liabilities | |
|---|---|---|---|
| Loans | $1,200,000 | Deposits | $1,000,000 |
| Reserves | $100,000 | | |

Figure 14-3 shows First Street Bank's financial position. The loans First Street Bank has made are on the left side because they're assets: they represent funds that those who have borrowed from the bank are expected to repay. The bank's only other assets, in this simplified example, are its reserves, which, as we've learned, can take the form either of cash in the bank's vault or deposits at the Federal Reserve. On the right side we show the bank's liabilities, which in this example consist entirely of deposits made by customers at First Street Bank. These are liabilities because they represent funds that must ultimately be repaid to depositors.

Notice, by the way, that in this example First Street Bank's assets are larger than its liabilities. That's the way it's supposed to be! In fact, as we'll see shortly, banks are required by law to maintain assets larger by a specific percentage than their liabilities.

In this example, First Street Bank holds reserves equal to 10% of its customers' bank deposits. The fraction of bank deposits that a bank holds as reserves is its **reserve ratio.** In the modern American system, the Federal Reserve—which, among other things, regulates banks operating in the United States—sets a minimum required reserve ratio that banks are required to maintain. To understand why banks are regulated, let's consider a problem banks can face: bank runs.

## The Problem of Bank Runs

A bank can lend out most of the funds deposited in its care because in normal times only a small fraction of its depositors want to withdraw their funds on any given day. But what would happen if, for some reason, all or at least a large fraction of its depositors did try to withdraw their funds during a short period of time, such as a couple of days?

If a significant share of its depositors demand their money back at the same time, the bank wouldn't be able to raise enough cash to meet those demands. The reason is that banks convert most of their depositors' funds into loans made to borrowers; that's how banks earn revenue—by charging interest on loans.

Bank loans, however, are illiquid: they can't easily be converted into cash on short notice. To see why, imagine that First Street Bank has lent $100,000 to Drive-A-Peach Used Cars, a local dealership. To raise cash to meet demands for withdrawals, First Street Bank can sell its loan to Drive-A-Peach to someone else—another bank or an individual investor. But if First Street Bank tries to sell the loan quickly, potential buyers will be wary: they will suspect that First Street Bank wants to sell the loan because there is something wrong and the loan might not be repaid. As a result, First Street Bank can sell the loan quickly only by offering it for sale at a deep discount—say, a discount of 40%, for a sale price of $60,000.

The upshot is that if a significant number of First Street Bank's depositors suddenly decided to withdraw their funds, the bank's efforts to raise the necessary cash quickly would force it to sell off its assets very cheaply. Inevitably, this leads to a *bank failure:* the bank would be unable to pay off its depositors in full.

The **reserve ratio** is the fraction of bank deposits that a bank holds as reserves.

A **bank run** is a phenomenon in which many of a bank's depositors try to withdraw their funds due to fears of a bank failure.

**Deposit insurance** guarantees that a bank's depositors will be paid even if the bank can't come up with the funds, up to a maximum amount per account.

What might start this whole process? That is, what might lead First Street Bank's depositors to rush to pull their money out? A plausible answer is a spreading rumor that the bank is in financial trouble. Even if depositors aren't sure the rumor is true, they are likely to play it safe and get their money out while they still can. And it gets worse: a depositor who simply thinks that *other* depositors are going to panic and try to get their money out will realize that this could "break the bank." So he or she joins the rush. In other words, fear about a bank's financial condition can be a self-fulfilling prophecy: depositors who believe that other depositors will rush to the exit will rush to the exit themselves.

A **bank run** is a phenomenon in which many of a bank's depositors try to withdraw their funds due to fears of a bank failure. Moreover, bank runs aren't bad only for the bank in question and its depositors. Historically, they have often proved contagious, with a run on one bank leading to a loss of faith in other banks, causing additional bank runs. The upcoming Economics in Action describes an actual case of just such a contagion, the wave of bank runs that swept across the United States in the early 1930s. In response to that experience and similar experiences in other countries, the United States and most other modern governments have established a system of bank regulations that protect depositors and prevent most bank runs. We'll encounter bank runs again in Chapter 17, which contains an in-depth analysis of financial crises and their aftermath.

## Bank Regulation

Should you worry about losing money in the United States due to a bank run? No. After the banking crises of the 1930s, the United States and most other countries put into place a system designed to protect depositors and the economy as a whole against bank runs. This system has four main features: *deposit insurance*, *capital requirements*, *reserve requirements*, and, in addition, banks have access to the *discount window*, a source of cash when it's needed.

**1. Deposit Insurance** Almost all banks in the United States advertise themselves as a "member of the FDIC"—the Federal Deposit Insurance Corporation. As we learned in Chapter 10, the FDIC provides **deposit insurance,** a guarantee that depositors will be paid even if the bank can't come up with the funds, up to a maximum amount per account. The FDIC currently guarantees the first $250,000 per depositor, per insured bank.

It's important to realize that deposit insurance doesn't just protect depositors if a bank actually fails. The insurance also eliminates the main reason for bank runs: since depositors know their funds are safe even if a bank fails, they have no incentive to rush to pull them out because of a rumor that the bank is in trouble.

**2. Capital Requirements** Deposit insurance, although it protects the banking system against bank runs, creates a well-known incentive problem. Because depositors are protected from loss, they have no incentive to monitor their bank's financial health, allowing risky behavior by the bank to go undetected. At the same time, the owners of banks have an incentive to engage in overly risky investment behavior, such as making questionable loans at high interest rates. That's because if all goes well, the owners profit; if things go badly, the government covers the losses through federal deposit insurance.

To reduce the incentive for excessive risk taking, regulators require that the owners of banks hold substantially more assets than the value of bank deposits. That way, the bank will still have assets larger than its deposits even if some of its loans go bad, and losses will accrue against the bank owners' assets, not the government. The excess of a bank's assets over its bank deposits and other liabilities is called the *bank's capital*. For example, First Street Bank has capital of $300,000, equal to $300,000/($1,200,000 + $100,000) = 23% of the total value of its assets. In practice, banks' capital is required to equal at least 7% of the value of their assets.

**3. Reserve Requirements**  Another regulation used to reduce the risk of bank runs is **reserve requirements,** rules set by the Federal Reserve that specify the minimum reserve ratio for banks. For example, in the United States, the minimum reserve ratio for checkable bank deposits is 10%.

**4. The Discount Window**  One final protection against bank runs is the fact that the Federal Reserve, which we'll discuss more thoroughly later in this chapter, stands ready to lend money to banks in trouble, an arrangement known as the **discount window.** The ability to borrow money means a bank can avoid being forced to sell its assets at fire-sale prices in order to satisfy the demands of a sudden rush of depositors demanding cash. Instead, it can turn to the Fed and borrow the funds it needs to pay off depositors.

> **Reserve requirements** are rules set by the Federal Reserve that determine the minimum reserve ratio for banks.
>
> The **discount window** is an arrangement in which the Federal Reserve stands ready to lend money to banks in trouble.

## ECONOMICS ❯ *IN ACTION*

### IT'S A WONDERFUL BANKING SYSTEM

**N**ext Christmastime, it's a sure thing that at least one TV channel will show the 1946 film *It's a Wonderful Life*, featuring Jimmy Stewart as George Bailey, a small-town banker whose life is saved by an angel. The movie's climactic scene is a run on Bailey's bank, as fearful depositors rush to take their funds out.

When the movie was made, such scenes were still fresh in Americans' memories. There was a wave of bank runs in late 1930, a second wave in the spring of 1931, and a third wave in early 1933. By the end, more than a third of the nation's banks had failed. To bring the panic to an end, on March 6, 1933, the newly inaugurated president, Franklin Delano Roosevelt, declared a national "bank holiday," closing all banks for a week to give bank regulators time to close unhealthy banks and certify healthy ones.

Since then, regulation has protected the United States and other wealthy countries against most bank runs. In fact, the scene in *It's a Wonderful Life* was already out of date when the movie was made. But recent decades have seen several waves of bank runs in developing countries. For example, bank runs played a role in an economic crisis that swept Southeast Asia in 1997–1998 and in the severe economic crisis in Argentina that began in late 2001. And as explained in Chapter 17, a "panic" with strong resemblance to a wave of bank runs swept world financial markets in 2008.

Notice that we said "most bank runs." There are some limits on deposit insurance; in particular, in the United States currently only the first $250,000 of an individual depositor's funds in an insured bank is covered. As a result, there can still be a run on a bank perceived as troubled. In fact, that's exactly what happened to IndyMac in July 2008, a Pasadena-based lender that had made a large number of questionable home loans. As questions about IndyMac's financial soundness were raised, depositors began pulling out funds, forcing federal regulators to step in and close the bank. In Britain the limits on deposit insurance are much lower, which

In July 2008, panicky IndyMac depositors lined up to pull their money out of the troubled California bank.

*Gabriel Bouys/AFP/Getty Images*

exposed the bank Northern Rock to a classic bank run that same year. Unlike in the bank runs of the 1930s, however, most depositors at both IndyMac and Northern Rock got all their funds back—and the panics at these banks didn't spread to other institutions.

**CHECK YOUR UNDERSTANDING   14-2**

1. Suppose you are a depositor at First Street Bank. You hear a rumor that the bank has suffered serious losses on its loans. Every depositor knows that the rumor isn't true, but each thinks that most other depositors believe the rumor. Why, in the absence of deposit insurance, could this lead to a bank run? How does deposit insurance change the situation?

2. A con artist has a great idea: he'll open a bank without investing any capital and lend all the deposits at high interest rates to real estate developers. If the real estate market booms, the loans will be repaid and he'll make high profits. If the real estate market goes bust, the loans won't be repaid and the bank will fail—but he will not lose any of his own wealth. How would modern bank regulation frustrate his scheme?

Solutions appear at back of book.

# Determining the Money Supply

**W**ithout banks, there would be no checkable deposits, so the quantity of currency in circulation would equal the money supply. In that case, the money supply would be solely determined by whoever controls government minting and printing presses. But banks do exist, and through their creation of checkable bank deposits they affect the money supply in two ways. First, banks remove some currency from circulation: dollar bills that are sitting in bank vaults, as opposed to sitting in people's wallets, aren't part of the money supply. Second, and much more importantly, banks create money by accepting deposits and making loans—that is, they make the money supply larger than just the value of currency in circulation. Our next topic is how banks create money and what determines the amount of money they create.

## How Banks Create Money

To see how banks create money, let's examine what happens when someone decides to deposit currency in a bank. Consider the example of Silas, a miser, who keeps a shoebox full of cash under his bed. Suppose Silas realizes that it would be safer, as well as more convenient, to deposit that cash in the bank and to use his debit card when shopping. Assume that he deposits $1,000 into a checkable account at First Street Bank. What effect will Silas's actions have on the money supply?

Panel (a) of Figure 14-4 shows the initial effect of his deposit. First Street Bank credits Silas with $1,000 in his account, so the economy's checkable bank deposits rise by $1,000. Meanwhile, Silas's cash goes into the vault, raising First Street's reserves by $1,000 as well.

This initial transaction has no effect on the money supply. Currency in circulation, part of the money supply, falls by $1,000; checkable bank deposits, also part of the money supply, rise by the same amount.

But this is not the end of the story because First Street Bank can now lend out part of Silas's deposit. Assume that it holds 10% of Silas's deposit—$100—in reserves and lends the rest out in cash to Silas's neighbor, Maya. The effect of this second stage is shown in panel (b). First Street's deposits remain unchanged, and so does the value of its assets. But the composition of its assets changes: by

## FIGURE 14-4 Effect on the Money Supply of Turning Cash into a Checkable Deposit at First Street Bank

**(a) Initial Effect Before Bank Makes a New Loan**

| Assets | | Liabilities | |
|---|---|---|---|
| Loans | No change | Checkable deposits | +$1,000 |
| Reserves | +$1,000 | | |

**(b) Effect When Bank Makes a New Loan**

| Assets | | Liabilities |
|---|---|---|
| Loans | +$900 | No change |
| Reserves | −$900 | |

When Silas deposits $1,000 (which had been stashed under his bed) into a checkable bank account, there is initially no effect on the money supply: currency in circulation falls by $1,000, but checkable bank deposits rise by $1,000. The corresponding entries on the bank's T-account, depicted in panel (a), show deposits initially rising by $1,000 and the bank's reserves initially rising by $1,000. In

the second stage, depicted in panel (b), the bank holds 10% of Silas's deposit ($100) as reserves and lends out the rest ($900) to Maya. As a result, its reserves fall by $900 and its loans increase by $900. Its liabilities, including Silas's $1,000 deposit, are unchanged. The money supply, the sum of checkable bank deposits and currency in circulation, has now increased by $900—the $900 now held by Maya.

making the loan, it reduces its reserves by $900, so that they are only $100 larger than they were before Silas made his deposit. In the place of the $900 reduction in reserves, the bank has acquired an IOU, its $900 cash loan to Maya.

So by putting $900 of Silas's cash back into circulation by lending it to Maya, First Street Bank has, in fact, increased the money supply. That is, the sum of currency in circulation and checkable bank deposits has risen by $900 compared to what it had been when Silas's cash was still under his bed. Although Silas is still the owner of $1,000, now in the form of a checkable deposit, Maya has the use of $900 in cash from her borrowings.

And this may not be the end of the story. Suppose that Maya uses her cash to buy a television and a DVD player from Acme Merchandise. What does Anne Acme, the store's owner, do with the cash? If she holds on to it, the money supply doesn't increase any further. But suppose she deposits the $900 into a checkable bank deposit—say, at Second Street Bank. Second Street Bank, in turn, will keep only part of that deposit in reserves, lending out the rest, creating still more money.

Assume that Second Street Bank, like First Street Bank, keeps 10% of any bank deposit in reserves and lends out the rest. Then it will keep $90 in reserves and lend out $810 of Anne's deposit to another borrower, further increasing the money supply.

Table 14-1 shows the process of money creation we have described so far. At first the money supply consists only of Silas's $1,000. After he deposits the cash into a checkable bank deposit and the bank makes a loan, the money supply rises to $1,900. After the second deposit and the second loan, the money supply rises to $2,710. And the process will, of course, continue from there. (Although we have considered the case in which Silas places his cash in a checkable bank deposit, the results would be the same if he put it into any type of near-money.)

This process of money creation may sound familiar. In Chapter 11 we described the *multiplier process:* an initial increase in real GDP leads to a rise

### TABLE 14-1 How Banks Create Money

| | Currency in circulation | Checkable bank deposits | Money supply |
|---|---|---|---|
| **First stage:** Silas keeps his cash under his bed. | $1,000 | $0 | $1,000 |
| **Second stage:** Silas deposits cash in First Street Bank, which lends out $900 to Maya, who then pays it to Anne Acme. | 900 | 1,000 | 1,900 |
| **Third stage:** Anne Acme deposits $900 in Second Street Bank, which lends out $810 to another borrower. | 810 | 1,900 | 2,710 |

**Excess reserves** are a bank's reserves over and above its required reserves.

in consumer spending, which leads to a further rise in real GDP, which leads to a further rise in consumer spending, and so on. What we have here is another kind of multiplier—the *money multiplier*. Next, we'll learn what determines the size of this multiplier.

## Reserves, Bank Deposits, and the Money Multiplier

In tracing out the effect of Silas's deposit in Table 14-1, we assumed that the funds a bank lends out always end up being deposited either in the same bank or in another bank—so funds disbursed as loans come back to the banking system, even if not to the lending bank itself.

In reality, some of these loaned funds may be held by borrowers in their wallets and not deposited in a bank, meaning that some of the loaned amount "leaks" out of the banking system. Such leaks reduce the size of the money multiplier, just as leaks of real income into savings reduce the size of the real GDP multiplier. (Bear in mind, however, that the "leak" here comes from the fact that borrowers keep some of their funds in currency, rather than the fact that consumers save some of their income.)

But let's set that complication aside for a moment and consider how the money supply is determined in a "checkable-deposits-only" monetary system, where funds are always deposited in bank accounts and none are held in wallets as currency. That is, in our checkable-deposits-only monetary system, any and all funds borrowed from a bank are immediately deposited into a checkable bank account. We'll assume that banks are required to satisfy a minimum reserve ratio of 10% and that every bank lends out all of its **excess reserves,** reserves over and above the amount needed to satisfy the minimum reserve ratio.

Now suppose that for some reason a bank suddenly finds itself with $1,000 in excess reserves. What happens? The answer is that the bank will lend out that $1,000, which will end up as a checkable bank deposit somewhere in the banking system, launching a money multiplier process very similar to the process shown in Table 14-1.

In the first stage, the bank lends out its excess reserves of $1,000, which becomes a checkable bank deposit somewhere. The bank that receives the $1,000 deposit keeps 10%, or $100, as reserves and lends out the remaining 90%, or $900, which again becomes a checkable bank deposit somewhere. The bank receiving this $900 deposit again keeps 10%, which is $90, as reserves and lends out the remaining $810. The bank receiving this $810 keeps $81 in reserves and lends out the remaining $729, and so on. As a result of this process, the total increase in checkable bank deposits is equal to a sum that looks like:

$$\$1,000 + \$900 + \$810 + \$729 + \ldots$$

We'll use the symbol *rr* for the reserve ratio. More generally, the total increase in checkable bank deposits that is generated when a bank lends out $1,000 in excess reserves is:

**(14-1)** Increase in checkable bank deposits from $1,000 in excess reserves =
$\$1,000 + (\$1,000 \times (1 - rr)) + (\$1,000 \times (1 - rr)^2) + (\$1,000 \times (1 - rr)^3) + \ldots$

As we saw in Chapter 11, an infinite series of this form can be simplified to:

**(14-2)** Increase in checkable bank deposits from $1,000 in excess reserves =
$\$1,000/rr$

Given a reserve ratio of 10%, or 0.1, a $1,000 increase in excess reserves will increase the total value of checkable bank deposits by $1,000/0.1 = $10,000. In fact, in a checkable-deposits-only monetary system, the total value of checkable bank deposits will be equal to the value of bank reserves divided by the reserve ratio. Or to put it a different way, if the reserve ratio is 10%, each $1 of reserves held by a bank supports $1/$rr$ = $1/0.1 = $10 of checkable bank deposits.

> The **monetary base** is the sum of currency in circulation and bank reserves.

## The Money Multiplier in Reality

In reality, the determination of the money supply is more complicated than our simple model suggests because it depends not only on the ratio of reserves to bank deposits but also on the fraction of the money supply that individuals choose to hold in the form of currency. In fact, we already saw this in our example of Silas depositing the cash under his bed: when he chose to hold a checkable bank deposit instead of currency, he set in motion an increase in the money supply.

To define the money multiplier in practice, it's important to recognize that the Federal Reserve controls the *sum* of bank reserves and currency in circulation, called the *monetary base,* but it does not control the allocation of that sum between bank reserves and currency in circulation. Consider Silas and his deposit one more time: by taking the cash from under his bed and depositing it in a bank, he reduced the quantity of currency in circulation but increased bank reserves by an equal amount—leaving the *monetary base,* on net, unchanged. The **monetary base,** which is the quantity the monetary authorities control, is the sum of currency in circulation and reserves held by banks.

The monetary base is different from the money supply in two ways. First, bank reserves, which are part of the monetary base, aren't considered part of the money supply. A $1 bill in someone's wallet is considered money because it's available for an individual to spend, but a $1 bill held as bank reserves in a bank vault or deposited at the Federal Reserve isn't considered part of the money supply because it's not available for spending. Second, checkable bank deposits, which are part of the money supply because they are available for spending, aren't part of the monetary base.

Figure 14-5 shows the two concepts schematically. The circle on the left represents the monetary base, consisting of bank reserves plus currency in circulation.

FIGURE **14-5** The Monetary Base and the Money Supply

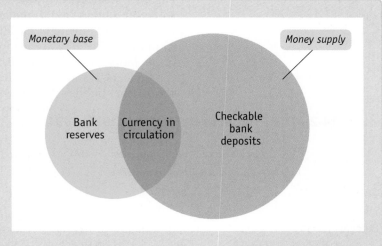

The monetary base is equal to bank reserves plus currency in circulation. It is different from the money supply, consisting mainly of checkable or near-checkable bank deposits plus currency in circulation. Each dollar of bank reserves backs several dollars of bank deposits, making the money supply larger than the monetary base.

The **money multiplier** is the ratio of the money supply to the monetary base.

The circle on the right in Figure 14-5 represents the money supply, consisting mainly of currency in circulation plus checkable or near-checkable bank deposits. As the figure indicates, currency in circulation is part of both the monetary base and the money supply. But bank reserves aren't part of the money supply, and checkable or near-checkable bank deposits aren't part of the monetary base. In practice, most of the monetary base actually consists of currency in circulation, which also makes up about half of the money supply.

Now we can formally define the **money multiplier:** it's the ratio of the money supply to the monetary base. In normal times the money multiplier in the United States, using M1 as our measure of money, has fluctuated between 3.0 and 1.5. During the recession of 2007–2009, it fell to about 0.7. Even in normal times, that's a lot smaller than 1/0.1 = 10, the money multiplier in a checkable-deposits-only system with a reserve ratio of 10% (the minimum required ratio for most checkable deposits in the United States). The reason the actual money multiplier is so small arises from the fact that people hold significant amounts of cash, and a dollar of currency in circulation, unlike a dollar in reserves, doesn't support multiple dollars of the money supply. In fact, currency in circulation normally accounts for more than 90% of the monetary base. However, in January 2012, currency in circulation was $1,069 billion, compared with a monetary base of $2,659 billion—just about 40%. What had happened?

Notice that earlier we said "in normal times." As explained later in this chapter, and at greater length in Chapter 17, a very abnormal situation developed after Lehman Brothers, a key financial institution, failed in September 2008. Banks, seeing few opportunities for safe, profitable lending, began parking large sums at the Federal Reserve in the form of deposits—deposits that counted as part of the monetary base. As a result, currency in circulation in January 2012 made up only 40% of the monetary base, and in 2011 the monetary base was actually larger than M1, with the money multiplier therefore less than 1.

## ECONOMICS ▶ IN ACTION

### MULTIPLYING MONEY DOWN

In our hypothetical example illustrating how banks create money, we described Silas the miser taking the currency from under his bed and turning it into a checkable bank deposit. This led to an increase in the money supply, as banks engaged in successive waves of lending backed by Silas's funds. It follows that if something happened to make Silas revert to old habits, taking his money out of the bank and putting it back under his bed, the result would be less lending and, ultimately, a decline in the money supply. That's exactly what happened as a result of the bank runs of the 1930s.

Table 14-2 shows what happened between 1929 and 1933, as bank failures shook the public's confidence in the banking system. The second column shows the public's holdings of currency. This increased sharply, as many Americans decided that money under the bed was safer than money in the bank after all. The third column shows the value of checkable bank deposits. This fell sharply, through the multiplier process we have just analyzed, when individuals pulled their cash out of banks. Loans also fell because banks that survived the waves of bank runs increased their excess reserves, just in case another wave began. The fourth column shows the value of M1, the first of the monetary

**TABLE 14-2 The Effects of Bank Runs, 1929–1933**

| | Currency in circulation | Checkable bank deposits | M1 |
|---|---|---|---|
| | (billions of dollars) | | |
| 1929 | $3.90 | $22.74 | $26.64 |
| 1933 | 5.09 | 14.82 | 19.91 |
| Percent change | +31% | −35% | −25% |

Source: U.S. Census Bureau (1975), *Historical Statistics of the United States.*

aggregates we described earlier. It fell sharply because the total reduction in checkable or near-checkable bank deposits was much larger than the increase in currency in circulation.

### CHECK YOUR UNDERSTANDING    14-3

1. Assume that total reserves are equal to $200 and total checkable bank deposits are equal to $1,000. Also assume that the public does not hold any currency. Now suppose that the required reserve ratio falls from 20% to 10%. Trace out how this leads to an expansion in bank deposits.

2. Take the example of Silas depositing his $1,000 in cash into First Street Bank and assume that the required reserve ratio is 10%. But now assume that each time someone receives a bank loan, he or she keeps half the loan in cash. Trace out the resulting expansion in the money supply.

*Solutions appear at back of book.*

# The Federal Reserve System

Who's in charge of ensuring that banks maintain enough reserves? Who decides how large the monetary base will be? The answer, in the United States, is an institution known as the Federal Reserve (or, informally, as "the Fed"). The Federal Reserve is a **central bank**—an institution that oversees and regulates the banking system and controls the monetary base. Other central banks include the Bank of England, the Bank of Japan, and the European Central Bank, or ECB. The ECB acts as a common central bank for 17 European countries: Austria, Belgium, Cyprus, Estonia, Finland, France, Germany, Greece, Ireland, Italy, Luxembourg, Malta, the Netherlands, Portugal, Slovakia, Slovenia, and Spain. The world's oldest central bank, by the way, is Sweden's Sveriges Rijksbank, which awards the Nobel Prize in economics.

## The Structure of the Fed

The legal status of the Fed, which was created in 1913, is unusual: it is not exactly part of the U.S. government, but it is not really a private institution either. Strictly speaking, the Federal Reserve system consists of two parts: the Board of Governors and the 12 regional Federal Reserve Banks.

The Board of Governors, which oversees the entire system from its offices in Washington, D.C., is constituted like a government agency: its seven members are appointed by the president and must be approved by the Senate. However, they are appointed for 14-year terms, to insulate them from political pressure in their conduct of monetary policy. (Why this is a potential problem will become clear in Chapter 16, when we discuss inflation.) Although the chairman is appointed more frequently—every four years—it's traditional for chairmen to be reappointed and serve much longer terms. For example, William McChesney Martin was chairman of the Fed from 1951 until 1970. Alan Greenspan, appointed in 1987, served as the Fed's chairman until 2006.

The 12 Federal Reserve Banks each serve a region of the country, providing various banking and supervisory services. One of their jobs, for example, is to audit the books of private-sector banks to ensure their financial health. Each regional bank is run by a board of directors chosen from the local banking and business community. The Federal Reserve Bank of New York plays a special role: it carries out *open-market operations,* usually the main tool of monetary policy.

A **central bank** is an institution that oversees and regulates the banking system and controls the monetary base.

FIGURE **14-6**
## The Federal Reserve System

The Federal Reserve system consists of the Board of Governors in Washington, D.C., plus 12 regional Federal Reserve Banks. This map shows each of the 12 Federal Reserve districts.

*Source:* Board of Governors of the Federal Reserve System.

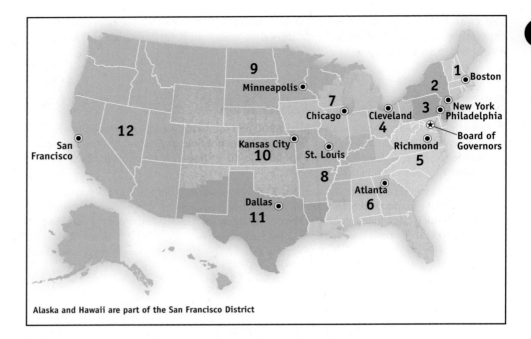

Alaska and Hawaii are part of the San Francisco District

Figure 14-6 shows the 12 Federal Reserve districts and the city in which each regional Federal Reserve Bank is located.

Decisions about monetary policy are made by the Federal Open Market Committee, which consists of the Board of Governors plus five of the regional bank presidents. The president of the Federal Reserve Bank of New York is always on the committee, and the other four seats rotate among the 11 other regional bank presidents. The chairman of the Board of Governors normally also serves as the chairman of the Open Market Committee.

The effect of this complex structure is to create an institution that is ultimately accountable to the voting public because the Board of Governors is chosen by the president and confirmed by the Senate, all of whom are themselves elected officials. But the long terms served by board members, as well as the indirectness of their appointment process, largely insulate them from short-term political pressures.

## What the Fed Does: Reserve Requirements and the Discount Rate

The Fed has three main policy tools at its disposal: *reserve requirements,* the *discount rate,* and, most importantly, *open-market operations.*

In our discussion of bank runs, we noted that the Fed sets a minimum reserve ratio requirement, currently equal to 10% for checkable bank deposits. Banks that fail to maintain at least the required reserve ratio on average over a two-week period face penalties.

What does a bank do if it looks as if it has insufficient reserves to meet the Fed's reserve requirement? Normally, it borrows additional reserves from other banks via the **federal funds market,** a financial market that allows banks that fall short of the reserve requirement to borrow reserves (usually just overnight) from banks that are holding excess reserves. The interest rate in this market is determined by supply and demand—but the supply and demand for bank reserves are both strongly affected by Federal Reserve actions. As we'll see in the next chapter, the **federal funds rate,** the interest rate at which funds are borrowed and lent in the federal funds market, plays a key role in modern monetary policy.

The **federal funds market** allows banks that fall short of the reserve requirement to borrow funds from banks with excess reserves.

The **federal funds rate** is the interest rate determined in the federal funds market.

Alternatively, banks in need of reserves can borrow from the Fed itself via the *discount window*. The **discount rate** is the rate of interest the Fed charges on those loans. Normally, the discount rate is set 1 percentage point above the federal funds rate in order to discourage banks from turning to the Fed when they are in need of reserves. Beginning in the fall of 2007, however, the Fed reduced the spread between the federal funds rate and the discount rate as part of its response to an ongoing financial crisis, described in the upcoming Economics in Action. As a result, by the spring of 2008 the discount rate was only 0.25 percentage point above the federal funds rate. And by January 2012 the discount rate was still only 0.65 percentage point above the federal funds rate.

In order to alter the money supply, the Fed can change reserve requirements, the discount rate, or both. If the Fed reduces reserve requirements, banks will lend a larger percentage of their deposits, leading to more loans and an increase in the money supply via the money multiplier. Alternatively, if the Fed increases reserve requirements, banks are forced to reduce their lending, leading to a fall in the money supply via the money multiplier. If the Fed reduces the spread between the discount rate and the federal funds rate, the cost to banks of being short of reserves falls; banks respond by increasing their lending, and the money supply increases via the money multiplier. If the Fed increases the spread between the discount rate and the federal funds rate, bank lending falls—and so will the money supply via the money multiplier.

Under current practice, however, the Fed doesn't use changes in reserve requirements to actively manage the money supply. The last significant change in reserve requirements was in 1992. The Fed normally doesn't use the discount rate either, although, as we mentioned earlier, there was a temporary surge in lending through the discount window beginning in 2007 in response to a financial crisis. Ordinarily, normal monetary policy is conducted almost exclusively using the Fed's third policy tool: open-market operations.

The **discount rate** is the rate of interest the Fed charges on loans to banks.

An **open-market operation** is a purchase or sale of government debt by the Fed.

## Open-Market Operations

Like the banks it oversees, the Federal Reserve has assets and liabilities. The Fed's assets normally consist of holdings of debt issued by the U.S. government, mainly short-term U.S. government bonds with a maturity of less than one year, known as U.S. Treasury bills. Remember, the Fed isn't exactly part of the U.S. government, so U.S. Treasury bills held by the Fed are a liability of the government but an asset of the Fed. The Fed's liabilities consist of currency in circulation and bank reserves. Figure 14-7 summarizes the normal assets and liabilities of the Fed in the form of a T-account.

In an **open-market operation** the Federal Reserve buys or sells U.S. Treasury bills, normally through a transaction with *commercial banks*—banks that mainly make business loans, as opposed to home loans. The Fed never buys U.S. Treasury bills directly from the federal government. There's a good reason for this: when a central bank buys government debt directly from the government, it is lending directly to the government—in effect, the central bank is printing money to finance the government's budget deficit. As we'll

**FIGURE   14-7   The Federal Reserve's Assets and Liabilities**

The Federal Reserve holds its assets mostly in short-term government bonds called U.S. Treasury bills. Its liabilities are the monetary base—currency in circulation plus bank reserves.

| Assets | Liabilities |
|---|---|
| Government debt (Treasury bills) | Monetary base (currency in circulation + bank reserves) |

see later in the book, this has historically been a formula for disastrously high levels of inflation.

The two panels of Figure 14-8 show the changes in the financial position of both the Fed and commercial banks that result from open-market operations. When the Fed buys U.S. Treasury bills from a commercial bank, it pays by crediting the bank's reserve account by an amount equal to the value of the Treasury bills. This is illustrated in panel (a): the Fed buys $100 million of U.S. Treasury bills from commercial banks, which increases the monetary base by $100 million because it increases bank reserves by $100 million. When the Fed sells U.S. Treasury bills to commercial banks, it debits the banks' accounts, reducing their reserves. This is shown in panel (b), where the Fed sells $100 million of U.S. Treasury bills. Here, bank reserves and the monetary base decrease.

You might wonder where the Fed gets the funds to purchase U.S. Treasury bills from banks. The answer is that it simply creates them with a stroke of the pen—or, these days, a click of the mouse—that credits the banks' accounts with extra reserves. (The Fed prints money to pay for Treasury bills only when banks want the additional reserves in the form of currency.) Remember, the modern dollar is fiat money, which isn't backed by anything. So the Fed can create additional monetary base at its own discretion.

The change in bank reserves caused by an open-market operation doesn't directly affect the money supply. Instead, it starts the money multiplier in motion. After the $100 million increase in reserves shown in panel (a) of Figure 14-8, commercial banks would lend out their additional reserves, immediately increasing the money supply by $100 million. Some of those loans would be deposited back into the banking system, increasing reserves again and permitting a further round of loans, and so on, leading to a rise

FIGURE **14-8** Open-Market Operations by the Federal Reserve

| **(a) An Open-Market Purchase of $100 Million** | | | | |
|---|---|---|---|---|
| | **Assets** | | **Liabilities** | |
| **Federal Reserve** | Treasury bills | +$100 million | Monetary base | +$100 million |

| | **Assets** | | **Liabilities** | |
|---|---|---|---|---|
| **Commercial banks** | Treasury bills | −$100 million | No change | |
| | Reserves | +$100 million | | |

| **(b) An Open-Market Sale of $100 Million** | | | | |
|---|---|---|---|---|
| | **Assets** | | **Liabilities** | |
| **Federal Reserve** | Treasury bills | −$100 million | Monetary base | −$100 million |

| | **Assets** | | **Liabilities** | |
|---|---|---|---|---|
| **Commercial banks** | Treasury bills | +$100 million | No change | |
| | Reserves | −$100 million | | |

In panel (a), the Federal Reserve increases the monetary base by purchasing U.S. Treasury bills from private commercial banks in an open-market operation. Here, a $100 million purchase of U.S. Treasury bills by the Federal Reserve is paid for by a $100 million addition to private bank reserves, generating a $100 million increase in the monetary base. This will ultimately lead to an increase in the money supply via the money multiplier as banks lend out some of these new reserves. In panel (b), the Federal Reserve reduces the monetary base by selling U.S. Treasury bills to private commercial banks in an open-market operation. Here, a $100 million sale of U.S. Treasury bills leads to a $100 million reduction in private bank reserves, resulting in a $100 million decrease in the monetary base. This will ultimately lead to a fall in the money supply via the money multiplier as banks reduce their loans in response to a fall in their reserves.

## FOR INQUIRING MINDS

### WHO GETS THE INTEREST ON THE FED'S ASSETS?

As we've just learned, the Fed owns a lot of assets—Treasury bills—that it bought from commercial banks in exchange for monetary base in the form of credits to banks' reserve accounts. These assets pay interest. Yet the Fed's liabilities consist mainly of the monetary base, liabilities on which the Fed normally *doesn't* pay interest. So the Fed is, in effect, an institution that has the privilege of borrowing funds at a zero interest rate and lending them out at a positive interest rate. That sounds like a pretty profitable business. Who gets the profits?

The answer is, you do—or rather, U.S. taxpayers do. The Fed keeps some of the interest it receives to finance its operations but turns most of it over to

the U.S. Treasury. For example, in 2010 the Federal Reserve system received $79.301 billion in interest income (most of it in interest on its holdings of Treasury bills and on government-sponsored mortgage-backed securities), of which $79.268 billion was returned to the Treasury.

We can now finish the chapter's opening story—the impact of those forged $100 bills allegedly printed in North Korea. When a fake $100 bill enters circulation, it has the same economic effect as a real $100 bill printed by the U.S. government. That is, as long as nobody catches the forgery, the fake bill serves, for all practical purposes, as part of the monetary base.

Meanwhile, the Fed decides on the size of the monetary base based on economic considerations—in particular, the Fed doesn't let the monetary base get too large because that can cause higher inflation. So every fake $100 bill that enters circulation basically means that the Fed prints one less real $100 bill. When the Fed prints a $100 bill legally, however, it gets Treasury bills in return—and the interest on those bills helps pay for the U.S. government's expenses. So a counterfeit $100 bill reduces the amount of Treasury bills the Fed can acquire and thereby reduces the interest payments going to the Fed and the U.S. Treasury. Taxpayers, then, bear the real cost of counterfeiting.

in the money supply. An open-market sale has the reverse effect: bank reserves fall, requiring banks to reduce their loans, leading to a fall in the money supply.

Economists often say, loosely, that the Fed controls the money supply—checkable deposits plus currency in circulation. In fact, it controls only the monetary base—bank reserves plus currency in circulation. But by increasing or reducing the monetary base, the Fed can exert a powerful influence on both the money supply and interest rates. This influence is the basis of monetary policy, the subject of our next chapter.

## The European Central Bank

As we noted earlier, the Fed is only one of a number of central banks around the world, and it's much younger than Sweden's Sveriges Rijksbank and Britain's Bank of England. In general, other central banks operate in much the same way as the Fed. That's especially true of the only other central bank that rivals the Fed in terms of importance to the world economy: the European Central Bank.

The European Central Bank, known as the ECB, was created in January 1999 when 11 European nations abandoned their national currencies and adopted the euro as their common currency and placed their joint monetary policy in the ECB's hands. (Six more countries have joined since 1999.) The ECB instantly became an extremely important institution: although no single European nation has an economy anywhere near as large as that of the United States, the combined economies of the eurozone, the group of countries that have adopted the euro as their currency, are roughly as big as the U.S. economy. As a result, the ECB and the Fed are the two giants of the monetary world.

Like the Fed, the ECB has a special status: it's not a private institution, but it's not exactly a government agency either. In fact, it can't be a government agency because there is no pan-European government! Luckily for puzzled Americans, there are strong analogies between European central banking and the Federal Reserve system.

First of all, the ECB, which is located in the German city of Frankfurt, isn't really the counterpart of the whole Federal Reserve system: it's the equivalent of the Board of Governors in Washington. The European counterparts of the regional Federal Reserve Banks are Europe's national central banks: the Bank of France, the Bank of Italy, and so on. Until 1999, each of these national banks was its country's equivalent to the Fed. For example, the Bank of France controlled the French monetary base.

Today these national banks, like regional Feds, provide various financial services to local banks and businesses and conduct open-market operations, but the making of monetary policy has moved upstream to the ECB. Still, the various European national central banks aren't small institutions: in total, they employ more than 50,000 people; in December 2010, the ECB employed only 1,607.

In the eurozone, each country chooses who runs its own national central bank. The ECB's Executive Board is the counterpart of the Fed's Board of Governors; its members are chosen by unanimous consent of the eurozone national governments. The counterpart of the Federal Open Market Committee is the ECB's Governing Council. Just as the Fed's Open Market Committee consists of the Board of Governors plus a rotating group of regional Fed presidents, the ECB's Governing Council consists of the Executive Board plus the heads of the national central banks.

Like the Fed, the ECB is ultimately answerable to voters but given the fragmentation of political forces across national boundaries, it appears to be even more insulated than the Fed from short-term political pressures.

## ECONOMICS ▶ IN ACTION

### THE FED'S BALANCE SHEET, NORMAL AND ABNORMAL

Figure 14-7 showed a simplified version of the Fed's balance sheet. Here, liabilities consisted entirely of the monetary base and assets consisted entirely of Treasury bills. This is an oversimplification because the Fed's operations are more complicated in reality and its balance sheet contains a number of additional things. But, in normal times, Figure 14-7 is a reasonable approximation: the monetary base typically accounts for 90% of the Fed's liabilities, and 90% of its assets are in the form of claims on the U.S. Treasury (as in Treasury bills).

But in late 2007 it became painfully clear that we were no longer in normal times. The source of the turmoil was the bursting of a huge housing bubble, described in Chapter 10, which led to massive losses for financial institutions that had made mortgage loans or held mortgage-related assets. This led to a widespread loss of confidence in the financial system.

As we'll describe in more detail in the next section, not only standard deposit-taking banks were in trouble, but also non-depository financial institutions—financial institutions that did not accept customer deposits. Because they carried a lot of debt, faced huge losses from the collapse of the housing bubble, and held illiquid assets, panic hit these "nonbank banks." Within hours the financial system was frozen as financial institutions experienced what were essentially bank runs. For example, in 2008, many investors became worried about the health of Bear Stearns, a Wall Street non-depository financial institution that engaged in complex financial deals, buying and selling financial assets with borrowed funds. When confidence in Bear Stearns dried up, the firm found itself unable to raise the funds it needed to deliver on its end of these deals and it quickly spiraled into collapse.

The Fed sprang into action to contain what was becoming a meltdown across the entire financial sector. It greatly expanded its discount window—making huge loans to deposit-taking banks as well as non-depository financial institutions such as Wall Street financial firms. This gave financial institutions the liquidity that the financial market had now denied them. And as these firms took advantage of the ability to borrow cheaply from the Fed, they pledged their assets on hand as collateral—a motley collection of real estate loans, business loans, and so on.

Examining Figure 14-9, we see that starting in mid-2008, the Fed sharply reduced its holdings of traditional securities like Treasury bills, as its lending to financial institutions skyrocketed. "Lending to financial institutions" refers to discount window lending, but also loans the Fed made directly to firms like Bear Stearns. "Liquidity to key credit markets" covers purchases by the Fed of assets like corporate bonds, which was necessary to keep interest rates on loans to firms from soaring. Finally, "Federal agency debt" is the debt of Fannie Mae and Freddie Mac, the government-sponsored home mortgage agencies, which the Fed was also compelled to buy in order to prevent collapse in the mortgage market.

As the crisis subsided in late 2009, the Fed didn't return to its traditional asset holdings. Instead, it shifted into long-term Treasury bills and increased its purchases of Federal agency debt. The whole episode was very unusual—a major departure from the way in which the Fed normally conducts business, but one that it deemed necessary to stave off financial and economic collapse. It was also a graphic illustration of the fact that the Fed does much more than just determine the size of the monetary base.

**FIGURE 14-9 The Federal Reserve's Assets**

Source: Federal Reserve Bank of Cleveland.

---

**CHECK YOUR UNDERSTANDING    14-4**

1. Assume that any money lent by a bank is always deposited back in the banking system as a checkable deposit and that the reserve ratio is 10%. Trace out the effects of a $100 million open-market purchase of U.S. Treasury bills by the Fed on the value of checkable bank deposits. What is the size of the money multiplier?

Solution appears at back of book.

**▼ Quick Review**

● The Federal Reserve is America's **central bank,** overseeing banking and making monetary policy.

● The Fed sets the required reserve ratio. Banks borrow and lend reserves in the **federal funds market.** The interest rate determined in this market is the **federal funds rate.** Banks can also borrow from the Fed at the **discount rate.**

● Although the Fed can change reserve requirements or the discount rate, in practice, monetary policy is conducted using **open-market operations.**

● An open-market purchase of Treasury bills increases the monetary base and therefore the money supply. An open-market sale reduces the monetary base and the money supply.

# The Evolution of the American Banking System

Up to this point, we have been describing the U.S. banking system and how it works. To fully understand that system, however, it is helpful to understand how and why it was created—a story that is closely intertwined with the story of how and when things went wrong. For the key elements of twenty-first-century U.S. banking weren't created out of thin air: efforts to change both the regulations that govern banking and the Federal Reserve system that began in 2008 have propelled financial reform to the forefront. This reform promises to continue reshaping the financial system well into future years.

## The Crisis in American Banking in the Early Twentieth Century

The creation of the Federal Reserve system in 1913 marked the beginning of the modern era of American banking. From 1864 until 1913, American banking was dominated by a federally regulated system of national banks. They alone were allowed to issue currency, and the currency notes they issued were printed by the federal government with uniform size and design. How much currency a national bank could issue depended on its capital. Although this system was an improvement on the earlier period in which banks issued their own notes with no uniformity and virtually no regulation, the national banking regime still suffered numerous bank failures and major financial crises—at least one and often two per decade.

The main problem afflicting the system was that the money supply was not sufficiently responsive: it was difficult to shift currency around the country to respond quickly to local economic changes. (In particular, there was often a tug-of-war between New York City banks and rural banks for adequate amounts of currency.) Rumors that a bank had insufficient currency to satisfy demands for withdrawals would quickly lead to a bank run. A bank run would then spark a contagion, setting off runs at other nearby banks, sowing widespread panic and devastation in the local economy. In response, bankers in some locations pooled their resources to create local clearinghouses that would jointly guarantee a member's liabilities in the event of a panic, and some state governments began offering deposit insurance on their banks' deposits.

However, the cause of the Panic of 1907 was different from those of previous crises; in fact, its cause was eerily similar to the roots of the 2008 crisis. Ground zero of the 1907 panic was New York City, but the consequences devastated the entire country, leading to a deep four-year recession.

The crisis originated in institutions in New York known as trusts, bank-like institutions that accepted deposits but that were originally intended to manage only inheritances and estates for wealthy clients. Because these trusts were supposed to engage only in low-risk activities, they were less regulated, had lower reserve requirements, and had lower cash reserves than national banks.

However, as the American economy boomed during the first decade of the twentieth century, trusts began speculating in real estate and the stock market, areas of speculation forbidden to national banks. Less regulated than national banks, trusts were able to pay their depositors higher returns. Yet trusts took a free ride on national banks' reputation for soundness, with depositors considering them equally safe. As a result, trusts grew rapidly: by 1907, the total assets of trusts in New York City were as large as those of national banks. Meanwhile, the trusts declined to join the New York Clearinghouse, a consortium of New York City national banks that guaranteed one anothers' soundness; that would have required the trusts to hold higher cash reserves, reducing their profits.

The Panic of 1907 began with the failure of the Knickerbocker Trust, a large New York City trust that failed when it suffered massive losses in unsuccessful stock market speculation. Quickly, other New York trusts came under pressure, and frightened depositors began queuing in long lines to withdraw their funds. The New York Clearinghouse declined to step in and lend to the trusts, and even healthy trusts came under serious assault. Within two days, a dozen major trusts had gone under. Credit markets froze, and the stock market fell dramatically as stock traders were unable to get credit to finance their trades and business confidence evaporated.

Fortunately, New York City's wealthiest man, the banker J. P. Morgan, quickly stepped in to stop the panic. Understanding that the crisis was spreading and

In both the Panic of 1907 and the financial crisis of 2008, large losses from risky speculation destabilized the banking system.

would soon engulf healthy institutions, trusts and banks alike, he worked with other bankers, wealthy men such as John D. Rockefeller, and the U.S. Secretary of the Treasury to shore up the reserves of banks and trusts so they could withstand the onslaught of withdrawals. Once people were assured that they could withdraw their money, the panic ceased. Although the panic itself lasted little more than a week, it and the stock market collapse decimated the economy. A four-year recession ensued, with production falling 11% and unemployment rising from 3% to 8%.

## Responding to Banking Crises: The Creation of the Federal Reserve

Concerns over the frequency of banking crises and the unprecedented role of J. P. Morgan in saving the financial system prompted the federal government to initiate banking reform. In 1913 the national banking system was eliminated and the Federal Reserve system was created as a way to compel all deposit-taking institutions to hold adequate reserves and to open their accounts to inspection by regulators. The Panic of 1907 convinced many that the time for centralized control of bank reserves had come. In addition, the Federal Reserve was given the sole right to issue currency in order to make the money supply sufficiently responsive to satisfy economic conditions around the country.

Although the new regime standardized and centralized the holding of bank reserves, it did not eliminate the potential for bank runs because banks' reserves were still less than the total value of their deposits. The potential for more bank runs became a reality during the Great Depression. Plunging commodity prices hit American farmers particularly hard, precipitating a series of bank runs in 1930, 1931, and 1933, each of which started at midwestern banks and then spread throughout the country.

After the failure of a particularly large bank in 1930, federal officials realized that the economy-wide effects compelled them to take a less hands-off approach and to intervene more vigorously. In 1932, the Reconstruction Finance Corporation (RFC) was established and given the authority to make loans to banks in order to stabilize the banking sector. Also, the Glass-Steagall Act of 1932, which created federal deposit insurance and increased the ability of banks to borrow from the Federal Reserve system, was passed. A loan to a leading Chicago bank from the Federal Reserve appears to have stopped a major banking crisis in 1932. However, the beast had not yet been tamed. Banks became fearful of borrowing from the RFC because doing so signaled weakness to the public.

During the catastrophic bank run of 1933, the new president, Franklin Delano Roosevelt, was inaugurated. He immediately declared a "bank holiday," closing all banks until regulators could get a handle on the problem.

In March 1933, emergency measures were adopted that gave the RFC extraordinary powers to stabilize and restructure the banking industry by providing capital to banks through either loans or outright purchases of bank shares. With the new rules, regulators closed nonviable banks and recapitalized viable ones by allowing the RFC to buy preferred shares in banks (shares that gave the U.S. government more rights than regular shareholders) and by greatly expanding banks' ability to borrow from the Federal Reserve. By 1933, the RFC had invested over $16.2 billion (2010 dollars) in bank capital—one-third of the total capital of all banks in the United States at that time—and purchased shares in almost one-half of all banks. The RFC loaned more than $32.4 billion (2010 dollars) to banks during this period.

Economic historians uniformly agree that the banking crises of the early 1930s greatly exacerbated the severity of the Great Depression, rendering

Official White House Photo by Pete Souza

Like FDR, President Obama, shown here meeting with economic advisers, was faced with a major financial crisis upon taking office.

monetary policy ineffective as the banking sector broke down and currency, withdrawn from banks and stashed under beds, reduced the money supply.

Although the powerful actions of the RFC stabilized the banking industry, new legislation was needed to prevent future banking crises. The Glass-Steagall Act of 1933 separated banks into two categories, **commercial banks,** depository banks that accepted deposits and were covered by deposit insurance, and **investment banks,** which engaged in creating and trading financial assets such as stocks and corporate bonds but were not covered by deposit insurance because their activities were considered more risky.

Regulation Q prevented commercial banks from paying interest on checking accounts in the belief that this would promote unhealthy competition between banks. In addition, investment banks were much more lightly regulated than commercial banks. The most important measure for the prevention of bank runs, however, was the adoption of federal deposit insurance (with an original limit of $2,500 per deposit).

These measures were clearly successful, and the United States enjoyed a long period of financial and banking stability. As memories of the bad old days dimmed, Depression-era bank regulations were lifted. In 1980, Regulation Q was eliminated; by 1999, the Glass-Steagall Act had been so weakened that offering services like trading financial assets was no longer off-limits to commercial banks.

## The Savings and Loan Crisis of the 1980s

Along with banks, the banking industry also included **savings and loans** (also called S&Ls or **thrifts**), institutions designed to accept savings and turn them into long-term mortgages for home-buyers. S&Ls were covered by federal deposit insurance and were tightly regulated for safety. However, trouble hit in the 1970s, as high inflation led savers to withdraw their funds from low-interest-paying S&L accounts and put them into higher-interest-paying money market accounts. In addition, the high inflation rate severely eroded the value of the S&Ls' assets, the long-term mortgages they held on their books.

In order to improve S&Ls' competitive position vis-à-vis banks, Congress eased regulations to allow S&Ls to undertake much more risky investments in addition to long-term home mortgages. However, the new freedom did not bring with it increased oversight, leaving S&Ls with less oversight than banks. Not surprisingly, during the real estate boom of the 1970s and 1980s, S&Ls engaged in overly risky real estate lending. Also, corruption occurred as some S&L executives used their institutions as private piggy banks.

Unfortunately, during the late 1970s and early 1980s, political interference from Congress kept insolvent S&Ls open when a bank in a comparable situation would have been quickly shut down by bank regulators. By the early 1980s, a large number of S&Ls had failed. Because accounts were covered by federal deposit insurance, the liabilities of a failed S&L were now liabilities of the federal government, and depositors had to be paid from taxpayer funds. From 1986 through 1995, the federal government closed over 1,000 failed S&Ls, costing U.S. taxpayers over $124 billion dollars.

In a classic case of shutting the barn door after the horse has escaped, in 1989 Congress put in place comprehensive oversight of S&L activities. It also empowered Fannie Mae and Freddie Mac to take over much of the home mortgage lending previously done by S&Ls. Fannie Mae and Freddie Mac are quasi-governmental agencies created during the Great Depression

A **commercial bank** accepts deposits and is covered by deposit insurance.

An **investment bank** trades in financial assets and is not covered by deposit insurance.

A **savings and loan (thrift)** is another type of deposit-taking bank, usually specialized in issuing home loans.

to make homeownership more affordable for low- and moderate-income households. It has been calculated that the S&L crisis helped cause a steep slowdown in the finance and real estate industries, leading to the recession of the early 1990s.

## Back to the Future: The Financial Crisis of 2008

The financial crisis of 2008 shared features of previous crises. Like the Panic of 1907 and the S&L crisis, it involved institutions that were not as strictly regulated as deposit-taking banks as well as excessive speculation. Like the crises of the early 1930s, it involved a U.S. government that was reluctant to take aggressive action until the scale of the devastation became clear. In addition, by the late 1990s, advances in technology and financial innovation had created yet another systemic weakness that played a central role in 2008. The story of Long-Term Capital Management, or LTCM, highlights these problems.

**Long-Term Capital (Mis)Management** Created in 1994, LTCM was a hedge fund, a private investment partnership open only to wealthy individuals and institutions. Hedge funds are virtually unregulated, allowing them to make much riskier investments than mutual funds, which are open to the average investor. Using vast amounts of **leverage**—that is, borrowed money—in order to increase its returns, LTCM used sophisticated computer models to make money by taking advantage of small differences in asset prices in global financial markets to buy at a lower price and sell at a higher price. In one year, LTCM made a return as high as 40%.

LTCM was also heavily involved in derivatives, complex financial instruments that are constructed—derived—from the obligations of more basic financial assets. Derivatives are popular investment tools because they are cheaper to trade than basic financial assets and can be constructed to suit a buyer's or seller's particular needs. Yet their complexity can make it extremely hard to measure their value. LTCM believed that its computer models allowed it to accurately gauge the risk in the huge bets that it was undertaking in derivatives using borrowed money.

However, LTCM's computer models hadn't factored in a series of financial crises in Asia and in Russia during 1997 and 1998. Through its large borrowing, LTCM had become such a big player in global financial markets that attempts to sell its assets depressed the prices of what it was trying to sell. As the markets fell around the world and LTCM's panic-stricken investors demanded the return of their funds, LTCM's losses mounted as it tried to sell assets to satisfy those demands. Quickly, its operations collapsed because it could no longer borrow money and other parties refused to trade with it. Financial markets around the world froze in panic.

The Federal Reserve realized that allowing LTCM's remaining assets to be sold at panic-stricken prices presented a grave risk to the entire financial system through the **balance sheet effect:** as sales of assets by LTCM depressed asset prices all over the world, other firms would see the value of their balance sheets fall as assets held on these balance sheets declined in value. Moreover, falling asset prices meant the value of assets held by borrowers on their balance sheets would fall below a critical threshold, leading to a default on the terms of their credit contracts and forcing creditors to call in their loans. This in turn would lead to more sales of assets as borrowers tried to raise cash to repay their loans, more credit defaults, and more loans called in, creating a **vicious cycle of deleveraging.**

The Federal Reserve Bank of New York arranged a $3.625 billion bailout of LTCM in 1998, in which other private institutions took on shares of LTCM's assets and obligations, liquidated them in an orderly manner, and eventually

A financial institution engages in **leverage** when it finances its investments with borrowed funds.

The **balance sheet effect** is the reduction in a firm's net worth due to falling asset prices.

A **vicious cycle of deleveraging** takes place when asset sales to cover losses produce negative balance sheet effects on other firms and force creditors to call in their loans, forcing sales of more assets and causing further declines in asset prices.

**Subprime lending** is lending to home-buyers who don't meet the usual criteria for being able to afford their payments.

In **securitization,** a pool of loans is assembled and shares of that pool are sold to investors.

turned a small profit. Quick action by the Federal Reserve Bank of New York prevented LTCM from sparking a contagion, yet virtually all of LTCM's investors were wiped out.

**Subprime Lending and the Housing Bubble** After the LTCM crisis, U.S. financial markets stabilized. They remained more or less stable even as stock prices fell sharply from 2000 to 2002 and the U.S. economy went into recession. During the recovery from the 2001 recession, however, the seeds for another financial crisis were planted.

The story begins with low interest rates: by 2003, U.S. interest rates were at historically low levels, partly because of Federal Reserve policy and partly because of large inflows of capital from other countries, especially China. These low interest rates helped cause a boom in housing, which in turn led the U.S. economy out of recession. As housing boomed, however, financial institutions began taking on growing risks—risks that were not well understood.

Traditionally, people were only able to borrow money to buy homes if they could show that they had sufficient income to meet the mortgage payments. Home loans to people who don't meet the usual criteria for borrowing, called **subprime lending,** were only a minor part of overall lending. But in the booming housing market of 2003–2006, subprime lending started to seem like a safe bet. Since housing prices kept rising, borrowers who couldn't make their mortgage payments could always pay off their mortgages, if necessary, by selling their homes. As a result, subprime lending exploded.

Who was making these subprime loans? For the most part, it wasn't traditional banks lending out depositors' money. Instead, most of the loans were made by "loan originators," who quickly sold mortgages to other investors. These sales were made possible by a process known as **securitization:** financial institutions assembled pools of loans and sold shares in the income from these pools. These shares were considered relatively safe investments, since it was considered unlikely that large numbers of home-buyers would default on their payments at the same time.

But that's exactly what happened. The housing boom turned out to be a bubble, and when home prices started falling in late 2006, many subprime borrowers were unable either to meet their mortgage payments or sell their houses for enough to pay off their mortgages. As a result, investors in securities backed by subprime mortgages started taking heavy losses. Many of the mortgage-backed assets were held by financial institutions, including banks and other institutions playing bank-like roles. Like the trusts that played a key role in the Panic of 1907, these "nonbank banks" were less regulated than commercial banks, which allowed them to offer higher returns to investors but left them extremely vulnerable in a crisis. Mortgage-related losses, in turn, led to a collapse of trust in the financial system.

Figure 14-10 shows one measure of this loss of trust: the TED spread, which is the difference between the interest rate on three-month loans that banks make to each other and the interest rate the federal government pays on three-month bonds. Since government bonds are considered extremely safe, the TED spread shows how much risk banks think they're taking on when lending to each other. Normally the spread is around a quarter of a percentage point, but it shot up in August 2007 and surged to an unprecedented 4.58 percentage points in October 2008, before returning to more normal levels in mid-2009.

**Crisis and Response** The collapse of trust in the financial system, combined with the large losses suffered by financial firms, led to a severe cycle of deleveraging and a credit crunch for the economy as a whole. Firms found it difficult to borrow, even for short-term operations; individuals found home loans unavailable and credit card limits reduced.

*"Honey, we're homeless."*

FIGURE **14-10** The TED Spread

The TED spread is the difference between the interest rate at which banks lend to each other and the interest rate on U.S. government debt. It's widely used as a measure of financial stress. The TED spread soared as a result of the financial crisis of 2007–2008.

*Sources:* British Bankers' Association; Federal Reserve Bank of St. Louis.

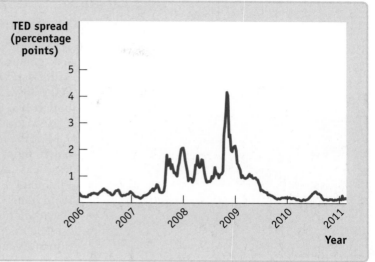

Overall, the negative economic effect of the financial crisis bore a distinct and troubling resemblance to the effects of the banking crisis of the early 1930s, which helped cause the Great Depression. Policy makers noticed the resemblance and tried to prevent a repeat performance. Beginning in August 2007, the Federal Reserve engaged in a series of efforts to provide cash to the financial system, lending funds to a widening range of institutions and buying private-sector debt. The Fed and the Treasury Department also stepped in to rescue individual firms that were deemed too crucial to be allowed to fail, such as the investment bank Bear Stearns and the insurance company AIG.

In September 2008, however, policy makers decided that one major investment bank, Lehman Brothers, could be allowed to fail. They quickly regretted the decision. Within days of Lehman's failure, widespread panic gripped the financial markets, as illustrated by the surge in the TED spread shown in Figure 14-10. In response to the intensified crisis, the U.S. government intervened further to support the financial system, as the U.S. Treasury began "injecting" capital into banks. Injecting capital, in practice, meant that the U.S. government would supply cash to banks in return for shares—in effect, partially nationalizing the financial system.

By the fall of 2010, the financial system appeared to be stabilized, and major institutions had repaid much of the money the federal government had injected during the crisis. It was generally expected that taxpayers would end up losing little if any money. However, the recovery of the banks was not matched by a successful turnaround for the overall economy: although the recession that began in December 2007 officially ended in June 2009, unemployment remained stubbornly high.

The Federal Reserve responded to this troubled situation with novel forms of open-market operations. Conventional open-market operations are limited to short-term government debt, but the Fed believed that this was no longer enough. It provided massive liquidity through discount window lending, as well as buying large quantities of other assets, mainly long-term government debt and debt of Fannie Mae and Freddie Mac, government-sponsored agencies that support home lending. This explains the surge in Fed assets after September 2008 visible in Figure 14-9.

Like earlier crises, the crisis of 2008 led to changes in banking regulation, most notably the Dodd-Frank financial regulatory reform bill enacted in 2010. We describe that bill briefly in the Economics in Action that follows.

## ECONOMICS ➤ IN ACTION

### REGULATION AFTER THE 2008 CRISIS

In July 2010, President Obama signed the Wall Street Reform and Consumer Protection Act—generally known as Dodd-Frank, after its sponsors in the Senate and House, respectively—into law. It was the biggest financial reform enacted since the 1930s—not surprising given that the nation had just gone through the worst financial crisis since the 1930s. How did it change regulation?

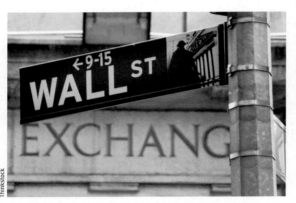

The Wall Street Reform and Consumer Protection Act of 2010 was an attempt to extend the spirit of old-fashioned bank regulation to today's more complex financial system.

For the most part, it left regulation of traditional deposit-taking banks more or less as it was. The main change these banks would face was the creation of a new agency, the Bureau of Consumer Financial Protection, whose mission was to protect borrowers from being exploited through seemingly attractive financial deals they didn't understand.

The major changes came in the regulation of financial institutions other than banks—institutions that, as the fall of Lehman Brothers showed, could trigger banking crises. The new law gave a special government committee, the Financial Stability Oversight Council, the right to designate certain institutions as "systemically important" even if they weren't ordinary deposit-taking banks. These systemically important institutions would be subjected to bank-style regulation, including relatively high capital requirements and limits on the kinds of risks they could take. In addition, the federal government would acquire "resolution authority," meaning the right to seize troubled financial institutions in much the same way that it routinely takes over troubled banks.

Beyond this, the law established new rules on the trading of derivatives, those complex financial instruments that sank LTCM and played an important role in the 2008 crisis as well: most derivatives would henceforth have to be bought and sold on exchanges, where everyone could observe their prices and the volume of transactions. The idea was to make the risks taken by financial institutions more transparent.

Overall, Dodd-Frank is probably best seen as an attempt to extend the spirit of old-fashioned bank regulation to the more complex financial system of the twenty-first century. Will it succeed in heading off future banking crises? Stay tuned.

### ▼ Quick Review

- The Federal Reserve system was created in response to the Panic of 1907.

- Widespread bank runs in the early 1930s resulted in greater bank regulation and the creation of federal deposit insurance. Banks were separated into two categories: **commercial** (covered by deposit insurance) and **investment** (not covered).

- In the **savings and loan (thrift)** crisis of the 1970s and 1980s, insufficiently regulated S&Ls incurred huge losses from risky speculation.

- During the mid-1990s, the hedge fund LTCM used huge amounts of **leverage** to speculate in global markets, incurred massive losses, and collapsed. In selling assets to cover its losses, LTCM caused **balance sheet effects** for firms around the world. To prevent a **vicious cycle of deleveraging,** the New York Fed coordinated a private bailout.

- In the mid-2000s, loans from **subprime lending** spread through the financial system via **securitization,** leading to a financial crisis. The Fed responded by injecting cash into financial institutions and buying private debt.

- In 2010, the Dodd-Frank bill revised financial regulation in an attempt to prevent repeats of the 2008 crisis.

### CHECK YOUR UNDERSTANDING   14-5

1. What are the similarities between the Panic of 1907, the S&L crisis, and the crisis of 2008?

2. Why did the creation of the Federal Reserve fail to prevent the bank runs of the Great Depression? What measures stopped the bank runs?

3. Describe the balance sheet effect. Describe the vicious cycle of deleveraging. Why is it necessary for the government to step in to halt a vicious cycle of deleveraging?

Solutions appear at back of book.

# BUSINESS CASE : The Perfect Gift: Cash or a Gift Card?

Richard B. Levine/Alamy

It's always nice when someone shows his or her appreciation by giving you a gift. Over the past few years, more and more people have been showing their appreciation by giving gift cards, prepaid plastic cards issued by a retailer that can be redeemed for merchandise. The best-selling single item for more than 80% of the top 100 American retailers, says GiftCardUSA.com, is their gift cards. What could be more simple and useful, so the thinking goes, than allowing the recipient to choose what he or she wants? And isn't a gift card more personal than cash or a check stuffed in an envelope? (And they have pretty pictures, too.)

Yet several websites are now making a profit from the fact that gift card recipients are often willing to sell their cards at a discount—sometimes at a fairly sizable discount—to turn them into cold, impersonal dollars and cents.

PlasticJungle.com is one such site. At the time of writing, it offers to pay cash to a seller of a Whole Foods gift card equivalent to 90% of the card's face value (for example, the seller of a card with a value of $100 would receive $90 in cash). But it offers cash equal to only 70% of a Gap card's face value. PlasticJungle.com profits by reselling the card at a premium over what it paid; for example, it buys a Gap card for 70% of its face value and then resells it for 88% of its face value.

Many consumers may be willing to sell at a sizable discount to turn their gift cards into cash, but retailers are eager to promote the use of gift cards over cash. According to GiftCardUSA.com, 5% to 15% of gift cards are never redeemed. Those unredeemed dollars accrue to the retailer, making gift cards a highly profitable line of business. The Tower Group, a financial consulting firm, placed the value of "breakage," the amount of a gift card that accrues to the retailer rather than to the card holder, at about $5 billion in 2009.

How does breakage occur? People lose cards. Or they spend only $47 of a $50 gift card, figuring it's not worth the effort to return to the store to spend that last $3. Also, retailers impose fees on the use of the card or make cards subject to expiration dates, which customers forget about. And if a retailer goes out of business, the value of any outstanding gift cards disappears with it.

In addition to breakage, retailers benefit when customers intent on using up the value of their gift card find that it is too difficult to spend exactly the amount of the card; instead, they spend more than the card's face value, sometimes even spending more than they would have in the absence of the gift card.

Gift cards are so beneficial to retailers that those which used to reward customer loyalty with rebate checks have largely switched to dispensing gift cards. As one commentator noted in explaining why retailers prefer gift cards to rebate checks, "Nobody neglects to spend cash."

However, the future may not be quite so profitable for gift card issuers: during the difficult economic times of 2009–2010, industry analysts found that a growing percentage of gift cards were being completely spent down by their holders. In 2010, breakage was down by half (to $2.5 billion) compared to the year before.

## QUESTIONS FOR THOUGHT

1. Why are gift card owners willing to sell their cards for a cash amount less than their face value?

2. Why do gift cards for retailers like Walmart, Home Depot, and Whole Foods sell for a smaller discount than those for retailers like the Gap and Aeropostale?

3. Use your answer from Question 2 to explain why cash never "sells" at a discount.

4. Explain why retailers prefer to reward loyal customers with gift cards instead of rebate checks.

5. Recent legislation restricted retailers' ability to impose fees and expiration dates on their gift cards and mandated greater disclosure of their terms. Why do you think Congress enacted this legislation?

1. **Money** is any asset that can easily be used to purchase goods and services. **Currency in circulation** and **checkable bank deposits** are both considered part of the **money supply.** Money plays three roles: it is a **medium of exchange** used for transactions, a **store of value** that holds purchasing power over time, and a **unit of account** in which prices are stated.

2. Over time, **commodity money,** which consists of goods possessing value aside from their role as money, such as gold and silver coins, was replaced by **commodity-backed money,** such as paper currency backed by gold. Today the dollar is pure **fiat money,** whose value derives solely from its official role.

3. The Federal Reserve calculates two measures of the money supply. M1 is the narrowest **monetary aggregate,** containing only currency in circulation, traveler's checks, and checkable bank deposits. M2 includes a wider range of assets called **near-moneys,** mainly other forms of bank deposits, that can easily be converted into checkable bank deposits.

4. Banks allow depositors immediate access to their funds, but they also lend out most of the funds deposited in their care. To meet demands for cash, they maintain **bank reserves** composed of both currency held in vaults and deposits at the Federal Reserve. The **reserve ratio** is the ratio of bank reserves to bank deposits. A **T-account** summarizes a bank's financial position, with loans and reserves counted as assets and deposits counted as liabilities.

5. Banks have sometimes been subject to **bank runs,** most notably in the early 1930s. To avert this danger, depositors are now protected by **deposit insurance,** bank owners face capital requirements that reduce the incentive to make overly risky loans with depositors' funds, and banks must satisfy **reserve requirements.**

6. When currency is deposited in a bank, it starts a multiplier process in which banks lend out **excess reserves,** leading to an increase in the money supply— so banks create money. If the entire money supply consisted of checkable bank deposits, the money supply would be equal to the value of reserves divided by the reserve ratio. In reality, much of the **monetary base** consists of currency in circulation, and the **money multiplier** is the ratio of the money supply to the monetary base.

7. The monetary base is controlled by the Federal Reserve, the **central bank** of the United States. The Fed regulates banks and sets reserve requirements. To meet those requirements, banks borrow and lend reserves in the **federal funds market** at the **federal funds rate.** Through the **discount window** facility, banks can borrow from the Fed at the **discount rate.**

8. **Open-market operations** by the Fed are the principal tool of monetary policy: the Fed can increase or reduce the monetary base by buying U.S. Treasury bills from banks or selling U.S. Treasury bills to banks.

9. In response to the Panic of 1907, the Fed was created to centralize the holding of reserves, inspect banks' books, and make the money supply sufficiently responsive to varying economic conditions.

10. The Great Depression sparked widespread bank runs in the early 1930s, which greatly worsened and lengthened it. Federal deposit insurance was created, and the government recapitalized banks by lending to them and by buying shares of banks. By 1933, banks had been separated into two categories: **commercial banks** (covered by deposit insurance) and **investment banks** (not covered). Public acceptance of deposit insurance finally stopped the bank runs of the Great Depression.

11. The **savings and loan (thrift)** crisis of the 1980s arose because insufficiently regulated S&Ls engaged in overly risky speculation and incurred huge losses. Depositors in failed S&Ls were compensated with taxpayer funds because they were covered by deposit insurance. The crisis caused steep losses in the financial and real estate sectors, resulting in a recession in the early 1990s.

12. During the mid-1990s, the hedge fund LTCM used huge amounts of **leverage** to speculate in global financial markets, incurred massive losses, and collapsed. LTCM was so large that, in selling assets to cover its losses, it caused **balance sheet effects** for firms around the world, leading to the prospect of a **vicious cycle of deleveraging.** As a result, credit markets around the world froze. The New York Fed coordinated a private bailout of LTCM and revived world credit markets.

13. **Subprime lending** during the U.S. housing bubble of the mid-2000s spread through the financial system via **securitization.** When the bubble burst, massive losses by banks and nonbank financial institutions led to widespread collapse in the financial system. To prevent another Great Depression, the Fed and the U.S. Treasury expanded lending to bank and nonbank institutions, provided capital through the purchase of bank shares, and purchased private debt. Because much of the crisis originated in nontraditional bank institutions, the crisis of 2008 indicated that a wider safety net and broader regulation are needed in the financial sector. The 2010 Dodd-Frank bill, the biggest financial reform since the 1930s, is an attempt to prevent another crisis.

## PROBLEMS

1. For each of the following transactions, what is the initial effect (increase or decrease) on M1? On M2?

   a. You sell a few shares of stock and put the proceeds into your savings account.

   b. You sell a few shares of stock and put the proceeds into your checking account.

   c. You transfer money from your savings account to your checking account.

   d. You discover $0.25 under the floor mat in your car and deposit it in your checking account.

   e. You discover $0.25 under the floor mat in your car and deposit it in your savings account.

2. There are three types of money: commodity money, commodity-backed money, and fiat money. Which type of money is used in each of the following situations?

   a. Bottles of rum were used to pay for goods in colonial Australia.

   b. Salt was used in many European countries as a medium of exchange.

   c. For a brief time, Germany used paper money (the "Rye Mark") that could be redeemed for a certain amount of rye, a type of grain.

   d. The town of Ithaca, New York, prints its own currency, the Ithaca HOURS, which can be used to purchase local goods and services.

3. The table below shows the components of M1 and M2 in billions of dollars for the month of December in the years 2000 to 2010 as published in the 2011 Economic Report of the President. Complete the table by calculating M1, M2, currency in circulation as a percentage of M1, and currency in circulation as a percentage of M2. What trends or patterns about M1, M2, currency in circulation as a percentage of M1, and currency in circulation as a percentage of M2 do you see? What might account for these trends?

| Year | Currency in circulation | Traveler's checks | Checkable deposits | Savings deposits | Time deposits | Money market funds | M1 | M2 | Currency in circulation as a percentage of M1 | Currency in circulation as a percentage of M2 |
|------|------|------|------|------|------|------|------|------|------|------|
| 2000 | $531.2 | $8.3 | $547.7 | $1,878.0 | $1,046.0 | $902.0 | ? | ? | ? | ? |
| 2001 | 581.1 | 8.0 | 592.9 | 2,309.5 | 974.5 | 962.5 | ? | ? | ? | ? |
| 2002 | 626.2 | 7.8 | 585.7 | 2,773.4 | 894.5 | 887.5 | ? | ? | ? | ? |
| 2003 | 662.5 | 7.7 | 636.2 | 3,162.8 | 817.8 | 777.0 | ? | ? | ? | ? |
| 2004 | 697.7 | 7.6 | 671.1 | 3,508.8 | 827.9 | 694.7 | ? | ? | ? | ? |
| 2005 | 724.1 | 7.2 | 643.5 | 3,606.0 | 993.1 | 699.4 | ? | ? | ? | ? |
| 2006 | 749.6 | 6.7 | 610.0 | 3,694.6 | 1,205.3 | 799.0 | ? | ? | ? | ? |
| 2007 | 759.7 | 6.3 | 607.6 | 3,872.6 | 1,275.0 | 972.7 | ? | ? | ? | ? |
| 2008 | 815.0 | 5.5 | 782.1 | 4,106.1 | 1,455.7 | 1,080.5 | ? | ? | ? | ? |
| 2009 | 861.5 | 5.1 | 827.0 | 4,836.9 | 1,177.4 | 820.8 | ? | ? | ? | ? |
| 2010 | 915.7 | 4.7 | 911.7 | 5,357.6 | 926.6 | 700.0 | ? | ? | ? | ? |

*Source:* 2011 Economic Report of the President.

4. Indicate whether each of the following is part of M1, M2, or neither:
   a. $95 on your campus meal card
   b. $0.55 in the change cup of your car
   c. $1,663 in your savings account
   d. $459 in your checking account
   e. 100 shares of stock worth $4,000
   f. A $1,000 line of credit on your Sears credit card

5. Tracy Williams deposits $500 that was in her sock drawer into a checking account at the local bank.
   a. How does the deposit initially change the T-account of the local bank? How does it change the money supply?
   b. If the bank maintains a reserve ratio of 10%, how will it respond to the new deposit?
   c. If every time the bank makes a loan, the loan results in a new checkable bank deposit in a different bank equal to the amount of the loan, by how much could the total money supply in the economy expand in response to Tracy's initial cash deposit of $500?
   d. If every time the bank makes a loan, the loan results in a new checkable bank deposit in a different bank equal to the amount of the loan and the bank maintains a reserve ratio of 5%, by how much could the money supply expand in response to Tracy's initial cash deposit of $500?

6. Ryan Cozzens withdraws $400 from his checking account at the local bank and keeps it in his wallet.
   a. How will the withdrawal change the T-account of the local bank and the money supply?
   b. If the bank maintains a reserve ratio of 10%, how will it respond to the withdrawal? Assume that the bank responds to insufficient reserves by reducing the amount of deposits it holds until its level of reserves satisfies its required reserve ratio. The bank reduces its deposits by calling in some of its loans, forcing borrowers to pay back these loans by taking cash from their checking deposits (at the same bank) to make repayment.
   c. If every time the bank decreases its loans, checkable bank deposits fall by the amount of the loan, by how much will the money supply in the economy contract in response to Ryan's withdrawal of $400?
   d. If every time the bank decreases its loans, checkable bank deposits fall by the amount of the loan and the bank maintains a reserve ratio of 20%, by how much will the money supply contract in response to a withdrawal of $400?

7. The government of Eastlandia uses measures of monetary aggregates similar to those used by the United States, and the central bank of Eastlandia imposes a required reserve ratio of 10%. Given the following information, answer the questions below.
   Bank deposits at the central bank = $200 million
   Currency held by public = $150 million
   Currency in bank vaults = $100 million
   Checkable bank deposits = $500 million
   Traveler's checks = $10 million
   a. What is M1?
   b. What is the monetary base?
   c. Are the commercial banks holding excess reserves?
   d. Can the commercial banks increase checkable bank deposits? If yes, by how much can checkable bank deposits increase?

8. In Westlandia, the public holds 50% of M1 in the form of currency, and the required reserve ratio is 20%. Estimate how much the money supply will increase in response to a new cash deposit of $500 by completing the accompanying table. (*Hint:* The first row shows that the bank must hold $100 in minimum reserves—20% of the $500 deposit—against this deposit, leaving $400 in excess reserves that can be loaned out. However, since the public wants to hold 50% of the loan in currency, only $400 × 0.5 = $200 of the loan will be deposited in round 2 from the loan granted in round 1.) How does your answer compare to an economy in which the total amount of the loan is deposited in the banking system and the public doesn't hold any of the loan in currency? What does this imply about the relationship between the public's desire for holding currency and the money multiplier?

| Round | Deposits | Required reserves | Excess reserves | Loans | Held as currency |
|---|---|---|---|---|---|
| 1 | $500.00 | $100.00 | $400.00 | $400.00 | $200.00 |
| 2 | 200.00 | ? | ? | ? | ? |
| 3 | ? | ? | ? | ? | ? |
| 4 | ? | ? | ? | ? | ? |
| 5 | ? | ? | ? | ? | ? |
| 6 | ? | ? | ? | ? | ? |
| 7 | ? | ? | ? | ? | ? |
| 8 | ? | ? | ? | ? | ? |
| 9 | ? | ? | ? | ? | ? |
| Total after 10 rounds | ? | ? | ? | ? | ? |

9. What will happen to the money supply under the following circumstances in a checkable-deposits-only system?
   a. The required reserve ratio is 25%, and a depositor withdraws $700 from his checkable bank deposit.
   b. The required reserve ratio is 5%, and a depositor withdraws $700 from his checkable bank deposit.
   c. The required reserve ratio is 20%, and a customer deposits $750 to her checkable bank deposit.
   d. The required reserve ratio is 10%, and a customer deposits $600 to her checkable bank deposit.

10. Although the U.S. Federal Reserve doesn't use changes in reserve requirements to manage the money supply, the central bank of Albernia does. The commercial banks of Albernia have $100 million in reserves

and $1,000 million in checkable deposits; the initial required reserve ratio is 10%. The commercial banks follow a policy of holding no excess reserves. The public holds no currency, only checkable deposits in the banking system.

**a.** How will the money supply change if the required reserve ratio falls to 5%?

**b.** How will the money supply change if the required reserve ratio rises to 25%?

**11.** Using Figure 14-6, find the Federal Reserve district in which you live. Go to http://www.federalreserve.gov/bios/pres.htm and click on your district to identify the president of the Federal Reserve Bank in your district. Go to http://www.federalreserve.gov/fomc/ and determine if the president of the regional Federal Reserve bank in your district is currently a voting member of the Federal Open Market Committee (FOMC).

**12.** Show the changes to the T-accounts for the Federal Reserve and for commercial banks when the Federal Reserve buys $50 million in U.S. Treasury bills. If the public holds a fixed amount of currency (so that all loans create an equal amount of deposits in the banking system), the minimum reserve ratio is 10%, and banks hold no excess reserves, by how much will deposits in the commercial banks change? By how much will the money supply change? Show the final changes to the T-account for commercial banks when the money supply changes by this amount.

**13.** Show the changes to the T-accounts for the Federal Reserve and for commercial banks when the Federal Reserve sells $30 million in U.S. Treasury bills. If the public holds a fixed amount of currency (so that all new loans create an equal amount of checkable bank deposits in the banking system) and the minimum reserve ratio is 5%, by how much will checkable bank deposits in the commercial banks change? By how much will the money supply change? Show the final changes to the T-account for the commercial banks when the money supply changes by this amount.

**14.** The Congressional Research Service estimates that at least $45 million of counterfeit U.S. $100 notes produced by the North Korean government are in circulation.

**a.** Why do U.S. taxpayers lose because of North Korea's counterfeiting?

**b.** As of August 2011, the interest rate earned on one-year U.S. Treasury bills was 0.11%. At a 0.11% rate of interest, what is the amount of money U.S. taxpayers are losing per year because of these $45 million in counterfeit notes?

**15.** As shown in Figure 14-9, the portion of the Federal Reserve's assets made up of U.S. Treasury bills has declined since 2007. Go to www.federalreserve.gov. Under "Select Statistical Releases," click on "All Statistical Releases." Under the heading "Money Stock and Reserve Balances," click on "Factors Affecting Reserve Balances." Click on the date of the current release.

**a.** Under "Statement of Condition of Each Federal Reserve Bank," look in the "Total" column. What is the amount displayed next to "Total assets"? What is the amount displayed next to "U.S. Treasury securities"? What percentage of the Federal Reserve's total assets are currently made up of U.S. Treasury bills?

**b.** Do the Federal Reserve's assets consist primarily of U.S. Treasury securities, as they did in January 2007, the beginning of the graph in Figure 14-9, or does the Fed still own a large number of other assets, as it did in mid-2011, the end of the graph in Figure 14-9?

**16.** The accompanying figure shows new U.S. housing starts, in thousands of units per month, between January 1980 and August 2011. The graph shows a large drop in new housing starts in 1984–1991 and 2006–2009. New housing starts are related to the availability of mortgages.

**a.** What caused the drop in new housing starts in 1984–1991?

**b.** What caused the drop in new housing starts in 2006–2009?

**c.** How could better regulation of financial institutions have prevented these two instances?

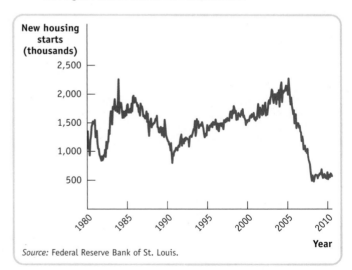

*Source:* Federal Reserve Bank of St. Louis.

# CHAPTER 15

# Monetary Policy

## PERSON OF THE YEAR

© Dan Winters

As Fed chairman, Ben Bernanke has more influence over the economy's ups and downs than the president.

❭ What the **money demand curve** is

❭ Why the **liquidity preference model** determines the interest rate in the short run

❭ How the Federal Reserve implements monetary policy, moving the interest rate to affect aggregate output

❭ Why monetary policy is the main tool for stabilizing the economy

❭ How the behavior of the Federal Reserve compares to that of other central banks

❭ Why economists believe in **monetary neutrality**—that monetary policy affects only the price level, not aggregate output, in the long run

"A BALD MAN WITH A GRAY beard and tired eyes is sitting in his oversize Washington office, talking about the economy. He doesn't have a commanding presence. He isn't a mesmerizing speaker. He has none of the look-at-me swagger or listen-to-me charisma so common among men with oversize Washington offices. His arguments aren't partisan or ideological; they're methodical, grounded in data and the latest academic literature. When he doesn't know something, he doesn't bluster or bluff. He's professorial, which makes sense, because he spent most of his career as a professor."

So began *Time* magazine's profile of Ben Bernanke, whom the magazine named Person of the Year for 2009. Who is this mild-mannered man, and why does he matter so much? The answer is that Bernanke is the chairman of the Board of Governors of the Federal

Reserve System—the body that controls *monetary policy.*

People sometimes say that Bernanke decides how much money to print. That's not quite true: for one thing, the Fed doesn't literally print money, and beyond that, monetary decisions are actually made by a committee rather than by one man. But as we learned in Chapter 14, the Federal Reserve can use open-market operations and other actions, such as changes in reserve requirements, to alter the money supply—and Ben Bernanke has more influence over these actions than anyone else in America.

And these actions matter a lot. Roughly half of the recessions the United States has experienced since World War II can be attributed, at least in part, to the decisions of the Federal Reserve to tighten policy to fight inflation. In a number of other cases, the Fed has played a key role in fighting slumps

and promoting recovery. The financial crisis of 2008 put the Fed at center stage. Bernanke's aggressive response to the crisis, which, as we saw in Chapter 14, included a tripling of the monetary base, inspired both praise (including his designation as Person of the Year) and condemnation.

In this chapter we'll learn how monetary policy works—how actions by the Federal Reserve can have a powerful effect on the economy. We'll start by looking at the *demand for money* from households and firms. Then we'll see how the Fed's ability to change the *supply of money* allows it to move interest rates in the short run and thereby affect real GDP. We'll look at U.S. monetary policy in practice and compare it to the monetary policy of other central banks. We'll conclude by examining the long-run effects of monetary policy. ■

# The Demand for Money

I n Chapter 14 we learned about the various types of monetary aggregates: M1, the most commonly used definition of the money supply, consists of currency in circulation (cash), plus checkable bank deposits, plus traveler's checks; and M2, a broader definition of the money supply, consists of M1 plus deposits that can easily be transferred into checkable deposits. We also learned why people hold money—to make it easier to purchase goods and services. Now we'll go deeper, examining what determines how much money individuals and firms want to hold at any given time.

## The Opportunity Cost of Holding Money

Most economic decisions involve trade-offs at the margin. That is, individuals decide how much of a good to consume by determining whether the benefit they'd gain from consuming a bit more of any given good is worth the cost. The same decision process is used when deciding how much money to hold.

There is a price to be paid for the convenience of holding money.

Individuals and firms find it useful to hold some of their assets in the form of money because of the convenience money provides: money can be used to make purchases directly, but other assets can't. But there is a price to be paid for that convenience: money normally yields a lower rate of return than nonmonetary assets.

As an example of how convenience makes it worth incurring some opportunity costs, consider the fact that even today—with the prevalence of credit cards, debit cards, and ATMs—people continue to keep cash in their wallets rather than leave the funds in an interest-bearing account. They do this because they don't want to have to go to an ATM to withdraw money every time they want to buy lunch from a place that doesn't accept credit cards or won't accept them for small amounts because of the processing fee. In other words, the convenience of keeping some cash in your wallet is more valuable than the interest you would earn by keeping that money in the bank.

Even holding money in a checking account involves a trade-off between convenience and earning interest. That's because you can earn a higher interest rate by putting your money in assets other than a checking account. For example, many banks offer certificates of deposit, or CDs, which pay a higher interest rate than ordinary bank accounts. But CDs also carry a penalty if you withdraw the funds before a certain amount of time—say, six months—has elapsed. An individual who keeps funds in a checking account is forgoing the higher interest rate those funds would have earned if placed in a CD in return for the convenience of having cash readily available when needed.

So making sense of the demand for money is about understanding how individuals and firms trade off the benefit of holding cash—that provides convenience but no interest—versus the benefit of holding interest-bearing nonmonetary assets—that provide interest but not convenience. And that trade-off is affected by the interest rate. (As before, when we say *the interest rate* it is with the understanding that we mean a nominal interest rate—that is, it's unadjusted for inflation.) Next, we'll examine how that trade-off changed dramatically from June 2007 to June 2008, when there was a big fall in interest rates.

Table 15-1 illustrates the opportunity cost of holding money in a specific month, June 2007. The first row shows the interest rate on one-month certificates of deposit—that is, the interest rate individuals could get if they were willing to tie their funds up for one month. In June 2007, one-month CDs yielded 5.30%. The second row shows the interest rate on interest-bearing demand deposits (specifically, those included in M2, minus small time deposits). Funds in these accounts were more accessible than those in CDs, but the price of that convenience was a

**TABLE  15-1  Selected Interest Rates, June 2007**

| | |
|---|---|
| One-month certificates of deposit (CDs) | 5.30% |
| Interest-bearing demand deposits | 2.30% |
| Currency | 0 |

*Source:* Federal Reserve Bank of St. Louis.

much lower interest rate, only 2.30%. Finally, the last row shows the interest rate on currency—cash in your wallet—which was, of course, zero.

Table 15-1 shows the opportunity cost of holding money at one point in time, but the opportunity cost of holding money changes when the overall level of interest rates changes. Specifically, when the overall level of interest rates falls, the opportunity cost of holding money falls, too.

Table 15-2 illustrates this point by showing how selected interest rates changed between June 2007 and June 2008, a period when the Federal Reserve was slashing rates in an (unsuccessful) effort to fight off a rapidly worsening recession. A comparison between interest rates in June 2007 and June 2008 illustrates what happens when the opportunity cost of holding money falls sharply. Between June 2007 and June 2008, the federal funds rate, which is the rate the Fed controls most directly, fell by 3.25 percentage points. The interest rate on one-month CDs fell almost as much, 2.8 percentage points. These interest rates are **short-term interest rates**—rates on financial assets that come due, or mature, within less than a year.

> **Short-term interest rates** are the interest rates on financial assets that mature within less than a year.
>
> **Long-term interest rates** are interest rates on financial assets that mature a number of years in the future.

As short-term interest rates fell between June 2007 and June 2008, the interest rates on money didn't fall by the same amount. The interest rate on currency, of course, remained at zero. The interest rate paid on demand deposits did fall, but by much less than short-term interest rates. As a comparison of the two columns of Table 15-2 shows, the opportunity cost of holding money fell. The last two rows of Table 15-2 summarize this comparison: they give the differences between the interest rates on demand deposits and on currency and the interest rate on CDs. These differences—the opportunity cost of holding money rather than interest-bearing assets—declined sharply between June 2007 and June 2008. This reflects a general result: *The higher the short-term interest rate, the higher the opportunity cost of holding money; the lower the short-term interest rate, the lower the opportunity cost of holding money.*

**TABLE 15-2** Interest Rates and the Opportunity Cost of Holding Money

|  | June 2007 | June 2008 |
|---|---|---|
| Federal funds rate | 5.25% | 2.00% |
| One-month certificates of deposit (CDs) | 5.30% | 2.50% |
| Interest-bearing demand deposits | 2.30% | 1.24% |
| Currency | 0 | 0 |
| **CDs minus interest-bearing demand deposits (percentage points)** | **3.00** | **1.26** |
| **CDs minus currency (percentage points)** | **5.30** | **2.50** |

*Source:* Federal Reserve Bank of St. Louis.

The fact that the federal funds rate in Table 15-2 and the interest rate on one-month CDs fell by almost the same percentage is not an accident: all short-term interest rates tend to move together, with rare exceptions. The reason short-term interest rates tend to move together is that CDs and other short-term assets (like one-month and three-month U.S. Treasury bills) are in effect competing for the same business. Any short-term asset that offers a lower-than-average interest rate will be sold by investors, who will move their wealth into a higher-yielding short-term asset. The selling of the asset, in turn, forces its interest rate up, because investors must be rewarded with a higher rate in order to induce them to buy it.

Conversely, investors will move their wealth into any short-term financial asset that offers an above-average interest rate. The purchase of the asset drives its interest rate down when sellers find they can lower the rate of return on the asset and still find willing buyers. So interest rates on short-term financial assets tend to be roughly the same because no asset will consistently offer a higher-than-average or a lower-than-average interest rate.

Table 15-2 contains only short-term interest rates. At any given moment, **long-term interest rates**—rates of interest on financial assets that mature, or come due, a number of years into the future—may be different from short-term interest rates. The difference between short-term and long-term interest rates is sometimes important as a practical matter. Moreover, it's short-term rates rather than long-term rates that affect money demand, because the decision to hold money involves trading off the convenience of holding cash versus the payoff from holding assets that mature in the short term—a year or less. For the moment, however, let's ignore the distinction between short-term and long-term rates and assume that there is only one interest rate.

The **money demand curve** shows the relationship between the interest rate and the quantity of money demanded.

# The Money Demand Curve

Because the overall level of interest rates affects the opportunity cost of holding money, the quantity of money individuals and firms want to hold is, other things equal, negatively related to the interest rate. In Figure 15-1, the horizontal axis shows the quantity of money demanded and the vertical axis shows the interest rate, $r$, which you can think of as a representative short-term interest rate such as the rate on one-month CDs. (As we discussed in Chapter 10, it is the nominal interest rate, not the real interest rate, that influences people's money allocation decisions. Hence, $r$ in Figure 15-1 and all subsequent figures is the nominal interest rate.)

The relationship between the interest rate and the quantity of money demanded by the public is illustrated by the **money demand curve,** $MD$, in Figure 15-1. The money demand curve slopes downward because, other things equal, a higher interest rate increases the opportunity cost of holding money, leading the public to reduce the quantity of money it demands. For example, if the interest rate is very low—say, 1%—the interest forgone by holding money is relatively small. As a result, individuals and firms will tend to hold relatively large amounts of money to avoid the cost and nuisance of converting other assets into money when making purchases.

By contrast, if the interest rate is relatively high—say, 15%, a level it reached in the United States in the early 1980s—the opportunity cost of holding money is high. People will respond by keeping only small amounts in cash and deposits, converting assets into money only when needed.

You might ask why we draw the money demand curve with the interest rate—as opposed to rates of return on other assets, such as stocks or real estate—on the vertical axis. The answer is that for most people the relevant question in deciding how much money to hold is whether to put the funds in the form of other assets that can be turned fairly quickly and easily into money. Stocks don't fit that definition because there are significant transaction fees when you sell stock (which is why stock market investors are advised not to buy and sell too often). Real estate doesn't fit the definition either because selling real estate involves even larger fees and can take a long time as well. So the relevant comparison is with assets that are "close to" money—fairly liquid assets like CDs. And as we've already seen, the interest rates on all these assets normally move closely together.

**FIGURE 15-1** The Money Demand Curve

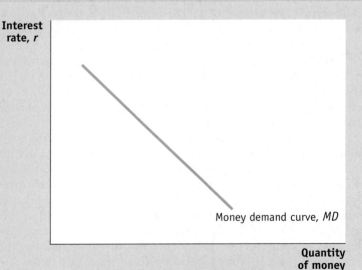

The money demand curve illustrates the relationship between the interest rate and the quantity of money demanded. It slopes downward: a higher interest rate leads to a higher opportunity cost of holding money and reduces the quantity of money demanded. Correspondingly, a lower interest rate reduces the opportunity cost of holding money and increases the quantity of money demanded.

Interest rate, $r$

Money demand curve, $MD$

Quantity of money

## Shifts of the Money Demand Curve

A number of factors other than the interest rate affect the demand for money. When one of these factors changes, the money demand curve shifts. Figure 15-2 shows shifts of the money demand curve: an increase in the demand for money corresponds to a rightward shift of the *MD* curve, raising the quantity of money demanded at any given interest rate; a decrease in the demand for money corresponds to a leftward shift of the *MD* curve, reducing the quantity of money demanded at any given interest rate. The most important factors causing the money demand curve to shift are changes in the aggregate price level, changes in real GDP, changes in credit markets and banking technology, and changes in institutions.

**Changes in the Aggregate Price Level**  Americans keep a lot more cash in their wallets and funds in their checking accounts today than they did in the 1950s. One reason is that they have to if they want to be able to buy anything: almost everything costs more now than it did when you could get a burger, fries, and a drink at McDonald's for 45 cents and a gallon of gasoline for 29 cents. So, other things equal, higher prices increase the demand for money (a rightward shift of the *MD* curve), and lower prices decrease the demand for money (a leftward shift of the *MD* curve).

We can actually be more specific than this: other things equal, the demand for money is *proportional* to the price level. That is, if the aggregate price level rises by 20%, the quantity of money demanded at any given interest rate, such as $r_1$ in Figure 15-2, also rises by 20%—the movement from $M_1$ to $M_2$. Why? Because if the price of everything rises by 20%, it takes 20% more money to buy the same basket of goods and services. And if the aggregate price level falls by 20%, at any given interest rate the quantity of money demanded falls by 20%—shown by the movement from $M_1$ to $M_3$ at the interest rate $r_1$. As we'll see later, the fact that money demand is proportional to the price level has important implications for the long-run effects of monetary policy.

**Changes in Real GDP**  Households and firms hold money as a way to facilitate purchases of goods and services. The larger the quantity of goods and services they buy, the larger the quantity of money they will want to hold at any given interest rate. So an increase in real GDP—the total quantity of goods and services produced and sold in the economy—shifts the money demand curve rightward. A fall in real GDP shifts the money demand curve leftward.

**FIGURE  15-2  Increases and Decreases in the Demand for Money**

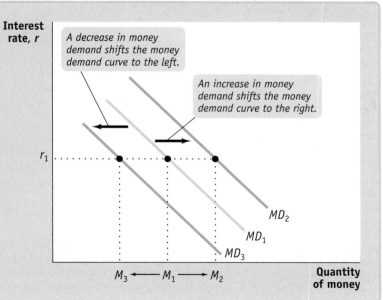

The demand curve for money shifts when non-interest rate factors that affect the demand for money change. An increase in money demand shifts the money demand curve to the right, from $MD_1$ to $MD_2$, and the quantity of money demanded rises at any given interest rate. A decrease in money demand shifts the money demand curve to the left, from $MD_1$ to $MD_3$, and the quantity of money demanded falls at any given interest rate.

Interest rate, *r*

A decrease in money demand shifts the money demand curve to the left.

An increase in money demand shifts the money demand curve to the right.

$r_1$

$MD_2$

$MD_1$

$MD_3$

$M_3 \longleftarrow M_1 \longrightarrow M_2$

Quantity of money

**Changes in Credit Markets and Banking Technology** Credit cards are everywhere in American life today, but it wasn't always so. The first credit card that allowed customers to carry a balance from month to month (called a "revolving balance") was issued in 1959. Before then, people had to either pay for purchases in cash or pay off their balance every month. The invention of revolving-balance credit cards allowed people to hold less money in order to fund their purchases and decreased the demand for money. In addition, changes in banking technology that made credit cards widely available and widely accepted magnified the effect, making it easier for people to make purchases without having to convert funds from their interest-bearing assets, further reducing the demand for money.

**Changes in Institutions** Changes in institutions can increase or decrease the demand for money. For example, until Regulation Q was eliminated in 1980, U.S. banks weren't allowed to offer interest on checking accounts. So the interest you would forgo by holding funds in a checking account instead of an interest-bearing asset made the opportunity cost of holding funds in checking accounts very high. When banking regulations changed, allowing banks to pay interest on checking account funds, the demand for money rose and shifted the money demand curve to the right.

## ECONOMICS > *IN ACTION*

### A YEN FOR CASH

Japan, say financial experts, is still a "cash society." Visitors from the United States or Europe are surprised at how little use the Japanese make of credit cards and how much cash they carry around in their wallets. Yet Japan is an economically and technologically advanced country and, according to some measures, ahead of the United States in the use of telecommunications and information technology. So why do the citizens of this economic powerhouse still do business the way Americans and Europeans did a generation ago? The answer highlights the factors affecting the demand for money.

One reason the Japanese use cash so much is that their institutions never made the switch to heavy reliance on plastic. For complex reasons, Japan's retail sector is still dominated by small mom-and-pop stores, which are reluctant to invest in credit card technology. Japan's banks have also been slow about pushing transaction technology; visitors are often surprised to find that ATMs close early in the evening rather than staying open all night.

But there's another reason the Japanese hold so much cash: there's little opportunity cost to doing so. Short-term interest rates in Japan have been below 1% since the mid-1990s. It also helps that the Japanese crime rate is quite low, so you are unlikely to have your wallet full of cash stolen. So why not hold cash?

No matter what they are shopping for, Japanese consumers tend to pay with cash rather than plastic.

▼ **Quick Review**

• Money offers a lower rate of return than other financial assets. We usually compare the rate of return on money with **short-term**, not **long-term, interest rates.**

• Holding money provides liquidity but incurs an opportunity cost that rises with the interest rate, leading to the downward slope of the **money demand curve.**

• Changes in the aggregate price level, real GDP, credit markets and banking technology, and institutions shift the money demand curve. An increase in the demand for money shifts the money demand curve rightward; a decrease in the demand for money shifts the money demand curve leftward.

**CHECK YOUR UNDERSTANDING** 15-1

1. Explain how each of the following would affect the quantity of money demanded. Does the change cause a movement along the money demand curve or a shift of the money demand curve?
   a. Short-term interest rates rise from 5% to 30%.
   b. All prices fall by 10%.
   c. New wireless technology automatically charges supermarket purchases to credit cards, eliminating the need to stop at the cash register.
   d. In order to avoid paying a sharp increase in taxes, residents of Laguria shift their assets into overseas bank accounts. These accounts are harder for tax authorities to trace but also harder for their owners to tap and convert funds into cash.

2. Which of the following will increase the opportunity cost of holding cash? Reduce it? Have no effect? Explain.
   a. Merchants charge a 1% fee on debit/credit card transactions for purchases of less than $50.
   b. To attract more deposits, banks raise the interest paid on six-month CDs.
   c. It's the holiday shopping season and retailers have temporarily slashed prices to unexpectedly low levels.
   d. The cost of food rises significantly.

*Solutions appear at back of book.*

> According to the **liquidity preference model of the interest rate,** the interest rate is determined by the supply and demand for money.
>
> The **money supply curve** shows how the quantity of money supplied varies with the interest rate.

# Money and Interest Rates

*The Federal Open Market Committee decided today to lower its target for the federal funds rate 75 basis points to 2¼ percent.*

*Recent information indicates that the outlook for economic activity has weakened further. Growth in consumer spending has slowed and labor markets have softened. Financial markets remain under considerable stress, and the tightening of credit conditions and the deepening of the housing contraction are likely to weigh on economic growth over the next few quarters.*

So read the beginning of a press release from the Federal Reserve issued on March 18, 2008. (A basis point is equal to 0.01 percentage point. So the statement implies that the Fed lowered the target from 3% to 2.25%.) We learned about the federal funds rate in Chapter 14: it's the rate at which banks lend reserves to each other to meet the required reserve ratio. As the statement implies, at each of its eight-times-a-year meetings, a group called the Federal Open Market Committee sets a target value for the federal funds rate. It's then up to Fed officials to achieve that target. This is done by the Open Market Desk at the Federal Reserve Bank of New York, which buys and sells short-term U.S. government debt, known as Treasury bills, to achieve that target.

As we've already seen, other short-term interest rates, such as the rates on CDs, move with the federal funds rate. So when the Fed reduced its target for the federal funds rate from 3% to 2.25% in March 2008, many other short-term interest rates also fell by about three-quarters of a percentage point.

How does the Fed go about achieving a *target federal funds rate*? And more to the point, how is the Fed able to affect interest rates at all?

## The Equilibrium Interest Rate

Recall that, for simplicity, we're assuming there is only one interest rate paid on nonmonetary financial assets, both in the short run and in the long run. To understand how the interest rate is determined, consider Figure 15-3, which illustrates the **liquidity preference model of the interest rate;** this model says that the interest rate is determined by the supply and demand for money in the market for money. Figure 15-3 combines the money demand curve, *MD*, with the **money supply curve,** *MS*, which shows how the quantity of money supplied by the Federal Reserve varies with the interest rate.

In Chapter 14 we learned how the Federal Reserve can increase or decrease the money supply: it usually does this through *open-market operations*, buying or selling Treasury bills, but it can also lend via the *discount window* or change *reserve requirements*. Let's assume for simplicity that the Fed, using one or more of these methods, simply chooses the level of the money supply that it believes will achieve its interest rate target. Then the money supply curve is a vertical line, *MS* in Figure 15-3, with a horizontal intercept corresponding to the money supply chosen by the Fed, $\overline{M}$. The money market equilibrium is at *E*, where *MS* and *MD* cross. At this point the quantity of money demanded equals the money supply, $\overline{M}$, leading to an equilibrium interest rate of $r_E$.

**FIGURE** **15-3** Equilibrium in the Money Market

The money supply curve, *MS*, is vertical at the money supply chosen by the Federal Reserve, $\overline{M}$. The money market is in equilibrium at the interest rate $r_E$: *the quantity of money demanded by the public is equal to* $\overline{M}$, *the quantity of money supplied.*

At a point such as *L*, the interest rate, $r_L$, is below $r_E$ and the corresponding quantity of money demanded, $M_L$, exceeds the money supply, $\overline{M}$. In an attempt to shift their wealth out of nonmoney interest-bearing financial assets and raise their money holdings, investors drive the interest rate up to $r_E$. At a point such as *H*, the interest rate $r_H$ exceeds $r_E$ and the corresponding quantity of money demanded, $M_H$, is less than the money supply, $\overline{M}$. In an attempt to shift out of money holdings into nonmoney interest-bearing financial assets, investors drive the interest rate down to $r_E$.

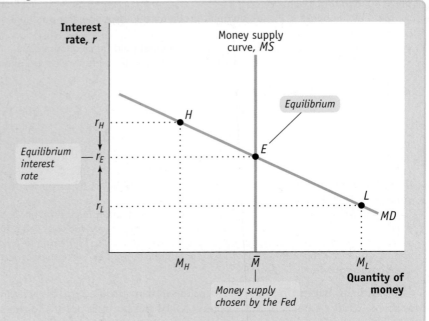

To understand why $r_E$ is the equilibrium interest rate, consider what happens if the money market is at a point like *L*, where the interest rate, $r_L$, is below $r_E$. At $r_L$ the public wants to hold the quantity of money $M_L$, an amount larger than the actual money supply, $\overline{M}$. This means that at point *L*, the public wants to shift some of its wealth out of interest-bearing assets such as CDs into money.

This has two implications. One is that the quantity of money demanded is *more* than the quantity of money supplied. The other is that the quantity of interest-bearing money assets demanded is less than the quantity supplied. So those trying to sell nonmoney assets will find that they have to offer a higher interest rate to attract buyers. As a result, the interest rate will be driven up from $r_L$ until the public wants to hold the quantity of money that is actually available, $\overline{M}$. That is, the interest rate will rise until it is equal to $r_E$.

Now consider what happens if the money market is at a point such as *H* in Figure 15-3, where the interest rate $r_H$ is above $r_E$. In that case the quantity of money demanded, $M_H$, is less than the quantity of money supplied, $\overline{M}$. Correspondingly, the quantity of interest-bearing nonmoney assets demanded is greater than the quantity supplied. Those trying to sell interest-bearing nonmoney assets will find that they can offer a lower interest rate and still find willing buyers. This leads to a fall in the interest rate from $r_H$. It falls until the public wants to hold the quantity of money that is actually available, $\overline{M}$. Again, the interest rate will end up at $r_E$.

## Two Models of Interest Rates?

You might have noticed that this is the second time we have discussed the determination of the interest rate. In Chapter 10 we studied the *loanable funds model* of the interest rate; according to that model, the interest rate is determined by the equalization of the supply of funds from lenders and the demand for funds by borrowers in the market for loanable funds. But here we have described a seemingly different model in which the interest rate is determined by the equalization of the supply and demand for money in the money market. Which of these models is correct?

The answer is both. We explain how the models are consistent with each other in the appendix to this chapter. For now, let's put the loanable funds model to one side and concentrate on the liquidity preference model of the interest rate. The most important insight from this model is that it shows us how monetary policy—actions by the Federal Reserve and other central banks—works.

The **target federal funds rate** is the Federal Reserve's desired federal funds rate.

## Monetary Policy and the Interest Rate

Let's examine how the Federal Reserve can use changes in the money supply to change the interest rate. Figure 15-4 shows what happens when the Fed increases the money supply from $\overline{M}_1$ to $\overline{M}_2$. The economy is originally in equilibrium at $E_1$, with an equilibrium interest rate of $r_1$ and money supply $\overline{M}_1$. An increase in the money supply by the Fed to $\overline{M}_2$ shifts the money supply curve to the right, from $MS_1$ to $MS_2$, and leads to a fall in the equilibrium interest rate to $r_2$. Why? Because $r_2$ is the only interest rate at which the public is willing to hold the quantity of money actually supplied, $\overline{M}_2$.

So an increase in the money supply drives the interest rate down. Similarly, a reduction in the money supply drives the interest rate up. By adjusting the money supply up or down, the Fed can set the interest rate.

In practice, at each meeting the Federal Open Market Committee decides on the interest rate to prevail for the next six weeks, until its next meeting. The Fed sets a **target federal funds rate,** a desired level for the federal funds rate. This target is then enforced by the Open Market Desk of the Federal Reserve Bank of New York, which adjusts the money supply through the purchase and sale of Treasury bills until the actual federal funds rate equals the target rate. The other tools of monetary policy, lending through the discount window and changes in reserve requirements, aren't used on a regular basis (although the Fed used discount window lending in its efforts to address the 2008 financial crisis).

Figure 15-5 shows how this works. In both panels, $r_T$ is the target federal funds rate. In panel (a), the initial money supply curve is $MS_1$ with money supply $\overline{M}_1$, and the equilibrium interest rate, $r_1$, is above the target rate. To lower the interest rate to $r_T$, the Fed makes an open-market

**FIGURE** **15-4**  The Effect of an Increase in the Money Supply on the Interest Rate

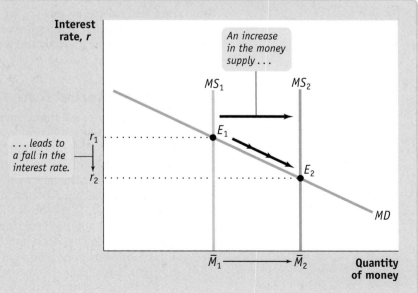

The Federal Reserve can lower the interest rate by increasing the money supply. Here, the equilibrium interest rate falls from $r_1$ to $r_2$ in response to an increase in the money supply from $\overline{M}_1$ to $\overline{M}_2$. In order to induce people to hold the larger quantity of money, the interest rate must fall from $r_1$ to $r_2$.

FIGURE **15-5** Setting the Federal Funds Rate

The Federal Reserve sets a target for the federal funds rate and uses open-market operations to achieve that target. In both panels the target rate is $r_T$. In panel (a) the initial equilibrium interest rate, $r_1$, is above the target rate. The Fed increases the money supply by making an open-market purchase of Treasury bills, pushing the money supply curve rightward, from $MS_1$ to $MS_2$, and driving the interest rate down to $r_T$. In panel (b) the initial equilibrium interest rate, $r_1$, is below the target rate. The Fed reduces the money supply by making an open-market sale of Treasury bills, pushing the money supply curve leftward, from $MS_1$ to $MS_2$, and driving the interest rate up to $r_T$.

purchase of Treasury bills. As we learned in Chapter 14, an open-market purchase of Treasury bills leads to an increase in the money supply via the money multiplier. This is illustrated in panel (a) by the rightward shift of the money supply curve from $MS_1$ to $MS_2$ and an increase in the money supply to $\overline{M}_2$. This drives the equilibrium interest rate down to the target rate, $r_T$.

Panel (b) shows the opposite case. Again, the initial money supply curve is $MS_1$ with money supply $\overline{M}_1$. But this time the equilibrium interest rate, $r_1$, is below the target federal funds rate, $r_T$. In this case, the Fed will make an open-market sale of Treasury bills, leading to a fall in the money supply to $\overline{M}_2$ via the money multiplier. The money supply curve shifts leftward from $MS_1$ to $MS_2$, driving the equilibrium interest rate up to the target federal funds rate, $r_T$.

## Long-Term Interest Rates

Earlier in this chapter we mentioned that *long-term interest rates*—rates on bonds or loans that mature in several years—don't necessarily move with short-term interest rates. How is that possible, and what does it say about monetary policy?

Consider the case of Millie, who has already decided to place $10,000 in U.S. government bonds for the next two years. However, she hasn't decided whether to put the money in one-year bonds, at a 4% rate of interest, or two-year bonds, at a 5% rate of interest. If she buys the one-year bond, then in one year, Millie will receive the $10,000 she paid for the bond (the *principal*) plus interest earned. If instead she buys the two-year bond, Millie will have to wait until the end of the second year to receive her principal and her interest.

You might think that the two-year bonds are a clearly better deal—but they may not be. Suppose that Millie expects the rate of interest on one-year bonds to rise sharply next year. If she puts her funds in one-year bonds this year, she will be able to reinvest the money at a much higher rate next year. And this could give her a two-year rate of return that is higher than if she put her funds into the two-year bonds today. For example, if the rate of interest on one-year bonds rises from 4% this year to 8% next year, putting her funds in a one-year bond today and in another one-year bond a year from now will give her an annual rate of return over the next two years of about 6%, better than the 5% rate on two-year bonds.

The same considerations apply to all investors deciding between short-term and long-term bonds. If they expect short-term interest rates to rise, investors may buy short-term bonds even if long-term bonds bought today offer a higher interest rate today. If they expect short-term interest rates to fall, investors may buy long-term bonds even if short-term bonds bought today offer a higher interest rate today.

As this example suggests, long-term interest rates largely reflect the average expectation in the market about what's going to happen to short-term rates in the future. When long-term rates are higher than short-term rates, as they were in 2010, the market is signaling that it expects short-term rates to rise in the future.

This is not, however, the whole story: risk is also a factor. Return to the example of Millie, deciding whether to buy one-year or two-year bonds. Suppose that there is some chance she will need to cash in her investment after just one year—say, to meet an emergency medical bill. If she buys two-year bonds, she would have to sell those bonds to meet the unexpected expense. But what price will she get for those bonds? It depends on what has happened to interest rates in the rest of the economy. As we learned in Chapter 10, bond prices and interest rates move in opposite directions: if interest rates rise, bond prices fall, and vice versa.

This means that Millie will face extra risk if she buys two-year rather than one-year bonds, because if a year from now bond prices fall and she must sell her bonds in order to raise cash, she will lose money on the bonds. Owing to this risk factor, long-term interest rates are, on average, higher than short-term rates in order to compensate long-term bond purchasers for the higher risk they face (although this relationship is reversed when short-term rates are unusually high).

As we will see later in this chapter, the fact that long-term rates don't necessarily move with short-term rates is sometimes an important consideration for monetary policy.

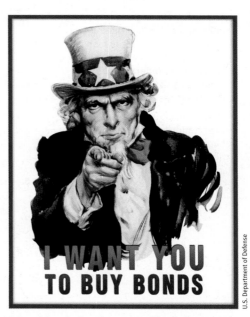

Advertising during the two world wars increased the demand for government long-term bonds from savers who might have been otherwise reluctant to tie up their funds for several years.

## ECONOMICS ▶ IN ACTION

### THE FED REVERSES COURSE

We began this section with the Fed's announcement of March 18, 2008, that it was cutting its target interest rate. This particular action was part of a larger story: a dramatic reversal of Fed policy that began in September 2007.

Figure 15-6 shows two interest rates from the beginning of 2004 to mid-2011: the target federal funds rate, decided by the Federal Open Market Committee, and the effective, or actual, rate in the market. As you can see, the Fed raised its target rate in a series of steps from late 2004 until the middle of 2006; it did this to head off the possibility of an overheating economy and rising inflation (more on that later in this chapter). But the Fed dramatically reversed course beginning in September 2007, as falling housing prices triggered a growing

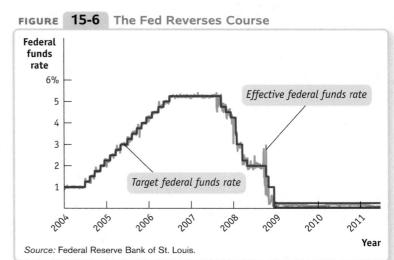

**FIGURE 15-6** The Fed Reverses Course

*Source:* Federal Reserve Bank of St. Louis.

financial crisis and ultimately a severe recession. And in December 2008, the Fed decided to allow the federal funds rate to move inside a target band between 0% and 0.25%. From 2009 to mid-2011, the Fed funds rate was kept close to zero in response to a very weak economy and high unemployment.

Figure 15-6 also shows that the Fed doesn't always hit its target. There were a number of days, especially in 2008, when the effective federal funds rate was significantly above or below the target rate. But these episodes didn't last long, and overall the Fed got what it wanted, at least as far as short-term interest rates were concerned.

### CHECK YOUR UNDERSTANDING  15-2

1. Assume that there is an increase in the demand for money at every interest rate. Using a diagram, show what effect this will have on the equilibrium interest rate for a given money supply.

2. Now assume that the Fed is following a policy of targeting the federal funds rate. What will the Fed do in the situation described in Question 1 to keep the federal funds rate unchanged? Illustrate with a diagram.

3. Frannie must decide whether to buy a one-year bond today and another one a year from now, or buy a two-year bond today. In which of the following scenarios is she better off taking the first action? The second action?
   a. This year, the interest on a one-year bond is 4%; next year, it will be 10%. The interest rate on a two-year bond is 5%.
   b. This year, the interest rate on a one-year bond is 4%; next year, it will be 1%. The interest rate on a two-year bond is 3%.

Solutions appear at back of book.

## Monetary Policy and Aggregate Demand

In Chapter 13 we saw how fiscal policy can be used to stabilize the economy. Now we will see how monetary policy—changes in the money supply, and the interest rate—can play the same role.

### Expansionary and Contractionary Monetary Policy

In Chapter 12 we learned that monetary policy shifts the aggregate demand curve. We can now explain how that works: through the effect of monetary policy on the interest rate.

Figure 15-7 illustrates the process. Suppose, first, that the Federal Reserve wants to reduce interest rates, so it expands the money supply. As you can see in the top portion of the figure, a lower interest rate, in turn, will lead, other things equal, to more investment spending. This will in turn lead to higher consumer spending, through the multiplier process, and to an increase in aggregate output demanded. In the end, the total quantity of goods and services demanded at any given aggregate price level rises when the quantity of money increases, and the *AD* curve shifts to the right. Monetary policy that increases the demand for goods and services is known as **expansionary monetary policy.**

Suppose, alternatively, that the Federal Reserve wants to increase interest rates, so it contracts the money supply. You can see this process illustrated in the bottom portion of the diagram. Contraction of the money supply leads to a higher interest rate. The higher interest rate leads to lower investment spending, then to lower consumer spending, and then to a decrease in aggregate output demanded. So the total quantity of goods and services demanded falls when the money supply is reduced, and the *AD* curve shifts to the left. Monetary policy that decreases the demand for goods and services is called **contractionary monetary policy.**

*"I told you the Fed should have tightened."*

**Expansionary monetary policy** is monetary policy that increases aggregate demand.

**Contractionary monetary policy** is monetary policy that decreases aggregate demand.

FIGURE **15-7** Expansionary and Contractionary Monetary Policy

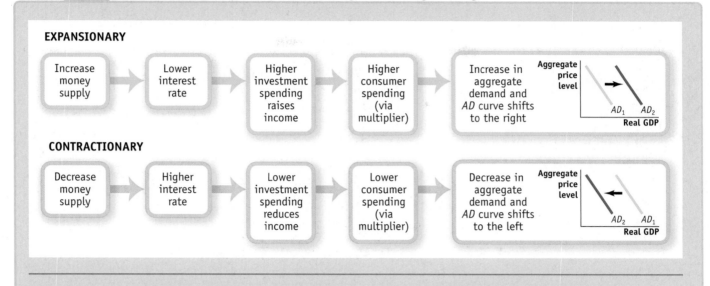

The top portion shows what happens when the Fed adopts an expansionary monetary policy and increases the money supply. Interest rates fall, leading to higher investment spending, which raises income, which, in turn, raises consumer spending and shifts the *AD* curve to the right. The bottom portion shows what happens when the Fed adopts a contractionary monetary policy and reduces the money supply. Interest rates rise, leading to lower investment spending and a reduction in income. This lowers consumer spending and shifts the *AD* curve to the left.

## Monetary Policy in Practice

How does the Fed decide whether to use expansionary or contractionary monetary policy? And how does it decide how much is enough? In Chapter 6 we learned that policy makers try to fight recessions, as well as try to ensure *price stability*: low (though usually not zero) inflation. Actual monetary policy reflects a combination of these goals.

In general, the Federal Reserve and other central banks tend to engage in expansionary monetary policy when actual real GDP is below potential output. Panel (a) of Figure 15-8 shows the U.S. output gap, which we defined in Chapter 12 as the percentage difference between actual real GDP and potential output, versus the federal funds rate since 1985. (Recall that the output gap is positive when actual real GDP exceeds potential output.) As you can see, the Fed has tended to raise interest rates when the output gap is rising—that is, when the economy is developing an inflationary gap—and cut rates when the output gap is falling.

The big exception was the late 1990s, when the Fed left rates steady for several years even as the economy developed a positive output gap (which went along with a low unemployment rate). One reason the Fed was willing to keep interest rates low in the late 1990s was that inflation was low. Panel (b) of Figure 15-8 compares the inflation rate, measured as the rate of change in consumer prices excluding food and energy, with the federal funds rate. You can see how low inflation during the mid-1990s, the early 2000s, and the late 2000s helped encourage loose monetary policy in the late 1990s, in 2002–2003, and again beginning in 2008.

## The Taylor Rule Method of Setting Monetary Policy

In 1993 Stanford economist John Taylor suggested that monetary policy should follow a simple rule that takes into account concerns about both the business cycle and inflation. He also suggested that actual monetary policy often looks as if the Federal Reserve was, in fact, more or less following the proposed rule. A **Taylor rule for monetary policy** is a rule for setting interest rates that takes

A **Taylor rule for monetary policy** is a rule that sets the federal funds rate according to the level of the inflation rate and either the output gap or the unemployment rate.

**FIGURE** **15-8** Tracking Monetary Policy Using the Output Gap and Inflation

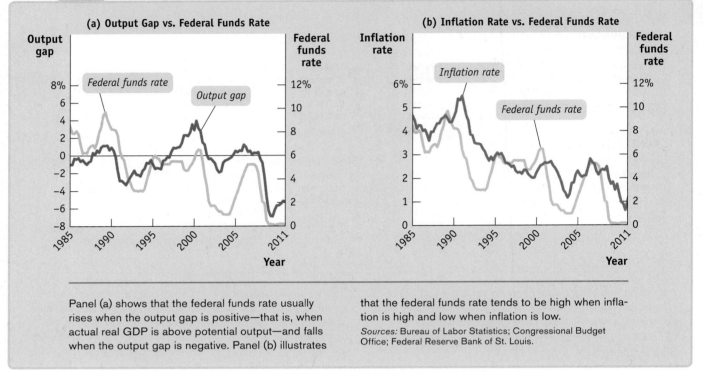

Panel (a) shows that the federal funds rate usually rises when the output gap is positive—that is, when actual real GDP is above potential output—and falls when the output gap is negative. Panel (b) illustrates that the federal funds rate tends to be high when inflation is high and low when inflation is low.

*Sources:* Bureau of Labor Statistics; Congressional Budget Office; Federal Reserve Bank of St. Louis.

into account the inflation rate and the output gap or, in some cases, the unemployment rate.

A widely cited example of a Taylor rule is a relationship among Fed policy, inflation, and unemployment estimated by economists at the Federal Reserve Bank of San Francisco. These economists found that between 1988 and 2008 the Fed's behavior was well summarized by the following Taylor rule:

$$\text{Federal funds rate} = 2.07 + 1.28 \times \text{inflation rate} - 1.95 \times \text{unemployment gap}$$

where the inflation rate was measured by the change over the previous year in consumer prices excluding food and energy, and the unemployment gap was the difference between the actual unemployment rate and Congressional Budget Office estimates of the natural rate of unemployment.

Figure 15-9 compares the federal funds rate predicted by this rule with the actual federal funds rate from 1985 to early 2011. As you can see, the Fed's decisions were quite close to those predicted by this particular Taylor rule from 1988 through the end of 2008. We'll talk about what happened after 2008 shortly.

## Inflation Targeting

Until January 2012, the Fed did not explicitly commit itself to achieving a particular inflation rate. However, in January 2012, Bernanke announced that the Fed would set its policy to maintain an approximately 2% inflation rate per year. With that statement, the Fed joined a number of other central banks that have explicit inflation targets. So rather than using a Taylor rule to set monetary policy, they instead announce the inflation rate that they want to achieve—the *inflation target*—and set policy in an attempt to hit that target. This method of setting monetary policy, called **inflation targeting,** involves having the central bank announce the inflation rate it is trying to achieve and set policy in an attempt to

**Inflation targeting** occurs when the central bank sets an explicit target for the inflation rate and sets monetary policy in order to hit that target.

FIGURE    **15-9**    The Taylor Rule and the Federal Funds Rate

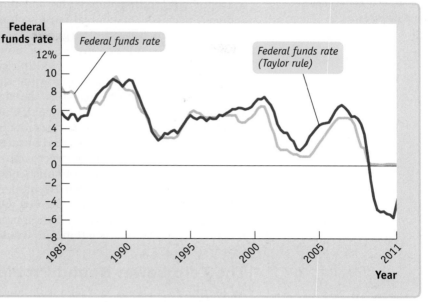

The blue line shows the federal funds rate predicted by the San Francisco Fed's version of the Taylor rule, which relates the interest rate to the inflation rate and the unemployment rate. The red line shows the actual federal funds rate. The actual rate tracked the predicted rate quite closely through the end of 2008. After that, however, the Taylor rule called for negative interest rates, which aren't possible.

*Sources:* Bureau of Labor Statistics; Congressional Budget Office; Federal Reserve Bank of St. Louis; Glenn D. Rudebusch, "The Fed's Monetary Policy Response to the Current Crisis," *FRBSF Economic Letter* #2009-17 (May 22, 2009).

hit that target. The central bank of New Zealand, which was the first country to adopt inflation targeting, specified a range for that target of 1% to 3%.

Other central banks commit themselves to achieving a specific number. For example, the Bank of England has committed to keeping inflation at 2%. In practice, there doesn't seem to be much difference between these versions: central banks with a target range for inflation seem to aim for the middle of that range, and central banks with a fixed target tend to give themselves considerable wiggle room.

One major difference between inflation targeting and the Taylor rule method is that inflation targeting is forward-looking rather than backward-looking. That is, the Taylor rule method adjusts monetary policy in response to *past* inflation, but inflation targeting is based on a forecast of future inflation.

## GLOBAL COMPARISON    INFLATION TARGETS

This figure shows the target inflation rates of six central banks that have adopted inflation targeting. The central bank of New Zealand introduced inflation targeting in 1990. Today it has an inflation target range of from 1% to 3%. The central banks of Canada and Sweden have the same target range but also specify 2% as the precise target. The central banks of Britain and Norway have specific targets for inflation, 2% and 2.5%, respectively. Neither states by how much they're prepared to miss those targets. Since 2012, the U.S. Federal Reserve also targets inflation at 2%.

In practice, these differences in detail don't seem to lead to any significant difference in results. New Zealand aims for the middle of its range, at 2% inflation; Britain, Norway, and the United States allow themselves considerable wiggle room around their target inflation rates.

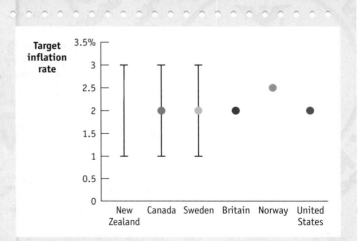

The **zero lower bound for interest rates** means that interest rates cannot fall below zero.

Advocates of inflation targeting argue that it has two key advantages over a Taylor rule: *transparency* and *accountability*. First, economic uncertainty is reduced because the central bank's plan is transparent: the public knows the objective of an inflation-targeting central bank. Second, the central bank's success can be judged by seeing how closely actual inflation rates have matched the inflation target, making central bankers accountable.

Critics of inflation targeting argue that it's too restrictive because there are times when other concerns—like the stability of the financial system—should take priority over achieving any particular inflation rate. Indeed, in late 2007 and early 2008 the Fed cut interest rates much more than either a Taylor rule or inflation targeting would have dictated because it feared that turmoil in the financial markets would lead to a major recession. (In fact, it did.)

Many American macroeconomists have had positive things to say about inflation targeting—including Ben Bernanke, the current chairman of the Federal Reserve. And in January 2012 the Fed declared that what it means by the "price stability" it seeks is 2 percent inflation, although there was no explicit commitment about when this inflation rate would be achieved.

## The Zero Lower Bound Problem

As Figure 15-9 shows, a Taylor rule based on inflation and the unemployment rate does a good job of predicting Federal Reserve policy from 1988 through 2008. After that, however, things go awry, and for a simple reason: with very high unemployment and low inflation, the same Taylor rule called for an interest rate less than zero, which isn't possible.

Why aren't negative interest rates possible? Because people always have the alternative of holding cash, which offers a zero interest rate. Nobody would ever buy a bond yielding an interest rate less than zero because holding cash would be a better alternative.

The fact that interest rates can't go below zero—called the **zero lower bound for interest rates**—sets limits to the power of monetary policy. In 2009 and 2010, inflation was low and the economy was operating far below potential, so the Federal Reserve wanted to increase aggregate demand. Yet the normal way it does this—open-market purchases of short-term government debt to expand the money supply—had run out of room to operate because short-term interest rates were already at or near zero.

In November 2010 the Fed began an attempt to circumvent this problem, which went by the somewhat obscure name "quantitative easing." Instead of purchasing only short-term government debt, it began buying longer-term government debt—five-year or six-year bonds, rather than three-month Treasury bills. As we have already pointed out, long-term interest rates don't exactly follow short-term rates. At the time the Fed began this program, short-term rates were near zero, but rates on longer-term bonds were between 2% and 3%. The Fed hoped that direct purchases of these longer-term bonds would drive down interest rates on long-term debt, exerting an expansionary effect on the economy.

This policy may have given the economy some boost in 2011, but as of early 2012, recovery remained painfully slow.

## ECONOMICS ▸ IN ACTION

### WHAT THE FED WANTS, THE FED GETS

What's the evidence that the Fed can actually cause an economic contraction or expansion? You might think that finding such evidence is just a matter of looking at what happens to the economy when interest rates go up or down. But it turns out that there's a big problem with that approach: the Fed usually changes interest rates in an attempt to tame the business cycle, raising rates if the economy is expanding and reducing rates if the economy is slumping. So in the actual data, it often looks as if low interest rates go along with a weak economy and high rates go along with a strong economy.

In a famous 1994 paper titled "Monetary Policy Matters," the macroeconomists Christina Romer and David Romer solved this problem by focusing on episodes in which monetary policy wasn't a reaction to the business cycle. Specifically, they used minutes from the Federal Open Market Committee and other sources to identify episodes "in which the Federal Reserve in effect decided to attempt to create a recession to reduce inflation." As we'll learn in Chapter 16, rather than just using monetary policy as a tool of macroeconomic stabilization, sometimes it is used to eliminate *embedded* inflation—inflation that people believe will persist into the future. In such a case, the Fed needs to create a recessionary gap—not just eliminate an inflationary gap—to wring embedded inflation out of the economy.

Figure 15-10 shows the unemployment rate between 1952 and 1984 (orange) and also identifies five dates on which, according to Romer and Romer, the Fed decided that it wanted a recession (vertical red lines). In four out of the five cases, the decision to contract the economy was followed, after a modest lag, by a rise in the unemployment rate. On average, Romer and Romer found, the unemployment rate rises by 2 percentage points after the Fed decides that unemployment needs to go up.

So yes, the Fed gets what it wants.

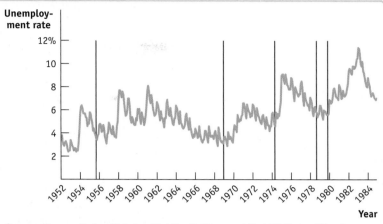

**FIGURE 15-10** When the Fed Wants a Recession

*Sources:* Bureau of Labor Statistics; Christina D. Romer and David H. Romer, "Monetary Policy Matters," *Journal of Monetary Economics* 34 (August 1994): 75–88.

---

**CHECK YOUR UNDERSTANDING  15-3**

1. Suppose the economy is currently suffering from an output gap and the Federal Reserve uses an expansionary monetary policy to close that gap. Describe the short-run effect of this policy on the following.
   **a.** The money supply curve
   **b.** The equilibrium interest rate
   **c.** Investment spending
   **d.** Consumer spending
   **e.** Aggregate output

2. In setting monetary policy, which central bank—one that operates according to a Taylor rule or one that operates by inflation targeting—is likely to respond more directly to a financial crisis? Explain.

*Solutions appear at back of book.*

## Money, Output, and Prices in the Long Run

Through its expansionary and contractionary effects, monetary policy is generally the policy tool of choice to help stabilize the economy. However, not all actions by central banks are productive. In particular, as we'll see in the next chapter, central banks sometimes print money not to fight a recessionary gap but to help the government pay its bills, an action that typically destabilizes the economy.

▼ **Quick Review**

- The Federal Reserve can use **expansionary monetary policy** to increase aggregate demand and **contractionary monetary policy** to reduce aggregate demand. The Federal Reserve and other central banks generally try to tame the business cycle while keeping the inflation rate low but positive.

- Under a **Taylor rule for monetary policy,** the target federal funds rate rises when there is high inflation and either a positive output gap or very low unemployment; it falls when there is low or negative inflation and either a negative output gap or high unemployment.

- In contrast, some central banks set monetary policy by **inflation targeting,** a forward-looking policy rule, rather than by using the Taylor rule, a backward-looking policy rule. Although inflation targeting has the benefits of transparency and accountability, some think it is too restrictive. Until 2008, the Fed followed a loosely defined Taylor rule. Starting in early 2012, it began inflation targeting with a target of 2% per year.

- There is a **zero lower bound for interest rates**—they cannot fall below zero—that limits the power of monetary policy.

- Because it is subject to fewer lags than fiscal policy, monetary policy is the main tool for macroeconomic stabilization.

What happens when a change in the money supply pushes the economy away from, rather than toward, long-run equilibrium? We learned in Chapter 12 that the economy is self-correcting in the long run: a demand shock has only a temporary effect on aggregate output. If the demand shock is the result of a change in the money supply, we can make a stronger statement: in the long run, changes in the quantity of money affect the aggregate price level, but they do not change real aggregate output or the interest rate. To see why, let's look at what happens if the central bank permanently increases the money supply.

## Short-Run and Long-Run Effects of an Increase in the Money Supply

To analyze the long-run effects of monetary policy, it's helpful to think of the central bank as choosing a target for the money supply rather than the interest rate. In assessing the effects of an increase in the money supply, we return to the analysis of the long-run effects of an increase in aggregate demand, first introduced in Chapter 12.

Figure 15-11 shows the short-run and long-run effects of an increase in the money supply when the economy begins at potential output, $Y_1$. The initial short-run aggregate supply curve is $SRAS_1$, the long-run aggregate supply curve is $LRAS$, and the initial aggregate demand curve is $AD_1$. The economy's initial equilibrium is at $E_1$, a point of both short-run and long-run macroeconomic equilibrium because it is on both the short-run and the long-run aggregate supply curves. Real GDP is at potential output, $Y_1$.

Now suppose there is an increase in the money supply. Other things equal, an increase in the money supply reduces the interest rate, which increases investment spending, which leads to a further rise in consumer spending, and so on. So an increase in the money supply increases the quantity of goods and services

## FIGURE 15-11 The Short-Run and Long-Run Effects of an Increase in the Money Supply

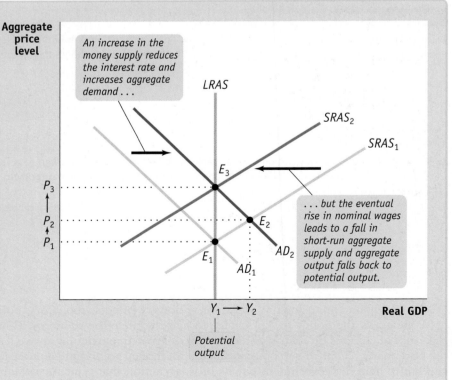

When the economy is already at potential output, an increase in the money supply generates a positive short-run effect, but no long-run effect, on real GDP.

Here, the economy begins at $E_1$, a point of short-run and long-run macroeconomic equilibrium. An increase in the money supply shifts the $AD$ curve rightward, and the economy moves to a new short-run macroeconomic equilibrium at $E_2$ and a new real $GDP$ of $Y_2$. But $E_2$ is not a long-run equilibrium: $Y_2$ exceeds potential output, $Y_1$, leading over time to an increase in nominal wages. In the long run, the increase in nominal wages shifts the short-run aggregate supply curve leftward, to a new position at $SRAS_2$.

The economy reaches a new short-run and long-run macroeconomic equilibrium at $E_3$ on the $LRAS$ curve, and output falls back to potential output, $Y_1$. When the economy is already at potential output, the only long-run effect of an increase in the money supply is an increase in the aggregate price level from $P_1$ to $P_3$.

demanded, shifting the *AD* curve rightward, to $AD_2$. In the short run, the economy moves to a new short-run macroeconomic equilibrium at $E_2$. The price level rises from $P_1$ to $P_2$, and real GDP rises from $Y_1$ to $Y_2$. That is, both the aggregate price level and aggregate output increase in the short run.

But the aggregate output level, $Y_2$, is above potential output. As a result, nominal wages will rise over time, causing the short-run aggregate supply curve to shift leftward. This process stops only when the *SRAS* curve ends up at $SRAS_2$ and the economy ends up at point $E_3$, a point of both short-run and long-run macroeconomic equilibrium. The long-run effect of an increase in the money supply, then, is that the aggregate price level has increased from $P_1$ to $P_3$, but aggregate output is back at potential output, $Y_1$. In the long run, a monetary expansion raises the aggregate price level but has no effect on real GDP.

We won't describe the effects of a monetary contraction in detail, but the same logic applies. In the short run, a fall in the money supply leads to a fall in aggregate output as the economy moves down the short-run aggregate supply curve. In the long run, however, the monetary contraction reduces only the aggregate price level, and real GDP returns to potential output.

> According to the concept of **monetary neutrality,** changes in the money supply have no real effects on the economy.

## Monetary Neutrality

How much does a change in the money supply change the aggregate price level in the long run? The answer is that a change in the money supply leads to an equal proportional change in the aggregate price level in the long run. For example, if the money supply falls 25%, the aggregate price level falls 25% in the long run; if the money supply rises 50%, the aggregate price level rises 50% in the long run.

How do we know this? Consider the following thought experiment: Suppose all prices in the economy—prices of final goods and services and also factor prices, such as nominal wage rates—double. And suppose the money supply doubles at the same time. What difference does this make to the economy in real terms? The answer is none. All real variables in the economy—such as real GDP and the real value of the money supply (the amount of goods and services it can buy)—are unchanged. So there is no reason for anyone to behave any differently.

We can state this argument in reverse: If the economy starts out in long-run macroeconomic equilibrium and the money supply changes, restoring long-run macroeconomic equilibrium requires restoring all real values to their original values. This includes restoring the real value of the money supply to its original level. So if the money supply falls 25%, the aggregate price level must fall 25%; if the money supply rises 50%, the price level must rise 50%; and so on.

This analysis demonstrates the concept known as **monetary neutrality,** in which changes in the money supply have no real effects on the economy. In the long run, the only effect of an increase in the money supply is to raise the aggregate price level by an equal percentage. Economists argue that *money is neutral in the long run.*

This is, however, a good time to recall the dictum of John Maynard Keynes: "In the long run we are all dead." In the long run, changes in the money supply don't have any effect on real GDP, interest rates, or anything else except the price level. But it would be foolish to conclude from this that the Fed is irrelevant. Monetary policy does have powerful real effects on the economy in the short run, often making the difference between recession and expansion. And that matters a lot for society's welfare.

## Changes in the Money Supply and the Interest Rate in the Long Run

In the short run, an increase in the money supply leads to a fall in the interest rate, and a decrease in the money supply leads to a rise in the interest rate. In the long run, however, changes in the money supply don't affect the interest rate.

FIGURE **15-12** The Long-Run Determination of the Interest Rate

In the short run, an increase in the money sup-ply from $\overline{M}_1$ to $\overline{M}_2$ pushes the interest rate down from $r_1$ to $r_2$ and the economy moves to $E_2$, a short-run equilibrium. In the long run, however, the aggregate price level rises in proportion to the increase in the money supply, leading to an increase in money demand at any given interest rate in proportion to the increase in the aggre-gate price level, as shown by the shift from $MD_1$ to $MD_2$. The result is that the quantity of money demanded at any given interest rate rises by the same amount as the quantity of money supplied. The economy moves to long-run equilibrium at $E_3$ and the interest rate returns to $r_1$.

Figure 15-12 shows why. It shows the money supply curve and the money demand curve before and after the Fed increases the money supply. We assume that the economy is initially at $E_1$, in long-run macroeconomic equilibrium at potential output, and with money supply $\overline{M}_1$. The initial equilibrium interest rate, determined by the intersection of the money demand curve $MD_1$ and the money supply curve $MS_1$, is $r_1$.

Now suppose the money supply increases from $\overline{M}_1$ to $\overline{M}_2$. In the short run, the economy moves from $E_1$ to $E_2$ and the interest rate falls from $r_1$ to $r_2$. Over time, however, the aggregate price level rises, and this raises money demand, shifting the money demand curve rightward from $MD_1$ to $MD_2$. The economy moves to a new long-run equilibrium at $E_3$, and the interest rate rises to its original level at $r_1$.

And it turns out that the long-run equilibrium interest rate is the original interest rate, $r_1$. We know this for two reasons. First, due to monetary neutral-ity, in the long run the aggregate price level rises by the same proportion as the money supply; so if the money supply rises by, say, 50%, the price level will also rise by 50%. Second, the demand for money is, other things equal, proportional to the aggregate price level. So a 50% increase in the money supply raises the aggregate price level by 50%, which increases the quantity of money demanded at any given interest rate by 50%. As a result, the quantity of money demanded at the initial interest rate, $r_1$, rises exactly as much as the money supply—so that $r_1$ is still the equilibrium interest rate. In the long run, then, changes in the money supply do not affect the interest rate.

## ECONOMICS ▸ IN ACTION

### INTERNATIONAL EVIDENCE OF MONETARY NEUTRALITY

These days monetary policy is quite similar among wealthy countries. Each major nation (or, in the case of the euro, the euro area) has a central bank that is insu-lated from political pressure. All of these central banks try to keep the aggregate price level roughly stable, which usually means inflation of at most 2% to 3% per year.

But if we look at a longer period and a wider group of countries, we see large differences in the growth of the money supply. Between 1970 and the present, the money supply rose only a few percent per year in some countries, such as Switzerland and the United States, but rose much more rapidly in some poorer countries, such as South Africa. These differences allow us to see whether it is really true that increases in the money supply lead, in the long run, to equal percent rises in the aggregate price level.

Figure 15-13 shows the annual percentage increases in the money supply and average annual increases in the aggregate price level—that is, the average rate of inflation—for a sample of countries during the period 1970–2010, with each point representing a country. If the relationship between increases in the money supply and changes in the aggregate price level were exact, the points would lie precisely on a 45-degree line. In fact, the relationship isn't exact, because other factors besides money affect the aggregate price level. But the scatter of points clearly lies close to a 45-degree line, showing a more or less proportional relationship between money and the aggregate price level. That is, the data support the concept of monetary neutrality in the long run.

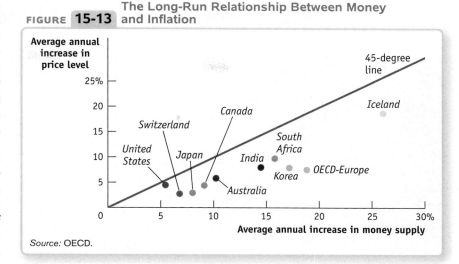

**FIGURE 15-13**  The Long-Run Relationship Between Money and Inflation

*Source:* OECD.

### CHECK YOUR UNDERSTANDING    15-4

1. Assume the central bank increases the quantity of money by 25%, even though the economy is initially in both short-run and long-run macroeconomic equilibrium. Describe the effects, in the short run and in the long run (giving numbers where possible), on the following.
   a. Aggregate output
   b. Aggregate price level
   c. Interest rate

2. Why does monetary policy affect the economy in the short run but not in the long run?

*Solutions appear at back of book.*

# BUSINESS CASE : PIMCO Bets on Cheap Money

Pacific Investment Management Company, generally known as PIMCO, is one of the world's largest investment companies. Among other things, it runs PIMCO Total Return, the world's largest mutual fund. Bill Gross, shown at left, who heads PIMCO, is legendary for his ability to predict trends in financial markets, especially bond markets, where PIMCO does much of its investing.

In the fall of 2009, Gross decided to put more of PIMCO's assets into long-term U.S. government bonds. This amounted to a bet that long-term interest rates would fall. This bet was especially interesting because it was the opposite of the bet many other investors were making. For example, in November 2009 the investment bank Morgan Stanley told its clients to expect a sharp rise in long-term interest rates.

What lay behind PIMCO's bet? Gross explained the firm's thinking in his September 2009 commentary. He suggested that unemployment was likely to stay high and inflation low. "Global policy rates," he asserted—meaning the federal funds rate and its equivalents in Europe and elsewhere—"will remain low for extended periods of time."

PIMCO's view was in sharp contrast to those of other investors: Morgan Stanley expected long-term rates to rise in part because it expected the Fed to raise the federal funds rate in 2010.

Who was right? PIMCO, mostly. As Figure 15-14 shows, the federal funds rate stayed near zero, and long-term interest rates fell through much of 2010, although they rose somewhat very late in the year as investors became somewhat more optimistic about economic recovery. Morgan Stanley, which had bet on rising rates, actually apologized to investors for getting it so wrong.

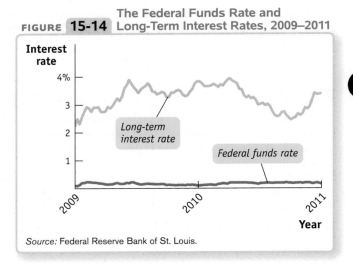

**FIGURE 15-14** The Federal Funds Rate and Long-Term Interest Rates, 2009–2011

*Source:* Federal Reserve Bank of St. Louis.

Bill Gross's foresight, however, was a lot less accurate in 2011. Anticipating a significantly stronger U.S. economy by mid-2011 that would result in inflation, Gross bet heavily against U.S. government bonds early that year. But this time he was wrong, as weak growth continued. By late summer 2011, Gross realized his mistake as U.S. bonds rose in value and the value of his funds sank. He admitted to the *Wall Street Journal* that he had "lost sleep" over his bet, and called it a "mistake."

## QUESTIONS FOR THOUGHT

1. Why did PIMCO's view that unemployment would stay high and inflation low lead to a forecast that policy interest rates would remain low for an extended period?

2. Why would low policy rates suggest low long-term interest rates?

3. What might have caused long-term interest rates to rise in late 2010, even though the federal funds rate was still zero?

## SUMMARY

1. The **money demand curve** arises from a trade-off between the opportunity cost of holding money and the liquidity that money provides. The opportunity cost of holding money depends on **short-term interest rates,** not **long-term interest rates.** Changes in the aggregate price level, real GDP, technology, and institutions shift the money demand curve.

2. According to the **liquidity preference model of the interest rate,** the interest rate is determined in the money market by the money demand curve and the **money supply curve.** The Federal Reserve can change the interest rate in the short run by shifting the money supply curve. In practice, the Fed uses open-market operations to achieve a **target federal funds rate,** which other short-term interest rates generally track. Although long-term interest rates don't necessarily move with short-term interest rates, they reflect expectations about what's going to happen to short-term rates in the future.

3. **Expansionary monetary policy** reduces the interest rate by increasing the money supply. This increases investment spending and consumer spending, which in turn increases aggregate demand and real GDP in the short run. **Contractionary monetary policy** raises the interest rate by reducing the money supply. This reduces investment spending and consumer spending, which in turn reduces aggregate demand and real GDP in the short run.

4. The Federal Reserve and other central banks try to stabilize the economy, limiting fluctuations of actual output around potential output, while also keeping inflation low but positive. Under a **Taylor rule for monetary policy,** the target federal funds rate rises when there is high inflation and either a positive output gap or very low unemployment; it falls when there is low or negative inflation and either a negative output gap or high unemployment. Some central banks (including the Fed as of January 2012) engage in **inflation targeting,** which is a forward-looking policy rule, whereas the Taylor rule method is a backward-looking policy rule. Because monetary policy is subject to fewer implementation lags than fiscal policy, it is the preferred policy tool for stabilizing the economy. Because interest rates cannot fall below zero—the **zero lower bound for interest rates**—the power of monetary policy is limited.

5. In the long run, changes in the money supply affect the aggregate price level but not real GDP or the interest rate. Data show that the concept of **monetary neutrality** holds: changes in the money supply have no real effect on the economy in the long run.

## KEY TERMS

Short-term interest rates, p. 449
Long-term interest rates, p. 449
Money demand curve, p. 450
Liquidity preference model of the interest rate, p. 453

Money supply curve, p. 453
Target federal funds rate, p. 455
Expansionary monetary policy, p. 458
Contractionary monetary policy, p. 458
Taylor rule for monetary policy, p. 459

Inflation targeting, p. 460
Zero lower bound for interest rates, p. 462
Monetary neutrality, p. 465

## PROBLEMS

1. Go to the FOMC page of the Federal Reserve Board's website (http://www.federalreserve.gov/FOMC/) to find the statement issued after the most recent FOMC meeting. (Click on "Meeting calendars and information" and then click on the most recent statement listed in the calendar.)

   a. What is the target federal funds rate?

   b. Is the target federal funds rate different from the target federal funds rate in the previous FOMC statement? If yes, by how much does it differ?

   c. Does the statement comment on current macroeconomic conditions in the United States? How does it describe the U.S. economy?

2. How will the following events affect the demand for money? In each case, specify whether there is a shift of the demand curve or a movement along the demand curve and its direction.

   a. There is a fall in the interest rate from 12% to 10%.

   b. Thanksgiving arrives and, with it, the beginning of the holiday shopping season.

   c. McDonald's and other fast-food restaurants begin to accept credit cards.

   d. The Fed engages in an open-market purchase of U.S. Treasury bills.

3. a. Go to www.treasurydirect.gov. Under "Individuals," go to "Learn about Treasury Bills, Notes, Bonds, and TIPS." Click on "Treasury bills." Under "at a glance," click on "rates in recent auctions." What is the investment rate for the most recently issued 26-week T-bills?

**b.** Go to the website of your favorite bank. What is the interest rate for six-month CDs?

**c.** Why are the rates for six-month CDs higher than for 26-week Treasury bills?

**4.** Go to www.treasurydirect.gov. Under "Individuals," go to "Learn about Treasury Bills, Notes, Bonds, and TIPS." Click on "Treasury notes." Under "at a glance," click on "rates in recent auctions." Use the list of Recent Note, Bond, and TIPS Auction Results to answer the following questions.

**a.** What are the interest rates on 2-year and 10-year notes?

**b.** How do the interest rates on the 2-year and 10-year notes relate to each other? Why is the interest rate on the 10-year note higher (or lower) than the interest rate on the 2-year note?

**5.** An economy is facing the recessionary gap shown in the accompanying diagram. To eliminate the gap, should the central bank use expansionary or contractionary monetary policy? How will the interest rate, investment spending, consumer spending, real GDP, and the aggregate price level change as monetary policy closes the recessionary gap?

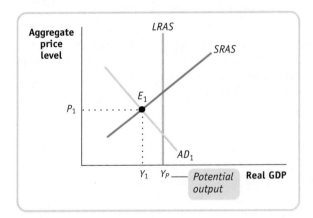

**6.** An economy is facing the inflationary gap shown in the accompanying diagram. To eliminate the gap, should the central bank use expansionary or contractionary monetary policy? How will the interest rate, investment spending, consumer spending, real GDP, and the aggregate price level change as monetary policy closes the inflationary gap?

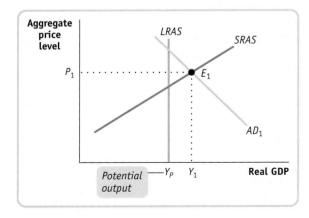

**7.** In the economy of Eastlandia, the money market is initially in equilibrium when the economy begins to slide into a recession.

**a.** Using the accompanying diagram, explain what will happen to the interest rate if the central bank of Eastlandia keeps the money supply constant at $\overline{M}_1$.

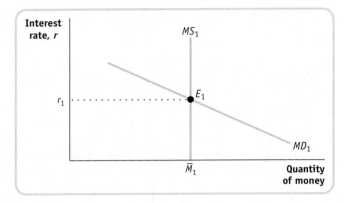

**b.** If the central bank is instead committed to maintaining an interest rate target of $r_1$, then as the economy slides into recession, how should the central bank react? Using your diagram from part a, demonstrate the central bank's reaction.

**8.** Suppose that the money market in Westlandia is initially in equilibrium and the central bank decides to decrease the money supply.

**a.** Using a diagram like the one in Problem 7, explain what will happen to the interest rate in the short run.

**b.** What will happen to the interest rate in the long run?

**9.** An economy is in long-run macroeconomic equilibrium with an unemployment rate of 5% when the government passes a law requiring the central bank to use monetary policy to lower the unemployment rate to 3% and keep it there. How could the central bank achieve this goal in the short run? What would happen in the long run? Illustrate with a diagram.

**10.** According to the European Central Bank website, the treaty establishing the European Community "makes clear that ensuring price stability is the most important contribution that monetary policy can make to achieve a favourable economic environment and a high level of employment." If price stability is the only goal of monetary policy, explain how monetary policy would be conducted during recessions. Analyze both the case of a recession that is the result of a demand shock and the case of a recession that is the result of a supply shock.

**11.** The effectiveness of monetary policy depends on how easy it is for changes in the money supply to change interest rates. By changing interest rates, monetary policy affects investment spending and the aggregate demand curve. The economies of Albernia and Brittania have very different money demand curves, as shown in the accompanying diagram. In which economy will changes in the money supply be a more effective policy tool? Why?

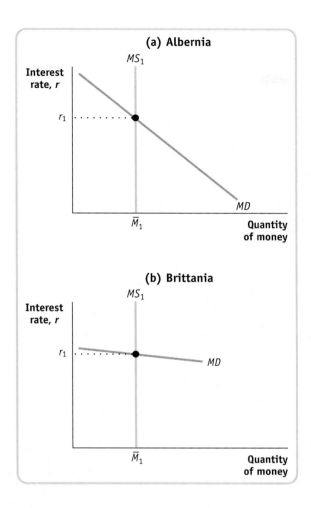

**(a) Albernia**

**(b) Brittania**

12. During the Great Depression, businesspeople in the United States were very pessimistic about the future of economic growth and reluctant to increase investment spending even when interest rates fell. How did this limit the potential for monetary policy to help alleviate the Depression?

13. Because of the economic slowdown associated with the 2007–2009 recession, the Federal Open Market Committee of the Federal Reserve, between September 18, 2007 and December 16, 2008, lowered the federal funds rate in a series of steps from a high of 5.25% to a rate between zero and 0.25%. The idea was to provide a boost to the economy by increasing aggregate demand.

  **a.** Use the liquidity preference model to explain how the Federal Open Market Committee lowers the interest rate in the short run. Draw a typical graph that illustrates the mechanism. Label the vertical axis "Interest rate" and the horizontal axis "Quantity of money." Your graph should show two interest rates, $r_1$ and $r_2$.

  **b.** Explain why the reduction in the interest rate causes aggregate demand to increase in the short run.

  **c.** Suppose that in 2013 the economy is at potential output but that this is somehow overlooked by the Fed, which continues its monetary expansion. Demonstrate the effect of the policy measure on the *AD* curve. Use the *LRAS* curve to show that the effect of this policy measure on the *AD* curve, other things equal, causes the aggregate price level to rise in the long run. Label the vertical axis "Aggregate price level" and the horizontal axis "Real GDP."

# Reconciling the Two Models of the Interest Rate

In the liquidity preference model of the interest rate developed in Chapter 15, at the equilibrium interest rate the quantity of money demanded equals the quantity of money supplied. Yet, in the loanable funds model of the interest rate developed in Chapter 10, the equilibrium interest rate matches the quantity of loanable funds supplied by savers with the quantity of loanable funds demanded for investment spending. Can these two models of the interest rate be reconciled? Yes, they can. We will do this in two steps, focusing first on the short run and then on the long run.

## The Interest Rate in the Short Run

As explained in Chapter 15, a fall in the interest rate leads to a rise in investment spending, *I*, which then leads to a rise in both real GDP and consumer spending, *C*. The rise in real GDP doesn't lead only to a rise in consumer spending, however. It also leads to a rise in savings: at each stage of the multiplier process, part of the increase in disposable income is saved. How much do savings rise? In Chapter 10 we introduced the *savings–investment spending identity:* total savings in the economy is always equal to investment spending. *This tells us that when a fall in the interest rate leads to higher investment spending, the resulting increase in real GDP generates exactly enough additional savings to match the rise in investment spending.* To put it another way, after a fall in the interest rate, the quantity of savings supplied rises exactly enough to match the quantity of savings demanded. Understanding this relationship is the key to reconciling the two models of the interest rate.

Figure 15A-1 illustrates how the two models of the interest rate are reconciled in the short run. Panel (a) shows the liquidity preference model of the interest rate where $MS_1$ and $MD_1$ are the initial supply and demand curves for money, and $r_1$, the initial equilibrium interest rate, equalizes the quantity of money supplied to the quantity of money demanded in the money market. Panel (b) shows the loanable funds model of the interest rate where $S_1$ is the initial supply curve, $D$ is the demand curve for loanable funds, and $r_1$, the initial equilibrium interest rate, equalizes the quantity of loanable funds supplied to the quantity of loanable funds demanded in the market for loanable funds.

In Figure 15A-1 both the money market and the market for loanable funds are initially in equilibrium at $E_1$ with the same interest rate, $r_1$. You might think that this would only happen by accident, but in fact it will always be true. To see why, consider what happens in panel (a), the money market, when the Fed increases the money supply from $\overline{M}_1$ to $\overline{M}_2$, pushing the money supply curve rightward, to $MS_2$, reducing the equilibrium interest rate in the market to $r_2$, and moving the economy to a short-run equilibrium at $E_2$. What happens in panel (b), the market for loanable funds? In the short run, the fall in the interest rate due to the increase in the money supply leads to a rise in real GDP, which generates a rise in savings through the multiplier process. This rise in savings shifts the supply curve for loanable funds rightward, from $S_1$ to $S_2$, moving the equilibrium in the loanable funds market from $E_1$ to $E_2$ and reducing the equilibrium interest rate in the loanable funds market. Since the rise in savings must exactly match the rise in investment spending, the equilibrium rate in the loanable funds market must fall to $r_2$, the same as the new equilibrium interest rate in the money market.

In the short run, then, the supply and demand for money determine the interest rate, and the loanable funds market follows the lead of the money market

**FIGURE 15A-1** The Short-Run Determination of the Interest Rate

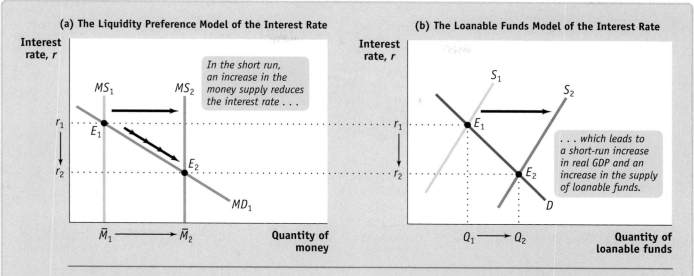

Panel (a) shows the liquidity preference model of the interest rate: the equilibrium interest rate matches the money supply to the quantity of money demanded. In the short run, the interest rate is determined in the money market, where an increase in the money supply, from $\overline{M}_1$ to $\overline{M}_2$, pushes the equilibrium interest rate down, from $r_1$ to $r_2$. Panel (b) shows the loanable funds model of the interest rate. The fall in the interest rate in the money market leads, through the multiplier effect, to an increase in real GDP and savings; to a rightward shift of the supply curve of loanable funds, from $S_1$ to $S_2$; and to a fall in the interest rate, from $r_1$ to $r_2$. As a result, the new equilibrium interest rate in the loanable funds market matches the new equilibrium interest rate in the money market at $r_2$.

until the equilibrium interest rate in the loanable funds market is the same as the equilibrium interest rate in the money market.

Notice our use of the phrase "in the short run." Changes in aggregate demand affect aggregate output only in the short run. In the long run, aggregate output is equal to potential output. So our story about how a fall in the interest rate leads to a rise in aggregate output, which leads to a rise in savings, applies only to the short run. In the long run, as we'll see next, the determination of the interest rate is quite different, because the roles of the two markets are reversed. In the long run, the loanable funds market determines the equilibrium interest rate, and it is the market for money that follows the lead of the loanable funds market.

## The Interest Rate in the Long Run

In the short run an increase in the money supply leads to a fall in the interest rate, and a decrease in the money supply leads to a rise in the interest rate. In the long run, however, changes in the money supply don't affect the interest rate.

Figure 15A-2 shows why. As in Figure 15A-1, panel (a) shows the liquidity preference model of the interest rate and panel (b) shows the supply and demand for loanable funds. We assume that in both panels the economy is initially at $E_1$, in long-run macroeconomic equilibrium at potential output with the money supply equal to $\overline{M}_1$. The demand curve for loanable funds is $D$, and the initial supply curve for loanable funds is $S_1$. The initial equilibrium interest rate in both markets is $r_1$.

Now suppose the money supply rises from $\overline{M}_1$ to $\overline{M}_2$. As in Figure 15A-1, this initially reduces the interest rate to $r_2$. According to the neutrality of money, in the long run the aggregate price level rises by the same proportion as the increase in the money supply. And we also know that a rise in the aggregate price level increases money demand by the same proportion. So in the long run the money demand curve shifts out to $MD_2$ as money demand responds to

FIGURE **15A-2** The Long-Run Determination of the Interest Rate

Panel (a) shows the liquidity preference model long-run adjustment to an increase in the money supply from $\overline{M}_1$ to $\overline{M}_2$; panel (b) shows the corresponding long-run adjustment in the loanable funds market. Both panels start from $E_1$, a long-run macroeconomic equilibrium at potential output and with interest rate $r_1$. As we discussed in Figure 15A-1, the increase in the money supply reduces the interest rate from $r_1$ to $r_2$, increases real GDP, and increases savings in the short run. This is shown in panel (a) and panel (b) as the movement from $E_1$ to $E_2$. In the long run, however, the increase in the money supply raises wages and other nominal prices. This shifts the money demand curve in panel (a) from $MD_1$ to $MD_2$, leading to an increase in the interest rate from $r_2$ to $r_1$ as the economy moves from $E_2$ to $E_3$. The rise in the interest rate causes a fall in real GDP and a fall in savings, shifting the loanable funds supply curve back to $S_1$ from $S_2$ and moving the loanable funds market from $E_2$ back to $E_1$. In the long run, the equilibrium interest rate is determined by matching the supply and demand for loanable funds that arises when real GDP equals potential output.

higher prices, and moving the equilibrium interest rate rises back to its original level, $r_1$.

Panel (b) of Figure 15A-2 shows what happens in the market for loanable funds. As before, an increase in the money supply leads to a short-run rise in real GDP, and this shifts the supply of loanable funds rightward from $S_1$ to $S_2$. In the long run, however, real GDP falls back to its original level as wages and other nominal prices rise. As a result, the supply of loanable funds, $S$, which initially shifted from $S_1$ to $S_2$, shifts back to $S_1$.

In the long run, then, changes in the money supply do not affect the interest rate. So what determines the interest rate in the long run—$r_1$ in Figure 15A-2? The answer is the supply and demand for loanable funds. More specifically, in the long run the equilibrium interest rate matches the supply and demand for loanable funds that arise at potential output.

## PROBLEMS

1. Using a figure similar to Figure 15A-1, explain how the money market and the loanable funds market react to a reduction in the money supply in the short run.

2. Contrast the short-run effects of an increase in the money supply on the interest rate to the long-run effects of an increase in the money supply on the interest rate. Which market determines the interest rate in the short run? Which market does so in the long run? What are the implications of your answers for the effectiveness of monetary policy in influencing real GDP in the short run and the long run?

# CHAPTER 16

# Inflation, Disinflation, and Deflation

WHAT YOU WILL LEARN IN THIS CHAPTER

## BRINGING A SUITCASE TO THE BANK

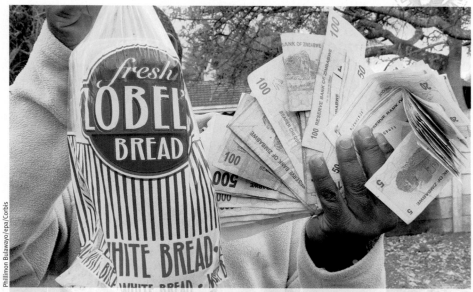

In 2008, the Zimbabwe dollar was so devalued by extreme inflation that this much currency was needed to pay for a single loaf of bread.

*Phillimon Bulawayo/epa/Corbis*

**WHAT YOU WILL LEARN IN THIS CHAPTER**

❯ Why efforts to collect an **inflation tax** by printing money can lead to high rates of inflation and hyperinflation

❯ What the **Phillips curve** is and how it describes the short-run trade-off between inflation and unemployment

❯ Why there is no long-run trade-off between inflation and unemployment

❯ Why expansionary policies are limited due to the effects of expected inflation

❯ Why even moderate levels of inflation can be hard to end

❯ Why deflation is a problem for economic policy and leads policy makers to prefer a low but positive inflation rate

❯ Why the nominal interest rate cannot go below the **zero bound** and the danger a **liquidity trap** poses

I N 2008, THE AFRICAN NATION OF Zimbabwe achieved a dubious distinction: it exhibited one of the highest inflation rates ever recorded, peaking at around 500 billion percent. Although the government kept introducing ever-larger denominations of the Zimbabwe dollar—for example, in May 2008 it introduced a half-billion-dollar bill—it still took a lot of currency to pay for the necessities of life: a stack of Zimbabwean cash worth $100 U.S. dollars weighed about 40 pounds. Zimbabwean currency was worth so little that some people withdrawing funds from banks brought suitcases along, in order to be able to walk away with enough cash to pay for ordinary living expenses. In the end, the Zimbabwe dollar lost all value—literally. By October 2008, the currency more or less vanished from circulation, replaced by U.S. dollars and South African rands.

Zimbabwe's experience was shocking, but not unprecedented. In 1994 the inflation rate in Armenia hit 27,000%. In 1991 Nicaraguan inflation exceeded 60,000%. And Zimbabwe's experience was more or less matched by history's most famous example of extreme inflation, which took place in Germany in 1922–1923. Toward the end of the German hyperinflation, prices were rising 16% a *day,* which—through compounding—meant an increase of approximately 500 billion percent over the course of five months. People became so reluctant to hold paper money, which lost value by the hour, that eggs and lumps of coal began to circulate as currency. German firms would pay their workers several times a day so that they could spend their earnings before they lost value (lending new meaning to the term *hourly wage*). Legend has it that men sitting down at a bar would order two beers at a time, out of fear that the price of a beer would rise before they could order a second round!

The United States has never experienced that kind of inflation. The worst U.S. inflation in modern times took place at the end of the 1970s, when consumer prices were rising at an annual rate of 13%. Yet inflation at even that rate was profoundly troubling to the American public, and the policies the Federal Reserve pursued in order to get U.S. inflation back down to an acceptable rate led to the deepest recession since the Great Depression.

What causes inflation to rise and fall? In this chapter, we'll look at the underlying reasons for inflation. We'll see that the underlying causes of very high inflation, the type of inflation suffered by Zimbabwe, are quite different from the causes of more moderate inflation. We'll also learn why *disinflation,* a reduction in the inflation rate, is often very difficult. Finally, we'll discuss the special problems associated with a falling price level, or deflation. ■

According to the **classical model of the price level,** the real quantity of money is always at its long-run equilibrium level.

# Money and Inflation

A s we'll see later in this chapter, moderate levels of inflation such as those experienced in the United States—even the double-digit inflation of the late 1970s—can have complex causes. But very high inflation is always associated with rapid increases in the money supply.

To understand why, we need to revisit the effect of changes in the money supply on the overall price level. Then we'll turn to the reasons governments sometimes increase the money supply very rapidly.

## The Classical Model of Money and Prices

In Chapter 15, we learned that in the short run an increase in the money supply increases real GDP by lowering the interest rate and stimulating investment spending and consumer spending. However, in the long run, as nominal wages and other sticky prices rise, real GDP falls back to its original level. So in the long run, an increase in the money supply does not change real GDP. Instead, other things equal, it leads to an equal percent rise in the overall price level; that is, the prices of all goods and services in the economy, including nominal wages and the prices of intermediate goods, rise by the same percentage as the money supply. And when the overall price level rises, the aggregate price level—the prices of all final goods and services—rises as well. As a result, a change in the *nominal* money supply, $M$, leads in the long run to a change in the aggregate price level that leaves the *real* quantity of money, $M/P$, at its original level. As a result, there is no long-run effect on aggregate demand or real GDP. For example, when Turkey dropped six zeros from its currency, the Turkish lira, in January 2005, Turkish real GDP did not change. The only thing that changed was the number of zeros in prices: instead of something costing 2,000,000 lira, it cost 2 lira.

This is, to repeat, what happens in the long run. When analyzing large changes in the aggregate price level, however, macroeconomists often find it useful to ignore the distinction between the short run and the long run. Instead, they work with a simplified model in which the effect of a change in the money supply on the aggregate price level takes place instantaneously rather than over a long period of time. You might be concerned about this assumption given that in previous chapters we've emphasized the difference between the short run and the long run. However, for reasons we'll explain shortly, this is a reasonable assumption to make in the case of high inflation.

A simplified model in which the real quantity of money, $M/P$, is always at its long-run equilibrium level is known as the **classical model of the price level** because it was commonly used by "classical" economists who wrote before the work of John Maynard Keynes. To understand the classical model and why it is useful in the context of high inflation, let's revisit the *AD–AS* model and what it says about the effects of an increase in the money supply. (Unless otherwise noted, we will always be referring to changes in the *nominal* supply of money.)

Figure 16-1 reviews the effects of an increase in the money supply according to the *AD–AS* model. The economy starts at $E_1$, a point of short-run and long-run macroeconomic equilibrium. It lies at the intersection of the aggregate demand curve, $AD_1$, and the short-run aggregate supply curve, $SRAS_1$. It also lies on the long-run aggregate supply curve, *LRAS*. At $E_1$, the equilibrium aggregate price level is $P_1$.

Now suppose there is an increase in the money supply. This is an expansionary monetary policy, which shifts the aggregate demand curve to the right, to $AD_2$, and moves the economy to a new short-run macroeconomic equilibrium at $E_2$. Over time, however, nominal wages adjust upward in response to the rise in the aggregate price level, and the *SRAS* curve shifts to the left, to $SRAS_2$. The new long-run macroeconomic equilibrium is at $E_3$, and real GDP returns to its initial

**FIGURE  16-1**  The Classical Model of the Price Level

Starting at $E_1$, an increase in the money supply shifts the aggregate demand curve rightward, as shown by the movement from $AD_1$ to $AD_2$. There is a new short-run macroeconomic equilibrium at $E_2$ and a higher price level at $P_2$. In the long run, nominal wages adjust upward and push the $SRAS$ curve leftward to $SRAS_2$. The total percent increase in the price level from $P_1$ to $P_3$ is equal to the percent increase in the money supply. In the *classical model of the price level*, we ignore the transition period and think of the price level as rising to $P_3$ immediately. This is a good approximation under conditions of high inflation.

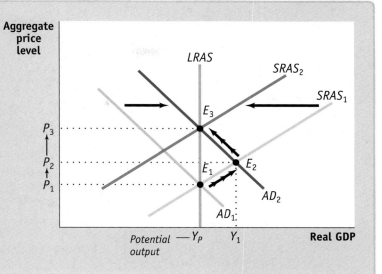

level. As we learned in Chapter 15, the long-run increase in the aggregate price level from $P_1$ to $P_3$ is proportional to the increase in the money supply. As a result, in the long run changes in the money supply have no effect on the real quantity of money, $M/P$, or on real GDP. In the long run, money—as we learned—is *neutral*.

The classical model of the price level ignores the short-run movement from $E_1$ to $E_2$, assuming that the economy moves directly from one long-run equilibrium to another long-run equilibrium. In other words, it assumes that the economy moves directly from $E_1$ to $E_3$ and that real GDP never changes in response to a change in the money supply. In effect, in the classical model the effects of money supply changes are analyzed as if the short-run as well as the long-run aggregate supply curves were vertical.

In reality, this is a poor assumption during periods of low inflation. With a low inflation rate, it may take a while for workers and firms to react to a monetary expansion by raising wages and prices. In this scenario, some nominal wages and the prices of some goods are sticky in the short run. As a result, under low inflation there is an upward-sloping $SRAS$ curve, and changes in the money supply can indeed change real GDP in the short run.

But what about periods of high inflation? In the face of high inflation, economists have observed that the short-run stickiness of nominal wages and prices tends to vanish. Workers and businesses, sensitized to inflation, are quick to raise their wages and prices in response to changes in the money supply. This implies that under high inflation there is a quicker adjustment of wages and prices of intermediate goods than occurs in the case of low inflation. So the short-run aggregate supply curve shifts leftward more quickly and there is a more rapid return to long-run equilibrium under high inflation. As a result, the classical model of the price level is much more likely to be a good approximation of reality for economies experiencing persistently high inflation.

The consequence of this rapid adjustment of all prices in the economy is that in countries with persistently high inflation, changes in the money supply are quickly translated into changes in the inflation rate. Let's look at Zimbabwe. Figure 16-2 shows the annual rate of growth in the money supply and the annual rate of change of consumer prices from 2003 through April 2008. As you can see, the surge in the growth rate of the money supply coincided closely with a roughly equal surge in the inflation rate. Note that to fit these very large percentage increases—several thousand of percent—onto the figure, we have

FIGURE **16-2** Money Supply Growth and Inflation in Zimbabwe

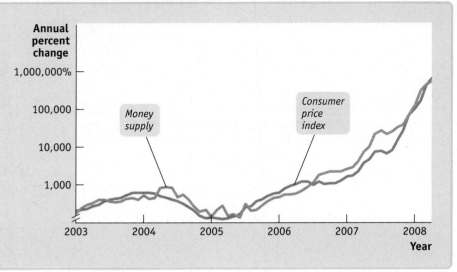

This figure, drawn on a logarithmic scale, shows the annual rates of change of the money supply and the price level in Zimbabwe from 2003 through April 2008. The surges in the money supply were quickly reflected in a roughly equal surge in the price level.

*Source:* International Monetary Fund.

drawn the vertical axis using a logarithmic scale that allows us to draw equal-sized percent changes as the same size.

What leads a country to increase its money supply so much that the result is an inflation rate in the millions, or even billions, of percent?

## The Inflation Tax

Modern economies use fiat money—pieces of paper that have no intrinsic value but are accepted as a medium of exchange. In the United States and most other wealthy countries, the decision about how many pieces of paper to issue is placed in the hands of a central bank that is somewhat independent of the political process. However, this independence can always be taken away if politicians decide to seize control of monetary policy.

So what is to prevent a government from paying for some of its expenses not by raising taxes or borrowing but simply by printing money? Nothing. In fact, governments, including the U.S. government, do it all the time. How can the U.S. government do this, given that the Federal Reserve issues money, not the U.S. Treasury? The answer is that the Treasury and the Federal Reserve work in concert. The Treasury issues debt to finance the government's purchases of goods and services, and the Fed *monetizes* the debt by creating money and buying the debt back from the public through open-market purchases of Treasury bills. In effect, the U.S. government can and does raise revenue by printing money.

For example, in August 2007 the U.S. monetary base—bank reserves plus currency in circulation—was $600 billion larger than it had been a year earlier. This occurred because, over the course of that year, the Federal Reserve had issued $20 billion in money or its electronic equivalent and put it into circulation through open-market operations. To put it another way, the Fed created money out of thin air and used it to buy valuable government securities from the private sector. It's true that the U.S. government pays interest on debt owned by the Federal Reserve—but the Fed, by law, hands the interest payments it receives on government debt back to the Treasury, keeping only enough to fund its own operations. In effect, then, the Federal Reserve's actions enabled the government to pay off $600 billion in outstanding government debt by printing money.

An alternative way to look at this is to say that the right to print money is itself a source of revenue. Economists refer to the revenue generated by the government's right to print money as *seignorage*, an archaic term that goes back to the Middle Ages. It refers to the right to stamp gold and silver into coins, and charge a fee for doing so, that medieval lords—seigneurs, in France—reserved for themselves.

Seignorage normally accounts for only a tiny fraction (less than 1%) of the U.S. government's budget. Furthermore, concerns about seignorage don't have any influence on the Federal Reserve's decisions about how much money to print; the Fed is worried about inflation and unemployment, not revenue. But this hasn't always been true, even in America: both sides relied on seignorage to help cover budget deficits during the Civil War. And there have been many occasions in history when governments turned to their printing presses as a crucial source of revenue. According to the usual scenario, a government finds itself running a large budget deficit—and lacks either the competence or the political will to eliminate this deficit by raising taxes or cutting spending. Furthermore, the government can't borrow to cover the gap because potential lenders won't extend loans given the fear that the government's weakness will continue and leave it unable to repay its debts.

In such a situation, governments end up printing money to cover the budget deficit. But by printing money to pay its bills, a government increases the quantity of money in circulation. And as we've just seen, increases in the money supply sooner or later translate into equally large increases in the aggregate price level. So printing money to cover a budget deficit leads to inflation.

Who ends up paying for the goods and services the government purchases with newly printed money? The people who currently hold money pay. They pay because inflation erodes the purchasing power of their money holdings. In other words, a government imposes an **inflation tax,** the reduction in the value of the money held by the public, by printing money to cover its budget deficit and creating inflation.

It's helpful to think about what this tax represents. If the inflation rate is 5%, then a year from now $1 will buy goods and services worth only $0.95 today. So a 5% inflation rate in effect imposes a tax rate of 5% on the value of all money held by the public.

But why would any government push the inflation tax to rates of hundreds or thousands of percent? We turn next to the logic of hyperinflation.

## The Logic of Hyperinflation

Inflation imposes a tax on individuals who hold money. And, like most taxes, it will lead people to change their behavior. In particular, when inflation is high, people will try to avoid holding money and will instead substitute real goods as well as interest-bearing assets for money. In this chapter's opening story, we described how, during the German hyperinflation, people began using eggs or lumps of coal as a medium of exchange. They did this because lumps of coal maintained their real value over time but money didn't. Indeed, during the peak of German hyperinflation, people often burned paper money, which was less valuable than wood. Moreover, people don't just reduce their nominal money holdings—they reduce their *real* money holdings, cutting the

> The **inflation tax** is the reduction in the value of money held by the public caused by inflation.

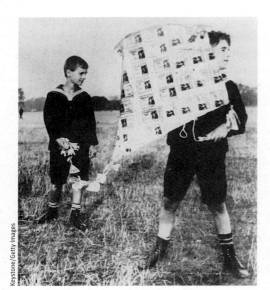

In the 1920s, hyperinflation made German currency worth so little that children made kites from banknotes.

amount of money they hold so much that it actually has less purchasing power than the amount of money they would hold if inflation were low. They do this by using the money to buy goods that last over time or assets that hold their value like gold. Why? Because the more real money holdings they have, the greater the real amount of resources the government captures from them through the inflation tax.

We are now prepared to understand how countries can get themselves into situations of extreme inflation. High inflation arises when the government must print a large quantity of money, imposing a large inflation tax, to cover a large budget deficit.

Now, the seignorage collected by the government over a short period—say, one month—is equal to the change in the money supply over that period. Let's use $M$ to represent the money supply and use the symbol $\Delta$ to mean "monthly change in." Then:

**(16-1)** Seignorage $= \Delta M$

The money value of seignorage, however, isn't very informative by itself. After all, the whole point of inflation is that a given amount of money buys less and less over time. So it's more useful to look at *real* seignorage, the revenue created by printing money divided by the price level, $P$:

**(16-2)** Real seignorage $= \Delta M/P$

Equation 16-2 can be rewritten by dividing and multiplying by the current level of the money supply, $M$, giving us:

**(16-3)** Real seignorage $= (\Delta M/M) \times (M/P)$

or

Real seignorage = Rate of growth of the money supply × Real money supply

But as we've just explained, in the face of high inflation the public reduces the real amount of money it holds, so that the far right-hand term in Equation 16-3, $M/P$, gets smaller. Suppose that the government needs to print enough money to pay for a given quantity of goods and services—that is, it needs to collect a given *real* amount of seignorage. Then, as the real money supply, $M/P$, falls as people hold smaller amounts of real money, the government has to respond by accelerating the rate of growth of the money supply, $\Delta M/M$. This will lead to an even higher rate of inflation. And people will respond to this new higher rate of inflation by reducing their real money holdings, $M/P$, yet again. As the process becomes self-reinforcing, it can easily spiral out of control. Although the amount of real seignorage that the government must ultimately collect to pay off its deficit does not change, the inflation rate the government needs to impose to collect that amount rises. So the government is forced to increase the money supply more rapidly, leading to an even higher rate of inflation, and so on.

Here's an analogy: imagine a city government that tries to raise a lot of money with a special fee on taxi rides. The fee will raise the cost of taxi rides, and this will cause people to turn to easily available substitutes, such as walking or taking the bus. As taxi use declines, the government finds that its tax revenue declines and it must impose a higher fee to raise the same amount of revenue as before. You can imagine the ensuing vicious circle: the government imposes fees on taxi rides, which leads to less taxi use, which causes the government to raise the fee on taxi rides, which leads to even less taxi use, and so on.

Substitute the real money supply for taxi rides and the inflation rate for the increase in the fee on taxi rides, and you have the story of hyperinflation. A race develops between the government printing presses and the public: the presses churn out money at a faster and faster rate, to try to compensate for the fact that the public is reducing its real money holdings. At some point the inflation rate explodes into hyperinflation, and people are unwilling to hold any money at all (and resort to trading in eggs and lumps of coal). The government is then forced to abandon its use of the inflation tax and shut down the printing presses.

## ECONOMICS ▶ IN ACTION

### ZIMBABWE'S INFLATION

**A**s we noted in this chapter's opening story, Zimbabwe offers a recent example of a country experiencing very high inflation. Figure 16-2 showed that surges in Zimbabwe's money supply growth were matched by almost simultaneous surges in its inflation rate. But looking at rates of change doesn't give a true feel for just how much prices went up.

Figure 16-3 shows Zimbabwe's consumer price index from January 2000 to July 2008, with the January 2000 level set equal to 100. As in Figure 16-2, we also use a logarithmic scale. Over the course of just over eight years, consumer prices rose by approximately 80 trillion percent.

Why did Zimbabwe's government pursue policies that led to runaway inflation? The reason boils down to political instability, which in turn had its roots in Zimbabwe's history. Until the 1970s, Zimbabwe had been ruled by its small white minority; even after the shift to majority rule, many of the country's farms remained in the hands of whites. Eventually Robert Mugabe, Zimbabwe's president, tried to solidify his position by seizing these farms and turning them over to his political supporters. But because this seizure disrupted production, the result was to undermine the country's economy and its tax base. It became impossible for the country's government to balance its budget either by raising taxes or by cutting spending. At the same time, the regime's instability left Zimbabwe unable to borrow money in world markets. Like many others before it, Zimbabwe's government turned to the printing press to cover the gap—leading to massive inflation.

**FIGURE 16-3** Consumer Prices in Zimbabwe, 2000–2008

*Source:* International Monetary Fund.

**CHECK YOUR UNDERSTANDING 16-1**

1. Suppose there is a large increase in the money supply in an economy that previously had low inflation. As a consequence, aggregate output expands in the short run. What does this say about situations in which the classical model of the price level applies?

2. Suppose that all wages and prices in an economy are indexed to inflation—that is, wages and prices are automatically adjusted to incorporate the latest inflation figures. Can there still be an inflation tax?

Solutions appear at back of book.

## Moderate Inflation and Disinflation

**T**he governments of wealthy, politically stable countries like the United States and Britain don't find themselves forced to print money to pay their bills. Yet over the past 40 years both countries, along with a number of other nations, have experienced uncomfortable episodes of inflation. In the United States, the inflation rate peaked at 13% at the beginning of the 1980s. In

Britain, the inflation rate reached 26% in 1975. Why did policy makers allow this to happen?

The answer, in brief, is that in the short run, policies that produce a booming economy also tend to lead to higher inflation, and policies that reduce inflation tend to depress the economy. This creates both temptations and dilemmas for governments.

First, imagine yourself as a politician facing an election in a year or two, and suppose that inflation is fairly low at the moment. You might well be tempted to pursue expansionary policies that will push the unemployment rate down, as a way to please voters, even if your economic advisers warn that this will eventually lead to higher inflation. You might also be tempted to find different economic advisers who will tell you not to worry: in politics, as in ordinary life, wishful thinking often prevails over realistic analysis.

Conversely, imagine yourself as a politician in an economy suffering from inflation. Your economic advisers will probably tell you that the only way to bring inflation down is to push the economy into a recession, which will lead to temporarily higher unemployment. Are you willing to pay that price? Maybe not.

This political asymmetry—inflationary policies often produce short-term political gains, but policies to bring inflation down carry short-term political costs—explains how countries with no need to impose an inflation tax sometimes end up with serious inflation problems. For example, that 26% rate of inflation in Britain was largely the result of the British government's decision in 1971 to pursue highly expansionary monetary and fiscal policies. Politicians disregarded warnings that these policies would be inflationary and were extremely reluctant to reverse course even when it became clear that the warnings had been correct.

But why do expansionary policies lead to inflation? To answer that question, we need to look first at the relationship between output and unemployment.

## The Output Gap and the Unemployment Rate

In Chapter 12 we introduced the concept of *potential output*, the level of real GDP that the economy would produce once all prices had fully adjusted. Potential output typically grows steadily over time, reflecting long-run growth. However, as we learned from the aggregate demand–aggregate supply model, actual aggregate output fluctuates around potential output in the short run: a recessionary gap arises when actual aggregate output falls short of potential output; an inflationary gap arises when actual aggregate output exceeds potential output. Recall from Chapter 12 that the percentage difference between the actual level of real GDP and potential output is called the *output gap*. A positive or negative output gap occurs when an economy is producing more than or less than what would be "expected" because all prices have not yet adjusted. And wages, as we've learned, are the prices in the labor market.

Meanwhile, we learned in Chapter 8 that the unemployment rate is composed of cyclical unemployment and natural unemployment, the portion of the unemployment rate unaffected by the business cycle. So there is a relationship between the unemployment rate and the output gap. This relationship is defined by two rules:

1. When actual aggregate output is equal to potential output, the actual unemployment rate is equal to the natural rate of unemployment.

2. When the output gap is positive (an inflationary gap), the unemployment rate is *below* the natural rate. When the output gap is negative (a recessionary gap), the unemployment rate is *above* the natural rate.

*In other words, fluctuations of aggregate output around the long-run trend of potential output correspond to fluctuations of the unemployment rate around the natural rate.*

This makes sense. When the economy is producing less than potential output—when the output gap is negative—it is not making full use of its productive resources. Among the resources that are not fully utilized is labor, the economy's most important resource. So we would expect a negative output gap to be associated with unusually high unemployment. Conversely, when the economy is producing more than potential output, it is temporarily using resources at higher-than-normal rates. With this positive output gap, we would expect to see lower-than-normal unemployment.

Figure 16-4 confirms this rule. Panel (a) shows the actual and natural rates of unemployment, as estimated by the Congressional Budget Office (CBO). Panel (b) shows two series. One is cyclical unemployment: the difference between the actual unemployment rate and the CBO estimate of the natural rate of unemployment, measured on the left. The other is the CBO estimate of the output gap, measured on the right. To make the relationship clearer, the output gap series is inverted—shown upside down—so that the line goes down if actual output rises above potential output and up if actual output falls below potential output. As you can see, the two series move together quite closely, showing the strong relationship between the output gap and cyclical unemployment. Years of high cyclical unemployment, like 1982, 1992, or 2009,

**FIGURE 16-4 Cyclical Unemployment and the Output Gap**

Panel (a) shows the actual U.S. unemployment rate from 1949 to the middle of 2011, together with the Congressional Budget Office estimate of the natural rate of unemployment. The actual rate fluctuates around the natural rate, often for extended periods. Panel (b) shows cyclical unemployment—the difference between the actual unemployment rate and the natural rate of unemployment—and the output gap, also estimated by the CBO. The unemployment rate is measured on the left vertical axis, and the output gap is measured with an inverted scale on the right vertical axis. With an inverted scale, it moves in the same direction as the unemployment rate: when the output gap is positive, the actual unemployment rate is below its natural rate; when the output gap is negative, the actual unemployment rate is above its natural rate. The two series track one another closely, showing the strong relationship between the output gap and cyclical unemployment.

*Sources:* Congressional Budget Office; Bureau of Labor Statistics; Bureau of Economic Analysis.

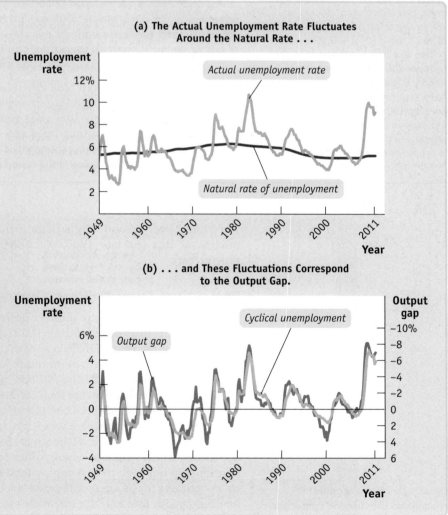

## ☁ FOR INQUIRING MINDS

### OKUN'S LAW

Although cyclical unemployment and the output gap move together, cyclical unemployment seems to move *less* than the output gap. For example, the output gap reached −8% in 1982, but the cyclical unemployment rate reached only 4%. This observation is the basis of an important relationship originally discovered by Arthur Okun, John F. Kennedy's chief economic adviser.

Modern estimates of **Okun's law**—the negative relationship between the output gap and the unemployment rate—typically find that a rise in the output gap of 1 percentage point reduces the unemployment rate by about ½ of a percentage point.

For example, suppose that the natural rate of unemployment is 5.2% and that the economy is currently producing at only 98% of potential output. In that case, the output gap is −2%, and Okun's law predicts an unemployment rate of $5.2\% - \frac{1}{2} \times (-2\%) = 6.2\%$.

The fact that a 1% rise in output reduces the unemployment rate by only ½ of 1% may seem puzzling: you might have expected to see a one-to-one relationship between the output gap and unemployment. Doesn't a 1% rise in aggregate output require a 1% increase in employment? And shouldn't that take 1% off the unemployment rate?

The answer is no: there are several well-understood reasons why the relationship isn't one-to-one. For one thing, companies often meet changes in demand in part by changing the number of hours their existing employees work. For example, a company that experiences a sudden increase in demand for its products may cope by asking (or requiring) its workers to put in longer hours, rather than by hiring more workers. Conversely, a company that sees sales drop will often reduce workers' hours rather than lay off employees. This behavior dampens the effect of output fluctuations on the number of workers employed.

Also, the number of workers looking for jobs is affected by the availability of jobs. Suppose that the number of jobs falls by 1 million. Measured unemployment will rise by less than 1 million because some unemployed workers become discouraged and give up actively looking for work. (Recall from Chapter 8 that workers aren't counted as unemployed unless they are actively seeking work.) Conversely, if the econ-

omy adds 1 million jobs, some people who haven't been actively looking for work will begin doing so. As a result, measured unemployment will fall by less than 1 million.

Finally, the rate of growth of labor productivity generally accelerates during booms and slows down or even turns negative during busts. The reasons for this phenomenon are the subject of some dispute among economists. The consequence, however, is that the effects of booms and busts on the unemployment rate are dampened.

---

were also years of a strongly negative output gap. Years of low cyclical unemployment, like the late 1960s or 2000, were also years of a strongly positive output gap.

## The Short-Run Phillips Curve

We've just seen that expansionary policies lead to a lower unemployment rate. Our next step in understanding the temptations and dilemmas facing governments is to show that there is a short-run trade-off between unemployment and inflation—lower unemployment tends to lead to higher inflation, and vice versa. The key concept is that of the *Phillips curve*.

The origins of this concept lie in a famous 1958 paper by the New Zealand–born economist A.W.H. Phillips. Looking at historical data for Britain, he found that when the unemployment rate was high, the wage rate tended to fall, and when the unemployment rate was low, the wage rate tended to rise. Using data from Britain, the United States, and elsewhere, other economists soon found a similar apparent relationship between the unemployment rate and the rate of inflation—that is, the rate of change in the aggregate price level. For example, Figure 16-5 shows the U.S. unemployment rate and the rate of consumer price inflation over each subsequent year from 1955 to 1968, with each dot representing one year's data.

**Okun's law** is the negative relationship between the output gap and cyclical unemployment.

FIGURE **16-5** Unemployment and Inflation, 1955–1968

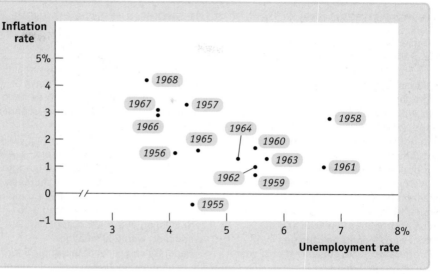

Each dot shows the average U.S. unemployment rate for one year and the percentage increase in the consumer price index over the subsequent year. Data like this lay behind the initial concept of the Phillips curve.

*Source:* Bureau of Labor Statistics.

Looking at evidence like Figure 16-5, many economists concluded that there is a negative short-run relationship between the unemployment rate and the inflation rate, which is called the **short-run Phillips curve,** or *SRPC*. (We'll explain the difference between the short-run and the long-run Phillips curve soon.) Figure 16-6 shows a hypothetical short-run Phillips curve.

Early estimates of the short-run Phillips curve for the United States were very simple: they showed a negative relationship between the unemployment rate and the inflation rate, without taking account of any other variables. During the 1950s and 1960s this simple approach seemed, for a while, to be adequate. And this simple relationship is clear in the data in Figure 16-5.

Even at the time, however, some economists argued that a more accurate short-run Phillips curve would include other factors. In Chapter 12 we discussed the effect of *supply shocks*, such as sudden changes in the price of oil, which shift the short-run aggregate supply curve. Such shocks also shift the short-run Phillips curve: surging oil prices were an important factor in the inflation of

The **short-run Phillips curve** is the negative short-run relationship between the unemployment rate and the inflation rate.

FIGURE **16-6** The Short-Run Phillips Curve

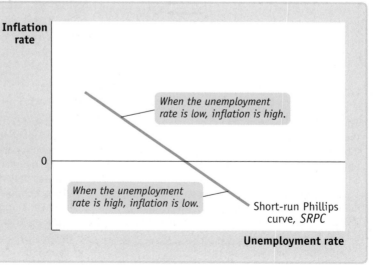

The short-run Phillips curve, SRPC, slopes downward because the relationship between the unemployment rate and the inflation rate is negative.

## FOR INQUIRING MINDS

### THE AGGREGATE SUPPLY CURVE AND THE SHORT-RUN PHILLIPS CURVE

In earlier chapters we made extensive use of the *AD–AS* model, in which the short-run aggregate supply curve—a relationship between real GDP and the aggregate price level—plays a central role. Now we've introduced the concept of the short-run Phillips curve, a relationship between the unemployment rate and the rate of inflation. How do these two concepts fit together?

We can get a partial answer to this question by looking at panel (a) of Figure 16-7, which shows how changes in the aggregate price level and the output gap depend on changes in aggregate demand. Assume that in year 1 the aggregate demand curve is $AD_1$, the long-run aggregate supply curve is *LRAS,* and the short-run aggregate supply curve is *SRAS*. The initial macroeconomic equilibrium is at $E_1$, where the price level is 100 and real GDP is $10 trillion. Notice that at $E_1$ real GDP is equal to potential output, so the output gap is zero.

Now consider two possible paths for the economy over the next year. One is that aggregate demand remains unchanged and the economy stays at $E_1$. The other is that aggregate demand shifts rightward to $AD_2$ and the economy moves to $E_2$.

At $E_2$, real GDP is $10.4 trillion, $0.4 trillion more than potential output—a 4% output gap. Meanwhile, at $E_2$ the aggregate price level is 102—a 2% increase. So panel (a) tells us that in this example a zero output gap is associated with zero inflation and a 4% output gap is associated with 2% inflation.

Panel (b) shows what this implies for the relationship between unemployment and inflation. Assume that the natural rate of unemployment is 6% and that a rise of 1 percentage point in the output gap causes a fall of ½ percentage point in the unemployment rate per Okun's law, described in the previous For Inquiring Minds. In that case, the two cases shown in panel (a)—aggregate demand either

staying put or rising—correspond to the two points in panel (b). At $E_1$, the unemployment rate is 6% and the inflation rate is 0%. At $E_2$, the unemployment rate is 4%, because an output gap of 4% reduces the unemployment rate by 4% × 0.5 = 2% below its natural rate of 6%—and the inflation rate is 2%. So there is a negative relationship between unemployment and inflation.

So does the short-run aggregate supply curve say exactly the same thing as the short-run Phillips curve? Not quite. The short-run aggregate supply curve seems to imply a relationship between the *change* in the unemployment rate and the inflation rate, but the short-run Phillips curve shows a relationship between the *level* of the unemployment rate and the inflation rate. Reconciling these views completely would go beyond the scope of this book. The important point is that the short-run Phillips curve is a concept that is closely related, though not identical, to the short-run aggregate supply curve.

**FIGURE** **16-7** The *AD–AS* Model and the Short-Run Phillips Curve

**(a) An Increase in Aggregate Demand . . .**

**(b) . . . Leads to Both Inflation and a Fall in the Unemployment Rate.**

The short-run Phillips curve is closely related to the short-run aggregate supply curve. In panel (a), the economy is initially in equilibrium at $E_1$, with the aggregate price level at 100 and aggregate output at $10 trillion, which we assume is potential output. Now consider two possibilities. If the aggregate demand curve remains at $AD_1$, there is an output gap of zero and 0% inflation. If the aggregate demand curve shifts

out to $AD_2$, there is an output gap of 4%—reducing unemployment to 4%—and 2% inflation. Assuming that the natural rate of unemployment is 6%, the implications for unemployment and inflation are as follows, shown in panel (b): if aggregate demand does not increase, 6% unemployment and 0% inflation will result; if aggregate demand does increase, 4% unemployment and 2% inflation will result.

**FIGURE** **16-8** The Short-Run Phillips Curve and Supply Shocks

A negative supply shock shifts the *SRPC* up, and a positive supply shock shifts the *SRPC* down.

A negative supply shock shifts *SRPC* up.

A positive supply shock shifts *SRPC* down.

Inflation rate

Unemployment rate

$SRPC_1$

$SRPC_0$

$SRPC_2$

the 1970s and also played an important role in the acceleration of inflation in 2007–2008. In general, a negative supply shock shifts *SRPC* up as the inflation rate increases for every level of the unemployment rate, and a positive supply shock shifts it down as the inflation rate falls for every level of the unemployment rate. Both outcomes are shown in Figure 16-8.

But supply shocks are not the only factors that can change the inflation rate. In the early 1960s, Americans had little experience with inflation because inflation rates had been low for decades. But by the late 1960s, after inflation had been steadily increasing for a number of years, Americans had come to expect future inflation. In 1968 two economists—Milton Friedman of the University of Chicago and Edmund Phelps of Columbia University—independently set forth a crucial hypothesis: that expectations about future inflation directly affect the present inflation rate. Today most economists accept that the *expected inflation rate*—the rate of inflation that employers and workers expect in the near future—is the most important factor, other than the unemployment rate, affecting inflation.

## Inflation Expectations and the Short-Run Phillips Curve

The expected rate of inflation is the rate of inflation that employers and workers expect in the near future. One of the crucial discoveries of modern macroeconomics is that changes in the expected rate of inflation affect the short-run trade-off between unemployment and inflation and shift the short-run Phillips curve.

Why do changes in expected inflation affect the short-run Phillips curve? Put yourself in the position of a worker or employer about to sign a contract setting the worker's wages over the next year. For a number of reasons, the wage rate they agree to will be higher if everyone expects high inflation (including rising wages) than if everyone expects prices to be stable. The worker will want a wage rate that takes into account future declines in the purchasing power of earnings. He or she will also want a wage rate that won't fall behind the wages of other workers. And the employer will be more willing to agree to a wage increase now if hiring workers later will be even more expensive. Also, rising prices will make paying a higher wage rate more affordable for the employer because the employer's output will sell for more.

For these reasons, an increase in expected inflation shifts the short-run Phillips curve upward: the actual rate of inflation at any given unemployment rate is higher when the expected inflation rate is higher. In fact, macroeconomists believe that the relationship between changes in expected inflation and changes in actual inflation is one-to-one. That is, when the expected inflation rate increases, the actual inflation rate at any given unemployment rate will increase by the same amount. When the expected inflation rate falls, the actual inflation rate at any given level of unemployment will fall by the same amount.

Figure 16-9 shows how the expected rate of inflation affects the short-run Phillips curve. First, suppose that the expected rate of inflation is 0%. $SRPC_0$ is the short-run Phillips curve when the public expects 0% inflation. According to $SRPC_0$, the actual inflation rate will be 0% if the unemployment rate is 6%; it will be 2% if the unemployment rate is 4%.

**FIGURE    16-9    Expected Inflation and the Short-Run Phillips Curve**

An increase in expected inflation shifts the short-run Phillips curve up. $SRPC_0$ is the initial short-run Phillips curve with an expected inflation rate of 0%; $SRPC_2$ is the short-run Phillips curve with an expected inflation rate of 2%. Each additional percentage point of expected inflation raises the actual inflation rate at any given unemployment rate by 1 percentage point.

Alternatively, suppose the expected rate of inflation is 2%. In that case, employers and workers will build this expectation into wages and prices: at any given unemployment rate, the actual inflation rate will be 2 percentage points higher than it would be if people expected 0% inflation. $SRPC_2$, which shows the Phillips curve when the expected inflation rate is 2%, is $SRPC_0$ shifted upward by 2 percentage points at every level of unemployment. According to $SRPC_2$, the actual inflation rate will be 2% if the unemployment rate is 6%; it will be 4% if the unemployment rate is 4%.

What determines the expected rate of inflation? In general, people base their expectations about inflation on experience. If the inflation rate has hovered around 0% in the last few years, people will expect it to be around 0% in the near future. But if the inflation rate has averaged around 5% lately, people will expect inflation to be around 5% in the near future.

Since expected inflation is an important part of the modern discussion about the short-run Phillips curve, you might wonder why it was not in the original formulation of the Phillips curve. The answer lies in history. Think back to what we said about the early 1960s: at that time, people were accustomed to low inflation rates and reasonably expected that future inflation rates would also be low. It was only after 1965 that persistent inflation became a fact of life. So only then did it become clear that expected inflation would play an important role in price-setting.

## ECONOMICS ➤ IN ACTION

### FROM THE SCARY SEVENTIES TO THE NIFTY NINETIES

Figure 16-5 showed that the American experience during the 1950s and 1960s supported the belief in the existence of a short-run Phillips curve for the U.S. economy, with a short-run trade-off between unemployment and inflation.

After 1969, however, that relationship appeared to fall apart according to the data. Figure 16-10 plots the track of U.S. unemployment and inflation rates from 1961 to 1990. As you can see, the track looks more like a tangled piece of yarn than like a smooth curve.

Through much of the 1970s and early 1980s, the economy suffered from a combination of above-average unemployment rates coupled with inflation rates unprecedented in modern American history. This condition came to be known as *stagflation*—for stagnation combined with high inflation. In the late 1990s, by contrast, the economy was experiencing a blissful combination of low unemployment and low inflation. What explains these developments?

Part of the answer can be attributed to a series of negative supply shocks that the U.S. economy suffered during the 1970s. The price of oil, in particular, soared as wars and revolutions in the Middle East led to a reduction in oil supplies and as oil-exporting countries deliberately curbed production to drive up prices. Compounding the oil price shocks, there was also a slowdown in labor productivity growth. Both of these factors shifted the short-run Phillips curve upward. During the 1990s, by contrast, supply shocks were positive. Prices of oil and other raw materials were generally falling, and productivity growth accelerated. As a result, the short-run Phillips curve shifted downward.

Equally important, however, was the role of expected inflation. As mentioned earlier in the chapter, inflation accelerated during the 1960s. During the 1970s the public came to expect high inflation, and this also shifted the short-run Phillips curve up. It took a sustained and costly effort during the 1980s to get inflation back down. The result, however, was that expected inflation was very low by the late 1990s, allowing actual inflation to be low even with low rates of unemployment.

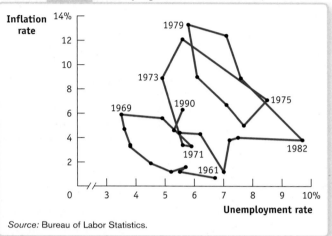

FIGURE **16-10** Unemployment and Inflation, 1961–1990

*Source:* Bureau of Labor Statistics.

### CHECK YOUR UNDERSTANDING    16-2

1. Explain how the short-run Phillips curve illustrates the negative relationship between cyclical unemployment and the actual inflation rate for a given level of the expected inflation rate.

2. Which way does the short-run Phillips curve move in response to a fall in commodities prices? To a surge in commodities prices? Explain.

Solutions appear at back of book.

## Inflation and Unemployment in the Long Run

The short-run Phillips curve says that at any given point in time there is a trade-off between unemployment and inflation. According to this view, policy makers have a choice: they can choose to accept the price of high inflation in order to achieve low unemployment. In fact, during the 1960s many economists believed that this trade-off represented a real choice.

### ▼ Quick Review

- **Okun's law** describes the relationship between the output gap and cyclical unemployment.

- The **short-run Phillips curve** illustrates the negative relationship between unemployment and inflation.

- A negative supply shock shifts the short-run Phillips curve upward, but a positive supply shock shifts it downward.

- An increase in the **expected rate of inflation** pushes the short-run Phillips curve upward: each additional percentage point of expected inflation pushes the actual inflation rate at any given unemployment rate up by 1 percentage point.

- In the 1970s, a series of negative supply shocks and a slowdown in labor productivity growth led to *stagflation* and an upward shift in the short-run Phillips curve.

However, this view was greatly altered by the later recognition that expected inflation affects the short-run Phillips curve. In the short run, expectations often diverge from reality. In the long run, however, any consistent rate of inflation will be reflected in expectations. If inflation is consistently high, as it was in the 1970s, people will come to expect more of the same; if inflation is consistently low, as it has been in recent years, that, too, will become part of expectations.

So what does the trade-off between inflation and unemployment look like in the long run, when actual inflation is incorporated into expectations? Most macroeconomists believe that there is, in fact, no long-run trade-off. That is, it is not possible to achieve lower unemployment in the long run by accepting higher inflation. To see why, we need to introduce another concept: the *long-run Phillips curve*.

## The Long-Run Phillips Curve

Figure 16-11 reproduces the two short-run Phillips curves from Figure 16-9, $SRPC_0$ and $SRPC_2$. It also adds an additional short-run Phillips curve, $SRPC_4$, representing a 4% expected rate of inflation. In a moment, we'll explain the significance of the vertical long-run Phillips curve, $LRPC$.

Suppose that the economy has, in the past, had a 0% inflation rate. In that case, the current short-run Phillips curve will be $SRPC_0$, reflecting a 0% expected inflation rate. If the unemployment rate is 6%, the actual inflation rate will be 0%.

Also suppose that policy makers decide to trade off lower unemployment for a higher rate of inflation. They use monetary policy, fiscal policy, or both to drive the unemployment rate down to 4%. This puts the economy at point A on $SRPC_0$, leading to an actual inflation rate of 2%.

Over time, the public will come to expect a 2% inflation rate. *This increase in inflationary expectations will shift the short-run Phillips curve upward* to $SRPC_2$. Now, when the unemployment rate is 6%, the actual inflation rate will be 2%. Given this new short-run Phillips curve, policies adopted to keep the unemployment rate at 4% will lead to a 4% actual inflation rate—point B on $SRPC_2$—rather than point A with a 2% actual inflation rate.

Eventually, the 4% actual inflation rate gets built into expectations about the future inflation rate, and the short-run Phillips curve shifts upward yet again to

**FIGURE 16-11** The NAIRU and the Long-Run Phillips Curve

$SRPC_0$ is the short-run Phillips curve when the expected inflation rate is 0%. At a 4% unemployment rate, the economy is at point A with an actual inflation rate of 2%. The higher inflation rate will be incorporated into expectations, and the $SRPC$ will shift upward to $SRPC_2$. If policy makers act to keep the unemployment rate at 4%, the economy will be at B and the actual inflation rate will rise to 4%. Inflationary expectations will be revised upward again, and $SRPC$ will shift to $SRPC_4$. At a 4% unemployment rate, the economy will be at C and the actual inflation rate will rise to 6%. Here, an unemployment rate of 6% is the NAIRU, or nonaccelerating inflation rate of unemployment. As long as unemployment is at the NAIRU, the actual inflation rate will match expectations and remain constant. An unemployment rate below 6% requires ever-accelerating inflation. The long-run Phillips curve, $LRPC$, which passes through $E_0$, $E_2$, and $E_4$, is vertical: no long-run trade-off between unemployment and inflation exists.

$SRPC_4$. To keep the unemployment rate at 4% would now require accepting a 6% actual inflation rate, point $C$ on $SRPC_4$, and so on. In short, a persistent attempt to trade off lower unemployment for higher inflation leads to *accelerating* inflation over time.

*To avoid accelerating inflation over time, the unemployment rate must be high enough that the actual rate of inflation matches the expected rate of inflation.* This is the situation at $E_0$ on $SRPC_0$: when the expected inflation rate is 0% and the unemployment rate is 6%, the actual inflation rate is 0%. It is also the situation at $E_2$ on $SRPC_2$: when the expected inflation rate is 2% and the unemployment rate is 6%, the actual inflation rate is 2%. And it is the situation at $E_4$ on $SRPC_4$: when the expected inflation rate is 4% and the unemployment rate is 6%, the actual inflation rate is 4%. As we'll learn in Chapter 18, this relationship between accelerating inflation and the unemployment rate is known as the *natural rate hypothesis.*

The unemployment rate at which inflation does not change over time—6% in Figure 16-11—is known as the **nonaccelerating inflation rate of unemployment,** or **NAIRU** for short. Keeping the unemployment rate below the NAIRU leads to ever-accelerating inflation and cannot be maintained. Most macroeconomists believe that there is a NAIRU and that there is no long-run trade-off between unemployment and inflation.

We can now explain the significance of the vertical line $LRPC$. It is the **long-run Phillips curve,** the relationship between unemployment and inflation in the long run, after expectations of inflation have had time to adjust to experience. It is vertical because any unemployment rate below the NAIRU leads to ever-accelerating inflation. In other words, the long-run Phillips curve shows that there are limits to expansionary policies because an unemployment rate below the NAIRU cannot be maintained in the long run. Moreover, there is a corresponding point we have not yet emphasized: any unemployment rate above the NAIRU leads to decelerating inflation.

The **nonaccelerating inflation rate of unemployment,** or **NAIRU,** is the unemployment rate at which inflation does not change over time.

The **long-run Phillips curve** shows the relationship between unemployment and inflation after expectations of inflation have had time to adjust to experience.

## The Natural Rate of Unemployment, Revisited

Recall the concept of the natural rate of unemployment, the portion of the unemployment rate unaffected by the swings of the business cycle. Now we have introduced the concept of the *NAIRU.* How do these two concepts relate to each other?

The answer is that the NAIRU is another name for the natural rate. The level of unemployment the economy "needs" in order to avoid accelerating inflation is equal to the natural rate of unemployment.

In fact, economists estimate the natural rate of unemployment by looking for evidence about the NAIRU from the behavior of the inflation rate and the unemployment rate over the course of the business cycle. For example, the way major European countries learned, to their dismay, that their natural rates of unemployment were 9% or more was through unpleasant experience. In the late 1980s, and again in the late 1990s, European inflation began to accelerate as European unemployment rates, which had been above 9%, began to fall, approaching 8%.

In Figure 16-4 we cited Congressional Budget Office estimates of the U.S. natural rate of unemployment. The CBO has a model that predicts changes in the inflation rate based on the deviation of the actual unemployment rate from the natural rate. Given data on actual unemployment and inflation, this model can be used to deduce estimates of the natural rate—and that's where the CBO numbers come from. As of April 2012, the CBO estimate of the U.S. natural rate was 5.5%.

## The Costs of Disinflation

Through experience, policy makers have found that bringing inflation down is a much harder task than increasing it. The reason is that once the public has come to expect continuing inflation, bringing inflation down is painful.

## GLOBAL COMPARISON | DISINFLATION AROUND THE WORLD

The great disinflation of the 1980s wasn't unique to the United States. A number of other advanced countries also experienced high inflation during the 1970s, then brought inflation down during the 1980s at the cost of a severe recession. This figure shows the annual rate of inflation in Britain, Italy, and the United States from 1970 to 2010. All three nations experienced high inflation rates following the two oil shocks of 1973 and 1979, with the U.S. inflation rate the least severe of the three. All three nations then weathered severe recessions in order to bring inflation down. Since the 1980s, inflation has remained low and stable in all wealthy nations.

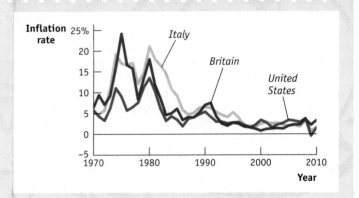

*Source:* OECD.

A persistent attempt to keep unemployment below the natural rate leads to accelerating inflation that becomes incorporated into expectations. To reduce inflationary expectations, policy makers need to run the process in reverse, adopting contractionary policies that keep the unemployment rate above the natural rate for an extended period of time. The process of bringing down inflation that has become embedded in expectations is known as **disinflation.**

Disinflation can be very expensive. As the following Economics in Action documents, the U.S. retreat from high inflation at the beginning of the 1980s appears to have cost the equivalent of about 18% of a year's real GDP, the equivalent of roughly $2.6 trillion today. The justification for paying these costs is that they lead to a permanent gain. Although the economy does not recover the short-term production losses caused by disinflation, it no longer suffers from the costs associated with persistently high inflation. In fact, the United States, Britain, and other wealthy countries that experienced inflation in the 1970s eventually decided that the benefit of bringing inflation down was worth the required suffering—the large reduction in real GDP in the short term.

Some economists argue that the costs of disinflation can be reduced if policy makers explicitly state their determination to reduce inflation. A clearly announced, credible policy of disinflation, they contend, can reduce expectations of future inflation and so shift the short-run Phillips curve downward. Some economists believe that the clear determination of the Federal Reserve to combat the inflation of the 1970s was credible enough that the costs of disinflation, huge though they were, were lower than they might otherwise have been.

## ECONOMICS ▶ IN ACTION

### THE GREAT DISINFLATION OF THE 1980s

**A**s we've mentioned several times in this chapter, the United States ended the 1970s with a high rate of inflation, at least by its own peacetime historical standards—13% in 1980. Part of this inflation was the result of one-time events, especially a world oil crisis. But expectations of future inflation at 10% or more per year appeared to be firmly embedded in the economy.

**Disinflation** is the process of bringing down inflation that is embedded in expectations.

FIGURE **16-12** The Great Disinflation

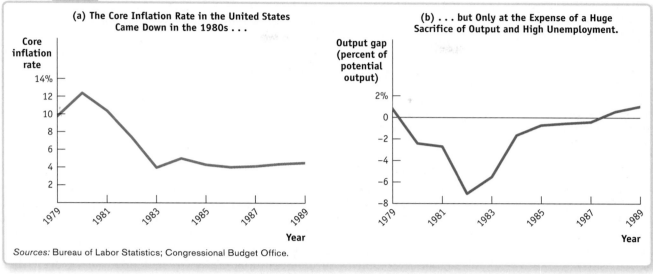

**(a) The Core Inflation Rate in the United States Came Down in the 1980s . . .**

**(b) . . . but Only at the Expense of a Huge Sacrifice of Output and High Unemployment.**

*Sources:* Bureau of Labor Statistics; Congressional Budget Office.

By the mid-1980s, however, inflation was running at about 4% per year. Panel (a) of Figure 16-12 shows the annual rate of change in the "core" consumer price index (CPI)—also called the *core inflation rate.* This index, which excludes volatile energy and food prices, is widely regarded as a better indicator of underlying inflation trends than the overall CPI. By this measure, inflation fell from about 12% at the end of the 1970s to about 4% by the mid-1980s.

How was this disinflation achieved? At great cost. Beginning in late 1979, the Federal Reserve imposed strongly contractionary monetary policies, which pushed the economy into its worst recession since the Great Depression. Panel (b) shows the Congressional Budget Office estimate of the U.S. output gap from 1979 to 1989: by 1982, actual output was 7% below potential output, corresponding to an unemployment rate of more than 9%. Aggregate output didn't get back to potential output until 1987.

Our analysis of the Phillips curve tells us that a temporary rise in unemployment, like that of the 1980s, is needed to break the cycle of inflationary expectations. Once expectations of inflation are reduced, the economy can return to the natural rate of unemployment at a lower inflation rate. And that's just what happened.

But the cost was huge. If you add up the output gap over 1980–1987, you find that the economy sacrificed approximately 18% of an average year's output over the period. If we had to do the same thing today, that would mean giving up roughly $2.6 trillion worth of goods and services.

### CHECK YOUR UNDERSTANDING 16-3

**1.** Why is there no long-run trade-off between unemployment and inflation?

**2.** British economists believe that the natural rate of unemployment in that country rose sharply during the 1970s, from around 3% to as much as 10%. During that period, Britain experienced a sharp acceleration of inflation, which for a time went above 20%. How might these facts be related?

**3.** Why is disinflation so costly for an economy? Are there ways to reduce these costs?

Solutions appear at back of book.

---

**▼ Quick Review**

● Policies that keep the unemployment rate below the **NAIRU,** the **nonaccelerating rate of inflation,** will lead to accelerating inflation as inflationary expectations adjust to higher levels of actual inflation. The NAIRU is equal to the natural rate of unemployment.

● The **long-run Phillips curve** is vertical and shows that an unemployment rate below the NAIRU cannot be maintained in the long run. As a result, there are limits to expansionary policies.

● **Disinflation** imposes high costs— unemployment and lost output—on an economy. Governments do it to avoid the costs of persistently high inflation.

**Debt deflation** is the reduction in aggregate demand arising from the increase in the real burden of outstanding debt caused by deflation.

There is a **zero bound** on the nominal interest rate: it cannot go below zero.

The economy is in a **liquidity trap** when conventional monetary policy is ineffective because nominal interest rates are up against the zero bound.

# Deflation

Before World War II, *deflation*—a falling aggregate price level—was almost as common as inflation. In fact, the U.S. consumer price index on the eve of World War II was 30% lower than it had been in 1920. After World War II, inflation became the norm in all countries. But in the 1990s, deflation reappeared in Japan and proved difficult to reverse. Concerns about potential deflation played a crucial role in U.S. monetary policy in the early 2000s and again in the aftermath of the 2008 financial crisis.

Why is deflation a problem? And why is it hard to end?

## Debt Deflation

Deflation, like inflation, produces both winners and losers—but in the opposite direction. Due to the falling price level, a dollar in the future has a higher real value than a dollar today. So lenders, who are owed money, gain under deflation because the real value of borrowers' payments increases. Borrowers lose because the real burden of their debt rises.

In a famous analysis at the beginning of the Great Depression, Irving Fisher (who first analyzed the *Fisher effect* of expected inflation on interest rates, described in Chapter 10) claimed that the effects of deflation on borrowers and lenders can worsen an economic slump. Deflation, in effect, takes real resources away from borrowers and redistributes them to lenders. Fisher argued that borrowers, who lose from deflation, are typically short of cash and will be forced to cut their spending sharply when their debt burden rises. Lenders, however, are unlikely to increase spending sharply when the values of the loans they own rise. The overall effect, said Fisher, is that deflation reduces aggregate demand, deepening an economic slump, which, in a vicious circle, may lead to further deflation. The effect of deflation in reducing aggregate demand, known as **debt deflation,** probably played a significant role in the Great Depression.

## Effects of Expected Deflation

Like expected inflation, expected deflation affects the nominal interest rate. Look back at Figure 10-7, which demonstrated how expected inflation affects the equilibrium interest rate. In Figure 10-7, the equilibrium nominal interest rate is 4% if the expected inflation rate is 0%. Clearly, if the expected inflation rate is –3%—if the public expects deflation at 3% per year—the equilibrium nominal interest rate will be 1%.

But what would happen if the expected rate of inflation is –5%? Would the nominal interest rate fall to –1%, in which lenders are paying borrowers 1% on their debt? No. Nobody would lend money at a negative nominal rate of interest because they could do better by simply holding cash. This illustrates what economists call the **zero bound** on the nominal interest rate: it cannot go below zero.

This zero bound can limit the effectiveness of monetary policy. Suppose the economy is depressed, with output below potential output and the unemployment rate above the natural rate. Normally the central bank can respond by cutting interest rates so as to increase aggregate demand. If the nominal interest rate is already zero, however, the central bank cannot push it down any further. Banks refuse to lend and consumers and firms refuse to spend because, with a negative inflation rate and a 0% nominal interest rate, holding cash yields a positive real return: with falling prices, a given amount of cash buys more over time. Any further increases in the monetary base will either be held in bank vaults or held as cash by individuals and firms, without being spent.

A situation in which conventional monetary policy to fight a slump—cutting interest rates—can't be used because nominal interest rates are up against the zero bound is known as a **liquidity trap.** A liquidity trap can occur whenever there is a sharp reduction in demand for loanable funds—which is exactly what

FIGURE  **16-13**  The Zero Bound in U.S. History

This figure shows U.S. short-term interest rates, specifically the interest rate on three-month Treasury bills, from 1920 to 2011. As shown by the shaded area at left, for much of the 1930s, interest rates were very close to zero, leaving little room for expansionary monetary policy. After World War II, persistent inflation generally kept interest rates well above zero. However, in late 2008, in the wake of the housing bubble bursting and the financial crisis, the interest rate on three-month Treasury bills was again virtually zero.

*Source:* Federal Reserve Bank of St. Louis.

happened during the Great Depression. Figure 16-13 shows the interest rate on short-term U.S. government debt from 1920 to December 2011. As you can see, from 1933 until World War II brought a full economic recovery, the U.S. economy was either close to or up against the zero bound. After World War II, when inflation became the norm around the world, the zero bound largely vanished as a problem as the public came to expect inflation rather than deflation.

However, the recent history of the Japanese economy, shown in Figure 16-14, provides a modern illustration of the problem of deflation and the liquidity trap. Japan experienced a huge boom in the prices of both stocks and real estate in the late 1980s, then saw both bubbles burst. The result was a prolonged period of economic stagnation, the so-called Lost Decade, which gradually reduced the inflation rate and eventually led to persistent deflation. In an effort to fight the weakness of the economy, the Bank of Japan—the equivalent of the Federal

FIGURE  **16-14**  Japan's Lost Decade

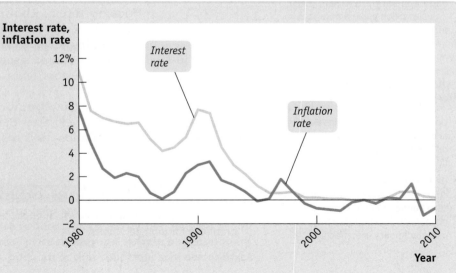

A prolonged economic slump in Japan led to deflation from the late 1990s on. The Bank of Japan responded by cutting interest rates—but eventually ran up against the zero bound.

*Source:* OECD.

Reserve—repeatedly cut interest rates. Eventually, it arrived at the ZIRP: the zero interest rate policy. The call money rate, the equivalent of the U.S. federal funds rate, was literally set equal to zero. Because the economy was still depressed, it would have been desirable to cut interest rates even further. But that wasn't possible: Japan was up against the zero bound.

In the aftermath of the 2008 financial crisis, the Federal Reserve also found itself up against the zero bound, with the interest rate on short-term U.S. government debt virtually at zero. As discussed in the following Economics in Action, this led to fears of a Japan-type trap and spurred the Fed to take some unconventional action.

## ECONOMICS ▷ IN ACTION

### THE DEFLATION SCARE OF 2010

Ever since the financial crisis of 2008, U.S. policy makers have been worried about the possibility of "Japanification"—that is, they have worried that, like Japan since the 1990s, the United States might find itself stuck in a deflationary trap. Indeed, Ben Bernanke, the chairman of the Federal Reserve, studied Japan intensively before he went to the Fed and has sought to do better than his Japanese counterparts did.

Fears of deflation were particularly intense in the summer and early fall of 2010. Figure 16-15 shows why, by tracking two numbers the Fed watches carefully when making policy. One of these numbers is the "core" inflation rate over the past year—the percentage rise in a measure of consumer prices (the personal consumption expenditure deflator) that excludes volatile food and energy prices. The Fed normally regards this core inflation rate as its best guide to underlying inflation and tries to keep it at around 2%. The other number is a measure of expected inflation derived by calculating the difference between the interest rate on ordinary government bonds and the rate on government bonds whose yield is protected against inflation.

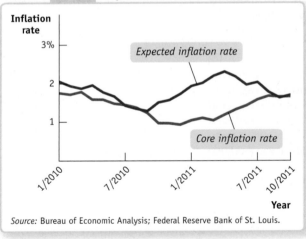

**FIGURE 16-15** Expected vs. Actual Inflation, 2010

*Source:* Bureau of Economic Analysis; Federal Reserve Bank of St. Louis.

As you can see, by the late summer of 2010 both actual inflation and expected inflation were sliding to levels well below the Fed's 2% target. Fed officials were worried, and they took action. In August 2010 Ben Bernanke gave a speech at the annual Fed meeting in Jackson Hole, Wyoming, signaling that he would take special actions to head off the deflationary threat. And in November the Fed, which normally buys only short-term government debt, began a program of long-term bond purchases, in the hope that this would give the economy a boost.

Figure 16-15 shows that Bernanke's speech and the Fed's action led to a major change in expectations, as investors' fears of deflation ebbed. Actual inflation also picked up significantly.

What was far from clear, however, was whether the Fed had achieved more than a temporary reprieve. A year after Bernanke's big speech, expected inflation was sagging again, and deflation fears were again on the rise.

### ▼ Quick Review

- Unexpected deflation helps lenders and hurts borrowers. This can lead to **debt deflation,** which has a contractionary effect on aggregate demand.

- Deflation makes it more likely that interest rates will end up against the **zero bound.** When this happens, the economy is in a **liquidity trap,** and monetary policy is ineffective.

### CHECK YOUR UNDERSTANDING 16-4

1. Why won't anyone lend money at a negative nominal rate of interest? How can this pose problems for monetary policy?

Solution appears at back of book.

## BUSINESS CASE • Licenses to Print Money

Alamy

People sometimes talk about profitable companies as having a "license to print money." Well, the British firm De La Rue actually does. In 1930, De La Rue, printer of items such as postage stamps, expanded into the money-printing business, producing banknotes for the then-government of China. Today it produces the currencies of about 150 countries.

De La Rue's business received some unexpected attention in 2011 when Muammar Gaddafi, the dictator who had ruled Libya since 1969, was fighting to suppress a fierce popular uprising. To finance his efforts, he turned to seignorage, ordering around $1.5 billion worth of Libyan dinars printed. But Libyan banknotes weren't printed in Libya; they were printed in Britain at one of De La Rue's facilities. The British Government, an enemy of the Gaddafi regime, seized the new banknotes before they could be flown to Libya, refusing to release them until Gaddafi had been overthrown.

Why do so many countries turn to private companies like De La Rue and its main rival, the German firm Giesecke and Devrient, to print their currencies? The short answer is that printing money isn't as easy as it sounds: producing high-quality banknotes that are hard to counterfeit requires highly specialized equipment and expertise. Large, wealthy nations like the United States can easily afford to do this for themselves: U.S. currency is printed by the Bureau of Engraving and Printing, a division of the Treasury Department. But smaller, poorer countries do better by turning to experts like De La Rue, which can include high-tech features like security threads and holography to fight counterfeiters.

Actually, De La Rue has had its own problems with quality control: a scandal erupted in 2010, when it emerged that one of its plants had been producing defective security paper and that employees had covered up the problems. Nonetheless, many countries will surely continue relying on expert private firms to produce their currency.

### QUESTIONS FOR THOUGHT

1. How can a government obtain revenue by printing money when someone else actually prints the money?

2. Why, exactly, would Gaddafi have resorted to the printing press in early 2011?

3. Were there risks to the Libyan economy in releasing those dinars to the new government?

## SUMMARY

1. In analyzing high inflation, economists use the **classical model of the price level,** which says that changes in the money supply lead to proportional changes in the aggregate price level even in the short run.

2. Governments sometimes print money in order to finance budget deficits. When they do, they impose an **inflation tax,** generating tax revenue equal to the inflation rate times the money supply, on those who hold money. Revenue from the real inflation tax, the inflation rate times the real money supply, is the real value of resources captured by the government. In order to avoid paying the inflation tax, people reduce their real money holdings and force the government to increase inflation to capture the same amount of real inflation tax revenue. In some cases, this leads to a vicious circle of a shrinking real money supply and a rising rate of inflation, leading to hyperinflation and a fiscal crisis.

3. The output gap is the percentage difference between the actual level of real GDP and potential output. A positive output gap is associated with lower-than-normal unemployment; a negative output gap is associated with higher-than-normal unemployment. The relationship between the output gap and cyclical unemployment is described by **Okun's law.**

4. Countries that don't need to print money to cover government deficits can still stumble into moderate inflation, either because of political opportunism or because of wishful thinking.

5. At a given point in time, there is a downward-sloping relationship between unemployment and inflation known as the **short-run Phillips curve.** This curve is shifted by changes in the expected rate of inflation. The **long-run Phillips curve,** which shows the relationship between unemployment and inflation once expectations have had time to adjust, is vertical. It defines the **nonaccelerating inflation rate of unemployment,** or **NAIRU,** which is equal to the natural rate of unemployment. *Stagflation*, a combination of high unemployment and high inflation, reflects an upward shift of the short-run Phillips curve.

6. Once inflation has become embedded in expectations, getting inflation back down can be difficult because **disinflation** can be very costly, requiring the sacrifice of large amounts of aggregate output and imposing high levels of unemployment. However, policy makers in the United States and other wealthy countries were willing to pay that price of bringing down the high inflation of the 1970s.

7. Deflation poses several problems. It can lead to **debt deflation,** in which a rising real burden of outstanding debt intensifies an economic downturn. Also, interest rates are more likely to run up against the **zero bound** in an economy experiencing deflation. When this happens, the economy enters a **liquidity trap,** rendering conventional monetary policy ineffective.

## KEY TERMS

Classical model of the price level, p. 476
Inflation tax, p. 479
Okun's law, p. 484
Short-run Phillips curve, p. 485
Nonaccelerating inflation rate of unemployment (NAIRU), p. 491
Long-run Phillips curve, p. 491
Disinflation, p. 492
Debt deflation, p. 494
Zero bound, p. 494
Liquidity trap, p. 494

## PROBLEMS

1. In the economy of Scottopia, policy makers want to lower the unemployment rate and raise real GDP by using monetary policy. Using the accompanying diagram, show why this policy will ultimately result in a higher aggregate price level but no change in real GDP.

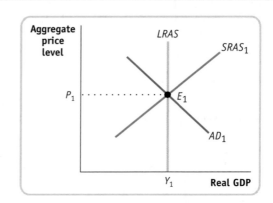

2. In the following examples, would the classical model of the price level be relevant?

   a. There is a great deal of unemployment in the economy and no history of inflation.

   b. The economy has just experienced five years of hyperinflation.

   c. Although the economy experienced inflation in the 10% to 20% range three years ago, prices have recently been stable and the unemployment rate has approximated the natural rate of unemployment.

3. The Federal Reserve regularly releases data on the U.S. monetary base. You can access that data at various websites, including the website for the Federal Reserve Bank of St. Louis. Go to http://research.stlouisfed.org/fred2/ and click on "Money, Banking, & Finance," then on "Monetary Data," then on "Monetary Base," and then on "Board of Governors Monetary Base, Adjusted for Changes in Reserve Requirements" for the latest report. Then click on "View Data."

   a. The last two numbers in the column show the levels of the monetary base in the last year. How much did it change?

   b. How did this help in the government's efforts to finance its deficit?

   c. Why is it important for the central bank to be independent from the part of the government responsible for spending?

4. Answer the following questions about the (real) inflation tax, assuming that the price level starts at 1.

   a. Maria Moneybags keeps $1,000 in her sock drawer for a year. Over the year, the inflation rate is 10%. What is the real inflation tax paid by Maria for this year?

   b. Maria continues to keep the $1,000 in her drawer for a second year. What is the real value of this $1,000 at the beginning of the second year? Over the year, the inflation rate is again 10%. What is the real inflation tax paid by Maria for the second year?

   c. For a third year, Maria keeps the $1,000 in the drawer. What is the real value of this $1,000 at the beginning of the third year? Over the year, the inflation rate is again 10%. What is the real inflation tax paid by Maria for the third year?

   d. After three years, what is the cumulative real inflation tax paid?

   e. Redo parts a through d with an inflation rate of 25%. Why is hyperinflation such a problem?

5. The inflation tax is often used as a significant source of revenue in developing countries where the tax collection and reporting system is not well developed and tax evasion may be high.

   a. Use the numbers in the accompanying table to calculate the inflation tax in the United States and India (Rp = rupees).

| | Inflation in 2010 | Money supply in 2010 (billions) | Central government receipts in 2010 (billions) |
|---|---|---|---|
| India | 1.65% | Rp16,318 | Rp7,943 |
| United States | 1.4% | $1,838 | $2,430 |

*Sources:* Bureau of Economic Analysis; Federal Reserve Bank of St. Louis; Controller General of Accounts (India); Reserve Bank of India; International Monetary Fund.

   b. How large is the inflation tax for the two countries when calculated as a percentage of government receipts?

6. Concerned about the crowding-out effects of government borrowing on private investment spending, a candidate for president argues that the United States should just print money to cover the government's budget deficit. What are the advantages and disadvantages of such a plan?

7. The accompanying scatter diagram shows the relationship between the unemployment rate and the output gap in the United States from 1990 to 2004. Draw a straight line through the scatter of dots in the figure. Assume that this line represents Okun's law:

   Unemployment rate = $b - (m \times$ Output gap) where $b$ is the vertical intercept and $-m$ is the slope

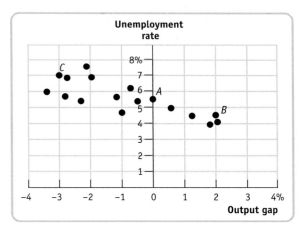

What is the unemployment rate when aggregate output equals potential output? What would the unemployment rate be if the output gap were 2%? What if the output gap were –3%? What do these results tell us about the coefficient $m$ in Okun's law?

8. After experiencing a recession for the past two years, the residents of Albernia were looking forward to a decrease in the unemployment rate. Yet after six months of strong positive economic growth, the unemployment rate has fallen only slightly below what it was at the

end of the recession. How can you explain why the unemployment rate did not fall as much although the economy was experiencing strong economic growth?

9. Due to historical differences, countries often differ in how quickly a change in actual inflation is incorporated into a change in expected inflation. In a country such as Japan, which has had very little inflation in recent memory, it will take longer for a change in the actual inflation rate to be reflected in a corresponding change in the expected inflation rate. In contrast, in a country such as Zimbabwe, which has recently had very high inflation, a change in the actual inflation rate will immediately be reflected in a corresponding change in the expected inflation rate. What does this imply about the short-run and long-run Phillips curves in these two types of countries? What does this imply about the effectiveness of monetary and fiscal policy to reduce the unemployment rate?

10. a. Go to www.bls.gov. Click on link "Subject Areas"; on the left, under "Inflation & Prices," click on the link "Consumer Price Index." Scroll down to the section "CPI Tables," and find the link "Consumer Price Index Detailed Report, Tables Annual Averages 2009 (PDF)." What is the value of the percent change in the CPI from 2008 to 2009?

b. Now go to www.treasury.gov and click on "Resource Center." From there, click on "Data and Charts Center." Then click on "Interest Rate Statistics," followed by "TextView." In the scroll-down windows, select "Daily Treasury Bill Rates" and "2009." Examine the data in "4 Weeks Bank Discount." What is the maximum? The minimum? Then do the same for 2007. How do the data for 2009 and 2007 compare? How would you relate this to your answer in part (a)? From the data on Treasury bill interest rates, what would you infer about the level of the inflation rate in 2007 compared to 2009? (You can check your answer by going back to the www.bls.gov website to find the percent change in the CPI from 2006 to 2007.)

c. How would you characterize the change in the U.S. economy from 2007 to 2009?

11. The accompanying table provides data from the United States on the average annual rates of unemployment and inflation. Use the numbers to construct a scatter plot similar to Figure 16-5. Discuss why, in the short run, the unemployment rate rises when inflation falls.

| Year | Unemployment rate | Inflation rate |
|------|-------------------|----------------|
| 2000 | 4.0% | 3.4% |
| 2001 | 4.7 | 2.8 |
| 2002 | 5.8 | 1.6 |
| 2003 | 6.0 | 2.3 |
| 2004 | 5.5 | 2.7 |
| 2005 | 5.1 | 3.4 |
| 2006 | 4.6 | 3.2 |
| 2007 | 4.6 | 2.9 |
| 2008 | 5.8 | 3.8 |
| 2009 | 9.3 | −0.4 |
| 2010 | 9.6 | 1.6 |

*Source:* Bureau of Labor Statistics.

12. The economy of Brittania has been suffering from high inflation with an unemployment rate equal to its natural rate. Policy makers would like to disinflate the economy with the lowest economic cost possible. Assume that the state of the economy is not the result of a negative supply shock. How can they try to minimize the unemployment cost of disinflation? Is it possible for there to be no cost of disinflation?

13. Who are the winners and losers when a mortgage company lends $100,000 to the Miller family to buy a house worth $105,000 and during the first year prices unexpectedly fall by 10%? What would you expect to happen if the deflation continued over the next few years? How would continuing deflation affect borrowers and lenders throughout the economy as a whole?

# CHAPTER 17

# Crises and Consequences

## FROM PURVEYOR OF DRY GOODS TO DESTROYER OF WORLDS

The collapse of Lehman Brothers, the once-venerable investment bank, set off a chain of events that led to a worldwide financial panic.

**WHAT YOU WILL LEARN IN THIS CHAPTER**

❱ How depository banks and **shadow banks** differ

❱ Why, despite their differences, both types of banks are subject to bank runs

❱ What happens during **financial panics** and **banking crises**

❱ Why the effects of panics and crises on the economy are so severe and long-lasting

❱ How regulatory loopholes and the rise of **shadow banking** led to the financial crisis of 2008

❱ How the new regulatory framework seeks to avoid another crisis

IN 1844 HENRY LEHMAN, A GERMAN immigrant, opened a dry goods store in Montgomery, Alabama. Over time, Lehman and his brothers, who followed him to America, branched out into cotton trading, then into a variety of financial activities. By 1850, Lehman Brothers was established on Wall Street; by 2008, thanks to its skill at trading financial assets, Lehman Brothers was one of the nation's top investment banks. Unlike commercial banks, investment banks trade in financial assets and don't accept deposits from customers.

In September 2008, Lehman's luck ran out. The firm had invested heavily in subprime mortgages—loans to home buyers with too little income or too few assets to qualify for standard (also called "prime") mortgages. In the summer and fall of 2008, as the U.S. housing market plunge intensified and investments related to subprime mortgages lost much of their value, Lehman was hit hard.

Lehman had been borrowing heavily in the short-term credit market—often using overnight loans that must be repaid the next business day—to finance its ongoing operations and trading. As rumors began to spread about how heavily Lehman was exposed to the tanking housing market, its sources of credit dried up. On September 15, 2008, the firm declared bankruptcy, the largest bankruptcy to date in the United States. What happened would shock the world.

When Lehman fell, it set off a chain of events that came close to taking down the entire world financial system. Because Lehman had hidden the severity of its vulnerability, its failure came as a nasty surprise. Through securitization (a concept we defined in Chapter 14) financial institutions throughout the world were exposed to real estate loans that were quickly deteriorating in value as default rates on those loans rose. Credit markets froze because those with funds to lend decided it was better to sit on the funds rather than lend them out and risk losing them to a borrower who might go under like Lehman had. Around the world, borrowers were hit by a global *credit crunch:* they either lost their access to credit or found themselves forced to pay drastically higher interest rates. Stocks plunged, and within weeks the Dow had fallen almost 3,000 points.

Nor were the consequences limited to financial markets. The U.S. economy was already in recession when Lehman fell, but the pace of the downturn accelerated drastically in the months that followed. By the time U.S. employment bottomed out in early 2010, more than 8 million jobs had been lost. Europe and Japan were also suffering their worst recessions since the 1930s, and world trade plunged even faster than it had in the first year of the Great Depression.

All of this came as a great shock because few people imagined that such events were possible in twenty-first-century America. Yet economists who knew their history quickly recognized what they were seeing: it was a modern version of a *financial panic*, a sudden and widespread disruption of financial markets. Financial panics were a regular feature of the U.S. financial system before World War II. As we discussed in Chapter 14, the financial panic that hit the United States in 2008

shared many features with the Panic of 1907, whose devastation prompted the creation of the Federal Reserve system. Financial panics almost always include a *banking crisis*, in which a significant portion of the banking sector ceases to function.

On reflection, the panic following Lehman's collapse was not unique, even in the modern world. The failure of Long-Term Capital Management in 1998 also precipitated a financial panic: global financial markets froze until the Federal Reserve rode to the rescue and coordinated a winding-down of the firm's operations. Because the Federal Reserve resolved the LTCM crisis quickly, its fall didn't result in a blow to the economy at large.

Financial panics and banking crises have happened fairly often, sometimes with disastrous effects on output and employment. Chile's 1981 banking cri-

sis was followed by a 19% decline in real GDP per capita and a slump that lasted through most of the following decade. Finland's 1990 banking crisis was followed by a surge in the unemployment rate from 3.2% to 16.3%. Japan's banking crisis of the early 1990s led to more than a decade of economic stagnation.

In this chapter, we'll examine the causes and consequences of banking crises and financial panics, expanding on the discussion of this topic in Chapter 14. We'll begin by examining what makes banking vulnerable to a crisis and how this can mutate into a full-blown financial panic. Then we'll turn to the history of such crises and their aftermath, exploring why they are so destructive to the economy. Finally, we'll look at how governments have tried to limit the risks of financial crises. ■

## Banking: Benefits and Dangers

As we learned in earlier chapters, banks perform an essential role in any modern economy. In Chapter 14 we defined commercial banks and savings and loans as financial intermediaries that provide liquid financial assets in the form of deposits to savers and uses its funds to finance the illiquid investment spending needs of borrowers. Deposit-taking banks perform the important functions of providing liquidity to savers and directly influencing the level of the money supply.

Lehman Brothers, however, was not a deposit-taking bank. Instead, it was an investment bank (also defined in Chapter 14)—in the business of speculative trading for its own profit and the profit of its investors. Yet Lehman got into trouble in much the same way that a deposit-taking bank does: it experienced a loss of confidence and something very much like a bank run—a phenomenon in which many of a bank's depositors try to withdraw their funds due to fears of a bank failure. Lehman was part of a larger category of institutions called shadow banks. *Shadow banking*, a term coined by the economist Paul McCulley of the giant bond fund Pimco, is composed of a wide variety of types of financial firms: investment banks like Lehman, hedge funds like Long-Term Capital Management (LTCM), and money market funds. (As we will explain in more detail later, "shadow" refers to the fact that before the 2008 crisis these financial institutions were neither closely watched nor effectively regulated.) Like deposit-taking banks, shadow banks are vulnerable to bank runs because they perform the same economic task: *maturity tranformation,* the transformation of short-term liabilities into long-term assets. From now on, we will use the term *depository banks* for banks that accept deposits (commercial banks and savings and loans) to better distinguish them from shadow banks (investment banks, hedge funds, and money market funds) which do not.

## The Trade-off Between Rate of Return and Liquidity

Imagine that you live in a world without any banks. Further imagine that you have saved a substantial sum of money that you don't plan on spending anytime soon. What can you do with those funds?

One answer is that you could simply store the money—say, put it under your bed or in a safe. The money would always be there if you need it, but it would just sit there, not earning any interest.

Alternatively, you could lend the money out, say, to a growing business. This would have the great advantage of putting your money to work, both for you, since the loan would pay interest, and for the economy, since your funds would help pay for investment spending. There would, however, be a potential disadvantage: if you needed the money before the loan was paid off, you might not be able to recover it.

It's true that we asked you to assume that you had no plans for spending the money soon. But it's often impossible to predict when you will want or need to make cash outlays; for example, your car could break down or you could be offered an exciting opportunity to study abroad. Now, a loan is an asset, and there are ways to convert assets into cash. For example, you can try to sell the loan to someone else. But this can be difficult, especially if you need cash on short notice. So, in a world without banks, it's better to have some cash on hand when an unexpected financial need arises.

In other words, without banks, savers face a trade-off when deciding how much of their funds to lend out and how much to keep on hand in cash: a tradeoff between liquidity, the ability to turn one's assets into cash on short notice, and the rate of return, in the form of interest or other payments received on one's assets. Without banks, people would make this trade-off by keeping a large fraction of their wealth idle, sitting in safes rather than helping pay for productive investment spending. Banking, however, changes that by allowing people ready access to their funds even while those funds are being used to make loans for productive purposes.

## The Purpose of Banking

Banking, as we know it, emerged from a surprising place: it was originally a sideline business for medieval goldsmiths. By the nature of their business, goldsmiths needed vaults in which to store their gold. Over time, they realized that they could offer safekeeping services for their customers, too, because a wealthy person might prefer to leave his stash of gold and silver with a goldsmith rather than keep it at home, where thieves might snatch it.

Someone who deposited gold and silver with a goldsmith received a receipt that could be redeemed for those precious metals at any time. And a funny thing happened: people began paying for their purchases not by cashing in their receipts for gold and then paying with the gold, but simply by handing over their precious metal receipts to the seller. Thus, an early form of paper money was born.

Meanwhile, goldsmiths realized something else: even though they were obligated to return a customer's precious metals on demand, they didn't actually need to keep all of the treasure on their premises. After all, it was unlikely that all of their customers would want to lay hands on their gold and silver on the same day, especially if customers were using receipts as a means of payment. So a goldsmith could safely put some of his customers' wealth to work by lending it out to other businesses, keeping only enough on hand to pay off the few customers likely to demand their precious metals on short notice—plus some additional reserves in case of exceptional demand.

And so banking was born. In a more abstract form, depository banks today do the same thing those enterprising goldsmiths learned to do: they accept the savings of individuals, promising to return them on demand, but put most of those funds to work by taking advantage of the fact that not everyone will want access to those funds at the same time. A typical bank account lets you withdraw as much of your funds as you want, anytime you want—but the bank doesn't actually keep everyone's

**Maturity transformation** is the conversion of short-term liabilities into long-term assets.

A **shadow bank** is a nondepository financial institution that engages in maturity transformation.

cash in its safe or even in a form that can be turned quickly into cash. Instead, the bank lends out most of the funds placed in its care, keeping limited reserves to meet day-to-day withdrawals. And because deposits can be put to use, banks don't charge you (or charge very little) for the privilege of keeping your savings safe. Depending on the type of account you have, they might even pay you interest on your deposits.

More generally, what depository banks do is borrow on a short-term basis from depositors (who can demand to be repaid at any time) and lend on a long-term basis to others (who cannot be forced to repay until the end date of their loan). This is what economists call **maturity transformation:** converting short-term liabilities (deposits in this case) into long-term assets (bank loans that earn interest). Shadow banks, such as Lehman Brothers, also engage in maturity transformation, but they do it in a way that doesn't involve taking deposits.

Instead of taking deposits, Lehman borrowed funds in the short-term credit markets and then invested those funds in longer-term speculative projects. Indeed, a **shadow bank** is any financial institution that does not accept deposits but does engage in maturity transformation—borrowing over the short term and lending or investing over the longer term. And just as bank depositors benefit from the liquidity and higher return that banking provides compared to sitting on their money, lenders to shadow banks like Lehman benefit from liquidity (their loans must be repaid quickly, often overnight) and higher return compared to other ways of investing their funds.

A generation ago, depository banks accounted for most banking. After about 1980, however, there was a steady rise in shadow banking. Shadow banking has grown so popular because it has not been subject to the regulations, such as capital requirements and reserve requirements, that are imposed on depository banking. So, like the unregulated trusts that set off the Panic of 1907, shadow banks can offer their customers a higher rate of return on their funds. As of July 2007, generally considered the start of the financial crisis that climaxed when Lehman fell in September 2008, the U.S. shadow banking sector was about 1.5 times larger, in terms of dollars, than the formal, deposit-taking banking sector.

As we pointed out in Chapter 14, things are not always simple in banking. There we learned why depository banks can be subject to bank runs. As the cases of Lehman and LTCM so spectacularly illustrate, the same vulnerability afflicts shadow banks. Next we explore why.

## Shadow Banks and the Re-emergence of Bank Runs

Because a depository bank keeps on hand just a small fraction of its depositors' funds, a bank run typically results in a bank failure: the bank is unable to meet depositors' demands for their money and closes its doors. Ominously, bank runs can be self-fulfilling prophecies: although a bank may be in fine financial shape, if enough depositors believe it is in trouble and try to withdraw their money, their beliefs end up dooming the bank.

To prevent such occurrences, after the 1930s the United States (and most other countries) adopted wide-ranging banking regulation in the form of regular audits by the Federal Reserve, deposit insurance, capital requirements and reserve requirements, and provisions allowing troubled banks to borrow from the Fed's discount window.

Shadow banks, though, don't take deposits. So how can they be vulnerable to a bank run? The reason is that a shadow bank, like a depository bank, engages in maturity transformation: it borrows short term and lends or invests longer term. If a shadow bank's lenders suddenly decide one day that it's no longer safe to lend it money, the shadow bank can no longer fund its operations. Unless it can sell its assets immediately to raise cash, it will quickly fail. This is exactly what happened to Lehman.

Lehman borrowed funds in the overnight credit market (also known as the *repo* market), funds that it was required to repay the next business day, in order to fund its trading operations. So Lehman was on a very short leash: every day it had to be able to convince its creditors that it was a safe place to park their funds. And one day, that ability was no longer there. The same phenomenon happened at LTCM: the hedge fund was enormously leveraged (that is, it had borrowed huge amounts of money)—also, like Lehman, to fund its trading operations. One day its credit simply dried up, in its case because creditors perceived that it had lost huge amounts of money during the Asian and Russian financial crises of 1997–1998.

Bank runs are destructive to everyone associated with a bank: its shareholders, its creditors, its depositors and loan customers, and its employees. But a bank run that spreads like a contagion is extraordinarily destructive, causing depositors at other banks to also lose faith, leading to a cascading sequence of bank failures and a banking crisis. This is what happened in the United States during the early 1930s as Americans in general rushed out of bank deposits—the total value of bank deposits fell by 35%—and started holding currency instead. Until 2008, it had never happened again in the United States. Our next topic is to explore how and why bank runs reappeared.

## ECONOMICS ➤ *IN ACTION*

### THE DAY THE LIGHTS WENT OUT AT LEHMAN

On Friday night, September 12, 2008, an urgent meeting was held in the New York Federal Reserve Bank's headquarters on Wall Street. Attending was the outgoing Bush Administration's Treasury Secretary, Hank Paulson, and then head of the New York Fed, Tim Geithner (later the Treasury Secretary in the Obama Administration), along with the heads of the country's largest investment banks. Lehman Brothers was rapidly imploding and Paulson called the meeting in the hope of pressing the investment bankers into a deal that would, like the LTCM bailout described in Chapter 14, avert a messy bankruptcy.

Since the forced sale of the nearly bankrupt investment bank Bear Stearns six months earlier to a healthier bank, Lehman had been under increasing pressure. Like Bear Stearns, Lehman had invested heavily in sub-prime mortgages and other assets tied to real estate. And when Bear Stearns fell as its creditors began calling in its loans and other banks refused to lend to it, many wondered if Lehman would fall next.

In July 2008, Lehman reported a $2.8 billion loss for the second quarter of 2008 (the months April–June), precipitating a 54% fall in its stock price. As its share price fell, Lehman's sources of credit began to dry up and its trading operations withered. CEO of Lehman, Richard Fuld, began a desperate search for a healthier bank to buy shares of Lehman and provide desperately needed funding. By early September 2008, Lehman's loss for the third quarter had risen to $3.9 billion. On September 9, J.P. Morgan Chase, a far healthier investment bank that had been Lehman's major source of financing for its trades, demanded $5 billion in cash as extra collateral or it would freeze Lehman's accounts and cut off its credit. Unable to come up with the cash, Lehman teetered on the edge of bankruptcy.

In the September 12 meeting, Treasury Secretary Paulson urged the investment bankers to put together a package to purchase Lehman's bad assets. But, fearing for their own survival in an extremely turbulent market, they refused unless Paulson would give them a government guarantee on the value of Lehman's assets. The Treasury had made the Bear Stearns sale possible by arranging a huge loan from the New York Fed to its purchaser. This time, facing a backlash from Congress over "bailing out profligate bankers," Paulson refused to provide government help. And in the wee hours of Monday morning, September 15, 2008, Lehman went down, declaring the most expensive bankruptcy in history.

Yet, as Fuld had earlier warned Paulson, the failure of Lehman unleashed the furies. That same day the U.S. stock market fell 504 points, triggering an increase in bank borrowing costs and a run on money-market funds and financial institutions

Richard Fuld, the head of Lehman, testified before a congressional panel on how the collapse of Lehman precipitated a financial panic.

around the world. By Tuesday, Paulson agreed to an $85 billion bailout of another major corporation, the foundering American International Group, at the time the world's largest insurer. Before the markets stabilized months later, the U.S. government made $250 billion of capital infusions to bolster major U.S. banks. Whether or not Paulson made a catastrophic mistake by not acting to save Lehman is a matter likely to be debated for years to come.

●●◁

### CHECK YOUR UNDERSTANDING    17-1

1. Which of the following are examples of maturity transformations? Which are subject to a bank-run-like phenomenon in which fear of a failure becomes a self-fulfilling prophecy? Explain.
    a. You sell tickets to a lottery in which each ticket holder has a chance of winning a $10,000 jackpot.
    b. Dana borrows on her credit card to pay her living expenses while she takes a year-long course to upgrade her job skills. Without a better-paying job, she will not be able to pay her accumulated credit card balance.
    c. An investment partnership invests in office buildings. Partners invest their own funds and can redeem them only by selling their partnership share to someone else.
    d. The local student union savings bank offers checking accounts to students and invests those funds in student loans.

Solutions appear at back of book.

# Banking Crises and Financial Panics

Bank failures are common: even in a good year, several U.S. banks typically go under for one reason or another. And shadow banks sometimes fail, too. **Banking crises**—episodes in which a large part of the depository banking sector or the shadow banking sector fails or threatens to fail—are relatively rare by comparison. Yet they do happen, often with severe negative effects on the broader economy. What would cause so many of these institutions to get into trouble at the same time? Let's take a look at the logic of banking crises, then review some of the historical experiences.

## The Logic of Banking Crises

When many banks—either depository banks or shadow banks—get into trouble at the same time, there are two possible explanations. First, many of them could have made similar mistakes, often due to an *asset bubble*. Second, there may be *financial contagion*, in which one institution's problems spread and create trouble for others.

**Shared Mistakes** In practice, banking crises usually owe their origins to many banks making the same mistake of investing in an *asset bubble*. In an **asset bubble,** the price of some kind of asset, such as housing, is pushed to an unreasonably high level by investors' expectations of further price gains. For a while, such bubbles can feed on themselves. A good example is the savings and loan crisis of the 1980s, when there was a huge boom in the construction of commercial real estate, especially office buildings. Many banks extended large loans to real estate developers, believing that the boom would continue indefinitely. By the late 1980s, it became clear that developers had gotten carried away, building far more office space than the country needed. Unable to rent out their space or forced to slash rents, a number of developers defaulted on their loans—and the result was a wave of bank failures.

A similar phenomenon occurred between 2002 and 2006, when rapidly rising housing prices led many people to borrow heavily to buy a house in the belief that prices would keep rising. This process accelerated as more buyers rushed into the

A **banking crisis** occurs when a large part of the depository banking sector or the shadow banking sector fails or threatens to fail.

In an **asset bubble,** the price of an asset is pushed to an unreasonably high level due to expectations of further price gains.

market and pushed housing prices up even faster. Eventually the market runs out of new buyers and the bubble bursts. At this point asset prices fall; in some parts of the United States, housing prices fell by half between 2006 and 2009. This, in turn, undermines confidence in financial institutions that are exposed to losses due to falling asset prices. This loss of confidence, if it's sufficiently severe, can set in motion the kind of economy-wide vicious downward spiral that marks a financial contagion.

**Financial Contagion**   In especially severe banking crises, a vicious downward spiral of **financial contagion** occurs among depository banks or shadow banks: each institution's failure worsens depositors' or lenders' fears and increases the odds that another bank will fail.

As already noted, one underlying cause of contagion arises from the logic of bank runs. In the case of depository banks, when one bank fails, depositors are likely to become nervous about others. Similarly in the case of shadow banks, when one fails, lenders in the short-term credit market become nervous about lending to others. The shadow banking sector, because it is largely unregulated, is especially prone to fear- and rumor-driven contagion.

There is also a second channel of contagion: asset markets and the vicious cycle of deleveraging, a phenomenon we learned about in Chapter 14. When a financial institution is under pressure to reduce debt and raise cash, it tries to sell assets. To sell assets quickly, though, it often has to sell them at a deep discount. The contagion comes from the fact that other financial institutions own similar assets, whose prices decline as a result of the "fire sale." This decline in asset prices hurts the other financial institutions' financial positions, too, leading their creditors to stop lending to them. This knock-on effect forces more financial institutions to sell assets, reinforcing the downward spiral of asset prices. This kind of downward spiral was clearly evident in the months immediately following Lehman's fall: prices of a wide variety of assets held by financial institutions, from corporate bonds to pools of student loans, plunged as everyone tried to sell assets and raise cash. Later, as the severity of the crisis abated, many of these assets saw at least a partial recovery in prices.

Combine an asset bubble with a huge, unregulated shadow banking system and a vicious cycle of deleveraging and it is easy to see, as the U.S. economy did in 2008, how a full-blown **financial panic**—a sudden and widespread disruption of financial markets that happens when people suddenly lose faith in the liquidity of financial institutions and markets—can arise. A financial panic almost always involves a banking crisis, either in the depository banking sector, or the shadow banking sector, or both.

Because banking provides much of the liquidity needed for trading financial assets like stocks and bonds, severe banking crises almost always lead to disruptions of the stock and bond markets. Disruptions of these markets, along with a headlong rush to sell assets and raise cash, lead to a vicious circle of deleveraging. As the panic unfolds, savers and investors come to believe that the safest place for their money is under their bed, and their hoarding of cash further deepens the distress.

So what can history tell us about banking crises and financial panics?

## Historical Banking Crises: The Age of Panics

Between the Civil War and the Great Depression, the United States had a famously crisis-prone banking system. Even then, banks were regulated: most banking was carried out by "national banks" that were regulated by the federal government and subject to rules involving reserves and capital, of the kind described below. However, there was no system of guarantees for depositors. As a result, bank runs were common, and banking crises, also known at the time as panics, were fairly frequent.

Table 17-1 shows the dates of these nationwide banking crises and the number of banks that failed in each episode. Notice that the table is divided into two parts. The first part is devoted to the "national banking era," which preceded the 1913 creation of the Federal Reserve—which was supposed to put an end to such crises. It failed. The second part of the table is devoted to the epic waves of bank failures that took place in the early 1930s.

A **financial contagion** is a vicious downward spiral among depository banks or shadow banks: each bank's failure worsens fears and increases the likelihood that another bank will fail.

A **financial panic** is a sudden and widespread disruption of the financial markets that occurs when people suddenly lose faith in the liquidity of financial institutions and markets.

TABLE **17-1** Number of Bank Failures: National Banking Era and Great Depression

| National Banking era (1863–1912) | | Great Depression (1929–1941) | |
|---|---|---|---|
| **Panic dates** | **Number of failures** | **Panic dates** | **Number of failures** |
| September 1873 | 101 | November–December 1930 | 806 |
| May 1884 | 42 | April–August 1931 | 573 |
| November 1890 | 18 | September–October 1931 | 827 |
| May–August 1893 | 503 | June–July 1932 | 283 |
| October–December 1907 | 73* | February–March 1933 | Bank holiday |

*This understates the scale of the 1907 crisis because it doesn't take into account the role of trusts.

The events that sparked each of these panics differed. In the nineteenth century, there was a boom-and-bust cycle in railroad construction somewhat similar to the boom-and-bust cycle in office building construction during the 1980s. Like modern real estate companies, nineteenth-century railroad companies relied heavily on borrowed funds to finance their investment projects. And railroads, like office buildings, took a long time to build. This meant that there were repeated episodes of overbuilding: competing railroads would invest in expansion, only to find that collectively they had laid more track than the demand for rail transport warranted. When the overbuilding became apparent, business failures, debt defaults, and an overall banking crisis followed. The Panic of 1873 began when Jay Cooke and Co., a financial firm with a large stake in the railroad business, failed. The Panic of 1893 began with the failure of the overextended Philadelphia and Reading Railroad.

As we'll see later in this chapter, the major financial panics of the nineteenth and early twentieth centuries were followed by severe economic downturns. However, the banking crises of the early 1930s made previous crises seem minor by comparison. In four successive waves of bank runs from 1930 to 1932, about 40% of the banks in America failed. In the end, Franklin Delano Roosevelt declared a temporary closure of all banks—the so-called "bank holiday"—to put an end to the vicious circle. Meanwhile, the economy plunged, with real GDP shrinking by a third and a sharp fall in prices as well.

There is still considerable controversy about the banking crisis of the early 1930s. In part, this controversy is about cause and effect: did the banking crisis cause the wider economic crisis, or vice versa? (No doubt causation ran in both directions, but the magnitude of these effects remains disputed.) There is also controversy about the extent to which the banking crisis could have been avoided. Milton Friedman and Anna Schwartz, in their famous study *Monetary History of the United States*, argued that the Federal Reserve could and should have prevented the banking crisis—and that if it had, the Great Depression itself could also have been prevented. However, this view has been disputed by other economists.

In the United States, the experience of the 1930s led to banking reforms that prevented a replay for more than 70 years. Outside the United States, however, there were a number of major banking crises.

A typical scene outside a bank during the banking crises of the Great Depression.

## Modern Banking Crises Around the World

Around the world, banking crises are relatively frequent events. However, the ways in which they occur differ according to the banking sector's particular institutional framework. According to a 2008 analysis by the International Monetary Fund (IMF), no fewer than 127 banking crises occurred around the world between 1970 and 2007. Most of these were in small, poor countries that lack the regulatory safeguards found in advanced countries. In poorer countries, banks generally get in trouble in much the same way: insufficient capital, poor accounting, too many loans and, often, corruption. But banks in advanced countries can also make the same mistakes—for example, there was the Savings and Loan crisis in the United States during the 1980s (described in Chapter 14).

In more advanced countries, banking crises almost always occur as a consequence of an asset bubble—typically in real estate. Between 1985 and 1995, three advanced countries—Finland, Sweden, and Japan—experienced banking crises due to the bursting of a real estate bubble. Banks in the three countries lent heavily into a real estate bubble that their lending helped to inflate. Figure 17-1 shows real estate prices, adjusted for inflation, in Finland, Sweden, and Japan from 1985 to 1995. As you can see, in each country a sharp rise was followed by a drastic fall, leading many borrowers to default on their real estate loans, pushing large parts of each country's banking system into insolvency.

**FIGURE   17-1   Real Housing Prices in Three Banking Crises**

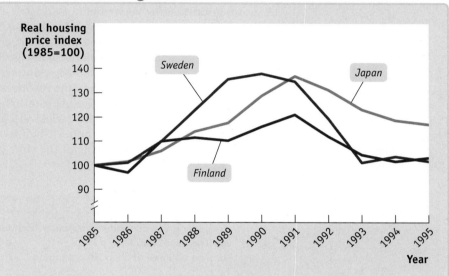

During the period 1985 to 1995, Finland, Sweden, and Japan each experienced a banking crisis due to a real estate bubble. Here you can see how real housing prices (housing prices adjusted for inflation) in each country rose dramatically and then fell sharply. The sharp fall in housing prices pushed a significant part of each country's banking sector into insolvency.

*Sources:* Bank of Finland; Statistics Sweden; Japan Real Estate Institute; Bank for international Settlements; OECD.

In the United States, the fall of Lehman in September 2008 precipitated a banking crisis in the shadow banking sector that included financial contagion as well as financial panic, but left the depository banking sector largely unaffected. As we discussed in the opening story, the financial crisis of 2008 was devastating because of securitization, which had distributed sub-prime mortgage loans throughout the entire shadow banking sector both in the United States and abroad.

At the time of writing, the market for securitization has not yet recovered and the shadow banking sector is a shadow of its former self. Since 2008, investors have rediscovered the benefits of regulation, and the depository banking sector has grown at the expense of the shadow banking sector. In the next section, we will learn how troubles in the banking sector soon translate into troubles for the broader economy.

## ECONOMICS > *IN ACTION*

### ERIN GO BROKE

For much of the 1990s and 2000s, Ireland was celebrated as an economic success story: the "Celtic Tiger" was growing at a pace the rest of Europe could only envy. But the miracle came to an abrupt halt in 2008, as Ireland found itself facing a huge banking crisis.

Like the earlier banking crises in Finland, Sweden, and Japan, Ireland's crisis grew out of excessive optimism about real estate. Irish housing prices began rising in the 1990s, in part a result of the economy's strong growth. However, real estate developers began betting on ever-rising prices, and Irish banks were all too willing to lend these developers large amounts of money to back their speculations. Housing prices tripled between 1997 and 2007, home construction quadrupled over the same period, and total credit offered by banks rose far faster than in any other European nation. To raise the cash for their lending spree, Irish banks supplemented the funds of depositors with large amounts of "wholesale" funding—short-term borrowing from other banks and private investors.

In 2007 the real estate boom collapsed. Home prices started falling, and home sales collapsed. Many of the loans that banks had made during the boom went into default. Now, so-called ghost estates, new housing developments full of unoccupied, crumbling homes, dot the landscape. In 2008, the troubles of the Irish banks threatened to turn into a sort of bank run—not by depositors, but by lenders who had provided the banks with short-term funding through the wholesale interbank lending market. To stabilize the situation, the Irish government stepped in, guaranteeing repayment of all bank debt.

This created a new problem because it put Irish taxpayers on the hook for potentially huge bank losses. Until the crisis struck, Ireland had seemed to be in good fiscal shape, with relatively low government debt and a budget surplus. The banking crisis, however, led to serious questions about the solvency of the Irish government—whether it had the resources to meet its obligations—and forced the government to pay high interest rates on funds it raised in international markets.

Like most banking crises, Ireland's led to a severe recession. The unemployment rate rose from less than 5% before the crisis to more than 14.8% in January 2012—and it was still rising at the time of writing.

**CHECK YOUR UNDERSTANDING   17-2**

1. Regarding the Economics in Action "Erin Go Broke," identify the following:
   a. The asset bubble
   b. The channel of financial contagion

2. Again regarding "Erin Go Broke," why do you think the Irish government tried to stabilize the situation by guaranteeing the debts of the banks? Why was this a questionable policy?

   Solutions appear at back of book.

# The Consequences of Banking Crises

I f banking crises affected only banks, they wouldn't be as serious a concern. In fact, however, banking crises are almost always associated with recessions, and severe banking crises are associated with the worst economic slumps. Furthermore, history shows that recessions caused in part by banking crises inflict sustained economic damage, with economies taking years to recover.

## Banking Crises, Recessions, and Recovery

A severe banking crisis is one in which a large fraction of the banking system either fails outright (that is, goes bankrupt) or suffers a major loss of confidence and must be bailed out by the government. Such crises almost invariably lead to deep recessions, which are usually followed by slow recoveries. Figure 17-2 illustrates this phenomenon by tracking unemployment in the aftermath of two banking crises widely separated in space and time: the Panic of 1893 in the United States and the Swedish banking crisis of 1991. In the figure, *t* represents the year of the crisis: 1893 for the United States, 1991 for Sweden. As the figure shows, these crises on

## FIGURE  17-2  Unemployment Rates, Before and After a Banking Crisis

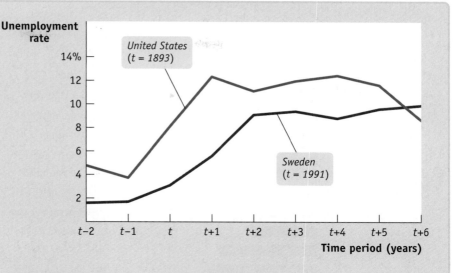

This figure tracks unemployment in the wake of two banking crises: the Panic of 1893 in the United States and the Swedish banking crisis of 1991. *t* represents the year of the crisis—1893 for the United States, 1991 for Sweden. *t* − 2 is the date two years before the crisis hit; *t* + 5 is the date five years after. In both cases, the economy suffered severe damage from the banking crisis: unemployment shot up and came down only slowly and erratically. In both cases, five years after the crisis the unemployment rate remained high compared to pre-crisis levels.

*Sources:* Christina D. Romer, "Spurious Volatility in Historical Unemployment Data," *Journal of Political Economy* 94, no. 1 (1986): 1–37; Eurostat.

different continents, almost a century apart, produced similarly devastating results: unemployment shot up and came down only slowly and erratically so that, even five years after the crisis, the number of jobless remained high by pre-crisis standards.

These historical examples are typical. Figure 17-3, taken from a widely cited study by the economists Carmen Reinhart and Kenneth Rogoff, compares employment performance in the wake of a number of severe banking crises. The bars on the left show the rise in the unemployment rate during and following the crisis; the bars on the right show the time it took before unemployment began to fall. The numbers are shocking: on average, severe banking crises have been followed by a 7 percentage point rise in the unemployment rate, and in many cases it has taken four years or more before the unemployment rate even begins to fall, let alone returns to pre-crisis levels.

## Why Are Banking-Crisis Recessions So Bad?

It's not difficult to see why banking crises normally lead to recessions. There are three main reasons: a *credit crunch* arising from reduced availability of credit, financial distress caused by a *debt overhang*, and the loss of monetary policy effectiveness.

1. *Credit crunch.* The disruption of the banking system typically leads to a reduction in the availability of credit called a **credit crunch,** in which potential borrowers either can't get credit at all or must pay very high interest rates. Unable to borrow or unwilling to pay higher interest rates, businesses and consumers cut back on spending, pushing the economy into a recession.

2. *Debt overhang.* A banking crisis typically pushes down the prices of many assets through a vicious circle of deleveraging, as distressed borrowers try to sell assets to raise cash, pushing down asset prices and causing further financial distress. As we have already seen, deleveraging is a factor in the spread of the crisis, lowering the value of the assets banks hold on their balance sheets and so undermining their solvency. It also creates problems for other players in the economy. To take an example all too familiar from recent events, falling housing prices can leave consumers substantially poorer, especially because they are still stuck with the debt they incurred to buy their homes. A banking crisis, then, tends to leave consumers and businesses with a **debt overhang:** high debt but diminished assets. Like a credit crunch, this also leads to a fall in spending and a recession as consumers and businesses cut back in order to reduce their debt and rebuild their assets.

In a **credit crunch,** potential borrowers either can't get credit at all or must pay very high interest rates.

A **debt overhang** occurs when a vicious circle of deleveraging leaves a borrower with high debt but diminished assets.

FIGURE **17-3** Episodes of Banking Crises and Unemployment

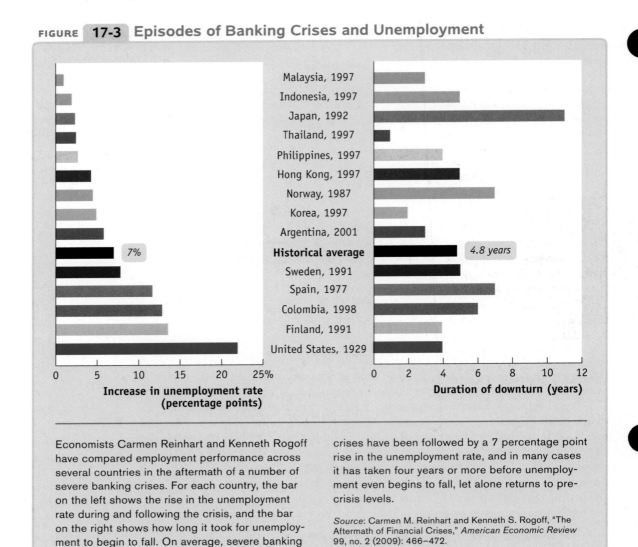

Economists Carmen Reinhart and Kenneth Rogoff have compared employment performance across several countries in the aftermath of a number of severe banking crises. For each country, the bar on the left shows the rise in the unemployment rate during and following the crisis, and the bar on the right shows how long it took for unemployment to begin to fall. On average, severe banking crises have been followed by a 7 percentage point rise in the unemployment rate, and in many cases it has taken four years or more before unemployment even begins to fall, let alone returns to pre-crisis levels.

*Source*: Carmen M. Reinhart and Kenneth S. Rogoff, "The Aftermath of Financial Crises," *American Economic Review* 99, no. 2 (2009): 466–472.

3. *Loss of monetary policy effectiveness.* A key feature of banking-crisis recessions is that when they occur, monetary policy—the main tool of policy makers for fighting negative demand shocks caused by a fall in consumer and investment spending—loses much of its effectiveness. The ineffectiveness of monetary policy makes banking-crisis recessions especially severe and long-lasting.

Recall from Chapter 14 how the Fed normally responds to a recession: it engages in open-market operations, purchasing short-term government debt from banks. This leaves banks with excess reserves, which they lend out, leading to a fall in interest rates and causing an economic expansion through increased consumer and investment spending.

Under normal conditions, this policy response is highly effective. In the aftermath of a banking crisis, though, the whole process tends to break down. Banks, fearing runs by depositors or a loss of confidence by their creditors, tend to hold on to excess reserves rather than lend them out. Meanwhile, businesses and consumers, finding themselves in financial difficulty due to the plunge in asset prices, may be unwilling to borrow even if interest rates fall. As a result, even very low interest rates may not be enough to push the economy back to full employment.

In Chapter 16 we described the problem of the economy's falling into a liquidity trap, when even pushing short-term interest rates to zero isn't enough. In fact, all the historical episodes in which the zero bound on interest rates became an important constraint on policy—the 1930s, Japan in the 1990s, and a number of countries after 2008—have occurred after a major banking crisis.

The inability of the usual tools of monetary policy to offset the macroeconomic devastation caused by banking crises is the major reason such crises produce deep, prolonged slumps. The obvious solution is to look for other policy tools. In fact, governments do typically take a variety of special steps when banks are in crisis.

> A **lender of last resort** is an institution, usually a country's central bank, that provides funds to financial institutions when they are unable to borrow from the private credit markets.

## Governments Step In

Before the Great Depression, policy makers often adopted a laissez-faire attitude toward banking crises, allowing banks to fail in the belief that market forces should be allowed to work. Since the catastrophe of the 1930s, though, almost all policy makers have believed that it's necessary to take steps to contain the damage from bank failures. In general, central banks and governments take three main kinds of action in an effort to limit the fallout from banking crises:

1. They act as the *lender of last resort*.
2. They offer guarantees to depositors and others with claims on banks.
3. An extreme crisis, a central bank will step in and provide financing to private credit markets.

**1. Lender of Last Resort**  A **lender of last resort** is an institution, usually a country's central bank, that provides funds to financial institutions when they are unable to borrow from the private credit markets. In particular, the central bank can provide cash to a bank that is facing a run by depositors but is fundamentally solvent, making it unnecessary for the bank to engage in fire sales of its assets to raise cash. This acts as a lifeline, working to prevent a loss of confidence in the bank's solvency from turning into a self-fulfilling prophecy.

Did the Federal Reserve act as a lender of last resort in the 2008 financial crisis? Very much so. Figure 17-4 shows borrowing by banks from the Fed between 2005 and 2010: commercial banks borrowed negligible amounts from the central bank before the crisis, but their borrowing rose to $700 billion in the months

FIGURE  **17-4**  **Total Borrowings of Depository Institutions from the Federal Reserve**

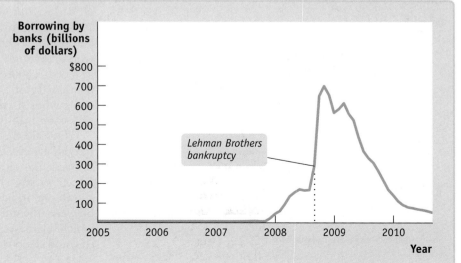

Although commercial banks borrowed negligible amounts from the Fed before the crisis hit in 2008, in the months after Lehman's collapse their borrowing surged to $700 billion—an amount 14 times total bank reserves before the crisis.

*Source:* Federal Reserve Bank of St. Louis.

following Lehman's failure. To get a sense of how large this borrowing was, note that total bank reserves before the crisis were less than $50 billion—so these loans were 14 times the banks' initial reserves.

**2. Government Guarantees** There are limits, though, to how much a lender of last resort can accomplish: it can't restore confidence in a bank if there is good reason to believe the bank is fundamentally insolvent. If the public believes that the bank's assets aren't worth enough to cover its debts even if it doesn't have to sell these assets on short notice, a lender of last resort isn't going to help much. And in major banking crises there are often good reasons to believe that many banks are truly bankrupt.

In such cases, governments often step in to guarantee banks' liabilities. In 2007, a bank run hit the British bank, Northern Rock, ceasing only when the British government stepped in and guaranteed all deposits at the bank, regardless of size. Ireland's government eventually stepped in to guarantee repayment of not just deposits at all of the nation's banks, but all bank debts. Sweden did the same thing after its 1991 banking crisis.

When governments take on banks' risk, they often demand a quid pro quo—namely, they often take ownership of the banks they are rescuing. Northern Rock was nationalized in 2008. Sweden nationalized a significant part of its banking system in 1992. In the United States, the Federal Deposit Insurance Corporation routinely seizes banks that are no longer solvent; it seized 140 banks in 2009. Ireland, however, chose not to seize any of the banks whose debts were guaranteed by taxpayers.

These government takeovers are almost always temporary. In general, modern governments want to save banks, not run them. So they "reprivatize" nationalized banks, selling them to private buyers, as soon as they believe they can.

**3. Provider of Direct Financing** As we learned in Chapter 14, during the depths of the 2008 financial crisis the Federal Reserve expanded its operations beyond the usual measures of open-market operations and lending to depository banks. It also began lending to shadow banks and buying commercial paper—short-term bonds issued by private companies—as well as buying the debt of Fannie Mae and Freddie Mac, the government-sponsored home mortgage agencies. In this way, the Fed provided credit to keep the economy afloat when private credit markets had dried up.

## ECONOMICS > IN ACTION

### BANKS AND THE GREAT DEPRESSION

According to the official business-cycle chronology, the United States entered a recession in August 1929, two months before that year's famous stock market crash. Although the crash surely made the slump worse, through late 1930 it still seemed to be a more or less ordinary recession. Then the bank failures began. A majority of economists believe that the banking crisis is what turned a fairly severe but not catastrophic recession into the Great Depression.

How did the banking crisis hurt the wider economy? Largely by creating a credit crunch, in which businesses in particular either could not borrow or found themselves forced to pay sharply higher interest rates. Figure 17-5 shows one indicator of this credit crunch: the difference between the interest rates—known as the "spread"—at which businesses with good but not great credit could borrow and the borrowing costs of the federal government.

**FIGURE 17-5** The 1930s Banking Crisis and Credit Crunch

*Source:* Federal Reserve Bank of St. Louis.

Baa corporate bonds are those that Moody's, the credit rating agency, considers "medium-grade obligations"—debts of companies that should be able to pay but aren't completely reliable. ("Baa" refers to the specific rating assigned to the bonds of such companies.) Until the banking crisis struck, Baa borrowers borrowed at interest rates only about 2 percentage points higher than the interest rates the government borrowed at, and this spread remained low until the summer of 1931. Then it surged, peaking at more than 7 percentage points in 1932. Bear in mind that this is just one indicator of the credit crunch: many would-be borrowers were completely shut out.

One striking fact about the banking crisis of the early 1930s is that the Federal Reserve, although it had the legal ability to act as a lender of last resort, largely failed to do so. Nothing like the surge in bank borrowing from the Fed that took place in 2007–2009 occurred. In fact, bank borrowing from the Fed throughout the 1930s banking crisis was at levels lower than those reached in 1928–1929.

Meanwhile, neither the Fed nor the federal government did anything to rescue failing banks until 1933. So the early 1930s offer a clear example of a banking crisis that policy makers more or less allowed to take its course. It's not an experience anyone wants to repeat.

*"Scuse me, Buddy, is this the bread line or a run on a bank?"*

**CHECK YOUR UNDERSTANDING** 17-3

1. Explain why, as of late 2010, the Federal Reserve was able to prevent the crisis of 2008 from turning into another Great Depression but was unable to significantly reduce the surge in unemployment that occurred.

2. Explain why, in the aftermath of a severe banking crisis, a very low interest rate—even as low as 0%—may be unable to move the economy back to full employment.

*Solutions appear at back of book.*

# The 2008 Crisis and Its Aftermath

As we've just seen, banking crises have typically been followed by major economic problems. How did the aftermath of the financial crisis of 2008 compare with this historical experience? The answer, unfortunately, is that history has proved a very good guide: once again, the economic damage from the financial crisis was both large and prolonged. And aftershocks from the crisis continue to shake the world economy today, after Lehman's 2008 fall.

## Severe Crisis, Slow Recovery

Figure 17-6 shows real GDP in the United States and the European Union, the world's two largest economies, during the crisis and aftermath, with the peak pre-crisis quarter—the last quarter of 2007 for the United States US, the first quarter of 2008 for the EU—set equal to 100. What you can see is that both economies suffered severe downturns, shrinking more than 5%, followed by relatively slow recoveries. As of early 2012, Europe had not yet regained its pre-crisis level of output, and the United States was barely above its previous peak.

▼ **Quick Review**

● Banking crises almost always result in recessions, with severe banking crises associated with the worst economic slumps. Historically, severe banking crises have resulted, on average, in a 7-percentage-point rise in the unemployment rate.

● Recessions caused by banking crises are especially severe because they involve a **credit crunch,** a vicious circle of deleveraging coupled with a **debt overhang,** leading households and businesses to cut spending, further deepening the downturn.

● Slumps induced by bank crises are so severe and prolonged because they make monetary policy ineffective: even though the central bank can lower interest rates, financially distressed households and businesses may still be unwilling to borrow and spend.

● Central banks and governments use two main types of policies to limit the damage from a banking crisis: acting as the **lender of last resort** and offering guarantees that the banks' liabilities will be repaid. In the aftermath of a bank rescue, governments sometimes nationalize the bank and then later reprivatize it. In an extreme crisis, the central bank will provide direct financing to private credit markets.

FIGURE **17-6** Crisis and Recovery in the United States and the European Union

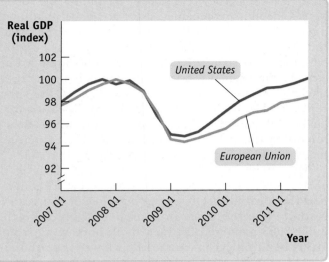

In the aftermath of the 2008 financial crisis, aggregate output in the European Union and in the United States fell dramatically. Real GDP, shown here as an index with each economy's peak pre-crisis quarter set to 100, declined by more than 5%. By late 2011, real GDP in the United States had only barely recovered to pre-crisis levels, and aggregate output in the European Union had still not reached its pre-crisis peak.

*Sources*: Bureau of Economic Analysis; Eurostat.

The severe slump and the slow recovery were very bad news for workers, since a healthy job market depends on an economy growing fast enough to accommodate both a growing workforce and rising productivity. Figure 17-7 shows two indicators of unemployment in the United States—the overall unemployment rate and the percentage of the unemployed who had been out of work 27 weeks or more. Both measures shot up during the crisis and remained very high years later, indicating a labor market in which it remained very hard to find a job.

This outcome was, sad to say, about what one should have expected given the severity of the initial financial shock and the historical experience with such shocks. In fact, the U.S. experience with unemployment almost exactly matched the average performance of past economies that had suffered major banking disruptions. America, observed Kenneth Rogoff (whose work we cited earlier), was experiencing a "garden variety severe financial crisis."

FIGURE **17-7** Unemployment in the Aftermath of the 2008 Crisis

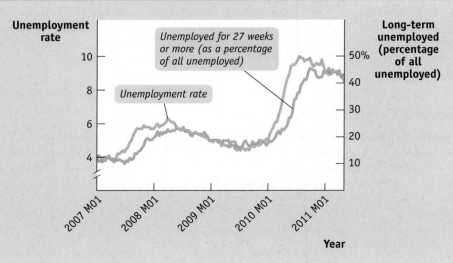

After 2008, the unemployment rate increased dramatically and remained high. Long-term unemployment, measured by the percentage of the unemployed who were out of work for 27 weeks or longer, increased at the same time. By 2011, almost half of all unemployed workers were long-term unemployed.

*Source:* Bureau of Labor Statistics.

## Aftershocks in Europe

One important factor bedeviling hopes for recovery was the emergence of special difficulties in several European nations—difficulties that repeatedly raised the specter of a second financial crisis.

The 2008 crisis was caused by problems with private debt, mainly home loans, which then triggered a crisis of confidence in banks. In 2011 and 2012, fears of a second crisis were focused on public debt, specifically the public debts of Southern European countries plus Ireland.

Europe's troubles first surfaced in Greece, a country with a long history of fiscal irresponsibility. In late 2009, it was revealed that a previous Greek government had understated the size of the budget deficits and the amount of government debt, prompting lenders to refuse further loans to Greece. Other European countries provided emergency loans to the Greek government in return for harsh budget cuts. But these budget cuts depressed the Greek economy, and by late 2011 there was general agreement that Greece could not pay back its debts in full.

By itself, this was probably a manageable shock for the European economy since Greece accounts for less than 3% of European GDP. Unfortunately, foot-dragging by European officials in confronting Greece's problems and the effects of the harsh budget cuts on the Greek economy spooked investors. By the fall of 2011, the crisis had spread beyond the Greek borders, hitting two major European economies: Spain and Italy.

Figure 17-8 shows a measure of pressure on Italy and Spain during the 2008 and 2011 crises: the difference between interest rates on 10-year bonds issued by the two nations' governments and interest rates on German debt, which most people consider a safe investment. Because all three countries use the same currency, the euro, these rates would all be the same if Italian and Spanish government debt were considered as safe as German government debt. The rise in "spreads" therefore indicates a growing perception of risk.

Spain's fiscal problems were mainly fallout from the 2008 crisis. Before that crisis, Spain seemed to be in very good fiscal condition, with low debt and a budget surplus. However, Spain, like Ireland, had a huge housing bubble between 2000 and 2007. When the bubble burst, the Spanish economy fell into a deep slump, depressing tax receipts and causing large budget deficits. At the same time, there were worries that the Spanish government might eventually have to spend large amounts bailing out banks. As a result, investors began worrying about the solvency of the Spanish government and a possible default, driving up interest rates.

FIGURE   **17-8**   Interest Spread Against German 10-Year Bonds

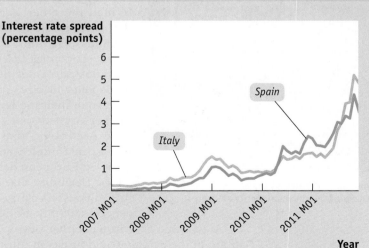

One indicator of investors' perceptions of the risk of government default is the spread of interest rates on government bonds between that country and a country that is perceived as a safe investment. The spread of the interest rates on 10-year government bonds for Italy and Spain, measured against the interest rate on German bonds, rose as investors' fears of default by Italy and Spain increased.

*Source:* Eurostat.

Italy's case was somewhat different. Italy has long had high levels of public debt as a percentage of GDP, but it has not run large deficits in recent years; as late as the spring of 2010 its fiscal position looked fairly stable. At that point, however, investors began to have doubts about the Italian government's solvency, in part because in the aftermath of the 2008 crisis the Italian economy was growing very slowly—too slowly, it was feared, to generate enough tax revenue to repay its public debt. These doubts drove up interest rates on Italian public debt, and this in turn created a vicious circle: higher interest payments, caused by fears about Italian government solvency, worsened Italy's fiscal position even further and pushed it closer to the edge.

At the time of writing, Greece had defaulted on its government bonds, Spanish youth unemployment was over 50%, and it was unclear how much worse the European situation would get. But Europe's difficulties reinforced the sense that the damage from the 2008 financial crisis was by no means over.

## The Stimulus–Austerity Debate

The persistence of economic difficulties after the 2008 financial crisis led to fierce debates about appropriate policy responses. Broadly speaking, economists and policy makers were divided as to whether the situation called for more fiscal stimulus—expansionary fiscal measures such as more government spending and possibly tax cuts to promote spending and reduce unemployment—or for fiscal "austerity," contractionary fiscal measures such as spending cuts and possibly tax increases to reduce budget deficits.

The proponents of more stimulus pointed to the continuing poor performance of major economies, arguing that the combination of high unemployment and relatively low inflation clearly pointed to the need for expansionary policies. And since monetary policy was limited by the zero bound on interest rates, stimulus proponents advocated expansionary fiscal policy to fill the gap.

The austerity camp took a very different view. Strongly influenced by the solvency troubles of Greece, Ireland, Spain, and Italy, they argued that the common source of all the problems were high levels of government deficits and debts. In their view, countries like the United States that continued to run large government deficits several years after the 2008 crisis were at risk of suffering a similar loss of investor confidence in their ability to repay their debts. Moreover, austerity advocates claimed that cuts in government spending would not actually be contractionary because they would improve investor confidence and keep interest rates on government debt low.

Each side of the debate argued that recent experience refuted the other side's claims. Austerity proponents argued that the persistence of high unemployment despite the fiscal stimulus programs adopted by the United States and other major economies in 2009 showed that stimulus doesn't work. Stimulus advocates argued that these programs were simply inadequate in size, pointing out that many economists had warned of their inadequacy from the start. Stimulus advocates further argued that warnings about the dangers of deficits were overblown, that far from rising, borrowing costs for Japan, the United States, and Britain—nations that, unlike the troubled European debtors, still had their own currencies with all the flexibility that implies—had fallen to record lows. And they dismissed claims that spending cuts would raise confidence as mainly fantasy.

The British economy was decimated by the aftermath of the 2008 crisis coupled with government austerity measures.

At the time of writing, neither side was giving much ground. Clearly, any resolution of the debate would hinge on future economic developments and how they were interpreted.

## The Lesson of the Post-Crisis Slump

Almost all major economies had great difficulty dealing with the aftermath of the 2008 financial crisis—high unemployment, low growth and, for some, solvency concerns, and high interest rates on public debt.

Clearly, then, the best way to avoid the terrible problems that arise after a financial crisis is not to have a crisis in the first place. How can you do that? In part, one might hope, through better regulation of financial institutions. We turn next to attempts at regulatory reform.

## ECONOMICS ➤ IN ACTION

### AUSTERITY BRITAIN

An election in May 2010 led to a shift in power in Britain, with a Labour Party government replaced by a coalition dominated by the Conservative Party under the new prime minister, David Cameron. The new government was firmly committed to the austerity side of the great post-crisis policy debate, and it changed policy accordingly.

Unlike Greece or Ireland, Britain wasn't under any immediate pressure to slash its budget deficit. Like the U.S. government, the British government was still able to borrow cheaply despite its large deficit. And the British economy was, if anything, even more depressed than the U.S. one, with fewer signs of recovery. The Cameron government believed, however, that preemptive cuts in public spending combined with some tax increases were necessary to preserve investor confidence and also that such cuts could boost the economy by improving confidence.

How have these policies performed? As of early 2012, the experiment in austerity had yielded disappointing results. British economic growth was weak—in fact, considerably weaker than in the United States, even though U.S. performance was lackluster. And as Figure 17-9 shows, the hoped-for surge in business confidence that austerity measures were supposed to generate had failed to materialize.

FIGURE **17-9** Business Confidence in Britain

*Source:* Grant Thornton, UK Business Confidence Monitor.

### ▼ Quick Review

- Economic damage from the financial crisis of 2008 was both large and prolonged. Aftershocks from the crisis continue to shake the world economy.

- The world's two largest economies, in the United States and the European Union, suffered severe downturns, shrinking more than 5%, followed by relatively slow recoveries. The severe slump and the slow recovery were very bad news for workers.

- The persistence of economic difficulties after the 2008 financial crisis led to severe solvency concerns for several European countries. A fierce debate erupted over whether fiscal stimulus or fiscal austerity was the right policy prescription.

### CHECK YOUR UNDERSTANDING    17-4

1. In November 2011, the government of France announced that it was reducing its forecast for economic growth in 2012. It was also reducing its estimates of tax revenue for 2012, since a weaker economy would mean smaller tax receipts. To offset the effect of lower revenue on the budget deficit, the government also announced a new package of tax increases and spending cuts. Which side of the stimulus–austerity debate was France taking?

## Regulation in the Wake of the Crisis

By late 2009, interventions by governments and central banks around the world had restored calm to financial markets. However, huge damage had been done to the global economy. In much of the advanced world, countries suffered their deepest slumps since the 1930s. And all indications were that the typical pattern of slow recovery after a financial crisis would be repeated, with unemployment remaining high for years to come.

The banking crisis of 2008 demonstrated, all too clearly, that financial regulation is a continuing process—that regulations will and should change over time to keep up with a changing world. The dependence on very short-term loans (called repo), the lack of regulation, and being outside the lender-of-last-resort system made the shadow-banking sector vulnerable to crises and panics. So what changes will the most recent crisis bring? One thing that became all too clear in the 2008 crisis was that the traditional scope of banking regulation was too narrow. Regulating only depository institutions was clearly inadequate in a world in which a large part of banking, properly understood, is undertaken by the shadow banking sector.

In the aftermath of the crisis, then, an overhaul of financial regulation was clearly needed. And in 2010 the U.S. Congress enacted a bill that represented an effort to respond to the events of the preceding years. Like most legislation, the Wall Street Reform and Consumer Protection Act—often referred to as the Dodd-Frank bill—is complex in its details. But it contains four main elements:

1. Consumer protection
2. Derivatives regulation
3. Regulation of shadow banks
4. Resolution authority over nonbank financial institutions that face bankruptcy

**1. Consumer Protection** One factor in the financial crisis was the fact that many borrowers accepted offers they didn't understand, such as mortgages that were easy to pay in the first two years but required sharply higher payments later on. In an effort to limit future abuses, the new law creates a special office, the Consumer Financial Protection Bureau, dedicated to policing financial industry practices and protecting borrowers.

**2. Derivatives Regulation** Another factor in the crisis was the proliferation of derivatives, complex financial instruments that were supposed to help spread risk but arguably simply concealed it. Under the new law, most derivatives have to be bought and sold in open, transparent markets, hopefully limiting the extent to which financial players can take on invisible risk.

**3. Regulation of Shadow Banks** A key element in the financial crisis, as we've seen, was the rise of institutions that didn't fit the conventional definition of a bank but played the role of banks and created the risk of a banking crisis. How can regulation be extended to such institutions? Dodd-Frank does not offer an explicit new definition of what it means to be a bank. Instead, it offers a sort of financial version of "you know it when you see it." Specifically, it gives a special panel the ability to designate financial institutions as "systemically important," meaning that their activities have the potential to create a banking crisis. Such institutions will be subject to bank-like regulation of their capital, their investments, and so on.

**4. Resolution Authority** The events of 2008 made it clear that governments would often feel the need to guarantee a wide range of financial institution debts in a crisis, not just deposits. Yet how can this be done without creating huge incentive problems, motivating financial institutions to undertake overly risky behavior in the knowledge that they will be bailed out by the government if they get into trouble? Part of the answer is to empower the government to seize control of financial institutions that require a bailout, the way it already does with failing commercial banks and thrifts. This new power, known as resolution authority, should be viewed as solving a problem that seemed acute in early 2009, when several major financial institutions were teetering on the brink. Yet it wasn't clear whether Washington had the legal authority to orchestrate a rescue that was fair to taxpayers.

All this is now law in the United States, but two things remain unclear. (1) How will these regulations be worked into the international financial system? Will other nations adopt similar policies? If they do, how will conflicts among different national policies be resolved? (2) Will these regulations do the trick? Post-1930s bank regulation produced decades of stability, but will that happen again? Or will the new system fail in the face of a serious test?

Nobody knows the answers to these questions. We'll just have to wait and see.

## ECONOMICS > IN ACTION

### BENT BREAKS THE BUCK

In 1970 a financial innovator named Bruce Bent introduced a new concept to American finance: the money market mutual fund. Most mutual funds offer ways for small investors to buy stocks: when you buy a share in a mutual fund like Fidelity or Vanguard, you are indirectly acquiring a diversified mix of stocks. Bent, however, created a mutual fund that invests only in short-term assets, such as Treasury bills and commercial paper issued by highly rated corporations, which carry a low risk of default. The idea was to give people a safe place to park their money, but one that offered a higher interest rate than a bank deposit. Many people eventually began seeing their investments in money market funds as equivalent to bank accounts, but better.

But money placed in money market funds was different from money deposited in a bank in one crucial dimension: money market funds weren't federally insured. And on September 16, 2008, the day after Lehman Brothers fell, it became known that one major money market fund had lost heavily on money placed with Lehman, to such an extent that it had "broken the buck"; that is, it no longer had enough assets to pay off all the people who had placed their money at its disposal. As a result, the fund had to suspend withdrawals; in effect, a "bank" had suddenly shut its doors.

In September 2008, the $65 billion Reserve Primary Fund broke the buck after it was caught with bankrupt Lehman Brothers debt, leaving investors in a panic.

And which fund was in this predicament? Reserve Primary Fund, controlled by none other than Bruce Bent. Panicked money market mutual fund customers pulled hundreds of billions of dollars out of money market funds over a two-day period.

The federal government stemmed the panic by instituting a temporary insurance scheme for money market funds, giving them the same protected status as bank deposits. But the money fund panic was an object lesson in the extent to which financial innovation had undermined the traditional bank safety net.

### CHECK YOUR UNDERSTANDING 17-5

1. Why does the use of short-term borrowing and being outside of the lender-of-last-resort system make shadow banks vulnerable to events similar to bank runs?

2. How do you think the crisis of 2008 would have been mitigated if there had been no shadow banking sector but only the formal depository banking sector?

3. Describe the incentive problem facing the U.S. government in responding to the 2007–2009 crisis with respect to the shadow banking sector. How did the Dodd-Frank bill attempt to address those incentive problems?

Solutions appear at back of book.

### ▼ Quick Review

- When the panic hit after Lehman's fall, governments and central banks around the world stepped in to fight the crisis and calm the markets. Most advanced economies experienced their worst slump since the 1930s.

- In 2010 Congress enacted the Dodd-Frank bill to remedy the regulatory oversights exposed by the crisis of 2007–2009. It created the Consumer Financial Protection Bureau to protect borrowers and consumers, implemented stricter regulation of derivatives, extended the reach of regulation to the shadow banking sector, and empowered the government to seize control of any financial institution requiring a bailout.

## SUMMARY

1. Without banks, people would make the trade-off between liquidity and rate of return by holding a large fraction of their wealth in idle cash. Banks engage in **maturity transformation,** transforming short-term liabilities into long-term assets. Banking improves savers' welfare, allowing them immediate access to their funds as well as paying them interest on those funds.

2. **Shadow banks** have grown greatly since 1980. Largely unregulated, they can pay savers a higher rate of return than depository banks. Like depository banks, shadow banks engage in maturity transformation, depending on short-term borrowing to operate and investing in long-term assets. Therefore, shadow banks can also be subject to bank runs.

3. Although **banking crises** are rare, they typically inflict severe damage on the economy. They have two main sources: shared mistakes, such as investing in an **asset bubble,** and **financial contagion.** Contagion is spread through bank runs or via a vicious cycle of deleveraging. When unregulated, shadow banking is particularly vulnerable to contagion. In 2008, a **financial panic** hit the United States, arising from the combination of an asset bubble, a huge shadow banking sector, and a vicious cycle of deleveraging.

4. The United States has suffered numerous banking crises and financial panics, each followed by a severe downturn. The crisis of the 1930s spurred bank reform that prevented another crisis until 2008. Banking crises occur frequently throughout the world, mostly in small, poor countries. In the recent past, though, several advanced countries have had banking crises driven by real estate bubbles.

5. Severe banking crises almost invariably lead to deep and long recessions, with unemployment remaining high for several years after the crisis began. There are three main reasons why banking crises are so damaging to the economy: they result in a **credit crunch,** the vicious circle of deleveraging leads to a **debt overhang,** and monetary policy is rendered ineffective as the economy falls into a liquidity trap. As a result, households and businesses are either unable or unwilling to spend, deepening the downturn.

6. Unlike during the Great Depression, governments now step in to try to limit the damage from a banking crisis by acting as the **lender of last resort** and by guaranteeing the banks' liabilities. Sometimes, but not always, governments nationalize the banks and then later reprivatize them. In an extreme crisis, the central bank may directly finance commercial transactions.

7. Economic damage from the financial crisis of 2008 was large and prolonged. The world's two largest economies, the United States and the European Union, suffered severe downturns, shrinking more than 5%, followed by relatively slow recoveries. The persistence of economic difficulties after 2008 led to fierce debates about appropriate policy responses between economists and policy makers calling for more fiscal stimulus—more government spending and possibly tax cuts to promote spending and reduce unemployment—and those favoring fiscal austerity—spending cuts and possibly tax increases to reduce budget deficits.

8. The banking regulatory system put in place during the 1930s has eroded due to the rise of shadow banking. The dependence on short-term financing (repo) the lack of regulation, and being outside the lender-of-last-resort system makes the shadow banking sector vulnerable to a banking panic.

9. The crisis of 2008 began as the shadow banking sector suffered high losses when a real estate bubble burst. Despite the fact that governments and central banks around the world stepped in to fight the crisis and the downturn, most advanced countries experienced their worst slump since the 1930s. Persistently high unemployment is likely to endure for years to come.

10. In the aftermath of the crisis, the U.S. Congress enacted the Dodd-Frank bill in the hope of preventing a replay of the crisis. The main elements of the new reform are stronger consumer protection, greater regulation of derivatives, regulation of shadow banking, and resolution authority for a variety of financial institutions. We have yet to see whether these changes will be adequate or whether they will also be adopted by other countries.

## KEY TERMS

Maturity transformation, p. 504
Shadow bank, p. 504
Banking crisis, p. 506

Asset bubble, p. 506
Financial contagion, p. 507
Financial panic, p. 507

Credit crunch, p. 511
Debt overhang, p. 511
Lender of last resort, p. 513

## PROBLEMS

1. Which of the following are examples of debt overhang? Which examples are likely to lead to a cutback in spending? Explain.

   a. Your uncle starts a restaurant, borrowing to fund his investment. The restaurant fails, and your uncle must shut down but still must pay his debt.

   b. Your parents take out a loan to buy a house. Your father is transferred to a new city, and now your parents must sell the house. The value of the house has gone up during the time your family has lived there.

   c. Your friend's parents take out a loan to buy her a condo to live in while she is at college. Meanwhile, the housing market plummets. By the time your friend leaves college, the condo is worth significantly less than the value of the loan.

   d. You finish college with an honors degree in a field with many good job prospects and with $25,000 in student loans that you must repay.

2. Which of the following are *not* examples of a vicious cycle of deleveraging? Explain.

   a. Your university decides to sell several commercial buildings in the middle of town in order to upgrade buildings on campus.

   b. A company decides to sell its large and valuable art collection because other asset prices on its balance sheet have fallen below a critical level, forcing creditors to call in their loans to the company because of provisions written into the original loan contract.

   c. A company decides to issue more stock in order to voluntarily pay off some of its debt.

   d. A shadow bank must sell its holdings of corporate bonds because falling asset prices have led to a default on the terms of its loans with some creditors.

3. In the following figure showing the Case–Shiller U.S. Home Price Index from 2000 to 2010, did housing prices peak before or after the financial crisis in the United States? Explain your answer.

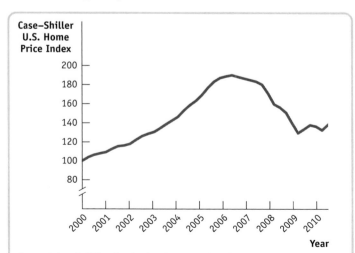

*Source*: Robert J. Shiller, *Irrational Exuberance*, 2nd ed. (Princeton, NJ: Princeton University Press 2005); data retrieved from http://www.econ.yale.edu/~shiller/data.htm.

4. Figure 17-2 tracks the unemployment rate in the years before and after the Panic of 1893 in the United States and the banking crisis of 1991 in Sweden.

   a. In Figure 17-2, how many years after the Panic of 1893 did unemployment peak in the United States?

   b. In Figure 17-2, how many years after the banking crisis of 1991 did unemployment peak in Sweden?

5. In 2007–2009, the Federal Reserve, acting as a lender of last resort, stepped in to provide funds when private markets were unable to do so. The Fed also took over many banks. In 2007, it seized 3 banks; in 2008, it seized 25 banks; and in 2009, it seized 140 banks. Go to www.fdic.gov; under "Bank Closing Information," click on "Complete Failed Bank List." Then count the number of banks that the Federal Reserve has seized so far this year. Have bank failures decreased since the crisis in 2008?

6. During the financial crisis in October 2008, the federal government could borrow at a rate of 2.73% (the yield on five-year Treasury securities). During October 2008, though, Baa borrowers (corporate borrowers rated by Moody's as not being completely reliable) had to pay 8.88%.

   a. What was the difference in borrowing costs for these corporate borrowers and the federal government?

   b. Go to research.stlouisfed.org/fred2/categories/22. Click on the link for "Treasury constant maturity" and find the most recent interest rate on 10-year U.S. Treasury bonds. Then click on the link for "Corporate bonds" and find the rate for Baa corporate bonds. What is the current difference in borrowing costs between corporate borrowers and the U.S. government?

   c. Has this difference in borrowing costs increased or decreased since the height of the financial crisis in October of 2008? Why?

7. Go to www.federalreserve.gov and click on the tab "Banking Information & Regulation." Then select the links "Banking Data" followed by "Large Commercial Banks." Once there, choose the latest release of quarterly data.

   a. Which bank has the largest consolidated assets?

   b. Which bank has the largest domestic assets?

   c. What percent of U.S. GDP are the domestic assets of the bank listed in part b? (*Hint:* You can find U.S. GDP at http://research.stlouisfed.org/fred2/series/GDP?cid=106 using the links "Gross Domestic Product (GDP)" and then "Current-dollar and 'real' GDP.")

8. Go to www.fdic.gov and click on the tab "Industry Analysis" and then on the link "Research & Analysis." Under "Historical Perspectives," select "The First Fifty Years: A History of the FDIC 1933–1983." Open Chapter 3, "Establishment of the FDIC," and scroll

down to the section entitled "The Banking Crisis of 1933" and the section entitled "Federal Deposit Insurance Legislation." Read the section and then answer these questions.

**a.** President Roosevelt was sworn in on March 4, 1933. What was one of his first official acts in response to the banking crisis?

**b.** How many banks suspended operations during 1933?

**c.** Who was the chief proponent of federal deposit insurance in Congress?

**d.** How much coverage did the temporary fund for federal deposit insurance provide?

**9.** The U.S. Government Accountability Office (GAO) does research to support congressional decision making. After the Long Term Capital Management (LTCM) crisis, the GAO produced a summary of the events of the crisis located at http://www.gao.gov/products/GGD-00-3. Read the summary and then answer the following questions.

**a.** How much of its capital did LTCM lose in 1998?

**b.** Why did the GAO conclude that LTCM was able to establish leveraged trading positions of a size that posed systemic risk to the banking system?

**c.** What was the recommendation of the President's Working Group regarding the Securities and Exchange Commission (SEC) and the Commodity Futures Trading Commission (CFTC)?

# CHAPTER 18

# Macroeconomics: Events and Ideas

## A TALE OF TWO SLUMPS

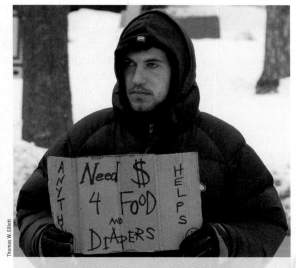

The breakthroughs in macroeconomics that occurred in the wake of the Great Depression are being revived today to confront the difficulties created by the Great Recession.

I N NOVEMBER 2002, THE FEDERAL Reserve held a special conference to honor Milton Friedman on the occasion of his 90th birthday. Among those delivering tributes was Ben Bernanke, who had recently moved to the Fed from Princeton University and would later become the Fed's chairman. In his tribute, Bernanke surveyed Friedman's intellectual contributions, with particular focus on the argument made by Friedman and his collaborator Anna Schwartz that the Great Depression of the 1930s could have been avoided if only the Fed had done its job properly.

At the close of his talk, Bernanke directly addressed Friedman and Schwartz, who were sitting in the audience: "Let me end my talk by abusing slightly my status as an official representative of the Federal Reserve. I would like to say to Milton and Anna: Regarding the Great Depression. You're right, we did it. We're very sorry. But thanks to you, we won't do it again."

Today, in the aftermath of a devastating financial crisis that continues to inflict high unemployment, those words ring somewhat hollow. Avoiding severe economic downturns, it turned out, wasn't as easy as Friedman, Schwartz, and Bernanke had believed. Yet, as bad as they were, the crisis of 2008 and its aftermath were less devastating than the Great Depression. It can be reasonably argued that part of the reason was that macroeconomics had evolved in the 78 years from 1930 to 2008. As a result, policy makers knew more about the causes of depressions and how to fight them than they did during the Great Depression.

In this chapter we'll trace the development of macroeconomic ideas over the past 80 years. As we'll see, this development has been strongly influenced by economic events, from the Great Depression of the 1930s, to the stagflation of the 1970s, to the surprising period of economic stability achieved between 1985 and 2007. And as we'll also see, the process contin-

### WHAT YOU WILL LEARN IN THIS CHAPTER

❱ **Why classical macroeconomics was inadequate for the problems posed by the Great Depression**

❱ **How Keynes and the experience of the Great Depression legitimized macroeconomic policy activism**

❱ What **monetarism** is and why monetarists claim there are limits to the use of **discretionary monetary policy**

❱ How challenges led to a revision of **Keynesian economics** and the emergence of the **new classical macroeconomics**

❱ Why the **Great Moderation consensus** was challenged by the **2008 financial crisis,** leading to fierce debates among economists about the best use of fiscal and monetary policy during challenging economic times

ues, as the economic difficulties since 2008 have spurred many macroeconomists to rethink what they thought they knew. ■

# Classical Macroeconomics

The term *macroeconomics* appears to have been coined in 1933 by the Norwegian economist Ragnar Frisch. The date, during the worst year of the Great Depression, is no accident. Still, there were economists analyzing what we now consider macroeconomic issues—the behavior of the aggregate price level and aggregate output—before then.

## Money and the Price Level

In Chapter 16, we described the classical *model of the price level.* According to the classical model, prices are flexible, making the aggregate supply curve vertical even in the short run. In this model, an increase in the money supply leads, other things equal, to an equal proportional rise in the aggregate price level, with no effect on aggregate output. As a result, increases in the money supply lead to inflation, and that's all. Before the 1930s, the classical model of the price level dominated economic thinking about the effects of monetary policy.

Did classical economists really believe that changes in the money supply affected only aggregate prices, without any effect on aggregate output? Probably not. Historians of economic thought argue that before 1930 most economists were aware that changes in the money supply affect aggregate output as well as aggregate prices in the short run—or, to use modern terms, they were aware that the short-run aggregate supply curve slopes upward. But they regarded such short-run effects as unimportant, stressing the long run instead. It was this attitude that led John Maynard Keynes to scoff at the focus on the long run, in which, as he said, "we are all dead."

## The Business Cycle

Classical economists were, of course, also aware that the economy did not grow smoothly. The American economist Wesley Mitchell pioneered the quantitative study of business cycles. In 1920 he founded the National Bureau of Economic Research, an independent, nonprofit organization that to this day has the official role of declaring the beginnings of recessions and expansions. Thanks to Mitchell's work, the *measurement* of business cycles was well advanced by 1930. But there was no widely accepted *theory* of business cycles.

In the absence of any clear theory, conflicts arose among policy makers on how to respond to a recession. Some economists favored expansionary monetary and fiscal policies to fight a recession. Others believed that such policies would worsen the slump or merely postpone the inevitable. For example, in 1934 Harvard's Joseph Schumpeter, now famous for his early recognition of the importance of technological change, warned that any attempt to alleviate the Great Depression with expansionary monetary policy "would, in the end, lead to a collapse worse than the one it was called in to remedy." When the Great Depression hit, policy was paralyzed by this lack of consensus. In many cases, economists now believe, policy moved in the wrong direction.

Necessity was, however, the mother of invention. As we'll explain next, the Great Depression provided a strong incentive for economists to develop theories that could serve as a guide to policy—and economists responded.

## ECONOMICS ▸ *IN ACTION*

### WHEN DID THE BUSINESS CYCLE BEGIN?

The official chronology of past U.S. business cycles maintained by the National Bureau of Economic Research goes back only to 1854. There are two reasons for this. One is that the farther back in time you go, the less economic data are available. The other is that business cycles, in the modern sense, may have not occurred in the United States before 1854.

In the first half of the nineteenth century the United States had an overwhelmingly rural, agricultural economy. Figure 18-1 shows estimates of the changing percentages of GDP coming from agriculture and from manufacturing and mining over the period from 1840 to 1900. The figure shows that agriculture dwarfed manufacturing in 1840 and that manufacturing didn't overtake agriculture in economic importance until the 1880s.

Why does this matter? Fluctuations in aggregate output in agricultural economies are very different from the business cycles we know today. That's because prices of agricultural goods tend to be highly flexible. As a result, the short-run aggregate supply curve of a mainly agricultural economy is probably close to vertical, so demand shocks don't cause output fluctuations. Instead, fluctuations on the farm are driven mainly by weather, making shifts of the short-run aggregate supply curve the primary source of fluctuations. In contrast, modern business cycles are largely the result of shifts in the aggregate demand curve.

The modern business cycle probably originated in Britain—home of the Industrial Revolution—which was already a largely industrial and urban society by 1820. The British recession of 1846–1847 had a particularly modern feel: it followed a bout of overoptimism in which firms spent heavily on an exciting new technology—railroads—and then realized they had overdone it.

**FIGURE 18-1** The Changing Character of the Nineteenth-Century Economy

Source: Robert E. Gallman, "Economic Growth and Structural Change in the Long Nineteenth Century," in Stanley L. Engerman and Robert E. Gallman, eds., *The Cambridge Economic History of the United States, vol. II: The Long Nineteenth Century* (Cambridge, UK: Cambridge University Press, 2000).

---

**CHECK YOUR UNDERSTANDING 18-1**

1. When Ben Bernanke, in his tribute to Milton Friedman, said that "Regarding the Great Depression . . . we did it," he was referring to the fact that the Federal Reserve at the time did not pursue expansionary monetary policy. Why would a classical economist have thought that action by the Federal Reserve would not have made a difference in the length or depth of the Great Depression?

Solutions appear at back of book.

> **▼ Quick Review**
>
> ● Classical macroeconomists focused on the long-run effects of monetary policy on the aggregate price level, ignoring any short-run effects on aggregate output.
>
> ● By the time of the Great Depression, the measurement of business cycles was well advanced, but there was no widely accepted theory about why they happened.

# The Great Depression and the Keynesian Revolution

The Great Depression demonstrated, once and for all, that economists cannot safely ignore the short run. Not only was the economic pain severe; it threatened to destabilize societies and political systems. In particular, the economic plunge helped Adolf Hitler rise to power in Germany.

The whole world wanted to know how this economic disaster could be happening and what should be done about it. But because there was no widely accepted theory of the business cycle, economists gave conflicting and, we now believe, often harmful advice. Some believed that only a huge change in the economic system—such as having the government take over much of private industry and replace markets with a command economy—could end the slump. Others argued that slumps were natural—even beneficial—and that nothing should be done.

Some economists, however, argued that the slump both could and should be cured—without giving up on the basic idea of a market economy. In 1930 the British economist John Maynard Keynes compared the problems of the U.S.

and British economies to those of a car with a defective starter. Getting the economy running, he argued, would require only a modest repair, not a complete overhaul.

Nice metaphor. But what was the nature of the trouble?

## Keynes's Theory

In 1936 Keynes presented his analysis of the Great Depression—his explanation of what was wrong with the economy's starter—in a book titled *The General Theory of Employment, Interest, and Money*. In 1946 the great American economist Paul Samuelson wrote that "it is a badly written book, poorly organized. . . . Flashes of insight and intuition intersperse tedious algebra. . . . We find its analysis to be obvious and at the same time new. In short, it is a work of genius." *The General Theory* isn't easy reading, but it stands with Adam Smith's *The Wealth of Nations* as one of the most influential books on economics ever written.

As Samuelson's description suggests, Keynes's book is a vast stew of ideas. *Keynesian economics* is principally based on two innovations. First, Keynes emphasized the short-run effects of changes in aggregate demand on aggregate output, rather than the long-run determination of the aggregate price level. As Keynes's famous remark about being dead in the long run suggests, until his book appeared most economists had treated short-run macroeconomics as a minor issue. Keynes focused the attention of economists on situations in which the short-run aggregate supply curve slopes upward and shifts in the aggregate demand curve affect aggregate output and employment as well as aggregate prices.

Figure 18-2 illustrates the difference between Keynesian and classical macroeconomics. Both panels of the figure show the short-run aggregate supply curve, *SRAS*; in both it is assumed that for some reason the aggregate demand curve shifts leftward from $AD_1$ to $AD_2$—let's say in response to a fall in stock market prices that leads households to reduce consumer spending.

**FIGURE** **18-2** **Classical versus Keynesian Macroeconomics**

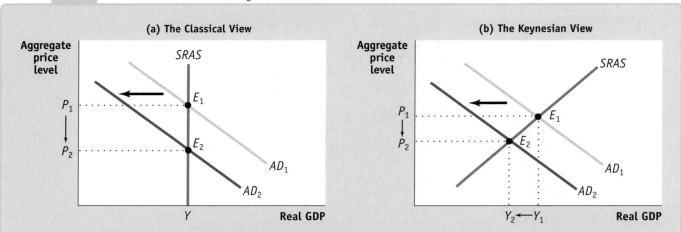

**(a) The Classical View**

**(b) The Keynesian View**

One important difference between classical and Keynesian economics involves the short-run aggregate supply curve. Panel (a) shows the classical view: the *SRAS* curve is vertical, so shifts in aggregate demand affect the aggregate price level but not aggregate output. Panel (b) shows the Keynesian view: in the short run the *SRAS* curve slopes upward, so shifts in aggregate demand affect aggregate output as well as aggregate prices.

Panel (a) shows the classical view: the short-run aggregate supply curve is vertical. The decline in aggregate demand leads to a fall in the aggregate price level, from $P_1$ to $P_2$, but no change in aggregate output. Panel (b) shows the Keynesian view: the short-run aggregate supply curve slopes upward, so the decline in aggregate demand leads to both a fall in the aggregate price level, from $P_1$ to $P_2$, and a fall in aggregate output, from $Y_1$ to $Y_2$.

As we've already explained, many classical macroeconomists would have agreed that panel (b) was an accurate story in the short run—but they regarded the short run as unimportant. Keynes disagreed. [Just to be clear, there isn't any diagram that looks like panel (b) of Figure 18-2 in Keynes's *General Theory*. But Keynes's discussion of aggregate supply, translated into modern terminology, clearly implies an upward-sloping *SRAS* curve.]

Classical economists emphasized the role of changes in the money supply in shifting the aggregate demand curve, paying little attention to other factors. Keynes's second innovation was his argument that other factors, especially changes in "animal spirits"—these days usually referred to with the bland term *business confidence*—are mainly responsible for business cycles. Before Keynes, economists often argued that a decline in business confidence would have no effect on either the aggregate price level or aggregate output, as long as the money supply stayed constant. Keynes offered a very different picture.

**Keynesian economics** has penetrated deeply into the public consciousness, to the extent that many people who have never heard of Keynes, or have heard of him but think they disagree with his theory, use Keynesian ideas all the time. For example, suppose that a business commentator says something like this: "Because of a decline in business confidence, investment spending slumped, causing a recession." Whether the commentator knows it or not, that statement is pure Keynesian economics.

**Keynesian economics** rests on two main tenets: changes in aggregate demand affect aggregate output, employment, and prices; and changes in business confidence cause the business cycle.

## FOR INQUIRING MINDS

### THE POLITICS OF KEYNES

The term Keynesian economics is sometimes used as a synonym for left-wing economics: authors seem to believe that because Keynes offered a rationale for some kinds of government activism, he was a leftist of some kind, maybe even a socialist. But the truth is more complicated.

As we explain in the text, Keynesian ideas have actually been accepted across a broad range of the political spectrum. In 2004 the president was a conservative, as was his top economist, N. Gregory Mankiw; but Mankiw is also the editor of a collection of readings titled *New Keynesian Economics.*

And Keynes himself was no socialist—and not much of a leftist. At the time *The General Theory* was published, many intellectuals in Britain believed that the Great Depression was the final crisis of the capitalist economic system and that only a government takeover of industry

Some people consider *Keynesian economics* a synonym for *left-wing economics*. But this is misguided because in reality the ideas of John Maynard Keynes have been accepted across a broad sweep of the political spectrum.

could save the economy. Keynes, in contrast, argued that all the system needed was a narrow technical fix. In that sense, his ideas were pro-capitalist and politically conservative.

What is true is that the rise of Keynesian economics in the 1940s, 1950s, and 1960s went along with a general enlargement of the role of government in the economy, and those who favored a larger role for government tended to be enthusiastic Keynesians. Conversely, a swing of the pendulum back toward free-market policies in the 1970s and 1980s was accompanied by a series of challenges to Keynesian ideas, which we describe later in this chapter. But it's perfectly possible to have conservative political preferences while respecting Keynes's contribution and equally possible to be very liberal while questioning Keynes's ideas.

**Macroeconomic policy activism**
is the use of monetary and fiscal
policy to smooth out the business
cycle.

Keynes himself more or less predicted that his ideas would become part of what
"everyone knows." In another famous passage, this from the end of *The General
Theory*, he wrote: "Practical men, who believe themselves to be quite exempt from
any intellectual influences, are usually the slaves of some defunct economist."

## Policy to Fight Recessions

The main practical consequence of Keynes's work was that it legitimized **macroeconomic policy activism**—the use of monetary and fiscal policy to smooth
out the business cycle.

Macroeconomic policy activism wasn't something completely new. Before
Keynes, many economists had argued for using monetary expansion to fight
economic downturns—though others were fiercely opposed. Some economists
had even argued that temporary budget deficits were a good thing in times of
recession—though others disagreed strongly. In practice, during the 1930s many
governments followed policies that we would now call Keynesian. In the United
States, the administration of Franklin Roosevelt engaged in modest deficit spending in an effort to create jobs.

But these efforts were half-hearted. In fact, in 1937 Roosevelt gave in to advice
from non-Keynesian economists who urged him to balance the budget and raise
interest rates, even though the economy was still depressed. The result was a
renewed slump.

After World War II, Keynesian ideas were broadly accepted by U.S. economists. There were, however, a series of challenges to those ideas, which led to
a considerable shift in views even among those economists who continued to
believe that Keynes was broadly right about the causes of recessions. In the
upcoming section, we'll learn about those challenges and the schools, *new classical economics* and *new Keynesian economics*, that emerged.

## ECONOMICS ▸ *IN ACTION*

### THE END OF THE GREAT DEPRESSION

It would make a good story if Keynes's ideas had led to a change in economic policy that brought the Great Depression to an end. Unfortunately,
that's not what happened. Still, the way the Depression ended did a lot to
convince economists that Keynes was right.

The basic message many of the young
economists who adopted Keynes's ideas in
the 1930s took from his work was that economic recovery requires aggressive fiscal
expansion—deficit spending on a large scale
to create jobs. And that is what they eventually got, but it wasn't because politicians
were persuaded. Instead, what happened
was a very large and expensive war, World
War II.

Figure 18-3 shows the U.S. unemployment rate and the federal budget deficit as a
share of GDP from 1930 to 1947. As you can
see, deficit spending during the 1930s was on
a modest scale. In 1940, as the risk of war
grew larger, the United States began a large
military buildup, moving the budget deep
into deficit. After the attack on Pearl Harbor

FIGURE  **18-3**  Fiscal Policy and the End of the Great Depression

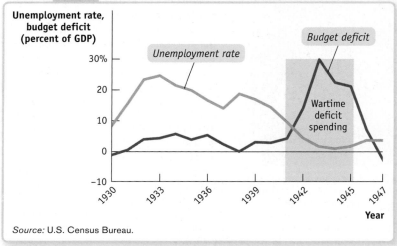

*Source:* U.S. Census Bureau.

on December 7, 1941, the country began deficit spending on an enormous scale: in fiscal 1943, which began in July 1942, the deficit was 30% of GDP. Today that would be equivalent to a deficit of $4.3 trillion.

And the economy recovered. World War II wasn't intended as a Keynesian fiscal policy, but it demonstrated that expansionary fiscal policy can, in fact, create jobs in the short run.

### CHECK YOUR UNDERSTANDING   18-2

1. In a press release from early 2012, the National Federation of Independent Business, which calculates the Small Business Optimism Index, stated "The Small Business Optimism Index rose just 0.1 points in January. . . . Historically, optimism remains at recession levels. While small business owners appeared less pessimistic about the outlook for business conditions and real sales growth, that optimism did not materialize in hiring or increased inventories plans." Would this statement seem familiar to a Keynesian economist? Which conclusion would a Keynesian economist draw for the need for public policy?

Solution appears at back of book.

## Challenges to Keynesian Economics

Keynes's ideas fundamentally changed the way economists think about business cycles. They did not, however, go unquestioned. In the decades that followed the publication of *The General Theory*, Keynesian economics faced a series of challenges. As a result, the consensus of macroeconomists retreated somewhat from the strong version of Keynesianism that prevailed in the 1950s. In particular, economists became much more aware of the limits to macroeconomic policy activism.

### The Revival of Monetary Policy

Keynes's *General Theory* suggested that monetary policy wouldn't be very effective in depression conditions. Many modern macroeconomists agree: in Chapter 16 we introduced the concept of a *liquidity trap,* a situation in which monetary policy is ineffective because the interest rate is down against the zero bound. In the 1930s, when Keynes wrote, interest rates were, in fact, very close to 0%. (The term *liquidity trap* was first introduced by the British economist John Hicks in a 1937 paper, "Mr. Keynes and The Classics: A Suggested Interpretation," that summarized Keynes's ideas.)

But even when the era of near-0% interest rates came to an end after World War II, many economists continued to emphasize fiscal policy and downplay the usefulness of monetary policy. Eventually, however, macroeconomists reassessed the importance of monetary policy. A key milestone in this reassessment was the 1963 publication of *A Monetary History of the United States, 1867–1960* by Milton Friedman, of the University of Chicago, and Anna Schwartz, of the National Bureau of Economic Research. Friedman and Schwartz showed that business cycles had historically been associated

Milton Friedman and his co-author Anna Schwartz played a key role in convincing macroeconomists of the importance of monetary policy.

**Monetarism** asserts that GDP will grow steadily if the money supply grows steadily.

**Discretionary monetary policy** is the use of changes in the interest rate or the money supply to stabilize the economy.

with fluctuations in the money supply. In particular, the money supply fell sharply during the onset of the Great Depression. Friedman and Schwartz persuaded many, though not all, economists that the Great Depression could have been avoided if the Federal Reserve had acted to prevent that monetary contraction. They persuaded most economists that monetary policy should play a key role in economic management.

The revival of interest in monetary policy was significant because it suggested that the burden of managing the economy could be shifted away from fiscal policy—meaning that economic management could largely be taken out of the hands of politicians. Fiscal policy, which must involve changing tax rates or government spending, necessarily involves political choices. If the government tries to stimulate the economy by cutting taxes, it must decide whose taxes will be cut. If it tries to stimulate the economy with government spending, it must decide what to spend the money on.

Monetary policy, in contrast, does not involve such choices: when the central bank cuts interest rates to fight a recession, it cuts everyone's interest rate at the same time. So a shift from relying on fiscal policy to relying on monetary policy makes macroeconomics a more technical, less political issue. In fact, as we learned in Chapter 14, monetary policy in most major economies is set by an independent central bank that is insulated from the political process.

## Monetarism

After the publication of *A Monetary History,* Milton Friedman led a movement that sought to eliminate macroeconomic policy activism while maintaining the importance of monetary policy. **Monetarism** asserts that GDP will grow steadily if the money supply grows steadily. The monetarist policy prescription was to have the central bank target a constant rate of growth of the money supply, such as 3% per year, and maintain that target regardless of any fluctuations in the economy.

It's important to realize that monetarism retained many Keynesian ideas. Like Keynes, Friedman asserted that the short run is important and that short-run changes in aggregate demand affect aggregate output as well as aggregate prices. Like Keynes, he argued that policy should have been much more expansionary during the Great Depression.

Monetarists argued, however, that most of the efforts of policy makers to smooth out the business cycle actually make things worse. In Chapter 13 we discussed concerns over the usefulness of *discretionary fiscal policy*—changes in taxes or government spending, or both, in response to the state of the economy. As we explained, government perceptions about the economy often lag behind reality, and there are further lags in changing fiscal policy and in its effects on the economy. As a result, discretionary fiscal policies intended to fight a recession often end up feeding a boom, and vice versa. According to monetarists, **discretionary monetary policy,** changes in the interest rate or the money supply by the central bank in order to stabilize the economy, faces the same problem of lags as fiscal policy, but to a lesser extent.

Friedman also argued that if the central bank followed his advice and refused to change the money supply in response to fluctuations in the economy, fiscal policy would be much less effective than Keynesians believed. In Chapter 10 we analyzed the phenomenon of *crowding out,* in which government deficits drive up interest rates and lead to reduced investment spending. Friedman and others pointed out that if the money supply is held fixed while the government pursues an expansionary fiscal policy, crowding out will occur and will limit the effect of the fiscal expansion on aggregate demand.

Figure 18-4 illustrates this argument. Panel (a) shows aggregate output and the aggregate price level. $AD_1$ is the initial aggregate demand curve and $SRAS$ is the short-run aggregate supply curve. At the initial equilibrium, $E_1$, the level of aggregate output is $Y_1$ and the aggregate price level is $P_1$. Panel (b) shows

FIGURE  **18-4**  Fiscal Policy with a Fixed Money Supply

**(a) The Increase in Aggregate Demand from an Expansionary Fiscal Policy Is Limited When the Money Supply Is Fixed...**

**(b) ...Because the Increase in Money Demand Drives up the Interest Rate, Crowding out Some Investment Spending.**

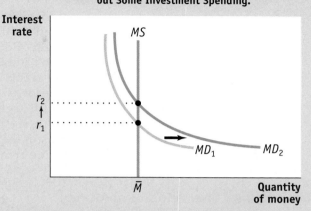

In panel (a) an expansionary fiscal policy shifts the *AD* curve rightward, driving up both the aggregate price level and aggregate output. However, this leads to an increase in the demand for money. If the money supply is held fixed, as in panel (b), the increase in money demand drives up the interest rate, reducing investment spending and offsetting part of the fiscal expansion. So the shift of the *AD* curve is less than it would otherwise be: fiscal policy becomes less effective when the money supply is held fixed.

the money market. *MS* is the money supply curve and $MD_1$ is the initial money demand curve, so the initial interest rate is $r_1$.

Now suppose the government increases purchases of goods and services. We know that this will shift the *AD* curve rightward, as illustrated by the shift from $AD_1$ to $AD_2$, and that aggregate output will rise, from $Y_1$ to $Y_2$, and the aggregate price level will rise, from $P_1$ to $P_2$. Both the rise in aggregate output and the rise in the aggregate price level will, however, increase the demand for money, shifting the money demand curve rightward from $MD_1$ to $MD_2$. This drives up the equilibrium interest rate to $r_2$. Friedman's point was that this rise in the interest rate reduces investment spending, partially offsetting the initial rise in government spending. As a result, the rightward shift of the *AD* curve is smaller than the multiplier analysis in Chapter 13 indicated. And Friedman argued that with a constant money supply, the multiplier is so small that there's not much point in using fiscal policy, even in a depressed economy.

But Friedman didn't favor activist monetary policy either. He argued that the problems of time lags that limit the ability of discretionary fiscal policy to stabilize the economy also apply to discretionary monetary policy. Friedman's solution was to put monetary policy on "autopilot." The central bank, he argued, should follow a **monetary policy rule,** a formula that determines its actions and leaves it relatively little discretion. During the 1960s and 1970s, most monetarists favored a monetary policy rule of slow, steady growth in the money supply. Underlying this view was the concept of the **velocity of money,** the ratio of nominal GDP to the money supply. Velocity is a measure of the number of times the average dollar bill in the economy turns over per year between buyers and sellers (e.g., I tip the Starbucks barista a dollar, she uses it to buy lunch, and so on). This concept gives rise to the *velocity equation:*

**(18-1)** $M \times V = P \times Y$

Where *M* is the money supply, *V* is velocity, *P* is the aggregate price level, and *Y* is real GDP.

A **monetary policy rule** is a formula that determines the central bank's actions.

The **velocity of money** is the ratio of nominal GDP to the money supply.

Monetarists believed, with considerable historical justification, that the velocity of money was stable in the short run and changes only slowly in the long run. As a result, they claimed, steady growth in the money supply by the central bank would ensure steady growth in spending, and therefore in GDP.

Monetarism strongly influenced actual monetary policy in the late 1970s and early 1980s. It quickly became clear, however, that steady growth in the money supply didn't ensure steady growth in the economy: the velocity of money wasn't stable enough for such a simple policy rule to work. Figure 18-5 shows how events eventually undermined the monetarists' view. The figure shows the velocity of money, as measured by the ratio of nominal GDP to M1, from 1960 through late 2011. As you can see, until 1980 velocity followed a fairly smooth, seemingly predictable trend. After the Fed began to adopt monetarist ideas in the late 1970s and early 1980s, however, the velocity of money began moving erratically—probably due to financial market innovations.

**FIGURE** **18-5** The Velocity of Money

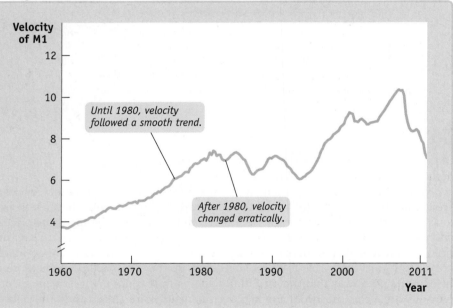

From 1960 to 1980, the velocity of money was stable, leading monetarists to believe that steady growth in the money supply would lead to a stable economy. After 1980, however, velocity began moving erratically, undermining the case for traditional monetarism. As a result, traditional monetarism fell out of favor.

*Source:* Federal Reserve Bank of St. Louis.

Traditional monetarists—those who believe that GDP will grow steadily if the money supply grows steadily—are hard to find among today's macroeconomists. As we'll see later in the chapter, however, the concern that originally motivated the monetarists—that too much discretionary monetary policy can actually destabilize the economy—has become widely accepted.

## Inflation and the Natural Rate of Unemployment

At the same time that monetarists were challenging Keynesian views about how macroeconomic policy should be conducted, other economists—some, but not all of them, monetarists—were emphasizing the limits to what activist macroeconomic policy could achieve.

In the 1940s and 1950s, many Keynesian economists believed that expansionary fiscal policy could be used to achieve full employment on a permanent basis. In the 1960s, however, many economists realized that expansionary policies could cause problems with inflation, but they still believed policy makers could choose to trade off low unemployment for higher inflation even in the long run.

In 1968, however, Milton Friedman and Edmund Phelps of Columbia University, working independently, proposed the concept of the natural rate of unemployment, which we discussed in Chapter 8. And in Chapter 16 we showed that the natural rate of unemployment is also the nonaccelerating inflation rate of unemployment, or NAIRU. According to the **natural rate hypothesis,** because inflation is eventually embedded into expectations, to avoid accelerating inflation over time, the unemployment rate must be high enough that the actual inflation rate equals the expected rate of inflation. Attempts to keep the unemployment rate below the natural rate will lead the expected inflation rate to exceed the actual inflation rate, and generate an ever-rising inflation rate.

The natural rate hypothesis limits the role of activist macroeconomic policy compared to earlier theories. Because the government can't keep unemployment below the natural rate, its task is not to keep unemployment low but to keep it *stable*—to prevent large fluctuations in unemployment in either direction.

The Friedman–Phelps hypothesis made a strong prediction: that the apparent trade-off between unemployment and inflation would not survive an extended period of rising prices. Once inflation was embedded into the public's expectations, it would continue even in the face of high unemployment. Sure enough, that's exactly what happened in the 1970s. This accurate prediction was one of the triumphs of macroeconomic analysis, and it convinced the great majority of economists that the natural rate hypothesis was correct. In contrast to traditional monetarism, which declined in influence as more evidence accumulated, the natural rate hypothesis has become almost universally accepted among macroeconomists, with a few qualifications. (Some macroeconomists believe that at very low or negative rates of inflation the hypothesis doesn't work.)

## The Political Business Cycle

One final challenge to Keynesian economics focused not on the validity of the economic analysis but on its political consequences. A number of economists and political scientists pointed out that activist macroeconomic policy lends itself to political manipulation.

Statistical evidence suggests that election results tend to be determined by the state of the economy in the months just before the election. In the United States, if the economy is growing rapidly and the unemployment rate is falling in the six months or so before Election Day, the incumbent party tends to be re-elected even if the economy performed poorly in the preceding three years.

This creates an obvious temptation to abuse activist macroeconomic policy: pump up the economy in an election year, and pay the price in higher inflation and/or higher unemployment later. The result can be unnecessary instability in the economy, a **political business cycle** caused by the use of macroeconomic policy to serve political ends.

An often-cited example is the combination of expansionary fiscal and monetary policy that led to rapid growth in the U.S. economy just before the 1972 election and a sharp acceleration in inflation after the election. Kenneth Rogoff, a highly respected macroeconomist who served as chief economist at the International Monetary Fund, has proclaimed Richard Nixon, the president at the time, "the all-time hero of political business cycles."

As we learned in Chapter 14, one way to avoid a political business cycle is to place monetary policy in the hands of an independent central bank, insulated from political pressure. The political business cycle is also a reason to limit the use of discretionary fiscal policy to extreme circumstances.

According to the **natural rate hypothesis,** because inflation is eventually embedded into expectations, to avoid accelerating inflation over time the unemployment rate must be high enough that the actual inflation rate equals the expected inflation rate.

A **political business cycle** results when politicians use macroeconomic policy to serve political ends.

## ECONOMICS ➤ *IN ACTION*

### THE FED'S FLIRTATION WITH MONETARISM

In the late 1970s and early 1980s the Federal Reserve flirted with monetarism. For most of its prior existence, the Fed had targeted interest rates, adjusting its target based on the state of the economy. In the late 1970s, however, the Fed adopted a monetary policy rule and began announcing target ranges for several measures of the money supply. It also stopped setting targets for interest rates. Most people interpreted these changes as a strong move toward monetarism.

In 1982, however, the Fed turned its back on monetarism. Since 1982 the Fed has pursued a discretionary monetary policy, which has led to large swings in the money supply. At the end of the 1980s, the Fed returned to conducting monetary policy by setting target levels for the interest rate.

Why did the Fed flirt with monetarism, then abandon it? The turn to monetarism largely reflected the events of the 1970s, when a sharp rise in inflation broke the perceived trade-off between inflation and unemployment and discredited traditional Keynesianism. The accuracy of Friedman's prediction of a worsening trade-off between inflation and unemployment increased his prestige and that of his followers. As a result, policy makers adopted Friedman's proposals.

The turn away from monetarism also reflected events: as we saw in Figure 18-5, the velocity of money, which had followed a smooth trend before 1980, became erratic after 1980. This made monetarism seem like a much less good idea.

### CHECK YOUR UNDERSTANDING 18-3

1. Consider Figure 18-5.
   a. If the Federal Reserve had pursued a monetarist policy of a constant rate of growth in the money supply, what would have happened to output beginning in 2008 according to the velocity equation?
   b. In fact, the Federal Reserve accelerated the rate of growth in M1 rapidly beginning in 2008, partly in order to counteract a large increase in unemployment. Would a monetarist have agreed with this policy? What limits are there, according to a monetarist point of view, to changing the unemployment rate?
2. What are the limits of macroeconomic policy activism?

*Solutions appear at back of book.*

## Rational Expectations, Real Business Cycles, and New Classical Macroeconomics

As we have seen, one key difference between classical economics and Keynesian economics is that classical economists believed that the short-run aggregate supply curve is vertical, while Keynesian economics claims that the aggregate supply curve slopes upward in the short run. As a result of the upward-sloping demand curve, Keynes argued that demand shocks—shifts in the aggregate demand curve—can cause fluctuations in aggregate output.

The challenges to Keynesian economics that arose in the 1950s and 1960s from monetarists and from natural rate theorists didn't rely on classical economics ideas. In other words, the challengers still accepted that an increase in aggregate demand leads to a rise in aggregate output in the short run and that a decrease in aggregate demand leads to a fall in aggregate output in the short run. Instead, they argued that the policy medicine—activist macroeconomic policy—would worsen the disease—economic fluctuations.

In the 1970s and 1980s, however, some economists developed an approach to the business cycle known as **new classical macroeconomics,** which revived the classical view that shifts in the aggregate demand curve affect only the aggregate price level, not aggregate output. The new approach evolved in two steps. First, some economists challenged traditional arguments about the slope of the short-run aggregate supply curve based on the concept of *rational expectations.* Second, some economists suggested that changes in productivity cause economic fluctuations, a view known as *real business cycle theory.*

## Rational Expectations

In the 1970s a concept known as *rational expectations* had a powerful impact on macroeconomics. **Rational expectations,** originally introduced by John Muth in 1961, is the view that individuals and firms make decisions optimally, using all available information.

For example, workers and employers bargaining over long-term wage contracts need to estimate the inflation rate they expect over the life of that contract. Rational expectations says that in making estimates of future inflation, they won't just look at past rates of inflation; they will also take into account available information about monetary and fiscal policy. Suppose that prices didn't rise last year, but that the monetary and fiscal policies announced by policy makers make it clear to economic analysts that there will be substantial inflation over the next few years. According to rational expectations, long-term wage contracts will be adjusted today to reflect this future inflation, even though prices didn't rise in the past.

Adopting rational expectations can significantly alter policy makers' beliefs about the effectiveness of government policy. According to the original version of the natural rate hypothesis, a government attempt to trade off higher inflation for lower unemployment would work in the short run but would eventually fail because higher inflation would get built into expectations. According to rational expectations, we should remove the word *eventually* and replace it with *immediately:* if it's clear that the government intends to trade off higher inflation for lower unemployment, the public will understand this, and expected inflation will immediately rise. So, under rational expectations, government intervention fails in the short run and the long run.

In the 1970s Robert Lucas of the University of Chicago, in a series of highly influential papers, used the logic of rational expectations to argue that monetary policy can change the level of output and unemployment only if it comes as a surprise to the public. Otherwise, attempts to lower unemployment will simply result in higher prices. According to Lucas's **rational expectations model** of the economy, monetary policy isn't useful in stabilizing the economy after all. In 1995 Lucas won the Nobel Prize in economics for this work, which remains widely admired. However, many—perhaps most—macroeconomists, especially those advising policy makers, now believe that his conclusions were overstated. The Federal Reserve certainly thinks that it can play a useful role in economic stabilization.

Why, in the view of many macroeconomists, doesn't Lucas's rational expectations model of macroeconomics accurately describe how the economy actually behaves? **New Keynesian economics,** a set of ideas that became influential in the 1990s, provides an explanation. It argues that market imperfections interact to make many prices in the economy temporarily sticky. For example, one new Keynesian argument points out that monopolists don't have to be too careful about setting prices exactly "right": if they set a price a bit too high, they'll lose some sales but make more profit on each sale; if they set the price too low, they'll reduce the profit per sale but sell more. As a result, even small costs to changing prices can lead to substantial price stickiness and make the economy as a whole behave in a Keynesian fashion.

Over time, new Keynesian ideas combined with actual experience have reduced the practical influence of the rational expectations concept. Nonetheless, the idea of rational expectations served as a useful caution for macroeconomists who had become excessively optimistic about their ability to manage the economy.

**New classical macroeconomics** is an approach to the business cycle that returns to the classical view that shifts in the aggregate demand curve affect only the aggregate price level, not aggregate output.

**Rational expectations** is the view that individuals and firms make decisions optimally, using all available information.

According to the **rational expectations model** of the economy, expected changes in monetary policy have no effect on unemployment and output and only affect the price level.

According to **new Keynesian economics,** market imperfections can lead to price stickiness for the economy as a whole.

**Real business cycle theory** claims that fluctuations in the rate of growth of total factor productivity cause the business cycle.

## Real Business Cycles

In Chapter 9 we introduced the concept of *total factor productivity*, the amount of output that can be generated with a given level of factor inputs. Total factor productivity grows over time, but that growth isn't smooth. In the 1980s a number of economists argued that slowdowns in productivity growth, which they attributed to pauses in technological progress, are the main cause of recessions. **Real business cycle theory** claims that fluctuations in the rate of growth of total factor productivity cause the business cycle.

Believing that the aggregate supply curve is vertical, real business cycle theorists attribute the source of business cycles to shifts of the aggregate supply curve: a recession occurs when a slowdown in productivity growth shifts the aggregate supply curve leftward, and a recovery occurs when a pickup in productivity growth shifts the aggregate supply curve rightward. In the early days of real business cycle theory, the theory's proponents denied that changes in aggregate demand—and, likewise, macroeconomic policy activism—have any effect on aggregate output.

This theory was strongly influential, as shown by the fact that two of the founders of real business cycle theory, Finn Kydland of Carnegie Mellon University and Edward Prescott of the Federal Reserve Bank of Minneapolis, won the 2004 Nobel Prize in economics. The current status of real business cycle theory, however, is somewhat similar to that of rational expectations. The theory is widely recognized as having made valuable contributions to our understanding of the economy, and it serves as a useful caution against too much emphasis on aggregate demand. But many of the real business cycle theorists themselves now acknowledge that their models need an upward-sloping aggregate supply curve to fit the economic data—

## FOR INQUIRING MINDS

### SUPPLY-SIDE ECONOMICS

During the 1970s a group of economic writers began propounding a view of economic policy that came to be known as "supply-side economics." The core of this view was the belief that reducing tax rates, and so increasing the incentives to work and invest, would have a powerful positive effect on the growth rate of potential output. The supply-siders urged the government to cut taxes without worrying about matching spending cuts: economic growth, they argued, would offset any negative effects from budget deficits. Some supply-siders even argued that a cut in tax *rates* would have such a miraculous effect on economic growth that tax *revenues*—the total amount taxpayers pay to the government—would actually rise. That is, some supply-siders argued that the United States was on the wrong side of the *Laffer curve*, a hypothetical relationship between tax rates and total tax revenue that slopes upward at low tax rates but turns downward when tax rates are very high.

In the 1970s supply-side economics was enthusiastically supported by the editors of the *Wall Street Journal* and other figures in the media, and it became popular with politicians. In 1980 Ronald Reagan made supply-side economics the basis of his presidential campaign.

Because supply-side economics emphasizes supply rather than demand, and because the supply-siders themselves are harshly critical of Keynesian economics, it might seem as if supply-side theory belongs in our discussion of new classical macroeconomics. But unlike rational expectations and real business cycle theory, supply-side economics is generally dismissed by economic researchers.

The main reason for this dismissal is lack of supporting evidence. Almost all economists agree that tax cuts increase incentives to work and invest. But attempts to estimate these incentive effects indicate that at current U.S.

Although many have claimed that the Reagan tax cuts were pro-growth, data from the Congressional Budget Office and others show no sign of an acceleration in growth after the cuts were implemented.

tax levels, the positive incentive effects aren't nearly strong enough to support the strong claims made by supply-siders. In particular, the supply-side doctrine implies that large tax cuts, such as those implemented by Ronald Reagan in the early 1980s, should sharply raise potential output. Yet estimates of potential output by the Congressional Budget Office and others show no sign of an acceleration in growth after the Reagan tax cuts.

and that this gives aggregate demand a potential role in determining aggregate output. And as we have seen, policy makers strongly believe that aggregate demand policy has an important role to play in fighting recessions.

## ECONOMICS ➤ *IN ACTION*

### TOTAL FACTOR PRODUCTIVITY AND THE BUSINESS CYCLE

**R**eal business cycle theory argues that fluctuations in the rate of growth of total factor productivity are the principal cause of business cycles. Although many macroeconomists dispute that claim, the theory did draw attention to the fact that there is a strong correlation between the rate of total factor productivity growth and the business cycle. Figure 18-6 shows the annual rate of total factor productivity growth estimated by the Bureau of Labor Statistics. The shaded areas represent recessions. Clearly, recessions tend also to be periods in which the growth of total factor productivity slows sharply or even turns negative. And real business cycle theorists deserve a lot of credit for drawing economists' attention to this fact.

**FIGURE 18-6**  Total Factor Productivity and the Business Cycle

There are, however, disputes about how to interpret this correlation. In the early days of real business cycle theory, proponents argued that productivity fluctuations are entirely the result of uneven technological progress. Critics pointed out, however, that in really severe recessions, like those of 1974–1975 or the early 1980s, total factor productivity actually declines. If real business cycle theorists were correct, then technology actually regressed during those periods—something that is hard to believe.

So what accounts for declining total factor productivity during recessions? Some economists argue that it is a result, not a cause, of economic downturns. An example may be helpful. Suppose we measure productivity at the local post office by the number of pieces of mail handled, divided by the number of postal workers. Since the post office doesn't lay off workers whenever there's a slow mail day, days in which there is a fall in the amount of mail to process will seem to be days in which workers are especially unproductive. In other words, the slump in business is causing the apparent decline in productivity, not the other way around.

It's now widely accepted that some of the correlation between total factor productivity and the business cycle is the result of the effect of the business cycle on productivity, rather than the reverse. But the main direction of causation is a subject of continuing research.

### CHECK YOUR UNDERSTANDING   18-4

**1.** In late 2008, as it became clear that the United States was experiencing a recession, the Fed reduced its target for the federal funds rate to near zero, as part of a larger aggressively expansionary monetary policy stance (including what the Fed called "quantitative easing"). Most observers agreed that the Fed's aggressive monetary expansion helped reduce the length and severity of the 2007–2009 recession.
  **a.** What would rational expectations theorists say about this conclusion?
  **b.** What would real business cycle theorists say?

*Solutions appear at back of book.*

▼ **Quick Review**

● According to **new classical macro-economics,** the short-run aggregate supply curve is vertical after all. It contains two branches: *the rational expectations model* and *real business cycle theory*.

● **Rational expectations** claims that people take all information into account. The **rational expectations model** of the economy claims that only unexpected changes in monetary policy affect aggregate output and employment; expected changes only alter the price level.

● **New Keynesian economics** argues that due to market imperfections that create price stickiness, the aggregate supply curve is upward-sloping; therefore changes in aggregate demand affect aggregate output and employment.

● **Real business cycle theory** argues that fluctuations in the rate of productivity growth cause the business cycle.

● New Keynesian ideas and events have diminished the acceptance of the rational expectations model, while real business cycle theory has been undermined by its implication that technology regresses during deep recessions. It is now generally believed that the aggregate supply curve is upward-sloping.

The **Great Moderation** is the period from 1985 to 2007 when the U.S. economy experienced relatively small fluctuations and low inflation.

The **Great Moderation consensus** combines a belief in monetary policy as the main tool of stabilization, with skepticism toward the use of fiscal policy, and an acknowledgement of the policy constraints imposed by the natural rate of unemployment and the political business cycle.

# Consensus and Conflict in Modern Macroeconomics

The 1970s and the first half of the 1980s were a stormy period for the U.S. economy (and for other major economies, too). There was a severe recession in 1974–1975, then two back-to-back recessions in 1979–1982 that sent the unemployment rate to almost 11%. At the same time, the inflation rate soared into double digits—and then plunged. As we have seen, these events left a strong mark on macroeconomic thought.

After about 1985, however, the economy settled down. The recession of 1990–1991 was much milder than the 1974–1975 recession or the double-dip slump from 1979 to 1982, and the inflation rate generally stayed below 4%. The period of relative calm in the economy from 1985 to 2007 came to be known as the **Great Moderation.** And the calmness of the economy was to a large extent marked by a similar calm in macroeconomic policy discussion. In fact, it seemed that a broad consensus had emerged about several key macroeconomic issues.

The Great Moderation was, unfortunately, followed by the *Great Recession,* the severe and persistent slump that followed the 2008 financial crisis. We'll talk shortly about the policy disputes caused by the Great Recession. First, however, let's examine the apparent consensus that emerged during the Great Moderation, which we call the **Great Moderation consensus.** It combines a belief in monetary policy as the main tool of stabilization, with skepticism toward the use of fiscal policy, and an acknowledgement of the policy constraints imposed by the natural rate of unemployment and the political business cycle. To understand where it came from and what still remains in dispute, we'll look at how macroeconomists have changed their answers to five key questions about macroeconomic policy. The five questions and the various answers given by schools of macroeconomics over the decades are summarized in Table 18-1. (In the table, new classical economics is subsumed under classical economics, and new Keynesian economics is subsumed under the Great Moderation consensus.) Notice that classical macroeconomics said no to each question; basically, classical macroeconomists didn't think macroeconomic policy could accomplish very much. But let's go through the questions one by one.

**TABLE 18-1** Five Key Questions About Macroeconomic Policy

| | Classical macroeconomics | Keynesian macroeconomics | Monetarism | Great Moderation consensus |
|---|---|---|---|---|
| 1. Is expansionary monetary policy helpful in fighting recessions? | No | Not very | Yes | Yes, except in special circumstances |
| 2. Is expansionary fiscal policy effective in fighting recessions? | No | Yes | No | Yes |
| 3. Can monetary and/or fiscal policy reduce unemployment in the long run? | No | Yes | No | No |
| 4. Should fiscal policy be used in a discretionary way? | No | Yes | No | No, except possibly in special circumstances |
| 5. Should monetary policy be used in a discretionary way? | No | Yes | No | Still in dispute |

## Question 1: Is Expansionary Monetary Policy Helpful in Fighting Recessions?

As we've seen, classical macroeconomists generally believed that expansionary monetary policy was ineffective or even harmful in fighting recessions. In the early years of Keynesian economics, macroeconomists weren't against monetary expansion during recessions, but they tended to believe that it was of doubtful effectiveness. Milton Friedman and his followers convinced economists that monetary policy is effective after all.

Nearly all macroeconomists now agree that monetary policy can be used to shift the aggregate demand curve and to reduce economic instability. The classical view that changes in the money supply affect only aggregate prices, not aggregate output, has few supporters today. The view held by early Keynesian economists—that changes in the money supply have little effect—has equally few supporters. Now it is generally agreed that monetary policy is ineffective only in the case of a liquidity trap.

## Question 2: Is Expansionary Fiscal Policy Effective in Fighting Recessions?

Classical macroeconomists were, if anything, even more opposed to fiscal expansion than monetary expansion. Keynesian economists, on the other hand, gave fiscal policy a central role in fighting recessions. Monetarists argued that fiscal policy was ineffective if the money supply was held constant. But that strong view has become relatively rare.

Most macroeconomists now agree that fiscal policy, like monetary policy, can shift the aggregate demand curve. Most macroeconomists also agree that the government should not seek to balance the budget regardless of the state of the economy: they agree that the role of the budget as an automatic stabilizer helps keep the economy on an even keel.

## Question 3: Can Monetary and/or Fiscal Policy Reduce Unemployment in the Long Run?

Classical macroeconomists didn't believe the government could do anything about unemployment. Some Keynesian economists moved to the opposite extreme, arguing that expansionary policies could be used to achieve a permanently low unemployment rate, perhaps at the cost of some inflation. Monetarists believed that unemployment could not be kept below the natural rate.

Almost all macroeconomists now accept the natural rate hypothesis. This hypothesis leads them to accept sharp limits to what monetary and fiscal policy can accomplish. Effective monetary and fiscal policy, most macroeconomists believe, can limit the size of fluctuations of the actual unemployment rate around the natural rate, but they can't be used to keep unemployment below the natural rate.

## Question 4: Should Fiscal Policy Be Used in a Discretionary Way?

As we've already seen, views about the effectiveness of fiscal policy have gone back and forth, from rejection by classical macroeconomists, to a positive view by Keynesian economists, to a negative view once again by monetarists. Today most macroeconomists believe that tax cuts and spending increases are at least somewhat effective in increasing aggregate demand.

Many, but not all, macroeconomists, however, believe that *discretionary fiscal policy* is usually counterproductive, for the reasons discussed in Chapter 13: the lags in adjusting fiscal policy mean that, all too often, policies intended to fight a slump end up intensifying a boom.

As a result, the macroeconomic consensus gives monetary policy the lead role in economic stabilization. Some, but not all, economists believe that fiscal policy must be brought back into the mix under special circumstances, in particular when interest rates are at or near the zero lower bound and the economy is in a liquidity trap. As we'll see shortly, the proper role of fiscal policy became a huge point of contention after 2008.

## Question 5: Should Monetary Policy Be Used in a Discretionary Way?

Classical macroeconomists didn't think that monetary policy should be used to fight recessions; Keynesian economists didn't oppose discretionary monetary policy, but they were skeptical about its effectiveness. Monetarists argued that discretionary monetary policy was doing more harm than good. Where are we today? This remains an area of dispute. Today, under the Great Moderation consensus, most macreconomists agree on these three points:

- Monetary policy should play the main role in stabilization policy.
- The central bank should be independent, insulated from political pressures, in order to avoid a political business cycle.
- Discretionary fiscal policy should be used sparingly, both because of policy lags and because of the risks of a political business cycle.

However, the Great Moderation was up-ended by events that posed very difficult questions—questions that rage as this book goes to press. We'll now examine what happened and why the ongoing debate is so fierce.

## Crisis and Aftermath

The Great Recession shattered any sense among macroeconomists that they had entered a permanent era of agreement over key policy questions. Given the nature of the slump, however, this should not have come as a surprise. Why? Because the severity of the slump arguably made the policies that seemed to work during the Great Moderation inadequate.

Under the Great Moderation consensus, there had been broad agreement that the job of stabilizing the economy was best carried out by having the Federal Reserve and its counterparts abroad raise or lower interest rates as the economic situation warranted. But what should be done if the economy is deeply depressed, but the interest rates the Fed normally controls are already close to zero and can go no lower (that is, when the economy is in a liquidity trap)? Some economists called for the aggressive use of discretionary fiscal policy and/or unconventional monetary policies that might achieve results despite the zero lower bound. Others strongly opposed these measures, arguing either that they would be ineffective or that they would produce undesirable side effects.

**The Debate over Fiscal Policy** In 2009 a number of governments, including that of the United States, responded with expansionary fiscal policy, or "stimulus," generally taking the form of a mix of temporary spending measures and temporary tax cuts. From the start, however, these efforts were highly controversial.

Supporters of fiscal stimulus offered three main arguments for breaking with the normal presumption against discretionary fiscal policy:

1. They argued that discretionary fiscal expansion was needed because the usual tool for stabilizing the economy, monetary policy, could no longer be used now that interest rates were near zero.
2. They argued that one normal concern about expansionary fiscal policy— that deficit spending would drive up interest rates, crowding out private

investment spending—was unlikely to be a problem in a depressed economy. Again, this was because interest rates were close to zero and likely to stay there as long as the economy was depressed.

3. Finally, they argued that another concern about discretionary fiscal policy—that it might take a long time to get going—was less of a concern than usual given the likelihood that the economy would be depressed for an extended period.

These arguments generally won the day in early 2009. However, opponents of fiscal stimulus raised two main objections:

1. They argued that households and firms would see any rise in government spending as a sign that tax burdens were likely to rise in the future, leading to a fall in private spending that would undo any positive effect. (This is the *Ricardian equivalence* argument that we encountered in Chapter 13.)

2. They also warned that spending programs might undermine investors' faith in the government's ability to repay its debts, leading to an increase in long-term interest rates despite loose monetary policy.

In fact, by 2010 a number of economists were arguing that the best way to boost the economy was actually to cut government spending, which they argued would increase private-sector confidence and lead to a rise in output and employment. This notion, often referred to as the doctrine of "expansionary austerity," was especially popular in Europe, where it was supported by officials at the European Central Bank and became the official policy of the Cameron government in Britain, which took office in the spring of 2010.

One might have hoped that events would resolve this dispute. At the time this book went to press, however, the debate was still raging. Critics of fiscal stimulus pointed out that the U.S. stimulus had failed to deliver a convincing fall in unemployment; stimulus advocates, however, had warned from the start that this was likely to happen because the stimulus was too small compared with the depth of the slump. Meanwhile, austerity programs in Britain and elsewhere had also failed to deliver an economic turnaround and, in fact, had seemed to deepen the slump; supporters of these programs, however, argued that they were nonetheless necessary to head off a potential collapse of confidence.

One thing that was clear, however, was that those who had predicted a sharp rise in U.S. interest rates due to budget deficits, leading to conventional crowding out, had been wrong: by the fall of 2011, U.S. long-term rates were hitting record lows despite continuing large deficits.

### The Debate over Monetary Policy

As we saw in Chapter 16, a central bank that wants to increase aggregate demand normally does this by buying short-term government debt, pushing short-term interest rates down and causing spending to rise. By the fall of 2008, however, this conventional form of monetary policy had already reached its limit because the relevant interest rates were close to zero. The question then became whether there were other things the Federal Reserve and other central banks could do.

In 2008–2009 and again in the fall of 2010, the Fed pursued one such alternative, known as "quantitative easing," which involved buying assets other than short-term government debt, notably long-term debt whose interest rate was still significantly above zero. For example, in November 2010 the Fed began buying $600 billion worth of longer-term U.S. debt in a program generally referred to as "QE2"

In 2008, the Fed took a series of unconventional monetary policy actions in response to the deepening recession and financial crisis.

Brendan Smialowski/Bloomberg News/Getty Images

(quantitative easing 2). The idea was to drive down longer-term interest rates, which arguably matter more for private spending than short-term rates. In September 2011 the Fed announced another program, this time one that would involve selling shorter-term assets with interest rates already near zero and buying longer-term assets instead.

The policy of quantitative easing was controversial, facing criticisms both from those who believed that the Fed was doing too much and from those who believed it was doing too little. Those who believed that the Fed was doing too much were concerned about possible future inflation; they argued that the Fed would find its unconventional measures hard to reverse as the economy recovered and that the end result would be a much too expansionary monetary policy.

Critics from the other side argued that the Fed's actions were likely to be ineffective: long-term interest rates, they suggested, mainly reflected expectations about future short-term rates, and even large purchases of long-term bonds by the Fed would have little impact.

*"I'll pause for a moment so you can let this information sink in."*

Many of those calling on the Fed for even more active policy advocated an official rise in the Fed's inflation target. Recall from Chapters 8 and 10 the distinction between the nominal interest rate, which is the number normally cited, and the *real* interest rate—the nominal rate minus expected inflation—which is what should matter for investment decisions. Advocates of a higher inflation target argued that by promising to raise prices over, say, the next 10 years by an annual average rate of 3% or 4%, the Fed could push the real interest rate down even though the nominal rate was up against the zero lower bound.

Such proposals, however, led to fierce disputes. Some economists pointed out that the Fed had fought hard to drive inflation expectations down and argued that changing course would undermine hard-won credibility. Others argued that given the enormous economic and human damage being done by high unemployment, it was time for extraordinary measures, and inflation-fighting could no longer be given first priority.

At the time of writing, these disputes were still raging, and it seemed unlikely that a new consensus about macroeconomic policy would emerge any time soon.

## ECONOMICS ▶ IN ACTION

### AN IRISH ROLE MODEL?

Over the course of 2010 and 2011 a fierce debate raged, among both economists and policy makers, about whether countries suffering large budget deficits should move quickly to reduce those deficits if they were also suffering from high unemployment. Many economists argued that spending cuts and/or tax increases should be delayed until economies had recovered. As we explained in the text, however, others argued that fast action on deficits would actually help the economy even in the short run, by improving confidence—a claim that came to be known as "expansionary austerity."

How could this dispute be settled? Researchers turned their attention to historical episodes, in particular to cases in which nations had managed to combine sharp reductions in budget deficits with strong economic growth. One case in particular became a major intellectual battleground: Ireland in the second half of the 1980s.

Panel (a) of Figure 18-7 shows why Ireland's experience drew attention. It compares Ireland's cyclically adjusted budget deficit as a percentage of GDP with

**FIGURE** **18-7** Economic Indicators for Ireland

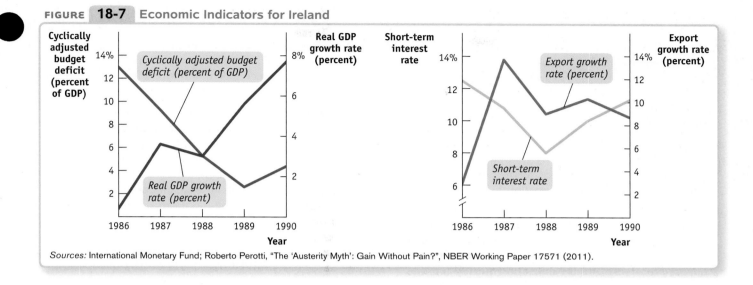

*Sources:* International Monetary Fund; Roberto Perotti, "The 'Austerity Myth': Gain Without Pain?", NBER Working Paper 17571 (2011).

its growth rate. Between 1986 and 1989 Ireland drastically reduced its underlying deficits with a combination of spending cuts and tax hikes, and the Irish economy's growth sharply accelerated. A number of observers suggested that nations facing large deficits in the aftermath of the 2008 financial crisis should seek to emulate that experience.

A closer look, however, suggested that Ireland's situation in the 1980s was very different from that facing Western economies in 2010 and 2011. Panel (b) of Figure 18-7 shows two other economic indicators for Ireland from 1986 to 1990: short-term interest rates and export growth. Ireland entered into fiscal austerity with high interest rates, which fell sharply between 1986 and 1988 as investors gained more confidence in its solvency (although they rose thereafter). At the same time, Ireland had a major export boom, partly due to rapid economic growth in neighboring Britain. Both factors helped offset any contractionary effects from lower spending and higher taxes.

The point was that these "cushioning" factors would not be available if, say, the United States were to slash spending. Short-term interest rates were already near zero and couldn't fall further, and America had no booming neighbors to export to.

By the end of 2011 careful study of the historical record had convinced most, though not all, economists studying the issue that hopes for expansionary austerity were probably misplaced. However, the debate about what the United States and other troubled economies should actually do raged on.

### CHECK YOUR UNDERSTANDING    18-5

**1.** Why did the Great Recession lead to the decline of the Great Moderation consensus? Given events, why is it predictable that a new consensus has not emerged?

Solutions appear at back of book.

**▼ Quick Review**

● The **Great Moderation,** the period of relative economic calm from 1985 to 2007, produced the **Great Moderation consensus.**

● According to the Great Moderation consensus: monetary policy should be the main stabilization tool; to avoid a political business cycle, the central bank should be independent and fiscal policy should not be used, except possibly in exceptional circumstances such as a liquidity trap; and the natural rate of unemployment limits how much policy activism can reduce the unemployment rate.

● The Great Moderation consensus was severely challenged by the Great Recession. Active fiscal policy was revived given the ineffectiveness of monetary policy in the midst of a liquidity trap. Fiercely debated, fiscal stimulus in the United States failed to deliver a significant fall in unemployment. Critics cited this as evidence that fiscal policy doesn't work, while supporters countered that the size of the stimulus was too small. However, crowding out failed to materialize as critics had warned that it would.

● Monetary policy was also deeply controversial in the wake of the Great Recession, as the Fed pursued "quantitative easing" and other unconventional policies. Critics claimed the Fed was doing too much and too little, while some advocated the adoption of a higher inflation target to push the real interest rate down.

## SUMMARY

1. Classical macroeconomics asserted that monetary policy affected only the aggregate price level, not aggregate output, and that the short run was unimportant. By the 1930s, measurement of business cycles was a well-established subject, but there was no widely accepted theory of business cycles.

2. Keynesian economics attributed the business cycle to shifts of the aggregate demand curve, often the result of changes in business confidence. Keynesian economics also offered a rationale for **macroeconomic policy activism.**

3. In the decades that followed Keynes's work, economists came to agree that monetary policy as well as fiscal policy is effective under certain conditions. **Monetarism,** a doctrine that called for a **monetary policy rule** as opposed to **discretionary monetary policy** and that argued—based on a belief that the **velocity of money** was stable—that GDP would grow steadily if the money supply grew steadily, was influential for a time but was eventually rejected by many macroeconomists.

4. The **natural rate hypothesis** became almost universally accepted, limiting the role of macroeconomic policy to stabilizing the economy rather than seeking a permanently lower unemployment rate. Fears of a **political business cycle** led to a consensus that monetary policy should be insulated from politics.

5. **Rational expectations** claims that individuals and firms make decisions using all available information. According to the **rational expectations model** of the economy, only unexpected changes in monetary policy affect aggregate output and employment; expected changes merely alter the price level. **Real business cycle theory** claims that changes in the rate of growth of total factor productivity are the main cause of business cycles. Both of these versions of **new classical macroeconomics** received wide attention and respect, but policy makers and many economists haven't accepted the conclusion that monetary and fiscal policy are ineffective in changing aggregate output.

6. **New Keynesian economics** argues that market imperfections can lead to price stickiness, so that changes in aggregate demand have effects on aggregate output after all.

7. The **Great Moderation** from 1985 to 2007 generated the **Great Moderation consensus:** belief in monetary policy as the main tool of stabilization; skepticism toward use of fiscal policy, except possibly in exceptional circumstances such as a liquidity trap; and acknowledgement of the policy constraints imposed by the natural rate of unemployment and the political business cycle. But the Great Moderation consensus was challenged by the post-2008 crisis events, as monetary policy lost its effectiveness in the midst of a liquidity trap. As a result, many advocated the use of fiscal policy to address the deep recession.

8. In 2009, a number of governments, including the United States, used fiscal stimulus to support their deeply depressed economies in the face of a liquidity trap. The use of fiscal policy remained highly controversial. In the United States, it failed to significantly reduce unemployment, with critics citing that as proof of its general ineffectiveness, while supporters argued the size of the stimulus was too small. Yet the crowding out predicted by its critics failed to occur.

9. Monetary policy was also hotly debated in the wake of the Great Recession, as the Fed pursued "quantitative easing" and other unconventional monetary policies to address the liquidity trap. Critics claimed the Fed was doing too much and would sacrifice its hard-won credibility as an inflation fighter. Others countered that the Fed was doing too little, yet others claimed the Fed's actions would have little impact. Some proposed the Fed adopt a higher inflation target to push the real interest rate down.

## KEY TERMS

Keynesian economics, p. 529
Macroeconomic policy activism, p. 530
Monetarism, p. 532
Discretionary monetary policy, p. 532
Monetary policy rule, p. 533

Velocity of money, p. 533
Natural rate hypothesis, p. 535
Political business cycle, p. 535
New classical macroeconomics, p. 537
Rational expectations, p. 537

Rational expectations model, p. 537
New Keynesian economics, p. 537
Real business cycle theory, p. 538
Great Moderation, p. 540
Great Moderation consensus, p. 540

## PROBLEMS

1. Since the crash of its stock market in 1989, the Japanese economy has seen little economic growth and some deflation. The accompanying table from the Organization for Economic Cooperation and Development (OECD) shows some key macroeconomic data for Japan for 1991 (a "normal" year) and 1995–2003.

   **a.** From the data, determine the type of policies Japan's policy makers undertook at that time to promote growth.

   **b.** We can safely consider a short-term interest rate that is less than 0.1% to effectively be a 0% interest rate. What is this situation called? What does it imply about the effectiveness of monetary policy? Of fiscal policy?

| Year | Real GDP annual growth rate | Short-term interest rate | Government debt (percent of GDP) | Government budget deficit (percent of GDP) |
|------|------|------|------|------|
| 1991 | 3.4% | 7.38% | 64.8% | −1.81% |
| 1995 | 1.9 | 1.23 | 87.1 | 4.71 |
| 1996 | 3.4 | 0.59 | 93.9 | 5.07 |
| 1997 | 1.9 | 0.60 | 100.3 | 3.79 |
| 1998 | −1.1 | 0.72 | 112.2 | 5.51 |
| 1999 | 0.1 | 0.25 | 125.7 | 7.23 |
| 2000 | 2.8 | 0.25 | 134.1 | 7.48 |
| 2001 | 0.4 | 0.12 | 142.3 | 6.13 |
| 2002 | −0.3 | 0.06 | 149.3 | 7.88 |
| 2003 | 2.5 | 0.04 | 157.5 | 7.67 |

2. The National Bureau of Economic Research (NBER) maintains the official chronology of past U.S. business cycles. Go to its website at http://www.nber.org/cycles/cyclesmain.html to answer the following questions.

   **a.** How many business cycles have occurred since the end of World War II in 1945?

   **b.** What was the average duration of a business cycle when measured from the end of one expansion (its peak) to the end of the next? That is, what was the average duration of a business cycle in the period from 1945 to 2001?

   **c.** When and what was the last announcement by the NBER's Business Cycle Dating Committee, and what was it?

3. The fall of America's military rival, the Soviet Union, in 1989 allowed the United States to significantly reduce its defense spending in subsequent years. Using the data in the following table from the Economic Report of the President, replicate Figure 18-3 for the 1990–2000 period. Given the strong economic growth in the United States during the late 1990s, why would a Keynesian see the reduction in defense spending during the 1990s as a good thing?

| Year | Budget deficit (percent of GDP) | Unemployment rate |
|------|------|------|
| 1990 | 3.9% | 5.6% |
| 1991 | 4.5 | 6.8 |
| 1992 | 4.7 | 7.5 |
| 1993 | 3.9 | 6.9 |
| 1994 | 2.9 | 6.1 |
| 1995 | 2.2 | 5.6 |
| 1996 | 1.4 | 5.4 |
| 1997 | 0.3 | 4.9 |
| 1998 | −0.8 | 4.5 |
| 1999 | −1.4 | 4.2 |
| 2000 | −2.4 | 4.0 |

4. In the modern world, central banks are free to increase or reduce the money supply as they see fit. However, some people harken back to the "good old days" of the gold standard. Under the gold standard, the money supply could expand only when the amount of available gold increased.

   **a.** Under the gold standard, if the velocity of money were stable when the economy was expanding, what would have had to happen to keep prices stable?

   **b.** Why would modern macroeconomists consider the gold standard a bad idea?

5. Monetarists believed for a period of time that the velocity of money was stable within a country. However, with financial innovation, the velocity began shifting around erratically after 1980. As would be expected, the velocity of money is different across countries depending upon the sophistication of their financial systems—velocity of money tends to be higher in countries with developed financial systems. The accompanying table provides money supply and GDP information in 2005 for six countries.

| Country | National currency | M1 (billions in national currency) | Nominal GDP (billions in national currency) |
|------|------|------|------|
| Egypt | Egyptian pounds | 101 | 539 |
| South Korea | Korean won | 77,274 | 806,622 |
| Thailand | Thai baht | 863 | 7,103 |
| United States | U.S. dollars | 1,369 | 12,456 |
| Kenya | Kenyan pounds | 231 | 1,415 |
| India | Indian rupees | 7,213 | 35,314 |

*Source:* Datastream.

**a.** Calculate the velocity of money for each of the countries. The accompanying table shows GDP per capita for each of these countries in 2005 in U.S. dollars.

| Country | Nominal GDP per capita (U.S. dollars) |
|---|---|
| Egypt | $1,270 |
| South Korea | 16,444 |
| Thailand | 2,707 |
| United States | 41,886 |
| Kenya | 572 |
| India | 710 |

*Source:* IMF.

**b.** Rank the countries in descending order of per capita income and velocity of money. Do wealthy countries or poor countries tend to "turn over" their money more times per year? Would you expect wealthy countries to have more sophisticated financial systems?

**6.** The chapter explains that Kenneth Rogoff proclaimed Richard Nixon "the all-time hero of political business cycles." Using the following table of data from the *Economic Report of the President*, explain why Nixon may have earned that title. (*Note:* Nixon entered office in January 1969 and was reelected in November 1972. He resigned in August 1974.)

| Year | Government receipts (billions of dollars) | Government spending (billions of dollars) | Government budget balance (billions of dollars) | M1 growth | M2 growth | 3-month Treasury bill rate |
|---|---|---|---|---|---|---|
| 1969 | $186.9 | $183.6 | $3.2 | 3.3% | 3.7% | 6.68% |
| 1970 | 192.8 | 195.6 | −2.8 | 5.1 | 6.6 | 6.46 |
| 1971 | 187.1 | 210.2 | −23.0 | 6.5 | 13.4 | 4.35 |
| 1972 | 207.3 | 230.7 | −23.4 | 9.2 | 13.0 | 4.07 |
| 1973 | 230.8 | 245.7 | −14.9 | 5.5 | 6.6 | 7.04 |

**7.** The economy of Albernia is facing a recessionary gap, and the leader of that nation calls together five of its best economists representing the classical, Keynesian, monetarist, real business cycle, and Great Moderation consensus views of the macroeconomy. Explain what policies each economist would recommend and why.

**8.** Which of the following policy recommendations are consistent with the classical, Keynesian, monetarist, and/or Great Moderation consensus views of the macroeconomy?

**a.** Since the long-run growth of GDP is 2%, the money supply should grow at 2%.

**b.** Decrease government spending in order to decrease inflationary pressure.

**c.** Increase the money supply in order to alleviate a recessionary gap.

**d.** Always maintain a balanced budget.

**e.** Decrease the budget deficit as a percent of GDP when facing a recessionary gap.

**9.** Using a graph like Figure 18-4, show how a monetarist can argue that a contractionary fiscal policy need not lead to a fall in real GDP given a fixed money supply. Explain.

# CHAPTER 19

# Open-Economy Macroeconomics

## SWITZERLAND DOESN'T WANT YOUR MONEY

In 2011, the Swiss National Bank undertook extraordinary actions to protect itself from the consequences of being an open economy.

**WHAT YOU WILL LEARN IN THIS CHAPTER**

❭ The meaning of the **balance of payments accounts**

❭ The determinants of international capital flows

❭ The role of the **foreign exchange market** and the **exchange rate**

❭ The importance of **real exchange rates** and their role in the **current account**

❭ Considerations that lead countries to choose different **exchange rate regimes,** such as **fixed exchange rates** and **floating exchange rates**

❭ Why open-economy considerations affect macroeconomic policy under floating exchange rates

**P**ARKING YOUR MONEY IN A Swiss bank is no way to get rich, given the low interest rates Swiss bankers offer. Recently, in fact, Swiss banks have paid negative interest on deposits, charging customers for the service of keeping their funds.

But for generations, Swiss bank accounts have been seen as a way to *stay* rich, a safe place to store your wealth. In the troubled years that followed the 2008 financial crisis, the Swiss reputation for safety became especially important. European investors, in particular, poured money into Switzerland.

And the Swiss hated it—the result of the inflow of foreign funds was a surge in the value of the Swiss franc that wreaked havoc with Swiss exports.

At the beginning of 2008, one Swiss franc traded for about 0.6 euro. By mid-2011, the franc was trading for around 0.9 euro. That meant that Swiss exports, other things equal, had seen a 50% rise in their labor costs relative to competitors elsewhere in Europe. Thanks

to its reputation for quality, Switzerland has been remarkably successful over the years at selling goods to the world market, despite high labor costs. Nobody expects to get a bargain on Swiss watches or Swiss chocolate. But this was pushing matters to the breaking point.

So what was to be done? Starting in early 2009, the Swiss National Bank, Switzerland's equivalent of the Federal Reserve, began selling francs on the foreign exchange market in an attempt to hold down the franc's value. In return for these francs, it received other currencies, mainly dollars and euros, which it added to its reserves. We're talking about a *lot* of sales: over a period of 2½ years, the bank added $180 billion to its foreign exchange reserves, which was about a third of Switzerland's GDP—the equivalent for the United States of selling $5 trillion dollars.

Yet even that wasn't enough to stop the franc's rise. In September 2011, as the franc seemed headed for a value of 1 euro or more, the Swiss National Bank announced

that it would do whatever it took—sell an unlimited amount of francs—to keep the franc below a maximum of 0.833 euro per franc (that is, 1.2 francs per euro, which was the way the target was stated). That announcement finally seemed to stop the franc's rise, at least at first.

What the extraordinary efforts of the Swiss National Bank illustrated was the importance of a dimension of macroeconomics that we haven't emphasized so far—the fact that modern national economies are *open economies* that trade goods, services, and assets with the rest of the world. Open-economy macroeconomics is a branch of macroeconomics that deals with the relationships between national economies. In this chapter we'll learn about some of the key issues in open-economy macroeconomics: the determinants of a country's *balance of payments,* the factors affecting *exchange rates,* the different forms of *exchange rate policy* adopted by various countries, and the relationship between exchange rates and macroeconomic policy. ■

# Capital Flows and the Balance of Payments

In 2010 people living in the United States sold about $3.5 trillion worth of stuff to people living in other countries and bought about $3.5 trillion worth of stuff in return. What kind of stuff? All kinds. Residents of the United States (including firms operating in the United States) sold airplanes, bonds, wheat, and many other items to residents of other countries. Residents of the United States bought cars, stocks, oil, and many other items from residents of other countries.

How can we keep track of these transactions? In Chapter 7 we learned that economists keep track of the domestic economy using the national income and product accounts. Economists keep track of international transactions using a different but related set of numbers, the *balance of payments accounts*.

## Balance of Payments Accounts

A country's **balance of payments accounts** are a summary of the country's transactions with other countries.

To understand the basic idea behind the balance of payments accounts, let's consider a small-scale example: not a country, but a family farm. Let's say that we know the following about how last year went financially for the Costas, who own a small artichoke farm in California:

- They made $100,000 by selling artichokes.
- They spent $70,000 on running the farm, including purchases of new farm machinery, and another $40,000 buying food, paying utility bills, replacing their worn-out car, and so on.
- They received $500 in interest on their bank account but paid $10,000 in interest on their mortgage.
- They took out a new $25,000 loan to help pay for farm improvements but didn't use all the money immediately. So they put the extra in the bank.

How could we summarize the Costas' year? One way would be with a table like Table 19-1, which shows sources of cash coming in and money going out, characterized under a few broad headings. The first row of Table 19-1 shows sales and purchases of goods and services: sales of artichokes; purchases of groceries, heating oil, that new car, and so on. The second row shows interest payments: the interest the Costas received from their bank account and the interest they paid on their mortgage. The third row shows cash coming in from new borrowing versus money deposited in the bank.

**TABLE 19-1** The Costas' Financial Year

| | Sources of cash | Uses of cash | Net |
|---|---|---|---|
| **Purchases or sales of goods and services** | Artichoke sales: $100,000 | Farm operation and living expenses: $110,000 | –$10,000 |
| **Interest payments** | Interest received on bank account: $500 | Interest paid on mortgage: $10,000 | –$9,500 |
| **Loans and deposits** | Funds received from new loan: $25,000 | Funds deposited in bank: $5,500 | +$19,500 |
| **Total** | **$125,500** | **$125,500** | **$0** |

In each row we show the net inflow of cash from that type of transaction. So the net in the first row is –$10,000, because the Costas spent $10,000 more than they earned. The net in the second row is –$9,500, the difference between the interest the Costas received on their bank account and the interest they paid on the mortgage. The net in the third row is $19,500: the Costas brought in $25,000 with their new loan but put only $5,500 of that sum in the bank.

The last row shows the sum of cash coming in from all sources and the sum of all cash used. These sums are equal, by definition: every dollar has a source, and every dollar received gets used somewhere. (What if the Costas hid money under the mattress? Then that would be counted as another "use" of cash.)

A country's balance of payments accounts summarize its transactions with the world with a table basically similar to the way we just summarized the Costas' financial year.

Table 19-2 shows a simplified version of the U.S. balance of payments accounts for 2010. Where the Costa family's accounts show sources and uses of cash, the balance of payments accounts show payments from foreigners—in effect, sources of cash for the United States as a whole—and payments to foreigners.

Row 1 of Table 19-2 shows payments that arise from sales and purchases of goods and services. For example, the value of U.S. wheat exports and the fees foreigners pay to U.S. consulting companies appear in the second column; the value of U.S. oil imports and the fees American companies pay to Indian call centers—the people who often answer your 1-800 calls—appear in the third column.

Row 2 shows *factor income*—the income countries pay for the use of factors of production owned by residents of other countries. Mostly this means investment income: interest paid on loans from overseas, the profits of foreign-owned corporations, and so on. For example, the profits earned by Disneyland Paris, which is owned by the U.S.-based Walt Disney Company, appear in the second column; the profits earned by the U.S. operations of Japanese auto companies appear in the third column. This category also includes some labor income. For example, the wages of an American engineer who works temporarily on a construction site in Dubai are counted in the second column.

Row 3 shows *international transfers*—funds sent by residents of one country to residents of another. The main element here is the remittances that immigrants, such as the millions of Mexican-born workers employed in the United States, send to their families in their country of origin. Notice that Table 19-2 only shows the net value of transfers. That's because the U.S. government only provides an estimate of the net, not a breakdown between payments to foreigners and payments from foreigners.

The next two rows of Table 19-2 show payments resulting from sales and purchases of assets, broken down by who is doing the buying and selling. Row 4 shows transactions that involve governments or government agencies, mainly central banks. As we'll learn later, in 2010 most of the U.S. sales in this category involved the accumulation of *foreign exchange reserves* by the central bank of China and oil-exporting countries. Row 5 shows private sales and purchases of assets. For example, the 2010 purchase of Ford Motor Company's Volvo brand by the Chinese company Greely Automobile would show up in the second column of row 5; purchases of European stocks by U.S. investors show up in the third column.

In laying out Table 19-2, we have separated rows 1, 2, and 3 into one group and rows 4 and 5 into another. This reflects a fundamental difference in how these two groups of transactions affect the future.

TABLE **19-2**  The U.S. Balance of Payments in 2010 (billions of dollars)

| | | Payments from foreigners | Payments to foreigners | Net |
|---|---|---|---|---|
| 1 | Sales and purchases of goods and services | $1,838 | $2,338 | –$500 |
| 2 | Factor income | 663 | 498 | 165 |
| 3 | Transfers | — | — | –136 |
| | Current account (1 + 2 + 3) | | | –471 |
| 4 | Official asset sales and purchases | 350 | –6 | 356 |
| 5 | Private sales and purchases of assets | 910 | 1,011 | –101 |
| | Financial account (4 + 5) | | | 255 |
| | Total | — | — | –216 |

*Source:* Bureau of Economic Analysis.

A country's **balance of payments on current account,** or **current account,** is its balance of payments on goods and services plus net international transfer payments and factor income.

A country's **balance of payments on goods and services** is the difference between its exports and its imports during a given period.

The **merchandise trade balance,** or **trade balance,** is the difference between a country's exports and imports of goods.

A country's **balance of payments on financial account,** or simply its **financial account,** is the difference between its sales of assets to foreigners and its purchases of assets from foreigners during a given period.

When a U.S. resident sells a good such as wheat to a foreigner, that's the end of the transaction. But a financial asset, such as a bond, is different. Remember, a bond is a promise to pay interest and principal in the future. So when a U.S. resident sells a bond to a foreigner, that sale creates a liability: the U.S. resident will have to pay interest and repay principal in the future. The balance of payments accounts distinguish between transactions that don't create liabilities and those that do.

Transactions that don't create liabilities are considered part of the **balance of payments on current account,** often referred to simply as the **current account:** the balance of payments on goods and services plus net international transfer payments and factor income. The balance of row 1 of Table 19-2, –$500 billion, corresponds to the most important part of the current account: the **balance of payments on goods and services,** the difference between the value of exports and the value of imports during a given period.

By the way, if you read news reports on the economy, you may well see references to another measure, the **merchandise trade balance,** sometimes referred to as the **trade balance** for short. This is the difference between a country's exports and imports of goods alone—not including services. Economists sometimes focus on the merchandise trade balance, even though it's an incomplete measure, because data on international trade in services aren't as accurate as data on trade in physical goods, and they are also slower to arrive.

The current account, as we've just learned, consists of international transactions that don't create liabilities. Transactions that involve the sale or purchase of assets, and therefore do create future liabilities, are considered part of the **balance of payments on financial account,** or the **financial account** for short. (Until a few years ago, economists often referred to the financial account as the *capital account*. We'll use the modern term, but you may run across the older term.)

So how does it all add up? The shaded rows of Table 19-2 show the bottom lines: the overall U.S. current account and financial account for 2010. As you can see, in 2010 the United States ran a current account deficit: the amount it paid to foreigners for goods, services, factors, and transfers was more than the amount it received. Simultaneously, it ran a financial account surplus: the value of the assets it sold to foreigners was more than the value of the assets it bought from foreigners.

In the 2010 official data, the U.S. current account deficit and financial account surplus didn't offset each other: the financial account surplus in 2010 was $216 billion smaller than the current account deficit. But that's just a statistical error, reflecting the imperfection of official data. (That $216 billion discrepancy probably reflected foreign purchases of U.S. assets that official data somehow missed.) In fact, it's a basic rule of balance of payments accounting that the current account and the financial account must sum to zero:

**(19-1)** Current account ($CA$) + Financial account ($FA$) = 0

or

$$CA = -FA$$

Why must Equation 19-1 be true? We already saw the fundamental explanation in Table 19-1, which showed the accounts of the Costa family: in total, the sources of cash must equal the uses of cash. The same applies to balance of payments accounts. Figure 19-1, a variant on the circular-flow diagram we have found useful in discussing domestic macroeconomics, may help you visualize how this adding up works. Instead of showing the flow of money

FIGURE    **19-1**    The Balance of Payments

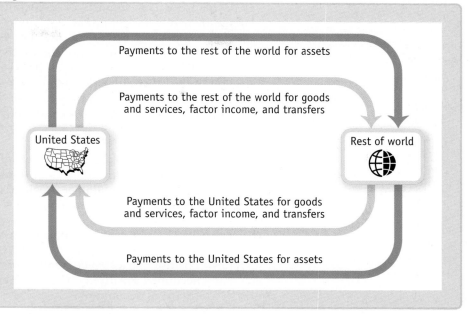

The green arrows represent payments that are counted in the current account. The red arrows represent payments that are counted in the financial account. Because the total flow into the United States must equal the total flow out of the United States, the sum of the current account plus the financial account is zero.

Payments to the rest of the world for assets

Payments to the rest of the world for goods and services, factor income, and transfers

United States

Rest of world

Payments to the United States for goods and services, factor income, and transfers

Payments to the United States for assets

*within* a national economy, Figure 19-1 shows the flow of money *between* national economies.

Money flows into the United States from the rest of the world as payment for U.S. exports of goods and services, as payment for the use of U.S.-owned factors of production, and as transfer payments. These flows (indicated by the lower green arrow) are the positive components of the U.S. current account. Money also flows into the United States from foreigners who purchase U.S. assets (as shown by the lower yellow arrow)—the positive component of the U.S. financial account.

## FOR INQUIRING MINDS

### GDP, GNP, AND THE CURRENT ACCOUNT

When we discussed national income accounting in Chapter 7, we derived the basic equation relating GDP to the components of spending:

$$Y = C + I + G + X - IM$$

where $X$ and $IM$ are exports and imports, respectively, of goods and services. But as we've learned, the balance of payments on goods and services is only one component of the current account balance. Why doesn't the national income equation use the current account as a whole?

The answer is that gross domestic product, $Y$, is the value of goods and services produced domestically. So

it doesn't include international factor income and international transfers, two sources of income that are included in the calculation of the current account balance. The profits of Ford Motors U.K. aren't included in America's GDP, and the funds Latin American immigrants send home to their families aren't subtracted from GDP.

Shouldn't we have a broader measure that does include these sources of income? Actually, gross *national* product—GNP—does include international factor income. Estimates of U.S. GNP differ slightly from estimates of GDP because GNP adds in items such as the earnings of U.S. companies

abroad and subtracts items such as the interest payments on bonds owned by residents of China and Japan. There isn't, however, any regularly calculated measure that includes transfer payments.

Why do economists use GDP rather than a broader measure? Two reasons. First, the original purpose of the national accounts was to track production rather than income. Second, data on international factor income and transfer payments are generally considered somewhat unreliable. So if you're trying to keep track of movements in the economy, it makes sense to focus on GDP, which doesn't rely on these unreliable data.

At the same time, money flows from the United States to the rest of the world as payment for U.S. imports of goods and services, as payment for the use of foreign-owned factors of production, and as transfer payments. These flows, indicated by the upper green arrow, are the negative components of the U.S. current account. Money also flows from the United States to purchase foreign assets, as shown by the upper yellow arrow—the negative component of the U.S. financial account. As in all circular-flow diagrams, the flow into a box and the flow out of a box are equal. This means that the sum of the red and green arrows going into the United States is equal to the sum of the red and green arrows going out of the United States. That is,

**(19-2)** Positive entries on current account (lower green arrow) + Positive entries on financial account (lower red arrow) = Negative entries on current account (upper green arrow) + Negative entries on financial account (upper red arrow)

Equation 19-2 can be rearranged as follows:

**(19-3)** Positive entries on current account – Negative entries on current account + Positive entries on financial account – Negative entries on financial account = 0

Equation 19-3 is equivalent to Equation 19-1: the current account plus the financial account—both equal to positive entries minus negative entries—is equal to zero.

But what determines the current account and the financial account?

## Modeling the Financial Account

A country's financial account measures its net sales of assets to foreigners. There is, however, another way to think about the financial account: it's a measure of *capital inflows,* of foreign savings that are available to finance domestic investment spending.

What determines these capital inflows?

Part of our explanation will have to wait for a little while because some international capital flows are carried out by governments and central banks, which sometimes act very differently from private investors. But we can gain insight into the motivations for capital flows that are the result of private decisions by using the *loanable funds model* we developed in Chapter 10. In using this model, we make two important simplifications:

- We simplify the reality of international capital flows by assuming that all flows are in the form of loans. In reality, capital flows take many forms, including purchases of shares of stock in foreign companies and foreign real estate as well as *direct foreign investment,* in which companies build factories or acquire other productive assets abroad.

- We also ignore the effects of expected changes in *exchange rates,* the relative values of different national currencies. We analyze the determination of exchange rates later in the chapter.

## GLOBAL COMPARISON  BIG SURPLUSES

As we've seen, the United States generally runs a large deficit in its current account. In fact, America leads the world in its current account deficit; other countries run bigger deficits as a share of GDP, but they have much smaller economies, so the U.S. deficit is much bigger in absolute terms.

For the world as a whole, however, deficits on the part of some countries must be matched with surpluses on the part of other countries. So who are the surplus nations offsetting U.S. deficits, and what if anything do they have in common?

The accompanying figure shows the average current account surplus of the six countries that ran the largest surpluses over the decade from 2001 to 2010. You may not be surprised to learn that China tops the list. As we explain later in this chapter, China's surplus is largely due to its policy of keeping its currency weak relative to other currencies. But what about the others?

Japan and Germany run current account surpluses for more or less the same reasons: both are rich nations with high savings rates, giving them a lot of money to invest. Since some of that money goes abroad, the result is that they run deficits on the financial account and surpluses on current account.

The other three countries are all major oil exporters. (You may not think of Russia or Norway as "petro-economies," but Russia derives about two-thirds of its export revenue from oil, and Norway owns huge oil fields in the North Sea.) These countries are all deliberately building up assets abroad to help them sustain their spending when the oil runs out.

All in all, the surplus countries are a diverse group. If your picture of the world is simply one of American deficits versus Chinese surpluses, you're missing a large part of the story.

**Average current account balance (billions of 2010 dollars)**

| Country | Balance |
|---|---|
| China | $210 |
| Japan | $148 |
| Germany | $143 |
| Russia | $105 |
| Saudi Arabia | $70 |
| Norway | $53 |

*Source:* International Monetary Fund.

---

Figure 19-2 recaps the loanable funds model for a closed economy. Equilibrium corresponds to point $E$, at an interest rate of 4%, where the supply of loanable funds curve, $S$, intersects the demand for loanable funds curve, $D$. But if international capital flows are possible, this diagram changes and $E$ may no longer be the equilibrium. We can analyze the causes and effects of international capital flows using Figure 19-3, which places the loanable funds market diagrams for two countries side by side.

Figure 19-3 illustrates a world consisting of only two countries, the United States and Britain. Panel (a) shows the loanable funds market in the United States, where the equilibrium in the absence of international capital flows is at point $E_{US}$ with an interest rate of 6%. Panel (b) shows the loanable funds market in Britain, where the equilibrium in the absence of international capital flows is at point $E_B$ with an interest rate of 2%.

Will the actual interest rate in the United States remain at 6% and that in Britain at 2%? Not if it is easy for British residents to make loans to Americans. In that case, British lenders, attracted by high American interest rates, will send some of their loanable funds to the United States. This capital inflow will increase the quantity of loanable funds supplied to American borrowers, pushing the U.S. interest rate down. At the same time, it will reduce the quantity of loanable funds supplied to British borrowers, pushing the British interest rate up. So international capital flows will narrow the gap between U.S. and British interest rates.

FIGURE   **19-2**   The Loanable Funds Model Revisited

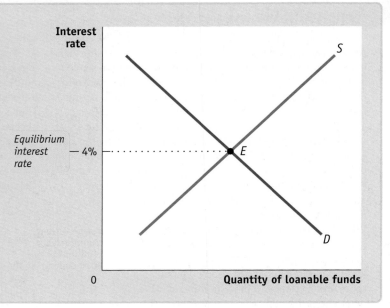

According to the loanable funds model of the interest rate, the equilibrium interest rate is determined by the intersection of the supply of loanable funds curve, *S*, and the demand for loanable funds curve, *D*. At point *E*, the equilibrium interest rate is 4%.

Let's further suppose that British lenders regard a loan to an American as being just as good as a loan to one of their own compatriots, and American borrowers regard a debt to a British lender as no more costly than a debt to an American lender. In that case, the flow of funds from Britain to the United States will continue until the gap between their interest rates is eliminated. In other words, when residents of the two countries believe that a foreign asset is as good as a domestic one and that a foreign liability is as good as a domestic one, then international capital flows will equalize the interest rates in the two countries.

FIGURE   **19-3**   Loanable Funds Markets in a Two-Country World

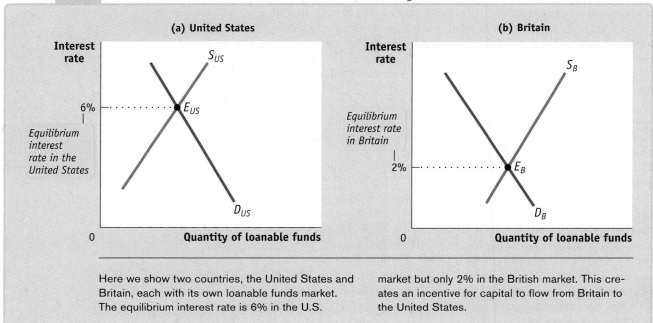

Here we show two countries, the United States and Britain, each with its own loanable funds market. The equilibrium interest rate is 6% in the U.S. market but only 2% in the British market. This creates an incentive for capital to flow from Britain to the United States.

FIGURE  **19-4**  International Capital Flows in a Two-Country World

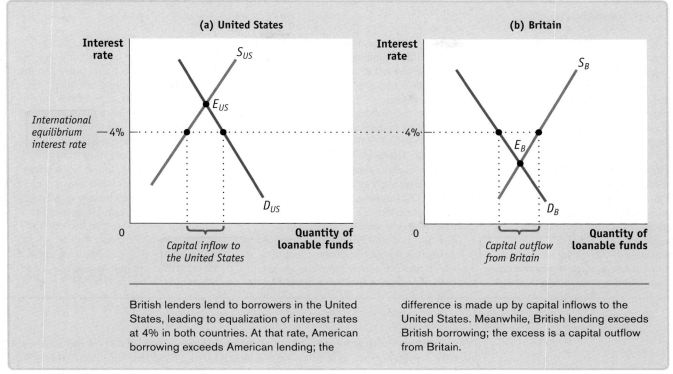

British lenders lend to borrowers in the United States, leading to equalization of interest rates at 4% in both countries. At that rate, American borrowing exceeds American lending; the

difference is made up by capital inflows to the United States. Meanwhile, British lending exceeds British borrowing; the excess is a capital outflow from Britain.

Figure 19-4 shows an international equilibrium in the loanable funds markets where the equilibrium interest rate is 4% in both the United States and Britain. At this interest rate, the quantity of loanable funds demanded by American borrowers exceeds the quantity of loanable funds supplied by American lenders. This gap is filled by "imported" funds—a capital inflow from Britain. At the same time, the quantity of loanable funds supplied by British lenders is greater than the quantity of loanable funds demanded by British borrowers. This excess is "exported" in the form of a capital outflow to the United States. And the two markets are in equilibrium at a common interest rate of 4%—at that interest rate, the total quantity of loans demanded by borrowers across the two markets is equal to the total quantity of loans supplied by lenders across the two markets.

In short, international flows of capital are like international flows of goods and services. Capital moves from places where it would be cheap in the absence of international capital flows to places where it would be expensive in the absence of such flows.

## Underlying Determinants of International Capital Flows

The open-economy version of the loanable funds model helps us understand international capital flows in terms of the supply and demand for funds. But what underlies differences across countries in the supply and demand for funds? Why, in the absence of international capital flows, would interest rates differ internationally, creating an incentive for international capital flows?

International differences in the demand for funds reflect underlying differences in investment opportunities. In particular, a country with a rapidly growing economy, other things equal, tends to offer more investment opportunities

## FOR INQUIRING MINDS

### A GLOBAL SAVINGS GLUT?

In the early years of the twenty-first century, the United States moved into massive deficit on current account, which meant that it became the recipient of huge capital inflows from the rest of the world (especially China, other Asian countries, and the Middle East). Why did that happen?

In an influential speech early in 2005, Ben Bernanke—who was at that time a governor of the Federal Reserve and who would soon become the Fed's chairman—offered a hypothesis: the United States wasn't responsible. The "principal causes of the U.S. current account deficit," he declared, lie "outside the country's borders." Specifically, he argued that special factors had cre-

ated a "global savings glut" that had pushed down interest rates worldwide and thereby led to an excess of investment spending over savings in the United States.

What caused this global savings glut? According to Bernanke, the main cause was the series of financial crises that began in Thailand in 1997; ricocheted across much of Asia; then hit Russia in 1998, Brazil in 1999, and Argentina in 2002. The ensuing fear and economic devastation led to a fall in investment spending and a rise in savings in a number of relatively poor countries. As a result, a number of these countries, which had previously been the recipients of capital inflows from advanced

countries like the United States, began experiencing large capital outflows. For the most part, the capital flowed to the United States, perhaps because "the depth and sophistication of the country's financial markets" made it an attractive destination.

When Bernanke gave his speech, it was viewed as reassuring: basically, he argued that the United States was responding in a sensible way to the availability of cheap money in world financial markets. Later, however, it would become clear that the cheap money from abroad helped fuel a housing bubble, which caused widespread financial and economic damage when it burst.

than a country with a slowly growing economy. So a rapidly growing economy typically—though not always—has a higher demand for capital and offers higher returns to investors than a slowly growing economy. As a result, capital tends to flow from slowly growing to rapidly growing economies.

The classic example, described in the upcoming Economics in Action, is the flow of capital from Britain to the United States, among other countries, between 1870 and 1914. During that era, the U.S. economy was growing rapidly as the population increased and spread westward and as the nation industrialized. This created a demand for investment spending on railroads, factories, and so on. Meanwhile, Britain had a much more slowly growing population, was already industrialized, and already had a railroad network covering the country. This left Britain with savings to spare, much of which were lent out to the United States and other New World economies.

International differences in the supply of funds reflect differences in savings across countries. These may be the result of differences in private savings rates, which vary widely among countries. For example, in 2010 gross private savings were 28.5% of Japan's GDP but only 19.2% of U.S. GDP. They may also reflect differences in savings by governments. In particular, government budget deficits, which reduce overall national savings, can lead to capital inflows.

### Two-Way Capital Flows

The loanable funds model helps us understand the direction of *net* capital flows—the excess of inflows into a country over outflows, or vice versa. The direction of net flows, other things equal, is determined by differences in interest rates between countries. As we saw in Table 19-2, however, *gross* flows take place in both directions: for example, the United States both sells assets to foreigners and buys assets from foreigners. Why does capital move in both directions?

The answer to this question is that in the real world, as opposed to the simple model we've just learned, there are other motives for international capital flows besides seeking a higher rate of interest.

Individual investors often seek to diversify against risk by buying stocks in a number of countries. Stocks in Europe may do well when stocks in the United States do badly, or vice versa, so investors in Europe try to reduce their risk by buying some U.S. stocks, as investors in the United States try to reduce their risk by buying some European stocks. The result is capital flows in both directions.

Meanwhile, corporations often engage in international investment as part of their business strategy—for example, auto companies may find that they can compete better in a national market if they assemble some of their cars locally. Such business investments can also lead to two-way capital flows, as, say, European car makers build plants in the United States even as U.S. computer companies open facilities in Europe.

Finally, some countries, including the United States, are international banking centers: people from all over the world put money in U.S. financial institutions, which then invest many of those funds overseas.

The result of these two-way flows is that modern economies are typically both debtors (countries that owe money to the rest of the world) and creditors (countries to which the rest of the world owes money). Due to years of both capital inflows and outflows, at the end of 2010, the United States had accumulated foreign assets worth $20.3 trillion, and foreigners had accumulated assets in the United States worth $22.8 trillion.

## ECONOMICS ➤ IN ACTION

### THE GOLDEN AGE OF CAPITAL FLOWS

Technology, it's often said, shrinks the world. Jet planes have put most of the world's cities within a few hours of one another; modern telecommunications transmit information instantly around the globe. So you might think that international capital flows must now be larger than ever.

But if capital flows are measured as a share of world savings and investment, that belief turns out not to be true. The golden age of capital flows actually preceded World War I—from 1870 to 1914.

These capital flows went mainly from European countries, especially Britain, to what were then known as "zones of recent settlement," countries that were attracting large numbers of European immigrants. Among the big recipients of capital inflows were Australia, Argentina, Canada, and the United States.

The large capital flows reflected differences in investment opportunities. Britain, a mature industrial economy with limited natural resources and a slowly growing population, offered relatively limited opportunities for new investment. The zones of recent settlement, with rapidly growing populations and abundant natural resources, offered investors a higher return and attracted capital inflows. Estimates suggest that over this period Britain sent about 40% of its savings abroad, largely to finance railroads and other large projects. No country has matched that record in modern times.

Why can't we match the capital flows of our great-great-grandfathers? Economists aren't completely sure, but they have pointed to two causes: migration restrictions and political risks.

During the golden age of capital flows, capital movements were complementary to population movements: the big recipients of capital from Europe were also places to which large numbers of Europeans were moving. These large-scale population movements were possible before World War I because there were few legal restrictions on immigration. In today's world, by contrast, migration is limited by extensive legal barriers, as anyone considering a move to the United States or Europe can tell you.

The other factor that has changed is political risk. Modern governments often limit foreign investment because they fear it will diminish their national autonomy. And due to political or security concerns, governments sometimes seize foreign property, a risk that deters investors from sending more than a relatively modest share of their wealth abroad. In the nineteenth century such actions were rare, partly because some major destinations of investment were still European colonies, partly because in those days governments had a habit of sending troops and gunboats to enforce the claims of their investors.

### CHECK YOUR UNDERSTANDING 19-1

1. Which of the balance of payments accounts do the following events affect?
    a. Boeing, a U.S.-based company, sells a newly built airplane to China.
    b. Chinese investors buy stock in Boeing from Americans.
    c. A Chinese company buys a used airplane from American Airlines and ships it to China.
    d. A Chinese investor who owns property in the United States buys a corporate jet, which he will keep in the United States so he can travel around America.

2. What effect do you think the collapse of the U.S. housing bubble and the ensuing recession had on international capital flows into the United States?

*Solutions appear at back of book.*

## The Role of the Exchange Rate

We've just seen how differences in the supply of loanable funds from savings and the demand for loanable funds for investment spending lead to international capital flows. We've also learned that a country's balance of payments on current account plus its balance of payments on financial account add to zero: a country that receives net capital inflows must run a matching current account deficit, and a country that generates net capital outflows must run a matching current account surplus.

The behavior of the financial account—reflecting inflows or outflows of capital—is best described by equilibrium in the international loanable funds market. At the same time, the balance of payments on goods and services, the main component of the current account, is determined by decisions in the international markets for goods and services. So given that the financial account reflects the movement of capital and the current account reflects the movement of goods and services, what ensures that the balance of payments really does balance? That is, what ensures that the two accounts actually offset each other?

Not surprisingly, a price is what makes these two accounts balance. Specifically, that price is the *exchange rate,* which is determined in the *foreign exchange market.*

### Understanding Exchange Rates

In general, goods, services, and assets produced in a country must be paid for in that country's currency. American products must be paid for in dollars; European products must be paid for in euros; Japanese products must be paid for in yen. Occasionally, sellers will accept payment in foreign currency, but they will then exchange that currency for domestic money.

Currencies are traded in the **foreign exchange market.**

The prices at which currencies trade are known as **exchange rates.**

When a currency becomes more valuable in terms of other currencies, it **appreciates.**

When a currency becomes less valuable in terms of other currencies, it **depreciates.**

International transactions, then, require a market—the **foreign exchange market**—in which currencies can be exchanged for each other. This market determines **exchange rates,** the prices at which currencies trade. (The foreign exchange market is, in fact, not located in any one geographic spot. Rather, it is a global electronic market that traders around the world use to buy and sell currencies.)

Table 19-3 shows exchange rates among the world's three most important currencies as of 5:55 P.M., EDT, on September 24, 2011. Each entry shows the price of the "row" currency in terms of the "column" currency. For example, at that time US$1 exchanged for €0.7412, so it took €0.7412 to buy US$1. Similarly, it took US$1.3492 to buy €1. These two numbers reflect the same rate of exchange between the euro and the U.S. dollar: 1/1.3492 = 0.7412.

There are two ways to write any given exchange rate. In this case, there were €0.7412 to US$1 and US$1.3492 to €1. Which is the correct way to write it? The answer is that there is no fixed rule. In most countries, people tend to express the exchange rate as the price of a dollar in domestic currency. However, this rule isn't universal, and the U.S. dollar–euro rate is commonly quoted both ways. The important thing is to be sure you know which one you are using! See the Pitfalls that follows.

When discussing movements in exchange rates, economists use specialized terms to avoid confusion. When a currency becomes more valuable in terms of other currencies, economists say that the currency **appreciates.** When a currency becomes less valuable in terms of other currencies, it **depreciates.** Suppose, for example, that the value of €1 went from $1 to $1.25, which means that the value of US$1 went from €1 to €0.80 (because 1/1.25 = 0.80). In this case, we would say that the euro appreciated and the U.S. dollar depreciated.

Movements in exchange rates, other things equal, affect the relative prices of goods, services, and assets in different countries. Suppose, for example, that the price of an American hotel room is US$100 and the price of a French hotel room is €100. If the exchange rate is €1 = US$1, these hotel rooms have the same price. If the exchange rate is €1.25 = US$1, the French hotel room is 20% cheaper than the American hotel room. If the exchange rate is €0.80 = US$1, the French hotel room is 25% more expensive than the American hotel room.

But what determines exchange rates? Supply and demand in the foreign exchange market.

## The Equilibrium Exchange Rate

Imagine, for the sake of simplicity, that there are only two currencies in the world: U.S. dollars and euros. Europeans wanting to purchase American goods, services, and assets come to the foreign exchange market, wanting to exchange euros for U.S. dollars. That is, Europeans demand U.S. dollars from the foreign exchange market and, correspondingly, supply euros to that market. Americans wanting to buy European goods, services, and assets come to the foreign exchange market to exchange U.S. dollars for euros. That is, Americans supply U.S. dollars to the foreign exchange market and, correspondingly, demand euros from that market. (International transfers and payments of factor income also enter into the foreign exchange market, but to make things simple we'll ignore these.)

Figure 19-5 shows how the foreign exchange market works. The quantity of dollars demanded and supplied at any given euro–U.S.

**TABLE 19-3 Exchange Rates, September 24, 2011, 5:55 P.M**

| | U.S. dollars | Yen | Euros |
|---|---|---|---|
| One U.S. dollar exchanged for | 1 | 76.6850 | 0.7412 |
| One yen exchanged for | 0.0130 | 1 | 0.0097 |
| One euro exchanged for | 1.3492 | 103.4596 | 1 |

⚠️ **PITFALLS**

**WHICH WAY IS UP?**
Suppose someone says, "The U.S. exchange rate is up." What does that person mean?

It isn't clear. Sometimes the exchange rate is measured as the price of a dollar in terms of foreign currency, sometimes as the price of foreign currency in terms of dollars. So the statement could mean either that the dollar appreciated or that it depreciated!

You have to be particularly careful when using published statistics. Most countries other than the United States state their exchange rates in terms of the price of a dollar in their domestic currency—for example, Mexican officials will say that the exchange rate is 10, meaning 10 pesos per dollar. But Britain, for historical reasons, usually states its exchange rate the other way. On September 24, 2011, US$1 was worth £0.64620, and £1 was worth US$1.5475. More often than not, this number is reported as an exchange rate of 1.5475. In fact, on occasion, professional economists and consultants embarrass themselves by getting the direction in which the pound is moving wrong!

By the way, Americans generally follow other countries' lead: we usually say that the exchange rate against Mexico is 10 pesos per dollar but that the exchange rate against Britain is 1.55 dollars per pound. But this rule isn't reliable; exchange rates against the euro are often stated both ways.

So it's always important to check before using exchange rate data: which way is the exchange rate being measured?

**FIGURE** **19-5** **The Foreign Exchange Market**

The foreign exchange market matches up the demand for a currency from foreigners who want to buy domestic goods, services, and assets with the supply of a currency from domestic residents who want to buy foreign goods, services, and assets. Here the equilibrium in the market for dollars is at point *E*, corresponding to an equilibrium exchange rate of €0.74 per US$1.

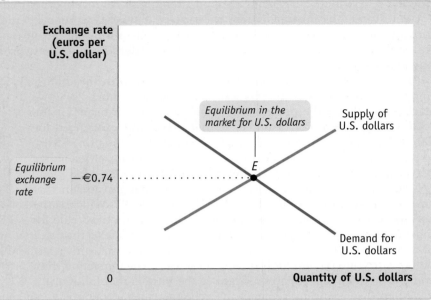

dollar exchange rate is shown on the horizontal axis, and the euro–U.S. dollar exchange rate is shown on the vertical axis. The exchange rate plays the same role as the price of a good or service in an ordinary supply and demand diagram.

The figure shows two curves, the demand curve for U.S. dollars and the supply curve for U.S. dollars. The key to understanding the slopes of these curves is that the level of the exchange rate affects exports and imports. When a country's currency appreciates (becomes more valuable), exports fall and imports rise. When a country's currency depreciates (becomes less valuable), exports rise and imports fall. To understand why the demand curve for U.S. dollars slopes downward, recall that the exchange rate, other things equal, determines the prices of American goods, services, and assets relative to those of European goods, services, and assets. If the U.S. dollar rises against the euro (the dollar appreciates), American products will become more expensive to Europeans relative to European products. So Europeans will buy less from the United States and will acquire fewer dollars in the foreign exchange market: the quantity of U.S. dollars demanded falls as the number of euros needed to buy a U.S. dollar rises. If the U.S. dollar falls against the euro (the dollar depreciates), American products will become relatively cheaper for Europeans. Europeans will respond by buying more from the United States and acquiring more dollars in the foreign exchange market: the quantity of U.S. dollars demanded rises as the number of euros needed to buy a U.S. dollar falls.

A similar argument explains why the supply curve of U.S. dollars in Figure 19-5 slopes upward: the more euros required to buy a U.S. dollar, the more dollars Americans will supply. Again, the reason is the effect of the exchange rate on relative prices. If the U.S. dollar rises against the euro, European products look cheaper to Americans—who will demand more of them. This will require Americans to convert more dollars into euros.

The **equilibrium exchange rate** is the exchange rate at which the quantity of U.S. dollars demanded in the foreign exchange market is equal to the quantity of U.S. dollars supplied. In Figure 19-5, the equilibrium is at point *E*, and the equilibrium exchange rate is 0.74. That is, at an exchange rate of €0.74

The **equilibrium exchange rate** is the exchange rate at which the quantity of a currency demanded in the foreign exchange market is equal to the quantity supplied.

per US$1, the quantity of U.S. dollars supplied to the foreign exchange market is equal to the quantity of U.S. dollars demanded.

To understand the significance of the equilibrium exchange rate, it's helpful to consider a numerical example of what equilibrium in the foreign exchange market looks like. A hypothetical example is shown in Table 19-4. The first row shows European purchases of U.S. dollars, either to buy U.S. goods and services or to buy U.S. assets. The second row shows U.S. sales of U.S. dollars, either to buy European goods and services or to buy European assets. At the equilibrium exchange rate, the total quantity of U.S. dollars Europeans want to buy is equal to the total quantity of U.S. dollars Americans want to sell.

Remember that the balance of payments accounts divide international transactions into two types. Purchases and sales of goods and services are counted in the current account. (Again, we're leaving out transfers and factor income to keep things simple.)

**TABLE 19-4 A Hypothetical Equilibrium in the Foreign Exchange Market**

| European purchases of U.S. dollars (trillions of U.S. dollars) | To buy U.S. goods and services: 1.0 | To buy U.S. assets: 1.0 | Total purchases of U.S. dollars: 2.0 |
|---|---|---|---|
| U.S. sales of U.S. dollars (trillions of U.S. dollars) | To buy European goods and services: 1.5 | To buy European assets: 0.5 | Total sales of U.S. dollars: 2.0 |
| | U.S. balance of payments on current account: −0.5 | U.S. balance of payments on financial account: +0.5 | |

Purchases and sales of assets are counted in the financial account. At the equilibrium exchange rate, then, we have the situation shown in Table 19-4: the sum of the balance of payments on current account plus the balance of payments on financial account is zero.

Now let's briefly consider how a shift in the demand for U.S. dollars affects equilibrium in the foreign exchange market. Suppose that for some reason capital flows from Europe to the United States increase—say, due to a change in the preferences of European investors. The effects are shown in Figure 19-6. The demand for U.S. dollars in the foreign exchange market increases as European investors convert euros into dollars to fund their new investments in the United States. This is shown by the shift of the demand curve from $D_1$ to $D_2$. As a result, the U.S. dollar appreciates against the euro: the number of euros per U.S. dollar at the equilibrium exchange rate rises from $XR_1$ to $XR_2$.

**FIGURE 19-6 An Increase in the Demand for U.S. Dollars**

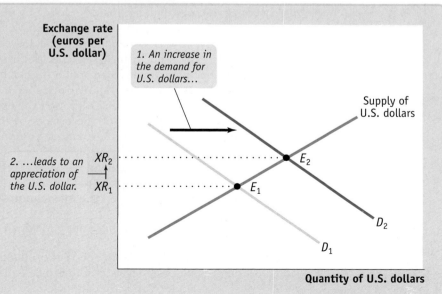

An increase in the demand for U.S. dollars might result from a change in the preferences of European investors. The demand curve for U.S. dollars shifts from $D_1$ to $D_2$. So the equilibrium number of euros per U.S. dollar rises—the dollar appreciates against the euro. As a result, the balance of payments on current account falls as the balance of payments on financial account rises.

What are the consequences of this increased capital inflow for the balance of payments? The total quantity of U.S. dollars supplied to the foreign exchange market still must equal the total quantity of U.S. dollars demanded. So the increased capital inflow to the United States—an increase in the balance of payments on financial account—must be matched by a decline in the balance of payments on current account. What causes the balance of payments on current account to decline? The appreciation of the U.S. dollar. A rise in the number of euros per U.S. dollar leads Americans to buy more European goods and services and Europeans to buy fewer American goods and services.

Table 19-5 shows a hypothetical example of how this might work. Europeans are buying more U.S. assets, increasing the balance of payments on financial account from 0.5 to 1.0. This is offset by a reduction in European purchases of U.S. goods and services and a rise in U.S. purchases of European goods and services, both the result of the dollar's appreciation. *So any change in the U.S. balance of payments on financial account generates an equal and opposite reaction in the balance of payments on current account.* Movements in the exchange rate ensure that changes in the financial account and in the current account offset each other.

**TABLE 19-5** **A Hypothetical Example of Effects of Increased Capital Inflows**

| European purchases of U.S. dollars (trillions of U.S. dollars) | To buy U.S. goods and services: 0.75 (down 0.25) | To buy U.S. assets: 1.5 (up 0.5) | Total purchases of U.S. dollars: 2.25 |
|---|---|---|---|
| U.S. sales of U.S. dollars (trillions of U.S. dollars) | To buy European goods and services: 1.75 (up 0.25) | To buy European assets: 0.5 (no change) | Total sales of U.S. dollars: 2.25 |
| | U.S. balance of payments on current account: −1.0 (down 0.5) | U.S. balance of payments on financial account: +1.0 (up 0.5) | |

Let's briefly run this process in reverse. Suppose there is a reduction in capital flows from Europe to the United States—again due to a change in the preferences of European investors. The demand for U.S. dollars in the foreign exchange market falls, and the dollar depreciates: the number of euros per U.S. dollar at the equilibrium exchange rate falls. This leads Americans to buy fewer European products and Europeans to buy more American products. Ultimately, this generates an increase in the U.S. balance of payments on current account. So a fall in capital flows into the United States leads to a weaker dollar, which in turn generates an increase in U.S. net exports.

## Inflation and Real Exchange Rates

In 1993 one U.S. dollar exchanged, on average, for 3.1 Mexican pesos. By 2011, the peso had fallen against the dollar by almost 75%, with an average exchange rate in 2011 of 12.4 pesos per dollar. Did Mexican products also become much cheaper relative to U.S. products over that 18-year period? Did the price of Mexican products expressed in terms of U.S. dollars also fall by almost 75%? The answer is no, because Mexico had much higher inflation than the United States over that period. In fact, the relative price of U.S. and Mexican products changed little between 1993 and 2011, although the exchange rate changed a lot.

To take account of the effects of differences in inflation rates, economists calculate **real exchange rates,** exchange rates adjusted for international differences in aggregate price levels. Suppose that the exchange rate we are looking at is the number of Mexican pesos per U.S. dollar. Let $P_{US}$ and $P_{Mex}$ be indexes of the aggregate price levels in the United States and Mexico, respectively. Then the real exchange rate between the Mexican peso and the U.S. dollar is defined as:

**(19-4)** Real exchange rate = Mexican pesos per U.S. dollar $\times \dfrac{P_{US}}{P_{Mex}}$

To distinguish it from the real exchange rate, the exchange rate unadjusted for aggregate price levels is sometimes called the *nominal* exchange rate.

**Real exchange rates** are exchange rates adjusted for international differences in aggregate price levels.

To understand the significance of the difference between the real and nominal exchange rates, let's consider the following example. Suppose that the

Mexican peso depreciates against the U.S. dollar, with the exchange rate going from 10 pesos per U.S. dollar to 15 pesos per U.S. dollar, a 50% change. But suppose that at the same time the price of everything in Mexico, measured in pesos, increases by 50%, so that the Mexican price index rises from 100 to 150. At the same time, suppose that there is no change in U.S. prices, so that the U.S. price index remains at 100. Then the initial real exchange rate is:

$$\text{Pesos per dollar before depreciation} \times \frac{P_{US}}{P_{Mex}} = 10 \times \frac{100}{100} = 10$$

After the peso depreciates and the Mexican price level increases, the real exchange rate is:

$$\text{Pesos per dollar after depreciation} \times \frac{P_{US}}{P_{Mex}} = 15 \times \frac{100}{150} = 10$$

In this example, the peso has depreciated substantially in terms of the U.S. dollar, but the *real* exchange rate between the peso and the U.S. dollar hasn't changed at all. And because the real peso–U.S. dollar exchange rate hasn't changed, the nominal depreciation of the peso against the U.S. dollar will have no effect either on the quantity of goods and services exported by Mexico to the United States or on the quantity of goods and services imported by Mexico from the United States.

To see why, consider again the example of a hotel room. Suppose that this room initially costs 1,000 pesos per night, which is $100 at an exchange rate of 10 pesos per dollar. After both Mexican prices and the number of pesos per dollar rise by 50%, the hotel room costs 1,500 pesos per night—but 1,500 pesos divided by 15 pesos per dollar is $100, so the Mexican hotel room still costs $100. As a result, a U.S. tourist considering a trip to Mexico will have no reason to change plans.

The same is true for all goods and services that enter into trade: *the current account responds only to changes in the real exchange rate, not the nominal exchange rate.* A country's products become cheaper to foreigners only when that country's currency depreciates in real terms, and those products become more expensive to foreigners only when the currency appreciates in real terms. As a consequence, economists who analyze movements in exports and imports of goods and services focus on the real exchange rate, not the nominal exchange rate.

Figure 19-7 illustrates just how important it can be to distinguish between nominal and real exchange rates. The line labeled "Nominal exchange rate" shows the number of pesos it took to buy a U.S. dollar from November 1993 to December

FIGURE **19-7** Real versus Nominal Exchange Rates, 1993–2011

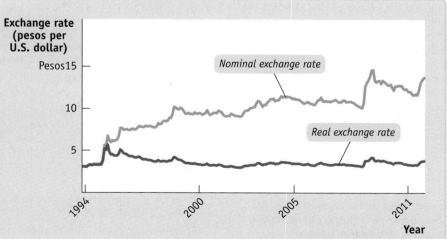

Between November 1993 and December 2011, the price of a dollar in Mexican pesos increased dramatically. But because Mexico had higher inflation than the United States, the real exchange rate, which measures the relative price of Mexican goods and services, ended up roughly where it started.

*Source:* Federal Reserve Bank of St. Louis.

The **purchasing power parity** between two countries' currencies is the nominal exchange rate at which a given basket of goods and services would cost the same amount in each country.

2011. As you can see, the peso depreciated massively over that period. But the line labeled "Real exchange rate" shows the real exchange rate: it was calculated using Equation 19-4, with price indexes for both Mexico and the United States set so that 1993 = 100. In real terms, the peso depreciated between 1994 and 1995, but not by nearly as much as the nominal depreciation. By the end of 2011, the real peso–U.S. dollar exchange rate was just about back where it started.

## Purchasing Power Parity

A useful tool for analyzing exchange rates, closely connected to the concept of the real exchange rate, is known as *purchasing power parity*. The **purchasing power parity** between two countries' currencies is the nominal exchange rate at which a given basket of goods and services would cost the same amount in each country. Suppose, for example, that a basket of goods and services that costs $100 in the United States costs 1,000 pesos in Mexico. Then the purchasing power parity is 10 pesos per U.S. dollar: at that exchange rate, 1,000 pesos = $100, so the market basket costs the same amount in both countries.

Calculations of purchasing power parities are usually made by estimating the cost of buying broad market baskets containing many goods and services—everything from automobiles and groceries to housing and telephone calls. But as the For Inquiring Minds below explains, once a year the magazine *The Economist* publishes a list of purchasing power parities based on the cost of buying a market basket that contains only one item—a McDonald's Big Mac.

Nominal exchange rates almost always differ from purchasing power parities. Some of these differences are systematic: in general, aggregate price levels

## FOR INQUIRING MINDS

### BURGERNOMICS

For a number of years the British magazine *The Economist* has produced an annual comparison of the cost in different countries of one particular consumption item that is found around the world—a McDonald's Big Mac. The magazine finds the price of a Big Mac in local currency, then computes two numbers: the price of a Big Mac in U.S. dollars using the prevailing exchange rate and the exchange rate at which the price of a Big Mac would equal the U.S. price. If purchasing power parity held for Big Macs, the dollar price of a Big Mac would be the same everywhere. If purchasing power parity is a good theory for the long run, the exchange rate at which a Big Mac's price matches the U.S. price should offer some guidance about where the exchange rate will eventually end up.

Table 34-6 shows the *Economist* estimates for selected countries as of July 28, 2011, ranked in increasing order of the dollar price of a Big Mac. The countries with the cheapest Big Macs, and therefore by this measure

with the most undervalued currencies, are India and China, both developing countries. But not all developing countries have low-priced Big Macs: the price of a Big Mac in Brazil, converted into dollars, is considerably higher than in the United States. This reflects a sharp appreciation of the *real*, Brazil's currency, in recent years

as the country has become a favorite of international investors. And topping the list, with a Big Mac some 75% more expensive than in the United States, is Switzerland—the nation that, as we described in this chapter's opening story, took extraordinary action later in 2011 in an effort to depreciate its currency.

**TABLE 19-6** Purchasing Power Parity and the Price of a Big Mac

| Country | Big Mac price | | Local currency per dollar | |
| --- | --- | --- | --- | --- |
| | In local currency | In U.S. dollars | Implied PPP | Actual exchange rate |
| India | Rupee 84.0 | 1.6642 | 20.7 | 50.475 |
| China | Yuan 14.7 | 2.289 | 3.6 | 6.422 |
| Mexico | Peso 32.0 | 2.2988 | 7.87 | 13.9205 |
| Britain | £ 2.39 | 3.7233 | 0.59 | 0.6419 |
| United States | $4.07 | 4.07 | — | 1 |
| Japan | ¥ 320 | 4.1503 | 78.7 | 77.103 |
| Euro area | € 3.44 | 4.6032 | 0.85 | 0.7473 |
| Brazil | Real 9.50 | 5.1271 | 2.34 | 1.8529 |
| Switzerland | SFr 6.5 | 7.1539 | 1.6 | 0.9086 |

FIGURE **19-8** Purchasing Power Parity versus the Nominal Exchange Rate, 1990–2011

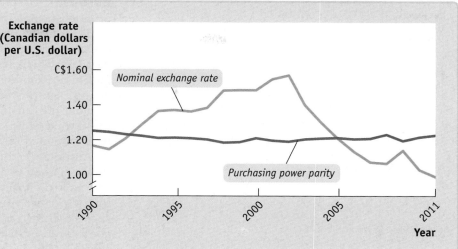

The purchasing power parity between the United States and Canada—the exchange rate at which a basket of goods and services would have cost the same amount in both countries—changed very little over the period shown, staying near C$1.20 per US$1. But the nominal exchange rate fluctuated widely.

are lower in poor countries than in rich countries because services tend to be cheaper in poor countries. But even among countries at roughly the same level of economic development, nominal exchange rates vary quite a lot from purchasing power parity. Figure 19-8 shows the nominal exchange rate between the Canadian dollar and the U.S. dollar, measured as the number of Canadian dollars per U.S. dollar, from 1990 to 2011, together with an estimate of the purchasing power parity exchange rate between the United States and Canada over the same period. The purchasing power parity didn't change much over the whole period because the United States and Canada had about the same rate of inflation. But at the beginning of the period the nominal exchange rate was below purchasing power parity, so a given market basket was more expensive in Canada than in the United States. By 2002 the nominal exchange rate was far above the purchasing power parity, so a market basket was much cheaper in Canada than in the United States.

Over the long run, however, purchasing power parities are pretty good at predicting actual changes in nominal exchange rates. In particular, nominal exchange rates between countries at similar levels of economic development tend to fluctuate around levels that lead to similar costs for a given market basket. In fact, by July 2005 the nominal exchange rate between the United States and Canada was C$1.22 per US$1—just about the purchasing power parity. And by 2011 the cost of living was once again higher in Canada than in the United States.

## ECONOMICS ➤ IN ACTION

### LOW-COST AMERICA

**D**oes the exchange rate matter for business decisions? And how. Consider what European auto manufacturers were doing in 2008. One report from the University of Iowa summarized the situation as follows:

> While luxury German carmakers BMW and Mercedes have maintained plants in the American South since the 1990s, BMW aims to expand U.S. manufacturing in South Carolina by 50% during the next 5 years. Volvo of Sweden is in negotiations to build a plant in New Mexico. Analysts at Italian carmaker Fiat determined that it needs to build a North American factory to profit from the upcoming re-launch of its Alfa Romeo model. Tennessee recently closed a deal with Volkswagen to build a $1 billion factory by offering $577 million in incentives.

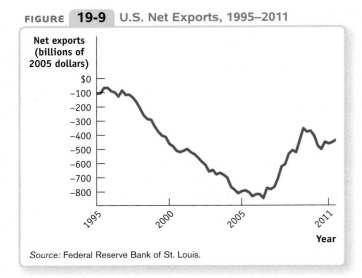

**FIGURE   19-9**   U.S. Net Exports, 1995–2011

Net exports (billions of 2005 dollars)

*Source:* Federal Reserve Bank of St. Louis.

Why were European automakers flocking to America? To some extent because they were being offered special incentives, as the case of Volkswagen in Tennessee illustrates. But the big factor was the exchange rate. In the early 2000s one euro was, on average, worth less than a dollar; by the summer of 2008 the exchange rate was around €1 = $1.50. This change in the exchange rate made it substantially cheaper for European car manufacturers to produce in the United States than at home—especially if the cars were intended for the U.S. market.

Automobile manufacturing wasn't the only U.S. industry benefiting from the weak dollar; across the board, U.S. exports surged after 2006 while import growth fell off. Figure 19-9 shows one measure of U.S. trade performance, real net exports of goods and services: exports minus imports, both measured in 2005 dollars. As you can see, this balance, after a long slide, turned sharply upward in 2006. There was a modest reversal in 2009–2010, as an economy recovering from the 2007–2009 recession pulled in more imports, but a major narrowing of the trade gap remained in place.

### CHECK YOUR UNDERSTANDING   19-2

1. Mexico discovers huge reserves of oil and starts exporting oil to the United States. Describe how this would affect the following.
   **a.** The nominal peso–U.S. dollar exchange rate
   **b.** Mexican exports of other goods and services
   **c.** Mexican imports of goods and services

2. A basket of goods and services that costs $100 in the United States costs 800 pesos in Mexico, and the current nominal exchange rate is 10 pesos per U.S. dollar. Over the next five years, the cost of that market basket rises to $120 in the United States and to 1,200 pesos in Mexico, although the nominal exchange rate remains at 10 pesos per U.S. dollar. Calculate the following.
   **a.** The real exchange rate now and five years from now, if today's price index in both countries is 100
   **b.** Purchasing power parity today and five years from now

Solutions appear at back of book.

# Exchange Rate Policy

The nominal exchange rate, like other prices, is determined by supply and demand. Unlike the price of wheat or oil, however, the exchange rate is the price of a country's money (in terms of another country's money). Money isn't a good or service produced by the private sector; it's an asset whose quantity is determined by government policy. As a result, governments have much more power to influence nominal exchange rates than they have to influence ordinary prices.

The nominal exchange rate is a very important price for many countries: the exchange rate determines the price of imports and the price of exports; in economies where exports and imports are large percentages of GDP, movements in the exchange rate can have major effects on aggregate output and the aggregate price level. What do governments do with their power to influence this important price?

The answer is, it depends. At different times and in different places, governments have adopted a variety of *exchange rate regimes.* Let's talk about these regimes, how they are enforced, and how governments choose a regime. (From now on, we'll adopt the convention that we mean the nominal exchange rate when we refer to the exchange rate.)

## Exchange Rate Regimes

An **exchange rate regime** is a rule governing policy toward the exchange rate. There are two main kinds of exchange rate regimes. A country has a **fixed exchange rate** when the government keeps the exchange rate against some other currency at or near a particular target. For example, Hong Kong has an official policy of setting an exchange rate of HK$7.80 per US$1. In contrast, a country has a **floating exchange rate** when the government lets market forces determine the exchange rate. This is the policy followed by Britain, Canada, and the United States.

Fixed exchange rates and floating exchange rates aren't the only possibilities. At various times, countries have adopted compromise policies that lie somewhere between fixed and floating exchange rates. These include exchange rates that are fixed at any given time but are adjusted frequently, exchange rates that aren't fixed but are "managed" by the government to avoid wide swings, and exchange rates that float within a "target zone" but are prevented from leaving that zone. In this book, however, we'll focus on the two main exchange rate regimes.

The immediate question about a fixed exchange rate is how it is possible for governments to fix the exchange rate when the exchange rate is determined by supply and demand.

Exchange rates play a very important role in the global economy.

## How Can an Exchange Rate Be Held Fixed?

To understand how it is possible for a country to fix its exchange rate, let's consider a hypothetical country, Genovia, which for some reason has decided to fix the value of its currency, the geno, at US$1.50.

The obvious problem is that $1.50 may not be the equilibrium exchange rate in the foreign exchange market: the equilibrium rate may be either higher or lower than the target exchange rate. Figure 19-10 shows the foreign exchange market for genos, with the quantities of genos supplied and demanded on the horizontal axis and the exchange rate of the geno, measured in U.S. dollars per geno, on the vertical axis. Panel (a) shows the case in which the equilibrium value of the geno is *below* the target exchange rate. Panel (b) shows the case in which the equilibrium value of the geno is *above* the target exchange rate.

Consider first the case in which the equilibrium value of the geno is below the target exchange rate. As panel (a) shows, at the target exchange rate of $1.50 per geno, there is a surplus of genos in the foreign exchange market, which would normally push the value of the geno down. How can the Genovian government support the value of the geno to keep the rate where it wants? There are three possible answers, all of which have been used by governments at some point.

One way the Genovian government can support the geno is to "soak up" the surplus of genos by buying its own currency in the foreign exchange market. Government purchases or sales of currency in the foreign exchange market are called **exchange market intervention.** To buy genos in the foreign exchange market, of course, the Genovian government must have U.S. dollars to exchange for genos. In fact, most countries maintain **foreign exchange reserves,** stocks of foreign currency (usually U.S. dollars or euros) that they can use to buy their own currency to support its price.

An **exchange rate regime** is a rule governing policy toward the exchange rate.

A country has a **fixed exchange rate** when the government keeps the exchange rate against some other currency at or near a particular target.

A country has a **floating exchange rate** when the government lets market forces determine the exchange rate.

Government purchases or sales of currency in the foreign exchange market are **exchange market intervention.**

**Foreign exchange reserves** are stocks of foreign currency that governments maintain to buy their own currency on the foreign exchange market.

FIGURE **19-10** Exchange Market Intervention

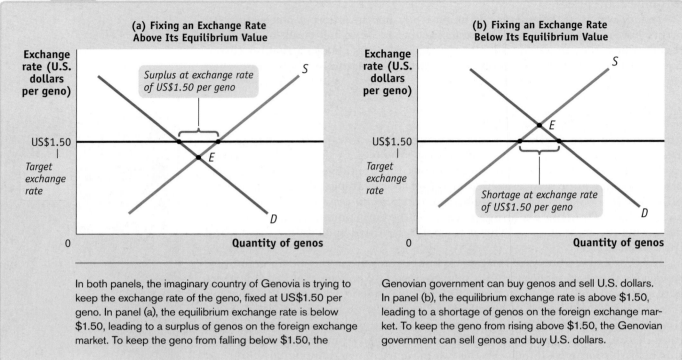

**(a) Fixing an Exchange Rate Above Its Equilibrium Value**

**(b) Fixing an Exchange Rate Below Its Equilibrium Value**

In both panels, the imaginary country of Genovia is trying to keep the exchange rate of the geno, fixed at US$1.50 per geno. In panel (a), the equilibrium exchange rate is below $1.50, leading to a surplus of genos on the foreign exchange market. To keep the geno from falling below $1.50, the

Genovian government can buy genos and sell U.S. dollars. In panel (b), the equilibrium exchange rate is above $1.50, leading to a shortage of genos on the foreign exchange market. To keep the geno from rising above $1.50, the Genovian government can sell genos and buy U.S. dollars.

We mentioned earlier in the chapter that an important part of international capital flows is the result of purchases and sales of foreign assets by governments and central banks. Now we can see why governments sell foreign assets: they are supporting their currency through exchange market intervention. As we'll see in a moment, governments that keep the value of their currency *down* through exchange market intervention must *buy* foreign assets. First, however, let's talk about the other ways governments fix exchange rates.

A second way for the Genovian government to support the geno is to try to shift the supply and demand curves for the geno in the foreign exchange market. Governments usually do this by changing monetary policy. For example, to support the geno the Genovian central bank can raise the Genovian interest rate. This will increase capital flows into Genovia, increasing the demand for genos, at the same time that it reduces capital flows out of Genovia, reducing the supply of genos. So, other things equal, an increase in a country's interest rate will increase the value of its currency.

Third, the Genovian government can support the geno by reducing the supply of genos to the foreign exchange market. It can do this by requiring domestic residents who want to buy foreign currency to get a license and giving these licenses only to people engaging in approved transactions (such as the purchase of imported goods the Genovian government thinks are essential). Licensing systems that limit the right of individuals to buy foreign currency are called **foreign exchange controls.** Other things equal, foreign exchange controls increase the value of a country's currency.

So far we've been discussing a situation in which the government is trying to prevent a depreciation of the geno. Suppose, instead, that the situation is as shown in panel (b) of Figure 19-10, where the equilibrium value of the geno is *above* the target exchange rate of $1.50 per geno and there is a shortage of genos. To maintain the target exchange rate, the Genovian government can apply the same three basic options in the reverse direction. It can intervene in the foreign

**Foreign exchange controls** are licensing systems that limit the right of individuals to buy foreign currency.

exchange market, in this case *selling* genos and acquiring U.S. dollars, which it can add to its foreign exchange reserves. It can *reduce* interest rates to increase the supply of genos and reduce the demand. Or it can impose foreign exchange controls that limit the ability of foreigners to buy genos. All of these actions, other things equal, will reduce the value of the geno.

As we said, all three techniques have been used to manage fixed exchange rates. But we haven't said whether fixing the exchange rate is a good idea. In fact, the choice of exchange rate regime poses a dilemma for policy makers, because fixed and floating exchange rates each have both advantages and disadvantages.

## The Exchange Rate Regime Dilemma

Few questions in macroeconomics produce as many arguments as that of whether a country should adopt a fixed or a floating exchange rate. The reason there are so many arguments is that both sides have a case.

To understand the case for a fixed exchange rate, consider for a moment how easy it is to conduct business across state lines in the United States. There are a number of things that make interstate commerce trouble-free, but one of them is the absence of any uncertainty about the value of money: a dollar is a dollar, in both New York City and Los Angeles.

By contrast, a dollar isn't a dollar in transactions between New York City and Toronto. The exchange rate between the Canadian dollar and the U.S. dollar fluctuates, sometimes widely. If a U.S. firm promises to pay a Canadian firm a given number of U.S. dollars a year from now, the value of that promise in Canadian currency can vary by 10% or more. This uncertainty has the effect of deterring trade between the two countries. So one benefit of a fixed exchange rate is certainty about the future value of a currency.

There is also, in some cases, an additional benefit to adopting a fixed exchange rate: by committing itself to a fixed rate, a country is also committing itself not to engage in inflationary policies. For example, in 1991 Argentina, which has a long history of irresponsible policies leading to severe inflation, adopted a fixed exchange rate of US$1 per Argentine peso in an attempt to commit itself to non-inflationary policies in the future. (Argentina's fixed exchange rate regime collapsed disastrously in late 2001. But that's another story.)

The point is that there is some economic value in having a stable exchange rate. Indeed, as the upcoming For Inquiring Minds explains, the presumed benefits of stable exchange rates motivated the international system of fixed exchange rates created after World War II. It was also a major reason for the creation of the euro.

However, there are also costs to fixing the exchange rate. To stabilize an exchange rate through intervention, a country must keep large quantities of foreign currency on hand—usually a low-return investment. Furthermore, even large reserves can be quickly exhausted when there are large capital flows out of a country. If a country chooses to stabilize an exchange rate by adjusting monetary policy rather than through intervention, it must divert monetary policy from other goals, notably stabilizing the economy and managing the inflation rate. Finally, foreign exchange controls, like import quotas and tariffs, distort incentives for importing and exporting goods and services. They can also create substantial costs in terms of red tape and corruption.

So there's a dilemma. Should a country let its currency float, which leaves monetary policy available for macroeconomic stabilization but creates uncertainty for business? Or should it fix the exchange rate, which eliminates the uncertainty but means giving up monetary policy, adopting exchange controls,

## FOR INQUIRING MINDS

### FROM BRETTON WOODS TO THE EURO

In 1944, while World War II was still raging, representatives of Allied nations met in Bretton Woods, New Hampshire, to establish a postwar international monetary system of fixed exchange rates among major currencies. The system was highly successful at first, but it broke down in 1971. After a confusing interval during which policy makers tried unsuccessfully to establish a new fixed exchange rate system, by 1973 most economically advanced countries had moved to floating exchange rates.

In Europe, however, many policy makers were unhappy with floating exchange rates, which they believed created too much uncertainty for business. From the late 1970s onward they tried several times to create a system of more

or less fixed exchange rates in Europe, culminating in an arrangement known as the Exchange Rate Mechanism. (The Exchange Rate Mechanism was, strictly speaking, a "target zone" system—European exchange rates were free to move within a narrow band, but not outside it.) And in 1991 they agreed to move to the ultimate in fixed exchange rates: a common European currency, the euro. To the surprise of many analysts, they pulled it off: today most of Europe has abandoned national currencies for the euro.

Figure 19-11 illustrates the history of European exchange rate arrangements. It shows the exchange rate between the French franc and the German mark, measured as francs per mark, from 1971 until their replacement by the euro.

The exchange rate fluctuated widely at first. The "plateaus" you can see in the data—eras when the exchange rate fluctuated only modestly—are periods when attempts to restore fixed exchange rates were in process. The Exchange Rate Mechanism, after a couple of false starts, became effective in 1987, stabilizing the exchange rate at about 3.4 francs per mark. (The wobbles in the early 1990s reflect two *currency crises*—episodes in which widespread expectations of imminent devaluations led to large but temporary capital flows.)

In 1999 the exchange rate was "locked"—no further fluctuations were allowed as the countries prepared to switch from francs and marks to the euro. At the end of 2001, the franc and the mark ceased to exist.

The transition to the euro has not been without costs. Countries that adopted the euro sacrificed some important policy tools: they could no longer tailor monetary policy to their specific economic circumstances, and they could no longer lower their costs relative to other European nations simply by letting their currencies depreciate. At the time this book went to press, the euro area was under serious stress, with several nations—including Greece, Spain, and Italy, three big economies—facing widespread skepticism about their ability to make needed economic adjustments without defaulting on their debts and abandoning the euro.

FIGURE **19-11** The Road to the Euro

The exchange rate between the French franc and the German mark tells the tale of Europe's long march to a common currency. European nations made several attempts to fix exchange rates in the 1970s and 1980s. The first two attempts failed, but from 1987 on they were mostly successful. The exchange rate was "locked" in the late 1990s, and at the end of 2001 the franc and the mark were replaced by the euro.

*Source:* Federal Reserve Bank of St. Louis.

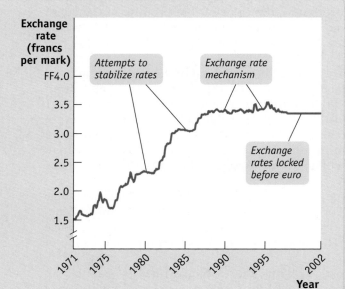

or both? Different countries reach different conclusions at different times. Most European countries, except for Britain, have long believed that exchange rates among major European economies, which do most of their international trade with each other, should be fixed. But Canada seems happy with a floating exchange rate with the United States, even though the United States accounts for most of Canada's trade.

Fortunately we don't have to resolve this dilemma. For the rest of the chapter, we'll take exchange rate regimes as given and ask how they affect macroeconomic policy.

## ECONOMICS ➤ IN ACTION

### CHINA PEGS THE YUAN

In the early years of the twenty-first century, China provided a striking example of the lengths to which countries sometimes go to maintain a fixed exchange rate. Here's the background: China's spectacular success as an exporter led to a rising surplus on current account. At the same time, non-Chinese private investors became increasingly eager to shift funds into China, to invest in its growing domestic economy. These capital flows were somewhat limited by foreign exchange controls—but kept coming in anyway. As a result of the current account surplus and private capital inflows, China found itself in the position described by panel (b) of Figure 19-10: at the target exchange rate, the demand for yuan exceeded the supply. Yet the Chinese government was determined to keep the exchange rate fixed at a value below its equilibrium level. Although China allowed a small revaluation of the yuan in 2005, at the time of this writing in 2011, many economists estimated the level of the undervaluation of the yuan at 15 to 25%.

China provides a striking example of the lengths to which countries sometimes go to maintain a fixed exchange rate.

To keep the rate fixed, China had to engage in large-scale exchange market intervention, selling yuan, buying up other countries' currencies (mainly U.S. dollars) on the foreign exchange market, and adding them to its reserves. In 2010, China added $450 billion to its foreign exchange reserves, and by the summer of 2011, those reserves had risen to $3.2 trillion. To get a sense of how big these totals are, in 2010 China's GDP was approximately $5.9 trillion. This means that in 2010 China bought U.S. dollars and other currencies equal to about 7½% of its GDP, making its accumulated reserves equal to more than half its GDP. That's as if the U.S. government had bought well over $1 trillion worth of yen and euros in a single year, even though it was already sitting on an $8 trillion pile of foreign currencies. Not surprisingly, China's exchange rate policy has led to some friction with its trading partners who feel that it has had the effect of subsidizing Chinese exports.

### CHECK YOUR UNDERSTANDING    19-3

1. Draw a diagram, similar to Figure 19-10, representing the foreign exchange situation of China when it kept the exchange rate fixed. (*Hint:* Express the exchange rate as U.S. dollars per yuan.) Then show with a diagram how each of the following policy changes might eliminate the disequilibrium in the market.
   **a.** An appreciation of the yuan
   **b.** Placing restrictions on foreigners who want to invest in China
   **c.** Removing restrictions on Chinese who want to invest abroad
   **d.** Imposing taxes on Chinese exports, such as shipments of clothing, that are causing a political backlash in the importing countries

Solutions appear at back of book.

### ▼ Quick Review

- Countries choose different **exchange rate regimes.** The two main regimes are **fixed exchange rates** and **floating exchange rates.**

- Exchange rates can be fixed through **exchange market intervention,** using **foreign exchange reserves.** Countries can also use domestic policies to shift supply and demand in the foreign exchange market (usually monetary policy), or they can impose **foreign exchange controls.**

- Choosing an exchange rate regime poses a dilemma: Stable exchange rates are good for business. But holding large foreign exchange reserves is costly, using domestic policy to fix the exchange rate makes it hard to pursue other objectives, and foreign exchange controls distort incentives.

# Exchange Rates and Macroeconomic Policy

When the euro was created in 1999, there were celebrations across the nations of Europe—with a few notable exceptions. You see, some countries chose not to adopt the new currency. The most important of these was Britain, but other European countries, such as Sweden, also decided that the euro was not for them.

A **devaluation** is a reduction in the value of a currency that is set under a fixed exchange rate regime.

A **revaluation** is an increase in the value of a currency that is set under a fixed exchange rate regime.

Why did Britain say no? Part of the answer was national pride: if Britain gave up the pound, it would also have to give up currency that bears the portrait of the queen. But there were also serious economic concerns about giving up the pound in favor of the euro. British economists who favored adoption of the euro argued that if Britain used the same currency as its neighbors, the country's international trade would expand and its economy would become more productive. But other economists pointed out that adopting the euro would take away Britain's ability to have an independent monetary policy and might lead to macroeconomic problems.

As this discussion suggests, the fact that modern economies are open to international trade and capital flows adds a new level of complication to our analysis of macroeconomic policy. Let's look at three policy issues raised by open-economy macroeconomics.

## 1. Devaluation and Revaluation of Fixed Exchange Rates

Historically, fixed exchange rates haven't been permanent commitments. Sometimes countries with a fixed exchange rate switch to a floating rate, as Argentina did in 2001. In other cases, they retain a fixed rate but change the target exchange rate. Such adjustments in the target were common during the Bretton Woods era described in the preceding For Inquiring Minds. For example, in 1967 Britain changed the exchange rate of the pound against the U.S. dollar from US$2.80 per £1 to US$2.40 per £1. A modern example is Argentina, which maintained a fixed exchange rate against the dollar from 1991 to 2001 but switched to a floating exchange rate at the end of 2001.

A reduction in the value of a currency that is set under a fixed exchange rate regime is called a **devaluation.** As we've already learned, a *depreciation* is a downward move in a currency. A devaluation is a depreciation that is due to a revision in a fixed exchange rate target. An increase in the value of a currency that is set under a fixed exchange rate regime is called a **revaluation.**

A devaluation, like any depreciation, makes domestic goods cheaper in terms of foreign currency, which leads to higher exports. At the same time, it makes foreign goods more expensive in terms of domestic currency, which reduces imports. The effect is to increase the balance of payments on current account. Similarly, a revaluation makes domestic goods more expensive in terms of foreign currency, which reduces exports, and makes foreign goods cheaper in domestic currency, which increases imports. So a revaluation reduces the balance of payments on current account.

Devaluations and revaluations serve two purposes under fixed exchange rates. First, they can be used to eliminate shortages or surpluses in the foreign exchange market. For example, in 2010 some economists and politicians were urging China to revalue the yuan because they believed that China's exchange rate policy unfairly aided Chinese exports.

Second, devaluation and revaluation can be used as tools of macroeconomic policy. A devaluation, by increasing exports and reducing imports, increases aggregate demand. So a devaluation can be used to reduce or eliminate a recessionary gap. A revaluation has the opposite effect, reducing aggregate demand. So a revaluation can be used to reduce or eliminate an inflationary gap.

## 2. Monetary Policy Under Floating Exchange Rates

Under a floating exchange rate regime, a country's central bank retains its ability to pursue independent monetary policy: it can increase aggregate demand by cutting the interest rate or decrease aggregate demand by raising the interest rate.

But the exchange rate adds another dimension to the effects of monetary policy. To see why, let's return to the hypothetical country of Genovia and ask what happens if the central bank cuts the interest rate.

Just as in a closed economy, a lower interest rate leads to higher investment spending and higher consumer spending. But the decline in the interest rate also affects the foreign exchange market. Foreigners have less incentive to move funds into Genovia because they will receive a lower interest rate on their loans. As a result, they have less need to exchange U.S. dollars for genos, so the demand for genos falls. At the same time, Genovians have *more* incentive to move funds abroad because the interest rate on loans at home has fallen, making investments outside the country more attractive. As a result, they need to exchange more genos for U.S. dollars, so the supply of genos rises.

Figure 19-12 shows the effect of an interest rate reduction on the foreign exchange market. The demand curve for genos shifts leftward, from $D_1$ to $D_2$, and the supply curve shifts rightward, from $S_1$ to $S_2$. The equilibrium exchange rate, as measured in U.S. dollars per geno, falls from $XR_1$ to $XR_2$. That is, a reduction in the Genovian interest rate causes the geno to *depreciate*.

FIGURE **19-12** Monetary Policy and the Exchange Rate

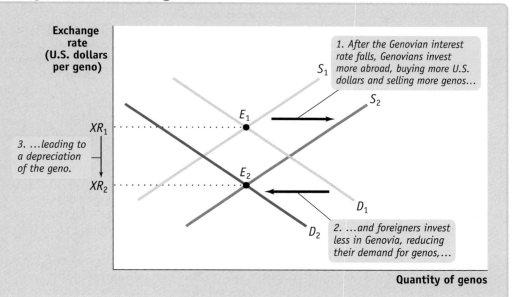

Here we show what happens in the foreign exchange market if Genovia cuts its interest rate. Residents of Genovia have a reduced incentive to keep their funds at home, so they invest more abroad. As a result, the supply of genos shifts rightward, from $S_1$ to $S_2$. Meanwhile, foreigners have less incentive to put funds into Genovia, so the demand for genos shifts leftward, from $D_1$ to $D_2$. The geno depreciates: the equilibrium exchange rate falls from $XR_1$ to $XR_2$.

1. After the Genovian interest rate falls, Genovians invest more abroad, buying more U.S. dollars and selling more genos...

3. ...leading to a depreciation of the geno.

2. ...and foreigners invest less in Genovia, reducing their demand for genos,...

The depreciation of the geno, in turn, affects aggregate demand. We've already seen that a devaluation—a depreciation that is the result of a change in a fixed exchange rate—increases exports and reduces imports, thereby increasing aggregate demand. A depreciation that results from an interest rate cut has the same effect: it increases exports and reduces imports, increasing aggregate demand.

In other words, monetary policy under floating rates has effects beyond those we've described in looking at closed economies. In a closed economy, a reduction in the interest rate leads to a rise in aggregate demand because it leads to more investment spending and consumer spending. In an open economy with a floating exchange rate, the interest rate reduction leads to increased investment spending and consumer spending, but it also increases aggregate demand in another way: it leads to a currency depreciation, which increases exports and reduces imports, and further increases aggregate demand.

## 3. International Business Cycles

Up to this point, we have discussed macroeconomics, even in an open economy, as if all demand shocks originate from the domestic economy. In reality, however, economies sometimes face shocks coming from abroad. For example, recessions in the United States have historically led to recessions in Mexico.

The key point is that changes in aggregate demand affect the demand for goods and services produced abroad as well as at home: other things equal, a recession leads to a fall in imports and an expansion leads to a rise in imports. And one country's imports are another country's exports. This link between aggregate demand in different national economies is one reason business cycles in different countries sometimes—but not always—seem to be synchronized. The prime example is the Great Depression, which affected countries around the world.

The extent of this link depends, however, on the exchange rate regime. To see why, think about what happens if a recession abroad reduces the demand for Genovia's exports. A reduction in foreign demand for Genovian goods and services is also a reduction in demand for genos in the foreign exchange market. If Genovia has a fixed exchange rate, it responds to this decline with exchange market intervention. But if Genovia has a floating exchange rate, the geno depreciates. Because Genovian goods and services become cheaper to foreigners when the demand for exports falls, the quantity of goods and services exported doesn't fall by as much as it would under a fixed rate. At the same time, the fall in the geno makes imports more expensive to Genovians, leading to a fall in imports. Both effects limit the decline in Genovia's aggregate demand compared to what it would have been under a fixed exchange rate.

One of the virtues of a floating exchange rate, according to advocates of such exchange rates, is that they help insulate countries from recessions originating abroad. This theory looked pretty good in the early 2000s: Britain, with a floating exchange rate, managed to stay out of a recession that affected the rest of Europe, and Canada, which also has a floating rate, suffered a less severe recession than the United States.

In 2008, however, a financial crisis that began in the United States led to a recession in virtually every country. In this case, it appears that the international linkages among financial markets were much stronger than any insulation from overseas disturbances provided by floating exchange rates.

## ECONOMICS ▶ IN ACTION

### THE JOY OF A DEVALUED POUND

Earlier in the chapter, we mentioned the Exchange Rate Mechanism, the system of European fixed exchange rates that paved the way for the creation of the euro in 1999. Britain joined that system in 1990 but dropped out in 1992. The story of Britain's exit from the Exchange Rate Mechanism is a classic example of open-economy macroeconomic policy.

Britain originally fixed its exchange rate for both the reasons we described earlier in the chapter: British leaders believed that a fixed exchange rate would help promote international trade, and they also hoped that it would help fight inflation. But by 1992 Britain was suffering from high unemployment: the unemployment rate in September 1992 was over 10%. And as long as the country had a fixed exchange rate, there wasn't much the government could do. In particular, the government wasn't able to cut interest rates because it was using high interest rates to help support the value of the pound.

In the summer of 1992, investors began speculating against the pound—selling pounds in the expectation that the currency would drop in value. As its foreign reserves dwindled, this speculation forced the British government's hand. On September 16, 1992, Britain abandoned its fixed exchange rate. The pound promptly dropped 20% against the German mark, the most important European currency at the time.

At first, the devaluation of the pound greatly damaged the prestige of the British government. But the Chancellor of the Exchequer—the equivalent of the U.S. Treasury Secretary—claimed to be happy about it. "My wife has never before heard me singing in the bath," he told reporters. There were several reasons for his joy. One was that the British government would no longer have to engage in large-scale exchange market intervention to support the pound's value. Another was that devaluation increases aggregate demand, so the pound's fall would help reduce British unemployment. Finally, because Britain no longer had a fixed exchange rate, it was free to pursue an expansionary monetary policy to fight its slump.

Indeed, events made it clear that the chancellor's joy was well founded. British unemployment fell over the next two years, even as the unemployment rate rose in France and Germany. One person who did not share in the improving employment picture, however, was the chancellor himself. Soon after his remark about singing in the bath, he was fired.

## CHECK YOUR UNDERSTANDING   19-4

1. Look at the data in Figure 19-11. Where do you see devaluations and revaluations of the franc against the mark?

2. In the late 1980s Canadian economists argued that the high interest rate policies of the Bank of Canada weren't just causing high unemployment—they were also making it hard for Canadian manufacturers to compete with the United States. Explain this complaint, using our analysis of how monetary policy works under floating exchange rates.

*Solutions appear at back of book.*

### ▼ Quick Review

- Countries can change fixed exchange rates. **Devaluation** or **revaluation** can help reduce surpluses or shortages in the foreign exchange market and can increase or reduce aggregate demand.

- In an open economy with a floating exchange rate, interest rates also affect the exchange rate, and so monetary policy affects aggregate demand through the effects of the exchange rate on imports and exports.

- Because one country's imports are another country's exports, business cycles are sometimes synchronized across countries. However, floating exchange rates may reduce this link.

# BUSINESS CASE : War of the Earthmovers

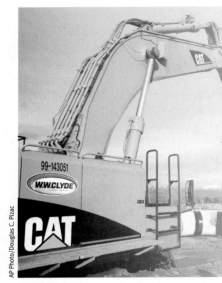

AP Photo/Douglas C. Pizac

Visit a construction site almost anywhere in the world, and odds are that the earthmoving equipment you see—the tractors, dump trucks, excavators, graders, scrapers, and so on—is made by one of two companies, America's Caterpillar or Japan's Komatsu. Caterpillar and Komatsu both rely heavily on exports, rather than selling only to their domestic markets, and have been fierce competitors for three decades, with first one company, then the other, seemingly on the ropes.

Ask the companies' leaders to explain the course of this seesawing competitive struggle, and they will tell a tale of corporate cultures and management decisions. Caterpillar, the story goes, entered the 1980s filled with complacency thanks to its longtime dominance of the earthmoving industry, only to face a shock from Komatsu that almost drove it to the brink. Then Caterpillar reformed its management practices, regaining the upper hand in the 1990s, and Komatsu found itself in danger of failing, until reinvigorated management stabilized the company again.

But is this the whole story? Not exactly. Management decisions were no doubt crucial to both firms, but so were movements in the exchange rate. Figure 19-13 shows the real exchange rate between the United States and Japan, using consumer prices, from 1980 to 2011. The figure immediately suggests one reason Caterpillar was able to recover from the shock of competition in the 1980s: a sharp appreciation of the Japanese yen beginning in 1985. And Komatsu's ability to survive Caterpillar's resurgence was surely helped by the slide in the yen after 1995, and especially after 2000.

At the time of writing, the two companies seemed to have settled into relatively stable positions, with Caterpillar the bigger firm but Komatsu also doing well thanks in part to rapid growth in demand from China. But Japanese executives at Komatsu (and other firms) were getting worried about the effects of a yen that was once again on the rise.

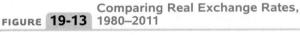

**FIGURE 19-13 Comparing Real Exchange Rates, 1980–2011**

*Source:* Federal Reserve Bank of St. Louis.

## QUESTIONS FOR THOUGHT

**1.** Why does the yen–dollar exchange rate matter so much for the fortunes of Caterpillar and Komatsu?

**2.** Why does the figure present the real rather than the nominal exchange rate? Do you think this makes an important difference to the story?

**3.** In 2011, Japanese policy makers were discussing possible sales of yen on the foreign exchange market. How would this affect the Caterpillar/Komatsu rivalry?

## SUMMARY

1. A country's **balance of payments accounts** summarize its transactions with the rest of the world. The **balance of payments on current account,** or **current account,** includes the **balance of payments on goods and services** together with balances on factor income and transfers. The **merchandise trade balance,** or **trade balance,** is a frequently cited component of the balance of payments on goods and services. The **balance of payments on financial account,** or **financial account,** measures capital flows. By definition, the balance of payments on current account plus the balance of payments on financial account is zero.

2. Capital flows respond to international differences in interest rates and other rates of return; they can be usefully analyzed using an international version of the loanable funds model, which shows how a country where the interest rate would be low in the absence of capital flows sends funds to a country where the interest rate would be high in the absence of capital flows. The underlying determinants of capital flows are international differences in savings and opportunities for investment spending.

3. Currencies are traded in the **foreign exchange market;** the prices at which they are traded are **exchange rates.** When a currency rises against another currency, it **appreciates;** when it falls, it **depreciates.** The **equilibrium exchange rate** matches the quantity of that currency supplied to the foreign exchange market to the quantity demanded.

4. To correct for international differences in inflation rates, economists calculate **real exchange rates,** which multiply the exchange rate between two countries' currencies by the ratio of the countries' price levels. The current account responds only to changes in the real exchange rate, not the nominal exchange rate. **Purchasing power parity** is the exchange rate that makes the cost of a basket of goods and services equal in two countries. While purchasing power parity and the nominal exchange rate almost always differ, purchasing power parity is a good predictor of actual changes in the nominal exchange rate.

5. Countries adopt different **exchange rate regimes,** rules governing exchange rate policy. The main types are **fixed exchange rates,** where the government takes action to keep the exchange rate at a target level, and **floating exchange rates,** where the exchange rate is free to fluctuate. Countries can fix exchange rates using **exchange market intervention,** which requires them to hold **foreign exchange reserves** that they use to buy any surplus of their currency. Alternatively, they can change domestic policies, especially monetary policy, to shift the demand and supply curves in the foreign exchange market. Finally, they can use **foreign exchange controls.**

6. Exchange rate policy poses a dilemma: there are economic payoffs to stable exchange rates, but the policies used to fix the exchange rate have costs. Exchange market intervention requires large reserves, and exchange controls distort incentives. If monetary policy is used to help fix the exchange rate, it isn't available to use for domestic policy.

7. Fixed exchange rates aren't always permanent commitments: countries with a fixed exchange rate sometimes engage in **devaluations,** a reduction in the target value of the currency, or **revaluations,** an increase in the target value of the currency. In addition to helping eliminate a surplus of domestic currency on the foreign exchange market, a devaluation increases aggregate demand. Similarly, a revaluation reduces shortages of domestic currency and reduces aggregate demand.

8. Under floating exchange rates, expansionary monetary policy works in part through the exchange rate: cutting domestic interest rates leads to a depreciation, and through that to higher exports and lower imports, which increases aggregate demand. Contractionary monetary policy has the reverse effect.

9. The fact that one country's imports are another country's exports creates a link between the business cycle in different countries. Floating exchange rates, however, may reduce the strength of that link.

## KEY TERMS

1. How would the following transactions be categorized in the U.S. balance of payments accounts? Would they be entered in the current account (as a payment to or from a foreigner) or the financial account (as a sale of assets to or purchase of assets from a foreigner)? How will the balance of payments on the current and financial accounts change?

   **a.** A French importer buys a case of California wine for $500.

   **b.** An American who works for a French company deposits her paycheck, drawn on a Paris bank, into her San Francisco bank.

   **c.** An American buys a bond from a Japanese company for $10,000.

   **d.** An American charity sends $100,000 to Africa to help local residents buy food after a harvest shortfall.

2. The accompanying diagram shows foreign-owned assets in the United States and U.S.-owned assets abroad, both as a percentage of foreign GDP. As you can see from the diagram, both increased around fivefold from 1980 to 2010.

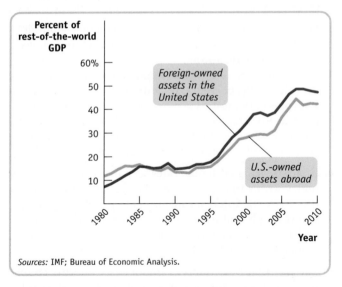

*Sources:* IMF; Bureau of Economic Analysis.

   **a.** As U.S.-owned assets abroad increased as a percentage of foreign GDP, does this mean that the United States, over the period, experienced net capital outflows?

   **b.** Does this diagram indicate that world economies were more tightly linked in 2010 than they were in 1980?

3. In the economy of Scottopia in 2010, exports equaled $400 billion of goods and $300 billion of services, imports equaled $500 billion of goods and $350 billion of services, and the rest of the world purchased $250 billion of Scottopia's assets. What was the merchandise trade balance for Scottopia? What was the balance of payments on current account in Scottopia? What was the balance of payments on financial account? What was the value of Scottopia's purchases of assets from the rest of the world?

4. In the economy of Popania in 2010, total Popanian purchases of assets in the rest of the world equaled $300 billion, purchases of Popanian assets by the rest of the world equaled $400 billion, and Popania exported goods and services equal to $350 billion. What was Popania's balance of payments on financial account in 2010? What was its balance of payments on current account? What was the value of its imports?

5. Suppose that Northlandia and Southlandia are the only two trading countries in the world, that each nation runs a balance of payments on both current and financial accounts equal to zero, and that each nation sees the other's assets as identical to its own. Using the accompanying diagrams, explain how the demand and supply of loanable funds, the interest rate, and the balance of payments on current and financial accounts will change in each country if international capital flows are possible.

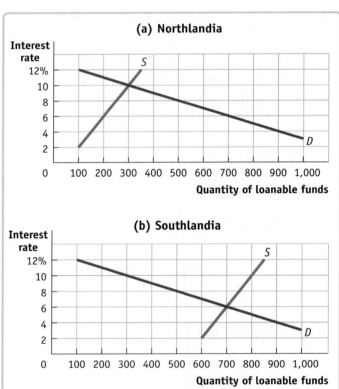

**6.** Based on the exchange rates for the first trading days of 2011 and 2012 shown in the accompanying table, did the U.S. dollar appreciate or depreciate during 2011? Did the movement in the value of the U.S. dollar make American goods and services more or less attractive to foreigners?

| January 3, 2011 | January 3, 2012 |
|---|---|
| US$1.55 to buy 1 British pound sterling | US$1.57 to buy 1 British pound sterling |
| 29.08 Taiwan dollars to buy US$1 | 30.28 Taiwan dollars to buy US$1 |
| US$0.99 to buy 1 Canadian dollar | US$1.01 to buy 1 Canadian dollar |
| 81.56 Japanese yen to buy US$1 | 76.67 Japanese yen to buy US$1 |
| US$1.34 to buy 1 euro | US$1.31 to buy 1 euro |
| 0.93 Swiss franc to buy US$1 | 0.93 Swiss franc to buy US$1 |

**7.** Go to http://fx.sauder.ubc.ca. Using the table labeled "The Most Recent Cross-Rates of Major Currencies," determine whether the British pound (GBP), the Canadian dollar (CAD), the Japanese yen (JPY), the euro (EUR), and the Swiss franc (CHF) have appreciated or depreciated against the U.S. dollar (USD) since January 3, 2012. The exchange rates on January 3, 2012, are listed in the table in Problem 6 above.

**8.** Suppose the United States and Japan are the only two trading countries in the world. What will happen to the value of the U.S. dollar if the following occur, other things equal?

**a.** Japan relaxes some of its import restrictions.

**b.** The United States imposes some import tariffs on Japanese goods.

**c.** Interest rates in the United States rise dramatically.

**d.** A report indicates that Japanese cars last much longer than previously thought, especially compared with American cars.

**9.** From January 1, 2001, to June 2003, the U.S. federal funds rate decreased from 6.5% to 1%. During the same period, the marginal lending facility rate at the European Central Bank decreased from 5.75% to 3%.

**a.** Considering the change in interest rates over the period and using the loanable funds model, would you have expected funds to flow from the United States to Europe or from Europe to the United States over this period?

**b.** The accompanying diagram shows the exchange rate between the euro and the U.S. dollar from

January 1, 2001, through September 2008. Is the movement of the exchange rate over the period January 2001 to June 2003 consistent with the movement in funds predicted in part a?

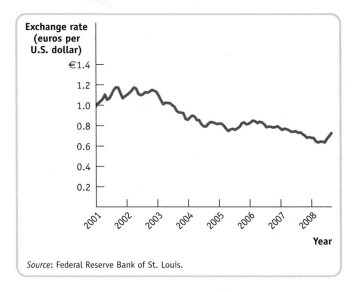

Source: Federal Reserve Bank of St. Louis.

**10.** In each of the following scenarios, suppose that the two nations are the only trading nations in the world. Given inflation and the change in the nominal exchange rate, which nation's goods become more attractive?

**a.** Inflation is 10% in the United States and 5% in Japan; the U.S. dollar–Japanese yen exchange rate remains the same.

**b.** Inflation is 3% in the United States and 8% in Mexico; the price of the U.S. dollar falls from 12.50 to 10.25 Mexican pesos.

**c.** Inflation is 5% in the United States and 3% in the euro area; the price of the euro falls from $1.30 to $1.20.

**d.** Inflation is 8% in the United States and 4% in Canada; the price of the Canadian dollar rises from US$0.60 to US$0.75.

**11.** Starting from a position of equilibrium in the foreign exchange market under a fixed exchange rate regime, how must a government react to an increase in the demand for the nation's goods and services by the rest of the world to keep the exchange rate at its fixed value?

**12.** Suppose that Albernia's central bank has fixed the value of its currency, the bern, to the U.S. dollar (at a rate of US$1.50 to 1 bern) and is committed to that exchange rate. Initially, the foreign exchange market for the bern is also in equilibrium, as shown in the accompanying diagram. However, both Albernians and Americans begin to believe that there are big risks in holding Albernian assets; as a result, they become unwilling to hold Albernian assets unless they receive a higher rate of return on them than they do on U.S. assets. How would this affect the diagram? If the Albernian central bank tries to keep the exchange rate fixed using monetary policy, how will this affect the Albernian economy?

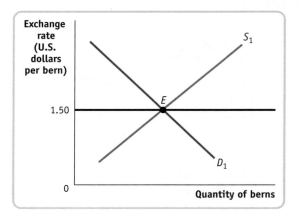

13. Your study partner asks you, "If central banks lose the ability to use discretionary monetary policy under fixed exchange rates, why would nations agree to a fixed exchange rate system?" How do you respond?

# MACROECONOMIC
# DATA TABLES

# Table I.
# MACROECONOMIC DATA FOR THE UNITED STATES 1929–2010[1]

| | 1929 | 1933 | 1939 | 1945 | 1950 | 1955 | 1960 |
|---|---|---|---|---|---|---|---|
| **Nominal GDP and Its Components** | | | | | | | |
| 1. + Consumer spending (C) | 77.4 | 45.9 | 67.2 | 120.0 | 192.2 | 258.8 | 331.7 |
| 2. + Investment spending (I) | 16.5 | 1.7 | 9.3 | 10.8 | 54.1 | 69.0 | 78.9 |
| 3. + Government purchases of goods and services (G) | 9.4 | 8.7 | 14.8 | 93.0 | 46.8 | 86.5 | 111.6 |
| 4. + Exports (X) | 5.9 | 2.0 | 4.0 | 6.8 | 12.4 | 17.7 | 27.0 |
| 5. – Imports (IM) | 5.6 | 1.9 | 3.1 | 7.5 | 11.6 | 17.2 | 22.8 |
| 6. = **Gross domestic product (GDP)** | **103.6** | **56.4** | **92.2** | **223.1** | **293.8** | **414.8** | **526.4** |
| 7. + Income from abroad earned by Americans | 1.1 | 0.4 | 0.7 | 0.8 | 2.2 | 3.5 | 4.9 |
| 8. – Income paid to foreigners | 0.4 | 0.1 | 0.3 | 0.5 | 0.7 | 1.1 | 1.8 |
| 9. = **Gross national product** | **104.4** | **56.7** | **92.5** | **223.4** | **295.2** | **417.2** | **529.5** |
| 10. National income | 94.2 | 48.9 | 82.2 | 198.4 | 264.4 | 372.7 | 474.9 |
| 11. Government transfers | 1.2 | 1.7 | 2.5 | 5.6 | 14.0 | 15.7 | 25.7 |
| 12. Taxes | 1.7 | 0.8 | 1.5 | 19.4 | 18.9 | 32.9 | 46.1 |
| 13. Disposable income | 83.4 | 46.1 | 71.4 | 152.2 | 210.1 | 283.3 | 365.4 |
| 14. Private savings | 3.8 | −0.7 | 3.2 | 31.1 | 15.1 | 19.7 | 26.7 |
| **Real GDP and Growth Measures** | | | | | | | |
| 15. Real GDP (billions of 2000 dollars) | 865.2 | 635.5 | 950.7 | 1,786.3 | 1,777.3 | 2,212.8 | 2,501.8 |
| 16. Real GDP growth (percent change from previous year) | - | −1.3% | 8.1% | −1.1% | 8.7% | 7.1% | 2.5% |
| 17. Real GDP per capita (2000 dollars) | 7,099 | 5,056 | 7,256 | 12,766 | 11,717 | 13,389 | 13,840 |
| 18. Real GDP per capita growth (percent change from previous year) | - | −1.9% | 7.2% | −2.2% | 6.9% | 5.3% | 0.4% |
| **Prices and Inflation** | | | | | | | |
| 19. Consumer Price Index (1982 – 1984 = 100) | 17.1 | 13.0 | 13.9 | 18.0 | 24.1 | 26.8 | 29.6 |
| 20. CPI inflation rate | - | −5.1% | −1.4% | 2.3% | 1.3% | −0.4% | 1.7% |
| 21. Producer Price Index (all commodities, 1982 = 100) | 16.4 | 11.4 | 13.3 | 18.2 | 27.3 | 29.3 | 31.7 |
| 22. PPI inflation rate | - | 1.8% | −1.5% | 1.7% | 3.8% | 0.0% | 0.0% |
| 23. GDP deflator (2000 = 100) | 11.9 | 8.9 | 9.7 | 12.5 | 16.5 | 18.7 | 21.0 |
| 24. GDP deflator inflation rate | - | −2.6% | −1.2% | 2.6% | 0.8% | 1.5% | 1.4% |
| **Population and Employment** | | | | | | | |
| 25. Population (thousands) | 121,878 | 125,690 | 131,028 | 139,928 | 151,684 | 165,275 | 180,760 |
| 26. Labor force (thousands)[2] | 49,180 | 51,590 | 55,230 | 53,860 | 62,208 | 65,023 | 69,628 |
| 27. Unemployed (thousands)[2] | 1,550 | 12,830 | 9,480 | 1,040 | 3,288 | 2,852 | 3,852 |
| 28. Unemployment rate | 3.2% | 24.9% | 17.2% | 1.9% | 5.3% | 4.4% | 5.5% |
| **Government Finance and Money** | | | | | | | |
| 29. Government (federal, state and local) budget balance | 2.6 | −0.5 | −0.1 | −27.4 | 6.8 | 9.2 | 11.5 |
| 30. Budget balance (percent of GDP) | 2.5% | −0.9% | −0.1% | −12.3% | 2.3% | 2.2% | 2.2% |
| 31. M1 | - | - | - | - | - | - | 140.3 |
| 32. M2 | - | - | - | - | - | - | 304.3 |
| 33. Federal funds rate (yearly average) | - | - | - | - | - | 1.8% | 3.2% |
| **International Trade** | | | | | | | |
| 34. Current account balance | - | - | - | - | - | - | 2.8 |

*Sources:* Bureau of Economic Analysis, Bureau of Labor Statistics, Federal Reserve Bank of St. Louis.

1. Data in billions of current dollars unless otherwise stated. Only select dates shown for 1929 through 1965; annual data supplied for 1965 through 2010.
2. Until 1947, includes workers 14 years and older; 1948 and after, includes workers 16 years and older.

| | 1965 | 1966 | 1967 | 1968 | 1969 | 1970 | 1971 | 1972 | 1973 | 1974 | 1975 |
|---|---|---|---|---|---|---|---|---|---|---|---|
| | 443.8 | 480.9 | 507.8 | 558 | 605.1 | 648.3 | 701.6 | 770.2 | 852 | 932.9 | 1,033.80 |
| | 118.2 | 131.3 | 128.6 | 141.2 | 156.4 | 152.4 | 178.2 | 207.6 | 244.5 | 249.4 | 230.2 |
| | 151.5 | 171.8 | 192.5 | 209.3 | 221.4 | 233.7 | 246.4 | 263.4 | 281.7 | 317.9 | 357.7 |
| | | | | | | | | | | | |
| | 37.1 | 40.9 | 43.5 | 47.9 | 51.9 | 59.7 | 63 | 70.8 | 95.3 | 126.7 | 138.7 |
| | 31.5 | 37.1 | 39.9 | 46.6 | 50.5 | 55.8 | 62.3 | 74.2 | 91.2 | 127.5 | 122.7 |
| | **719.1** | **787.8** | **832.4** | **909.8** | **984.4** | **1,038.30** | **1,126.80** | **1,237.90** | **1,382.30** | **1,499.50** | **1,637.70** |
| | 7.9 | 8.1 | 8.7 | 10.1 | 11.8 | 12.8 | 14 | 16.3 | 23.5 | 29.8 | 28 |
| | | | | | | | | | | | |
| | 2.6 | 3.0 | 3.3 | 4 | 5.7 | 6.4 | 6.4 | 7.7 | 10.9 | 14.3 | 15 |
| | **724.4** | **792.9** | **837.8** | **915.9** | **990.5** | **1,044.70** | **1,134.40** | **1,246.40** | **1,394.90** | **1,515.00** | **1,650.70** |
| | 653.4 | 711.0 | 750.4 | 821.2 | 888.5 | 929.5 | 1,005.60 | 1,110.30 | 1,246.10 | 1,341.50 | 1,444.00 |
| | 36.2 | 39.6 | 50.3 | 58.4 | 64.1 | 77.3 | 92.2 | 103 | 115.2 | 135.9 | 171.3 |
| | 57.7 | 66.4 | 73 | 87 | 104.5 | 103.1 | 101.7 | 123.6 | 132.4 | 151 | 147.6 |
| | 498.1 | 537.5 | 575.1 | 624.7 | 673.8 | 735.5 | 801.4 | 869 | 978.1 | 1,071.70 | 1,187.30 |
| | 43.0 | 44.4 | 54.2 | 52.5 | 52.5 | 69.4 | 80.4 | 77.5 | 102.9 | 114.2 | 125.9 |
| | | | | | | | | | | | |
| | 3,191.1 | 3,399.1 | 3,484.60 | 3,653.33 | 3,766.82 | 3,773.97 | 3,900.72 | 4,107.89 | 4,345.92 | 4,321.96 | 4,312.77 |
| | 6.4% | 6.5% | 2.5% | 4.8% | 3.1% | 0.2% | 3.4% | 5.3% | 5.8% | −0.6% | −0.2% |
| | | | | | | | | | | | |
| | 16,420 | 17,290 | 17,533 | 18,199.46 | 18,580.42 | 18,402.76 | 18,781.95 | 19,569.50 | 20,506.43 | 20,206.79 | 19,969.02 |
| | 5.1% | 5.3% | 1.4% | 3.8% | 2.1% | −1.0% | 2.1% | 4.2% | 4.8% | −1.5% | −1.2% |
| | | | | | | | | | | | |
| | 31.5 | 32.4 | 33.4 | 34.8 | 36.7 | 38.8 | 40.5 | 41.8 | 44.4 | 49.3 | 53.8 |
| | | | | | | | | | | | |
| | 1.6% | 2.9% | 3.1% | 4.2% | 5.5% | 5.7% | 4.4% | 3.2% | 6.2% | 11.0% | 9.1% |
| | 32.3 | 33.3 | 33.4 | 34.2 | 35.6 | 36.9 | 38.1 | 39.8 | 45.0 | 53.5 | 58.4 |
| | | | | | | | | | | | |
| | 2.2% | 3.1% | 0.3% | 2.4% | 4.1% | 3.7% | 3.3% | 4.5% | 13.1% | 18.9% | 9.2% |
| | 22.5 | 23.2 | 23.9 | 24.9 | 26.1 | 27.5 | 28.9 | 30.1 | 31.8 | 34.7 | 38.0 |
| | 1.8% | 2.8% | 3.1% | 4.2% | 4.9% | 5.3% | 5.0% | 4.3% | 5.5% | 9.1% | 9.5% |
| | | | | | | | | | | | |
| | 194,347 | 196,599 | 198,664 | 200,664 | 202,649 | 204,982 | 207,589 | 209,838 | 211,857 | 213,815 | 215,891 |
| | 74,455 | 75,770 | 77,348 | 78,710 | 80,705 | 82,796 | 84,376 | 87,011 | 89,411 | 91,976 | 93,770 |
| | 3,366 | 2,875 | 2,972 | 2,797 | 2,830 | 4,127 | 5,022 | 4,876 | 4,359 | 5,173 | 7,940 |
| | 4.5% | 3.8% | 3.8% | 3.6% | 3.5% | 5.0% | 6.0% | 5.6% | 4.9% | 5.6% | 8.5% |
| | | | | | | | | | | | |
| | 9.9 | 10 | −2.3 | 5.1 | 16.5 | −8.4 | −22.2 | −9.3 | 3.9 | −5.2 | −68.2 |
| | | | | | | | | | | | |
| | 1.4% | 1.3% | −0.3% | 0.6% | 1.7% | −0.8% | −2.0% | −0.8% | 0.3% | −0.3% | −4.2% |
| | 163.4 | 171.0 | 177.7 | 190.1 | 201.4 | 209.1 | 223.1 | 239.0 | 256.3 | 269.1 | 281.3 |
| | 442.5 | 471.4 | 503.6 | 545.3 | 578.7 | 601.5 | 674.4 | 758.2 | 831.8 | 880.6 | 963.5 |
| | 4.1% | 5.1% | 4.2% | 5.7% | 8.2% | 7.2% | 4.7% | 4.4% | 8.7% | 10.5% | 5.8% |
| | | | | | | | | | | | |
| | 5.4 | 3.0 | 2.6 | 0.6 | 0.4 | 2.3 | −1.4 | −5.8 | 7.1 | 2.0 | 18.1 |

(continued on next page)

# MACROECONOMIC DATA FOR THE UNITED STATES 1929–2010[1]

| | 1976 | 1977 | 1978 | 1979 | 1980 | 1981 | 1982 |
|---|---|---|---|---|---|---|---|
| **Nominal GDP and Its Components** | | | | | | | |
| 1. + Consumer spending (C) | 1,151.30 | 1,277.80 | 1,427.60 | 1,591.20 | 1,755.80 | 1,939.50 | 2,075.50 |
| 2. + Investment spending (I) | 292 | 361.3 | 438 | 492.9 | 479.3 | 572.4 | 517.2 |
| 3. + Government purchases of goods and services (G) | 383 | 414.1 | 453.6 | 500.7 | 566.1 | 627.5 | 680.4 |
| 4. + Exports (X) | 149.5 | 159.4 | 186.9 | 230.1 | 280.8 | 305.2 | 283.2 |
| 5. – Imports (IM) | 151.1 | 182.4 | 212.3 | 252.7 | 293.8 | 317.8 | 303.2 |
| 6. = Gross domestic product (GDP) | 1,824.60 | 2,030.10 | 2,293.80 | 2,562.20 | 2,788.10 | 3,126.80 | 3,253.20 |
| 7. + Income from abroad earned by Americans | 32.4 | 37.2 | 46.3 | 68.3 | 79.1 | 92 | 101 |
| 8. – Income paid to foreigners | 15.5 | 16.9 | 24.7 | 36.4 | 44.9 | 59.1 | 64.5 |
| 9. = Gross national product | 1,841.40 | 2,050.40 | 2,315.30 | 2,594.20 | 2,822.30 | 3,159.80 | 3,289.70 |
| 10. National income | 1,609.80 | 1,797.40 | 2,027.90 | 2,248.30 | 2,433.00 | 2,729.80 | 2,851.40 |
| 11. Government transfers | 184.3 | 195.9 | 210.9 | 236 | 281.7 | 318.1 | 354.7 |
| 12. Taxes | 172.3 | 197.5 | 229.4 | 268.7 | 298.9 | 345.2 | 354.1 |
| 13. Disposable income | 1,302.30 | 1,435.00 | 1,607.30 | 1,790.90 | 2,002.70 | 2,237.10 | 2,412.70 |
| 14. Private savings | 122.8 | 125.3 | 142.4 | 157.5 | 196.3 | 236.7 | 263.9 |
| **Real GDP and Growth Measures** | | | | | | | |
| 15. Real GDP (billions of 2000 dollars) | 4,544.17 | 4,753.11 | 5,018.18 | 5,174.97 | 5,160.83 | 5,291.82 | 5,189.03 |
| 16. Real GDP growth (percent change from previous year) | 5.4% | 4.6% | 5.6% | 3.1% | –0.3% | 2.5% | –1.9% |
| 17. Real GDP per capita (2000 dollars) | 20,837.89 | 21,577.72 | 22,542.05 | 22,990.19 | 22,663.14 | 23,007.86 | 22,346.71 |
| 18. Real GDP per capita growth (percent change from previous year) | 4.4% | 3.6% | 4.5% | 2.0% | –1.4% | 1.5% | –2.9% |
| **Prices and Inflation** | | | | | | | |
| 19. Consumer Price Index (1982 – 1984 = 100) | 56.9 | 60.6 | 65.2 | 72.6 | 82.4 | 90.9 | 96.5 |
| 20. CPI inflation rate | 5.8% | 6.5% | 7.6% | 11.3% | 13.5% | 10.3% | 6.2% |
| 21. Producer Price Index (all commodities, 1982 = 100) | 61.1 | 64.9 | 69.9 | 78.7 | 89.8 | 98.0 | 100.0 |
| 22. PPI inflation rate | 4.6% | 6.2% | 7.7% | 12.6% | 14.1% | 9.1% | 2.0% |
| 23. GDP deflator (2000 = 100) | 40.2 | 42.7 | 45.7 | 49.5 | 54.0 | 59.1 | 62.7 |
| 24. GDP deflator inflation rate | 5.7% | 6.4% | 7.0% | 8.3% | 9.1% | 9.4% | 6.1% |
| **Population and Employment** | | | | | | | |
| 25. Population (thousands) | 217,999 | 220,193 | 222,525 | 225,003 | 227,622 | 229,916 | 232,128 |
| 26. Labor force (thousands)[2] | 96,151 | 98,984 | 102,233 | 104,961 | 106,974 | 108,676 | 110,244 |
| 27. Unemployed (thousands)[2] | 7,398 | 6,967 | 6,187 | 6,135 | 7,671 | 8,276 | 10,715 |
| 28. Unemployment rate | 7.7% | 7.1% | 6.1% | 5.9% | 7.2% | 7.6% | 9.7% |
| **Government Finance and Money** | | | | | | | |
| 29. Government (federal, state and local) budget balance | –46.3 | –33 | –10.2 | –1 | –47.8 | –49.2 | –137.5 |
| 30. Budget balance (percent of GDP) | –2.5% | –1.6% | –0.4% | 0.0% | –1.7% | –1.6% | –4.2% |
| 31. M1 | 297.2 | 319.9 | 346.2 | 372.6 | 395.7 | 425.0 | 453.0 |
| 32. M2 | 1,086.5 | 1,221.2 | 1,322.2 | 1,425.7 | 1,540.2 | 1,679.3 | 1,832.6 |
| 33. Federal funds rate (yearly average) | 5.1% | 5.5% | 7.9% | 11.2% | 13.4% | 16.4% | 12.3% |
| **International Trade** | | | | | | | |
| 34. Current account balance | 4.3 | –14.3 | –15.1 | –0.3 | 2.3 | 5.0 | –5.5 |

*Sources:* Bureau of Economic Analysis, Bureau of Labor Statistics, Federal Reserve Bank of St. Louis.

1. Data in billions of current dollars unless otherwise stated. Only select dates shown for 1929 through 1965; annual data supplied for 1965 through 2010.
2. Until 1947, includes workers 14 years and older; 1948 and after, includes workers 16 years and older.

| | 1983 | 1984 | 1985 | 1986 | 1987 | 1988 | 1989 | 1990 | 1991 | 1992 | 1993 |
|---|---|---|---|---|---|---|---|---|---|---|---|
| | 2,288.60 | 2,501.10 | 2,717.60 | 2,896.70 | 3,097.00 | 3,350.10 | 3,594.50 | 3,835.50 | 3,980.1 | 4,236.9 | 4,483.6 |
| | 564.3 | 735.6 | 736.2 | 746.5 | 785 | 821.6 | 874.9 | 861 | 802.9 | 864.8 | 953.3 |
| | 733.4 | 796.9 | 878.9 | 949.3 | 999.4 | 1,038.90 | 1,100.60 | 1,181.70 | 1,236.1 | 1,273.5 | 1,294.8 |
| | | | | | | | | | | | |
| | 277 | 302.4 | 302 | 320.3 | 363.8 | 443.9 | 503.1 | 552.1 | 596.6 | 635.0 | 655.6 |
| | 328.6 | 405.1 | 417.2 | 452.9 | 508.7 | 554 | 591 | 629.7 | 623.5 | 667.8 | 720.0 |
| | **3,534.60** | **3,930.90** | **4,217.50** | **4,460.10** | **4,736.40** | **5,100.40** | **5,482.10** | **5,800.50** | **5,992.1** | **6,342.3** | **6,667.4** |
| | 101.9 | 121.9 | 112.4 | 111 | 122.8 | 151.6 | 177.2 | 188.5 | 168.1 | 151.8 | 155.2 |
| | | | | | | | | | | | |
| | 64.8 | 85.6 | 85.9 | 93.4 | 105.2 | 128.3 | 151.2 | 154.1 | 138.2 | 122.7 | 124.0 |
| | **3,571.70** | **3,967.20** | **4,244.00** | **4,477.70** | **4,754.00** | **5,123.80** | **5,508.10** | **5,835.00** | **6,022.0** | **6,371.4** | **6,698.5** |
| | 3,070.90 | 3,461.30 | 3,696.30 | 3,871.50 | 4,150.00 | 4,522.30 | 4,800.50 | 5,059.50 | 5,217.9 | 5,517.1 | 5,784.7 |
| | 382.5 | 395.3 | 420.4 | 446.6 | 464.4 | 493.6 | 538.1 | 592.4 | 628.9 | 756.3 | 804.6 |
| | 352.3 | 377.4 | 417.3 | 437.2 | 489.1 | 504.9 | 566.1 | 592.7 | 586.6 | 610.5 | 646.5 |
| | 2,599.80 | 2,891.50 | 3,079.30 | 3,258.80 | 3,435.30 | 3,726.30 | 3,991.40 | 4,254.00 | 4,444.9 | 4,736.7 | 4,921.6 |
| | 226.9 | 296.3 | 253.6 | 246.5 | 223.4 | 256.6 | 265 | 276.7 | 313.2 | 348.1 | 285.4 |
| | | | | | | | | | | | |
| | 5,423.51 | 5,813.21 | 6,053.79 | 6,263.44 | 6,463.90 | 6,729.59 | 6,970.00 | 7,100.81 | 7,084.2 | 7,324.6 | 7,533.5 |
| | 4.5% | 7.2% | 4.1% | 3.5% | 3.2% | 4.1% | 3.6% | 1.9% | −0.2% | 3.4% | 2.9% |
| | | | | | | | | | | | |
| | 23,145.75 | 24,592.69 | 25,382.90 | 26,024.61 | 26,618.59 | 27,461.83 | 28,176.02 | 28,383.73 | 27,944 | 28,510 | 28,945 |
| | 3.6% | 6.3% | 3.2% | 2.5% | 2.3% | 3.2% | 2.6% | 0.7% | −1.6% | 2.0% | 1.5% |
| | | | | | | | | | | | |
| | 99.6 | 103.9 | 107.6 | 109.6 | 113.6 | 118.3 | 124.0 | 130.7 | 136.2 | 140.3 | 144.5 |
| | | | | | | | | | | | |
| | 3.2% | 4.3% | 3.6% | 1.9% | 3.6% | 4.1% | 4.8% | 5.4% | 4.2% | 3.0% | 3.0% |
| | 101.3 | 103.7 | 103.2 | 100.2 | 102.8 | 106.9 | 112.2 | 116.3 | 116.5 | 117.2 | 118.9 |
| | | | | | | | | | | | |
| | 1.3% | 2.4% | −0.5% | −2.9% | 2.6% | 4.0% | 5.0% | 3.7% | 0.2% | 0.6% | 1.5% |
| | 65.2 | 67.6 | 69.7 | 71.2 | 73.3 | 75.8 | 78.7 | 81.7 | 84.6 | 86.6 | 88.5 |
| | 4.0% | 3.8% | 3.0% | 2.2% | 2.9% | 3.4% | 3.8% | 3.9% | 3.5% | 2.4% | 2.2% |
| | | | | | | | | | | | |
| | 234,247 | 236,307 | 238,416 | 240,593 | 242,751 | 244,968 | 247,286 | 250,047 | 253,392 | 256,777 | 260,146 |
| | 111,515 | 113,532 | 115,467 | 117,846 | 119,853 | 121,671 | 123,851 | 125,857 | 126,352 | 128,099 | 129,185 |
| | 10,694 | 8,529 | 8,313 | 8,245 | 7,414 | 6,697 | 6,524 | 7,061 | 8,640 | 9,611 | 8,927 |
| | 9.6% | 7.5% | 7.2% | 7.0% | 6.2% | 5.5% | 5.3% | 5.6% | 6.9% | 7.5% | 6.9% |
| | | | | | | | | | | | |
| | −171.4 | −147.5 | −156.3 | −173.9 | −137.4 | −121.2 | −113.8 | −170.3 | −224.2 | −303.9 | −281.2 |
| | | | | | | | | | | | |
| | −4.8% | −3.8% | −3.7% | −3.9% | −2.9% | −2.4% | −2.1% | −2.9% | −3.7% | −4.8% | −4.2% |
| | 503.2 | 538.6 | 587.0 | 666.3 | 743.6 | 774.8 | 782.2 | 810.6 | 859.0 | 965.9 | 1,078.4 |
| | 2,056.9 | 2,221.2 | 2,419.0 | 2,615.8 | 2,786.0 | 2,936.2 | 3,059.7 | 3,227.4 | 3,347.1 | 3,409.0 | 3,444.7 |
| | 9.1% | 10.2% | 8.1% | 6.8% | 6.7% | 7.6% | 9.2% | 8.1% | 5.7% | 3.5% | 3.0% |
| | | | | | | | | | | | |
| | −38.7 | −94.3 | −118.2 | −147.2 | −160.7 | −121.2 | −99.5 | −79.0 | 2.9 | −51.6 | −84.8 |

(continued on next page)

| | 1994 | 1995 | 1996 | 1997 | 1998 | 1999 | 2000 |
|---|---|---|---|---|---|---|---|
| **Nominal GDP and Its Components** | | | | | | | |
| 1. + Consumer spending (C) | 4,750.8 | 4,987.3 | 5,273.6 | 5,570.6 | 5,918.5 | 6,342.8 | 6,830.4 |
| 2. + Investment spending (I) | 1,097.3 | 1,144.0 | 1,240.2 | 1,388.7 | 1,510.8 | 1,641.5 | 1,772.2 |
| 3. + Government purchases of goods and services (G) | 1,329.8 | 1,374.0 | 1,421.0 | 1,474.4 | 1,526.1 | 1,631.3 | 1,731.0 |
| 4. + Exports (X) | 720.7 | 811.9 | 867.7 | 954.4 | 953.9 | 989.3 | 1,093.2 |
| 5. − Imports (IM) | 813.4 | 902.6 | 964.0 | 1,055.8 | 1,115.7 | 1,251.4 | 1,475.3 |
| 6. = **Gross domestic product (GDP)** | **7,085.2** | **7,414.7** | **7,838.5** | **8,332.4** | **8,793.5** | **9,353.5** | **9,951.5** |
| 7. + Income from abroad earned by Americans | 184.1 | 229.3 | 245.8 | 279.5 | 286.2 | 319.5 | 380.5 |
| 8. − Income paid to foreigners | 160.0 | 199.6 | 214.2 | 256.1 | 268.9 | 291.7 | 342.8 |
| 9. = **Gross national product** | **7,109.2** | **7,444.3** | **7,870.1** | **8,355.8** | **8,810.8** | **9,381.3** | **9,989.2** |
| 10. National income | 6,181.3 | 6,522.3 | 6,931.7 | 7,406.0 | 7,875.6 | 8,358.0 | 8,938.9 |
| 11. Government transfers | 839.9 | 882.4 | 929.2 | 954.6 | 978.1 | 1,014.9 | 1,071.5 |
| 12. Taxes | 690.5 | 743.9 | 832.0 | 926.2 | 1,026.4 | 1,107.5 | 1,232.3 |
| 13. Disposable income | 5,184.3 | 5,457.0 | 5,759.6 | 6,074.6 | 6,498.9 | 6,803.3 | 7,327.2 |
| 14. Private savings | 270.7 | 286.3 | 281.1 | 280.4 | 341.5 | 207.8 | 213.1 |
| **Real GDP and Growth Measures** | | | | | | | |
| 15. Real GDP (billions of 2000 dollars) | 7,840.4 | 8,037.5 | 8,338.2 | 8,709.8 | 9,089.1 | 9,527.8 | 9,922.2 |
| 16. Real GDP growth (percent change from previous year) | 4.1% | 2.5% | 3.7% | 4.5% | 4.4% | 4.8% | 4.1% |
| 17. Real GDP per capita (2000 dollars) | 29,762 | 30,152 | 30,916 | 31,910 | 32,915 | 34,111 | 35,135 |
| 18. Real GDP per capita growth (percent change from previous year) | 2.8% | 1.3% | 2.5% | 3.2% | 3.1% | 3.6% | 3.0% |
| **Prices and Inflation** | | | | | | | |
| 19. Consumer Price Index (1982 – 1984 = 100) | 148.2 | 152.4 | 156.9 | 160.5 | 163.0 | 166.6 | 172.2 |
| 20. CPI inflation rate | 2.6% | 2.8% | 3.0% | 2.3% | 1.6% | 2.2% | 3.4% |
| 21. Producer Price Index (all commodities, 1982 = 100) | 120.4 | 124.7 | 127.7 | 127.6 | 124.4 | 125.5 | 132.7 |
| 22. PPI inflation rate | 1.3% | 3.6% | 2.4% | −0.1% | −2.5% | 0.9% | 5.7% |
| 23. GDP deflator (2000 = 100) | 90.4 | 92.3 | 94.0 | 95.7 | 96.8 | 98.2 | 100.3 |
| 24. GDP deflator inflation rate | 2.1% | 2.1% | 1.9% | 1.8% | 1.1% | 1.5% | 2.2% |
| **Population and Employment** | | | | | | | |
| 25. Population (thousands) | 263,325 | 266,458 | 269,581 | 272,822 | 276,022 | 279,195 | 282,296 |
| 26. Labor force (thousands)[2] | 131,047 | 132,315 | 133,951 | 136,301 | 137,680 | 139,380 | 142,586 |
| 27. Unemployed (thousands)[2] | 7,976 | 7,407 | 7,231 | 6,729 | 6,204 | 5,879 | 5,685 |
| 28. Unemployment rate | 6.1% | 5.6% | 5.4% | 4.9% | 4.5% | 4.2% | 4.0% |
| **Government Finance and Money** | | | | | | | |
| 29. Government (federal, state and local) budget balance | −212.2 | −197 | −125.3 | −23.8 | 80.5 | 140.6 | 226.5 |
| 30. Budget balance (percent of GDP) | −3.0% | −2.7% | −1.6% | −0.3% | 0.9% | 1.5% | 2.3% |
| 31. M1 | 1,145.2 | 1,143.0 | 1,106.8 | 1,070.2 | 1,080.7 | 1,102.3 | 1,103.7 |
| 32. M2 | 3,490.6 | 3,562.9 | 3,735.7 | 3,924.2 | 4,203.7 | 4,514.0 | 4,784.2 |
| 33. Federal funds rate (yearly average) | 4.2% | 5.8% | 5.3% | 5.5% | 5.4% | 5.0% | 6.2% |
| **International Trade** | | | | | | | |
| 34. Current account balance | −121.6 | −113.6 | −124.8 | −140.7 | −215.1 | −300.8 | −416.4 |

*Sources:* Bureau of Economic Analysis, Bureau of Labor Statistics, Federal Reserve Bank of St. Louis.

1. Data in billions of current dollars unless otherwise stated. Only select dates shown for 1929 through 1965; annual data supplied for 1965 through 2010.
2. Until 1947, includes workers 14 years and older; 1948 and after, includes workers 16 years and older.

| 2001 | 2002 | 2003 | 2004 | 2005 | 2006 | 2007 | 2008 | 2009 | 2010 |
|---|---|---|---|---|---|---|---|---|---|
| 7,148.8 | 7,439.2 | 7,804.0 | 8,285.1 | 8,819.0 | 9,322.7 | 9,806.3 | 10,104.5 | 10,001.3 | 10,349.1 |
| 1,661.9 | 1,647.0 | 1,729.7 | 1,968.6 | 2,172.2 | 2,327.2 | 2,295.2 | 2,096.7 | 1,589.2 | 1,827.5 |
| 1,846.4 | 1,983.3 | 2,112.6 | 2,232.8 | 2,369.9 | 2,518.4 | 2,674.2 | 2,878.3 | 2,914.9 | 3,000.2 |
| | | | | | | | | | |
| 1,027.7 | 1,003.0 | 1,041.0 | 1,180.2 | 1,305.1 | 1,471.0 | 1,661.7 | 1,843.4 | 1,578.4 | 1,837.5 |
| 1,398.7 | 1,430.2 | 1,545.1 | 1,798.9 | 2,027.8 | 2,240.3 | 2,375.7 | 2,553.8 | 1,964.7 | 2,353.9 |
| **10,286.2** | **10,642.3** | **11,142.1** | **11,867.8** | **12,638.4** | **13,398.9** | **14,061.8** | **14,369.1** | **14,119.0** | **14,660.4** |
| 323.0 | 313.5 | 353.3 | 448.6 | 573.0 | 721.1 | 871.0 | 839.2 | 629.8 | 706.2 |
| | | | | | | | | | |
| 271.1 | 264.4 | 284.6 | 357.4 | 475.9 | 648.6 | 747.7 | 664.7 | 483.6 | 517.9 |
| **10,338.1** | **10,691.4** | **11,210.8** | **11,959.0** | **12,735.5** | **13,471.3** | **14,185.1** | **14,543.6** | **14,265.3** | **14,848.7** |
| 9,185.2 | 9,408.5 | 9,840.2 | 10,534.0 | 11,273.8 | 12,031.2 | 12,396.4 | 12,557.8 | 12,225.0 | 12,828.2 |
| 1,169.0 | 1,280.9 | 1,354.8 | 1,440.1 | 1,534.9 | 1,631.0 | 1,743.4 | 1,902.7 | 2,164.9 | 2,333.3 |
| 1,234.8 | 1,050.4 | 1,000.3 | 1,047.8 | 1,208.6 | 1,352.4 | 1,488.7 | 1,438.2 | 1,140.0 | 1,166.8 |
| 7,648.5 | 8,009.7 | 8,377.8 | 8,889.4 | 9,277.3 | 9,915.7 | 10,423.6 | 10,952.9 | 11,034.9 | 11,379.9 |
| 204.9 | 282.2 | 289.8 | 303.7 | 127.7 | 235.0 | 214.7 | 447.9 | 655.3 | 659.2 |
| | | | | | | | | | |
| 10,029.3 | 10,211.2 | 10,465.5 | 10,839.4 | 11,170.5 | 11,469.1 | 11,692.4 | 11,692.3 | 11,384.6 | 11,709.5 |
| 1.1% | 1.8% | 2.5% | 3.6% | 3.1% | 2.7% | 1.9% | 0.0% | −2.6% | 2.9% |
| | | | | | | | | | |
| 35,151 | 35,441 | 35,984 | 36,933 | 37,711 | 38,353 | 38,716 | 38,359 | 37,026 | 37,762 |
| 0.0% | 0.8% | 1.5% | 2.6% | 2.1% | 1.7% | 0.9% | −0.9% | −3.5% | 2.0% |
| | | | | | | | | | |
| 177.1 | 179.9 | 184.0 | 188.9 | 195.3 | 201.6 | 207.342 | 215.303 | 214.537 | 218.056 |
| | | | | | | | | | |
| 2.8% | 1.6% | 2.3% | 2.7% | 3.4% | 3.2% | 2.8% | 3.8% | −0.4% | 1.6% |
| 134.2 | 131.1 | 138.1 | 146.7 | 157.4 | 164.7 | 172.6 | 189.6 | 172.9 | 184.8 |
| | | | | | | | | | |
| 1.1% | −2.3% | 5.3% | 6.2% | 7.3% | 4.6% | 4.8% | 9.8% | −8.8% | 6.9% |
| 102.6 | 104.3 | 106.5 | 109.5 | 113.2 | 116.9 | 120.3 | 122.9 | 124.1 | 125.3 |
| 2.3% | 1.6% | 2.2% | 2.8% | 3.3% | 3.3% | 2.9% | 2.2% | 0.9% | 1.0% |
| | | | | | | | | | |
| 285,216 | 288,019 | 290,733 | 293,389 | 296,115 | 298,930 | 301,903 | 304,718 | 307,374 | 309,997 |
| 143,769 | 144,856 | 146,500 | 147,380 | 149,289 | 151,409 | 153,126 | 154,331 | 154,206 | 153,893 |
| 6,830 | 8,375 | 8,770 | 8,140 | 7,579 | 6,991 | 7,077 | 8,962 | 14,319 | 14,825 |
| 4.7% | 5.8% | 6.0% | 5.5% | 5.1% | 4.6% | 4.6% | 5.8% | 9.3% | 9.6% |
| | | | | | | | | | |
| 24.6 | −306.9 | −415.2 | −387.8 | −257.1 | −152.7 | −233 | −663.6 | −1,271.90 | −1,299.20 |
| | | | | | | | | | |
| 0.2% | −2.9% | −3.7% | −3.3% | −2.0% | −1.1% | −1.7% | −4.6% | −9.0% | −8.9% |
| 1,140.3 | 1,196.3 | 1,273.5 | 1,344.2 | 1,371.6 | 1,374.2 | 1,372.2 | 1,433.1 | 1,636.8 | 1,743.6 |
| 5,201.9 | 5,594.3 | 5,978.7 | 6,257.9 | 6,523.9 | 6,866.5 | 7,299.2 | 7,818.3 | 8,434.3 | 8,631.1 |
| 3.9% | 1.7% | 1.1% | 1.4% | 3.2% | 5.0% | 5.0% | 1.9% | 0.2% | 0.2% |
| | | | | | | | | | |
| −397.2 | −458.1 | −520.7 | −630.5 | −747.6 | −802.6 | −718.1 | −668.9 | −378.4 | −470.2 |

# Table II.
# MACROECONOMIC DATA FOR SELECT COUNTRIES
## GDP (Billions of U.S. Dollars)

| Country | 1985 | 1986 | 1987 | 1988 | 1989 | 1990 | 1991 | 1992 | 1993 |
|---|---|---|---|---|---|---|---|---|---|
| Argentina | 88.18 | 106.04 | 108.72 | 127.34 | 81.70 | 141.33 | 189.58 | 228.76 | 236.49 |
| Australia | 176.88 | 183.57 | 216.18 | 274.38 | 310.98 | 328.20 | 328.79 | 321.64 | 312.89 |
| Austria | 68.03 | 96.53 | 120.71 | 132.41 | 132.06 | 165.26 | 172.78 | 193.52 | 188.39 |
| Bangladesh | 21.34 | 22.37 | 24.68 | 26.64 | 29.34 | 30.50 | 31.43 | 31.44 | 32.95 |
| Belgium | 85.76 | 118.88 | 147.79 | 160.47 | 162.45 | 203.31 | 208.53 | 231.79 | 222.26 |
| Brazil | 253.08 | 293.58 | 319.55 | 356.98 | 490.05 | 507.78 | 445.24 | 426.52 | 478.62 |
| Bulgaria | 27.39 | 24.24 | 28.10 | 45.92 | 46.77 | 20.62 | 2.02 | 8.20 | 4.45 |
| Canada | 355.71 | 368.87 | 421.53 | 498.16 | 555.52 | 582.74 | 598.20 | 579.52 | 563.68 |
| Chile | 16.49 | 17.72 | 20.90 | 24.64 | 28.39 | 31.56 | 36.43 | 44.47 | 47.69 |
| China | 307.02 | 297.59 | 323.97 | 404.15 | 451.31 | 390.28 | 409.17 | 488.22 | 613.22 |
| Colombia | 48.68 | 48.75 | 50.75 | 54.71 | 55.17 | 56.19 | 57.54 | 68.75 | 77.85 |
| Cyprus | 2.43 | 3.09 | 3.71 | 4.27 | 4.56 | 5.59 | 5.77 | 6.91 | 6.61 |
| Czech Republic | n/a | n/a | n/a | n/a | n/a | n/a | n/a | n/a | n/a |
| Denmark | 61.20 | 86.37 | 107.37 | 113.23 | 110.06 | 135.84 | 136.70 | 150.20 | 140.63 |
| Dominican Republic | 6.49 | 7.88 | 8.30 | 7.60 | 8.58 | 7.99 | 9.79 | 11.49 | 12.95 |
| Ecuador | 16.18 | 11.87 | 11.10 | 10.55 | 10.36 | 10.52 | 11.80 | 12.90 | 15.07 |
| Egypt | 46.45 | 51.43 | 73.57 | 88.00 | 109.71 | 91.38 | 46.06 | 42.01 | 47.10 |
| Estonia | n/a | n/a | n/a | n/a | n/a | n/a | n/a | n/a | 1.73 |
| Finland | 55.25 | 72.33 | 90.12 | 107.26 | 116.73 | 139.12 | 125.66 | 110.72 | 87.39 |
| France | 547.90 | 761.35 | 923.68 | 1,004.44 | 1,009.84 | 1,248.56 | 1,249.22 | 1,374.07 | 1,292.12 |
| Germany | 639.70 | 913.64 | 1,136.93 | 1,225.73 | 1,216.80 | 1,547.03 | 1,815.06 | 2,066.73 | 2,005.56 |
| Ghana | 5.33 | 6.03 | 4.76 | 5.15 | 5.94 | 6.53 | 6.85 | 6.66 | 5.97 |
| Greece | 45.13 | 53.10 | 61.78 | 71.95 | 74.56 | 92.20 | 99.42 | 109.56 | 102.61 |
| Guatemala | 10.39 | 5.62 | 6.50 | 7.04 | 8.12 | 7.07 | 8.70 | 9.60 | 10.46 |
| Hungary | 21.14 | 24.35 | 26.77 | 29.29 | 29.90 | 33.89 | 34.27 | 38.19 | 39.57 |
| Iceland | 2.94 | 3.93 | 5.44 | 6.02 | 5.59 | 6.36 | 6.80 | 6.97 | 6.12 |
| India | 229.56 | 252.45 | 278.20 | 304.46 | 302.14 | 325.93 | 289.36 | 291.86 | 285.33 |
| Ireland | 20.99 | 28.14 | 33.36 | 36.55 | 37.70 | 47.77 | 48.42 | 54.44 | 50.44 |
| Israel | 25.32 | 31.17 | 37.23 | 46.06 | 46.81 | 55.09 | 62.10 | 69.03 | 69.19 |
| Italy | 437.10 | 619.08 | 777.01 | 860.86 | 895.34 | 1,135.54 | 1,198.99 | 1,271.91 | 1,022.66 |
| Jamaica | 2.16 | 2.57 | 2.90 | 3.46 | 4.01 | 5.06 | 4.75 | 4.25 | 5.92 |
| Japan | 1,352.06 | 2,003.32 | 2,429.60 | 2,950.00 | 2,951.77 | 3,030.05 | 3,464.93 | 3,781.78 | 4,340.89 |
| Kenya | 8.75 | 10.39 | 11.39 | 11.81 | 11.71 | 12.18 | 11.50 | 11.33 | 7.87 |
| Korea | 98.50 | 113.74 | 143.38 | 192.11 | 236.23 | 270.41 | 315.58 | 338.17 | 372.21 |
| Latvia | n/a | n/a | n/a | n/a | n/a | n/a | n/a | 1.55 | 2.47 |

*Source:* International Monetary Fund, World Economic Outlook Database, October 2010.
2010 is estimated as of 4/13/2011.

| 1994 | 1995 | 1996 | 1997 | 1998 | 1999 | 2000 | 2001 | 2002 | 2003 | 2004 |
|---|---|---|---|---|---|---|---|---|---|---|
| 257.43 | 258.02 | 272.22 | 292.99 | 299.08 | 283.76 | 284.54 | 269.10 | 102.72 | 129.54 | 153.01 |
| 356.64 | 382.25 | 428.03 | 428.44 | 382.28 | 413.57 | 400.87 | 379.42 | 426.47 | 543.19 | 658.55 |
| 201.64 | 238.55 | 234.23 | 207.13 | 212.44 | 211.21 | 191.76 | 190.32 | 206.68 | 252.52 | 289.42 |
| 35.80 | 39.58 | 41.52 | 43.39 | 44.76 | 46.53 | 47.05 | 47.19 | 49.56 | 54.48 | 59.12 |
| 242.62 | 284.79 | 275.17 | 249.76 | 255.57 | 254.38 | 233.14 | 232.34 | 253.29 | 311.70 | 360.98 |
| 596.76 | 769.74 | 840.05 | 871.52 | 841.30 | 573.12 | 642.42 | 552.84 | 500.27 | 555.54 | 665.55 |
| 7.82 | 13.11 | 9.90 | 10.37 | 12.85 | 12.98 | 12.60 | 13.60 | 15.60 | 19.99 | 24.65 |
| 564.48 | 590.50 | 613.78 | 637.53 | 616.78 | 661.25 | 724.91 | 715.44 | 734.65 | 865.90 | 992.23 |
| 55.16 | 71.35 | 75.77 | 82.81 | 79.37 | 72.99 | 75.20 | 68.56 | 67.25 | 73.99 | 95.65 |
| 559.22 | 727.95 | 856.08 | 952.65 | 1,019.48 | 1,083.28 | 1,198.48 | 1,324.81 | 1,453.83 | 1,640.96 | 1,931.65 |
| 97.87 | 110.81 | 120.00 | 112.70 | 109.12 | 96.89 | 100.36 | 98.75 | 98.23 | 94.97 | 118.86 |
| 7.45 | 9.25 | 9.35 | 8.90 | 9.56 | 9.78 | 9.32 | 9.68 | 10.56 | 13.32 | 15.82 |
| n/a | 55.26 | 62.01 | 57.14 | 61.85 | 60.19 | 56.72 | 61.84 | 75.28 | 91.36 | 109.53 |
| 153.59 | 181.99 | 184.44 | 170.44 | 173.65 | 173.94 | 160.08 | 160.48 | 173.88 | 212.62 | 244.73 |
| 13.99 | 15.52 | 17.07 | 19.19 | 20.08 | 21.48 | 23.72 | 24.62 | 24.93 | 20.18 | 21.56 |
| 18.59 | 20.22 | 21.29 | 23.66 | 23.28 | 16.69 | 15.95 | 21.27 | 24.72 | 28.41 | 32.65 |
| 51.88 | 60.16 | 67.63 | 75.87 | 84.82 | 89.94 | 99.16 | 95.40 | 87.51 | 81.38 | 78.80 |
| 2.42 | 3.78 | 4.73 | 5.05 | 5.59 | 5.71 | 5.68 | 6.24 | 7.32 | 9.85 | 12.03 |
| 100.99 | 130.85 | 128.28 | 123.07 | 129.84 | 130.39 | 122.07 | 124.67 | 135.56 | 164.44 | 189.17 |
| 1,366.16 | 1,572.38 | 1,574.32 | 1,425.80 | 1,474.24 | 1,458.37 | 1,333.28 | 1,341.25 | 1,463.46 | 1,804.41 | 2,060.58 |
| 2,151.03 | 2,524.95 | 2,439.35 | 2,163.23 | 2,187.48 | 2,146.43 | 1,905.80 | 1,892.60 | 2,024.06 | 2,446.89 | 2,748.82 |
| 5.45 | 6.46 | 6.93 | 6.89 | 7.48 | 7.72 | 4.98 | 5.32 | 6.17 | 7.63 | 8.88 |
| 109.82 | 128.90 | 136.27 | 133.13 | 133.87 | 137.83 | 127.60 | 131.14 | 147.91 | 194.99 | 231.02 |
| 11.84 | 13.32 | 14.20 | 16.09 | 17.31 | 16.49 | 17.19 | 18.70 | 20.78 | 21.92 | 23.96 |
| 42.55 | 45.79 | 46.59 | 47.18 | 48.75 | 49.13 | 47.29 | 53.37 | 66.77 | 83.88 | 102.61 |
| 6.29 | 7.01 | 7.31 | 7.42 | 8.27 | 8.73 | 8.68 | 7.90 | 8.91 | 10.97 | 13.23 |
| 323.94 | 367.73 | 378.99 | 424.14 | 427.55 | 456.52 | 479.87 | 491.44 | 514.25 | 595.44 | 690.32 |
| 55.35 | 67.13 | 74.09 | 81.29 | 88.12 | 96.42 | 97.04 | 104.91 | 123.21 | 158.33 | 185.68 |
| 78.37 | 96.06 | 105.37 | 108.39 | 109.89 | 110.79 | 124.75 | 123.06 | 113.01 | 118.90 | 126.84 |
| 1,054.90 | 1,126.63 | 1,259.95 | 1,193.62 | 1,218.67 | 1,202.40 | 1,100.56 | 1,118.32 | 1,223.24 | 1,510.06 | 1,730.10 |
| 7.66 | 5.81 | 7.84 | 8.20 | 8.62 | 8.76 | 8.95 | 9.13 | 9.56 | 9.49 | 10.17 |
| 4,778.99 | 5,264.38 | 4,642.55 | 4,261.84 | 3,857.03 | 4,368.73 | 4,667.45 | 4,095.48 | 3,918.33 | 4,229.10 | 4,605.94 |
| 9.42 | 11.94 | 12.05 | 13.28 | 13.77 | 12.88 | 12.32 | 13.06 | 13.19 | 15.04 | 16.09 |
| 435.59 | 531.14 | 573.00 | 532.24 | 357.51 | 461.81 | 533.39 | 504.58 | 575.93 | 643.76 | 721.98 |
| 4.15 | 4.96 | 5.68 | 6.25 | 6.73 | 7.29 | 7.83 | 8.31 | 9.32 | 11.19 | 13.76 |

(continued on next page)

# MACROECONOMIC DATA FOR SELECT COUNTRIES
## GDP (Billions of U.S. Dollars)

| Country | 2005 | 2006 | 2007 | 2008 | 2009 | 2010 |
|---|---|---|---|---|---|---|
| Argentina | 183.00 | 214.04 | 262.04 | 328.03 | 310.06 | 351.02 |
| Australia | 738.08 | 783.67 | 951.77 | 1,058.05 | 994.25 | 1,219.72 |
| Austria | 303.45 | 322.64 | 372.83 | 416.62 | 382.07 | 366.26 |
| Bangladesh | 61.13 | 65.20 | 73.97 | 84.46 | 94.60 | 105.40 |
| Belgium | 377.77 | 399.98 | 459.25 | 506.72 | 472.10 | 461.33 |
| Brazil | 890.05 | 1,093.49 | 1,366.22 | 1,635.52 | 1,574.04 | 2,023.53 |
| Bulgaria | 27.19 | 31.66 | 39.55 | 49.90 | 47.10 | 44.84 |
| Canada | 1,133.76 | 1,278.61 | 1,424.07 | 1,499.11 | 1,336.07 | 1,563.66 |
| Chile | 118.22 | 146.75 | 164.21 | 170.86 | 161.62 | 199.18 |
| China | 2,256.92 | 2,712.92 | 3,494.24 | 4,519.95 | 4,984.73 | 5,745.13 |
| Colombia | 146.62 | 161.01 | 210.52 | 233.73 | 232.40 | 283.11 |
| Cyprus | 17.00 | 18.42 | 21.84 | 25.38 | 23.60 | 22.75 |
| Czech Republic | 124.55 | 142.61 | 174.22 | 216.09 | 190.32 | 195.23 |
| Denmark | 257.68 | 274.38 | 310.72 | 340.80 | 310.09 | 304.56 |
| Dominican Republic | 33.53 | 35.67 | 40.99 | 45.52 | 46.71 | 50.87 |
| Ecuador | 36.94 | 41.71 | 45.50 | 54.28 | 55.55 | 61.49 |
| Egypt | 89.79 | 107.38 | 130.35 | 162.44 | 187.95 | 216.83 |
| Estonia | 13.90 | 16.81 | 21.69 | 23.70 | 19.31 | 19.22 |
| Finland | 195.97 | 207.99 | 246.31 | 271.75 | 238.61 | 231.98 |
| France | 2,147.77 | 2,270.36 | 2,598.77 | 2,865.23 | 2,656.38 | 2,555.44 |
| Germany | 2,793.23 | 2,921.27 | 3,333.93 | 3,651.62 | 3,338.68 | 3,305.90 |
| Ghana | 10.73 | 12.74 | 15.02 | 16.50 | 15.33 | 18.06 |
| Greece | 243.38 | 264.26 | 310.36 | 351.95 | 330.78 | 305.01 |
| Guatemala | 27.21 | 30.23 | 34.11 | 39.15 | 37.66 | 40.77 |
| Hungary | 110.17 | 112.91 | 138.37 | 155.48 | 129.54 | 132.28 |
| Iceland | 16.34 | 16.73 | 20.43 | 16.80 | 12.14 | 12.77 |
| India | 809.72 | 908.04 | 1,151.65 | 1,260.62 | 1,236.94 | 1,430.02 |
| Ireland | 202.20 | 222.68 | 259.56 | 264.89 | 222.36 | 204.14 |
| Israel | 134.26 | 145.84 | 168.00 | 202.30 | 195.39 | 201.25 |
| Italy | 1,780.78 | 1,865.11 | 2,119.25 | 2,307.43 | 2,118.26 | 2,036.69 |
| Jamaica | 11.08 | 11.97 | 12.90 | 13.53 | 12.64 | 13.74 |
| Japan | 4,552.19 | 4,362.58 | 4,377.96 | 4,886.95 | 5,068.89 | 5,390.90 |
| Kenya | 19.37 | 23.30 | 28.89 | 26.62 | 30.14 | 32.42 |
| Korea | 844.87 | 951.77 | 1,049.24 | 931.41 | 832.51 | 986.26 |
| Latvia | 16.04 | 19.94 | 28.80 | 33.87 | 25.93 | 23.39 |

Source: International Monetary Fund, World Economic Outlook Database, October 2010.
2010 is estimated as of 4/13/2011.

| Country | 1985 | 1986 | 1987 | 1988 | 1989 | 1990 | 1991 | 1992 | 1993 |
|---|---|---|---|---|---|---|---|---|---|
| Lithuania | n/a | n/a | n/a | n/a | n/a | n/a | n/a | 1.99 | 2.81 |
| Luxembourg | 4.57 | 6.65 | 8.26 | 9.36 | 9.96 | 12.71 | 13.77 | 15.42 | 15.81 |
| Malaysia | 31.77 | 28.24 | 32.18 | 35.27 | 38.85 | 44.03 | 49.88 | 60.05 | 67.90 |
| Mexico | 211.52 | 146.45 | 160.60 | 196.48 | 239.44 | 282.56 | 338.74 | 392.84 | 436.13 |
| Netherlands | 133.17 | 185.60 | 226.44 | 241.38 | 238.18 | 295.46 | 303.46 | 334.65 | 324.39 |
| New Zealand | 22.38 | 27.23 | 36.29 | 44.67 | 43.07 | 44.68 | 42.79 | 40.62 | 43.94 |
| Nigeria | 25.97 | 20.56 | 21.91 | 24.31 | 23.49 | 31.48 | 28.34 | 25.52 | 15.79 |
| Norway | 64.26 | 77.20 | 92.45 | 100.06 | 100.77 | 117.62 | 119.67 | 128.32 | 118.17 |
| Peru | 17.21 | 25.82 | 42.64 | 33.73 | 41.63 | 28.98 | 34.55 | 35.95 | 34.82 |
| Philippines | 30.73 | 29.87 | 33.20 | 37.89 | 42.65 | 44.16 | 45.32 | 52.98 | 54.37 |
| Poland | 70.78 | 73.68 | 63.71 | 68.61 | 66.90 | 62.08 | 80.45 | 88.71 | 90.37 |
| Portugal | 26.78 | 37.25 | 46.61 | 54.52 | 58.82 | 78.13 | 88.43 | 106.34 | 93.57 |
| Romania | 47.80 | 51.77 | 57.89 | 59.93 | 53.69 | 38.24 | 28.85 | 19.58 | 26.36 |
| Russia | n/a | n/a | n/a | n/a | n/a | n/a | n/a | 85.59 | 183.82 |
| Saudi Arabia | 103.89 | 86.95 | 85.70 | 88.26 | 95.34 | 116.78 | 131.34 | 136.30 | 132.15 |
| Singapore | 18.46 | 18.73 | 21.55 | 26.48 | 31.41 | 38.84 | 45.19 | 52.01 | 60.47 |
| South Africa | 57.27 | 65.42 | 85.79 | 92.24 | 95.98 | 112.00 | 120.24 | 130.53 | 130.45 |
| Spain | 176.69 | 244.48 | 309.75 | 363.91 | 401.39 | 520.71 | 560.80 | 613.02 | 514.95 |
| Sweden | 106.38 | 140.79 | 171.61 | 193.88 | 204.45 | 244.55 | 257.90 | 267.17 | 202.04 |
| Switzerland | 99.47 | 142.60 | 178.58 | 193.20 | 186.53 | 238.22 | 241.00 | 250.98 | 244.09 |
| Thailand | 38.90 | 43.10 | 50.54 | 61.67 | 72.25 | 85.64 | 96.19 | 109.43 | 121.80 |
| Turkey | 90.38 | 101.80 | 117.18 | 122.13 | 144.03 | 202.38 | 202.72 | 213.58 | 242.14 |
| Ukraine | n/a | n/a | n/a | n/a | n/a | n/a | n/a | 20.78 | 32.71 |
| United Arab Emirates | 27.35 | 21.67 | 23.80 | 24.19 | 27.92 | 35.99 | 33.19 | 33.49 | 36.72 |
| United Kingdom | 468.96 | 570.88 | 702.54 | 852.40 | 861.29 | 1,017.79 | 1,059.26 | 1,098.30 | 982.62 |
| United States | 4,217.48 | 4,460.05 | 4,736.35 | 5,100.43 | 5,482.13 | 5,800.53 | 5,992.10 | 6,342.30 | 6,667.33 |
| Vietnam | 15.00 | 33.87 | 42.05 | 23.23 | 6.29 | 6.47 | 7.64 | 9.87 | 13.18 |

(continued on next page)

# MACROECONOMIC DATA FOR SELECT COUNTRIES
## GDP (Billions of U.S. Dollars)

| Country | 1994 | 1995 | 1996 | 1997 | 1998 | 1999 | 2000 | 2001 | 2002 |
|---|---|---|---|---|---|---|---|---|---|
| Lithuania | 4.40 | 6.47 | 8.17 | 9.96 | 11.23 | 10.97 | 11.43 | 12.16 | 14.16 |
| Luxembourg | 17.59 | 20.70 | 20.59 | 18.54 | 19.38 | 21.22 | 20.33 | 20.22 | 22.66 |
| Malaysia | 75.61 | 90.17 | 102.38 | 101.68 | 73.27 | 80.34 | 93.79 | 92.78 | 100.85 |
| Mexico | 456.12 | 310.10 | 360.06 | 434.23 | 455.59 | 520.45 | 628.85 | 672.82 | 702.02 |
| Netherlands | 348.91 | 419.35 | 418.11 | 387.01 | 403.20 | 412.00 | 386.20 | 401.00 | 439.36 |
| New Zealand | 51.77 | 61.06 | 67.80 | 67.69 | 55.60 | 57.61 | 52.96 | 51.94 | 60.75 |
| Nigeria | 18.09 | 36.95 | 46.02 | 35.39 | 32.75 | 35.94 | 46.39 | 44.14 | 59.12 |
| Norway | 124.48 | 148.92 | 160.00 | 158.23 | 151.14 | 159.05 | 168.29 | 170.93 | 191.92 |
| Peru | 44.92 | 53.66 | 55.85 | 59.14 | 56.76 | 51.53 | 53.34 | 53.94 | 56.76 |
| Philippines | 64.08 | 75.53 | 84.37 | 83.74 | 66.60 | 76.16 | 75.91 | 71.22 | 76.81 |
| Poland | 103.68 | 139.10 | 156.66 | 157.08 | 172.00 | 167.79 | 171.26 | 190.42 | 198.21 |
| Portugal | 98.05 | 116.24 | 121.01 | 115.67 | 122.73 | 126.28 | 117.36 | 120.14 | 132.35 |
| Romania | 30.07 | 35.48 | 35.32 | 35.29 | 42.12 | 35.59 | 37.34 | 40.59 | 45.99 |
| Russia | 276.90 | 313.45 | 391.78 | 404.95 | 271.04 | 195.91 | 259.70 | 306.58 | 345.13 |
| Saudi Arabia | 134.33 | 142.46 | 157.74 | 164.99 | 145.97 | 161.17 | 188.69 | 183.26 | 188.80 |
| Singapore | 73.24 | 87.06 | 95.18 | 99.30 | 85.01 | 84.88 | 94.31 | 87.70 | 90.64 |
| South Africa | 135.82 | 151.12 | 143.83 | 148.84 | 134.22 | 133.11 | 132.96 | 118.56 | 111.36 |
| Spain | 516.72 | 597.28 | 622.65 | 573.38 | 601.63 | 618.69 | 582.38 | 609.63 | 688.68 |
| Sweden | 217.55 | 253.68 | 276.46 | 253.18 | 254.72 | 258.81 | 247.26 | 227.36 | 250.96 |
| Switzerland | 270.22 | 315.95 | 304.75 | 264.58 | 272.63 | 268.22 | 249.91 | 254.99 | 278.62 |
| Thailand | 144.31 | 168.02 | 181.95 | 150.89 | 111.86 | 122.63 | 122.73 | 115.54 | 126.88 |
| Turkey | 174.45 | 227.51 | 243.90 | 255.07 | 269.13 | 249.82 | 266.44 | 195.55 | 232.28 |
| Ukraine | 36.76 | 37.01 | 44.56 | 50.15 | 41.88 | 31.58 | 31.26 | 38.01 | 42.39 |
| United Arab Emirates | 37.44 | 40.73 | 48.01 | 51.22 | 48.51 | 55.18 | 70.22 | 69.23 | 74.30 |
| United Kingdom | 1,061.38 | 1,157.44 | 1,220.85 | 1,359.44 | 1,456.16 | 1,502.89 | 1,480.53 | 1,471.40 | 1,614.70 |
| United States | 7,085.15 | 7,414.63 | 7,838.48 | 8,332.35 | 8,793.48 | 9,353.50 | 9,951.48 | 10,286.18 | 10,642.30 |
| Vietnam | 16.28 | 20.80 | 24.69 | 26.89 | 27.23 | 28.70 | 31.18 | 32.52 | 35.10 |

*Source:* International Monetary Fund, World Economic Outlook Database, October 2010.
2010 is estimated as of 4/13/2011.

| 2003 | 2004 | 2005 | 2006 | 2007 | 2008 | 2009 | 2010 |
|---|---|---|---|---|---|---|---|
| 18.61 | 22.55 | 25.98 | 30.08 | 39.10 | 47.17 | 37.12 | 35.73 |
| 29.21 | 34.14 | 37.72 | 42.88 | 51.35 | 57.91 | 52.43 | 52.43 |
| 110.20 | 124.75 | 138.02 | 157.05 | 187.01 | 222.27 | 192.96 | 218.95 |
| 700.32 | 759.78 | 848.95 | 952.54 | 1,025.58 | 1,089.88 | 874.81 | 1,004.04 |
| 539.34 | 610.69 | 639.58 | 678.32 | 783.69 | 877.47 | 796.65 | 770.31 |
| 80.80 | 99.65 | 111.43 | 107.68 | 131.00 | 131.07 | 117.79 | 138.00 |
| 67.66 | 87.85 | 112.25 | 145.43 | 165.92 | 207.12 | 168.85 | 216.80 |
| 225.12 | 258.56 | 302.01 | 336.72 | 387.58 | 446.32 | 378.59 | 413.51 |
| 61.34 | 69.70 | 79.40 | 92.31 | 107.14 | 127.41 | 126.77 | 153.55 |
| 79.63 | 86.93 | 98.83 | 117.53 | 144.07 | 167.17 | 161.20 | 189.06 |
| 216.81 | 253.02 | 303.98 | 341.67 | 425.32 | 529.40 | 430.74 | 438.88 |
| 161.73 | 185.04 | 191.51 | 201.25 | 231.28 | 253.02 | 233.48 | 223.70 |
| 59.47 | 75.79 | 99.17 | 122.70 | 170.62 | 204.32 | 161.52 | 158.39 |
| 430.29 | 591.18 | 763.70 | 989.93 | 1,299.70 | 1,666.95 | 1,231.89 | 1,476.91 |
| 214.86 | 250.67 | 315.76 | 356.63 | 385.20 | 476.94 | 376.27 | 434.44 |
| 95.96 | 112.70 | 125.43 | 145.07 | 176.77 | 193.33 | 182.23 | 217.38 |
| 168.22 | 219.43 | 246.96 | 261.18 | 285.94 | 276.77 | 287.22 | 354.41 |
| 885.36 | 1,045.67 | 1,132.13 | 1,235.92 | 1,444.02 | 1,601.41 | 1,467.89 | 1,374.78 |
| 314.71 | 362.09 | 370.58 | 399.08 | 462.51 | 487.58 | 406.07 | 444.59 |
| 325.05 | 362.99 | 372.48 | 391.23 | 434.12 | 502.45 | 491.92 | 522.44 |
| 142.64 | 161.34 | 176.35 | 207.23 | 247.11 | 272.43 | 263.98 | 312.61 |
| 303.26 | 392.21 | 482.69 | 529.19 | 649.13 | 730.32 | 614.47 | 729.05 |
| 50.13 | 64.88 | 86.18 | 107.75 | 142.72 | 180.12 | 117.40 | 136.56 |
| 87.61 | 105.60 | 137.99 | 175.22 | 206.41 | 254.39 | 223.87 | 239.65 |
| 1,862.77 | 2,203.58 | 2,282.89 | 2,447.68 | 2,812.05 | 2,679.01 | 2,178.86 | 2,258.57 |
| 11,142.18 | 11,867.75 | 12,638.38 | 13,398.93 | 14,061.80 | 14,369.08 | 14,119.05 | 14,624.18 |
| 39.56 | 45.45 | 52.93 | 60.93 | 71.11 | 90.27 | 93.16 | 101.99 |

# Table III.
# MACROECONOMIC DATA FOR SELECT COUNTRIES
# GDP PER PERSON (U.S. dollars)

| Country | 1985 | 1986 | 1987 | 1988 | 1989 | 1990 | 1991 | 1992 | 1993 |
|---|---|---|---|---|---|---|---|---|---|
| Argentina | 2,905.51 | 3,449.53 | 3,496.89 | 4,046.48 | 2,564.37 | 4,344.56 | 5,750.17 | 6,845.08 | 6,972.55 |
| Australia | 11,183.47 | 11,438.51 | 13,264.12 | 16,552.99 | 18,459.18 | 19,114.91 | 18,909.99 | 18,294.44 | 17,617.49 |
| Austria | 9,000.85 | 12,758.60 | 15,933.79 | 17,455.89 | 17,332.21 | 21,524.07 | 22,280.00 | 24,680.90 | 23,830.11 |
| Bangladesh | 207.17 | 211.96 | 228.35 | 240.83 | 259.41 | 263.74 | 266.08 | 260.66 | 267.72 |
| Belgium | 8,690.74 | 12,042.73 | 14,959.01 | 16,158.07 | 16,330.38 | 20,377.96 | 20,821.48 | 23,052.22 | 22,018.45 |
| Brazil | 1,902.86 | 2,161.63 | 2,305.75 | 2,526.14 | 3,403.20 | 3,463.91 | 2,986.31 | 2,814.44 | 3,108.22 |
| Bulgaria | 3,056.86 | 2,711.70 | 3,156.34 | 5,187.98 | 5,321.33 | 2,365.24 | 233.86 | 958.73 | 525.83 |
| Canada | 13,779.84 | 14,149.88 | 15,965.78 | 18,621.91 | 20,412.25 | 21,088.87 | 21,374.10 | 20,460.27 | 19,673.56 |
| Chile | 1,368.47 | 1,447.21 | 1,678.64 | 1,945.73 | 2,203.77 | 2,409.14 | 2,734.64 | 3,283.03 | 3,463.35 |
| China | 290.05 | 276.81 | 296.41 | 364.01 | 400.44 | 341.35 | 353.27 | 416.68 | 517.41 |
| Colombia | 1,580.94 | 1,550.93 | 1,581.29 | 1,669.79 | 1,649.49 | 1,646.60 | 1,651.75 | 1,935.07 | 2,150.17 |
| Cyprus | 4,492.97 | 5,641.41 | 6,694.01 | 7,640.24 | 8,042.04 | 9,647.73 | 9,697.76 | 11,322.67 | 10,562.59 |
| Czech Republic | n/a | n/a | n/a | n/a | n/a | n/a | n/a | n/a | n/a |
| Denmark | 11,974.67 | 16,880.56 | 20,950.32 | 22,075.41 | 21,454.88 | 26,451.43 | 26,560.90 | 29,095.51 | 27,144.62 |
| Dominican Republic | 1,017.32 | 1,206.08 | 1,238.83 | 1,108.08 | 1,224.38 | 1,117.44 | 1,345.60 | 1,556.04 | 1,729.10 |
| Ecuador | 1,778.51 | 1,272.70 | 1,160.39 | 1,077.26 | 1,032.55 | 1,024.51 | 1,123.61 | 1,201.21 | 1,372.53 |
| Egypt | 997.96 | 1,077.02 | 1,507.61 | 1,767.07 | 2,155.49 | 1,779.26 | 878.62 | 785.04 | 862.41 |
| Estonia | n/a | n/a | n/a | n/a | n/a | n/a | n/a | n/a | 1,144.63 |
| Finland | 11,249.99 | 14,684.85 | 18,247.74 | 21,649.39 | 23,467.10 | 27,832.32 | 24,986.08 | 21,902.56 | 17,209.10 |
| France | 9,910.66 | 13,706.55 | 16,546.25 | 17,898.68 | 17,897.45 | 22,017.09 | 21,925.58 | 24,005.52 | 22,484.47 |
| Germany | 8,405.08 | 11,996.27 | 14,925.38 | 15,993.71 | 15,720.09 | 19,610.39 | 22,713.25 | 25,703.34 | 24,795.78 |
| Ghana | 422.86 | 466.03 | 358.82 | 378.62 | 425.84 | 456.27 | 467.04 | 442.89 | 386.81 |
| Greece | 4,543.20 | 5,325.16 | 6,174.09 | 7,163.53 | 7,387.00 | 9,073.37 | 9,701.56 | 10,581.02 | 9,802.05 |
| Guatemala | 1,432.21 | 755.05 | 852.62 | 900.56 | 1,012.88 | 860.72 | 1,034.67 | 1,112.81 | 1,181.69 |
| Hungary | 1,994.90 | 2,306.36 | 2,547.02 | 2,799.19 | 2,869.34 | 3,266.35 | 3,303.76 | 3,681.66 | 3,817.42 |
| Iceland | 12,137.93 | 16,098.36 | 21,968.44 | 23,881.42 | 22,020.74 | 24,873.07 | 26,173.66 | 26,553.26 | 23,100.27 |
| India | 296.30 | 318.80 | 343.82 | 368.31 | 357.86 | 378.04 | 328.74 | 324.86 | 311.26 |
| Ireland | 5,928.40 | 7,947.96 | 9,407.19 | 10,351.70 | 10,741.39 | 13,626.12 | 13,732.85 | 15,314.37 | 14,112.47 |
| Israel | 6,171.41 | 7,480.52 | 8,797.63 | 10,700.08 | 10,645.01 | 12,204.03 | 13,328.51 | 14,291.12 | 13,796.30 |
| Italy | 7,724.27 | 10,938.18 | 13,729.40 | 15,207.03 | 15,804.94 | 20,029.19 | 21,129.68 | 22,403.30 | 17,997.61 |
| Jamaica | 952.72 | 1,122.37 | 1,256.68 | 1,488.94 | 1,723.04 | 2,138.61 | 2,007.47 | 1,796.23 | 2,499.47 |
| Japan | 11,192.50 | 16,495.61 | 19,909.75 | 24,072.15 | 23,992.61 | 24,547.04 | 27,959.09 | 30,408.22 | 34,791.19 |
| Kenya | 440.14 | 504.64 | 534.26 | 535.29 | 513.27 | 517.14 | 473.71 | 453.40 | 306.68 |
| Korea | 2,413.94 | 2,759.70 | 3,444.79 | 4,570.73 | 5,565.10 | 6,307.66 | 7,288.84 | 7,729.98 | 8,422.05 |
| Latvia | n/a | n/a | n/a | n/a | n/a | n/a | n/a | 580.22 | 925.32 |

*Source:* International Monetary Fund, World Economic Outlook Database, October 2010.
As of 4/13/2011, 2010 is estimated.

| 1994 | 1995 | 1996 | 1997 | 1998 | 1999 | 2000 | 2001 | 2002 | 2003 | 2004 |
|---|---|---|---|---|---|---|---|---|---|---|
| 7,493.51 | 7,418.73 | 7,734.46 | 8,229.00 | 8,306.54 | 7,795.95 | 7,735.45 | 7,242.35 | 2,738.14 | 3,420.78 | 4,002.64 |
| 19,866.96 | 21,007.40 | 23,237.05 | 23,022.91 | 20,318.73 | 21,723.22 | 20,800.18 | 19,423.73 | 21,570.51 | 27,143.21 | 32,517.69 |
| 25,407.63 | 30,012.70 | 29,429.96 | 25,994.61 | 26,632.13 | 26,426.20 | 23,935.54 | 23,664.72 | 25,572.99 | 31,104.80 | 35,426.97 |
| 285.09 | 309.01 | 317.86 | 325.86 | 329.85 | 336.60 | 334.23 | 329.36 | 339.92 | 367.38 | 392.24 |
| 23,959.92 | 28,077.11 | 27,057.22 | 24,505.34 | 25,021.15 | 24,844.32 | 22,716.46 | 22,535.48 | 24,461.05 | 29,982.38 | 34,556.38 |
| 3,814.87 | 4,844.95 | 5,207.26 | 5,321.32 | 5,060.36 | 3,396.19 | 3,750.70 | 3,180.47 | 2,836.12 | 3,103.85 | 3,665.23 |
| 934.04 | 1,579.64 | 1,203.66 | 1,269.92 | 1,584.72 | 1,608.63 | 1,546.08 | 1,723.30 | 1,988.37 | 2,561.75 | 3,175.83 |
| 19,491.61 | 20,179.05 | 20,756.80 | 21,345.18 | 20,474.85 | 21,775.27 | 23,653.36 | 23,100.42 | 23,466.71 | 27,402.39 | 31,103.90 |
| 3,941.21 | 5,020.86 | 5,254.90 | 5,663.02 | 5,354.81 | 4,860.15 | 4,943.71 | 4,451.12 | 4,314.00 | 4,698.20 | 5,981.58 |
| 466.60 | 601.01 | 699.48 | 770.59 | 817.15 | 861.21 | 945.60 | 1,038.04 | 1,131.80 | 1,269.83 | 1,486.02 |
| 2,654.98 | 2,955.78 | 3,149.58 | 2,919.74 | 2,783.75 | 2,440.62 | 2,491.52 | 2,419.86 | 2,376.85 | 2,269.41 | 2,805.54 |
| 11,664.17 | 14,338.35 | 14,246.56 | 13,360.48 | 14,152.07 | 14,322.69 | 13,492.90 | 13,874.97 | 14,965.10 | 18,631.71 | 21,665.13 |
| n/a | 5,348.65 | 6,011.54 | 5,545.14 | 6,033.68 | 5,880.87 | 5,548.48 | 6,077.48 | 7,401.06 | 8,974.90 | 10,742.47 |
| 29,556.47 | 34,891.63 | 35,123.93 | 32,309.47 | 32,796.45 | 32,735.73 | 30,033.99 | 29,999.92 | 32,389.91 | 39,495.21 | 45,339.87 |
| 1,843.49 | 2,017.01 | 2,187.81 | 2,425.07 | 2,501.54 | 2,637.74 | 2,870.64 | 2,926.64 | 2,910.91 | 2,315.29 | 2,430.13 |
| 1,656.84 | 1,764.01 | 1,819.83 | 1,982.04 | 1,912.04 | 1,344.85 | 1,261.24 | 1,749.73 | 1,952.33 | 2,212.13 | 2,506.02 |
| 930.63 | 1,057.35 | 1,162.07 | 1,277.18 | 1,397.39 | 1,450.67 | 1,566.42 | 1,474.48 | 1,325.85 | 1,209.27 | 1,148.71 |
| 1,637.68 | 2,607.15 | 3,316.00 | 3,592.78 | 4,015.81 | 4,141.60 | 4,139.67 | 4,565.18 | 5,380.73 | 7,260.34 | 8,905.06 |
| 19,806.46 | 25,571.65 | 24,993.62 | 23,909.01 | 25,164.25 | 25,213.82 | 23,561.05 | 23,998.34 | 26,038.26 | 31,503.61 | 36,123.79 |
| 23,693.93 | 27,183.03 | 27,131.27 | 24,495.14 | 25,244.77 | 24,853.95 | 22,574.15 | 22,551.09 | 24,434.17 | 29,922.03 | 33,927.70 |
| 26,458.85 | 30,934.66 | 29,807.01 | 26,395.70 | 26,675.98 | 26,166.43 | 23,220.16 | 23,039.41 | 24,590.61 | 29,697.87 | 33,366.36 |
| 344.14 | 398.31 | 416.53 | 403.72 | 427.40 | 429.90 | 270.63 | 281.47 | 318.41 | 384.32 | 436.04 |
| 10,383.31 | 12,077.84 | 12,676.58 | 12,311.89 | 12,323.38 | 12,639.03 | 11,661.88 | 11,950.44 | 13,446.40 | 17,692.57 | 20,922.08 |
| 1,302.34 | 1,426.10 | 1,481.22 | 1,634.38 | 1,712.17 | 1,588.87 | 1,531.10 | 1,625.82 | 1,762.06 | 1,813.32 | 1,933.79 |
| 4,111.21 | 4,430.16 | 4,514.34 | 4,580.14 | 4,741.95 | 4,791.44 | 4,626.82 | 5,231.78 | 6,562.39 | 8,270.33 | 10,142.61 |
| 23,558.97 | 26,159.28 | 27,086.75 | 27,226.44 | 29,988.74 | 31,299.76 | 30,620.91 | 27,566.39 | 30,902.26 | 37,743.87 | 45,075.15 |
| 346.47 | 385.80 | 390.22 | 428.80 | 424.58 | 445.47 | 460.27 | 463.46 | 477.00 | 543.40 | 620.08 |
| 15,434.63 | 18,639.10 | 20,431.52 | 22,184.24 | 23,795.57 | 25,769.39 | 25,607.31 | 27,269.11 | 31,454.28 | 39,781.12 | 45,901.32 |
| 15,070.23 | 17,875.72 | 19,040.69 | 19,072.88 | 18,877.51 | 18,607.53 | 20,504.11 | 19,813.45 | 17,841.75 | 18,423.14 | 19,297.47 |
| 18,557.95 | 19,819.03 | 22,164.10 | 20,985.09 | 21,433.76 | 21,129.57 | 19,293.34 | 19,541.08 | 21,317.48 | 26,308.26 | 30,119.03 |
| 3,139.30 | 2,351.98 | 3,145.77 | 3,254.03 | 3,392.79 | 3,440.54 | 3,484.89 | 3,525.27 | 3,663.65 | 3,605.50 | 3,846.28 |
| 38,196.39 | 41,968.58 | 36,930.26 | 33,821.23 | 30,526.86 | 34,511.71 | 36,800.44 | 32,214.33 | 30,756.08 | 33,134.47 | 36,058.72 |
| 358.16 | 443.68 | 437.42 | 471.61 | 478.82 | 438.03 | 409.18 | 423.09 | 418.53 | 467.47 | 490.45 |
| 9,757.49 | 11,778.76 | 12,586.60 | 11,582.11 | 7,723.84 | 9,906.50 | 11,346.66 | 10,654.82 | 12,093.73 | 13,451.10 | 15,028.82 |
| 1,579.60 | 1,982.47 | 2,300.75 | 2,557.51 | 2,781.22 | 3,037.84 | 3,294.83 | 3,516.14 | 3,970.89 | 4,798.01 | 5,933.75 |

(continued on next page)

# MACROECONOMIC DATA FOR SELECT COUNTRIES
## GDP PER PERSON (U.S. dollars)

| Country | 2005 | 2006 | 2007 | 2008 | 2009 | 2010 |
|---|---|---|---|---|---|---|
| Argentina | 4,741.91 | 5,492.40 | 6,658.16 | 8,253.18 | 7,725.46 | 8,662.99 |
| Australia | 35,926.70 | 37,543.54 | 44,761.03 | 48,706.88 | 45,285.02 | 54,868.92 |
| Austria | 36,892.02 | 39,022.92 | 44,913.74 | 49,975.21 | 45,685.88 | 43,723.32 |
| Bangladesh | 399.21 | 419.42 | 468.89 | 527.89 | 583.16 | 640.85 |
| Belgium | 35,940.82 | 37,787.60 | 43,102.15 | 47,224.21 | 43,794.31 | 42,596.55 |
| Brazil | 4,832.39 | 5,892.81 | 7,281.00 | 8,625.58 | 8,220.36 | 10,470.90 |
| Bulgaria | 3,522.32 | 4,122.32 | 5,301.52 | 6,560.72 | 6,223.25 | 5,954.72 |
| Canada | 35,204.73 | 39,301.50 | 43,302.01 | 45,051.11 | 39,657.92 | 45,887.74 |
| Chile | 7,285.82 | 8,940.63 | 9,901.11 | 10,200.76 | 9,515.93 | 11,587.09 |
| China | 1,726.05 | 2,063.87 | 2,644.56 | 3,403.53 | 3,734.61 | 4,282.89 |
| Colombia | 3,418.72 | 3,709.42 | 4,792.52 | 5,258.21 | 5,167.05 | 6,220.60 |
| Cyprus | 22,686.38 | 24,039.80 | 28,044.01 | 32,161.20 | 29,619.50 | 27,721.84 |
| Czech Republic | 12,175.43 | 13,892.90 | 16,880.48 | 20,734.15 | 18,256.16 | 18,721.63 |
| Denmark | 47,617.09 | 50,553.52 | 57,043.54 | 62,237.76 | 56,263.43 | 55,112.71 |
| Dominican Republic | 3,712.32 | 3,879.03 | 4,378.59 | 4,776.68 | 4,815.80 | 5,152.05 |
| Ecuador | 2,795.47 | 3,080.13 | 3,314.28 | 3,899.22 | 3,935.26 | 4,295.64 |
| Egypt | 1,282.77 | 1,505.96 | 1,771.00 | 2,160.04 | 2,450.39 | 2,771.41 |
| Estonia | 10,317.77 | 12,499.60 | 16,160.24 | 17,651.19 | 14,402.46 | 14,416.52 |
| Finland | 37,287.22 | 39,414.66 | 46,468.58 | 51,020.39 | 44,581.06 | 43,134.00 |
| France | 35,104.94 | 36,858.07 | 41,940.89 | 45,991.04 | 42,412.63 | 40,591.43 |
| Germany | 33,922.40 | 35,512.83 | 40,570.06 | 44,524.95 | 40,831.66 | 40,511.83 |
| Ghana | 513.76 | 594.51 | 683.57 | 732.16 | 663.39 | 761.98 |
| Greece | 21,997.32 | 23,835.36 | 27,930.40 | 31,601.66 | 29,634.92 | 27,264.83 |
| Guatemala | 2,142.56 | 2,322.56 | 2,557.00 | 2,863.23 | 2,687.57 | 2,839.03 |
| Hungary | 10,910.85 | 11,205.35 | 13,746.16 | 15,477.50 | 12,914.01 | 13,210.40 |
| Iceland | 54,471.92 | 54,374.91 | 65,181.13 | 53,107.81 | 37,991.40 | 39,562.89 |
| India | 716.18 | 791.15 | 988.58 | 1,066.46 | 1,031.59 | 1,176.06 |
| Ireland | 48,914.67 | 52,521.45 | 59,820.87 | 59,901.95 | 49,863.42 | 45,642.49 |
| Israel | 20,062.28 | 21,413.04 | 24,134.52 | 28,437.13 | 26,874.40 | 27,085.13 |
| Italy | 30,662.59 | 31,917.69 | 35,992.66 | 38,887.23 | 35,435.15 | 33,828.55 |
| Jamaica | 4,172.01 | 4,483.25 | 4,808.00 | 5,024.31 | 4,683.71 | 5,055.00 |
| Japan | 35,633.04 | 34,150.33 | 34,267.77 | 38,271.30 | 39,740.27 | 42,325.23 |
| Kenya | 579.05 | 684.49 | 833.69 | 754.86 | 840.00 | 887.92 |
| Korea | 17,550.88 | 19,706.59 | 21,653.27 | 19,161.95 | 17,074.33 | 20,164.85 |
| Latvia | 6,955.25 | 8,689.98 | 12,622.47 | 14,912.93 | 11,465.61 | 10,377.78 |

Source: International Monetary Fund, World Economic Outlook Database, October 2010.
As of 4/13/2011, 2010 is estimated.

| Country | 1985 | 1986 | 1987 | 1988 | 1989 | 1990 | 1991 | 1992 | 1993 |
|---|---|---|---|---|---|---|---|---|---|
| Lithuania | n/a | n/a | n/a | n/a | n/a | n/a | n/a | 531.34 | 743.92 |
| Luxembourg | 12,469.15 | 18,059.15 | 22,284.20 | 25,026.75 | 26,386.38 | 33,267.96 | 35,561.42 | 39,298.54 | 39,723.15 |
| Malaysia | 2,026.29 | 1,753.14 | 1,946.87 | 2,082.17 | 2,238.90 | 2,431.97 | 2,713.63 | 3,200.32 | 3,470.94 |
| Mexico | 2,802.90 | 1,901.55 | 2,044.18 | 2,452.40 | 2,931.82 | 3,395.13 | 3,994.92 | 4,548.33 | 4,958.68 |
| Netherlands | 9,189.30 | 12,736.41 | 15,441.07 | 16,353.76 | 16,040.23 | 19,760.56 | 20,136.83 | 22,119.79 | 21,286.59 |
| New Zealand | 6,891.89 | 8,310.97 | 10,975.98 | 13,388.89 | 12,778.44 | 13,098.57 | 12,222.46 | 11,483.85 | 12,274.65 |
| Nigeria | 331.05 | 254.85 | 263.86 | 284.38 | 266.90 | 347.63 | 304.17 | 266.62 | 160.53 |
| Norway | 15,449.40 | 18,496.04 | 22,020.51 | 23,706.45 | 23,805.31 | 27,677.27 | 27,999.23 | 29,848.03 | 27,323.01 |
| Peru | 881.80 | 1,293.35 | 2,088.49 | 1,616.57 | 1,953.19 | 1,331.97 | 1,557.50 | 1,590.72 | 1,513.25 |
| Philippines | 562.18 | 533.36 | 578.33 | 645.41 | 709.60 | 718.11 | 719.38 | 822.70 | 825.01 |
| Poland | 1,895.37 | 1,960.94 | 1,687.17 | 1,815.14 | 1,767.95 | 1,625.24 | 2,100.56 | 2,310.23 | 2,346.24 |
| Portugal | 2,673.82 | 3,713.27 | 4,644.50 | 5,438.56 | 5,873.95 | 7,816.33 | 8,868.71 | 10,671.01 | 9,381.23 |
| Romania | 2,073.64 | 2,233.82 | 2,483.98 | 2,558.08 | 2,283.52 | 1,624.61 | 1,227.46 | 836.15 | 1,132.02 |
| Russia | n/a | n/a | n/a | n/a | n/a | n/a | n/a | 575.22 | 1,236.98 |
| Saudi Arabia | 8,732.75 | 6,960.55 | 6,532.88 | 6,407.38 | 6,592.09 | 7,689.19 | 8,235.57 | 8,042.29 | 7,648.99 |
| Singapore | 6,748.29 | 6,853.03 | 7,767.00 | 9,303.40 | 10,715.16 | 12,745.06 | 14,412.55 | 16,099.09 | 18,240.07 |
| South Africa | 1,735.62 | 1,937.54 | 2,485.04 | 2,614.36 | 2,662.24 | 3,039.44 | 3,192.05 | 3,389.85 | 3,315.64 |
| Spain | 4,600.34 | 6,347.03 | 8,022.62 | 9,405.61 | 10,353.62 | 13,407.90 | 14,401.90 | 15,691.09 | 13,140.00 |
| Sweden | 12,726.98 | 16,804.10 | 20,413.72 | 22,959.79 | 24,048.59 | 28,543.17 | 29,899.78 | 30,791.92 | 23,148.90 |
| Switzerland | 15,373.83 | 21,923.98 | 27,285.00 | 29,301.51 | 28,062.55 | 35,490.19 | 35,441.76 | 36,504.10 | 35,179.84 |
| Thailand | 750.97 | 813.60 | 938.09 | 1,122.03 | 1,306.77 | 1,518.17 | 1,686.61 | 1,899.10 | 2,087.83 |
| Turkey | 1,837.97 | 2,024.85 | 2,281.01 | 2,416.97 | 2,810.23 | 3,859.52 | 3,788.04 | 3,915.63 | 4,355.54 |
| Ukraine | n/a | n/a | n/a | n/a | n/a | n/a | n/a | 400.70 | 632.56 |
| United Arab Emirates | 19,818.48 | 15,051.53 | 15,865.98 | 13,513.74 | 15,011.58 | 19,514.64 | 17,220.53 | 16,652.45 | 17,628.87 |
| United Kingdom | 8,292.22 | 10,071.35 | 12,367.79 | 14,976.44 | 15,090.29 | 17,782.06 | 18,441.42 | 19,072.63 | 17,025.60 |
| United States | 17,689.60 | 18,537.76 | 19,511.17 | 20,820.82 | 22,169.18 | 23,197.70 | 23,647.57 | 24,699.63 | 25,629.13 |
| Vietnam | 251.20 | 556.02 | 674.88 | 365.89 | 97.16 | 98.03 | 113.65 | 144.15 | 189.26 |

(continued on next page)

# MACROECONOMIC DATA FOR SELECT COUNTRIES
## GDP PER PERSON (U.S. dollars)

| Country | 1994 | 1995 | 1996 | 1997 | 1998 | 1999 | 2000 | 2001 | 2002 |
|---|---|---|---|---|---|---|---|---|---|
| Lithuania | 1,168.11 | 1,741.55 | 2,268.54 | 2,787.02 | 3,163.68 | 3,113.15 | 3,267.38 | 3,492.73 | 4,082.09 |
| Luxembourg | 43,570.22 | 50,515.36 | 49,539.13 | 44,037.74 | 45,439.25 | 49,053.28 | 46,360.39 | 45,789.99 | 50,781.69 |
| Malaysia | 3,759.35 | 4,358.45 | 4,836.12 | 4,693.25 | 3,303.27 | 3,537.53 | 4,029.68 | 3,863.93 | 4,111.69 |
| Mexico | 5,093.73 | 3,402.30 | 3,889.58 | 4,623.09 | 4,783.03 | 5,388.50 | 6,419.10 | 6,713.54 | 6,912.25 |
| Netherlands | 22,742.86 | 27,187.80 | 26,985.21 | 24,860.92 | 25,756.79 | 26,141.54 | 24,249.91 | 24,990.55 | 27,206.45 |
| New Zealand | 14,269.23 | 16,579.55 | 18,123.50 | 17,871.13 | 14,558.72 | 15,003.34 | 13,708.73 | 13,343.55 | 15,338.96 |
| Nigeria | 178.95 | 355.76 | 431.26 | 322.73 | 290.68 | 310.48 | 389.95 | 361.11 | 470.70 |
| Norway | 28,626.25 | 34,077.70 | 36,424.60 | 35,853.71 | 34,036.54 | 35,554.37 | 37,390.55 | 37,821.70 | 42,206.16 |
| Peru | 1,953.74 | 2,298.39 | 2,356.06 | 2,456.54 | 2,322.06 | 2,076.04 | 2,115.87 | 2,107.06 | 2,183.50 |
| Philippines | 949.21 | 1,104.99 | 1,206.14 | 1,170.32 | 910.44 | 1,018.88 | 986.56 | 906.42 | 957.57 |
| Poland | 2,686.41 | 3,603.96 | 4,056.01 | 4,064.24 | 4,448.54 | 4,339.99 | 4,453.74 | 4,978.57 | 5,184.50 |
| Portugal | 9,814.38 | 11,603.35 | 12,049.01 | 11,483.23 | 12,139.97 | 12,442.64 | 11,511.28 | 11,712.97 | 12,813.29 |
| Romania | 1,299.35 | 1,542.01 | 1,543.54 | 1,550.48 | 1,859.90 | 1,579.31 | 1,664.36 | 1,811.50 | 2,110.08 |
| Russia | 1,864.66 | 2,116.48 | 2,641.77 | 2,749.13 | 1,852.62 | 1,345.51 | 1,793.52 | 2,095.58 | 2,376.90 |
| Saudi Arabia | 7,588.63 | 7,855.13 | 8,489.58 | 8,667.04 | 7,483.87 | 8,065.43 | 9,216.39 | 8,736.41 | 8,785.13 |
| Singapore | 21,419.97 | 24,702.00 | 25,929.64 | 26,158.10 | 21,647.26 | 21,441.38 | 22,790.80 | 21,001.23 | 22,027.88 |
| South Africa | 3,382.24 | 3,684.84 | 3,439.25 | 3,495.07 | 3,100.05 | 3,029.06 | 2,986.45 | 2,632.83 | 2,445.22 |
| Spain | 13,149.72 | 15,164.36 | 15,772.03 | 14,485.63 | 15,146.23 | 15,495.85 | 14,464.24 | 14,971.13 | 16,811.64 |
| Sweden | 24,750.02 | 28,710.50 | 31,238.76 | 28,591.84 | 28,750.48 | 29,188.77 | 27,841.74 | 25,531.88 | 28,090.69 |
| Switzerland | 38,637.47 | 44,874.60 | 43,093.25 | 37,323.36 | 38,344.56 | 37,544.78 | 34,786.15 | 35,284.34 | 38,246.93 |
| Thailand | 2,441.76 | 2,825.74 | 3,037.52 | 2,496.14 | 1,828.67 | 1,984.94 | 1,966.75 | 1,835.78 | 1,999.30 |
| Turkey | 3,084.88 | 3,956.36 | 4,170.26 | 4,390.31 | 4,560.43 | 4,169.85 | 4,245.22 | 3,064.26 | 3,581.58 |
| Ukraine | 716.46 | 727.45 | 884.10 | 1,003.56 | 845.35 | 642.99 | 642.40 | 787.90 | 886.45 |
| United Arab Emirates | 16,788.85 | 16,891.58 | 19,650.32 | 19,850.98 | 17,118.62 | 18,193.68 | 23,446.15 | 21,858.84 | 22,184.77 |
| United Kingdom | 18,343.34 | 19,947.19 | 20,989.85 | 23,312.43 | 24,902.18 | 25,609.93 | 25,142.25 | 24,891.24 | 27,218.78 |
| United States | 26,906.53 | 27,826.60 | 29,076.55 | 30,541.33 | 31,857.84 | 33,501.68 | 35,251.93 | 36,064.52 | 36,949.99 |
| Vietnam | 229.85 | 288.87 | 337.52 | 361.91 | 360.93 | 374.72 | 401.57 | 413.34 | 440.21 |

*Source:* International Monetary Fund, World Economic Outlook Database, October 2010.
As of 4/13/2011, 2010 is estimated.

| 2003 | 2004 | 2005 | 2006 | 2007 | 2008 | 2009 | 2010 |
|---|---|---|---|---|---|---|---|
| 5,387.33 | 6,562.97 | 7,608.24 | 8,863.07 | 11,582.13 | 14,047.47 | 11,115.07 | 10,765.34 |
| 64,675.97 | 74,516.56 | 81,092.71 | 90,714.82 | 106,983.25 | 118,570.05 | 105,917.79 | 104,390.27 |
| 4,409.42 | 4,898.40 | 5,318.53 | 5,950.56 | 6,967.10 | 8,142.62 | 6,950.47 | 7,754.99 |
| 6,807.90 | 7,294.27 | 8,167.17 | 9,084.16 | 9,694.42 | 10,216.02 | 8,133.87 | 9,243.03 |
| 33,241.45 | 37,507.13 | 39,189.91 | 41,497.70 | 47,838.63 | 53,354.89 | 48,208.83 | 46,418.33 |
| 20,016.70 | 24,333.02 | 26,902.63 | 25,685.01 | 30,927.30 | 30,652.74 | 27,258.94 | 31,588.78 |
| 524.26 | 662.47 | 823.82 | 1,038.76 | 1,153.40 | 1,401.24 | 1,111.75 | 1,389.31 |
| 49,228.14 | 56,219.31 | 65,203.29 | 72,074.46 | 82,086.88 | 93,235.22 | 78,178.34 | 84,543.44 |
| 2,323.97 | 2,600.45 | 2,916.98 | 3,339.59 | 3,796.51 | 4,445.84 | 4,356.04 | 5,195.98 |
| 972.59 | 1,040.35 | 1,159.13 | 1,351.39 | 1,624.13 | 1,848.02 | 1,747.82 | 2,011.00 |
| 5,675.00 | 6,626.66 | 7,964.70 | 8,958.02 | 11,157.27 | 13,886.66 | 11,302.08 | 11,521.64 |
| 15,539.29 | 17,665.23 | 18,188.19 | 19,040.18 | 21,820.44 | 23,830.05 | 21,969.76 | 21,030.61 |
| 2,736.09 | 3,497.02 | 4,586.27 | 5,684.47 | 7,921.82 | 9,501.33 | 7,523.11 | 7,390.71 |
| 2,967.51 | 4,099.70 | 5,321.98 | 6,932.30 | 9,139.96 | 11,739.11 | 8,681.41 | 10,521.79 |
| 9,758.02 | 11,126.52 | 13,657.95 | 15,049.63 | 15,858.75 | 19,156.86 | 14,744.61 | 16,641.41 |
| 23,029.40 | 26,418.80 | 28,497.52 | 31,615.67 | 36,526.53 | 39,266.25 | 36,378.74 | 42,652.76 |
| 3,656.18 | 4,722.82 | 5,266.90 | 5,511.06 | 5,975.57 | 5,684.68 | 5,823.58 | 7,100.81 |
| 21,250.10 | 24,693.89 | 26,305.39 | 28,244.15 | 32,468.29 | 35,364.24 | 32,030.27 | 29,875.09 |
| 35,096.99 | 40,218.82 | 40,997.73 | 43,946.23 | 50,558.90 | 52,882.38 | 43,668.36 | 47,667.02 |
| 44,291.00 | 49,112.67 | 50,084.28 | 52,275.88 | 57,490.59 | 65,699.35 | 63,535.95 | 67,074.31 |
| 2,228.54 | 2,479.01 | 2,708.51 | 3,174.43 | 3,758.91 | 4,107.79 | 3,940.97 | 4,620.71 |
| 4,602.81 | 5,862.20 | 7,108.45 | 7,766.97 | 9,422.08 | 10,484.26 | 8,711.16 | 10,206.79 |
| 1,056.72 | 1,377.56 | 1,843.51 | 2,318.97 | 3,089.69 | 3,921.02 | 2,568.65 | 3,002.80 |
| 24,672.25 | 28,076.55 | 33,607.69 | 41,433.45 | 45,990.64 | 53,388.04 | 45,614.54 | 47,406.66 |
| 31,277.10 | 36,820.75 | 37,897.81 | 40,399.45 | 46,118.06 | 43,651.55 | 35,257.45 | 36,298.39 |
| 38,324.38 | 40,450.62 | 42,680.64 | 44,822.96 | 46,577.19 | 47,155.32 | 45,934.47 | 47,131.95 |
| 489.03 | 554.07 | 636.91 | 724.05 | 835.08 | 1,047.54 | 1,068.26 | 1,155.57 |

# Solutions to Check Your Understanding Questions

This section offers suggested answers to the "Check Your Understanding" questions found within chapters.

## Chapter One

### 1-1 CHECK YOUR UNDERSTANDING

**1. a.** This illustrates the concept of opportunity cost. Given that a person can only eat so much at one sitting, having a slice of chocolate cake requires that you forgo eating something else, such as a slice of coconut cream pie.

**b.** This illustrates the concept that resources are scarce. Even if there were more resources in the world, the total amount of those resources would be limited. As a result, scarcity would still arise. For there to be no scarcity, there would have to be unlimited amounts of everything (including unlimited time in a human life), which is clearly impossible.

**c.** This illustrates the concept that people usually exploit opportunities to make themselves better off. Students will seek to make themselves better off by signing up for the tutorials of teaching assistants with good reputations and avoiding those teaching assistants with poor reputations. It also illustrates the concept that resources are scarce. If there were unlimited spaces in tutorials with good teaching assistants, they would not fill up.

**d.** This illustrates the concept of marginal analysis. Your decision about allocating your time is a "how much" decision: how much time spent exercising versus how much time spent studying. You make your decision by comparing the benefit of an additional hour of exercising to its cost, the effect on your grades of one fewer hour spent studying.

**2. a.** Yes. The increased time spent commuting is a cost you will incur if you accept the new job. That additional time spent commuting—or equivalently, the benefit you would get from spending that time doing something else—is an opportunity cost of the new job.

**b.** Yes. One of the benefits of the new job is that you will be making $50,000. But if you take the new job, you will have to give up your current job; that is, you have to give up your current salary of $45,000. So $45,000 is one of the opportunity costs of taking the new job.

**c.** No. A more spacious office is an additional benefit of your new job and does not involve forgoing something else. So it is not an opportunity cost.

### 1-2 CHECK YOUR UNDERSTANDING

**1. a.** This illustrates the concept that markets usually lead to efficiency. Any seller who wants to sell a book for at least $30 does indeed sell to someone who is willing to buy a book for $30. As a result, there is no way to change how used textbooks are distributed among buyers and sellers in a way that would make one person better off without making someone else worse off.

**b.** This illustrates the concept that there are gains from trade. Students trade tutoring services based on their different abilities in academic subjects.

**c.** This illustrates the concept that when markets don't achieve efficiency, government intervention can improve society's welfare. In this case the market, left alone, will permit bars and nightclubs to impose costs on their neighbors in the form of loud music, costs that the bars and nightclubs have no incentive to take into account. This is an inefficient outcome because society as a whole can be made better off if bars and nightclubs are induced to reduce their noise.

**d.** This illustrates the concept that resources should be used as efficiently as possible to achieve society's goals. By closing neighborhood clinics and shifting funds to the main hospital, better health care can be provided at a lower cost.

**e.** This illustrates the concept that markets move toward equilibrium. Here, because books with the same amount of wear and tear sell for about the same price, no buyer or seller can be made better off by engaging in a different trade than he or she undertook. This means that the market for used textbooks has moved to an equilibrium.

**2. a.** This does not describe an equilibrium situation. Many students should want to change their behavior and switch to eating at the restaurants. Therefore, the situation described is not an equilibrium. An equilibrium will be established when students are equally as well off eating at the restaurants as eating at the dining hall—which would happen if, say, prices at the restaurants were higher than at the dining hall.

**b.** This does describe an equilibrium situation. By changing your behavior and riding the bus, you would not be made better off. Therefore, you have no incentive to change your behavior.

### 1-3 CHECK YOUR UNDERSTANDING

**1. a.** This illustrates the principle that government policies can change spending. The tax cut would increase people's after-tax incomes, leading to higher consumer spending.

**b.** This illustrates the principle that one person's spending is another person's income. As oil companies increase their spending on labor by hiring more workers, or pay existing workers higher wages, those workers' incomes rise. In turn, these workers increase their consumer spending, which becomes income to restaurants and other consumer businesses.

**c.** This illustrates the principle that overall spending sometimes gets out of line with the economy's productive capacity. In this case, spending on housing was too high relative to the economy's capacity to create new housing. This first led to a rise in house prices, and then—as a result—to a rise in overall prices, or *inflation*.

## Chapter Two

### 2-1 CHECK YOUR UNDERSTANDING

**1. a.** False. An increase in the resources available to Boeing for use in producing Dreamliners and small jets changes the production possibility frontier by shifting it outward. This is because Boeing can now produce more small jets and Dreamliners than before. In the accompanying figure, the line labeled "Boeing's original *PPF*" represents Boeing's original production possibility frontier, and the line labeled "Boeing's new *PPF*" represents the new production possibility frontier that results from an increase in resources available to Boeing.

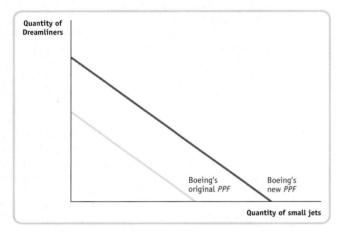

**b.** True. A technological change that allows Boeing to build more small jets for any amount of Dreamliners built results in a change in its production possibility frontier. This is illustrated in the accompanying figure: the new production possibility frontier is represented by the line labeled "Boeing's new *PPF*," and the original production frontier is represented by the line labeled "Boeing's original *PPF*." Since the maximum quantity of Dreamliners that Boeing can build is the same as before, the new production possibility frontier intersects the vertical axis at the same point as the original frontier. But since the maximum possible quantity of small jets is now greater than before, the new frontier intersects the horizontal axis to the right of the original frontier.

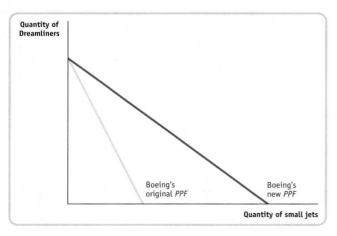

**c.** False. The production possibility frontier illustrates how much of one good an economy must give up to get more of another good only when resources are used efficiently in production. If an economy is producing inefficiently—that is, inside the frontier—then it does not have to give up a unit of one good in order to get another unit of the other good. Instead, by becoming more efficient in production, this economy can have more of both goods.

**2. a.** The United States has an absolute advantage in automobile production because it takes fewer Americans (6) to produce a car in one day than Italians (8). The United States also has an absolute advantage in washing machine production because it takes fewer Americans (2) to produce a washing machine in one day than Italians (3).

**b.** In Italy the opportunity cost of a washing machine in terms of an automobile is $3/8$: $3/8$ of a car can be produced with the same number of workers and in the same time it takes to produce 1 washing machine. In the United States the opportunity cost of a washing machine in terms of an automobile is $2/6 = 1/3$: $1/3$ of a car can be produced with the same number of workers and in the same time it takes to produce 1 washing machine. Since $1/3 < 3/8$, the United States has a comparative advantage in the production of washing machines: to produce a washing machine, only $1/3$ of a car must be given up in the United States but $3/8$ of a car must be given up in Italy. This means that Italy has a comparative advantage in automobiles. This can be checked as follows. The opportunity cost of an automobile in terms of a washing machine in Italy is $8/3$, equal to $2\,2/3$: $2\,2/3$ washing machines can be produced with the same number of workers and in the time it takes to produce 1 car in Italy. And the opportunity cost of an automobile in terms of a washing machine in the United States is $6/2$, equal to 3: 3 washing machines can be produced with the same number of workers and in the time it takes to produce 1 car in the United States. Since $2\,2/3 < 3$, Italy has a comparative advantage in producing automobiles.

**c.** The greatest gains are realized when each country specializes in producing the good for which it has a comparative advantage. Therefore, the United States should specialize in washing machines and Italy should specialize in automobiles.

**3.** At a trade of 10 U.S. large jets for 15 Brazilian small jets, Brazil gives up less for a large jet than it would if it were building large jets itself. Without trade, Brazil gives up 3 small jets for each large jet it produces. With trade, Brazil gives up only 1.5 small jets for each large jet from the United States. Likewise, the United States gives up less for a small jet than it would if it were producing small jets itself. Without trade, the United States gives up $3/4$ of a large jet for each small jet. With trade, the United States gives up only $2/3$ of a large jet for each small jet from Brazil.

**4.** An increase in the amount of money spent by households results in an increase in the flow of goods to households. This, in turn, generates an increase in demand for factors of production by firms. So, there is an increase in the number of jobs in the economy.

## 2-2 CHECK YOUR UNDERSTANDING

**1. a.** This is a normative statement because it stipulates what should be done. In addition, it may have no "right" answer. That is, should people be prevented from all dangerous personal behavior if they enjoy that behavior—like skydiving? Your answer will depend on your point of view.

   **b.** This is a positive statement because it is a description of fact.

**2. a.** True. Economists often have different value judgments about the desirability of a particular social goal. But despite those differences in value judgments, they will tend to agree that society, once it has decided to pursue a given social goal, should adopt the most efficient policy to achieve that goal. Therefore economists are likely to agree on adopting policy choice B.

   **b.** False. Disagreements between economists are more likely to arise because they base their conclusions on different models or because they have different value judgments about the desirability of the policy.

   **c.** False. Deciding which goals a society should try to achieve is a matter of value judgments, not a question of economic analysis.

## Chapter Three

## 3-1 CHECK YOUR UNDERSTANDING

**1. a.** The quantity of umbrellas demanded is higher at any given price on a rainy day than on a dry day. This is a rightward *shift of* the demand curve, since at any given price the quantity demanded rises. This implies that any specific quantity can now be sold at a higher price.

   **b.** The quantity of weekend calls demanded rises in response to a price reduction. This is a *movement along* the demand curve for weekend calls.

   **c.** The demand for roses increases the week of Valentine's Day. This is a rightward *shift of* the demand curve.

   **d.** The quantity of gasoline demanded falls in response to a rise in price. This is a *movement along* the demand curve.

## 3-2 CHECK YOUR UNDERSTANDING

**1. a.** The quantity of houses supplied rises as a result of an increase in prices. This is a *movement along* the supply curve.

   **b.** The quantity of strawberries supplied is higher at any given price. This is a rightward *shift of* the supply curve.

   **c.** The quantity of labor supplied is lower at any given wage. This is a leftward *shift of* the supply curve compared to the supply curve during school vacation. So, in order to attract workers, fast-food chains have to offer higher wages.

   **d.** The quantity of labor supplied rises in response to a rise in wages. This is a *movement along* the supply curve.

   **e.** The quantity of cabins supplied is higher at any given price. This is a rightward *shift of* the supply curve.

## 3-3 CHECK YOUR UNDERSTANDING

**1. a.** The supply curve shifts rightward. At the original equilibrium price of the year before, the quantity supplied exceeds the quantity demanded. This is a case of surplus. The price of grapes will fall.

   **b.** The demand curve shifts leftward. At the original equilibrium price, the quantity of hotel rooms supplied exceeds the quantity demanded. This is a case of surplus. The rates for hotel rooms will fall.

   **c.** The demand curve for second-hand snowblowers shifts rightward. At the original equilibrium price, the quantity of second-hand snowblowers demanded exceeds the quantity supplied. This is a case of shortage. The equilibrium price of second-hand snowblowers will rise.

## 3-4 CHECK YOUR UNDERSTANDING

**1. a.** The market for large cars: this is a rightward shift in demand caused by a decrease in the price of a complement, gasoline. As a result of the shift, the equilibrium price of large cars will rise and the equilibrium quantity of large cars bought and sold will also rise.

   **b.** The market for fresh paper made from recycled stock: this is a rightward shift in supply due to a technological innovation. As a result of this shift, the equilibrium price of fresh paper made from recycled stock will fall and the equilibrium quantity bought and sold will rise.

   **c.** The market for movies at a local movie theater: this is a leftward shift in demand caused by a fall in the price of a substitute, on-demand films. As a result of this shift, the equilibrium price of movie tickets will fall and the equilibrium number of people who go to the movies will also fall.

**2.** Upon the announcement of the new chip, the demand curve for computers using the earlier chip shifts leftward, as demand decreases, and the supply curve for these computers shifts rightward, as supply increases.

   **a.** If demand decreases relatively more than supply increases, then the equilibrium quantity falls, as shown here:

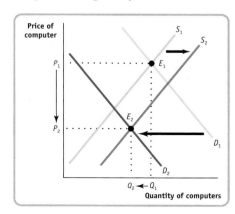

**b.** If supply increases relatively more than demand decreases, then the equilibrium quantity rises, as shown here:

In both cases, the equilibrium price falls.

# Chapter Four

## 4-1 CHECK YOUR UNDERSTANDING

**1. a.** Fewer homeowners are willing to rent out their driveways because the price ceiling has reduced the payment they receive. This is an example of a fall in price leading to a fall in the quantity supplied. It is shown in the accompanying diagram by the movement from point $E$ to point $A$ along the supply curve, a reduction in quantity of 400 parking spaces.

**b.** The quantity demanded increases by 400 spaces as the price decreases. At a lower price, more fans are willing to drive and rent a parking space. It is shown in the diagram by the movement from point $E$ to point $B$ along the demand curve.

**c.** Under a price ceiling, the quantity demanded exceeds the quantity supplied; as a result, shortages arise.

In this case, there will be a shortage of 800 parking spaces. It is shown by the horizontal distance between points $A$ and $B$.

**d.** Price ceilings result in wasted resources. The additional time fans spend to guarantee a parking space is wasted time.

**e.** Price ceilings lead to inefficient allocation of a good—here, the parking spaces—to consumers.

**f.** Price ceilings lead to black markets.

**2. a.** False. By lowering the price that producers receive, a price ceiling leads to a decrease in the quantity supplied.

**b.** True. A price ceiling leads to a lower quantity supplied than in an efficient, unregulated market. As a result, some people who would have been willing to pay the market price, and so would have gotten the good in an unregulated market, are unable to obtain it when a price ceiling is imposed.

**c.** True. Those producers who still sell the product now receive less for it and are therefore worse off. Other producers will no longer find it worthwhile to sell the product at all and so will also be made worse off.

## 4-2 CHECK YOUR UNDERSTANDING

**1. a.** Some gas station owners will benefit from getting a higher price. $Q_F$ indicates the sales made by these owners. But some will lose; there are those who make sales at the market equilibrium price of $P_E$ but do not make sales at the regulated price of $P_F$. These missed sales are indicated on the graph by the fall in the quantity demanded along the demand curve, from point $E$ to point $A$.

**b.** Those who buy gas at the higher price of $P_F$ will probably receive better service; this is an example of *inefficiently high quality* caused by a price floor as gas station owners compete on quality rather than price. But opponents are correct to claim that consumers are generally worse off—those who buy at $P_F$ would have been happy to buy at $P_E$, and many who were willing to buy at a price between $P_E$ and $P_F$ are now unwilling to buy. This is indicated on the graph by the fall in the quantity demanded along the demand curve, from point $E$ to point $A$.

**c.** Proponents are wrong because consumers and some gas station owners are hurt by the price floor. Every price floor creates "missed opportunities"—desirable transactions between consumers and station owners that never take place. Moreover, the inefficiency of wasted resources arises as consumers spend time and money driving to other states. The price floor also tempts people to engage in black market activity. With the price floor, only $Q_F$ units are sold. But at prices between $P_E$ and $P_F$, there are drivers who cumulatively want to buy more than $Q_F$ and owners who are willing to sell to them, a situation likely to lead to illegal activity.

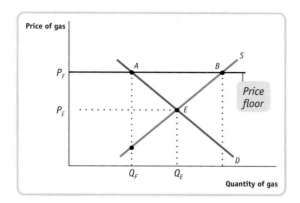

## 4-3    CHECK YOUR UNDERSTANDING

**1. a.** The price of a ride is $7 since the quantity demanded at this price is 6 million: $7 is the *demand price* of 6 million rides. This is represented by point $A$ in the accompanying figure.

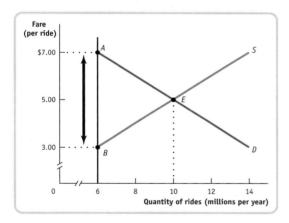

**b.** At 6 million rides, the supply price is $3 per ride, represented by point $B$ in the figure. The wedge between the demand price of $7 per ride and the supply price of $3 per ride is the quota rent per ride, $4. This is represented in the figure above by the vertical distance between points $A$ and $B$.

**c.** At 9 million rides, the demand price is $5.50 per ride, indicated by point $C$ in the accompanying figure, and the supply price is $4.50 per ride, indicated by point $D$. The quota rent is the difference between the demand price and the supply price: $1.

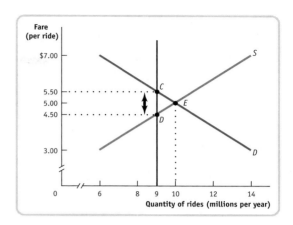

**2.** The accompanying figure shows a decrease in demand by 4 million rides, represented by a leftward shift of the demand curve from $D_1$ to $D_2$: at any given price, the quantity demanded falls by 4 million rides. (For example, at a price of $5, the quantity demanded falls from 10 million to 6 million rides per year.) This eliminates the effect of a quota limit of 8 million rides. At point $E_2$, the new market equilibrium, the equilibrium quantity is equal to the quota limit; as a result, the quota has no effect on the market.

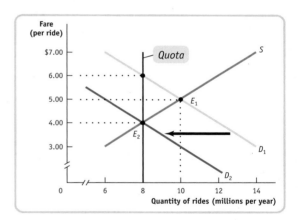

## Chapter Five

## 5-1    CHECK YOUR UNDERSTANDING

**1. a.** To determine comparative advantage, we must compare the two countries' opportunity costs for a given good. Take the opportunity cost of 1 ton of corn in terms of bicycles. In China, the opportunity cost of 1 bicycle is 0.01 ton of corn; so the opportunity cost of 1 ton of corn is 1/0.01 bicycles = 100 bicycles. The United States has the comparative advantage in corn since its opportunity cost in terms of bicycles is 50, a smaller number.

Similarly, the opportunity cost in the United States of 1 bicycle in terms of corn is 1/50 ton of corn = 0.02 ton of corn. This is greater than 0.01, the Chinese opportunity cost of 1 bicycle in terms of corn, implying that China has a comparative advantage in bicycles.

**b.** Given that the United States can produce 200,000 bicycles if no corn is produced, it can produce 200,000 bicycles × 0.02 ton of corn/bicycle = 4,000 tons of corn when no bicycles are produced. Likewise, if China can produce 3,000 tons of corn if no bicycles are produced, it can produce 3,000 tons of corn × 100 bicycles/ton of corn = 300,000 bicycles if no corn is produced. These points determine the vertical and horizontal intercepts of the U.S. and Chinese production possibility frontiers, as shown in the accompanying diagram.

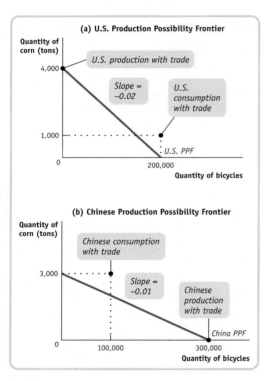

**c.** The diagram shows the production and consumption points of the two countries. Each country is clearly better off with international trade because each now consumes a bundle of the two goods that lies outside its own production possibility frontier, indicating that these bundles were unattainable in autarky.

**2. a.** According to the Heckscher–Ohlin model, this pattern of trade occurs because the United States has a relatively larger endowment of factors of production, such as human capital and physical capital, that are suited to the production of movies, but France has a relatively larger endowment of factors of production suited to wine-making, such as vineyards and the human capital of vintners.

**b.** According to the Heckscher–Ohlin model, this pattern of trade occurs because the United States has a relatively larger endowment of factors of production, such as human and physical capital, that are suited to making

machinery, but Brazil has a relatively larger endowment of factors of production suited to shoe-making, such as unskilled labor and leather.

# 5-2 CHECK YOUR UNDERSTANDING

**1.** In the accompanying diagram, $P_A$ is the U.S. price of grapes in autarky and $P_W$ is the world price of grapes under international trade. With trade, U.S. consumers pay a price of $P_W$ for grapes and consume quantity $Q_D$, U.S. grape producers produce quantity $Q_S$, and the difference, $Q_D - Q_S$, represents imports of Mexican grapes. As a consequence of the strike by truckers, imports are halted, the price paid by American consumers rises to the autarky price, $P_A$, and U.S. consumption falls to the autarky quantity, $Q_A$.

**a.** Before the strike, U.S. consumers enjoyed consumer surplus equal to areas $W + X + Z$. After the strike, their consumer surplus shrinks to $W$. So consumers are worse off, losing consumer surplus represented by $X + Z$.

**b.** Before the strike, U.S. producers had producer surplus equal to the area $Y$. After the strike, their producer surplus increases to $Y + X$. So U.S. producers are better off, gaining producer surplus represented by $X$.

**c.** U.S. total surplus falls as a result of the strike by an amount represented by area $Z$, the loss in consumer surplus that does not accrue to producers.

**2.** Mexican grape producers are worse off because they lose sales of exported grapes to the United States, and Mexican grape pickers are worse off because they lose the wages that were associated with the lost sales. The lower demand for Mexican grapes caused by the strike implies that the price Mexican consumers pay for grapes falls, making them better off. U.S. grape pickers are better off because their wages increase as a result of the increase of $Q_A - Q_S$ in U.S. sales.

# 5-3 CHECK YOUR UNDERSTANDING

**1. a.** If the tariff is $0.50, the price paid by domestic consumers for a pound of imported butter is $0.50 + $0.50 = $1.00, the same price as a pound of domestic butter. Imported butter will no longer have a price advantage over domestic butter, imports will cease, and domestic producers will capture all the feasible sales to domestic consumers, selling amount $Q_A$ in the accompanying figure. But if the tariff is less than

$0.50—say, only $0.25—the price paid by domestic consumers for a pound of imported butter is $0.50 + $0.25 = $0.75, $0.25 cheaper than a pound of domestic butter. American butter producers will gain sales in the amount of $Q_2 - Q_1$ as a result of the $0.25 tariff. But this is smaller than the amount they would have gained under the $0.50 tariff, the amount $Q_A - Q_1$.

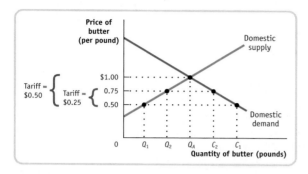

   **b.** As long as the tariff is at least $0.50, increasing it more has no effect. At a tariff of $0.50, all imports are effectively blocked.

**2.** All imports are effectively blocked at a tariff of $0.50. So such a tariff corresponds to an import quota of 0.

# 5-4 CHECK YOUR UNDERSTANDING

**1.** There are many fewer businesses that use steel as an input than there are consumers who buy sugar or clothing. So it will be easier for such businesses to communicate and coordinate among themselves to lobby against tariffs than it will be for consumers. In addition, each business will perceive that the cost of a steel tariff is quite costly to its profits, but an individual consumer is either unaware of or perceives little loss from tariffs on sugar or clothing. The tariffs were indeed lifted at the end of 2003.

**2.** Countries are often tempted to protect domestic industries by claiming that an import poses a quality, health, or environmental danger to domestic consumers. A WTO official should examine whether domestic producers are subject to the same stringency in the application of quality, health, or environmental regulations as foreign producers. If they are, then it is more likely that the regulations are for legitimate, non–trade protection purposes; if they are not, then it is more likely that the regulations are intended as trade protection measures.

# Chapter Six

## 6-1 CHECK YOUR UNDERSTANDING

**1. a.** This is a microeconomic question because it addresses decisions made by consumers about a particular product.

   **b.** This is a macroeconomic question because it addresses consumer spending in the overall economy.

   **c.** This is a macroeconomic question because it addresses changes in the overall economy.

   **d.** This is a microeconomic question because it addresses changes in a particular market, in this case the market for geologists.

   **e.** This is a microeconomic question because it addresses choices made by consumers and producers about which mode of transportation to use.

   **f.** This is a microeconomic question because it addresses changes in a particular market.

   **g.** This is a macroeconomic question because it addresses changes in a measure of the economy's overall price level.

**2. a.** When people can't get credit to finance their purchases, they will be unable to spend money. This will weaken the economy, and as others see the economy weaken, they will also cut back on their spending in order to save for future bad times. As a result, the credit shortfall will spark a compounding effect through the economy as people cut back their spending, making the economy worse, leading to more cutbacks in spending, and so on.

   **b.** If you believe the economy is self-regulating, then you would advocate doing nothing in response to the slump.

   **c.** If you believe in Keynesian economics, you would advocate that policy makers undertake monetary and fiscal policies to stimulate spending in the economy.

## 6-2 CHECK YOUR UNDERSTANDING

**1.** We talk about business cycles for the economy as a whole because recessions and expansions are not confined to a few industries—they reflect downturns and upturns for the economy as a whole. In downturns, almost every sector of the economy reduces output and the number of people employed. Moreover, business cycles are an international phenomenon, sometimes moving in rough synchrony across countries.

**2.** Recessions cause a great deal of pain across the entire society. They cause large numbers of workers to lose their jobs and make it hard to find new jobs. Recessions hurt the standard of living of many families and are usually associated with a rise in the number of people living below the poverty line, an increase in the number of people who lose their houses because they can't afford their mortgage payments, and a fall in the percentage of Americans with health insurance. Recessions also hurt the profits of firms.

## 6-3 CHECK YOUR UNDERSTANDING

**1.** Countries with high rates of population growth will have to maintain higher growth rates of overall output than countries with low rates of population growth in order to achieve an increased standard of living per person because aggregate output will have to be divided among a larger number of people.

**2.** No, Argentina is not poorer than it was in the past. Both Argentina and Canada have experienced long-run growth. However, after World War II, Argentina did not make as much progress as Canada, perhaps because of political instability and bad macroeconomic policies. Canada's economy grew much faster than Argentina's.

Although Canada is now about three times as rich as Argentina, Argentina still had long-run growth of its economy.

# 6-4 CHECK YOUR UNDERSTANDING

**1. a.** As some prices have risen but other prices have fallen, there may be overall inflation or deflation. The answer is ambiguous.

   **b.** As all prices have risen significantly, this sounds like inflation.

   **c.** As most prices have fallen and others have not changed, this sounds like deflation.

# 6-5 CHECK YOUR UNDERSTANDING

**1. a.** This situation reflects comparative advantage. Canada's comparative advantage results from the development of oil—Canada now has an abundance of oil.

   **b.** This situation reflects comparative advantage. China's comparative advantage results from an abundance of labor; China is good at labor-intensive activities such as assembly.

   **c.** This situation reflects macroeconomic forces. Germany has been running a huge trade surplus because of underlying decisions regarding savings and investment spending with its savings in excess of its investment spending.

   **d.** This situation reflects macroeconomic forces. The United States was able to begin running a large trade deficit because the technology boom made the United States an attractive place to invest, with investment spending outstripping U.S. savings.

# Chapter Seven
## 7-1 CHECK YOUR UNDERSTANDING

**1.** Let's start by considering the relationship between the total value added of all domestically produced final goods and services and aggregate spending on domestically produced final goods and services. These two quantities are equal because every final good and service produced in the economy is either purchased by someone or added to inventories. And additions to inventories are counted as spending by firms. Next, consider the relationship between aggregate spending on domestically produced final goods and services and total factor income. These two quantities are equal because all spending that is channeled to firms to pay for purchases of domestically produced final goods and services is revenue for firms. Those revenues must be paid out by firms to their factors of production in the form of wages, profit, interest, and rent. Taken together, this means that all three methods of calculating GDP are equivalent.

**2.** Firms make sales to other firms, households, the government, and the rest of the world. Households are linked to firms through the sale of factors of production to firms, through purchases from firms of final goods and services, and through lending funds to firms in the financial markets. Households are linked to the gov-

ernment through their payment of taxes, their receipt of transfers, and their lending of funds to the government via the financial markets. Finally, households are linked to the rest of the world through their purchases of imports and transactions with foreigners in financial markets.

**3.** You would be counting the value of the steel twice—once as it was sold by American Steel to American Motors and once as part of the car sold by American Motors.

## 7-2 CHECK YOUR UNDERSTANDING

**1. a.** In 2011 nominal GDP was (1,000,000 × $0.40) + (800,000 × $0.60) = $400,000 + $480,000 = $880,000. A 25% rise in the price of french fries from 2011 to 2012 means that the 2012 price of french fries was 1.25 × $0.40 = $0.50. A 10% fall in servings means that 1,000,000 × 0.9 = 900,000 servings were sold in 2012. As a result, the total value of sales of french fries in 2012 was 900,000 × $0.50 = $450,000. A 15% fall in the price of onion rings from 2011 to 2012 means that the 2012 price of onion rings was 0.85 × $0.60 = $0.51. A 5% rise in servings sold means that 800,000 × 1.05 = 840,000 servings were sold in 2012. As a result, the total value of sales of onion rings in 2012 was 840,000 × $0.51 = $428,400. Nominal GDP in 2012 was $450,000 + $428,400 = $878,400. To find real GDP in 2012, we must calculate the value of sales in 2012 using 2011 prices: (900,000 french fries × $0.40) + (840,000 onion rings × $0.60) = $360,000 + $504,000 = $864,000.

   **b.** A comparison of nominal GDP in 2011 to nominal GDP in 2012 shows a decline of (($880,000 – $878,400) / $880,000) × 100 = 0.18%. But a comparison using real GDP shows a decline of (($880,000 – $864,000) / $880,000) × 100 = 1.8%. That is, a calculation based on real GDP shows a drop 10 times larger (1.8%) than a calculation based on nominal GDP (0.18%). In this case, the calculation based on nominal GDP underestimates the true magnitude of the change.

**2.** A price index based on 2005 prices will contain a relatively high price of electronics and a relatively low price of housing compared to a price index based on 2010 prices. This means that a 2005 price index used to calculate real GDP in 2012 will magnify the value of electronics production in the economy, but a 2010 price index will magnify the value of housing production in the economy.

## 7-3 CHECK YOUR UNDERSTANDING

**1.** This market basket costs, pre-frost, (100× $0.20) + (50 × $0.60) + (200 × $0.25) = $20 + $30 + $50 = $100. The same market basket, post-frost, costs (100 × $0.40) + (50 × $1.00) + (200 × $0.45) = $40 + $50 + $90 = $180. So the price index is ($100/$100) × 100 = 100 before the frost and ($180/$100) × 100 = 180 after the frost, implying a rise in the price index of 80%. This increase in the price index is less than the 84.2% increase calculated in the text. The reason for this difference is that the new market basket of 100 oranges, 50 grapefruit, and 200 lemons contains proportionately more of the items that have experienced relatively lower price increases (the lemons, whose price has increased by 80%) and proportionately fewer of the items that have experienced relatively large price increases (the oranges, whose price has increased by 100%). This shows that the price index can be very sensitive to the composition of the market basket. If the market basket contains a large proportion of goods whose prices have risen faster than the prices of other goods, it will lead to a higher estimate of the increase in the price level. If it contains a large proportion of goods whose prices have risen more slowly than the prices of other goods, it will lead to a lower estimate of the increase in the price level.

**2. a.** A market basket determined 10 years ago will contain fewer cars than at present. Given that the average price of a car has grown faster than the average prices of other goods, this basket will underestimate the true increase in the cost of living because it contains relatively too few cars.

**b.** A market basket determined 10 years ago will not contain broadband Internet access. So cannot track the fall in prices of Internet access over the past few years. As a result, it will overestimate the true increase in the cost of living.

**3.** Using Equation 7-3, the inflation rate from 2009 to 2010 is $((218.056 - 214.537)/214.537) \times 100 = 1.6\%$.

# Chapter Eight

## 8-1 CHECK YOUR UNDERSTANDING

**1.** The advent of websites that enable job-seekers to find jobs more quickly will reduce the unemployment rate over time. However, websites that induce discouraged workers to begin actively looking for work again will lead to an increase in the unemployment rate over time.

**2. a.** Rosa is not counted as unemployed because she is not actively looking for work, but she is counted in broader measures of labor underutilization as a discouraged worker.

**b.** Anthony is not counted as unemployed; he is considered employed because he has a job.

**c.** Grace is unemployed; she is not working and is actively looking for work.

**d.** Sergio is not unemployed, but underemployed; he is working part time for economic reasons. He is counted in broader measures of labor underutilization.

**e.** Natasha is not unemployed, but marginally attached. She is counted in broader measures of labor underutilization.

**3.** Both parts a and b are consistent with the relationship, illustrated in Figure 8-5, between above-average or below-average growth in real GDP and changes in the unemployment rate: during years of above-average growth, the unemployment rate falls, and during years of below-average growth, the unemployment rate rises. However, part c is not consistent: it implies that a recession is associated with a fall in the unemployment rate, which is correct.

## 8-2 CHECK YOUR UNDERSTANDING

**1. a.** When the pace of technological advance quickens, there will be higher rates of job creation and destruction as old industries disappear and new ones emerge. As a result, frictional unemployment will be higher as workers leave jobs in declining industries in search of jobs in expanding industries.

**b.** When the pace of technological advance quickens, there will be greater mismatch between the skills employees have and the skills employers are looking for, leading to higher structural unemployment.

**c.** When the unemployment rate is low, frictional unemployment will account for a larger share of total unemployment because other sources of unemployment will be diminished. So the share of total unemployment composed of the frictionally unemployed will rise.

**2.** A binding minimum wage represents a price floor below which wages cannot fall. As a result, actual wages cannot move toward equilibrium. So a minimum wage causes the quantity of labor supplied to exceed the quantity of labor demanded. Because this surplus of labor reflects unemployed workers, it affects the unemployment rate. Collective bargaining has a similar effect—unions are able to raise the wage above the equilibrium level to a level like $W_U$ in the accompanying diagram. This will act like a minimum wage by causing the number of job-seekers to be larger than the number of workers firms are willing to hire. Collective bargaining causes the unemployment rate to be higher than it otherwise would be, as shown in the accompanying diagram.

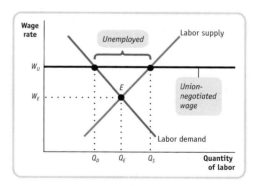

**3.** An increase in unemployment benefits at the peak of the business cycle reduces the cost to individuals of being unemployed, causing them to spend more time searching for new jobs. So the natural rate of unemployment would increase.

## 8-3 CHECK YOUR UNDERSTANDING

**1.** Shoe-leather costs as a result of inflation will be lower because it is now less costly for individuals to manage their assets in order to economize on their money holdings. This reduction in the costs associated with converting other assets into money translates into lower shoe-leather costs.

**2.** If inflation came to an unexpected and complete stop over the next 15 or 20 years, the inflation rate would be zero, which of course is less than the expected inflation rate of 2% to 3%. Because the real interest rate is the nominal interest rate minus the inflation rate, the real interest rate on a loan would be higher than expected, and lenders would gain at the expense of borrowers. Borrowers would have to repay their loans with funds that have a higher real value than had been expected.

## Chapter Nine

### 9-1 CHECK YOUR UNDERSTANDING

1. Economic progress raises the living standards of the average resident of a country. An increase in overall real GDP does not accurately reflect an increase in an average resident's living standard because it does not account for growth in the number of residents. If, for example, real GDP rises by 10% but population grows by 20%, the living standard of the average resident falls: after the change, the average resident has only (110/120) × 100 = 91.6% as much real income as before the change. Similarly, an increase in nominal GDP per capita does not accurately reflect an increase in living standards because it does not account for any change in prices. For example, a 5% increase in nominal GDP per capita generated by a 5% increase in prices implies that there has been no change in living standards. Real GDP per capita is the only measure that accounts for both changes in the population and changes in prices.

2. Using the Rule of 70, the amount of time it will take for China to double its real GDP per capita is (70/8.9) = 8 years; India, (70/4.2) = 17 years; Ireland, (70/3.1) = 23 years; the United States, (70/1.7) = 41 years; France, (70/l.3) = 54 years; and Argentina (70/1.2) = 58 years. Since the Rule of 70 can only be applied to a positive growth rate, we cannot apply it to the case of Zimbabwe, which experienced negative growth. If India continues to have a higher growth rate of real GDP per capita than the United States, then India's real GDP per capita will eventually surpass that of the United States.

3. The United States began growing rapidly over a century ago, but China and India have begun growing rapidly only recently. As a result, the living standard of the typical Chinese or Indian household has not yet caught up with that of the typical American household.

### 9-2 CHECK YOUR UNDERSTANDING

1. a. Significant technological progress will result in a positive growth rate of productivity even though physical capital per worker and human capital per worker are unchanged.

 b. The growth rate of productivity will fall but remain positive due to diminishing returns to physical capital.

2. a. If output has grown 3% per year and the labor force has grown 1% per year, then productivity—output per person—has grown at approximately 3% – 1% = 2% per year.

 b. If physical capital has grown 4% per year and the labor force has grown 1% per year, then physical capital per worker has grown at approximately 4% – 1% = 3% per year.

 c. According to estimates, each 1% rise in physical capital, other things equal, increases productivity by 0.3%. So, as physical capital per worker has increased by 3%, productivity growth that can be attributed to an increase in physical capital per worker is 0.3 × 3% = 0.9%. As a percentage of total productivity growth, this is 0.9%/2% × 100% = 45%.

 d. If the rest of productivity growth is due to technological progress, then technological progress has contributed 2% – 0.9% = 1.1% to productivity growth. As a percentage of total productivity growth, this is 1.1%/2% × 100% = 55%.

3. It will take a period time for workers to learn how to use the new computer system and to adjust their routines. And because there are often setbacks in learning a new system, such as accidentally erasing your computer files, productivity at Multinomics may decrease for a period of time.

### 9-3 CHECK YOUR UNDERSTANDING

1. A country that has high domestic savings is able to achieve a high rate of investment spending as a percent of GDP. This, in turn, allows the country to achieve a high growth rate.

2. It is likely that the United States will experience a greater pace of creation and development of new drugs because closer links between private companies and academic research centers will lead to work more directly focused on producing new drugs rather than on pure research.

3. It is likely that these events resulted in a fall in the country's growth rate because the lack of property rights would have dissuaded people from making investments in productive capacity.

### 9-4 CHECK YOUR UNDERSTANDING

1. The conditional version of the convergence hypothesis says that countries grow faster, other things equal, when they start from relatively low GDP per capita. From this we can infer that they grow more slowly, other things equal, when their real GDP per capita is relatively higher. This points to lower future Asian growth. However, other things might not be equal: if Asian economies continue investing in human capital, if savings rates continue to be high, if governments invest in infrastructure, and so on, growth might continue at an accelerated pace.

2. The regions of East Asia, Western Europe, and the United States support the convergence hypothesis because a comparison among them shows that the growth rate of real GDP per capita falls as real GDP per capita rises. Eastern Europe, West Asia, Latin America, and Africa do not support the hypothesis because they all have much lower real GDP per capita than the United States but have either approximately the same growth rate (West Asia and Eastern Europe) or a lower growth rate (Africa and Latin America).

3. The evidence suggests that both sets of factors matter: better infrastructure is important for growth, but so is political and financial stability. Policies should try to address both areas.

# 9-5 CHECK YOUR UNDERSTANDING

1. Economists are typically more concerned about environmental degradation than resource scarcity. The reason is that in modern economies the price response tends to alleviate the limits imposed by resource scarcity through conservation and the development of alternatives. However, because environmental degradation involves a negative externality—a cost imposed by individuals or firms on others without the requirement to pay compensation—effective government intervention is required to address it. As a result, economists are more concerned about the limits to growth imposed by environmental degradation because a market response would be inadequate.

2. Growth increases a country's greenhouse gas emissions. The current best estimates are that a large reduction in emissions will result in only a modest reduction in growth. The international burden sharing of greenhouse gas emissions reduction is contentious because rich countries are reluctant to pay the costs of reducing their emissions only to see newly emerging countries like China rapidly increase their emissions. Yet most of the current accumulation of gases is due to the past actions of rich countries. Poorer countries like China are equally reluctant to sacrifice their growth to pay for the past actions of rich countries.

# Chapter Ten
## 10-1 CHECK YOUR UNDERSTANDING

**1. a.** As there is a net capital inflow into the economy, the supply of loanable funds increases. This is illustrated by the shift of the supply curve from $S_1$ to $S_2$ in the accompanying diagram. As the equilibrium moves from $E_1$ to $E_2$, the equilibrium interest rate falls from $r_1$ to $r_2$, and the equilibrium quantity of loanable funds increases from $Q_1$ to $Q_2$.

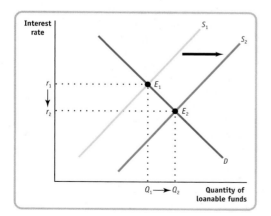

**b.** Savings fall due to the higher proportion of retired people, and the supply of loanable funds decreases. This is

illustrated by the leftward shift of the supply curve from $S_1$ to $S_2$ in the accompanying diagram. The equilibrium moves from $E_1$ to $E_2$, the equilibrium interest rate rises from $r_1$ to $r_2$, and the equilibrium quantity of loanable funds falls from $Q_1$ to $Q_2$.

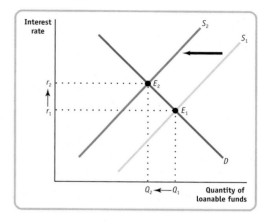

2. We know from the loanable funds market that as the interest rate rises, households want to save more and consume less. But at the same time, an increase in the interest rate lowers the number of investment spending projects with returns at least as high as the interest rate. The statement "households will want to save more money than businesses will want to invest" cannot represent an equilibrium in the loanable funds market because it says that the quantity of loanable funds offered exceeds the quantity of loanable funds demanded. If that were to occur, the interest rate must fall to make the quantity of loanable funds offered equal to the quantity of loanable funds demanded.

**3. a.** The real interest rate will not change. According to the Fisher effect, an increase in expected inflation drives up the nominal interest rate, leaving the real interest rate unchanged.

**b.** The nominal interest rate will rise by 3%. Each additional percentage point of expected inflation drives up the nominal interest rate by 1 percentage point.

**c.** As we saw in Figure 25-7, as long as inflation is expected, it does not affect the equilibrium quantity of loanable funds. Both the supply and demand curves for loanable funds are pushed upward, leaving the equilibrium quantity of loanable funds unchanged.

## 10-2 CHECK YOUR UNDERSTANDING

1. The transaction costs for (a) a bank deposit and (b) a share of a mutual fund are approximately equal because each can typically be accomplished by making a phone call, going online, or visiting a branch office. Transaction costs are highest for (c) a share of a family business, since finding a buyer for the share consumes time and resources. The level of risk is lowest for (a) a bank deposit, since these deposits are insured by the Federal Deposit Insurance Corporation (FDIC) up to $250,000; somewhat higher for (b) a share of a mutual fund, since despite diversification, there is still risk associated with holding mutual funds; and highest for

(c) a share of a family business, since this investment is not diversified. The level of liquidity is highest for (a) a bank deposit, since withdrawals can usually be made immediately; somewhat lower for (b) a share of a mutual fund, since it may take a few days between selling your shares and the payment being processed; and lowest for (c) a share of a family business, since it can only be sold with the unanimous agreement of other members and it will take some time to find a buyer.

2. Economic development and growth are the result of, among other factors, investment spending on physical capital. Since investment spending is equal to savings, the greater the amount saved, the higher investment spending will be, and so the higher growth and economic development will be. So the existence of institutions that facilitate savings will help a country's growth and economic development. As a result, a country with a financial system that provides low transaction costs, opportunities for diversification of risk, and high liquidity to its savers will experience faster growth and economic development than a country that doesn't.

## 10-3 CHECK YOUR UNDERSTANDING

1. **a.** Today's stock prices reflect the market's expectation of future stock prices, and according to the efficient markets hypothesis, stock prices always take account of all available information. The fact that this year's profits are low is not new information, so it is already built into the share price. However, when it becomes known that the company's profits will be high next year, the price of a share of its stock will rise today, reflecting this new information.

   **b.** The expectations of investors about high profits were already built into the stock price. Since profits will be lower than expected, the market's expectations about the company's future stock price will be revised downward. This new information will lower the stock price.

   **c.** When other companies in the same industry announce that sales are unexpectedly slow this year, investors are likely to conclude that sales will also be unexpectedly slow for this company. As a result, investors will revise downward their expectations of future profits and of the future stock price. This new information will result in a lower stock price today.

   **d.** This announcement will either have no effect on the company's stock price or will increase it only slightly. It does not add any new information, beyond removing some uncertainty about whether the profit forecast was correct. It should therefore result in either no increase or only a small increase in the stock price.

2. The efficient markets hypothesis states that all available information is immediately taken into account in stock prices. So if investors consistently bought stocks the day after the Dow rose by 1%, a smart investor would *sell* on that day because demand—and so stock prices—would be high. If a profit can be made that way, eventually many investors would be selling, and it would no longer be true that investors always bought stocks the day after the Dow rose by 1%.

## Chapter Eleven

# 11-1 CHECK YOUR UNDERSTANDING

1. A decline in investment spending, like a rise in investment spending, has a multiplier effect on real GDP—the only difference in this case is that real GDP falls instead of rises. The fall in $I$ leads to an initial fall in real GDP, which leads to a fall in disposable income, which leads to lower consumer spending, which leads to another fall in real GDP, and so on. So consumer spending falls as an indirect result of the fall in investment spending.

2. When the $MPC$ is 0.5, the multiplier is equal to $1/(1 - 0.5) = 1/0.5 = 2$. When the $MPC$ is 0.8, the multiplier is equal to $1/(1 - 0.8) = 1/0.2 = 5$.

3. The greater the share of GDP that is saved rather than spent, the lower the $MPC$. Disposable income that goes to savings is like a "leak" in the system, reducing the amount of spending that fuels a further expansion. So it is likely that Amerigo will have the larger multiplier.

# 11-2 CHECK YOUR UNDERSTANDING

1. **a.** Angelina's autonomous consumer spending is $8,000. When her current disposable income rises by $10,000, her consumer spending rises by $12,000 – $8,000 = $4,000. So her $MPC$ is $4,000/$10,000 = 0.4 and her consumption function is $c = \$8{,}000 + 0.4 \times yd$. Felicia's autonomous consumer spending is $6,500. When her current disposable income rises by $10,000, her consumer spending rises by $14,500 – $6,500 = $8,000. So her $MPC$ is $8,000/$10,000 = 0.8 and her consumption function is $c = \$6{,}500 + 0.8 \times yd$. Marina's autonomous consumer spending is $7,250. When her current disposable income rises by $10,000, her consumer spending rises by $14,250 – $7,250 = $7,000. So her $MPC$ is $7,000/$10,000 = 0.7 and her consumption function is $c = \$7{,}250 + 0.7 \times yd$.

   **b.** The aggregate autonomous consumer spending in this economy is $8,000 + $6,500 + $7,250 = $21,750. A $30,000 increase in disposable income (3 × $10,000) leads to a $4,000 + $8,000 + $7,000 = $19,000 increase in consumer spending. So the economy-wide $MPC$ is $19,000/$30,000 = 0.63 and the aggregate consumption function is $C = \$21{,}750 + 0.63 \times YD$.

2. If you expect your future disposable income to fall, you would like to save some of today's disposable income to tide you over in the future. But you cannot do this if you cannot save. If you expect your future disposable income to rise, you would like to spend some of tomorrow's higher income today. But you cannot do this if you cannot borrow. If you cannot save or borrow, your expected future disposable income will have no effect on your consumer spending today. In fact, your $MPC$ must always equal 1: you must consume all your current disposable income today, and you will be unable to smooth your consumption over time.

# 11-3 CHECK YOUR UNDERSTANDING

1. **a.** An unexpected increase in consumer spending will result in a reduction in inventories as producers sell items from their inventories to satisfy this short-term increase in demand. This is negative unplanned

inventory investment: it reduces the value of producers' inventories.

**b.** A rise in the cost of borrowing is equivalent to a rise in the interest rate: fewer investment spending projects are now profitable to producers, whether they are financed through borrowing or retained earnings. As a result, producers will reduce the amount of planned investment spending.

**c.** A sharp increase in the rate of real GDP growth leads to a higher level of planned investment spending by producers, according to the accelerator principle, as they increase production capacity to meet higher demand.

**d.** As sales fall, producers sell less, and their inventories grow. This leads to positive unplanned inventory investment.

2.  Since the marginal propensity to consume is less than 1—because consumers normally spend part but not all of an additional dollar of disposable income—consumer spending does not fully respond to fluctuations in current disposable income. This behavior diminishes the effect of fluctuations in the economy on consumer spending. In contrast, by the accelerator principle, investment spending is directly related to the expected future growth rate of GDP. As a result, investment spending will magnify fluctuations in the economy: a higher expected future growth rate of real GDP leads to higher planned investment spending; a lower expected future growth rate of real GDP leads to lower planned investment spending.

3.  When consumer spending is sluggish, firms with excess production capacity will cut back on planned investment spending because they think their existing capacities are sufficient for expected future sales. Similarly, when consumer spending is sluggish and firms have a large amount of unplanned inventory investment, they are likely to cut back their production of output because they think their existing inventories are sufficient for expected future sales. So an inventory overhang is likely to depress current economic activity as firms cut back on their planned investment spending and on their output.

# 11-4

1.  A slump in planned investment spending will lead to a fall in real GDP in response to an unanticipated increase in inventories. The fall in real GDP will translate into a fall in households' disposable income, and households will respond by reducing consumer spending. The decrease in consumer spending leads producers to further decrease output, further lowering disposable income and leading to further reductions in consumer spending. So although the slump originated in investment spending, it will cause a reduction in consumer spending.

2. **a.** After an autonomous fall in planned aggregate spending, the economy is no longer in equilibrium: real GDP is greater than planned aggregate spending. The accompanying figure shows this autonomous fall in planned aggregate spending by the shift of the aggregate spending curve from $AE_1$ to $AE_2$. The difference between the

two results in positive unplanned inventory investment: there is an unanticipated increase in inventories. Firms will respond by reducing production. This will eventually move the economy to a new equilibrium. In the accompanying figure, this is illustrated by the movement from the initial income–expenditure equilibrium at $E_1$ to the new income–expenditure equilibrium at $E_2$. As the economy moves to its new equilibrium, real GDP falls from its initial income–expenditure equilibrium level at $Y_1^*$ to its new lower level, $Y_2^*$.

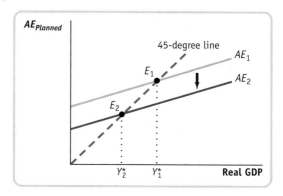

**b.** We know that the change in income–expenditure equilibrium GDP is given by Equation 11-17: $\Delta Y^* = $ Multiplier $\times \Delta AAE_{Planned}$. Here, the multiplier = $1/(1 - 0.5) = 1/0.5 = 2$. So a $300 million autonomous reduction in planned aggregate spending will lead to a $2 \times $300$ million = $600 million ($0.6 billion) fall in income–expenditure equilibrium GDP. The new $Y^*$ will be $500 billion – $0.6 billion = $499.4 billion.

# Chapter Twelve
# 12-1

1. **a.** This is a shift of the aggregate demand curve. A decrease in the quantity of money raises the interest rate, since people now want to borrow more and lend less. A higher interest rate reduces investment and consumer spending at any given aggregate price level. So the aggregate demand curve shifts to the left.

**b.** This is a movement up along the aggregate demand curve. As the aggregate price level rises, the real value of money holdings falls. This is the interest rate effect of a change in the aggregate price level: as the value of money falls, people want to hold more money. They do so by borrowing more and lending less. This leads to a rise in the interest rate and a reduction in consumer and investment spending. So it is a movement along the aggregate demand curve.

**c.** This is a shift of the aggregate demand curve. Expectations of a poor job market, and so lower average disposable incomes, will reduce people's consumer spending today at any given aggregate price level. So the aggregate demand curve shifts to the left.

**d.** This is a shift of the aggregate demand curve. A fall in tax rates raises people's disposable income. At any given aggregate price level, consumer spending is now higher. So the aggregate demand curve shifts to the right.

**e.** This is a movement down along the aggregate demand curve. As the aggregate price level falls, the real value of assets rises. This is the wealth effect of a change in the aggregate price level: as the value of assets rises, people will increase their consumption plans. This leads to higher consumer spending. So it is a movement along the aggregate demand curve.

**f.** This is a shift of the aggregate demand curve. A rise in the real value of assets in the economy due to a surge in real estate values raises consumer spending at any given aggregate price level. So the aggregate demand curve shifts to the right.

## 12-2 CHECK YOUR UNDERSTANDING

**1. a.** This represents a movement along the *SRAS* curve because the CPI—like the GDP deflator—is a measure of the aggregate price level, the overall price level of final goods and services in the economy.

**b.** This represents a shift of the *SRAS* curve because oil is a commodity. The *SRAS* curve will shift to the right because production costs are now lower, leading to a higher quantity of aggregate output supplied at any given aggregate price level.

**c.** This represents a shift of the *SRAS* curve because it involves a change in nominal wages. An increase in legally mandated benefits to workers is equivalent to an increase in nominal wages. As a result, the *SRAS* curve will shift leftward because production costs are now higher, leading to a lower quantity of aggregate output supplied at any given aggregate price level.

**2.** You would need to know what happened to the aggregate price level. If the increase in the quantity of aggregate output supplied was due to a movement along the *SRAS* curve, the aggregate price level would have increased at the same time as the quantity of aggregate output supplied increased. If the increase in the quantity of aggregate output supplied was due to a rightward shift of the *LRAS* curve, the aggregate price level might not rise. Alternatively, you could make the determination by observing what happened to aggregate output in the long run. If it fell back to its initial level in the long run, then the temporary increase in aggregate output was due to a movement along the *SRAS* curve. If it stayed at the higher level in the long run, the increase in aggregate output was due to a rightward shift of the *LRAS* curve.

## 12-3 CHECK YOUR UNDERSTANDING

**1. a.** An increase in the minimum wage raises the nominal wage and, as a result, shifts the short-run aggregate supply curve to the left. As a result of this negative supply shock, the aggregate price level rises and aggregate output falls.

**b.** Increased investment spending shifts the aggregate demand curve to the right. As a result of this positive demand shock, both the aggregate price level and aggregate output rise.

**c.** An increase in taxes and a reduction in government spending both result in negative demand shocks, shifting the aggregate demand curve to the left. As a

result, both the aggregate price level and aggregate output fall.

**d.** This is a negative supply shock, shifting the short-run aggregate supply curve to the left. As a result, the aggregate price level rises and aggregate output falls.

**2.** As the rise in productivity increases potential output, the long-run aggregate supply curve shifts to the right. If, in the short run, there is now a recessionary gap (aggregate output is less than potential output), nominal wages will fall, shifting the short-run aggregate supply curve to the right. This results in a fall in the aggregate price level and a rise in aggregate output. As prices fall, we move along the aggregate demand curve due to the wealth and interest rate effects of a change in the aggregate price level. Eventually, as long-run macroeconomic equilibrium is reestablished, aggregate output will rise to be equal to potential output.

## 12-4 CHECK YOUR UNDERSTANDING

**1. a.** An economy is overstimulated when an inflationary gap is present. This will arise if an expansionary monetary or fiscal policy is implemented when the economy is currently in long-run macroeconomic equilibrium. This shifts the aggregate demand curve to the right, in the short run raising the aggregate price level and aggregate output and creating an inflationary gap. Eventually nominal wages will rise and shift the short-run aggregate supply curve to the left, and aggregate output will fall back to potential output. This is the scenario envisaged by the speaker.

**b.** No, this is not a valid argument. When the economy is not currently in long-run macroeconomic equilibrium, an expansionary monetary or fiscal policy does not lead to the outcome described above. Suppose a negative demand shock has shifted the aggregate demand curve to the left, resulting in a recessionary gap. An expansionary monetary or fiscal policy can shift the aggregate demand curve back to its original position in long-run macroeconomic equilibrium. In this way, the short-run fall in aggregate output and deflation caused by the original negative demand shock can be avoided. So, if used in response to demand shocks, fiscal or monetary policy is an effective policy tool.

**2.** Those within the Fed who advocated lowering interest rates were focused on boosting aggregate demand in order to counteract the negative demand shock caused by the collapse of the housing bubble. Lowering interest rates will result in a rightward shift of the aggregate demand curve, increasing aggregate output but raising the aggregate price level. Those within the Fed who advocated holding interest rates steady were focused on the fact that fighting the slump in aggregate demand in the face of a negative supply shock could result in a rise in inflation. Holding interest rates steady relies on the ability of the economy to self-correct in the long run, with the aggregate price level and aggregate output only gradually returning to their levels before the negative supply shock.

# Chapter Thirteen

## 13-1 CHECK YOUR UNDERSTANDING

**1. a.** This is a contractionary fiscal policy because it is a reduction in government purchases of goods and services.

   **b.** This is an expansionary fiscal policy because it is an increase in government transfers that will increase disposable income.

   **c.** This is a contractionary fiscal policy because it is an increase in taxes that will reduce disposable income.

**2.** Federal disaster relief that is quickly disbursed is more effective than legislated aid because there is very little time lag between the time of the disaster and the time it is received by victims. So it will stabilize the economy after a disaster. In contrast, legislated aid is likely to entail a time lag in its disbursement, potentially destabilizing the economy.

**3.** This statement implies that expansionary fiscal policy will result in crowding out of the private sector, and that the opposite, contractionary fiscal policy, will lead the private sector to grow. Whether this statement is true or not depends upon whether the economy is at full employment; it is only then that we should expect expansionary fiscal policy to lead to crowding out. If, instead, the economy has a recessionary gap, then we should expect instead that the private sector grows along with the fiscal expansion, and contracts along with a fiscal contraction.

## 13-2 CHECK YOUR UNDERSTANDING

**1.** A $500 million increase in government purchases of goods and services directly increases aggregate spending by $500 million, which then starts the multiplier in motion. It will increase real GDP by $500 million × $1/(1 - MPC)$. A $500 million increase in government transfers increases aggregate spending only to the extent that it leads to an increase in consumer spending. Consumer spending rises by $MPC × \$1$ for every $1 increase in disposable income, where $MPC$ is less than 1. So a $500 million increase in government transfers will cause a rise in real GDP only $MPC$ times as much as a $500 million increase in government purchases of goods and services. It will increase real GDP by $500 million × $MPC/(1 - MPC)$.

**2.** This is the same issue as in Problem 1, but in reverse. If government purchases of goods and services fall by $500 million, the initial fall in aggregate spending is $500 million. If there is a $500 million reduction in government transfers, the initial fall in aggregate spending is $MPC × \$500$ million, which is less than $500 million.

**3.** Boldovia will experience greater variation in its real GDP than Moldovia because Moldovia has automatic stabilizers while Boldovia does not. In Moldovia the effects of slumps will be lessened by unemployment insurance benefits that will support residents' incomes, while the effects of booms will be diminished because tax revenues will go up. In contrast, incomes will not be supported in Boldovia during slumps because there is no unemployment insurance. In addition, because Boldovia has lump-sum taxes, its booms will not be diminished by increases in tax revenue.

## 13-3 CHECK YOUR UNDERSTANDING

**1.** The actual budget balance takes into account the effects of the business cycle on the budget deficit. During recessionary gaps, it incorporates the effect of lower tax revenues and higher transfers on the budget balance; during inflationary gaps, it incorporates the effect of higher tax revenues and reduced transfers. In contrast, the cyclically adjusted budget balance factors out the effects of the business cycle and assumes that real GDP is at potential output. Since, in the long run, real GDP tends to potential output, the cyclically adjusted budget balance is a better measure of the long-run sustainability of government policies.

**2.** In recessions, real GDP falls. This implies that consumers' incomes, consumer spending, and producers' profits also fall. So in recessions, states' tax revenue (which depends in large part on consumers' incomes, consumer spending, and producers' profits) falls. In order to balance the state budget, states have to cut spending or raise taxes. But that deepens the recession. Without a balanced-budget requirement, states could use expansionary fiscal policy during a recession to lessen the fall in real GDP.

## 13-4 CHECK YOUR UNDERSTANDING

**1. a.** A higher growth rate of real GDP implies that tax revenue will increase. If government spending remains constant and the government runs a budget surplus, the size of the public debt will be less than it would otherwise have been.

   **b.** If retirees live longer, the average age of the population increases. As a result, the implicit liabilities of the government increase because spending on programs for older Americans, such as Social Security and Medicare, will rise.

   **c.** A decrease in tax revenue without offsetting reductions in government spending will cause the public debt to increase.

   **d.** Public debt will increase as a result of government borrowing to pay interest on its current public debt.

**2.** In order to stimulate the economy in the short run, the government can use fiscal policy to increase real GDP. This entails borrowing, increasing the size of the public debt further and leading to undesirable consequences: in extreme cases, governments can be forced to default on their debts. Even in less extreme cases, a large public debt is undesirable because government borrowing crowds out borrowing for private investment spending. This reduces the amount of investment spending, reducing the long-run growth of the economy.

**3.** Fiscal austerity is the same as a contractionary fiscal policy. It reduces government spending, which in turn reduces income and reduces tax revenue. With less tax revenue, the government is less able to pay its debts. Also, a failing economy causes lenders to have less confidence that a government is able to pay its debts and leads them to raise interest rates on the debt. Higher interest rates on the debt make it even less likely the government can repay.

# Chapter Fourteen

## 14-1 CHECK YOUR UNDERSTANDING

1. The defining characteristic of money is its liquidity: how easily it can be used to purchase goods and services. Although a gift certificate can easily be used to purchase a very defined set of goods or services (the goods or services available at the store issuing the gift certificate), it cannot be used to purchase any other goods or services. A gift certificate is therefore not money, since it cannot easily be used to purchase all goods and services.

2. Again, the important characteristic of money is its liquidity: how easily it can be used to purchase goods and services. M1, the narrowest definition of the money supply, contains only currency in circulation, traveler's checks, and checkable bank deposits. CDs aren't checkable—and they can't be made checkable without incurring a cost because there's a penalty for early withdrawal. This makes them less liquid than the assets counted in M1.

3. Commodity-backed money uses resources more efficiently than simple commodity money, like gold and silver coins, because commodity-backed money ties up fewer valuable resources. Although a bank must keep some of the commodity—generally gold and silver—on hand, it only has to keep enough to satisfy demand for redemptions. It can then lend out the remaining gold and silver, which allows society to use these resources for other purposes, with no loss in the ability to achieve gains from trade.

## 14-2 CHECK YOUR UNDERSTANDING

1. Even though you know that the rumor about the bank is not true, you are concerned about other depositors pulling their money out of the bank. And you know that if enough other depositors pull their money out, the bank will fail. In that case, it is rational for you to pull your money out before the bank fails. All depositors will think like this, so even if they all know that the rumor is false, they may still rationally pull their money out, leading to a bank run. Deposit insurance leads depositors to worry less about the possibility of a bank run. Even if a bank fails, the FDIC will currently pay each depositor up to $250,000 per account. This will make you much less likely to pull your money out in response to a rumor. Since other depositors will think the same, there will be no bank run.

2. The aspects of modern bank regulation that would frustrate this scheme are *capital requirements* and *reserve requirements*. Capital requirements mean that a bank has to have a certain amount of capital—the difference between its assets (loans plus reserves) and its liabilities (deposits). So the con artist could not open a bank without putting any of his own wealth in because the bank needs a certain amount of capital—that is, it needs to

hold more assets (loans plus reserves) than deposits. So the con artist would be at risk of losing his own wealth if his loans turn out badly.

## 14-3 CHECK YOUR UNDERSTANDING

1. Since they only have to hold $100 in reserves, instead of $200, banks now lend out $100 of their reserves. Whoever borrows the $100 will deposit it in a bank, which will lend out $100 × (1 − $rr$) = $100 × 0.9 = $90. Whoever borrows the $90 will put it into a bank, which will lend out $90 × 0.9 = $81, and so on. Overall, deposits will increase by $100/0.1 = $1,000.

2. Silas puts $1,000 in the bank, of which the bank lends out $1,000 × (1 − $rr$) = $1,000 × 0.9 = $900. Whoever borrows the $900 will keep $450 in cash and deposit $450 in a bank. The bank will lend out $450 × 0.9 = $405. Whoever borrows the $405 will keep $202.50 in cash and deposit $202.50 in a bank. The bank will lend out $202.50 × 0.9 = $182.25, and so on. Overall, this leads to an increase in deposits of $1,000 + $450 + $202.50 + . . . But it decreases the amount of currency in circulation: the amount of cash is reduced by the $1,000 Silas puts into the bank. This is offset, but not fully, by the amount of cash held by each borrower. The amount of currency in circulation therefore changes by −$1,000 + $450 + $202.50 + . . . The money supply therefore increases by the sum of the increase in deposits and the change in currency in circulation, which is $1,000 − $1,000 + $450 + $450 + $202.50 + $202.50 + . . . and so on.

## 14-4 CHECK YOUR UNDERSTANDING

1. An open-market purchase of $100 million by the Fed increases banks' reserves by $100 million as the Fed credits their accounts with additional reserves. In other words, this open-market purchase increases the monetary base (currency in circulation plus bank reserves) by $100 million. Banks lend out the additional $100 million. Whoever borrows the money puts it back into the banking system in the form of deposits. Of these deposits, banks lend out $100 million × (1 − $rr$) = $100 million × 0.9 = $90 million. Whoever borrows the money deposits it back into the banking system. And banks lend out $90 million × 0.9 = $81 million, and so on. As a result, bank deposits increase by $100 million + $90 million + $81 million + . . . = $100 million/$rr$ = $100 million/0.1 = $1,000 million = $1 billion. Since in this simplified example all money lent out is deposited back into the banking system, there is no increase of currency in circulation, so the increase in bank deposits is equal to the increase in the money supply. In other words, the money supply increases by $1 billion. This is greater than the increase in the monetary base by a factor of 10: in this simplified model in which deposits are the only component of the money supply and in which banks hold no excess reserves, the money multiplier is 1/$rr$ = 10.

## 14-5 CHECK YOUR UNDERSTANDING

1. The Panic of 1907, the S&L crisis, and the crisis of 2008 all involved losses by financial institutions that were less regulated than banks. In the crises of 1907 and

2008, there was a widespread loss of confidence in the financial sector and collapse of credit markets. Like the crisis of 1907 and the S&L crisis, the crisis of 2008 exerted a powerful negative effect on the economy.

2. The creation of the Federal Reserve failed to prevent bank runs because it did not eradicate the fears of depositors that a bank collapse would cause them to lose their money. The bank runs eventually stopped after federal deposit insurance was instituted and the public came to understand that their deposits were now protected.

3. The balance sheet effect occurs when asset sales cause declines in asset prices, which then reduce the value of other firms' net worth as the value of the assets on their balance sheets declines. In the vicious cycle of deleveraging, the balance sheet effect on firms forces their creditors to call in their loan contracts, forcing the firms to sell assets to pay back their loans, leading to further asset sales and price declines. Because the vicious cycle of deleveraging occurs across different firms and no single firm can stop it, it is necessary for the government to step in to stop it.

## Chapter Fifteen

# 15-1    CHECK YOUR UNDERSTANDING

1. a. By increasing the opportunity cost of holding money, a high interest rate reduces the quantity of money demanded. This is a movement up and to the left along the money demand curve.

   b. A 10% fall in prices reduces the quantity of money demanded at any given interest rate, shifting the money demand curve leftward.

   c. This technological change reduces the quantity of money demanded at any given interest rate. So it shifts the money demand curve leftward.

   d. This will increase the demand for money at any given interest rate. With more of the economy's assets in over-seas bank accounts that are difficult to access, people will want to hold more cash to finance purchases.

2. a. A 1% processing fee on debit/credit card transactions for purchases less than $50 reduces the opportunity cost of holding cash because consumers will save money by paying with cash.

   b. An increase in the interest paid on six-month CDs raises the opportunity cost of holding cash because holding cash requires forgoing the higher interest paid.

   c. This reduces the opportunity cost of holding cash because it can now be used to fund purchases at very low prices, and compensating its owner for any interest forgone by holding cash.

   d. Because many purchases of food are made in cash, a significant increase in the cost of food reduces the opportunity cost of holding cash.

# 15-2    CHECK YOUR UNDERSTANDING

1. In the accompanying diagram, the increase in the demand for money is shown as a rightward shift of the

money demand curve, from $MD_1$ to $MD_2$. This raises the equilibrium interest rate from $r_1$ to $r_2$.

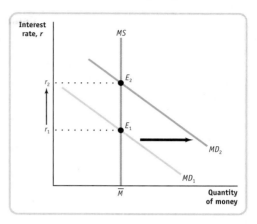

2. In order to prevent the interest rate from rising, the Federal Reserve must make an open-market purchase of Treasury bills, shifting the money supply curve right-ward. This is shown in the accompanying diagram as the move from $MS_1$ to $MS_2$.

3. a. Frannie is better off buying a one-year bond today and a one-year bond tomorrow because this allows her to get the higher interest rate one year from now.

   b. Frannie is better off buying a two-year bond today because it gives her a higher interest rate in the second year than if she bought two one-year bonds.

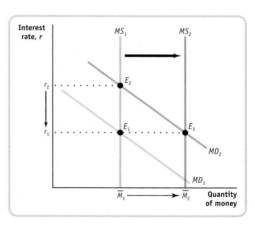

# 15-3    CHECK YOUR UNDERSTANDING

1. a. The money supply curve shifts to the right.

   b. The equilibrium interest rate falls.

   c. Investment spending rises, due to the fall in the interest rate.

   d. Consumer spending rises, due to the multiplier process.

   e. Aggregate output rises because of the rightward shift of the aggregate demand curve.

2. The central bank that uses a Taylor Rule is likely to respond more directly to a financial crisis than one that

uses inflation targeting because with a Taylor Rule the central bank does not have to set policy to meet a pre-specified inflation target.

# 15-4 CHECK YOUR UNDERSTANDING

**1. a.** Aggregate output rises in the short run, then falls back to equal potential output in the long run.

**b.** The aggregate price level rises in the short run, but by less than 25%. It rises further in the long run, for a total increase of 25%.

**c.** The interest rate falls in the short run, then rises back to its original level in the long run.

**2.** In the short run, a change in the interest rate alters the economy because it affects investment spending, which in turn affects aggregate demand and real GDP through the multiplier process. However, in the long run, changes in consumer spending and investment spending will eventually result in changes in nominal wages and the nominal prices of other factors of production. For example, an expansionary monetary policy will eventually cause a rise in factor prices; a contractionary policy will eventually cause a fall in factor prices. In response, the short-run aggregate supply curve will shift to move the economy back to long-run equilibrium. So in the long run monetary policy has no effect on the economy.

# Chapter Sixteen
# 16-1 CHECK YOUR UNDERSTANDING

**1.** The inflation rate is more likely to quickly reflect changes in the money supply when the economy has had an extended period of high inflation. That's because an extended period of high inflation sensitizes workers and firms to raise nominal wages and prices of intermediate goods when the aggregate price level rises. As a result, there will be little or no increase in real output in the short run after an increase in the money supply, and the increase in the money supply will simply be reflected in an equal-sized percent increase in prices. In an economy where people are not sensitized to high inflation because of low inflation in the past, an increase in the money supply will lead to an increase in real output in the short run. This illustrates the fact that the classical model of the price level best applies to economies with *persistently* high inflation, not those with little or no history of high inflation even though they may currently have high inflation.

**2.** Yes, there can still be an inflation tax because the tax is levied on people who hold money. As long as people hold money, regardless of whether prices are indexed or not, the government is able to use seignorage to capture real resources from the public.

# 16-2 CHECK YOUR UNDERSTANDING

**1.** When real GDP equals potential output, cyclical unemployment is zero and the unemployment rate is equal to the natural rate. This is given by point $E_1$ in

Figure 16-7. Assuming a 0% expected inflation rate, this also corresponds to a 6% unemployment rate on curve $SRPC_0$ in Figure 16-9. Any unemployment in excess of this 6% rate, or less than the 6% rate, represents cyclical unemployment. An increase in aggregate demand leads to a fall in the unemployment rate below the natural rate (negative cyclical unemployment) and an increase in the inflation rate. This is given by the movement from $E_1$ to $E_2$ in Figure 16-7 and traces a movement upward along the short-run Phillips curve. A reduction in aggregate demand leads to a rise in the unemployment rate above the natural rate (positive cyclical unemployment) and a fall in the inflation rate. This would be represented by a movement down along the short-run Phillips curve from point $E_1$. So for a given expected inflation rate, the short-run Phillips curve illustrates the relationship between cyclical unemployment and the actual inflation rate.

**2.** A fall in commodities prices leads to a positive supply shock, which lowers the aggregate price level and reduces inflation. As a result, any given level of unemployment can be sustained with a lower inflation rate now—meaning that the short-run Phillips curve has shifted downward. In contrast, a surge in commodities prices leads to a negative supply shock, which raises the aggregate price level and increases inflation. Any given level of unemployment can be sustained only with a higher inflation rate—meaning that the short-run Phillips curve has shifted upward.

# 16-3 CHECK YOUR UNDERSTANDING

**1.** There is no long-run trade-off between inflation and unemployment because once expectations of inflation adjust, wages will also adjust, returning employment and the unemployment rate to their equilibrium (natural) levels. This implies that once expectations of inflation fully adjust to any change in actual inflation, the unemployment rate will return to the natural rate of unemployment, or NAIRU. This also implies that the long-run Phillips curve is vertical.

**2.** There are two possible explanations for this. First, negative supply shocks (for example, increases in the price of oil) will cause an increase in unemployment and an increase in inflation. Second, it is possible that British policy makers attempted to peg the unemployment rate below the natural rate of unemployment. Any attempt to peg unemployment below the natural rate will result in an increase in inflation.

**3.** Disinflation is costly because to reduce the inflation rate, aggregate output in the short run must typically fall below potential output. This, in turn, results in an increase in the unemployment rate above the natural rate. In general, we would observe a reduction in real GDP. The costs of disinflation can be reduced by not allowing inflation to increase in the first place. Second, the costs of any disinflation will be lower if the central bank is credible and it announces in advance its policy to reduce inflation. In this situation, the adjustment to the disinflationary policy will be more rapid, resulting in a smaller loss of aggregate output.

# 16-4 CHECK YOUR UNDERSTANDING

1. If the nominal interest rate is negative, an individual is better off simply holding cash, which has a 0% nominal rate of return. If the options facing an individual are to lend and receive a negative nominal interest rate or to hold cash and receive a 0% nominal interest rate, the individual will hold cash. Such a scenario creates the possibility of a liquidity trap, in which monetary policy is ineffective because the nominal interest rate cannot fall below zero. Once the nominal interest rate falls to zero, further increases in the money supply will lead firms and individuals to simply hold the additional cash.

## Chapter Seventeen
# 17-1 CHECK YOUR UNDERSTANDING

**1. a.** This is not an example of maturity transformation because no short-term liabilities are being turned into long-term assets. So it is not subject to a bank run.

**b.** This is an example of maturity transformation: Dana incurs a short-term liability, credit card debt, to fund the acquisition of a long-term asset, better job skills. It can result in a bank-run-like phenomenon if her credit card lender becomes fearful of her ability to repay and stops lending to her. If this happens, she will not be able to finish her course and, as a result, will not be able to get the better job that would allow her to pay off her credit card loans.

**c.** This is not an example of maturity transformation because there are no short-term liabilities. The partnership itself has no obligation to repay an individual partner's investment and so has no liabilities, short term or long term.

**d.** This is an example of maturity transformation: the checking accounts are short-term liabilities of the student union savings bank, and the student loans are long-term assets.

# 17-2 CHECK YOUR UNDERSTANDING

**1. a.** The asset bubble occurred in Irish real estate.

**b.** The channel of the financial contagion was the short-term lending that Irish banks depended on from the wholesale interbank lending market. When lenders began to worry about the soundness of the Irish banks, they refused to lend any more money, leading to a type of bank run and putting the Irish banks at great risk of failure.

**2.** Because the bank run started with fears among lenders to Irish banks, the Irish government sought to eliminate those fears by guaranteeing the lenders that they would be repaid in full. It was a question-

able strategy, though, because it put the Irish taxpayers on the hook for potentially very large losses, so large that they threatened the solvency of the Irish government.

# 17-3 CHECK YOUR UNDERSTANDING

**1.** The Federal Reserve was able to prevent a replay of the Great Depression because, unlike in the 1930s, it acted as a lender of last resort to stabilize the banking sector and halt the contagion. But it was unable to significantly reduce the surge in unemployment because the United States experienced a credit crunch and a vicious circle of deleveraging, leaving monetary policy relatively ineffective.

**2.** In the aftermath of a severe banking crisis, businesses and households have high debt and reduced assets. They cut back on spending to try to reduce their debt. So they are unwilling to borrow regardless of how low the interest rate is.

# 17-4 CHECK YOUR UNDERSTANDING

**1.** According to standard macroeconomics, a government should adopt expansionary policies to increase aggregate demand to address an economic slump. France, however, did just the opposite, responding to a weaker economy with a contractionary fiscal policy that would make the economy even weaker. This shows that the French government had adopted the austerity view, believing that it was more important to try to assure markets of its solvency than to support the economy.

# 17-5 CHECK YOUR UNDERSTANDING

**1.** Because shadow banks like Lehman relied on short-term borrowing to fund their operations, fears about their soundness could quickly lead lenders to immediately cut off their credit and force them into failure. And without membership in the lender-of-last-resort system, shadow banks like Lehman could not borrow from the Federal Reserve to make up for the short-term loans it had lost.

**2.** If there had been only a formal depository banking sector, several factors would have mitigated the potential and scope of a banking crisis. First, there would have been no repo financing; the only short-term liabilities would have been customers' deposits, and these would have been largely covered by deposit insurance. Second, capital requirements would have reduced banks' willingness to take on excessive risk, such as holding onto subprime mortgages. Also, direct oversight by the Federal Reserve would have prevented so much concentration of risk within the banking sector. Finally, depository banks are within the lender-of-last-resort system; as a result, depository banks had another layer of protection against the fear of depositors and other creditors that they couldn't meet their obligations. All of these factors would have reduced the potential and scope of a banking crisis.

**3.** Because the shadow banking sector had become such a critical part of the U.S. economy, the crisis of 2008 made it clear that in the event of another crisis the government would find it necessary to guarantee a wide range of financial institution debts, including those of shadow banks as well as depository banks. This created an incentive problem because it would induce shadow banks to take more risk, knowing that the government would bail them out in the event of a meltdown. To counteract this, the Dodd-Frank bill gave the government the power to regulate "systemically important" shadow banks (those likely to require bailing out) in order to reduce their risk taking. It also gave the government the power to seize control of failing shadow banks in a way that was fair to taxpayers and didn't unfairly enrich the owners of the banks.

# Chapter Eighteen
## 18-1 CHECK YOUR UNDERSTANDING

1. A classical economist would have said that although expansionary monetary policy would probably have some effect in the short run, the short run was unimportant. Instead, a classical economist would have stressed the long run, claiming expansionary monetary policy would result only in an increase in the aggregate price level without affecting aggregate output.

## 18-2 CHECK YOUR UNDERSTANDING

1. The statement would seem very familiar to a Keynesian economist. According to Keynes, business confidence (which he called "animal spirits") is mainly responsible for recessions. If business confidence is low, a Keynesian economist would think of this as a case for macroeconomic policy activism: that the government should use expansionary monetary and fiscal policy to help the economy recover.

## 18-3 CHECK YOUR UNDERSTANDING

1. a. According to the velocity equation, $M \times V = P \times Y$, where $M$ is the money supply, $V$ the velocity of money, $P$ the aggregate price level, and $Y$ real GDP. If the Federal Reserve had pursued a monetary policy rule of constant money supply growth, the collapse in the velocity of money beginning in 2008 and visible in Figure 18-5 would have resulted in a dramatic decline in aggregate output.

   b. Although monetarists generally believe that monetary policy is not only effective but, in fact, more effective than fiscal policy, they also generally do not favor macroeconomic policy activism. Instead, monetarists generally advocate monetary policy rules, such as a low but constant rate of money supply growth. In addition, the natural rate hypothesis states that although monetary policy may be effective in helping return unemployment to its natural rate, it cannot permanently reduce unemployment below the natural rate.

2. Fiscal policy is limited by time lags in recognizing economic problems, forming a response, passing legislation, and implementing the policies. Monetary policy is also limited by time lags, but these lags are not as severe as those for fiscal policy because the Federal Reserve tends to act more quickly than Congress. Attempts to reduce unemployment below the natural rate via both fiscal and monetary policy are limited by predictions of the natural rate hypothesis: that these attempts will result in accelerating inflation. Also, both fiscal and monetary policy are limited by concerns about the political business cycle: that they will be used to satisfy political ends and will end up destabilizing the economy.

## 18-4 CHECK YOUR UNDERSTANDING

1. a. Rational expectations theorists would argue that only unexpected changes in the money supply would have any short-run effect on economic activity. They would also argue that expected changes in the money supply would affect only the aggregate price level, with no short-run effect on aggregate output. So such theorists would give credit to the Fed for limiting the severity of the 2007–2009 recession only if the Fed's monetary policy had been more aggressive than individuals expected during this period.

   b. Real business cycle theorists would argue that the Fed's policy had no effect on ending the 2007–2009 recession because they believe that fluctuations in aggregate output are caused largely by changes in total factor productivity.

## 18-5 CHECK YOUR UNDERSTANDING

1. The liquidity trap brought on by the Great Recession greatly diminished the Great Moderation consensus because it considered monetary policy to be the main policy tool and monetary policy was now largely ineffective. The continuing disagreements over fiscal policy were now brought to the forefront as fiscal policy was used by policy makers to support their deeply depressed economies. A new consensus is unlikely to emerge anytime soon because results of the various policies have been unclear or disappointing: fiscal stimulus has failed to bring down unemployment substantially (although some say the stimulus was too small); conventional monetary policy does not work; and the Fed's unconventional monetary policy seemed to have relatively little effect.

# Chapter Nineteen
## 19-1 CHECK YOUR UNDERSTANDING

1. a. The sale of the new airplane to China represents an export of a good to China and so enters the current account.

   b. The sale of Boeing stock to Chinese investors is a sale of a U.S. asset and so enters the financial account.

   c. Even though the plane already exists, when it is shipped to China it is an export of a good from the United States. So the sale of the plane enters the current account.

   d. Because the plane stays in the United States, the Chinese investor is buying a U.S. asset. So this is identical to the answer to part b: the sale of the jet enters the financial account.

2. The collapse of the U.S. housing bubble and the ensuing recession led to a dramatic fall in interest rates in the United States because of the deeply depressed economy. Consequently, capital inflows into the United States dried up.

# 19-2 CHECK YOUR UNDERSTANDING

**1. a.** The increased purchase of Mexican oil will cause U.S. individuals (and firms) to increase their demand for the peso. To purchase pesos, individuals will increase their supply of U.S. dollars to the foreign exchange market, causing a rightward shift in the supply curve of U.S. dollars. This will cause the peso price of the dollar to fall (the amount of pesos per dollar will fall). The peso has appreciated and the U.S. dollar has depreciated as a result.

**b.** This appreciation of the peso means it will take more U.S. dollars to obtain the same quantity of Mexican pesos. If we assume that the price level (measured in Mexican pesos) of other Mexican goods and services does not change, other Mexican goods and services become more expensive to U.S. households and firms. The dollar cost of other Mexican goods and services will rise as the peso appreciates. So Mexican exports of goods and services other than oil will fall.

**c.** U.S. goods and services become cheaper in terms of pesos, so Mexican imports of goods and services will rise.

**2. a.** The real exchange rate equals

$$\text{Pesos per U.S. dollar} \times \frac{\text{Aggregate price level in the U.S.}}{\text{Aggregate price level in Mexico}}$$

Today, the aggregate price levels in both countries are both equal to 100. The real exchange rate today is 10 × (100/100) = 10. The aggregate price level in five years in the U.S. will be 100 × (120/100) = 120, and in Mexico it will be 100 × (1,200/800) = 150. The real exchange rate in five years, assuming the nominal exchange rate does not change, will be 10 × (120/150) = 8.

**b.** Today, a basket of goods and services that costs $100 costs 800 pesos, so the purchasing power parity is 8 pesos per U.S. dollar. In five years, a basket that costs $120 will cost 1,200 pesos, so the purchasing power parity will be 10 pesos per U.S. dollar.

# 19-3 CHECK YOUR UNDERSTANDING

1. The accompanying diagram shows the supply of and demand for the yuan, with the U.S. dollar price of the yuan on the vertical axis. In 2005, prior to the revaluation, the exchange rate was pegged at 8.28 yuan per U.S. dollar or, equivalently, 0.121 U.S. dollars per yuan ($0.121). At the target exchange rate of $0.121, the quantity of yuan demanded exceeded the quantity of yuan supplied, creating the shortage depicted in the diagram. Without any intervention by the Chinese government, the U.S. dollar price of the yuan would be bid up, causing an appreciation of the

yuan. The Chinese government, however, intervened to prevent this appreciation.

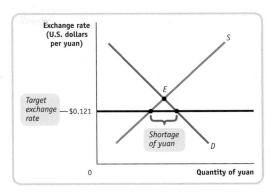

**a.** If the exchange rate were allowed to move freely, the U.S. dollar price of the exchange rate would move toward the equilibrium exchange rate (labeled $XR^*$ in the accompanying diagram). This would occur as a result of the shortage, when buyers of the yuan would bid up its U.S. dollar price. As the exchange rate increases, the quantity of yuan demanded would fall and the quantity of yuan supplied would increase. If the exchange rate were to increase to $XR^*$, the disequilibrium would be entirely eliminated.

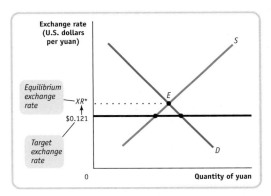

**b.** Placing restrictions on foreigners who want to invest in China would reduce the demand for the yuan, causing the demand curve to shift in the accompanying diagram from $D_1$ to something like $D_2$. This would cause a reduction in the shortage of the yuan. If demand fell to $D_3$, the disequilibrium would be completely eliminated.

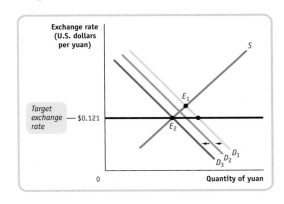

c. Removing restrictions on Chinese who wish to invest abroad would cause an increase in the supply of the yuan and a rightward shift in the supply curve. This increase in supply would also cause a reduction in the size of the shortage. If, for example, supply increased from $S_1$ to $S_2$, the disequilibrium would be eliminated completely in the accompanying diagram.

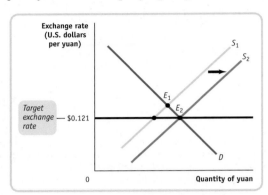

d. Imposing a tax on exports (Chinese goods sold to foreigners) would raise the price of these goods and decrease the amount of Chinese goods purchased. This would also decrease the demand for the yuan. The graphical analysis here is virtually identical to that found in the figure accompanying part b.

# 19-4 CHECK YOUR UNDERSTANDING

1. The devaluations and revaluations most likely occurred in those periods when there was a sudden change in the franc–mark exchange rate: 1974, 1976, the early 1980s, 1986, and 1993–1994.

2. The high Canadian interest rates would likely have caused an increase in capital inflows to Canada. To obtain these assets (which yielded a relatively higher interest rate) in Canada, investors would first have had to obtain Canadian dollars. The increase in the demand for the Canadian dollar would have caused the Canadian dollar to appreciate. This appreciation of the Canadian currency would have raised the price of Canadian goods to foreigners (measured in terms of the foreign currency). This would have made it more difficult for Canadian firms to compete in other markets.

*Italicized terms* within definitions are key terms that are defined elsewhere in this glossary.

## A

**absolute advantage** the advantage conferred on an individual or country in an activity if the individual or country can do it better than others. A country with an absolute advantage can produce more output per worker than other countries.

**absolute value** the value of a number without regard to a plus or minus sign.

**accelerator principle** the proposition that a higher rate of growth in *real GDP* results in a higher level of planned *investment spending*, and a lower growth rate in real GDP leads to lower planned investment spending.

**actual investment spending** the sum of *planned investment spending* and *unplanned inventory investment*.

**AD–AS model** the basic model used to understand fluctuations in *aggregate output* and the *aggregate price level*. It uses the *aggregate supply curve* and the *aggregate demand curve* together to analyze the behavior of the *economy* in response to shocks or government policy.

**aggregate consumption function** the relationship for the *economy* as a whole between aggregate current *disposable income* and aggregate *consumer spending*.

**aggregate demand curve** a graphical representation that shows the relationship between the *aggregate price level* and the quantity of *aggregate output* demanded by *households*, *firms*, the government, and the rest of the world. The aggregate demand curve has a negative slope due to the *wealth effect of a change in the aggregate price level* and the *interest rate effect of a change in the aggregate price level*.

**aggregate output** the total quantity of *final goods and services* the *economy* produces for a given time period, usually a year. *Real GDP* is the numerical measure of aggregate output typically used by economists.

**aggregate price level** a single number that represents the overall price level for *final goods and services* in the *economy*.

**aggregate production function** a hypothetical function that shows how productivity (*real GDP* per worker) depends on the quantities of *physical capital* per worker and *human capital* per worker as well as the state of *technology*.

**aggregate spending** the total flow of funds into markets for domestically produced *final goods and services*; the sum of *consumer spending, investment spending, government purchases of goods and services,* and *exports* minus *imports*.

**aggregate supply curve** a graphical representation that shows the relationship between the *aggregate price level* and the total quantity of *aggregate output* supplied.

**appreciation** a rise in the value of one currency in terms of other currencies.

**asset bubble** the price of an asset pushed to an unreasonably high level due to expectations of further price gains.

**autarky** a situation in which a country does not trade with other countries.

**automatic stabilizers** government spending and taxation rules that cause *fiscal policy* to be automatically expansionary when the *economy* contracts and automatically contractionary when the economy expands without requiring any deliberate actions by policy makers. Taxes that depend on *disposable income* are the most important example of automatic stabilizers.

**autonomous change in aggregate spending** an initial rise or fall in *aggregate spending* at a given level of *real GDP*.

## B

**balance of payments accounts** a summary of a country's transactions with other countries, including two main elements: the *balance of payments on current account* and the *balance of payments on financial account*.

**balance of payments on current account (current account)** transactions that don't create liabilities; a country's *balance of payments on goods and services* plus net international transfer payments and factor income.

**balance of payments on financial account (financial account)** international transactions that involve the sale or purchase of assets, and therefore create future liabilities.

**balance of payments on goods and services** the difference between the value of *exports* and the value of *imports* during a given period.

**balance sheet effects** the reduction in a firm's net worth from falling asset prices.

**bank** a *financial intermediary* that provides *liquid* assets in the form of *bank deposits* to lenders and uses those funds to finance the *illiquid* investments or *investment spending* needs of borrowers.

**bank deposit** a claim on a *bank* that obliges the bank to give the depositor his or her cash when demanded.

**bank reserves** currency held by *banks* in their vaults plus their deposits at the Federal Reserve.

**bank run** a phenomenon in which many of a *bank*'s depositors try to withdraw their funds due to fears of a bank failure.

**banking crisis** episode when a large part of the depository banking sector or the shadow banking sector fails or threatens to fail.

**bar graph** a graph that uses bars of varying heights or lengths to show the comparative sizes of different observations of a *variable*.

**barter** the direct exchange of goods or services for other goods or services without the use of money.

**black market** a market in which goods or services are bought and sold illegally, either because it is illegal to sell them at all or because the prices charged are legally prohibited by a *price ceiling*.

**bond** a legal document based on borrowing in the form of an IOU that pays interest.

**budget balance** the difference between tax revenue and government spending. A positive budget balance is referred to as a *budget surplus*; a negative budget balance is referred to as a *budget deficit*.

**budget deficit** the difference between tax revenue and government spending when government spending exceeds tax revenue; dissaving by the government in the form of a budget deficit is a negative contribution to *national savings*.

**budget surplus** the difference between tax revenue and government spending when tax revenue exceeds government spending; saving by the government in the form of a budget surplus is a positive contribution to *national savings*.

**business cycle** the short-run alternation between economic downturns, known as *recessions*, and economic upturns, known as *expansions*.

**business-cycle peak** the point in time at which the *economy* shifts from *expansion* to *recession*.

**business-cycle trough** the point in time at which the *economy* shifts from *recession* to *expansion*.

## C

**causal relationship** the relationship between two *variables* in which the value taken by one variable directly influences or determines the value taken by the other variable.

**central bank** an institution that oversees and regulates the banking system and controls the *monetary base*.

**chained dollars** method of calculating *real GDP* that splits the difference between growth rates calculated using early base years and the growth rate calculated using a late base year.

**checkable bank deposits** *bank* accounts on which people can write checks.

**circular-flow diagram** a diagram that represents the transactions in an *economy* by two kinds of flows around a circle: flows of physical things such as goods or labor in one direction and flows of money to pay for these physical things in the opposite direction.

**classical model of the price level** a simplified financial model of the price level in which the real quantity of money, *M/P*, is always at its long-run *equilibrium* level. This model ignores the distinction between the short run and the long run but is useful for analyzing the case of high *inflation*.

**commercial bank** a *bank* that accepts deposits and is covered by *deposit insurance*.

**commodity money** a *medium of exchange* that is a good, normally gold or silver, that has intrinsic value in other uses.

**commodity-backed money** a *medium of exchange* that has no intrinsic value whose ultimate value is guaranteed by a promise that it can be converted into valuable goods on demand.

**comparative advantage** the advantage conferred on an individual or country in producing a good or service if the *opportunity cost* of producing the good or service is lower for that individual or country than for other producers.

**competitive market** a market in which there are many buyers and sellers of the same good or service, none of whom can influence the price at which the good or service is sold.

**complements** pairs of goods for which a rise in the price of one good leads to a decrease in the demand for the other good.

**consumer price index (CPI)** a measure of prices; calculated by surveying market prices for a *market basket* intended to represent the consumption of a typical urban American family of four. The CPI is the most commonly used measure of prices in the United States.

**consumer spending** *household* spending on goods and services from domestic and foreign *firms*.

**consumer surplus** a term often used to refer both to *individual consumer surplus* and to *total consumer surplus*.

**consumption function** an equation showing how an individual *household's consumer spending* varies with the household's current *disposable income*.

**contractionary fiscal policy** *fiscal policy* that reduces aggregate demand by decreasing government purchases, increasing taxes, or decreasing transfers.

**contractionary monetary policy** *monetary policy* that, through the raising of the interest rate, reduces aggregate demand and therefore output.

**convergence hypothesis** a principle of economic growth that holds that international differences in *real GDP* per capita tend to narrow over time because countries that start with lower real GDP per capita tend to have higher growth rates.

**cost (of potential seller)** the lowest price at which a seller is willing to sell a good.

**credit crunch** a reduction in the availability of credit in which potential borrowers can't get credit at all or must pay very high interest rates.

**crowding out** the negative effect of *budget deficits* on private investment, which occurs because government borrowing drives up interest rates.

**currency in circulation** actual cash held by the public.

**current account (balance of payments on current account)** transactions that don't create liabilities; a country's *balance of payments on goods and services* plus net international transfer payments and factor income.

**curve** a line on a graph, which may be curved or straight, that depicts a relationship between two *variables*.

**cyclical unemployment** the difference between the actual rate of *unemployment* and the *natural rate of unemployment* due to downturns in the business cycle.

**cyclically adjusted budget balance** an estimate of what the *budget balance* would be if *real GDP* were exactly equal to *potential output*.

## D

**debt deflation** the reduction in aggregate demand arising from the increase in the real burden of outstanding debt caused by *deflation*; occurs because borrowers, whose real debt rises as a result of deflation, are likely to cut spending sharply, and lenders, whose real assets are now more valuable, are less likely to increase spending.

**debt overhang** high debt but diminished assets, resulting from a vicious circle of deleveraging.

**debt–GDP ratio** government debt as a percentage of GDP, frequently used as a measure of a government's ability to pay its debts.

**default** the failure of a bond issuer to make payments as specified by the bond contract.

**deflation** a fall in the overall level of prices.

**demand curve** a graphical representation of the *demand schedule*, showing the relationship between *quantity demanded* and price.

**demand price** the price of a given quantity at which consumers will demand that quantity.

**demand schedule** a list or table showing how much of a good or service consumers will want to buy at different prices.

**demand shock** an event that shifts the *aggregate demand curve*. A positive demand shock is associated with higher demand for *aggregate output* at any price level and shifts the curve to the right. A negative demand shock is associated with lower demand for aggregate output at any price level and shifts the curve to the left.

**dependent variable** the determined *variable* in a *causal relationship*.

**deposit insurance** a guarantee that a *bank's* depositors will be paid even if the bank can't come up with the funds, up to a maximum amount per account.

**depreciation** a fall in the value of one currency in terms of other currencies.

**devaluation** a reduction in the value of a currency that is set under a *fixed exchange rate regime*.

**diminishing returns to physical capital** in an *aggregate production function* when the amount of *human capital* per worker and the state of technology are held fixed, each successive increase in the amount of *physical capital* per worker leads to a smaller increase in productivity.

**discount rate** the rate of interest the Federal Reserve charges on loans to *banks* that fall short of *reserve requirements*.

**discount window** a protection against *bank runs* in which the Federal Reserve stands ready to lend money to *banks* in trouble.

**discouraged workers** individuals who want to work but who have stated to government researchers that they aren't currently searching for a job because they see little prospect of finding one given the state of the job market.

**discretionary fiscal policy** *fiscal policy* that is the direct result of deliberate actions by policy makers rather than rules.

**discretionary monetary policy** policy actions, either changes in interest rates or changes in the *money supply*, undertaken by the *central bank* based on its assessment of the state of the *economy*.

**disinflation** the process of bringing down *inflation* that has become embedded in expectations.

**disposable income** income plus *government transfers* minus taxes; the total amount of *household* income available to spend on consumption and to save.

**diversification** investment in several different assets with unrelated, or independent, risks, so that the possible losses are independent events.

**domestic demand curve** a *demand curve* that shows how the quantity of a good demanded by domestic consumers depends on the price of that good.

**domestic supply curve** a *supply curve* that shows how the quantity of a good supplied by domestic producers depends on the price of that good.

### E

**economic growth** the growing ability of the *economy* to produce goods and services.

**economics** the social science that studies the production, distribution, and consumption of goods and services.

**economy** a system for coordinating society's productive activities.

**efficiency wages** wages that employers set above the *equilibrium* wage rate as an incentive for workers to deliver better performance.

**efficient** description of a market or *economy* that takes all opportunities to make some people better off without making other people worse off.

**efficient markets hypothesis** a principle of asset price determination that holds that asset prices embody all publicly available information. The hypothesis implies that *stock* prices should be unpredictable, or follow a *random walk*, since changes should occur only in response to new information about fundamentals.

**employment** the total number of people currently employed for pay in the *economy*, either full time or part time.

**equilibrium** an economic situation in which no individual would be better off doing something different.

**equilibrium exchange rate** the *exchange rate* at which the quantity of a currency demanded in the *foreign exchange market* is equal to the quantity supplied.

**equilibrium price** the price at which the market is in *equilibrium*, that is, the quantity of a good or service demanded equals the quantity of that good or service supplied; also referred to as the *market-clearing price*.

**equilibrium quantity** the quantity of a good or service bought and sold at the *equilibrium* (or *market-clearing*) price.

**equity** fairness; everyone gets his or her fair share. Since people can disagree about what's "fair," equity isn't as well defined a concept as efficiency.

**European Union (EU)** a customs union among 27 European nations.

**excess reserves** a *bank*'s *reserves* over and above the reserves required by law or regulation.

**exchange market intervention** government purchases or sales of currency in the *foreign exchange market*.

**exchange rate** the price at which currencies trade, determined by the *foreign exchange market*.

**exchange rate regime** a rule governing policy toward the *exchange rate*.

**expansion** period of economic upturn in which output and employment are rising; most economic numbers are following their normal upward trend; also referred to as a recovery.

**expansionary fiscal policy** *fiscal policy* that increases aggregate demand by increasing government purchases, decreasing taxes, or increasing transfers.

**expansionary monetary policy** *monetary policy* that, through the lowering of the interest rate, increases aggregate demand and therefore output.

**exporting industries** industries that produce goods or services that are sold abroad.

**exports** goods and services sold to other countries.

### F

**factor intensity** the difference in the ratio of factors used to produce a good in various industries. For example, oil refining is capital-intensive compared to auto seat production because oil refiners use a higher ratio of capital to labor than do producers of auto seats.

**factor markets** markets in which *firms* buy the *resources* they need to produce goods and services.

**factors of production** the *resources* used to produce goods and services. Labor and capital are examples of factors.

**federal funds market** the *financial market* that allows *banks* that fall short of *reserve requirements* to borrow funds from banks with *excess reserves*.

**federal funds rate** the interest rate at which funds are borrowed and lent in the *federal funds market*.

**fiat money** a *medium of exchange* whose value derives entirely from its official status as a means of payment.

**final goods and services** goods and services sold to the final, or end, user.

**financial account (balance of payments on financial account)** international transactions that involve the sale of purchase of assets, and therefore create future liabilities.

**financial asset** a paper claim that entitles the buyer to future income from the seller. *Loans, stocks, bonds,* and *bank deposits* are types of financial assets.

**financial contagion** a vicious downward spiral among *depository banks* or *shadow banks:* each bank's failure worsens fears and increases the likelihood that another bank will fail.

**financial intermediary** an institution, such as a *mutual fund, pension fund, life insurance company,* or *bank,* that transforms the funds it gathers from many individuals into *financial assets*.

**financial markets** the banking, *stock*, and *bond* markets, which channel *private savings* and foreign lending into *investment spending*, *government borrowing*, and foreign borrowing.

**financial panic** a sudden and widespread disruption of the *financial markets* that occurs when people suddenly lose faith in the liquidity of financial institutions and markets.

**financial risk** uncertainty about future outcomes that involve financial losses or gains.

**firm** an organization that produces goods and services for sale.

**fiscal policy** changes in government spending and taxes designed to affect overall spending.

**fiscal year** the time period used for much of government accounting, running from October 1 to September 30. Fiscal years are labeled by the calendar year in which they end.

**Fisher effect** the principle by which an increase in expected future *inflation* drives up the *nominal interest rate*, leaving the expected *real interest rate* unchanged.

**fixed exchange rate** an *exchange rate regime* in which the government keeps the *exchange rate* against some other currency at or near a particular target.

**floating exchange rate** an *exchange rate regime* in which the government lets market forces determine the *exchange rate*.

**forecast** a simple prediction of the future.

**foreign exchange controls** licensing systems that limit the right of individuals to buy foreign currency.

**foreign exchange market** the market in which currencies can be exchanged for each other.

**foreign exchange reserves** *stocks* of foreign currency that governments can use to buy their own currency on the *foreign exchange market*.

**free trade** *trade* that is unregulated by government *tariffs* or other artificial barriers; the levels of *exports* and *imports* occur naturally, as a result of supply and demand.

**frictional unemployment** *unemployment* due to time workers spend in *job search*.

### G

**gains from trade** gains achieved by dividing tasks and trading; in this way people can get more of what they want through *trade* than they could if they tried to be self-sufficient.

**GDP deflator** a price measure for a given year that is equal to 100 times the ratio of *nominal GDP* to *real GDP* in that year.

**GDP per capita** GDP divided by the size of the population; equivalent to the average GDP per person.

**globalization** the phenomenon of growing economic linkages among countries.

**government borrowing** the total amount of funds borrowed by federal, state, and local governments in *financial markets* to buy goods and services.

**government purchases of goods and services** total purchases by federal, state, and local governments on goods and services.

**government transfers** payments by the government to individuals for which no good or service is provided in return.

**Great Moderation** the period from 1985 to 2007 when the U.S. *economy* experienced small fluctuations and low *inflation*.

**Great Moderation consensus** a belief in *monetary policy* as the main tool of stabilization combined with skepticism toward the use of *fiscal policy* and an acknowledgment of the policy constraints imposed by the *natural rate of unemployment* and the *political business cycle*.

**gross domestic product (GDP)** the total value of all *final goods and services* produced in the *economy* during a given period, usually a year.

**growth accounting** estimates the contribution of each of the major factors (*physical* and *human capital*, labor, and *technology*) in the *aggregate production function*.

### H

**Heckscher–Ohlin model** a *model* of international trade in which a country has a *comparative advantage* in a good whose production is intensive in the factors that are abundantly available in that country.

**horizontal axis** the horizontal number line of a graph along which values of the *x*-variable are measured; also referred to as the *x-axis*.

**horizontal intercept** the point at which a *curve* hits the *horizontal axis*; it indicates the value of the *x*-variable when the value of the *y*-variable is zero.

**household** a person or a group of people who share their income.

**human capital** the improvement in labor created by the education and knowledge embodied in the workforce.

### I

**illiquid** describes an asset that cannot be quickly converted into cash with relatively little loss of value.

**implicit liabilities** spending promises made by governments that are effectively a debt despite the fact that they are not included in the usual debt statistics. In the United States, the largest implicit liabilities arise from Social Security and Medicare, which promise transfer payments to current and future retirees (Social Security) and to the elderly (Medicare).

**import quota** a legal limit on the quantity of a good that can be imported.

**import-competing industries** industries that produce goods or services that are also imported.

**imports** goods and services purchased from other countries.

**incentive** anything that offers rewards to people who change their behavior.

**income distribution** the way in which total income is divided among the owners of the various *factors of production*.

**income–expenditure equilibrium** a situation in which *aggregate output*, measured by *real GDP*, is equal to *planned aggregate spending* and *firms* have no incentive to change output.

**income–expenditure equilibrium GDP** the level of *real GDP* at which real GDP equals *planned aggregate spending*.

**independent variable** the determining *variable* in a *causal relationship*.

**individual choice** the decision by an individual of what to do, which necessarily involves a decision of what not to do.

**individual consumer surplus** the net gain to an individual buyer from the purchase of a good; equal to the difference between the buyer's *willingness to pay* and the price paid.

**individual demand curve** a graphical representation of the relationship between *quantity demanded* and price for an individual consumer.

**individual producer surplus** the net gain to an individual seller from selling a good; equal to the difference between the price received and the seller's *cost*.

**individual supply curve** a graphical representation of the relationship between *quantity supplied* and price for an individual producer.

**inefficient allocation of sales among sellers** a form of inefficiency in which sellers who would be willing to sell a good at the lowest price are not always those who actually manage to sell it; often the result of a *price floor*.

**inefficient allocation to consumers** a form of inefficiency in which people who want a good badly and are willing to pay a high price don't get it, and those who care relatively little about the good and are only willing to pay a low price do get it; often a result of a *price ceiling*.

**inefficiently high quality** a form of inefficiency in which sellers offer high-quality goods at a high price even though buyers would prefer a lower quality at a lower price; often the result of a *price floor*.

**inefficiently low quality** a form of inefficiency in which sellers offer low-quality goods at a low price even though buyers would prefer a higher quality at a higher price; often a result of a *price ceiling*.

**inferior good** a good for which a rise in income decreases the demand for the good.

**inflation** a rise in the overall level of prices.

**inflation rate** the annual percent change in a price index—typically the *consumer price index*. The inflation rate is positive when the *aggregate price level* is rising (*inflation*) and negative when the aggregate price level is falling (*deflation*).

**inflation targeting** an approach to *monetary policy* that requires that the *central bank* try to keep the *inflation rate* near a predetermined target rate.

**inflation tax** the reduction in the value of money held by the public caused by *inflation*.

**inflationary gap** exists when *aggregate output* is above *potential output*.

**infrastructure** *physical capital*, such as roads, power lines, ports, information networks, and other parts of an *economy*, that provides the underpinnings, or foundation, for economic activity.

**input** a good or service used to produce another good or service.

**interaction (of choices)** my choices affect your choices, and vice versa; a feature of most economic situations. The results of this interaction are often quite different from what the individuals intend.

**interest rate** the price, calculated as a percentage of the amount borrowed, that a lender charges a borrower for the use of their savings for one year.

**interest rate effect of a change in the aggregate price level** the effect on *consumer spending* and *investment spending* caused by a change in the purchasing power of consumers' money holdings when the *aggregate price level* changes. A rise (fall) in the aggregate price level decreases (increases) the purchasing power of consumers' money holdings. In response, consumers try to increase (decrease) their money holdings, which drives up (down) interest rates, thereby decreasing (increasing) consumption and investment.

**intermediate goods and services** goods and services—bought from one *firm* by another firm—that are inputs for production of *final goods and services*.

**international trade agreements** treaties by which countries agree to lower *trade protections* against one another.

**inventories** stocks of goods and raw materials held to facilitate business operations.

**inventory investment** the value of the change in total *inventories* held in the *economy* during a given period. Unlike other types of *investment spending*, inventory investment can be negative, if inventories fall.

**investment bank** a *bank* that trades in *financial assets* and is not covered by *deposit insurance*.

**investment spending** spending on productive *physical capital*—such as machinery and construction of buildings—and on changes to *inventories*.

**invisible hand** a phrase used by Adam Smith to refer to the way in which an individual's pursuit of self-interest can lead, without the individual's intending it, to good results for society as a whole.

**J**

**job search** when workers spend time looking for *employment*.

**jobless recovery** a period in which GDP growth rate is positive but the *unemployment rate* is still rising.

**K**

**Keynesian cross** a diagram that identifies *income–expenditure equilibrium* as the point where the *planned aggregate spending* line crosses the 45-degree line.

**Keynesian economics** a school of thought emerging out of the works of John Maynard Keynes; according to Keynesian economics, a depressed *economy* is the result of inadequate spending and government intervention can help a depressed economy through *monetary policy* and *fiscal policy*.

**L**

**labor force** the sum of *employment* and *unemployment*; that is, the number of people who are currently working plus the number of people who are currently looking for work.

**labor force participation rate** the percentage of the population age 16 or older that is in the *labor force*.

**labor productivity** output per worker; also referred to as simply *productivity*. Increases in labor productivity are the only source of *long-run economic growth*.

**law of demand** the principle that a higher price for a good or service, other things equal, leads people to demand a smaller quantity of that good or service.

**lender of last resort** an institution, usually a country's *central bank*, that provides funds to financial institutions when they are unable to borrow from private credit markets.

**leverage** the degree to which a financial institution is financing its investments with borrowed funds.

**liability** a requirement to pay income in the future.

**license** the right, conferred by the government or an owner, to supply a good.

**life insurance company** a *financial intermediary* that sells policies guaranteeing a payment to a policyholder's beneficiaries when the policyholder dies.

**linear relationship** the relationship between two *variables* in which the *slope* is constant and therefore is depicted on a graph by a *curve* that is a straight line.

**liquid** describes an asset that can be quickly converted into cash with relatively little loss of value.

**liquidity preference model of the interest rate** a model of the market for money in which the interest rate is determined by the supply and demand for money.

**liquidity trap** the economy is in a liquidity trap when *monetary policy* is ineffective because *nominal interest rates* are up against the *zero bound*.

**loan** a lending agreement between an individual lender and an individual borrower. Loans are usually tailored to the individual borrower's needs and ability to pay but carry relatively high *transaction costs.*

**loan-backed securities** assets created by pooling individual *loans* and selling shares in that pool.

**loanable funds market** a hypothetical market that brings together those who want to lend money (savers) and those who want to borrow (*firms* with *investment spending* projects).

**long-run aggregate supply curve** a graphical representation that shows the relationship between the *aggregate price level* and the quantity of *aggregate output* supplied that would exist if all prices, including *nominal wages*, were fully flexible. The long-run aggregate supply curve is vertical because the aggregate price level has no effect on aggregate output in the long run; in the long run, aggregate output is determined by the *economy's potential output.*

**long-run economic growth** the sustained rise in the quantity of goods and services the *economy* produces.

**long-run macroeconomic equilibrium** the point at which the *short-run macroeconomic equilibrium* is on the *long-run aggregate supply curve;* so *short-run equilibrium aggregate output* is equal to *potential output.*

**long-run Phillips curve** a graphical representation of the relationship between *unemployment* and *inflation* in the long run after expectations of inflation have had time to adjust to experience.

**long-term interest rate** the interest rate on *financial assets* that mature a number of years into the future.

**lump-sum taxes** taxes that don't depend on the taxpayer's income.

### M

**macroeconomic policy activism** the use of *monetary policy* and *fiscal policy* to smooth out the *business cycle.*

**macroeconomics** the branch of *economics* that is concerned with the overall ups and downs in the *economy.*

**marginal analysis** the study of *marginal decisions.*

**marginal decision** a decision made at the "margin" of an activity to do a bit more or a bit less of that activity.

**marginal propensity to consume (*MPC*)** the increase in *consumer spending* when *disposable income* rises by $1. Because consumers normally spend part but not all of an additional dollar of disposable income, *MPC* is between 0 and 1.

**marginal propensity to save (*MPS*)** the fraction of an additional dollar of *disposable income* that is saved; *MPS* is equal to $1 - MPC$.

**marginally attached workers** nonworking individuals who say they would like a job and have looked for work in the recent past but are not currently looking for work.

**market basket** a hypothetical consumption bundle of consumer purchases of goods and services, used to measure changes in overall price level.

**market economy** an *economy* in which decisions about production and consumption are made by individual producers and consumers.

**market failure** the failure of a market to be efficient.

**market-clearing price** the price at which the market is in *equilibrium,* that is, the quantity of a good or service demanded equals the quantity of that good or service supplied; also referred to as the *equilibrium price.*

**markets for goods and services** markets in which *firms* sell goods and services that they produce to *households.*

**maturity transformation** the conversion of short-term liabilities into long-term assets.

**maximum** the highest point on a *nonlinear curve,* where the *slope* changes from positive to negative.

**medium of exchange** an asset that individuals acquire for the purpose of trading for goods and services rather than for their own consumption.

**menu cost** the real cost of changing a listed price.

**merchandise trade balance (trade balance)** the difference between a country's *exports* and *imports* of goods alone—not including services.

**microeconomics** the branch of *economics* that studies how people make decisions and how those decisions interact.

**minimum** the lowest point on a *nonlinear curve,* where the *slope* changes from negative to positive.

**minimum wage** a legal floor on the wage rate. The wage rate is the market price of labor.

**model** a simplified representation of a real situation that is used to better understand real-life situations.

**monetarism** a theory of *business cycles,* associated primarily with Milton Friedman, that asserts that GDP will grow steadily if the *money supply* grows steadily.

**monetary aggregate** an overall measure of the *money supply.* The most common monetary aggregates in the United States are M1, which includes *currency in circulation,* traveler's checks, and *checkable bank deposits,* and M2, which includes M1 as well as *near-moneys.*

**monetary base** the sum of *currency in circulation* and *bank reserves.*

**monetary neutrality** the concept that changes in the *money supply* have no real effects on the *economy* in the long run and only result in a proportional change in the price level.

**monetary policy** changes in the quantity of money in circulation designed to alter *interest rates* and affect the level of overall spending.

**monetary policy rule** a formula that determines the *central bank's* actions.

**money** any asset that can easily be used to purchase goods and services.

**money demand curve** a graphical representation of the relationship between the interest rate and the quantity of money demanded. The money demand curve slopes downward because, other things equal, a higher interest rate increases the *opportunity cost* of holding money.

**money multiplier** the ratio of the *money supply* to the *monetary base.*

**money supply** the total value of *financial assets* in the *economy* that are considered *money.*

**money supply curve** a graphical representation of the relationship between the quantity of money supplied by the Federal Reserve and the interest rate.

**movement along the demand curve** a change in the *quantity demanded* of a good that results from a change in the price of that good.

**movement along the supply curve** a change in the *quantity supplied* of a good that results from a change in the price of that good.

**multiplier** the ratio of total change in *real GDP* caused by an *autonomous change in aggregate spending* to the size of that autonomous change.

**mutual fund** a *financial intermediary* that creates a *stock* portfolio by buying and holding shares in companies and then selling shares of this portfolio to individual investors.

### N

**national income and product accounts** method of calculating and keeping track of *consumer spending*, sales of producers, business *investment spending*, government purchases, and a variety of other flows of money between different sectors of the *economy*; also referred to as *national accounts*.

**national savings** the sum of *private savings* and the government's *budget balance;* the total amount of savings generated within the *economy*.

**natural rate hypothesis** the hypothesis that because *inflation* is eventually embedded into expectations, to avoid accelerating inflation over time the *unemployment rate* must be high enough that the actual inflation rate equals the expected inflation rate.

**natural rate of unemployment** the normal *unemployment rate* around which the actual unemployment rate fluctuates; the unemployment rate that arises from the effects of *frictional* and *structural unemployment*.

**near moneys** financial assets that can't be directly used as a *medium of exchange* but can be readily converted into cash or *checkable bank deposits*.

**negative relationship** a relationship between two *variables* in which an increase in the value of one variable is associated with a decrease in the value of the other variable. It is illustrated by a *curve* that slopes downward from left to right.

**net capital inflow** the total inflow of funds into a country minus the total outflow of funds out of a country.

**net exports** the difference between the value of *exports* and the value of *imports*. A positive value for net exports indicates that a country is a net exporter of goods and services; a negative value indicates that a country is a net importer of goods and services.

**new classical macroeconomics** an approach to the *business cycle* that returns to the classical view that shifts in the *aggregate demand curve* affect only the *aggregate price level*, not *aggregate output*.

**new Keynesian economics** theory that argues that market imperfections can lead to price stickiness for the *economy* as a whole.

**nominal GDP** the value of all *final goods and services* produced in the *economy* during a given year, calculated using the prices current in the year in which the output is produced.

**nominal interest rate** the *interest rate* in dollar terms.

**nominal wage** the dollar amount of any given wage paid.

**nonaccelerating inflation rate of unemployment (NAIRU)** the *unemployment rate* at which, other things equal, *inflation* does not change over time.

**nonlinear curve** a *curve* in which the *slope* is not the same between every pair of points.

**nonlinear relationship** the relationship between two *variables* in which the *slope* is not constant and therefore is depicted on a graph by a *curve* that is not a straight line.

**normal good** a good for which a rise in income increases the demand for that good—the "normal" case.

**normative economics** the branch of economic analysis that makes prescriptions about the way the *economy* should work.

**North American Free Trade Agreement (NAFTA)** a *trade* agreement among the United States, Canada, and Mexico.

### O

**offshore outsourcing** the practice of businesses hiring people in another country to perform various tasks.

**Okun's law** the negative relationship between the *output gap* and the *unemployment rate*, whereby each additional percentage point of output gap reduces the unemployment rate by about ½ of a percentage point.

**omitted variable** an unobserved *variable* that, through its influence on other variables, creates the erroneous appearance of a direct *causal relationship* among those variables.

**open economy** an *economy* that trades goods and services with other countries.

**open-market operation** a purchase or sale of U.S. Treasury bills by the Federal Reserve, normally through a transaction with a *commercial bank*.

**opportunity cost** the real cost of an item: what you must give up in order to get it.

**origin** the point where the axes of a two-*variable* graph meet.

**other things equal assumption** in the development of a model, the assumption that all relevant factors except the one under study remain unchanged.

**output gap** the percentage difference between actual *aggregate output* and *potential output*.

### P

**pension fund** a type of *mutual fund* that holds assets in order to provide retirement income to its members.

**physical asset** a claim on a tangible object that can be used to generate future income.

**physical capital** manufactured resources, such as buildings and machines.

**pie chart** a circular graph that shows how some total is divided among its components, usually expressed in percentages.

**planned aggregate spending** the total amount of planned spending in the *economy*; includes *consumer spending* and *planned investment spending*.

**planned investment spending** the *investment spending* that *firms* intend to undertake during a given period. Planned investment spending may differ from actual investment spending due to *unplanned inventory investment*.

**political business cycle** a *business cycle* that results from the use of macroeconomic policy to serve political ends.

**positive economics** the branch of economic analysis that describes the way the *economy* actually works.

**positive relationship** a relationship between two *variables* in which an increase in the value of one variable is associated with an increase in the value of the other variable. It is illustrated by a *curve* that slopes upward from left to right.

**potential output** the level of *real GDP* the *economy* would produce if all prices, including *nominal wages*, were fully flexible.

**present value** (of X) the amount of money needed today in order to receive X at a future date given the interest rate.

**price ceiling** the maximum price sellers are allowed to charge for a good or service; a form of *price control*.

**price controls** legal restrictions on how high or low a market price may go.

**price floor** the minimum price buyers are required to pay for a good or service; a form of *price control*.

**price index** a measure of the cost of purchasing a given *market basket* in a given year, where that cost is normalized so that it is equal to 100 in the selected base year; a measure of overall price level.

**price stability** a situation in which the overall cost of living is changing slowly or not at all.

**private savings** *disposable income* minus *consumer spending*; *disposable income* that is not spent on consumption but rather goes into *financial markets*.

**producer price index (PPI)** a measure of the cost of a typical basket of goods and services purchased by producers. Because these commodity prices respond quickly to changes in demand, the PPI is often regarded as a leading indicator of changes in the *inflation rate*.

**producer surplus** a term often used to refer to either *individual producer surplus* or *total producer surplus*.

**production possibility frontier** a model that illustrates the trade-offs facing an *economy* that produces only two goods. It shows the maximum quantity of one good that can be produced for any given quantity produced of the other.

**productivity** output per worker; a shortened form of the term *labor productivity*.

**protection** policies that limit *imports*; an alternative term for *trade protection*.

**public debt** government debt held by individuals and institutions outside the government.

**purchasing power parity (between two countries' currencies)** the nominal *exchange rate* at which a given basket of goods and services would cost the same amount in each country.

### Q

**quantity control** an upper limit, set by the government, on the quantity of some good that can be bought or sold; also referred to as a *quota*.

**quantity demanded** the actual amount of a good or service consumers are willing to buy at some specific price.

**quantity supplied** the actual amount of a good or service producers are willing to sell at some specific price.

**quota** an upper limit, set by the government, on the quantity of some good that can be bought or sold; also referred to as a *quantity control*.

**quota limit** the total amount of a good under a *quota* or *quantity control* that can be legally transacted.

**quota rent** the difference between the *demand price* and the *supply price* at the *quota limit;* this difference, the earnings that accrue to the license holder, is equal to the market price of the *license* when the license is traded.

### R

**random walk** the movement over time of an unpredictable *variable*.

**rational expectations** a theory of expectation formation that holds that individuals and *firms* make decisions optimally, using all available information.

**rational expectations model** a model of the *economy* in which expected changes in *monetary policy* have no effect on *unemployment* and output and only affect the price level.

**real business cycle theory** a theory of *business cycles* that asserts that fluctuations in the growth rate of *total factor productivity* cause the business cycle.

**real exchange rate** the *exchange rate* adjusted for international differences in *aggregate price levels*.

**real GDP** the total value of all *final goods and services* produced in the *economy* during a given year, calculated using the prices of a selected base year.

**real income** income divided by the price level.

**real interest rate** the *nominal interest rate* minus the *inflation rate*.

**real wage** the wage rate divided by the price level.

**recession** a downturn in the *economy*.

**recessionary gap** exists when *aggregate output* is below *potential output*.

**research and development (R&D)** spending to create new technologies and prepare them for practical use.

**reserve ratio** the fraction of *bank deposits* that a *bank* holds as reserves. In the United States, the minimum required reserve ratio is set by the Federal Reserve.

**reserve requirements** rules set by the Federal Reserve that set the minimum *reserve ratio* for *banks*. For *checkable bank deposits* in the United States, the minimum reserve ratio is set at 10%.

**resource** anything, such as land, labor, and capital, that can be used to produce something else; includes natural resources (from the physical environment) and human resources (labor, skill, intelligence).

**revaluation** an increase in the value of a currency that is set under a *fixed exchange rate regime*.

**reverse causality** the error committed when the true direction of causality between two *variables* is reversed, and the *independent variable* and the *dependent variable* are incorrectly identified.

**Ricardian model of international trade** a model that analyzes international *trade* under the assumption that *opportunity costs* are constant.

**Rule of 70** a mathematical formula that states that the time it takes *real GDP* per capita, or any other *variable* that grows gradually over time, to double is approximately 70 divided by that variable's annual growth rate.

### S

**savings and loans (thrifts)** deposit-taking *banks*, usually specialized in issuing home loans.

**savings–investment spending identity** an accounting fact that states that savings and *investment spending* are always equal for the *economy* as a whole.

**scarce** in short supply; a *resource* is scarce when there is not enough of the resource available to satisfy all the various ways a society wants to use it.

**scatter diagram** a graph that shows points that correspond to actual observations of the *x*- and *y*-variables; a *curve* is usually fitted to the scatter of points to indicate the trend in the data.

**securitization** the pooling of loans and mortgages made by a financial institution and the sale of shares in such a pool to other investors.

**self-correcting** describes an *economy* in which shocks to aggregate demand affect *aggregate output* in the short run but not in the long run.

**self-regulating economy** an *economy* in which problems such as *unemployment* are resolved without government intervention, through the working of the *invisible hand*, and in which government attempts to improve the economy's performance would be ineffective at best, and would probably make things worse.

**shadow bank** a nondepository financial institution that engages in *maturity transformation*.

**shift of the demand curve** a change in the *quantity demanded* at any given price, represented graphically by the change of the original *demand curve* to a new position, denoted by a new demand curve.

**shift of the supply curve** a change in the *quantity supplied* of a good or service at any given price, represented graphically by the change of the original *supply curve* to a new position, denoted by a new supply curve.

**shoe-leather costs** (of inflation) the increased costs of transactions caused by *inflation*.

**shortage** the insufficiency of a good or service that occurs when the *quantity demanded* exceeds the *quantity supplied*; shortages occur when the price is below the *equilibrium price*.

**short-run aggregate supply curve** a graphical representation that shows the positive relationship between the *aggregate price level* and the quantity of *aggregate output* supplied that exists in the short run, the time period when many production costs, particularly *nominal wages*, can be taken as fixed. The short-run aggregate supply curve has a positive slope because a rise in the aggregate price level leads to a rise in profits, and therefore output, when production costs are fixed.

**short-run equilibrium aggregate output** the quantity of *aggregate output* produced in *short-run macroeconomic equilibrium*.

**short-run equilibrium aggregate price level** the *aggregate price level* in *short-run macroeconomic equilibrium*.

**short-run macroeconomic equilibrium** the point at which the quantity of *aggregate output* supplied is equal to the *quantity demanded*.

**short-run Phillips curve** a graphical representation of the negative short-run relationship between the *unemployment rate* and the *inflation rate*.

**short-term interest rate** the interest rate on *financial assets* that mature within less than a year.

**slope** a measure of how steep a line or *curve* is. The slope of a line is measured by "rise over run"—the change in the *y*-variable between two points on the line divided by the change in the *x*-variable between those same points.

**social insurance** government programs—like Social Security, Medicare, unemployment insurance, and food stamps—intended to protect families against economic hardship.

**specialization** the situation in which each person specializes in the task that he or she is good at performing.

**stabilization policy** the use of government policy to reduce the severity of *recessions* and to rein in excessively strong *expansions*. There are two main tools of stabilization policy: *monetary policy* and *fiscal policy*.

**stagflation** the combination of *inflation* and falling *aggregate output*.

**sticky wages** *nominal wages* that are slow to fall even in the face of high *unemployment* and slow to rise even in the face of labor shortages.

**stock** a share in the ownership of a company held by a shareholder.

**store of value** an asset that is a means of holding purchasing power over time.

**structural unemployment** *unemployment* that results when there are more people seeking jobs in a particular labor market than there are jobs available at the current wage rate, even when the economy is at the peak of the business cycle.

**subprime lending** lending to homebuyers who don't meet the usual criteria for borrowing.

**substitutes** pairs of goods for which a rise in the price of one of the goods leads to an increase in the demand for the other good.

**supply and demand model** a model of how a *competitive market* behaves.

**supply curve** a graphical representation of the *supply schedule*, showing the relationship between *quantity supplied* and price.

**supply price** the price of a given quantity at which producers will supply that quantity.

**supply schedule** a list or table showing how much of a good or service producers will supply at different prices.

**supply shock** an event that shifts the *short-run aggregate supply curve*. A negative supply shock raises production costs and reduces the *quantity supplied* at any *aggregate price level*, shifting the curve leftward. A positive supply shock decreases production costs and increases the quantity supplied at any aggregate price level, shifting the curve rightward.

**surplus** the excess of a good or service that occurs when the *quantity supplied* exceeds the *quantity demanded*; surpluses occur when the price is above the *equilibrium price*.

**sustainable long-run economic growth** is long-run growth that can continue in the face of the limited supply of natural resources and the impact of growth on the environment.

**T**

**T-account** a simple tool that summarizes a business's financial position by showing, in a single table, the business's assets and liabilities, with assets on the left and liabilities on the right.

**tangent line** a straight line that just touches a *nonlinear curve* at a particular point; the *slope* of the tangent line is equal to the slope of the nonlinear curve at that point.

**target federal funds rate** the Federal Reserve's desired level for the *federal funds rate*. The Federal Reserve adjusts the *money supply* through the purchase and sale of Treasury bills until the actual rate equals the desired rate.

**tariff** a tax levied on *imports*.

**Taylor rule for monetary policy** a rule that sets the *federal funds rate* according to the level of the *inflation rate* and either the *output gap* or the *unemployment rate*.

**technological progress** an advance in the technical means of production of goods and services.

**technology** the technical means for producing goods and services.

**time-series graph** a two-*variable* graph that has dates on the *horizontal axis* and values of a variable that occurred on those dates on the *vertical axis*.

**total consumer surplus** the sum of the *individual consumer surpluses* of all the buyers of a good in a market.

**total factor productivity** the amount of output that can be produced with a given amount of factor inputs.

**total producer surplus** the sum of the *individual producer surpluses* of all the sellers of a good in a market.

**total surplus** the total net gain to consumers and producers from trading in a market; the sum of the *consumer surplus* and the *producer surplus*.

**trade** the practice, in a *market economy*, in which individuals provide goods and services to others and receive goods and services in return.

**trade balance (merchandise trade balance)** the difference between a country's *exports* and *imports* of goods alone—not including services.

**trade deficit** when the value of the goods and services bought from foreigners is more than the value of the goods and services sold to consumers abroad.

**trade protection** policies that limit *imports*; also known simply as *protection*.

**trade surplus** when the value of goods and services bought from foreigners is less than the value of the goods and services sold to them.

**trade-off** a comparison of costs and benefits of doing something.

**transaction costs** the expenses of negotiating and executing a deal.

**truncated** cut; in a truncated axis, some of the range of values are omitted, usually to save space.

### U

**underemployment** the number of people who work part time because they cannot find full-time jobs.

**unemployment** the total number of people who are actively looking for work but aren't currently employed.

**unemployment rate** the percentage of the total number of people in the *labor force* who are unemployed, calculated as *unemployment/(unemployment + employment)*.

**unit of account** a measure used to set prices and make economic calculations.

**unit-of-account costs (of inflation)** costs arising from the way *inflation* makes money a less reliable unit of measurement.

**unplanned inventory investment** unplanned changes in *inventories*, which occur when actual sales are more or less than businesses expected.

### V

**value added (of a producer)** the value of a producer's sales minus the value of its purchases of intermediate goods and services.

**variable** a quantity that can take on more than one value.

**velocity of money** the ratio of *nominal GDP* to the *money supply*.

**vertical axis** the vertical number line of a graph along which values of the *y*-variable are measured; also referred to as the *y-axis*.

**vertical intercept** the point at which a *curve* hits the *vertical axis*; it shows the value of the *y*-variable when the value of the *x*-variable is zero.

**vicious cycle of deleveraging** describes the sequence of events that takes place when a *firm*'s asset sales to cover losses produce negative *balance sheet effects* on other firms and force creditors to call in their *loans*, forcing sales of more assets and causing further declines in asset prices.

### W

**wasted resources** a form of inefficiency in which people expend money, effort, and time to cope with the shortages caused by a *price ceiling*.

**wealth (of a household)** the value of accumulated savings.

**wealth effect of a change in the aggregate price level** the effect on *consumer spending* caused by the change in the purchasing power of consumers' assets when the *aggregate price level* changes. A rise in the aggregate price level decreases the purchasing power of consumers' assets, so consumers decrease their consumption; a fall in the aggregate price level increases the purchasing power of consumers' assets, so consumers increase their consumption.

**wedge** the difference between the *demand price* of the quantity transacted and the *supply price* of the quantity transacted for a good when the supply of the good is legally restricted. Often created by a *quantity control*, or *quota*.

**willingness to pay** the maximum price a consumer is prepared to pay for a good.

**world price** the price at which a good can be bought or sold abroad.

**World Trade Organization (WTO)** an international organization of member countries that oversees *international trade agreements* and rules on disputes between countries over those agreements.

### X

**x-axis** the horizontal number line of a graph along which values of the *x*-variable are measured; also referred to as the *horizontal axis*.

### Y

**y-axis** the vertical number line of a graph along which values of the *y*-variable are measured; also referred to as the *vertical axis*.

### Z

**zero bound** the lower bound of zero on the *nominal interest rate*.

**zero lower bound for interest rates** statement of the fact that interest rates cannot fall below zero.